Community-Based
CORRECTIONS

Titles of Related Interest

Tibbetts and Hemmens: *Criminological Theory: A Text/Reader*

Stohr, Walsh, and Hemmens: *Corrections: A Text/Reader*

Spohn and Hemmens: *Courts: A Text/Reader*

Barton-Bellessa/Hanser: *Community Corrections: A Text/Reader*

Lawrence and Hemmens: *Juvenile Justice: A Text/Reader*

Lilly, Cullen, and Ball: *Criminological Theory* (5th ed.)

Pratt, Franklin, and Gau: *Key Ideas in Criminology and Criminal Justice*

Wright, Tibbetts, and Daigle: *Criminals in the Making*

Walsh and Ellis: *Criminology: An Interdisciplinary Perspective*

Hagan: *Introduction to Criminology* (7th ed.)

Crutchfield, Kubrin, Weiss, and Bridges: *Crime: Readings* (3rd ed.)

Maguire and Okada: *Critical Issues in Criminology and Criminal Justice*

Felson: *Crime and Everyday Life* (5th ed.)

Hagan: *Crime Types and Criminals*

Hanser: *Community Corrections*

Pratt: *Addicted to Incarceration*

Scaramella, Cox, and McAmey: *Introduction to Policing*

Bachman and Schutt: *The Practice of Research in Criminology and Criminal Justice* (4th ed.)

Bachman and Schutt: *Fundamentals of Research in Criminology and Criminal Justice* (3rd ed.)

Mosher, Miethe, and Hart: *The Mismeasure of Crime* (2nd ed.)

Gabbidon and Greene: *Race and Crime* (2nd ed.)

Helfgott: *Criminal Behavior*

Bartol and Bartol: *Forensic Psychology* (3rd ed.)

Banks: *Criminal Justice Ethics* (3rd ed.)

Fox and Levin: *Extreme Killing* (3rd ed.)

Gerstenfeld: *Hate Crimes* (2nd ed.)

Holmes and Holmes: *Profiling Violent Crime* (4th ed.)

Holmes and Holmes: *Sex Crimes* (3rd ed.)

Howell: *Preventing and Reducing Juvenile Delinquency* (2nd ed.)

Cox, Allan, Hanser, and Conrad: *Juvenile Justice* (7th ed.)

Martin: *Understanding Terrorism* (3rd ed.)

Martin: *Essentials of Terrorism* (2nd ed.)

Martin: *Terrorism and Homeland Security*

Community-Based
CORRECTIONS
A Text/Reader

Shannon M. Barton-Bellessa
Indiana State University

Robert D. Hanser
University of Louisiana at Monroe

Los Angeles | London | New Delhi
Singapore | Washington DC

For information:

SAGE Publications, Inc.
2455 Teller Road
Thousand Oaks, California 91320
E-mail: order@sagepub.com

SAGE Publications Ltd.
1 Oliver's Yard
55 City Road
London EC1Y 1SP
United Kingdom

SAGE Publications India Pvt. Ltd.
B 1/I 1 Mohan Cooperative Industrial Area
Mathura Road, New Delhi 110 044
India

SAGE Publications Asia-Pacific Pte. Ltd.
33 Pekin Street #02-01
Far East Square
Singapore 048763

Printed in the United States of America

Library of Congress Cataloging-in-Publication Data

Barton-Bellessa, Shannon M.
Community-based corrections: a text/reader / Shannon M. Barton-Bellessa, Robert D. Hanser.
     p. cm.
Includes bibliographical references and index.
ISBN 978-1-4129-8746-2 (pbk.)
   1. Community-based corrections. 2. Criminals—Rehabilitation. I. Hanser, Robert D. II. Title.

HV9275.B37 2012
364.6'8—dc22   2010035402

This book is printed on acid-free paper.

10 11 12 13 14   10 9 8 7 6 5 4 3 2 1

Acquisitions Editor:	Jerry Westby
Associate Editor:	Aja Baker
Editorial Assistant:	Nichole O'Grady
Production Editor:	Catherine M. Chilton
Copy Editor:	Megan Markanich
Typesetter:	C&M Digitals (P) Ltd.
Proofreader:	Annette R. Van Deusen
Indexer:	Molly Hall
Cover Designer:	Bryan Fishman
Marketing Manager:	Erica DeLuca

Brief Contents

Detailed Contents

    Andrew von Hirsch

       In this essay, Andrew von Hirsch explored the ethical dilemmas
        faced by increasing the use of noncustodial sanctions.

Foreword

You hold in your hands a book that we think is something new. It is billed as a "text/reader." What that means is we have taken the two most commonly used types of books, the textbook and the reader, and blended them in a way that we anticipate will appeal to both students and faculty.

Our experience as teachers and scholars has been that textbooks for the core classes in criminal justice (or any other social science discipline) leave many students and professors cold. The textbooks are huge, crammed with photographs, charts, highlighted material, and all sorts of pedagogical devices intended to increase student interest. Too often, though, these books end up creating a sort of sensory overload for students and suffer from a focus on "bells and whistles," such as fancy graphics, at the expense of coverage of the most current research on the subject matter.

Readers, on the other hand, are typically comprised of recent and classic research articles on the subject matter. They generally suffer, however, from an absence of meaningful explanatory material. Articles are simply lined up and presented to the students, with little or no context or explanation. Students, particularly undergraduate students, are often confused and overwhelmed.

This text/reader represents our attempt to take the best of both the textbook and reader approaches. This book comprises research articles on corrections. This text/reader is intended to serve either as a supplement to a core textbook or as a stand-alone text. The book includes a combination of previously published articles and textual material introducing these articles and providing some structure and context for the selected readings. The book is divided into a number of sections. The sections of the book track the typical content and structure of a textbook on the subject. Each section of the book has an introductory section that serves to introduce, explain, and provide context for the readings that follow. The readings are a selection of the best recent research that has appeared in academic journals, as well as some classic readings. The articles are edited as necessary to make them accessible to students. This variety of research and perspectives will provide the student with a grasp of the development of research, as well as an understanding of the current status of research in the subject area. This approach gives the student the opportunity to learn the basics (in the textbook-like introductory portion of each section) and to read some of the most interesting research on the subject.

There is also an introductory section explaining the organization and content of the book and providing context for the articles that follow. This introductory section provides a framework for the text and articles that follow, as well as introducing relevant themes, issues, and concepts. This will assist the student in understanding the articles.

Each section will include a summary of the material covered. There will also be a selection of discussion questions, placed after each reading. These summaries and discussion questions should facilitate student thought and class discussion of the material.

It is our belief that this method of presenting the material will be more interesting for both students and faculty. We acknowledge that this approach may be viewed by some as more challenging than the traditional textbook. To that we say, "Yes! It is!" But we believe that, if we raise the bar, our students will rise to the challenge. Research shows that students and faculty often find textbooks boring to read. It is our belief that many criminal justice instructors would welcome the opportunity to teach without having to rely on a "standard" textbook that covers only the most basic information and that lacks both depth of coverage and an attention to current research. This book provides an alternative for instructors who want to get more out of the basic criminal justice courses and curriculum than one can get from a typical textbook that is aimed at the lowest common denominator and filled with flashy but often useless features that merely serve to drive up its cost. This book is intended for instructors who want to go beyond the ordinary, standard coverage provided in textbooks.

We also believe students will find this approach more interesting. They are given the opportunity to read current, cutting-edge research on the subject, while also being provided with background and context for this research.

We hope that this unconventional approach will be more interesting and thus make learning and teaching more fun—and hopefully more useful as well. Students need not only content knowledge but also an understanding of the academic skills specific to their discipline. Criminal justice is a fascinating subject, and the topic deserves to be presented in an interesting manner. We hope you will agree.

Craig Hemmens, JD, PhD
Department of Criminal Justice
Boise State University

Preface

This book is intended as a text/reader examining community-based alternatives to imprisonment. Although a number of very good texts exist on the subject, this book offers a unique approach combining both descriptive material along with some of the most relevant journal articles examining the effectiveness of community-based alternatives. In addition, this book is unique to many other community-based corrections texts in its organization and efforts to expand upon some of the newer techniques in the field devoting entire sections to topics such as restorative justice and assessment and risk prediction. We also make special effort to tie this work into the practical uses that the majority of our students will be utilizing. This includes discussions on qualifications of specific types of officers, stressors confronted in the daily work, and examples of instruments that will be used in the field. Finally each section includes the Applied Theory Section box that ties in the material in that section that supports why these methods should be used. These elements of the book make this text/reader unique in its presentation and format. As community corrections has moved into the new millennium, so has the need for using statistical procedures, writing, and best practices in the field. The organization of the book follows a logical flow through the system from the historical development of community-based alternatives, to pretrial release and diversion, restorative justice, treatment, assessment and risk prediction, probation and case planning, intermediate sanctions both residential and nonresidential, parole, juvenile offenders in the community, and dealing with special populations.

One of the difficulties in completing this text/reader was narrowing down the journal articles for inclusion in the text. For some topics, there was an overabundance of great research for inclusion, for others practically nothing existed. This divergence in available materials exemplifies the need for more research and progress in the area of community-based corrections. The majority of the articles were chosen based upon their timeliness, their thoroughness, empirical data, keeping the targeted audience in mind, and making every effort to complement the text/reader. In reviewing these articles, we believe that they represent the best examples of community-based corrections research. At the end of the first section, students are presented with an example of how to read a research article. These paragraphs are intended to assist the student with not only those included in this text/reader but for their future courses and any additional assigned materials.

Despite the importance and relevance of each of the journal articles, one must keep in mind that they are written for a professional audience. To accommodate the student, whether an undergraduate or a graduate, we have edited these articles to include the purpose of the study, the methods used to collect the data (where relevant), the findings, and the implications of the study. That being said, efforts were made to reduce the length of the articles for inclusion to make them as student friendly as possible. This means that many of the articles have tables and the results sections omitted. We have made every effort to edit these materials without losing the core concepts, the findings, and policy implications of the studies. Anyone wishing to review the complete journal article(s) may find a link to them on the SAGE companion website.

This book is intended to serve as a stand-alone text for undergraduate students, and as either a primary or supplementary book for graduate students. For a graduate course, the book introduces students to the core concepts of community-based corrections. The addition of the journal articles with their online availability may serve as a starting point for extended research and lectures.

⬛ Structure of the Book

In reviewing community corrections texts, there are a variety of different orders including those where the historical development of community-based corrections is combined with probation and parole and those that are separated. Because of the limited space and the order that we typically teach the course, we have divided these sections into distinct and separate categories. Although this does not diminish the fact that the majority of all community-based sanctions developed within a similar time frame, we have found it is easier for students to understand this as a separate entity. In addition, this book offers a unique framework not only in the inclusion of the articles but also with the introduction of more practically related materials and innovative strategies such as restorative justice, presentence investigations (PSIs), risk and needs assessments, prediction instruments, and dealing with special populations such as substance abusers, sex offenders, and the mentally ill.

This text/reader is divided into 11 sections covering the primary topics in community-based corrections. A similar format is used with a beginning paragraph highlighting what the reader should expect to see in the section along with a conclusion summarizing the section. Additionally, there are key terms, discussion questions, a section summary, and web resources at the end of each of the sections. A summary of the 11 sections follows.

Section I. History and Development of Community-Based Corrections

This section of the text serves as an introduction and overview to the historical development of community-based corrections. This includes a brief overview of the philosophical underpinnings of punishment and how they apply to alternative sanctions in the community, suggested theoretical approaches to reintegration and treatment, and new developments in legislation that have directly impacted how offenders are supervised and released.

Section II. Pretrial Release and Diversion

In this section, we discuss how offenders awaiting trial or sentencing are either supervised or diverted from the system completely. An examination of more innovative approaches to dealing with specialized offender populations with the advent and implementation of drug courts, mental health courts, and reentry courts are discussed. This section sets the foundation for collaborative models between courts and community-based alternatives.

Section III. Restorative Justice

In this section, we discuss the various types of restorative justice programs being used by courts and community-based personnel. As a mechanism for reducing costs but also keeping less serious offenders out of the system while recognizing the rights of the victim, these programs offer viable alternatives to traditional sentences. A review of innovative alternative programs such as family conferences, teen courts, reintegrative shaming, community justice, and victim–offender mediation are included in this section.

Section IV. The Viability of Treatment Perspectives

In this section, we discuss the viability of treatment as an option for community-based sanctions. A review of the impact of Robert Martinson's "Nothing Works" proposition is included along with a discussion on the relative influence of this approach to treating offenders. A review of the role of treatment staff is included in this section along with a review of some of the more frequently used alternatives in the community.

Section V. Assessment and Risk Prediction

This section may be one of the more valuable to those individuals seeking a career in the field of community corrections. Here we review not only the historical development of assessment and classification but provide examples of those instruments often utilized in the field. A review and discussion of the PSI and the role of this instrument is also included in this section.

Section VI. Probation Management and Case Planning

In this section, we discuss the evolution of probation beginning with recognizance and suspended sentences through modern-day uses. This section also includes a variety of different types of probation administrative models that include not only the qualifications of officers but the supervisory strategies and responsibilities of offenders. Issues of revocation and legal procedures are also included.

Section VII. Community-Based Residential Intermediate Sanctions

In this section, we cover only residentially based intermediate sanctions. These include halfway houses, community residential treatment centers, shock incarceration, and boot camps. This section is intended to provide the reader with an overview of the most restrictive forms of community sanctions within the continuum of options.

Section VIII. Community-Based Nonresidential and Economic Intermediate Sanctions

In this section, we cover those intermediate sanctions that do not have a residential component. Rather these alternatives include the most rigorous sanctions that allow the offender to remain within their home environment and to maintain employment without being incarcerated. These include both restrictive and financial options such as fines, fees, forfeiture and restitution, community service, intensive supervision, electronic monitoring, home detention, day reporting centers, and testing technologies.

Section IX. Parole Management, Case Planning, and Reentry

In this section, we discuss the evolution of parole beginning with the European system through modern-day evolution. This section also includes a variety of different types of parole administrative models that include not only the qualifications of officers but the supervisory strategies and responsibilities of offenders. The use of prerelease planning and mechanisms, along with the parole board use and revocation, are also included.

Section X. Juvenile Offenders

In this section, we provide a very brief overview to the supervision strategies used for juvenile offenders in the community. These include probation, the juvenile court system, the role of juvenile records, child protective services, residential programs, restorative justice techniques, and dealing with gangs.

Section XI. Specialized and Problematic Offender Typologies in a Changing Era

In this final section, we include a discussion on the supervisory strategies used for a special offender population, which includes sex offenders, substance abusers, mentally ill offenders, and mentally retarded offenders. This growing population in the community offers special concerns for community safety and strategies to supervise. This section addresses some of these issues as well as provides suggestions for effective supervisory strategies.

Ancillaries

To enhance the text/reader and to assist in the use of this book, a variety of different ancillaries have been created. Each of these is briefly described:

Instructor's Resource CD. A variety of instructor's materials is available. For each section, this includes summaries, PowerPoint slides, chapter activities, web resources, and a complete set of test questions.

Student Study Site. This comprehensive student study site features chapter outlines students can print for class, flash cards, interactive quizzes, web exercises, links to additional journal articles, links to *Frontline* videos and NPR and PBS radio shows, and more.

⬛ Acknowledgments

We would first like to thank Jerry Westby, executive editor. Jerry's continued support and faith in this project have been an inspiration and is greatly appreciated, as are those efforts and support of Craig Hemmens and Jerry's developmental assistant, Aja Baker. These individuals were able to maintain a three-way dialogue among the authors, editors, and reviewers, which resulted in this project being the best it could be. We would also like to thank Erin Conley, who wrote "How to Read a Research Article." This guide has proven to be very useful in other text/readers in this series and we believe will continue to be extremely helpful and useful with this book. We would also like to thank our copy editor, Megan Markanich.

Shannon M. Barton-Bellessa:
I would also like to thank the various people who made this project—and ultimately my career—possible. First, I would like to thank Ken Ayers, my undergraduate professor at Kentucky Wesleyan College, without whose advice and guidance the possibilities of a PhD and writing would have never been possible. I would also like to thank those professors at the University of Cincinnati who shaped the core values and beliefs in

treatment and reformation in criminal justice. These include Francis Cullen and Patricia VanVoorhis. I would like to offer a very special thank-you for my mentor Edward Latessa, who opened my eyes to the possibilities of community-based alternatives and the possibilities to make a difference through evaluation research and community involvement. Words can never truly express my gratitude to these individuals who have shaped my career. Finally, there are a number of people whom I owe an inordinate amount of thanks for their support, friendship, and advice throughout not only this process but many others as well. These people include Nancy Hogan, Phillip Shon, Eric Lambert, Velmer Burton, Sudipto Roy, DeVere Woods, and all my other colleagues in the Department of Criminology and Criminal Justice at Indiana State University including the administrative support staff of Peggy Strobel, Linda Everly, and Brenda Starkey. Without their patience and support throughout this process, none of it would have been possible. I would also like to thank my coauthor Robert Hanser for allowing such generous usage and alteration of his *Community Corrections* text. Although this text/reader is different in nature, without his foundational work this task would have been overwhelming.

Finally, I owe the most gratitude to my husband, Darin; my children, Drake and Brady; and my mother, Betty Barton, for their generosity, patience, and the sacrifices of time away from them and what they enjoy while I worked on this project. Without them, this truly would not have been possible, nor would it be meaningful.

Robert D. Hanser:
I would like to give thanks as well. I would like to thank my wife, Penny, and my three children, Amy, Tiffany, and Adam. They have provided continued patience and understanding while I spent hours in the study, typing away on one project or another. I would also like to thank my granddaughter, Abigail, for being the wonderful source of joy that she is. Lastly, I would like to extend special gratitude to all of the correctional practitioners who carry out the daily tasks of our correctional system, whether it be institutional or community based. These individuals deserve the highest praise as they work in a field that is demanding and undervalued. I thank you all for the contributions that you make to our society.

Both of us are grateful to the many reviewers who spent time reading the document and making a considerable number of recommendations that helped to shape the final product. Every effort was made to incorporate those ideas. We fully believe these suggestions and insights only helped to improve the final product. A special thanks goes out to the following experts: Gaylene Armstrong, Sam Houston State University; Kristie R. Blevins, University of North Carolina at Charlotte; J. Michael Botts, Arkansas State University; Mark Brown, University of South Carolina; Michael Brown, Ball State University; Gary Cornelius, George Mason University; Tanya M. Grant, Sacred Heart University; Mario L. Hesse, Saint Cloud State University; Verna R. Jones, Jackson State University; Eric Metchik, Salem State College; Stephen S. Owen, Radford University; and Donald R. Trapp, Portland State University.

◼ Dedication

Shannon M. Barton-Bellessa: I dedicate this book to my parents, Betty and Gerald Barton, who have made all of this and more possible. To my boys Drake and Brady, you are truly the light of my life. To my husband, Darin, thank you for bringing a smile to my face every day.

Robert D. Hanser: I dedicate this book to my wife, Penny; my children, Amy, Tiffany, and Adam; and my granddaughter, Abigail. I love you all very much.

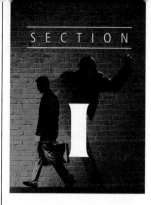

SECTION

I

History and Development of Community-Based Corrections

Learning Objectives

1. Define **community corrections** and understand the reasons for its emergence.
2. Identify early historical precursors to probation and parole.
3. Identify and discuss the various philosophical underpinnings associated with sentencing and the administration of offender supervision within the community.
4. Understand the various suggested theoretical approaches to reintegrating the offender in the community.
5. Identify some of the more recent legislative responses to supervising offenders in the community.
6. Identify the four main purposes of punishment and explain how each serves as a guide in agency **policy** and practice.

As states and the federal government continue to experience an unprecedented growth in the prison population with diminished resources, the development of alternative-based punishments both before and after incarceration have become a necessity rather than a luxury (Steen & Bandy, 2007). Also known as community-based corrections, the necessity for these alternatives and best practices comes at a time when our knowledge of those programs most effective at reducing recidivism while addressing the individual needs of the offender is at an all-time high. Unlike other correctional options, community corrections are designed to minimize the penetration of the offender into the correctional system. At year-end 2008, more than 7.3 million adults (1 in every 31) were under some form of correctional supervision (Glaze & Bonczar, 2009; Sabol, West, & Cooper, 2009). This number included more than 5 million supervised in the community (probation and parole) and over 2.3 million confined in either prison or jail (Glaze & Bonczar, 2009). The term *community corrections* itself elicits many different thoughts and perceptions of individuals depending upon your personal experiences, backgrounds, traditions, and the social context of the day (Rothman, 1980). For instance, some people may view community corrections as consisting of only probation and parole while others might see community corrections as being more related to community service and other such programs. Yet others tend to equate community corrections with being "easy" on crime. Certainly, the first two examples are (objectively speaking) actual tools used within the field of community corrections. However, the third example demonstrates that perceptions may negatively impact the notion of community corrections, even when the term is considered on a mere conceptual level. This is important because the perceptions that persons have of community corrections will, in fact, have a direct impact on how effective community-based programs are likely to be. Thus, a positive community perception is actually quite relevant and important for evidence-based programs especially in a time when "get tough" policies continue to get political representatives elected and being seen as "soft" on crime equates to a political death sentence. As noted by Michael Tonry (1999), the United States has a tendency to be so egocentric that we fail to examine what policies have been successful in other countries that may be useful and easily transferrable to the United States. Community-based alternatives such as day fines, prosecutorial fines, community service orders, and sentencing guidelines have offered options for courts, offenders, victims, and the communities that meet the **goals** of **retribution** while advancing rehabilitative strategies (Tonry, 1999). These various alternatives and their relative policy impacts will be discussed throughout the text using both materials and the selected readings to accomplish these goals.

⬛ Community Corrections Defined

With it being clear that community perceptions are important to the overall effectiveness of community corrections, this begs the question: How does the community envision a community corrections program, and how would we define such a program? Therefore, what is meant by the term *community corrections*? For purposes of this text/reader, community corrections includes all non-incarcerating correctional sanctions imposed upon an offender for the purposes of reintegrating that offender within the community. The use of this definition is important for several reasons.

First, this definition acknowledges that community corrections consists of those programs that do not employ incarceration. Yet this definition does not contend that these sanctions simply exist due to a need for alternatives to incarceration. This is a very important point that deserves elaboration. It is undoubtedly true that there is a need for alternatives to jail and/or prison simply due to the fact that both types of facilities tend to be overcrowded in various areas of the United States. In truth, the need for options to avoid further jail and prison construction is probably the main impetus behind the proliferation of community corrections programs that occurred during the later 1990s and has continued on into the 21st century. As states continue to struggle for the appropriate resources to house those offenders sentenced to longer periods of incarceration, the need to explore alternatives that allow for the goals of punishment and **rehabilitation** to be met point to an increased use of reintegration strategies that include programs such as work release and community transition. Community corrections, therefore, provides alternatives at both the front end and the back end of the correctional system. With respect to front end alternatives, probation has been used as a means of avoiding further crowding in jails and prisons. Indeed, many chief judges and court administrators are acutely aware of population capacities in the jails that are run by their corresponding sheriff's office. At the back end of the correctional process, parole systems have continued to act as release valves upon prison system populations, allowing correctional systems to ease overcrowding through the use of early release mechanisms that keep offenders under supervision until the expiration of their original sentence. Additionally, many states have begun to use **split sentencing** alternatives that allow for the offenders to be sentenced to a term of imprisonment and probation to be served at the end of the confinement period rather than being placed on parole. Again, this action serves to reduce the need for a separate supervising agency while continuing to meet the public's perception of "getting tough" on crime.

Thus, to say that community correction provides an alternative to incarceration is not necessarily wrong, but it limits the intent and use of community corrections sanctions. This also further implies that if there were enough prison space community corrections might not exist. This is simply not the case since community corrections is often implemented in jurisdictions that do not have overcrowding problems. Rather, community corrections, in and of itself, holds value as a *primary* sanction, regardless of whether jail or prison space is abundant. In times past, this may not have been the case: such sanctions being restricted to a set of options only used in lieu of prison sanctions. However, it should instead be considered that the contemporary use of community corrections often exists as a first choice among sanctions and that these programs are now used because they have been shown to be more effective than sentencing schemes that are over-reliant on incarceration. Thus, almost by accident, the criminal justice system has found that community-based programs actually work better than incarceration and are therefore the preferred modality of sanctioning in many cases of offender processing. Through data-driven analyses of outcomes and comparisons in recidivism rates, it has been found that these programs are often superior in promoting long-term public safety agendas. This is largely due to the fact that these sanctions tend to work better with the less serious offender population, particularly those who are not violent. The nonviolent offender population happens to be the larger segment of those on community supervision. To be sure, jails and prisons do still have their place in corrections, but there are a large number of offenders who fare better in terms of recidivism if they are spared the debilitating effects of prison but yet are made to be accountable for their crime to the community. This then derives a quasi-therapeutic benefit that leads to a long-term reduction in future criminality. This also leads into the second aspect of the community corrections definition that was provided by this text/reader; community corrections has a definite reintegration component.

The reintegrative nature of community corrections is important from both society's perspective and the perspective of the offender. First, if the offender is successfully reintegrated, it is more likely that the offender will produce something of material value (through gainful employment) for society. The mere payment of taxes, coupled with a lack of further cost to society from the commission of further crimes, itself is a benefit extending to the whole of society. Further, offenders who are employed are able to generate payment for court fines, treatment programs, and victim compensation—none of these benefits are realized within the prison environment. Likewise, a truly reintegrated offender can provide contributions through effective parenting of one's own children. This is actually a very important issue. **Female offenders** are often the primary caretakers of their children (with at least 70% of such offenders having children) while male offenders are often absent from the lives of their children (further adding to problems associated with father absenteeism). Known as collateral consequences of incarceration, the social costs associated with foster homes are staggering, not to mention the fact that these children are likely to have a number of emotional problems that stem from their chaotic childhoods (Parke & Clarke-Stewart, 2003). Offenders who are reintegrated can stop this trend and can perhaps counter intergenerational cycles that persist in some family systems (Eddy & Reid, 2003). This alone is a substantial social benefit that makes reintegrative aspects all the more valuable.

Additional social benefits might also come in the way of offender community **involvement**. Reintegrated offenders may be involved in religious institutions, volunteer **activities**, or even anti-crime activities with youth who might be at risk of crime (prior offenders can provide insight on the hazards of criminal lifestyles in school or other settings). The potential benefits for society may not be apparent from a budgetary perspective, but they can reap enormous benefits in the way of relationships that build community cohesion. Further, prevention efforts can be aided through the input of prior offenders involved with various community programs. Thus, it is clear that there are financial, familial, and community benefits associated with offender reintegration that can be realized by society.

From the perspective of the offender, the potential benefits should be clear. Such offenders do not have their liberty as restricted as is the case while being incarcerated. Further, such offenders are still able to maintain contact with family (particularly their children), and these offenders are able to maintain meaningful connections with the community. This is exclusive of the fact that these individuals are spared the trauma and debilitating effects associated with prison life. Rather, such offenders are spared the pains of imprisonment, being able to develop relations with significant others, maintain contact with their children, pursue vocational and educational goals, and so forth. It is clear that such options are likely to be perceived as more beneficial by nonviolent offenders than a prison sentence might be. Thus, the reintegrative nature of community corrections holds value in and of itself, regardless of the holding capacity of incarcerating facilities.

When talking about the development of community corrections, there are several historical antecedents that occurred that are important to understand. This section will provide the student with an examination of some alternatives to incarceration that existed in the early history of corrections and punishment sentencing. Just like the evolution of the legal system and law enforcement, much of what we do in modern day community-based corrections is derived from European methodologies, in particular England. In providing this broad historical backdrop, it will be made apparent that early alternatives to incarceration had a therapeutic or reintegrative intent rather than a desire to save space or resources in correctional programs. Indeed, overcrowding was not a concern in the early history of corrections since there were no regulations regarding an inmate's quality of life and since deplorable conditions were (at one time) considered standard fare within a prison setting. In essence, unhealthy and unsafe conditions were considered part and parcel to any jail or prison. Thus, the desire to save space or expenses was not of any appreciable concern when providing offenders with alternatives to incarceration. Although probation was one of the earliest uses of genuine community supervision in the United States, a cursory review of this sanction will be included in this section while a more in-depth discussion on the historical development of this sanction will be reserved for Section VI.

◪ Early Alternative Sanctions

The historical development of community-based alternatives can be traced back to the four specific sanctions used in European countries: **sanctuary**, **benefit of clergy**, **judicial reprieve**, and **recognizance**. Each of these sanctions along with a brief discussion of their origins will be presented in this section.

Sanctuary

One of the earliest forms of leniency was known as sanctuary. Sanctuary came in two forms—one that was largely secular in nature and the other that had its roots in Christian religion. The secular form of sanctuary existed through the identification of various cities or regions (most often cities) that were set aside as a form of neutral ground from criminal prosecution. Accused criminals could escape prosecution by fleeing to these cities and maintaining their residence there. Though it might have been a bit difficult to reach these cities of sanctuary, they were widely known by the populace to be places of refuge for suspected criminals and provided a means for accused criminals to essentially "self-select" themselves for a self-imposed banishment within these neutral regions. Thus, it is clear that this type of sanctuary was mainly intended to protect the accused from capricious forms of punishment, but this also indicates that some crimes required mitigation efforts that eliminated the need for incarcerative sanctions.

The second type of sanctuary began during the 4th century and was grounded in European Christian **beliefs** that appealed to the kind mercy of the church. This type of sanctuary consisted of a place—usually a church—where the king's soldiers were forbidden to enter for purposes of taking an accused criminal into custody. In such cases, sanctuary was provided until some form of negotiation could be arranged or until the accused was ultimately smuggled out of the area. If while in sanctuary the accused confessed to their crime, they were typically granted abjuration (Cromwell, Del Carmen, & Alarid, 2002). Abjuration required that the offender promise to leave England with the understanding that any return to England without explicit permission from the Crown would lead to immediate punishment (Cromwell et al., 2002).

▲ **Photo 1.1** Before the separation of church and state, churches were sometimes a source of temporary sanctuary for many offenders.

This form of leniency lasted for well over a thousand years in European history and was apparently quite common in England. Even if they did not confess to their crime as a means of seeking abjuration, the accused could still be granted sanctuary. Over time, however, specific rules were placed upon the use of this form of leniency. For instance, during the 13th century, felons who sought sanctuary could stay up to 40 days or, before the expiration of that time, could agree to leave the kingdom. If they remained past the 40 days, "they risked being forced out of sanctuary through starvation" (Sahagun, 2007, p. 1). Eventually, sanctuary lost its appeal in Europe and, "in the 15th century, several parliamentary petitions sought to restrict the right of sanctuary in England. In the next century, King Henry VIII reduced the number of sanctuaries by about half" (Sahagun, 2007, p. 1). From roughly 1750 onward, countries throughout Europe began to abolish sanctuary provisions as secular courts gained power over ecclesiastical courts. The process of eliminating sanctuary was a long and protracted one that took nearly 100 years before sanctuary ultimately disappeared as an option of leniency for accused offenders (Sahagun, 2007, p. 1).

Benefit of Clergy

The second early alternative sanction, benefit of clergy, was initially a form of exemption to criminal punishment that was provided for clergy in Europe during the 12th century. This benefit was originally implemented for the benefit of members of various churches, including clerics, monks, and nuns who might be accused of crimes. This alternative to typical punishment required church representatives to be delivered to church authorities for punishment, avoiding criminal processing through the secular court system. When originally implemented, the ecclesiastical courts (church courts) were very powerful (particularly in regard to religious matters or issues that could be connected to matters of religion), and these courts had the power to enact life sentences, if so desired. This was, however, a rarity since the church clergy members involved in crimes (clerics, monks, nuns) were often purported to have religious convictions, moral considerations, or ethical binds that mitigated their various offenses.

In addition, the ecclesiastical courts viewed negative behavior as being more a result of sin—thereby being an offense against God—rather than being purely a crime that was an offense against men or the Crown. Given this fact, and that the biblical leanings toward repentance, forgiveness, and mercy might sometimes be provided as the underlying basis for sentencing, it was common that church clergy members would be given sentences that were less punitive and more reformative in nature.

Though this might seem to be an effort to simply integrate compassion in the sentencing process, the origins of benefit of clergy had their genesis in a feudal power struggle between the Crown and the Holy Roman Catholic Church in England (Dressler, 1962). During this period, King Henry II desired more control over the church in England and wished to diminish the influence that the ecclesiastical church had on the decision-making powers of the Crown (Dressler, 1962). It was the specific desire of Henry II to subject the clerics and monks of the church to the will of the king's court (Dressler, 1962; Latessa & Allen, 1999). In doing so, the Crown would then hold dominion over the church, and power would be centralized under a secular court controlled by the king. Thus, the benefit of clergy was the churches' attempt to thwart the efforts of King Henry II and to maintain power within England. This is interesting because this is an early example of how political power struggles can impact justice-making decisions. As will be seen in later sections of this text, many of the programs that are implemented in both prison and community corrections systems are steeped in ideology or have their beginnings attributed to some form of political debate over crime and punishment. The benefit of clergy is a very early example of how ideology and public policy become intertwined and how both are shaped and crafted due to power struggles between opposing parties. This also demonstrates that justice, in its purest form, is manipulated by the underlying desires of those in power. Further, this demonstrates that social forces can impact sanctions that are utilized on a widespread basis. This will be an important point in later sections as well, demonstrating that history does indeed repeat itself and likewise makes clear the fact that community corrections does not operate in a social vacuum.

Through benefit of clergy, ordained clerics, monks, and nuns were transferred to what was referred to as the bishop's court of the Holy Roman Catholic Church. Though it was initially reserved for church clergy members, by the 14th century this form of leniency had been made available to all who were literate (Latessa & Allen, 1999). Judges in secular courts provided this option but required offenders to demonstrate that they were indeed literate. The test of literacy required that the offender read the text of Psalm 51 out loud in front of the judge. However, criminals being a fairly wily and crafty lot began to memorize the verse. Many criminals who were not literate at all but were able to stand before a judge looked at the page with Psalm 51 and recited the verses from memory, all without being able to actually read the verses in front of them. Presuming the criminal could master the verses—word for word—and could recite them when before witnesses, a lighter sentence was theirs to be had. Naturally, one could test their ability to read by requiring the accused to point at specific words within the text ,and this is precisely what occurred in later years as judges became aware of the past deception that had occurred in their courts.

However, it is the case that most who were literate at this time were also financially well off. Thus, this benefit tended to aid those who had power meanwhile ignoring the plight of the poor who were more vulnerable. Rather, it was typically the poor and the underclasses who were most often given incarcerative sanctions (not much different from today's socioeconomic sentencing demographic). This was an especially important option given England's penchant for the death penalty during the centuries that followed. Benefit of clergy was thus a means of escaping a very tough sentencing scheme for minor crimes. Over time, the English criminal law did achieve a much better sense of parity or proportionality. Because of these changes, the benefit of clergy was effectively abolished in 1827 since it was no longer necessary to safeguard persons from an unwieldy and brutal sentencing structure.

Judicial Reprieve

Later, during the last part of the 1700s, it became increasingly common for judges in England to utilize the third alternative method of punishment known as judicial reprieve. The use of judicial reprieves was actually at the full discretion of judges, and they were used in cases where judges did not believe that incarceration was proportionate to the crime or in cases where no productive benefit was expected. The judicial reprieve simply suspended sentences of incarceration as an act of mercy or leniency. Naturally, as might be expected, this option was reserved for offenders who had committed minor infractions of the law and who did not have prior records. While the offender was on reprieve, the offender retained their liberties and freedoms. Upon the expiration of a specified period of time, the offender was then able to apply to the Crown of England for a full pardon (Cromwell et al., 2002).

In these cases, judges made decisions based on their own hunches as to the likelihood of offender outcomes, and this was regardless of the number of inmates in their local jail. In fact, jailers often received a substantial income from fees obtained through the provision of goods and services to inmates within their charge. In a literal sense, a jailer's income was enhanced when they had high numbers of inmates in their facility; therefore, the more inmates in a facility, the more income that was produced for the jailer. Thus, it was not at all in the jailer's best interest to limit the number of inmates, particularly when one considers that there were no standards of care that jailers had to meet. Simply put, inmates could be crammed into jail facilities without any concern of public or court reprisal. Therefore, jailers had everything to gain and nothing at all to lose when overcrowding their jail facility.

Then, it is clear that jailers would not have desired widespread use of reprieves since this would essentially block their income. Thus, when judges did use reprieves it was simply due to their own genuine concern for the inmate's welfare rather than pressure related to overfilled facilities. Cromwell et al. (2002) went so far as to note that judicial reprieves were a method by which judges "recognized

▲ **Photo 1.2**   Stan Davis (left), Brother Jim Fogerty (middle), and Willie J. R. Fleming all work in an area of Chicago known as Cabrini Green. This area has been plagued with high crime and has a disproportionate amount of it. Cabrini Green is known for having serious gang problems. These three men work with gang offenders, providing faith-based and community-based interventions. These men are prime examples of how church-based interventions work with modern day offender populations.

that not all offenders are dangerous, evil persons" (p. 27) and thus sought to avoid prescribing the specified punishment when such punishment was simply out of sync with the judge's perception of the offender's temperament or demeanor. This is again important because it demonstrates that, at base, reprieves were actually provided as a form of compassion in the hope that the offender would be deterred from criminal activity in the future. Such a perspective is nothing less than a rehabilitative perspective whereby the reintegration of the offender is given priority over mere desires for punishment.

Recognizance

Finally, recognizance in the United States is often traced to the case of *Commonwealth v. Chase* (1830) in which Judge Thacher of Boston, Massachusetts, found a woman named Jerusha Chase guilty of stealing from inside a home (Grinnel, 1941). Ms. Chase pleaded her guilt but did have numerous friends who also pleaded for mercy from the court. This resulted in her release "at large" on her own recognizance until which time she was called to appear before the court (Begnaud, 2007). The accused was likewise acquitted before the same court of another charge of larceny and was only sentenced for her prior 1830 crime (Begnaud, 2007; Grinnel, 1941).

Begnaud (2007) contended that this use of recognizance in the United States is the first antecedent to probation given that the convicted was released into society but if subsequent criminal act were charged could then be charged further for the original crime that led to their initial contact with the court. Latessa and Allen (1999) supported this contention by demonstrating that ever more aspects of modern probation began to also appear in the use of recognizance in England. This practice, also known as "binding over," involved the use of

> a bond or obligation entered into by a defendant, who is bound to refrain from doing, or is bound to do, something for a stipulated period, and to appear in court on a specified date for trial or for final disposition of the case. (Dressler, 1962, p. 9; Latessa & Allen, 1999, p. 108)

As with judicial reprieves, this alternative to incarceration was usually only used with offenders who had committed petty crimes. If the offender violated the terms of this agreement, the binding was claimed by the state, and the offender might then face incarceration or some other form of punishment—often including physical sanctions (Latessa & Allen, 1999).

Latessa and Allen (1999) noted that this sanction has sometimes been thought to consist of the very beginnings of community supervision because this sanction included the supervision of a sentence and provided conditional freedom that was leveraged against possible revocation of the offender's recognizant release.

⊠ Philosophical Basis of Community Corrections—Both Probation and Parole

Within the field of corrections itself, four goals or philosophical orientations of punishment are generally recognized. These are retribution, **deterrence** (both general and specific), **incapacitation**, and rehabilitation. Two of these orientations focus on the offender (rehabilitation and **specific deterrence**) while the other orientations (**general deterrence**, retribution, and incapacitation) are thought to generally focus more on the crime that was committed. The diversity and interaction of these goals typically reflect not only the desire to punish the offender but also serve as a reflection of the true causes of criminal behavior (Woodahl & Garland, 2009). The intent of this section is to present philosophical bases specifically related to community corrections and offender reintegration. However, it is useful to first provide a quick and general overview of the four primary philosophical bases of punishment. Each of these philosophical bases of punishment will be discussed in greater detail in Section IV of this text, but a quick introduction to these concepts is provided here for student reference when completing the remainder of the current section.

Retribution is often referred to as the "eye for an eye" mentality and simply implies that offenders committing a crime should be punished in a like fashion or in a manner that is commensurate with the severity of the crime that they have committed. In other words, retribution implies proportionality of punishments to the seriousness of the crime committed. Deterrence includes general and specific deterrence. General deterrence is intended to cause vicarious learning whereby observers see that offenders are punished for a given crime and therefore themselves are discouraged from committing a like mannered crime due to fear of similar punishment. Specific deterrence is simply the infliction of a punishment upon a specific offender in the hope that the particular offender will be discouraged from committing future crimes. Incapacitation simply deprives the offender of their liberty and removes them from society with the intent of ensuring that society cannot be further victimized by that offender during the offender's term of incarceration. Lastly, rehabilitation implies that an offender should be provided the means to fulfill a constructive level of functioning in society, with an implicit expectation that such offenders will be deterred from reoffending due to their having worthwhile stakes in legitimate society—stakes that they will not wish to lose as a consequence of criminal offending.

Numerous authors and researchers associated with the field of community corrections have noted that the underlying philosophical basis of both probation and parole is that of rehabilitating offenders and reintegrating them into society (Abadinsky, 2003; Clear & Cole, 2003; Latessa & Allen, 1999). As we go through the text, it will become more clear that notable figures such as John Augustus (the Father of Probation) and Alexander Maconochie (the Father of Parole) were more concerned with the potential reformation of the offender when determining suitability for either sanction. The earliest theoretical and philosophical bases for both probation and parole lie in the work of Cesare Beccaria's classic treatise entitled *An Essay on Crimes and Punishments* (1764). Beccaria is also held out to be the Father of Classical Criminology, which was instrumental in shifting views on crime and punishment toward a more humanistic means of response. Among other things, Beccaria advocated for proportionality between the crime that was committed by an offender and the specific sanction that was given. Since not all crimes are equal, the use of progressively greater sanctions becomes an instrumental component in achieving this proportionality. Naturally, community-based perspectives that utilize a continuum of sanctions (Clear & Cole, 2003) fit well with the tenets of proportionality.

The key differences between earlier approaches in processing offenders (i.e., harsh and publicly displayed punishments) and the emerging reformation emphasis that occurred during the last part of the late 1700s were grounded in the way that offenders were viewed as well as the decided intent of the criminal law (Latessa & Allen, 1999). Specifically, "the focus shifted to dealing with individual offenders, rather than focusing on the crime that had been committed" (Latessa & Allen, 1999, p. 111). The need for individualization of treatment and punishment began to be realized, with the tenets of classical criminology being central to the implementation of treatment and punishment schemes.

Classical criminology, in addition to proportionality, emphasized that punishments must be useful, purposeful, and reasonable. Rather than employing barbaric public displays (itself being a deterrent approach) designed to frighten people into obedience through deterrence, reformers called for more moderate correctional responses. Beccaria, in advocating this shift in offender processing, contended that humans were hedonistic—seeking pleasure while wishing to avoid pain—and that this required an appropriate amount of punishment to counterbalance the rewards derived from criminal behavior. It will become clear in subsequent pages that this emphasis on proportional rewards and punishments dovetails well with behavioral psychology's views on the use of reinforcements (rewards) and punishments. Behavioral and learning theories will likewise be presented as the primary theoretical bases to effective community corrections interventions since they gibe well with the tenets of classical criminology, are easily assessed and evaluated, and are able to be easily integrated with most criminal justice program **objectives**.

Applied Theory Section 1.1

Classical Criminology, Behavioral Psychology, and Community Corrections

In addition to Cesare Beccaria, another noteworthy figure associated with classical criminology was Jeremy Bentham. Bentham is known for advocating that punishments should be swift, severe, and certain. This has been widely touted by classical criminologists and even by many modern day criminologists who have leanings toward classical and/or rational choice theories on crime. Essentially, Bentham believed that a delay in the amount of time between the crime and the punishment impaired the likely deterrent value of the punishment in the future. Likewise, Bentham held that punishments must be severe enough in consequence as to deter persons from engaging in criminal behavior. Lastly, Bentham noted that the punishment must be assured, otherwise people will simply become more clever at hiding their crimes once they know that the punishment can be avoided.

Current research actually supports some aspects of classical criminology while refuting other points. In particular, it has been found that the certainty of the punishment does indeed lower the likelihood of recidivism. Likewise, the less time between the crime and the punishment, the less likely offenders will reoffend in the future. However, it has not been found to be true that the severity of the punishment is successful in reducing crime. In fact, there has been substantial historical research on the death penalty that seems to indicate that general deterrence is not achieved with the death penalty, even though it is the most severe punishment that can be given.

Further, research on the use of prisons has shown that prisons may actually increase the likelihood of future recidivism for many offenders. Obviously, this is counterproductive to the desire of the criminal justice system. While some offenders are simply too dangerous to have released into the community, others who are not so dangerous will ultimately be returned. Among those, the goal of any sanction should be to reduce the likelihood that they will commit crime—not increase that likelihood. The research of Smith, Goggin, and Gendreau (2002) provides evidence that the prison environment may simply increase the likelihood for recidivism among many offenders. Smith et al. (2002) conducted a meta-analysis of various recidivism studies and concluded that prisons could indeed be considered "schools of crime" (p. 21). Further, they found that the longer the term of imprisonment, the more likely offenders were to recidivate. Thus, severity of the punishment does not reduce crime, and in actuality it does indeed increase the likelihood of future crime. Other studies substantiate this research.

This alone presents a valid argument against the unnecessary use of prisons—particularly when community corrections can provide effective supervision and sanctions without the reliance on prison facilities. Community corrections sanctions can be swifter in implementation, and they are much more certain in their application. For example, many offenders may be given a certain number of years in prison but will later be released early, reducing the certainty (and severity) that they will be held to serve their intended punishment. Further, the plea bargaining system in the United States provides the opportunity for the convicted to avoid incarceration entirely, even though a prison sentence would have been given for the crime that they had committed. It is then clear that the use of such pleas detracts from the certainty of the sentence.

In addition, overcrowding may delay the time during which an offender may be placed in prison, with law enforcement jail facilities holding the offender during the interim. Further, offenders are able to avoid the assumption of responsibility for their crimes when they are simply given a sentence and allowed to serve their time without being accountable to the victim and/or society. Community corrections sentencing, on the other hand, has a number of additional conditions and programs that often require that the offender make restitution, provide services, and/or pay fines to victims and/or the community (examples of these conditions will be presented in later sections). Thus, the flexibility of this type of sanctioning provides an element of certainty that offenders will be held accountable and these types of sanctions can be administered quite quickly.

In addition, many behavioral **psychologists** note that if punishment is to be effective, certain considerations must be taken into account. These considerations, summarized by Davis and Palladino (2002), are presented here:

1. The punishment should be delivered immediately after the undesirable behavior occurs (similar to the "swiftness" requirement of classical criminologists).

2. The punishment should be strong enough to make a real difference to that particular organism. This is similar to the "severity" requirement of classical criminologists, but this point also illustrates that "severity" may be perceived differently from one person to another.

3. The punishment should be administered after each and every undesired response. *This is similar to the "certainty" requirement of classical criminologists.*

4. The punishment must be applied uniformly with no chance of undermining or escaping the punishment. When considering our justice system, it is clear that this consideration is undermined by the plea-bargaining process.

5. If excessive punishment occurs and/or is not proportional to the aberrant behavior committed, the likelihood of aggressive responding increases. *In a similar vein and as noted earlier, excessive prison sentences simply increase crime, including violent crime.*

(Continued)

(Continued)

6. To ensure that positive changes are permanent, provide an alternative behavior that can gain reinforcement for the person. In other words, the use of reintegrative efforts to instill positive behaviors and activities must be supplemented for those that are criminal in nature. (pp. 262–263)

From this presentation it can be seen that there is a great deal of similarities between classical criminologists and behavioral psychologists on the dynamics associated with the use of punishment. This is actually important because it demonstrates that both criminological and psychological **theory** can provide a clear basis as to how correctional practices (particularly community corrections practices) should be implemented. The second consideration demonstrates the need for severity, but it illustrates a point often overlooked; severity of a punishment is in the eye of the beholder. For instance, some offenders would prefer to simply "do flat time" in prison rather than complete the various requirements of community supervision. This is particularly true for offenders who have become habituated to prison life. In these cases, the goal should not be to acclimate the offender to prison life but instead should be to have them acclimated to community life as responsible and productive citizens. Community corrections encourages this outcome and utilizes a range of sanctions that can be calibrated to be more or less "severe" as is needed by the individual offender. In other words, community corrections utilizes techniques from behavioral psychology/classical criminology in a manner that individualizes punishment for the offender. It is this aspect that makes community corrections a superior punishment and reintegration tool over prison. It is also for this reason that prison should be utilized only for those offenders who are simply not receptive to change and/or the assumption of responsibility for their crimes.

Though it is certain that there are exceptions, classical criminology does continue to serve as the basic underlying theoretical foundation of our criminal justice system in the United States, including the correctional components. It is indeed presumed that offenders can (and do) learn from their transgressions through a variety of reinforcement and punishment schedules that institutional and community-based corrections may provide. Not only was this presumed by John Augustus when implementing the beginning prototypes of what would later be known as formal probation, but Alexander Maconochie and Sir Walter Crofton likewise held similar beliefs when using their mark systems and methods of classifying offenders, as we will see in later sections.

It is not at all surprising that these forefathers of community corrections were affected by the work of Cesare Beccaria. Beccaria's treatise was highly regarded and publicized throughout Europe and the United States and predated each of these person's own innovations. In fact, classical criminology and Beccaria's own thoughts on crime and punishment served as the primary theoretical and philosophical basis to all forms of community corrections that existed during their time. Further, as will be seen, the works of Beccaria, the tenets of classical criminology, the contentions of each of the father figures in the early history of community corrections, the use of indeterminate forms of sanctioning as leverage and motivation in obtaining offender compliance, and the later developments in behavioral and learning psychology all share views that complement one another and are likewise congruent in nature. This then provides the primary set of theoretical and philosophical perspectives on community corrections for this text, thereby providing a consistent connection between the past and present practice of community corrections.

Thus, community corrections (probation and parole) was initially implemented to reform or reintegrate the offender. Further, if assessment of likely offender reformation is accurate, then public safety will be automatically enhanced. The job of the criminal justice system in general and that of the correctional section in particular is public safety. When further dividing the correctional section of the criminal justice system between institutional and community-based corrections, it is perhaps best explained that institutional corrections seeks public safety through incapacitation while community corrections seeks public safety through reintegration. Both are tasked with public safety as the primary function, yet each goes about achieving such protection in a different manner. Thus, as with all criminal justice functions, protection of the public is paramount, and when community corrections is concerned, the primary function is the reintegration/rehabilitation of the offender to achieve this goal.

If probation and parole are the pre- and post-incarcerative sanctions most frequently associated with community corrections, and if the philosophical basis for each is primarily one of reintegration or rehabilitation, then one must ascertain the specific theoretical approaches that should be used when achieving this function. Abadinsky (2003), in describing rehabilitation as the primary function of probation and parole, notes that there are three basic theoretical models for rehabilitation in probation and parole. These are (1) the social casework model, (2) the use of reality therapy, and (3) behavioral and/or learning theory. This text will, for the most part, incorporate Abadinsky's theoretical perspective on probation and parole for two reasons. First, the author of this current book has noted in previous publications that clinical/mental health perspectives used in the community are the best choice to use when reintegrating offenders (Hanser, 2007a). Second, the author of this text has previously pointed toward the importance of assessment and evaluation in improving current community-based correctional programs (Hanser, 2007a). Abadinsky (2003) also emphasized these points when providing his own theoretical perspective on probation and parole.

⬚ Suggested Theoretical Approach to Reintegration and Offender Treatment

According to Abadinsky, social casework provides concrete services to persons in need as a means of solving problems. The importance of social casework in probation and parole starts with theory and extends into the very skills and professional training that helping professionals are provided. These skills include such factors as effective interviewing, fact-finding in the offender's background, and the ability to identify and distinguish surface from underlying problems. These skills aid the clinician in getting a good baseline of the offender's challenges to effective reintegration. With this in mind, Abadinsky (2003) noted that there are three key components practiced in social casework, which are as follows:

1. Assessment: Gathering and analyzing relevant information upon which a treatment and a supervision plan should be based

2. Evaluation: Consisting of the organization of facts into a meaningful goal-oriented explanation

3. Intervention: Implementing the treatment plan. (p. 295)

Assessment is intended to provide the clinician and the community supervision officer (CSO) with a clear understanding of the client's current level of functioning. The presentence investigation report (PSI)—which will be discussed later in this text—is perhaps a very effective and pragmatic assessment, being a compilation of numerous areas of functioning that must be considered for each offender. This is also a good example of how supervision and treatment plans may work hand in hand to augment one another (Hanser, 2007a). Assessment includes the gathering of information from documents and through interviews with the offender as well as other persons who are familiar with the offender (Abadinsky, 2003). The need for effective assessment will be discussed in greater detail later in this text, but for the time being it is sufficient to state that assessment serves as the foundation to everything else that follows, both in relation to treatment and public safety. Thus, assessment is the cornerstone to meeting the manifest factor related to offender reintegration and the latent factor of public safety.

Evaluation is the process whereby assessment data are incorporated into the planning process to assist in goal setting for the offender. Perlman (1957) suggested that this phase of social casework includes

1. The nature of the problem and the goals sought by the client, in their relationship to

2. The nature of the person who bears the problem, his or her social and psychological situation and functioning, and who needs help with his or her problem, in relation to

3. The nature and purpose of the agency and the kind of help it can offer or make available. (pp. 168–169)

The evaluation plan takes into account both the processes and the desired outcomes for effective offender reintegration. These components must be clearly defined at the outset and both require consistent monitoring throughout the entire period of offender supervision. The most effective form of evaluation design will include a pretest (once the offender begins supervision) and a posttest (when the offender has successfully completed their sentence) to determine progress that can be attributed to either interventions that are employed or supervision regimens that are maintained.

Lastly, intervention involves activities, assignments, and routines that are designed to bring about behavior change in a systematic manner, resulting in goal-directed behavior toward the desired community supervision outcome. The specific relationship between the CSO and the offender is actually quite important. One might be surprised to find that many offenders do develop some degree of affinity for their supervision officer. Naturally, the CSO does have authority over the client and must ensure that the client maintains requirements of their supervision. Regardless of any collaboration between the offender and the officer, it is the officer's task to maintain close watch over the offender and ensure that compliance is maintained.

Reality therapy is based on the notion that all persons have two specific psychological needs: (1) the need to belong and (2) the need for self-worth and recognition. Therapists operating from a reality therapy theoretical perspective seek to engage the offender in various social groups and to motivate them in achievement-oriented activities. Each of these helps meet the two psychological needs that are at the heart of most all human beings. Further, therapists maintain a warm and caring approach, but reality therapy rejects irresponsible behavior. Therapists are expected to confront irresponsible or maladaptive behavior and are even expected to set the tone for "right" or "wrong" behavior. This is an unorthodox approach when compared to other theoretical perspectives in counseling and psychotherapy since it is often thought that therapy should be self-directed by the client. Reality therapy encourages—indeed it expects—the therapist to be directive.

In addition, reality therapy has been used in a number of correctional contexts, both institutional and community based. Indeed, the tenets of reality therapy are complementary to community supervision where direct interventions are often necessary and where a client may have to be told that they have committed a "wrong" behavior. Lastly, William Glasser (the founder of reality therapy) has expressed a great deal of support for correctional agencies in general and for CSOs in particular, but he does caution against the excessive use of punishments to correct offender behavior, especially among juvenile offenders (note that this is consistent with classical criminological concepts). This is because punishment can often serve as a justification or rationalization for further antisocial behavior, particularly if it is not proportional to the offense (especially technical offenses) and the criminogenic peer group will likely reinforce these faulty justifications. On the other hand, when a given penalty is actually proportional and is consistent with the listed sanctions, such countereffects do not seem to occur.

— Lastly, one primary theoretical orientation used in nearly all treatment programs associated with community corrections is operant conditioning. This form of behavioral modification is based on the notion that certain environmental consequences occur that strengthen the likelihood of a given behavior and that other consequences tend to lessen the likelihood that a given behavior is repeated. A primary category of behavior modification occurs through operant conditioning. Those consequences that strengthen a given behavior are called reinforcers. Reinforcers can be both positive and negative, with **positive reinforcers** being rewards for a desired behavior. An example might be if we provided a certificate of achievement for offenders who completed a life skills program. **Negative reinforcers** are unpleasant stimuli that are removed when a desired behavior occurs. An example might be if we agreed to remove the requirement of wearing **electronic monitoring** (EM) devices when offenders successfully maintained their scheduled meetings and appointments for one full year without any lapse in attendance.

Consequences that weaken a given behavior are known as punishments. Punishments, as odd as this may sound, can be either positive or negative. A **positive punishment** is one where a stimulus is applied to the offender when the offender commits an undesired behavior. For instance, we might require the offender to pay an additional late fee if they are late in paying their restitution to the victim of their crime. A **negative punishment** is the removal of a valued stimulus when the offender commits an undesired behavior. An example might be when we remove the offender's ability to leave their domicile for recreational or personal purposes (placed on house arrest) if they miss any of their scheduled appointments or meetings.

The key in distinguishing between reinforcers and punishments to keep in mind is that reinforcers are intended to *increase* the likelihood of a *desired* behavior whereas punishments are intended to *decrease* the likelihood of an *undesired* behavior. In operant conditioning, the term *positive* refers to the addition of a stimulus rather than the notion that something is good or beneficial. Likewise, the term *negative* refers to the removal of a stimulus rather than being used to denote something that is bad or harmful.

Operant conditioning tends to work best if the reinforcer or the punishment is applied immediately after the behavior (again, similar to classical criminology). Likewise, reinforcers work best when they are intermittent in nature rather than continual since the offender must exhibit a desired behavior with reward given at unpredictable points, thereby instilling a sense of delayed gratification (rather than instant gratification). Punishments, on the other hand, have been found to work best when they are in close proximal time of the undesired behavior (swift), sufficient enough to prevent repeating the behavior (severe), and when there is no means of escaping the punisher (certain). These findings have been determined through empirical research and are consistent with the notions of classical criminology, which was previously discussed. Lastly, behavioral psychologists have found that excessive punishments can (and often do) breed hostility among subjects: specific hostility toward the punisher in particular and general hostility that is generalized within the environment. Thus, this is support for Beccaria's point that punishments should not be excessive but should be proportional to the crime. To do more may unwittingly create a more hostile future offender.

◼ Legislative Response to the Community

Although the classical school may provide the foundation for many of the sentencing policies we currently utilize, legislature and policy makers continue to look for options that allow for the punishment of offenders combined with continued community safety. In spite of community sentiment that limits the ability for legislators to get reelected if seen as being too "soft on crime," no individual wants to support mechanisms that may in fact enhance criminal activity once the offender is released from an institution. Therefore, in an effort to enhance the reintegration of offenders into communities, two specific acts hold particular importance in these efforts: the Community Corrections Act (CCA) and the Second Chance Act. Each of these acts will briefly be reviewed next.

Community Corrections Act

During the early 1970s, as part of a larger commitment to involving local communities in handling offenders and an overall loss of faith by both conservatives and liberals to trust state governments to uphold rehabilitative efforts, CCAs were developed and passed. These acts specifically attempt to address the needs of local communities and the value of partnerships between state and local governments (Cromwell et al., 2002; Harris, 1996). Harris (1996) defined CCAs as "a statewide mechanism included in legislation for involving citizens and granting funds to local units of government and community agencies to plan, to develop, and to deliver correctional sanctions and services at the local level" (p. 199). The first CCA was passed in Minnesota in 1973 (Harris, 1996). Since that time, nearly all states have enacted legislation to implement community corrections agencies at the local level. Four models have been offered for states to follow: Minnesota model, Iowa model, Colorado model, and "Southern" model. There are common explicit and implicit goals within each of these models. The common goals include the following:

- Increasing public safety
- Improving local programs
- Promoting collaboration between states and the local communities
- Promoting creative options and flexibility within the community
- Providing a wide range of options within the community

Likewise, a central component of these programs is to decentralize the authority so that programs can be tailored to the local needs and citizens. CCAs also provide opportunities for local citizen involvement. For example, the state of Indiana's Community Correction legislation allows for probation and parole to be governed by the Department of Correction (DOC) directly, and these services are provided in support of that mission. (See Section VII for an example of Indiana's Community Corrections Program Elements—Indiana Criminal Code 11-12-1 et. seq.) These components require local planning supported by state funding (Harris, 1996). Although these agencies differ in terms of their responsibilities, they are designed to provide alternative reintegration strategies both at the front end and back end of the system.

Second Chance Act

Every year, over 600,000 prisoners reenter communities. In 2007, the then president Bush signed the Second Chance Act into legislation as a way to provide local communities with support in assisting offenders in a safe and successful transition back into the community from the prison. The focus of this effort is on "job training, housing, and mental health and substance abuse treatment" (Schultz, 2006, p. 22). The Second Chance Act is specifically designed to expand upon previous efforts related to offender reentry projects. Federal funds have been designated to establish the National Adult and Juvenile Offender Reentry Resource Center. Grant monies are to be distributed to local communities to assist with reducing the overlap in services, enhance mentoring programs for offenders returning to their communities, provide more drug treatment at the local level, and enhance family bonds particularly with children. Because this act is so new, no research on the effectiveness of these legislative efforts has been conducted. This effort does, however, demonstrate the commitment by federal, state, and local officials to address the needs of overcrowding within the correctional system and the need for responding to the families of those incarcerated in an effort to reduce future offending.

Community-Based Options

Fortunately for offenders and the community, alternatives to incarceration and ways to enhance reintegration back into communities continue to evolve rather than remain stagnant. As mentioned previously in this section, the need to supervise offenders in the community derives not only from issues addressing overcrowding but also the recognition that 95% of individuals entering prison return to their communities. Ultimately, the question that arises is what type of offender do you want in your community? Do you want someone with skill sets such as job retraining and who has received mental health and substance abuse counseling, when necessary, or someone who essentially was forgotten by society for an extended time period and expected to reintegrate flawlessly? Additionally, as you have seen, communities have increased the number of alternatives that give offenders the opportunities to remain in residence. Known as a continuum of sanctions, the options available allow those in the criminal justice system the opportunity to oversee these offenders in such a way to simultaneously ensure the successful reintegration of offenders and ensure community safety. Throughout this text you will be presented with a variety of different ideologies and responses to criminal behavior. DiMascio (1997) offered a general description of potential continuum of sanctions offered in communities.

> First, **probation** is viewed as the least severe sanction. This option may be used in conjunction with a suspended sentence and any other options. For this sanction, offenders meet with their probation officer periodically, albeit in person or via call-in supervision.
>
> **Intensive supervision** is an enhanced version of regular probation. With this option, offenders have increased contacts with their probation officer. Typically, these contacts begin with three to five times a week with regular drug and alcohol screenings. Contacts are diminished as the offender demonstrates success on this option.
>
> **Restitution** and **fines** are typically used in conjunction with probation, although they may be used as stand-alone sanctions. Fines are the most frequently used sanction. European countries have begun to expand the use of this sanction with the concept of proportionality in mind with the creation of day fines.
>
> **Community service** is one sanction also used as a stand-alone option or in conjunction with other community-based alternatives. This option requires offenders to voluntarily donate their time back to serving their community in many unique ways.

Substance abuse treatment referrals are often provided when the offense either includes some substance or there is evidence during the intake process that an offender needs such a referral.

Day reporting centers in theory require that offenders report to a centralized location on a daily basis to receive treatment and/or education. This alternative provides increased supervision of the offender without incarceration.

House confinement and EM programs are typically used in conjunction with some form of intensive probation supervision. Offenders are monitored very closely, being required to remain in their homes unless leaving for work, school, doctor appointments, or court appointments.

Halfway houses are used in residential settings. Although based in the community, offenders are required to remain in the house at night but are allowed to obtain employment in their respective communities. This option provides assistance for a seemingly seamless transition back into the community.

Boot camp alternatives incorporate the rigorous military style punishments. These programs are designed as short-term residential options whereby offenders are given acceptable punishments and discipline.

Prisons and **jails** serve as the final option on the continuum of sanctions. This option is used as a last resort, whereby offenders who are unable to successfully navigate the community-based options may have their sentences revoked with a short- or long-term stay in a confined setting.

Each of these options will be covered in more detail throughout the text. They are to be used as a basis for understanding the types of sanctions and alternatives utilized in the community.

◪ Conclusion

It is clear that community corrections have gone through a long and complicated process of development. Throughout this process, the specific purpose of community corrections has not always been clear. Indeed, many recognized experts, authors, and researchers offer competing views on the purpose of community corrections, resulting in a great deal of confusion and uncertainty related to the effectiveness of community-based sanctions. The importance of a clear definition as well as a clear rationale for the use of community corrections sanctions has been illustrated. Further, this section has traced the historical developments and philosophical precursors to both probation and parole. These developments help to make sense of the various challenges associated with community corrections sanctions and also provide guidance for future uses of these sanctions. Lastly, it is clear that there is a great deal of variety from state to state in regard to the community supervision process. The implementation of probation and parole comes in many shapes, forms, and methods, creating a rich yet challenging process of offender supervision in communities throughout the United States.

◪ Section Summary

- Community-based corrections includes all non-incarcerating correctional sanctions imposed upon an offender for the purposes of reintegrating that offender within the community.
- Community corrections extends beyond an alternative to incarceration to include primary sanctions as well as alternatives.

- Individuals who are reintegrated back into their communities are more likely to produce something of material value: pay restitution, court fines, victim compensation, etc. In addition, they may be involved in prosocial activities. Their informal social controls are enhanced, and their liberty is not restricted. Offenders will be able to maintain or obtain employment and seek treatment, and the effects of collateral consequences are diminished.

- The historical development of community-based corrections can be traced back to four European sanctions: (1) sanctuary, (2) benefit of clergy, (3) judicial reprieve, and (4) recognizance.

- Community-based corrections has a grounding in the four philosophies of punishment: (1) retribution, (2) deterrence, (3) incapacitation, and (4) rehabilitation. Rehabilitation and specific deterrence are geared toward the offender while general deterrence, retribution, and incapacitation are aimed toward the crime.

- Community-based correctional sanctions should incorporate the elements of social casework, which include assessment, evaluation, and intervention.

- Two legislative acts were highlighted as those influencing community-based corrections in the 21st century: CCA and the Second Chance Act.

- Community-based corrections operates on the assumption of a continuum of sanctions whereby offenders depending upon their actions may be moved up or down the continuum of level of supervision/intrusiveness.

KEY TERMS

Benefit of clergy	Incapacitation	Recognizance
Cesare Beccaria	John Augustus	Rehabilitation
Community corrections	Judicial reprieve	Retribution
Community Corrections Act (CCA)	Negative punishment	Sanctuary
	Negative reinforcers	Second Chance Act
Continuum of sanctions	Positive punishment	Specific deterrence
General deterrence	Positive reinforcers	

DISCUSSION QUESTIONS

1. How did early alternative sanctions administered in Europe influence community-based corrections as we know it today?

2. Which philosophy of punishment best describes community-based corrections? Why?

3. It can be argued that the skills necessary to supervise offenders in the community are based on the social casework model of assessment, evaluation, and intervention. What are these elements, and why are they important to incorporate into community-based corrections?

4. What are CCAs? Does your state have a CCA/division? If so, how is it structured?

5. When thinking about community-based corrections, what does it mean to say that a continuum of sanctions is used for keeping offenders within your community?

WEB RESOURCES

Council on Crime and Justice:

http://crimeandjustice.org/

Center for Community Corrections:

http://centerforcommunitycorrections.org/?page_id=78

ACT Community Coalition on Corrections:

http://www.correctionscoalitionact.org.au/

Comprehensive Community Corrections Act and Pretrial Services Act Annual Report to the Legislature July 2005–June 2006:

http://www.dcjs.virginia.gov/corrections/pretrial/annualReportFY2006.pdf

Second Chance Act—Reentry Policy:

http://www.reentrypolicy.org/government_affairs/second_chance_act

Second Chance Act of 2007:

http://www.govtrack.us/congress/bill.xpd?bill=h110-1593

National Reentry Resource Center—Second Chance Act:

http://nationalreentryresourcecenter.org/about/second-chance-act

States Want Second Chance Act Funded:

http://www.stateline.org/live/details/story?contentId=357802

Families Against Mandatory Minimums:

http://www.famm.org/Repository/Files/032008_FAQ_Second_Chance_ActFINAL.pdf

Criminon of Maine:

http://criminalrehabilitation.org/

Please refer to the student study site for web resources and additional resources.

How To Read A Research Article

As you travel through your criminal justice and criminology studies, you will soon learn that some of the best-known and emerging explanations of crime and criminal behavior come from research articles in academic journals. This book is full of research articles, and you may be asking yourself, how do I read a research article? It is my hope to answer this question with a quick summary of the key elements of any research article, followed by the questions you should be answering as you read through the assigned sections.

Every research article published in a social science journal will have the following elements: (1) introduction, (2) literature review, (3) methodology, (4) results, and (5) discussion/conclusion.

In the introduction, you will find an overview of the purpose of the research. Within the introduction, you will also find the **hypothesis** or hypotheses. A hypothesis is most easily defined as an educated statement or guess. In most hypotheses, you will find that the format usually followed is if X, Y will occur. For example, a simple hypothesis may be the following: If the price of gas increases, more people will ride bikes. This is a testable statement that the researcher wants to address in his or her study. Usually authors will state the hypothesis directly but not always. Therefore, you must be aware of what the author is actually testing in the research project. If you are unable to find the hypothesis, ask yourself what is being tested or manipulated and what are the expected results.

The next section of the research article is the literature review. At times, the literature review will be separated from the text in its own section, and at other times, it will be found within the introduction. In any case, the literature review is an examination of what other researchers have already produced in terms of the research question on prices and bike riding; we may find that five researchers have previously conducted studies on the increase of gas prices. In the literature review, the author will discuss their findings and then discuss what his or her study will add to the existing research. The literature review may also be used as a platform of support for the hypothesis. For example, one researcher may have already determined that an increase in gas prices causes more people to roller-skate to work. The author can use this study as evidence to support his or her hypothesis that increased gas prices will lead to more bike riding.

The methods used in the research design are found in the next section of the research article. In the methodology section, you will find the following: who/what was studied, how many subjects were studied, the research tool (e.g., interview, survey, or observation), how long the subjects were studied, and how the data that were collected were processed. The methods section is usually very concise, with every step of the research project recorded. This is important because a major goal of the researcher is **reliability**; describing exactly how the research was done allows it to be repeated. Reliability is determined by whether the results are the same.

The results section is an analysis of the researcher's findings. If the researcher conducted a quantitative study, using numbers or statistics to explain the research, you will find statistical tables and analyses that explain whether or not the researcher's hypothesis is supported. If the researcher conducted a qualitative study—non-numerical research for the purpose of theory construction—the results will usually be displayed as a theoretical analysis or interpretation of the research question.

The research article will conclude with a discussion and summary of the study. In the discussion, you will find that the hypothesis is usually restated, and there may be a small discussion of why this was the hypothesis. You will also find a brief overview of the methodology and results. Finally, the discussion section looks at the implications of the research and what future research is still needed.

Now that you know the key elements of a research article, let us examine a sample article from your text.

⊠ What Influences Offenders' Willingness to Serve Alternative Sanctions?

David C. May and Peter B. Wood

1. What is the thesis, or main idea, from this article?

   - The thesis, or main idea, of this article can be found in the introductory paragraph. In this study, the authors argue that much of the literature relative to offenders serving their sentence in the community is related to community satisfaction. In this study, the authors contend that successful completion of a sentence may be contingent upon the offenders' perception of the severity of the sanction, therefore calling into question the viability of a continuum of sanctions that is being used within community-based corrections.

2. What is the hypothesis?

   - Again, the hypothesis can be found in the introductory paragraph and later at the end of the literature review in the form of research questions. In this study, the hypothesis is stated as "What demographic, correctional experience, and attitudinal indicators make one more likely to avoid a sanction altogether?" and "What demographic, correctional experience, and attitudinal indicators help predict the amount of an alternative offenders will endure to avoid one year of imprisonment?"

3. Is there any prior literature related to the hypothesis?

   - This article does have a section devoted to the previous literature. Albeit brief, May and Wood select those studies that have assessed offenders' willingness to serve non-incarcerative sanctions. They use the previous works to identify the weaknesses in the research and to develop their research questions and hypotheses.

4. What methods are used to support the hypothesis?

   - May and Woods' research methodology is referred to as cross-sectional survey methodology. In this study, they identify 800 offenders serving nonviolent sentences in the Oklahoma DOC for inclusion on the study. A survey was administered to each of these offenders by their case managers. Just over 51% agreed to participate ($n = 415$). The authors argue that this is a comparative sample to other studies conducted on this subject.

5. Is this a qualitative study or quantitative study?

   - To determine whether the study is qualitative or quantitative, you must look to the statistical analysis and the results. In this study, the authors use a multivariate statistical analysis to explore what influences the offenders' willingness to serve. Because May and Wood use numerical statistics to examine the hypothesis, it is safe to say that this study is quantitative.

6. What are the results, and how do the authors present the results?

   - Because this is a quantitative study, the results are found in the results section, the discussion, and further summarized in the conclusion. The results are presented in the original article in table format with detailed explanation in the text of how the authors conducted the statistics and the results. The results are then interpreted in the discussion section by variable. For this study, the key findings suggested that younger inmates, those with higher levels of education, women, those who were married, and those who had served the proposed alternative previously were more likely to agree to the various presented sanctions than their counterparts. This study points to the need to further examine community-based sanctions as being viewed as "soft" on crime. As illustrated by one fourth of participants refusing to serve any time in the community and the mixed results of those who consider it, the overall intrusion in the lives of offenders combined with relatively generous good time and release policies may be worth the gamble to offenders to avoid being supervised in the community. Likewise, those with the greatest bonds to their communities and those with the most to lose if incarcerated appear to be willing to make the sacrifice of serving their sanction in the community and avoiding the stigmatization of serving time behind bars.

7. Do you believe that the authors provided a persuasive argument? Why or why not?

   - This answer is ultimately up to the reader to decide by examining the research questions/hypotheses, the methods employed, and the ultimate findings. We believe based upon the methodology and the results that the authors do present a persuasive argument that the idea of a continuum of sanctions may not truly exist. Further, with an understanding of other theoretical literature, the finding that those offenders who have the greatest bonds to society are most willing to serve the sentences there are also those offenders who are least likely to recidivate.

8. Who is the intended audience of this article?

   - When reading the article, you must ask yourself who/whom is/are the authors intending to read this study and how might it inform those individuals. After reading this article, you should be able to ascertain that May and Wood are writing for students, professors, criminologists, agency personnel, and policy makers.

9. What does the article add to your knowledge of the subject?

   - Again, this question is best left to the reader to decide. However, one way to answer the question is as such: Previous research has explored the public satisfaction with offenders serving their sentences in the community. This study expands that literature by asking those serving these sentences not only were they willing to serve them but what factors increased their likelihood of willingness to serve a particular sentence. The results offer some insight to policy makers on how to reconcile not only community sentiment for punishment but increase the likelihood for successful reintegration and rehabilitation of the offender.

10. What are the implications for criminal justice policy that can be derived from this article?

- The implications of the study can be found in the conclusion. In this study, the authors explicitly identify three policy implications. To summarize, first, they contend that the results call into question whether a continuum of sanctions actually exists and whether it is successful. Second, they find that perceptions of the sanction may differ based upon which sanctions are being proposed to a particular offender. The offenders' willingness to serve a particular sanction may be based more on their personal circumstances (e.g., job, family, or physical prowess) than the mere existence of options. So these external circumstances should be taken into consideration. The third and final implication of the research addresses the use of multivariate statistics and the ability to expand the literature by exploring the relationship between factors such as demographics, education, etc., and the offenders' willingness to serve. The results reveal that the relationship is rather complex and the administering of sanctions should not be completed with a one size fits all mentality.

Now that we have gone through the elements of a research article, it is your turn to continue through your text, reading the various articles and answering the same questions. You may find that some articles are easier to follow than others, but do not be dissuaded. Remember that each article will follow the same format: introduction, literature review, methods, results, and discussion. If you have any problems, refer to this introduction for guidance.

READING

In this essay, Andrew von Hirsch explored the ethical dilemmas faced by increasing the use of noncustodial sanctions. The author identified two specific areas of ethical concerns faced by those administering noncustodial sanctions: (1) proportionality (just deserts) and (2) the level of intrusiveness into the privacy of one's life—particularly for third parties. In terms of proportionality, von Hirsch pointed to the disjuncture between what "works" and the severity of the sanction. As illustrated by the previous research, most programs are considered effective if the offender does not return to the attention of the system. This, however, does not consider the punitiveness of the sanction relative to the harm caused to society. This is particularly troublesome when the use of alternatives such as intermediate sanctions essentially turns the individuals' home into a prison. Although attractive in their presentation, these sentences may not serve to meet the proportionality needs of the system, the victim, or the offender.

When considering the fallacies of intrusiveness, von Hirsch pointed to the flaws in the arguments that anything is better than prison and that intrusiveness is a matter of technology and issue of legalism. Based upon his review of both the proportionality of sanctions and the intrusiveness into the daily lives of individuals, von Hirsch devised what he termed the acceptable penal content. It is within this framework that he argued we should consider both custodial and noncustodial sanctions. In his conclusion, von Hirsch cautioned policy makers to consider as we further develop the use of community-based alternatives that we may in fact be creating a mechanism for further humiliating and damaging the lives of offenders than the use of incarceration strategies.

The Ethics of Community-Based Sanctions

Andrew von Hirsch

Imprisonment is a severe punishment, suited only for grave offenses. Crimes of lesser and intermediate gravity should receive nonincarcerative sanctions. Such sanctions long were underdeveloped in the United States, and it is gratifying that they are now attracting interest. Noncustodial penalties, however, raise their own ethical questions. Is the sanction proportionate to the gravity of the crime? Is it unduly intrusive, upon either defendants' human dignity or the privacy of third persons?

In the enthusiasm for community-based sanctions, such issues are easily overlooked. Harsh as imprisonment is, its deprivations are manifest—and so, therefore, is the need for limits on its use. Noncustodial penalties seem humane by comparison, and their apparent humanity can lead us to ignore the moral issues. As Allen (1964) warned us two decades ago, it is precisely when we seem to ourselves to be "doing good" for offenders that we most need to safeguard their rights.

SOURCE: von Hirsch, A. (1990). The ethics of community-based sanctions. *Crime & Delinquency, 36*(1), 162–173. Copyright © 1990 by Sage Publications, Inc.

This essay will address two kinds of ethical issues involved in noncustodial sanctions. One concerns just deserts: that is, the proportionality of the sanction to the gravity of the crime of conviction. The other issue—or, as we will see, cluster of issues—concerns the "intrusiveness" of the sanction, that is, the constraints that are needed to prevent punishments in the community from degrading the offender or threatening the rights of third parties.

⊠ Proportionality and Desert

The issue of proportionality in community-based sanctions has suffered a double neglect. Desert theorists, when writing on proportionality and its requirements, tended to focus on the use and limits of imprisonment, paying little attention to community sanctions. Reformers involved in developing these sanctions, meanwhile, gave little thought to proportionality.

The disregard of proportionality has reinforced a tendency to assess community-based sanctions principally in terms of their effectiveness. If a program (e.g., an intensive supervision scheme) seems to "work" in the sense of its participants having a low rate of return to crime, then it is said to be a good program. Seldom considered are questions of the sanction's severity and of the seriousness of the crimes of those recruited into the program.

Imprisonment is obviously a severe punishment, and its manifestly punitive character brings questions of proportionality into sharp relief. Noncustodial measures, however, are also punishments—whether their proponents characterize them as such or not. A sanction levied in the community, like any other punishment, visits deprivation on the offender under circumstances that convey disapproval or censure of his or her conduct. Like any other blaming sanction, its degree of severity should reflect the degree of blameworthiness of the criminal conduct.[1] In other words, the punishment should comport with the seriousness of the crime.

The punitive character of noncustodial sanctions, however, is often less visible to those who espouse them. Because these sanctions are often advertised as more humane alternatives to the harsh sanction of imprisonment, the deprivations they themselves involve are often overlooked. Because the offender no longer has to suffer the pains of confinement, why cavil at the pains the new program makes him or her suffer in the community?

Such attitudes are particularly worrisome when it comes to the newer noncustodial sanctions, which include such measures as intensive supervision, community service, home detention, and day-fines.[2] These sanctions often involve substantial deprivations: intensive supervision and home detention curtail an offender's freedom of movement, a community-service program exacts enforced labor, a day-fine may inflict substantial economic losses. Part of the attraction of these programs has been that their more punitive character gives them greater public credibility than routine probation and, hence, makes them plausible substitutes for imprisonment. In short, these are sanctions of intermediate severity. But then it must be asked: Are the offenses involved serious enough to make the sanction a proportionate response? Often, the answer to this question is no. Clear (this issue) points out that intensive supervision programs tend to be applied to offenders convicted of the least serious felonies because program organizers feel that such persons would be more likely to "cooperate."

When devising community penalties, reformers should ask themselves about the proportionality of the sanction. They might begin by posing a few simple questions. First, how serious are the crimes that the proposed sanction would punish? Seriousness is a complex topic (see von Hirsch, 1985, ch. 6), but rough-and-ready assessments should be possible. For example, several sentencing commissions (most notably, those of Minnesota, Washington, and Pennsylvania) have explicitly ranked the gravity of crimes on a rating scale (von Hirsch, Knapp, and Tonry, 1987); those rankings could be drawn upon, supplemented by common-sense arguments about the appropriateness of particular rankings.

Second, how severe is the proposed sanction? Severity is likewise a complex topic (see von Hirsch, Wasik, and Greene, 1989), but, again, a common-sense assessment is possible. If one assumes routine probation to be lenient and imprisonment to be severe, one can make a comparative judgment of the onerousness of the proposed sanction. This would involve inquiring about the extent of restriction of freedom of movement, of monetary deprivation, etc., and it should yield a rough assessment of whether the sanction is mild, intermediate, or more severe. In assessing severity, the preventive as well as punitive aspects of the sanction should be considered. An intensive supervision program that, for example, involves curfews or periods of home detention invades personal liberty to a significant extent, and is therefore quite severe. This holds true whether the purpose of the detention is to punish or to restrain or cure.

Asking such questions will put reformers in the position to begin to make judgments about commensurability. Potential mismatches will begin to become apparent, for example, the imposition of sanctions of intermediate or higher severity on lesser crimes.

There are more sophisticated models available for gauging commensurability that are applicable to noncustodial penalties. One actual project—the Vera Institute's day-fine project in Staten Island, New York—has developed explicit standards: Crimes are rated on a seriousness scale, and monetary penalties are arrayed accordingly (Greene, 1988). Theoretical models are also beginning to develop. I refer interested readers to a general account of how desert principles apply to community punishments (von Hirsch et al., 1989), as space does not permit me to summarize these views here.

✍ Common Fallacies of "Intrusiveness"

When we consider the potential intrusiveness of sanctions, we enter less-explored territory. Whereas an extensive literature on desert exists,[3] less thought has been devoted to what makes a punishment unacceptably humiliating or violative of others' privacy. We might begin by clearing away the underbrush, that is, putting aside some commonly heard fallacies.

One fallacy is the anything-but-prison theory. Intervention in the community is tolerable irrespective of its intrusiveness, this theory asserts, as long as the resulting sanction is less onerous than imprisonment. This is tantamount to a carte blanche: Because imprisonment (at least for protracted periods) is harsher than almost any other community punishment, one could virtually never object.

The anything-but-prison theory is a version of the wider misconception that an individual cannot complain about how he or she is being punished if there is something still worse that might have been done instead. The idea bedeviled prison policy for years: Prisoners should not complain of conditions because they might have fared worse—been held longer or in nastier conditions, or even been executed. The short answer is that a sanction needs to be justified in its own right, not merely by comparison with another—possibly more onerous—punishment.

The theory also rests on the mistaken factual supposition that all those who receive the proposed community sanction would otherwise have been imprisoned. That is almost never the case. Many, if not the bulk, of those receiving the new community sanctions are likely to be persons who otherwise would have received a conventional noncustodial sanction such as probation instead.

A second fallacy is that intrusiveness is a matter of technology. The installation of an electronic monitor on an offender's telephone elicits comparisons to "Big Brother," but no similar issues of privacy are assumed to arise from home visits by enforcement agents. The mistake should be obvious: Orwell's totalitarian state may have relied on two-way television screens, but the Czarist secret police achieved plenty of intrusion without newfangled gadgetry. The same point holds for noncustodial sanctions. Intrusion depends not on technology but on the extent to which the practice affects the dignity and privacy of those intruded upon. Frequent, unannounced home visits may be more disturbing than an electronic telephone monitor that verifies the offender's presence in the home but cannot see into it.

A third fallacy is legalism. Intrusiveness, in this view, is a matter of whether the practice infringes on specific constitutional requirements. The U.S. Constitution does not give much consideration to the treatment of convicted offenders, and such provisions as are germane have been restrictively interpreted. Those provisions do not exhaust the ethical requirements the state should abide by in the treatment of offenders. This has been understood where proportionality is concerned. The Eighth Amendment (as now construed) outlaws only the most grossly dispropor-tionate punishments,[4] but the state should (and some jurisdictions have) gone further in safeguarding desert requirements.[5] The same should hold true for the pre-sent issues of "intrusiveness." When a program is devel-oped, its sponsors should ask themselves not only whether it passes constitutional muster but whether there are any substantial ethical grounds for consider-ing it humiliating or intrusive.

⊠ Dignity and "Acceptable Penal Content"

The idea of "intrusiveness" is actually a cluster of concepts, and we need to identify its component elements. One important element is the idea of dignity—that offenders should not be treated in a humiliating or degrading fashion. We need to inquire why convicted criminals should be punished with dignity and how this idea can be put into operation in fashioning punishments.

The Rationale for "Dignity" in Punishment

To inquire into the rationale for the idea, we might begin with a passage from the philosopher Jeffrie Murphy:

> A punishment will be unjust (and thus banned on principle) if it is of such a nature as to be degrading or dehumanizing (inconsistent with human dignity). The values of justice, rights and desert make sense, after all, only on the assumption that we are dealing with creatures who are autonomous, responsible, and deserving of the special kind of treatment due that status. . . . A theory of just punishment, then, must keep this special status of persons and the respect it deserves at the center of attention. (Murphy, 1979, p. 233)

What this passage reflects is the idea that convicted offenders are still members of the moral community and that they remain persons and should

be treated as such. Someone's status as a person would ordinarily militate against any sort of insulting or demeaning treatment. With offenders, however, there is a complication—the nature of punishment itself. Punishment not only serves as a deprivation but also conveys blame or censure (von Hirsch, 1985, ch. 3). Blame, because it embodies disapproval of the offender for his or her conduct, is necessarily unflattering. What is left, then, of the idea that punishment should not humiliate its recipient?

The answer lies in the communicative character of blaming. Blame, Duff (1986) has pointed out, conveys disapproval addressed to a rational agent. The function of the disapproval is not only to express our judgment of the wrongfulness of the act but to communicate that judgment to offenders in the hope that they will reflect upon it and reevaluate their actions. We may wish offenders to feel ashamed of what they have done, but the shame we are trying to elicit is their own shame at the conduct, not merely a sense of being abased by what we are doing to them. The more one treats wrongdoers in a demeaning fashion, the more this entire moral process is short-circuited. When prisoners are made to walk the lockstep—to shuffle forward, with head down and eyes averted—they are humiliated irrespective of any judgment they might make about the propriety of their conduct. The shame comes not from any accep-tance of the social judgment of censure but simply from the fact that they are being treated as inferior beings.

Punishments, therefore, should be of the kind that can be endured with self-possession by persons of rea-sonable fortitude. These individuals should be able to undergo the penalty (unpleasant as it inevitably is) with dignity, protesting their innocence if they feel they are innocent or acknowledging their guilt if they feel guilty—but acknowledging it as a person, not a slave, would do. A person can endure the deprivation of various goods and liberties with dignity, but it is hard to be dig-nified while having to carry out rituals of self-abase-ment, whether the lockstep, the stocks, or newer rituals.

Acceptable Penal Content

How do we apply this idea of dignity? One way would be to try to identify and list the various kinds of intrusions we wish to rule out as undignified. But as intrusion on dignity is a matter of degree, this would be no easy task. It would be particularly difficult for non-custodial sanctions because these may be so numerous and variable in character.

A better approach, I think, is through the idea of "acceptable penal content." The penal content of a sanction consists of those deprivations imposed in order to achieve its punitive and preventive ends. Acceptable penal content, then, is the idea that a sanction should be devised so that its intended penal deprivations are those that can be administered in a manner that is clearly consistent with the offender's dignity. If the penal deprivation includes a given imposition, X, then one must ask whether that can be undergone by offenders in a reasonably self-possessed fashion. Unless one is confident that it can, it should not be a part of the sanction.

Where prisons are concerned, we already have the kernel of this idea, expressed in the maxim that imprisonment should be imposed as punishment but not for punishment. The idea is that the deprivation of freedom of movement should be the main intended penal deprivation—that while it is severe (and hence suitable only for serious crimes), such deprivation per se can be endured without self-abasement. According to this maxim, the intended penal content should not include various possible sanctions within the prison because we have no guarantee that these can be undergone with dignity. It thus would be inappropriate, for example, to prescribe solitary confinement as the punishment for designated crimes. And notice that one need not determine whether each possible sanction-within-the-prison is unduly humiliating. The idea that prison exists only as and not for punishment serves precisely as a prophylactic rule, to endorse only that deprivation—of liberty—that we think can be decently imposed and not to authorize all kinds of further impositions whose moral acceptability is in doubt. Granted, the reality of American prisons is different, with numerous unconscionable deprivations occurring. But we consider them unconscionable precisely because they lie outside the sanction's acceptable penal content.

Once we have specified the acceptable penal content of the sanction, we may also have to permit certain ancillary deprivations as necessary to carry the sanction out. Imprisonment, for example, involves maintaining congregate institutions and preventing escapes or attacks on other inmates and staff. Segregation of some violent or easily victimized offenders for limited periods may be necessary for such purposes, even if not appropriate as part of the intended penal content in the first place. But these ancillary deprivations must truly be essential to maintaining the sanction.

Can these ideas be carried over to noncustodial penalties? I think they can. The first step would be to try to identify the acceptable penal content for such penalties. Certain kinds of impositions, I think, can be undergone with a modicum of self-possession, and thus would qualify. These would include deprivations of property (if not impoverishing); compulsory labor, if served under humane conditions (community service, but not chain-gang work); and limitation of freedom of movement. Clearly excluded, for example, would be punitive regimes purposely designed to make the offender appear humbled or ridiculous. An example is compulsory self-accusation, e.g., making convicted drunken drivers carry bumper stickers indicating their drinking habits. There is no way a person can, with dignity, go about in public with a sign admitting himself or herself to be a moral pariah. We may wish the offender to feel ashamed of what he or she has done—but not act as though he or she is ashamed, whatever he or she actually feels. This list of acceptable and unacceptable intrusions is far from complete, and I shall not try to complete it. I am merely suggesting a mode of analysis.

That analysis should be applied not only to the expressly punitive but also to the supposed rehabilitative features of a program. Deprivations administered for treatment are still penal deprivations and can be no less degrading than deprivations imposed for expressly punitive or deterrent ends. I would, for example, consider suspect a drug program in the community that involves compulsory attitudinizing. One may wish to persuade the offender of the evils of drug use and, for that purpose, deny him or her access to drugs or other stimulants. But if we try to compel the offender, as part of the program, to endorse attitudes about drug use that he or she does not necessarily subscribe to, we are bypassing his or her status as a rational agent.

After we have specified the acceptable penal content, there comes the question of ancillary enforcement measures. These are measures that are not part of the primary sanction—the intended penal deprivation—but are necessary to ensure that that sanction is carried out. An example is home visits. Such visits are not a part of acceptable penal content: It is not plausible to assert that, without any other need for it, the punishment for a given type of crime should be that state agents will periodically snoop into one's home. The visits could be justified only as a mechanism to help enforce another sanction that does meet our suggested standard of acceptable penal content.

What might such a sanction be? Consider the sanction of community service, which I have suggested does meet the primary standard. To assure attendance at work sites and check on excuses for absences, occasional home visits may be necessary and indeed are part of the enforcement routine of the Vera Institute's community service project (McDonald, 1986). Because home visits are justified only as an ancillary enforcement mechanism, their scope must be limited accordingly, that is, be no more intrusive than necessary to enforce the primary sanction. If home visits are ancillary to community service, they should occur only when the participant has failed to appear for work, and their use should be restricted to ascertaining the offender's whereabouts and checking on any claimed excuse. The less connected the visits are with such enforcement and the more intrusive they become, the more they are suspect. General, periodic searches of the offender's home could not be sustained on this theory.

Telephone monitoring can be analyzed in similar fashion. A phone monitor, used to enforce a sentence of home detention, would be an acceptable ancillary measure if designed so that the defendant can simply register his or her presence. Repeated and searching verbal phone inquiries would be another matter.

Unresolved Issues

The analysis still has a number of loose ends. Thus:

1. Are there any principled limits on the ancillary enforcement sanctions, other than their being essential to enforce the primary penalty? Enforcement sanctions that are grossly humiliating should be ruled out, even if needed as an enforcement tool for a particular kind of primary sanction. If X is an acceptable sanction but needs Y—a morally repulsive one—to enforce it, then the appropriate solution would be to give up X in favor of some other sanction that can be enforced less intrusively. I leave to future discussion how we might specify more clearly such a limit on enforcement measures.

2. Can one ever argue for intrusions on dignity in order to create noncustodial sanctions with a punitive "bite" comparable to that of imprisonment? Consider a range of fairly serious crimes for which imprisonment would normally be the sanction. May one substitute home detention, with specially intrusive conditions designed to make the sanction "equivalent" to the prison? My instinct would be to resist such a suggestion if those conditions are sufficiently demeaning to infringe on the principles just described. For here, imprisonment is not an undeserved response, given the seriousness of the conduct. The alternative is objectionable because of its degrading character.

3. What of choices of evils? Suppose a jurisdiction inappropriately uses imprisonment for crimes of intermediate or lesser severity and is prepared to substitute a noncustodial sentence only if it is made highly intrusive. Here, proportionality concerns collide with concerns about dignity—and may require one to decide which value should be accorded higher importance, Such an apparent choice, however, is most likely to arise in poorly regulated sentencing systems in which proportionality constraints and controls over discretion are weak. That, however, is precisely the kind of system in which such purported "alternatives" to incarceration so easily become, instead, substitutes for traditional and less noxious noncustodial penalties.

⊠ The Rights of Third Parties

The prison segregates the offender. The segregation, whatever its other ills, means the rights of third parties are not directly affected. If X goes to prison, this does not restrain Y's rights of movement, privacy, etc. Granted, Y still suffers if he or she is attached to X or economically dependent. But Y, nevertheless, is not restrained.

Noncustodial penalties reintroduce the punished offender into settings in which others live their own existence. As a result, the offender's punishment spills over into the lives of others. Home visits, or an electronic telephone monitor ringing at all hours of the day, affects not only the defendant but any other persons residing at the apartment—and it is their as well as his or her dwelling place.[6]

The third-party question is distinct from the issue of the offender's dignity, as discussed earlier. That is true even when the latter issue is affected by the presence of third parties. Consider home visits. Such visits may be potentially shaming to the defendant in part because of the presence of unconvicted third-party witnesses, that is, the other residents of the home. But the visits also affect those other residents, diminishing their own sense of privacy.

However, such other persons, are often affected because they have some consensual[7] relation to the defendant, for example, they share the defendant's home. Here lies the difficulty: Granted that the quality of their lives may suffer, but have they not in some sense assumed that risk? When A chooses to live with B, will not A inevitably suffer indirectly from whatever adverse consequences legitimately befall B as a consequence of his or her behavior? It is this issue—the extent to which third parties lose their right to complain—that requires more reflection. I have not been able to think of a general answer to this relinquishment-of-rights question. The following modest steps, however, might help to reduce the impact of noncustodial punishments on third parties:

1. Often, it is not the primary sanction itself but its ancillary enforcement mechanism that intrudes into the lives of third parties (to cite a previous example, home visits used to enforce community service). In such cases, the enforcement mechanism should be limited to enforcing the primary sanction and should not be used to investigate the general extent to which other persons abide by the law. When the defendant's home is visited to check on his or her excuse for being absent at the work site, for example, that should not be used as an occasion to gather evidence of law violations by others in the apartment.

2. The impact on third persons should be one of the criteria used in choosing among noncustodial penalties. Often, the sanctioners may have several sanctions of approximately equal severity to choose from, any of which would comport with crimes of a given degree of seriousness. Where that choice is available, the sanctioner should, other things being equal, choose the sanction that affects third parties least. Suppose, for example, that the choice lies between home detention (enforced by a telephone monitor) and a fairly stiff schedule of community service (enforced by home visits to check the offender's presence, but only when he or she fails to appear at the work site). Suppose, for the sake of argument, that the penalties have been calibrated to be of approximately equal severity (see von Hirsch et al., 1989). If we conclude that the occasional home visits used to enforce community service are less disturbing to other residents than a (frequently ringing) telephone monitor used with home detention, that would be reason for preferring community service.

✑ Conclusions

This essay provides more questions than answers. Concerning the first issue, that of proportionality, I have some sense of confidence because there has been an extensive literature on desert. Concerning the second issue, that relating to dignity and humiliation, I have tried to offer the rudiments of a theory, but it stands in need of development. Concerning the third, intrusion into the rights of third parties, I have done little more than raise some issues.

Because innovative noncustodial penalties are only beginning to be explored in this country, little thought has been devoted to limits on their use. Such thinking is now urgently necessary. With adequate ethical limits, community-based sanctions may become a means of creating a less inhumane and unjust penal system. Without adequate limits, however, they could become just another menace and extend the network of state intrusion into citizens' lives. We should not, to paraphrase David Rothman,[8] decarcerate the prisons to make a prison of our society.

Notes

1. For a discussion of how the idea of censure or blame underlies the principle of proportionality, see von Hirsch (1985, chs. 3, 5).

2. For a survey of such penalties, see Tonry & Will (1989).

3. See e.g., von Hirsch (1976, 1985), Singer (1979), and Duff (1986).

4. See e.g., Rummel v. Estelle, 445 U.S. 263 (1980), Solem v. Helm, 463 U.S. 277 (1983).

5. In particular, the states that have adopted sentencing guidelines that emphasize desert principles. See von Hirsch, Knapp, and Tonry (1987, chs. 2, 5). Some foreign jurisdictions—most notably Sweden—have also adopted statutes on choice of sentence, stressing ideas of proportionality and desert. See von Hirsch (1987) and, for the English-language text of the statute as enacted, von Hirsch and Jareborg (1989).

6. For a brief previous discussion of this question of third parties, see von Hirsch and Hanrahan (1979, pp. 109–12).

7. Any children present will not have actually consented, however.

8. The original quotation appears in von Hirsch (1976, pp. xxxv–xxxvi).

References

Allen, Francis A. 1964. *The Borderland of Criminal Justice*. Chicago: University of Chicago Press.

Duff, R. A. 1986. *Trials and Punishments*. Cambridge, England: Cambridge University Press.

Green, Judith A. 1988. "Structuring Criminal Fines: Making an 'Intermediate Penalty' More Useful and Equitable." *Justice System Journal* 13:37.

McDonald, Douglas C. 1986. *Punishment Without Walls: Community Service Sentences in New York City*. New Brunswick, NJ: Rutgers University Press.

Murphy, Jeffrie G. 1979. *Retribution, Justice, and Therapy*. Dordrecht, Netherlands: D. Riedel.

Singer, Richard G. 1979. *Just Deserts: Sentencing Based on Equality and Desert*. Cambridge, MA: Ballinger.

Tonry, Michael and R. Will. 1989. *Intermediate Sanctions*. Washington, DC: Government Printing Office.

von Hirsch, Andrew. 1976. *Doing Justice: The Choice of Punishments*. New York: Hill & Wang. Reprinted 1986, Boston: Northeastern University Press.

———. 1985. *Past or Future Crimes: Deservedness and Dangerousness in the Sentencing of Criminals*. New Brunswick, NJ: Rutgers University Press.

———. 1987. "Principles for Choosing Sanctions: Sweden's Proposed Sentencing Statute." *New England Journal on Criminal and Civil Confinement* 13:171.

——— and K.J. Hanrahan. 1979. *The Question of Parole: Retention, Reform, or Abolition?* Cambridge, MA: Ballinger.

——— and N. Jareborg. 1989. Sweden's Sentencing Statute Enacted. *Criminal Law Review* :275.

DISCUSSION QUESTIONS

1. What does von Hirsch mean by the use of "acceptable penal content"? According to the author, how should this shape the current sentencing structure in the United States?

2. According to von Hirsch, how do noncustodial sentences impact third parties?

3. What can be done to increase the privacy of third parties when noncustodial sentences are administered?

4. Given that individuals who are sentenced have committed offenses not only against the victim but society as a whole, why should we be concerned with the ethics of community-based sanctions?

READING

In their seminal work, May and Wood explored the impact of demographic, correctional experience, and attitudinal indicators on the willingness of offenders to serve community-based sanctions in lieu of one year of incarceration. A total of 800 offenders serving time in the Oklahoma correctional system were surveyed with 415 (51%; 181 male, 224 female, and 10 not reporting sex) agreeing to participate. Because at the time of the study Oklahoma had the third highest female incarceration rate in the United States, women were oversampled by 50%. Survey participants were presented with descriptions of alternatives to incarceration and asked to report how many months of the alternative sanction they would be willing to serve to avoid incarceration. Overall, the results indicate that 25% of the survey participants (1 in 4) refused to participate in any form of community-based alternative. Of those who did agree, results suggested that education, age, sex, the amount of time served, previous experience with the alternative, and reported bonds to their community influenced their decisions to participate and the overall reported length of time. Younger inmates, those with higher levels of education, women, those who were married, and those who had served the proposed alternative previously were more likely to agree to the various presented sanctions than their counterparts. This study points to the need to further examine community-based sanctions as being viewed as "soft" on crime. As illustrated by one fourth of participants refusing to serve any time in the community and the mixed results of those who consider it, the overall intrusion in the lives of offenders combined with relatively generous good time and release policies may be worth the gamble to offenders to avoid being supervised in the community. Likewise, those with the greatest bonds to their communities and those with the most to lose if incarcerated appear to be willing to make the sacrifice of serving their sanction in the community and avoiding the stigmatization of serving time behind bars.

What Influences Offenders' Willingness to Serve Alternative Sanctions?

David C. May and Peter B. Wood

Alternatives to incarceration have become increasingly popular in an attempt to deal with rising costs and overcrowded conditions of prisons in the United States. Although many alternative sanctions are no more effective in reducing recidivism than prison (see Marion, 2002, for review), lawmakers, judges, and the public generally support the notion of a continuum of punishment options with graduated levels of supervision and punishment severity (Morris & Tonry, 1990; Petersen & Palumbo, 1997). To date, few studies have examined the opinions of those most affected by the punishment continuum, the offenders

SOURCE: May, D. C., & Wood, P. B. (2005). What influences offenders' willingness to serve alternative sanctions? *The Prison Journal*, 85(2), 145–167. Copyright © 2005 by Sage Publications, Inc.

(Apospori & Alpert, 1993; Crouch, 1993; McClelland & Alpert, 1985; Petersilia, 1990; Petersilia & Deschenes, 1994a, 1994b; Spelman, 1995; Wood & Grasmick, 1999; Wood & May, 2003). Prior research has tended to present uni- and bivariate data analysis that focuses on demographic correlates of offenders' perceptions of the relative severity of a wide range of sanctions when compared to imprisonment. As such, the available literature (with the possible exception of Spelman, 1995) does not include the study of offenders' perceptions of the severity of alternative sanctions in a multivariate context. The current study helps fill this gap in the literature by using demographic, correctional experience, and attitudinal indicators to predict the amount of regular probation, community service, and boot camp that offenders will serve to avoid 1 year of actual imprisonment. Analysis is based on a survey of 415 male and female inmates serving prison terms for nonviolent crimes.

Experience in correctional settings—their longest sentence served and the total amount of time they have spent in prisons and jails—was also collected. We also included a race identification item in the pretest survey but were counseled by personnel from the Oklahoma Department of Corrections (ODOC) to delete it. At the time of the survey, the ODOC was conducting a racial balance study of its inmate population. ODOC personnel were concerned that race-specific findings might be politically sensitive and might discourage some inmates from participating in the survey. Although the inclusion of race-specific findings was of interest to us, we submitted to their request and removed the race item from the instrument. Finally, based on offenders' comments regarding their reluctance to enroll in alternative sanctions, we included items examining reasons why an offender might participate in an alternative and reasons why an offender might avoid participation.

By the end of 1955 (the year of the survey), there were 17,983 inmates serving time in Oklahoma correctional centers. Approximately 2,800 of these inmates met our selection criteria. Our initial sample of 875 accounts for approximately 31% of these inmates, and approximately 5% of the total inmate population.

Although the sample consisted of 875 male and female inmates who met our criteria (nonviolent controlling offense, no history of violence, and less than a 5-year sentence), we determined that slightly fewer than 800 inmates were available to participate in the survey. Some had been released by the time the survey was administered, some had been transferred to another institution, and some were serving an administrative sanction and were unable to participate in the survey. Many inmates who were eligible simply refused to participate in the survey. We concluded data collection with 415 respondents (181 men, 224 women, and 10 who did not report their gender) representing better than a 50% response rate based on those inmates available for participation. This response rate compares very favorably with other voluntary, self-administered surveys conducted in correctional centers (Wood & Grasmick, 1999).

In 1995, Oklahoma claimed the third highest incarceration rate in the nation, and the highest female incarceration rate of all 50 states—a distinction we felt was significant enough to warrant special attention. Furthermore, a review of the published literature on the relative punitiveness of punishments revealed no previous work examining female offenders' perceptions of the severity of alternative sanctions. Consequently, we oversampled women so they made up one half of our sample and just more than 50% of our survey respondents.

During October, the survey was administered in classroom settings to small groups of inmates who met the selection criteria, had been randomly sampled, and who voluntarily agreed to participate. All data analysis reported here is based on an initial sample of 415 inmates.

⬛ Dependent Variable

Respondents were presented with descriptions of several alternative sanctions and then were asked to consider how many months of the alternative they were willing to serve to avoid 12 months of actual imprisonment. In the current study, we focused on respondents' perceptions of the relative severity of probation, community service, and boot camp when compared to 12 months incarceration in a medium-security prison. We assume that if a respondent will serve fewer than 12 months of an alternative sanction to avoid 12 months of imprisonment, the alternative is perceived as more punitive than prison. If the respondent will serve more than 12 months of the alternative to avoid 12 months of imprisonment, then imprisonment is viewed as more punitive.

Recent work (Wood & Grasmick, 1999; Wood & May, 2003) suggests that the alternatives examined in the current study are viewed by people under correctional supervision as among the least punitive (regular probation and community service) and among the most punitive (boot camp) alternatives available. As the primary purpose of the current study was to examine offenders' perceptions of the severity of sanctions in a multivariate context, we felt it would be useful to compare sanctions viewed as less and more severe than prison to see if the impact of demographic, experiential, and attitudinal indicators varies by type of alternative.

Demographic and Correctional Experience Predictors

A number of demographic and experiential variables are represented in the models that follow. These include respondents' gender, age, education (years), marital status, number of children, total time spent in prison (months), and the length of their longest prison stay (months). In addition, we controlled for whether the respondent had previously served the alternative in question (regular probation, community service, or boot camp), and the total number of different alternatives they have ever served. We hypothesized that those respondents who are female, older, married, more educated, have children, have less prison experience, and have previous experience with the sanction in question will (a) be more likely to serve an alternative and (b) endure a longer duration of each alternative rather than serve 1 year of imprisonment.

Attitudinal Predictors

Three scales were created to reflect offenders' attitudes about alternative sanctions. First, respondents were asked to indicate the importance of eight statements as reasons for choosing to avoid participation in an alternative sanction. Responses to the statements were coded so that a higher score on the Avoidance Scale reflects greater agreement with reasons to avoid alternative sanctions We expect those scoring at the high end of the Avoidance Scale will be more likely to avoid alternative sanctions and will view alternative sanctions as more punitive when compared to prison than those scoring at the lower end of the scale.

Second, respondents were asked to indicate the importance of six statements (very important, pretty important, somewhat important, not at all important) as reasons for choosing to participate in an alternative sanction. Response to the statements were coded so that a higher score on the Participation Scale reflects greater agreement with reasons to participate in alternative sanctions We expect those scoring at the high end of the Participation Scale will be more likely to participate in alternative sanctions and will view alternative sanctions as less punitive when compared to prison than those scoring at the lower end of the scale.

Third, respondents were asked to rate the importance (very important, pretty important, somewhat important, not at all important) of three community bonds (i.e., having a job, spouse, and/or children outside prison) as reasons to participate in alternatives. Responses to the statements were coded so that a higher score on the Community Bond Scale reflects greater agreement that such bonds are important reasons to participate in alternatives We expect those scoring at the high end of the Community Bond Scale will be more willing to participate in alternative sanctions and will view alternative sanctions as less punitive than those scoring at the lower end of the scale.

Multivariate Results

Recent work suggests that some offenders view alternative sanctions as unacceptable options, no matter what the length of the sentence, and would rather be sentenced to prison than serve any length of an alternative (Spelman, 1995; Wood & Grasmick, 1999; Wood & May, 2003). Given this finding, it seems important to determine what factors contribute to an offender's refusal to serve any amount of an alternative sanction, or conversely, to agree to participate in an alternative.

Logistic regression results suggest that, as expected, offenders with higher levels of education were significantly more likely to choose to participate in probation and boot camp than their counterparts who were less educated. Furthermore, younger respondents were significantly more likely to agree to participate in regular probation, community service, and boot camp. In addition, those with prior experience serving boot camp and community service (but not probation) were significantly more likely to agree to participate in those sanctions compared to offenders with no prior experience while those respondents who scored higher on the Participation Scale were significantly more likely to agree to participate in boot camp and community service (but not probation). Respondents who had served fewer alternatives were also significantly more likely to indicate that they would participate in community service, as were those who scored higher on the Community Bond Scale. Neither of these variables had a significant association with the choice to participate in either probation or boot camp.

Finally, offenders who scored higher on the Avoidance Scale were significantly less likely to participate in all of the alternative sanctions in question. Thus, the associations between the demographic, experiential, and attitudinal predictors and the respondent's choice to participate in alternatives were in the hypothesized direction, and with the exception of gender and total prison time, each variable had a statistically significant impact on the decision to participate in at least one of the alternative sanctions under study. The only notable exception involves married individuals, who were significantly more likely to say they would serve some probation, but significantly less likely to say they would participate in boot camp—an association likely due to the restrictive visitation and home visit regulations governing boot camp. More will be said of this finding in the concluding section.

It appears, then, that the variables included in the models do a better job of predicting the choice to participate in community service than probation and boot camp. Furthermore, the impact of the demographic, experiential, and attitudinal predictors—with the exception of age and the Avoidance Scale—appears contingent on the type of sanction in question.

The OLS regression results from the reduced model predicting the duration of each alternative (measured in months) that respondents would serve to avoid 12 months imprisonment. Offenders who refused to serve any duration of the alternative were deleted from the analysis. It is immediately obvious that while gender had no effect on whether an individual chose to participate in an alternative sanction, it is one of the better predictors of the amount of each alternative offenders are willing to serve, as females would serve longer durations of probation, community service, and boot camp to avoid 12 months in prison than would males.

In addition, the results indicate that offenders with higher levels of education will serve fewer months of probation to avoid 12 months imprisonment than those with less education. Similarly, older prisoners will serve fewer months of community service to avoid 12 months imprisonment than their younger counterparts. Both of these associations achieve statistical significance.

Regarding correctional experience indicators, inmates with more time in prison were willing to serve more community service than offenders with less cumulative time in prison. In addition, those inmates who had served a greater variety of alternative sanctions will serve fewer months of probation and community service to avoid imprisonment than those who had experienced fewer alternative sanctions.

The association between the amount of an alternative sanction the individual was willing to serve and the three attitudinal scale measures (avoidance, participation, and community bond) also proved to be interesting. Offenders who scored higher on the Avoidance Scale would serve fewer months of probation than those with more favorable views of alternative sanctions but were willing to serve more months of boot camp to avoid 12 months imprisonment. Although this may appear counterintuitive, the discussion below makes a number of suggestions for its occurrence. In addition, while the Participation Scale and the Community Bond Scale were important predictors of whether offenders chose to serve any duration of certain alternative sanctions, their explanatory power diminishes greatly when considering the length of time an individual would serve to avoid imprisonment. Analysis generated only one significant—and potentially counterintuitive—association as those individuals who scored higher on the Participation Scale were likely to serve fewer months of boot camp to avoid imprisonment than those with less favorable views of alternatives. This finding is discussed below.

Discussion

This research offers the first multivariate study of offenders' perceptions of the severity of alternative sanctions compared to prison and, by extension, identifies some of the factors that influence offenders' willingness to serve alternatives. Based on the review of the research in this area, a number of hypotheses were tested in this study. Of those hypotheses, most were supported for at least one alternative sanction and, in some cases, for all three alternative sanctions. The effects of demographic, experiential, and attitudinal predictors on offenders' perceptions of the punitiveness of probation, boot camp, and community service are presented below.

Education

No previous research has examined the relationship between the education level of a person under correctional supervision and her or his perception of the relative severity of criminal justice sanctions while controlling for other relevant factors. Results indicate that inmates with higher levels of education were significantly more likely to agree to participate in boot camp and probation but not community service. However, when asked to compare the length of time they would be willing to serve to avoid 1 year of imprisonment, those with higher levels of education would

endure fewer months of probation than their less educated counterparts. This inverse relationship contrasts directly with the expected relationship between education and the choice of whether to participate in probation. It is apparent those inmates with greater levels of education are willing to serve some probation but would not serve as much of it as those with less education. Possibly these individuals are more discriminating in realizing the value of serving an alternative while also recognizing that the risk of revocation increases with time spent serving an alternative (see Wood & Grasmick, 1999; Wood & May, 2003). As such, it may be that inmates with more education employ a more conservative cost-benefit analysis that encourages them to participate in probation to avoid prison but also takes into account the gamble associated with serving more time in an alternative.

Age

Results indicate that age affects both the decision to engage in alternative sanctions and the amount of an alternative offenders are willing to serve to avoid imprisonment. Younger inmates are significantly more likely to agree to participate in all the alternative sanctions and more likely to agree to serve more community service than older inmates. We suggest two possible explanations for this finding. First, older prisoners may view alternative sanctions as more of a gamble than younger ones. They may feel that the chances of revocation are too high and realize that if they fail to complete the sanction they will be returned to prison to serve out their original sentence, thus extending their time under correctional supervision. Consequently, they may feel that their total time under correctional supervision may be shorter if they avoid alternative sanctions altogether and go directly to prison to serve out their term. An alternative explanation is that older prisoners may have become accustomed to incarceration, now view it as less severe compared to when they were younger, and thus feel more comfortable serving their time incarcerated than in the community. This analysis does not offer a conclusive finding in this regard, and future research should attempt to explore the intricacies of this dynamic.

Gender

One of the most interesting findings from the current study concerns the relationship between gender and our dependent variables. While gender had no significant impact on whether an inmate decided to participate in an alternative sanction, it had a significant effect on the length of time an individual was willing to serve to avoid imprisonment. Females were willing to serve more months of each of the three sanctions to avoid imprisonment than were men. Multivariate analyses suggest that the impact of gender on an offender's choice to engage in alternative sanctions is mediated by other variables in the model, while the impact of gender on the amount of the alternative remains, even when controlling for other relevant factors. Thus, these findings lend qualified support to the widely accepted belief that females may prefer alternative sanctions because they tend to have stronger ties to family and community than do men. For example, 79.5% of the women in our sample have children; however, only 19.3% are married. It is possible that many women may opt for longer durations of alternatives to avoid imprisonment to retain custody of or contact with children. Further study of the unique circumstances of female inmates may shed light on this issue.

Marital Status

Married respondents were significantly more likely to agree to participate in probation but significantly less likely to agree to do any amount of time in boot camp. Thus, something about either marriage, boot camp, or probation induces married respondents to refuse to serve boot camp but not probation. Among those willing to serve an alternative sanction, marital status had no impact on the length of time an individual was willing to serve in that alternative sanction. We suspect that the restrictive nature of boot camp (limited visitation rights, limited or no phone calls, limited or no mail privileges, no community release, etc.) may discourage married persons who wish to maintain regular community ties from participating. The married inmate may view boot camp as much harsher than prison and choose not to engage in any duration of that sanction. Thus, it could be that although married respondents

are more likely to agree to participate in some alternative sanctions, the fact that boot camp requires that the offender be separated from family in a highly stressful environment may affect the decision to participate in boot camp. Inmates in the sample were twice as likely to refuse to participate in boot camp as the other two sanctions. We suggest that the more intrusive nature of boot camp makes it more likely to be an unpopular alternative sanction among inmates in general, but particularly among married inmates.

Total Prison Time Served

Individuals with more experience in a prison setting were more likely to agree to participate in community service; however, the overall impact of incarceration does not make an individual more likely to agree to participate in alternative sanctions than those with less prison experience. We suspect the effect of total time served is highly associated with the effect of age. As noted above, older inmates are less likely to serve alternatives, and it is those inmates who have served more time. Findings indicate that persons with more prison experience are less willing to serve alternative sanctions and would prefer to serve prison instead. This finding contradicts the idea of the traditional probation to prison severity continuum; if prison were perceived by inmates as significantly more punitive than alternatives, then persons with more prison experience should be more willing to serve alternative sanctions and to serve longer lengths of alternative sanctions to avoid imprisonment. With the exception of the length of time inmates would endure on community service, this was not the case.

Number and/or Variety of Alternative Sanctions Served

Those individuals who had the most experience with alternative sanctions were significantly less likely to agree to participate in any length of community service than their counterparts who had less experience with alternative sanctions. In addition, when those who refused to participate in alternative sanctions were excluded, those who had the most experience with a variety of intermediate sanctions would serve less time in probation and community service than offenders who had less experience with alternative sanctions. This finding again challenges the concept of the probation to prison severity continuum.

Avoidance Scale

As expected, results indicate that inmates who agreed most strongly with reasons to avoid alternative sanctions were significantly less likely to participate in probation, community service, and boot camp. When asked how much of an alternative they would serve to avoid imprisonment, however, those who scored higher on the avoidance index would serve shorter lengths of probation but longer lengths of boot camp. Although this relationship may appear to be counterintuitive, there is at least one possible explanation. Those individuals with more negative views toward alternative sanctions were less likely to agree to participate in them; nevertheless, this model included those respondents willing to serve some duration of the alternative sanction. As such, it may be that when individuals who refuse to serve the three alternatives are removed from the analysis (23.6% for boot camp, 12.3% for probation, and 9.4% for community service), the equation changes somewhat. It may be that although still opposed to boot camp for the reasons mentioned in the index, the offender understands that the time served in boot camp will be much shorter than 12 months in prison if he or she successfully completes the sentence. Only 4% of the sample agreed to do as much as 12 months boot camp to avoid 12 months imprisonment while almost two thirds (64.8%) of the sample said they would be willing to do less than seven months boot camp to avoid 12 months in prison. It seems likely that some offenders who oppose alternative sanctions are willing to spend a few months in boot camp simply because they want the extra 2 to 5 months of their life they would gain in comparison to 12 months imprisonment. Future studies should explore exactly why offenders choose to avoid alternative sanctions in an attempt to provide substantive explanations for findings such as this.

Participation Scale

As expected, inmates who agreed more strongly with reasons to participate in alternative sanctions were

significantly more likely to participate in boot camp and community service. However, after removing those offenders who refused to participate in any amount of boot camp, offenders scoring higher on the participation scale would serve fewer months of boot camp. This again appears counterintuitive. It could be that the negative stigma and conditions that surround boot camp discussed earlier make it an anomaly when it comes to alternative sanctions. The statements used to compose the index do not deal directly with any specific alternative sanction; as such, when the inmates were stating their views of alternative sanctions in general, they may not have been thinking about boot camp as one of the alternative sanctions. Consequently, when asked about their willingness to participate in boot camp specifically, they agreed to do so but are not willing to invest a large amount of time in boot camp when compared to the alternative of prison. Although prison still carries a negative stigma, it may not be as negative as that attached to boot camp, and offenders may believe that the so-called "easier" time might be in prison than in boot camp.

Community Bond Scale

As expected, inmates who were more likely to agree that community bonds were important reasons to serve alternative sanctions were more willing to participate in community service. However, contrary to expectations, this index had nonsignificant effects on all other dependent variables. Thus, the nature of the offender's social bond may not be as important in structuring the decision to participate in alternative sanctions as the other elements included in the proalternative sanctions scale. However, there may be other dimensions of community and family ties that are not represented in our measure, and more effort should be made to identify community and family bonds that might influence offenders' perceptions of alternative sanctions.

Previous Experience With the Alternative in Question

Having served the particular alternative sanction in question influences the decision whether to serve that alternative again and the amount of time the offender is willing to invest in that sanction (except in the case of probation). Individuals with prior boot camp experience were significantly more likely to agree to participate in boot camp and to serve more of it to avoid imprisonment than their counterparts who had not previously served boot camp; these relationships were replicated for community service. This may be due to at least two reasons: (a) inmates with prior experience with the sanction had success with the specific sanction previously and are willing to try it again and/or (b) inmates are now more willing to participate in the alternative sanction because it is no longer an unknown. Inmates with no prior experience may fear an unknown alternative sanction. These relationships deserve to be examined in future studies.

◼ Conclusion

Implications from the current study are threefold. First, the findings presented here again call into question the idea of a continuum of alternative sanctions with probation as the least punitive sanction and prison as the most punitive sanction. One in four inmates refused to participate in any amount of boot camp to avoid 12 months in prison; furthermore, in certain circumstances, some offenders would rather do prison than either probation or community service, two sanctions most often placed at the lenient end of the sanction continuum. At the very least, results call for further exploration into the perceived severity of criminal justice sanctions.

Second, it appears that the associations between demographic, experiential, and attitudinal predictors and perceptions of sanction severity are contingent on the type of sanction in question. Boot camp is perceived by inmates as a significant gamble, with a high likelihood of revocation, and 23.6% of inmates in the sample refused to serve any duration of boot camp to avoid a brief prison term. One of the reasons boot camp is such an unpopular option is probably due to the nature of boot camps in general. At least one former inmate has suggested that boot camp amounted to "institutionalized embarrassment" wherein one's very

manhood is questioned constantly by being forced to do things one would not do otherwise. The military regimen and the total authority, and influence boot camp drill instructors have over prisoners (even more than prison) also play a role. Many prisoners view boot camp as the embodiment of every forced treatment program they have encountered and will avoid it at all cost. According to some inmates, those who volunteer for boot camp are "punks" who are willing to subject themselves to institutionalized embarrassment and who are afraid to serve time in the general prison population. Relatedly, one might expect that persons with no prior prison experience might be more willing to do boot camp, and to do more of it to avoid imprisonment. Boot camp, therefore, is not only viewed as highly punitive with a strong likelihood of revocation but also carries a strong stigma among many inmates. As one ex-convict responded when questioned about boot camp, asking a prisoner to choose between prison and boot camp is similar to asking a political scientist from a democracy to choose between communism and fascism; in one, you lose control over your economic situation (prison) and in the other, you lose control over every aspect of your life (boot camp). Differences in offenders' perceptions of alternative sanctions may, therefore, depend partly on the type of sanction in question. In this respect, boot camp may be deserving of a special category when speaking of alternative sanctions.

Finally, use of multivariate procedures like those used in the current study allows a more comprehensive look at factors that influence offenders' perceptions of the severity of a range of criminal justice sanctions. Larger samples across several jurisdictions and the inclusion of a wider variety of predictors are likely to offer a better understanding of these dynamics. Furthermore, we would argue that the nature of the relationships uncovered in the current study is complex; as such, future research should attempt to include open-ended, qualitative research to more fully understand offenders' reasons to choose to participate in or avoid alternative sanctions. In sum, then, as the popularity and application of alternative sanctions increases, it might help judges, prosecutors, and legislators to be cognizant of how offenders view the severity of prison when compared to alternative sanction. By doing so, sentencing strategies could be devised that protect society, potentially deter crime, and reduce the cost to taxpayers to fund imprisonment.

☒ References

Apospori, E., & Alpert, G. (1993). Research note: The role of differential experience with the criminal justice system in changes in perception of severity of legal sanctions over time. *Crime & Delinquency, 39,* 184–194.

Crouch, B. M. (1993). Is incarceration really worse? Analysis of offenders' preferences for prison over probation. *Justice Quarterly, 10,* 67–88.

Marciniak, L. M. (1999). The use of day reporting as an intermediate sanction: A study of offender targeting and program termination. *The Prison Journal, 79*(2), 205–225.

Marion, N. (2002). Effectiveness of community-based correctional programs: A case study. *The Prison Journal, 52*(4), 478–497.

McClelland, K. A., & Alpert, G. (1985). Factor analysis applied to magnitude estimates of punishment seriousness: Patterns of individual differences. *Journal of Quantitative Criminology, 1,* 307–318.

Morris, N., & Tonry, M. (1990). *Between prison and probation: Intermediate punishments in a rational sentencing system.* New York: Oxford University Press.

National Institute of Justice. (1993). *Intermediate sanctions (Research In Brief).* Washington, DC: Office of Justice Programs, U.S. Department of Justice.

National Institute of Justice. (1995). *National assessment program: 1994 survey results.* Washington, DC: Office of Justice Programs, U.S. Department of Justice.

Petersen, R. D., & Palumbo, D. J. (1997). The social construction of intermediate punishments. *The Prison Journal, 77,* 77–92.

Petersilia, J. (1990). When probation becomes more dreaded than prison. *Federal Probation, 54,* 23–27.

Petersilia, J., & Deschenes, E. P. (1994a). Perceptions of punishment: Inmates and staff rank the severity of prison versus intermediate sanctions. *The Prison Journal, 74,* 306–328.

Petersilia, J., & Deschenes, E. P. (1994b). What punishes? Inmates rank the severity of prison vs. intermediate sanctions. *Federal Probation, 58,* 3–8.

Spelman, W. (1995). The severity of intermediate sanctions. *Journal of Research in Crime and Delinquency, 32,* 107–135.

Wood, P. B., & Grasmick, H. G. (1999). Toward the development of punishment equivalencies: Male and female inmates rate the severity of alternative sanctions compared to prison. *Justice Quarterly, 16,* 19–50.

Wood, P. B., & May, D. C. (2003). Race differences in perceptions of the severity of sanctions: A comparison of prison with alternatives. *Justice Quarterly, 20,* 605–631.

DISCUSSION QUESTIONS

1. What factors specifically influenced an offenders' decision to serve alternative sanctions?

2. What significance was there in the finding that one quarter of all survey respondents reported they would not choose to serve any form of community-based alternative to imprisonment?

3. Based upon the findings of the study, should offenders be allowed to serve the same community-based sanction? Why or why not?

4. Based upon the findings, should offenders be given different sanctions based upon their sex, age, race, and education level?

5. What do the findings suggest for judges when sentencing offenders to community-based alternatives?

READING

In this reading, the authors pointed to the necessary conversations that states need to entertain regarding the need for policy reform in light of diminishing resources and the pursuit of punishment and enhanced public safety. More specifically, the authors overviewed the three goals of punishment (expressive, utilitarian, and managerial) and combine those with the current state of punishment. A sample of six states that at the time of the study were considering reforming their sentencing laws as well as their responses to crime was taken. A review of major newspapers revealed a shift in policy approaches from a more retributive response of increased imprisonment to considerations for budgetary and economic responses to crime. The authors further pointed to the opportunities for reformers to enter into conversations with legislative bodies about how to reform the system in difficult economic times.

When the Policy Becomes the Problem

Criminal Justice in the New Millennium

Sara Steen and Rachel Bandy

⧉ Introduction

The importance of state legislatures in the development, oversight, and funding of US criminal justice policy cannot be overstated. Over the past 30 years, legislatures have become increasingly responsible for setting crime and punishment agendas, agendas that have been marked by a return to a corrections model based on the philosophy of retributive justice. Because most crimes fall under state jurisdictions, state legislatures' development of policies reflective of retributive justice has had far-reaching consequences, most notably the unprecedented growth in incarceration rates and the concomitant growth in state corrections expenditures (Snell et al., 2003). As many states today face their largest budget crises in recent history, legislators are now forced to consider whether, and if so how, adherence to a criminal justice philosophy of retribution can be sustained in light of diminishing resources.

The scope of the criminal justice enterprise in the United States has increased dramatically since the mid-1970s. The incarceration rate for state and federal prisoners (excluding offenders held in local jails) has almost doubled each decade, increasing from 135 per 100,000 US residents in 1978 to 244 in 1988 to 460 in 1998. Growth has slowed since then, reaching a national incarceration rate of 482 in 2003 (Harrison and Beck, 2004). Including prisoners held in local jails, the incarceration rate reached 714 in 2003, which translates into one in every 140 US residents being confined in a state or federal prison or a local jail. As a result of this rapid expansion in incarceration, state corrections expenditures were the second fastest growing component of state budgets during the 1990s (Snell et al., 2003).

In 1970, spending on prisons accounted for 1.5 per cent of state and local spending, compared to 4.3 per cent in 2000 (Ziedenberg and Schiraldi, 2002). Throughout this period, there were also national shifts

SOURCE: Sara Steen and Rachel Bandy (2007). When the policy becomes the problem: Criminal justice in the new millennium. *Punishment & Society, 9*(1), 5–26.

in the philosophy of punishment away from rehabilitation and treatment toward just deserts and retribution. Grasmick et al. (1992) identify two watershed cases that served to augur in an era of retributive crime policy: Furman v. Georgia in 1972 and Gregg v. Georgia in 1976. Both of these cases were argued before the US Supreme Court and addressed, specifically, the use of capital punishment and, broadly, the role of retribution in punishment. While the Furman ruling invalidated the use of capital punishment and later the Gregg ruling reinstated its use, at the core of each ruling (and found in both majority and dissenting opinions) was the appropriate role of retribution in US penal policy. While the role of retribution in deciding penal policy was a divisive issue for the justices, the prevailing sentiment was that 'public opinion, including the public's presumed desire for retribution, can be a legitimate basis for penal policy' (Grasmick et al., 1992: 21). From this point in modern history, Grasmick et al. mark the formal adoption of retribution as a guiding principle in criminal justice policy-making.

The rise in retribution as a guiding principle for punishment contributed to the development of, support for, and ultimately passage of state policies such as Three-Strikes and mandatory sentencing laws, both of which have generated great costs to corrections budgets. In addition, the federal government encouraged retributive policies by offering states financial incentives to implement certain laws (e.g., Truth in Sentencing laws) and to construct new prisons.

It is increasingly clear that, left unchecked and unchallenged, retributive sentiments can easily result in extremely costly systems of punishment; systems that in the current economic climate have proven to be no longer sustainable. This article originated with the recognition that economic concerns may have re-opened conversations about the wisdom and viability of retributive policies, conversations that have been stifled for almost three decades. Legislators who spent the cash-rich '90s passing 'Tough on Crime' policies based almost exclusively on concerns about retribution and public safety are now having to revisit those policies to determine whether or not they represent a fiscally appropriate response to crime. We begin with the proposition that the economic crisis of the early 21st century has created a context in which old ideas about punishment may have become unconvincing, and new ideas (or old ideas that have been ignored in recent decades) may have newfound validity.

Our primary interest in this article is in how advocates for reform speak about less retributive sentencing practices in a time of fiscal constraint, and in how this might be changing public discourse about crime and punishment more generally. To analyze conversations about reform, we identify the terms and issues used to frame recent debates in a sample of newspaper articles published during 2003 legislative sessions in six sample states. Specifically, we examine arguments set forth by a variety of reform advocates in states which are seeking to change their sentencing structures in times of fiscal constraint.

◾ Theoretical Background

Recent scholarship has begun to explore what Stanley Cohen (1985) termed 'visions' of social control. David Garland (1990: 180) argues that historically there have been two dominant visions of social control—'the passionate desire to punish' (expressive in nature) and 'the rationalistic concern to manage' (instrumental in nature). While there are elements of each vision in any system of punishment, Garland argues that, at any given time and place, one vision is more likely to resonate with the populace than the other. For the purpose of this article, the issue is not whether penal policy itself is expressive or instrumental, but rather whether under present budgetary circumstances policymakers perceive certain types of reform arguments as likely to be more palatable than others to a public that has become accustomed to retributive rhetoric.

In this section of the article, we first briefly contrast the beliefs underlying both expressive/passionate and instrumental/rational policies as a way of framing our analyses of conversations about punishment. We also briefly review recent scholarship on the managerial model of punishment, which provides a third way to think about punishment. We then describe the conclusions reached by scholars about the relative weight of instrumental and expressive concerns in our system of punishment over the past 30 years as a point of departure for our analyses of public conversations about legislative reforms taking place in 2003.

☒ Goals of Punishment

Expressive Goals

From a Durkheimian perspective, punishment is first and foremost a mechanism through which moral values are taught and enforced. Durkheim theorized that 'the essence of punishment is not rationality or instrumental control—though these ends are superimposed upon it—the essence of punishment is irrational, unthinking emotion fixed by a sense of the sacred and its violation' (Garland, 1990: 32). Indeed, whether a particular form of punishment is successful in reducing crime is essentially irrelevant according to Durkheim. It is the cultural content of punishment, rather than its outcome, that is its defining feature, and cost is not a logical consideration.

> The expressive mode [of reasoning] is . . . overtly moralistic, uncompromising, and concerned to assert the force of sovereign power. The penal measures associated with this expressive, sovereign approach tend to be fueled by collective outrage and a concern for symbolic statement. . . . [This way of thinking] presses the imperatives of punishing criminals and protecting the public, 'whatever the cost'. (Garland, 1990: 191)

According to legal scholar and former justice Robert Bork, the need to express moral outrage and to seek retribution is:

> indispensable . . . in the criminal justice system. The mixture of reprobation and expiation in retribution is sometimes required as a dramatic mark of our sense of great evil and to reinforce our respect for ourselves and the dignity of others. (2005)

Utilitarian Goals

In contrast to the expressive mode of reasoning, utilitarian models recognize crime control as the paramount goal of punishment. Utilitarian reasoning does not privilege one form of punishment over another; rather, it advocates for punishment that most effectively and efficiently controls crime. Absent knowledge regarding their efficacy in controlling crime, rehabilitation, deterrence, and incapacitation are all, therefore, equally viable goals and strategies. In summarizing the relationship between utilitarianism and justice, Nolan (2001: 162) says that 'the principal aim of punishment is the utilitarian concern of promoting the well-being of society, not justice pet se'.

Managerial Goals

Managerial goals privilege the management of an offender population over all other punishment goals. While frequently consistent with utilitarian models of punishment, an emphasis on management shifts the focus from the individual offender to offenders in the aggregate, with the task for criminal justice agents being to sort those offenders according to their risk to society and then manage them accordingly. Cohen (1985: 147) says that:

> For some time, now, the few criminologists who have looked into the future have argued that 'the game is up' for all policies directed to the criminal as an individual, either in terms of detection (blaming and punishing) or causation (finding motivational and causal chains). The technological paraphernalia previously directed at the individual will now be invested in cybernetics, management, systems analysis, surveillance, information gathering, and opportunity reduction.

☒ The Current State of Punishment

In trying to understand the dramatic increase in rates of incarceration that has occurred over the past three decades, a number of scholars have pointed to ideological shifts in popular and professional views of punishment (Tonry, 1996; Beckett, 1997; Garland, 2001). Garland (2001), for example, talks about recent laws as representing attempts to act out 'punitive urges' (p. 173), and suggests that the prison has become much more explicitly 'a mechanism of exclusion and control' (p. 177). Similarly, Tonry (1996: 3) argues that virtually all states and the federal government have passed laws since the 1980s based on 'the premise that harsher penalties will reduce crime rates'. This premise is supported by a shift in the underlying view of punishment:

> Some other governing rationale for sentencing policy was bound to take the place left empty when rehabilitation lost favor. In both academic and policy circles, that place was taken (sometimes implicitly) by retribution or 'just deserts'. (Tonry 1996: 3)

Most accounts suggest that, between the 1970s and the beginning of the 21st century, systems of punishment in the United States moved sharply away from utilitarian goals (such as rehabilitation) toward more expressive goals of punishment (specifically, retribution). This shift—toward retribution and a concomitant shift in the power to punish away from criminal justice decision-makers to popularly elected legislative bodies (Garland, 2001)—resulted in unprecedented increases in the scope of the punishment apparatus in the United States.

In the 1970s, all state and federal systems were based on indeterminate sentencing. In an indeterminate system, decision makers (both judges and correctional officials) have a great deal of discretion, allowing them to tailor sentences to individual offenders. Under indeterminate sentencing, the primary goal of punishment is generally rehabilitation, so sentence type and length vary depending on the needs and progress of the individual. In the mid-1970s, amidst growing disillusionment with treatment and growing distrust of the state correctional system, a justice or just deserts model of punishment began to gain support (MacKenzie, 2001). Under this model, the driving ideal was that the punishment should fit the crime rather than the criminal.

While at its purest, this model is strictly retributionist and punishment is not required to serve any utilitarian purpose (von Hirsch et al., 1976), many viewed the justice model (particularly in relation to the treatment model that preceded it) as serving the utilitarian goal of deterrence. By mandating certain penalties for crimes, reformers hoped to increase the deterrent capacity of the law, thereby increasing effective crime control. While one of the fundamental principles of the justice model was 'a commitment to the most stringent limits on incarceration' (von Hirsch et al., 1976: xxxix), the model was more frequently used to justify harsher penalties in the name of deterrence.

With the move from rehabilitation to just deserts came shifts at both the state and federal levels of government from indeterminate sentencing systems to determinate sentencing systems, whereby specific crimes warranted specific sentences and judicial discretion was sharply reduced. Both a cause and a result of this change was the shift in the power to punish away from criminal justice decision makers toward legislative bodies. It was at this juncture, according to Franklin Zimring, that 'punishment became a political issue' (Beiser, 2001). In a study of the politics of law and order, for example, Stuart Scheingold (1991: 15) talks about 'the cultural resonance of punitive values' and argues that politicians have increasingly turned to crime policy as a venue for increasing their political currency. David Garland (2001) argues that the intensified role of legislators in the conversations pertaining to the goals of justice and the means of achieving them increased the likelihood that expressive goals would supersede instrumental goals. He argues that, as the criminal justice system 'became more politicized in the 1980s and 1990s, the balance of forces often shifted away from the logic of administration and expert decision-making towards a more political and populist style' (Garland, 2001: 113).

The importance of this shift in explaining the retributive policies passed in the 1980s and 1990s cannot be overstated. Expressive policies designed to convince the disgruntled American public that something was being done to address the crime problem rendered the symbolic functions of punishment (what people believe about punishment) more important than its instrumental functions (what punishment actually accomplishes). With widespread disillusionment about the ability of the criminal justice system to accomplish such lofty goals as rehabilitation, attention shifted to incapacitation as a means of controlling crime (if offenders are locked up, they cannot commit crimes on the outside). Incapacitation was appealing in that it also served the symbolic function of establishing criminal offenders as 'others' and removing them from law-abiding society. Indeed, Zimring and Hawkins argue that, during the 1980s, incapacitation came to be seen as 'the *dominant justifying aim* of all incarceration' (Zimring and Hawkins, 1991: 88, italics added).

Numerous examples of criminal justice reforms passed over the past 25 years could be characterized as explicitly expressive reforms, and many are also focused on incapacitating offenders. Garland (2001: 173) argues that:

> [Laws like Megan's Law and Three Strikes] represent a kind of retaliatory law-making, acting out the punitive urges and controlling anxieties of expressive justice. Its chief aims are to assuage popular outrage, reassure the public, and restore the credibility of the system, all of which are political rather than penological concerns.

These political concerns are derived largely from an increased fear of crime and a belief in what Scheingold (1984) calls 'the myth of crime and punishment'. Harkening back to Durkheim, Scheingold suggests that 'there is . . . a strong affective side to the attractions of the myth of crime and punishment, and this affective component provides the real key to understanding the attractions of the myth of crime and punishment in times of crisis' (1984: 65).

In this article we look at the possibility that the sense of crisis (as it relates specifically to crime) may have abated enough to allow for consideration of non-retributive policies. We also explore the possibility that the economic crisis faced by most states in the early 21st century has eclipsed the earlier crisis, and that conversations about crime and punishment have expanded to explicitly consider the costs of punishment as a relevant factor in sentencing policy.

▧ Data and Methods

Sample

For the current study, we have chosen six states on which to focus our attention. We used a number of criteria to select these states. First, and most importantly, we wanted to find states in which a reasonable amount of sentencing reform activity was happening during the 2003 legislative session. This required that more than one or two isolated sentencing reform bills were introduced and debated. Using summary reports from the Justice Policy Institute, the Sentencing Project, and the Drug Policy Alliance, we identified those states entertaining sentencing reform measures and sought to build a sample that consisted of diverse reform initiatives. We also wanted a sample that was geographically representative, leading us to select at least one state each from the Northeast, the Southeast, the Midwest/Central region, the Pacific Northwest, and the West. Our sample states include New York, Arkansas, Wisconsin, Iowa, Washington, and Nevada.

The newspapers chosen as data sources were selected based on the following criteria: they posted their articles on Lexus Nexus, they had a wide readership (relative to other newspapers in the state), and they regularly covered the legislative session. Several newspapers per state were reviewed for data.

While most states started their legislative sessions in early to mid-January, the ending dates varied across sample states. This is important because it means that our sampling frame varied, and we gathered more articles from some states (particularly NY and WI) than others (particularly AR and WA). Additionally, we see that only the states of Wisconsin and Iowa did not call for special legislative sessions; a move made by the other sample states so that budget issues could be finalized. Legislative discussions which occurred during special sessions were considered within this research.

While not included as formal criteria for inclusion in the sample, we also looked at the size of state prison populations, state rankings of budget crises, and the extent of prison overcrowding in each state to get a sense of the context in which these legislative conversations were occurring.

The states in our sample vary widely in the number of state prisoners they house (ranging from approximately 8000 in Iowa to over 67,000 in New York). Part of this difference, of course, is related to differences in population. Prison population rates (column 3) adjust for state population, and show states ranging from 259 prisoners per 100,000 population (WA) to almost 500 prisoners per 100,000 population (NV). There is less variation in prison capacity—only two states in our sample (AR and NV) were not operating their prisons over their allotted capacity at the end of 2002. We also see considerable variation in the level of fiscal stress these states face; two of our sample states (NV and NY) ranked numbers 4 and 5 in terms of their budget deficits going into fiscal year 2003, while one of our other sample states (AR) ranked number 41.

Table 1.1 displays changes over time (1970-2003) in the amount of money spent in our sample states on corrections. All of our sample states saw huge increases in correctional expenditures during this time period, though the timing of the largest increases varies across states. Growth has slowed in recent years, however, particularly between 2000 and 2003, with the largest percentage growth being in Arkansas (11 per cent), and the smallest in Nevada (–2 per cent). Indeed, with one exception (New York between 1995 and 2000), this is the only time period in which ANY state experienced growth of less than 10 per cent. The largest increase occurred in Arkansas between 1970 and 1975 (335 per cent increase), but increases of more than 100 per cent over a 5-year period are not unusual. In the next section we describe the reform efforts being considered in each of our sample states as each state legislature worked to manage the collision between large prison populations and large budget deficits.

Data

The primary data sources for this article are newspaper articles pertaining to criminal justice reforms proposed during the 2003 legislative session in the six study states. We used a national database (Lexus Nexus Academic Universe) to identify relevant articles. For each state, the sample time frame is from 1 January 2003 (prior to the beginning of the legislative session) until one week after the end of each state's legislative session. Because we are specifically interested in the ways that state budgetary issues influence the conversation about punishment, we included the term 'budget' in all of our searches. We searched for articles with budget and one of several other search terms ('prison' or 'sentencing' or 'criminal justice'). Our search yielded 308 articles. From this, we narrowed our sample by excluding articles that were

| **Table 1.1** Department of Corrections Expenditures, per State, in Thousands of Dollars, 1970–2003 |||||||||

	1970	**1975**	**1980**	**1985**	**1990**	**1995**	**2000**	**2003**
AR	3255	14,159	28,254	53,182	81,060	160,878	275,158	305,803
IA	13,811	20,227	51,787	84,181	131,015	176,666	279,196	294,911
NV	5206	12,179	29,257	44,887	115,224	135,987	220,695	216,356
NY	128,236	240,059	462,952	1,139,288	1,858,799	2,272,887	2,440,336	2,535,996
WA	32,935	49,872	97,287	221,626	275,687	482,761	731,277	786,781
WI	35,083	45,604	92,536	186,159	274,736	509,551	837,496	906,725

SOURCES: "State Government Finances in 1970, 1975,1980, 1985." U.S. Department of Commerce, Bureau of the Census, GF70, GF75, GF80, GF85. No. 3; http:www.census.gov/govs/www/state95.html; www.census.gov/govs/www/state00.html; http:www.census.gov/govs/www/state03.html

repeated across newspapers (i.e., articles that appeared in one newspaper one day and another the following day) and articles that contained our search terms but were not actually about sentencing reform. Our final sample consists of 150 articles.

Analytic Method

To identify themes appearing in these articles, we utilized Atlas-ti, a program designed to aid researchers in qualitative analysis.

We have two different types of main codes. First, we coded information on the substance of the debate (i.e., what people were talking about). For this stage, we coded information in the following categories: Problem driving the need for reform; Nature of the problem; Implied/proposed solution; Support for proposed solution (Arguments, Types of support); Opposition to proposed solution (Arguments, Barriers to reform); and Outcome.

More importantly, we coded information on the nature of the debate (i.e., how people were talking about various reforms). For this stage, we coded arguments as falling into the following broad categories (all relating to punishment and reform): arguments about economics (cost), arguments about equity and fairness, arguments about effectiveness, and arguments about the impact of reform on the criminal justice system.

▧ Results

In this section, we outline the most prominent themes arising in published conversations about sentencing reform. While this represents only a snapshot of conversations about reform happening during the 2003 legislative session, it provides a window into some of the ways in which these conversations may be shifting. We first put the conversation in context by providing evidence that many reformers view the budget crisis as a welcome opportunity to discuss what they perceive as over reliance on incarceration in the United States. We then turn to pro-reform arguments based on critiques of existing laws (arguments about the effectiveness and fairness of these laws). We conclude with arguments justifying particular types of reforms (focusing primarily on treatment and reintegration). Throughout

this section, quotes that are not within quotation marks are directly from the article's author, while quotes within quotation marks are attributed to a source to whom the author spoke.

Timing of Conversation About Reform

Our results suggest that many reformers view the budget crisis as an opportunity to have an important conversation that is long overdue. States have made dramatic changes to their sentencing and corrections policies over the past three decades, changes that have almost universally toughened existing laws and increased reliance on incarceration as a response to crime. During this time, crime also moved to the forefront of public concerns, and politicians learned quickly that it could be politically lethal to question whether this heavy emphasis on incarceration was affordable, effective, or desirable (Garland, 2001; Beckett and Sasson, 2004).

In a 1995 article appearing in Time magazine, when an official in the Clinton administration was asked about why the president had not suggested any real alternative to the Tough on Crime proposals put forth in the Omnibus Crime Bill, the reply was:

> You can't appear soft on crime when crime hysteria is sweeping the country. Maybe the national temper will change, and maybe, if it does, we'll do it right later. (Kramer, 1994: 29)

We see similar statements in our sample of articles from 2003. Some public officials state explicitly that political concerns have prevented open discussion about punishment:

> [Wisconsin Attorney General Peg] Lautenschlager said one hurdle to an open discussion of revising sentencing practices is the fear that support of alternatives to prison will be seen as being soft on crime. 'In a way, this fear of political repercussion has stifled the debate about what's right and what's wrong'. (Associated Press, 2003a)

Vincent Schiraldi of the Justice Policy Institute, an organization that tracks sentencing policy, believes that lawmakers are now receptive to opening the discussion about punishment in ways that they have not been in the past. Indeed, Schiraldi stated that 'the atmosphere among state officials was the most receptive he'd seen during 23 years in the field' (Crary, Wisconsin, 6 March 2003).

✉ Critiques of Current Policies

Current Policies Are Ineffective

With the conversation about sentencing opening up to include voices critical of existing policies, some officials are publicly re-evaluating the utility of prisons. People are asking whether prisons accomplish the goals set out for them, and also whether the costs of incarceration (both financial and human) are worth the benefits. For example, Iowa Senator Jeff Angelo (R) is quoted as saying that 'Right now, we are just warehousing people' (Clayton, Nebraska, 1 November 2003), a statement that likely would have been politically difficult, if not impossible, to make during the 1990s. Similarly, Arkansas Senator Dave Bisbee (R) asked, 'Is society really getting this much worse, or are we doing something wrong with our prisons?' (Jefferson, Arkansas, 24 April 2003).

Others argue that we are over-incarcerating: that prison is an important tool, but that we are using it indiscriminately. Proponents of this position argue that we need to make distinctions between those who pose a real risk to public safety, and those who do not, and that prison should be reserved for the former group. This view is articulated by Nicholas Turner of the Vera Institute of Justice, and reiterated by the League of Women Voters.

> Those we are afraid of belong behind bars, but those we are angry at we can sanction in a different way that is less expensive. For the past 20 years, we've just relied on prisons to deal with both groups. (Broder, New York, 19 January 2003)

> The League believes jails and prisons must be viewed as a scarce and expensive resource, to be used only when necessary—i.e., to protect the public from violent and repeat offenders. (League of Women Voters, New York, 18 June 2003)

The suggestion that we should view prison cells as scarce resources flies in the face of many of the reforms passed over the past three decades, when legislators passed numerous policies that increased prison populations on the assumption that society would build as many prisons as are necessary to house the criminals deemed a threat to society (a category that expanded dramatically during this period).

Another area of concern for critics of current policies focuses on the drawbacks of incarceration of drug offenders and the tradeoffs that may be involved in this strategy. This piece of the conversation centers around the appropriate scope of punishment—questions about who should be punished, and how we can most rationally allocate our crime control resources. Reformers argue that we should focus our attention and resources on dangerous offenders, rather than taking up space and using resources to lock up nonviolent drug offenders. These arguments play on public fear of crime and suggest that the current response to crime actually has the potential to decrease public safety by wasting resources on drug offenders (particularly drug users—individuals engaged in so-called 'victimless crimes'). Arkansas state representative Sam Ledbetter (D) argued that:

> The cost of having someone in prison transcends the $ 15,000-a-year cost [of holding an inmate] to prisons. . . . If we don't be careful with the way we are doing this, we are going to end up with dangerous people that we don't have room for and people with an addiction taking up space. (Wickline, Arkansas, 17 March 2003)

In virtually all of the instances where arguments about the appropriate scope of punishment were made in our sample, reformers turned to images of danger and threat, images that have been used so successfully by people using the Tough on Crime rhetoric for the past 30 years. It is interesting to note that what are essentially scare tactics are being employed by reformers to fight many of the same laws that were created with the use of similar scare tactics.

Current Policies Are Unfair

Another criticism of current policies is that, regardless of their effectiveness, they are fundamentally unfair. The Rockefeller Drug Laws, in particular, are described time and time again as unjust (though notably not by legislators):

> 'The laws are so demonstrably a disastrous experiment . . . [and represent an] egregious miscarriage of justice' [said New York Court of Appeals Judge Joseph W. Bellacosa] (Caher, New York, 15 June 2003)

There are at least two strains of arguments about why the laws are so unfair. First, some argue that the laws themselves are unfair either because the punishment is disproportionate to the offense, or because judges are not allowed to take individual factors into account in sentencing. Others argue that it is the consequences of the laws that are unjust, in part because the individuals sentenced under the laws are not the offenders originally targeted by lawmakers, and in part because the laws have a disproportionately harsh impact on minority offenders and minority communities.

Punishment Is Unfair

One concern raised by opponents of the Rockefeller Drug Laws is that small-time drug offenders receive sentences that are much harsher than sentences handed out to serious violent offenders. In New York, individuals on both sides of reform efforts agree that the drug laws have produced disproportionate sentences:

> The Legislature and Gov. George E. Pataki have agreed that the Rockefeller-era drug laws are unduly harsh, mandating longer minimum sentences for some first-time, nonviolent drug offenses than for rape and manslaughter. (Purdy, New York, 12 February 2003)

A similar concern about disproportionality arises in comparing sentences for different drug offenders. The laws are structured so that it is the possession and/or sale of a drug that matters, not the amount of drug involved. Proponents of reform often evoke individual stories to illustrate the injustices.

A second set of concerns regarding the fairness of the Rockefeller Drug Laws has to do with judicial discretion. One of the primary goals behind the mandatory sentencing movement was to take discretionary power away from judges in order both to reduce sentencing disparities (e.g., by race) and to ensure that defendants were not receiving overly lenient sentences. To achieve these goals, reformers created laws designed to take the ability to consider individual circumstances of a particular case away from judges.

Some proponents of reform argue that one of the consequences of such laws has been a decrease in public faith in the criminal justice system:

> These statutes have had a deleterious effect on public trust in the justice system by imposing unduly harsh sentences on non-violent drug offenders, and by limiting the discretion of trial judges to address the unique circumstances of each case [said Lorraine Power Tharp, President of New York Bar Association.] (The Daily Record, 2003)

Concerns about the negative effects of restraining judicial discretion suggest that the distrust of the judiciary that led to sentencing guidelines and other reforms may have backfired, producing a system in which judgments are made by distant lawmakers, rather than by judges present to hear the circumstances of an individual case.

Consequences Are Unfair

Others have focused on the unfair consequences of the law. Referring again to the Rockefeller Drug Laws described above, one says:

> The tough terms were meant to nail drug kingpins, but instead they more commonly locked away lower-level drug carriers and users. (Buffalo News, 2003)

One consequence of these laws, then, has been to capture and harshly punish low-level drug offenders.

Indeed, one reformer, Robert Gangi, executive director of the Correctional Association of New York, argues that the laws actually create incentives for law enforcement personnel to focus on petty drug offenders rather than spending time going after the big dealers.

Another unjust consequence of drug laws (both in New York and elsewhere) has been the disproportionately harsh impact they have had on minorities. Claims of racial disproportionality tied specifically to drug laws arose in three of our study states (Iowa, Wisconsin, and New York). It is not only minority offenders who are hardest hit by the apparent differential enforcement of these laws. Critics also claim that minority communities are impacted as well.

✎ Advantages of Reforms: Smart on Crime

One theme that we see tying together a number of different arguments for reform is the claim that, by looking at the current costs and the future consequences of punishment, we can create criminal justice policies that are more rational than those passed under the Tough on Crime regime. Specifically, reformers argue that we should be more rational about how we allocate resources in the War on Crime. Part of the argument about rationality focuses on crime control, as described in the earlier section about the effectiveness of incarceration, while another frames proposed reforms as 'good investments'. Reformers argue that focusing more resources on treatment and reintegration of offenders will both reduce recidivism and help ex-offenders to become productive citizens and, specifically, taxpayers.

> The program, included in Doyle's proposed budget, would sentence certain nonviolent offenders who violate their probation or parole to 90 days of intensive reform and rehabilitation efforts. The plan seeks to avoid 'the most expensive and less-productive option of sending them to prison' according to Doyle's budget proposal. (Sheehan, Wisconsin, 9 March 2003)

Focusing on Treatment

In each of our six sample states, reformers were talking about changing laws dealing with drug offenders. The War on Drugs emerged in the 1970s and gained steam in the 1980s, with a number of states passing laws that mandated incarceration for relatively minor drug crimes (Baum, 1996). Reformers have targeted drug laws for a variety of reasons, one of which is the argument that incarceration is particularly ineffective at reforming drug offenders, many of whom commit crimes to support their addiction. A shift away from punishment toward treatment would more effectively address the underlying problem of addiction while also saving taxpayer dollars, a clear example of a policy that would be 'Smart on Crime'.

Our analysis shows reformers tying arguments for treatment to arguments about cost effectiveness as a way of communicating their message. For example, Kathryn Sowards, a senior research associate at the Center for Community Alternatives in Syracuse, frames her support for treatment in economic terms:

> Treatment is a highly profitable investment for society and is one of the most effective weapons in the real war on crime. (Sowards, New York, 17 April 2003)

The following summary of the proposal put forth by Wisconsin governor Doyle provides a clear example of how arguments for treatment combine assertions about economics with reassurances about public safety.

> Doyle wants to reduce the state's reliance on prisons by offering flexible sentencing and rehabilitation upturns. He said, by doing so, the state would make the justice system more effective and affordable while making residents safer. (Associated Press, 2003b)

Focusing on Reintegration

While arguments for treatment suggest replacing our current response to drug crime (incarceration) with a qualitatively different response, other reformers have focused on what happens after offenders are released from prison, and advocate increasing resources for reintegration. Whereas most policy reforms over the past 30 years have been highly exclusionary (e.g., by increasing reliance on incarceration and decreasing the services available to offenders to reintegrate after release), some reformers suggest that we should be more inclusionary when we think about the role of ex-offenders in society. Proponents of this view are pushing for concerns about the future to become a central consideration in criminal justice policy decisions. Referring to prisoner reintegration, Wisconsin DOC administrator, Kenneth Morgan, said:

> Not only is it part of the budget solution, it is part of what we're trying to do with offenders, and that's to make them valuable citizens and getting them back to where they belong. (Kertscher, Wisconsin, 23 March 2003)

Part of the impetus for this concern comes from rapidly escalating rates of parole revocation and recidivism in recent years.

> Wisconsin prisons released more than 7,600 men and women last year. But 3,087 ex-prisoners returned on parole revocations. Sure, some were incorrigible bad guys destined for another cell no matter how many touchy-feely support groups they attended on the outside. But others are caught in a cycle of release and revocation that has more to do with the many obstacles to rejoining community life than their own darker impulses. (Kelley, Wisconsin, 2 March 2003)

This excerpt clearly promotes the idea that recidivism is not simply the result of bad choices ('darker impulses') made by ex-offenders, but that it is also impacted by the resources a community devotes to reintegration.

Truth in Sentencing laws, one of the primary types of reform under the Tough on Crime regime, have had the unintended consequence of reducing the amount of time offenders spend on parole after being released from prison, and thereby decreasing opportunities to

provide them with assistance in reintegration. One of the ways Iowa lawmakers justified softening mandatory minimums for certain drug offenders was by talking about the importance of successful reintegration:

> [Iowa Republican Senator] Larson would support lowering the 85 percent mandatory sentence to 70 percent and require prisoners to serve the final part of their sentence being reintroduced into society. (Clayton, Nebraska, 11 January 2003)

Supporters say reducing the mandatory minimum would allow offenders to transition back to society through the community corrections system rather than then being released without supervision, which occurs under the current 85 per cent law (Eby, Iowa, 30 April 2003).

Part of the strategy behind focusing on reintegration seems to lie in shifting public attention away from the problem of crime onto a new problem (i.e., that of prisoner re-entry).

A final justification for encouraging more inclusionary policies is purely economic. Some lawmakers argue that policies should be designed with successful reintegration for offenders as a central goal in part so that ex-offenders can become taxpayers.

> 'In my view, something could be done' (director of the Arkansas DOC Larry] Norris said. 'It would save us a good deal of money. I think they should be locked up long enough to get cleaned up, straightened out and get an opportunity to go out and pay taxes'. (Blomeley, Arkansas, 20 February 2003)

⊠ Discussion and Conclusions

This article documents some of the shifts that occurred in public conversations about punishment during a period when both the costs of punishment and state budget deficits reached critical levels. While many of the reforms passed during the 1970s, 1980s, and 1990s were based largely on retributive principles with little attention paid to cost or effectiveness, reformers in the early 21st century have brought the economics of punishment back into the conversation. In this final section of the article, we describe what we see as the most significant themes coming out of the 2003 legislative session in six states, and speculate on how shifts in public conversations might impact criminal justice reform in the coming years.

One way to characterize changes in these conversations is to say that expressive goals of punishment are no longer being mobilized to the exclusion of economic concerns. Some of the extremely expensive criminal justice reforms passed in prior decades were justified almost entirely by their expressive aims. Garland (2001: 191) has argued that:

> This way of responding to crime confounds the cost-effectiveness considerations of the economic framework. The War on Drugs is a prominent example of this. So, too, are the mandatory sentences of the California Three Strikes laws, the recent prison works' policy of the UK government, and zero tolerance policing policies, all of which are very costly and, in crime control terms, of doubtful effectiveness. The adoption of a war mentality altogether defeats economic reasoning.

Because a war mentality encourages spending at virtually any cost, we believe legislators are rethinking the War on Drugs. Our analysis suggests that, while public officials who support sentencing reform are not actively working to deconstruct the War on Drugs, they are working to reconstruct drug crimes so that they come to be seen as different kinds of issues, in the hopes that a more effective, less costly, response will be seen as superior to widespread incarceration. What people in the articles we analyzed are arguing about drug offenders is not that what they are doing is not so wrong, but rather that they are not particularly dangerous and that they are taking up space and that this space is then not available for truly dangerous offenders. This kind of argument is consistent with the trend toward managerial goals playing a role in decision-making—that is, people are making decisions about what to do with individual offenders by looking at the criminal population at the aggregate level.

We would argue that budget issues have served as a catalyst for more widespread acceptance of the principles behind new penology, which 'replaces consideration of fault with predictions of dangerousness and safety management' (Feeley and Simon, 1992: 457). The argument that, rather than being 'tough on crime' we need to be 'smart on crime' is central to this shift. Reformers argue that, by moving toward treating rather than punishing drug offenders, we can reallocate resources so that our prison spending is going toward those offenders who present a danger to public safety, not toward those who are committing moral offenses.

Part of this shift toward new penology involves what we would call a redistribution of danger talk. Public officials interested in reform are trying to effect a change in the way we think about crime and danger by encouraging a symbolic separation between drug offenders and other (particularly violent offenders). In recent decades, public officials have been hugely successful at minimizing such a separation; drug offenders have been rhetorically paired with violent offenders as a threat to public safety for many years. One of the things we see in this article is that reformers are trying hard to decouple drug offenders from other criminals, and to establish them as a different kind of problem. It is highly relevant that the strategy for doing so relies heavily on 'danger talk' and that, rather than trying to diminish the sense of threat the public feels from criminals, reformers work to underline the threat posed by non-drug offenders, and to argue that this threat is exacerbated by incarcerating drug offenders.

This shift also involves a shift in focus toward the future. Retribution is oriented toward the past, with little concern for the future—people must be punished for the wrongs they have committed. Reformers suggest that a 'smart' response to crime involves thinking about what happens with offenders when their incarceration (or treatment) is complete. Significantly, one of the most common ways for this argument to be put forth is for reformers to talk about ex-offenders becoming productive citizens and, specifically, taxpayers. Indeed, one of our key findings is that reformers regularly connect proposals for qualitatively different ways of responding to crime to arguments about cost effectiveness.

This article started with curiosity about whether, and if so, how, a severe economic downturn would affect conversations about punishment that have been stuck in retributive mode for so many years. What our analyses show is that the economic crises of the early 21st century were, for many, a welcome opportunity to talk about the fairness, effectiveness, and cost of our current system of punishment. What we cannot conclude is that economic concerns caused these conversations to happen. We do not include in our analysis other possible explanatory variables, and can therefore not definitively assert a causal relationship between the economy and conversations about punishment. While prior research suggests that explanatory variables such as changes in the crime rate or fear of victimization are unlikely to effect such changes (e.g., Scheingold, 1984, 1991), it is possible that there were cultural changes in the early 21st century that changed the tenor of conversations about crime and punishment. For example, Scheingold's (1984: 38) argument that 'our response to crime may have less to do with the actual impact of crime on our lives than with the symbolic importance of crime in American culture' raises the possibility that, if crime decreased in symbolic importance, conversations about crime policy would also change. Unfortunately, our data do not allow us to evaluate this claim beside the claim that economic concerns were instrumental in shifting conversations about punishment.

One of the things that gives us confidence in our claim that the relationship between the economy and opportunities for reforming punishment, however, is that many of the reform advocates referred specifically to the economy in making their case for reform. Whether or not the economy opened the door to the conversations, reformers perceived it as a tool with which to convince people that reform was appropriate. The fact that reformers perceived economic problems as the element that allowed them the opportunity for talking about reform seems to us a crucial point. Furthermore, the reality is that four of our six sample states found it necessary to enter into special legislative session to determine how to balance rising costs of corrections with diminished state resources. These two factors contribute to our confidence in concluding that there is an important relationship between the economy and the ways we talk about punishment.

We see compelling possibilities for furthering this research, and specifically for examining the questions about causality raised earlier. Perhaps the most effective way to answer the question about whether economic concerns drive conversations about punishment would be to conduct a longitudinal study in which reform conversations are tracked over time. This would allow researchers, for example, to tentatively answer the question of whether a return to a bull economy would silence reform conversations. If economic concerns are the primary catalyst for reform, we would predict that a sharp economic upturn would have the effect of muting conversations about reform. We strongly suspect, however, that the relationship between the economy and punishment is a complicated one, and that such research would not produce definitive results. Indeed, while punishment has proved to be extraordinarily expensive, it continues to respond to the discontents of the public (Scheingold, 1984), and may therefore be exceedingly resistant to change.

This article represents a snapshot of a time when politicians are struggling to reconcile new economic conditions with old rhetoric about punishment, and it remains to be seen where this will lead. The fact that some of the reforms being debated in our analysis passed while others did not suggests that the effectiveness of the rhetorical shifts we document here is yet to be determined.

⊠ References

Associated Press (2003a) 'Judge says newly implemented guidelines will help', Oshkosh, Wisconsin, 10 February.

Associated Press (2003b) 'Doyle's budget plan would introduce new corrections plan', Madison, Wisconsin, 3 March.

Associated Press (2003c) 'House passes budget related bills', Olympia, Washington, 25 April.

Baum, Daniel (1996) *Smoke and mirrors: The war on drugs and the politics of failure*. New York: Little, Brown & Company.

Beckett, Katherine (1997) *Making crime pay: Law and order in contemporary American politics*. Oxford: Oxford University Press.

Beckett, Katherine and Theodore Sasson (2004) *The politics of injustice*, 2nd edition. Thousand Oaks, CA: Sage Publications.

Beiser, Vince (2001) 'How we got to two million', 10 July, special report to MotherJones.com.

Blomeley, S. (2003) 'State police, prisons fear shrinkage if budgets stall', Arkansas Democrat-Gazette, 20 February: 1.

Bork, R. H. (2005) 'Travesty time, again', *National Review*, 28 March: 17–18.

Bower, R. (2003) 'Funding for drug court dwindles', *Arkansas Democrat Gazette*, 3 March: 9.

Border, J. M. (2003) 'No hard time for prison budgets', *New York Times*, 19 January: 5.

Buffalo News (2003) 'Michigan steps away from mandatory sentencing: New York should follow', 5 January: F2.

Caher, J. (2003) 'Lowering the bars', *Newsday*, 15 June: A26.

Clayton, C. (2003) 'Budget creates bars to prison population; Lawmakers say changes in sentencing laws could help ease the crunch, Iowa prison population', *Omaha World Herald*, 11 January: 1A.

Cohen, Stanley (1985) *Visions of social control*. Cambridge: Polity Press.

The Columbian (2003) 'Opinion—in our view: Paper cuts and ex-cons', 13 March: C6.

Crary, D. (2003) Tough-on-crime policies getting softer in US: Budget problems force cuts', *Capital Times*, 6 March: 10A.

The Daily Record (2003) 'New York Bar Association presents 2003 legislative program', 14 April.

Eby, C. (2003) House gives final approval to sentencing reform package', *Sioux City Journal*, 30 April.

Feeley, Malcolm M. and Jonathan Simon (1992) 'The new penology: Notes on the emerging strategy of corrections and its implications', *Criminology* 30(4): 449–74.

Gangi, R. (2003) 'Drug law reform can help state cash woes', *The Times Union* (14 February): A13.

Garland, David (1990) *Punishment and modern society*. Chicago, IL: University of Chicago Press.

Garland, David (2001) *The culture of control*. Chicago, IL: University of Chicago Press.

Grasmick, H. G., E. Davenport, M.B. Chamlin, and R. J. Bursik, Jr. (1992) 'Protestant fundamentalism and the retributive doctrine of punishment', *Criminology* 30(1): 21-45.

Greenberg, D. (2003) 'Prosecutors are the wrong gatekeepers', *New York Law Journal* 229: 2.

Harrison, Paige M. and Allen J. Beck (November 2004) 'Bureau of Justice Statistics Bulletin: Prisoners in 2003', U.S. Department of Justice, Office of Justice Programs.

Harrison, Paige M. and Allen J. Beck (2003) 'Bureau of Justice Statistics Bulletin: Prisoners in 2002', July, U.S. Department of Justice, Office of Justice Programs.

Henican, E. (2003) 'Harsh justice, hard lessons', *Newsday*, 23 February: 8.

Jefferson, J. (2003) 'Agencies make compelling cases for additional funding', Associated Press, Little Rock, Arkansas, 24 February.

Kelley, T. (2003) 'When cons go free, how do they cope?' *Wisconsin State Journal*, 2 March: B3.

Kertscher, T. (2003) 'In Sturtevant, a different take on corrections; Complex aims to stop prisons' revolving doors', *Milwaukee Journal Sentinel*, 23 March: 01B.

Kramer, M. (1994) 'From Sarajevo to Needle Park', *Time*, 21 February; 29.

League of Women Voters (2003) 'Better ways than jail to punish the non-violent', *The Post-Standard*, 18 June: A13.

MacKenzie, Doris Layton (2001) *Sentencing and corrections in the 21st century: Setting the stage for the future*. Washington, DC: National Institute of Justice, U.S. Department of Justice.

Nolan, James, L., III (2001) *Reinventing Justice: The American Drug Court Movement*. Princeton, NJ: Princeton University Press.

Purdy, M. (2003) 'Our towns; So little cash for prisons, so much time', *New York Times*, 12 February: 1.

Scheingold, Stuart (1984) *The politics of law and order: Street crime and public policy*. New York: Longman.

Scheingold, Stuart (1991) *The politics of street crime: Criminal process and cultural obsession*. Philadelphia, PA: Temple University Press.

Sheehan, T. (2003) 'Doyle has plan for non-violent offenders', *Wisconsin State Journal*, 3 March: Al.

Snell, Ronald K., Corina Ecki, and Graham Williams (July 2003) *State spending in the 1990s*. A special report from the National Conference of State Legislatures.

Srateline.org (2003) 'State budget gaps: How does your state rank?', 11 February special report. http://www.Stateline.org

Sowards, K. (2003) 'Drug treatment for inmates more than pays for itself'. *Post Standard*, 17 April: All.

State and Local Sourcebook (2003) *Governing, v. 16*. Washington, DC: Congressional Quarterly.

Tonry, Michael (1996) *Sentencing matters*. Oxford: Oxford University Press.

Von Hirsch, Andrew and Committee for the Study of Incarceration (1976) *Doing justice: The choice of punishments. Report of the Committee for the Study of Incarceration*. New York: Hill and Wang.

Wickline, M. (2003) 'Legislators take aim at state's 70% law', *Arkansas Democrat-Gazette*, 17 March.

Zimring, Franklin E. and Gordon Hawkins (1991) *The scale of imprisonment*. Chicago, IL: University of Chicago Press.

Ziedenbert, Jason and Vincent Schiraldi (2002) *Cell blocks or classrooms? The funding of higher education and corrections and its impact on African American men*. Justice Policy Institute.

DISCUSSION QUESTIONS

1. According to the authors, what role does the economic system play in shaping our societal response to crime?

2. Given the importance of the budget and the downward economic trend, how might community-based alternatives seek to meet all of the punitive goals outlined in the article?

3. According to the authors, what is the current state of punishment in the United States?

4. Based on the current study, how might a review of newspaper articles before and after legislative hearings reveal information about the current state of punishment?

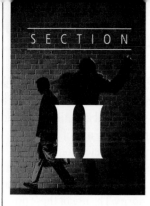

SECTION

II

Pretrial Release and Diversion

Learning Objectives

1. Understand the definition, purpose, and effectiveness of pretrial supervision.
2. Understand the definition, purpose, and effectiveness of **diversion.**
3. Be able to identify the **five essential elements of specialized courts.**
4. Identify the purpose and objectives of drug courts.
5. Identify the role of mental health courts in addressing the needs of this specific population.
6. Understand the purpose and objectives of **reentry courts.**

A s you saw in Section I of the text, community-based corrections is administered in many different forms ranging from probation through residential confinement. The use of these sanctions, however, is not strictly limited to responses by the court system via formal sanctions. Rather, one way to decrease recidivism and formal involvement in the system is through the use of pretrial release, diversionary programs, and specialized courts. Research indicates that pretrial detention of the accused may decrease the likelihood of obtaining adequate defense and increasing the severity of the sentence (Demuth & Steffensmeier, 2004). Likewise, there is evidence to suggest that pretrial release based upon the ability to pay may restrict opportunities for offenders who are poor and minority. The use of these programs including diversionary alternatives rely very heavily on the ability of law enforcement officials and prosecutors to screen out or divert those individuals who may be in need of more services rather than punishment. This section of the text will review three types of programs aimed at diverting individuals from the formal criminal justice system and toward community-based alternatives: (1) pretrial supervision, (2) diversion, and (3) specialized court-based programs.

▧ Pretrial Supervision

The need for an alternative to detaining individuals arrested and charged with minor or first-time offenses came to the forefront of attention during the 1960s. It was during this time period that those working in release programs noticed that many offenders who had been arrested, charged, and not initially released continued to recycle through the process. It was the belief that if programs could be developed that specifically addressed the causes of the arrest, then recidivism could be reduced (*Pretrial Diversion Abstract*, 1998). Likewise, it was the belief that the creation of an alternative program could assist with reducing the stigmatization given to those coming to the attention of the court system. Legally those who have been arrested have the right to appear in front of a judge within a 24-hour time period (72 hours maximum including weekends). Failure to appear during that specified range may result in the case being removed from the system. Although this time period may seem short, given the number of cases officially processed through the system and resulting in conviction it becomes apparent that many of those awaiting their first appearance do not need to be detained. This coupled with the destigmatization movement of the mid-20th century led policy makers to seek alternatives to address these areas. One such response was the creation of pretrial release and supervision.

What Is Pretrial Supervision?

The first pretrial release program began in 1961 with the Manhattan Bail Project. This project was designed to assist judges in identifying defendants who were eligible to be released on their own recognizance (ROR). Modeled after the recognizance programs in Europe discussed in the previous section, this program became so successful that over the next 2 decades more than 200 cities had some version of pretrial release in place (Pretrial Justice Institute, 2009). This program and similar programs today continue to be designed as prosecutor-centered approaches. By 1982, federal legislation had been passed with the enactment of the Pretrial Services Act of 1982 (18 US.C. 3152) calling for the creation of a separate federal agency designed to oversee the prerelease and detention of the accused as well as other pretrial services (Lowenkamp & Whetzel, 2009). These services were so successful that they were further extended to include a community component with the Federal Bail Reform Act of 1984 (Alarid, Del Carmen, & Cromwell, 2007; Lowenkamp

& Whetzel, 2009). This act called for community safety to be considered when releasing an offender under pretrial supervision. Despite these efforts for community safety consideration, the Bail Reform Act did not specify any risk criteria to be used in making these determinations. Therefore, federal pretrial service officers relied on subjective measures such as previous experience, criminal histories, and other criminogenic factors that might contribute to additional criminal offending (Lowenkamp & Whetzel, 2009). States utilizing the pretrial release process have expanded the use of the measures to include quantitative measures such as actuarial risk assessment tools (Alarid et al., 2007; Lowenkamp & Whetzel, 2009).

Purpose of Pretrial Supervision

Today, the National Association of Pretrial Services Agencies (NAPSA) (2008) defines the purpose of pretrial diversion/intervention as being a "voluntary option which provides alternative criminal case processing for a defendant charged with a crime that ideally, upon successful completion of an individualized program plan results in a dismissal of the charge(s)" (p. vi). Additionally, the standards set forth by NAPSA call for these programs to address the root causes of crime through the use of programs with prosecutorial merit. Over the past 20 years, pretrial diversion services have witnessed the evolution and expansion of these ideas into court-centered approaches such as the creation and expanded use of drug and specialized courts, which will be discussed later in this section (NAPSA, 2008).

Effectiveness of Pretrial Supervision

Studies assessing the effectiveness of these programs have been limited. The majority of studies assessing the effectiveness have focused on localized assessments or the ability to predict success or failure while on pretrial. In a study conducted by Lowenkamp and Whetzel (2009), the authors examined whether one could identify risk factors predicting success or failure using an actuarial instrument for those individuals entering the federal system. A study of 565,178 defendants (all those entering the system between FY2001 to FY2007) revealed that there were specific static and dynamic factors that predicted success while on pretrial. Static factors included those intuitive measures utilized previously by federal pretrial service workers such as criminal history and current offense. They also found dynamic factors such as substance use, home ownership, educational attainment, and employment status did predict accurately whether an individual would succeed or fail on these sanctions (p. 34). Additionally, Demuth and Steffensmeier (2004), in your first reading for this section, sought to answer whether sex and **race** made a difference in determining success while released prior to trial. A review of the nation's 75 most populous counties between 1990 and 1996 revealed that white females were the most likely to be released, and Hispanic males were the least likely (p. 222).

Efforts to further examine the implementation of pretrial services programs are limited. In fact, the most recent national review completed in August 2009 is only the fourth national study to be conducted. Administered by the National Pretrial Service Institute of 171 jurisdictions, results indicated that the programs are more likely to serve multiple counties in a single jurisdiction serving populations of 100,001 to 500,000. Almost half of all programs (49%) served a mixture of rural and urban communities. Although this is a consistent finding from previous studies, an interesting revelation was that newer programs are being created in rural areas as opposed to more urban approaches. These programs have an average staff size of 22 with about half of all programs having less than 5 staff. Further, this report suggests there are continued efforts to continue the use of these programs on smaller budgets (Pretrial Justice Institute, 2009). For those working in the system, this occurrence is not surprising. Most agency personnel are being asked to do more with less. While pretrial supervision continues to be at the forefront of addressing issues such as jail overcrowding and reducing the number of offenders coming to the attention of the courts multiple times, research in this is lacking. Other programs, such as division that seeks to keep offenders out of the system, continue to be used and expanded with both juvenile and adult offenders.

⬕ Diversion

Following the use of pretrial supervision, those individuals who have been convicted or adjudicated may qualify for a diversionary program. These diversionary alternatives by their very nature are controversial. Specifically designed for juvenile offenders but used for adults as well, these programs offer assistance at four different points in the system: (1) diversion from arrest, (2) **diversion from prosecution**, (3) diversion from jail, and (4) diversion from imprisonment. Each of these different diversionary processes will be discussed next. One thing to keep in mind as we consider diversion as a viable alternative to further exposure to the system is the intent of its existence: Is it to shield youth/adults from the stigmatizing effects of the system? Or is diversion used as a mechanism for widening the net to include more individuals under the broad scope of the criminal justice system?

What Is Diversion?

The term *diversion* has several different meanings. Broadly defined, diversion is a process whereby someone— either an adult or child—is referred to a program (usually external to the official system) for counseling or care of some form in lieu of referral to the official court (Houston & Barton, 2005, p. 170). The nature of the act or the offense may determine where, if at all, in the system the individual may be diverted.

Typically diversion is used with juvenile first-time offenders charged with status or misdemeanant offenses or those in treatment (Houston & Barton, 2005; Sarri & Vinter, 1975). Diversion from the system occurs at various times within the process ranging from police contact to first appearance in front of the judge. The idea behind this form of community alternative is to minimize penetration into the system. By diverting offenders to community-based treatment facilities, or in some cases allowing the offender to be informally supervised, participation in these alternatives may be the very element necessary to reduce future criminal offending. There are programs specifically designed for adult offenders; however, the majority of diversionary program alternatives for adults, particularly for those programs dealing with the mentally ill, are found in larger communities with populations over 100,000 (Steadman, Cocozza, & Veysey, 1999). Restorative justice and mediation options also exist as a diversionary tactic for both juvenile and adult offenders. These responses to the system will be discussed in more detail in Section III.

Types of Diversion Programs

Clear and Dammer (2000) summarize the four different types of diversionary programs. The types of programs are as follows: (1) diversion from arrest, (2) diversion from prosecution, (3) diversion from jail, and (4) diversion from imprisonment. Diversion from arrest is oftentimes used with juvenile offenders but may be used with adults as well. In these instances, law enforcement officers are typically called to the scene of an event where all evidence suggests that a crime has occurred and asked to respond accordingly. In these circumstances, officers have wide latitude to decide what to do and how best to respond. Additionally, diversion from arrest also may occur in domestic violence calls for service. In those jurisdictions with preferred arrest policies, officers may electively choose to separate the parties involved rather than making a formal arrest. This discretion toward diversion is eliminated in domestic violence cases in states and/or jurisdictions with mandatory arrest policies.

Diversion from prosecution may also fall under the category of pretrial release. In these cases, offenders are formally charged and diverted to programs outside of the court system. Individuals successfully completing their programs would have their charges dropped, and depending upon the state and the offense, they could potentially have their records expunged.

Diversion from jail is also a pretrial mechanism to keep offenders out of the system. As reviewed in the previous discussion, offenders who have been summoned to court can await their trial date at home. This provides them with an opportunity to maintain gainful employment—if they have a job—and bonds to their community, which are especially important if children are present.

Finally, diversion from imprisonment includes a variety of different sanctions, which will be discussed in later sections and next. These alternatives can include suspending the sentence of offenders in lieu of probation, release on parole, early release, or other intermediate sanctions. Other options include diversionary or specialized courts such as drug courts, whereby individuals charged with drug- or alcohol-related offenses can have their cases heard and processed in a drug court that allows for treatment as opposed to punishment.

Effectiveness of Diversion Programs

The majority of studies assessing the effectiveness of diversionary programs specifically focus on their usefulness in the juvenile justice system. One exception may be found in the study by Steadman et al. (1999). In this study, the authors assessed the efficacy of using one such program for diverting offenders with mental illnesses out of the formal system or process. Results from this study indicate that there were no significant differences in the recidivism rates of those offenders who were processed through the diversion court versus those who were detained. One important finding, however, was that those who were not processed in the diversion tended to never get released from custody versus those who were processed. This finding could point to the need for further enhancement of programs to not only address the mental health issues of those coming to the attention of both institutional and community-based corrections but also reduce the costs of confinement since those individuals appear to

▲ **Photo 2.1** The Monroe office for state probation and parole coordinates supervision efforts with various treatment facilities in the area such as Rays of Sonshine as well as the local courthouse of Ouachita Parish.

never get out of the system. Overall, the results of studies assessing the effectiveness of diversionary alternatives reveal that it is possible to divert offenders out of the system. However, agency officials must be mindful to not widen the net in attempting to resolve issues of crime and delinquency within their communities.

⬚ Specialized Court-Based Programs

There are numerous types of treatment programs that exist for a wide variety of offenders. From a community corrections standpoint, it is first the courthouse that sets the tone as to the particular programs that operate within a given jurisdiction. It is also the courthouse where many community supervision officers (CSOs) will have initial interface with the offender's sentence, including treatment-related aspects of that sentence. Because of this, this section first reviews two of the more common court-based treatment programs that exist throughout the United States. These are the drug courts and the mental health courts that typically involved community supervision of offenders processed within their jurisdictions.

In discussing court-based programs, the term **therapeutic jurisprudence** is often used to describe these programs and their orientation toward case processing. Therapeutic jurisprudence is the study of the role of the law as a therapeutic agent. Essentially, therapeutic jurisprudence focuses on the law's impact on emotional life and on psychological well-being (Wexler & Winick, 2008). In this regard, therapeutic jurisprudence focuses on the human, emotional, and psychological side of law and the legal process. Specific examples would include mental health courts and/or drug courts. This is important because it demonstrates a treatment-minded approach to jurisprudence and this provides additional justification for a reintegrative approach to offender supervision. Miller (2007) provided an analysis of therapeutic jurisprudence and noted that there are two distinct means of viewing this type of court operation. First, there is the managerial mode, where a court will seek to "identify the range of problems facing its target clientele and ameliorate those problems by matching clients with the available social resources" (Miller, 2007, p. 127). This perspective is very similar to the case management model to be described in Section VI. This is a point worth noting because this demonstrates that most all aspects of community supervision tend to follow a case management method of operation, regardless of whether this consists of courthouse programs or the supervision agency (which is typically corollary to the court). Second, Miller (2007) described an interventionist mode of therapeutic jurisprudence whereby "the court seeks to intervene to change the way in which ex-offenders perceive themselves as responsible agents, as a means to preclude socially disfavored conduct" (p. 127).

For the most part, court programs engaged in therapeutic jurisprudence have borrowed and adapted their ideas from the drug court model. According to Miller (2007), "drug court judges often point to intervention in the offender's antisocial lifestyle as its core therapeutic feature" (p. 128). As an example, in drug court, the judge may be the informal leader of a team of professionals who are committed to the rehabilitation of the drug-addicted offender. In this respect, the judge utilizes a dynamic, personal relationship with each offender, which holds the offender accountable, on the one hand, yet ensures that the offender is placed in treatment whenever this is a feasible option. In essence, the judge plays the role of a high-powered treatment team leader or perhaps an authoritative case manager of a sort. The main point is that this follows the same theme and concepts that have been presented throughout this text in regard to offender reintegration.

Much of the therapeutic jurisprudence movement has occurred in response to specialized types of offenders since they are in need of detailed treatment resources. Neubauer (2002) spoke to this, noting that courts have created numerous specialized courts that deal with specialized type of offenses and/or offenders. Common examples of specialized courts include the widely touted drug court but also included innovations such as domestic violence courts, drunk driving courts, elder courts, and so on. These specialized courts are often tailored with a therapeutic justice orientation in mind. Neubauer (2002) identified five essential elements of specialized courts. They are as follows:

1. Immediate intervention

2. Non-adversarial adjudication

3. Hands-on judicial involvement

4. Treatment programs with clear rules and structured goals

5. A team approach that brings together the judge, prosecutors, defense counsel, treatment provider, and correctional staff

Some court applications are better known than others. This section will provide brief discussions on drug courts and mental health courts. As noted previously, drug courts are one of the best-known applications of therapeutic justice. Drug courts vary widely in structure, target populations, and treatment programs. The least distinctive way of creating a drug court is to establish one section of court that processes all minor drug cases; the primary goal is to speed up case dispositions of drug cases and at the same time free other judges to expedite their own dockets. Another type of drug court concentrates on drug defendants accused of serious crimes who also have major prior criminal records. These cases are carefully monitored by court administrators to ensure that all other charges are consolidated before a single judge and no unexpected developments interfere with the scheduled trial date. Still, other drug courts emphasize treatment. The assumption is that treatment will reduce the likelihood that convicted drug abusers will be rearrested. These courts will often mandate extensive treatment plans that are supervised by the probation officer. The sentencing judge, however, as opposed to the probation officer, monitors the offender's behavior. All in all, drug courts are thought to be a relatively successful method of combining both aspects of the punitive and rehabilitative components of the criminal justice system.

Drug Courts

Established as a result of court and prison overcrowding, special drug courts have proven popular. In 1989, a special drug court was established by judicial order in Miami. This high-volume court expanded on traditional drug-defendant diversion programs by offering a year or more of court-run treatment; defendants who complete this option have their criminal cases dismissed. Between 1991 and 1993, Miami influenced officials in more than 20 other jurisdictions to establish drug courts (Abadinsky, 2003). Within a decade, drug courts moved from the experimental stage to being recognized as well-established programs. The government now lists over 325 drug courts across 43 states (Neubauer, 2002).

Although they vary widely, common features of drug courts include a non-adversarial approach to integrating substance abuse treatment with criminal justice case processing. The focus is on early identification of eligible substance abusers and prompt placement in treatment, combined with frequent drug testing.

In discussing the objectives of drug courts, McNeece, Springer, and Arnold (2002) illuminated eight key objectives:

1. Drug courts integrate alcohol and other drug treatment services with justice system case processing.

2. Using a non-adversarial approach, prosecution and defense counsel promote public safety while protecting participants' due process rights.

▲ **Photo 2.2** The Ouachita Parish Courthouse runs a large drug court program. Local facilities such as Southern Oaks Addiction Recovery and Rays of Sonshine routinely coordinate with this courthouse.

3. Eligible participants are identified early and promptly placed in the drug court program.

4. Drug courts provide access to a continuum of alcohol, drug, and other related treatment and rehabilitation services.

5. Abstinence is monitored by frequent alcohol and other drug testing.

6. A coordinated strategy governs drug court responses to participants' compliance.

7. Ongoing judicial interaction with each drug court participant is essential.

8. Monitoring and evaluation measure the achievement of program goals and gauge effectiveness.

These features are among those that are thought to constitute an "ideal" model of drug court, though few meet these requirements (McNeece et al., 2002). In general, an offender is placed in a drug court program for 9 to 12 months. On successfully completing that program, the offender will be continued on probation for another year. In some jurisdictions, the offender's criminal record may be expunged if all of the court's conditions for treatment are satisfied (McNeece et al., 2002).

The role of the judge is crucial in a drug court. Judges are free to openly chastise or praise clients for their behavior during the courtroom proceedings. Beyond that, judges may issue court orders requiring that a client attend treatment, submit to urinalysis, seek employment, meet with a probation officer, avoid associations with drug-abusing friends, etc. (McNeece et al., 2002). Failure to comply with these judicial determinations may place the offender in contempt of court or in jail, or they may be transferred to a regular criminal court. Judges are provided with continuous feedback on the offender's performance by the other drug court participants. Because of this, there is little room for the offender to evade accountability within the program.

Research assessing the effectiveness of drug courts reveals an encouraging finding. Overall, as an innovative tool to deal with drug-involved offenders, drug courts seemingly do reduce recidivism of participants, increase treatment retention, and are a cost-effective alternative to incarceration (Nored & Carlan, 2008). Although these factors are true, there still exists a high failure rate among participants (Hepburn & Harvey, 2007). One explanation for this occurrence could be the types of offenders being placed in those programs. For example, Saum and Hiller (2008) found in their study of 452 offenders assigned to a post-plea drug court that those with violent charges are most likely to recidivate. However, one caveat to this finding is that when controlling for previous offense, time at risk, number of lifetime charges, sociodemographics, and drug court discharge status that there were no significant differences (Saum & Hiller, p. 303). This finding suggests that although violent offenders should not automatically be eliminated from participation in these programs that the methods for selection should be considered. It further suggests that those offenders who may be at lowest risk of offending in the first place are the ones who are most likely to succeed anyway. Efforts to administer these programs may also affect their success or failure. For example, as your third reading by Heck and Roussell (2007) illustrates, the most important factor in administering any drug court program is the input and involvement from all state-level **stakeholders**.

Mental Health Courts

Mental health courts, on the other hand, are designed to ensure that nonviolent mentally ill offenders are not warehoused in prisons; however, at the same time, the goal of these courts is to ensure that these offenders are not being a nuisance for the community. Often these offenders commit petty crimes and are homeless. Because of this, and because the vast majority of mentally ill offenders are not violent, informal interventions such as mental health courts are considered a much more effective method of intervention. These courts provide the offender with treatment and also provide the police and other community responders a venue to utilize when processing these offenders. Mental health courts are adept at working with local agencies both to address the needs of the offender and to protect the public's safety. Intervention and treatment specialists work with the judge to ensure that services are effectively delivered to the offender. This, like other previous examples, is reflective of an integrative casework model of intervention.

Reentry Courts

While drug court and mental health courts are created for specific offender issues (i.e., substance abuse and mental health concerns), there are other types of courts that have been implemented to specifically address the offender population that faces release from prison. These courts are called reentry courts. Reentry courts are courts that provide comprehensive services to offenders who return from prison to the community by utilizing comprehensive services provided by a network of agencies in the surrounding area. The focus of reentry courts recognizes that offenders need to be held strictly accountable but yet are in serious need of assistance as they return to communities. Importantly, the concept of the reentry court does not envision any change in the timing of decisions regarding a prisoner's release. In other words, reentry courts are not used as leverage tools to obtain offender compliance. They are instead tools to ensure public safety, at one extreme, and that offenders receive the necessary case management services, at the opposite extreme. These courts address the conflict between public safety and offender reintegration, acting as the moderator between the two competing interests. Further, the use of reentry courts acknowledge that most offenders eventually return to the community. These courts focus on the work of prisons in preparing offenders for release and presume that a reentry court will actively involve the state corrections agency and others, as outlined next. The core elements of a reentry court are the following (see National Criminal Justice Resources and Statistics, 1999):

1. *Assessment and Planning.* It is envisioned that correctional administrators, ideally with a reentry judge, would meet with inmates prior to release to explain the reentry process. The state corrections agency, and, where available, the parole agency, working in consultation with the reentry court, would identify those inmates to be released under the auspices of the reentry court to assess the inmates' needs upon release and begin building linkages to a constellation of social services, family counseling, health and mental health services, housing, job training, and work opportunities that would support successful reintegration.

2. *Active Oversight.* The reentry court would see prisoners released into the community with a high degree of frequency—probably once a month—beginning right after release and continuing until the end of parole (or other form of supervision). It is critical that the judge see offenders who are making progress as well as those who have failed to perform. The judge would also actively engage the parole officer or other supervising authority and the **community policing** officer responsible for the parolee's neighborhood in assessing progress. In the drug court experience, acknowledgment of the successful achievement of milestones by participants provides encouragement to others who observe them.

3. *Management of Supportive Services.* The reentry court must have at its disposal a broad array of supportive resources, including substance abuse treatment services, job training programs, private employers, faith institutions, family members, housing services, and community organizations. These support systems would be marshaled by the court, drawing upon existing community resources where possible. At the core, the court would again actively engage the parole officer or other supervising authority, as well as the community policing officer responsible for the parolee's neighborhood. In the drug court experience, judges and others have become very effective service brokers and advocates on behalf of participants. An important lesson from the drug court experience is that this brokerage function requires the development of a case management function accountable to the court. To be successful, a reentry court would have to develop a similar case management capacity.

4. *Accountability to Community.* A jurisdiction might consider creating a citizen advisory board to work with the reentry court to develop both community service and support opportunities as well as accountability mechanisms for successful reentry of released inmates. Accountability mechanisms might include ongoing restitution orders and participation in victim impact panels. It may also be appropriate to involve the crime victims and victims' organizations as part of the reentry process. The advisory board should broadly represent the community. Other mechanisms for drawing upon diverse community perspectives should also be considered.

5. *Graduated and Parsimonious Sanctions.* The reentry court would establish and articulate a predetermined range of sanctions for violations of the conditions of release. These would not automatically require return to prison; in fact, this would be reserved for new crimes or egregious violations. As with drug courts, it would be important for the reentry court to arrange for an array of relatively low-level sanctions that could be swiftly, predictably, and universally applied. Jurisdictions interested in piloting a reentry court must clearly outline how graduated sanctions would be imposed and the array of sanctions that would be used.

6. *Rewards for Success.* The reentry court also would need to incorporate positive judicial reinforcement—rewarding success, perhaps by negotiating early release from parole after established goals are achieved or by conducting graduation ceremonies akin to those seen in drug courts. The successful completion of parole should be seen as an important life event for an offender, and the court can help acknowledge that accomplishment. Courts provide powerful public forums for encouraging positive behavior and for acknowledging the individual effort in achieving reentry goals. Jurisdictions are required to outline milestones in the reentry process that would trigger recognition and an appropriate reward.

Importantly, these courts address the needs of all returning offenders, not just those who have drug abuse or mental health issues. Also, these types of programs are very important because they address those offenders who are perhaps in the most profound need, going through a transition from prison to release that is often much more difficult to navigate than is the adjustment for offenders placed on probation.

Though these court-based treatment models are comprehensive and provide a unique blend between criminal justice and therapeutic responses, it should be obvious that there are several approaches other than a court model that can provide a vehicle to serve the reentry management role. The structure of such a program is limited only by one's imagination. Further, partnerships between different agencies and/or components of the criminal justice system can and should work in tandem to optimize potential outcomes. For example, the Office of Justice Programs (OJP) has tested the use of law enforcement, corrections, and community partnerships to manage reentry. Such partnerships have proven central to the reentry court as well. The use of partnerships will be discussed in additional detail in a later section. However, it is important to note here that the issue of partnerships is one that continues to be a recurring theme throughout this text, recognizing their usefulness to the supervision and treatment of offenders.

Students should note that again, in the current section, the need for both agency and community partnerships is integral to the success of specialized programs such as drug courts, mental health courts, and reentry courts. Beyond this point, communities that wish to establish reentry courts will find that collaborative work on the part of agencies and concerned community members can lead to creative methods of drawing upon existing resources and may even lead to additional funding sources. Likewise, collaborative efforts aid in providing a range of essential reentry support services for offenders and mechanisms for ensuring easy access to them. As has been noted earlier in this section, volunteers and other collaborators can effectively fill in the gaps by assisting with transportation and other informal services that ensure that services are realistically reachable for offenders that may have limited resources. This is a particularly relevant concern for offenders returning from periods of incarceration.

Applied Theory Section 2.1

Social Disorganization, Collective Efficacy, and Community Supervision

The work of Robert Sampson, Stephen Raudenbush, and Felton Earls (1997) shows that crime and recidivism is much lower in communities that have their fair share of **collective efficacy**. Collective efficacy refers to a concept where communities that experience disorderly conduct or criminal behavior possess citizens who have the cohesiveness to act in an "effective" means to solve the crime problem in their area. This then means that collective efficacy is a resource possessed by the community wherein the community acts as a "self-starter," so to speak. Rather than waiting on a formal means of thwarting criminal behavior, the community itself is actively involved in the process of fighting crime.

This concept of collective efficacy is important since it reflects a healthy community and since this describes the specific characteristics that community supervision agencies seek within communities where partnerships are formed. Communities with high levels of collective efficacy are ideal for aiding agencies in providing additional human supervision of offenders. Further, offenders who might otherwise reoffend are less likely to do so due to the high level of collective efficacy in a neighborhood, the result being that the offender is watched much more carefully by members of that community.

Communities with strong collective efficacy have well-developed forms of informal social control. In other words, non-law enforcement controls from churches, schools, civic groups, and other such informal social institutions will be in place. Further, these communities will tend to have a high degree of social cohesion and trust, both among each other and (ideally) with their community supervision agency. What this means for community supervision agencies is that in addition to educating citizens on the effectiveness of treatment programs, agencies must engage their communities so that the citizens are involved in the reintegration process. Doing so will enhance the collective efficacy that exists. In cases where communities do not exhibit strong collective efficacy, it should be the first order of business among criminal justice agencies to instill this in communities through various public outreach campaigns and initiatives. Doing so will produce benefits and rewards that will positively impact the agency and the community alike, while also reducing likely recidivism rates in the future.

⬚ Conclusion

At the outset of this section, we intended to provide the reader with an overview of pretrial, diversionary, and court-based programs designed to keep offenders or the accused in the communities. Overall, the programs reviewed suggest that offenders—even those convicted of violent felony offenses and offenders with mental health problems—can remain in the community while under supervision. The key to success lies in early detection and intervention. Incorporating the use of actuarial instruments may provide those working in the system with an opportunity to identify such offenders and respond accordingly. Maintaining ties and assisting offenders to find gainful employment may provide the most meaningful alternative yet.

⬚ Section Summary

- Community-based corrections include more than just the formal sanctions. Pretrial supervision, diversionary alternatives, and specialized courts offer creative sanctioning/handling options for either the accused or those convicted.
- Pretrial supervision serves as a voluntary option for offenders awaiting a court appearance. Ideally, those charged would complete some form of individualized treatment program before being released.
- Studies assessing the effectiveness of pretrial supervision reveal no difference in demographic characteristics of offenders who are given the opportunity for pretrial release. However, white females are most likely to be released with Hispanic males being the least likely.
- Diversion programs are typically used for juvenile offenders but are being expanded into greater use with adult offenders. Diversion can occur at four different points in the system: (1) diversion from arrest, (2) diversion from prosecution, (3) diversion from jail, and (4) diversion from imprisonment.
- Diversionary programs have been extended to courts dealing with the mentally ill. In these instances, research suggests that diversion to a community-based program does not increase the likelihood of success.
- Specialized court-based programs include therapeutic jurisprudence, drug courts, mental health courts, and reentry courts.
- Therapeutic jurisprudence is the study of the role of the law as a therapeutic agent.
- Drug courts have been used since the late 1980s into the early 1990s. These courts vary in the purpose ranging from non-adversarial to including court processing.
- Research assessing the effectiveness of drug courts reveals they may reduce recidivism of participants, increase treatment retention, and offer a cost-effective alternative.
- Mental health courts are a more recent innovation to deal with the mentally ill.
- Reentry courts are designed to provide comprehensive treatment to those leaving prison while ensuring public safety.

KEY TERMS

Diversion	Drug courts	Pretrial supervision
Diversion from arrest	Graduated sanctions	Reentry courts
Diversion from imprisonment	Mental health courts	Specialized courts
Diversion from jail	Parsimonious	Therapeutic
Diversion from prosecution	sanctions	jurisprudence

DISCUSSION QUESTIONS

1. Based on what we know about pretrial services, do they serve as a successful alternative to detention? Explain your response.

2. Should diversionary programs be utilized in lieu of harsher penalties? What are the pros and cons of extended use of such programs?

3. What type of special issues do those diagnosed with mental health problems present to those working in both a confined and community-based setting?

4. What is the value in evaluating diversionary programs for adults as opposed to simply offering descriptions of the programs?

5. What are the strengths and weaknesses of having centralized drug court management versus decentralized management?

6. What role does politics play in funding drug court programs?

7. Given the current economic and politic climates, create a policy using one of the alternative models discussed in this section.

WEB RESOURCES

American Bar Association Pretrial Release:

http://www.abanet.org/crimjust/standards/pretrialrelease_toc.html

Brevard County Florida Pretrial Release Program:

http://www.brevardcounty.us/criminal_justice/cjs_pretrial_rel.cfm

Center for Court Innovation:

http://www.communityjustice.org/

Pretrial Justice Institute (covers all types of pretrial services including diversion):

http://www.pretrial.org/Pages/Default.aspx

Pretrial Diversion Program:

http://www.justice.gov/usao/eousa/foia_reading_room/usam/title9/22mcrm.htm

Diversion Programs and Overview:

http://www.ncjrs.gov/html/ojjdp/9909-3/div.html

Juvenile Diversion Programs in Phoenix, Arizona:

http://phoenix.gov/PRL/arythjv.html

Northern Star Council: Boy Scouts of America Juvenile Diversion Program

http://www.northernstarbsa.org/YouthPrograms/JuvenileDiversion/

Office of National Drug Control Policy:

http://www.whitehousedrugpolicy.gov/enforce/drugcourt.html

National Institute of Justice Statewide Drug Courts:

http://www.ojp.usdoj.gov/nij/topics/courts/drug-courts/welcome.htm

National Drug Court Institute:

http://www.ndci.org/ndci-home/

Bureau of Justice Programs Mental Health Courts:

http://www.ojp.usdoj.gov/BJA/grant/mentalhealth.html

PBS Frontline New Asylums:

http://www.pbs.org/wgbh/pages/frontline/shows/asylums/special/courts.html

National Center for State Courts: Mental Health Resource Guide:

http://www.ncsconline.org/wc/CourTopics/ResourceGuide.asp?topic=MenHea

http://www.ncsconline.org/wc/courtopics/statelinks.asp?id=60&topic=menhea

U.S. Department of Justice Reentry Courts:

http://www.reentry.gov/publications/courts.html

http://www.reentrypolicy.org/announcements/reentry_courts_emerging_trend

Indiana Reentry Courts:

http://www.in.gov/judiciary/pscourts/reentry.html

Center for Court Innovation Reentry Courts:

http://www.courtinnovation.org/index.cfm?fuseaction=Page.ViewPage&PageID=595&currentTopTier2
=true

Please refer to the student study site for web resources and additional resources.

READING

In this study, Demuth and Steffensmeier explored the impact of race, **ethnicity**, and gender on the decision to release eligible offenders pretrial and the actual outcome of that decision (i.e., actually being released). Recognizing a significant gap in the literature, the authors employed a dual focus by examining both the pretrial release process and outcome data to assess whether receiving the opportunity for pretrial equated to actual release. Felony defendant records from a large data set from the 75 most populous counties in the United States were reviewed. These data accounted for pretrial records collected over a 6-year span (1990–1996) at 2-year intervals. A total of 6,120 individuals were included in the analysis. These findings suggest there are no differences by race, ethnicity, or gender in who is most likely to receive the opportunity for pretrial release. Rather, results did indicate that being white and female increased the defendants' likelihood for being released prior to trial while those who were male and Hispanic were least likely to be released. Policy makers and those working in the system cannot ignore the fact that receiving a particular sentence or opportunity for release does not always mean they are released. The findings of this study are particularly relevant for those making decisions on who and how to release defendants. These results could potentially point to the disparities in the system based on economic eligibility and opportunity more so than sex, race, and ethnicity.

The Impact of Gender and Race-Ethnicity in the Pretrial Release Process

Stephen Demuth and Darrell Steffensmeier

An assessment of the research on gender disparities in the case processing of criminal defendants highlights two major shortcomings. First, in addition to the relative paucity of studies examining the treatment of women in the courts, there is in particular a lack of research on decision making at earlier stages of the criminal case process (e.g., pretrial release). Indeed, most of what we know about the treatment of women in the criminal courts is based on the impact of gender at the sentencing stage. This narrow research focus on sentencing is not limited to studies involving gender, but rather is also a notable limitation of prior studies examining race and ethnicity in the courts. Data are more readily available for examinations of sentencing, in part because sentencing is (1) more proximate to jail and prison and is viewed as where the "real" punishments are meted out and (2) more visible and more highly regulated than other stages.

Second, there is a scarcity of research examining possible interactive effects between gender and race, and even more so, interactive effects between gender and ethnicity—i.e., the inclusion of Hispanic defendants. Despite a rapidly growing Hispanic imputation in the United States, research on case processing has been slow to examine the treatment of this ethnic minority group. Prior sentencing research (Steffensmeier, Ulmer, and Kramer 1998) demonstrates the importance of considering the joint effects of social statuses such as race and gender. Not only may the joint effects of race and gender be considerably larger than either single main effect, but an examination of interactive effects may also reveal extra-legal disparities that are otherwise masked when examining additive models. At issue, in particular, is the question of whether gender differences in case processing outcomes for criminal defendants are similar/different across different racial and ethnic groups.

The present study addresses these gaps in the literature by using felony defendant data collected in large urban courts by the State Court Processing Statistics (SCPS) program of the Bureau of Justice Statistics for the years 1990–1996 to examine the intersection of gender and race-ethnicity on decision making at the pretrial release stage. Importantly, the present study includes white, black, and Hispanic defendants in its sampling framework and also clarifies various dimensions of the pretrial release process, notably a dual focus on both pretrial release decisions (e.g., option for bail, bail amount) and pretrial release outcomes (e.g., pretrial detention or release). We pursue this dual focus because an examination limited to legal outcomes ignores the important underlying process of decision making by which these outcomes are achieved. As our findings reveal, similar/different decisions made throughout the pretrial release process often produce different/similar outcomes across defendant subgroups. The central empirical issue is whether early criminal case processing is influenced by ascribed statuses like gender and race-ethnicity once other legally allowable factors have been taken into account.

◢ Prior Research

Pretrial release practices receive less research and public attention than sentencing practices. This lack of attention is unfortunate for several reasons. First, pretrial detention is punishment before conviction. Even

SOURCE: Stephen Demuth and Darrell Steffensmeier (2004). The impact of gender and race-ethnicity in the pretrial release process. *Social Problems, 51*(2), 222–242. Copyright © 2004 by Society for the Study of Social Problems, Inc.

temporary incarceration is potentially disruptive to family, employment, and community ties and negatively stigmatizes the defendant (Irwin 1985; LaFree 1985). In addition, there is evidence that pretrial detention may interfere with the defendant's ability to prepare an adequate defense (Foote 1954) and may lead to more severe sanctions upon conviction (Goldkamp 1979).

Second, judicial and prosecutorial discretion that involves financial considerations also could produce disparities in pretrial release outcomes. If poor and minority defendants are less able to pay bail, then this disparate impact may amount to a form of de facto racial and ethnic discrimination.

Third, discretion and therefore disparity are more likely at early stages of criminal case processing than at final sentencing (Hagan 1974; Steffensmeier 1980). Decisions made at pretrial stages are less visible than decisions to convict or incarcerate, the criteria used for making pretrial release decisions are less restrictive than the criteria considered legally relevant for making sentencing decisions, and currently-invoked legislative mandates and determinate or guidelines sentencing militate against discretionary adjustments to sentencing outcomes once defendants are convicted. These restrictions on sentencing decisions also may encourage making greater use of discretionary options early in the process. Thus, it is anticipated that the greater informality, the lesser visibility, and the fewer legal constraints surrounding pretrial decision making may facilitate undue disparity at the pretrial stage, including that based on gender and race-ethnicity.

⬛ Conceptual Framework

Legal decision making is complex, repetitive, and frequently constrained by time and resources in ways that may produce considerable ambiguity or uncertainty for arriving at a "satisfactory" decision (Albonetti 1991; Farrell and Holmes 1991). The complexity and uncertainty stem partly from the difficulty inherent in predicting the risk of recidivism or failure to reappear at subsequent court hearings. At the pretrial release stage in particular, there oftentimes is very little definitive information on the background and character of the

defendant that might aid in calibrating those risks. As an adaptation to these constraints, a "perceptual shorthand" (see Steffensmeier et al. 1998) for decision making emerges among judges and other court actors that utilizes attributions about case and defendant characteristics to manage the uncertainty and the case flow. Then, once in place and continuously reinforced, such patterned ways of thinking and acting are resistant to change. Indeed, prior studies examining the decisions of "courtroom workgroups" provide evidence that an inability to internalize crime attributions threatens the effectiveness of an overloaded court system (Eisenstein and Jacob 1977; Nardulli, Eisenstein, and Flemming 1988). As a result, although legal agents may rely mainly on the defendant's current offense and criminal history, their decision making may also be influenced by attributions linked to the defendant's race/ethnicity or gender (Albonetti 1991; Steffensmeier 1980; Steffensmeier et al. 1993). On the basis of these attributions, judges may project behavioral expectations about such things as the offenders' risk of recidivism or danger to the community or risk of flight that, in turn, result in racial/ethnic or gender biases in criminal case processing in general and in pretrial release decision making in particular.

Steffensmeier and associates (1980, 1998, 2000, 2001) suggest that judges are guided by three focal concerns in reaching sentencing decisions: blameworthiness, protection of the community, and practical constraints and consequences. Blameworthiness is associated with defendant culpability. Protection of the community draws on similar concerns but emphasizes incapacitating dangerous offenders or reducing the risk of recidivism. Practical constraints and consequences include concerns about the organizational costs incurred by the criminal justice system and the disruption of ties to children or other family members. Importantly, they report that all of these focal concerns may be influenced by legally irrelevant extra-legal factors, such as race-ethnicity and gender (see Steffensmeier et al. 1998).

Regarding gender, more lenient pretrial release decisions may be imposed on women because judges and other court actors view females as less dangerous and less of a public safety risk than males, and tend to see women's crimes as an outgrowth of their own victimization (e.g., by coercive men or drugs); they may also result from judges' beliefs that the social costs of detaining women are higher since they are more likely than males to have child care responsibilities and mental or health problems that could not be treated in a jail setting (Steffensmeier et al. 1993). Also, women are perceived to maintain community ties more so than males (e.g., with children, parents) and are more closely bonded to conventional institutions that serve to reduce both the likelihood of "flight" as well as future involvement with the criminal justice system (see also Daly 1994).

Concerning race-ethnicity, less lenient pretrial release decisions are likely to be imposed on black and Hispanic defendants than white defendants because of court actors' beliefs that blacks and Hispanics are more dangerous, more likely to recidivate, and less likely to be deterred. Research on labeling and stereotyping of black and Hispanic offenders reveals that court officials (and society-at-large) often view them as violent-prone, threatening, disrespectful of authority, and more criminal in their lifestyles (Bridges and Steen 1998; Hagan and Palloni 1999; Spohn and Beichner 2000; Swigert and Farrell 1976). Also, legal agents may fear that the risk of flight is higher among Hispanic and black male defendants—who may tend to have fewer community ties and may also be illegal immigrants.

Additionally, John Hagan and Alberto Palloni (1999) provide evidence that the government and public perceive immigrants as more criminally involved than citizens. They also show that this perception of a strong link between immigration and crime (which turns out to be a misperception) appears to lead to higher levels of detention among Hispanic immigrants at the pretrial release stage. Their findings suggest the possibility that Hispanics may suffer an especially increased burden at the pretrial release stage, both as Hispanic and as immigrant. In the present study, it is likely that many of the Hispanic defendants are also immigrants. Therefore, any differences in the decisions or outcomes surrounding Hispanics at the pretrial release stage may be partially a function of their citizenship status rather than just their ethnicity. Unfortunately, we have no way of disentangling the effects of ethnicity and citizenship status in the present study. Future research (discussed below) needs to explore the individual and combined effects of ethnicity and citizenship status on decisions and outcomes in the criminal justice system.

These considerations, along with our review of prior studies of gender and race-ethnicity effects at the sentencing stage of the criminal justice process, highlight the importance of testing for intersections among gender and race/ethnicity on criminal case-processing outcomes, and to do so across earlier as well as later stages of the criminal justice system. The failure to consider such interaction may result in misleading conclusions about the effect of these variables.

▧ Hypotheses

Three key hypotheses guide our analysis of pretrial decision making in felony cases:

1. Female defendants will receive more favorable pretrial treatment than male defendants, net of controls for legal, extralegal, and contextual factors. That is, female defendants will be more likely to receive pretrial decisions that encourage pretrial release (e.g., nonfinancial release options, lower bail amounts) than male defendants. It is important to note that if female defendants are more likely to be impoverished than male defendants, then getting lower bail amounts than males may not make a difference for the ability to post bail. However, female defendants may have more access to financial resources through their access to family or social networks willing to post bail or greater success with bail bondsmen for purposes of making bail. Overall, female defendants will be more likely to gain pretrial release than male defendants.

2. Black and especially Hispanic defendants will receive less favorable treatment than white defendants, net of controls for legal, extralegal, and contextual factors. That is, black and Hispanic defendants will be more likely to

receive pretrial decisions that discourage pre-trial release (e.g., financial release options, higher bail amounts) than white defendants. As a result, black and Hispanic defendants will be less likely to gain pretrial release than white defendants.

3. The gender effect on pretrial decision making will persist, and do so in a generally uniform way, across the racial-ethnic comparison groups.

Hypothesis 3 anticipating a small or negligible interaction effect between gender and race-ethnicity is at odds with the view of some writers that white women, but not necessarily black or Hispanic women, are advantaged and will receive preferential treatment in the criminal justice system because they benefit from chivalrous attitudes and because they tend to be more deferential to legal functionaries than black or Hispanic women (Belknap 1996; Farnworth and Teske 1995; Klein and Kress 1976). As Joanne Belknap (1996) writes, "women of color may not receive the chivalry according white women" [because women of color] "may not appear and behave in ways perceived by men as deserving of protection" (p. 70). Drawing instead on the focal concerns perspective, along with several recent studies showing a persistent gender effect in sentencing outcomes across subgroup comparisons (Daly 1994; Spohn and Beichner 2000; Steffensmeier et al. 1998), we expect all female defendants to benefit from beliefs viewing them as less culpable, as less likely to recidivate or to flee (partly because of stronger ties to kin/family including children), and as more essential for providing child care.

Data and Procedures

In the present study, we use individual-level data compiled by the State Court Processing Statistics (SCPS) program of the Bureau of Justice Statistics on the processing of a sample of formally charged felony defendants in the state courts of the nation's 75 most populous counties in 1990, 1992, 1994, and 1996. The SCPS data are well-suited for the proposed analysis because they (1) offer extensive information on the processing of defendants, including detailed information about pretrial release decisions and outcomes; (2) provide important demographic, case, and contextual information such as gender, ethnicity, age, criminal history, arrest and conviction offense, and jurisdiction that might affect decisions at various stages of the process; (3) furnish adequate numbers of cases across all gender and racial/ethnic groups of interest at the pretrial stage of case processing; and (4) permit considerable generalizability of findings since the counties sampled represent courts that handle a substantial proportion of felony cases in the United States.

We restrict the original data sample to include only white, black, and Hispanic defendants. Defendants belonging to the "other" race-ethnicity category represent a small number of cases (i.e., comprise less than 1 percent of the total sample) and are not distributed evenly across counties, thus making data analysis and interpretation of findings difficult. Depending on the county, defendants categorized as "other" may be Asian, Native American, or some other non-white, -black, or -Hispanic racial or ethnic identity. The analytic sample contains 39,435 defendants.

Independent and Control Variables

Gender is measured using a single dummy variable. Race and ethnicity are measured using three dummy variable categories: non-Hispanic white, non-Hispanic black, and Hispanic of any race. Age is measured using a continuous variable. An age-squared component (that is centered and orthogonal to the linear component) is also included. The results of past sentencing studies suggest that age has a nonlinear relationship with incarceration and term length outcomes (see Steffensmeier, Kramer, and Ulmer 1995). It is possible that a similar relationship exists at the pretrial release stage.

Measures of legal variables like offense severity and criminal history are critical for any analysis of criminal case process decision making since these two variables are the best predictors of court decisions in the processing of criminal defendants. For this analysis, offense severity is measured using a set of 10 dummy variables representing the specific offense type of the most serious felony arrest charge (e.g., murder, assault, drug trafficking).

Criminal history is measured in several different ways. The first set of measures are used to indicate prior contact with the criminal justice system. Dummy variable (yes/no) measures are used to address each of the following questions: Has the defendant ever been arrested for a felony?, Has the defendant ever been convicted of a felony?, Has the defendant ever been in jail?, Has the defendant ever been in prison? The second measure of criminal history is a dummy variable indicating whether the defendant has ever failed to appear (FTA) in court pending disposition in the past. The third measure of criminal history is a dummy variable indicating the criminal justice status of the defendant at the time of the most recent arrest (i.e., the arrest recorded in the current data set). Defendants who are on release pending another case, on probation, on parole, or in custody when arrested have active criminal justice statuses.

Because there is significant variation in case processing outcomes across counties, dummy variables for each of the counties in the sample are included in regression models to control for contextual effects such as variation in criminal justice practices across the jurisdictions represented in the SCPS program. Inclusion of these variables controls for mean differences in outcomes across counties. Dummy variables representing the filing year are also included in the regression models.

◪ Dependent Variables

In this study of pretrial release, we examine five different dependent variables. The most general pretrial release variable is a dummy variable indicating whether the defendant is detained or released pending case disposition. However, whether the defendant is ultimately detained or released also depends on the outcomes of a series of decisions made both by agents of the court (e.g., judge, pretrial release officer) and by the defendant (see Goldkamp 1979). These intermediate decisions constitute the remaining four dependent variables.

At the first stage, the judge determines whether the defendant is eligible for pretrial release or should be preventively detained for public safety or flight-risk reasons. The dependent variable representing this decision is a dummy variable indicating whether the defendant was denied bail or given some other release option.

At the second stage, if the defendant is eligible for release, the judge decides whether a financial or nonfinancial release option is most appropriate. To simplify the analysis, specific release options (e.g., ROR, full cash bond) have been combined into two general categories: nonfinancial release and financial release. The dependent variable representing this decision is a dummy variable indicating whether the defendant is given a financial or nonfinancial release option.

At the third stage, for defendants given a financial release option, the amount of bail is set. The dependent variable representing this decision is a continuous variable indicating the number of dollars set for bail. Because the distribution of bail amount is skewed, the natural log of bail amount is used in regression analyses.

At the fourth stage, the defendant who is offered bail either posts bail and is released or does not post bail and remains in jail. Although the ability to pay bail is not technically a criminal justice decision (i.e., made by a legal agent), it is a direct consequence of wise process decision making. In this sense, a financial release option may amount to preventive detention for many defendants and indirectly create gender or racial-ethnic disparities in pretrial release outcomes. The dependent variable representing this outcome is a dummy variable indicating whether the defendant is held on bail or released on bail.

◪ Results

We present here the results of analyses examining the effects of gender and race-ethnicity on pretrial release.

First, we examine descriptive statistics at the pretrial release stage, focusing on differences between male and female white, black, and Hispanic defendant groups. Next, we present the results of multiple regression analyses examining the main effects of gender and race-ethnicity and other extralegal and legal factors on pretrial release decision and outcomes.

Descriptive Statistics

Female and white defendants are less likely to be detained than male, black, and Hispanic defendants. There also are noticeable differences in the arrest charges and criminal history profiles of the defendant groups. T-tests of statistical difference ($p < .001$) show that male defendants have more serious criminal records than female defendants for all measures of criminal history used in the present study. T-tests indicate that murder, rape, robbery, other violence, and burglary make up a greater percentage of criminal charges for males than females. Theft, other property, and other drug offenses make up a greater percentage of criminal charges for females than males ($p < .001$). There are no gender differences for assault and drug trafficking.

Looking at racial and ethnic differences, black and Hispanic defendants have more serious criminal histories than white defendants for all measures of criminal history (t-test, $p < .001$). Also, Hispanics especially are more likely than blacks and whites to be charged with drug offenses. Black defendants are the group most likely to be charged with violent offenses, while white defendants are the group most likely to be charged with property offenses ($p < .001$).

Main Effects of Gender and Race/Ethnicity

This section provides the results of multivariate regression analyses that examine whether differences in pretrial release decisions and outcomes among male and female white, black, and Hispanic defendants persist net of statistical controls for legal, extralegal, and contextual factors.

Similar to the findings of prior studies of pretrial release, an examination of standardized coefficients

(available from the authors upon request) reveals that legal factors are the strongest determinants of whether a defendant is released or detained. Defendants charged with more serious crimes and defendants with more extensive criminal backgrounds are more likely to be detained than other defendants.

Also, our findings concerning the age of the defendant are consistent with the results of past sentencing studies that find that age has a nonlinear relationship with incarceration and term length outcomes (see Steffensmeier and Demuth 2000). That is, age has an inverted-U relationship with the likelihood of pretrial detention. Younger and older defendants are less likely to be detained than are "peak age" defendants. These "peak age" defendants are the most likely to be required to pay bail and the least likely to be able to post bail. Interpreted within a focal concerns framework, these "peak age" defendants may be viewed by judges as less worthy of release because they are perceived as more culpable, more of a safety risk, or less likely to return to court for adjudication.

Turning to the main effects of gender, female defendants are significantly less likely to be detained than male defendants controlling for important extralegal, legal, and contextual factors. The odds of pretrial detention are about 37 percent less for female defendants than male defendants.

Regarding the main effects of race/ethnicity, black (odds = 1.553) and especially Hispanic (odds = 1.821) defendants are more likely to be detained than white defendants at the pretrial release stage. For black defendants, the increased likelihood detention appears to be primarily a result of decreased ability to pay bail. The odds of being held on bail are almost 2 times greater for black defendants than for white defendants. There are no statistical differences between black and white defendants concerning denial of bail, financial release, or amount. For Hispanic defendants, the increased likelihood of detention is not only a function of increased inability to pay bail (odds = 1.948), also because Hispanics are more likely to have bail for release (odds = 1.366) and also receive amounts that are about 7 percent higher than

There is no difference in preventive detention between Hispanic and white defendants.

So far, our findings are consistent with expectations. Female defendants receive more favorable pretrial treatment than male defendants. Indeed, at all decision points in the pretrial release process, female defendants are more likely than male defendants to receive pretrial decisions that encourage pretrial release. As a result, female defendants are considerably more likely to gain pretrial release than male defendants. Black and especially Hispanic defendants receive less favorable pretrial treatment than white defendants. Higher levels of detention among black defendants vis-à-vis white defendants is a result of black defendants' relative inability to post bail. There are no other statistically significant black-white differences in the pretrial release process. However, Hispanics are disadvantaged at many points in the pretrial release process resulting in the highest levels of overall pretrial detention among the three racial-ethnic defendant groups. Hispanics are the group most likely to receive financial release options and the group receiving the highest bail amounts. Also, similar to black defendants, Hispanic defendants are more likely to be held on bail than white defendants.

⬚ Summary

Our main goal in this analysis was to examine the intersection of defendants' gender and race-ethnicity on both pretrial release *decisions* and pretrial release *outcomes*. Drawing from the focal concerns perspective on decisions and practices of court officials, we expected that female defendants would receive more favorable pretrial treatment than male defendants, that white defendants would receive more favorable treatment than black or Hispanic defendants, and that this main effect would persist fairly uniformly across gender and racial-ethnic subgroup comparisons. In addition to the strong effects of prior record and offense seriousness on pretrial release decisions and outcomes (also

predicted by the focal concerns framework), our findings were generally supportive of these hypotheses. However, we also discovered some small but important gender-race/ethnicity interactions in both pretrial release decisions and outcomes. The observed influence of varied gender and race-ethnicity comparisons here can be viewed in alternative ways, depending on which group or subgroup combination one wants to emphasize.

The following findings represent important contributions to the literature on pretrial release outcomes and the decisions leading to those outcomes. Net of controls:

1. Each variable—gender and race-ethnicity—has a significant direct effect on pretrial release outcomes. Female defendants received more favorable pretrial treatment than male defendants. Females were more likely to receive pretrial decisions that encouraged pretrial release (e.g., nonfinancial release options, lower bail amounts) than male defendants and they were more likely to gain pretrial release than male defendants. Black and especially Hispanic defendants received less favorable treatment than white defendants. Black and Hispanic defendants were more likely to receive pretrial decisions that discourage pretrial release (e.g., financial release options, higher bail amounts) than white defendants and they were less likely to gain pretrial release than white defendants.

2. The gender effect on pretrial release outcomes is generally uniform across the racial ethnic comparison groups, but a small interactive effect exists. The gender difference is smallest among whites and largest among Hispanics with blacks placing in the middle.

3. The race-ethnicity effect on pretrial release outcomes is fairly consistent across gender but the effect is slightly greater among males than females.

4. White female defendants receive the most favorable pretrial release decisions in general (although there are a couple of small exceptions) and they are the defendant group most likely to be released prior to trial.

5. Hispanic male defendants, followed by black male defendants, receive the least favorable pretrial release decisions and they are least likely to be released prior to trial.

6. Very substantial differences in pretrial release outcomes exist when comparisons are made between the most dissimilar gender-race/ethnicity comparisons (e.g., Hispanic males are considerably more likely to be detained [prob = +23 percent] than white females); these differences are concealed when the analysis considers only main effects.

An important contribution of our study for research and theory on the pretrial phase of the criminal justice system involves the significance of (1) distinguishing the pretrial decision making process relative to the pretrial release outcome and in (2) analyzing the pretrial decisions as precursors for understanding how the eventual release outcomes might vary by gender and race-ethnicity. The following findings are key examples:

1. Even though Hispanic females and especially black females receive pretrial decisions that compare fairly favorably with those for white females (e.g., relative to whether the defendant is preventively detained, released on ROR, or bail amount), they (Hispanic and especially black females) are more likely to be detained prior to trial. The apparent reason is that they are less able to post bail (regardless of the amount). Stated differently, white female defendants are advantaged relative to non-white females primarily because they are better able to post bail, rather than because they are less likely to be preventively detained or are required to post higher bail amounts.

2. Black and especially Hispanic male defendants are disadvantaged at all points in the pretrial process—they (and, again, Hispanic males in particular) are more likely to be preventively detained, to receive a financial release option, to post a higher bail, and to be unable to post bail to secure their release. They therefore are more likely to be detained prior to trial than the other gender-racial/ethnic subgroups.

3. White male defendants are somewhat of an anomaly. Although they receive less favorable pretrial decisions than female defendants, they are only slightly more disadvantaged in these decisions than black male defendants (e.g., essentially no white-black difference in receiving the financial release option). Yet, white defendants are substantially less likely to be detained prior to trial than black male defendants (about 10 percent difference) as well as Hispanic male defendants (about 14 percent difference). The apparent reason is the greater ability of white male defendants to post bail.

Thus, an important finding to emerge from our analysis derives from differentiating between pretrial decisions and pretrial outcomes—namely, both female and male white defendants are advantaged at the pretrial stage in large part because of their greater ability to make bail. Relative to similarly-situated gender and race-ethnic subgroups, white defendants of both sexes apparently have greater financial capital or resources either in terms of their personal bankroll/resources, their access to family or social networks willing to post bail, or their greater access to bail bondsmen for purposes of making bail. In contrast, "being held on bail because one can't post it" is a main disadvantage facing Hispanic male defendants, black male defendants, black female defendants, and to a lesser extent Hispanic female defendants. In addition, male defendants who are black or Hispanic are also more likely to be preventively detained and less likely to be released on recognizance if not preventively detained.

Conclusion

So far as we know, this study is the first analysis of the pretrial release process that allows for a consideration of main and interactive effects of gender and race-ethnicity (white, black, Hispanic) on both pretrial release decisions and pretrial release outcomes. Our findings suggest at least four important implications for research on criminal case processing both in terms of the pretrial release stage and more generally at other decision points. First, the findings demonstrate the importance of including gender in studies of case processing and of testing not only for main effects but also for possible interactive effects of gender with other defendant statuses like race-ethnicity. For example, we found that gender differences are not necessarily the same for all racial-ethnic groups. In a similar vein, the results also demonstrate the necessity of considering not only defendants' race (i.e., black-white differences) in criminal case processing but the need to also include ethnicity (i.e., Hispanic-white and Hispanic-black differences). In general, Hispanic defendants are treated as or more harshly than black defendants and considerably more harshly than white defendants. Clearly, future studies in this area must distinguish among Hispanic, black, and white defendants as each group has unique experiences in the criminal justice system.

Second, research on gender and racial-ethnic disparities cannot neglect earlier stages of the criminal justice system. In the present study, gender and racial-ethnic differences are considerable at the pretrial release stage, suggesting that restricting our focus to later stages (e.g., sentencing) yields a misrepresentation of the roles of gender and race-ethnicity in the criminal case process. Unchecked prosecutorial and judicial discretion at earlier stages of the process create the potential for such factors as defendants' gender

and race-ethnicity as well as other extralegal characteristics to influence legal decision making and outcomes. Furthermore, it is likely that the outcomes of early decision making in the criminal case process affect later decisions made by judges and prosecutors.

Third, research needs to examine not only the pretrial decisions made by judges and court actors, but also the outcomes of such decisions. As shown in the present study, just because defendants are given the opportunity for pretrial release does not necessarily mean that they are actually released. Indeed, the apparent decision to grant release is frequently at odds with the actual outcome. For instance, we find that black and Hispanic defendants are considerably less able to pay bail to gain release from jail before adjudication. Future research on pretrial release needs to more closely consider the underlying socioeconomic reasons for this racial-ethnic discrepancy. Furthermore, researchers need to revisit the question of whether financial release options are truly necessary to ensure appearance in court and to maintain public safety (see Ares, Rankin, and Sturz 1963; Beeley 1927; Gottfredson and Gottfredson 1990). Given that minority defendants are less able to pay bail than white defendants, financial release options for these defendants may amount to de facto preventive detention decisions.

Fourth, research is needed that goes beyond the sort of statistical analysis reflected in this study to probe in depth how court officials arrive at pretrial decisions. Our findings lend credence to the focal concerns perspective that (1) judges and other court actors develop "patterned responses" that express both gender and race-ethnicity assessments relative to blameworthiness, dangerousness, risk of recidivism or flight and that (2) the defendant's gender and ethnicity may intertwine with the defendant's economic and social resources in ways that shape pretrial outcomes. But, field research and interviewing of court and bail officials are needed to better assess the focal concerns perspective and to better understand the overall harsher treatment of Hispanic male defendants at the pretrial stage. They not only are the group least likely to receive favorable (i.e., nonfinancial) release decisions, but Hispanic males are also the group least able to afford bail in order to gain release.

The observations and interviews should address whether, for example, the harsher treatment of Hispanic males is because (1) they lack the resources or power to resist imposition of harsh legal sanctions; (2) they are perceived as more dissimilar and threatening than white and even black defendants and hence most deserving of punishment; (3) they represent a greater risk of flight to a safe haven or "home country," especially since some Hispanic offenders will be illegal immigrants; and/or (4) some Hispanic defendants (especially recently immigrated Hispanic defendants) are disadvantaged by their difficulty with the English language, general ignorance about or distrust of the criminal justice system, and unwillingness to cooperate with authorities out of fear of deportation of family and friends. In light of their apparently harsher treatment at other case-processing stages (see, e.g., Steffensmeier and Demuth 2001), there is a pressing need for field research and interviewing that examines the unique factors and situations (e.g., language, color, citizenship differences) affecting the treatment of Hispanic defendants in the pretrial release process as well as in the larger criminal justice system.

We highlight one final and very important matter that is suggested from our findings, the importance of social and economic resources in shaping the effects of race-ethnicity on pretrial outcomes and (by extension) the playing out of the focal concerns—i.e., the defendant's ability to pay. Our analysis reveals that white defendants, whether female or male, are advantaged relative to non-white counterparts at the pretrial stage primarily because they are better able to post bail, rather than because they are less likely to be preventively detained or are required to post higher bail amounts. This finding in effect suggests that, even if there were no apparent gender or racial/ethnic disparities in pretrial release decisions, disparities in pretrial release outcomes might still emerge.

This possibility is troubling because these differences in early pretrial release outcomes may translate into unwarranted differences in decisions or outcomes at later stages (e.g., sentencing), as some writers suggest.

At issue is the often overlooked influence that poverty and social class have on sentencing and case-process decision making. As Andrew von Hirsch(1976) notes, "As long as a substantial segment of the population is denied adequate opportunities for a livelihood, any scheme for punishing must be morally flawed" (p. 149). Von Hirsch's concern about achieving "just deserts in an unjust society" (p. 142) seems particularly noteworthy as regards pretrial release decisions and outcomes since, as much more so than elsewhere in the case process, it is at the pretrial stage that one's freedom is so often intertwined with one's money.

⊠ References

Albonetti, Celesta A. 1991. "An Integration of Theories to Explain Judicial Discretion." *Social Problems* 38:247–66.

Albonetti, Celesta A., Robert M. Hauser, John Hagan, and Ilene H. Nagel. 1989. "Criminal Justice Decision Making as a Stratification Process: The Role of Race and Stratification Resources in Pretrial Release." *Journal of Quantitative Criminology* 5:57–82.

Ares, Charles E., Anne Rankin, and Herbert Sturz. 1963. 'The Manhattan Bail Project: An Interim Report on the Use of Pre-Trial Parole." *New York University Law Review* 38:67–95.

Beeley, Arthur L. 1927. *The Bail System in Chicago.* Chicago: University of Chicago Press.

Belknap, Joanne. 1996. *The Invisible Woman: Gender, Crime, and Criminal Justice.* Belmont, CA: Wadsworth.

Belsley, David A. 1991. *Conditioning Diagnostics: Collinearity and Weak Data in Regression.* New York: Wiley and Sons.

Berk, Richard A. 1983. "An Introduction to Sample Selection Bias in Sociological Data." *American Sociological Review* 48:386–98.

Bickle, Gayle S. and Ruth D. Peterson. 1991. "The Impact of Gender-Based Family Roles on Criminal Sentencing." *Social Problems* 38:372–94.

Bobo, Lawrence and Vincent Hutchings. 1996. "Perceptions of Racial Group Competition: Extending Blumer's Theory of Group Position to a Multiracial Social Context." *American Sociological Review* 61:951–72.

Bridges, George S. and Sara Steen. 1998. "Racial Disparities in Official Assessments of Juvenile Offenders: Attributional Stereotypes Mediating Mechanisms." *American Sociological Review* 63:55

Bureau of Justice Statistics. 1999. *Felony Defendants in Large Counties, 1996.* Washington, DC: Department of Justice

Clogg, Clifford C, Eva Petkova, and Adamantios Harif "Statistical Methods for Comparing Regression Between Models." *American Journal of Sociology*

Crawford, Charles. 2000. "Gender, Race, and Habitual Offender Sentencing in Florida." *Criminology* 38:263–80.

Crawford, Charles, Ted Chiricos, and Gary Kleck. 1998. "Race, Racial Threat, and Sentencing of Habitual Offenders." *Criminology* 36:481–511.

Daly, Kathleen. 1987. "Discrimination in the Courts: Family. Gender, and the Problem of Equal Treatment." *Social Forces* 66:152–75.

———. 1994. *Gender, Crime, and Punishment.* New Haven, CT: Yale University Press.

Daly, Kathleen and Rebecca L. Bordt. 1995. "Sex Effects and Sentencing: An Analysis of the Statistical Literature." *Justice Quarterly* 12:143–77.

Eisenstein, James and Herbert Jacob. 1977. *Felony Justice: An Organizational Analysis of Felony Courts.* Boston: Little, Brown.

Farnworth, Margaret and Raymond Teske, Jr. 1995. "Gender Differences in Felony Court Processing: Three Hypotheses of Disparity." *Women and Criminal Justice* 62:23–44.

Farnworth, Margaret, Raymond H. C. Teske, Jr., and Gina Thurman. 1991. "Ethnic, Racial, and Minority Disparity in Felony Court Processing." Pp. 54–70 in *Race and Criminal Justice,* edited by Michael J. Lynch and E. Britt Patterson. New York: Harrow and Heston.

Farrell, Ronald A. and Malcolm D. Holmes. 1991. "The Social and Cognitive Structure of Legal Decision-Making." *Sociological Quarterly* 32:529–42.

Foote, Caleb. 1954. "Compelling Appearance in Court: Administration of Bail in Philadelphia." *University of Pennsylvania Law Review* 102:1031–79.

Goldkamp, John S. 1979. *Two Classes of Accused: A Study of Bail and Detention in American Justice.* Cambridge, MA: Ballinger.

Gottfredson, Michael R. and Don M. Gottfredson. 1990. *Decision Making in Criminal Justice: Toward the Rational Exercise of Discretion,* 2nd ed. New York: Plenum.

Hagan, John. 1974. "Extra-Legal Attributes and Criminal Sentencing: An Assessment of a Sociological Viewpoint." *Law and Society Review* 8:357–83.

Hagan, John and Kristin Bumiller. 1983. "Making Sense of Sentencing: A Review and Critique of Sentencing Research." Pp. 1–54 in *Research on Sentencing; The Search for Reform,* edited by A. Blumstein, J. Cohen, and S. Martin. Washington, DC: National Academy Press.

Hagan, John and Alberto Palloni. 1999. "Sociological Criminology and the Mythology of Hispanic Immigration and Crime." *Social Problems* 46:617–32.

Hanushek, Eric A. and John Jackson. 1977. *Statistical Methods for Social Scientists.* New York: Academic Press.

Holmes, Malcolm, Harmon Hosch, Howard Daudistel, Delores Perez, and Joseph Graves. 1996. "Ethnicity, Legal Resources, and Felony Dispositions in Two Southwestern Jurisdictions." *Justice Quarterly* 13:11–30.

Irwin, John. 1985. *The Jail: Managing the Underclass in American Society.* Berkeley: University of California Press.

Katz, Charles M. and Cassia C. Spohn. 1995. "The Effect of Race and Gender on Bail Outcomes: A Test of an Interactive Model." *American Journal of Criminal Justice* 19:161–84.

Kleck, Gary. 1981. "Racial Discrimination in Criminal Sentencing: A Critique Evaluation of the Evidence with Additional Evidence on the Death Penalty." *American Sociological Review* 46:783–805.

Klein, Dorie and June Kress. 1976. "Any Women's Blues: A Critical Overview of Women, Crime, and the Criminal Justice System." *Crime and Social Justice* 5:34–59.

Kruttschnitt, Candace. 1984. "Sex and Criminal Court Dispositions: The Unresolved Controversy." *Journal of Research in Crime and Delinquency* 21:213–32.

LaFree, Gary D. 1985. "Official Reactions to Hispanic Defendants in the Southwest." *Journal of Research in Crime and Delinquency* 22:213–37.

Little, Roderick J. A. and Donald B. Rubin. 1987. *Statistical Analysis with Missing Data.* New York: Wiley.

Nagel, Ilene H. 1983. "The Legal/Extra-Legal Controversy: Judicial Decisions in Pretrial Release." *Law and Society Review* 17:481–515.

Nardulli, Peter F., James Eisenstein, and Roy B. Flemming. 1988. *The Tenor of Justice: Criminal Courts and the Guilty Plea Process.* Urbana, IL: University of Illinois Press.

Paternoster, Raymond, Robert Brame, Paul Mazerolle, and Alex Piquero. 1998. "Using the Correct Statistical Test for the Equality of Regression Coefficients." *Criminology* 36:859–66.

Patterson, E. Britt and Michael J. Lynch. 1991. "Bias in Formalized Bail Procedures." Pp. 36–53 in *Race and Criminal Justice,* edited by Michael Lynch and Britt Patterson. Albany, NY: Harrow and Heston.

Peterson, Ruth D. and John Hagan. 1984. "Changing Conceptions of Race: Towards an Account of Anomalous Findings of Sentencing Research." *American Sociological Review* 49:56–70.

Pollard, Kelvin M. and William P. O'Hare. 1999. "America's Racial and Ethnic Minorities." *Population Bulletin* 54:1–48

Portes, Alejandro. 1990. "From South of the Border: Hispanic Minorities in the United States." Pp. 160–86 in *Immigration Reconsidered: History, Sociology, and Politics,* edited by Virginia Yans-McLaughlin. New York: Oxford University Press.

Schafer, Joseph L. 1997. *Analysis of Incomplete Multivariate Data.* New York: Chapman and Hall.

Schafer, Joseph L. and Maren K. Olsen. 1997. "Multiple Imputation for Multivariate Missing-Data Problems: A Data Analyst's Perspective." Department of Statistics, The Pennsylvania State University, University Park, PA. Unpublished manuscript.

Spohn, Cassia and Dawn Beichner. 2000. "Is Preferential Treatment of Female Offenders a Thing of the Past? A Multi-Site Study of Gender, Race, and Imprisonment." *Criminal Justice Policy Review* 11:149–84.

Spohn, Cassia and David Holleran. 2000. "The Imprisonment Penalty Paid by Young. Unemployed Black and Hispanic Male Offenders." *Criminology* 38: 281–306.

Steffensmeier, Darrell. 1980. "Assessing the Impact of the Women's Movement on Sex-Based Differences in the Handling of Adult Criminal Defendants." *Crime and Delinquency* 26:344–57.

Steffensmeier, Darrell and Stephen Demuth. 2000. "Ethnicity and Sentencing Outcomes in U.S. Federal Courts: Who is Punished More Harshly?" *American Sociological Review* 65:705–29.

———. 2001. "Ethnicity and Judges' Sentencing Decisions: Hispanic-Black-White Comparisons." *Criminology* 39:145-78.

Steffensmeier, Darrell, John Kramer, and Cathy Streifel. 1993. "Gender and Imprisonment Decisions." *Criminology* 31:411–46.

Steffensmeier, Darrell, John Kramer, and Jeffery Ulmer. 1995. "Age Differences in Sentencing." *Justice Quarterly* 12:583–602.

Steffensmeier, Darrell, Jeffery Ulmer, and John Kramer. 1998. "The Interaction of Race, Gender, and Age in Criminal Sentencing: The Punishment Cost of Being Young, Black, and Male." *Criminology* 36:763–98.

Swigert, Victoria and Ronald Farrell. 1976. *Murder, Inequality, and the Law: Differential Treatment in the Legal Process.* Lexington, MA: Heath.

von Hirsch, Andrew. 1976. *Doing Justice: The Choice of Punishments.* Boston, MA: Northeastern University Press.

Zatz, Marjorie S. 1987. "The Changing Forms of Racial/Ethnic Biases in Sentencing." *Journal of Research in Crime and Delinquency* 24:69–92.

DISCUSSION QUESTIONS

1. In the conclusion of this study, the authors offer four explanations for these results. As a pretrial release officer, how might these results influence your recommendations to the judge?

2. In the conclusion of this study, the authors offer four explanations for these results. As a judge, how might these results influence your recommendations to the judge?

3. Given the findings of this study, where else might disparities be occurring in the system that would account for no difference in the likelihood of opportunity for pretrial release? Why might this factor be important for policy?

READING

In this study, the authors examined the three models of drug court administration, funding, and legitimacy in states. As noted, when drug courts were originally created, many of them were done so with the assistance of federal funding and dollars. As this money dissipates, local communities become more reliant on states to continue to fund their existence. Given this trend, three drug court management models have emerged: "the executive branch model, the judicial branch model, and the collaborative model" (p. 421). To better understand the strengths and weaknesses of this process, the authors conducted semistructured interviews with 11 state drug court administrators. These interviews gave the researchers an opportunity to better understand the status of the state budget at the time of the interview and how the decision-making process for funding the programs occurred. Results from these studies supported the existence of the three models. Likewise they found that states embracing a collaborative model of drug court administration were most likely to have stability in funding and treatment options available. Based upon the results of their study, the researchers offered three recommendations for funding initiatives. First, they needed to have "enacting legislation supported by authoritative programmatic controls" (pp. 431–432). Second, there should be a joint oversight committee that allows for the inclusion of both judicial and executive branches of government. Finally, drug court advocates must collaborate with the legislature to ensure funding stability. This study has several policy implications based upon their findings and recommendations if states want to continue the movement toward using drug courts to specifically deal with substance abuse cases coming to the attention of the courts.

State Administration of Drug Courts

Exploring Issues of Authority, Funding, and Legitimacy

Cary Heck and Aaron Roussell

One of the largest problems for the U.S. criminal justice system in the past 30 years has been criminal offenders who frequently recidivate and seem unaffected by justice system sanctions. Repeat offenders represent a constant source of difficulty for law enforcement, the courts, and correctional institutions (Walker, 2001). Since 1989, drug courts have emerged as a means for dealing with this difficult population (Huddleston, Freeman-Wilson, & Boone, 2004; Marlowe, 2004). Judges and other criminal justice professionals originally designed drug courts to deal with low- to mid-level repeat offenders with co-occurring substance abuse disorders. Insofar as these offenders' recidivism stems directly from their substance abuse problems, successful drug and alcohol treatment could prevent future offenses (National Association of Drug Court Professionals, 1997). Conceptually, the drug court model is simple: Use appropriate tools to diagnose addiction severity, link offenders to appropriate treatment services, hold offenders accountable, and manage their behavior both within and outside the treatment setting through the systematic use of sanctions and incentives enforced by regular judicial status hearings.

The drug court model was originally formulated at the local court level, and it is there that it is best defined. Through national outreach, research, and training organizations, local programs have a great deal of technical and programmatic information available on which to rely in times of change or crisis. As drug courts become institutionalized, however, significant concerns remain about how best to administer drug courts at the state level. The executive branch can lay claim to drug court administration through treatment, law enforcement, and probation/parole. On the other hand, the judicial branch has more obvious jurisdiction over drug court through the judicial adjudicative and administrative process. As federal grants supporting local court programs expire and issues of funding and administration are increasingly being absorbed by states, this problem becomes ever more salient. And as governmental branches at the state level become more contentious over the issue, it is possible that local intervention will suffer.

To conceptualize the emerging problem of state drug court administration, this article will explore the modalities commonly used for managing drug court programs and attempt to answer several related questions. What are the mechanisms that states use to ensure effective delivery of public services (e.g., treatment) to clients? What are the strengths and weaknesses of each of these bureaucratic mechanisms? What factors influence funding stability? Finally, what recommendations can be drawn to accommodate diverse interests across states? This is not

SOURCE: Cary Heck and Aaron Roussell (2007). State administration of drug courts: Exploring issues of authority, funding and legitimacy. *Criminal Justice Policy Review, 18*(4), 418–433.

meant to be an exhaustive list of possible complications arising from interagency collaboration. Indeed, some issues raised herein may prove intractable even to the best intentioned, while other authors may wish to engage some issues for full philosophical satisfaction. Drug courts, however, are a practical response to a real problem—an article addressing their implementation must reflect the same. Our purpose here is to provide an outline of those pitfalls that are endemic to those wishing to establish or shift comprehensive statewide management of drug courts and some of the ways that they can be avoided, confronted, or defeated.

To accomplish these tasks, we reviewed relevant literature and operational examples and conducted interviews with a sample of state-level drug court program directors. Guided by these sources, we discovered that the issues relevant to a discussion of state drug court administration include sustainability, accountability, and program legitimacy. Further, legal and political challenges to drug courts at a state level often emanate from the lack of judicial authority, executive branch oversight of court-funded treatment, and inadequate evaluation and measurement of drug court activities. It is through these lenses that we will explore state drug court administration, funding, and legitimacy.

⬛ Defining the Models: Research and Methods

Fox and Wolfe (2004) developed three distinct categorical models of statewide drug court management: the executive branch model, the judicial branch model, and the collaborative model. Executive models are those that fund and manage their courts solely or largely through executive branch offices (generally the single state agency responsible for handling substance abuse and addiction problems). On the other hand, judicial models funnel authority through the state Administrative Offices of the Courts, also to varying degrees. These two models represent opposite ends of a continuum, with more collaborative approaches composing the middle. Where a state falls in

the spectrum depends on the agreed-on balance between judicial and executive branches over the administration of drug courts. Whereas "hard" executive or judicial models are easy to identify, collaborative models are "softer" and appear in a wide array of incarnations.

To better understand these models, we employed semistructured interviews with a number of state drug court administrators. There were some limitations in choosing interviewees. Not every state has a centralized management structure, nor did every state have a single person in charge and available to speak on these matters. Furthermore, whereas a majority of eligible states fell into the category of the judicial model, it was important to have all three models represented. A stratified sample was drawn from those available for inclusion, including, by design, states representative of each of the three drug court administrative modalities. These interviews were conducted by telephone with 11 state drug court program directors selected for their deep knowledge of their respective programs. These program directors are responsible for coordinating the disparate agencies that are involved in the drug court process, as well as interfacing between the local programs and state-level authorities. This puts them in the unique position of straddling the responsibilities between branches, as well as all levels of government, making them invaluable resources for this sort of inquiry.

The interviews comprised six open-ended questions regarding the modalities employed by states for administering drug court funding and programs. Also included were two Likert-type scaled questions regarding perceptions of the stability of state drug court funding specifically, as well as the stability of the overall state budget. Of the states that were surveyed, three used an executive model, six used a judicial model, and two used a collaborative approach. As is appropriate in a stratified sampling approach, this roughly reflects the national divide in drug court administrative structure. It is important to remember that the presence of a centralized management structure indicates a firm state commitment to drug court, which may indicate a difference between the interviewees and other states.

⬛ Model Strengths and Weaknesses

The administration and funding of drug courts takes various shapes throughout the country. Although we attempt to describe the various permutations of each model, the models themselves are ideal types. As such, specific strengths and weakness of each are reflected to varying degrees among their real-life counterparts. The interviews, as well as the authors' personal experience, were very helpful in this regard. The interviews revealed that the states' drug court administrative structures had been in place for different lengths of time and that this was reflected in their respective comfort levels with their chosen model. Several state contacts suggested that state oversight commissions, often a combination of executive, judicial, and even legislative branch partners, provided excellent oversight and credibility for the state drug court program in its entirety. Further, interviewees, regardless of model, made it clear that judges often felt more secure when supported in administrative function by the state supreme court and Administrative Offices of the Courts, whereas treatment providers felt more secure with executive branch oversight.

Executive Branch Model

A number of states that have centralized drug court management and oversight rely on executive branch agencies for drug court management The greatest strength of this model is the oversight available for treatment and supervision programs, due to the fact that funding is channeled through legislative appropriations directly to the executive branch. Whereas judges usually manage individual drug courts, programs revolve around high levels of treatment, frequent drug and alcohol testing, and supervision received by clients. Most drug court clients receive between 6 and 10 hours a week of counseling and treatment services. Counselors and treatment providers who are licensed by executive branch agencies usually provide these services. This connection provides the executive model drug court managers the ability to monitor the quality of treatment. Tellingly, one of the most common complaints made by local drug court judges is with regard to their ignorance of substance abuse treatment. State directors indicate that the executive branch model therefore reduces concerns about the nature of the treatment provided by drug court programs.

Still, this places executive management in the position of playing decision maker over what is ultimately a court program, thus invoking unease over separation-of-powers issues. The national Conference of State Court Administrators (COSCA) and Conference of Chief Justices, an organization on record in its support of problem-solving courts (COSCA, 2000), provides a powerful, practical perspective on this issue, suggesting that the separation-of-powers doctrine is based primarily on functional utility:

> Judicial independence is not an end in itself … but rather the means to ensure the primacy of the rule of law by guaranteeing the ability of the courts to protect individual rights, police the exercise of governmental powers and decide individual disputes impartially. Moreover, the doctrine of separation of powers contemplates some sharing of powers among the branches; indeed, the other branches are constitutionally empowered to determine the judicial branch's structure, jurisdiction and resources. (COSCA, 2001, p. 6)

This must be interpreted cautiously, as COSCA also asserts unequivocally the territory of the judiciary, stating that policy decisions involving the actual administration of justice must be the primary bailiwick of the judicial branch. This is not only a matter of "good governance" but also a strongly constitutional issue, because administration is inherently bound up in the adjudicative role of the courts (COSCA, 2001). Suggesting that outside regulation and accountability is both inevitable and desirable, COSCA (2001, p. 1) states that "with judicial governance comes the right and interest of the other branches of government and the public to hold the judiciary accountable for effective management of court business." Although courts do occupy a relatively independent position in American governance, they still must be accountable to the public for their institutional actions. Indeed, the late Chief Justice William H. Rehnquist (1996) opined in his *Year-End Report on the Federal Judiciary:*

> Once again this year—in my eleventh annual report on the state of the judiciary—I am struck by the paradox of judicial independence in the United States: we have as independent a judiciary as I know of in any democracy, and yet the judges are very much dependent on the legislative and executive branches for the enactment of laws to enable the judges to do a better job of administering justice. (p. 1)

The judicial branch is a separate, coequal branch of government, which has the constitutionally founded authority to make decisions about the actions of the legislative and executive branches. This authority is carefully guarded and protected against any advances made by agents of the other branches (American Bar Association, 1997). Indeed, the separation-of-powers doctrine requires that the three branches maintain distinct realms of authority largely to prevent abuse of power by any one branch. Yet, if this is ultimately a functional directive, as COSCA (2001) suggests, perhaps there is more room for overlap of authority than the separation-of-powers doctrine implies. This flexibility, however, must end at the point where the actual administration of justice begins (Rehnquist, 1996). Still, from the viewpoint of the most powerful state judicial leaders in the United States (i.e., COSCA and Conference of Chief Justices), executive control of judicial programs can be justified for the greater good under certain circumstances.

Beyond the philosophical, this problem is manifested in practical weaknesses of the executive branch model. Judges sometimes lament a lack of authority and oversight in the operation of their drug courts. Drug courts that have executive branch management and funding are precariously balanced between subjecting themselves to executive authority and maintaining their independence. Thus, as reported by state directors, drug court judges often feel as though they are operating programs on an island without the support of those systems designed to promote appropriate action within courts. In these cases, drug court judges are beholden to executive branch authorities to answer treatment and supervision questions and solve problems that they are often ill equipped to handle.

When executive model administrators grant authority to executive branch agencies to set rules and requirements for drug court program activity, the balance of power is imperiled. Fox and Wolfe (2004, p. 21) suggest that "as states have assumed more financial responsibility for drug courts, they have also begun taking on more policymaking authority." Thus, drug court programs that receive funding from executive agencies must also subject themselves to policies and rules established by these agencies. In essence, this acceptance of outside authority could go beyond the proscriptions set by COSCA and Rehnquist to actually determine the administration of justice. For many drug court judges, the value of the goals associated with successful treatment of addicted offenders outweighs the possible negative effects of having to follow rules established by the executive branch. Many see this as a mere technicality; others disagree. Should judges be forced to choose?

Were states to create third-party agencies comprising stakeholders from both (or all three) branches, it is possible that weaknesses relating to authority struggles and separations of power might be mitigated, while retaining the general executive model structure. Further, some states have seen the advantages of this sort of collaboration and have shifted varying amounts of their drug court authority to third-party agencies. Again, however, a full shift to a collaborative model may not be required—the improved judicial voice in executive decision making might mitigate concerns without the loss of the executive power majority and its related strengths.

Judicial Branch Model

Despite their collaborative nature, drug courts revolve around the judge and the courtroom. This links drug courts inextricably to the judicial system and is undoubtedly a major reason that the judicial model predominates across the United States. This model therefore has certain obvious strengths when it comes to drug court authority, not the least of which is legitimacy for all parties involved, including the program staff. Consistent with this are the results of a court study from Missouri (Myers, 2004) that conclude that most court administrators and staff would prefer a complete separation from the executive branch of government. In fact, more than three quarters of those surveyed wanted to report solely to the supervising judge (Myers, 2004). This suggests that judicial oversight is the most effective means of control of court employees and is an implicit argument for the efficacy of judicial management structures in general. Arguments for increased local control by executive officials therefore run counter to the orientation of the actual court employees, assuming that these findings are generalizable outside of Missouri. Consistent with Rehnquist (1996) and COSCA (2001), it was made clear by a majority of respondents that the executive branch should not involve itself in the judging of cases, and that the court structure should be separate from executive control (Myers, 2004). Taken together, this is a clear argument for a judicial approach from the ground up.

External legitimacy is also crucial. On the whole, state-level judicial budgets tend to be more consistent year to year than their executive branch counterparts, due to the legal requirements of the judiciary. These requirements usually force legislators to maintain funding stability over time. This, in turn, can create stability for court programs under judicial purview, such as drug court programs, but only when drug court funding is expressly a part of the judicial budget. Although the interviews suggest that funding stability is unrelated to choice of drug court administration model, strong ties to the more placid judicial branch may affect the perception of stability. It seems likely that the appearance of greater stability could actually lead to greater stability in the long run.

Legitimacy and the related issues of accountability and responsibility have driven changes at the state level in the past. The state of Louisiana, for example, shifted its funding for drug courts from the Office of Addictive Disorders to the state supreme court in 2001. This shift was driven by concerns about funding but also by the concerns of drug court judges, who felt isolated and abandoned in their roles without judicial support. This move was made possible due to the unified nature of Louisiana's courts and strong support from the state's supreme court justices. Further, the Louisiana Supreme Court alleviated executive branch concerns regarding this transition by contracting with the previous state director of treatment of the Office of Addictive Disorders to ensure that the quality of service would continue uninterrupted regardless of the administrative shift (Fox & Wolfe, 2004).

In 2005, the Wyoming State Substance Abuse Division conducted a series of drug court community meetings that provided the authors with information regarding the opinions of drug court judges on the subject of drug court administration. Similar to the situation in Louisiana, several judges mentioned similar concerns about their isolation. This isolation stemmed from a feeling that the drug court program is an "add-on" to traditional court functioning. This, combined with the lack of unified support and codified judicial rules for drug court, created the sense that programs were perpetually operating on an ad hoc basis and not as part of the overall judicial structure. Wyoming, like Louisiana before 2001, uses the executive model; it seems likely that this problem may have been mitigated through a similar shift to judicial branch oversight.

Still, the judicial branch model suffers from legal and philosophical challenges that are different yet as equally daunting as those with the executive branch approach. One of the major philosophical weaknesses of judicial branch administration of drug courts is the resolution of those legal claims that all legal interventions generate. Whereas state supreme courts are the highest legal authority in each state, the funding and administration of drug courts solely through the judicial branch creates an automatic conflict of interest in the adjudication of the lawsuits that inevitably arise. For example, in

Maricopa County, Arizona, the county attorney filed a case against two driving under the influence (DUI) court programs (Archibold, 2006). These programs were specifically tailored to meet the needs of Spanish-speaking and Native American offenders. The county attorney alleged that these programs violated both the U.S. Constitution and other laws "barring discrimination on the basis of race or ethnicity" (Archibold, 2006). Due to the nature of the allegations and the inherent conflict of interest, the case had to be filed in federal district court, which created an uncomfortable situation for the Arizona court system.

Accountability, though not a problem internally for a top-to-bottom judicial structure, becomes a salient interbranch issue. Drawn from a collaborative conference on the funding of state courts, Funding the State Courts (Tobin, 1996) deals with this theme: "The lack of clear guidelines for judges on how to deal with officials of the other branches, particularly in budgetary matters, exacerbates the[ir] isolation and lack of mutual education" (p. 4). Furthermore, attempts to extract more "accountability" from the judiciary are often met by stiff resistance, not from an inherent objection to the idea but because these attempts are often viewed as challenges to judicial power and independence. In these situations, the judiciary sometimes views accountability as a code word that contests judicial authority. Tobin (1996) suggests that a certain amount of tension with the legislature is created by this perception that the courts must be reined in. This can make it difficult for courts to obtain the resources they need to effectively perform their duties. A lack of communication between the legislature and the courts means that often courts can learn of unfavorable budgetary changes long after anything can be done about them. This strongly suggests that interbranch lines of communication should be open and continuous, rather than consisting solely of brief budgetary sessions. This is particularly true for drug courts because their funding could be seen as nonessential for the operation of state judicial structures.

Intermittent or contentious funding, especially as a by-product of judicial feuds with state legislatures, is at odds with the idea of ensuring quality drug court service. If legislatures are serious about institutionalizing

drug courts, then the funding issue must be permanently resolved, and in a way that enables consistent decision making through administrative stability. A cooperative, ongoing dialogue may be the best way to address this. It may further serve to insulate the court system from inevitable legislative crises and conflicts of interest. COSCA (2001) suggests that ongoing communication is fundamental for transparency and solidarity in a way that is consistent with this conclusion:

> By expanding and routinizing format and informal interbranch communications, state judiciaries can familiarize the other branches with the problems and needs of the courts. Productive working relationships, once established, foster an ethos of mutual understanding that reduces resistance and misunderstandings. Some examples of how this can be accomplished include: arranging informal meetings between the Chief Justice and the Governor to discuss basic concerns, or with legislative leaders . . . and scheduling meetings with groups of judges and legislators to exchange ideas and have a continuing dialogue on justice system issues. (p. 6, our emphasis)

However, despite the strained relationship between the legislature and the courts it pales beside the executive/judicial dynamic:

> Officials asserted that the executive branch interfered in financial administration, particularly in inhibiting the transfer of appropriations between budget categories and in conducting audits. Court officials felt that each new gubernatorial administration changed the ground rules and budget strategy, sometimes intruding into budget matters from which the governor is constitutionally excluded. (Tobin, 1996. p. 7, our emphasis)

Often, too, the politicization of various judicial matters—that is, crime and drugs—creates mandates from the executive branch that go unaccompanied by a commensurate increase in funding to cover the increased adjudicative activity. In terms of drug court specifically, Tobin's (1996) more general suggestion seems prudent: the formation of collaborative committees where these problems can be insulated from the governmental branches at large.

Finally, the judiciary, by definition and by choice, lacks overall program administration experience, particularly in the realm of substance abuse treatment. Although successful drug court judges usually acquire these skills through time and experience, there is no standardized accreditation process through which they can be trained. Thus, the learning curve for drug court judges is rather akin to "sink or swim." Although national trainings and programs have attempted to remedy this deficiency, there is no substitute for actual medical and clinical training. Thus, one primary function of the collaborative drug court team is to advise the judge on these matters. Perhaps this lesson can be applied also at the state administrative level, creating a model for the executive and judicial branches. Rather than the rotating cast of characters that is endemic to government at all levels, a permanent body empowered to undertake exactly those actions would provide for ongoing dialogue and an institutionalized presence for drug courts. Personal relationships, though valuable, disappear as the individuals involved matriculate or retire. An intermediary third-party agency could institutionalize the communication process. This could be an expedient way to prevent communication breakdowns between governmental branches. As with executive drug court models, judicial models must incorporate the input from their counterparts to successfully navigate the hurdles posed by their particular method of administration. Although there may be other ways to accomplish this, a third-party agency seems the most direct.

Collaborative Model

A collaborative approach can bring together the strengths of both the executive and judicial models. When the administrative structure at the top of the state hierarchy more closely reflects that of the "on the ground" practitioners, the members of the local drug court team can feel more secure in their respective hierarchical support. Mutual involvement from multiple branches of government allows for oversight of judicial functions (i.e., judges and in-court activities) and executive functions (i.e., substance abuse treatment and probation services) as well as enabling unified presentation to the legislature. However, this collaborative approach is comparatively difficult to enact, which reflects its relative scarcity.

Of the interviewees, Idaho and California reported having collaborative funding and oversight mechanisms. The Idaho model is statutorily defined and relies on a strong interagency agreement between the judicial and executive branches, which splits the drug court funding between the two. The executive branch manages all aspects of the substance abuse treatment programs, whereas the judicial branch manages funds for the rest of the drug court program activities. A statewide coordinating committee, which includes representatives from all three branches of government, as well as other program stakeholders (i.e., prosecutors, defense council, treatment providers, etc.), is responsible for the program as a whole. Program management is overseen by the Idaho Administrative Office of the Courts, whereas funding for treatment is managed exclusively by the executive branch. Funding for judicial functions comes from a dedicated surcharge on alcohol sales to support drug and family courts.

California's collaboration is manifested in the development of two divergent funding streams and the formation of strong interbranch committees to manage them. California's split drug court funding comes with a legislative requirement that it be "coadministered" by an Executive Steering Committee cochaired by the deputy director of the Department of Alcohol and Drug Programs (executive branch) and a judge from the Judicial Council (judicial brunch). Essentially, except for a $1 million line item directly to the judiciary, the rest of California's $21 million in drug court funding is jointly administered. In both cases, though funding comes from various sources to various agencies, the ultimate authority is a collaborative committee comprising those actors involved. Everyone has a voice.

While a strictly collaborative model appears to provide the best of both worlds, there are some potential weaknesses that arise from this approach. The first is the territoriality that automatically follows funding. Those state directors that reported a collaborative approach stated that this problem had to have been handled through strategic legislation at the inception of the programs or the model would not have been successful. Thus, this approach mandates legislative foresight and clear wording to prevent later problems. Additionally, the lack of an official final authority for these approaches is a concern. Although collaborative model states seem to have developed a good balance for handling difficult issues through their coordinating committees, these arrangements have yet to be seriously challenged. It became clear during the interviews that drug court programs bank on current goodwill between governmental branches and strong support of the drug court model by the current leaders in their respective branches. Interviewees reported no emerging reasons why this cooperation might collapse—indeed, it appears to grow stronger as time passes. However, if these elements are not preexistent in a particular state, it seems highly unlikely that the collaborative model would work effectively in times of conflict. Although potentially valuable for maximizing the strengths of appropriate agencies and avoiding structural controversy, a collaborative initiative must be approached with methodical deliberation and characterized by well-defined roles, extensive knowledge of drug courts, and clearly delineated authority.

Overall, even in states subscribing to noncollaborative models, a growing number of states are forming these legislatively required advisory committees comprising members of all three branches of government and other stakeholders. Those with collaborative models, of course, invest these committees with the bulk of the administrative decision-making and funding responsibility, but the idea is applicable across the board. The first obvious strength of this approach is that various administrative roles can still be fulfilled by the appropriate authority or agency, minimizing separation-of-powers issues. Second, through preexisting administrative mechanisms, each branch can provide accountability

and legitimacy for the components of the programs for which they are responsible. Thus, judges, probation officers, and treatment professionals are responsible to those respective agencies that have traditionally provided their funding and oversight. This alleviates concerns from both the judicial and executive models. Finally, there is the potential for disagreements to be resolved internally by the representative body to which the drug court answers, thus short-circuiting potential interbranch conflicts or destructive competition for legislative funding.

⬛ Stability of Drug Court Funding: A Legislative Issue

Important as the judicial and executive branches are in the administration and management of drug courts at the state level, funding ultimately comes from the state legislature. Clearly, the stability of funding is crucial to the smooth operation of drug court programs. Despite the importance of administrative model choice for drug courts, however, funding stability appears not to be strongly related to this variable. "Very stable" or "fairly stable" drug court funding was manifested in all three models in the interviews. The only qualification to this is that the only state directors to report nonstable drug court funding came from judicial model states. Although judicial models overall may appear to have more inherent stability, clearly this is not always the case and may depend on other variables. Both directors, for example, linked their funding instability to legislative insecurity about drug courts.

In general, however, state directors generally reported relatively stable drug court funding even when they saw the overall state budget as less predictable. Not surprisingly, those states with the greatest levels of stability suggested that this stability arose from strong legislation and well-defined, supportive leadership in all three state branches of government. In addition, court program stability appears to be partially a function of the age of each state program; as might be expected, older programs reported greater stability than did more recent ones. More important than which model a state chooses to enact, it is these factors that influence funding stability and in turn provide for better implementation and sustainability of drug courts. Tentatively, it appears that active cooperation of all three state branches of government often through a multilateral commission of some sort, can help ensure stable funding. Neither of those states that reported unstable funding employed multilateral commissions.

Finally, drug courts do not exist in a vacuum. Drug court money would be funneled elsewhere had drug courts never been implemented. Where that money would go is different for each state, but it should ultimately be a reflection of where drug courts' benefits are felt—that is, what part of the budget benefits the most from drug courts. When asked this hypothetical question, a substantial majority of state directors hypothesized that the money would return to the executive branch to be used for correctional purposes. Philosophically, this indicates that states are embracing the fact that drug courts save money that would otherwise be spent incarcerating participants. California, for example, statutorily requires regular cost/benefit analyses to support this claim. Even more important, this finding indicates that the money not saved by the establishment of drug courts would represent a drain for the executive branch, that is, through the Department of Corrections. Overall, this finding suggests that drug courts should maintain their strong links to executive administration and not be considered "just another court program."

⬚ Conclusions and Recommendations

Drug court is a relatively new innovation in jurisprudence that requires significant collaboration between arms of the government that are traditionally unaccustomed to working together. As such, considerable strategic consideration must be devoted to the issues of funding, management, oversight, and separation of powers. Although there is no silver bullet

in the administration of state drug court programs, each model presented here has separate strengths that may be suitable in different situations. Executive branch models provide strong support and oversight for the treatment and supervision components of drug courts while creating some philosophical and practical concerns about separation of powers. Judicial models partially resolve these issues and provide legitimacy for programs but often lack program management capability and expertise for nonjudicial components such as substance abuse treatment. The states that have been successful in maintaining satisfactory administrative control of programs over time tend to employ models that, like local programs, provide collaboration at the highest levels. If state administration of drug courts were viewed as a continuum, with fully judicial models on one side and fully executive models on the other, those in the middle tend to be the most successful. This does not necessarily mean that states must completely embrace the collaborative model, but perhaps simply a collaborative approach. For example, an administrative structure housed in the judicial branch might still use a steering committee comprising members from multiple branches of government and funding schemes that provide appropriate levels of continuity and oversight.

Three important recommendations emerge from this discussion. First, for states to have strong program stability, they must have specific enacting legislation that is supported by authoritative programmatic controls. Bluntly, the legislation must have teeth. It is not enough to simply define and provide blanket funding for drug courts. State drug court directors reported that legislation must also contain language pertaining to a second recommendation: the establishment of joint oversight committees with judicial and executive branch involvement and authority to create and enforce rules. It might also be helpful to include other relevant stakeholders, regardless of branch affiliation. This committee must have the ability to definitively answer specific legal and programmatic questions that arise during the course of drug court operations. Further, the committee must be invested with some legal authority to provide accountability and legitimacy for the program judges. Also, the committee should work to implement a third recommendation, namely, the creation of specific judicial rules regarding drug court operations. The rules must be broad enough to include the various systems employed by drug courts but should be specific enough so that judges can refer to them as unfamiliar issues arise. Finally, overall collaboration by drug court advocates with the legislature is crucial for eventual funding stability. Even in often-tumultuous state budgets, drug court program funding can achieve stability with full legislative buy-in to create strong and specific enabling legislation. All of these recommendations are critical, regardless of which model a state has enacted.

When designing, shifting, or revising a statewide drug court management plan, it is clear that state administrators, legislators, and judges must take a strategic approach. Program management infrastructure must be considered carefully and include issues of staffing, data collection, management, and funding. Guidelines must be incorporated to ensure adherence to the drug court model and the quality of services provided for program participants. Perhaps most important, the judicial framework must be crafted in such a way as to allow drug court judges to maintain their status as independent arbiters of the law while serving in this new role. The evidence strongly suggests that a judge's legal authority must be inviolate.

There are myriad pitfalls into which any well-intentioned branch of state government might fall in attempting to establish the administration of drug courts. Though certainly an admirable goal given diminishing federal funding, an honest appraisal of where the state should house its drug court authority is required. Whichever direction a state decides to go, it must, at all times, remember that drug court is a collaborative activity and that this must be reflected at every level of its implementation.

✉ References

American Bar Association. (1997). *Report of the ABA commission on separation of powers and judicial independence.* Washington, DC: Author.

Archibold, R. C. (2006, March 1). *A test of ethnic courts for drunken drivers.* New York Times, Late Edition. Final, p. A12.

Belenko, S. (1998). *Research on drug courts: A critical review.* National Drug Court Institute Review, 1(1), 1–42.

Belenko, S. (2001). *Research on drug courts: A critical review.* 2001 update. New York: National Center on Addiction and Substance Abuse at Columbia University.

Berman, G., & Feinblatt, J. (2005). *Good courts: The case for problem-solving justice.* New York: The New Press.

Conference of State Court Administrators. (2000, August). *In support of problem-solving courts.* Conference of Chief Justices Resolution 22, Conference of State Court Administrators Resolution IV. Adopted at Conference of Chief Justices, 52nd Annual Meeting.

Conference of State Court Administrators. (2001, December). *Position paper on effective judicial governance and accountability.* Arlington, VA: Author.

Fox, A., & Wolfe, R. V. (2004) *The future of drug courts: How states are mainstreaming the drug court model.* New York: Center for Court Innovation.

Goldkamp, J. S., White, M. D., & Robinson, J. B. (2002). *An honest chance: Perspectives on drug courts.* Federal Sentencing Reporter, 6, 369–372.

Government Accountability Office. (2005). *Adult drug courts: Evidence indicates recidivism reductions and mixed results for other outcomes.* Report to congressional committees. Washington, DC: Author.

Heck, C. (2006). *Local drug court research: Navigating performance measures and process evaluations* (Monograph Series 6). Alexandria, VA: National Drug Court Institute, National Association of Drug Court Professionals.

Huddleston, C. W., Freeman-Wilson, K., & Boone, D. (2004). *Painting the current picture: A national report card on drug courts and other problem solving courts,* 1, 1. Alexandria, VA: National Drug Court Institute, National Association of Drug Court Professionals.

Huddleston, C. W., Freeman-Wilson, K., Marlowe, D. B., & Roussell, A. (2005). *Painting the current picture: A national report card on drug courts and other problem solving courts,* 1, 2. Alexandria, VA: National Drug Court Institute, National Association of Drug Court Professionals.

Marlowe, D. B. (2004, September 9). Drug court efficacy vs. effectiveness. Retrieved May 10, 2007, from http://www.jointogether.org/sa/news/features/reader/0,1854,574745,00.html

Marlowe, D. B., Heck, C., Huddleston, C. W., & Casebolt, R. (2006). A national research agenda for drug courts: Plotting the course for second-generation scientific inquiry. *Drug Court Review*, 5(2), 1–27.

Myers, L. G. (2004). Judicial independence in the municipal court: Preliminary observations from Missouri. *Court Review*, 41, 26–31.

National Association of Drug Court Professionals. (1997, January). *Defining drug courts: The key components*. Washington, DC: Bureau of Justice Assistance, U.S. Department of Justice.

Rehnquist, W. H., U.S. Supreme Court. (1996). *Year-end report on the federal judiciary*. Washington, DC: Author. Retrieved April 11, 2006, from http://www.uscourxs.gov/cj96.htm

Tobin, R. W. (1996, July). *Funding the state courts: Issues and approaches*. Williamsburg, VA: National Center for State Courts, State Justice Institute.

Walker, S. (2001). *Sense and nonsense about crime and drugs: A policy guide*. Belmont, CA: Wadsworth.

DISCUSSION QUESTIONS

1. What are the strengths and weaknesses of each of the drug court management models discussed in the article?

2. Define and describe the three drug court management models. Which management model exists in your state? Why do you think this is the preferred management model?

3. What role do state oversight commissions play in the coordination, existence, and funding of drug court programs?

4. Given the findings of this study and what you have learned about drug courts, do you believe they are a good alternative to regular court processing? Explain your answer.

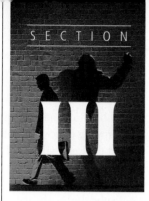

SECTION

III

Restorative Justice

Learning Objectives

1. Define **restorative justice** programming.

2. Understand how restorative justice programs differ from traditional sentencing strategies.

3. Understand and be able to differentiate the different types of restorative justice programs, such as family conferencing, **teen courts**, reintegrative shaming, and **community justice.**

4. Be able to explain the differences between restorative justice programs offered in the community and behind institutional walls.

5. Be able to discuss the benefits of restorative justice programming to both victims and offenders.

6. Understand the benefits and limitations of restorative justice.

Restorative justice approaches to offender sanctioning seek to restore the victim, the community, and the offender to a similar level of functioning that existed prior to the commission of the criminal act. Restorative justice initiatives require the offender to admit to their criminal behavior and demonstrate earnest and sincere remorse. Restitution is often made to the victim, and the victim provides direct input into the process. There are a number of such programs around the nation and even around the world (Hanser, 2006a, 2006b). In all cases, the attempt is made to heal the damage that has been done to the victim and the community, and it is the specific charge that the offender provides the action necessary for healing to occur. This integrative theoretical approach pulls together elements of labeling, social disorganization, **subcultural theory**, reality theory, etc., to provide a good overlay to community empowerment programs. Further, these programs are not designed to be a replacement for diversion; rather, they are designed as punishment and can be utilized at the various times in the process (i.e., police, probation, courts, corrections or parole) (Latimer, Dowden, & Muise, 2005, p. 126). This section of the text provides a definition of restorative justice, and provides examples of the various types of programs including family conferences, teen courts, reintegrative shaming, and victim–offender mediation (VOM). It also provides a discussion of the role of victims in the process.

⊠ Restorative Justice Defined

Restorative justice programs began in the 1970s as a grassroots initiative by practitioners who were disenchanted with how the criminal justice system operated (Dzur & Wertheimer, 2002; Wenzel, Okimoto, Feather, & Platow, 2008). As a hybrid movement, agency personnel along with victims rights advocates sought to minimize the existence of state victimization by including those harmed by the offender in the process while increasing the opportunity for meaningful responsibility of the perpetrator to the victim and encouraging forgiveness by their respective community (Braithwaite, 2000; Dzur & Wertheimer, 2002; Wenzel et al., 2008). As John Braithwaite (2002) contended, restorative justice programs must have top-down standards with bottom-up accountability and while ensuring human rights.

Restorative justice seeks to restore the victim and the community to its state of functioning prior to the criminal act, often involving numerous persons in the community in the reintegration of offenders and holding them accountable for their behavior. By bringing together victims, offenders, families, and other key stakeholders in a variety of settings, restorative justice helps offenders understand the implications of their actions and provides an opportunity for them to become reconnected to the community. Thus, restorative practices, while emphasizing the need for victim compensation and/or community healing, are essentially reintegrative approaches for the offender.

A review of the substantive literature on restorative justice reveals multiple definitions of the concept. For the purposes of this text, the definition of restorative justice is borrowed from researcher and advocate Thomas Quinn during his interview with the National Institute of Justice (1998). Specifically, restorative justice is a term for interventions that focus on restoring the health of the community, repairing the harm done, meeting victims' needs, and emphasizing that the offender can and must contribute to those repairs. Restorative justice considers the victims, communities, and offenders (in that order) as participants in the justice process. These participants are placed in active roles to work together to do the following:

- Empower victims in their search for closure
- Impress upon offenders the real human impact of their behavior
- Promote restitution to victims and communities

Since its inception, criminal justice practitioners have witnessed the evolution and expansion of these programs into three distinct categories: circles, conferences, and VOM (Latimer et al., 2005). Each of these will be described next. Although the names of the programs may range from VOM, victim reconciliation, teen courts, family conferencing, etc., they still fall under the auspices of repairing the harm caused by the offender to the victim and their respective communities. Furthermore, the process of these programs provides benefits to both the victim and the offender. For the victim, they receive redress, vindication, and healing by encouraging recompense. For the offender, they benefit from restorative justice initiatives through the process of reparation, fair treatment, and habilitation (Latimer et al., 2005, p. 129). These programs also provide opportunities for offenders to reintegrate into society while recognizing the harm they have done on a much more global basis (Dzur & Wertheimer, 2002, p. 5).

⊠ Types of Restorative Justice Programs

The most common and most established types of restorative justice are restitution and community service programs. These programs hold offenders personally accountable for their crimes and require that they make reparations to victims (either directly or indirectly). According to Schneider and Finkelstein (1998), there are three major types of restitution programs: community service, **monetary restitution**, and direct service to victims. Community service is work performed by an offender for the benefit of the community as a component of the offender's sentence. Community service is one means by which the offender is held accountable and required to provide amends for the harm caused by his or her criminal conduct. Monetary restitution is a process by which offenders are held partially or fully accountable for the financial losses suffered by the victims of their crimes. Restitution is typically ordered for property crimes or crimes where something of value was stolen or procured, such as with fraud, forgery, or theft. Restitution payments may also be used to reimburse victims of violent crime for expenses related to their physical and mental health recovery (Schneider & Finkelstein, 1998). Lastly and most rare is the use of restitution from the offender directly to the victim (Schneider & Finkelstein, 1998). According to Schneider and Finkelstein (1998), this is a type of reconciliation in which the offender and the victim meet in a supervised setting to determine how the offender can make restitution directly to the victim through the performance of some type of service. In same states, this may be referred to as victim–offender dialogues.

Although community service and restitution are the most frequently used forms of restorative justice, there are a variety of other programs specifically designed as a mechanism to repair the harm done by the offender to the victim. The following programs will be discussed: family conferences, teen courts, reintegrative shaming, community justice, and restorative justice behind institutional walls.

Family Conferences

Family group conferences are discussions that are facilitated and bring the victim, the victim's family, the offender, and the juvenile offender's family together to discuss the impact of a crime committed by the juvenile so that the group can decide how the juvenile is to be held accountable (Hanser, 2007a; Office of Juvenile Justice & Delinquency Prevention [OJJDP], 2007; Umbreit, 2000). Family group conferences originated in Australia and Oceana but were eventually adopted in various areas of the United States. Today, they are used as a formal juvenile sanction in Indiana, Florida Maine, Minnesota, Montana, New Mexico, Pennsylvania, Vermont, and Virginia (OJJDP, 2007). Group conferencing is consistent with the theoretical concepts of reintegrative shaming. This approach to offender reintegration contends that youth are generally deterred from committing crime by two informal forms of social control: fear of social disapproval and conscience (Braithwaite, 1989; OJJDP, 2007). Braithwaite argued that the consequences imposed by family members, friends, or other individuals important to an offender are more meaningful and are therefore more effective than those imposed by the legal system. Further, Braithwaite contended that once shamed the effects can be stigmatizing unless specific efforts are made by persons in the community to draw the juvenile back into the mainstream community (see the section on Reintegrative Shaming for more information). The key is to eliminate the behavior, not the offending person.

A typical conference begins when the victim, the offender, and each of their supporters are brought together with a trained facilitator to discuss the incident and the harm it has caused. This proceeds with the offender describing the incident and each participant describing the impact of the incident on his or her life (OJJDP, 2007; Umbreit, 2000). The purpose of this process is for the offender to acknowledge the human impact of his or her crime (Umbreit, 2000). From this point, victims are then given the chance to express feelings, ask questions about the offense, or explain their own desired outcomes from the conference. At the end of the conference, all participants must reach a mutual agreement on how the juvenile should make amends to the victim, and the juvenile offender then must sign a reparation agreement (OJJDP, 2007; Umbreit, 2000). The reparation agreement most often includes an apology as well as an outline of the specific type of restitution to be made to the victim (OJJDP, 2007).

▲ **Photo 3.1** The Center for Children and Families provides therapeutic services for youth and their families of origin. Family Foundations is a subdivision of the center that provides aftercare services for youth who are released from state custody. Note the Family Justice Center sign farther back in the photo. This center provides services for victims of domestic violence. The two agencies are adjacent to one another and represent the partnering emphasized in this text. The author of this text is on the steering committee for the Family Justice Center and is also involved in the preliminary stages of a research evaluation project with Family Foundations.

Teen Courts

Teen courts are much like traditional courts in that there are prosecutors and defense attorneys, offenders and victims, and judges and juries, but other youth rather than adults fill these roles and these youth even determine the disposition of the case (OJJDP, 2007). Similar to restorative justice precepts, the primary goal of teen courts is to hold young offenders accountable for their behavior while requiring reparation for the harm inflicted against the victim and the community: "The basic theory behind the use of young people in court is that youths will respond better to prosocial peers than to adult authority figures" (OJJDP, 2007, p. 3). This peer justice approach assumes that, similar to the way in which an association with delinquent peers is highly correlated with the onset of delinquent behavior (Surgeon General, 2001), peer pressure from prosocial peers may serve as a protective factor that pulls youth away from antisocial behavior and toward prosocial behavior (Butts, Buck, & Coggeshall, 2002; OJJDP, 2007). The primary function of most teen courts is to determine a fair and appropriate disposition for a youth who has already admitted to the charge (Butts, Buck, & Coggeshall, 2002; OJJDP, 2007). Teen courts utilize a number of innovative dispositions that allow the disposition to best fit the case and the crime committed by the processed juvenile. Resulting dispositions may include paying restitution, performing community service, writing formal apologies, or serving on a subsequent teen court jury (OJJDP, 2007). Teen courts may also require that sentenced juveniles attend classes to improve decision-making skills, enhance victim empathy, or deter them from future recidivism (Butts, Buck, & Coggeshall, 2002; OJJDP, 2007).

Reintegrative Shaming

Expanding and incorporating the premises of restorative justice, Braithwaite (1989) expanded these ideas to include the concept of reintegrative shaming. The notion behind this premise is that stigmatizing an offender is counterproductive to the reintegration process. The more stigmatizing the offense, the more likely the offender is to reoffend (Braithwaite, 2000). Rather, societies should utilize the process of reintegrative shaming to hold offenders accountable for their actions while simultaneously the community should forgive their transactions through the use of both formal and informal social controls. It is his contention that societies that continue to stigmatize offenders rather than "forgive" their transgressions experience the highest crime rates. Within this framework, Braithwaite argued, moral clarity is an important concept. Those individuals with whom individuals are closest are the ones most likely to exact shamefulness. Subsequently, individuals with fewer informal social controls are at greatest risk for committing future criminal acts. Therefore, a society that continues to criminalize more behavior and enhance penalties may further disenfranchise individuals from their communities who may have otherwise served to mitigate criminal activity. The concept and implementation of retributive policies (stigmatization) may encourage the creation of criminal subcultures as individuals seeking acceptance and approval turn to others who are similarly fitted to them.

Braithwaite (1989, 2000) drew on the experiences of communitarian societies such as the Nanante and Japanese to illustrate his theory. These cultures utilize reintegrative shaming as a mechanism for brining offenders, victims, and communities together. In general, offenders come forward in various ways showing remorse for their actions to the victim and their families. Following these overtures, the victim, the victims' family, and their community forgive the offender, allowing him or her to reintegrate back into the community (see Braithwaite, 2006 for a more detailed explanation of these communitarian societies).

The theoretical concepts of reintegration incorporate both normative and explanatory theories of crime (Braithwaite, 1989, 2000). The theory of shaming relies on both macro- and micro-level suppositions. At the macro-level is the belief that communities and individuals are interdependent upon one another. Societies with increased residential mobility and urbanization experience decreases in informal social controls. Therefore, the lack of communitarianism serves to enhance criminal activity rather than decrease it. On the micro-level, it is the effect of stigmatizing and breaking down the informal social controls that may have the reverse effect (Cullen & Agnew, 2006). Keep in mind that Braithwaite did not call for the complete elimination of shaming. Rather, he stated the shaming process itself should be reintegrative whereby society is willing and able to forgive the transgressions and the transgressor, while simultaneously the accused takes responsibility and seeks redemption (Cullen & Agnew, 2006). (See Applied Theory Section 3.1 for a summary of Braithwaite's theory of reintegrative shaming.) Through this process, repentant offenders are given a chance to be forgiven after taking public responsibility for their actions—a process that then allows them and even encourages them to reconnect with their friends, family, and community. This then makes the entire justice experience one that is productive rather than destructive—a primary desire in the field of both adult and juvenile corrections.

Applied Theory Section 3.1

Juvenile Offending, Labeling, and Reintegrative Shaming

It is clear that early juvenile advocates were concerned that a juvenile offender's initial acts of offending might negatively affect his or her future possibilities in adulthood, even when he or she might otherwise have stopped offending. This is also true today, and it serves as one primary basis for having youths' records sealed and for preventing public view of the proceedings. These concerns reflect the general ideas of labeling theory. **Labeling theory** holds that when individuals are labeled as criminals they will become stabilized in those roles, developing criminal identities that separate them from the mainstream population and exclude them from conventional roles. It should be obvious to the student that engagement in conventional activities and/or roles is a protective factor for further juvenile offending. If youth are excluded from such activities due to labeling, then it is clear that labeling does, in fact, further enmesh them in lifestyles of offending. In short, labeling can be a risk factor to continued juvenile offending.

The work of John Braithwaite provides an alternate view of labeling that is perhaps more balanced in approach. Basically, Braithwaite's primary point is that criminal behavior will increase when shaming is stigmatizing and will be lessened when shaming is reintegrative. This helps to explain why some persons reoffend more than others. Further, Braithwaite notes that shaming has the most profound impact on individuals with few social bonds to conventional society. Braithwaite notes that this is especially true for young, unmarried, unemployed males. This describes many juvenile offenders in today's society.

Although labeling theorists claim that no labeling should occur, Braithwaite offers another view to the shaming and offending connection. Essentially, he holds that a degree of shaming is useful for social control but that it should include some form of reintegrative process. Offenders should be connected back with society; the key issue is what follows after they have been shamed by the community for their actions. Reintegration is essential because shamed youth are at a turning point in their lives. This is a time when they will either become reconnected with society or further entrenched in criminal behavior. The reactions of the community are instrumental in the final outcome. Thus restorative forms of justice serve to fulfill this process of reconnection. When a degree of forgiveness is coupled with accountability to the victim and to the community, there is then the possibility of reintegrative shaming. The use of restorative justice therefore closely mirrors the underlying concepts of Braithwaite's version of labeling theory. Through this process, repentant offenders are given a chance to be forgiven after taking public responsibility for their actions, a process that then allows them and even encourages them to reconnect with their friends, family, and community. The entire justice experience thus becomes productive rather than destructive, a primary desire in the field of juvenile corrections. As Cullen and Agnew (2006) argue, there are several key reasons why reintegrative shaming works. These include the process of informal controls, whereby shame in the eyes of intimates is more effective than formal punishment. Unlike most punishments, it functions as both a specific and a general deterrent, working most effectively for those with the greatest number of attached relationships. Ultimately, the process of stigmatization can break attachments, but reintegrative shaming may provide social support, ultimately enhancing prosocial behavior. Shaming is the social process that leads to the cognition and development of consciousness that certain behaviors are wrong, thereby creating an anxiety response to wrongful actions. The combination of shaming and repentance is more powerful than shaming alone.

The role of citizens cannot be underscored too heavily. Participation in the process of shaming creates an atmosphere in which citizens are instruments for change rather than just targets. Likewise this process creates and reinforces the need to frame certain activities within a moral code. The process of public shaming further reinforces and in some instances redefines the general notion of wrongdoing to meet modern-day definitions. Societies incorporating reintegrative shaming into their methods of punishment have a smoother transition from practices within the family (private shaming) and socialization to the wider society (public shaming). The process of understanding that you do not have to be shamed to your face to reduce wrongful behavior is equally effective. It is the process of knowing and understanding that shaming and the need for forgiveness is occurring. Therefore, one that is confident that he or she can be accepted as a member of the larger society is more likely to positively respond to the "gossip" and prosocially reintegrate back into society. Finally, shaming is often more effective when aimed not only at the individual but at the family or company (when applicable). The process of collectively shaming an individual will encourage family members or companies to transmit the shame to the individual in a manner that is as reintegrative as possible.

Community Justice

Community supervision programs around the nation must learn to modify, update, and revise their use of probation as a sanction. Community corrections experts have long advocated for the increased use of community partnerships to fill the gaps in routine community supervision processes (Abadinsky, 2003). The development of these partnerships emphasizes a need for increased and enhanced community involvement as a means of securing public safety. Though much of the literature does not connect this current contention with the past history of criminal justice (at least not in most cases), it is interesting to note that experts are coming back again to the contributions of the individual community member to aid in resolving many of the challenges that have been encountered by the criminal justice system.

However, the "broken windows" thesis goes beyond simply asking for community volunteerism. It calls for the improvement and upkeep of communities that are not well kept and/or maintained. Such communities convey a sense of chaos and disorganization, and this opens the door to problematic populations that thrive in such conditions. The broken windows thesis contends that neighborhood citizens can reduce crime, including recidivism, by improving the physical and structural elements of their community. This then integrates both a crime-prevention and a community-supervision orientation. This also reflects what has been called a "community justice" approach to addressing crime (Clear & Cole, 2003; Clear & Karp, 2000).

Community justice is, in a general sense, a philosophy on justice that is based on the pursuit of justice that goes beyond the traditional tasks of the criminal justice system—apprehension, conviction, and punishment (Clear & Cole, 2003). Community justice approaches seek to improve the quality of life in a given community, and this is especially the case for communities that have been hard-hit by crime (consider, for example, gang-infested communities). In essence, there is a deliberate attempt to develop a sense of "collective efficacy" within the neighborhood (Cullen & Agnew, 2003). The term *collective efficacy* refers to a sense of cohesion within a given community whereby citizens have close and interlocking relationships with one another. These relationships tend to cement the community together—psychologically, sociologically, and perhaps even spiritually.

It is obvious that collective efficacy is the opposite of social disorganization. The process of taking a socially disorganized community and instilling a sense of collective efficacy is accomplished through a three-part strategy of justice that has been most aptly presented by Clear and Cole (2003). According to these authors, the means by which the formal criminal justice system can assist communities in reclamation, build collective efficacy, and integrate a community justice framework consists of **environmental crime prevention** efforts, the implementation and maintenance of community policing, and the use of restorative justice case processing.

Environmental crime prevention is simply a term that involves improvements of the community structure and landscape to deter the likelihood of criminal offending in that given area. Target-hardening techniques are utilized to enhance the security of a given area (i.e., more effective street and business lighting, ensuring that business/domicile entry points are visible from other locations, effective placement of landscaping, parking, and/or fencing). Such efforts can be implemented in very specific locations rather than throughout an entire city and can have impressive results. This stems from the fact that in some urban areas, nearly "70 percent of crime occurs in 20 percent of the city's locations" (Clear & Cole, 2003). This is an important point because it demonstrates that well-placed and targeted efforts can truly offset major areas of crime production.

▲ **Photo 3.2**   Community supervision officers (CSOs) may have clients from a variety of diverse backgrounds and communities. In some communities, ethnic and cultural identity is important. Probation and parole officers conducting home visits in these communities must understand the importance of cultural identity among offenders on their caseload.

Community policing is an approach to law enforcement that uses problem-solving strategies that involve community participants in the process. Community meetings, advisory boards, and other committee-based forms of civilian input are sought by both the police and the community supervision agency. Community policing seeks to encourage a sense of community involvement in an effort to build a rapport with the community. Programs such as citizen's police academies, National Night Out, and Neighborhood Watch help serve this function. In addition, police make themselves visible (both in uniform and otherwise) within the community as a means of integrating the officer staff with the law-abiding community that it is tasked to serve and protect. Such an approach is preventive in nature and goes beyond the simple arrest of offenders. Further, this approach tends to build a list of investigative leads from law-abiding witnesses throughout the community who feel a sense of personal commitment to the officer or the agency. Lastly, this type of rapport can greatly enhance security of the neighborhood and the degree of human contact that offenders on community supervision will receive in these communities.

Community justice approaches are based in the neighborhood and are focused on solving crime problems. Amidst this, the incorporation of the community is a central tenet to success. Clear and Cole (2003) noted a general process of implementing a community justice orientation to a community as follows:

1. Crime-mapping is used to identify where criminal activity is most problematic.

2. Citizen advisory groups are used to prioritize community concerns.

3. Working citizen partnerships between criminal justice agencies and citizen groups should be formed.

4. Integrated collaboration between police agencies, the court system, and community supervision agencies should be cultivated, and information sharing should be emphasized.

5. Citizens and victims are encouraged to be involved in the sentencing and even the supervision process of the offender.

6. Community supervision of the offenders is designed to restore victims and the community.

7. In the process of restoring the victim and community, the offender is given community support to adequately reintegrate into the community (both emotionally and economically).

This seven-stage process, adapted from Clear and Cole (2003) but including modification as a means of refining its applicability to the current discussion, demonstrates the exact manner by which programs should be implemented within a community. It should be clear that community supervision personnel and agencies are likely to be at the center of such a process. Nearly each of these stages also utilize some form of theoretical basis, and it is clear that this entire approach is intended to reintegrate the victim through a process of restoring the damage that they have done to their victims and the community. Thus, this approach is much more comprehensive in nature, improves supervision of the offender (more eyes are on the offender with increased community involvement), holds the offender accountable for their criminal offense, and meets the goals of restorative justice. Such an approach grounded in a strong theoretical background is practical to implement and is not, as critics might contend, soft on crime.

Restorative Justice Behind Institutional Walls

The concept of restorative justice has been given a lot of attention for offenders housed in the community. As we have already seen in Section I, however, 95% of all those incarcerated will leave prison at some point. Given the increase in length of sentences and the reduction in good time experienced both nationally and federally, services for the victim should not stop at the **sentencing stage**. Rather, victims should have an opportunity to testify at parole hearings (when such hearings exist) and should be provided with services after the process ends. Albeit limited, the development of restorative justice programming behind institutional walls and post-incarceration has been emerging over the past 10 to 15 years. Unlike programs offered in the community, programs offered behind institutional walls focus heavily on the ability of the offender to reintegrate post-release. Two such programs showing promise, restorative circles and victim wraparound programs, will be described.

Restorative Circles

Restorative circles serve as another program variation in the evolution of restorative justice. Unlike restorative justice programs that are focused on the needs of individuals and communities, restorative circles are solution-based by nature focusing on the offender rather than the victim (Walker, Sakai, & Brady, 2006). Restorative circles are administered by a therapist. Used historically in school-based programs (Boulton, 2006), they are now being expanded into institutional settings. A reentry program in Hawaii, for example, requires a 3-hour meeting where the offender meets with their family or directly affected parties in their personal lives, their prison counselor, and are observed by the warden, parole board, as well as other prison **counselors**. During this 3-hour session, the inmate takes responsibility for their behavior, outlines how they plan to remain crime free, and their particular plan for their future. Facilitators of the circle do not offer solutions for the offender and their families; rather, their purpose is to ask questions to guide the inmate on developing a realistic plan following release. Research assessing inmate satisfaction with this program revealed that, following completion of the circle, inmates were supportive of the program and believed that participation helped them in forgiving themselves and others and would set the foundation for a positive reintegration back into society. Although this study was cross-sectional rather than longitudinal, the results did suggest at least some level of responsibility being taken by those committing crimes and a desire to live a crime-free life (Walker, Sakai, & Brady, 2006). Ultimately, meeting the goals of restorative justice and suggesting a need for further expansion and exploration, the use of the restorative circle model has been further expanded into the use of **victim wraparound services**/programs for institutionalized offenders.

Victim Wraparound Services

Prompted by victim's services, many states have been successful at instituting restorative justice-type programs in the release process known as victim wraparound services. These efforts are an enhanced recognition that victims' needs and concerns do not stop once the offender receives and begins to serve their sentence. In fact, for many victims, once the offender is released they begin to relive the emotions suffered post-victimization, some suffer post-traumatic stress disorder, and others must deal with issues such as child support and visitation upon the offender's release. These services appear to be even more important for offenders serving longer sentences. One explanation for this is because offenders become more removed from the crime and their victims, and they tend to have limited contact if any with their families, therefore making reintegration more difficult. To date, there appears to be no standardization of victim wraparound programs designed to assist both the victim and offender behind bars (Hurley, 2009). As Hurley (2009) contended, these services can provide "opportunities for victims to develop safety plans, identify notification needs with law enforcement, assistance with obtaining information on the release of the offender, assistance with appropriate exchange of information between the offender and victim, and assistance in obtaining restitution" (p. 20). Overall, these programs extend the use and function of restorative justice not only at the front end but post-incarceration as well. These efforts can serve the purpose of both retribution and restoration by assisting the offender with taking responsibility for their actions.

The use of restorative justice principles holds promise with parolees because they are often individually tailored to the victim and, at the same time, they are likewise tailored to the offender. The offender has specific acts of redemption that are required to meet his/her sentencing requirements, and these acts are derived from the agreed-upon contract established by the victim and the offender. This means that this reintegration plan heals the victim, the offender, and the community and thus ensures that all parties work in congruence rather than conflict.

Victim–Offender Mediation

VOM represents one form of restorative justice that has been in existence for approximately 30 years in the United States. Borrowing from restorative justice ideology, both the victim and the offender play a crucial role in determining the outcome—that is, sentence. A trained mediator serves as the official facilitator of the encounter. Cases are referred to the program, sometimes known as victim–offender reconciliation, via the courts, probation, prosecutors, defense attorneys, and victims advocates. In some cases, unlike other forms of restorative justice, VOM referrals may be a true form of diversion (Bazemore & Umbreit, 2001). Many of these programs are used for work with juvenile offenders. This process seeks to meet the goal of destigmatization and reparation set forth by the juvenile justice system. In the adult system, programs are offered many times as a probationary alternative but can also be used at the various points in the criminal justice system as well (Wemmers & Cyr, 2005). It is during these mediation sessions that the victim is allowed to confront the offender (accused) and to let them know how the crime has impacted them. According to Bazemore and Umbreit (2001), the three goals of offender mediation include the following:

1. Supporting the healing process of victims by providing a safe, controlled setting for them to meet and speak with offenders on a strictly voluntary basis.

2. Allowing offenders to learn about the impact of their crimes on the victims and take direct responsibility for their behavior.

3. Providing an opportunity for the victim and offender to develop a mutually acceptable plan that addresses the harm caused by the crime. (pp. 2–3)

Victim empowerment is key to the success of a VOM program. By allowing the victim to choose the where, when, how, order, and why of the process, they gain control over essentially their role in the process. Unlike civil or commercial mediation where "guilt" may not be determined prior to the mediation session, each of the actors (victim and offender) understand their role (Bazemore & Umbreit, 2001).

Evaluations assessing the effectiveness of these programs suggest that VOM programs can work. As illustrated by Wemmers and Cyr (2005), in their study of 59 victims in Quebec, procedural justice can facilitate healing whenever victims feel they have been treated fairly. Gerkin (2009) arrived at similar conclusions in observations of a VOM program servicing more than 400 cases per year. In this instance, the higher levels of participation by the victim equated to higher levels of overall success. One potential shortcoming of this approach is that offenders are coerced into taking responsibility in a manner that may not coalesce with the transgression. Furthermore, mediators must be mindful to take into account the needs of the offender as well as the victim. Even when responsible for enacting harm on the victim, if a needs-based approach is not taken for both parties then crime and recourse may increase (Gerkin, 2009).

Even with the increased attention given to programs such as VOM, as of 2004 only 23 states had a specific reference to mediation or some form of conferencing allowed (Lightfoot & Umbreit, 2004). As Lightfoot and Umbreit (2004) noted in their review of statutory legislation recognizing VOM programs, for these such alternatives to exist and to continue to be funded at the state level, it is imperative that language referencing these programs be included in legislation.

▨ Victims and Restorative Justice

In recent years, there has been a continued emphasis on the use of restorative justice techniques within the U.S. criminal justice system. Much of the reasons for this have perhaps been due to the corresponding victim's rights movement as well as the emergence of the field of victimology. Likewise, there has increasingly been a desire for accountability among offenders, regardless of whether they do (or do not) receive incarceration. Indeed, in times past (particularly during the rehabilitative model and the medical model eras of corrections), victims were for the most part overlooked. Rather than having a system that sought to repair the damage to the victim, the primary emphasis of our justice system was to find the offender and to ensure that they received their punishment. While punishment may indeed be rightfully in store for offenders, this did little to ameliorate the plight of the victim. An ongoing debate over the role of the victim in the process and the outcome of that participation continues. Some argue that victim participation increases the punitive/retributive response of the system while others argue that the system becomes more efficient and streamlined (Hurley, 2009; Mika, Achilles, Halbert, Amstutz, & Zehr, 2004).

Ideally, the full reintegration of the offender requires that the offender be fully accountable for their transgressions and that this accountability be made directly to the victim or their family, not some amorphous agency that collects their monetary fine and payment. Naturally, if the victim does not wish to have such services, then their desires should of course be primary and their wishes should be respected. Indeed, Lehman and colleagues (2002) noted that any "victim centered" approach to reentry partnerships must recognize the "us and them" feelings that victims may have about offenders, yet simultaneously they must also account for the fact that victims would prefer to have a voice in issues that affect their own livelihood. Because of this, Lehman and colleagues (2002), contended that the victim impact statement is a critical component to restorative justice approaches, both from the perspective of the victim and from the perspective of offender reintegration. See Focus Topic 3.1.

Focus Topic 3.1

Victim Impact Statement in the State of Iowa

Victim Impact Statement (915.21)

1. A victim may present a victim impact statement to the court using one or more of the following methods: A victim may file a signed victim impact statement with the county attorney. This filed impact statement shall be included in the presentence investigation report. If a presentence investigation report is not ordered by the court, a filed victim impact statement shall be provided to the court prior to sentencing.

   a. A victim may orally present a victim impact statement at the sentencing hearing, in the presence of the defendant, and at any hearing regarding reconsideration of sentence.

   b. If the victim is unable to make an oral or written statement because of the victim's age, or mental, emotional, or physical incapacity, the victim's attorney or a designated representative shall have the opportunity to make a statement on behalf of the victim.

2. A victim impact statement shall include the identification of the victim of the offense, and may include the following:

   a. Itemization of any economic loss suffered by the victim as a result of the offense. For purposes of this paragraph, a pecuniary damages statement prepared by a county attorney pursuant to section 910.3 may serve as the itemization of economic loss.

   b. Identification of any physical injury suffered by the victim as a result of the offense with detail as to its seriousness and permanence.

   c. Description of any change in the victim's personal welfare or familial relationships as a result of the offense.

   d. Description of any request for psychological services initiated by the victim or the victim's family as a result of the offense.

   e. Any other information related to the impact of the offense upon the victim.

Anne Seymour, a victim's rights advocate, identified five distinct rights for victims within a restorative justice framework that must be maintained for these programs to be effective. These rights include victim notification, victim impact statements, victim/witness protection, restitution, and victim information referrals (Seymour, 2000). First, victim notification has been noted as the most important service provided to the victim (Bazemore & Seymour, 1998). This process goes beyond the obvious notification of the offenders' status to include notification of rights, process, right to a victim impact state, victim impact panels, etc. Essentially, this act of notification provides an opportunity to empower the victim at the various stages of the process. Second, victim impact statements, which will be explained in more detail, give the opportunity for the victim to inform the court of how the crime affected them on a more personal level. Third, the process of victim/witness protection is paramount. Victims/witnesses should feel safe to tell their story and should be informed of the various protections available to them ranging from personal protection orders to the more extreme case of relocation. Fourth, victim restitution, as covered previously, may be the largest "black hole" of victims' rights. Although strides have been made in victims' rights efforts to reimburse victims of monetary loss, these reimbursements oftentimes fail in comparison to actual loss. Loss of employment/income, loss of life, or costs related to hospitalization can devastate a victim and/or their respective family members. Agencies at the community level, including probation departments, advocacy groups, etc., must strive to assist with restitution compensation. Efforts at the state and federal level have been created to eliminate some of the burden imposed upon victims of crime but still need to be improved. Finally, practitioners are not expected to know or be experts in the field of victims' rights. They should, however, be knowledgeable in victim information referrals services. Most communities have services established either formally or on a voluntary basis to assist victims with their particular needs. Practitioners must strive to become more informed of these services to not only help the victim but potentially help the processing of the case. Victims who feel more empowered, safer, and have more services at their disposal are more apt to participate more fully in the system and feel justice has been served. This approach to the handling of cases improves rather than mars both the victim's criminal justice experience as well as the communities.

Bazemore and O'Brien (2002) noted that significant evidence exists that restorative practices can have a significant impact on recidivism. They contend that the overwhelming majority of the research shows that such programs either cause improvements in certain areas of offender reformation or, at worse, simply seem to work as well (and by proxy, no worse) than other traditional programs. This is important because this approach helps to inform and educate the community about the specific issues facing offenders.

Hanser (2007b) has also shown that the use of restorative justice can be quite effective, even with higher risk offenders on intensive forms of community supervision, presuming that appropriate safeguards are utilized. Hanser's (2007b) analysis examined the use of restorative justice with domestic abusers and sex offenders. His analysis likewise compared this type of approach in the United States and Canada. From his analysis, he concluded that restorative justice principles can augment both community involvement in the supervision process and offender accountability. Though he made it clear that restorative justice is no panacea, it does nevertheless provide a viable option, particularly when offenders are making genuine efforts to successfully complete their parole sentence. With this in mind, Hanser (2007b) provided three specific recommendations that are expected to improve public safety, offender reintegration, and the plight of the victim. His recommendations are as follows:

1. *Concerns for the victim(s) must remain paramount:* This is not to say that such considerations are not given primary concern in most programs, but there is typically strong resistance to the notion of using such approaches between perpetrators and victims of certain crimes such as those associated with domestic violence. The resistance to these approaches is largely centered around concern for the victim's—

welfare and safety. If the safety of the victim is at all compromised by a restorative justice approach, then such an alternate form of processing domestic violence cases should simply not be allowed (Hanser, 2007b). This is perhaps the strongest argument against a restorative justice approach. Thus, safety planning practices for victims, appropriate security measures (both during and after the dialogue with the offender), as well as other pragmatic methods of ensuring victim safety will have to be fully implemented if such approaches will be accepted with violent offenders. Likewise, various power-dynamics between the perpetrator and the victim will need to be identified and addressed to ensure that victims are not intimidated, manipulated, or exploited during or after the process (Hanser, 2007a, 2007b).

2. *The public must be educated on restorative justice and offender reentry:* Specifically, jurisdictions should consider public bulletins, media campaigns, and citizen training programs to disseminate knowledge of the potential benefits of a restorative justice approach in the community. It will be necessary that the public is made fully aware that offenders processed through restorative justice processes are held accountable for their crimes. The fact that many victims tend to report more closure, compensation, and sense of satisfaction from these approaches will also be important if this type of orientation is ever likely to obtain full support in the United States. This recommendation augments the points made in Section II where both community education and community involvement are imperative in optimizing offender supervision and public safety.

3. *High-risk offenders will need to be appropriately identified and supervised:* This does seemingly reflect the same concern noted in the first recommendation. However, this goes a step further since much of this lies more with the function of community supervision agencies than with restorative justice programs. In other words, community supervision programs will need to correctly assess offender dangerousness (points toward the need for effective assessment and classification processes) and will likewise need to use intensive forms of supervision that are likely to be technologically enhanced, such as with GPS tracking and other such modern innovations (Champion, 2002; Schmidt, 1994). These and other forms of tight supervision have been shown to be more effective for high-risk offenders than less rigorous supervision schemes (Champion, 2002; Hanser, 2007a, 2007b; Schmidt, 1994). Conversely, intensive forms of supervision have been shown to be counterproductive for low-risk populations (Champion, 2002; Hanser, 2007a, 2007b). Thus, intensive supervision schemes will need to be well integrated as an adjunct backdrop to any restorative justice program that processes violent offenders.

⊠ Criticisms of Restorative Justice

An important criticism of restorative justice focuses on the definition of community. What constitutes a community? Can the terms *community* and *neighborhood* be used interchangeably? This idea becomes even more relevant when you seek to develop programs where groups—for example, African Americans—have historically been disenfranchised (Takagi & Shank, 2004). In addition, Mika and his colleagues (2004), in their study of teams representing victim advocates and restorative justice programs in seven states, raised concern over the efficacy of victims programs to deliver on their intended goals/purposes. Three specific areas of concerns were advanced. First, the use of mediation programs by their definition excludes some victims from participation where no identified offender exists. Second, programs requiring restitution as a key element for success may not be appropriate for all offenses, particularly personal crimes such as domestic violence. Finally, questions arise regarding who constitutes the victim: the state or the individual. With this, victims who have not been identified will be ignored by the system and process because of the nature of the implementation.

◪ Conclusion

Restorative justice practices seek to reconnect the victim, offender, and community in meaningful ways through the process of forgiveness and redemption. Although there are many different forms of restorative justice, each has the ultimate goal of reducing recidivism through acceptance and reparation. As shown in this section, these goals can be effectively accomplished while meeting the needs of all involved parties. Findings from studies assessing the effectiveness of these programs have definite implications for policy.

◪ Section Summary

- Restorative justice programs began in the 1970s as a grassroots effort designed to restore the victim, the community, and the offender to a similar level of functioning that existed prior to the commission of the criminal act.
- Restorative justice programs may be collapsed into one of three categories: conferences, circles, and VOM.
- The most common forms of restorative justice are community service and restitution.
- Other forms of restorative justice include family conferences, teen courts, reintegrative shaming, community justice, restorative circles, victim wraparound services, and VOM.
- Family conferences are designed to address juvenile offenders. The victim, the victim's family, the offender, and their family are brought together to discuss the offense and develop a reparation agreement.
- Teen courts are used with juvenile offenders. The majority are designed as dispositional alternatives, although some do allow for adjudication. These courts provide for creative disposition alternatives.
- John Braithwaite developed this integrative theoretical perspective on the premise that offenders who are stigmatized by shaming (the offense and the repercussions following sentencing) are most likely to continue criminal activity. He further argued that offenders who experience reintegrative shaming by their act, primarily by informal social controls, are least likely to recidivate.
- Reintegrative shaming calls for remorse by the offender, a forgiveness of the act by the victim and their communities, and the opportunity for the offender to essentially receive a worry-free pass back into society.
- Community justice is a restorative justice program that relies on the broken windows thesis. These programs encourage citizen responsibility and involvement in reducing and responding to crime and deviance.
- Restorative circles are conducted behind institutional walls prior to the offender being released into their community. These programs bring the offender, their families, prison counselors, and other interested parties together for the offender to seek forgiveness and redemption and to build a plan for their future post-release.
- Victim wraparound services are similar to restorative circles except they extend services to the victim post-offender release.
- VOM programs are another form of restorative justice whereby the victim and the offender have definitive roles going into the process—that is, guilt has already been determined. These programs are administered by a mediator who seeks to find a resolution between the victim and the offender. Agreements are binding and may be used in lieu of a formal sanction.

KEY TERMS

Broken windows thesis

Community justice

Community service

Family conferences

Monetary restitution

Reintegrative shaming

Restorative circles

Restorative justice

Stigmatization

Teen courts

Victim impact statement

Victim–offender mediation (VOM)

Victim wraparound services

DISCUSSION QUESTIONS

1. Should forgiveness be a central component of the criminal justice system?

2. John Braithwaite, in his discussion of reintegrative shaming, laid the foundation for a successful restorative justice program. What are some of the impediments in the United States to implementing these programs nationally? How might these programs be implemented?

3. What role does politics and economics play in instituting restorative justice programs?

4. Given what you have read and learned regarding restorative justice programming, should communities seek to develop these types of alternatives? Why or why not?

WEB RESOURCES

Restorative Justice Online:

http://www.restorativejustice.org/

National Institute of Justice on Restorative Justice:

http://www.ojp.usdoj.gov/nij/topics/courts/restorative-justice/welcome.htm

Resolutions Northwest: Restorative Justice Programs:

http://www.resolutionsnorthwest.org/restorative_justice

Transforming Conflict—Restorative Justice in School:

http://www.transformingconflict.org/Restorative_Justice_in_School.htm

International Institute for Restorative Practices:

http://www.iirp.org/article_detail.php?article_id=NDMz

The Child Welfare Group & Policy Practice:

http://www.childwelfaregroup.org/documents/FTC_History.pdf

Edna McConnell Clark Foundation Handbook for Family Team Conferencing:

http://www.cssp.org/uploadFiles/Family_Team_Conferencing_Handbook.pdf

Victim–Offender Reconciliation Program:

http://www.vorp.com/

Victim Offender Mediation Association:

http://www.voma.org/

Guidelines for Victim-Sensitive VOM: Restorative Justice Through Dialogue:

http://www.ojp.usdoj.gov/ovc/publications/infores/restorative_justice/96517-gdlines_victims-sens/welcome.html

Dispute Resolution Program Services:

http://www.sccgov.org/portal/site/drps/agencyarticle?path=%2Fv7%2FDispute%20Resolution%20Program%20Services%20%28PRG%29%2FMediation%20Programs%2FJuvenile%20Justice&contentId=b05818e77f5c4010VgnVCMP230004adc4a92_____

Directory of VOM Programs in the United States:

http://www.ojp.usdoj.gov/ovc/publications/infores/restorative_justice/96521-dir_victim-offender/welcome.html

National Association of Youth Courts:

http://www.youthcourt.net/

National Center for State Courts:

http://www.ncsconline.org/WC/Publications/KIS_JuvJus_Trends02_TeenPub.pdf

The Impact of Teen Court on Young Offenders:
http://www.urban.org/UploadedPDF/410457.pdf

READING

One area of restorative justice programming that appears to be lacking is the creation and study of victim wraparound programs in institutional settings and at release. Hurley, in her research, considered the efficacy of restorative justice wraparound programs for offenders in an institutional setting. As illustrated in her study, very few programs of this nature exist. These programs are designed to extend the level of acknowledgment and responsibility of the offenders. Results of this study reveal that these programs are most effective with offenders serving long terms of incarceration. One explanation for this finding is that these offenders potentially have desensitized the crime, removed themselves from the offense, and have lost many contacts from their previous life, making the transition back into their community more difficult. Several states have instituted the use of these types of program alternatives for their parole populations. Overall, Hurley contended that these programmatic alternatives may reduce recidivism of participants, increase victim satisfaction in the process, increase accountability of the offender, and better meet the needs of the victims. The results of this study, although exploratory in nature, have implications for future policy decisions about handling victims and offenders post incarceration.

AUTHOR'S NOTE: The paper was supported by funding from the Illinois Long Term Offender Committee and a previous version of this paper was presented to the Illinois Long-Term Offender Committee in Chicago, Illinois, August 2007.

SOURCE: Hurley, M. H. (2009). Restorative practices in institutional settings and at release: Victim wrap around programs. *Federal Probation, 73*(1), 16–22.

Restorative Practices in Institutional Settings and at Release

Victim Wrap Around Programs

Martha Henderson Hurley

Over the last three decades, a growing social movement has advocated for an increased role for victims in the criminal justice system process. Debate over the extent to which victims should be included in criminal justice processes continues to divide scholars, practitioners, offenders, victims, and other correctional advocates. Some argue that the inclusion of victims in criminal justice processes has created more punitive and retributive correctional policies, whereas others think that greater involvement of victims creates a more efficient, justice oriented and restorative process (Mika, Achilles, Halbert, Amstutz, and Zehr, 2004). While the debate continues to rage, it should be recognized that the federal government and most states have legislative mandates that acknowledge a basic role for victims within the criminal justice system process. Central to the debate is an understanding of why victims matter.

Why Crime Victims Matter

There are several reasons why crime victim participation in criminal justice system processing is of concern. First, the sheer size of the victim population in the United States requires some recognition of the role of victims. In 2005, U.S. residents age 12 and older were the victims of more than 23 million crimes, with at least 5.2 million of those offenses being violent in nature (Criminal Victimization in the United States, 2005).

Second, while we are still learning about the long-term impact of crime on victims, a significant body of literature details the negative impact that victimization has on victim perceptions of the government and

their community (Mika et al. 2004; National Center for Victims of Crime, 2005). More important for some types of victimization, such as crimes against children, victimization is associated not just with negative perceptions of government and community but also with future offending (Cartwright, 2000). Third, the criminal justice system is dependent upon the cooperation and participation of victims in coming forward to convict offenders. In addition, some criminal justice officials recognize that criminal victimization has psychological impacts potentially leading to depression, anxiety, increased fear, and other disorders that can reduce functioning. Evidence of this recognition can be seen by recent developments in Victim Wrap Around programs and the creation of victim services units within each state. Finally, research suggests that victim participation in some criminal justice processes reveals promising results for the reduction of recidivism rates with certain types of offenders under certain conditions (Armour 2006; Marshall, 2005; Parker, 2005). Consequently, few correctional officials would argue that there is no role for victims within larger criminal justice processes.

While earlier efforts to increase victim involvement emphasized changes within early stages of the criminal justice system, recent efforts have emphasized the need for greater involvement of victims within institutional settings and during the reentry process. The most recent avenue of exploration for policy changes within institutional environments that include victims' perspectives has been the desire to implement restorative justice practices within institutional settings for adult offenders (see information available from The Pennsylvania Prison Society at http://www.prisonsociety.org/progs/rj.shtml). In addition to the push for implementation of restorative practices behind prison walls, several state correctional systems have incorporated victim wrap around services within the parole process. The next section discusses the literature and reviews some of the programs that have been developed as part of restorative justice practices behind prison walls and victim wrap around services incorporated into the reentry process for inmates.

⊠ Defining Restorative Justice Practices Within Institutional Contexts

The next question then, is just what is restorative justice? Howard Zehr refers to restorative justice as "a process to involve, to the extent possible, those who have a stake in a specific offense and to collectively identify and address the harms, needs, and obligations, in order to heal and put things as right as possible" (Zehr, 2002, p. 37). Restorative justice has also been referred to as "restoring through a facilitated process that brings together all affected parties, the dignity and well-being of those involved in and harmed by a criminal incident" (Smith and Robinson 2006: 59). According to Armour, the author of Bridges to Life (2006, p. 2), "restorative justice seeks to elevate the role of crime victims and community members, hold offenders directly accountable to the people they have violated, and restore the emotional and material losses of victims by providing a range of opportunities for dialogue, negotiation, and problem solving that can lead to a greater sense of community safety, conflict resolution, and healing for all involved." The Pennsylvania Prison Society describes restorative justice as:

> An approach to justice that actively involves all who are impacted by crime—victims, offenders, their communities of care, and the broader community—and seeks to promote accountability, healing, and the common good. (http://www.prisonsociety.org/progs/rj.html)

While definitions of restorative justice vary, certain common themes are associated with restorative practices. First, restorative justice is a philosophy that emphasizes the need to repair the harm caused by crime. Reparation is not something that can only be done by punishing the offender. True reparation requires the participation of all stakeholders (victims, offenders, the community, and criminal justice officials) in the development of plans to repair the harms caused by criminality. Second, restorative practices are predicated upon the idea that offenders must be held accountable for their actions. Thus, consequences must be applied when offenders fail to follow through with restorative activities. Third, when all stakeholders participate in the process, healing occurs, the potential for future harm is reduced, and offenders can be restored back into society. A critical element is the fact that restorative justice is a process that cannot be captured through a single program or event.

Two camps exist within the restorative justice paradigm. One group views restorative justice as requiring the direct involvement of all stakeholders to promote change. This group views assisting victims, addressing victim needs, helping victims work through their issues, and encouraging victims to participate in criminal justice processes as the primary goal (Mika, Achilles, Halbert, Amstutz, and Zehr, 2004). A second group, which is growing in number, embraces the concept of offender-oriented restorative justice. Offender oriented restorative justice reflects the needs of offenders and victims along with emphasizing the fact that the offender must make amends, change, and engage in rehabilitative efforts (Mika, Achilles, Halber, Amstutz, and Zehr, 2004). Many in the offender-oriented group have focused their attention on adding restorative justice practices to institutional environments and parole processes.

The approach used to discuss restorative justice practices within institutional contexts in this article is consistent with the framework set forth by the Pennsylvania Prison Society and is considered offender-oriented. The Pennsylvania Prison Society discusses restorative justice through the use of the web of relationships metaphor (http://www.prbonsociety .org/progs/rj.shtml). This is a framework where restorative justice programs can:

- Engage offenders on restorative justice, accountability, personal healing and growth, among other restorative themes.
- Support offenders who have been crime victims and provide services to meet their needs as victims.
- Invite direct and indirect dialogue between victims and offenders.
- Bring together victims, offenders, and community into conversation around restorative themes.
- Address issues of release and reintegration through the restorative justice lens.
- Serve or transform the prison in a way that promotes restorative values and principles. (Toews, 2006a, pg. 3)

⊠ Restorative Justice Programs Within Institutional Contexts

There is a limited amount of publicly available research literature on the restorative justice practices in adult institutional settings.

Institutional restorative justice programs are typically viewed as a means for empowering offenders to take responsibility, to repair the harm to victims and communities, and to generate pro-social behaviors during incarceration and upon release (Toews, 2006a; 2006b.). Table 3.1 reveals the many different levels at which institutional-based programs can operate.

According to Fraley (2001, p. 62), restorative justice programs within institutional contexts may be more important for the mental health and well-being of long-term inmates than of short term inmates. Inmates with only a short time to serve have an opportunity to repair the harm for their criminal behavior upon release. Those serving short sentences

Table 3.1   Levels of Restorative Justice Practices Within Institutions

I. Individual—Focuses on how individuals are impacted by their experiences, what they need for accountability and healing and ways in which they can transform their lives to wholeness.

II. Relational—Focuses on the relationships between individuals, the role and nature of accountability and healing in those relationships and ways in which to repair the relationship. These relationships may be, for instance, between victim and offender or offender and his or her family.

III. Daily life—Focuses on the values, assumptions and ways in which people interact with each other in their social lives, ways in which to make restorative justice a way of life and transformation of the prison culture. This may include daily relationships with family and friends, prison staff and other prisoners.

IV. Prison Operations—Focuses on the use of restorative justice philosophy and practices in prison operations and programs. There is also an element of systemic transformation. This level may include, for instance, using mediation in grievance procedures or offering services to people when they become crime victims while incarcerated.

V. Community—Focuses on the community role in crime and justice, its needs for accountability and healing and building bridges between offenders and community.

VI. Criminal Justice Systems—Focuses on transforming the foundation of the criminal justice system, incorporating restorative practices into the system at all levels and building partnerships with all justice participants. There is a policy element to this level.

SOURCE: Toews (2006a, p. 4).

who wish to take responsibility for their actions and reconcile with victims, friends, or family have an opportunity to do so within the community. In contrast, "It is a given that those of us [long-term inmates] serving long sentences will have no opportunity (or one that is long delayed) to reconcile with those to whom we have brought pain and suffering" (Fraley, p. 62). Long-term inmates over time are much more disconnected from the crime, their victims, their families, and the community. Consequently, repairing the harm to victims, family, and community is less likely without the inclusion of restorative programming during incarceration and upon release.

Review of the Research on Restorative Justice Practices Within Institutions

The implementation of restorative justice programs in institutions varies widely. The majority of the published restorative justice programs in institutions appear to focus on adult male offenders within prisons and typically require voluntary participation. Only one study reported results for an adult female prison population. In most cases, participation in the restorative justice program did not affect the status of the inmate (i.e., participation does not translate into early release). Restorative justice programs in prisons lack standardized implementation.

- Some programs include only inmates and correctional staff. Others include inmates, victims, and community members.
- Significant differences exist in the length and number of restorative sessions that take place.
- There is no uniform method of service delivery across the restorative practices. Each program used direct mediation, indirect mediation, or some form of conferencing alone or in combination.

Limitations of Research

The research available on institutional restorative justice programs has several significant limitations. The majority of the studies have small sample sizes that reduce the generalizability of results. Experimental designs were also typically not utilized. Moreover, only two of the evaluative studies presented assessed post-release recidivism. Thus, at the present time no definitive conclusions can be drawn about the impact of institution-based restorative justice programs on the behavior of offenders in the community. The literature also reveals that while institutional restorative justice programs are growing in popularity overseas, few states have been willing to implement and evaluate such programs in the United States. Thus, while restorative justice practices in institutions have increased in visibility and appear promising, more research and greater implementation is required in the United States.

Victim Wrap Around and Parole Processes

While most states have implemented legislation increasing victim involvement in criminal justice processes, many recognize that more work needs to be done. In recent years, victims' advocates have achieved some success in getting state correctional and parole authorities to recognize the need to address victims' issues during the parole and reentry process (National Center for Victims of Crime, 2005). Several states now have implemented parole and reentry processes that attempt to address the needs of victims and include victims as full participants in the release process (National Center for Victims of Crime, 2005).

Why Has There Been a Call for Greater Inclusion in the Release Process and Parole?

Activist calls for greater victim involvement at these latter stages of justice are related to four factors. First is the open acknowledgement that released inmates return back to a small number of communities. According to an Urban Institute report, two-thirds of released prisoners return to major metropolitan areas in the United States. Often these returning offenders are concentrated in a few neighborhoods in the central city (Lynch & Sabol, 2001; Petersilia 2003). For example, in Illinois returning inmates are concentrated in Chicago, with 51 percent of those returning to the city. The largest share (34 percent) of returning offenders in Illinois reside in six neighborhoods—Austin, Humboldt Park, North Lawndale, Englewood, West Englewood, and East Garfield Park.

Second, more people now recognize that the fates of victims and offenders are intertwined. As a report by the National Center for Victims of Crimes (2005) highlights, offenders and their victims live and work in the same neighborhoods and have similar social and economic experiences. Thus, "the mere proximity of many victims and their returning offenders highlights the importance of considering the needs of victims and offenders together and involving victim services providers as reentry initiatives are developed and implemented" (p. 2).

Moreover, current legislation inadequately addresses victim issues. A recent Reentry Policy Council report reveals that while legislation has been passed increasing the role of victims in the parole process, only 15 states notify all victims about the scheduling of parole hearings and 6 still do not permit victims to appear at parole hearings (Reentry Policy Council Chapter 23).

Victim advocates are also calling for increased participation at later stages of the criminal justice process, because the needs of victims at later stages of the criminal justice system can differ from the needs of victims upon initial incarceration. Victims at the sentencing stage may be more concerned with punishing the offender and addressing their own emotional needs. At the release stage, victim safety, PTSD, child support and visitation rights, and offender rehabilitation may be of greater concern for victims (National Center for Victims of Crime, 2005). According to the National Center for Victims of Crime Report for Victim Services (2000), a balanced release process would recognize "that while correctional agencies are 'offender-directed,' they can also be 'victim-centered.'" Victim

Wrap Around Programs represent the latest attempt to incorporate restorative practices prior to release.

What Does Victim Wrap Around Mean?

When an offender is released back into the community, victims are likely to be concerned about their safety, may experience resurgence in emotional trauma, and may experience confusion regarding their rights. "The primary function of Victim Wrap Around programs is the provision of services to support the victim at the time of the offender's re-entry into the community" (Report of The Advisory Committee on Geriatric and Seriously Ill Inmates, 2005); they can include the following:

1. The development of a safety plan to enhance victim and community safety when an offender is in the community. The safety plan may provide for the delineation of geographic conditions that address both the needs of the offender and the safety needs of the victim; the examination of the victim's home to identify and address crime prevention needs; obtaining civil orders (e.g., a protection from abuse order) that address safety, residence and custody issues; identifying victims.

2. Notification needs and planning for intervention by police and other law enforcement agencies to ensure the safety of the victim.

3. Assistance in obtaining information on the status of the offender.

4. Assistance in the exchange of information between the victim and the offender as deemed appropriate and necessary by both parties.

5. Assistance in obtaining restitution.

6. Assistance in linking the victim to other needed services. (Report of The Advisory Committee on Geriatric and Seriously Ill Inmates, 2005, p. 109)

While the above services focus primarily on victim safety and emotional security, for these programs to fully incorporate restorative practices, all major stakeholders (victims, law enforcement, correctional officials, and offenders) must participate in the release process. Thus, Victim Wrap Around programs around the country have included victim input into the conditions of release imposed on an offender, meetings between victims and offenders, meetings between victims and parole officers, victim notification, and community involvement in conditions of release.

⊠ Review of Victim Wrap Around Programs

Victim Wrap Around Programs have taken various forms. The Washington State Department of Corrections was the first to implement a Victim Wrap Around program and serves as a model for most other locations (Lehman, 1999; see also www.doc.wa.gov/stories/victimwrap.htm). In the Washington program, victims, corrections staff, parole authority members, law enforcement, victim advocates, and community-based service providers form a workgroup that determines all aspects of the release process for the offender and how best to meet the needs of the victim. More important, victims have a direct impact on the release process by their input into the release conditions for offenders. As many victims may be concerned about their safety upon release of an offender back into the community, the work group helps alleviate some victim anxiety related to personal safety by devising a safety plan for the victim prior to the release of the offender back into the community.

Responding to the literature that discusses how the release process can cause further harm to victims, the Washington program provides additional wrap around services to victims by working with the victim to determine his or her other victim-related needs prior to release. The program then utilizes a formal process for connecting victims with agencies in the community capable of addressing those needs in a timely manner. This process is not one simply of referral but of connecting victims with services directly. For example, if the victim states that he or she is experiencing emotional distress as a result of the release of the offender back into the community, then the victim

is directly connected to service providers offering counseling and support.

While Washington serves as a model for other states, not all aspects of the program have been implemented elsewhere. Each of the states incorporated the workgroup aspect of Victim-Wrap-Around by including victims, corrections staff, parole officers, law enforcement, victim advocates, and community service providers in the reentry process. However, Washington appears to be the only state where victims have a direct impact on the parole process. A few states have expanded the role of victims by providing additional services, such as victim/offender mediation and other services, to the wrap around process.

⊠ Conclusions

Despite the minimal amount of information available, two points can be made. First, it is clear that restorative justice practices behind institutional walls and Victim Wrap Around programs represent new avenues for exploration in the quest to increase victim involvement within the criminal justice process. Second, such programs may represent promising approaches and have the potential to reduce recidivism, increase victim satisfaction with the release process, provide an additional opportunity to meet the needs of victims, increase accountability on the part of offenders, and provide an additional avenue for meeting the needs of offenders at the same time. Unfortunately, more empirical research on outcomes for victims, offenders, institutional behavior, and public safety impacts is needed before such programs can be considered "best practices" in corrections.

⊠ References

Armour, M. (2006). Bridges to Life: A Promising In Prison Restorative Justice Intervention. http://www.restorativejustice.org/editions/2006/june06/2006-05-2s.6472027063

Baker, L. (2007). Sycamore Tree Project Impact Evaluation for Prison Fellowship New Zealand. Retrieved April 26, 2007 from http://www.sdrjmp.org/pdf/051107%20ST%20Evaluation%20-%20-BakkeT%20(2).pdf

Burns, H. (2001). Citizens, Victims, & Offenders: Restoring Justice Project Minnesota Correctional Facility for Women at Shakopee. Center for Restorative Justice & Peacemaking.

Burns, H. (2002). Citizens, Victims, & Offenders Restoring Justice Project MCF-Lino Lakes. Center for Restorative Justice & Peacemaking.

Cartwright, H. (2000). "Including Victims in the American Criminal Justice Process." Retrieved April 16, 2007 from http://www .unafei.or.jp/english/pdf/PDF_rms/no56/56-16.pdf

Criminal Victimization in the United States. (2005). Criminal Victimization in the United States-Statistical Tables. Retrieved May 1, 2007 from http://www.ojp.usdoj.gov/bjs/abstract/cvusst.htm

Forget, M. (2005). Restorative Justice in Prisons. Presented at Ancillary Meeting #40. Eleventh United Nations Congress on Crime Prevention and Criminal Justice, Bangkok, Thailand.

Fraley, Stephen (2001). The Meaning of Reconciliation for Prisoners Serving Long Sentences. *Contemporary Justice Review* 4(1).

LaVigne, N. G., Mamalian, C. A., Travis, J., and Visher, C. (2003). A Portrait of Prisoner Reentry in Illinois. Urban Institute, http:// www.urban.org/url.cfm?ID=410662

Lehman, J. (1999). Reinventing Community Corrections in Washington State. *Corrections Management Quarterly* 5(3). See also www.doc.wa.gov/stories/victimwrap.htm

Lynch, J. P., and Sabol, J. (2001). *Prisoner Re-entry in Perspective*. Washington, D.C.: The Urban Institute.

Marshall, M. (2005). A Consideration of the Sycamore Tree Programme and Survey: Results from the Perspective of a Restorative Justice Practitioner.

Mika, H., Achilles, M., Halbert B., Amstutz, L., and Zehr, H. (2004). Listening to Victims—A Critique of Restorative Justice Policy and Practice in the United States. *Federal Probation* 68(1). Retrieved March 20, 2007 from http://www.uscourts.gov/fed-prob/June_2004/listening.html

National Center for Victims of Crime (2005). *Bringing Victims and Victim Service Providers into Reentry Planning in New Jersey*. The National Center for Victims of Crime.

National Center for Victims of Crime (1999). Promising Practices and Strategies for Victim Services in Corrections. The National Center for Victims of Crime http://www.ncvc.org/ncvc/main .aspx?dbName=DocumentViewer &DocumentID=32565

Parker, L. (2005). RSVP: Restorative Justice in a County Jail. http://www.restoratrvejustice.org/editions/2005/decem ber05/rsvp/

Petersilia, J. (2003). *When Prisoners Come Home: Parole and Prisoner Reentry*. Oxford University Press: New York.

Report of the Advisory Committee on Geriatric and Seriously Ill Inmates (2005). General Assembly of the Commonwealth of Pennsylvania. http://jsg.legis.state.pa.us/lnmates%20Report .PDF

Report of the Re-Entry Policy Council Charting the Safe and Successful Return of Prisoners to the Community. (2005). Council of State Governments. Reentry Policy Council. New York: Council of State Governments. http://www.reentryrpolicy.org/Report/ PartII/ChapterII-D/PolicyStatement23

Shepland, J., Atkinson, A., Atkinson, H., Chapman. B., Colledge, E., Dignan, J., Howes, M., Johnstone, J., Robinson, G. and Sorsby, A. (2006). *Restorative Justice in Practice: The Second Report of the Evaluation of Three Schemes*. Centre for Criminological Research, University of Sheffield, http://www.Sheffield.ac.uk/ccr

Smith, L., Robinson. B. (2006). *Beyond the Holding Tank: Pathways to Rehabilitative and Restorative Prison Policy*. The Salvation Army Policy Unit.

Toews, B. (2006a). Creating Prison-Based Restorative Justice Projects: A Prisoners' Guide for Getting Started. Retrieved April 25, 2007 from http://www.prisonsociety.org/pdf/rj_ Guide.pdf

Toews, B. (2006b). Restorative Justice: Rebuilding the Web of Relationships. Resources for Restorative Justice Education in Prison. Retrieved April 25, 2007 from http://www.prisorisoci ety.org/pdf/rj_workbook.pdf

Umbreit, M. A. and Vos, B. (2000). Homicide Survivors Meet the Offender Prior to Execution: Restorative Justice through Dialogue. *Homicide Studies* 4 (l):63–87.

Umbreit, M., Coates, R. B., and Vos, B. (2007). Restorative Justice Dialogue: A Multi-Dimensional, Evidence-Based Practice Theory. *Contemporary Justice Review* 10(1): 23–41.

Walker, L., Sakai, T., and Brady, K. (2006). Restorative Circles: A Solution-Focused Reentry Planning Process for Inmates. *Federal Probation* 70:1.

Zehr, H. (2002). *The Little Book of Restorative Justice*. Intercourse, PA: Good Books.

DISCUSSION QUESTIONS

1. How do institutionally based restorative justice programs differ from those offered in the community?

2. What are some of the pros and cons of victim wraparound programs in an institutional setting?

3. What are some of the difficulties of assessing institutionally based victim wraparound programs?

READING

In 2005, Latimer, Dowden, and Muise published their meta-analysis assessing the effectiveness of restorative justice programs. This seminal work was and continues to be important to the burgeoning field of restorative justice because of the ever-expanding trend toward the use of alternative-based programs, especially in light of diminished resources and criminalization of behavior. To conduct their analyses, they decided to review the literature for 25 years. They only included studies assessing voluntary programs that sought to bring together the victim, the offender, and the community to repair the harm done. Furthermore, they only included studies that compared restorative justice programs with traditional sentences. Because of the difficulty with defining recidivism with one set outcome, they accepted varying definitions of recidivism for inclusion. Overall, the results of the study were very encouraging for future restorative justice programs. Results indicated that victims who participated in restorative justice programs were more satisfied with the process than those having their cases processed through the traditional court system. Offenders also appeared to be more satisfied than their counterparts, but the relationship was weak. Participation in restorative justice programs did appear to reduce recidivism and increase compliance. Overall, the results suggested restorative justice programs were effective at achieving their stated goals. These results carry forward encouraging policy implications. Given the choice between traditional sentencing and restorative justice programming, these options could effectively be made available for victims.

The Effectiveness of Restorative Justice Practices

A Meta-Analysis

Jeff Latimer, Craig Dowden, and Danielle Muise

Current activity at governmental and community levels suggests that restorative justice, in its many forms, is emerging as an increasingly important element in mainstream criminological practice. Although first discussed in the 1970s by Barnett (1977) and Eglash (1977) in the context of restitution, restorative justice has been more clearly integrated into criminological thinking through such works as Braithwaite (1989), Marshall (1985), Umbreit (1994b), and Zehr (1990). Rather than focusing on the traditional rehabilitation versus retribution debate, many researchers and policy makers now consider restorative justice and, more precisely the concept of restoration, as a valid third alternative (Zehr, 1990). Numerous countries have adopted restorative approaches including Canada, England, Australia, Scotland, New Zealand, Norway, the United States, Japan, and several European countries (Hughes & Mossman, 2001).

Despite the increased attention given to restorative justice, the concept still remains somewhat problematic to define as numerous responses to criminal

SOURCE: Latimer, J., Dowden, C. & Muise, D. (2005). The effectiveness of restorative justice practices: A meta-analysis. *The Prison Journal, 85*(2), 127–144.

behavior may fall under the so-called restorative umbrella. The term has been used interchangeably with such concepts as community justice, transformative justice, peacemaking criminology, and relational justice (Bazemore & Walgrave, 1999). Although a universally accepted and concise definition of the term has yet to be established, Tony F. Marshall's (1996) definition appears to encompass the main principles of restorative justice: "Restorative justice is a process whereby all the parties with a stake in a particular offence come together to resolve collectively how to deal with the aftermath of the offence and its implications for the future" (p. 37; cf. Braithwaite, 1999. p. 5).

——The fundamental premise of the restorative justice paradigm is that crime is a violation of people and relationships (Zehr, 1990) rather than merely a violation of law. The most appropriate response to criminal behavior, therefore, is to repair the harm caused by the wrongful act (Law Commission, 2000). As such, the criminal justice system should provide those most closely affected by the crime (the victim, the offender, and the community) an opportunity to come together to discuss the event and attempt to arrive at some type of understanding about what can be done to provide appropriate reparation.

According to Llewellyn and Howse (1998), the main elements of the restorative process involve voluntariness, truth telling, and a face-to-face encounter. Consequently, the process should be completely voluntary for all participants; the offender needs to accept responsibility for the harm and be willing to openly and honestly discuss the criminal behaviour; and the participants should meet in a safe and organized setting to collectively agree on an appropriate method of repairing the harm.

Models of restorative justice can be grouped into three categories: circles, conferences, and victim-offender mediations. Although somewhat distinct in their practices, the principles employed in each model remain similar. A restorative justice program may be initialed at any point in the criminal justice system and need not be used simply for diversionary purposes. Currently, there are five identified entry points into the criminal justice

system where offenders may be referred to a restorative justice program:

- Police (precharge)
- Crown (postcharge)
- Courts (presentence)
- Corrections (postsentence)
- Parole (prerevocation)

Proponents of restorative justice claim that the process is beneficial to victims and offenders by emphasizing recovery of the victim through redress, vindication, and healing and by encouraging recompense by the offender through reparation, fair treatment, and habilation (Van Ness & Strong, 1997). In the process of joining together to restore relationships, the community is also provided with an opportunity to heal through the reintegration of victims and offenders (Llewellyn & Howse, 1998).

Despite the intuitive appeal of restorative justice, it is imperative to fully evaluate the impact of this approach on several important outcomes. Previous evaluation research focusing on this area has ranged from purely anecdotal accounts to more rigorous designs using comparison groups and, in SOOH cases, random assignment into control and/or treatment groups (Bonta, Wallace-Capretta, & Rooney, 1998). These studies have examined the impact of restorative justice on victim and offender satisfaction, restitution compliance, recidivism, procedural fairness, and several others.

Given that the field of restorative justice research has been maturing, there existed a need to aggregate the present body of empirical knowledge. In this regard, several authors have provided comprehensive literature reviews of this area of research (Braithwaite, 1999; Latimer & Kleinknecht, 2000: Marshall, 1999). Summarizing the research through narrative or qualitative approaches, however, may fail to objectively analyze the available data and draw the appropriate conclusions. Cooper and Rosenthal (1980) directly tested the reliability of synthesizing literature through narrative reviews by providing test participants with a set of seven studies that measured the relationship between two variables. Despite the fact that the set of studies showed a clear statistically significant relationship between the variables, 73% of the reviewers found limited or no support for the hypothesis. This suggested that traditional narrative reviews suffer a considerable loss of power and that the incidence of Type II errors may be common. In addition, the criteria for selecting literature for a narrative review are rarely systematic and consistent. The introduction of meta-analytic techniques, however, has marked a major step forward in summarizing research by providing a more objective method of aggregating knowledge.

Method

Following the techniques of Rosenthal (1991), a meta-analysis was designed to test the effectiveness of restorative justice practices. One of the major issues in conducting this form of research is agreeing on a definition of restorative justice. Generally, it is much easier to identify a nonrestorative approach than it is to provide a precise definition of what constitutes restorative justice. For the purpose of this meta-analysis, the following operational definition was developed: Restorative justice is a voluntary, community-based response to criminal behavior that attempts to bring together the victim, the offender, and the community, in an effort to address the harm caused by the criminal behavior.

Although this may be open to debate, an operational definition is necessary for the purposes of conducting research. Therefore, for the current meta-analysis, programs that contained so-called restorative elements, such as restitution or community service, but did not attempt to bring together the victim, the offender, and the community were not considered. This definition provided us with a guide for the study selection process and ensured that we were examining a consistent response to criminal behavior.

We also needed to identify appropriate outcomes that were measurable and linked directly to the goals of restorative justice. Although several outcome measures have been used, we selected victim and offender satisfaction, recidivism, and restitution compliance as these were the only ones that were sufficiently

available to be subjected to a meta-analysis. Furthermore, these four outcomes are clear and quantifiable determinants of the effectiveness of restorative justice.

Literature Review: Study Identification Criteria

To gather eligible studies for the meta-analysis, a comprehensive search was conducted on the restorative justice literature over the past 25 years. The studies were primarily drawn from the Internet, social science journals, and governmental and nongovernmental reports. A secondary search was conducted using the bibliographies of the identified studies and by contacting researchers active in the field to identify new, unpublished and/or undiscovered research. An explicit set of criteria was established to select studies for inclusion in the meta-analysis:

1. The study evaluated a restorative justice program that fell within our wording definition.

2. The study used a control group or a comparison group that did not participate in a restorative justice program.

3. At least one of the following four outcomes was reported for the treatment and control and/or comparison group: recidivism, victim satisfaction, offender satisfaction, and/or restitution compliance.

4. Sufficient statistical information was reported to calculate an effect size.

Results

Twenty-two unique studies that examined the effectiveness of 35 individual restorative justice programs generated 66 effect sizes.

The vast majority of the effect sizes were derived from programs that targeted predominantly male (94%), young (74%) offenders. It is interesting to note, a large proportion of the effect sizes were drawn from studies that were not published in peer-reviewed academic journals (55%), which, as discussed previously, is typically not the case in meta-analytic work. Studies commonly included one or more of the following outcome measures: victim satisfaction, offender satisfaction, restitution compliance, and recidivism reduction. Each of these issues will be discussed accordingly in the following subsections.

Victim Satisfaction

Participation in a restorative justice program resulted in higher victim satisfaction ratings when compared to a comparison group in all but one of the 13 programs examined. It should be noted that the one negative result was found in the only program that operated at the post-sentence (or corrections) entry point. Compared to victims who participated in the traditional justice system, victims who participated in restorative processes were significantly more satisfied, $t(12) = 3.89, p < .01$.

Offender Satisfaction

Although offenders who participated in restorative justice programs displayed higher satisfaction with the process than their comparisons, the one-sample t test indicated that this difference was not statistically significant. The 95% CI for these values included zero, which further decreased our confidence that these programs have any discernible impact on offender satisfaction.

The difference in offender satisfaction between restorative and nonrestorative participation also becomes significant, $t(11) = 4.52\ p < .01$. It is interesting to note, the $-.71$ effect size was drawn from the same postsentence entry point program as the only negative victim satisfaction effect size.

Restitution Compliance

One of the potential advantages of a restorative justice approach is that it could be more effective in ensuring offender compliance with restitution agreements. This would be a significant contribution as the victims would have a greater likelihood of receiving compensation for the harm caused by the criminal activity and the offenders would be actively accepting responsibility.

Size of $+.33$ (SD $= .24$) was quite high, indicating that offenders who participated in restorative justice programs tended to have substantially higher compliance rates than offenders exposed to other arrangements. Compared to the comparison and/or control groups not participating in a restorative justice program, offenders in the treatment groups were significantly more likely to complete restitution agreements, $t(7) = 3.87, p < .01$.

Recidivism

Arguably, one of the most important outcome variables for any form of criminal justice intervention is recidivism. In other words, restorative justice programs, on average, yielded reductions in recidivism compared to nonrestorative approaches to criminal behavior. In fact, compared to the comparison and/or control groups who did not participate in a restorative justice program, offenders in the treatment groups were significantly more successful during the follow-up periods, $t(31) = 2.88, p < .01$.

Moderator Analysis

Given the relatively wide range of effect sizes, additional analyses were conducted to explore whether characteristics of the study sample or methodological considerations could explain this variability. Initially we had hoped to explore a relatively large number of potential moderators such as gender, ethnicity, criminal history, offense type, facilitator characteristics, and so on. Unfortunately, the relative homogeneity of the offenders used in the studies, as well as the large amount of missing data, rendered many of these analyses untenable. Moreover, because of the low number of restitution compliance effect sizes and the offender satisfaction outlier issue, we only conducted moderating analyses on victim satisfaction and recidivism using the following six variables: random assignment, offender age, publication source, restorative justice model, entry point, and control and/or comparison group type.

The results, however, did not yield any significant between-group differences. One noteworthy difference, albeit not statistically significant, was that for victim satisfaction and recidivism the mean effect sizes from published peer-reviewed studies (+.30 and +.12) were noticeably higher than the mean effect sizes found in unpublished sources (+.16 and +.02). Although this lends support to the file-drawer criticism of meta-analytic work, this problem has been addressed in the current meta-analysis by conducting searches of governmental and nongovernmental reports, graduate theses, and dissertations and by directly contacting researchers active in the field for unpublished research.

◤ Discussion

Generally, compared to traditional nonrestorative approaches, restorative justice was found to be more successful at achieving each of its four major goals. In other words, based on the findings of the current meta-analysis, restorative justice programs are a more effective method of improving victim and/or offender satisfaction, increasing offender compliance with restitution, and decreasing the recidivism of offenders when compared to more traditional criminal justice responses (i.e., incarceration, probation, court-ordered restitution, etc.). In fact, restorative programs were significantly more effective than these approaches across all four outcomes (when the offender satisfaction outlier is excluded).

Self-Selection Bias

The positive results of this meta-analysis are mitigated, however, by the self-selection bias evident in controlled outcome studies on restorative justice programs. Restorative justice, by its very nature, is a voluntary process. This creates a treatment group of participants (offenders and victims) who have chosen to participate in the program and may, therefore, be more motivated than the control group. This concern is elevated by the high rate of attrition within many of the studies in the current meta-analysis. McCold and Wachtel (1998), for example, found clear differences in the recidivism rates of restorative justice participants (20%) versus individuals who refused participation in the program (48%) versus the comparison group (35%). In fact, these authors argued that there was no treatment effect on

recidivism from participation in restorative justice beyond a self-selection effect.

Self-selection bias is an inherent problem in restorative justice research as it is not possible to truly randomly assign participants to treatment and control conditions. When an individual is forced to participate in a restorative justice program, most would argue that the program is no longer truly restorative. Given this, we believe that an alternative method of determining the effectiveness of restorative justice is necessary. We recommend administering questionnaires designed to measure participants' motivation prior to program participation This would allow researchers to examine the motivation of the control group, restorative justice participants, and those who refused participation. This type of research design would provide a comparison of highly motivated, moderately motivated, and unmotivated individuals in each group. If the satisfaction or recidivism rates, for example, were improved in the restorative justice group, and motivation was controlled for in the analysis, we would be more convinced that there is a treatment effect from participation in restorative justice processes.

Notwithstanding this issue of self-selection bias, the results of the current meta-analysis, at present, represent the best indicator of the effectiveness of restorative justice practices. At the very least, those individuals who choose to participate in restorative justice programs find the process satisfying, tend to display lower recidivism rates, and are more likely to adhere to restitution agreements.

Appropriate Treatment

Although the effects of restorative justice participation on recidivism remain somewhat uncertain because of the self-selection bias, many argue that it may be naive to believe that a time-limited intervention such as victim-offender mediation will have a dramatic effect on altering criminal and delinquent behaviour (Umbreit, 1994a). Additional factors, such as antisocial peers, substance abuse, and criminogenic communities, which have been linked to criminal behavior (Hawkins et al., 1998; Lipsey & Derzon, 1998), are not adequately addressed in the restorative process. Andrews and Bonta (1998) identified several criminogenic needs that they maintained are imperative to address in the treatment of offenders to effectively reduce recidivism.

In addition to those listed above, they identified antisocial attitudes, poor self-control and/or self-management, personality factors, family factors, and low levels of educational and employment attainment.

Previous meta-analytic work conducted by Dowden (1998) and Andrews et al. (1990) found that so-called appropriate correctional treatment (i.e., those programs that adhered to the clinically relevant principles of risk, need, and responsivity),[1] displayed an appreciably higher mean effect size (+.26 and .30, respectively) for recidivism compared to the findings for restorative justice programs (+.07) presented here. In other words, although restorative justice programs may yield reductions in recidivism compared to more traditional criminal justice responses to crime, they did not have nearly as strong an impact on reoffending as psychologically informed treatment.

It has been argued, however, that restorative justice and rehabilitation are rather complementary approaches (Crowe, 1998). The utilization, therefore, of restorative and rehabilitative components as a comprehensive response to criminal behavior would be a valuable and theoretically directed experiment. This combination would enable both approaches to capitalize on each of their strengths while minimizing their weaknesses. More specifically, the restorative processes could increase victim and/or offender satisfaction and restitution compliance while the rehabilitative processes could have a significant impact on recidivism.

Moderating Variables

Unfortunately, there were several questions that we were unable to answer because of a lack of data reported in the literature. For example, we were interested in exploring whether the characteristics of the facilitator had a significant moderating impact on restorative justice program effectiveness. However, very few, if any, of the studies provided information concerning the education, professional background, or training of the facilitators. This is particularly noteworthy as facilitators within restorative justice programs can have a significant impact on the outcome of a session. Support for this assertion may be found within the correctional treatment literature where program staff characteristics and behaviors have been found to have a significant impact on program effectiveness (Dowden & Andrews, 2004). There was also rather limited data on additional important variables such as the criminal history of the offenders (i.e., first-time offenders vs. repeat offenders), the specific offenses (i.e., minor vs. serious offenses, property vs. violent offenses), and the relationship between offenders and victims (i.e., family, neighbor, stranger).

In general, we were unable to provide an adequate explanation for the large range of reported effect sizes in each of the outcomes. It is possible that the significant factors in determining a more successful restorative justice program are those that were not reported in the literature (i.e., facilitator characteristics, offense types, criminal history). To facilitate a better understanding of the effectiveness of restorative justice, we recommend that future studies report outcomes, such as recidivism or satisfaction, separately for groups of offenders using such variables as gender, age, criminal history, offense types, and relationship between victim and offender. In addition, we recommend that studies provide more detailed information on the processes used within the restorative justice program and the facilitators.

Additional Research Issues

One issue that future studies may wish to explore is the effect that offender compliance with restitution agreements has on victim satisfaction. The restrictions of meta-analytic procedures precluded such an analysis. Morris and Maxwell (1998), however, did report that the reason most frequently reported for victim dissatisfaction in an evaluation of a family-group conference program in New Zealand was a failure to receive the appropriate restitution. More empirical research into the restitution conditions (i.e., type of restitution, size of restitution, length of time given to comply) that lead to successful compliance would also be appropriate. Moreover, the same type of analysis could be completed on restitution conditions and victim and/or offender satisfaction. And finally, there is no research in the literature that examines the longer term effects for victims who participate in a restorative justice process. An examination of whether victims still feel that they have experienced some closure and healing 6 months or a year after the restorative process would be beneficial.

It is surprising to note, given the current level of activity, there were no appropriate empirical evaluations of circle sentencing models or healing circles. This is likely because of our selection criteria, which required the use of a control and/or comparison group. In addition, as with a large proportion of criminal justice research, there was a dearth of information on the effectiveness of restorative justice for female offenders.

Conclusion

The current meta-analysis provides the most comprehensive empirical synthesis of the restorative justice literature to date. Despite some methodological limitations, the results provide notable support for the effectiveness of these programs in increasing offender/victim satisfaction and restitution compliance, and decreasing offender recidivism. The next critical step for research and program development is to obtain a better understanding of the effect of self-selection bias that diminishes our confidence in these results. To more definitively claim restorative justice an effective response to criminal behavior, we need to be able to address this limitation inherent in restorative justice research methods.

Note

1. For a detailed description of the principles of risk, need, and responsivity and their role in delivering effective correctional treatment, see Andrews and Bourn (1998).

References

Andrews, D. A., & Bonta, J. (1998). *Psychology of criminal conduct* (2nd ed.). Cincinnati, OH: Anderson.

Andrews, D. A., Zinger, I., Hoge, R., Bonta, J., Gendreau, P., & Cullen, F. (1990). Does correctional treatment work? A clinically relevant and psychologically informed meta-analysis. *Criminology, 28,* 369–404

Barnett, R. (1977). Restitution: A new paradigm of criminal justice. *Ethics,* 87, 279–301.

Bazemore, G., & Walgrave, L (1999). *Restorative juvenile justice: Repairing the harm of youth crime.* Monsey, NY: Criminal Justice Press.

Bonta, J., Law, M., & Hanson, R. K. (1998). The prediction of criminal and violent recidivism among mentally disordered offenders: A meta-analysis. *Psychological Bulletin,* 123, 123–142.

Bonta, J., Wallace-Capretta, S., & Rooney, J. (1998). *Restorative justice: An evaluation of the Restorative Resolutions Project.* Ottawa: Solicitor General Canada.

Braithwaite, J. (1989). *Crime, shame and reintegration.* Cambridge, UK: Cambridge University Press.

Braithwaite, J. (1999). *Restorative justice: Assessing optimistic and pessimistic accounts.* In M. Tonry (Ed.), Crime and justice: A review of research (pp. 1–127). Chicago: University of Chicago Press.

Cooper, H., & Rosenthal, R (1980) Statistical versus traditional procedures for summarizing research findings. *Psychological Bulletin,* 87, 442–449.

Crowe, A. H. (1998). Restorative justice and offender rehabilitation: A meeting of the minds. Perspectives: *Journal of the American Probation and Parole Association,* 22, 28–41.

Dowden, C. (1998). A meta-analytic examination of the risk, need and responsivity principles and their importance within the rehabilitation debate. Unpublished M.A. thesis, Ottawa, Canada, Carleton University, Psychology Department.

Dowden, C., & Andrews, D. A. (1999). What works for female offenders: A meta-analytic review. *Crime & Delinquency,* 45, 438–452.

Dowden, C., & Andrews, D.A. (2000). Effective correctional treatment and violent re-offending: A meta-analysis. *Canadian Journal of Criminology,* 42, 449–476.

Dowden, C., & Andrews, D. A. (2004). The importance of staff characteristics in delivering effective correctional treatment: A meta-analytic review of core correctional practice. International *Journal of Offender Therapy and Comparative Criminology,* 48, 203–215.

Dowden, C., & Brown, S. L. (2002). The role of substance abuse factors in predicting recidivism: A meta-analysis. *Psychology, Crime, and Law,* 8, 1–22.

Eglash, A. (1977). Beyond restitution: Creative restitution. In J. Hudson & B. Galaway (Eds.), *Restitution in criminal justice* (pp. 91–129). Lexington, MA: D.C. Heath.

Gendreau, P., Little, T., & Goggin, C. (1996). A meta-analysis of the predictors of adult offender recidivism: What works! *Criminology,* 34, 575–607.

Glass, G., McGaw, B., & Smith, M. (1981). *Meta-analysis in social research.* Newbury Park, CA: Sage.

Hanson, R. K., & Bussiere, M. (1998). Predicting relapse: A meta-analysis of sexual offender recidivism studies. *Journal of Consulting and Clinical Psychology*, 66, 348–362.

Hawkins. J. D., Herrenkohl, T., Farrington, D. P., Browser, D., Catalano, R. P., & Harachi, T. W. (1998). A review of predictors of youth violence. In R. Loeber & D. P. Farrington (Eds.), *Serious and violent juvenile offenders: Risk factors and successful interventions* (pp. 106–146). London: Sage.

Hughes, P., & Mossman, M. J. (2001). *Rethinking access to criminal justice in Canada: A critical review of needs and responses.* Ottawa: Research and Statistics Division, Department of Justice Canada.

Latimer, J. (2001). A meta analytic examination of youth delinquency, family treatment and recidivism. *Canadian Journal of Criminology*, 43, 237–253.

Latimer, J., & Kleinknecht, S. (2000). *The effects of restorative justice programming: A review of the empirical research literature.* Ottawa: Research and Statistics Division, Department of Justice Canada.

Law Commission. (2000). From restorative justice to transformative justice. Discussion paper, Ottawa: Law Commission of Canada.

Lipsey, M. W. (1995). What do we learn from 400 research studies on the effectiveness of treatment with juvenile delinquents? In J. McGuire (Ed.), *What works: Reducing reoffending- Guidelines from research and practice* (pp. 63–78). Chichester, UK: Wiley & Sons.

Lipsey, M. W., & Derzon, J. (1998). Predictors of violent or serious delinquency in adolescence and early adulthood: A synthesis of longitudinal research. In R. Loeber & D. P. Farrington (Eds.), *Serious and violent juvenile offenders: Risk factors and successful interventions* (pp. 86–105). London: Sage.

Lipsey, M. W., & Wilson, D. (1993). The efficacy of psychological, educational, and behavioral treatment: Confirmation from meta-analysis. *American Psychologist*, 48, 1181–1209.

Llewellyn, J., & Howse, R. (1998). *Restorative justice: A conceptual framework.* Ottawa: Law Commission of Canada.

Marshall, T. (1985). *Alternatives to criminal courts: The potential for non-judicial dispute resolution.* Brookfield, VT: Gower.

Marshall, T. F. (1996). The evolution of restorative justice in Britain. *European Journal of Criminal Policy and Research*, 4, 21–42.

Marshall, T. (1999). *Restorative justice: An overview.* London: Home Office, Research Development and Statistics Directorate.

McCold, P., & Wachtel, B. (1998). *Restorative policing experiment; The Bethlehem Pennsylvania Police Family Group Conferencing Project-Summary.* Pipersville, PA: Community Service Foundation.

Morris, A., & Maxwell, G. (1998). *Restorative justice in New Zealand: Family group conferences as a case study.* Western Criminology Review, 1, 1–19.

Rosenthal, R. (1991). *Meta-analytic procedures for social research.* Newbury Park, CA: Sage.

Roy, S. (1993). Two types of juvenile restitution programs in two midwestern counties: A comparative study. *Federal Probation*, 57, 48–53.

Schneider, A. L. (3986). Restitution and recidivism rates of juvenile offenders: Results from four experimental studies. *Criminology*, 24, 533–552.

Sherman, L. W., & Strang, H. (2000). *Recidivism patterns in the Canberra Reintegrate Shaming Experiments (RISE).* Canberra: Centre for Restorative Justice, Research School of Social Sciences, Australian National University.

Umbreit, M. S. (1994a). Crime victims confront their offenders: The impact of a Minneapolis mediation program. *Research on Social Work Practice*, 4, 436–447.

Umbreit, M. S. (1994b). *Victim meets offender: The impact of restorative justice and mediation.* Monsey, NY: Criminal Justice Press.

Van Ness, D., & Strong, K. H. (1997). *Restoring justice.* Cincinnati, OH: Anderson.

Whitehead, J. T., & Lab, S. P. (1989). A meta-analysis of juvenile correctional treatment. *Journal of Research on Crime and Delinquency*, 26, 276–295.

Zehr, H. (1990). *Changing lenses: A new focus for time and justice.* Scottsdale, PA: Herald Press.

DISCUSSION QUESTIONS

1. Given the results from Latimer, Dowden and Muise's meta-analysis, to what extent do restorative justice programs function as an appropriate alternative to traditional sentencing?

2. In this study, the authors identified three models of restorative programs. Identify these three models. What are their similarities and differences? Is one model more effective than the other?

3. Based on the findings of this study and your knowledge of restorative justice programming, create a policy aimed at reducing recidivism and increasing satisfaction for all interested parties (i.e., victims, offenders, and the community). Be sure to discuss the characteristics of the target audiences.

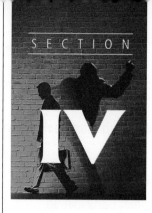

IV

The Viability of Treatment Perspectives

Section Highlights

- The Martinson Report—Revisited
- The Need for Community-Based Treatment and the Pitfalls of Treatment Programs in Institutional Settings
- Suggested Theoretical Approach to Reintegration and Offender Treatment
- Community Supervision Staff and Treatment Staff: Effective Alliances
- Different Types of Treatment Modalities/Orientations in Therapy
- Different Types of Treatment Programs
- Treatment Professionals
- Community Partnerships and Agency Alliances
- Treatment Staff, Referrals, and Increased Human Supervision
- Progress in Treatment Programs and the Likelihood for Recidivism
- Educating the Community About Treatment Benefits and Integrating Citizen and Agency Involvement
- Conclusion

Learning Objectives

1. Compare current evaluations of treatment programs with the outdated **Martinson report.**

2. Describe the types of treatment modalities.

3. Understand how different therapist characteristics impact treatment.

4. Demonstrate the importance of agency partnerships and volunteer participation.

5. Know how treatment approaches can be integrated within the community.

6. Describe the various means by which agencies and community volunteers can aid the treatment process.

7. Understand why public knowledge of treatment approaches is important.

Treatment programs for offenders abound around the country. The proliferation of treatment programs would lead one to believe that there should be relatively little crime if such programs do indeed work well. Often, critics of treatment-oriented policies will note this as proof that treatment is not effective. However, this is a misleading and misinformed observation on the utility of treatment. Treatment is not prevention, and one cannot simply overlook this point. Prevention programs are designed to eliminate crime *before* the crime ever has a chance to take place. Treatment programs, on the other hand, are designed to decrease the likelihood of crime *after* a crime or aberrant behavior has been detected and processed. Thus, the initial activity of offending that brings an offender into treatment is one that is a prevention agenda and not necessarily a treatment agenda. Over generations, one would presume that the reduction in offending would be transmitted to the offender's children and community, but there are a huge variety of sociological variables that impede and undermine treatment effects once a person leaves the structure of a treatment program.

Further, treatment is not a panacea for all criminals and all criminal behavior. There are indeed some offenders who are simply not amenable to treatment. Extremely hardcore offenders (i.e., psychopaths, certain types of serial murderers and serial rapists, and perhaps some hardened gang members) may simply be beyond the reach of current treatment techniques and processes. In short, treatment cannot work with everyone all of the time, and no truly knowledgeable treatment professional would claim otherwise. Treatment is one of a variety of responses to criminal offending, but it should not be viewed as the *only* response to criminal offending.

Lastly, punishment schemes that do not integrate treatment have been tried extensively throughout correctional history. It is clear that these approaches do not "work" very well either. Indeed, if punishment was working so well, one would presume that criminal behavior would have been eradicated long ago. However, crime continues to occur around the globe, regardless of how stiff the penalties may be. Though certainty of detection may reduce some crime, it does not reduce it all, and even organized criminals may "factor in" some prison time throughout their career as part of the overhead in doing business within the criminal world. Given that prisons are full and that death penalty prone jurisdictions tend to have high crime rates, it is clear that punishment is not working well.

In that light, one must ask why treatment should not be integrated into the correctional response. After all, it just might work and, given that state budgets are completely drained from expensive criminal justice budgets, it may seem that we have little choice. Though this last point may seem to be a pessimistic means of justifying treatment, it is nonetheless a possible truth. But added to this would be an additional question: What would society be like if we had no treatment at all? Would it actually be safer? From the research during the past decade, it is clear that our society would be in worse hands with no treatment programs. Though skeptics from the 1970s might have believed that they had a legitimate claim in eschewing treatment, it has become clear since then that they were misled by faulty research, faulty reporting, and personal biases that essentially disabled the true effectiveness of our correctional system.

▧ The Martinson Report—Revisited

In 1974, Robert Martinson published the now infamous "What Works?—Question and Answers About Prison Reform" in *Public Interest*. His conclusions drew into question the veracity of treatment approaches compared to incarceration. In a review of 231 evaluation studies published between 1945 and 1967, he concluded that

> With few and isolated exceptions, the rehabilitative efforts that have been reported so far have had no appreciable effect on recidivism. Studies that have been done since our survey was completed do not present any major grounds for altering that original conclusion. (Martinson, 1974, p. 25)

At the time that the Martinson report was published, both liberals and conservatives had lost faith in the state to implement treatment programs (liberals) or effectively punish offenders (conservatives) (Cullen & Gilbert, 1982). Those interpreting the Martinson report findings touted them as the absolute example that a shift in the current system was needed. The long-range impact of those findings and subsequent shift in policy could not have been forecasted to be so extreme. The ultimate results of the Martinson report have been quite detrimental to those persons who do support a treatment approach. In particular, although recognition does exist that there are programs that may be effective and few researchers or politicians questioned the methodology employed for assessing program effectiveness, most interpreted Martinson as proclaiming "nothing works" (for examples, see Cullen, 2007; Gendreau, Smith, & Thériault, 2009; Lipsey, 2009; Palmer, 1975; Sarre, 2001). Much of this is because Martinson's report was largely misquoted. It is not so much that Martinson said that treatment does not work; rather, he noted that no single treatment modality works in every single circumstance. Since that time, a number of meta-analytical studies have been conducted with differing results. In sum, the results suggest that treatment success depends on the offender, the type of treatment used, and the person delivering the treatment.

The idea of treatment and rehabilitation as the guiding philosophy of corrections (both institutional and community based) continues to generate a lot of attention by agency personnel and policy makers alike. The appropriateness of punishment versus treatment is an argument that in all likelihood will continue long past the merits of this text. Cullen (2007) contended that criminologists, practitioners, and policy makers alike should stand together and reaffirm that rehabilitation should be the guiding philosophy of corrections regardless of whether it is in an institutional or community-based setting. He offered five assertions supporting the revitalization of rehabilitation. They are summarized as follows: (1) rejecting rehabilitation was a mistake, (2) punishment does not work, (3) rehabilitation does work, (4) the public likes rehabilitation . . . even if it is a liberal idea, and (5) rehabilitation is the moral thing to do (pp. 718–721).

As Latessa, Cullen, and Gendreau (2002) noted, the lack of focus on treatment is often guided by what they referred to as "correctional quackery." Although oftentimes this "quackery" is created by a lack of support for professionalism within the field of corrections, there is also a seeming lack of trust between those who work in the field for those who have not (i.e., academics and criminologists). More specifically, they identified four sources of known correctional quackery. They include (1) failure to use research in designing programs, (2) failure to follow appropriate assessment and classification practices, (3) failure to use effective treatment models, and (4) failure to evaluate what we do (Latessa et al., 2002, pp. 44–46). In spite of the fact that research continues to be conducted and a growing body of literature demonstrates the necessary principles for effective treatment, many communities still rely on programming such as punitive-oriented programs (e.g., boot camps, scared straight), control-oriented programs (e.g., intensive supervision), or non-intervention programs (e.g., labeling theory) that have no empirical support for their effectiveness (Cullen, 2007; Latessa et al., 2002). More specifically, Latessa et al. (2002, p. 45) listed the eight principles necessary for effective correctional intervention (see Table 4.1 for a list of these principles and their definitions). As reported in a multitude of articles (see Gendreau et al., 2009; Lipsey, 2009 for examples), programs whereby these principles are endorsed and incorporated into the programming do experience meaningful reductions in recidivism and successful programmatic outcomes. Likewise, programs that fail to incorporate these principles appear to either experience no reductions in recidivism or have the reverse effect on participants (Latessa et al., 2002). We now turn our attention to some of the research that demonstrates how and when treatment programs have been found to be effective.

According to Janet Firshein, treatment does indeed work. Drug treatment is a particularly important area of research since the majority of the offender population has drug treatment issues. In examining drug treatment programs, Firshein noted that data released from the National Institute on Drug Abuse (NIDA) make it quite clear that treatment works, stating that

> NIDA tracked 10,000 drug abusers in 100 treatment programs around the U.S. from 1991 to 1993 and found that methadone treatment cut heroin use by 70 percent. Only 28 percent of patients in outpatient methadone treatment programs reported weekly or more frequent heroin use, down from 89.4 percent prior to admission. The study also found that long-term abstinence-based treatment resulted in 50 percent reductions in weekly or more frequent cocaine use after one year of follow-up. (Firshein, 1998, p. 1)

This is especially good news since this also means that in many cases other corollary crimes (such as theft, assault, and prostitution) also decrease with lowered rates of drug addiction. Further, this study is obviously large in scale and therefore easily rivals the earlier research presented by Martinson in his fateful report. While the results reported by Firshein (1998) are indeed promising, it is important to look at a number of treatment programs and orientations when determining the efficacy of treatment perspectives.

Consider the research by Babcock (2006), who conducted a meta-analytic review that examined the findings of 22 studies evaluating treatment efficacy for domestically violent males. The outcome literature of controlled quasi-experimental and experimental studies was reviewed to test the relative impact of the Duluth model, cognitive behavioral therapy (CBT), and other types of treatment on subsequent recidivism of violence. Babcock tested study design and type of treatment as moderators, and she found that treatment design tended to have only a small influence on effect size. Her overall conclusion was that the effects due to treatment were small, meaning that the current interventions have a minimal impact on reducing recidivism beyond the effect of being arrested. Analogies to treatment for other populations are presented for comparison.

Other researchers have examined the efficacy of programs that provide therapeutic interventions for sex offenders. One research project examined the effectiveness of treatment by summarizing data from

Table 4.1 Eight Principles of Effective Correctional Intervention

1. **Organizational Culture.** Effective organizations have well-defined goals, ethical principles, and a history of efficiently responding to issues that have an impact on the treatment facilities. Staff cohesion, support service training, self-evaluation and use of outside resources also characterize the organization.

2. **Program Implementation/Maintenance.** Programs are based on empirically-defined needs and are consistent with the organization's values. The program is fiscally responsible and congruent with stakeholder's values. Effective programs also are based on thorough reviews of the literature (i.e., meta-analyses), undergo pilot trials, and maintain the staff's professional credentials.

3. **Management/Staff Characteristics.** The program director and treatment staff are professionally trained and have previous experience working in offender treatment programs. Staff selection is based on their holding beliefs supportive of rehabilitation and relationship styles and therapeutic skill factors typical of effective therapies.

4. **Client Risk/Need Practices.** Offender risk is assessed using psychometric instruments of proven predictive validity. The risk instrument consists of a wide range of dynamic risk factors or criminogenic needs (e.g., anti-social attitudes and values). The assessment also takes into account the responsivity of offenders to different styles and modes of service. Changes in risk level over time (e.g., 3 to 6 months) are routinely assessed in order to measure intermediate changes in risk/need levels that may occur as a result of planned interventions.

5. **Program Characteristics.** The program targets for change a wide variety of criminogenic needs (factors that predict recidivism), using empirically valid behavioral/social/learning/cognitive behavioral therapies that are directed to higher-risk offender. The ratio of rewards to punishers is at least 4:1. Relapse prevention strategies are available once offenders complete the formal treatment phase.

6. **Core Correctional Practice.** Program therapists engage in the following therapeutic practices: anti-criminal modeling, effective enforcement and disapproval, problem-solving techniques, structured learning procedures for skill building, effective use of authority, cognitive self-change, relationship practices, and motivational interviewing.

7. **Inter-Agency Communication.** The agency aggressively makes referrals and advocates for its offenders in order that they receive high quality services in the community.

8. **Evaluation.** The agency routinely conducts program audits, consumer satisfaction surveys, process evaluation of changes in criminogenic need, and follow-ups of recidivism rates. The effectiveness of the program is evaluated by comparing the respective recidivism rates of risk-control comparison groups of other treatments or those of a minimal treatment group.

43 studies with a combined total population of 9,454 sex offenders (Hanson et al., 2002). These researchers found that most forms of treatment operating prior to 1980 appeared to have little effect. However, when averaged across all studies, the sexual offense recidivism rate was lower for the treatment groups than for those sex offenders who remained untreated (Hanson et al., 2002). Programs with modalities and data reflective of 2000 and beyond were associated with reductions in sexual recidivism and general recidivism. In these cases, the recidivism rates for treated sex offenders were lower than the recidivism rates of untreated sex offenders. Studies comparing treatment completers to those who did not complete the therapeutic program consistently found higher recidivism rates for the dropouts, regardless of the type of treatment provided (Hanson et al., 2002).

From the research just presented by Hanson et al. (2002), it would appear that treatment programs for sex offenders have improved over the years. This is not surprising since these offenders have drawn considerable attention during the past 2 decades. Also interesting is the fact that research methodology (and especially statistical applications) has improved during the past 2 to 3 decades, and these improvements are likely to effectively differentiate between programs. Nevertheless, the fact that sex offenders do have some success in treatment demonstrates that, at least on some occasions, therapy can and does work.

Further, when considering specialized populations, it would again seem that treatment does work, but making such a determination is complicated. For instance, a study examining treatment programs for female offenders was conducted by Andrews and Dowden (2002). They reported the following:

> Although little has been understood about "what works" for female offenders, the findings of this meta-analysis outline a theoretically based and empirically validated set of guidelines for delivering effective correctional treatment to this population. Subject to additional research, we conclude now that the principles of case classification, integrity and core correctional practice are highly relevant to program design and delivery with female offenders.

These researchers found that, in general, hardcore female offenders benefited more from highly structured and tightly supervised forms of intervention. In comparison, less serious female offenders tended to do better when the treatment regimen was more flexible in orientation. This then again shows that treatment can and does work, particularly when the appropriate type of intervention is matched with the appropriate type of offender. Further still, there is abundant evidence that female offenders have better prognoses when they have contact with their children. Thus, we can conclude that female offenders are receptive to treatment. If the treatment is implemented correctly, then it is indeed likely to provide successful outcomes that clearly identify what works for female offenders.

With juvenile offenders, it has been widely shown that therapeutic interventions can and do work. Lipsey, Wilson, and Cothern (2000) noted that research tends to clearly indicate that intervention programs can reduce overall recidivism rates among juvenile offenders, but they examine this further by explaining treatment outcomes with serious juvenile offenders. These authors conducted a meta-analysis of programs under the banner of the Office of Juvenile Justice and Delinquency Prevention (OJJDP). Their research sought to address two key questions: (1) Can intervention programs reduce recidivism rates among serious delinquents? (2) If so, what types of programs are most effective? These two questions cut to the chase when considering the widely noted slant of the ill-fated Martinson report that was previously discussed. While there were many details to this study (as there are with any meta-analysis), Lipsey et al. (2000) found that "effects measured across the 200 studies reviewed varied considerably, there was an overall decrease of 12 percent in recidivism for serious juvenile offenders who received treatment interventions" (p. 1). Further, these researchers were able to pinpoint aspects of programs that tended to make them particularly successful. They found that the most effective interventions included interpersonal skills training, individual counseling, and behavioral programs for noninstitutionalized offenders and interpersonal skills training and community-based, family-type group homes for institutionalized offenders. Thus, even with serious juvenile offenders, there has been clear and solid research that demonstrates the efficacy of treatment.

Even further, Hanser and Mire (2008) researched treatment programs of juvenile sex offenders, these offenders having all of the complicated treatment characteristics of hardcore juvenile offenders as well as the characteristics of adult offenders. Their research not only examined this specialized and difficult group of offenders but it examined these types of offenders in both the United States and Australia. From their research, it was clear that juvenile sex offending could be effectively treated. To be sure, not all such offenders can be effectively treated, but the majority benefited from interventions in the research by Hanser and Mire (2008).

While the previous discussion on treatment intervention effectiveness is by no means exhaustive, it does demonstrate one key point: Treatment does indeed work, if it is allowed to. This is quite clear from the research presented, and it should also be pointed out that each of the studies presented were meta-analyses. Further, this is important because this means that each of these studies examined a number of other studies. This means that the results presented are likely to be robust, being grounded in the research of numerous other researchers. It would appear that over time, the quality of treatment services has indeed improved, resulting in lowered rates of recidivism: the ultimate litmus test of effectiveness in the criminal justice system. It is because of improved intervention and evaluation techniques that the pendulum of correctional policy has changed in the direction of a "what works" rather than a "nothing works" orientation. The contemporary emphasis, as pointed out in the preceding discussion, is grounded in years of research that has emerged since the seminal study conducted by Martinson (1974). Figure 4.1 provides an illustration of the back-and-forth view on treatment and rehabilitation in correctional policy throughout the past few decades.

▧ The Need for Community-Based Treatment and the Pitfalls of Treatment Programs in Institutional Settings

Naturally, the slant of this text is one in favor of the use of community corrections. This same slant is likewise held in relation to offender treatment programs. It is important that the student understand that there are a number of logical reasons for favoring treatment perspectives. The use of community corrections is conducive to better treatment outcomes, and this alone makes it a preferred method of supervising offenders in treatment when compared to programs within the institution.

Students should understand that most treatment programs in the community tend to have more face-to-face contacts between treatment providers and participants. This is true for a number of reasons. First, the offender has more options in making contact with helping professionals, and helping professionals have more latitude in aiding offenders since they are able to maintain contact at scheduled and unscheduled points of the day or night. The typical administrative limitations associated with the institutional environment are not present in community-based settings. Though ethical constraint and professional decorum always applies, treatment providers can typically be available in a more flexible manner when they are in the community and when the offender has suitable mobility to access assistance during different times throughout the day or night. While it might intuitively seem that inmates in prison would have more contact with treatment providers, this is usually not the case. In fact, they tend to have very limited contact that is highly structured, being limited by the physical facilities and security to prevent flexible contact.

Further, prison treatment staff tend to be overloaded with demands from heavy caseloads and are hampered by the restrictions associated with the custodial environment. In addition, the security culture that is attributed to prison institutions often undermines any true treatment orientation. Thus, the prison environment tends to be less than ideal. Add to this the fact that the inmate subculture tends to look down on those persons who do disclose and/or trust others (such as therapists) and it becomes clear that the environment in prisons works in opposition to treatment strategies. All of these same restrictions and/or negative perceptions of the treatment process do not exist to the same magnitude, if at all, within community programs. Because of this, it is typically considered that community-based treatment programs tend to have better results than those within a secure facility.

In addition, if the offender is not located within a criminogenic region of the community, they are less likely to have routine contact with other offenders. In prison facilities, inmates are in constant contact with

Figure 4.1 Pendulum Shifts and Swings in Correctional Policy

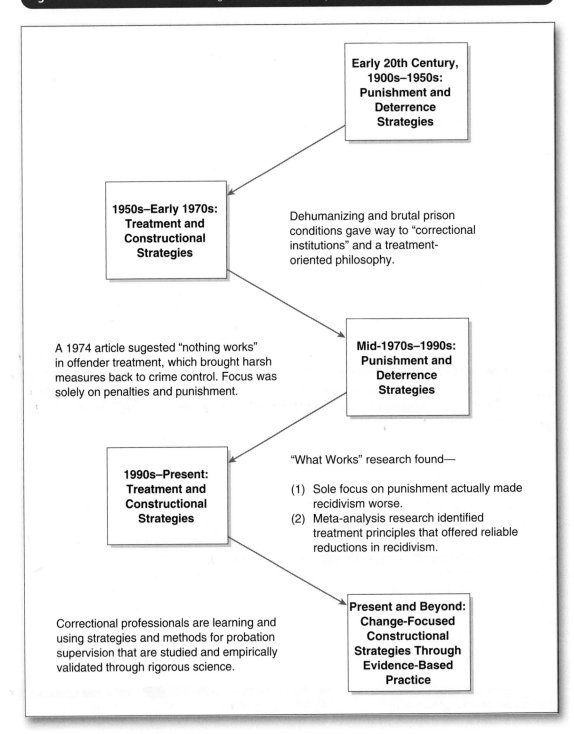

other criminals, and this tends to contaminate the efforts of treatment staff. Thus, existence within the community can aid in separating the offender from other problematic friends and/or criminal associates, improving the ability of treatment programs. While separation between the offender and old associates is not guaranteed, community supervision officers (CSOs) can aid in observing contacts that the offender makes and in providing the appropriate structure that eliminates much of the opportunity for the further commission of crime.

Lastly, case managers tend to have more options in the community when addressing offender needs. There tends to be a wider variety of services that caseworkers can coordinate with, and there also tends to be many more choices between each type of service. This alone aids greatly in the treatment process. The end result is a comprehensive set of services that, while not all being collected within one single facility, allows for choice and specificity in the selection of various services. Add to this improved access to one's therapist, improved opportunities for corollary services (job placement, medical services, and so forth), and removal from noxious social influences and it is clear that the community-oriented process of intervention is a superior choice in many cases. While there are certainly some offenders that simply cannot be released into the community due to their level of dangerousness, most are able to make much better use of intervention programs located in the community than those located in the institution. It is for all of these reasons that this text presents community interventions as superior to those offered within the custodial institution.

As previously noted in Section I, the primary basis for most community-based alternatives, particularly probation and parole, is one of reintegration or rehabilitation. As we just saw, the idea of keeping an individual convicted of a less serious or first time offense out of a correctional institution may serve to mitigate the harshness of the penalty and allow for offenders to be productive members of society. If this is true, then one must ascertain the specific theoretical approaches that should be used when achieving this function. Abadinsky (2003), in describing rehabilitation as the primary function of probation and parole, noted that there are three basic theoretical models for rehabilitation in probation and parole. These are (1) the social casework model, (2) the use of **reality therapy,** and (3) behavioral and/or learning theory. This text will, for the most part, incorporate Abadinsky's theoretical perspective on probation and parole. Abadinsky (2003) also emphasizes these points when providing his own theoretical perspective on probation and parole.

▧ Suggested Theoretical Approach to Reintegration and Offender Treatment

According to Abadinsky, social casework provides concrete services to persons in need as a means of solving problems. The importance of social casework in probation and parole starts with theory and extends into the very skills and professional training that helping professionals are provided. These skills include such factors as effective interviewing, fact-finding in the offender's background, and the ability to identify and distinguish surface from underlying problems. These skills aid the clinician in getting a good baseline of the offender's challenges to effective reintegration. With this in mind, Abadinsky (2003) noted that there are three key components practiced in social casework, which are as follows:

1. *Assessment:* Gathering and analyzing relevant information upon which a treatment and a supervision plan should be based.

2. *Evaluation*: Consisting of the organization of facts into a meaningful goal-oriented explanation.

3. *Intervention*: Implementation of the treatment plan. (p. 295)

Assessment is intended to provide the clinician and the CSO with a clear understanding of the client's current level of functioning. The **presentence investigation report (PSI),** which will be discussed in the next section of this text, is perhaps a very effective and pragmatic assessment, being a compilation of numerous areas of functioning that must be considered for each offender. This is also a good example of how supervision and treatment plans may work hand in hand to augment one another (Hanser, 2007a). Assessment includes the gathering of information from documents and through interviews with the offender as well as other persons that are familiar with the offender (Abadinsky, 2003). The need for effective assessment will be discussed in greater detail later in this text, but for the time being, it is sufficient to state that assessment serves as the foundation to everything else that follows, both in relation to treatment and public safety. Thus, assessment is the cornerstone to meeting the manifest factor related to offender reintegration and the latent factor of public safety.

Evaluation is the process whereby assessment data are incorporated into the planning process to assist in goal-setting for the offender. Perlman (1957) suggested that this phase of social casework includes

1. The nature of the problem and the goals sought by the client, in their relationship to

2. The nature of the person who bears the problem, his or her social and psychological situation and functioning, and who needs help with his or her problem, in relation to

3. The nature and purpose of the agency and the kind of help it can offer or make available. (pp. 168–169)

The evaluation plan takes into account both the processes and the desired outcomes for effective offender reintegration. These components must be clearly defined at the outset, and both require consistent monitoring throughout the entire period of offender supervision. The most effective form of evaluation design will include a pretest (once the offender begins supervision) and a posttest (when the offender has successfully completed their sentence) to determine progress that can be attributed to either interventions that are employed or supervision regimens that are maintained.

Lastly, *intervention* involves activities, assignments, and routines that are designed to bring about a behavior change in a systematic manner, resulting in goal-directed behavior toward the desired community supervision outcome. The specific relationship between the CSO and the offender is actually quite important. One might be surprised to find that many offenders do develop some degree of affinity for their supervision officer. Naturally, the CSO does have authority over the client and must ensure that the client maintains requirements of their supervision. Regardless of any collaboration between the offender and the officer, it is the officer's task to maintain close watch over the offender and ensure that compliance is maintained.

Reality therapy is based on the notion that all persons have two specific psychological needs: (1) the need to belong and (2) the need for self-worth and recognition. Therapists operating from a reality therapy theoretical perspective seek to engage the offender in various social groups and to motivate them in achievement-oriented activities. Each of these help meet the two psychological needs that are at the heart of most all human beings. Further, therapists maintain a warm and caring approach, but reality therapy rejects irresponsible behavior. Therapists are expected to confront irresponsible or maladaptive behavior and are even expected to set the tone for "right" or "wrong" behavior. This is an unorthodox approach when compared to other theoretical perspectives in counseling and psychotherapy since it is often thought that therapy should be self-directed by the client. Reality therapy encourages—indeed it expects—the therapist to be directive.

In addition, reality therapy has been used in a number of institutional and community-based correctional contexts. Indeed, the tenets of reality therapy are complementary to community supervision where direct interventions are often necessary and where a client may have to be told that they have committed a "wrong" behavior. Lastly, William Glasser (the founder of reality therapy) has expressed a great deal of support for correctional agencies in general and for CSOs in particular, but he does caution against the excessive use of punishments to correct offender behavior, especially among juvenile offenders (note that this is consistent with classical criminological concepts). This is because punishment can often serve as a justification or rationalization for further antisocial behavior, particularly if it is not proportional to the offense (especially technical offenses) and the criminogenic peer group will likely reinforce these faulty justifications. On the other hand, when a given penalty is actually proportional and is consistent with the listed sanctions, such countereffects do not seem to occur.

Lastly, one primary theoretical orientation used in nearly all treatment programs associated with community corrections is behavioral and/or learning theory through the use of operant conditioning. This form of behavioral modification is based on the notion that certain environmental consequences occur that strengthen the likelihood of a given behavior and that other consequences tend to lessen the likelihood that a given behavior is repeated. A primary category of behavior modification occurs through operant conditioning. Those consequences that strengthen a given behavior are called reinforcers. Reinforcers can be both positive and negative, with positive reinforcers being a reward for a desired behavior. An example might be if we provided a certificate of achievement for offenders that completed a life skills program. Negative reinforcers are unpleasant stimuli that are removed when a desired behavior occurs. An example might be if we agreed to remove the requirement of wearing electronic monitoring (EM) devices when offenders successfully maintained their scheduled meetings and appointments for one full year without any lapse in attendance.

Consequences that weaken a given behavior are known as punishments. Punishments, as odd as this may sound, can be either positive or negative. A positive punishment is one where a stimulus is applied to the offender when the offender commits an undesired behavior. For instance, we might require the offender to pay an additional late fee if they are late in paying their restitution to the victim of their crime. A negative punishment is the removal of a valued stimulus when the offender commits an undesired behavior. An example might be when we remove the offender's ability to leave their domicile for recreational or personal purposes (placed on house arrest) if they miss any of their scheduled appointments or meetings.

The key in distinguishing between reinforcers and punishments to keep in mind is that reinforcers are intended to *increase* the likelihood of a *desired* behavior whereas punishments are intended to *decrease* the likelihood of an *undesired* behavior. In operant conditioning, the term *positive* refers to the addition of a stimulus rather than the notion that something is good or beneficial. Likewise, the term *negative* refers to the removal of a stimulus rather than being used to denote something that is bad or harmful.

Operant conditioning tends to work best if the reinforcer or the punishment is applied immediately after the behavior (again, similar to classical criminology). Likewise, reinforcers work best when they are intermittent in nature rather than continual since the offender must exhibit a desired behavior with reward given at unpredictable points, thereby instilling a sense of delayed gratification (rather than instant gratification). Punishments, on the other hand, have been found to work best when they are in close proximal time of the undesired behavior (swift), sufficient enough to prevent repeating the behavior (severe), and when there is no means of escaping the punisher (certain). These findings have been determined through empirical research and are consistent with the notions of classical criminology which was previously discussed. Lastly, behavioral psychologists have found that excessive punishments can (and often do) breed hostility among subjects—specific hostility toward the punisher in particular and general hostility that is generalized within the environment.

Community Supervision Staff and Treatment Staff: Effective Alliances

The main point to this section is to further emphasize that CSOs have a strong impact on the ultimate outcome of the offender's supervision process. There are a variety of different dynamics likely to be experienced during the first encounter between an officer and an offender. As noted at that time, this can be a time of serious discomfort for the offender who will likely be anxious during this encounter and will likely have a difficult time trusting the officer. These dynamics are actually true among CSOs and all offenders new to the community supervision process. This mutual appraisal process, though quite informal, is an important first step in the process of relationship building.

CSOs who build a good rapport with offenders on their caseloads are in a much better position to guide offenders toward effective reform. Since resistance will not likely exist between the officer and the offender, this means that such CSOs can better aid in encouraging offenders to actually apply techniques that they learn while participating in treatment programs. While CSOs have the authority to coerce attendance, they typically have a difficult time ensuring that offenders actually participate in earnest while attending various treatment services. If the CSO can encourage the offender to earnestly participate in treatment, all the while with the understanding that the officer could resort to coercive mechanisms (but yet chooses not to force the offender into compliant participation), then this is likely to build trust and compliance between the two. This also increases the likelihood that the offender's prognosis will be positive. It is in this manner that CSOs can aid treatment providers in maximizing the intervention programs available to offenders.

▲ **Photo 4.1** Dr. Hanser stands in his office and describes abusive patterns of behavior as being rooted in faulty cognitions and socialization. While explaining this, he has found a resource to provide to a client.

Further, treatment staff who work in unison with supervision officers also provide effective insight into the supervision process. This allows supervision officers to track the behavior of offenders and to also determine if their reintegration extends beyond the mere elimination of recidivism. This is an important point since there may be a number of other measures that are important regardless of recidivism rates. For instance, offenders who successfully engage in a job training program may actually recidivate by committing a minor crime but, rather than using restrictive methods, it may be that they could be given a fine or some other such sanction that does not preclude their continued supervision and participation in their program. In fact, officers could even strive to have sanctions dovetail and complement attendance in treatment by assigning community services in treatment agencies. Constructive use of sanctions can improve offender participation while also utilizing the treatment service provider with the ability to observe the offender's progress. This then works to increase the amount of human supervision that the offender is given. This is even truer in many group counseling or group treatment programs where participating members are also expected to maintain contact with one another. It is in this manner that treatment providers and supervision officers can work hand in hand to improve security standards (through increased human contacts) and treatment outcomes: by motivating both attendance and actual participation. Table 4.2 provides an overview of some of the primary functions associated with the reintegration process, demonstrating that these functions often overlap between community supervision personnel and treatment personnel. Likewise, Figure 4.2 illustrates the interfacing between treatment staff and community supervision personnel.

Before proceeding further, students should understand that the infusion of treatment-based personnel and supervision personnel is actually quite consistent with the overall emphasis of this text. Throughout this text, it has been stressed that it is important for community supervision agencies to have interrelationships between individuals within the community and among a variety of professions. In addition to the inclusion of volunteers, there has been an emphasis on networking with other agencies such as will be presented in Section VIII on case management planning and implementation. Thus, the true means by which

Table 4.2 Functions of Both Community Supervision Personnel and Treatment Personnel in Offender Reintegration

Primary Functions in Offender Reintegration	Community Supervision Officer	Treatment Specialist
Build collaborative relationships that both motivate and hold offenders accountable for their actions.	X	X
Target supervision and treatment resources to offenders who are at a higher risk of reoffending.	X	X
Target factors that predict crime and that can be changed.	X	
Help improve the offender's self-control by encouraging natural talents and interests, talking about what worked for an offender in the past, and identifying and/or role-playing difficult situations.	X	X
Enlarge the offender's connections to other parts of the community through employment, faith communities, and other types of civic participation.	X	
Encourage an offender to change "playgrounds and playmates"—that is, to stay away from criminal friends and criminal behaviors.	X	X
Tailor interactions and interventions to offender characteristics such as motivation, learning style, and intelligence.	X	X

Figure 4.2 The Interface Between Treatment and Supervision Staff

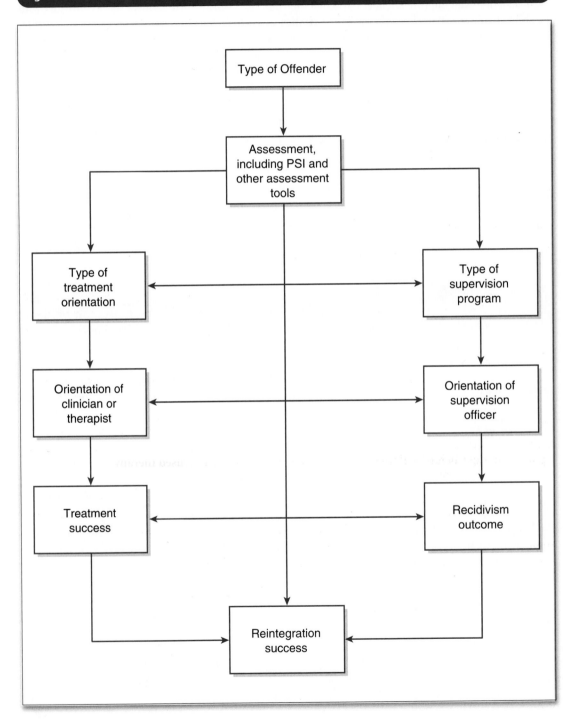

offenders are to be reintegrated into the community resides with a multivariate set of circumstances that require assistance from a variety of persons. The reintegration of the offender, as it turns out, is not a task left to the supervision agency alone. This was made clear in Section II and has been noted throughout this text. True offender reintegration requires supervision personnel, treatment personnel, and case managers to coordinate the resources throughout various agencies; a number of personnel from various agencies; and involvement from community members themselves. It is clear that reintegration must include comprehensive and varied services that are systematic in implementation. Any failure to observe this is likely to leave critical offender needs unattended, thereby increasing the likelihood of criminal activity in the future.

▧ Different Types of Treatment Modalities/Orientations in Therapy

There are a multitude of treatment modalities that exist among treatment providers. Many of these modalities are grounded in their own distinct theoretical bases while others are grounded in theoretical frameworks that are similar to those discussed in earlier sections (i.e., cognitive behavioral modalities). Further, the existence of this variety of modalities makes it difficult to assess the efficacy of treatment because there are a number of different approaches to be assessed. This was a major challenge to Martinson's research and is another reason that meta-analyses of treatment programs are preferable to other forms of evaluation; they allow for comparisons between various studies that may use any number of different modalities of service delivery. With this in mind, it is important that the student have at least a minimal exposure to these modalities to better understand how some fit quite well within the realm of correctional treatment while others do not seem to fit at all.

The purpose of this section is to orient the student to the basic modalities and theoretical orientations associated with therapeutic interventions. The main emphasis of this text is on the supervision of offenders and their reintegration into society. The following list of treatment modalities and/or orientations are those that are likely to be used in the criminal justice system. While not an all-encompassing list, it does provide a fairly good overview of what practitioners might encounter among treatment agencies that network and collaborate with community corrections agencies. The most common types of correctional therapy include **cognitive therapy, behavioral therapy**, reality therapy, and **solution-focused therapy**. Each of these are described in the following paragraphs.

First, the cognitive therapy approach is based on the belief that faulty thinking patterns and belief systems cause psychological problems and that changing our thoughts improves our mental and emotional health and results in changes in behavior. Cognitive therapy challenges all-or-nothing thinking, antisocial attitudes, impulsivity, egocentrisms, fatalistic thinking, and overgeneralizations. Dosage and strength of the treatment are higher than most programs. The program is designed to be administered by nonprofessional staff who have completed intensive training. Groups of 4 to 10 participants meet for 35 two-hour sessions. Group facilitators use a variety of techniques such as journaling, group discussions, videos, etc., to lead the discussion. The most popular version of this program, Thinking for a Change, has been adopted in several community corrections locations because of the ease of implementation. Research demonstrates that this program works best with offenders over the age of 25, who are classified as higher risk, substance abusers, sex offenders, and domestic batterers. This program has not been found to work well with those under the age of 25 or property offenders (Gaes, Flanagan, Motiuk, & Stewart, 1999). (See Applied Theory Section 4.1 for more information on cognitive therapies in corrections.)

Behavioral therapy holds that long-term change is accomplished through action and that disorders are learned means of behaving that are maladaptive. The premise to this method of intervention is that if the offender practices the new behavior long enough, then feelings will begin to change as well. This type of therapy may also incorporate elements of social learning and models in learning new behavior. This type of therapy is used extensively and is a preferred modality among criminal justice agencies because it can be easily observed and measured.

Reality therapy uses forms of involvement between counselor and client to teach the client to be self-responsible. The therapist rejects irresponsible and unrealistic behavior and insists that the client assume responsibility free of denial or excuse making. Lastly, the therapist teaches and instructs the offender–client to fulfill their needs within the limits set by reality.

Finally, solution-focused treatment begins from the observation that most psychological problems are present only intermittently. This type of therapy assists the client to notice when symptoms are diminished or absent and use this knowledge as a foundation for recovery. If a patient insists that the symptoms are constant and unrelieved, the therapist works with him or her to find exceptions and make this exception more frequent, predictable, and controllable.

The less common types of therapy include **family systems therapy, feminist therapy,** and **faith-based therapy.** These will be described next as well.

First, family systems therapy looks at the entire family as a system with its own customs, roles, beliefs, and dynamics that affect and impact the offender more routinely than any other group. Each family member plays a part in the system, and family systems therapy helps an individual discover how their family operates, their role in that system, and how this affects their relationships inside and outside that family system. This type of intervention has been found to be particularly effective with alcoholics and other substance abusers and should be a mandatory form of therapy for families of early childhood offenders and juvenile offenders. This type of therapy should augment individual counseling and is very effective in getting the family involved in the offender's treatment. It is likewise effective with female offenders, particularly those with children.

Feminist therapy focuses on empowering women by strengthening their communication skills, sense of assertiveness, self-esteem, and relationships. This is useful with female offenders since so many of these offenders were themselves victims at an early age (childhood sexual abuse) or during adulthood (domestically abusive relationships).

Finally, faith-based forms of therapy often blend cognitive and behavioral techniques grounded in scriptural instructions on the appropriate form of cognition or behavior. These types of programs are becoming increasingly more popular and have been particularly effective with substance abusing clients.

Note that in addition to each of these modalities, most every therapist will utilize the basic techniques associated with **client-centered therapy,** though the full use and undiluted version of this type of therapy is not usually used with the offending population. The main point is that client-centered techniques maintain that the therapist must be genuine, accepting, and empathetic to the offender–client. The therapist attempts to create a safe environment where the offender–client feels free to talk about his/her issues and is free to gain insight from them.

It is clear that there are numerous types of therapy that can be used, and they all have a set of characteristics that make them more useful in one situation as opposed to another. Further, some therapists may have a certain therapeutic orientation, or they may have specialized training with one type of offender population but not with another. Thus, a "one therapist fits all" approach is not likely to be effective at integrating offenders. It is with that in mind that we again find that an effective case manager is critical to success since they are the primary official responsible for connecting an offender to an appropriate treatment program.

Applied Theory Section 4.1

Cognitive Behavioral Therapies in the Community

As previously mentioned, one of the most frequently used therapies in the community have a cognitive orientation. These programs assert that offenders differ from the law-abiding population in their ability to properly process information and cope with their environment. One of the advantages to these programs is that they could and should be used in conjunction with other approaches such as substance abuse treatment, vocational programming, etc. (Gaes et al., 1999). More specifically, cognitive programs target change through the use of "cognitive restructuring, coping skills, cognitive skills, problem solving, moral development, and reasoning" (MacKenzie, 2006, p. 113). Further, these programs are designed to be implemented by community nonprofessional staff who have been trained in the desired program. The goal of therapy is to "help offenders improve in interpersonal skills of problem solving, critical reasoning, and planning" (MacKenzie, 2006, p. 113). Because of the relative ease of implementation, the reduced costs, and the successful reduction in recidivism, these programs have widely been instituted throughout the United States and internationally. One of the more frequently implemented programs was developed by Ross and Fabiano in 1985 called Reasoning and Rehabilitation (R&R). Unlike other programs, the R&R program recognizes that criminal behavior does not occur in a vacuum. Rather it is a compilation of economic, social, cognitive, and behavioral factors that converge to influence the decision-making process. As Ross and Fabiano noted, most criminal activity is not well thought out. Most offenders have experienced developmental delays that have led to their inappropriate cognitive reasoning. Therefore, they experience difficulty in problem solving and coping skills, social skills, and social perspective. They often act without thinking (impulsivity); believe that the world revolves around them (egocentric); utilize illogical reasoning patterns; and have antisocial attitudes, values, and associates. With this program, the ultimate goal is to get offenders to essentially stop and think before they act, to consider the impact of their actions on others, and to think of alternatives other than criminal activity.

> This program consists of 35 sessions, running eight to twelve weeks. The program occurs in a group setting of six to eight participants. A mixture of audio-visual presentations, games, puzzles, reasoning exercises, role playing, modeling, and group discussion techniques and strategies are used. (MacKenzie, 2006, p. 122)

Meta-analyses do indicate that this program can be successful for reducing crime and delinquent activities. With the proper implementation, ensuring that the goals and the objectives are being met (e.g., dosage and strength of the program), they can effectively meets the needs of the offender, the community, the victim, and resource shortages faced by many agencies.

⊠ Different Types of Treatment Programs

There are numerous types of treatment programs that exist for a wide variety of offenders. Though these court-based treatment models are comprehensive and provide a unique blend between criminal justice and therapeutic responses, it should be obvious that there are several approaches other than a court model that can provide a vehicle to serve the reentry management role. The structure of such a program is limited only by one's imagination. Further, partnerships between different agencies and/or components of the criminal justice system can and should work in tandem to optimize potential outcomes. For example, the Office of Justice Programs (OJP) has tested the use of law enforcement, corrections, and community partnerships to manage reentry. Such partnerships have proven central to the reentry court as well. In this section, we will discuss the use of partnerships in additional detail in a later section. However, the issue of partnerships is one that continues to be a recurring theme throughout this text, as critical to the supervision and treatment of offenders.

Aside from the courtroom components of different treatment programs, there are various types of programs themselves. In other words, some treatment programs may require offenders to stay at a facility while others may simply require the offender to attend during a prescribed number of hours per week. In most cases, these types of treatment programs are designed for substance abusing offenders. Indeed, with most other forms of mental health intervention, the offender will be required to simply meet their therapist for a set number of sessions with a set amount of time, as prescribed by the courts. The examples presented next have been adapted from the NIDA because they provide clear examples of the general categories of most treatment programs and because these are the most relevant types of programs to community corrections agencies in the United States.

First is the use of **outpatient drug-free treatment.** These treatments cost less than residential or inpatient treatment and often are more suitable for individuals who are employed or who have extensive social supports. Low-intensity programs may offer little more than drug education and admonition. Other outpatient models, such as intensive day treatment, can be comparable to residential programs in services and effectiveness, depending on the individual patient's characteristics and needs. In many outpatient programs, group counseling is emphasized. Some outpatient programs are designed to treat patients who have medical or mental health problems in addition to their drug disorder.

Second is the use of **short-term residential programs.** These programs provide intensive but relatively brief residential treatment based on a modified 12-step approach. These programs were originally designed to treat alcohol problems, but during the cocaine epidemic of the mid-1980s, many began to treat illicit drug abuse and addiction. The original residential treatment model consisted of a 3- to 6-week hospital-based inpatient treatment phase followed by extended outpatient therapy

▲ **Photo 4.2**   The Rays of Sonshine facility is a faith-based drug treatment program. Case management principles are routinely applied as offenders are guided through the recovery process.

and participation in a self-help group, such as Alcoholics Anonymous (AA). Reduced health care coverage for substance abuse treatment has resulted in a diminished number of these programs, and the average length of stay under managed care review is much shorter than in early programs.

Finally, is the use of **long-term residential treatment**. These facilities provide care 24 hours per day, generally in nonhospital settings. The best-known residential treatment model is the therapeutic community (TC), but residential treatment may also employ other models, such as CBT. TCs are residential programs with planned lengths of stay of 6 to 12 months. TCs focus on the "resocialization" of the individual and use the program's entire "community," including other residents, staff, and the social context as active components of treatment. Treatment is highly structured and can at times be confrontational, with activities designed to help residents examine damaging beliefs, self-concepts, and patterns of behavior and to adopt new, more harmonious and constructive ways to interact with others. Many TCs are quite comprehensive and can include employment training and other support services on site. Compared with offenders in other forms of treatment, the typical TC resident has more severe problems, with more co-occurring mental health problems and more criminal involvement.

Lastly, NIDA notes research has shown that a combination of criminal justice sanctions with treatment (particularly with drug treatments) can be an effective means of delivering treatment to the offender population. According to NIDA (National Institute on Drug Abuse [NIDA], 2005), "individuals under legal coercion tend to stay in treatment for a longer period of time and do as well as or better than others not under legal pressure" (p. 1). This is important because this naturally demonstrates the efficacy of programs such as drug courts, mental health courts, and other forms of innovative judicial and mental health intervention. Importantly, this also speaks to the initial discussion regarding Martinson's findings, presented at the beginning of this section. From current research, it would appear that "something" does indeed work when providing treatment to offenders after all.

▨ Treatment Professionals

Earlier in this section, students were provided an explanation of the different types of treatment professionals that are encountered in the field of community corrections. State laws often have different distinctions between types of therapeutic providers and the level of credential and/or license that they may hold. For, instance, while a person may be certified, this is not the same as **licensure. Certification** implies a certain level of oversight in that a minimum standard of competency exists, but it is licensure that provides the legal right to see clients and receive third-party billing. Third-party billing is when insurance companies, employment assistance programs, or state programs are billed to reimburse the therapist. Obviously, this is important for the therapeutic practitioner working in private practice or in a nonprofit but private facility. In addition, not all mental health specialists can give assessment tests. Many of the tests discussed in the next section require a fully licensed psychologist with a PhD (such as the MMPI-2) whereas the other tests may have little or no minimal criteria other than training to administer and score the test.

There are some additional important criteria worth noting when referencing the different types of treatment professionals. First, the more trained and educated the clinician, the more costly that he or she is likely to be. Because of this, agencies must be careful to make fiscally sound decisions, avoiding the possibility of paying an overqualified professional to do work that another, equally qualified but less expensive professional could effectively complete. Further still, as noted earlier in this section, the key to successful reintegration is to get the right treatment modality matched with the correct offender—a match with the correct treatment provider being the last key ingredient to therapeutic success. Thus, it is also important to get the correct type of treatment personnel matched with the type of offender receiving treatment. All of these factors contribute to agency effectiveness and individual treatment success.

Aside from types of expertise, it is also important to note that treatment professionals may vary in the modality that they use. Some may be cognitive behavioral in orientation while others may tend to professionally identify with other theoretical basis of service delivery. This is also another important consideration when networking with treatment providers. In some cases, theoretical differences between treatment providers may seem only a topical issue, but in others it may be quite important. While one therapist may use cognitive behavioral approaches, another might be more inclined toward solution-focused approaches. Each of these are valid treatment perspectives, but each have a different set of strengths and weaknesses. Indeed, solution-focused approaches are ideal for short-term therapy whereas cognitive behavioral approaches might be better suited for long-term therapy.

Further, the age of the treatment provider can be very important. With juvenile probationers in treatment, there is typically a stronger rapport if the therapist is younger and close to the youth's age. This is particularly true and is even further accentuated if the therapist has grown up in an area common to the other youths. A prime example might be juvenile street gang members on community supervision. Gang exit counseling programs are particularly well suited for this population when the treatment providers are near to the age of the offenders and/or if the treatment provider was a prior gang member. Understanding the vernacular, music, fashion, and other characteristics can be critical to developing an effective rapport with these types of offenders; a better rapport is directly linked to good treatment outcomes.

Likewise, the gender of the therapist can be important. This is particularly true when considering female offenders. Many of these offenders have challenges that are connected to their status as females within their own subculture as well as the role proscribed to them by broader society. Further, many female offenders have themselves been the victims of sexual assault or other forms of abuse (particularly domestic abuse), and it is often the case that they may feel awkward talking with male therapists about these and other issues. In addition, feminist therapy may be an effective modality for these offenders; it is typically the female therapist who is most skilled with this type of intervention, and thus again female therapists tend to be better able to leverage the social plight of women as a mechanism for empowerment and change.

Lastly, the race of the treatment provider may prove important. There has been considerable research that has demonstrated clients in therapy tend to identify better with therapists from similar backgrounds. Given that much of the offender population is classified as minority status, it may be that therapists from minority groups should be specifically identified and solicited for providing assistance. In fact, client–therapist racial/cultural matching is a sign of **cultural competen**ce among treatment agencies. Thus, the ability to provide treatment providers from similar racial and cultural groups as the offender caseload can be a definite advantage. Briefly, a number of authors have argued that African Americans are better served, especially by substance abuse services, when service delivery utilizes Afrocentric techniques. A study by King, Holmes, Henderson, and Latessa (2007) reports an evaluation of an Afrocentric treatment program for male, juvenile, felony offenders in one city. This evaluation used a two-group, **quasi-experimental design** to compare the 281 African American youths in the Afrocentric treatment program (called the Community Corrections Partnership) with a comparison group of 140 probation youths. Overall, the youths assigned to the Afrocentric treatment program performed slightly better than the probationers on 4 out of 15 measures of juvenile and adult.

It is clear from the previous examples that there are several different types of therapists and that each may have any number of distinct characteristics. Some therapists may specialize while others may simply vary by racial or ethnic background. Others may utilize differing therapeutic interventions and perspectives, and others may have different types of licensure and/or certification. Regardless, it is clear that one element of the equation to obtaining successful outcomes is to ensure that the treatment provider matches the various criteria that are needed within a community supervision agency's caseload. This again speaks directly to the Martinson report since at the time Martinson did his research it was found that the therapist–client relationship was an important factor in obtaining successful treatment outcomes for community supervision agencies. This was true in the past and continues to hold true even today.

▨ Community Partnerships and Agency Alliances

Throughout the text, it has been emphasized that the community must be considered a partner in the offender supervision process. It is clear that community corrections is not only correction that happens in the community but it is also corrections that happens with the aid of the community. Naturally, this is a theme throughout this text, and it is again brought up in this section for two reasons. First, this provides further clarity and is a reminder as to the integral nature of the community partnerships that are maintained with the community supervision agency. Second, the treatment perspective presented in this section benefits from a social environment that is conducive to reintegration; often this requires an adequate "buy in" among community members.

Having a healthy neighborhood environment helps to ensure that offender treatment outcomes are reinforced. Such environments are necessary if truly comprehensive forms of treatment are to be administered within a given community. Further, it is clear that agencies must network and collaborate on a routine basis if the case management process is to be adequately administered. Students have seen how various partnerships are integral to the case management process and to the effective reintegration of offenders on supervision. A variety of agencies have been considered, most dealing with treatment-related issues and/or some form of corollary service. However, there is one agency partner that does not immediately come to mind when considering the reintegration of the offender; this is the police.

▲ **Photo 4.3** Southern Oaks Addiction Recovery is a drug treatment facility that is well integrated with the surrounding community. This facility addresses addiction issues within the offender population and routinely coordinates treatment services with the local probation and parole office and the local courthouse.

Inclusion of the police in a reintegrative model of offender supervision may at first seem counterintuitive. This is because the police are naturally identified with enforcement and with the booking and extraction of offenders from the community. This is of course a necessary social function, and it would be a chaotic and lawless society if the police did not perform this function. However, such a view of the police is limited in scope and completely ignores other elements of policing that serve to prevent crime and deter offending. These elements of policing can actually aid both the supervision and the treatment process. While an agency partnering with the police might be effectively placed in other areas of this text, it is hoped that students will see that any form of partnership can have a positive impact on the efficacy of treatment programs—even those that involve partnerships with the police who are typically equated to a pure enforcement role. In fact, the Bureau of Justice Assistance (BJA) created a publication entitled *Building an Offender Reentry Program: A Guide for Law Enforcement* in which the police were specifically identified as effective partners in the reintegration process with offenders. Importantly, this document was drafted by a number of professional members of the International Association of Chiefs of Police (IACP).

This BJA publication is full of useful suggestions for practitioners in policing and illustrates that unlikely partnerships can emerge to be fruitful for the community, victims, and offenders. One example, the use of community-oriented policing (COP) houses, is particularly relevant to the prior discussion on socially disorganized communities that was presented in this section. The use of COP houses has been implemented in high crime, low socioeconomic areas of Racine, Wisconsin. These neighborhoods were chosen as focal points because a high number of offenders return to them. The houses serve as an extension of the collaboration already started between police and community corrections. Police and community corrections are located in the houses to serve as both a resource and crime deterrent in the community. This demonstrates how collaborative partnerships between the police and community corrections personnel can help to stabilize communities, providing environments that are more productive for offenders who are in the reintegration process. In this manner, COP houses provide a two-ply function, being both a deterrent to recidivism and being a source of support that gives offenders a social resource. In addition, the community as a whole benefits as crime is deterred and problematic areas are provided stability.

In further demonstration of the interlocking nature of these partnerships, consider that this same publication, oriented for policing agencies, emphasizes the need for the use of risk and needs assessments to be conducted on program participants. The most commonly used form of assessment is the Level of Service Inventory–Revised (LSI-R). These instruments have been tailored to specific populations including juveniles and females as a mechanism to both predict the risk of recidivism and to appropriately meet the needs of offenders. This information specifically ties into Section V, which will address the importance of assessment and risk prediction in community corrections. The LSI-R is praised in Section V of this text as a premiere instrument, and these claims are further validated by disparate sources that include policing organizations such as the IACP and federal agencies such as the BJA. This again demonstrates the interconnected nature of various components and ideas within the criminal justice system. These interlocking components and programs serve to further strengthen the landscape in which treatment programs must operate.

Next, police agencies can be very good partners in transitional/reentry planning. This is a logical extension of the assessment process and also dovetails well with partnerships that seek to stabilize communities that tend to draw prior offenders into their region. In this case, police personnel will be consulted so that they can provide input into the post-release supervision conditions of offenders. Police meet with corrections officials to share information on the offender's criminal history in the community and discuss their concerns for the offender's future. Some law enforcement officials make recommendations on which neighborhoods offenders should (or should not) be permitted to enter and/or associates with whom offenders may be restricted from seeing. While it may not be immediately apparent, this can actually have a substantive impact on treatment programs. Taking this concept one step further, it is likely to be beneficial for treatment professionals to also attend such reentry planning functions and directly collaborate with law enforcement. While guidelines and restrictions to confidentiality would need to be honored by treatment professionals, an initial meeting at the onset of the offender reintegration process can help to build agency rapport and ensure that all parties approach the process in a similar manner.

This idea is further reinforced by the fact that the IACP and the BJA note that policing agencies should be included in the operation of reentry courts. This again demonstrates that a variety of agencies and methods of intervention may be interlocked together to provide a seamless continuum of supervision and treatment services. In this regard, reentry courts can be envisioned as another crime prevention tool in that the court has the ability to order sanctions beyond the existing supervision conditions. Law enforcement experiences with these types of partnerships have been positive and are viewed as effective accountability tools. This again illustrates the overlap between supervision and treatment objectives. Each of these perspectives are necessary to maximize the reintegration process, and the seasoned treatment provider will realize that reinforcers and punishers in the community, when logically and skillfully utilized, help to augment therapeutic outcomes within the treatment program itself. In essence, agency partnerships provide the needed "training wheels" for offender behavior as they seek to implement the requirements of their treatment regimen.

Amidst this, treatment providers that have an effective rapport with local law enforcement will be privy to informal observations that police make when conducting their routine patrol activities. This can often be useful information for treatment providers who may wish to challenge manipulative offenders who are not fully honest and/or that may not be meeting aspects of their therapeutic contract. This again points toward the seamless nature of a truly integrated set of agency partnerships, demonstrating that enforcement functions can augment case management functions in the process of maintaining agency partnerships. The key is to have all parties involved as much as possible, and police agencies should not be left out of this picture.

One other recommendation that is worth mentioning includes the often touted idea of incorporating all community resources, specifically noting the need to tap into the policing, community, and partner volunteer programs. Volunteers can be used to support program activities and to spread the word about these programs. This naturally hearkens back to the ancient notion of the *hue and cry*, where citizens were involved in policing activities. This same point comes back full circle as we now consider notions of reintegration and treatment but do so from a different perspective. In this case, the emphasis is on integrating the policing agency into the background fabric of the treatment and reintegration process, with citizens again being the backbone of such interlocking community-based programs.

One other important point about the use of volunteers should be mentioned. The use of neighborhood watch programs should also be solicited. Members of these groups are often more than willing to observe and visit various locations to ensure that their locality is safe. Having these groups incorporated into the supervision process may be another additional way to further supervise the offender. Further, the members of this watch, being members of the community where the offender resides, may likely know the offender and his or her family, and thus they may be in a position to provide supervision that is structured more as a genuine visit of concern (more as a relapse prevention rather than a "you're busted" mentality) that may even be perceived as helpful by the offender and his or her family.

All of these mechanisms demonstrate that volunteers, employers, families, and probation departments can provide supervision that is comprehensive yet receptive to the reintegration of the offender population. This is important because both the components of care and supervision must be maintained. It is clear from the preceding examples that this obviously requires participation from the community. This is a pivotal point to this entire text. Without support from the community, the likelihood of reintegrating the offender is greatly impaired.

Naturally, a variety of agencies related to employment placement, medical services, educational attainment, and other such services should also be integrated into any reintegration network. This will be more clearly articulated in the Section IX on parole related to case management processes with the offender population. Indeed, these partnerships can be effective in both offender reintegration as well as treatment programs for victims of crime. This can then ensure a total and comprehensive response to crime and can further provide a community environment that is conducive to offender treatment and reintegration.

Lastly, in many cases, treatment services may not be provided by a single individual or agency. Consider, for example, an offender who is a domestic abuser and who has a substance abuse problem. This offender is likely to see a separate therapist for his or her domestic abuse issues while also seeing another service provider for his or her addiction issues. In fact, it is quite common that clinicians will not address a substance abuse issue in addition to other serious clinical issues. Rather, they will refer out or will require that the offender be referred to a substance abuse specialist. Because so many offenders do have substance abuse issues, it is actually quite common for them to have two separate therapists, particularly when they are dually diagnosed. This is an important point because this means that these practitioners and their agencies must stay in contact with one another so that comprehensive services can be provided. While this may seem to make intuitive sense (and it does indeed make good sense), this does not always occur. In fact, in many states, addictions professionals may be licensed and regulated under a board that is entirely different from those of other mental health providers, and this then means that each will have their own emphases, board of ethics, and standards or regulation of practice. This can be quite problematic.

Though it may not be new to many seasoned clinicians, community supervision personnel may make the surprising discovery that there is a schism that often exists between clinicians and addictions treatment providers. Often, the standards for treatment providers in the addictions field are less stringent than are those in other areas of service delivery. Because of this, some degree of conflict, elitism, and sense of authority gets convoluted into the process when clinicians from both camps attempt to work in a collaborative fashion. Indeed, it is not uncommon for addictions treatment providers to have been prior addicts at one time—this sometimes being referred to as the "wounded healer" treatment provider. This dynamic among these helping professionals has cast a cloud of skepticism over the field of addictions counseling and thereby increases the gap between these providers and the remaining clinical community. Though this may seem to be a topical or corollary problem, it is actually quite debilitating to the overall treatment process with a large proportion of the offender population. This is particularly true when one considers that over 60% of all offenders have some type of substance use at the point of arrest (Hanser, 2007a). Thus, addictions professionals are involved with the majority of the offender population.

Obviously, if addictions professionals are involved with more than half of the offender population and if they operate at odds with many members of the remaining circle of clinical professionals, a problem of considerable magnitude emerges. It is important that agencies look for these types of biases among treatment professionals. It is of course ironic that practitioners who are supposed to be associated with mental health and maturity would allow such differences to constrain their professional effectiveness, but this is nonetheless a frequent reality. It is important that collaborative partnerships ameliorate any differences that impair outcome effectiveness. A failure to do this only results in further risk to the community and also makes a mockery of the notion that actors in a given field of work are to be considered professionals—professionals whose goal should be to make society safer in the future, regardless of ideology, theoretical orientation, or their chosen areas of expertise.

◼ Treatment Staff, Referrals, and Increased Human Supervision

While correctional treatment professionals are responsible for the actual treatment and rehabilitation of the offender, it should be understood that the efforts of treatment professionals can be enhanced by the active involvement of various community members. The integration of both the community and the therapeutic service provider can work to provide offenders with treatment opportunities that might not otherwise exist. For example, consider that in some cases, treatment professionals might decide to assign "homework" that requires the offender to accomplish certain tasks that put them in contact with a variety of personnel in the community. An exercise in building self-esteem might require the offender to negotiate with a salesperson at a used car lot or in another environment where the offender must apply interaction skills that they have learned in their therapeutic sessions.

In substance abuse treatment, treatment specialists might work in tandem with self-help groups, such as AA and/or Narcotics Anonymous (NA). These groups typically include the use of a sponsor who acts as a mentor for the addicted person in recovery. Such a person is a community member who can be available to augment the treatment process, enhancing and supporting outcomes decided upon in the official therapeutic setting between correctional treatment staff and the offender. Another example might include the use of clergy members to support the offender; this is particularly useful for those offenders who note spiritual and religious beliefs as being important to them personally. When and where appropriate, religious institutions and the members of these institutions can provide a sense of integration for the offender, and they can assist the offender in meeting agreed-upon treatment objectives. This can also aid offenders of a variety of cultural backgrounds, being diversified to a wide range of religious affiliations. If offenders request such integration of treatment services, the use of religious support mechanisms can improve the overall treatment outcomes that might be realized.

In addition, treatment professionals may use family counseling perspectives to aid the offender in reintegration, with family members conducting a variety of roles in the offender's reformation. For instance, a juvenile offender might benefit from family counseling with his or her parents. A substance abuse offender might benefit by having their spouse and children involved in the treatment process. This goes beyond the mere contact and reporting process the family members might provide to probation agencies. Rather, family members are openly invited to assist in the treatment process, learning about the agreed-upon goals and objectives of the offender's treatment plan and participating in routines that aid the offender between therapeutic sessions. Caring family members can engage in exercises throughout the week that assist the offender in practicing prosocial skills and routines. Family members can also provide input to the offender and to the therapist regarding treatment processes, providing an informal support system for the therapeutic process. This also provides a sense of seamless support throughout the week so that the offender is reminded of their treatment objectives in between treatment sessions with their counselor. Inviting family members and friends of the offender to actual treatment sessions can help to further strengthen the integration of family and friends within the treatment program.

In addition, the use of family and friends in the treatment process provides yet another layer of human contact and accountability for the offender. This also helps to reinforce the partnerships between agencies and volunteers in the community. In all cases, the offender becomes meshed within the social system; the resulting support typically improving treatment outcomes. Family and friends will understand the offender's treatment plan and will be in a better position to aid the offender than will most other persons within the offender's network. Further, family and close friends will be around the offender during more personal points of the day and will have more depth in understanding the offender's personal characteristics, temperaments, habits, and tendencies. This helps to further fill in any gaps that may exist among agency partnerships and the use of community volunteers. With internal family support, the external support of community volunteers, and coordination of agency partnerships for services, the offender has both private and public assistance for their treatment regimen. This means that there are differing layers of support throughout the weeks and months of the offender's participation in treatment. This also means that the offender will have a variety of human contacts throughout that time, contacts that are in addition to those typically conducted by the community supervision agency. This then increases the amount of informal human supervision that the offender receives, providing a better treatment prognosis while also providing additional leverage for offender compliance to treatment and supervision requirements. The two objectives—treatment and supervision—then work together hand in hand once again, but in this manner they do so from the vantage of the treatment provider rather than from the vantage of a supervision perspective.

Consider also that treatment specialists can use other forms of community involvement that may include "corollary" forms of therapy that are not necessarily central to the offender's crime or even their special need but are nonetheless adaptive activities that the offender can benefit from. For example, the offender may smoke cigarettes or may be overweight. In this case, the strong urging at the behest of the therapist to join a group for smoking cessation or weight control may not be directly relevant to the crime but nonetheless are more beneficial than harmful for overall social integration purposes. Further, more community members are again supervising the offender, and the leaders of these programs can report progress to the treatment specialist. This again results in an increased number of weekly human contacts that the offender has. Thus, from a treatment perspective, the offender is constantly under the watchful eye of various persons who are tasked with addressing corollary treatment needs of the offender.

It should be clear that treatment specialists can provide another effective link with the community that simultaneously enhances both therapeutic objectives and supervision objectives. This is consistent with the notion of reintegration that was presented in earlier sections of this text. In fact, the therapeutic process is simply a micro version of human contact between the offender and another person, requiring that offenders engage in prosocial activities while also being under the observation of a clinician. This aids in the supervision of an offender but also provides depth in that supervision while also requiring a degree of transparency for the offender who must engage in the treatment process. The outcome is one where the activities of different persons (therapists, community volunteers, and community agency staff) serve as interlocking mechanisms to keep the offender's thoughts and behaviors routinely focused on their reintegration, providing a comprehensive treatment and supervision strategy that combines as a complementary process.

⬙ Progress in Treatment Programs and the Likelihood for Recidivism

The title of this subsection may seem to make intuitive sense and may not seem to warrant additional discussion. For persons working in treatment circles, this might actually be true, but for laypersons, the implications of treatment progress for recidivism rates might not be so clearly linked. In fact, it could also be said that progress in some areas of treatment may have little or no impact on future recidivism of offenders. The point is that the interconnections can be complicated and are sometimes not obvious, though intuitively one might think otherwise. To make this clear, some brief explanations are required.

First, when offenders successfully complete treatment programs, this often indicates a likelihood toward prosocial behaviors and a corresponding reduction in criminal behavior. Consider for example, an offender in a halfway house. While in the halfway house and even upon completion of the halfway house's treatment program, it is likely that the offender will experience a reduction in criminal activity. However, this would be true even if no real treatment intervention were applied due to the fact that the offender is under closer control than they would be when freely released to the community. Offenders in such a case may "fake good" in their behaviors and responses, knowing that their act is only temporary until they return to the community. This is, of course, where the public skepticism lies in regard to the treatment of the offender population. Concern with manipulation throughout the treatment regimen leads many members of the public to scoff at the validity of treatment perspectives.

On the other hand, even if offenders are genuinely committed to such programs, their return to their families and/or communities of origin may place them at risk of further offending. A lack of services during the reentry process and/or insufficient aftercare can ensure that over time the beneficial gains of treatment are diminished. Thus, the program itself can be quite effective but may only have residual effects when the props and support are removed from the offender. In fact, this is one of the shortcomings of a supervision-only approach to community corrections; once punitive leverage is removed, the offender has no incentive to remain crime free. Effective treatment programs seek to build a sense of internal regulation among offenders through insight and a variety of exercises and activities that reinforce that insight.

Likewise, negative treatment outcomes can be indicative of potential recidivism, even if the treatment regimen is corollary to the criminal behavior. Thus, even though the offender may have actually completed a specified number of treatment program sessions, this may not be a good marker of offender reform. In many court sentencing programs, offenders are required to participate for a defined number of weeks or months, basing success more on attendance rather than actual effort and/or progress in the treatment program. Court relationships with treatment providers must instead ensure that the input from treatment providers serves as the defining factor in completing their therapeutic requirements. When this leverage is provided, offenders are more likely to commit to treatment programs, and overall outcomes in recidivism are destined to be improved.

Lastly, a variety of assessment scales that are used in constructing treatment agendas can be used to predict the offender's likely treatment outcome by looking at corollary issues. For instance, some scales may measure the offender's likelihood of relapse for a mental health- or treatment-related issue but may also take additional measures of the offender's cognitive, motivational, and/or emotional characteristics. Some instruments may even measure the defensiveness and likely honesty of the offender that completes the instrument. Though these predictive mechanisms may be intended for therapeutic outcomes, it is sometimes the case that these same measures are consistent with likely recidivism. Indeed, offenders who are defensive or manipulative in therapy are also more likely to have such characteristics in regard to their likely criminal behavior. Thus, it may be that indirect measures intended for therapeutic purposes can also lead to effective prediction of recidivism among offenders, even though the intent of these items remains otherwise. While it would not be prudent to utilize instruments beyond their intended purposes, clinicians may find that they can provide additional insight and analysis of offender profiles so that community supervision officials will be better informed about the offender. This then demonstrates that therapeutic orientations can provide a public safety component over and above that which occurs when offenders are provided therapeutic services.

▧ Educating the Community About Treatment Benefits and Integrating Citizen and Agency Involvement

Since treatment is recommended for so many offenders and because treatment programs are often much more flexibly designed in the community, community partnerships serve as the continuum between the gaps that may emerge in various treatment strategies. As has been continuously emphasized throughout this text, community involvement improves the level of "human supervision" of the offender while also providing a much larger support network. This means that community support is greatly needed in the reintegration of the offender population, and this then means that community education is critical. Many community members may have no idea how specific treatment needs can directly impact the likelihood of offender reintegration. Further, these same people may not truly understand that offender recidivism—and the future crime rate—is directly impacted by the successful rehabilitation and reintegration of the offender.

Thus, the education of community members and the recruitment of community members in the treatment process can be very important. One benefit when including community members is the fact that these persons are then given the opportunity to make a direct contribution to the justice system by working directly with the victims and offenders who are involved. This ensures that volunteers are utilized in a manner that is significant and should show the volunteer that their contribution is not taken lightly. Indeed, when volunteers are utilized, the criminal justice system demonstrates a willingness to take their contributions seriously by involving them in a very important (yet fairly safe) and necessary task of "follow-up" in the community supervision process.

Many people in public may not understand basic issues related to criminal offending, and public service campaigns can work toward resolving this lack of understanding. Indeed, basic knowledge on different types of crime, their frequency, and the dynamics associated with each may not be widely known. This alone can provide insight as to the conditions that lead to crime-prone behavior, and this also can lead to public awareness of interventions that can prevent future behavior among persons likely to engage in criminal activity. Aside from prevention, the successful reformation of persons and/or family systems can eliminate future offending, and it is this aspect that should be emphasized in community awareness campaigns. Treatment groups and even criminal justice agencies must actively advertise this point to the public consumer. Lobbying actions in state legislatures, the use of media campaigns, community newsletters, and word of mouth can all aid in increasing awareness of treatment programs and their effectiveness in reducing criminal activity.

Further, when citizens are involved in reintegration activities, it is important that these activities are publicly showcased. This further demonstrates the need for public commitment and develops a sense of "buy-in" in regard to treatment perspectives. In many cases, it may be best to first showcase juvenile programs since many communities may be more empathetic to the plight of adolescent offenders than they are of adult offenders. By first gaining awareness and understanding of juvenile issues and the efficacy of treatment approaches, treatment advocates can gain a foot in the door, so to speak. This can be the first step in shifting public mentality from one that is skeptical of treatment orientations to one that is both understanding and supportive. Amidst this change process in community perceptions, it is also important that key community personnel be educated on the complexities involved in determining "what works" in treatment programs. This single issue is perhaps most important because it provides insight to community leaders as to why the beneficial effects of treatment approaches may not be immediately visible to the casual observer. Indeed, this is equally true for successful prevention programs; consider for a moment what the crime rate might look like if one did not engage in prevention at all. This same rationale should be presented for treatment approaches, noting that the social, economic, and personal costs of crime would be much higher than they currently may be.

Building social awareness of treatment programs and their efficacy can be very difficult, particularly in areas where criminal offending is pronounced and/or in regions of the United States that tend to be punitive in approach. Nevertheless, this is an important area of focus if one genuinely desires to improve current community supervision strategies. The simple reality is that we cannot afford to incarcerate the majority of our offender population, and added to this is the reality that the majority of offenders will commit crimes that do not warrant incarceration. Thus, offenders will remain in the community regardless of the modality that is utilized among agencies. While improvements in offender supervision are important, this is only one element of reducing recidivism. Such aspects are based on external compliance-based tactics. However, exclusive attention to these approaches completely ignores and overlooks internal incentives that may exist for many offenders. If community supervision processes are to be optimized, agencies and the community must also ensure that treatment approaches are given adequate focus and attention.

✑ Conclusion

This section demonstrates several points that further refine the reintegrative orientation of this text. First, it is clear that the widely touted conclusions from the Martinson report are likely to be outdated—the results of that report no longer being true to the circumstances of today. It is not necessarily clear if Martinson's findings were completely accurate to begin with, and it is also true that many persons have contorted the study's findings. This then demonstrates that more effective forms of research on treatment programs should be conducted and, as it turns out, there is an abundance of meta-analyses that have examined treatment efficacy in a much more careful, systematic, and rigorous manner. The results of this more contemporary research is that treatment programs do indeed work, depending on the objectives that are desired, the nature of the treatment, and the specific research questions that are asked. To say that "nothing works" is now an outdated, archaic, and incorrect assumption regarding treatment programs in corrections.

This section also demonstrates the need to have treatment programs in the community. This should be the first option when reintegration is the desired outcome. The use of institutional-based treatment programs tend to have drawbacks that can be avoided within programs that are set within the community. Because a treatment perspective is emphasized and because treatment programs are best administered in the community, community partnerships between agencies and volunteers become critical to the overall reintegration process. The integration of treatment professionals, community agencies, and community volunteers provides aids in reforming offenders and also provides for more human contact and interaction. In an indirect sense, this alone creates a process of seamless supervision as the offender remains in close proximity of one person or another. Since the offender is in contact with a variety of persons that are supportive of treatment, there is a chain of custody within the offender's daily interactions, leaving little time or possibility for offending that will go unnoticed. It is this aspect of increased human supervision that improves the treatment prognosis of the offender while also utilizing the community itself to maintain more effective supervision of the offender's behaviors and activities. It is in this manner that treatment staff and community members work together, hand in hand, to improve offender treatment outcomes.

✑ Section Summary

- Despite the far-reaching impact of Robert Martinson's (1974) "What Works?" article, support for treatment modalities and rehabilitation continues.
- Programs developed using the following eight principles appear to be most effective at reducing recidivism: (1) a well-defined organizational culture; (2) programs based on empirical evidence; (3) trained

staff; (4) programs that place offenders using the risk/need principles; (5) programs that target crimino-genic factors; (6) program therapists that utilize the core correctional practices of modeling prosocial behavior, problem solving techniques, motivational interviewing, etc.; (7) agencies that collaborate to make effective and meaningful referrals; and (8) evaluations conducted in accordance with the programs.

- The use of a social casework model for supervision provides much-needed support for both the offender and their community. This model relies on assessment, evaluation, and intervention.
- There are a variety of successful treatment interventions used in community-based corrections. These include the following forms of therapy: reality, cognitive, behavioral, solution-focused, family systems, faith-based, and feminist.
- It is important to develop relationships between the communities in which offenders reside and the agencies. These relationships will both enhance treatment and prevent future offending.
- Educating the public about the efficacy of programs is an important component of building successful reintegration programs.

KEY TERMS

Behavioral therapy

Client-centered therapy

Cognitive therapy

Community supervision officer (CSO)

Faith-based therapy

Family systems

Feminist therapy

Long-term residential treatment

Negative punishment

Negative reinforcers

Outpatient drug-free treatment

Positive punishment

Positive reinforcers

Reality therapy

Reentry courts

Short-term residential programs

Social casework

Solution-focused

Therapeutic interventions

Treatment specialist

DISCUSSION QUESTIONS

1. What role did Martinson's "What Works?" article play in shifting the focus from rehabilitation to a more punitive ideology?

2. Given what we know about the effectiveness of treatment programs, should treatment be provided in the community? Explain your response.

3. What is significant about the development of community partnerships and agency alliances? What are the pros and cons of developing and maintaining these community/agency partnerships and/or alliances?

4. Describe the various types of treatment programs offered in the community. What are the benefits of maintaining these programs?

5. What treatment programs are offered in your local community corrections department(s)? Are any of these programs mandated by law?

WEB RESOURCES

American Psychological Association:
http://www.apa.org/

National Institutes of Health:
http://www.nih.gov/

National Institute of Mental Health:
http://www.nimh.nih.gov/index.shtml

National Institute of Corrections (NIC)—Thinking for a CHANGE:
http://www.nicic.gov/T4C

National Association of Cognitive Behavioral Therapy:
http://www.nacbt.org/whatiscbt.htm

Please refer to the student study site for web resources and additional resources.

READING

In this study, Lowenkamp and colleagues evaluated the effectiveness of an often-used cognitive behavioral program known as Thinking for a Change (TFAC). With this program, participants are asked to confront their thinking errors during a series of 22 group sessions facilitated by trained community corrections personnel. This "real-world" application makes it different than others because offenders are referred to the program directly by the judge or their probation officer. A total of 217 felony probationers were included in the study ($n = 121$ treatment; $n = 96$ comparison). Success in the program is defined as a reduction in recidivism. Participants were followed up 6 months after completion of the program while the comparison was followed 6 months post-identification. Overall, the results indicated that the TFAC participants (23%) were significantly less likely to recidivate than the comparison group (36%). Using multivariate logistic regression, the researchers identified three characteristics most likely to predict recidivism: (1) age (younger), (2) risk category (higher risk), and (3) group membership (comparison group versus treatment group). These findings lend support for the argument that offenders should be placed in a cognitive behavioral program. As illustrated in the discussion, these programs can be administered at a relatively low cost to the courts by staff with minimal training. The authors further discussed the limitations of their study and made recommendations for future assessments.

SOURCE: Christopher T. Lowenkamp, Dana Hubbard, Matthew D. Markarios, & Edward J. Latessa (2009). A quasi-experimental evaluation of Thinking for a Change: A "real-world" application. *Criminal Justice and Behavior, 36*(2), 137–146. Copyright © 2009 Sage Publications. Published on behalf of the American Association for Correctional and Forensic Psychologists.

A Quasi-Experimental Evaluation of Thinking for a Change

A "Real-World" Application

Christopher T. Lowenkamp, Dana Hubbard,
Matthew D. Makarios, and Edward J. Latessa

Over the past three decades, much has been learned in regards to "what works" in reducing recidivism (Andrews, Bonta, & Hoge, 1990; Gendreau, 1996; Gendreau, French, & Taylor, 2002; Palmer, 1995). One finding that has consistently appeared is the effectiveness of cognitive behavioral therapy (CBT) in reducing recidivism (Landenberger & Lipsey, 2005). As a result, a variety of cognitive behavioral curricula that target criminal populations have surfaced. One such curriculum, Thinking for a Change (TFAC), has been developed by Bush, Glick, and Taymans (1997) with the support of the National Institute of Corrections. TFAC is becoming increasingly popular with implementation at some level in more than 45 states (personal communication with Steve Swisher, National Institute of Corrections, July 15, 2006). To date, however, very few evaluations of the TFAC program have been conducted (Reeves, 2006). In addition, although each study adds to the knowledge base on the effectiveness of TFAC, each study has limitations that are inherent in applied research.

Consequently, the purpose of the current study is to overcome some of the practical and methodological limitations of previous research using a quasi-experimental evaluation of the TFAC program. Practically, the program under evaluation was implemented and delivered by practitioners in the correctional system without the assistance and monitoring of an evaluator. Thus, this application of TFAC is a "real-world" application rather than a demonstration project. This has particular relevance because some research (see, for example, Lipsey, 1995) indicates that demonstration projects, managed by an involved evaluator or program designer, produce larger treatment effects than the same programs implemented in a "real-world"

setting. Furthermore, because the program was delivered by correctional practitioners that were a part of the justice system, this study will provide correctional agencies with a more realistic picture of the effectiveness of a readily available cognitive behavioral curriculum.

Reducing Recidivism in Community Supervision

One promising approach to reducing the recidivism of offenders on probation is to provide treatment services to offenders (for a review, see Cullen & Gendreau, 2000). Although probation alone is generally ineffective at reducing recidivism (Gendreau & Goggin. 1996), research indicates that if probation supervision is treatment focused, it can effectively reduce criminal behavior (Aos, Miller, & Drake, 2006; Hanley, 2002; Lowenkamp & Latessa, 2005; Petersilia & Turner, 1993; Taxman, Yancey, & Bilanin, 2006). However, it is important to note that not all treatment efforts are equally effective. Programs that adhere to specific principles of effective intervention have been shown to have the greatest impact on recidivism (Andrews, Zinger, et al., 1990) and should therefore serve as the basis of community supervision-based treatment services.

The three major principles of effective intervention—risk, need, and responsivity (Andrews, Zinger, et al., 1990; Andrews. Bonta, & Hoge, 1990; Andrews, Bonta, & Wormith, 2006; Lowenkamp & Latessa, 2005; Lowenkamp, Latessa, & Smith, 2006; Lowenkamp, Pealer, Latessa, & Smith, 2006)—are designed to provide a blueprint of effective intervention for correctional agencies to follow. Translated into practice, the principles of effective intervention suggest delivering behaviorally based programs (e.g., cognitive behavioral treatment), to higher risk offenders (those with the higher likelihood of recidivism), while focusing on relevant criminogenic needs (e.g., antisocial attitudes, values, and beliefs). Recent research suggests that probation agencies that follow these aspects have lower rates of recidivism than those which do not (Lowenkamp, Latessa, & Smith, 2006; Taxman et al., 2006).

At the core of providing effective correctional interventions in the community is delivering behaviorally based programming. Behavioral programming is based on the presumption that behavior is learned. Furthermore, once a particular behavior has been initiated, it is maintained or discouraged by the consequences of the behavior on one's attitudes, values, and beliefs (for a theoretical discussion, see Bandura, 1986; for an application to offending behavior, see Andrews & Bonta, 2006). For offenders to be retrained to exhibit prosocial behaviors, they must be given the opportunity to learn prosocial skills and attitudes. Meta-analytic reviews have consistently identified behavioral programs to be one of the most effective forms of correctional interventions aimed at reducing recidivism (e.g., Dowden & Andrews, 2000; Garrett, 1985; Lipsey, Chapman, & Landenberger, 2001; Wilson, Bouffard, & MacKenzie, 2005; Wilson, Gallagher, & MacKenzie, 2000).

◼ Cognitive Behavioral Therapy and Correctional Interventions

There are a number of justifications for using CBT with correctional populations (Andrews & Bonta, 2006). First, unlike many correctional programs that are based on so-called "common sense" approaches (Latessa, Cullen, & Gendreau, 2002), CBT is based on scientifically derived theories (cognitive and behavioral). Second, CBT is based on active learning, not talk therapy and consequently focuses on the *present* (how offenders currently think and behave), not past events that cannot be changed (Andrews & Bonta, 2006). Third, it targets major criminogenic needs in a structured group setting (Andrews & Bonta, 2006). Finally, cognitive behavioral programming has consistently been shown to reduce the recidivism of program participants (for a review, see Landenberger & Lipsey, 2005).

TFAC is a cognitive behavioral therapy developed to integrate cognitive skills and cognitive restructuring modalities of offender treatment. At its core, TFAC uses problem solving to teach offenders prosocial skills and attitudes. Consisting of 22 lessons, each lesson teaches participants important social skills, such as active listening and asking appropriate questions to more complex restructuring techniques, such as recognizing the types of thinking that leads them into trouble and understanding the feelings of others. As such, TFAC both stresses interpersonal communication skills development and confronts thought patterns that lead to problematic behaviors.

Landenberger and Lipsey's (2005) meta-analyses of cognitive behavioral programs provides some insight into the effectiveness of TFAC. They reviewed 58 studies of cognitive behavioral programs and found that, on average, these programs reduced recidivism by 25%. Furthermore, they examined several different cognitive behavioral curricula, including five evaluations of TFAC. Landenberger and Lipsey (2005) found that TFAC was effective in reducing recidivism, as the results indicated that the effects of the five studies were not different than that average reduction in recidivism of 25%. However, none of the studies included in the analysis had been published in peer reviewed journals, and they had other methodological limitations (such as short follow-up periods, lack of statistical controls, and small sample sizes). Furthermore, Landenberger and Lipsey (2005) encourage continued studies of CBT, as very few of the studies they were able to locate (6 out of 58) were randomized studies in "real-world" settings.

Recently, Golden, Gatchel, and Cahill (2006) provided the first published outcome evaluation of TFAC. They examined the effects of TFAC on a sample of probationers and found that, compared to those who did not attend the program, participants who completed the program experienced reductions in problem-solving skills and in proportion of the group who committed a new offense. Although informative, this research had a follow-up time limited to 1 year and used a three group analysis which excluded treatment dropouts from the experimental group.

A three-group analysis compares differences in the recidivism between participants who (a) completed treatment, (b) dropped out of treatment, and (c) received no treatment. The experimental group is separated into treatment completions and dropouts because it is assumed that individuals who did not get the full dose of treatment will "water down" the true treatment effect. Unfortunately, comparing treatment completions to a control group creates a selection bias, because offenders who are likely to drop out of treatment (because they are unmotivated to change or are higher risk) exist in both groups but are only eliminated from the treatment group. Furthermore, as the selection bias is created by eliminating unmotivated and/or higher risk individuals from the treatment group, this process will tend to inflate the treatment effect. To address this issue, the present research includes all individuals who attended at least one session of TFAC in the treatment group regardless of whether they successfully completed the treatment.

This research also offers two other methodological advances over prior evaluations of TFAC. To measure recidivism, this research uses the outcome of arrest which is superior to some of the previous evaluations of TFAC that used intermediate outcomes such as pre/post measures of attitudes (Reeves, 2006). Furthermore, the follow-up time for the outcome is longer than previous studies, and while variable, averages just more than 2 years. In sum, this research provides an evaluation of TFAC in a real-world setting, while addressing the methodological limitations of prior research by using (a) a two group analysis, (b) arrest as a measure of recidivism, and (c) an extended follow-up.

✎ Method

Research Location and Procedures

The Tippecanoe County probation department is located in central Indiana and provides services to adult offenders brought into the correctional system for a felony or misdemeanor offense. In addition to the probation department, Tippecanoe County also has a community corrections division that complements services provided by probation. Staff from both community corrections and probation provide TFAC services to offenders. The National Institute of Corrections

provided the initial training for the Tippecanoe County employees, after which the agency developed their own training program and provided subsequent training for new facilitators as the program grew and new staff were added.

Offenders were referred to the TFAC program directly from court (as a condition of their probation sentence) or from their probation officer as a sanction for violation behavior. Probationers enrolled in the TFAC program were expected to complete all 22 sessions. The number of sessions attended ranged from 2 to 22 with an average of 20. The high average was likely due to almost 75% of the treatment group completing all 22 sessions. The program was delivered over 11 weeks (2 sessions each week for a total of 22 sessions) with an average of 12 participants in each class (class size ranged from 5 to 20). The TFAC program was typically administered by two facilitators; however, with larger classes, as many as four facilitators were used.

Participants

The participants in this study $(n = 217)$ were individuals in Tippecanoe County that were placed on probation for a felony offense. Of the total, there were 121 treatment cases. Inclusion into the treatment group required that the individual on probation was referred to and attended at least one session of TFAC. Comparison cases $(n = 96)$ consist of offenders that were placed on probation during the same time period as the treatment cases but were not referred to TFAC. Cases were also required to have at least a 6-month follow-up period to be included in the study. For the treatment group, the follow-up requirement began 6 months from the time that they left the TFAC program, whereas the control group follow-up was based on the time they began probation. The two groups were very similar in terms of age, race, and gender, with no statistically significant differences detected. Overall, the sample was predominantly White (84%), male (71%), and on average 33.5 years old.

Measures

Since all offenders did not have a standardized risk/need assessment completed in their files, a risk measure was created that was based on factors used in prior analyses (Lowenkamp, Pealer, Latessa, & Smith, 2006; Lowenkamp & Latessa, 2005). Each offender was coded on seven factors based on file information. These factors included prior arrests (0 = *none,* 1 = *one or more),* prior prison commitments (0 = *none,* 1 = *one or more),* prior community supervision violation (0 = *none,* 1 = *one or more),* prior drug problem (0 = *no indication of a drug problem,* 1 = *some indication of a drug problem),* prior alcohol problem (0 = *no indication of an alcohol problem,* 1 = *some indication of an alcohol problem),* employed at arrest (0 = *unemployed at arrest,* 1 = *employed at arrest),* and education (0 = *completed less than Grade 12,* 1 = *high school graduate or above).* These factors were summed together to give a risk score that ranged in value from 0 to 7. Three categories (low, moderate, and high risk) were created based on the composite score.

The correlation between risk and any new arrest is 0.19 *(p* = .006). The recidivism rates by risk level were 20% for low-risk, 31% for moderate-risk, and 50% for high-risk (χ^2 = 7.938, *p* = .019). The two groups did differ significantly on this measure, with the treatment group scoring slightly higher than the comparison group (4.0 versus 3.5; *t* = 2.46; *p* = .015). Differences in risk between treatment and control groups may confound the final results, although the higher risk of the treatment groups suggests that the results would favor a null treatment effect. Still, to ensure the accuracy of the treatment effect, the final results control for differences in risk between the two groups.

Also, since offenders were followed for unequal periods of time, it was necessary to adjust for time at risk to recidivate. To do so, a variable was created that measured the number of months of follow-up time that recidivism was tracked. For the comparison group, the follow-up period began when the offender was placed on probation. For the treatment group, the follow-up period began when the offender entered the TFAC program; on average, the comparison group has a considerably longer follow-up period than the treatment group *(t* = 5.10; *p* = .000). Since differences in time at risk can also confound the final results, this measure was included in all multivariate models.

To operationalize recidivism, a dichotomous variable indicating whether the offender received an arrest for a new criminal charge (misdemeanor or felony offense) was created. These data were retrieved from county and local databases; worth noting is that the measure is limited to offenses that were reported only in Tippecanoe County.

Analysis

First, a bivariate analysis compared differences in the proportion of individuals who recidivated between the treatment and control group. Second, to adjust for potential confounding factors, we developed a multivariate model. Because of the dichotomous nature of the outcome and the desire to control for multiple confounding factors, logistic regression was used to estimate the odds of recidivism for the treatment and control groups. Based on the results of these models, we adjusted recidivism rates for the comparison group and the treatment group.

⚔ Results

Results from the bivariate analysis of the impact of participation in the TFAC program indicate that there is a statistically significant difference in the proportion of individuals who recidivated between the treatment and control groups. Specifically, 23% of the treatment group recidivated (i.e., were rearrested for new criminal behavior) whereas 36% of the comparison group recidivated (χ^2 = 3.93; *p* = .047). Thus, the difference in the odds of recidivating between the control and treatment groups indicates that the control group was 1.57 (or 57%) more likely to be arrested during the follow-up.

Since the groups differed significantly on several key variables, multivariate logistic regression was used to predict recidivism while controlling for time at risk, race, gender, age, and risk level. According to the results, the significant predictors of recidivism were age, risk category, and group membership. More specifically, younger offenders, higher-risk offenders, and offenders in the comparison group were more likely to be arrested for new criminal behavior during their follow-up.

The coefficient for group membership indicates that when controlling for confounding factors, the odds of the comparison group being arrested during the follow-up were almost double (Exp [B] = 1.95) that of the treatment group. Comparing the differences in odds of being arrested in the bivariate analysis (1.57) to those of the multivariate analysis (1.95) indicates that controlling for confounding factors produces increases in the treatment effect.

Figure 4.3 presents the adjusted recidivism rates for the treatment and comparison groups, holding all other independent variables constant. At 28%, the adjusted rate of recidivism for the treatment group is modestly lower than that of the comparison group's rate of 43%. This indicates that adjusting for the net effects of risk, age, race, gender, and follow-up time produces a recidivism rate of the treatment groups which is 15 percentage points lower than that of the comparison group.

⧄ Discussion

The results of the current study indicate that participation in the TFAC program, as delivered by the Tippecanoe County probation department, is associated with an appreciable reduction in recidivism. This shows that a specific cognitive behavioral curriculum that is readily available to correctional agencies can work to reduce recidivism. Furthermore, the program was delivered by community corrections staff that did not necessarily possess any exceptional qualifications or credentials aside from training on the facilitation of the TFAC program. Also, unlike many evaluations of cognitive programs, neither was this study a demonstration project nor was it delivered in an "optimal" or "artificial" environment. In sum, the current research indicates that a program that was delivered in a real-world setting was effective in reducing the recidivism of its participants.

While the results of this evaluation are encouraging, there are a number of limitations that should be noted. First and foremost, the participants in this study were not randomly assigned to the differing treatment conditions. Although the comparison and treatment groups were similar on most factors, there is still a possibility that there was some selection bias in assigning offenders

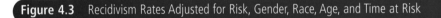

Figure 4.3 Recidivism Rates Adjusted for Risk, Gender, Race, Age, and Time at Risk

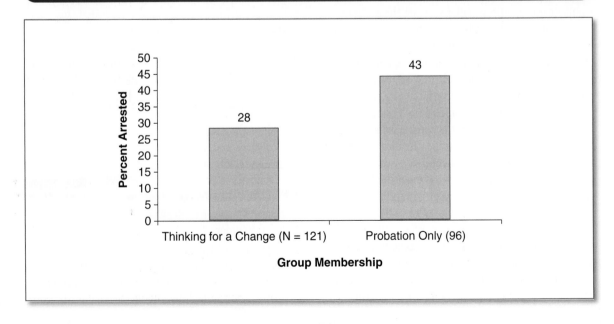

to the TFAC groups. Again, some of this concern is tempered by the fact that the two groups of offenders were similar on demographic characteristics except for risk—a difference which favored the comparison group. The other identified difference between the two groups, length of follow-up time, is another limitation. We would have preferred a standardized time frame and lengthier follow-up period; unfortunately, certain contextual factors and data limitations prohibited this from occurring.

While an experimental design with standardized follow-up would be preferred, this limitation is not fatal, as statistical controls were implemented to adjust for potentially confounding factors. Furthermore, the potential for bias due to risk favors the control group (who were of lower risk), suggesting that, if anything, differences in risk would produce conservative estimates. While the same cannot be said for time at risk (the control group spent more time at risk, which potentially could lead to artificial increases in the recidivism of the control group), our analyses that control for this factor show that time at risk failed to be a significant predictor of recidivism, indicating that this factor is not confounding the present results.

The current investigation indicates that probation and similar community supervision agencies may be able to use their staff to provide meaningful rehabilitative services that lead to reductions in recidivism. Furthermore, this research is consistent with recent research that suggests that TFAC in particular (Golden et al., 2006) and cognitive behavioral programs in general (Landenberger & Lipsey, 2005) can produce meaningful reductions in recidivism. This is important, because it suggests that community corrections agencies can work toward the goal of enhancing public safety through the implementation of programming which has been shown to be effective in a "real-world" setting.

No single study in social sciences is definitive, and the current investigation is no exception. Further research should seek to conduct randomized trials to investigate the impacts of the TFAC program. Furthermore, while effective on this sample of probationers in Tippecanoe County, Indiana, practitioners and scholars should not jump to conclusions about the generalizability of this research. Future evaluations, if conducted across multiple jurisdictions and with varied samples of offenders, would help to speak to the generalizability of TFAC in reducing recidivism. Also, continued testing of the efficacy of TFAC and other cognitive behavioral curricula will aid in the development of a base of knowledge to inform correctional agencies in making decisions regarding adoption and implementation of correctional programming.

◪ References

Andrews, D. A., & Bonta, J. (2006). *The psychology of criminal conduct* (4th ed). Cincinnati, OH: Anderson.

Andrews, D. A., Bonta, J., & Hoge, R. (1990). Classification for effective rehabilitation: Rediscovering psychology. *Criminal Justice & Behavior, 17,* 19–52.

Andrews, D. A., Bonia, J., & Womith, S. J. (2006). The recent past and near future of risk and/or need assessment. *Crime & Delinquency, 52,* 7–27.

Andrews, D. A., Zinger, I., Huge, R. D., Bonia, J., Gendreau, P., & Cullen, F. T. (1990). Does correctional treatment work? A clinically relevant and psychologically informed meta-analysis. *Criminology, 8,* 369–404.

Aos, S., Miller, M., & Drake, E. (2006). *Evidence-based public policy options to reduce future prison construction, criminal justice costs, and crime rates.* Olympia: Washington State Institute for Public Policy.

Bandura, A. (1986). *Social foundations of thought and action; A social cognitive theory.* Englewood Cliffs, NJ: Prentice-Hall.

Bush, J., Glick, B., & Taymans, J. (1997). *Thinking for a change: Integrated cognitive behavior change program.* National Institute of Corrections. Washington, DC: US. Department of Justice.

Cohen, R. L. (1995) *Probation and parole violators in state prison, 1991.* Washington, DC: Bureau of Justice Statistics.

Cullen, F. T., & Gendreau, P. (2000). Assessing correctional rehabilitation: Policy, practice, and prospects. In J. Horney (Ed.), *Criminal justice 2001, volume 3: Policies, processes, and decisions of the criminal justice system* (pp. 109–175). Washington, DC: National Institute of Justice.

Dowden, C., & Andrews, D. A. (2000). Effective correctional treatment and violent reoffending: A meta-analysis. *Canadian Journal of Criminology, 42,* 449–467.

Garrett, C. J. (1985). Effects of residential treatment on adjudicated delinquents: A meta-analysis. *Journal of Research in Crime & Delinquency, 22,* 287–308.

Gendreau, P. (1996). The principles of effective interventions with offenders. In A. T. Harland (Ed.), *Choosing correctional options that work: Defining the demand and evaluating the supply* (pp. 117–130). Thousand Oaks, CA: Sage.

Gendreau, P., & Goggin, C. (1996). Principles of effective correctional programming. *Forum on Corrections, 8,* 38–41.

Gendreau, P., French, S., & Taylor, A. (2002). *What works (what doesn't work)–revised 2002: The principles of effective correctional treatment.* Unpublished manuscript, University of New Brunswick at Saint John.

Gilford, S. (2002). *Justice expenditures and employment in the United States, 1999.* Washington, DC: Bureau of Justice Statistics.

Glaze, L. E., & Bonczar, T. P. (2006). *Probation and parole in the United States, 2005.* Washington, DC: U.S. Department of Justice.

Golden, L. S., Gatchel, R. J., & Cahill, M. A. (2006). Evaluating the effectiveness of the National Institute of Corrections' "Thinking for a Change" program among probationers. *Journal of Offender Rehabilitation, 42,* 55–73.

Hanley, D. (2002). *Risk differentiation and intensive supervision: A meaningful union?* Doctoral Dissertation. Division of Criminal Justice: University of Cincinnati. (UMI No. 3062606)

Harrison, P. M., & Beck, A. J. (2006). *Prisoners in 2005.* Washington. DC: United States Department of Justice.

Landenberger, N., & Lipsey, M. (2005). The positive effects of cognitive behavioral programs for offenders: A meta analysis of factors associated with effective treatment. *Journal of Experimental Criminology, 1,* 451–476.

Latessa, E. J., & Smith, P. (2007). *Corrections in the community.* Cincinnati, OH: Anderson.

Latessa, E. J., Cullen, F., & Gendreau, P. (2002). Beyond correctional quackery: Professionalism and the possibility of effective treatment. *Federal Probation, 66,* 43–49.

Lipsey, M. W. (1995). What have we learned from 400 research studies on the effectiveness of treatment with juvenile delinquents? In J. McGuire (Ed.), *What works? Reducing reoffending* (pp. 63–78). New York: John Wiley.

Lipsey, M. W., Chapman, G. L., & Landenberger, N. A. (2001). Cognitive behavioral programs for offenders. *Annals of the American Academy of Political and Social Science, 578,* 144–157.

Lowenkamp, C. T., & Latessa, E. J. (2005). *Evaluation of Ohio's CCA funded programs.* Unpublished Report, University of Cincinnati, Division of Criminal Justice.

Lowenkamp, C. T., Latessa, E. J., & Smith, P. (2006). Does correctional program quality really matter? The impact of adhering to the principles of effective interventions. *Criminology & Public Policy, 5,* 575–594.

Lowenkamp, C. T., Pealer, J., Latessa, E. J., & Smith, P. (2006). Adhering to the risk principle: Does it matter for supervision-based programs? *Federal Probation, 4,* 3–8.

Palmer, T. (1995). Programmatic and nonprogrammatic aspects of successful intervention: New directions for research. *Crime & Delinquency, 41,* 100–131.

Petersilia, J. (2000). *When prisoners return to the community: Political, economic, and social consequences.* Washington, DC: National Institute of Justice.

Petersilia, J., & Turner, S. (1993). Intensive probation and parole. In M. Tonry (Ed.), *Crime & Justice: A Review of Research* (pp. 281–335). Chicago: University of Chicago Press.

Public Safety Performance Project. (2007). *Public safety, public spending: Forecasting America's prison population, 2007–2011.* Washington, DC: The Pew Charitable Trusts.

Reeves, D. W. (2006). *Investigation of the impact of a cognitive skills educational program upon adult criminal offenders placed on supervised probation.* Doctoral Dissertation, Northern Arizona University. (UM1 No. 3213110)

Taxman, F. S., Yancey, C., & Bilanin, J. (2006). *Proactive community supervision in Maryland: Changing offender outcomes.* Baltimore: Maryland Division of Parole and Probation.

Weisfeld, N. E. (2007). *Realigning state-local relationships to save correctional dollars.* Washington, DC: The Pew Charitable Trusts.

Wilson, D. B., Bouffant, L. A., & MacKenzie, D. L. (2005). A quantitative review of structured, group-oriented, cognitive-behavioral programs for offenders. *Criminal Justice & Behavior, 32,* 172–204.

Wilson, D. B., Gallagher, C. A., & MacKenzie, D. L. (2000). A meta-analysis of corrections-based education, vocation, and work programs for adult offenders. *Journal on Research in Crime & Delinquency, 37,* 347–368.

DISCUSSION QUESTIONS

1. How do cognitive-based programs differ from other community-based treatments?

2. Given what we know about cognitive programs, should agencies continue to support their development and use? Why or why not?

3. What are some of the potential benefits and shortfalls of any community-based program such as TFC?

4. What are some of the potential shortcomings for implementing this type of program in a community-based setting?

READING

One argument made in the field of criminal justice is whether any treatment program referral made by an agency is truly voluntary. To better understand the impact of coercion on treatment effectiveness, Parhar and her colleagues conducted a meta-analysis of studies examining "the relationship between the level of treatment coerciveness and treatment outcome as measured by treatment retention and recidivism" (p. 1112). A total of 139 articles published between 1970 and 2005 met the search criteria for inclusion in the study. Overall, the findings revealed that more mandated and less voluntary programs had an increased likelihood of being found in the community. In spite of the lack of voluntary nature in the community, these programs appeared to have the greatest impact on reducing specific forms of recidivism and obtaining the desired treatment results as opposed to general recidivism. Furthermore, the findings revealed that mandated treatment had no effect on recidivism when administered in a custodial setting. Voluntary participation, however, did appear to reduce recidivism regardless of whether offered in the community or a custodial setting. The authors further concluded their study by reviewing the limitations of the meta-analysis process. There are several policy implications implied within the study and the findings.

Offender Coercion in Treatment

A Meta-Analysis of Effectiveness

Karen K. Parhar, J. Stephen Wormith, Dena M. Derkzen, and Adele M. Beauregard

The evidence that correctional treatment programs can be effective in reducing recidivism rates is now well established (e.g., Hollin, 1999; Lipsey, Chapman, & Landenberger, 2001; McGuire, 2002). More specifically, principles of effective correctional treatment—such as risk, need, and responsivity (RNR)—that increase the likelihood of success and decrease recidivism rates most dramatically have been well documented (e.g., Andrews, Bonta, & Hoge, 1990; Andrews, Bonta, & Wormith, 2006; Andrews, Zinger, et al., 1990). Consequently, there appears to be strong support for correctional treatment programs within correctional agencies (McGuire, 2004) and among many in the judiciary (W. Hall, 1997).

Perhaps because of this revived confidence in the effectiveness of correctional treatment, the use of court-ordered or legally mandated treatment, which is accompanied by "threats of legal consequences if individuals refuse to comply with a referral to treatment" (Polcin & Greenfield, 2003, p. 650), and coercive treatment, whereby refusal to participate in treatment results in negative consequences (Day, Tucker, & Howells, 2004), has become increasingly commonplace. For example, the number of legally mandated correctional treatment programs for substance abusers and

SOURCE: Karen K. Parhar, Stephen J. Wormith, Dena M. Derkzen, & Adele M. Beauregard. (2008). Offender coercion in treatment: A meta-analysis of effectiveness. *Criminal Justice and Behavior, 35*(9), 1109–1135. Copyright © 2008 Sage Publications. Published on behalf of the American Association for Correctional and Forensic Psychologists.

spousal assaulters has increased significantly within the past decade (Holtzworth-Munroe, 2001; Polcin, 1999; Rosenbaum & Geffner, 2002; Wells-Parker, 1994). Furthermore, court-ordered counseling for substance abusers has now become common practice in many regions and states of the United States (Shearer & Baletka, 1999).

Another possible explanation for the increased use of court-ordered programs is the belief that few offenders will enter treatment without some sort of external motivation (Farabee, Prendergast, & Anglin, 1998). Therefore, it may be argued that treatment should be legally mandated to safeguard the community. However, another perspective commonly held by clinicians is that treatment can be effective only if the participants choose to attend treatment because of their own internal motivations (Shearer & Baletka, 1999).

✵ Mandated and Nonmandated Offender Treatment

Although only a few studies have compared the recidivism rates of participants attending treatment under a legal mandate to those who attend voluntarily (e.g., "Principles of Drug Addiction," 2000), some evidence supports the concept of legally mandated treatment. After reviewing 11 empirical studies of compulsory substance abuse treatment programs, Farabee et al. (1998) concluded that legal referral to substance abuse treatment programs is an effective strategy for improving outcome and enhancing retention and compliance. This finding is supported by other drug treatment studies that have concluded that mandated treatment contributes to treatment completion (Rempel & Destefano, 2001; Siddall & Conway. 1988).

Moreover, comparative studies have found that those who are legally mandated to treatment are more likely to stay in treatment longer than those who are not legally mandated to treatment (e.g., Collins & Allison, 1983; Schnoll, Goldstein, Antes, & Rinella, 1980). For example, Rosenberg and Liftik (1976) compared retention rates between coerced and voluntary participants and found that offenders coerced to participate in an alcoholism treatment program had better attendance rates than did voluntary patients. In addition, Maxwell (2000) found that greater perceived legal threat increased retention in drug treatment, regardless of the client's actual legal status.

Other studies have found less favorable results for mandated treatment. Howard and McCaughrin (1996) found that organizations in which 75% of the cases were court mandated had a higher rate of treatment failure than did organizations with few court-mandated clients. Examining outcome studies of court-ordered treatment programs for spousal assaulters, Rosenfeld (1992) found that mandated treatment did not reduce recidivism. Rather, men who were arrested for spousal assault and were not treated were just as likely to recidivate as those who completed treatment. Moreover, court-mandated and nonmandated participants were equally likely to withdraw from treatment. Concerning two domestic violence treatment studies that found positive results for court-mandated treatment (i.e., Dutton, 1986; Waldo, 1988), Rosenfeld (1992) speculated that the participants who completed treatment were likely to have been the most motivated and least treatment resistant.

There is also evidence that nonmandated treatment programs are associated with treatment retention and compliance. Harford, Ungerer, and Kinsella (1976) found that offenders not under any legal pressure to attend drug abuse treatment remained in treatment for longer periods than did clients who were under legal pressure. Shearer and Ogan (2002) measured treatment resistance for voluntary and forced participants who were residing in a substance abuse treatment program, in a prerelease therapeutic community, or in a therapeutic community in a substance abuse treatment facility as a condition of probation. They found that treatment resistance was significantly lower among offenders who perceived they had volunteered for treatment.

Comparative studies have also found no differences between the effectiveness of mandated treatment and nonmandated treatment programs. Research on substance abuse treatment by the National Institute on Drug Abuse has found that involuntary treatment of offenders is just as effective as voluntary treatment ("Principles of Drug Addiction," 2000). More specifically, the report stated that "individuals who enter treatment under legal pressure have outcomes as favourable as those who enter treatment voluntarily" (p. 19). Similarly, Prendergast, Farabee, Cartier, and Henkin (2002) did not find any differences between voluntary and involuntary clients in a drug treatment program on most measures of psychosocial functioning. Moreover, a meta-analysis of the effects of coercion in a community sex offender treatment program found a negative, but nonsignificant, relationship between coercion and recidivism (Gray, 1998).

⚙ Research Issues

Existing comparisons of mandated and voluntary participation in correctional treatment may be misleading because these studies are plagued with conceptual and methodological problems. For example, truly voluntary participation does not exist in the criminal justice system because there is always some degree of external pressure (Wild, 1999). Wild (1999) concluded that the minimal difference found between mandated and nonmandated clients in substance abuse treatment may have occurred because he really compared mandated versus *coerced* clients and not mandated versus truly voluntary participants.

Furthermore, Farabee et al. (1998) identified a number of definitions of coercion, claiming that coercion can be used to refer to a range of situations, such as the following:

> a probation officer's recommendation to enter treatment, a drug court judge's offer of a choice between treatment or jail, a judge's requirement that the offender enter treatment as a condition of probation, or a correctional policy of sending inmates involuntarily to a prison treatment program in order to fill the beds. (p. 3)

Farabee et al. stated that even being involved in the criminal justice system alone is sufficient to be considered coercion.

Another conceptual difficulty occurs because some programs do not accept clients into treatment unless they are at least somewhat willing to participate, even if they are legally mandated to attend treatment (e.g., Dutton, 1986; Taylor, Davis, & Maxwell, 2001). In other words, mandated clients who enter treatment may actually volunteer to enter treatment even though they are legally required to participate. More specifically, in psychological rehabilitation programs, offenders cannot be physically forced to attend a treatment session; even if they do attend, they cannot be forced to participate fully, although they can be pressured (Day et al., 2004).

One of the most confounding difficulties in assessing the effectiveness of mandated versus voluntary treatment is the offender's motivation to attend treatment, regardless of mandate. One study found that more than three fourths of the patients who reported no control over their admission to an outpatient clinic planned to continue treatment when external pressure was removed and thereby appeared to have volunteered for treatment (Farabee, Shen, & Sanchez, 2002).

Consequently, discussions about mandated treatment evoke questions about client motivation. Motivation is commonly described on a continuum from external motivation to intrinsic motivation. According to McMurran (2002), externally motivated behavior occurs in the presence of an external reward or some other kind of external contingency, whereas intrinsically motivated behavior occurs in the absence of any external reward. A person undertakes intrinsically motivated behavior out of interest because it is optimally challenging and is based on innate psychological needs. When behavior change is the result of intrinsic motivation, the changes last longer; behavior change that is extrinsically motivated lasts only as long as the extrinsic controls are in place (Ryan & Deci, 2000). Consequently, offenders who are intrinsically motivated to desist from crime may be more likely to be successful in the long term. Intrinsic motivation has been associated with positive behavioral changes such as better learning, performance, and well-being (e.g., Benware & Deci, 1984; Deci, Schwartz, Sheinman, & Ryan, 1981; Grolnick & Ryan, 1987).

Generally speaking, mandated treatment provides external motivation to attend treatment, and those who voluntarily attend treatment are intrinsically motivated. Thus, it is not surprising that a large study of the general public, substance abuse counselors, probationers, and judges reported that all respondents believed that compulsory substance abuse treatment is less effective than voluntary treatment (Wild et al., 2001). In light of the evidence supporting the benefits of voluntary treatment attendance, it is hypothesized that nonmandated or voluntary treatment will have greater impact on recidivism and will correspond with lower rates of treatment attrition than mandated treatment.

Because most studies do not assess offender motivation for treatment, the present meta-analysis cannot directly address this issue. However, many offender treatment studies describe the legal context of their intervention and the conditions that may apply to their clientele in some detail. This should allow one to estimate the extent to which external pressure may be found in "voluntary" treatment (e.g., pressure from family) and internal motivation may be present even in mandated treatment (e.g., the offender would have volunteered regardless of mandate). Specifically, a 5-level coercion-voluntary scale, ranging from 1 *(mandated or involuntary)* to 5 *(nonmandated or voluntary)*, was used to assess the extent of coercion in a sample of treatment studies. In this manner, variations in the degree of coercion were established in an attempt to resolve Wild's (1999) concern regarding falsely classifying treatment participants into dichotomous categories of purely mandated and voluntary because categories fail to truly exist. Most interventions do not fall in either of these two extremes.

Another possible confound in the comparisons of mandated versus voluntary treatment concerns the effectiveness of the treatment strategy being adopted in any given study. In their meta-analysis, Andrews, Zinger, et al. (1990) recorded effectiveness of dramatically attenuated effect sizes between studies that adhered to the principles of RNR and those that did not. These findings have since been updated and supported (Andrews et al., 2006). It is quite possible that either mandated or voluntary treatment interventions are more or less effective, irrespective of the degree of voluntariness that is offered. Previous studies in this literature have not considered any other factors that might explain or camouflage differences in the effectiveness of voluntary or mandated interventions.

The goal of this article is to examine the relationship between the level of treatment coerciveness and treatment outcome as measured by treatment retention and recidivism. To achieve this objective, the degree of coercion was correlated with percentage of treatment dropouts, and unweighted treatment effect sizes and magnitudes of the treatment effect for mandated, coerced, and voluntary treatment programs were compared.

⊠ Method

Sample of Studies

A search for all relevant articles pertaining to mandated and nonmandated treatment of offenders was conducted through a number of key social scientific computerized databases. These included PsycINFO, Criminal Justice Abstracts, Medline, and Sociological Abstracts. The search was based on the following keywords used individually or in various combinations with each other: *mandatory, voluntary, compulsory, coercive, treatment, intervention, offender, criminal, inmate, recidivism, arrest, control,* and *comparison.* Finally, the bibliographies of articles published in 2004, 2005, and 2006 that met the inclusion criteria were searched for additional articles that might meet the inclusion criteria.[1]

Inclusion Criteria

The following information was required from each study to be included in the meta-analysis: Participants or the treatment in question were identified as either legally mandated or nonmandated, a comparison or control group was included in the study, and recidivism outcome measures were reported either as a Pearson product-moment correlation coefficient r (effect size) or in a manner that could be transformed into a Pearson r. In 31 cases, authors were contacted by e-mail or telephone when the information was present but clarification on any of the above criteria was required (e.g., when it was unclear if the treatment group was mandated or nonmandated or when specific recidivism information was needed to convert to r). That is, authors were contacted when there was enough information to code the items but some information was unclear or specific details were omitted from the article. Consequently, studies were excluded from the analyses if there was no indication of whether the program or participants in the treatment group were legally mandated or not mandated, the recidivism data could not be analyzed (e.g., only F statistics were reported), or no comparison or control group was included. In addition, studies comparing only mandated and nonmandated treatment participants, but with no control group, were excluded from the analyses because such a design does not afford an opportunity to compute a comparable effect size.

Study Characteristics and Coding

More than 500 studies were identified in the initial search and reviewed for possible inclusion. A total of 139 studies met the selection criteria. Of these, 46 (33.1%) studies involved exclusively mandated treatment programs, 83 (59.7%) involved exclusively nonmandated treatment programs, and 10 (7.2%) were mixed mandated and nonmandated treatment participants. A total of 69 items was used to code the articles. The item categories included background information (e.g., author, year, country, etc.), participants (e.g., gender, mean age, etc.), program information (e.g., location, research design, mandate, treatment type, treatment quality, sample size, treatment dropouts, etc.), and recidivism (e.g., length of follow-up, type of recidivism, number of rearrests, etc.).

The assessment of coercion and voluntariness was coded in three levels of specificity: a 2-level mandated-nonmandated variable, a 3-level mandated-coerced-voluntary variable, and a 5-point ordinal scale. The detailed, 5-point coercion-voluntary scale ranged from 1 *(mandated or involuntary)* to 5 *(nonmandated or voluntary)*. Each level of the scale was developed by the authors and subjectively ordered to reflect the variations in levels of coercion reported in the treatment studies based on the legal mandate of any available information regarding the level of perceived or actual coercion and/or implementation of the mandate. The most coercive end of the scale, *mandated or involuntary,* and the less coercive midrange scores of the scale (2 to 4) were defined similarly to the definitions provided by Klag, O'Callaghan, and Creed (2005) of compulsory and coerced treatment in their review of legal coercion in the treatment of substance abusers.

The 5 levels and their definitions were as follows: 1 = mandated involuntary (it is clear that offenders must take the program [if they do not attend treatment they face incarceration or other negative consequences]; it is a condition of their release; they are court referred; treatment is included in sentence), 2 = mandated coerced (offenders are mandated to treatment, but there is evidence that consequences are minimal or nil if they do not participate [e.g., they are not consistently punished]), 3 = nonmandated coerced with legal consequences (there is no mandate for offenders to participate in treatment [they are volunteers], but there are some legal consequences if they do not attend or complete treatment [e.g., get sent back to court]), 4 = nonmandated coerced (there is no mandate for offenders to participate in treatment, but they may receive incentives if they attend treatment, such as early release [this is usually in a parole or institutional setting]), and 5 = nonmandated or voluntary (offenders freely volunteer to attend treatment without evidence of any external costs or benefits).[2]

Ten articles reported mixed mandated and nonmandated treatment participants. However, because the mixed treatment studies could not be analyzed with the remaining studies without jeopardizing the integrity of the study, they were excluded from the analyses, resulting in a sample size of 129 studies. This 5-level coding scheme was then used to create the two simpler measures of coercion-voluntariness, the 2-level measure where scores of 1 to 2 *(mandated)* and 3 to 5 *(voluntary)* were collapsed, and the 3-level measure where scores of I *(mandated),* 2 to 4 *(coerced),* and 5 *(voluntary)* were recoded. These multiple levels of precision were used to gain a better understanding of previous findings.

Because correctional treatment programs that adhere to the principles of RNR produce greater effect sizes (Andrews, Zinger, et al., 1990), a treatment quality variable was created to assess the extent to which the treatment program adhered to the principles of RNR. Treatment studies that adhered to zero or one of the principles of RNR were coded as inappropriate and treatment programs that adhered to two or all three of the principles of RNR were coded as appropriate.

Meta-Analytic Strategy

Independence of Comparisons. The effect sizes collected for the meta-analysis report only independent comparisons in which a particular experimental group is statistically compared to just one comparison group. When several comparison groups were used in a single study, the highest quality comparison group was used. For example, random or matched-control groups were chosen over control groups composed of treatment dropouts. When more than one follow-up time was provided for the outcome data, comparisons based on the longest follow-up were used. Where studies reported more than one recidivism measure, recidivism was coded for arrest or the most inclusive recidivism measure reported. For example, if charges and convictions were reported, only charges were coded. Both general and specific (e.g., sexual, violent) recidivism rates were coded when reported.

⊠ Results

Study Characteristics

Of the 129 studies published between 1970 and 2005 *(Mdn = 1998)* that were used in the current analyses, the majority were conducted in the United States (80.6%) and Canada (14.7%). Most of the 118 studies (78.0%) reporting the age of the treatment participants involved participants exclusively in the adult justice system. More than half of the 120 studies (56.7%) that reported treatment setting took place exclusively in the community. More than half of the 113 studies (54.0%) reporting gender consisted of males only, whereas most of the remaining studies (42.5%) consisted of both males and females. More than half of the studies (55.0%) were classified as having a strong research design (random assignment or quasi-experimental). Nonmandated treatment programs were more common (64.3%) than mandated treatment programs (35.7%). Approximately half of the 126 studies (48.8%) that were coded for treatment quality were described as inappropriate and half were appropriate (51.2%).

The treatment programs included in the study addressed a variety of offender issues. The most frequently reported objectives targeted substance abuse (38.1%), sex offending (15.9%), juvenile delinquency (13.5%), and violence (13.5%). The most common treatment modality was cognitive-behavioral treatment (34.7%), followed by therapeutic community (20.2%), general counseling (15.3%), multisystemic therapy (10.5%), and psychoeducational treatment (8.9%).

Recidivism

A total of 106 (82.2%) articles included general recidivism information, and 52 (40.3%) articles included specific recidivism information that was directly related to the treatment in which offenders participated. Among the 106 studies reporting general recidivism, 104 indicated the source of the data; most were based on official records of recidivism (90.4%, $k = 94$), few were based on unofficial records (3.9%, $k = 5$) and both official and unofficial records (3.9%, $k = 5$). With respect to type of recidivism, 105 studies provided data, and arrest was used in half (49.5%, $k = 52$) of the studies, followed by incarceration (16.2%, $k = 17$) and convictions (12.4%, $k = 13$). Other types of recidivism reported were a combination of measures (5.7%, $k = 6$), charges (4.8%, $k = 5$), violations (3.8%, $k = 4$), court contact (2.9%, $k = 3$), other (2.9%, $k = 3$),[4] self-report (1.0%, $k = 1$), and unspecified (1.0%, $k = 1$).

Considering the 52 studies reporting specific recidivism, 50 reported the source of the data, and most were based on official recidivism (74.0%, $k = 37$); few were based on unofficial records (12.0%, $k = 6$) and both official and unofficial records (14.0%, $k = 7$). Of the 51 studies reporting type of recidivism data, arrest was the most common type of specific recidivism reported (29.4%, $k = 15$), followed by convictions (11.8%, $k = 6$), violations (9.8%, $k = 5$), and self-reported recidivism (9.8%, $k = 5$). Other types of recidivism reported were a combination of measures (7.8%, $k = 4$), charges (7.8%, $k = 4$), police records (5.9%, $k = 3$), drug use (5.9%, $k = 3$), other (3.9%, $k = 2$), unspecified (3.9%, $k = 2$), incarceration (2.0%, $k = 1$), and court contact (2.0%, $k = 1$).

Analysis of Study Variables by Level of Coercion

Prior to analyzing the mean effect sizes of the mandated $(k = 46)$ and nonmandated $(k = 83)$ treatment programs, analyses were conducted to determine whether there were differences between the two groups on study characteristics. Mandated treatment programs were significantly more likely to be located in the community,[5] $\chi^2(1, N= 120) = 9.51, p < .01$, and consist of juvenile offenders, $\chi^2(1, N = 118) = 14.75, p < .01$, than non-mandated treatment programs. Likewise, less voluntary treatment, as measured using the 5-point coercion-voluntary scale, was more likely to be located in the community, $t(128) = -4.26, p < .001$, and consist of juvenile offenders, $t(116) = -3.879, p < .001$, than more voluntary treatment. There were no significant differences between mandated and nonmandated treatment programs on quality of research design, $\chi^2 (1, N = 129) = 0.98, p > .05$, treatment quality (appropriate or inappropriate), $\chi^2(1, N = 125) = 0.13, p > .05$, sample size. $t(127) = -0.93, p > .05$, or percentage of treatment dropouts, $t(54) = 1.62, p > .05$. Similarly, no differences were found between level of coercion and research design, $t(127) = 1.028, p > .05$, treatment quality, $t(126) = .04, p > .05$, or sample size, $r(129) = .09, p > .05$, using the 5-point coercion-voluntary scale. Unweighted treatment effect size was not correlated with the number of RNR principles to which the treatment adhered for any, $r(126) = .10, p > .05$, general, $r(103) = .16, p > .05$, or specific recidivism, $r(51) = -.08, p > .05$.

Because two potentially confounding differences in study characteristics were found between mandated and nonmandated treatment, further analyses were conducted to determine whether these variables were related to treatment effect size. Treatment programs conducted in the community were more effective than treatment offered in custody as measured by unweighted effect sizes on any, $r(118) = 2.40, p = .02$, and specific recidivism, $r(46) = 2.03, p < .05$. but not general recidivism, $r(96) = 1.20, p > .05$. Moreover, an ordinal measure of setting, ranging from 1 to 3, consisting of community, mixed settings, and custodial settings, respectively, resulted in significant correlations on the unweighted effect sizes of any, $r(128) = -.21, p = .02$, and specific recidivism, $r(51) = -.28, p = .05$, but not general recidivism, $r(106) = -.12, p > .05$. No differences were found between the unweighted effect sizes for treatment offered to adult and juvenile offenders on any, $t(116) = -1.80, p > .05$, general, $t(30.83) = -0.88, p > .05$, or specific, $t(48) = 0.30, p > .05$, recidivism. Therefore, it was necessary for comparisons of treatment effectiveness between mandated and nonmandated treatment in the following analyses to consider treatment setting.

Relation Between Level of Coercion and Unweighted Effect Size Estimates

To examine the relationship between amount of coercion on the 5-point coercion-voluntary scale and magnitude of effect size, correlational analyses were conducted using the unweighted effect sizes of all studies (any recidivism), studies reporting general recidivism, and studies reporting specific recidivism, regardless of setting. Significant positive correlations were found between effect size and degree of voluntariness for any recidivism, $r(129) = .21, p = .02$, and general recidivism, $r(106) = .24, p = .01$, but not for specific recidivism, $r(52) = .13, p < .05$. These correlational analyses were repealed separately for custody and community settings. Significant positive correlations were found between unweighted effect sizes and degree of voluntariness in custody and community settings, respectively, for any recidivism, $r(52) = .41, p = .003$, $r(68) = .24, p = .05$, in custody only for general recidivism, $r(47) = .43, p = .003, r(51) = .20, p > .05$, and neither custody nor community for specific recidivism, $r(20) = .22, p > .05, r(28) = .18, p > .05$.

Mandated, Coerced, and Voluntary Treatment Effect Size Comparisons

Preliminary analyses comparing mandated and non-mandated treatment resulted in a similar pattern of results as comparisons among mandated, coerced, and voluntary treatment. In addition, only eight mandated treatment studies were nonmandated coerced and separating coerced treatment from voluntary and mandated treatment would be more informative than analysis of mandated versus nonmandated treatment. Therefore, mandated versus nonmandated comparisons were not reported to avoid redundancy and to provide a more detailed analysis of the impact of levels of coercion and treatment effectiveness. To assess the impact of the most extreme levels of coercion, the 5-point coercion-voluntary scale was collapsed into three groups as follows: 1 *(mandated involuntary),* 2 to 4 *(coerced),* and 5 *(nonmandated or voluntary).*

When the three levels of coercion were analyzed by treatment setting, custody settings were only effective in voluntary treatment using weighted and unweighted effect sizes for any, general, and specific recidivism. Community settings were effective for all three levels of coercion using any, general, and specific recidivism for all weighted and unweighted effect sizes.

⊠ Discussion

The research on mandated treatment programs for offenders has been complicated by many issues (see Seddon, 2007), one being definitional terminology. For example, the terms *coerced, compulsory, mandated, involuntary, legal pressure,* and *criminal justice referral* have all been used to discuss coerced treatment and sometimes even used interchangeably within the same article (Farabee et al., 1998). Not only has inconsistent terminology been used to define coerced treatment, but also the concept of mandated versus voluntary treatment covers a variety of formal and informal degrees of legal pressure (Prendergast, Farabee, et al., 2002).

The current investigation attempted to create a more precise measure of mandated and voluntary treatment that included various degrees of coercion rather than simply coding mandated and voluntary treatment in a dichotomous manner. It commenced with a review of the commentary provided in the offender treatment literature and was followed with the construction of a reliable coding scheme to rate the degree of treatment coercion on a 5-point coercion-voluntary scale. Correlational analyses were conducted on this most detailed scale, and comparative analyses were conducted on various degrees of coercion. Analyses were also conducted separately for treatment setting because it became apparent that the relationship between mandated-nonmandated treatment and treatment effect size was confounded by setting. Specifically, institutional programs were more voluntary, but community programs produced a larger mean treatment effect size.

Previous research on the effects of mandated and voluntary treatment has produced mixed and inconclusive results. For example, studies have found that mandated treatment is effective in reducing recidivism and increasing treatment retention (e.g., Farabee et al., 1998), that mandated treatment is less effective than nonmandated or voluntary treatment in retaining treatment participants (Harford et al., 1976), and that there is little or no difference between mandated and voluntary treatment (e.g., Wild, 1999). The current study attempted to provide more conclusive results by conducting a meta-analysis of a large number of studies using a variety of measures of coercion.

The results of this study partially support those studies that found no treatment effects for mandated programs (e.g., Rosenfeld, 1992), partially support reviews finding nonmandated or voluntary treatment superior to mandated treatment in outcome and retention (e.g., Harford et al., 1976), and partially support studies finding no differences between mandated and nonmandated treatment programs (e.g., "Principles of Drug Addiction," 2000). Our study also challenges a number of studies that concluded mandated treatment is effective and superior to nonmandated or voluntary treatment in outcome and retention (e.g., Farabee et al., 1998; Rempel & Destefano, 2001). But most important, the current study may provide an explanation for the inconclusive results of previous research.

Interpretation

Both weighted (including and excluding the outlier) and unweighted effect sizes are presented in the current study, with several differences emerging among them. Reminiscent of the differences in results that are often found when comparing effectiveness studies to efficacy studies (e.g., Lipsey, 1999; McGuire, 2002), smaller studies tended to have larger effect sizes.[6] Consequently, unweighted effect sizes tended to be larger than the weighted effect sizes, most notably in voluntary treatment excluding the outlier study. Larger effect sizes are needed to achieve significance in studies with small samples because of the decreased power associated with smaller samples (Rosenthal & DiMatteo, 2001). Moreover, studies that do not yield results that achieve statistical significance are less likely to be published (also known as the "file drawer problem");

studies with small sample sizes and large effect sizes are more likely to be published than studies with small sample sizes and small effect sizes, introducing possible selection bias into the sample. Moreover, the presence of one (voluntary) treatment study with an extremely large sample size, and an average to small effect size, further complicated our interpretation of the current findings. Consequently, it was not surprising to find the unweighted mean effect size was stronger than the weighted mean effect size for the total effect size and for voluntary treatment, on both any and general recidivism, and that the weighted mean effect sizes of the total and voluntary samples increased when the outlier was excluded. This finding also explains the significant differences found between mandated and voluntary treatment in the unweighted effect size analyses.

Most of the coerced interventions (35 of 43) were nonmandated treatment programs. This was one reason why the results reported analyses of mandated, coerced, and voluntary treatment rather than mandated versus nonmandated treatment. In fact, voluntary treatment was found to be effective regardless of treatment setting, whereas coerced treatment in custodial settings did not result in a treatment effect, similar to mandated treatment. Therefore, the findings of this meta-analysis indicate caution in providing treatment for what is most likely the most common treatment scenario in the criminal justice system, specifically conditions that are less than completely voluntary but are short of enforced treatment in terms of offenders' participation. It appears that some element of coercion may adversely affect the outcome of voluntary treatment.

The largest effect size across the three measures of outcome and three levels of voluntariness (i.e., .24) was found using unweighted effect sizes when voluntary treatment was applied to specific recidivism. When the studies were analyzed according to treatment setting, the largest effect size (i.e., .29) was found using unweighted effect sizes when voluntary treatment was applied to specific recidivism in community settings. This compares favorably with the other kinds of therapeutic intervention with offenders and with other clientele (Losel, 1995; McGuire, 2002; Pearson & Lipton, 1999). It is particularly encouraging to find such a strong treatment effect for what may prove to be the most vital kind of

treatment services for offenders (e.g., sex offender treatment, substance abuse offender treatment).

An examination of the effect sizes for general and specific recidivism reveals a similar pattern with one important difference. First, the overall effect size is larger for specific recidivism than general recidivism. Second, for general recidivism, the effect sizes for coerced and voluntary treatment in the three-group comparison are virtually the same, although modest in size, whereas the effect size for mandated treatment is low and not significantly different from zero (i.e., indicating a nil effect of treatment). Third, for specific recidivism, there is a consistent and relatively steady increase in the unweighted effect size as one goes from mandated to coerced to voluntary treatment, although these increases are not significant, quite possibly because of a lack of statistical power or difference in the types of recidivism measures reported. Most impressive, however, the strongest effect sizes in this study were found for voluntary treatment (without coercion), and the weakest effect sizes were found for mandated treatment.

One important finding of the current meta-analysis concerns the lack of treatment effect that mandated treatment had on general recidivism and custodial treatment, whereas voluntary treatment displayed a reliable impact on all offenders' recidivism regardless of treatment setting. Moreover, mandated treatment did have a significant effect on specific recidivism in spite of the small number of studies on which this mean effect size was based. As one might expect, studies that examined the treatment effect of mandated treatment on general recidivism included more studies with smaller effect sizes. On the other hand, nonmandated treatment consisted of more studies with a much larger sample size, providing more confidence for its effect on recidivism.

Several explanations may account for why voluntary treatment was effective regardless of treatment setting. Offenders in custodial settings mandated to attend treatment may perceive less personal choice to attend treatment than those in community settings. Therefore, custodial settings may increase the perception of forced treatment, whereas offenders mandated to treatment in community settings may perceive less force to attend treatment and perhaps more personal choice. According to the self-determination theory, intrinsic motivation is said to be fostered by personal autonomy, or behavior that is determined by oneself and under one's own control rather than the control of external forces (Deci & Ryan, 1991).

Other Considerations

Some might contend that effect sizes tended to be lower in mandated treatment because mandated treatment participants are more likely to be at higher risk for recidivism than nonmandated treatment participants. However, the risk principle, although counterintuitive to some, is supported by considerable empirical evidence demonstrating that larger treatment effects arc actually found with the higher risk offenders and in fact treatment can be iatrogenic with low-risk offenders (Andrews & Bonta, 2003). Because mandated and nonmandated treatment programs were not found to differ according to treatment quality, or the number of RNR principles the treatment adhered to, this explanation does not seem plausible. Furthermore, mandated studies were more likely to be conducted in community settings, and community settings were found to have greater effect sizes than custodial programs (Andrews, Zinger, et al., 1990). Therefore, if anything, mandated treatment would be expected to have an advantage in generating a positive treatment effect.

The present meta-analysis revealed that mandated treatment has no effect on recidivism when the program is administered in custodial settings. This implies that if offenders are being required by courts to attend treatment in custody settings, the treatment is likely to have no effect and cost the criminal justice system and the courts both time and money. On a positive note, coerced treatment produced effect sizes similar to voluntary treatment both in custody and in the community. Further research should be conducted on methods of motivating offenders to attend treatment on their own and/or increasing choice and reward for attending treatment (McMurran, 2002). On the other hand, it should not come as a surprise that community treatment is effective regardless of coercion and that voluntary treatment is effective regardless of treatment setting, although in both cases the degree of impact varies.

The current meta-analysis of offender treatment differs from previous ones in various ways. Being more recent, it includes some research that was not available in previous meta-analyses. It is more selective than the previous meta-analyses in that studies were excluded if there was insufficient information to rate the intervention on the coercion-voluntary dimension. Yet the mean unweighted effect size for all studies on any recidivism (.14) is consistent with those found in other analyses of offender treatment (e.g., Andrews, Zinger, et al., 1990; McGuire, 2002). The fact that the current overall effect size was comparable to those of previous meta-analyses suggests that the selection process that was necessary to investigate the impact of participant voluntariness did not distort or unduly bias the collection of studies in terms of their overall impact on offender treatment outcome.

A review of the ethics of coercion and the legality of mandated treatment for offenders was beyond the scope of the current investigation. Clearly, many jurisdictions have introduced mandated treatment of offenders, whereby their participation is required by law, particularly in the area of domestic violence treatment (Rosenbaum & Geffner, 2002). Many researchers, clinicians, and civil libertarians have questioned the wisdom and ethics of such services. One of the ethical arguments pertains to the provision of potentially ineffectual interventions. The current study, therefore, addressed not only the efficacy of mandated treatment but also, indirectly, the ethics of these services insofar as it may be deemed unethical to insist that offenders participate in interventions that have not been demonstrated to be effective. Required participation in offender treatment that targets general offending may be such a case. On the other hand, it is clear that treatment designed to address specialized kinds of outcome can have a positive effect on the desired outcomes and may not be considered unethical, at least in terms of requiring an offender to participate in unproven treatment.

Limitations

As is the case with any meta-analytic treatment study, the use of comparisons between groups of studies that share specific characteristics—in this case, the level of coercion—constitutes a correlational, as opposed to an experimental, design. In other words, the degree of voluntariness of offenders in treatment was correlated with the magnitude of the unweighted treatment effect for most of the analyses. But the specific reason for this positive correlation remains in question. It is unclear whether the difference in effect size was because of the act of volunteering or other client characteristics (e.g., motivation) or treatment characteristics (e.g., the intensity of the programs being offered). Another possibility may be that treatment facilitators are more responsive to clients who have volunteered and/or are motivated to attend treatment, thereby improving outcomes.

The concepts of mandated and voluntary treatment are neither simple nor discrete. In the current study, the determination of the degree of coercion was dependent on the information provided by the authors. Moreover, the motivation of each individual participant in the treatment programs was unknown. Some offenders who enter mandated treatment may do so voluntarily, regardless of their requirement to do so (Dutton, 1986; Taylor et al., 2001). Many offenders who enter voluntary treatment do so not only because of known systemic consequences imposed by the criminal justice system, including reduced security, parole, and other forms of early release, but also because of more subtle forms of coercion by family members and health care professionals (Polcin & Weisner, 1999). Furthermore, there may be inherent differences among types of programs targeting mostly mandated or voluntary treatment participants. Consequently, considerable effort was taken to consider the degree of coercion present in each treatment scenario. However, as a meta-analytic investigation, this was limited by the information provided by the authors and therefore generally done at the level of the individual study and not at the level of the individual offender.

The analyses conducted on any and general recidivism found significant differences among levels of coercion using unweighted effect sizes. Although there was an overall treatment effect on specific recidivism, there was no difference in the mean unweighted effect size for the different levels of coercion. In addition to there being truly no difference between the impact of different levels of coercion under these conditions of specific treatment, a statistical explanation is also possible. Because considerably fewer studies included in the current meta-analysis reported specific recidivism ($k = 52$), statistical power was considerably reduced in these comparisons, as evidenced by the large confidence intervals, particularly for mandated treatment ($k = 10$). Furthermore, the lack of significance found between different levels of coercive treatment when specific treatment was analyzed may be because of the reduced power associated with the small sample of studies, particularly when custody ($k = 3$) and community ($k = 7$) treatment were separately analyzed. Lack of power because of small sample sizes may have also caused greater levels of coercion associated with greater rates of treatment attrition overall, but not when custody and community treatment were separately analyzed. Further research should be conducted on the effects of specific versus general recidivism, and researchers should be encouraged to report both general and specific recidivism.

⌧ Conclusion

The practice of requiring offenders to participate in treatment is one of the most controversial aspects of service provision to offenders, in terms of both effectiveness and ethics (Day et al., 2004). The current meta-analysis was limited to an investigation of the impact of different levels of coercion to attend treatment on offender recidivism and attrition. Most notably, the study found that mandated treatment was ineffective, particularly when the treatment was located in custodial settings, whereas voluntary treatment produced significant treatment effect sizes regardless of setting.

⌧ Notes

1. The inclusion of a diverse set of offender treatment programs was deemed appropriate to avoid possible confounds due to selection bias.

2. An earlier version of the coercion-voluntary scale included six levels, where a score of 3 was mandated willing (offenders are mandated to participate in treatment, but there is evidence that they also took the treatment willingly or would have if it was not mandated); this level was excluded as none of the 129 studies included in the meta-analysis fit this description.

3. One study (Marshall, Eccles, & Barbaree, 1991) contributed two effect sizes that were calculated from the outcomes of two independent treatment groups.

4. Examples of the types of recidivism categorized as other include contact with any law enforcement agency, no further commitment (e.g., supervision, jail, prison), and rearraignment.

5. Treatment programs delivered in both custody and community settings (*n* = 8) were excluded from analyses conducted on community and custody settings.

6. Effectiveness studies, which are conducted in practical settings where operative variables are less controlled, typically yield effect sizes lower than those found in efficacy studies, which are assessed purely in scientific terms, such as randomized controlled trials.

⬛ References

References marked with an asterisk indicate studies included in the meta-analysis.

*Adams, R., & Vetter, H. J. (1981). Social structure and psychodrama outcome: A ten-year follow-up. *Journal of Offender Counseling, Services & Rehabilitation, 6,* 111–119.

*Alexander, C. N., Rainforth, M. V., Frank, P. R., Grant, J. D., Stade, C. V., & Walton, K. G. (2003). Walpole study of the transcendental meditation program in maximum security prisoners III: Reduced recidivism. *Journal of Offender Rehabilitation, 36*(1–4), 161–180.

Andrews, D. A., & Bonta, J. (2003). *The psychology of criminal conduct* (3rd ed.). Cincinnati, OH: Anderson.

Andrews, D. A., Bonta, J., & Hoge, R. D. (1990). Classification for effective rehabilitation: Rediscovering psychology. *Criminal Justice and Behavior, 17,* 19–52.

Andrews, D. A., Bonta, J., & Wormith, J. S. (2006). The recent past and near future of risk and/or need assessment. *Crime & Delinquency, 52,* 7–27.

Andrews, D. A., Zinger, I., Hoge, R. D., Bonta, J., Gendreau, R., & Cullen, F. T. (1990). Does correctional treatment work? A clinically relevant and psychologically informed meta-analysis. *Criminology, 28,* 369–404.

*Annis, H. M. (1979). Group treatment of incarcerated offenders with alcohol and drug problems: A controlled evaluation. *Canadian Journal of Criminology, 21,* 3–15.

*Aubertin, N., & Laporte, P. R. (1999). Contrecoups: A program of therapy for spousal and family violence. *Forum on Corrections Research, 11*(1), 3–5.

*Aytes, K. E., Olsen, S. S., Zakrajsek, T., Murray, P., & Ireson, R. (2001). Cognitive/behavioral treatment for sexual offenders: An examination of recidivism. *Sexual Abuse: A Journal of Research and Treatment, 13,* 223–231.

*Babcock, J. C., & Steiner, R. (1999). The relationship between treatment, incarceration, and recidivism of battering: A program evaluation of Seattle's coordinated community response to domestic violence. *Journal of Family Psychology, 13,* 46–59.

*Bahn, C., & Davis, J. F. (1997). An alternative to incarceration: The Fortune Society of New York. *Journal of Offender Rehabilitation, 24*(3–4), 163–181.

*Banks, D. C. (2001). The Baltimore city drug treatment court program; Drug court effect on time until rearrest (Doctoral dissertation, University of Maryland, 2001). *Dissertation Abstracts International, 62,* 4341.

*Barnes, J. M. (2001). Recidivism in sex offenders: A follow-up comparison of treated and untreated sex offenders released to the community in Kentucky (Doctoral dissertation, University of Louisville, 2001). *Dissertation Abstracts International, 62,* 535.

*Baro, A. L. (1999). Effects of a cognitive restructuring program on inmate institutional behavior. *Criminal Justice and Behavior, 26,* 466–484.

*Bavon, A. (2001). The effect of the Tarrant County drug court project on recidivism. *Evaluation and Program Planning, 24,* 13–22.

Benware, C., & Deci, E. L. (1984). Quality of learning with an active versus passive motivational set. *American Educational Research Journal, 21,* 755–765.

*Bleick, C. R., & Abrams, A. I. (1987). The transcendental meditation program and criminal recidivism in California. *Journal of Criminal Justice, 15,* 211–230.

*Borduin, C. M., Henggeler, S. W., Blaske, D. M., & Stein, R. J. (1990). Multisystemic treatment of adolescent sexual offenders. *International Journal of Offender Therapy and Comparative Criminology, 34,* 105–113.

*Borduin, C. M., Mann, B. J., Cone, L. T., Henggeler, S. W., Fucci, B. R., Blaske, D. M., et al. (1995). Multisystemic treatment of serious juvenile offenders: Long-term prevention of criminality and violence. *Journal of Consulting and Clinical Psychology, 63,* 569–578.

*Bourgon, G., & Armstrong, B. (2005). Transferring the principles of effective treatment into a "real world" prison setting. *Criminal Justice and Behavior, 32,* 3–25.

*Brier, N. (1994). Targeted treatment for adjudicated youth with learning disabilities: Effects on recidivism. *Journal of Learning Disabilities, 27,* 215–222.

*Butzin, C. A., Martin, S. S., & Inciardi, J. A. (2002). Evaluating component effects of a prison-based treatment continuum. *Journal of Substance Abuse Treatment, 22,* 63–69.

*Caldwell, M. F., & Van Rybroek, G. J. (2001). Efficacy of a decompression treatment model in the clinical management of violent juvenile offenders. *International Journal of Offender Therapy and Comparative Criminology, 45,* 469–477.

Collins, J. J., & Allison, M. (1983). Legal coercion and retention in drug abuse treatment. *Hospital and Community Psychiatry, 34,* 1145–1149.

Day, A., Tucker, K., & Howells, K. (2004). Coerced offender rehabilitation: A defensible practice? *Psychology, Crime & Law, 10,* 259–269.

Deci, E. L., & Ryan, R. M. (1991). A motivational approach to self: Integration in personality. In R. Dienstbier (Ed.), *Nebraska symposium on motivation. Vol. 38: Perspectives on motivation* (pp. 237–288). Lincoln: University of Nebraska Press.

Deci, E. L., Schwartz, A. J., Sheinman, L., & Ryan, R. M. (1981). An instrument to assess adults' orientations toward control versus autonomy with children. *Journal of Educational Psychology, 73,* 642–650.

*Dembo, R., Ramirez-Garnica, G., Schmeidler, J., Rollie, M., Livingston, S., & Hartsfield, A. (2001). Long-term impact of a family empowerment intervention on juvenile offender recidivism. *Journal of Offender Rehabilitation, 33*(1), 33–57.

*Deng, X. (1997). The deterrent effects of initial sanction on first-time apprehended shoplifters. *International Journal of Offender Therapy and Comparative Criminology, 41,* 284–297.

*Deschenes, E. P., & Greenwood, P. W. (1998). Alternative placements for juvenile offenders: Results from the evaluation of the Nokomis Challenge Program. *Journal of Research in Crime and Delinquency, 35,* 1–36.

*Donovan, D. M., Salzberg, P. M., Chaney, E. F., Queisser, H. R., & Marlatt, G. A. (1990). Prevention skills for alcohol-involved drivers. *Alcohol, Drugs and Driving, 6,* 169–187.

Dowden, C., Antonowicz, D., & Andrews, D. A. (2003). The effectiveness of relapse prevention with offenders; A meta-analysis. *International Journal of Offender Therapy and Comparative Criminology, 47,* 516–528.

*Dugan. J. R., & Everett, R. S. (1998). An experimental test of chemical dependency therapy for jail inmates. *International Journal of Offender Therapy and Comparative Criminology, 42,* 360–368.

*Dutton. D. G. (1986). The outcome of court-mandated treatment for wife assault: A quasi-experimental evaluation. *Violence and Victims, 1,* 163–175.

*Dwyer, S. M. (1997). Treatment outcome study: Seventeen years after sexual offender treatment. *Sexual Abuse: A Journal of Research and Treatment, 9,* 149–160.

*Eddy, J. M., Whaley, R. B., & Chamberlain, P. (2004). The prevention of violent behavior by chronic and serious male juvenile offenders: A 2-year follow-up study of a randomized clinical trial. *Journal of Emotional and Behavioral Disorders, 12,* 2–8.

*Employment research project. Volume I: Unemployment, crime and vocational counseling. (1980). *The Prison Journal, 60,* 7–64.

Farabee, D., Prendergast, M. L., & Anglin, M. D. (1998). The effectiveness of coerced treatment for drug-abusing offenders. *Federal Probation, 62(1),* 3–10.

Farabee, D., Shen, H., & Sanchez, S. (2002). Perceived coercion and treatment need among mentally ill parolees. *Criminal Justice and Behavior, 29,* 76–86.

*Feder, L., & Horde, D. R. (2000). *A test of the efficacy of court-mandated counseling for domestic violence offenders: The Broward experiment* (NCJ 184752). Rockville, MD: National Institute of Justice.

*Federoff, P. J., Wisner-Carlson, R., Dean, S., & Berlin, F. S. (1992). Medroxy-progesterone acetate in the treatment of paraphilic sexual disorders: Rate of relapse in paraphilic men treated in long-term group psychotherapy with or without medroxy-progesterone acetate. *Journal of Offender Rehabilitation, 19*(3–4), 109–123.

Field, A. P. (2001). Meta-analysis of correlation coefficients: A Monte Carlo comparison of fixed- and random-effects methods. *Psychological Methods, 6,* 161–180.

*Field, G. (1992). Oregon prison drug treatment programs. *NIDA Research Monograph, 18,* 142–155.

*Fielding, J. E., Tye, G., Ogawa, P. L., Imam, I. J., & Long, A. M. (2002). Los Angeles County drug court programs: Initial results. *Journal of Substance Abuse Treatment, 23,* 217–224.

*Friendship, C., Blud, L., Erikson, M., Travers, R., & Thornton, D. (2003). Cognitive-behavioral treatment for imprisoned offenders: An evaluation of HM Prison Service's cognitive skills programmes. *Legal and Criminological Psychology, 8,* 103–114.

*Friendship, C., Mann, R. E., & Beech, A. R. (2003). Evaluation of a national prison-based treatment program for sexual offenders in England and Wales. *Journal of Interpersonal Violence, 18,* 744–759.

Gendreau, P., & Smith, P. (2007). Influencing the "people who count": Some perspectives on the reporting of meta-analytic results for prediction and treatment outcomes with offenders. *Criminal Justice and Behavior, 34,* 1536–1559.

*Goldkamp, J. S. (1994). Miami's treatment drug court for felony defendants: Some implications of assessment findings. *The Prison Journal, 73,* 110–166.

*Gordon, J. A. (1996). An evaluation of Paint Creek Youth Center (Doctoral dissertation, University of Cincinnati, 1996). *Dissertation Abstracts International, 57,* 4549.

Gray, G. A. (1998). Does coercion play a significant role in community treatment programs that reduce offender recidivism? (Doctoral dissertation. University of New Brunswick, 1998). *Dissertation Abstracts International, 37,* 1035.

*Griffith, I. L. (1999). Prison-based substance abuse treatment, residential aftercare, and risk classification: A cost-effectiveness analysis (Doctoral dissertation, Texas Christian University, 1999). *Dissertation Abstracts International, 60,* 5773.

Grolnick, W. S., & Ryan, R. M. (1987). Autonomy in children's learning: An experimental and individual difference investigation. *Journal of Personality and Social Psychology, 52,* 890–898.

*Hagan, M. P., Cho, M. E., Jensen, J. A., & King, R. P. (1997). An assessment of the effectiveness of an intensive treatment program for severely mentally disturbed juvenile offenders. *International Journal of Offender Therapy and Comparative Criminology, 41,* 340–350.

*Hall, E. A., Prendergast, M. L., Wellisch, J., Patten, M., & Cao, Y. (2004). Treating drug-abusing women prisoners: An outcomes evaluation of the Forever Free program. *The Prison Journal, 84,* 81–105.

Hall, W. (1997). The role of legal coercion in the treatment of offenders with .alcohol and heroin problems. *Australian and New Zealand Journal of Criminology, 30,* 103–120.

Harford, R. J., Ungerer, J. C., & Kinsella, J. K. (1976). Effects of legal pressure on prognosis for treatment of drug dependence. *American Journal of Psychiatry, 133,* 1399–1404.

*Henggeler, S. W., Clingempel, G. W., Brondino, M. J., & Pickrel, S. G. (2002). Four-year follow-up of multisystematic therapy with substance-abusing and substance-dependent juvenile offenders. *Journal of the American Academy of Child & Adolescent Psychiatry, 41,* 868–874.

*Henggeler, S. W., Melton, G. B., & Smith, L. A. (1992). Family preservation using multisystemic therapy: An effective alternative to incarcerating serious juvenile offenders. *Journal of Consulting and Clinical Psychology, 60,* 953–961.

*Henning, K. R., & Frueh, B. C. (1996). Cognitive-behavioral treatment of incarcerated offenders: An evaluation of the Vermont Department of Corrections' cognitive self-change program. *Criminal Justice and Behavior, 23,* 523–541.

*Hiller, M. L., Knight, K., Devereux, J., & Hathcoat, M. (1996). Posttreatment outcomes for substance-abusing probationers mandated to residential treatment. *Journal of Psychoactive Drugs, 28,* 291–296.

* Hiller, M. L., Knight, K., & Simpson, D. D. (1999). Prison-based substance abuse treatment, residential aftercare, and recidivism. *Addiction, 94,* 833–842.

Hollin, C. R. (1999). Treatment programs for offenders: Meta-analysis, "what works," and beyond. *International Journal of Law and Psychiatry, 22,* 361–372.

Holzworth-Munroe, A. (2001). Standards for batterer treatment programs: How can research inform our decisions? *Journal of Aggression, Maltreatment and Trauma, 5*(2), 165–180.

Howard, D. L., & McCaughrin, W. C. (1996). The treatment effectiveness of outpatient substance misuse treatment organizations between court-mandated and voluntary clients. *Substance Use & Misuse, 31,* 895–926.

*Howitt, P. S., & Moore, E. A. (1991). The efficacy of intensive early intervention an evaluation of the Oakland County probate court early offender program. *Juvenile and Family Court Journal, 42*(3), 25–36.

Hunter, J. E., & Schmidt, F. L. (2004). *Methods of meta-analysis: Correcting error and bias in research findings* (2nd ed.). Thousand Oaks, CA: Sage.

*Inciardi, J. M., Martin, S. S., & Butzin, C. A. (2004). Five-year outcomes of therapeutic community treatment of drug-involved offenders after release from prison. *Crime & Delinquency, 50,* 55–107.

*Inciardi, J. A., Martin, S. S., Butzin, C. A., Hooper, R. M., & Harrison, L. D. (1997). An effective model of prison-based treatment for drug-involved offenders. *Journal of Drug Issues, 27,* 261–278.

*lnciardi, J. A., Martin, S. S., & Surrat, H. L. (2001). Therapeutic communities in prisons and work release: Effective modalities for drug-involved offenders. In B. Rawlings & R. Yates (Eds.), *Therapeutic communities for the treatment of drug users* (pp. 241–256). London: Jessica Kingsley.

*Josi, D. A., & Sechrest, D. K. (1999). A pragmatic approach to parole aftercare: Evaluation of a community reintegration program for high-risk youthful offenders. *Justice Quarterly, 16,* 52–79.

*Kempinen, C. A., & Kurlychek, M. C. (2003). An outcome evaluation of Pennsylvania's boot camp: Does rehabilitative programming within a disciplinary setting reduce recidivism? *Crime & Delinquency, 49,* 581–602.

Klag, S., O'Callaghan, F., & Creed, P. (2005). The use of legal coercion in the treatment of substance abusers: An overview and critical analysis of thirty years of research. *Substance Use & Misuse, 40,* 1777–1795.

*Knight, K., Hiller, M. L., Simpson, D. D., & Broome, K. M. (1998). The validity of self-reported cocaine use in a criminal justice treatment sample. *American Journal of Drug and Alcohol Abuse, 24,* 647–660.

*Knight, K., Simpson, D. D., Chatham, L. R., & Camacho, L. M. (1997). An assessment of prison-based drug treatment: Texas' in-prison therapeutic community program. *Journal of Offender Rehabilitation, 24*(3–4), 75–100.

*Knight, K., Simpson, D. D., & Hiller, M. L. (1999). Three-year reincarceration outcomes for in-prison therapeutic community treatment in Texas. *The Prison Journal, 79,* 337–351.

*Lab, S. R., Shields, G., & Schondel, C. (1993). Research note: An evaluation of juvenile sexual offender treatment. *Crime & Delinquency, 39,* 543–553.

*Langworthy, R. H., & Latessa, E. J. (1993). Treatment of chronic drunk drivers: The Turning Point project. *Journal of Criminal Justice, 21,* 265–276.

*Langworthy, R. H., & Latessa, E. J. (1996). Treatment of chronic drunk drivers: A four-year follow-up of the Turning Point project. *Journal of Criminal Justice, 24,* 273–281.

*Latessa, E. J., & Travis, L. R. III. (1988). The effects of intensive supervision with alcoholic probationers. *Journal of Offender Counseling, Services and Rehabilitation, 12*(2), 175–190.

*Lattimore, P. K., Witte, A. D., & Baker, J. R. (1990). Experimental assessment of the effect of vocational training on youthful property offenders. *Evaluation Review, 14,* 115–133.

*Leeman, L. W., Gibbs, J. C. & Fuller, D. (1993). Evaluation of a multi component group treatment program for juvenile delinquents. *Aggressive Behavior, 19,* 281–292.

*Leiber, M. J., & Mawhorr, T. L. (1995). Evaluating the use of social skills training and employment with delinquent youth. *Journal of Criminal Justice, 23,* 127–141.

*Leschied, A. W., & Cunningham, A. (2000). Intensive community-based services can influence re-offending rates of high-risk youth: Preliminary results of the multisystemic therapy clinical trials in Ontario. *Empirical and Applied Criminal Justice Research, 1,* 1–27.

*Leve, L. D., Chamberlain, P., & Reid, J. B. (2005). Intervention outcomes for girls referred from juvenile justice: Effects on delinquency. *Journal of Consulting and Clinical Psychology, 73,* 1181–1185.

*Lewis, R. V. (1983). Scared straight-California style: Evaluation of the San Quentin Squires Program. *Criminal Justice and Behavior, 10,* 209–226.

*Liau, A. K., Shively, R., Horn, M., Landau. J., Barriga, A., & Gibbs, J. C. (2004). Effects of psychoeducation for offenders in a community correctional facility. *Journal of Community Psychology, 32,* 543–558.

*Lindforss, L., & Magnusson, D. (1997). Solution-focused therapy in prison. *Contemporary Family Therapy, 19,* 89–103.

Lipsey, M. W. (1999). Can rehabilitative programs reduce the recidivism of juvenile offenders? An inquiry into the effectiveness of practical programs. *Virginia Journal of Social Policy & the Law, 6,* 611–641.

Lipsey, M. W., Chapman, G. L., & Landenberger, N. A. (2001). Cognitive-behavioral programs for offenders. *Annals of the American Academy of Political and Social Science, 578,* 144–157.

*Looman, J., Abracen, J., & Nicholaichuk, T. P. (2000). Recidivism among treated sexual offenders and matched controls: Data from the Regional Treatment Centre (Ontario). *Journal of Interpersonal Violence, 15,* 279–290.

Lösel, F. (1995). The efficacy of correctional treatment: A review and synthesis of meta-evaluations. In J. McGuire (Ed.), *What works: Reducing reoffending—Guidelines from research and practice* (pp. 79–111). New York: John Wiley.

*Lucker, G. W., & Osti, J. R. (1997). Reduced recidivism among first-time DWI offenders as a correlate of pre-trial intervention. *Journal of Offender Rehabilitation, 24*(3–4), 1–17.

*Mackenzie, D. L., & Shaw, J. W. (1993). The impact of shock incarceration on technical violations and new criminal activities. *Justice Quarterly, 10,* 463–487.

*Mander, A. M., Atrops, M. E., Barnes, A. R., & Munafo, R. (1996). *Sex offender treatment program; Initial recidivism study.* Anchorage: Alaska Department of Corrections and Alaska Justice Statistical Analysis Unit.

*Marques, J. K., Day, D. M., Nelson, C., & West, M. A. (1994). Effects of cognitive-behavioral treatment on sex offender recidivism. *Criminal Justice and Behavior, 21,* 28–54.

*Marques, J. K., & Nelson, C. (1992). The relapse prevention model: Can it work with sex offenders? In R. D. Peters, R. J. McMahon, & V. L. Quinsey (Eds.), *Aggression and violence throughout the life span* (pp. 222–243). Thousand Oaks, CA: Sage.

*Marques, J. K., Nelson, C., West, M. A., & Day, D. M. (1994). The relationship between treatment goals and recidivism among child molesters. *Behaviour Research and Therapy, 32,* 577–588.

*Marshall, W. L., & Barbaree, H. E. (1988). The long-term evaluation of a behavioural treatment program for child molesters. *Behaviour and Research Therapy, 26,* 499–511.

*Marshall, W. L., Eccles, A., & Barbaree, H. B. (1991). The treatment of exhibitionists: A focus on sexual deviance versus cognitive and relationship features. *Behaviour and Research Therapy, 29,* 129–135.

*Martin, S. S., Butzin, C. A., Saum, C. A., & Inciardi, J. A. (1999). Three-year outcomes of therapeutic community treatment for drug-involved offenders in Delaware: From prison to work release to aftercare. *The Prison Journal, 79,* 294–320.

Maxwell, S. R. (2000). Sanction threats in court-ordered programs: Examining their effects on offenders mandated into drug treatment. *Crime & Delinquency, 46,* 542–563.

*McCarty, D., & Argeriou, M. (1986). Rearrest following residential treatment for repeat offender drunken drivers. *Journal of Studies on Alcohol, 49,* 1–7.

*McCollister, K. E., French, M. T, Prendergast, M., Wexler, H., Stacks, S., & Hall, E. (2003). Is in-prison treatment enough? A cost-effectiveness analysis of prison-based treatment and aftercare services for substance-abusing offenders. *Law & Policy, 25,* 63–82.

McGuire, J. (2002). Integrating findings from research reviews. In J. McGuire (Ed.), *Offender rehabilitation and treatment: Effective programmes and policies to reduce re-offending* (pp. 3–38). Chichester, UK: Wiley.

McGuire, J. (2004). Commentary: Promising answers, and the next generation of questions. *Psychology, Crime & Law, 10,* 335–345.

McMurran, M. (Ed.). (2002). *Motivating offenders to change: A guide to enhancing engagement in therapy.* Chichester, UK: Wiley.

*Meyer, W. J., Cole, C., & Emory, E. (1992). Depo provera treatment for sex offending behavior; An evaluation of outcome. *Bulletin of the American Academy of Psychiatry and the Law, 20,* 249–259.

*Miller, L. C. (1970). Southfields: Evaluation of a short-term inpatient treatment center for delinquents. *Crime &. Delinquency, 16,* 305–316.

*Miner, M. H., Marques, J. K., Day, D. M., & Nelson, C. (1990). Impact of relapse prevention in treating sex offenders: Preliminary findings. *Annals of Sex Research, 3,* 165–185.

*Moody, E. E. (1997). Lessons from pair counseling with incarcerated juvenile delinquents. *Journal of Addictions and Offender Counseling, 18,* 10–24.

*Moon, M. M., & Latessa, E. J. (1994). Drug treatment in adult probation: An evaluation of an outpatient and acupuncture program. *Evaluation and Program Planning, 17,* 217–226.

*Myers, W. C., Burton, P. R., Sanders, P. D., Donat, K. M., Cheney, J., Fitzpatrick, T. M., et al. (2000). Project back-on-track at 1 year: A delinquency treatment program for early-career juvenile offenders. *Journal of the American Academy of Child and Adolescent Psychiatry, 39,* 1127–1134.

*Nicholaichuck, T., Gordon, A., Gu, D., & Wong, S. (2000). Outcome of an institutional sexual offender treatment program: A comparison between treated and matched untreated offenders. *Sexual Abuse: A Journal of Research and Treatment, 12,* 139–153.

*Nielson, A. L., Scarpitti, F. R., & Inciardi, J. A. (1996). Integrating the therapeutic community and work release for drug-involved offenders. *Journal of Substance Abuse Treatment, 13,* 349–358.

*Niemeyer, M., & Shichor, D. (1996). A preliminary study of a large victim/offender reconciliation program. *Federal Probation, 60*(3), 30–38.

*Palmer, S. E., Brown, R. A., & Barrera, M. E. (1992). Group treatment program for abusive husbands: Long-term evaluation. *American Journal of Orthopsychiatry, 62,* 276–283.

*Pealer, J. A. (2004). A community of peers: Promoting behaviour change. The effectiveness of a therapeutic community for juvenile male offenders in reducing recidivism (Doctoral dissertation, University of Cincinnati, 2004). *Dissertation Abstracts International, 65,* 3580.

Pearson, F. S., & Lipton, D. S. (1999). A meta-analytic review of the effectiveness of corrections-based treatments for drug abuse. *The Prison Journal, 79,* 384–410.

*Pelissier, B., Rhodes, W., Saylor, W., Gaes, G., Camp, S. D., Vanyur, S. D., et al. (2000). *TRIAD Drug Treatment Evaluation Project. Final report of three-year outcomes: Part I.* Washington, DC: Federal Bureau of Prisons, Office of Research and Evaluation.

*Pelissier, B., Rhodes, W., Saylor, W., Gaes, G., Camp, S. D., Vanyur, S. D., et al. (2001). Triad drug treatment evaluation project. *Federal Probation, 65*(3), 3–7.

*Pelissier, B., Wallace, S., O'Neil, J. A., Gaes, G. G., Camp, S., Rhodes, W., et al. (2001). Federal prison residential drug treatment reduces substance use and arrests after release. *American Journal of Drug and Alcohol Abuse, 27,* 315–337.

*Pelissier, M. M., Camp, S. D., Gaes, G. G., Saylor, W. G., & Rhodes, W. (2003). Gender differences in outcomes from prison-based residential treatment. *Journal of Substance Abuse Treatment, 24,* 149–160.

*Peters, R. H., & Murrin, M. R. (2000). Effectiveness of treatment-based drug courts in reducing criminal recidivism. *Criminal Justice and Behavior, 27,* 72–96.

*Phillips, M. T., Tejaratchi, A., & Nehwadowich, W. (2002). *Estimating jail displacement for alternative-to-incarceration programs in New York City.* New York: New York City Criminal Justice Agency.

*Polaschek, D. L. L., Wilson, N. J., Townsend, M. R., & Daly, L. R. (2005). Cognitive-behavioural rehabilitation for high-risk violent offenders: An outcome evaluation of the violence prevention unit. *Journal of Interpersonal Violence, 20,* 1611–1627.

Polcin, D. L. (1999). Criminal justice coercion in the treatment of alcohol problems: An examination of two client subgroups. *Journal of Psychoactive Drugs, 31,* 137–143.

Polcin, D. L., & Greenfield, T. K. (2003). Factors associated with probation officers' use of criminal justice coercion to mandate alcohol treatment. *American Journal of Drug and Alcohol Abuse, 29,* 647–670.

Polcin, D. L., & Weisner, C. (1999). Factors associated with coercion in entering treatment for alcohol problems. *Drug and Alcohol Dependence, 54,* 63–68.

*Porporino, F. J., Robinson, D., Millson, B., & Weekes, J. R. (2002). An outcome evaluation of prison-based treatment programming for substance users. *Substance Use & Misuse, 37,* 1047–1077.

*Prendergast, M. L., Farabee, D., Cartier, J., & Henkin, S. (2002). Involuntary treatment within a prison setting; Impact on psychosocial change during treatment. *Criminal Justice and Behavior, 29,* 5–26.

*Prendergast, M., Hall, E., & Wellisch, J. (2002). *An outcome evaluation of the Forever Free substance abuse treatment program; One-year post-release outcomes* (NCJ 199685). Rockville, MD: National Institute of Justice.

*Prendergast, M., Hall, E., & Wexler, H. (2003). Multiple measures of outcome in assessing a prison-based drug treatment program. *Journal of Offender Rehabilitation, 37*(3–4), 65–94.

*Prendergast, M., Hall, E., Wexler, H., Melnick, G., & Cao, Y. (2004). Amity prison-based therapeutic community: Five-year outcomes. *The Prison Journal, 84,* 36–60.

Principles of drug addiction treatment: A research-based guide. (2000). *Spectrum: The Journal of State Government, 73*(2), 16–69.

*Quinsey, V. L., Khanna, A., & Malcolm, P. B. (1998). A retrospective evaluation of the regional treatment centre sex offender treatment program. *Journal of Interpersonal Violence, 13,* 621–644.

*Rainforth, M. V., Alexander, C. N., & Cavanaugh, K. L. (2003). Effects of the transcendental meditation program on recidivism among former inmates of Folsom Prison: Survival analysis of 15-year follow-up data. *Journal of Offender Rehabilitation, 36*(1–4), 181–203.

Rempel, M., & Destefano, C. D. (2001). Predictors of engagement in court-mandated treatment: Findings at the Brooklyn Treatment Court. 1996-2000. *Journal of Offender Rehabilitation, 33*(4), 87–124.

*Rice, M. E., Harris, G. T., & Cormier, C. A. (1992). An evaluation of a maximum security therapeutic community for psychopaths and other mentally disordered offenders. *Law and Human Behavior, 16,* 399–412.

*Robinson, D. (1995). *The impact of cognitive skills training on post-release recidivism among Canadian federal offenders* (Research Report No. R-41). Ottawa, Ontario: Correctional Service of Canada.

Rosenbaum, A., & Geffner, R. A. (2002). Future directions in mandated standards for domestic violence offenders. *Journal of Aggression, Maltreatment and Trauma, 5*(2), 287–293.

Rosenberg, C. M., & Liftik, J. (1976). Use of coercion in the outpatient treatment of alcoholism. *Journal of Studies on Alcohol, 37,* 58–65.

Rosenfeld, B. D. (1992). Court-ordered treatment of spouse abuse. *Clinical Psychology Review, 12,* 205–226.

Rosenthal, R., & DiMatteo, M. R. (2001). Meta-analysis: Recent developments in quantitative methods for literature reviews. *Annual Review of Psychology, 52,* 59–82.

*Ross, R. R., Fabiano, E. A., & Ewles, C. D. (1988). Reasoning and rehabilitation. *International Journal of Offender Therapy and Comparative Criminology, 32*(1), 29–35.

Ryan, R. M, & Deci, E. L. (2000). The darker and brighter sides of human existence: Basic psychological needs as a unifying concept. *Psychological Inquiry, 11,* 319–338.

*Sacks, S., Sacks, J., McKendrick, K., Banks, S., & Siommel, J. (2004). Modified therapeutic community for MICA offenders: Crime outcomes. *Behavioral Sciences & the Law, 22,* 477–501.

Schnoll, S. H., Goldstein, M. R., Antes, D. E., & Rinella, V. C. (1980). The impact of legal involvement on substance abusers in a residential treatment setting. *Corrective and Social Psychiatry and Journal of Behavior Technology. Methods and Therapy, 26,* 21–28.

*Sealock, M. D., Gottfredson, D. C., & Gallagher, C. A. (1997). Drug treatment for juvenile offenders: Some good and bad news. *Journal of Research in Crime and Delinquency, 34,* 210–236.

Seddon, T. (2007). Coerced drug treatment in the criminal justice system: Conceptual, ethical and criminological issues. *Criminology & Criminal Justice, 7,* 269–286.

Shearer, R. A., & Baletka, D. M. (1999). Counseling substance abusing offenders: Issues and strategies. *Texas Counseling Association Journal, 27*(2), 71–77.

Shearer, R. A., & Ogan, G. D. (2002). Voluntary participation and treatment resistance in substance abuse treatment programs. *Journal of Offender Rehabilitation, 34*(3), 31–45.

Siddall, J. W., & Conway, G. L. (1988). Interactional variables associated with retention and success in residential drug treatment. *International Journal of the Addictions, 23,* 1241–1254.

*Simons, R. L., Whitbeck, L. B., & Bales, A. (1989). Life on the streets: Victimization and psychological distress among the adult homeless. *Journal of Interpersonal Violence, 4,* 482–501.

*Spohn, C., Piper, R. K., Martin, T., & Frenzel, E. D. (2001). Drug courts and recidivism: The results of an evaluation using two comparison groups and multiple indicators of recidivism. *Journal of Drug Issues, 31,* 149–176.

*Sung, H. (2003). Differential impact of deterrence vs. rehabilitation as drug interventions on recidivism after 36 months. *Journal of Offender Rehabilitation, 57*(3–4), 95–108.

*Taylor, B. G., Davis, R. C., & Maxwell, C. D. (2001). The effects of a group batterer treatment program: A randomized experiment in Brooklyn. *Justice Quarterly, 18,* 171–201.

*Thanner, M. H., & Taxman, F. S. (2003). Responsivity: The value of providing intensive services to high-risk offenders. *Journal of Substance Abuse Treatment, 24,* 137–147.

*Trulson, C., Triplett, R., & Snell, C. (2001). Social control in a school setting: Evaluating a school-based boot camp. *Crime & Delinquency, 47,* 573–609.

*Turley, A., Thornton, T., Johnson, C., & Azzolino, S. (2004). Jail drug and alcohol treatment program reduces recidivism in nonviolent offenders: A longitudinal study of Monroe County, New York's, jail treatment drug and alcohol program. *International Journal of Offender Therapy and Comparative Criminology, 48,* 721–728.

*Turner, B. W., Bingham, J. E., & Andrasik, F. (2000). Short-term community-based treatment for sexual offenders: Enhancing effectiveness. *Sexual Addiction & Compulsivity, 7,* 211–223.

*Van Stelle, K. R., & Moberg, D. P. (2000). *Outcome evaluation of the Wisconsin residential substance abuse treatment program: The Mental Illness-Chemical Abuse (MICA) Program at Oshkosh Correctional Institution.* Madison: University of Wisconsin Medical School.

*Van Voorhis, P., Spruance, L. M., Ritchey, P. N., Johnson Listwan, S., & Seabrook, R. (2004). The Georgia cognitive skills experiment: A replication of reasoning and rehabilitation. *Criminal Justice and Behavior, 31,* 282–305.

*Vaughn, M. S., Deng, F., & Lee, L. (2003). Evaluating a prison-based drug treatment program in Taiwan. *Journal of Drug Issues, 33,* 357–384.

*Vigilante, K. C., Flynn, M. M., Affleck, P. C., Stunkle, J. C., Merriman, N. A., Flanigan, T. P., et al. (1999). Reduction of recidivism of incarcerated women through primary care, peer counseling, and discharge planning. *Journal of Women's Health, 8,* 409–415.

*Vito, G. F. (1989). The Kentucky Substance Abuse Program: A private program to treat probationers and parolees. *Federal Probation, 53*(1), 65–73.

*Vito, G. F., & Tewksbury, R. A. (1998). The impact of treatment: The Jefferson County (Kentucky) drug court program. *Federal Probation, 62*(2), 46–51.

*Waldo, M. (1988). Relationship enhancement counseling groups for wife abusers. *Journal of Mental Health Counseling, 10,* 37–45.

*Walters, G. D. (1999). Short-term outcome of inmates participating in the lifestyle change program. *Criminal Justice and Behavior, 26,* 322–337.

Wells-Parker, E. (1994). Mandated treatment: Lessons from research with drinking and driving offenders. *Alcohol Health and Research World, 18,* 302–306.

*Wexler, H. K., De Leon, G., Thomas, G., Kressel, D., & Peters, J. (1999). The Amity Prison TC evaluation: Reincarceration outcomes. *Criminal Justice and Behavior, 26,* 147–167.

*Wexler, H. K., Falkin, G. P., & Lipton, D. S. (1990). Outcome evaluation of a prison therapeutic community for substance abuse treatment. *Criminal Justice and Behavior, 17,* 71–92.

*Wexler, H. K., Melnick, G., Lowe, L., & Peters, J. (1999). Three-year reincarceration outcomes for Amity in-prison therapeutic community and aftercare in California. *The Prison Journal, 79,* 321–336.

Wild, T. C. (1999). Compulsory substance-user treatment and harm reduction: A critical analysis. *Substance Use & Misuse, 34,* 83–102.

Wild, T. C., Newton-Taylor, B., Ogborne, A. C., Mann, R., Erickson, P., & Macdonald, S. (2001). Attitudes toward compulsory substance abuse treatment: A comparison of the public, counselors, probationers and judges' views. *Drugs: Education, Prevention & Policy, 8,* 33–45.

*Wille, R., & Beier, K. M. (1989). Castration in Germany. *Annals of Sex Research, 2,* 103–133.

*Worling, J. R., & Curwen. T. (2000). Adolescent sexual offender recidivism: Success of specialized treatment and implications for risk prediction. *Child Abuse & Neglect, 24,* 965–982.

*Wormith, J. S. (1984). Attitude and behavior change of correctional clientele: A three year follow-up. *Criminology, 22,* 595–618.

*Young, D., Fluellen, R., & Belenko, S. (2004). Criminal recidivism in three models of mandatory drug treatment. *Journal of Substance Abuse Treatment, 27,* 313–323.

*Zimring, F. E. (1977). Determinants of the death rate from robbery: A Detroit time study. *Journal of Legal Studies, 6,* 317–332.

DISCUSSION QUESTIONS

1. Why is it important to understand the relative level of coerciveness toward offenders to participate in treatment programming?

2. How does the concept of coercion potentially influence the level of responsivity of an offender placed in a treatment program?

3. Given the findings of the study, what are some of the policy implications for coercive treatment in a custodial/confined setting?

4. How might an agency respond differently for treatment referrals given the type of setting? What potential implications do these findings have for aftercare programs?

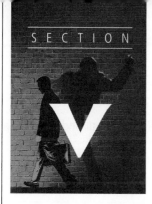

SECTION

V

Assessment and Risk Prediction

Learning Objectives

1. Understand the importance of the presentence investigation report (PSI) and why accurate information is critical to later supervision and treatment needs of the offender.
2. Understand basic concepts inherent to assessment.
3. Know a **false positive, false negative, true positive,** and **true negative**.
4. Understand the difference between **static risk factors** and **dynamic risk factors**.
5. Identify subjective and objective means of assessment and risk prediction.
6. Be familiar with the **Wisconsin risk assessment system** and the flaws associated with that instrument.

(Continued)

(Continued)

7. Be familiar with the **Level of Service Inventory–Revised (LSI-R)**, and understand the strengths associated with that instrument.

8. Understand the reasons why the MMPI-2 Criminal Justice and Correctional Report is presented as a premier instrument.

Because of concerns with public safety, it is imperative that correctional agencies be as adept as possible at accurately assessing the future prognosis of any offender under its supervision. For purposes of this text, the term **prognosis** refers to the likelihood that an offender will successfully reform and to simultaneously refrain from further criminal activity. Thus, there is both a treatment component (reform) and a public safety (likelihood of further criminal activity) component contained within an offender's prognosis. Both must be considered simultaneously if the correctional agency is to fulfill its mission in a satisfactory manner.

The Presentence Investigation Report

Intake is the process that occurs when the offender is initially entered into the correctional system post conviction. This process is heavily tied to information obtained from the PSI that the probation department will provide to the presiding judge of an offender's case. The PSI includes a wide range of background information on the offender, such as demographics and vocational, educational, and personal information on the offender as well as records on their prior offending patterns and the probation department's recommendation as to the appropriate type of sentencing and supervision for the offender in question. In many respects, the PSI is the initial point of assessment, and it will often be utilized during assessment in the institutional setting or when the offender is officially placed under the jurisdiction of the probation department. The primary purpose of the PSI is to provide the court with the necessary information from which a sentencing decision can be derived. Likewise, the PSI tends to serve as a basic foundation for supervision and treatment planning throughout the future of the offender's sentence. It is quite often the case that this document will serve as a reference point for placing the offender in a variety of programs. Among other things, the PSI will contain information related to the character and behavior of the offender. This then means that the probation officer's impressions of the offender can greatly impact the outcome of the PSI. The federal probation system has set forth some clear and simplified guidelines for completing the PSI. These guidelines are as follows:

1. *Brevity:* Avoid repetition. For clarity and interest, use short sentences and paragraphs without risking the ability to acquire information that is required.

2. *Language:* It is important not to take the offender's statements out of context. Also, direct quoting of the offender should be used if such gives a clearer picture of the situation or context.

3. *Sources of information:* PSI reporting officers should verify the facts contained in their report from some other source than the offender. If unverified information is included, it should be clearly designated as being unverified. It is important to note that unverified information can and does cause

serious harm to the offender and also negatively impacts supervision and/or treatment programs in the future.

4. *Technical words and phrases:* The PSI reporting officer should use technical words and phrases only if they are commonly known among practitioners in the criminal justice and/or court system.

5. *Style and format:* The report should be kept as simple and direct as possible. Likewise, emotional appraisals and other such comments from the officer should not be included as content.

The PSI is conducted after a defendant is found guilty of a charge (whether by pleading or court finding) but prior to the point of sentencing. There are three primary reasons why this reported is conducted post-conviction rather than pre-conviction. First, if a conviction is not obtained, conducting a PSI becomes a waste of time and resources for the officer and the department. Second, the defendants' right to privacy may be compromised if a non-guilty verdict is reached. For some of the accused, the lengthy and intrusive process of collecting information for completing the PSI may result in loss of employment, loss of good standing in the community, and a loss of privacy. Finally, when completing the PSI, many states have rules of confidentiality when gathering privileged information for the PSI as well as regulations regarding the disclosure of that information once it has been included in the final report. However, the conversations between the probation officer and the defendant are not considered privileged, and such information may be subject to disclosure. This information along with a recommendation will aid the judge, who must ultimately fashion a sentence as well as any corollary obligations attached to that sentence.

The PSI is typically conducted through an interview with the offender; therefore, it is important that community supervision officers (CSOs) have good interviewing skills. Further, the CSO will often conduct interviews with family members, employers, and so forth to validate the information received by the offender. The written report should include the full police report related to the criminal incident, the defendant's version of the incident, the victim's input related to the offense, and a complete background on the offender. In being comprehensive, a report should contain certain bits of information that are germane to effective sentencing and offender placement. The typical PSI will also tend to have narrative components that are provided by the offender as well as others who are interviewed by the presentence investigator. When the conviction information is a matter of public record, probation officers may disclose this information to non-criminal justice agencies or other persons as long as this disclosure does not violate any agency regulations. As one might reasonably suspect, while in the course of their duty, probation officers may disclose an offender's information to criminal justice agencies on a need-to-know basis in most states. Courts will typically base their decision of disclosure on the type of crime that was committed as well as the probation officer's assessment of the offender's potential to harm other victims. Lastly, most states do allow the probation officer to provide information and/or records to the offender's victims, yet often these same records are not available to the general public. Figure 5.1 provides a good illustration of a typical PSI that may be submitted to a court prior to sentencing. This PSI form is very well structured and largely provides this information in a standardized format.

In *Williams v. New York* (337 U.S. 241), the U.S. Supreme Court upheld the confidentiality of the PSI. This is largely due to the perception of the court that the presentence investigator is a neutral and detached party with no real vested interest in the punishment of the offender. Indeed, the probation officer was considered to be a helping professional rather than one in league with prosecutorial efforts. Nevertheless, many states do allow defendants to view their PSI and have even passed regulations requiring that defendants be given the chance to review their PSI and to refute its contents before the sentence phase begins.

Figure 5.1 Presentence Investigation Report in the State of Kansas

2004 KANSAS SENTENCING GUIDELINES—PRESENTENCE INVESTIGATION REPORT
FACE SHEET

Judicial District: _____

County: _____

Case No: _____

Name: _____

A/K/A's: _____

D.O.B.: ___/___/___ **S.S.N. #:** _____

Age: _____ **K.B.L. No:** _____

Sex: ☐ Male ☐ Female **Race:** ☐ W ☐ B ☐ A.I. ☐ A

Ethnicity: ☐ Hispanic   ☐ Non-Hispanic

Address: _____
_____
_____

Citizenship: ☐ U.S. ☐ Citizen of: _____

DETAINER OR OTHER CHARGES PENDING? ☐YES ☐NO

SUBJECT IN CUSTODY AWAITING SENTENCING?
                              ☐ YES ☐ NO

begin _____ end _____

begin _____ end _____

IF OFFENDER WAS UNDER 18 YEARS OF AGE WHEN
CRIME(S) WAS COMMITTED AND WAS TRIED AS AN ADULT,
OFFENDER WAS:

☐ ADJUDICATED AS AN ADULT UNDER KSA 38-1636
☐ AUTOMATICALLY CONSIDERED AN ADULT
   BECAUSE OF A PRIOR FELONY

NAMES OF CO-DEFENDANTS, IF ANY _____
_____

NAME OF DEFENSE ATTORNEY: _____
_____

TYPE OF COUNSEL PRIOR TO SENTENCING:
☐ RETAINED ☐ APPOINTED ☐ SELF ☐ OTHER

NAME OF PROSECUTING ATTORNEY: _____
_____

NAME OF SENTENCING JUDGE: _____
_____

DATE OF GUILTY PLEA
OR JUDGMENT: ___/___/___

DATE OF SENTENCING: ___/___/___

NAME OF PRESENTENCE INVESTIGATOR:
_____

DATE ASSIGNED   ___/___/___

DATE SUBMITTED: ___/___/___

OFFENSES

NAME OF PRIMARY OFFENSE:
_____

K.S.A. No:_____ ☐ Felony ☐ Offgrid
                         ☐ Misd.   ☐ Nongrid

☐ Person   ☐ Drug   ☐ Attempt ☐ Conspiracy
☐ Nonperson ☐ Nondrug ☐ Solicitation

Severity Level: ___   **Criminal History Score:** ___

Sentencing Range:

Standard _____   ☐ Presumptive Prison

Aggravated _____   ☐ Presumptive Probation

Mitigated _____   ☐ Border Box

               ☐ Special Rule Applicable (see p. 4)

☐ Mandatory Drug Treatment ("SB 123")
☐ Drug Treatment with Court finding
☐ Not eligible for Drug Treatment due to criminal history

Postrelease Supervision Duration: ☐ 12 months ☐ 24 months
☐ 36 months ☐ 60 months ☐ No Postrelease - per K.S.A.
                                              22-3716 (e)

Probation Duration: ☐ 12 months   ☐ 18 months
☐ 24 months   ☐ 36 months   ☐ Other

NAME OF ADDITIONAL OFFENSE:
_____

K.S.A. No: _____ ☐ Felony   ☐ Offgrid
                              ☐ Misd.   ☐ Nongrid

☐ Person   ☐ Drug   ☐ Attempt ☐ Conspiracy
☐ Nonperson ☐ Nondrug ☐ Solicitation

Severity Level: _____ **Criminal History Score:** _____

Sentencing Range:

Standard _____   ☐ Presumptive Prison

Aggravated _____   ☐ Presumptive Probation

Mitigated _____   ☐ Border Box

               ☐ Special Rule Applicable (see p. 4)

☐ Mandatory Drug Treatment ("SB 123")
☐ Drug Treatment with Court finding
☐ Not eligible for Drug Treatment due to criminal history

Postrelease Supervision Duration: ☐ 12 months ☐ 24 months
☐ 36 months ☐ 60 months ☐ No Postrelease - per K.S.A. 22-3716 (e)

Probation Duration: ☐ 12 months   ☐ 18 months
☐ 24 months   ☐ 36 months   ☐ Other _____

Figure 5.1 (Continued)

2004 KANSAS SENTENCING GUIDELINES—PRESENTENCE INVESTIGATION REPORT
FACE SHEET SUPPLEMENTAL PAGE

NAME OF ADDITIONAL OFFENSE:

K.S.A. No: _____ ☐ Felony ☐ Offgrid
☐ Misd. ☐ Nongrid

☐ Person ☐ Drug ☐ Attempt ☐ Conspiracy
☐ Nonperson ☐ Nondrug ☐ Solicitation

Severity Level: _____ **Criminal History Score:** ___

Sentencing Range:

Standard _____ ☐ Presumptive Prison
Aggravated _____ ☐ Presumptive Probation
Mitigated _____ ☐ Border Box
☐ Special Rule Applicable (see p. 4)

☐ Mandatory Drug Treatment ("SB 123")
☐ Drug Treatment with Court finding
☐ Not eligible for Drug Treatment due to criminal history

Postrelease Supervision Duration: ☐ 12 months ☐ 24 months
☐ 36 months ☐ 60 months ☐ No Postrelease - per K.S.A.
22-3716 (e)

Probation Duration: ☐ 12 months ☐ 18 months
☐ 24 months ☐ 36 months ☐ Other

NAME OF ADDITIONAL OFFENSE:

K.S.A. No: _____ ☐ Felony ☐ Nongrid
☐ Misd. ☐ Offgrid

☐ Person ☐ Drug ☐ Attempt ☐ Conspiracy
☐ Nonperson ☐ Nondrug ☐ Solicitation

Severity Level: _____ **Criminal History Score:** ___

Sentencing Range:

Standard _____ ☐ Presumptive Prison
Aggravated _____ ☐ Presumptive Probation
Mitigated _____ ☐ Border Box
☐ Special Rule Applicable (see p. 4)

☐ Mandatory Drug Treatment ("SB 123")
☐ Drug Treatment with Court finding
☐ Not eligible for Drug Treatment due to criminal history

Postrelease Supervision Duration: ☐ 12 months ☐ 24 months
☐ 36 months ☐ 60 months ☐ No Postrelease - per K.S.A. 22-3716 (e)

Probation Duration: ☐ 12 months ☐ 18 months
☐ 24 months ☐ 36 months ☐ Other

NAME OF ADDITIONAL OFFENSE: _____

K.S A. No: _____ ☐ Felony ☐ Nongrid
☐ Misd. ☐ Offgrid

☐ Person ☐ Drug ☐ Attempt ☐ Conspiracy
☐ Nonperson ☐ Nondrug ☐ Solicitation

Severity Level: ____ **Criminal History Score:** ____

Sentencing Range:

Standard _____ ☐ Presumptive Prison
Aggravated _____ ☐ Presumptive Probation
Mitigated _____ ☐ Border Box
☐ Special Rule Applicable (see p. 4)

☐ Mandatory Drug Treatment ("SB 123")
☐ Drug Treatment with Court finding
☐ Not eligible for Drug Treatment due to criminal history

Postrelease Supervision Duration: ☐ 12 months ☐ 24 months
☐ 36 months ☐ 60 months ☐ No Postrelease - per K.S.A. 22-3716 (e)

Probation Duration: ☐ 12 months ☐ 18 months
☐ 24 months ☐ 36 months ☐ Other _____

NAME OF ADDITIONAL OFFENSE: _____

K.S A. No: _____ ☐ Felony ☐ Nongrid
☐ Misd. ☐ Offgrid

☐ Person ☐ Drug ☐ Attempt ☐ Conspiracy
☐ Nonperson ☐ Nondrug ☐ Solicitation

Severity Level: ____ **Criminal History Score:** ____

Sentencing Range:

Standard _____ ☐ Presumptive Prison
Aggravated _____ ☐ Presumptive Probation
Mitigated _____ ☐ Border Box
☐ Special Rule Applicable (see p. 4)

☐ Mandatory Drug Treatment ("SB 123")
☐ Drug Treatment with Court finding
☐ Not eligible for Drug Treatment due to criminal history

Postrelease Supervision Duration: ☐ 12 months ☐ 24 months
☐ 36 months ☐ 60 months ☐ No Postrelease - per K.S.A. 22-3716 (e)

Probation Duration: ☐ 12 months ☐ 18 months
☐ 24 months ☐ 36 months ☐ Other _____

KSG Desk Reference Manual 2004
Appendix D Page 2

(Continued)

Figure 5.1 (Continued)

KANSAS SENTENCING GUIDELINES—PRESENTENCE INVESTIGATION REPORT
CURRENT OFFENSE INFORMATION

OFFICIAL VERSION:

DEFENDANT'S VERSION:

VICTIM'S INJURY / DAMAGE / STATEMENT(S):

TOTAL RESTITUTION   _____

OWED TO   Name: _____
             Address: _____
                        _____
             Amount: _____

             Name: _____
             Address: _____
                        _____
             Amount: _____

             Name: _____
             Address: _____
                        _____
             Amount: _____

             Name: _____
             Address: _____
                        _____
             Amount: _____

             Name: _____
             Address: _____
                        _____
             Amount: _____

STATEMENT(S):

KSG Desk Reference Manual 2004
Appendix D Page 3

Figure 5.1 (Continued)

RECOMMENDED PLACEMENT: [The following is <u>not</u> a recommendation regarding the appropriate disposition to be imposed in this case, but is provided as the court services or community corrections officer's professional assessment if the court places the offender on probation or orders some form of community sanction.]

_____ COMMUNITY CORRECTIONS

_____ COURT SERVICES

_____ DEPARTMENT OF CORRECTIONS

[Indicate the criteria from K.S.A. 75-5291(a)(2) met by this defendant qualifying him/her for placement in Community Corrections.]

☐ Mandatory Drug Treatment ("SB 123")
☐ (a)(2)(A) Listed grid box (Border box, level 6 H or I, level 7 C-I)
☐ (a)(2)(B) Downward dispositional departure (presumptive prison)
☐ (a)(2)(C) Seventy level 7 or higher sex offender
☐ (a)(2)(D) Condition violator
☐ (a)(2)(E) Scored "high risk or needs, or both"
☐ (a)(2)(F) Follows successful completion of a conservation camp program

OFFICER'S ASSESSMENT OF CONDITIONS OF PROBATION:

K.S.A. 21-4610 and;   [Check All That Apply]
☐ (Alcohol) (Drug) (Mental Health) evaluation (follow recommendations)
☐ (In) (Out) Patient (Alcohol) (Drug) (Mental Health) treatment (Follow recommendations of counselor)
☐ (AA) (NA) Attendance
☐ No possession or consumption of alcohol or illegal drugs
☐ Submit to random (Breath) (Blood) (Urinalysis) testing at request of C.S.O. at defendant's own expense
☐ Community Service Work [_____ Hours]
☐ (Gain) (Maintain) employment
☐ Notify the C.S.O. of changes in employment, residence and phone number
☐ No contact with (victim) (co-defendant)
☐ Educational program - (G.E.D.) (Vocational) (Higher Education)
☐ Curfew Restriction: _____
☐ Travel Restriction: _____
☐ OTHER _____
☐ OTHER _____
☐ OTHER _____
☐ OTHER _____
☐ OTHER _____

PLEASE CHECK ANY SPECIAL SENTENCING RULES APPLICABLE TO THIS CASE:

☐ Person Felony Committed with a Firearm – K.S.A 21-4704 (h) (Shall be presumed imprisonment)
☐ Aggravated Battery on an L.E.O. – K.S.A. 21-4704 (g) (Shall be presumed imprisonment) (6-H or 6-I)
☐ Aggravated Assault on an L.E.O. – K.S.A. 21-4704 (g) (Shall be presumed imprisonment) (6-H or 6-I)
☐ Crime Committed for Benefit of Criminal Street Gang – K.S.A. 21-1704 (k) (Shall be presumed imprisonment)
☐ Persistent Sex Offender – K.S.A. 21-4704 (j) (Shall be presumed imprisonment)
☐ Felony DUI (third) – K.S.A 21-4704 (i)
☐ Felony DUI (fourth or subsequent) – K.S.A. S-1567 (g)
☐ Felony Criminal Deprivation of Property / Motor Vehicle [Crime committed prior to July 1, 1999.] – K.S.A. 21-3705 (b)
☐ Felony Domestic Battery – K.S.A. 21-3412a (b)(3)
☐ Crime Committed While Incarcerated and Serving a Felony Sentence, or While on Probation, Parole, Conditional Release or Postrelease Supervision for a Felony – K.S.A. 21-4603d (f) (New sentence shall be consecutive – K.S.A. 21-4608
☐ Crime Committed While on Felony Bond – K.S.A. 21-4603d (f) (Crime committed on or after 7/1/99 may sentence to prison
even if presumptive probation)

☐ Kansas Securities Act – K.S.A. 17-1267
☐ Extended Jurisdiction Juvenile Imposed – K.S.A. 38-1636
☐ Second or Subsequent Manufacture of a Controlled Substance Conviction – K.S.A. 21-4705 (e)
☐ Residential Burglary After a Prior Residential or Nonresidential or Agg. Burglary Conviction – K.S.A. 21-4704 (1)
(Shall be presumed imprisonment)

☐ Second Forgery – K.S.A. 21-3710 (b)(3)
☐ Third or Subsequent Forgery – K.S.A. 21-3710 (b)(4)
☐ Mandatory Drug Treatment – K.S.A. 21-4729 (SB 123)
☐ Other _____

KSG Desk Reference Manual 2004
Appendix D Page 4

SOURCE: Kansas Sentencing Commission. (2004). _Kansas sentencing guidelines: Presentence investigation report._ Topeka, KS: Author. Retrieved from http://www.kspace.org/bitstream/1984/69/7/Appendix_D_2004_PSI_Form.pdf.

▲ **Photo 5.1**   Probation and parole officer Chris Byrd and a court attorney discuss some of the content in an offender's PSI before the sentencing judge appears in the courtroom. In some cases, negotiations may be arranged by various court actors depending on the circumstances of the crime and the offender.

In the federal probation system, the contents of the PSI are disclosed to the defendant, the defendant's legal counsel, and the prosecuting attorney. Likewise, since the passage of the 1984 Sentencing Reform Act, the content of the PSI has determined the parameters of sentencing. This means that the central nature of the PSI to the sentencing process has become a source of scrutiny by defendants since it is important to the future sentence and since it serves as the basis for participation in specific programs offered within a prison system and/or community supervision agency. In many cases, the PSI serves as the basis of classification within both institutional- and community-based systems, and this is especially true in the federal system. Thus, the PSI is an important document for the offender, and its content must be closely guarded to ensure accuracy. From an assessment standpoint, this is an important consideration because this critical document is completed by one person (the presentence investigator), and this document allows for a great deal of discretion by that person. Given that this document will follow the offender throughout their sentence, it is perhaps one of the most important components of the community supervision process. The accuracy of information is critical to this stage of the community supervision process, and the information contained should pass the scrutiny of both the prosecution and the defense. Otherwise, this means of assessment/classification is greatly compromised.

This is actually an important point of discussion in relation to the PSI. Aside from the fact that the PSI will contain various information that is related to the supervision and treatment of the offender, the accuracy of the information is sometimes questionable and can actually impair the treatment outcomes of offenders. This is the primary concern in noting the use of the PSI. As will be seen later in this section, other departments (Travis County, Texas) have noted inefficiency in their presentence investigation process and have had to streamline and revamp their systems. Likewise, the completion of the PSI is a large part of the CSO's job design, and the excessive paperwork associated with the PSI and other documentation serves as a primary source of stress for CSOs. Thus, given the extensive detail required for these reports and given the heavy caseload burden that many CSOs face, it is no surprise that information may not always be accurate and that these inaccuracies lead to poor assessments, supervision schemes, and treatment outcomes. Given that judges tend to rely on the recommendation of PSI investigators when determining their sentence, it is clear that the PSI is a critical aspect of the community supervision process from both a reintegration perspective and a public safety perspective. More will be discussed regarding the PSI process later in this and other sections. Aside from understanding the basic information that is contained in a PSI, the fact that CSOs collect the information in the PSI, and the basic use of that information, the single most important factor for students to understand in regard to the PSI is that it is only as good as the investigator allows it to be.

The Sentencing Hearing and the Presentence Investigation Report

While procedures do vary from region to region, a sentencing phase will be conducted at some point during the processing of a criminal conviction. At this point, the defense counsel can have an impact on the overall process for the offender. Defense counsel may include having a private presentence investigation conducted at the defendant's expense, filing a sentencing memorandum with the court that highlights mitigating factors that might be favorable to the defendant, and even providing advice on the defendant's interaction with the probation staff that conduct the PSI (in particular, providing the names and addresses of persons favorable to the defendant) while challenging any inaccurate, incomplete, or misleading information that may end up in the PSI report. This last function of the defense counsel is actually quite critical. As one may recall, the PSI will follow the defendant well beyond the mere sentencing decision-making process. Indeed, the PSI will be used to classify the offender if they should be incarcerated and will also be used in future decisions regarding the supervision issues within the community. Thus, verification of the PSI's **validity** is crucial to the welfare of the defendant and keeps from creating scenarios that make an already bad situation worse.

From the standpoint of the CSO, the two most important sections of the PSI are the evaluation and the recommendation. There is typically a high degree of agreement between the probation officer's recommendations and the judge's decision when sentencing. However, it is not clear if it may be that the probation officer simply suggests sentences that are consistent with a certain judge's personality or professional leaning or if the judge actually tends to modify his or her decision making in favor of the probation officer's own judgment and impressions. Indeed, Neubauer (2002) presented the possibility that the plea bargaining process has actually supplanted the role of the probation officer, as the defense counsel and the prosecutor make their own terms as to sentencing agreements. This is not to infer that the probation officer is left out of the process; rather, instead the prosecutor and the defense will, in most cases, collaborate with the probation officer prior to the time when the PSI is submitted to the court. However, this collaboration may result in an after-the-fact justification of a sentence that is agreed upon. In such a case, the probation officer's impact is minimal, with his or her input being used to simply cement a form of justice that is not so much individualized as it is negotiated within an adversary system.

On the other hand, it is likely that those completing the PSI do have at least some impact on the justice process since their own narrative will affect subsequent outcomes that extend beyond the initial sentencing phase. Prosecutors and defense counsel are both aware of this and are not necessarily able to impact the input of the probation officer aside from the recommendations that are officially made to the judge. Proof of the fact that the PSI plays an important role in both the sentencing phase and in subsequent outcomes is given when one considers that if a defendant can afford such services, their defense counsel may purchase private services to construct a supplemental PSI to be considered by the court. Latessa and Allen (1999) noted that

> because most attorneys are not trained in behavioral sciences, retaining a "correctional expert" has been suggested as a more plausible approach and, although there are ethical issues involved, it appears that a social scientists can serve an important role in the sentencing process. (p. 189)

While privately obtained PSIs are allowed in several states as well as the federal court system they are not frequently used. They tend to be expensive, and there is a great deal of duplication in information between the privately constructed report and the report constructed by the probation agency. However, the private PSI can effectively argue on behalf of an offender and can also make suggestions that might not otherwise get included into the state-constructed PSI. In addition, the information in the private PSI may be used to refute or modify contentions made in the report provided by the probation agency. Though this may not affect the actual sentence, it can on rare occasions be of later use in classification and/or treatment decisions.

▧ The Basics of Risk Assessment

Before we can begin a discussion on specific instruments and inventories, it is important that the student understand the underlying presumptions behind risk prediction. In any type of risk assessment, there are some common principles that tend to run consistent throughout. If these basic statistical considerations and/or methodological processes are not honored during the construction of an instrument, the instrument is likely to be flawed and will therefore be less accurate in prediction. This places the public at risk and also improperly classifies offenders even when they are not in a position to be dangerous to the public. James Austin (2006) provided six basic suggestions for correctional officials who wish to know whether their instruments are effective.

First, the risk assessment instruments must be tested on your correctional population and separately normed for males and females. Because populations differ by jurisdiction (North versus South, Midwest versus West, etc.), it is imperative that the instrument be normed to the population you serve. This includes by sex as well as location since the issues leading to the criminality, types of crimes committed, and prognosis for treatment tend to be different from males to females.

Second, an inter-rater reliability test must be conducted by independent researchers who have no monetary or political incentive in regard to the testing outcome. Inter-rater reliability should consistently yield the same outcomes regardless of the person who is conducting the instrument, presuming that each person administering the assessment is competent in administering the instrument, that is.

Third, a validity test must be conducted. Validity simply ensures that the instrument is actually measuring what researchers believe that it is measuring. With respect to our current discussion, it is important that instruments actually measure recidivism (or perhaps reintegration, depending on our intent) rather than some other unknown variable.

Fourth, the instruments must allow for dynamic and static factors that have been well accepted and tested in a number of jurisdictions. The use of dynamic and static risk factors will be discussed in depth in a subsection that follows. Examples of dynamic risk factors would include characteristics such as age, marital status, and custody level. These characteristics can and do change over time. Static risk factors would include characteristics such as age at first arrest, crime seriousness, and prior convictions. Once established, these characteristics do not fluctuate over time.

Fifth, the instruments must be compatible with the skill level of your staff. As noted in the second suggestion, the accuracy of the assessment is also dependent on the skill of the person administering the assessment. Therefore, the instrument should be simplistic as necessary while ensuring the accuracy of the results. Staff must also be trained on and have experience in administering the instrument.

Finally, the risk assessment must have "face validity" and transparency with staff, prisoners, probationers, parolees, and policy makers. The instrument and the process of assessment must be understood and recognized as credible by all persons in the agency. Instruments that are only understood by eggheads and academics will never go over well with most practitioners. Further, if the instrument is perceived as being too "bookish" in nature and not applicable to the realities of the "street," so to speak, both practitioners and offenders will see the instrument as artificial and sterile, not really being able to probe the true reality to what an offender may (or may not) do. If the instrument appears to ask bogus questions or if it appears to do so in a naive manner, it will not be perceived as credible by practitioners and offenders alike.

False Positives and False Negatives

Agency administrators tend to assume that instruments are, in fact, valid and reliable and that staff can effectively use these instruments. To some extent, these administrators are forced to operate under these assumptions, as alternatives may be unavailable or unacceptable. Further, these administrators operate under these assumptions when making release decisions. But, as has just been discussed, when instruments are not normed appropriately, do not possess appropriate degrees of external validity, or lack other forms of appropriate methodological rigor in their manufacture, they tend to generate either underpredictions of future criminality or overpredictions of the same. Further, individuals using their own subjective opinions will also tend to over- and underpredict criminality. These forms of error are important to understand, and it is in this manner that false positives and false negatives are generated. The chronic occurrence of these two mistakes in risk prediction can lead to tragic consequences for society and/or costly expenditures for correctional agencies. When decision makers are making release decisions for offenders, they will ultimately have to decide if the offender will be allowed within the community or if the offender will remain behind bars. There are some implications to these decisions that may not be readily apparent to the casual observer, and these implications as well as the official professional terms associated with these implications should be understood by the student.

The true negative implies that the offender is predicted to not reoffend and the prediction turns out to be true. The false negative implies that the offender is predicted not to reoffend, but the prediction turns out to be false. The true positive implies that the offender is predicted to reoffend and that this prediction later turns out to be true. However, if another offender is likewise predicted to be likely to commit a crime but later the offender somehow is released onto community supervision and is found to never reoffend, this would be a false positive.

Naturally, the true positives and true negatives are what agencies hope to obtain as often as possible. These are perfect predictions of offender behavior. However, with things not being perfect, the false positive and false negative predictions are inevitable at some point.

Static and Dynamic Risk Factors

Not all risk factors are the same. Indeed, some risk factors are fairly permanent or at least they occur due to no fault or cause of the offender. Other risk factors, on the other hand, are solely due to the offender. Further, some risk factors are more suited for security, custody, and control of the offender whereas others are more designed for treatment. Factors such as age at first conviction, gender, sex, and even disabilities or mental impairments are not caused by the offender and are also unlikely to change. These permanent factors are inherent to the offender and are referred to as static risk factors (Van Voorhis, Braswell, & Lester, 2000). These characteristics are often the best basis for security determinations. Opposite of the static risk factor is the dynamic risk factor. Dynamic risk factors are those characteristics that can change and are more or less influenced or controlled by the offender, such as employment, motivation, drug use, and family relations (Van Voorhis et al., 2000). These characteristics are often most useful to treatment providers but are not really a sound basis for security determinations because they have the possibility of changing when certain stimuli are presented in the offender's life. Figure 5.2 provides an example of a risk assessment form that incorporates both static and dynamic scales for juvenile sex offenders who are assessed. The student should note the specific subscales and the separate scoring sections for static and dynamic scores when examining this insert.

Figure 5.2   Risk Assessment Form for Juvenile Sex Offenders

Juvenile Sex Offender Assessment Protocol-II Scoring Form

Scoring Code: 0 = Stable; 1= Moderate; 2 = Severe

Sexual Drive/Preoccupation Scale

1.	Prior Legally Charged Sex Offenses	0	1	2
2.	Number of Sexual Abuse Victims	0	1	2
3.	Male Child Victim	0	1	2
4.	Duration of Sex Offense History	0	1	2
5.	Degree of Planning in Sexual Offense(s)	0	1	2
6.	Sexualized Aggression	0	1	2
7.	Sexual Drive and Preoccupation	0	1	2
8.	Sexual Victimization History	0	1	2

Sexual Drive/Preoccupation Scale Total: _____

Impulsive/Antisocial Behavior Scale

9.	Caregiver Consistency	0	1	2
10.	Pervasive Anger	0	1	2
11.	School Behavior Problems	0	1	2
12.	History of Conduct Disorder	0	1	2
13.	Juvenile Antisocial Behavior	0	1	2
14.	Ever Charged or Arrested Before Age 16	0	1	2
15.	Multiple Types of Offenses	0	1	2
16.	History of Physical Assault and/or Exposure to Family Violence	0	1	2

Antisocial Behavior Scale Total: _____

Intervention Scale

17.	Accepting Responsibility for Offense(s)	0	1	2
18.	Internal Motivation for Change	0	1	2
19.	Understands Risk Factors	0	1	2
20.	Empathy	0	1	2
21.	Remorse and Guilt	0	1	2
22.	Cognitive Distortions	0	1	2
23.	Quality of Peer Relationships	0	1	2

Intervention Scale Total: _____

Community Stability/Adjustment Scale

24.	Management of Sexual Urges and Desire	0	1	2
25.	Management of Anger	0	1	2

Figure 5.2 (Continued)

26. Stability of Current Living Situation	0	1	2
27. Stability in School	0	1	2
28. Evidence of Positive Support Systems	0	1	2

Community Stability Scale Total: _____

Juvenile Sex Offender Assessment Protocol-II Summary Form

Static/Historical Scales

1. Sexual Drive/Preoccupation Scale Score:
   (Add Items 1–8 [range: 0–16]) _____/16 = _____

2. Impulsive-Antisocial Behavior Scale Score:
   (Add Items 9–16 [range: 0–16]) _____/16 = _____

Dynamic Scales

3. Intervention Scale Score:
   (Add Items 17–23 [range: 0–14]) _____/14 = _____

4. Community Stability Scale Score:
   (Add Items 24–28 [range: 0–10]) _____/10 = _____

Static Score

(Add items 1–16) _____/32 = _____

Dynamic Score

(Add items 17–28) _____/24 = _____

Total J-SOAP Score

(Add items 1–28) _____/56 = _____

The Appropriate Use of Subjective and Objective Assessments

If the offender is accurately assessed, then only those offenders who are a risk to public safety will be incarcerated. Indeed, those offenders who are either a low risk for recidivism or even those who are a high risk but are most likely to commit nuisance or nonviolent crimes should not be placed in prison. This is because such forms of custody are very expensive and are designed mainly to prevent the offender from hurting others in society. Despite the common notion that the loss of liberty (their punishment) is the basis for the prison, such a punishment can in fact be fulfilled as well through house arrest or some other form of secure supervision that does not require the expense incurred by prison. Thus, it is the basis of the offender's likelihood to comply with the mandate of their sentence, not the actual restriction of their liberty that should be the criteria of their receiving the added expense of a prison cell. Otherwise, financial resources are wasted and squandered unnecessarily on an offender who could have been just as severely punished for their wrongdoings at a fraction of the cost.

Further still, it should be noted that assessment is also critical because those offenders who have a high risk of committing violent crimes should not be placed on community supervision. This nonetheless occurs due to jail and prison overcrowding, which then places institutions in the precarious position of choosing the "least dangerous" of the violent offenders when releasing to the public. This is a very risky position that no administrator relishes, and this is also the most common source of criticism leveled at community release programs. Regardless of the correctional system's situation, it is a strong recommendation of this text that all security-level determinations be based solely on objective assessment instruments and that subjective criteria be avoided when issues of public safety are at stake. This is prudent for agency and personnel liability purposes, and this provides the most mathematically precise, consistent, and effective means of protecting public safety. On the other hand, when making determinations regarding treatment progress, the use of subjective criteria from the specific primary treatment provider should be utilized more than any other form of assessment. This subjective criteria should consist of feedback from both the clinical and the security staff who have had substantial face time with the offender.

Thus, offender supervision processes revolve around two key forms of response to the offending population: (1) incapacitation and (2) treatment. Incapacitation is the process of simply removing the offender from society so that they cannot cause further harm to the public. There is no goal beyond this with incapacitation nor is there any implied retribution or desire to deter other offenders from committing crime. On the other hand, treatment is the process whereby the offender is provided some form of intervention that will help them to function within society without resorting to criminal behavior. Both have the same goal of simply reducing the likelihood of future offending from that specific individual offender. In other words, each of these approaches have the same exact purpose (to prevent the offender from committing future criminal behavior), but both pursue this purpose in a different manner.

Subjective Assessment

One of the wisest investments for any correctional system desiring to ensure public safety is in the arena of assessment. More money and resources in assessment means that the subsequent stages (diagnostic, recidivism prediction, classification) in the equation will also operate better, resulting in increased public safety as the ultimate answer. One method of assessment, the **subjective assessment process** of interviewing and observation, is an important yet less structured method of determining the security and treatment needs of the offender. This process entails the use of professionals who use their sense of judgment and experience to determine the offender's possible dangerousness, treatment needs, likelihood of responding to treatment, and their likelihood of escaping. This is an important process that should not be overlooked. However, this process should not be the primary form of assessment, but it should serve as an integral part of a "two-pronged" assessment process.

There are some drawbacks to this process. For one, the process is subjective, which means that the determination is based upon the impressions of an individual. Thus, these assessments are likely to vary from one professional to another. Second, these assessments can be lengthy in nature and will thus not be useful for large facilities that do not have numerous well-qualified staff for such forms of assessment. Third, these forms of assessment require extensive skill from the staff that administer, and they are therefore only as good as the personnel administering them. This then means that these forms of assessment can be very costly since only highly educated and/or well-trained staff will be able to utilize this form of assessment.

To offset the potential capriciousness of a subjective assessment process, it is suggested that the use of a structured form of interview or observation process be utilized in all cases. A **subjective structured interview** is simply a process whereby an interviewer will ask a respondent a set of prearranged and open-ended questions so that the interview seems informal in nature (as if a conversation), yet because of the prearranged questions, a structure evolves throughout the conversation that ensures certain bits of desired data are gathered from the offender. These forms of interviews are useful since they guide clinicians and other staff who may conduct intakes. Further, the structure of these interviews provide for consistency and uniformity in record keeping, meaning that agencies can ensure similar criteria are considered despite the style and form of the individual interviewer. This provides a certain "baseline" of information by which all offenders are judged against. Lastly, this type of interview ensures that even less qualified staff can conduct an interview and that the interview will still contain that information that is considered critical for agency assessment.

Standardized interviews are designed to collect the same type of information from all the respondents. If it is a structured interview, all offenders are asked the same questions in the same order, and the answers are recorded identically (Drummond, 1996). In unscheduled interviews, the interviewer sometimes varies the sequence of the questions and the order of the topics so that the data can be compared and summarized. Advantages of the interviewing process include the following: (1) clients can be guided to answer items completely, (2) additional information or understanding can be pursued, and (3) nonverbal behavior and cues as well as affective behavior and voice tone and pitch can be observed and noted (Drummond, 1996). Again, this information should be noted only when the nature of the interview allows the clinician to focus on these behaviors as relevant. Like advantages, disadvantages occur as well. These disadvantages include the following: (1) success often depends on the skill of the interviewer to ask the right questions with the right timing and to correctly interpret the observations; (2) the communication of some individuals is inhibited, and clients may simply be unwilling to answer certain questions; they will then either refuse to answer or just provide a response that is a lie; and (3) the personality of the interviewer can greatly influence the outcome (Drummond, 1996).

Drummond (1996) noted that even though the reliability and the validity of interviewing may be questionable, this is sometimes the only way possible to gather certain types of information. Further, the interviewer can reword questions, add questions, seek clarification of information provided, focus on topics of clinical interest, and so forth. This means that information obtained from such a process will likely be much more relevant to the specific clinical focus, and it also means that helping professionals will have richer information to work with when consulting with the client's case file.

Objective Assessment

As noted earlier, when making determinations about security levels (especially when community supervision is involved) it is strongly recommended that determinations be based solely on objective assessment instruments. However, there are a variety of specific assessment instruments that are employed by agencies throughout the nation. These types of objective assessments can range from behavioral checklists that staff complete after a brief period of observation, a paper-and-pencil test completed by the offender, or assessment formats that characterize the offender's social, demographic, and criminal history (Van Voorhis et al., 2000). Regardless of the type of objective assessment (and some are better than others), the objective assessment should always be based upon the response of supervision staff and should never incorporate self-report data from the offender. Further, input from the victim (for example, in programs that utilize a restorative justice element) should not be considered when making decisions to release to the community.

Rather, the determination should be clearly restricted to objective mathematical "risk-factor" criteria devoid of all other considerations (i.e., prison or jail overcrowding, desires of the victim, apparent sincerity of the offender, and so forth).

Perhaps one of the best-known types of risk assessment systems is the Wisconsin risk assessment system. During the 1970s, the state of Wisconsin sought to develop a risk assessment scale that would assess an offender's likelihood for further unlawful or rule-violating behavior. To achieve this goal, outcome measures were based on arrests, misdemeanor convictions, felony convictions, absconsions from probation or parole, technical violations, and so forth. After randomly selecting a construction sample, the criminal history and other characteristics of these offenders were entered into a series of statistical analyses to determine the combination of variables that would best predict future behavior of offenders. At the close of this process, 10 specific factors were identified, isolated, and weighted. Many of these same factors appear on most other risk assessment instruments as well.

In addition to these 10 risk factors, this scale includes an administrative policy override. This override consists of an additional factor that entails prior or current assaultive offense history that is weighted in such a manner as to automatically classify an offender as high risk if they possess that factor (Connolly, 2003). These types of overrides are typically policy decisions that are made to classify all offenders with a certain characteristic (such as an assaultive offense history) as high risk, regardless of whether the statistical analysis determines that variable to actually be an indicator of likely recidivism. This is designed to address the consequences associated with that offender's potential criminal behavior rather than their actual likelihood of committing a crime. Thus, if an offender has a stable job with no prior criminal history but he is convicted of a violent sex offense, he may not score high in likelihood of reoffending, but if he were to reoffend, the consequences of his likely crime is considered too great to bear as a risk (Connolly, 2003).

This form of structured assessment has become the prototype for many probation and parole systems. Staff members use this instrument to score probationers on the predictors contained on the list, and from this point, they classify them into either high, medium, or low-risk categories (Van Voorhis et al., 2000). The items that are included on this list are all statistical predictors of likely failure while on probation. These predictors are all based on previous probation histories among probationers and are based on the premise that the best predictor of future aggregate probationer behavior is prior aggregate-level behavior of probationers. As a result of tracking probationers over time, this instrument has been able to find those factors that are associated with failure and success while on probation. Some of the factors that are examined include the following:

1. Number of address changes in the past 12 months

2. Percentage of time employed in the 12 months

3. Alcohol consumption problems

4. Other drug consumption problems

5. Offender attitude

6. Age at first conviction

7. Number of prior periods of probation/parole supervision

8. Number of prior probation/parole revocations

9. Number of prior felony convictions

10. Type of convictions or prior adjudications

An example of the Wisconsin risk assessment system is provided in Figure 5.3. Connolly (2003) noted that even though the Wisconsin risk assessment is one of the most commonly used instruments among agencies, there is very little comprehensive research that has been conducted on its predictive accuracy. However, of the research that does exist, there is considerable reason to question the validity of this assessment instrument. Because this scale is so widely used and because it has not been truly validated, this may be (at least in part) one reason for many of the error rates that have been found to occur throughout the nation. In fact, it is often the case that other textbooks on community corrections will present the Wisconsin risk assessment scale but do not go into detail as to the validity of that scale. This is a serious oversight among most textbooks and should be fully addressed within the field of community corrections.

Connelly (2003) conducted one of the most comprehensive examinations of risk assessment instruments in her dissertation, which was completed at the University of Texas at Austin. Connelly's examination of risk assessment instruments was of such caliber as to be funded by the U.S. Department of Justice. In her examination of the Wisconsin risk assessment scale, she provided research that clearly demonstrates the ineffective nature of this instrument. For example, one study by Harris (1994) examined a sample of adult felons on probation. This study sought to compare the predictive accuracy of the Wisconsin risk assessment with the client management classification (CMC) as well as a combination of the two instruments. Overall, Harris found that the Wisconsin risk assessment instrument had high prediction error rates, thereby demonstrating this instrument's lack of validity. In another study by Yacus (1998), the Wisconsin risk assessment scale and the Wisconsin needs assessment scale were examined for accuracy in the classification of adult felons in the state of Virginia. This study utilized a sample of 13,011 adult probation and parole offenders that were placed on supervision. Yacus (1998) also found high classification error rates for the Wisconsin risk assessment. As can be seen in Table 5.1, the results of both studies demonstrate some clear concern for the continued use of this instrument.

When examining Table 5.1, it can be seen that the study by Harris (1994), shows the false positive error rate to be very high (43%), which means the instrument tends to overpredict that offenders will fail on community supervision due to a resulting revocation of their probation or parole status. On the other hand, the Yacus (1998) study examined the likelihood of probation success. In this study, a true positive is therefore generated when an offender is predicted to be successful and they turn out to actually be successful in completing their probation. Conversely, a true negative for this study occurs when an offender is predicted to fail and does, in fact, fail. From the data in Table 5.1, it can be seen that the Wisconsin risk assessment instrument overpredicts that offenders will be successful. Each of these studies examines the instrument from an opposing vantage point. One study examines the instrument from the point of predicting that offenders will fail (Harris, 1994) while the other predicts that offenders will succeed (Yacus, 1998). In both cases, the Wisconsin risk assessment is found wanting, though of course the results are worse in the Harris study than the Yacus study.

Nevertheless, some serious questions have to be asked in regard to this tool, particularly since its predictive accuracy has not been established. In addition, the overprediction of offending should be considered a serious flaw, since this costs needless tax dollars, results in overstuffed prison systems, and is likely to expose offenders to environments that may actually increase the likelihood of reoffending (as noted in Section I, prison is sometimes equated to an educational camp for career criminals). One key

Figure 5.3 Wisconsin Risk Assessment Scale

RISK ASSESSMENT

NAME—LAST, FIRST	PROB. NO. X–	DPO	CL NO.	AO
DATE OF GRANT	EXPIRATION	DATE OF ASSESSMENT	BY	

Number of Address Changes in Last 12 Months: ___ (Prior to the offense)

- 0 None
- 2 One
- 3 Two or more

SCORE

_____

Percentage of Time Employed in Last 12 Months: ___ (Prior to the offense)

- 0 60% or more
- 1 40%–59%
- 2 Under 40%
- 0 Not applicable

_____

Alcohol Usage Problems: _____ (Prior to the offense)

- 0 No interference with functioning
- 2 Occasional abuse: some disruption of functioning
- 4 Frequent abuse: serious disruption: needs treatment

_____

Other Drug Usage Problems: _____ (Prior to the offense)

- 0 No interference with functioning
- 1 Occasional abuse: some disruption of functioning
- 2 Frequent abuse: serious disruption, needs treatment

_____

Attitude: _____

- 0 Motivated to change; receptive to assistance
- 3 Dependent or unwilling to accept responsibility
- 5 Rationalizes behavior; negative; not motivated to change

_____

Age at First Conviction: _____ (or Juvenile Adjudication)

- 0 24 or older
- 2 20–23
- 4 19 or younger

_____

Number of Prior Periods of Probation/Parole Supervision: _____ (Adult or Juvenile)

- 0 None
- 4 One or more

_____

Number of Prior Probation/Parole Revocations: _____ (Adult or Juvenile)

- 0 None
- 4 One or more

_____

Number of Prior Felony Convictions: _____ (or Juvenile Adjudications)

- 0 None
- 2 One
- 4 Two or more

_____

Convictions or Juvenile Adjudications for: _____ (Include current offense.)

- 2 Burglary, theft, auto theft, or robbery

_____

Convictions or Juvenile Adjudications for: _____ (Include current offense.)

- 3 NSF checks or forgery

_____

TOTAL _____

Table 5.1   Predictive Accuracy of the Wisconsin Risk Assessment

Study	False Positive	False Negative	True Positive	True Negative	Error Rate
Harris (1994)	43%	3%	13%	41%	54.5%
Yacus (1998)	22%	12%	57%	9%	34%

ingredient to this overprediction may be the use of administrative overrides. The use of these mechanisms creates enhanced likelihoods of false positives regardless of what the statistical analyses may otherwise indicate. This may explain much of the inaccuracy involved with the Wisconsin risk assessment and indicates that the system might be improved if such mechanisms were more carefully considered.

Another area of concern regarding the Wisconsin risk assessment revolves around problems with inter-rater reliability of the instrument. In brief, inter-rater reliability is simply a research term that describes the likelihood that multiple persons rating an instrument will derive similar ratings of that instrument. For a high inter-rater reliability to occur, a larger number of diverse rating experts must have similar judgments in reference to a given variable (such as the likelihood of an offender to continue using drugs). It is clear from past research that the Wisconsin risk assessment does not facilitate strong inter-rater reliability and thus indicates that the subjectivity of the rater can negatively impact the outcomes of the instrument. Indeed, the question related to the offender's attitude leaves a great deal to the discretion of the interviewer (ranging from 0 to 5), and attitude itself is a somewhat subjective concept. In addition, questions related to alcohol and drug usage also leave room for discretion that can be faulty. Different raters may rate the same offender(s) inconsistently, and this will then weaken the instrument's predictability (Connolly, 2003).

Since we have determined that reintegrative treatment is a necessary component of any community corrections strategy to reduce recidivism, it stands to reason that variables associated with reintegration must also be considered in the assessment process. In fact, it is often the case that the specific needs of the offender are intertwined with future recidivism. For example, a female offender who is unable to find suitable employment may resort to prostitution to make ends meet (particularly if they have one or more children to care for). In a similar vein, that same offender may have a drug habit that, when left untreated, can resort in further offending to sustain the drug habit. Likewise, mentally ill offenders may have medication and/or treatment needs to aid them in maintaining emotional balance. Without such needs being met, the likelihood of future offending is increased. Therefore, when discussing assessment, an additional distinction must be presented. This distinction rests between the understanding of **risk-principled-assessment** and the **needs-principled assessment** of offenders on community supervision.

With risk-principled assessment, the main concern revolves around the protection of society. Within the treatment scheme, the risk-principled assessment system will ensure that hardcore offenders are not in the same treatment regimen as less serious offenders. This may seem to be a topical distinction, but it can be critical to long-term success. For instance, in an anger management program, an offender who has problems with verbal abuse and verbal explosiveness may not benefit from being in an anger management group that has a majority of offenders who are severe domestic batterers. This would be even truer if these assaultive offenders had some form of a personality disorder to further aggravate their success. In this case, it is likely that the success of the offender with verbal anger problems might actually be impaired by repeat exposure to these other offenders. These offenders could therefore ruin any positive prognosis for change that the offender might have. In essence, the treatment program could ironically make the offender worse than he started! Though many students may be skeptical, this does in fact frequently happen in many community health service provider agencies. The same could be true in various substance abuse treatment groups and programs and any other treatment regimen that mixes offenders at various levels of therapeutic recovery.

Further still, research has shown that intensive correctional treatment programs are more successful with high-risk offenders than with low-risk offenders. Thus, it does not pay to place low-risk offenders in programs designed for high-risk offenders, and this could actually lower their likelihood of success due to negative influences from other high-risk members. Thus, treatment programs should distinguish between risk-principles in their assessment and future placement of offender clients. Indeed, according to Van Voorhis and colleagues (2000), the risk principle notes that low-risk offenders tend to do more poorly as a group on intensive treatment than if they had not been assigned to an intensive correctional intervention. Van Voorhis and colleagues (2000) went on to add that the treatment implications of the risk-principled assessment are as follows:

1. Identify the high, medium, and low-risk offenders.

2. Direct intensive treatment efforts (not just intensive security and supervision) to high-risk offenders.

3. Think carefully about intensive treatment interventions for low-risk offenders.

These three points clearly enunciate the importance of the risk-principled assessment and are specifically relevant to special needs offenders such as domestic batterers, differing types of sexual offenders (adult and juvenile, pedophile and rapist), substance abusers, mentally disordered offenders, and so forth.

Needs-principled assessment, on the other hand, is more concerned with factors specific to the effective treatment and reintegration of the special needs offender. Thus, needs-principled-assessment deals with the subjective and objective needs of the offender to maximize their potential for social reintegration and to reduce their likelihood of future recidivism. Needs-principled assessment takes into account factors such as substance addiction, medical assistance, mental health issues, job development, educational attainment, physical disabilities, and/or relationships with family and/or peers. The needs-principled assessment consists mostly of dynamic risk factors, but the needs-principled assessment will assess offenders based less on whether they possess a certain risk factor and more on the severity of that need or the seriousness of the affliction. For instance, substance abusers whose primary addiction problem revolves around pain relievers may be substantially different from those who abuse to have an elevated mood. Though all are addicts, the type of drug and the type of addiction severity may again warrant differing levels and/or types of treatment for that offender.

Needs-principled assessment is also multifaceted in nature and goes beyond looking at the main risk characteristic of concern. For instance, a substance abusing offender may have a wide range of other needs such as the settlement of legal issues, the maintenance of employment, and resolution of family-of-origin conflicts. Each of these issues are not specifically related to the offender's drug addiction, but each of these needs, if not properly addressed, can impair the offender's likelihood for further recovery. Rather, the failure to address one of these corollary needs can result in the likelihood of relapse since it is commonly known that drug offenders often resort to drug use during times of stress.

Thus, the multifaceted nature of needs-principled assessment will examine the offender's global likelihood of reintegration.

Many agencies classify their offenders both according to their likely risk of recidivating as well as their identified needs. In fact, one popular scale has also been developed by the state of Wisconsin and is often used in conjunction with the Wisconsin risk assessment. Aside from the desire to improve the likelihood of reintegration, the use of needs assessments also provides a measure to indicate the amount of time and effort that a CSO will spend on a given case in relation to their overall caseload. In addition, the use of needs-based assessments forces qualitative reviews of the offender's progress that go beyond simply determining if they have evaded detection for a technical violation or criminal action. The use of needs-based assessments and resulting classification schemes will be discussed later in this section since needs assessments are directly related to the casework model of community supervision. As noted in prior sections, the casework model of supervision is the primary orientation of offender supervision that is supported by this text. Figure 5.4 is provided as an early view of a commonly used needs-assessment scale.

Figure 5.4   Assessment of Client Needs

ASSESSMENT OF CLIENT NEEDS

Client Name (Last)	(First)	(MI)	Parole No.	SID No.
Release Date (Month, day, year)	Agent Name		Date	

Select the appropriate answer and enter the associated weight in the score column. Higher numbers indicate more severe problems. Total all scores. If client is to be referred to a community resource or to clinical services, check appropriate referral box.

ACADEMIC/VOCATIONAL SKILLS   **REFERRAL SCORE**

−1 High school   0 Adequate skills; able   +2 Low skill level   +4 Minimal skill level
   or above skill   to handle everyday   causing minor   causing serious
   level   requirements   adjustment problems   adjustment problems   ☐ _____

EMPLOYMENT

−1 Satisfactory   0 Secure   +3 Unsatisfactory   +6 Unemployed
   employment   employment; no   employment; or   and virtually
   for one year   difficulties reported;   unemployed but has   unemployable;   ☐ _____
   or longer   or homemaker,   adequate job skills   needs training
                      student or retired

FINANCIAL MANAGEMENT

−1 Long-standing   0 No current   +3 Situational or minor +5 Severe difficulties;
   pattern of   difficulties   difficulties   may include
   self-sufficiency;   garnishment, bad   ☐ _____
   e.g., good   checks or bankruptcy
   credit rating

(Continued)

Figure 5.4 (Continued)

MARITAL/FAMILY RELATIONSHIPS

−1 Relationships and support exceptionally strong   0 Relatively stable relationships   +3 Some disorganization or stress but potential for improvement   +5 Major disorganization or stress   ☐ _____

COMPANIONS

−1 Good support and influence   0 No adverse relationships   +2 Associations with occasional negative results   +4 Associations almost completely negative   ☐ _____

EMOTIONAL STABILITY

−2 Exceptionally well adjusted; accepts responsibility for actions   0 No symptoms of emotional instability; appropriate emotional responses   +4 Symptoms limit but do not prohibit adequate functioning; e.g., excessive anxiety   +7 Symptoms prohibit adequate functioning; e.g., lashes out or retreats into self   ☐ _____

ALCOHOL USAGE

0 No interference with functioning   +3 Occasional abuse; some disruption of functioning   +6 Frequent abuse; serious disruption; needs treatment   ☐ _____

OTHER DRUG USAGE

0 No interference with functioning   +3 Occasional substance abuse; some disruption of functioning   +5 Frequent substance abuse; serious disruption; needs treatment   ☐ _____

MENTAL ABILITY

0 Able to function independently   +3 Some need for assistance; potential for adequate adjustment; mild retardation   +6 Deficiencies severely limit independent functioning; moderate retardation   ☐ _____

HEALTH

0 Sound physical health; seldom ill   +1 Handicap or illness interferes with functioning on a recurring basis   +2 Serious handicap or chronic illness; needs frequent medical care   ☐ _____

SEXUAL BEHAVIOR

0 No apparent dysfunction   +3 Real or perceived situational or minor problems   +5 Real or perceived chronic or severe problems   ☐ _____

RECREATION/HOBBY

0 Constructive activities apparent   +1 Some constructive activities   +2 No constructive leisure-time activities or hobbies   ☐ _____

AGENT'S IMPRESSION OF CLIENT'S NEEDS

−1 Minimum   0 Low   +3 Medium   +5 Maximum   ☐ _____

Total: _____

⊠ Recidivism Prediction

Recidivism prediction is built off the information derived from the presentence interview. It is at this point that correctional personnel attempt to determine the risk involved with allowing the offender to be placed under community supervision. One key quasi-objective clinical inventory that is used to determine offender suitability is the LSI-R. This inventory was created by Don Andrews and James Bonta, and it has been found to be highly predictive of recidivism among a variety of correctional offender clients (Andrews & Bonta, 1994; Van Voorhis et al., 2000). The LSI-R is administered by case managers/counselors and/or mental health professionals. The assessment process includes a semistructured interview. As with the Wisconsin risk assessment system the LSI-R provides for reassessments of an offender's risk score. Reassessment of risk scores can be useful when assessing program effectiveness as well as facilitating program release decisions. In fact, it was found that the LSI-R predecessor, the LSI, was a better predictor of parolee recidivism than the Wisconsin risk assessment system. In a study by O'Keefe, Klebe, and Hromas (1998), it was found that initial classification levels based on the Wisconsin risk assessment indicated that 98% of offenders scored in the maximum supervision range. Similar to the previously discussed research by Connelly (2003), these researchers concluded that the Wisconsin system is strongly influenced by raters and may lead to overclassification O'Keefe et al., 1998). With overclassification, there occurs a waste of excess money due to more expensive security measures being used with offenders who do not require such extensive maintenance.

According to Andrews and Bonta (2003), the LSI-R inventory is a quantitative survey of offender attributes and their situations relevant to supervision levels and treatment decisions. The inventory was designed for offenders who are ages 16 and older; the LSI-R inventory aids in predicting parole outcome, success with offenders in halfway houses and aftercare facilities, and probation recidivism. This inventory consists of 54 items that are based on legal requirements and include relevant factors needed for making decisions about security risk levels and the likelihood of treatment success (Andrews & Bonta, 2003). The LSI-R inventory is designed for probation and parole officers to assist them with decisions about probation and parole placement, security-level classifications, and possible treatment progress.

The LSI-R screening version (LSI-R:SV) consists of eight items selected from the full LSI-R. Like the full version, LSI-R:SV samples both risk and needs, and the item content reflects four key risk factors: criminal history, criminal attitudes, criminal associates, and antisocial personality pattern (Andrews & Bonta, 2003). In addition, the LSI-R:SV inventory examines other factors such as employment, family, and substance abuse. The items included in the LSI-R:SV not only contribute to the predictive validity of the LSI-R:SV but they also include information that is important to offender treatment planning (Andrews & Bonta, 2003). Each of these items are rated either "yes/no" or "0 to 3" (0 = a very unsatisfactory situation with very clear and strong need for improvement and 3 = a satisfactory situation with little or no need for improvement).

It should be noted that the LSI-R is not intended to replace the professional judgment of the correctional worker. Rather, an objective risk-needs assessment enhances professional judgment, adds to the fairness of offender assessment, and alerts correctional staff to the need for a fuller offender risk-needs assessment (Andrews & Bonta, 2003). Research with the LSI-R shows that scores on the instrument have predicted a variety of outcomes important to offender management. Among probation samples, LSI-R scores have predicted violent recidivism and violations while under community supervision. Among incarcerated offenders, scores have predicted such varied outcomes as success in correctional halfway houses and institutional misconduct (Andrews & Bonta, 2003).

Andrews and Bonta (2003) made it clear that the LSI-R inventory is designed for use as a screening instrument in busy intake settings where, due to time constraints and insufficient staff resources, a complete LSI-R assessment may not be feasible for everyone. Lastly, the LSI-R also provides a summary of the static and dynamic risk factors that may require further assessment or further intervention from agency personnel.

In addition, the LSI-R fits a rather specific type of treatment model. Attitudes, criminal history, and associates are strong correlates among the entire offending population (Van Voorhis et al., 2000). As a risk-prediction inventory, the LSI-R fits best with programs that are based on clear cognitive behavioral and social learning treatment modalities. This is not a problem however, because most treatment programs in the criminal justice system are based on such orientations. But if clinicians desire an accurate assessment of the offender's likelihood of reforming, they must keep in mind that the LSI-R has limits that are grounded in cognitive behavioral approaches. Van Voorhis and colleagues (2000) pointed out that most research on cognitive behavioral and social learning approaches is showing that this modality is the most effective, overall, when dealing with the offender population. Thus, the LSI-R is ideally suited and designed for those programs that utilize the most effective modalities: cognitive behavioral and social learning. The LSI-R therefore dovetails nicely with these programs and lends further validity to the nature and intent of therapeutic treatment programs in the criminal justice field.

Focus Topic 5.1

The Confluence of Assessment, Classification, and Staff Attitudes in Determining Program Effectiveness

In the state of West Virginia, an ingenious study took place in 2006 that examined the use of effective assessment and classification systems implementing the LSI-R. Because of the evaluation's rigor, this alone would have been sufficient for inclusion as a focus topic in this chapter. However, the researchers—Stephen M. Haas, Cynthia A. Hamilton, and Dena Hanley—also examined the effects of staff culture and attitudes toward reentry and rehabilitative orientations. Specifically, these authors examined West Virginia's implementation of the West Virginia Offender Reentry Initiative (WVORI). In doing so, these authors pointed out that research consistently shows that correctional staff can have a strong influence on the predicted success or failure of a program that is implemented by a correctional agency. This is an important aspect of the classification process that is rarely (if ever) considered a variable in most assessment and/or classification systems. It may well be that staff attitudes could explain some of the variance that exists between predicted offender outcomes and those that occur and are different from what standardized instruments predict.

Thus, this research points to an underexplored area of assessment and treatment planning that may be applicable to any number of correctional programs. Some of the results that these researchers found are as follows:

1. Programs or interventions that depart substantially from the principles known to inform effective correctional programming are much less likely to observe reductions in recidivism.

2. Given that staff, such as case managers, counselors, and parole officers, interact with prisoners on a daily basis, they can determine the success or failure of any initiative undertaken by a correctional organization.

3. The identification of appropriate service and level of supervision after release should be contingent upon the accurate assessment of offender risk and needs.

4. Research has consistently shown that objective risk and needs assessments, based on statistical probabilities, more accurately predict the level of risk than personal or staff positions.

5. The success of a program can be significantly hampered by individual attitudes and personal opinions toward the new strategy, and the implementation of that strategy may be responsible for the success or failure of a new initiative.

6. Older organizations, with strong institutionalized organizational cultures and larger organizations with more layers of bureaucracy, have more difficulty with communication and coordination.

7. Conflict between individual values of the staff and the values of the organization negatively impacts implementation strategies.

8. Detachment between staff orientations and organizational values translates into role conflict. Role conflict produces stress and job dissatisfaction, contributing to a negative organizational culture.

9. Organizational culture drives staff behavior and knowledge of what is valued in the organization.

10. Staff tended to support the WVORI when they were supportive of rehabilitation, were more human service oriented, liked to work with others, liked their job, were empathetic toward inmates, and believed the department was committed to staff training and professional development.

11. A large majority of correctional staff were found to have a punitive orientation toward inmates, did not believe in the efficacy of rehabilitation, and were not oriented toward a human service career.

12. The initial report concluded that a substantial change in the human orientation of staff and greater support for rehabilitative efforts may be necessary for achieving greater support for reentry initiatives among correctional staff

(Continued)

(Continued)

This study is important because it illustrates that the predictions of offender behavior can be mitigated and/or aggravated by the actions of supervision and treatment staff within an agency. This observation is not, in and of itself, particularly astute. However, the fact that this was specifically linked to the assessment and classification process makes this research innovative and very useful. Further, these factors are important both for the prognosis of individual offenders and when evaluating agency outcomes. These authors, through this research approach, have found a common linking pin between individual offender treatment planning and agency evaluation outcomes. Because of this, it is perhaps a good recommendation that future classification systems take into account data input regarding the agency staff and its organizational culture since these factors are seldom assessed and since these factors have direct bearing on the success or failure of offenders who are released to community supervision.

The Link Between Theory and Risk Prediction

Connelly (2003) noted that in order for significant improvements in risk prediction to occur, instruments will need to be better grounded in theory. Specifically, actuarial prediction models to be used with serious offenders should be directly based on the discoveries made by research that empirically tests the ability of theories to explain and predict crime. Many students fail to appreciate the important connection between theoretical explanation of crime and its direct bearing on our ability to predict crime. In essence, theory is nothing less than a macro level form of assessment. What many laypersons and even experts in the field do not tend to realize is that many variables used to predict criminal behavior in theoretical tests are identical to those used in assessment instruments. This then means that there is a direct matching relationship between the research of theorists and the potential for improvement of risk assessment instruments. Indeed, as theoretical research continues, fertile ground is created for further refinement of instruments that use the same or similar variables. However, most current models are based on their simple ability to predict the likely outcome, but they do not explain the reason for criminal or noncriminal behavior (Connolly, 2003). This is problematic, particularly when one considers that needs-assessment variables are more related to explaining why recidivism might occur and since these variables are critical to the ultimate success of offender reintegration. Consider the point made by Krauss, Sales, Becker, and Figueredo (2000, p. 92), who argue that current risk assessment highlights those who are at greatest risk for recidivism rather than trying to explain why they are likely to recidivate. Explaining the "why" behind criminal behavior can therefore improve the treatment prognosis for most offenders (thus incorporating a needs-based approach that is best addressed through a casework model), which in turn improves their likely reintegration. While there is no single best theory to explain all crime, there are some common starting points that tend to lend themselves well to risk prediction. When considering these starting points, Connelly (2003) noted that the most promising research that has a direct application to the construction of adult offender risk prediction is based on one of the following three criminological theories: (1) the general theory of crime or self-control theory by Gottfredson and Hirschi, (2) the age-graded theory of informal social control by Sampson and Laub, and (3) **social learning theory** by Ronald Akers.

Applied Theory Section 5.1

Criminological Theory and Risk Prediction

Though this section makes it clear that theory aids in explaining the "why" behind criminal offending, it is important that students understand that the "why" also aids in predicting future criminal behavior. This is an important point because many persons may not be aware that criminological research examines variables that are quantified, measured, and examined for significance in likely criminal behavior. This is nothing less than a form of prediction.

The primary difference between purely theoretical research and pure risk prediction is that theoretical research starts with a hypothesis that is designed to test the efficacy of a theory in explaining criminal behavior; while on the other hand, risk prediction presumes these variable-based hypotheses are correct and uses them to predict the likelihood of criminal behavior in the future. It is in this manner that the two are interconnected—one with the other, in a circular relationship. Indeed, as practitioners use risk prediction devices, the effectiveness of these instruments will be established and over time will validate (or dispel) the theoretical bases that were initially used during their construction.

Nevertheless, risk prediction instruments are the practical outcome of widespread criminological and psychometric research. In other words, these instruments tend to combine findings from a wide range of theoretical approaches, with the single-minded purpose of predicting recidivism. It is in this manner that these instruments are a composite of a variety of theoretical components, ideally mixing and matching various constructs from multiple theoretical perspectives in a manner that optimizes prediction (leading to true positives and true negatives) and minimizes the likelihood of error (false negatives and false positives) in the risk assessment process.

◈ Classification

As has been pointed out in earlier sections, the presumption of this text is that recidivism can be more effectively reduced by ensuring that reintegrative efforts are maximized for offenders in the community. As was just pointed out, risk assessment of offenders is often simultaneously tied to their specific treatment needs. This means that security and treatment needs are not always easy to untangle from one another. Because of this, agencies must not only determine the general risk level of the inmate or offender on community supervision but the agency must also correctly "match up" the offender's treatment plan with the level of security determined by the LSI–R and other risk prediction tests and procedures. One primary tool used in corrections is an instrument known as the MMPI-2, which is the most widely used objective test instrument used in corrections. The **Minnesota Multiphasic Personality Inventory-2**, or **MMPI-2** is an objective personality adjustment inventory test that can be given to large numbers of offenders at the same time or individually as desired. The MMPI-2 has 567 true/false questions that require the offender to be able to read at the sixth grade level. Further, the MMPI-2 has been restandardized and is on tape for blind, illiterate, semiliterate, or disabled individuals. It is important to stress that the MMPI-2 is primarily a

▲ **Photo 5.2** An intake and classification worker enters information that will aid in determining an offender's eventual classification level, both in the jail and later on community supervision.

clinical tool used for detecting mental health disorders among abnormal populations.

This test has a number of "subscales" within it. These subscales are a series of questions that are embedded and camouflaged within the remainder of the 567 total questions and are dispersed at random points within the test. These questions are all designed to measure specific points of interest to provide a multi-profile view of the offender's personality. However, the MMPI-2 is very effective with the manipulative offender population because of three specific subscales that are included. These subscales of interest are the lie (L), infrequency (I), and the correction (K) scales.

The lie or "L" scale consists of 15 questions (out of 567 total questions) such as "I never get angry." The scale indicates whether the client is consciously or unconsciously presenting herself as a perfectionist. The I-scale consists of 64 questions (again, out of 567 questions) but does not measure a trait. Because the items are answered in a deviant direction by less than 10% of those who take the test, a high score indicates that the offender has endorsed a large number of serious psychological items. For offenders, this may be an attempt to look bad on the test or they may be confused or even having delusions (especially with mentally ill offenders). Lastly, the K or correction scale measures defensiveness as a test-taking attitude. The scale has 30 items that cover a wide range of content areas. Low scores usually indicate a deliberate attempt to appear bad, but sometimes a self-critical offender (an addict, some pedophiles, or an offender who feels remorse) may endorse responses that indicate pathological tendencies.

In addition to the MMPI-2, the **Minnesota Multiphasic Personality Inventory Criminal Justice and Correctional Report**, or **MMPI-2 CJCR** is based on decades of research and is designed to more closely fit the outcome data from the MMPI-2 to a classification scheme (Megargee, 2004).

The MMPI-2 CJCR is perfectly suited to match up the offender's treatment plan with the level of security and serves as an additional double check when making security decisions from the LSI-R. This report is used in conjunction with the MMPI-2 to provide information pertaining to the offender's needs assessment, risk assessment, and program planning within a correctional agency. The report is designed to identify those offenders who may suffer from thought disorders, serious depression, and substance abuse problems. It identifies those who may need mental health treatment as well as those who are most likely to be hostile, predatory, bullied, or victimized while incarcerated. This report also includes predictor items related to self-injury and suicide.

The MMPI-2 CJCR system was developed by Edwin Megargee and is fashioned around the well-regarded **Megargee offender classification system**. This system of classification is known to provide solid empirical support for classification and placement decisions. The Megargee system is especially effective in assisting criminal justice practitioners to deal with an offender population that is increasingly including the mentally ill or disordered within its ranks. Further, the Megargee system has been reported to effectively classify 90% to 95% of the MMPI-2 profiles encountered among most probation, parole, and institutional correctional settings. In fact, one federal institution used the system as a guide in providing offender cell assignments, and this process resulted in a 46% reduction in serious violence within that institution. The Megargee offender classification system is the basis for the MMPI-2 CJCR. The results from the MMPI-2 CJCR can be used to support important management, treatment, and programming decisions.

This includes the ability to do the following: First, reliably classify offenders at initial intake of incarceration to support important supervision and treatment issues. Second, identify offenders who may present less risk to the system, possibly allowing a downgrade in security level and improved placement on community supervision. Third, better understand an offender's background, attitudes, and abilities to determine whether the individual will benefit from substance abuse treatment, mental health programming, and other services. Fourth, identify offenders who may do well in prison work programs, based on their educational and vocational abilities. Fifth, address the readiness of the offender to leave the institution and to assist in developing effective aftercare programs. Finally, accurately evaluate and reclassify offenders over the course of their supervision to support programming or treatment decisions.

The **MMPI-2 Criminal Justice and Correctional Report** also consists of nine behavioral dimensions. These behavioral dimensions compare offenders to other offenders rather than to the general outside population to ensure that results are correctly normed. The nine behavioral dimensions of the MMPI-2 are (1) apparent need for further mental health assessment or programming; (2) apparent leadership ability (dominance); (3) indications of conflicts with or resentment of authorities; (4) likelihood of positive or favorable response to academic programming; (5) indications of socially deviant behavior or attitudes; (6) apparent need for social participation (extroversion); (7) likelihood of mature, responsible behavior and positive response to supervision; 8) likelihood of positive, favorable response to vocational programming; and (9) likelihood of hostile or antagonistic peer relations.

Further, the MMPI-2 CJCR identifies nine possible areas relevant to the offender. This provides treatment staff with indicators of difficulties that the offender may face. As with the other report components, the offender's problems are normed against a population of other offenders to ensure that comparisons are similar and that the test is valid for the offender population. The nine problem areas identified are as follows: difficulties with alcohol or other substance abuse, manipulation or exploitation of others, thought disorders, overcontrolled hostility, family conflict or alienation from family, depressive affect or mood disorder, awkward or difficult interpersonal relationships, anger control problems, and tendency to get sick or ill frequently.

When taken together, the MMPI-2 and the MMPI-2 CJCR provide a comprehensive means of classifying offenders based on both mental health and criminal justice categories of concern. The use of the LSI-R serves as an initial predictor of recidivism, and it is desirable to have one single instrument strictly for this purpose. The MMPI-2 and the MMPI-2 CJCR both go beyond mere recidivism prediction but instead include mental health and security classification determinations. The process described in this section would provide for optimal assessment, security, and treatment of offenders placed on community supervision. Simultaneously, the offender would also gain excellent treatment programming from a system that would address specific areas identified as possible "problem areas" in their effective reintegration.

⊠ Case Management

Case management as a function is relatively new in the mental health field. For the most part, this is where case management, as applied to community corrections, is derived. According to Enos and Southern (1996), the term *case management* began to appear in the common treatment literature during the mid to late 1970s. Other sources have also confirmed this to be the basic era during which case management emerged (Monchick, Scheyett, & Pfeifer, 2006). Case management is "seen as a way to connect clients with multiple needs to an increasingly complex social service delivery system" (Monchick et al., 2006, p. 5). This is an apt description of the process. Monchick and colleagues (2006) noted that case management has traditionally focused on the holistic needs of clients with particular attention to the basic needs of the client, such as those related to food, shelter, medical services, employment, and basic safety. These various factors all work together to provide a person with stability—the very stability that is missing from the lives of most offenders.

During the 1930s, federal legislation in regard to social security and other forms of social aid served as the impetus to programs that required the processing of persons through organized systems of welfare and support. As a means of effectively organizing the client case flow while also coordinating services from a number of agencies, the beginnings of the case management system began to emerge. However, the first direct and deliberate connection between networks of social assistance and the use of case management was perhaps presented by Froland, Pancoast, Chapman, and Kimboko (1981). These authors called for more active and overt links between a variety of social support systems for clients. Enos and Southern (1996) argued that this is perhaps the primary notion of case management.

During the 1950s, a variety of different researchers and criminologists became concerned about the welfare of patients in mental hospitals, and their works served as harbingers of the deinstitutionalization movement in the United States. During this time, a trend from hospitalization to community release was first set in motion in 1959, with nearly 559,000 mentally ill patients who were housed in state mental hospitals being progressively released over time (National Institute of Corrections, 2004).

The portrayal of mental hospitals as being ineffective (Goffman, 1961) coupled with the increased use of imprisonment led to the growing incarceration of those with special needs. Unfortunately, the training and qualifications of those involved most with these special needs offenders tended to be lacking at best but did illustrate the need for a greater use of paraprofessionals or those individuals grounded in the wisdom of those who are most acquainted with the daily routine of the client. This further demonstrates that treatment options progressively extended beyond the direct purview of the highly trained **psychiatrist** or psychologist and extended to other persons that could fill gaps that would otherwise occur in any comprehensive program designed to address multiple needs of the client.

The trend toward integrating paraprofessionals continued, coupled with a decrease in the use of secure mental health facilities. As the mentally ill clients were released into the community, it became clear that some sort of assistance would be necessary for these persons. Likewise, this was well beyond the ability or scope of practice for psychiatrists and psychologists who could not have routine community contact with large numbers of clients. Such an effort would prove to be both unwieldy and very costly. Rather, it was again the paraprofessional who became important in the follow-up coordination of care for those released during the deinstitutionalization movement. Deinstitutionalization then, with its emphasis on outpatient services, required a new method of service delivery, leading to the rise of the case management method (Enos & Southern, 1996).

During the time that these changes took place, one key piece of legislation was particularly important to correctional counselors (Enos & Southern, 1996). This was Public Law 89-793, which addressed community care rather than imprisonment for substance abusers. This law also emphasized a holistic approach to treatment and further cemented the notion of a multifaceted method of intervention. Because this law shifted treatment to community approaches and also recommended a broad range of services, the orientation toward case management perspectives continued to emerge. Further legislative developments occurred, and in 1975, Public Law 94-63 was passed. This was referred to as the Public Health Service Act Amendment and Special Revenue Sharing Act of 1975 and was the genesis for modern day case management approaches (Enos & Southern, 1996). This legislation emphasized the need for outreach efforts and coordination as a means of providing comprehensive health care and mental health services to those who were served (Enos & Southern, 1996).

Enos and Southern further noted that from the 1990s onward, case management is generally thought of as a "bridge and a system of networks resulting in the coordination and distribution of informal and formal services on behalf of someone in need" (Enos & Southern, 1996, p. 24). The use of paraprofessionals, including therapists, nurses, etc., further substantiates the need for treatment not just punishment. The sections that follow provide an overview of the tools used for case management and supervision strategies. (For a more in-depth discussion of the history and evolution of case management, see Hanser, 2009.)

Case Management Models

More recently, the work of Monchick and colleagues (2006) pointed toward the use of case management for the supervising offenders seeking drug treatment. In the community corrections field, this is a particularly important application because drug problems are often at the heart of an offender's difficulties—the tendency to relapse often being directly related to recidivism rates. Walsh (2000) presented four general case management models, these being the broker/generalist model, the strengths-based perspective, the assertive community treatment method, and the clinical/rehabilitation method. None of these models work in a completely unique manner, and each model has functions and purposes that overlap the other. Each agency utilizing case management processes must find the right balance between these models as determined by the needs of their clients and the resources that are available to the agency and/or the surrounding community. A brief presentation of each model is subsequently provided.

First, the **broker/generalist case management** is narrow in scope of action. This model focuses primarily on rapid linkage and referral. The case manager provides limited direct services other than the initial assessment to determine service needs, service referrals, and occasional monitoring of service provision. Where resources are scarce, this model allows for the provision of a limited number of services to the greatest number of participants.

Second, the **strengths-based perspective case management** involves assisting clients to examine and identify their own strengths and assets as the vehicle for resource acquisition and goal attainment. The case manager helps the client identify his or her strengths and assets, supports the client in defining goals, and helps identify ways the client's strengths can be used to reach these goals. The case manager provides support to the client so that he or she may assert direct control over his or her search for resources, such as housing and employment (Rapp, 1998).

Third, the **assertive community treatment case management** is an intensive case management model with low caseloads and frequent, community-based contact with clients. The model is grounded in a multidisciplinary team approach where all team members share the caseload and work together to provide proactive services, assertive outreach, and strong advocacy to clients. The case management team provides many services to the client directly, and, if referring to an outside agency, carefully monitors the relationship between the client and the service provider(s). Finally, in the **clinical/rehabilitation case management** approach, those providing case management services deliver the clinical treatment as well, providing both in an integrated manner. The case manager in this model has the primary responsibility for providing therapeutic intervention, including therapy, counseling, skills teaching, and other rehabilitative interventions along with case management services (Anthony, Cohen, & Farkas, 1990).

These four approaches to case management will be referred to from time to time throughout the section. As we progress further throughout the section, it will become clear that elements of each case management model are used in community corrections. Further, the more reintegrative the program, the more integral is the case management function.

Before proceeding further, it is important to distinguish between two key concepts. Both sound similar, but both are different from one another. These two conceptual terms, **case management** and **caseload management,** should not be confused with one another. For this text's purposes, case management is the process whereby an offender is provided fully comprehensive and coordinated services that address the offender's vocational, social, educational, and mental health functions. All aspects of the offender's needs, including basic medical needs, housing, and food accommodations, are provided within this coordinated program of service delivery. The goal is to address the offender's needs so that they are a fully functioning member of society. The previous description is what we mean when we refer to case management in this text. Caseload management, on the other hand, is the process that we use to assign supervision workloads to CSOs. This takes into account the number of offenders, the security risk of those offenders, and the specialized needs that those offenders may have. The more serious the security risk and/or the more profound the needs, the more intensive that offender is to supervise, resulting in fewer offenders under a balanced system of caseload management. Naturally, the less security risks and/or the fewer specialized needs of offenders would result in more such offenders being on a CSO's caseload.

Client Needs Assessment

Obviously, the needs of the offender are directly related to the process of case management. However, the needs of the offender are not just balanced against considerations of security risk but they are also counterbalanced by the resources that are available to the agency and the community. One primary aspect of accomplishing this has been through a process of offender classification. If existing resources are to be appropriately matched to offenders, and if future resources are to be intelligently planned (i.e., based on systemwide profiles and projections), then classification data gathering, recording, and initial decision making become critical. Existing technology and accumulated professional experience can make classification an effective tool of correctional management.

The failure to provide a reasonable level of "matching" of needs and programs has come under scrutiny both in prison conditions suits and in professional corrections. Court findings have addressed the harm that often results when offenders are indiscriminately housed in overly restrictive facilities and when needed services or special management are not provided. Correctional officials are also recognizing the financial and internal management implications of failing to assess realistically offender risk and special needs. For example, maximum security space, disproportionately costly, warrants very judicious use. The early identification of needs often can prevent deterioration—physical, psychological, and social—that may occur if left unchecked. From a humane point of view, deterioration is always costly. From a management perspective, unmet needs have widespread and predictable side effects regarding recidivism.

Parallel challenges exist in the areas of offender needs, management practices, and service provision specifically related to custody and security. The offender needs assessment is critical to the overall reduction of recidivism. In fact, it is likely that a primary reason for high recidivism rates during the first year to three years of offender release from prison has to do more with a lack of needs than anything else. In their research that occurred over 20 years ago, Clements, McKee, and Jones (1984) noted that one of the most serious challenges to effective program delivery is the development of effective objective screening devices. Clements and colleagues (1984) noted that with such instruments staff are able to apply standardized criteria that are uniformly weighted to identify the relative demands for services. Without this level of objectivity, it is less likely that all offenders who exhibit symptoms of need would be uniformly attended to. For this text's purposes, the term **needs assessment** will refer to those aspects of offender classification that seek to identify or determine the condition or state of individuals relative to some preestablished functional criteria. Those criteria may relate to more concrete attributes of adjustment (such as physical or psychological health), to behavioral skills that involve practical functioning (i.e., academic or vocational competence), or to more complex social situations in which deficits are measured relative to particular environments, conditions, or demands (e.g., vulnerability, personal/social skills).

When considering the appraisal of an offender's needs, it is important to distinguish among successively refined levels of assessment. Each level of assessment involves a more specific focus and a more individualized evaluation of the offender. This then allows for refined matching between the needs of the offender and the specific services or interventions that are given.

As demonstrated in Table 5.2, the refinement of the classification process correlates with the level of assessment. At a primary level, **intake screening of needs** should result in a series of judgments that subdivide offenders into broad categories of basic needs and/or deficits. This then points case managers in the general direction for referral of offenders to generalized service areas. From the first level of analysis, **dispositional needs assessment** provides additional information within one or more given need dimensions regarding the specific program or treatment that would benefit the offender. Finally, more **intensive needs assessment** would result in highly detailed intervention plans within a priority need area. Each level of assessment may require, in turn, the increased involvement of professionals who network with the community supervision agency, such as job placement programs, educational institutions, medical services, or mental health treatment providers. Further, it should be remembered that all people change over time; they also change as they encounter new experiences. This includes offenders as well. For better or worse, the offender is likely to have experienced some form of insight and/or addition to his or her repertoire of memories and experiences. This then means that a person's needs do not stay the same. Thus, the needs assessment should not be viewed as a "one shot" exercise but instead is a continual process of refinement that is repeated throughout an offender's supervision sentence. The basic principles of good assessment when determining offender needs would include the following: First, detect critical needs that would be problematic in any setting—for example, acute illness. Second, identify deficits or needs that may have influenced or been part of a pattern of law violation (criminality) or that may interfere with successful reintegration—that is, drug abuse, impulse control, and vocational deficits. Third, determine offenders' deficits, needs, traits, or behaviors that influence their adjustment or management while in prison—for example, vulnerability, personal/social skills. Finally, serve broader human needs—for example, for structure, activity, support, privacy, and so forth. Each purpose is usually associated with a different approach to assessment and intervention. Typically, these diverse needs are addressed by different agencies throughout the community.

Reliability and Validity of Needs Assessment Scales

As with risk assessment and prediction, the reliability and validity of needs-based assessment tools is important. The various necessary characteristics for good assessment scales are all the same; we are simply assessing a different concept or area of offender functioning when we assess their needs as opposed to their potential security level. With this said, students should keep the following subsections in mind as we close our discussion on the needs assessment process.

First, the assessment system should use highly reliable information, instruments, and techniques. Any substantial investment of time and resources is best served by using only those techniques or instruments that can be consistently administered. The goal is to achieve a degree of uniformity that tends to yield

Table 5.2   Levels of Assessment of Needs

Level or Type of Need	Scope	Decision or Function
Intake/screening of needs	Basic needs	Initial assignment, management, and basic referral decisions
Dispositional needs assessment	Specific program areas	Assignment to group or offender category for specific foci of intervention
Intensive needs assessment	Priority areas of need	Individualized treatment planning for the offender

comparable information from case to case. Moreover, officials, when relying on particular instruments or tests, must consider their inherent reliability characteristics. Finally, assessments should be conducted in settings and under conditions that are most conducive to obtaining full and accurate information.

Second, methods used that are specifically valid for and relevant to the assessments and decisions being made should be used. A given instrument or method is not inherently valid. Its relevance must be established for each specific purpose for which it is to be used. Needs assessment must move away from "shotgun" approaches in which information of widely varying reliability and validity is all fed into the "black box" of classification. In most instances, we need to limit sharply the generalization of information (or predictions) to those individual behaviors or conditions that have some known relationship to the assessment instrument or method.

Finally, assessment approaches must provide for the potential for change across time and settings. Some individual needs may be relatively static (e.g., physical disability) and may require a fairly constant response or management or environment. Still, other needs can be seen as recurring (e.g., exercise), thus requiring a continuing level of programming. Of more concern here, however, are those needs responsive to some degree of remediation or change. Since such changes should be measurable, follow-up assessments should be planned. Too, we must recognize that an individual's needs (especially in the interpersonal areas) may vary across settings. Clearly, then, descriptive labels should rarely be assigned to offenders on a permanent basis.

Cost-effectiveness is a commonsense concern. A very expensive system or an approach yielding little useful information is an obvious, and thankfully rare, waste of resources. A reduction in costs can be accomplished, for example, by developing a referral system in which only selected offenders are given higher-level diagnostic assessments—for example, for specific educational prescriptions. Effectiveness (often the forgotten side of the formula) can be enhanced through some of the principles previously cited, for example, by selecting only reliable and valid assessment instruments. Moreover, the effectiveness of needs assessment becomes moot if inadequate and insufficient management and treatment options exist.

Assessment

The principles of effective correctional intervention seek to target the highest-risk offenders. Prescreening assessments should be used by agencies to eliminate and divert lower-risk offenders. A good integrated case management system starts at the assessment interview thereby setting the tone for the offender's investment in the case management process. This process typically requires staff to change their approach to conducting an interview. For example, although many staff use the "interrogation interview," this process discounts the offender's "reality" and life situation. To discover this, staff must use motivational interviewing techniques and suspend judgment while gaining insight into how the offender thinks and acts. It is also important to remember to be very thorough in conducting the interview so that all necessary information is collected in order to complete the case management plan. Therefore, interviewers are responsible for understanding the offender's pattern of behavior, which includes knowing what led up to the offense(s), as well as the date of the charge and the disposition of the case. If you are going to change behavior, you must have a clear understanding of when the problem behavior is most likely to occur and when the offender is likely to be most vulnerable. In many ways, this step is analogous to the ABCs (antecedents, behavior, and consequences) of relapse prevention strategies.

In addition to conducting actuarial risk assessments, it is important to obtain data on personality traits either by performing assessments or gathering data from outside sources. There are a multitude of assessments, such as IQ tests, the Criminal Sentiments Scale, and Stages of Change, which also reveal pertinent information about an offender. Gathering this information directly or from collateral sources is important in developing programming tailored to the characteristics of the offender. Andrews and Bonta (2003) referred to this as the "responsivity principle" whereby the officer outlines the need to develop interventions and programming in a style and mode that is consistent with the ability and learning style of the offender to maximize the effectiveness of the programming.

The Supervision Plan

Once the assessments have been completed, the case management plan can be developed. The staff person needs to reflect back to the assessments and use the offender's descriptions of his circumstances and behaviors to design a plan that addresses the factors contributing to the problematic behavior. It is important that the case management plan stress the application of new techniques and skills learned in the appropriate programs. To have the offender participate in cognitive programming is one thing, but having the offender apply what he has learned in programming to real-life situations should be the goal when looking to long-term behavior change. The format of the supervision plan can vary as long as both agent and offender view the plan as a mutually agreed upon document.

Addressing Offender Needs Holistically

The goal of case management calls for comprehensive services that address all aspects of the offender's needs, including basic medical needs, housing, and food accommodations. All of these concerns are basic needs that do not even begin to address more complicated concerns related to treatment and/or recovery from substance abuse issues (a very common issue among the offender population). Such a goal is obviously well beyond the scope of a community supervision agency. When addressing the offender's needs holistically, it is important to again discuss the use of volunteers. Volunteers are able to assist offenders in obtaining their basic needs, but they are also able to do so much more. Volunteers may develop an informal bond with the offender that provides social capital that may prevent the offender from recidivating or relapsing during low emotional points in their supervision. A good volunteer network can fill in the gaps between the agency networking that occurs through the case management process.

The main point here is to simply demonstrate that once a need is assessed, then the offender must be connected with the source agency or person who is tasked with providing the service to fulfill that need.

However, many aspects of case management are often overlooked and, as some might say, the devil is in the details. For instance, transportation problems may occur, and the offender may not have the ability to find public transportation. Problems with other general and mundane services may occur that most other persons may take for granted on a daily basis. Offenders may have difficulty finding friends and socializing since their own prior friends may have all come from criminogenic backgrounds. In such cases, volunteers can help bridge the range of possibilities between that which exists among county and state agencies.

Many laypersons may view substance abuse issues at a topical level. This is largely due to a misunderstanding of the complex social, psychological, and physiological processes involved with long-term drug and/or alcohol abuse. Due to the need for comprehensive services, a number of programs have emerged around the nation to address this problem. The use of drug courts is perhaps the primary example, itself based on a case management model that strives to provide offenders with a comprehensive set of services and interventions. Because substance abuse is such a widespread problem among the offender population, it is with this in mind that we turn our attention to treatment screening and screening tools, keeping substance abuse issues as a primary area of attention but also considering corollary or comorbid issues associated with addiction.

Treatment Screening and Screening Tools

Treatment screening is simply a process where an offender is asked a number of questions, either orally or in written form, and the responses given by that offender determine whether the offender is in need of some sort of treatment. For this text's purposes, **screening** is the process by which an offender is determined to be appropriate for admission to a given intervention program. The means of determining whether the offender is eligible largely depend on the focus of the service, the specific client population that the service is designed to accommodate, as well as the funding requirements that fall within an agency.

As noted earlier, one of the key services that are relevant to offenders on community supervision is that of substance abuse intervention. However, in many cases offenders may not have an arrest or formal charge against them that is related to alcohol or drugs. But this still does not mean that they lack the need for services related to drug and alcohol abuse. In fact, roughly 60% to 70% of all offenders have some sort of drug and/or alcohol issue at the point of arrest, many being polydrug users. While this may not be the official charge against them (particularly after the plea bargaining process has been settled) it does highlight the fact that alcohol and drugs are a part of the offender lifestyle. Also keep in mind that those known to have substance abuse issues consist of those known to have such problems; many others are also likely to have such problems but have simply evaded detection. Thus, it is important in community supervision to be able to successfully and accurately screen for drug abuse. However, this alone is not effective because the offender may later be in denial or may simply claim to have used illicit substances much less frequently than is true.

Indeed, offenders typically do tend to avoid both substance abuse and mental health interventions if possible, due to the stigma and due to the desire to remain free from scrutiny. One instrument that is well suited in addressing these questions is the **Substance Abuse Subtle Screening Inventory (SASSI)**, which is a screening instrument that provides interpretations of client profiles and aids in developing hypotheses that clinicians or researchers may find useful in understanding persons in treatment. The SASSI is a brief and easily administered psychological screening measure that helps identify individuals who have a high probability of having a substance use disorder. What is quite unique about this screening tool is that the SASSI is designed to identify substance dependent offenders who may be unable or unwilling to acknowledge relevant substance-related behavior. The adult SASSI identifies substance dependence with an overall empirically tested accuracy of 93%. This aspect of the SASSI makes it ideal for the offender population.

Further, when the SASSI is used in combination with other available assessment information, SASSI profiles facilitate later treatment planning considerations.

Another instrument that is likewise used for substance abuse screening, intake, assessment, and evaluation is the **Maryland Addictions Questionnaire (MAQ)**. This instrument is an excellent treatment planning tool, but it is also an effective screening and assessment tool that takes into account many of the factors related to assessment. The MAQ is typically administered at intake, and it provides the evaluator with an idea of the severity of the addiction, the motivation of the client offender, and the likely risk of relapse for the offender. The MAQ also screens for cognitive and affective (anxiety and depression) difficulties that may complicate the treatment regimen. The MAQ is similar to the SASSI with its ability to detect when offenders may be deceptive and/or unwilling to truthfully provide details necessary for successful intervention. The MAQ is quick and easy to administer and thus does not require clinicians with extensive and costly licensures and/or certifications. This makes the MAQ a practical choice for agencies as well.

The last screening and/or assessment instrument to be discussed is the **Substance Abuse Relapse Assessment (SARA)**. The SARA is a structured interview designed as a treatment planning instrument for treatment professionals who work with substance abusers. It is especially helpful in developing relapse prevention goals for clients who tend to use multiple substances and in monitoring the achievement of these goals during treatment. The SARA helps the individual to identify the events that typically precede his/her substance use as well as the consequences that may reinforce that use. The SARA is designed for use with both juvenile and adult offenders who have a history of drug and/or alcohol abuse or whose ability to avoid relapse is in question. The SARA, unlike the SASSI and the MAQ, utilizes a subjective form of assessment since it is a structured interview. This instrument is likewise one that is less effective at the initial screening point but instead works well in determining likelihood of relapse, thereby aiding treatment planners in designing interventions aimed at the prevention of relapse.

Treatment Planning

After the appropriate screening and/or assessment process has been completed, various treatment staff will typically work to develop a plan of action for the offender's reintegration. This plan of action, usually therapeutic in nature, is often referred to as the treatment plan. Students do need to understand that treatment planning is not a one-time occurrence. Rather, treatment planning is a continual process that is refined over time as new challenges emerge and as the offender has successes and failures throughout the process. From this statement, it is clear then that it is expected that offenders will have some failures and it is up to the treatment staff to aid the client in the difficult transition to reform.

It is important that the treatment staff get a clear picture of the underlying issues relevant to the client. This may not always be what the client overtly states to the counselor. Indeed, the client may be manipulative and may desire to throw the treatment staff off course throughout the treatment process. Treatment providers must identify the needs of a client in an effective and realistic manner. As has been indicated throughout this section, it is important that the client's basic needs are met before they can be expected to effectively dwell on any meta-needs, such as belonging or actualization. Thus, basic needs must be attended to for most all correctional clients. It is important to keep in mind that when we talk about offender clients, we are typically referring to clients who have a lack of material resources, few job skills, a social stigma of being an offender working against them, likely housing problems, medical issues, and so forth. Any attempt to deliver services amidst this chaotic set of events will likely have dismal results unless effective interventions are in place.

In addition to the needs of the client, the strengths and resources that the client has must also be considered. In many cases, clients will not necessarily be aware of their own strengths and/or understand the resources that they have available. Sometimes this may be due to esteem issues (not recognizing their own strengths due to a negative self-image), and at other times it may be because they simply have not thought of a given strength or resource as being such. Naturally, caseworkers will want to ensure that the offender has clear objectives that are written. These objectives should of course be prioritized, but, just as importantly, the client should clearly understand why a given order of prioritization has been assigned to goals and objectives. This is also important because it teaches and reinforces a valuable skill that many offenders tend to lack—long-term and sequential planning. In addition, a list of steps for each objective should be made. While this may seem mundane and perhaps a bit overly detailed, this is important for clients who may not have had optimal socialization and/or educational training. Planning and organizing are critical skills to life success, and they should be emphasized when clients are in treatment.

In an ideal case, the correctional client fulfills all of their goals and objectives. In the real world, this seldom happens—at least initially. However, this does not mean that overall these clients are not successful with their programs; as pointed out earlier, there will be setbacks, and offenders will inevitably experience failures amidst their road to reintegration. Regardless, once the offender has met the criteria for program completion, they should be discharged. Naturally, the caseworker will need to, among other things, write a summary of the discharge elements as a means of recording the final outcome of the client while in the treatment program. In addition, the caseworker will need to have additional referrals available in case the offender has other issues or circumstances that they may wish to address. These may be corollary to the issues that the offender addressed with his or her counselor, and they may not be under any obligation to address such issues (often, court mandated treatment can be very specific, overlooking key areas of needed treatment). However, some offenders may wish to do so anyway. In such cases, it is important that agencies have an integrated system of services and resources available to aid the offender in their posttreatment functions and routines. If the offender is successful in arranging this, then it is likely that a continuum of care can be achieved for the offender, providing a seamless transition from the role of a criminal justice number to be processed to that of full-fledged prosocial member of society.

Progress Notes, Record Keeping, and Connecting the Case Plan With Supervision

One of the most important elements of the case management process—and directly addressed by ethical codes of conduct—is the accurate recording of notes pertaining to the activities of all counseling sessions. Recording and maintaining accurate records is important when guarding against potential liability concerns. In addition, case notes are vital to the process of treatment planning since they help keep interventions focused on pertinent issues of concern to the offender(s). To keep treatment planning and intervention work on track, case notes should reflect the offender's progress, or lack thereof, especially as it relates to the particular goals of an offender. Case notes provide one avenue for treatment planners to stay focused on particular issues as well as to verify compliance with legal issues. Accountability is a vital component of the counseling process that must be adhered to. The best way to ensure accountability is to accurately and ethically note all happenings of the treatment process and then record these notes in appropriate files.

Lastly, caseworkers must ensure that therapeutic staff and community supervision staff are apprised of the offender's programs, and appropriate insight as to the offender's progress should be shared. In like fashion, CSOs should ensure that treatment staff is informed about noteworthy developments throughout the supervision process. It is in this manner that both supervision and treatment staff can work together in tandem, thereby optimizing the offender's likely success. In essence, supervision staff can aid in ensuring offender compliance with attendance at treatment-related functions; caseworkers and treatment staff can provide supervision staff of a more detailed picture of the offender's actual progress in meeting the goals of their supervision. This then means that both the casework and security function of community corrections can aid one another, each being indispensable to achieving successful offender outcomes. Close communication and collaboration between both groups of practitioners and the integration of community assistance make the true ingredients of any successful reintegration program, the result being less recidivism and a safer community.

◩ Conclusion

The collection of information is an important first step in the intake and assessment process. It is critical that CSOs ensure that information included in the PSI is accurate since this document affects sentencing, later supervision levels, later treatment program participation, and release decisions that follow. In fact, it could be said that the PSI is a combined form of subjective and objective assessment document, and it is therefore fitting that it is discussed from the perspective of an assessment and/or classification perspective.

Both subjective and objective assessments should be used when making security and treatment decisions for special needs offenders. However, security decisions should be based solely on objective risk prediction criteria while treatment decisions should be based more upon subjective structured interviews and clinical diagnoses so as to capitalize upon the expertise of the clinician. The Wisconsin risk assessment system was presented as the recommended objective assessment scale for security-based decisions, while the use of subjective structured interviews based upon the *Diagnostic and Statistical Manual of Mental Disorders (DSM-IV-TR)* diagnosis criteria were recommended for purposes of treatment. The LSI-R was presented as the preferred instrument at the recidivism prediction stage due its utility with large populations, it quantitative aspect, the ease with which practitioners may use the instrument, and its ability to directly link with programs based on cognitive behavioral treatment programs (most dealing with special needs offenders will use some variety of cognitive behavioral intervention).

The problems and pitfalls associated with false positives and false negatives were noted to provide a general overview of the problems associated with inaccurate assessment in correctional systems. This demonstrates that it is an assessment that provides the basic building block to the success of community corrections as a whole. The MMPI-2 and the MMPI-2 CJCR were presented as the premier tools for effective classification of offenders based on their self-reported pathology and a variety of behavioral dimensions and problem areas that were identified. The use of these tools are specifically designed to be consistent with the Megargee offender classification system, which is presented as a premier classification system that would ideally be utilized with any agency that has a substantial population of special needs offenders.

Case management has a history that reaches back to early mental health treatment systems where clients were asked to provide their input into the treatment process. In addition, the use of multiple services led to the need for an organized approach of integration, leading to the process of case management. However, before case management can be effectively implemented, one must know the individual needs of a client to know which services are required of the client. This then calls for what is known as a needs assessment. The needs assessment compiles all of the different problems and challenges associated with an offender so that a list of needed services can be established. Both the caseworker and the offender provide input into this process, mirroring the early historical notions of case management. Further, these needs are prioritized, following any number of criteria to determine that priority. Once identified and prioritized, the treatment plan is constructed to address the various needs, in order of priority, as agreed upon between the caseworker and the offender.

While case management is a process designed primarily for offender reintegration and treatment, it is not entirely separate from the supervision concerns of the community supervision agency. In fact, quite the opposite is true; both work together in tandem to provide a coherent process of supervisory and treatment-based contact for the offender. Because case management and caseload assignment sound similar and because both work together, hand in hand, they can be confused with one another. Case management, associated more with providing basic needs and therapeutic treatment for the offender, is typically associated with social service and mental health practitioners. Caseload management is primarily a process of workload division between CSOs so that the supervision of offenders is accomplished with near to equitable levels among officers within the agency.

Classification is important to case management since it helps to determine priorities with different offender treatment plans and also classifies security levels for offender supervision. However, classification within the case management context is not identical to that *conducted* within the case management context.

Lastly, screening processes in treatment planning are important, and many are used when considering substance abuse interventions. Several were presented in this section, with two providing subtle screening that is designed to surreptitiously detect underlying issues that the offender might not otherwise report if asked directly. Further, these instruments are capable of detecting deceit, defensiveness, and manipulation among offenders. Because of these functions, these tools are considered superior to most screening processes that are overt and excessively face valid. Upon appropriate screening, offenders are provided a treatment plan for intervention, and it is at that point that actual therapeutic services are provided. Throughout the process, clinicians and supervision practitioners are both tasked with maintaining records to ensure the effective tracking of offender progress.

⊠ Section Summary

- The use of assessment and risk prediction is an increasing phenomenon in community-based corrections.
- The presentence investigation is a report conducted after conviction and presentencing. This report includes a plethora of information on the offenders' background, such as demographics, vocational, educational, and personal information as well as records on their prior offending.
- Typically, judges accept the recommendation of the reporting probation officers on sentencing.
- Risk assessments serve as a valuable tool in supervising offenders in the community. The most popular forms of instruments are some variation of the Wisconsin instrument and the LSI-R.
- The most meaningful instruments include some measure of both static and dynamic factors.
- Classification is another mechanism used to effectively manage offenders' populations in the community. Many agencies use the MMPI-2 to classify offenders.
- Many agencies utilize the case management model to supervise these offenders. This model includes the use of community resources to collaborate and supervise offenders.
- The use of progress notes and record keeping helps to facilitate the treatment progress of offenders in the community.

KEY TERMS

Assertive community treatment case management

Broker/generalist case management

Caseload management

Case management

Clinical/rehabilitation case management

Diagnostic and Statistical Manual of Mental Disorders (DSM-IV-TR)

Dispositional needs assessment

Dynamic risk factors

False negative

False positive

Incapacitation

Intensive needs assessment

Level of Service Inventory–Revised (LSI-R)

Maryland Addictions Questionnaire (MAQ)

Megargee offender classification system

Minnesota Multiphasic Personality Inventory (MMPI-2)

Minnesota Multiphasic Personality Inventory Criminal Justice and Correctional Report (MMPI-2 CJCR)

Needs assessment

Needs-principled assessment

Presentence investigation report (PSI)

Prognosis

Risk-principled assessment

Screening

Static risk factors

Strengths-based perspective case management

Subjective assessment process

Subjective structured interview

Substance Abuse Relapse Assessment (SARA)

Substance Abuse Subtle Screening Inventory (SASSI)

True negative

True positive

Wisconsin risk assessment system

DISCUSSION QUESTIONS

1. What is the importance of completing a thorough and accurate PSI? Why is accurate information critical to later supervision and treatment needs of the offender?

2. What are the basic concepts inherent to assessment?

3. What are the differences between false positives, false negatives, true positives, and true negatives? What are the pros and cons of wrongly identifying an offender?

4. What are the differences between static and dynamic risk factors?

5. What are the differences between subjective and objective means of assessment and risk prediction?

6. What are the advantages associated with the Wisconsin risk assessment and the flaws associated with that instrument?

7. Why is it important to conduct a client needs assessment before and during supervision?

8. Compare and contrast between case management and caseload assignment models.

9. What are the common aspects of classification within the case management context?

10. What is the importance of treatment planning to the reintegration process?

WEB RESOURCES

Risk and Assessment Instruments:

http://www.nhtsa.gov/people/injury/alcohol/juvenile/apac.html

Urban Institute: Development of an Empirically Based Assessment Instrument:

http://www.urban.org/publications/410892.html

ReEntry Policy Council:

http://tools.reentrypolicy.org/assessments/instruments/Recidivism+Risk

Virginia Department of Juvenile Justice Youth Assessment and Screening Instrument (YASI):

http://www.djj.virginia.gov/Initiatives/YASI.aspx

U.S. Legal Definitions:

http://definitions.uslegal.com/p/pre-sentence-investigation/

U.S. Probation Office Presentence Investigation:

http://www.vaept.uscourts.gov/Presentence-Investigation.aspx

Please refer to the student study site for web resources and additional resources.

READING

In this study, the authors sought to compare and validate two of the most frequently used third-generation risk assessment instruments: the LSI-R and the Correctional Offender Management Profiling for Alternative Sanctions (COMPAS). Using a cohort of 975 offenders, composed of primarily ethnic minorities from a Northeastern state, the authors sought to assess the validity of the instruments 12 months post–prison release. Results of this study reveal inconsistent findings based upon the ethnicity of the offender. Overall, the results predicted rearrest based upon criminogenic needs for all groups that were slightly better than chance. One disturbing finding of the results suggested that African Americans were more likely to be overclassified while whites and Hispanics were likely to be underclassified. Further, results of this study suggested that static factors, such as "juvenile and adult arrests, adult convictions, and parole violations" (p. 1106), were most predictive of rearrest within 12 months of release. This finding may call into question the necessity for including needs assessment used solely for predicting rearrest.

SOURCE: Tracy L. Fass, Kirk Heilbrun, David DeMatteo, & Ralph Fretz (2008). The LSI-R and the COMPAS: Validation data on two risk-needs tools. *Criminal Justice and Behavior, 35*(9), 1095–1108. Copyright © 2008 Sage Publications. Published on behalf of the American Association for Correctional and Forensic Psychologists.

The LSI-R and the COMPAS

Validation Data on Two Risk-Needs Tools

Tracy L. Fass, Kirk Heilbrun, David DeMatteo, and Ralph Fretz

Actuarial risk-needs assessment tools have become increasingly important in the field of criminal justice (Andrews & Bonta, 2003; Holsinger, Lowenkamp, & Latessa, 2006). Previously, the risk assessment of offenders incorporated professional judgment to a large extent (Andrews & Bonta, 2003; Holsinger et al., 2006). Over the past two decades, however, researchers have developed a number of empirically based risk assessment and classification tools (Andrews & Bonta, 2003). These tools are used with increasing frequency and have become an integral part of many correctional interventions (Holsinger et al., 2006; Whiteacre, 2006).

Bonta (1996) described three generations of risk assessment instruments. The first generation involved assessment conducted through an unstructured or semi structured interview, based largely on the assessor's experience and qualitative observations, which may involve gathering information with regard to relevant criminogenic variables (Holsinger et al., 2006). Second-generation assessments are empirically based risk instruments that use risk factors empirically related to future antisocial behavior. However, these assessments use primarily static risk factors and yield little information on rehabilitation needs. Third-generation assessments are also empirically based but incorporate both static and dynamic risk factors related to future antisocial behavior. Through ongoing assessment, third-generation tools can reflect risk-relevant change in the person and his or her situation.

More recently, researchers have described fourth-generation risk assessment tools (Andrews & Bonta, 2003). These tools are designed to follow the offender from intake through case closure (Andrews & Bonta, 2003; Andrews, Bonta, & Wormith, 2006). Such fourth-generation tools aim to further the principles of effective treatment and help design supervision that can protect society from recidivistic crime (Andrews et al., 2006).

There is a large and growing literature with regard to risk factors that are related to anti-social behavior.

A key distinction found in the literature is between "static" and "dynamic" risk factors. Static risk factors are typically historical, unlikely to change, and not amenable to intervention efforts; dynamic factors, by contrast, may change over time (Andrews & Bonta, 2003). In recent years, researchers have focused a great deal of attention on identifying static and dynamic factors that are predictive of violence and other forms of antisocial behavior (see Conroy & Murric, 2007, for a review). A review of the literature reveals several examples of empirically established static risk factors, including a history of violent and antisocial behavior, presence of psychopathy, age (with younger individuals being more at risk), and previous substance use. Although there is considerably less research on dynamic risk factors, recent research has identified several promising dynamic risk factors. In a recent comprehensive review of the relevant literature, Douglas and Skeem (2005) identified the following seven robust dynamic risk factors: impulsiveness, negative affect, psychosis, antisocial attitudes, current substance use, interpersonal relationship problems, and poor treatment compliance.

The Mac Arthur Violence Risk Assessment Study (Monahan et al., 2001) also provided valuable information with regard to risk factors that are most predictive of violent behavior. Monahan and colleagues studied more than 1,100 admissions to acute inpatient psychiatric facilities in three different cities and then conducted follow-up interviews every 10 weeks for 1 year after discharge. Out of the 134 risk factors examined in the study, psychopathy was more strongly associated with violence in the community after discharge than any other risk factor. Other robust risk factors found in the study included prior violence, a co-occurring diagnosis of substance abuse or dependence, and anger.

Other researchers have also examined the relationship between risk factors and antisocial behavior. Andrews and Bonta (2003) identified the most important of these factors and labeled them "the Big Four":

antisocial attitudes, antisocial associates, antisocial behavioral history, and antisocial personality. They further described "the Big Eight" risk factors that are relevant to criminal behavior. The Big Eight include the Big Four plus problems at home, problems at school or work, problems in leisure circumstances, and problems with substance abuse (Andrews & Bonta, 2003), all of which are risk factors that have been empirically related to criminal offending (e.g., Gendreau, Little, & Goggin, 1996).

Level of Service Inventory–Revised (LSI-R)

The LSI-R (Andrews & Bonta, 2001) is a third-generation assessment tool that measures offenders' characteristics and situations and is used to inform decisions concerning level of service necessary for a given offender. It measures the Big Eight and other relevant criminogenic factors through 54 items that are grouped into 10 subscales: Criminal History, Education/Employment, Finances, Family/Marital, Accommodations, Leisure/Recreation, Companions, Alcohol/Drug, Emotional/Personal, and Attitude Orientation. Unlike second-generation assessment tools, the LSI-R measures both static and dynamic risk factors (Andrews & Bonta, 2001). It was developed to assist correctional professionals in making decisions concerning necessary levels of supervision and can also aid in decisions concerning sentencing, program or institutional classification, release from institutional custody, bail, and security ratings (Kroner & Mills, 2001; Lowenkamp & Latessa, 2002). In addition, it is designed to provide an overall estimate of the risk of reoffending (Andrews & Bonta, 2001; Gendreau, Goggin, & Smith, 2002).

In 2002, Lowenkamp and Latessa conducted a validation study on the LSI-R in community-based correctional facilities in Ohio. They found that an increase in LSI-R composite score was positively related to the likelihood of an offender having a new arrest or a technical violation reported to the court, being sentenced to prison, or unsuccessfully terminating a community-based correctional facility program. In addition, they found that a larger percentage of higher risk individuals (as measured by LSI-R composite score) had negative outcomes (e.g., rearrest, technical violation reported to the court, incarcerated) than lower risk individuals,

although some of the increases were slight. Overall, they reported inconsistent results in terms of predictive validity across the programs they evaluated, with LSI-R scores from some programs predicting certain outcomes very well and LSI-R data from other programs performing less accurately. They attributed the variation in results to inconsistent data collection at some sites or the possibility that the outcome measure did not measure aberrant behavior as expected. They recommended that program sites develop specific cutoff scores based on their own populations (Lowenkamp & Latessa, 2002).

In another study of the validity of the LSI-R, Holsinger et al. (2006) reported that their data supported the predictive validity of the LSI-R for the whole sample but provided mixed results when the sample was divided by race. The results suggested that the LSI-R predicted rearrest most accurately for White offenders and male offenders overall and White men and White women compared with non-White (Native American) men and women (Holsinger et al., 2006).

Another recent study considered whether the LSI-R accurately classified African American, Caucasian, and Hispanic residents at a federal community corrections center, with the investigator seeking cutoff scores for each racial/ethnic group to minimize over- and underclassification (Whiteacre, 2006). He reported that the types and rates of classification errors depended on both cutoff score and outcome. When the predicted outcome was programmatic success, African Americans were more likely to be false positives than Caucasians or Hispanics. However, African Americans were more likely to be false negatives when predicting disciplinary incidents. Overall, the results reflected a consistent pattern of more classification errors for African Americans than for Caucasians or Hispanics. Whiteacre (2006) recommended that institutions evaluating risk assessment tools consider the appropriate cutoff score in light of their population, predicted outcome, and purpose for which the tool was used.

Correctional Offender Management Profiling for Alternative Sanctions (COMPAS)

The COMPAS (Brennan & Oliver, 2000) is one of the best known fourth-generation assessment instruments

(Andrews et al., 2006). It is a risk assessment tool that was created to measure key risk and needs factors in adult correctional populations in order to provide information to aid in decision making with regard to placement of offenders in the community. Unlike other risk assessment instruments, which provide a single risk score, the COMPAS provides separate risk estimates for violence, recidivism, failure to appear, and community failure. In addition to the Overall Risk Potential, as represented by those four scales, the COMPAS provides a Criminogenic and Needs Profile for the offender. This profile provides information about the offender with respect to criminal history, needs assessment, criminal attitudes, social environment, and additional factors such as socialization failure, criminal opportunity, criminal personality, and social support (Brennan & Oliver, 2000).

There are apparently no peer-reviewed published data with regard to the predictive validity of the COMPAS. The initial validation study, described in the COMPAS manual, followed a sample of 241 offenders from a New York probation sample released into the community and collected data on whether each offender was rearrested within 1 year of the date of COMPAS administration (Brennan & Oliver, 2000). The researchers reported that their sample offended at a rate of 24.7% during the outcome period. Using receiver operating characteristics (ROC) analysis, they described very good predictive validity (area under the curve [AUC] = .79) for the COMPAS recidivism scale. However, they noted that the AUC value may have been inflated because the same data set was used to develop and validate the data, and the data set was relatively small. This initial study did not include analyses using race/ethnicity or gender, however, so it is difficult to gauge its generalizability.

Purposes of This Study

This study had three main goals: first, to provide what was apparently the first empirical study on the COMPAS that was independent of its development; second, to describe the criminogenic variables most strongly related to rearrest within 1 year following release from prison in a relatively large (N = 975) sample with a substantial proportion of racial/ethnic minority offenders;

and third, to compare the predictive validities of the COMPAS recidivism score, the LSI-R composite score, and the relevant criminogenic variables, respectively, with regard to the performance of each in predicting rearrest within 1 year. Previous studies have provided data on the LSI-R in midwestern states in the United States (Lowenkamp & Latessa, 2002), in Canada (Andrews & Bonta, 2001, 2003), and with a primarily Native American sample (Holsinger, Lowenkamp, & Latessa, 2003; Holsinger et al., 2006). This study provides data using a U.S. sample from a northeastern, primarily urban population. The comparison of the LSI-R and the COMPAS is made to help gauge the accuracy of these respective tools. Using standard criminogenic variables compared with these tools gives some indication of how much the particular tools add to such accuracy, as contrasted with the consideration of separate variables that are well-recognized risk factors for criminal offending.

Method

Participants

The sample was made up of 975 male offenders (COMPAS N = 276; LSI-R N = 696; criminogenic variables N = 975) released from two assessment and treatment centers in New Jersey between 1999 and 2002. Approximately half of the offenders with COMPAS and half of the offenders with LSI-R scores came from each facility. The criminogenic variables were total number of previous adult arrests, total number of previous juvenile arrests, total number of previous adult convictions, and total number of prior parole violations. All participants were subsequently placed in community halfway houses in New Jersey.

Participants were randomly selected from a list of all male offenders released from the two facilities during the specified period. Researchers randomly chose a starting position on the list and then selected every other file. A power analysis revealed that for a logistic regression with four independent variables, with an alpha of .05, and a medium effect size (w = .3), 297 participants yielded power of .99. This indicates that with 975 participants, it is highly likely that a result was detected if it existed. Potential participants were eliminated if they did not have scores for the LSI-R or COMPAS (one of which, but not both, was administered to all participants, so the only cases eliminated on this basis were the few for whom LSI-R or COMPAS results were missing from the file). Participants were also eliminated if their files were missing information concerning the relevant criminogenic variables or if they had been released less than 12 months prior to data collection. Women were not included in this study because we intend to study these cohorts separately. Finally, participants who were not African American, Caucasian, or Hispanic were excluded because there was not a sufficient number of individuals of any other racial/ethnic group to perform statistical analyses.

Ages of the participants ranged from 18 to 63 years, with a mean of 32.5 years $(SD = 7.58)$. The racial/ethnic breakdown of the participants was as follows: 71.4% African American $(n = 696)$, 15.0% Hispanic or Latino $(n = 146)$, and 13.6% Caucasian $(n = 133)$. (Racial/ethnic status was recorded according to the individual's self-identified category.) The mean level of education completed was 11.21 years $(SD = 1.96)$, with 46.3% of the participants having completed either 12th grade or equivalent and 47.7% having completed less than 12th grade.

Materials

Participants' institutional files and New Jersey Department of Corrections (NJDOC) records were used for data collection purposes. Information in those files was collected as part of the routine assessment and classification procedure at both assessment and treatment facilities. These data were entered into a database created in SPSS 11.

Results

To determine whether participants differed based on racial group, a series of independent samples t tests was conducted. The dependent variables were the background variables (number of adult arrests, number of juvenile arrests, number of adult convictions), assessment data (LSI-R composite score and COMPAS recidivism score), and the outcome variable (rearrest within 12 months of release into the community). The results showed that on average, Caucasian participants had fewer previous parole violations than African American participants (equal variances not assumed). This remained significant after alpha was reduced to .002. African American participants also differed from Hispanic participants on number of previous parole violations. This did not remain significant after the Bonferroni correction. The results also showed that Caucasian participants obtained lower LSI-R composite scores than African American participants. This was no longer significant after alpha was adjusted with a Bonferroni correction. In addition, Caucasian participants had more previous adult arrests than Hispanic participants. African American participants also had more previous adult arrests than Hispanic participants. These, too, were no longer significant after the Bonferroni correction.

In terms of rearrest within 12 months of release into the community, Caucasian participants differed significantly from African American participants and African American participants differed significantly from Hispanic participants. Table 5.3 shows the descriptive information with regard to rearrest by race. Table 5.4 depicts the results of these significance tests.

Before conducting the main analyses, we calculated the base rate of offending for the entire sample. That base rate (0.21 or 21 %) was used as the predicted probability cutoff for the logistic regression analyses. With a predicted probability of 0.21, the LSI-R composite score correctly predicted outcomes for 48.4% of the sample as a whole, 80.4% of Caucasians, 43.4% of African Americans, and 82.4% of Hispanics. African Americans were more likely to be false positives than Caucasians or Hispanics (51.8% vs. 7.6% and 0%, respectively). In contrast, Hispanics and Caucasians were more likely to be false negatives than African Americans (17.7% and 12% vs. 4.78%, respectively). ROC analysis revealed an AUC of 0.6 with regard to the sample as a whole, with AUC values of 0.55 for Caucasians, 0.61 for African Americans, and 0.54 for Hispanics.

Data on the COMPAS may be used to compare predicted rearrest based on COMPAS recidivism score with actual rearrest within 1 year of community release. With a predicted probability of 0.21, the COMPAS recidivism score correctly predicted outcomes for 85%

Table 5.3 Participant Rearrest Within 12 Months of Release Into the Community

Race	# Rearrested	# Not Rearrested	Total
Caucasian	18 *lowest*	115 *lowest*	133 ↓
African American	165 *highest*	531 *highest*	696 *highest*
Hispanic	22	124	146

Table 5.4 Racial Differences in Rearrest Within 12 Months Following Release Into the Community

Sources	df	χ^2	p
Caucasian vs. African American	1	6.72	.010[a]
Caucasian vs. Hispanic	1	1.33	.715
African American vs. Hispanic	1	5.21	.022[a]

a. Indicates significant difference between groups, but not significant after Bonferroni correction of alpha to .002.

of the sample as a whole, 97.6% of Caucasians, 76.4% of African Americans, and 90.9% of Hispanics. African Americans were more likely to be false positives than Caucasians or Hispanics (7.32% vs. 0% and 0%), respectively). Likewise, African Americans were also more likely to be false negatives than Caucasians or Hispanics (16.2% vs. 2.4% and 9.1%. respectively). ROC analysis yielded an AUC of 0.53 with regard to the sample as a whole, with AUC values of 0.81 for Caucasians. 0.48 for African Americans, and 0.67 for Hispanics.

With a predicted probability of 0.21, the criminogenic variables correctly predicted outcomes for 59.6% of the sample as a whole, 78.2% of Caucasians, 37.2% of African Americans, and 78% of Hispanics. African Americans were more likely to be overclassified (false positives) than Caucasians or Hispanics (57.9% vs. 9.8% and 13%, respectively). In contrast, Caucasians were more likely to he underclassified (false negatives) than African Americans or Hispanics (12% vs. 4.9% and 8.9%, respectively). The ROC AUC value was 0.57 for the sample as a whole, 0.55 for Caucasians, 0.56 for African Americans, and 0.64 for Hispanics.

Logistic regression analysis was performed using rearrest within 1 year of community release as the dependent variable and number of previous adult arrests, number of previous juvenile arrests, number of previous adult convictions, and number of previous parole violations as predictors. A total of 975 cases was analyzed and the full model was significantly reliable. Of those who were not rearrested, 63.6% were correctly predicted to not be rearrested. However, only 44.4% of those who were rearrested were accurately predicted as such. Overall, 59.6% of cases were correctly predicted to either be rearrested or not rearrested, respectively.

Logistic regression analysis was also performed using the same dependent and predictor variables with the sample divided by race; a total of 146 Hispanic cases was included. Of those who were not rearrested, 84.7% were accurately predicted to not be rearrested. However, only 40.9% of those who were rearrested were accurately predicted to be rearrested. Overall, 78.1% of cases were correctly predicted to be either rearrested or not rearrested, respectively. A total of 133 Caucasian cases was included and the model was not significantly reliable

($\chi^2 = 4.24$, $df = 4$, $p = .374$). A total of 696 African American cases was included; again, the model was not significantly reliable ($\chi^2 = 6.86$, $df = 4$, $p = .143$).

To determine the relationship between LSI-R composite score and rearrest, logistic regression was run using rearrest as the dependent variable and LSI-R composite score as the predictor. Some 696 cases were included, and the full model was significantly reliable. Forty percent of the nonrearrested offenders were accurately predicted to not be rearrested, and 76.1 % of the rearrested offenders were successfully predicted to be rearrested. Overall, 48.4% of the cases were accurately predicted to either be rearrested or not, respectively.

When the LSI-R sample was divided by race, logistic regression with 92 Caucasian cases yielded a model that was not significantly reliable ($\chi^2 = 0.29$, $df = 1$, $p = .59$). In logistic regression with 502 African American cases yielded a model that was significantly reliable ($\chi^2 = 12.02$, $df = 1$, $p = .001$), of the variability in rearrest status. Of those who were not rearrested, 30.5% were correctly predicted to be not rearrested. In addition, 81.3% of the rearrested offenders were accurately predicted to be rearrested. Overall, 43.4% of cases were accurately predicted to either be rearrested or not, respectively. A logistic regression with 102 Hispanic cases resulted in a model that was not significantly reliable.

Finally, logistic regression analysis was conducted to assess the relationship between the COMPAS recidivism score and rearrest: 276 cases were included, and the full model was not significantly reliable ($\chi^2 = 0.21$, $df = 1$, $p = .645$).

When the sample was divided by race, logistic regression including 41 Caucasian cases yielded a model that was not significantly reliable ($\chi^2 = 1.613$, $df = 1$, $p = .204$). A logistic regression including 191 African American cases resulted in a model that was also not significantly reliable ($\chi^2 = 0.213$, $df = 1$, $p = .644$). Finally, a logistic regression including 44 Hispanic cases yielded a model that was not significantly reliable ($\chi^2 = 1.48$, $df = 1$, $p = .224$).

⬙ Discussion

Previous research has investigated the extent to which the LSI-R can predict future criminal behavior (Andrews & Bonta, 2003). However, there are limited data on the LSI-R using a northeastern U.S., primarily minority and urban cohort. To date, there are no published data on the predictive validity of the COMPAS. This study investigates the predictive abilities of the LSI-R, the COMPAS, and selected criminogenic variables for rearrest within 1 year of community release. This study used data drawn from a sample from a northeastern state that was substantially made up of minorities from urban areas.

The results indicate that the criminogenic variables predicted rearrest for the whole sample at a rate slightly better than chance. These criminogenic variables performed best for Hispanic individuals, correctly predicting approximately 78% of the outcomes.

These results suggest that there is predictive inaccuracy driven by racial/ethnic status. African Americans were more likely to be overclassified (predicted to be rearrested when they actually were not) than Caucasians or Hispanics across all three predictive approaches. By contrast, underclassification errors (predicting no rearrest when the participant was actually rearrested) varied by measure. For the LSI-R, Hispanics and Caucasians were more likely to be underclassificd than the other two groups. For the COMPAS, African Americans were more likely to be underclassified. For the criminogenic variables, Caucasians were more likely to be underclassified.

The results provide further support for previous empirical evidence that criminal history is strongly related to future offending (Andrews & Bonta, 2003). In this case, the results demonstrate that prior juvenile and adult arrests, adult convictions, and parole violations are predictive of rearrest within 12 months of community release from prison.

These results have potential implications for jurisdictions that include substantial proportions of minority offenders. Researchers have expressed concern with regard to the validity of risk-needs assessment tools as applied to certain specific populations, especially nonmajority populations (Holsinger et al., 2003, 2006; Whiteacre, 2006). These results provide further support for previous findings that the LSI-R yields mixed predictive validity when used with different clinic and racial populations (Holsinger et al., 2006; Whiteacre,

2006). In addition, this study suggests that the validity of the COMPAS and the criminogenic variables also varies with racial/ethnic group. It is possible that different groups may be influenced by different risk and needs factors that lead to recidivism. As part of the analysis, this study used contingency tables to test for racial/ethnic differences in prediction errors for the LSI-R composite score, COMPAS recidivism score, and four criminogenic variables. The results indicated an overall tendency to either over- or underclassify participants depending on ethnicity/race. This gives rise to concern about the use of different risk assessment instruments with certain specific populations.

In studies such as this, there is the possibility that the results of tools such as the LSI-R and the COMPAS would be available to parole officers in the community. This would be valuable for supervision and risk management purposes. However, it would also potentially contaminate the relationship between the risk-needs tool results and the risk of subsequent arrest, if parole officers were to focus more intensively on higher risk individuals and thus lower their reoffending risk. Because such results were not available to parole officers supervising this sample, however, this was not a problem in this study.

This study does have several limitations, however. First, it employed a relatively short outcome period of 12 months postrelease. Further research using these tools should expand that to include follow-up periods of varying length. Second, the outcome variable only represents rearrest records in a single jurisdiction (New Jersey). It is possible that some of the participants were rearrested in another state within the 1-year follow-up period. If that were so, then the base rate of offending would have been higher than was calculated. Third, the outcome in this study was rearrest. Although rearrest is commonly used and is often the only measure of recidivism available, it has been considered the least stringent of the possible recidivism measures (Holsinger et al., 2006). Perhaps, the major limitation to officially recorded rearrest is that some criminal offending that actually occurred will not be detected for the purposes of the study. Moreover, to the extent that there is racial bias in whether offenders are rearrested, this diminishes the sensitivity of rearrest as a measure of criminal

behavior. Further research should consider other measures of recidivism that may more accurately reflect actual antisocial behavior, including self-report and collateral report. Some of the subsamples for the COMPAS predictions were small, so replication is important before deciding whether and how to use this tool in practice. Fourth, the timing of the LSI-R and COMPAS administration may have affected the predictive accuracy of both tools. They were administered after participants had been released from prison and had entered a community-based assessment center, where they typically stayed for 6 to 9 months. To the extent that some dynamic risk factors changed while participants were treated in the center prior to full release into the community, the profiles yielded by the LSI-R and COMPAS would have been somewhat different. Finally, the results of this study may not be generalizable beyond the immediate cohort. This study used data on an all-male, mostly urban sample made up solely of Caucasians, African Americans, and Hispanics. Therefore, the results may not be generalizable to women or offenders of other racial/ethnic backgrounds. Further research should investigate how well the LSI-R and the COMPAS can predict recidivism in other populations. Likewise, future research should further examine the risk and needs factors that are relevant to different specific populations.

✉ References

Andrews, D. A., & Bonta, J. (2001). *Level of Service Inventory-Revised (LSI-R): User's manual.* North Tonawanda, NY: Multi-Health Systems.

Andrews, D. A., & Bonta, J. (2003). *The psychology of criminal conduct* (3rd ed). Cincinnati. OH: Anderson.

Andrews, D. A., Bonta, J., & Wormith, J. S. (2006). The recent past and near future of risk and/or need assessment. *Crime and Delinquency, 52,* 7–27.

Boata, J. (1996). Risk needs assessment and treatment. In A. Harland (Ed.), *Choosing correctional options that work: Defining the demand and evaluating the supply* (pp. 18–32). Thousand Oaks, CA: Sage.

Brennan, T., & Oliver, W. L. (2000). *Evaluation of reliability and validity of COMPAS scales: National aggregate sample.* Traverse City, MI: Northpointe Institute for Public Management.

Conroy, M. A., & Murrie, D. C. (2007). *Forensic assessment of violence risk: A guide for risk assessment and risk management.* Hoboken, NJ: John Wiley.

Douglas, K. S., & Skeem, J. L. (2005). Violence risk assessment: Getting specific about being dynamic. *Psychology, Public Policy, and Law, 11,* 347–383.

Gendreau, P., Goggin, C., & Smith, P. (2002). Is the PCL-R really the "unparalleled" measure of offender risk? *Criminal Justice and Behavior, 29,* 397–426.

Gendreau, P., Little, T., & Goggin, C. (1996). A meta-analysis of the predictors of adult offender recidivism: What works! *Criminology, 34,* 575–607.

Holsinger, A. M., Lowenkamp, C.T., & Latessa. E.J. (2003). Ethnicity, gender, and the Level of Service Inventory-Revised. *Journal of Criminal Justice, 31,* 309–320.

Holsinger, A. M., Lowenkamp, C. T., & Latessa, R. J. (2006). Exploring the validity of the Level of Service Inventory-Revised with Native American offenders. *Journal of Criminal Justice, 34,* 331–337.

Kroner, D. G., & Mills, J. F. (2001). The accuracy of five risk appraisal instruments in predicting institutional misconduct and new convictions. *Criminal Justice and Behavior, 28,* 471–489.

Lowenkamp, C. T., & Latessa, E. J. (2002). *Validating the level of service inventory revised in Ohio's community based correctional facilities.* Retrieved March 3, 2007, from http://www.uc.edu/criminaljustice/ProjectReports/OHIOCBCFLSI-R.pdf

Monahan, J., Steadman, H., Silver, E., Appelbaum, P., Robbins, P., Mulvey, E., et al. (2001). *Rethinking risk assessment: The MacArthur study of mental disorder and violence.* New York: Oxford University Press.

Whiteacre, K. W. (2006). Testing the Level of Service Inventory Revised (LSI-R) for racial/ethnic bias. *Criminal Justice Policy Review, 17,* 330–342.

DISCUSSION QUESTIONS

1. What are the potential implications for the use of dynamic factors in classifying offenders?

2. What are the pros and cons of using either the LSI-R or the COMPAS for predicting rearrest?

3. According to the authors, what are the limitations of their study? Why is it important to understanding these limitations when making recommendations on whether to use either the LSI-R or the COMPAS?

4. Given what you know about fourth-generation risk/needs assessment, how might the inclusion of long-term assessment alter the results of this study?

READING

In this article, Smith, Cullen and Latessa attempted to validate the use of the LSI-R on female offenders using a meta-analysis technique. Prior to the publication of this work, many researchers and practitioners questioned the validity of using the LSI-R on populations other than white males. A review of 25 published and unpublished studies including 14,737 females revealed that the LSI-R does in fact predict rearrest at the same rate for women as it does for men. Likewise, results indicated that effect sizes were greater for assessments with shorter follow-up periods and for those studies that were published. Results further revealed consistent findings with other meta-analyses reviewing similar groups. Overall, researchers provided policy recommendations for the continued use of this actuarial risk assessment. They further contended that assessments utilizing theoretical premises (i.e., social learning–cognitive theory of human behavior) are more effective at predicting long-term behavior than those based upon first-generation methods such as structured clinical interviews and should be continued. Furthermore, the authors argued that these results expanded the need for committing to long-term follow-up, care, and treatment of offenders to assist with reentry back into the offender's respective community.

SOURCE: Paula Smith, Francis T. Cullen, & Edward J. Latessa (April, 2009). Can 14,737 women be wrong? A meta-analysis of the LSI-R and recidivism for female offenders. *Criminology & Public Policy, 8*(1), 183–208. Copyright © 2009 by the American Society of Criminology.

Can 14,737 Women Be Wrong?

A Meta-Analysis of the LSI-R and Recidivism for Female Offenders

Paula Smith, Francis T. Cullen, and Edward J. Latessa

The dominant reality of U.S. corrections is the inordinate expansion of the correctional system. Since the early 1970s, prison and jail populations have increased from approximately 200,000 to more than 2.3 million (Sabol, Couture, and Harrison, 2007; Warren, 2008). On any given day, one in a hundred Americans is behind bars (Warren, 2008). Equally troubling, when probation and parole are considered, the number of individuals under state supervision exceeds 7 million (Glaze and Bonczar, 2006). As might be anticipated, a steady stream of books have been written documenting and seeking to understand this era of mass incarceration and community control (see Abramsky, 2007; Gottschalk, 2006; Lynch, 2007; Simon, 2007; Tonry, 2004). Regardless, DiIulio (1991) was prescient when he warned nearly two decades ago that there would be "no escape" from these correctional realities.

As Feeley and Simon (1992) point out, the growth of the correctional enterprise has created an organizational crisis as to how to house, feed, supervise, and ultimately release the large and unending stream of humanity that flows through the system (see also Simon, 1993). At its worst, this situation has led to a "new penology" in which a disturbing goal of displacement transpires—where the larger social purposes of corrections, such as rehabilitation, are replaced by the daily, pragmatic need to monitor and process correctional populations. In the best case scenario, a premium is placed on those correctional administrators who can confront challenging organizational conditions—the most obvious of which is intense overcrowding or large case loads—and in turn foster a safe environment and the delivery of human services (see DiIulio, 1987).

Although not new—they extend back to the work of Ernest Burgess in 1928 and to Sheldon and Eleanor Glueck in 1950 (Bonta, 1996; Jones, 1996)—offender assessment instruments are key tools in managing correctional populations. These instruments are employed primarily to measure the "risk" that an offender will recidivate if released into the community. These assessments coincide with new penology and managerial thinking in that they can be used to routinize and rationalize decision making that otherwise would be discretionary (e.g., who to release on parole and who to give probation). In this way, the correctional system gains in efficiency, and the community presumably gains in public safety. At the very least, it seems that criminal justice officials are taking credible steps to use science to manage risk, which includes dangerous offenders (Simon, 1993).

These instruments compile information about each offender, which in turn is used to predict the risk of recidivism. For the most part, the risk factors measured have been historical and "static" in nature (for a review, see Andrews and Bonta, 2006). That is, the instruments have focused on what has already occurred in an offender's life (historical) and on what cannot be changed (static). For example, a person's criminal history is an important predictor of future waywardness; still, an intervention cannot change a criminal record because it is, by its nature, in the past and thus unchangeable. This approach is not necessarily a problem if one wishes only to assess the risk of recidivism and to manage inmates or control offenders under community supervision. But as Bonta (1996:22) points out, instruments composed primarily of static factors provide "little direction for rehabilitation. . . . Rehabilitation is based on the premise that people can change, and if assessment is to contribute to rehabilitation efforts, it must be capable of measuring change."

In this context, an alternative approach to offender assessment has been developed by Canadian psychologists Don Andrews, James Bonta, Paul Gendreau, and others (Andrews and Bonta, 2006; Bonta, 1996; Gendreau, 1996); together, they are recognized as comprising the Canadians' school of correctional intervention (Cullen, 2002). Their ideas were developed within a correctional and national culture that was social-welfare oriented, and they were informed by professional ethics from their home discipline of psychology. Perhaps not surprisingly, their goal was to improve the lives of offenders; accordingly, they rejected the managerial, new-penology view of risk assessment prevailing in the United States during the "get tough" era of the 1980s and beyond (Simon, 1993). The Canadians' approach has three major features, which are outlined next.

First, building on the existing empirical evidence (see, e.g., Gendreau, Little, and Goggin, 1996), the approach argues that recidivism is predicted most accurately by including both static risk factors (e.g., criminal history) and dynamic risk factors. Dynamic risk factors, which are also called "criminogenic needs," are those predictors of recidivism that are potentially mutable. They would include, for example, antisocial attitudes, family functioning, and association with criminal peers.[1]

Second, rejecting new-penology thinking, the purpose of offender assessment should be not only risk management but also offender treatment. The inclusion of dynamic factors is critical because it is these "criminogenic needs" that rehabilitation programs will target for change. That is, by focusing on and changing these factors (e.g., reducing antisocial thinking), offenders' recidivism will be reduced. This strategy is referred to as the "need principle." Another principle of effective intervention set forth by Andrews and his colleagues is the "risk principle," which states that treatment should be devoted primarily to high-risk offenders. The "responsivity principle" asserts that treatment modalities should be used that can alter the criminogenic needs that underlie recidivism. Cognitive-behavioral programs are viewed as being particularly appropriate for this task (Andrews and Bonta 2006: Gendreau, Smith,

and French, 2006; Lipsey, Chapman, and Landenberger, 2001; see also MacKenzie, 2006).

Third, and of particular concern here, the Canadian scholars have developed an assessment instrument that predicts recidivism and can be used as the basis for effective intervention. This instrument is called the Level of Service Inventory or, the LSI as it is now commonly known; its revised version is termed the LSI-R (Andrews and Bonta, 2006; Bonta, 1996). The LSI-R consists of 54 items, most of which measure dynamic risk factors that are known as having criminogenic needs. Existing studies show that the LSI-R has predictive validity with regard to recidivism (Gendreau, Goggin, and Smith, 2002; Gendreau et al., 1996; Vose, Cullen, and Smith, 2008). Based on the extant research, Andrews and Bonta (2006:289) conclude that "all of the comparisons showed the LSI-R to predict as well or better than the other (assessment) instruments."

According to the Canadian scholars, the LSI-R is central to the delivery of effective offender treatment, whether in prison or in the community. Currently, correctional agencies often place offenders in rehabilitation programs either collectively (i.e., everyone receives the same program) or based on inaccurate clinical judgments about what might benefit an offender. By contrast, a core principle of effective intervention is that "responsive" interventions should be directed at high-risk offenders. This is the case for two reasons. First, low-risk offenders—those who would "go straight" on their own—either do not benefit from, or are made more criminogenic by, interventions. Second, high-risk offenders not only pose the greatest threat to the community but also can potentially experience substantial reductions in recidivism. Again, this means that a valid assessment of risk level is essential to an effective correctional intervention (Andrews and Bonta, 2006).

In this context, and given its empirical status, the LSI-R has emerged as perhaps the leading offender assessment instrument in corrections. Again, it gains

---

[1] According to Andrews and Bonta (2006), the major risk factors include the following: (1) antisocial/procriminal attitudes, values, and beliefs; (2) antisocial/procriminal peers; (3) temperament and personality factors such as being aggressive, impulsive, adventurous, and pleasure seeking; (4) a history of antisocial behaviors; (5) family factors such as family criminality, lack of caring and cohesiveness, as well as neglect and abuse; (6) low levels of educational, vocational, or financial achievement; (7) a lack of prosocial leisure activities; and (8) abuse of drugs and alcohol. Although these risk factors are all viewed as important, it is necessary to note that the first four items are referred to as the "Big Four" and are considered to be the most robust among the set (Andrews, Bonta, and Wormith, 2006).

added credibility because it is rooted in the empirical literature on predictors of recidivism and is integrated with a prominent paradigm of correctional treatment—which are the key principles of effective intervention (Cullen, 2002; see also Cullen and Gendreau, 2000; Gendreau et al., 2006; Ogloff and Davis, 2004). Across North America, the LSI-R is in use in more than 900 correctional agencies (Lowenkamp, Lovins, and Latessa, 2009; see also Listwan, Johnson, Cullen, and Latessa, 2008).

It is within this context that a recent, salient critique of the instrument takes on special importance: It is claimed that the LSI-R has predictive validity for males but not for females (Holtfreter and Cupp, 2007; Reisig, Holtfreter, and Morash, 2006). For Andrews, Bonta, and colleagues, the LSI-R is based on the general principles of social learning theory and cognitive psychology. In turn, they believe that the predictors of crime and recidivism are substantially the same for male and females; that is, the proximate causes of criminality are "general" rather than "gender specific" (for supportive meta-analytic evidence, see Dowden and Andrews, 1999; Gendreau et al., 1996; Hubbard and Pratt, 2002; Moffitt, Caspi, Rutter, and Silva, 2001; Simourd and Andrews, 1994). In this view, gender is important but to the extent that it shapes how and to what extent males and females are exposed to and/or acquire common risk factors (e.g., antisocial peers).

These observations have three important implications. First, treatment programs should have similar effects for males and females. Inappropriate programs (e.g., boot camps) will not be effective for either gender; by contrast, programs that adhere to the principles of effective intervention will work equally well for males and females. Evidence exists to support this claim (Andrews and Bonta, 2006). Second, gender may be important in the way in which treatments are delivered; this approach is termed "specific responsivity" (Andrews and Bonta, 2006). Thus, although cognitive-behavioral programs may be effective across genders, women may respond better if the treatment is delivered in a female-only group and where an emphasis is placed on creating "a community with a sense of connection" (Andrews and Bonta, 2006:465). And third, the LSI-R should predict recidivism and be used as an instrument assessing

offender change equally well for males and females. Notably, Andrews and Bonta (2006:301–302) recently presented data that show similar predictive validity across gender for a recent version of the LSI-R on a sample of 561 Ontario probationers followed for 3 years after release from supervision. Vose (2008) reports similar results regarding the predictive validity of the LSI-R across gender for probationers and parolees in Iowa.

The current critique of the LSI-R as being a male-specific assessment instrument is embedded within the larger criminological debate over whether the causes of crime are general (as most prevailing theories of crime claim) or are gender specific (as feminist scholars argue) (see Daigle, Cullen, and Wright, 2007; Miller and Mullins, 2006; Salisbury, 2007). Again, empirical research has shown, now for some time, a similarity in the causes of crime across gender (Simons, Miller, and Ainger, 1980; Smith and Paternoster, 1987). For example, based on their study in Dunedin, New Zealand, Moffitt et al. (2001:230) conclude that "the same risk factors predict antisocial behavior in both males and females; we did not detect any replicable sex-specific risk factors for antisocial behavior" (see also Farrington and Painter, 2004). Gender-specific theorists disagree, arguing that these more traditional approaches omit experiences—and thus risk factors—unique to women. Thus, they point to distinct differences by gender in socialization, development, and economic marginalization as the primary explanations for the gender differences in risk factors (Chesney-Lind, 1989; Daly, 1992, 1994; Reisig, Holtfreter, and Morash, 2002). For example, Covington and Bloom (1999:3) maintain that "the philosophy of criminogenic risk and needs does not consider factors such as economic marginalization, the role of patriarchy, sexual victimization, or women's place in society." These unique life-course trajectories that lead to criminal offending are referred to as "gendered pathways" (Daly, 1992, 1994; for a summary, see Miller and Mullins, 2006:228-232).

The construct of gendered pathways holds important implications for offender assessment and, ultimately, for treatment. If females predominantly enter crime for gender-specific reasons, then the LSI-R, which assumes the generality of crime causation, would not be of much value in predicting females' recidivism or in directing treatment interventions with women offenders. This possibility was poignantly suggested by the research of Reisig et al. (2006). Based on a sample of 235 female offenders under community supervision in Minnesota and Oregon, the authors examined the LSI-R's ability to predict recidivism across those who entered crimes for gender-neutral reasons (economic motivation) or gender-specific reasons (street women, harmed and harming women whose lives were filled with chaos and abuse/neglect, battered women, and drug-connected women). Their analysis revealed that although the LSI-R predicted recidivism for the economically motivated offenders, it misclassified and had low predictive validity for offenders who entered crime through gendered pathways. The economically motivated group, however, comprised only a quarter of the sample. The policy implications of this finding are clear. A "cause for concern" (Reisig et al., 2006:400) was found. The LSI-R risks endangering public safety and misallocating treatment resources by underclassifying some offenders (especially drug-connected females) and by overclassifying others. In short, the LSI-R may be appropriate to assess male offenders but not female offenders.

Our project attempts to use a meta-analysis of extant studies to bring additional evidence to bear on the ability of the LSI-R to predict recidivism for female offenders. This approach does not present a direct test of the gendered pathways model, because, with the exception of Reisig et al. (2006), current research does not divide offenders into pathway groups. Even so, critics of the LSI-R claim that because of its gender-specific nature, the ability of the LSI-R to predict recidivism for females should be low and, in addition, should be far lower than for males (Holtfreter and Cupp, 2007). Phrased alternatively, similar effects between the LSI-R and recidivism across gender groups would increase confidence that the instrument can be used to assess not only males but also females.

To assess these issues, we undertook a meta-analysis that involved 25 studies and 27 effect sizes representing data on 14,737 female offenders. In 16 studies, we calculated the effect sizes for both males and females. These data allowed us to conduct within-sample comparisons.

A meta-analysis involves the quantitative synthesis of research literatures, and it is now considered to be the review method of choice in several disciplines (Hunt,

1997), which include criminal justice. Furthermore, this statistical technique has been applied in several previous studies to evaluate the predictive validity of offender assessments (e.g., Campbell, French, and Gendreau, 2007; Gendreau et al., 2002). A meta-analysis expresses the outcome of interest (e.g., offender recidivism) from studies in a common metric, which is referred to as an effect size, and calculates an average. Variations in the magnitude of effect sizes can then be examined in relation to potential moderators. Many advantages are associated with this statistical technique. First, it standardizes the review process and generates a quantitative estimate of the magnitude of an effect. Second, it can highlight discrepancies and/or systematic shortcomings in a research literature. Third, it provides an estimate of the certainty of an effect through the use of fail-safe statistics. As a literature review technique, however, meta-analysis is not foolproof. Researcher biases can affect retrieval and coding decisions. In addition, meta-analytic reviews are often limited by the relative inconsistency with which descriptive information is included in individual primary studies.

⊠ Method

Sample

To collect studies and data relevant to the topic of the current investigation, searches of literature databases were conducted for all studies on the LSI-R, which include the Social Sciences Citation Index, PsycINFO, and the bulletins for the annual meetings of the Academy of Criminal Justice Sciences and the American Society of Criminology. Search terms included "Level of Service Inventory," "Level of Service Inventory–Revised," "LSI," "LSI-R," and "risk assessment." To obtain additional unpublished data, we also contacted researchers who had previously published articles on the LSI-R as well as researchers employed by correctional agencies that use the LSI-R. To be included in the current investigation, the primary study or unpublished data (1) had to include a prospective measure of recidivism and (2) were required to provide sufficient statistical information to allow for the calculation of the effect size statistic (Pearson's r or point biserial coefficient) for female offenders only. For each primary study or data set, the longest follow-up period and the most serious form of recidivism were used to calculate the effect size.

Coding of Studies

Several characteristics of each study or data set were coded.[2] These characteristics included publication information, sample demographics, follow-up information, recidivism measures, effect size, and sample size.

As recommended in the 2001 *APA Publication Manual* (American Psychological Association, 2001), 95% confidence intervals (CIs) were also calculated to assess the precision and magnitude of the effects. The CI specifies a range of values about the mean effect size that includes the respective population parameter for a specified percentage of the time (i.e., 95%). The utility of the CI lies in its interpretability: If the interval does not contain 0, then it can be concluded that the mean effect size is significantly different from 0 (i.e., better than chance alone). Similarly, if no overlap occurs between the 95% CIs, then the two mean effect sizes would be assessed as being statistically different from one another at the .05 level. In comparing the CIs of two different means, if no overlap occurs or the CIs barely touch, then $p < .01$. If the overlap is about half the average margin of error (i.e., the proportion overlap is about .50 or less), then $p < .05$ (see Cumming and Finch, 2005; Gendreau and Smith, 2007).

Finally, the primary utility of the CI rests in this study on the interpretation of its width. As the width of the CI increases, the precision of the estimate of μ decreases (or is associated with more uncertainty) (Hunter and Schmidt, 2004). The judgment of the width of the CI—which would lead to a conclusion that additional replication of the results is necessary before suggesting policy or clinical guidelines—is subjective; it depends on the internal width researchers in the various subdisciplines feel is relevant (Smithson, 2003). For a discussion of the different ways the CI can be interpreted, see Cumming and Finch (2005).

✄ Results

Study Characteristics

A total of 25 published and unpublished data sets were identified and included in the current analyses. These 25 data sets yielded a total of 27 distinct effect sizes of the relationship between the LSI-R and recidivism for female offenders. These 27 effect sizes represent data on a total of 14,737 female offenders.

Approximately half of the effect sizes (55%) were calculated from unpublished data/manuscripts/dissertations that had been collected between 2000 and 2009 (81%). A total of 14 effect sizes (52%) were calculated based on samples with no predominant racial group, whereas 6 effect sizes (22%) were generated with samples that were predominantly white. Sixty-seven percent of the effect sizes were generated based on samples where the average age was between 30 and 35 years.

In terms of outcome measures, most data sets tracked offenders for more than 2 years (32%), whereas a smaller percentage (30%) tracked offenders for 13 to 24 months, and only 5 studies (19%) followed offenders for 12 months or less. Thirty percent of the studies used reincarceration as the outcome measure, and 30% of the studies employed reconviction. A small percentage of studies used other measures of recidivism (e.g., self-report, rearrest, or community supervision violation).

Effect Sizes

The effect sizes generated using fixed-effects and random-effects models are presented. Note that the overall mean *r* values (fixed effects = .35; random effects = .34) and the *Z* values (fixed effects = .37; random effects = .35) are nearly identical in magnitude. The only notable differences are the widths of the CIs. The value of the *Q*-statistic ($Q = 273,916$, degrees of freedom [d.f.] $= 26, p = .000$) indicates significant variation in the effect sizes across the studies. Although this finding indicates that potential moderator variables might explain this variation, we did not have access to data on

---

[2] Effect sizes were initially coded and analyzed by Christopher T. Lowenkamp at the Center for Criminal Justice Research, University of Cincinnati. To establish inter-rater reliability, the published studies were then coded independently by the first author.

what we felt were theoretically important moderators (e.g., who administered the assessment, staff training, and other measures related to quality assurance that have been implicated in the use of dynamic risk assessments).

Nevertheless, two moderators, length of follow-up and publication status, were related to outcome. First, shorter follow-ups (i.e., 12 months or less) were associated with larger effect sizes $(r = .43, CI = .41$ to $.45)$ in comparison with longer time intervals (e.g., greater than 2 years, $r = .28, CI = .26$ to $.30$). This trend is not surprising given the fact that the LSI-R contains several dynamic items that are time sensitive. Second, published data (including journals, book chapters, conference presentations, and theses/dissertations) produced considerably larger effect sizes $(r = .44, CI = .42$ to $.46)$ than unpublished data $(r = .27, CI = .25$ to $.29)$. This finding is consistent with previous research that has documented a potential publication bias (Rothstein, Sutton, and Borenstein, 2005). It should be emphasized, however, that an r value of .27 (in the case of unpublished data) is considered to be both statistically and clinically significant. Finally, given the relatively small number of total effect sizes $(k = 27)$ and missing data in some cases, many moderators could not be tested with any meaningful interpretation. Future replications should extend this line of research.

Within-Study Comparison of Effect Sizes

Some critics have commented that within-sample comparisons yield more sensitive and accurate assessments of the predictive validity for males versus females. We identified 16 data sets that allowed for within-sample comparisons by gender. Once again, the mean r values for the fixed-effects and random-effects models were nearly identical. More important, the effect sizes for males and females were very similar, and in both cases, the 95% CIs overlapped. The Q statistics indicated significant variation in study effect sizes for both males $(Q = 147.323, \text{d.f.} = 15, p = .000)$ and females $(Q = 28.500, \text{d.f.} = 15, p = .019)$.

Comparison of Results With Previous Meta-Analyses

The results of the current analysis are comparable with the results of previous research that compared the predictive validities of the LSI-R in male versus female offenders.

Three previous meta-analyses that reported effect sizes for the LSI-R were identified in the existing research on risk prediction. These meta-analyses contained samples of males and females, although the samples included in the primary studies were predominantly males, which is important to note. The prior meta-analyses provide a way to place the current findings in the context of what is already known about the average t values generated from research on the predictive validity of the LSI-R with predominantly male samples.

First, Gendreau et al. (1996) investigated the average effect size of the LSI-R in predicting recidivism. The study included 28 effect sizes generated from data on 4,579 individuals. Notably, the point estimates from both the current study and the Gendreau et al. (1996) study are similar in magnitude, and the CIs overlap. This information suggests that the mean effect sizes are in fact sampled from the same distribution. Second, Gendreau, Goggin, and Law (1997) examined the relationship between the LSI-R and prison misconducts. Although not a study of recidivism per se, the point estimates for this study and our analysis are somewhat similar, and the CIs almost overlap. Third, Gendreau et al. (2002) produced a mean effect size for the LSI-R that was slightly higher than the effect size reported in the current study. Again, however, the intervals generated based on the data used in the Gendreau et al. (2002) study overlap with the CIs from the current investigation.

◪ Conclusion

Policy Recommendation

It has been demonstrated empirically that actuarial assessments in various fields (e.g., medicine, mental health, criminal justice, and education) are far superior to clinical assessments in their ability to predict outcomes and do so well beyond chance levels (Bonta, Law, and Hanson, 1998; Grove, Zald, Lebow, Snitz, and Nelson, 2000; Hanson and Bussiere, 1996; see also Ayres, 2007). In this context, the LSI-R has emerged as a significant actuarial instrument for assessing offenders within the realm of corrections. As recent meta-analyses have confirmed, the LSI rivals, if not surpasses, the predictive validity of other assessment instruments (Campbell et al., 2007; see also Andrews and Bonta, 2006; Gendreau et al., 2002).

The LSI-R's somewhat hidden, or at least often overlooked, value is that it promotes a progressive policy agenda. Unlike previous prediction instruments that relied mainly on static, historical factors, the LSI-R measures dynamic factors—criminogenic needs. This approach not only increases the predictive power of the LSI-R but also directs attention to sources of offender recidivism that can be changed and thus are amenable to treatment. In this model, therefore, offenders are not portrayed as super-predators who endanger the community but as clients whose involvement in crime can be reduced through interventions that are responsive to the factors that underlie recidivism. More generally, programs that adhere to the principles of effective intervention have the capacity to achieve meaningful reductions in recidivism for high-risk offenders.

Evidence-based corrections, however, demand that treatment practices, including offender assessment, be subjected to rigorous scrutiny (Cullen and Gendreau, 2000; MacKenzie, 2006). The value of the critical analysis by Reisig et al. (2006) is that it called into question the wisdom of using the LSI-R to categorize female offenders by risk level and, ultimately, to decide who should receive treatment resources. The notion of gendered pathways has traction because of the growing literature that supports its existence (Miller and Mullins, 2006; Salisbury, 2007); it undermines confidence in the LSI-R because Andrews and colleagues' approach to assessment is rooted in a general, social learning-cognitive theory of human behavior.

Still, in the end, it is inadvisable to reject the LSI-R's status as a valuable assessment instrument for female offenders based on a single study—however persuasive it is. Rather, our approach, which was inspired by Reisig et al. (2006), was to conduct the most systematic investigation of the issues at hand using meta-analysis to organize the extant knowledge. In this way, we propose that at this stage, the empirical status of the LSI-R should be based not on a sample of 235 offenders but on the 14,737 female offenders represented in the studies that were meta-analyzed.

Although the current research does not represent a direct test of the gendered pathways perspective, it should be noted that the variation in effect sizes for males was greater than for females. If the LSI-R only predicted recidivism for "economically motivated offenders" (who constituted just one quarter of the total sample of female offenders in the Reisig et al. study), then more variation would have been expected for females, and this trend should have attenuated the overall effect size.

More importantly, the results of the current investigation indicate that the relationship between the LSI-R and recidivism for females is statistically and practically similar to that for males. Furthermore, the results from the current study, which focuses on female offenders, are similar to the results that previous meta-analyses have generated when using mixed samples or samples dominated by male offenders. Based on the extant data, it seems that the LSI-R performs virtually the same for female offenders as it does for male offenders.

This finding is of practical and policy significance. It means that at this stage, correctional officials should be advised to use the LSI-R to assess not only male but also female offenders. This is especially the case for those agencies that currently have the LSI-R in place. The gender critique of the instrument cannot be dismissed fully, but the "best bet" for assessing female offenders remains the LSI-R. It also is instructive that little dispute surrounds the LSI-R's value in assessing risks and needs for male offenders.

Gender, Assessment, and Correctional Treatment

Corrections is often a dismal social domain, which is largely hidden from public view. It has a history of subjecting offenders to painful conditions and to well-intentioned but flawed rehabilitation programs that are best termed as "quackery" (Latessa, Cullen, and Gendreau, 2002; MacKenzie, 2006). When correctional interventions fail, it feeds the notion that "nothing works" to change offenders—an idea that in turn lends credence to new-penology thinking that offenders are merely human products in an overflowing assembly line that need to be managed efficiently and with minimal risk to public safety. Phrased differently, for corrections to have a higher social purpose (Allen, 1981), it must be shown that it can be a conduit for the delivery of effective, humane interventions that reform offenders and, in so doing, protect the community.

From an evidence-based perspective, the data we have presented support the continued use in correctional agencies of the LSI-R as a means for assessing male and female offenders and, in turn, for delivering treatment services. This recommendation, however, is provisional. As Merlon (1973) points out, a hallmark of science is "organized skepticism." Knowledge grows not through blind acceptance but through continued empirical investigation. Furthermore, and equally important, the LSI-R should not be viewed in narrow, technical terms. Beyond effect sizes and predictive validity, this instrument exists within a broader scholarly context in which an ongoing debate surrounds the role of gender in correctional treatment. We alluded to this debate previously, but we return to it now because it frames the choices researchers concerned with the treatment of female offenders will face in the time ahead.

The Canadians scholars' principles of effective intervention comprise a powerful correctional paradigm (Cullen, 2002). We use the term "paradigm" purposefully, because this approach integrates coherently criminological knowledge, prescriptions for the content of treatment, and the technology for delivering interventions (see also Kuhn, 1962). Their psychology of criminal conduct is enmeshed initially within a view of behavior drawn from social learning, cognitive, and personality theories—all frameworks that are supported by thousands of studies. They hold that these fundamental sources of human behavior are general. In particular, they recognize action as preceded by thought (i.e., cognition or attitudes), prior learning and current supportive associations, and personality (i.e., traits and temperament). Consistent with this theoretical approach, meta-analyses show that antisocial attitudes, antisocial peers, personality, and past involvement are the strongest predictors of recidivism. These factors are prominently featured in the LSI-R, which is an instrument used to assess offenders and shown—as in our study—to have predictive validity. Interventions

that target these empirically established predictors for change reveal large reductions in recidivism. Furthermore, in their *Psychology of Criminal Conduct*—which is now nearly 600 pages in its fourth edition—Andrews and Bonta (2006) compile in remarkable detail the evidence that supports this paradigm.

MacKenzie's (2006) systematic review in *What Works in Corrections* offers collateral support to the Canadians' targeting proximate factors for intervention. Based on the extant evidence, she concludes that escaping from crime must first involve "a cognitive transformation . . . within the individual" (2006:337). Programs that proved effective typically focused "on individual-level change"; in fact, such a change is "required before ties can be formed with social institutions" (2006:337).

The Canadians do not completely ignore gender, but they do relegate it to a place of secondary importance. In their view, gender is a "specific responsivity" factor, which means that how a treatment is delivered to males and females should consider gender (e.g., whether a cognitive intervention should use structured learning tasks or require sensitivity on the part of offenders) (Andrews and Bonta, 2006). The Canadians reject, however, gender-specific assessment and treatment interventions. They are persuaded that the proximate sources of criminal conduct are the same for men and women. "We have not found any evidence," conclude Andrews and Bonta (2006:467), "that the antisocial behavior of demographically defined groups is insensitive to personality, attitudes, associates, or behavioral history. Nor have we found that the impact of RNR [risk-needs-responsivity] adherence and breadth on future offending varies with age, race, or gender." In their model, gender differences may occur in more distal experiences, such as the degree of sexual victimization. But if so, such factors have their effects on criminal conduct by fostering criminogenic personality traits, attitudes, associates, and behavioral history—which are sometimes called "the Big Four" (as we noted in footnote 1). "A history of being victimized may well contribute to crime," observe Andrews and Bonta (2006:467-468), "but, in terms of the research reviewed in this text, it does so through the Big Four."

The Canadians' contentions can be criticized for being reductionist—for focusing on the Big Four and ignoring the complexity of factors that underlie female criminality. This reasoning is problematic. The Canadians are not offering a criminological theory but a *treatment theory*. Their goal is to identify those proximate, dynamic factors that, if changed, lower recidivism. Many facets of male and female criminality may differ dramatically but effective treatment—regardless of gender—will focus on the dynamic risk factors (or criminogenic needs) shown by the empirical evidence to predict recidivism. This is why, in their view, the LSI-R should have the content it does and should have similar predictive validity across gender.

The power of the Canadians' paradigm is that it has been constructed over the course of 30 years and is evidence based. When policy makers and practitioners must decide how to allocate scarce resources to fund treatment programs, it is risky to ignore the Canadians' principles of effective intervention and to implement programs that have little proven track record of reducing recidivism. This is not to say, however, that the issue of gender-specific offender rehabilitation is settled—far from it. Still, it does mean that systematic efforts must be taken to create the empirical base for moving forward in this direction.

First, from the emerging literature on gendered pathways, it will be important to produce meta-analyses that can demonstrate that, across many studies, gender-specific factors predict recidivism above and beyond those identified by the Canadians. Individual studies with striking findings may be illuminating, but they are just one data point. It is the organization of knowledge, especially its quantitative synthesis, which provides the empirical grounds to build a consensus that a given factor is a strong predictor of recidivism. Second, to form the basis of a treatment theory, these factors will have to be shown to be dynamic and not static as well as amenable to change through practical treatment modalities (e.g., cognitive-behavioral programs and skill building). Third, assessment instruments will have to be developed that can measure these factors and that have more predictive validity than the LSI-R. Fourth, carefully conducted experimental and quasi-experimental evaluation studies will need to be undertaken that can show across a variety of correctional contexts that these gender-specific interventions reduce recidivism more than programs based on the Canadians' principles of effective intervention.

Notably, important steps are being made in this direction. In conjunction with the National Institute of Justice, Patricia Van Voorhis and colleagues have been validating a series of new risk/need assessments for female offenders (see Van Voorhis, Salisbury, Wright, and Bauman, 2008; Van Voorhis, Wright, Salisbury, and Bauman, 2009). These assessments include items to evaluate both "gender-neutral" and "gender-responsive" factors (i.e., trauma and abuse, unhealthy relationships, parental stress, depression, andself-efficacy). In fact, the Women's Supplemental Risk/Needs Assessment is designed to supplement existing risk/needs assessments such as the LSI to expand the number of factors assessed (Van Voorhis et al., 2008). Based on a sample of 1,613 female offenders drawn from different correctional settings (i.e., prison, probation, and prerelease), the analysis revealed that gender-neutral factors have predictive validity. Even so, gender-specific factors improved the prediction of recidivism meaningfully. In our view, these findings support both the continued use of the LSI-R in correctional agencies and the ongoing, expanded efforts to incorporate gender-specific predictors into this assessment instrument.

In the end, effective intervention with offenders is an empirical, not an ideological, issue. Taking this evidence-based approach involves two imperatives. First, at any given time, it is incumbent on criminologists advising policy makers and practitioners to know fully the empirical status of competing treatment approaches. The approach with the strongest empirical support should be recommended as being the standard treatment in the field. Second, no treatment paradigm should be viewed as sacrosanct. The research and the construction of more effective interventions, which include assessment instruments, should be ongoing. We owe this to the offenders we bring under our auspices and to members of the public whose victimization we may have the power to prevent.

◪ References

*References marked with an asterisk (*) indicate studies included in the meta-analysis.

Abramsky, Sasha. 2007. *American furies: Crime, punishment, and vengeance in the age of mass incarceration*. Boston, MA: Beacon Press.

Allen, Francis A. 1981. *The decline of the rehabilitative ideal: Penal policy and social purpose.* New Haven, CT: Yale University Press.

American Psychological Association. 2001. *Publication manual of the American Psychological Association,* 5th Edition. Washington. DC: American Psychological Association.

*Andrews, Don A. 1984. *The Level of Service Inventory (LSI): The first follow-up.* Toronto, Canada: Ontario Ministry of Correctional Services.

Andrews, Don A. and James A. Bonta. 2006. *The psychology of criminal conduct,* 4th edition. Cincinnati, OH: Anderson.

Andrews, Don A., James A. Bonta, and Stephen Wormith. 2006. The recent past and near future of risk and/or need assessment. *Crime & Delinquency,* 52:7–27.

*Arnold, Tom. 2007. *Exploratory analysis of LSI-R: Results from a central Minnesota community corrections department.* Unpublished manuscript, St. Cloud State University, St. Cloud, Minnesota.

Ayres, Ian. 2007. *Super-crunchers: Why thinking-by-numbers is the new way to be smart.* New York: Bantam Books.

Bonta, James A. 1996. Risk-needs assessment and treatment. In (Alan T. Harland, ed.). *Choosing correctional options that work: Defining the demand and evaluating the supply.* Thousand Oaks, CA: Sage.

Bonta, James A., Moira Law, and R. Karl Hanson. 1998. The prediction of criminal and violent recidivism among mentally disordered offenders: A meta-analysis. *Psychological Bulletin,* 123:123–142.

*Brews, Albert and Stephen J. Wormith. 2007. *LSI-R and female offenders: Addressing issues of predictive validity.* Paper presented at the North American Correctional and Criminal Justice Conference, Ottawa, Ontario.

Campbell, Mary Ann, Sheila A. French, and Paul Gendreau. 2007. *Assessing the utility of risk assessment tools and personality measures in the prediction of violent recidivism for adult offenders.* Ottawa, Ontario: Department of Public Safety and Emergency Preparedness Canada.

Chesney-Lind, Meda. 1989. Girls' crime and woman's place: Toward a feminist model of female delinquency. *Crime & Delinquency,* 35:5–29.

*Coulson, Grant, Giorgio Ilacqua, Verna Nutbrown, Diana Giulekas, and Francis Cudjoe. 1996. Predictive utility of the LSI for incarcerated female offenders. *Criminal Justice and Behavior,* 23:427–439.

Covington, Stephanie and Barbara Bloom. 1999. *Gender-responsive programming and evaluation for women in the criminal justice system: A shift from what works? to what is the work?* Paper presented at the American Society of Criminology, Toronto, Ontario, Canada.

Cullen, Francis T. 2002. Rehabilitation and treatment programs. In (James Q Wilson and Joan Petersilia, eds.), *Crime: Public policies for crime control.* Oakland, CA: ICS Press.

Cullen, Francis T. and Paul Gendreau. 2000. Assessing correctional rehabilitation: Policy, practice, and prospects. In (Julie Homey, ed.), *Criminal justice 2000: Volume 3—Policies, processes, and decisions of the criminal justice system.* Washington, DC: National Institute of Justice, U.S. Department of Justice.

Cumming, Geoff and Sue Finch. 2005. Inference by eye: Confidence intervals and how to read pictures of data. *American Psychologist,* 60:170–180.

Daigle, Leah E., Francis T. Cullen, and John P. Wright. 2007. Gender differences in the predictors of juvenile delinquency: Assessing the generality-specificity debate. *Youth Violence and Juvenile Justice,* 5:254–286.

Daly, Kathleen. 1992. Women's pathways to felony court: Feminist theories of law-breaking and problems of representation. *Southern California Review of Law and Women's Studies.* 2:11–52.

Daly, Kathleen. 1994. *Gender, crime and punishment.* New Haven, CT: Yale University Press.

Dilulio, John, Jr. 1987. *Governing prisons: A comparative study of correctional management.* New York: The Free Press.

Dilulio, John, Jr. 1991. *No escape: The future of American corrections.* New York: Basic Books.

Dowden, Craig and Don A. Andrews. 1999. What works for female offenders: A meta-analytic review. *Crime & Delinquency,* 45:435–452.

Farrington, David P. and Kate Painter. 2004. *Gender differences in risk factors for offending.* Research, Development, and Statistics Directorate, London, UK. Retrieved March 15, 2008 from homeoffice.gov.uk/rds/onlinepubs1.html.

Feeley, Malcolm M. and Jonathan Simon. 1992. The new penology: Notes on the emerging strategy of corrections and its implications. *Criminology,* 30:449–474.

*Flores, Anthony W., Christopher T. Lowenkamp, Edward J. Latessa, and Paula Smith. 2006. Validating the Level of Service Inventory-Revised on a sample of federal probationers. *Federal Probation,* 70:44–48.

*Folsom, Jean and Jill L. Atkinson. 2007. The generalizability of the LSI-R and CAT to the prediction of recidivism in female offenders. *Criminal Justice and Behavior,* 34:1044–1056.

Gendreau, Paul. 1996. The principles of effective intervention with offenders. In (Alan T. Harland, ed.), *Choosing correctional options that work: Defining the demand and evaluating the supply.* Thousand Oaks, CA: Sage.

Gendreau, Paul, Claire Goggin, and Moira Law. 1997. Predicting prison misconducts. *Criminal Justice and Behavior,* 24: 414–431.

Gendreau, Paul, Claire Goggin, and Paula Smith. 2002. Is the PCL-R really the "unparalleled" measure of offender risk? *Criminal Justice and Behavior,* 29:397–426.

Gendreau, Paul, Tracy Little, and Claire Goggin. 1996. A meta-analysis of the predictors of adult offenders recidivism: What works! *Criminology,* 34:575–607.

Gendreau, Paul and Paula Smith. 2007. Influencing the "people who count": Some perspectives on the reporting of meta-analytic results for prediction and treatment outcomes with offenders. *Criminal Justice and Behavior,* 34:1536–1559.

Gendreau, Paul, Paula Smith, and Sheila A. French. 2006. The theory of effective correctional intervention: Empirical status and future directions. In (Francis T. Cullen, John P. Wright, and Kristie R. Blevins, eds.), *Taking stock: The status of criminological theory-Advances in criminological theory.* New Brunswick, NJ: Transaction.

Glaze, Lauren E. and Thomas P. Bonezar. 2006. *Probation and parole in the United States, 2005.* Washington, DC: Bureau of Justice Statistics, U.S. Department of Justice.

Gottschalk, Marie. 2006. *The prison and the gallows: The politics of mass incarceration in America.* New York: Cambridge University Press.

Grove, William M., David H. Zald, Boyd S. Lebow, Beth E. Snitz, and Chad Nelson. 2000. Clinical versus mechanical prediction: A meta-analysis. *Psychological Assessment,* 12:19–30.

Hanson, R. Karl and Monique T. Bussiere. 1996. *Predictors of sexual offender recidivism: A meta-analysis.* Ottawa: Solicitor General Canada.

Holtfreter, Kristy and Rhonda Cupp. 2007. Gender and risk assessment. *Journal of Contemporary Criminal Justice,* 23:363–382.

Hubbard, Dana and Travis C. Pratt. 2002. A meta-analysis of the predictors of delinquency among girls. *Journal of Offender Rehabilitation,* 34:1–13.

Hunt, Morton. 1997. *How science takes stock: The story of meta-analysis.* New York: Russell Sage Foundation.

Hunter, John E. and Frank L. Schmidt. 2004. *Methods of meta-analysis.* Newbury Park, CA: Sage.

Jones, Peter R. 1996. Risk prediction in criminal justice. In (Alan T. Harland, ed.), *Choosing correctional options that work: Defining the demand and evaluating the supply.* Thousand Oaks, CA: Sage.

*Jones-Hubbard, Dana. 2002. *Cognitive-behavioral treatment: An analysis of gender and other responsivity characteristics and their effects on success in offender rehabilitation.* Unpublished doctoral dissertation, University of Cincinnati.

*Kirkpatrick, Bonnie L. 1999. Exploratory research of female risk prediction and LSI-R. *Corrections Compendium,* 24:14–17.

Kuhn, Thomas S. 1962. *The structure of scientific revolutions.* Chicago, IL: University of Chicago Press.

Latessa, Edward J., Francis T. Cullen, and Paul Gendreau. 2002. Beyond correctional quackery: Professionalism and the possibility of effective treatment. *Federal Probation,* 66:43–49.

Lipsey, Mark, Gabrielle L. Chapman, and Nana Landenberger. 2001. Cognitive-behavioral programs for offenders. *ANNALS of the American Academy of Political and Social Science,* 578:144–157.

Listwan, Shelley Johnson, Cheryl Lero Johnson, Francis T. Cullen, and Edward J. Latessa. 2008. Cracks in the penal harm movement: Evidence from the field. *Criminology & Public Policy,* 7:423–465.

*Lowenkamp, Christopher T. 2007. LSI-R and recidivism—Delaware County, Ohio. Unpublished raw data.

*Lowenkamp, Christopher T. and Kristin Bechtel. 2006. LSI-R and recidivism—Iowa. Unpublished raw data.

*Lowenkamp, Christopher T., Alex M. Holsinger, and Edward J. Latessa. 2001. Risk/need assessment, offender classification, and the role of childhood abuse. *Criminal Justice and Behavior,* 28:543–563.

*Lowenkamp, Christopher T. and Edward J. Latessa. 2002a. *Validating the LSI-R in Ohio's community-based correctional facilities-Supplemental analysis.* Unpublished manuscript, University of Cincinnati.

*Lowenkamp, Christopher T. and Edward J. Latessa. 2005b. *Norming and validation study of the LSI-R: Maine community supervision sample.* Unpublished manuscript, University of Cincinnati.

*Lowenkamp, Christopher T. and Edward J. Latessa. 2006. *Norming and validation study of the Level of Service Inventory-Revised (LSI-R) and the Illinois Pre-Screen (IPS).* Unpublished manuscript, University of Cincinnati.

*Lowenkamp, Christopher T., Brian Lovins, and Edward J. Latessa. 2009. Validating the Level of Service Inventory–Revised and the Level of Service Inventory Screening Version with a sample of probationers. *Prison Journal.* In press.

Lynch, Michael J. 2007. *Big dreams, big prisons: Crime and the failure of America's penal system.* New Brunswick, NJ: Rutgers University Press.

MacKenzie, Doris L. 2006. *What works in corrections: Reducing the criminal activities of offenders and delinquents.* New York: Cambridge University Press.

*McConnell, Beth A. 1996. *The prediction of female federal offender recidivism with the Level of Supervision Inventory.* Unpublished honor's thesis, Queen's University, Kingston, Ontario.

Merton, Robert K. 1973. *The sociology of science: Theoretical and empirical investigations.* Chicago, IL: University of Chicago Press.

Miller, Jody and Christopher W. Mullins. 2006. The status of feminist theories in criminology. In (Francis T. Cullen, John P. Wright, and Kristie R. Blevins, eds.), *Taking stock: The status of criminological theory-Advances in criminological theory.* New Brunswick, NJ: Transaction.

Moffitt, Terrie E., Avshalom Caspi, Michael Rutter, and Phil A. Silva. 2001. *Sex differences in antisocial behavior: Conduct disorder, delinquency, and violence in the Dunedin longitudinal study.* Cambridge, UK: Cambridge University Press.

Ogloff, James R.P. and Michael R. Davis. 2004. Advances in offender assessment and rehabilitation: Contributions of the risk-need-responsivity approach. *Psychology, Crime, & Law,* 10:229–242.

Orwin, Robert G. 1983. A fail-safe N for effect size in meta-analysis. *Journal of Educational Statistics,* 8:157–159.

*Palmer, Emma J. and Clive R. Hollin. 2007. The Level of Service Inventory–Revised with English women prisoners: A needs and reconviction analysis. *Criminal Justice and Behavior,* 34:971–984.

*Raynor, Peter. 2006. Risk and need assessment in British probation: The contribution of the LSI-R. *Psychology, Crime, & Law,* 13:125–138.

*Raynor, Peter and Helen Miles. 2007. Evidence-based probation in a microstate: The British Channel Island of Jersey. *European Journal of Criminology,* 4:299–313.

Reisig, Michael D., Kristy Holtfreter, and Merry Morash 2002. Social capital among women offenders. *Journal of Contemporary Criminal Justice,* 18:167–187.

*Reisig, Michael D., Kristy Holtfreter, and Merry Morash. 2006. Assessing recidivism risk across female pathways to crime. *Justice Quarterly,* 23:384–405.

*Rettinger, Jill L. 1998. *A recidivism follow-up study investigating risk and need within a sample of provincially sentenced women.* Unpublished doctoral thesis, Carleton University.

Rosenthal, Robert. 1979. The "file drawer" problem and tolerance for negative results. *Psychological Bulletin,* 86:638–641.

Rothstein, Hannah R., Alexander J. Sutton, and Michael Borenstein. eds. 2005. *Publication bias in meta-analysis: Prevention, assessment, and adjustments.* Chichester, UK: Wiley.

Sabol, William J., Heather Couture, and Paige M. Harrison. 2007. *Prisoners in 2006.* Washington, DC: Bureau of Justice Statistics, U.S. Department of Justice.

Salisbury, Emily J. 2007. *Gendered pathways: An empirical investigation of women offenders' unique paths to crime.* Unpublished doctoral dissertation, University of Cincinnati.

Simon, Jonathan. 1993. *Poor discipline: Parole the social control of the underclass, 1890-1990.* Chicago, IL: University of Chicago Press.

Simon, Jonathan. 2007. *Governing through crime: How the war on crime transformed American democracy and created a culture of fear.* New York: Oxford University Press.

Simons, Ronald L., Martin O. Miller, and Stephen M. Aigner. 1980. Contemporary theories of deviance and female delinquency: An empirical test. *Journal of Research in Crime and Delinquency,* 17:42–57.

Simourd, Linda and Don A. Andrews. 1994. Correlates of delinquency: A look at gender differences. *Forum on Corrections Research,* 6:26–31.

Smith, Douglas A. and Raymond Paternoster. 1987. The gender gap in theories of deviance: Issues and evidence. *Journal of Research in Crime and Delinquency,* 24:140–172.

Smithson, Michael. 2003. *Confidence intervals.* Thousand Oaks, CA: Sage.

Tonry, Michael H. 2004. *Thinking about crime: Sense and sensibility in American penal culture.* New York: Oxford University Press.

Van Voorhis, Patricia, Emily Salisbury, Emily Wright, and Ashley Bauman. 2008. Achieving accurate pictures of risk and identifying gender responsive needs: Two new assessments for women offenders. *National Institute of Corrections Summary Report.*

Van Voorhis, Patricia, Emily Wright, Emily Salisbury, and Ashley Bauman. 2009. Women's risk factors and their contributions to existing risk/needs assessment: The current status of gender responsive assessment. *Criminal Justice and Behavior.* In press.

Vose, Brenda A. 2008. *Assessing the predictive validity of the Level of Service Inventory-Revised: Recidivism among Iowa parolees and probationers.* Unpublished doctoral dissertation. University of Cincinnati.

Vose, Brenda, Francis T. Cullen, and Paula Smith. 2008. The empirical status of the Level of Service Inventory. *Federal Probation,* 72:22–29.

Warren, Jenifer. 2008. *One in 100: Behind bars in America 2008.* Washington, DC: Pew Charitable Trusts.

*Washington State Institute for Public Policy. 2007. LSI-R and recidivism for female offenders. Unpublished raw data.

*Zajac, Gary. 2007. Pennsylvania Department of Corrections. Unpublished data.

DISCUSSION QUESTIONS

1. Summarize the policy implications of this study.

2. According to the authors, what are the strongest predictors of recidivism? Why is it important to understand these predictors in supervising offenders in the community?

3. What do the authors mean when they state that Canadian researchers "are not offering a criminological theory but a treatment theory"? Why is this important for community-based corrections?

4. Why is it imperative to use an empirical approach to supervising offenders, not just an ideological approach?

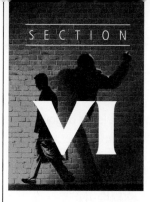

Probation Management and Case Planning

Learning Objectives

1. Understand the probation organization, primarily at the county and state levels of government.

2. Be aware of the objectives and advantages of probation.

3. Understand the future potential of **private probation** agencies.

4. Understand the importance of the presentence investigation report (PSI).

5. Understand the importance of the various courtroom actors when setting terms and conditions of probation.

6. Be cognizant of basic issues involved with probation evaluation.

7. Know the various forms of alternative probation sentences.

8. Understand various factors associated with the revocation of probation.

Probationers are criminal offenders who have been sentenced to a period of correctional supervision in the community in lieu of incarceration (Glaze & Bonczar, 2009). During the past few years, the overall population growth of probationers has continued; however, the rate of that growth has progressively slowed during the past several years. For instance, in 2008, the probation population grew by only 0.9%, or 36,446 probationers. The probation population accounted for approximately half of all growth in the overall correctional population throughout the nation (Glaze & Bonczar, 2009). Probationers continue to account for the largest proportion of all persons under corrections supervision, with 58% of all convicted offenders being on probation. At the close of 2008, the total probation population, when adding state and federal probationers, was 4,270,917 total probationers (Glaze & Bonczar, 2009). As the most frequently used alternative to incarceration, probation has its roots in England and in charity work addressing the needs of those prone to alcoholism. The historical development of probation along with the various issues surrounding it, including qualification, pay, job stress, and process, will be discussed in this section.

⊠ Evolution of Probation in the United States

As you recall from Section I, the earliest forms of non-incarcerative sanctions can be traced back to Europe with the development of four specific sanctions: (1) sanctuary, (2) benefit of clergy, (3) judicial reprieve, and (4) recognizance (see Section I for a review of these sanctions). The United States distinguished themselves from these practices through the use of recognizance and the suspended sentence.

Recognizance

Recognizance in the United States is often traced to the case of *Commonwealth v. Chase* (1830) in which Judge Thacher of Boston, Massachusetts, found a woman named Jerusha Chase guilty of stealing from inside a home (Grinnel, 1941). Ms. Chase pleaded her guilt but did have numerous friends that also pleaded for mercy from the court. This resulted in her release "at large" on her own recognizance until which time she was called to appear before the court (Begnaud, 2007). The accused was likewise acquitted before the same court of another charge of larceny and was only sentenced for her prior 1830 crime (Begnaud, 2007; Grinnel, 1941). These sentences were used as a means to avoid final conviction (Cromwell, Del Carmen, & Alarid, 2002). This is interesting because this again points toward the idea that many of the early alternatives to incarceration were implemented more for the reintegration of offenders rather than a concern over the population of the local jail facility.

Suspended Sentence

Suspended sentences were used as a way to mitigate the harshness of penalties. A sentence can be suspended in two separate ways: suspension of the imposition of the sentence or the suspension of the execution of the sentence. Suspending of the imposition of the sentence means a plea agreement is reached by the offender and the court whereby no sentence is pronounced if the offender remains crime free or completes a form of reformation during a specified amount of time. This process allows for the accused to maintain a crime-free record with all rights afforded to citizens. Suspending the execution of the sentence refers to the defendant being convicted of a crime followed by "the execution of a criminal sanction" (Alarid & Del Carmen, 2011, p. 80). These sanctions may be separate or used as an alternative. This form of sanctioning is still used today particularly with probation as a form of suspended sentence. The 1984 Federal Sentencing Reform Act further recognized probation as a form of sentencing whereby suspended sentences could be used in lieu of or a sentence of probation could be the formal sanction (18 U.S.C. 3561; Alarid & Del Carmen, 2011, p. 81; U.S. Courts Probation and Pretrial Services, 2010b).

▨ The Beginning of Probation in the United States

While many of the traditions and means of addressing issues associated with crime and punishment originated in England, the United States did have its own novel inventions. Probation is one such invention. John Augustus, a Boston bootmaker, is often recognized as the father of modern probation. Historical accounts are quick to note that Augustus did not recognize himself as being a member of a charitable organization. Rather, he had interest in Christian ideals and the reformation of mankind through charity work most notably with drunkards and abandoned children. His pursuits often led him to observe the workings of the local police court as a volunteer. In 1841, Augustus on one of his many visits to the police court observed a man who was noticeably there for intoxication. Through his keen sense of compassion, Augustus approached this man and did indeed find this was the case. Through his conversation and being inspired by the work of the Washington Total Abstinence Society in Boston (Alarid & Del Carmen, 2011; Panzarella, 2002), Augustus agreed to offer a pledge of bail for the man. Upon taking responsibility for him, he worked to ensure that the man refrained from alcohol consumption until his next appearance. Three weeks later, the man appeared in front of the judge, and in lieu of being incarcerated in the House of Correction, he was fined "one cent and costs, amounting in all to $3.76" (Alarid & Del Carmen, 2011, p. 82; Panzarella, 2002, p. 39). During the first 2 years of these endeavors, Augustus pledged his own money to bail out "drunkards." Because of his commitment to this task, his business as a bootmaker began to suffer. In 1843, he began accepting donations to support the bailout of individuals. Eventually (5 years after he first began assisting those in need), he lost his business and began relying on donations and the work of outside individuals to support this process. From his first intervention in 1841 until his death in 1859, Augustus, with the assistance of donors, continued to bail out numerous offenders, providing voluntary supervision and guidance until they were subsequently sentenced by the court. During his 18 years of activity, Augustus "bailed on probation" 1,152 male offenders and 794 female offenders (Barnes & Teeters, 1959, p. 554; Latessa & Allen, 1999). His rationale centered on his belief that "the object of the law is to reform criminals and to prevent crime and not to punish maliciously or from a spirit of revenge" (Dressler, 1962, p. 17). Thus, it was rehabilitation that Augustus ultimately sought to achieve, regardless of whether jails or houses of correction were considered humane (in fact, many were very inhumane).

It wasn't until 1878 that Massachusetts passed the first law providing for a paid probation officer. The passage of this law required the individual to report directly to the chief of police. Three years later, the law was revised so that the probation officer would report to the State Commissioners of Prisons and again in 1891 barring any active members of the police force from being probation officers (Panzarella, 2002, p. 42). With the rise of the Progressive Movement and further expansion of the *1870 Declaration of Principles*, which called for the use of indeterminate sentences, the use of probation became common practice between 1900 and 1920 (Rothman, 2002). It wasn't until 1925 that the federal government, under the auspices of President Coolidge, signed into law the National Probation Act. This act called for the hiring of a federal probation officer in every federal district. It was not, however, until 1927 that the first federal probation officer was actually appointed (U.S. Courts Probation and Pretrial Services, 2010a, 2010b) (see Focus Topic 6.1).

⊠ Probation From 1960 Onward

During the period from 1930 through the 1950s, correctional thought reflected what was then referred to as the "medical model," which centered on the use of rehabilitation and treatment of offenders. In general, support for the medical model of corrections began to dissipate during the late 1960s and had all but disappeared by the 1970s. The medical model presumed that criminal behavior was caused by social, psychological, or biological deficiencies that were correctable through treatment interventions. The 1950s were particularly given to the ideology of the medical model, with influential states such as Illinois, New York, and California falling under the treatment banner.

The 1970 U.S. Supreme Court case of *United States v. Birnbaum* (1970) made it clear that probation was a privilege and that it was not a right. Though this ruling may seem to address an issue that on the face of it should have been obvious, it did help to solidify the fact that community corrections in general and probation in particular are options of leniency. This then means that probation—and parole as well (to be covered in Section XI)—were considered discretionary means of processing offenders. In all cases, the rights of probationers and parolees are, in actuality, no different than those among persons that are incarcerated. It is simply due to the leniency of the courts that the offender is allowed to serve their sentence within the community.

Focus Topic 6.1

Historical Developments in Probation

1841   John Augustus becomes the "father of probation"

1869   First official probation program developed in Massachusetts (the home of probation)

1878   First law passed in Massachusetts providing for paid probation officers

1901   New York creates the first statute officially establishing adult probation services

1925	Federal probation is authorized by Congress (National Probation Act)
1927	Forty-nine states implement juvenile probation (all but Wyoming)
	First federal probation officer appointed in the District of Massachusetts
1930	Probation Act amended to include supervision of federal parolees
1943	PSIs formally created by federal probation system
1956	Mississippi is the 50th state to formally establish adult probation
1965	The birth of "shock probation" occurs in the state of Ohio
1979	Various risk/needs assessments are developed by the state of Wisconsin
1983	Intensive supervision probation (ISP) has its birth in Georgia.

As you recall from the introduction, at the close of 2008, the total probation population was 4,270,917 (4,248,169 state probationers; 22,748 federal probationers) (Glaze & Bonczar, 2009). Among the probation population, almost 1 out of 4 (24%) were female offenders. Further, more than half (56%) of all probationers were White Americans, almost a third (29%) were African American, and one eighth were Latino American. Persons of other racial orientations comprised about 2% of all probationers around the nation.

Overall, roughly 49% of all probationers were convicted of a felony offense with the misdemeanor population consisting of 48% of the probationer population. The remaining 2% were convicted of other types of offenses, such as city ordinances, county codes, and so forth. As Glaze and Bonczar (2009) indicated, the largest body of the probation population had been convicted of some form of drug-related violation (30%), followed with property offenses (25%), violent (19%), and public-order offenses (17%), which include DWIs. Though most probationers were on probation for nonviolent offenses, 3% were serving probation for sexual assault, another 6% were serving probation for some form of domestic violence, and 10% were on probation for a miscellaneous assault conviction (Glaze & Bonczar, 2009). Thus, about 1 in 5 probation offenders had committed acts of violence, and among these, many are not extreme acts. The remaining offenses tend to be fairly evenly distributed and include crimes, such as fraud, burglary, and minor (but probably repetitive) traffic violations (Glaze & Bonczar, 2009).

Not all probationers are required to report to their probation officer. Indeed, a certain proportion are simply kept on caseloads administratively and are checked from time to time, required to pay fees during the set amount of time, and so forth. So long as no word of violation is received or detected among other agencies, they finish out their probation with relative ease. In 2005, roughly 7 in 10 probationers were under active supervision, being required to regularly report to a probation authority in person, by mail, or by telephone (Glaze & Bonczar, 2009). This then means that roughly 30% of all probationers were on inactive administrative caseloads. In addition, roughly 11% of all probationers absconded during 2009. Though these individuals are still on probation caseloads, their whereabouts are completely unknown. This is a concern as this means that there are roughly 400,000 probation absconders across the nation. The rate of probation absconders has, during the past decade, slightly increased from 9% to 11% and, though slight, indicates a general need for improved methods of security over probationers.

◪ Models of Probation Administration

The specific means by which probation operates can vary considerably depending upon the level of government from which it is administered. Correctional systems, including community supervision components, can vary greatly from state to state. A bit more discussion on the organizational aspects of probation will be provided since this greatly impacts the operations of probations services within a given jurisdiction. One key characteristic involves the degree of centralization that exists within an agency. Indeed, adult probation in one state may be administered by a single, central state agency; by a variety of local agencies; or by a given combination of the two. When considering local levels of administration, agencies may operate at the county or even municipal level. However, these supposedly smaller jurisdictions should not be underestimated. Consider, for example, the probation departments in New York City, where felony and misdemeanor caseloads are larger than those of many entire state systems.

Further, probation services are delivered through one of two mechanisms: the executive or the judicial branch of government. In both cases, the probation agency will oversee the individual's compliance with conditions of their probation supervision. With this in mind, probation agencies administered through the executive branch may be part of the larger state correctional system or they may exist as an entirely separate system. In addition, these agencies may operate at local levels of government but again may be included within areas of government associated with the executive (enforcement) functions of government. While the sentencing courts, in these cases, may require probation agencies to provide reports on the subsequent supervision of the offender, the probation agencies are themselves outside of the judicial process.

On the other hand, probation agencies that are administered through the judicial branch work directly with the court system itself. In these cases, state and local courts will enforce compliance with the terms of probation through court judgments. In the process, court administrative offices or designated staff monitor various aspects of the probation process. Functions such as the collection of fees and/or fines, victim restitution, court-ordered child support, and so forth will be fulfilled through personnel that are tasked via judicial administrators or judges themselves.

Those who support the operation of probation services in the judicial branch contend that probation is more responsive to the courts when it is administered by the judiciary (Abadinsky, 2003; Nelson, Ohmart, & Harlow, 1978; Peak, 1995). Further, when probation personnel and court personnel operate in close proximity, an automatic feedback loop develops, thereby optimizing the performance of the dispositions that are given. In addition, the court will have better insight as to the challenges involved with administering probation supervision (Abadinsky, 2003; Nelson et al., 1978; Peak, 1995). With this in mind, it is then likely that judges would be more receptive to the needs and concerns of the probation agency, particularly since the agency would work in tandem with (and directly under) the supervision of the judiciary. This would also allow for better discretionary operations since the probation staff will not be members of an outside agency but instead will be aligned with the specific purposes of the court (Abadinsky, 2003; Nelson et al., 1978; Peak, 1995). Figure 6.1 provides an example of a probation department that is operated at the county level under a specific judicial court.

On the other hand, there are those who also oppose the operation of probation services in the judicial branch, noting several disadvantages. First, judges are trained in matters of legal interpretation rather than administration and are typically not appropriately equipped to administer probation services (Abadinsky, 2003; Nelson et al., 1978; Peak, 1995). Further, when under judicial control, services to persons on probation may receive a lower priority than services to the judge; such as with presentence investigations. Third, probation staff tend to be assigned to a variety of duties by judges, some of which are not related to probation

Figure 6.1 Example of a Locally Based Probation Organization That Is Under the Direction of a Judicial Court: Organization of the Allegheny County Probation Department

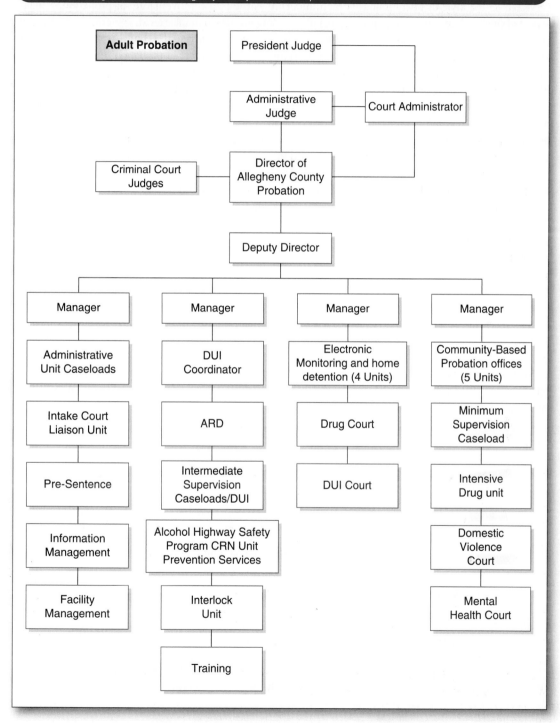

but are instead intended to help out other demands upon the courthouse (Abadinsky, 2003; Nelson et al., 1978; Peak, 1995). Fourth, the courts tend to be adjudicatory in nature and are therefore not oriented to a service-oriented style of operation. This then undermines the reintegrative nature of probation, a major aspect of this text's presentation of probation. Fifth, placing probation in the executive segment of state government would allow for better coordination of service provision and for budgetary considerations (Abadinsky, 2003; Nelson et al., 1978; Peak, 1995). Sixth, the centralization of probation services within the executive segment of government allows for a coordinated continuum of services to offenders (thereby improving reintegrative efforts) (Abadinsky, 2003; Nelson et al., 1978; Peak, 1995). Seventh and last, other human service agencies as well as institutional correctional systems tend to be placed in the executive branch as well (Abadinsky, 2003; Nelson et al., 1978; Peak, 1995). This then implies that probation would be better suited to coordinate with these agencies. Thus, as one can tell, there is an equally compelling argument for probation departments to be administered through the executive segment of state government as there is for administering them through the judicial branch.

Consider further that in many cases the administration of probation may be determined by the seriousness of the offense. For instance, felony offenses may be supervised by state-level personnel while misdemeanor cases may be supervised by local governmental probation agencies. For instance, in Michigan, adult felony probation is administered through the state's Department of Corrections (DOC) while adult misdemeanor probation is administered through the local district courts.

Further still, juvenile probation adds a whole new dimension of organizational considerations. Indeed, over half of all juvenile probation agencies are administered at the local level. To illustrate, juvenile probation may be provided through a separate agency or through a subdepartment of the large adult probation system. In over a dozen states, juvenile probation services are split, with the juvenile court administering services in urban jurisdictions and the state administering such services in rural areas. Lastly, some states have a statewide office of juvenile probation that is located in that state's executive branch (Siegel, 2003).

Lastly, Abadinsky (2003) noted that probation systems can be separated into six categories, with states having more than one system in operation simultaneously. The six categories of operation noted by Abadinsky (2003) are as follows:

1. *Juvenile:* This includes separate probation services for juveniles who are administered through county or municipal governments or on a statewide basis.

2. *Municipal:* These are independent probation agencies that are administered through lower courts or through the municipality itself.

3. *County:* The probation agency is governed by laws and/or guidelines established by the state, which empowers a county to operate its own probation agency.

4. *State:* One agency administers a centralized probation system that provides services throughout the state.

5. *State Combined P & P:* Probation and parole services are administered together on a statewide basis by a single agency.

6. *Federal:* Probation is administered nationally as a branch of the courts.

Much of the research on the organization of probation points toward the fact that probation would, in the most practical sense, be best administered through an executive segment of governmental administration. Moving probation within the executive segment of government requires that probation be operated from a centralized managerial scheme that would then naturally be administered at the state level (Peak, 1995). The coordination of centralized state-run probation systems tends to be much better and also allows for better integration of overall services (Nelson et al., 1978; Peak, 1995). While administrators will be more removed from the rank-and-file probation officer staff, the uniformity of services, elimination of widespread **disparity** in supervision, and the improved integration of services with other social service agencies is thought to offset concerns related to this type of administration (Peak, 1995).

⊠ An Overview and State-by-State Comparison of Community Supervision Models

States around the nation have varied methods of managing the organizational structure of their probation and parole programs. The National Institute of Corrections (NIC) has conducted extensive research on the organization of community supervision programs in the United States. The NIC conducted interviews with the head administrator of each state agency to determine the structure of each program, with primary emphasis being given to the implementation of probation. The organization of probation service delivery is quite important to understand before progressing into any in-depth study of community corrections for two key reasons.

First, probation is the single most common form of sanction that is used in correctional systems throughout the nation. Nearly 60% of all offenders in the United States are on probation, meaning that this sanction is much more common than prison sentences and is also much more common than the use of parole. Indeed, roughly 4,270,917 persons were on probation in 2008 compared to a mere 828,169 persons being on parole (Glaze & Bonczar, 2009).

Data from the NIC show that the most common organizational structure for probation consists of a state-level executive branch agency to oversee probation services throughout the entirety of the state (Krauth & Linke, 1999). Roughly 26 states provide probation services through executive branch agencies associated with the state-level (rather than county level) DOC (Krauth & Linke, 1999). Contrastly, three states (Iowa, New York, and Oregon), provide probation services through county agencies (rather than state agencies) in the executive branch. In eight states (Colorado, Connecticut, Hawaii, Kansas, Massachusetts, Nebraska, New Jersey, and South Dakota), probation services are administered through the state-level judicial branch. In five states, local agencies in the judicial branch administer probation services (including Arizona, Illinois, Indiana, Texas, and West Virginia). Lastly, probation services are delivered through multiple organizational models in Minnesota, Ohio, Pennsylvania, and California. In the first three of these states, there is a combination of state executive branch and local executive agencies that provide services. In California, probation services are always delivered by local agencies, but these agencies may be either executive or judicial in nature, depending on particular area of that state.

Equally important when examining the organization of community corrections from state to state is determining whether probation (a front-end sanction) and parole (a back-end sanction) are administered together by the same agency or separately. It has been found that states exhibit a great deal of variety in terms of probation service delivery and the delegation of other types of supervision caseloads, such as with paroled offenders and/or juvenile offenders. In the majority of states, the probation and parole functions are fully integrated with one another. In these states, officers usually have combined caseloads of both probationers and parolees. Only nine states have jurisdictions that deliver services solely to adult probationers.

In addition, adult and juvenile probation service delivery has been integrated in several states. These states include California, Colorado, Illinois, Indiana, Kansas, Nebraska, New Jersey, New York, South Dakota, and West Virginia. Another six states (Arizona, Minnesota, Ohio, Oregon, Pennsylvania, and Texas) combine adult and juvenile probation in some jurisdictions but not in others. Thus, there is a great deal of variety in supervision organizational structure from state to state when addressing adult and juvenile probationer caseloads.

Lastly, in a number of states, there is a combination of probation and parole services, but these states have abolished parole in years past. This combination of both types of community service sanction simply reflects the fact that there are residual offenders whose parole sanction has extended past the date of parole abolishment, and their supervision has been combined with probation agency caseloads, thereby eliminating the need for a specific parole agency in that state (Delaware, Minnesota, Mississippi, New Mexico, North Carolina, and Ohio). In other states where parole has been abolished, there is no combination of probation and parole services because no residual supervision has been necessary or it has been completely phased out through some sort of alternate means.

When taken together, the variation in state implementation of the day-to-day supervision of parolees (i.e., as a separate function or when being combined with probation caseloads) and the variation that exists among parole boards themselves, it is clear that the entire organizational structure can be quite complicated. While this may, on the face of it, appear to be the case, there is a great deal of similarity in the types of laws, forms of supervision, and regulations that are required throughout the nation. While each state naturally has the right and ability to administer community supervision functions in a manner that is most suitable for that state, it will become clear that there are as many similarities between probation and parole programs around the nation as there are differences.

⊠ Tasks and Nature of Work for Probation Officers

Probation officers (often also called community supervision officers [CSOs]), quite naturally, supervise those offenders who are placed on some form of probation and tend to spend more time monitoring the activities of these offenders than anything else. Probation officers most frequently maintain this supervision through personal contact with the offender, the offender's family, and the offender's employer. This point alone is worth expounding upon since the very nature of the word *contact* has changed greatly during the past decade. Prior to the 1990s, it was not uncommon for many probation officers to treat their job as if it were mainly a desk job. In these cases, probation officers would tend to stay within the familiar surroundings of their office and would simply require the probationer to visit during an agreed-upon appointment. Though this was naturally an easy way of maintaining contact with probationers, it did not ensure that probationers were being appropriately supervised, and it did not give the probation officer a true feel for the probationer's contextual experience and lifestyle routine. Though probation officers during this time might have conducted frequent phone contacts with employers and other such persons, this still did not give the probation officer sufficient perspective as to the family life and personal aspects of the probationer's lifestyle that might be important, both from a public safety and reintegrative standpoint.

During the mid-1990s this type of probation became commonly termed *fortress probation* among many experts in the field, so named because the probation officer would essentially sit within his or her "fortress" (the office) waiting for the probationer to approach him or her. Over time, there was a deliberate push to ensure that probation officers were in the field and that field visits were commonly conducted. This also led to a change in the work hours that many probation officers had become accustomed to. Indeed, because it was the intent to keep a more random and closer eye upon the offender, probation officers found themselves conducting visits in the evenings and even on weekends. No longer was probation a Monday through Friday, 8:00 a.m. to 5:00 p.m. job. This has had substantial impact on the field and on the work expectations of probation officers in particular and community supervision in general.

In addition to making contact with the offender through a combination of field visits and/or officer interviews, probation officers make routine contact with the offender's therapist(s), often having therapeutic reports either faxed or delivered to their office. These reports, providing the clinician's insight as to the offender's emotional progress and/or mental health, can be very important to the probation officer's assessment of the offender's progress. Typically, probation officers will work in what is called a casework fashion. This means that probation officers may coordinate job training, substance abuse counseling, community service involvement, and other elements of the offender reintegration process. In addition, offenders who are on electronic supervision require that the probation officer know how the equipment operates and the officer may be required to use such equipment to track the offender during odd points in the day or the night. For instance, supervision officers may drive by the probationer's home at night using EM devices to ensure that the offender is actually present at their home (indicated via electronic anklets that may be worn by certain offenders). Officers may also receive morning reports from automated "phone checks" that require the probationer to provide voice verification that they are at their premises during certain times in the evening. All of these functions are some of those performed by probation officer when fulfilling the public safety element of probation.

One other function of the probation officer ties in with the local court. In many cases, the probation officer will be tasked with investigating the background of the offender and writing what are known as PSIs. While doing this, probation officers may review sentencing recommendations with the offender and even (perhaps) with their family. Note that this is aside from any other arrangements that might be made throughout the plea bargaining process between the offender's counsel and that from the prosecutor's office. In some cases, probation officers may also be required to testify in court as to their findings and recommendation. They also will attend hearings for offenders on their caseload and will often update the court on the offender's efforts at rehabilitation and compliance with the terms of their sentences.

A large portion of a probation officer's time is spent completing PSIs. The investigative time that it takes to complete these detailed and comprehensive reports should not be underestimated. Probation officers must verify employment and the nature of relationships listed in the report. They must also amass educational and vocational records, complete interviews with family members (when applicable), and often obtain statements from victims and witnesses. In addition, various records such as the police report, prior mental health service case notes, court records, and the like must be gathered before the preparation of the PSI can truly begin. These various tasks naturally take up a great deal of time that may often go unaccounted since these tasks are not easy to observe, monitor, and measure in terms of work productivity analyses.

▲ **Photo 6.1** As a means of maintaining public safety, probation and parole officers may have to confiscate various types of contraband. Standing here is an officer who has confiscated both weapons and some elaborate drug paraphernalia while out in the field.

Further, many jurisdictions (particularly in rural regions) may not have much in the way of staff office support, and this simply makes the entire process even more difficult to organize and maintain. Since this is often the case, probation officers typically type up their own PSIs, meaning that they spend a substantial amount of time at a computer, making it understandable why the "fortress probation" mentality might indeed be tempting. Given the volume of paperwork and the emphasis on field visits, it is clear that probation officers tend to work long hours that may not actually be clearly or explicitly covered by their salary.

Aside from the completion of PSIs, probation officers can have very large caseloads. However, this is also a prime source of stress for many probation officers. The use of technological tools assist the probation officer in maintaining heavy caseloads, with computers, telephones, and fax machines being common working tools of probation. In fact, probation officers may conduct business from their own home via telephone and/or computer-based communications and form submission processes. Naturally, this can result in a blurring of distinctions between time at home and time at work, sometimes further compounding the stressful elements of the job.

The daily working conditions for probation officers can be quite safe when in the office but can also be fairly dangerous when conducting field visits. Some of the offenders who are on a probationer's caseload may themselves be more dangerous than their arrest record or actual conviction may indicate. Further, these offenders may still (in violation of their probation) continue to maintain contact with other associates who are more prone to violence than is the probationer. In many instances, the probationer may have to conduct fieldwork in high-crime areas.

This point should not be taken lightly, and it is unlikely that the average person can understand the true contextual feeling that is associated with such an experience when conducting casework. Often, members of the community may display negative nonverbal behavior toward the probation officer and may be evasive if the officer should happen to ask questions about the offender in their own neighborhood. In fact, in most cases, persons living next to the probationer may not disclose anything because they are also at cross-purposes with the law. In addition, family members are not always happy to have the probation officer visit the home and, while complying with the requirement, may openly resent the intrusion. Lastly, from time to time, the probation officer may make unannounced visits only to find the probationer in the company of unsavory sorts and/or in acts that are criminal in nature (i.e., drinking, trafficking drugs, or discussing various criminal opportunities). All of these issues can lead to some dangerous occurrences. This is even more true when one considers that most probation officers do not carry a firearm. The issue of firearm protection is a controversial one and will be discussed later in this section. However, it is safe to say at this point that there is a safety concern when meeting probationers on their own turf.

In addition, the travel may be quite extensive if the probation officer works in a large rural area of the nation. Some jurisdictions can be quite large, requiring substantial time on the road to reach probationers. The road time that may be involved can further exacerbate the stress since these same officers will be likely to have numerous court-imposed deadlines, PSIs, and other paperwork to complete, creating an even heavier caseload. Though probation officers are thought to generally work a 40-hour work week, the reality is that they may work much more than this, especially during crime-prone seasons of the year. Add to this the fact that most probationers are technically on call 24 hours a day to supervise and assist offenders and/or agency concerns, and it becomes clear that work in probation is not a cookie-cutter style of employment from day to day.

Though this work can be stressful, many probation officers do find the work rewarding. This is particularly true when probationers are successful on their probation and turn their lives around. Also, there tends to be solid benefits from working with local government agencies, as well as other perks that may not be available at other jobs. All in all, the work of a probation officer requires a person who is intrinsically rather than extrinsically motivated by their work. This means that persons likely to carve a successful career out of probation work will tend to thrive off the challenge of the job as well as the inherent reward of knowing that their work contributes to the reform of persons that may be in need and that their services contribute to society in a meaningful manner. Such persons will need to have this view inherently, regardless of what community members may (or may not) believe regarding the point and purpose of probation.

▧ Qualifications, Pay, and Demographics of Probation Officers

The field of community corrections in general and probation in particular has undergone a shift toward increased professionalization. Organizations such as the American Probation and Parole Association (APPA) as well as the American Correctional Association (ACA) have been instrumental in developing the field of community corrections into a professionalized form of service delivery. This has led to a number of on-site training conferences, correspondence, and online in-service training opportunities. While many states do not necessarily certify their probation and/or parole officers, some states do have various forms of certification that credential the skills of qualified professionals. For instance, the states of Illinois and Louisiana have a certification option for correctional workers known as the certified criminal justice professional. This certification, while not specific to probation and parole officers, is ideally suited for such workers since it requires a working knowledge of court procedures, casework, correctional supervision, and treatment planning. Most all of the skills for this certification dovetail with the requirements of most probation and parole officers.

At the point of recruitment, there are some basic background qualifications that are listed in the *Occupation Outlook Handbook*. The background qualifications for probation officers vary by state, but generally a bachelor's degree in criminal justice, social work, or a related field is required for initial consideration. Though this was not always the case in times past (some states allowed for less education when combined with experience), this is increasingly becoming the norm in most all states. Some employers may even require previous experience in corrections, casework, or a treatment-related field or a master's degree in criminal justice, social work, psychology, or a related discipline.

According to the *Occupation Outlook Handbook*, applicants are also usually administered a written, oral, psychological, and physical examination. Given the concern with job stress that is inherent to this field of work, it is no surprise that changes in screening mechanisms have been observed during the hiring phase (Champion, 2002). Indeed, practices "have changed to include psychological interviews and personality assessment inventories for the purpose of identifying those most able to handle the stress and psychological challenges of probation and parole work, with les emphasis on physical abilities" (Champion, 2002, p. 354). This demonstrates that agencies are aware of the unique challenges with this type of work and wish to identify those persons hearty enough to withstand the pressures that are inherent therein. This is of course a wise and prudent move on the part of agencies from a liability standpoint, a public safety standpoint, and from an employee–agency relations standpoint. Effective recruitment and selection at the forefront can prevent a host of problems that would likely be encountered by supervisors and agency leaders in the future.

Beyond recruitment and selection considerations, probation officers are also required to complete a training program sponsored by their particular state of employment. In some states, this may be similar to a police academy method of training. Indeed, many states essentially certify probation or parole officers as peace officers, though their specific jurisdiction remains with persons on community supervision rather than general law enforcement in the community. In such cases, officers must maintain qualifications that are identical to peace officers in that state, including handgun proficiency, physical standards, and in-service training. This type of training is especially true in states that have centralized training programs and/or that combine both probation and parole into one agency function. There is, at least to some extent, a concern with this model of training since much of the academy-level training that is encountered is more specific to policing than community supervision.

However, this drawback can be greatly offset, if agencies follow with sufficient on-the-job training and utilize effective mentoring between senior CSOs and those just graduating from the academy. In fact, when states do utilize standard police academy forms of instruction, this can be an instrumental means of creating camaraderie between policing professionals and community supervision professionals. Further, this provides the CSO with a much more comprehensive and in-depth understanding of their law enforcement function. And, as just noted, when local agency field offices provided a well-structured period of follow-up on-the-job training along with effective professional mentoring, the probation or parole officer will generally be more prepared for the challenges associated with their new function. Add to this an emphasis on in-service professional training through the APPA and the ACA as well as an emphasis on obtaining eventual certification as correctional treatment specialists and it is clear that such individuals are likely to be very well suited for their line of work.

During this period of mentoring, many agencies will have new probation officers work as trainees or on a probationary period for up to 1 year before being given a permanent position. This allows the agency to further assess the fit between the new-hire, the agency, and the line of work that is required. This is again a prudent move that can prevent many long-term problems likely to occur during later stages of that person's employment. In addition, many agencies will have several levels of probation and/or parole officers that can provide additional compensation as well as recognition of competency in the field. Indeed, agencies that do not have varying levels of staff classification should seriously consider adopting such a program, regardless of whether the compensation is greatly adjusted, since there is an inherent and intrinsic reward associated with the mere acknowledgment of the employee's expertise by the organization. This can go a long way in motivating and retaining experienced staff within the agency.

Entry-level probation officers should be in good physical and emotional condition. Most agencies require applicants to be at least 21 years old and, for federal employment, not older than 37 (U.S. Bureau of Labor Statistics, 2006). In many jurisdictions, persons who have been convicted of a felony may not be eligible for employment in this occupation (U.S. Bureau of Labor Statistics, 2006). Familiarity with the use of computers is typically expected given the increasing use of computer technology in probation and parole work (U.S. Bureau of Labor Statistics, 2006). Likewise, it is expected that candidates will be knowledgeable about laws and regulations pertaining to community supervision, though of course, much of this information will be provided during both the formal and informal training process. Probation officers should have strong writing skills because they are required to prepare many reports. In addition, a graduate degree in a related field, such as criminal justice, social work, counseling, or psychology, can aid an employee if advancing into supervisory positions within the agency (U.S. Bureau of Labor Statistics, 2006).

Community corrections agencies will also tend to have multiple levels of community supervision supervisors. Skill sets associated with supervisors of community corrections agencies can be quite demanding and can consist of a wide array of competencies ranging from the hiring of staff and coordination of training to offender case management and even including the maintenance of interagency community relationships. This last competency is directly related to the need for community involvement in goal setting, volunteering, and offender assistance. In addition, the need for interagency collaboration is also critical to the success of any type of case management and therefore is germane to the reintegrative process. Again, as noted before, reintegrative approaches are more likely to get the offender to internalize incentives and values that will encourage them to regulate their own behavior (rather than relying on external controls) and therefore desist from criminogenic lifestyles. It is imperative that supervisors in community corrections adopt this viewpoint and impart this upon their subordinate employees, building an agency culture that is reintegrative in nature. Thus, this area of competency (as well as others) is exceedingly important to the agency and the community.

One interesting aspect of probation work is the fact that the majority of probation staff tend to be female—roughly 57% or more, depending on the area of the United States (Champion, 2002). This is substantially different from fields such as law enforcement, where male officers tend to predominate; women tend to consist of less than 15% of the entire policing community (Shusta, Levine, Wong, & Harris, 2005). This is, in actuality, perhaps partly due to the nature of probation as compared to law enforcement. Indeed, even among police officers, women have been found to be highly effective in defusing conflict situations and/or providing less contact-prone means of response. The National Center for Women and Policing (2001) noted that female police officers tend to be inherently more suited to facilitate cooperation and trust in stressful contact situations and that they are less prone to use excessive force. Likewise, there tend to be fewer citizen complaints for female officers. Though these observations are related to female police officers, these same characteristics would seem to be well suited to probation work given the fact that probation has a reintegrative and supportive role with offenders on the officer's caseload.

On the other hand, most probation officers also tend to be white. This can be an important issue when one considers the fact that there is a disproportionate amount of minority representation on most client caseloads. Given that there is such a lack of minority representation among probation officers, it is likely that diversity-related training is all the more necessary and important in cultivating a rapport between community supervision personnel and those on community supervision. There is an abundance of literature that has examined issues related to therapist–client interactions when the two are of different racial and/or ethnic groups. Generally, the prognosis in mental health research does not tend to be as good as when there is a degree of matching or when specific training and consideration is given for racial or cross-cultural issues. Since community corrections has a reformative element, it is not unreasonable to presume that such observations could also be equally true among probation officers and their probationers.

Lastly, most probation officers have a college degree. This does mean that this group is, as a whole, a bit more educated than much of the general workforce. It may perhaps be true that this can mitigate some of the cross-cultural differences and this also may help to mitigate job dissatisfaction and stress since higher educated persons tend to, on the whole, be motivated by more than external reward. Though this is obviously not always the case, less emphasis on money does tend to correlate with better educated workforce members. Somewhat supporting this is the fact that several studies have found that probation work in general tends to be more enriching and challenging, requiring more of an emphasis on problem solving skills that are likely to mesh well with high-functioning and educated persons. From this, it is clear that probation work is becoming more professionalized and has been likened to an art where probation officers must be skilled at matching security and treatment issues with the particular offender's needs (Champion, 2002). This, as well as the helping aspects of the profession (despite the supervisory components of the profession), are likely to appeal to educated females who seek a professional track in their lives.

As of midyear 2004, the median annual earnings of probation officers was $39,600. The middle 50% of probation officers earned between $31,500 and $52,100 per year. Those within the lowest 10% of payment earned less than $26,310, and the highest 10% earned more than $66,000. As would be expected, higher wages are to be found in urban areas of the country and also tend to be found in states that tend to have higher, and more expensive, standards of living.

⧈ Role Confusion, Stress, and Burnout Related to the Job of Probation Officers

There is a dichotomy or duality of purpose that is associated with community corrections. On the one hand, the probation officer is expected to essentially act as a law enforcement agent, supervising and monitoring

▲ **Photo 6.2** They say a picture is worth a thousand words. In this case, body language of the CSO demonstrates the tension and stress that can take its toll on officers.

the offender. In this capacity, it is the charge of the probation officer to check on the probationer, interviewing and even interrogating them. Obviously, this serves an important public safety function, but this naturally impairs the sense of rapport that they are able to build with the offender. This sense of rapport is integral to any reintegrative approach and, as we have seen, the reintegrative process is perhaps what serves as the best likely means of ensuring that offenders do refrain from future criminality. Thus, there are competing interests that are inherent to the community corrections process. While this has already been mentioned, what has not been considered is the effect that this dichotomy of purpose has upon the actual CSO.

The competing interests associated with probation (and parole for that matter) have been found to cause a great deal of stress and uncertainty for many supervision officers. Indeed, ambiguity and uncertainty tend to generate stress for most persons because it is simply human nature to desire a sense of control and/or mastery over one's environment. Amidst ambiguous and competing messages, this sense of mastery or security is difficult to achieve. This then leads to a competing professional identity among probation officers. This has been termed **role identity confusion** and is a primary source of burnout among CSOs. Role identity confusion occurs when an officer is unclear about the expectations placed upon them as they attempt to juggle between the "policing" oriented nature of their work and the "reform" orientation to their work. If the agency is unclear or sends contradictory messages (such as noting that attention should be given to each offender's needs to prevent recidivism but yet weighing officers down with excessive caseloads), then the stress level for the officer is increased. Thus it may be that in some agencies the officer should strive to utilize each approach so that they can fulfill the multiple overt and covert expectations of the agency.

The stress associated with probation work has become a serious issue of concern to agencies and should likewise be an issue of concern for most communities. Public safety is directly impacted if officers are stressed to the point that supervision is not as effective as it otherwise would be. Finn and Kuck (2003) conducted what was perhaps one of the most comprehensive examinations of stress among community supervision personnel to date. In their report to the National Institute of Justice, they found that when considering stress associated with probation, there are three frequent and severe sources of stress; these are (1) high caseloads, (2) excessive paperwork, and (3) unreasonable deadlines.

Officers report that high caseloads create more stress for them than any other single aspect of their work. There is objective evidence to substantiate these officers' feelings. While there is no officially recommended maximum caseload number for probation and parole officers (a lot depends on the types of offenders they supervise), the average regular adult supervision caseload for probation officers in 1999 was 100 offenders. But even this "average" caseload size vastly understates the number of offenders the typical officer supervises because not all probation employees or even line officers supervise offenders.

Next to high caseloads, paperwork is the most significant source of stress for many officers. A study of federal probation officers found that paperwork was the most frequently mentioned of six sources of stress (Finn & Kuck, 2003). Even when extensive management information systems (MIS) have been introduced into an agency, the workload does not actually seem to disappear. Further, the introduction of technology then tends to bring its own unique set of problems as unwieldy data entry screens and outmoded databases prove to be equally onerous challenges for officers and supervisors.

Having to meet deadlines—many of them unexpected—is the third most common and serious source of stress for officers. Many officers must meet a variety of immutable deadlines, many of them unpredictable. For example, court hearings can cause interruptions in the officer's workload, particularly if one of their supervised offenders is arrested. Once this happens, the officer must quickly prepare associated paperwork to meet tight time limits in getting the arrest report finished prior to the hearing deadline; meanwhile their other work will then get backlogged.

High caseloads, excessive paperwork, and tight deadlines, while distinct sources of stress, typically combine to have widespread and frustrating results, both individually and, especially, cumulatively. This makes it difficult for many officers to find the time to supervise their caseloads properly (Finn & Kuck, 2003). Essentially, "many officers find that they are so burdened by huge caseloads that they are unable to help probationers and parolees avoid recidivating and thereby protect the public" (Finn & Kuck, 2003, p. 20). Roughly half of all probation officers in one notable survey reported that there was insufficient time to complete assigned and essential tasks of their job (Whitehead, 1986).

Another more recent study provided additional support for these earlier findings when a survey of federal probation officers found insufficient time for their workload was the most frequently reported cause of stress (Finn & Kuck, 2003).

Beyond caseloads, paperwork, and deadlines, Finn and Kuck (2003) also noted the following six issues were particularly stressful for CSOs:

1. *Lack of Promotional Opportunities:* Many probation officers have few options for promotion and feel stuck in their current service capacity.

2. *Low Salaries:* Many officers report that the low salaries they are paid contribute to their work-related stress. Because of their inadequate pay, many officers are forced to seek additional outside employment. Working lengthy hours can, of course, impair the officer's ability to function at optimal levels when supervising offenders.

3. *Danger to Officers:* The danger of assault, typically experienced during field contacts, is a significant source of stress for some officers. In a survey of federal probation and pretrial service officers, almost all (96%) expressed concern for their personal safety when making field contacts; almost 9% had experienced physical assaults (Lowry, 2000).

4. *Changing or Conflicting Policies and Procedures:* These frustrating policies and procedures tend to come from two sources. First, different judges may request different information and set different priorities, creating a lack of uniformity in the agency's operations. Second, probation and parole agencies may have their own conflicting or changing regulations.

5. *Personal Accountability for Offenders:* Sometimes officers feel that the community, the media, or agency administrators hold them personally accountable for an offender's misconduct or

criminal behavior while under their supervision. This may be a serious concern in some states, particularly when legislation has given just cause for such concern. For instance, in Washington State, the passage of the Offender Accountability Act provides legal recourse for victims of crime committed by recidivists by allowing personal liability lawsuits against state community corrections officers responsible for supervising that offender. In addition, many conscientious supervision officers may tend to feel personally responsible for their offenders' criminal behavior simply because they care about protecting the public and feel embarrassed to have an offender under their supervision harm the public.

6. *Courts and Judges:* In some cases, officers have voiced concern that the court system does not give adequate weight to the officers' reports. Interestingly, some supervision officers also express concern for perceived leniency on the part of the courts. This likewise adds stress to their own job and can undermine their motivation to maintain effective supervision.

Surveys of state parole or probation officers in New York, Pennsylvania, Texas, and Virginia have found that between 39% and 55% of probation or parole officers have been the victims of work-related violence or threats at some time during their careers (National Center for Victims of Crime, 1998).

In Pennsylvania, 38% of the total probation/parole workforce in the state have been victimized (e.g., assaulted, threatened, intimidated) at least once during their careers. Half of officers who actively supervise cases were victimized. Of the most serious incidents, 24% took place in an offender's or someone else's home, 22% in agency offices, 9% on the telephone or by mail, and 11% on the street. Almost 38% of the victimized officers reported being shaken up emotionally by the incident, with 11% experiencing physical symptoms such as headaches and stomachaches (Parsonage & Bushey, 1987).

Many probation and parole officers think their work has become more dangerous. There are good explanations for this perception. The increase in drug use and the severity of the type of drug among offenders on caseloads have resulted in individuals that have little hesitation in choosing to use violence (Finn & Kuck, 2003). More generally, people sentenced to probation and released on parole are more serious offenders than in the past in terms of seriousness of criminal acts, prior records, and drug abuse histories (Finn & Kuck, 2003). A second reason for the perception of increased danger is that roughly 72% of community supervision agencies have created increased expectations for field visits with officers spending more time in challenged neighborhoods and/or dangerous areas of a community than was the case in previous years. Naturally, fieldwork tends to be the most dangerous aspect of a supervision officer's line of work (McCoy, 2000). In 2003, for example, New York City probation officers were authorized to carry handguns because of a new policy that required an increased number of officers to make field visits (Finn & Kuck, 2003).

It is clear that the job of a probation officer has many challenges and associated stressors. This may paint a bleak picture for those who may consider such a line of employment. However, it should be pointed out that many officers successfully complete entire careers within this aspect of the criminal justice system. Further, the job of probation officer does provide many invaluable opportunities to network within the community. Probation officers do tend to be central figures within their community, particularly if a community probation model is implemented within the agency. It is often in such a capacity that officers can see the direct impact that they have upon their own community, thereby making a direct and observable social contribution that is rarely achievable in other service functions.

Applied Theory Section 6.1

General Strain Theory, the Offender, and the Probation Officer

General strain theory (GST) is based on the premise that persons experience strain when they are not able to obtain success goals that they desire. These goals can entail money, status, and even relationships. In some cases, persons may resort to criminal activities to alleviate this strain and/or to obtain their desired goal. However, strain is not caused only by the failure to achieve one's goals, often referred to as *goal blockage*, but strain can also occur when some type of *undesired stimuli* presents itself, or just as important, when some *valued stimulus* is taken away from the offender.

This theory, though not complicated, is important for probation officers to understand since most reasons that offenders give for their crimes reflect the basic tenets of this theory. This is then important both from a sanctioning level (determining the type of sanction to give an offender) and from a treatment planning perspective for helping professionals.

As an example, consider a young adolescent male named Tom who has limited access to quality higher education opportunities and has poor job prospects. He has a girlfriend named Kim. He likes her very much, but she is impressed with material goods. Kim has recently started talking about how bored she is since they cannot go out frequently due to a lack of money. Tom is worried about keeping Kim's interest. He cannot see any immediate rewards from education or employment opportunities. In order to maintain his relationship with her, he decides to engage in the burglary of a local business where money is sometimes kept and where goods and services are pawned. Tom commits the burglary, which is later reported in the local paper, and tells nobody about his activity. The police do not find any sufficient evidence, and the business writes off the loss. Tom secures enough money to keep his girlfriend occupied throughout future months ahead, thereby achieving his desired goal. Naturally, one can see that a degree of reinforcement also occurs with this example. Just as important, one should keep in mind that the goal of keeping the girlfriend is the reason for the youth's burglary, not his desire to accumulate money for personal greed. If Tom had been caught, it would be good for probation officers and treatment specialists to know the reasons behind the criminal activity. Treatment aspects might address self-esteem issues as well as healthy relationships, while the probation officers might pay attention to the youth's future choice of peers and significant others.

Likewise, one could again consider Tom as an example, who years later ends up marrying Kim. At an early age, they have a child together, Tom gets a full-time job, they get an apartment, and Kim stays home to take care of the child. During this time, finances are tight and the relationship sours. Further, a new gentleman moves into the apartment unit right next door. Tom comes home early from work one day and finds the other man in his living room talking with Kim. While neither person is apparently engaged in anything inappropriate, it is clear from the laughter that Tom hears (prior to entering his apartment) that the two are having a very good time joking and talking with one another. Tom enters and the other man,

(Continued)

(Continued)

Kevin, thanks Kim for letting him borrow some cooking ingredients, excuses himself, and exits the apartment. Later that day, Tom sees Kevin in the parking lot and confronts him. He punches Kevin in the face repeatedly, pushes Kevin against a vehicle, and says, "You stay away from my wife or I will kill you" followed with "If you say anything to anyone, I will break your legs. You keep quiet and stay away, you hear?" *This is where Tom experiences strain due to the presentation of a negative stimulus; in this case, the negative stimulus is Kevin and Tom resorts to violent crime in response to the presentation of Kevin in his life.*

Lastly, Kevin never does say anything, but he talks with the landlord about moving to another unit. He gives a bogus reason for the move but secretly wishes to put distance between himself and Tom. While moving to the other unit, Kim sees that Kevin has bruises and cuts on his face (from Tom punching him) and bemoans the fact that Kevin is moving to another section of the complex. She later notices that Tom has cuts on his knuckles, and she point blank asks, "Tom, did you beat Kevin up?" Tom says, "Uh-uh. Why would you ask such a thing?" Kim knows that Tom is lying, and she tells him that she is leaving him. She tells him, "I am going to go stay with my parents for a while. I am taking baby Jade with me."

Tom gets mad because he is about to lose a valued stimulus. As a result, he corners Kim in their bedroom, pulls her hair back and grabs her throat with his other hand. He tells her, "If you ever leave me or if I ever catch you with another man, I will kill you. You won't even know that it is coming when I do it." Tom has again resorted to violent crime, but this time it is to avoid the loss of a valued stimulus.

The scenarios just presented also demonstrate how the same type of criminal activity (i.e., violent behavior) can be used for different stimulus concerns. In one case, the presentation of a negative stimulus is the antecedent whereas in another it is the possible loss of a valued stimulus. In addition, Tom's sense of strain, throughout his lifetime, has led to a variety of crimes, namely burglary, assault, and battery, as well as a domestic assault and battery. Thus, strain theory can explain a diverse array of criminal behaviors, and probation officers will often find it beneficial to understand the circumstances that precede a crime, particularly when they construct PSIs. Though there are many other theoretical approaches to explaining criminal behavior, GST provides a versatile means of analyzing and categorizing the drives behind such behavior. Whether they know it or not, offenders are often engaged in behaviors that, at their base, verify the notions that are commonly espoused by GST. For the probation officer and/or correctional treatment specialist, this and other theories provide a coherent rationale for quantifying and/or categorizing the range of criminal behaviors that they observe.

◼ Setting Conditions for Supervision

According to Neubauer (2002), the public perceives the judge as the principal decision maker in criminal court. But, in actuality, the judge often is not the primary decision maker in regard to an offender's sentencing and/or probation conditions. This is not to say that the judge does not have ultimate authority over the court nor does it mean to imply that judges have a diminished sense of importance when presiding over their court. Rather, Neubauer demonstrated the collaborative nature of the various courtroom actors when processing offender caseloads. Throughout this process, judges will often voluntarily defer to the judgment of other members of the court, namely prosecutors, defense attorneys, victim's rights groups, and/or the probation agency. The role and importance of the courtroom workgroup cannot be denied.

Though other actors may be able to cause some problems in the courtroom, it is nevertheless clear that the judge ultimately has the real authority and is vested with the ability to use that authority to gain courtroom compliance. If, in the mind of the judge, actors in the courtroom are not being conducive to courtroom operations, the judge can put pressures upon the prosecutors and defense counsel through a number of mechanisms that place both parties in uneasy positions. Judges can be sticklers for detail and for timekeeping. They can sift through every administrative detail, ask annoying questions, and openly rebuke one or both parties in front of a public audience. All of these techniques may be employed to ensure that the courtroom actors stay in compliance.

Lastly, Neubauer (2002) noted that in larger court jurisdictions, a technique of judge selection may be common. Through a process of implementing motions of continuances and motions for a change of judge, defense attorneys may maneuver to have their case heard by a judge who is expected to be the most receptive to the offender's plight. Though judges do strive to remain within common guidelines in decisions and rulings, the fact of the matter is that they do tend to differ in terms of the sentences that are given, the manner by which they oversee their courtroom, and the number of cases that they have pending (Neubauer, 2002). An understanding of these tendencies can aid both the defense and the prosecutor in achieving a more favorable outcome consistent with their own particular desires.

Aside from each of the points just noted, the setting of conditions can actually be, at least in part, something that is often agreed upon prior to the judge's actual formal sentencing. Though the bargaining process may of course impact the final outcome of the probationer's sentence, their length of probation, and the conditions of that probation, the judge is always free to require additional conditions as he or she sees fit. The conditions that may be required are quite lengthy; some of the more commonly required conditions are noted as follows:

1. Refraining from associating with certain types of people (particularly those with a conviction) or frequenting certain locations known to draw criminal elements

2. Remaining sober and drug free; being restricted from using or being in possession of alcohol or drugs

3. Obeying restrictions on firearm ownership and/or possession

4. Obeying requirement to pay fines, restitution, and family support that may be due

5. Being willing to submit to drug tests as directed by the probation officer and/or representatives of the probation agency

6. Maintaining legitimate and steady employment

7. Refraining from obtaining employment in certain types of vocations (i.e., an embezzler being restricted from becoming a bookkeeper or a computer hacker being restricted from working with automated systems)

8. Maintaining a legal and legitimate residence with the requirement that the probation officer is notified of any change in residence prior to making such a change

9. Obeying the requirement that permission be requested to travel outside of the jurisdiction of the probation agency and/or to another state

10. Refraining from engaging in further criminal activity

Many of these listed conditions may be statutorily authorized by state legislators as a means of validating their application to probation sentences. This is reflective of the fact that most legislators desire some degree of uniformity and consistency in the supervision requirements and process. However, judges still may call for innovative and even controversial conditions to be added to certain probationers. This is certainly the case with sex offenders and other violent criminals. To date, these requirements have not been invalidated by the U.S. Supreme Court and, as the student may recall, it is unlikely that they ever will be invalidated if a convincing argument can be made that these conditions aid in the treatment process of the offender.

Regardless of the judges' own discretion with probation conditions, most states do have at least some statutorily required conditions for probation sentences, but these may vary considerably from state to state (Del Carmen, Barnhill, Bonham, Hignite, & Jermstad, 2001). Some states have only a few such requirements while others have an extensive list that clearly requires judges and probationers to structure probation sentences according to a certain prescribed template of conditions. Further, and related to the use of discretionary conditions imposed by judges, some legislators may also clearly note that judges are to be given deference in assigning specialized conditions on certain types of offenders; this is especially true with sex offenders and/or substance abuse offenders.

Abadinsky (2003) noted that the APPA "recommends that the only condition that should be imposed on every person sentenced to probation is that the probationer lead a law-abiding life during the period of probation" (p. 39). The APPA instead notes that other conditions should be left to the purview of the probation officer, who should primarily be responsible for setting conditions that are consistent with the circumstances of each case. Generally speaking, the APPA notes that aside from providing deterrent conditions to the commission of future recidivism, conditions should by and large be minimal. Further still, Del Carmen et al. (2001) noted that in general,

> a special condition of probation or parole is invalid only if it has all three of the following characteristics: (1) has no relationship to the crime, (2) relates to conduct that is not in itself criminal, and (3) forbids or requires conduct that is not reasonably related to the future criminality of the offender or does not serve the statutory ends of probation or parole. (p. 77)

Thus, it is clear that if put to the test, judges do have a great deal of discretion and latitude when assigning conditions to an offender on probation. So long as the condition has some relation to the crime or to the ability of the agency to monitor for potential future recidivism, then the condition is almost certain to be considered valid if it is later challenged.

⊠ Purpose of Probation, Evaluation, and Compliance With Conditions of Probation

As noted earlier, the purpose of probation is to reintegrate offenders into society, thereby improving public safety as offenders become less inclined to reoffend. Since our purpose is fairly well understood and defined, at least in a general sense, then it becomes important to ask if programs do, in fact, achieve these intended outcomes.

One primary means of determining success is simply by determining if offenders have recidivated. This is, in and of itself, one of the simplest means of determining success in community supervision agencies. But the definition of offending in and of itself lends itself to some degree of interpretation. For instance, should it be classified the same if one offender relapses with alcohol and is found to be drunk and disorderly, when another offender is caught burglarizing a home? Certainly, on the face of it, both offenses are not the same. Indeed, being drunk and disorderly may not be considered to be as serious as burglary. But consider that both offenses could be symptomatic of drug addiction; perhaps the first offender is an alcoholic that simply cannot seem to control his addiction (suffering from relapse and the corresponding behaviors associated with such difficulties), and in the other case, the offender might be a heroin addict who simply seeks something of material value as a means of supporting his habit. Neither offense is violent; however, it is possible that either offense could have turned violent at any point. What if the drunk and disorderly offender had been antagonized, startled, or himself assaulted? What if the homeowner had walked in on the burglar/heroin addict while his withdrawal symptoms and discomfort was at its height? In desperation, would he have attacked the homeowner? Might the homeowner have attacked the burglar? It is clear that the circumstances to an offense are important considerations.

Further, what if an agency has two offenders who are both pedophiles and one of the offenders is later arrested for molestation while the other offender is arrested for shoplifting. Naturally, both acts are illegal and both are criminal, but is this level of recidivism the same? Should we be equally concerned for each act? These scenarios demonstrate the difficulty that can be involved with determining the effectiveness of community supervision and in determining actual levels of compliance. Granted, offenders know that they are not supposed to commit criminal offenses, but if a convicted pedophile were to never commit another act of molestation while on supervision but yet they were found to have committed an act of shoplifting, it may well be that the supervision process was not an absolute failure. In some cases, certain types of recidivism may be the primary issue of concern and, presuming that other offenses are minimal and that they are not as serious as the primary offense of concern, it may be that supervision was at least partially successful. This is a very difficult notion to sell to the public.

Further complicating the picture is the fact that some conditions of probation result in what are often called **technical violations**. Technical violations are actions that do not comply with the conditions and requirements of a probationer's sentence, as articulated by the court that acted as the sentencing authority. Technical violations are not necessarily criminal, in and of themselves, and would likely be legal behaviors if the offender were not on probation. For instance, a condition of a drug offender's probation may be that he or she stay out of bars, nightclubs, and other places of business where the selling and consumption of alcohol is a primary attraction for customers frequenting the establishment. Another example might be if a sex offender is ordered to remain a certain distance from schools. For most citizens, going to nightclubs and/or setting foot on school grounds is not a violation of any sort, and neither of these acts are considered criminal. However, for the probationer, this can lead to the revocation of their probation.

A number of other behaviors can be technical violations. Though it may be clear that these violations are substantially different than those that carry a new and separate criminal conviction, they still do carry the weight of a revocation and may be used as recidivism measures in some agencies (Champion, 2002; Latessa & Allen, 1999). These indicators are obviously not comparable to a variety of criminal behaviors that offenders might commit.

⊠ Types of Probation Supervision

The variety of sanctions available, flexibility in administration, and the opportunity to individualize are what give probation its strength and make it so well suited for reintegrative efforts. This continuum of sanctions allows probation agencies to find suitable levels of supervision for different types of offenders, thereby aiding in the public safety element as well.

First, and most obviously, the sanction of **standard probation** is the basic form of supervision that is administered by most agencies. This type of sentence is actually little more than a baseline starting point for sanctioning. In reality, standard probation is not considered a form of supervision that is appropriate for any but the least serious of offenders. Though probation officers are required to oversee the offender's compliance with the various conditions of their probation, standard probation tends to have little face-to-face supervision of offenders. Typically, probation officers will have high caseloads if most of their probationers are on standard probation. Though this text has tended to recommend approximate caseloads of roughly 200 offenders on standard probation for every probation officer, it is not at all unusual for the number of offenders on a probation officer's caseload to greatly exceed this in urban jurisdictions. In fact, some caseloads may greatly exceed this general recommendation. This often is not due to any fault of the agency but is simply based on the reality that there are so many offenders and so few probation officers.

Further, standard probation is typically the type of probation that the community has in mind when forming the perception that probation is soft on crime. This is because of the comparatively lax forms of contact between the probation officer and the probationer. In many cases, the probationer may be free to simply contact their probation officer through a phone call. Likewise, the requirements attached to this type of probation are, quite naturally, much less stringent than other forms of probation. However, in the majority of cases, strict security is simply not necessary for probationers given this type of probation. But serious problems can develop when charges are pleaded down (especially if violent criminal charges are pleaded down to lesser or nonviolent offenses). In this case, it may be that some offenders may be on standard probation when they should be—due to the nature of their offense—on a more strict form of supervision. This can naturally end up compromising the security of the public. However, this is also a problem that the probation agency may inherit, with little ability to modify the situation until some sort of violation or other cause is provided to warrant an increase in supervision. But, when the offender is on standard probation, the terms are so lax that these offenders may recidivate and remain undetected, unless an actual arrest takes place. This particular dilemma is what has perhaps contributed the most to the negative public perception of probation.

Beyond the use of standard probation, there are a number of more secure sanctions that can be used to either enhance public safety or the reintegration of the offender. The following is a list of various alternative probation methods that are commonly utilized and will be further discussed in more detail in later sections: **probation with community service and restitution**, ISP, day reporting centers, home confinement with electronic monitoring (EM) and/or global positioning system (GPS), **residential treatment home**, halfway houses, boot camps, split sentencing, and **shock probation**.

The previous list of sanctions has been presented from the least to the most restrictive. In most cases, the use of a higher sanction subsumes the requirements of all the lower sanctions. Therefore, except in cases where it is unproductive, each sanction will also include the terms and conditions of the one before it. Thus, the probation arena has a variety of responses that are available, and this provides a range of options that exist both at the sentencing stage and even later when probationers violate the terms and conditions of their initial probation sentence. Probationers who are placed on, for example, standard probation and who prove to later do poorly on this sanction can then have that probation completely revoked or, as is often the case, the probationer can be placed on ISP. If, by some chance, the probationer should continue to have difficulties staying in compliance, home confinement, EM, and the use of day reporting centers may prove to be effective options. In addition, it may be that therapeutic obligations (especially drug treatment) or community service requirements may be modified or increased. If the offender should again prove intractable, they can be placed on shock probation. At this point, if the offender should be so stubborn as to persist in offending, it is certainly safe to say that a long-term prison stint may be the only option available to ensure the protection of the community. Effective or ineffective, useful or not, there is a hard reality that even the most ardent supporter of community corrections must contend—some offenders will simply not be amenable to probation and will therefore need to be restricted from continuing their sentence under such a sanction. It is with this in mind that we turn our attention to the revocation process itself, providing a brief discussion of this type of proceeding.

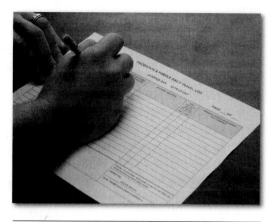

▲ **Photo 6.3** In this photo, a probation and parole officer begins to fill out a daily travel log. CSOs often alternate days in the field with those spent in the office. While out in the field, they will drive to and from the sites where their offender caseload must be visited. This log is used to record the distances and time traveled for each officer.

▨ Probation Revocation Procedures and Case Law Regarding Due Process During Revocation

Essentially, there are two primary cases that establish due process rights for probationers and parolees. The first case to emerge was *Morrissey v. Brewer* (1972), which dealt with revocation proceedings for parolees (Clear & Cole, 2003). The second case was *Gagnon v. Scarpelli* (1973), which extended the rights afforded to parolees under *Morrissey* to offenders on probation as well (Champion, 2002; Clear & Cole, 2003). Basically, the *Morrissey* court ruled that parolees facing revocation must be given due process through a prompt informal inquiry before an impartial hearing officer. The court required that this be through a two-step hearing process when revoking parole. The reason for this two-step process is to first screen for the reasonableness of holding the parolee since there is often a substantial delay between the point of arrest and the revocation hearing. This delay can be costly for both the justice system and the offender if it is based on circumstances that do not actually warrant full revocation. Specifically, the court stated that some minimal

> Inquiry should be conducted at or reasonably near the place of the alleged parole violation or arrest and as promptly as convenient after arrest while information is fresh and sources are available.... Such an inquiry should be seen as in the nature of a "preliminary hearing" to determine whether there is probable cause or reasonable ground to believe that the arrested parolee has committed acts that would constitute a violation of parole conditions. (*Gagnon v. Scarpelli* (1973)

The court also noted that this would need to be conducted by a neutral and detached party (a hearing officer), though the hearing officer did not necessarily need to be affiliated with the judiciary and this first step did not have to be formal in nature. The hearing officer is tasked with determining whether there is sufficient probable cause to justify the continued detention of the offender.

After the initial hearing, the revocation hearing would follow. It is interesting to point out that the court was quite specific on how the revocation hearings were to be conducted (Del Carmen et al., 2001). During this hearing, the parolee is entitled to the ability to contest charges and demonstrate that he or she did not, in fact, violate any of the conditions of their parole. If it should turn out that the parolee did, in fact, violate their parole requirements but that this violation was necessary due to mitigating circumstances, it may turn out that the violation does not warrant full revocation. The *Morrissey* court specified additional procedures during the revocation process that include the following:

1. Written notice of the claimed violation of parole

2. Disclosure to the parolee of evidence against him

3. An opportunity to be heard in person and to present witnesses and documentary evidence

4. The right to confront and cross-examine adverse witnesses

5. A "neutral and detached" hearing body, such as a traditional parole board, members of which need not be judicial officers or lawyers

6. A written statement by the fact finders as to the evidence relied on and reasons for revoking parole

The *Morrissey* case is obviously an example of judicial activism (much like *Miranda v. Arizona*) that has greatly impacted the field of community corrections. The court's clear and specific guidelines set forth in *Morrissey* have created specific standards and procedures that community supervision agencies must follow. Rather than ensuring that revocation proceedings include a just hearing and means of processing, the court laid out several pointed requirements that have continued to be relevant and binding to this day. While these specific requirements have been modified to meet a variety of circumstances that may not lend themselves to the strictest observance of the above procedures, the general spirit of the previously listed requirements has been honored. For instance, there is a great deal of variation from state to state in how offenders are provided written notice of their violation, and when notice is not able to be given because the offender cannot be located, failure to receive notice does not result in a violation of the offender's constitutional rights. Likewise, the right to confront witnesses can be foregone if the hearing officer specifically finds good cause for not allowing such confrontation. Thus, a sense of pragmatism has since developed in regard to the requirements established by *Morrissey*, with the general principles outlined by the court still being considered the gold standard of revocation proceedings, even today.

The next pivotal case dealing with revocation proceedings and community supervision is *Gagnon v. Scarpelli* (1973). In the simplest of terms, the U.S. Supreme Court ruled that all of the requirements for parole revocation proceedings noted in *Morrissey* also applied to revocation proceedings dealing with probationers. However, this case is important because it also addressed one other key and critical issues regarding revocation proceedings. In *Gagnon v. Scarpelli*, the court noted that offenders on community supervision do not have an absolute constitutional right to appointed counsel during revocation proceedings. Such proceedings are not considered to be true adversarial proceedings and therefore do not require official legal representation (Champion, 2002). Nevertheless, the court did note that some cases may warrant such representation when and if the offender can provide a substantive claim that may show that he or she did not commit the violation in question and/or when mitigating circumstances are involved that may impact the decision of the revocation body. Thus, the court basically held that there is no absolute right to counsel for offenders facing revocation proceedings. But, depending upon the circumstances, such representation may be offered on a case by case basis as determined by the circumstances.

It should be pointed out that there is a great deal of variation from state to state as to the specific standard of proof required to revoke parole. Some jurisdictions may require only slight evidence while others require a preponderance of the evidence. Likewise, the nature of the proof necessary for revocation may also vary. Some states may rely on the CSO's testimony as the sole or primary basis of revocation while others may not allow this to be sufficient without additional corroborating evidence of violation being produced by the officer. Nevertheless, Del Carmen et al. (2001) did note that CSOs should remain cognizant of the fact that their testimony and/or evidence may also be useful in court as later rebuttal evidence, for the purpose of impeachment, or to demonstrate the offender's state of mind. Further, if a CSO does not have personal knowledge of a given act that might lead to revocation, then it is unlikely that the officer's testimony will be sufficient to demonstrate the commission of a violation. But the use of prior arrests, prior criminal history, risk prediction instruments, or clinical assessments (related to relapse) can be used to prove the likelihood of the CSO's testimony. Thus, here again, it may well be that objective assessment and/or risk prediction data may prove useful in adding validity to an officer's testimony when supervising a probationer.

This last section addresses revocation from a nonlegal standpoint. This discussion is intended to present the use of revocation as a sanction and a component of the probation process in circumstances where offenders are not able to complete their initially given probation sentence. Previous research demonstrates that roughly 4 in 10 probationers fail to successfully complete the initial requirements of their probation (Bonczar, 1995; Clear & Cole, 2003; Glaze & Bonczar, 2007). Further, the most frequent reason that revocation hearings are initiated is due to a probationer's failure to maintain contact with their probation officer (Bonczar, 1995). Of those probationers who experience a disciplinary hearing, the most frequent reason tends to be absconding or the previously mentioned failure to contact their probation officer (Bonczar, 1995). Other reasons may include an arrest or conviction for a new offense, failure to pay fines/restitution, or failure to attend or complete an alcohol or drug treatment program (Bonczar, 1995). Among probationers who have revocation hearings initiated against them, almost half may be permitted to continue their probation sentence. For those who are allowed to continue, they will almost always have additional conditions imposed against them, and their type of supervision will typically be more restrictive (Bonczar, 1995; Clear & Cole, 2003).

In addition, some areas of the nation are more prone to revocation than others. Certain counties and/or communities may be more criminogenic in nature and will therefore tend to have more offending as well as more serious offenders who are processed through the local justice system. In such cases, it should not be surprising that probation departments in these areas will have higher rates of revocation proceedings that are generated. For example, consider a region where multiple neighborhoods are infested with gang activity. In these cases, the probation department is likely to have numerous gang offenders on the caseload as well as individuals who are peripheral to the gangs in that area. The recidivism rates for these individuals tend to be high, and it is therefore simply more likely that a probation department in this vicinity will contend with higher rates of revocation than would departments in other areas of the nation.

Generally, revocation proceedings are handled in three stages. First, the **preliminary hearing** examines the facts of the arrest to determine if probable cause does exist for a violation. Second, the **hearing stage** allows the probation agency to present evidence of the violation while the offender is given the opportunity to refute the evidence provided. Though the agency (or the local government) is not obligated to provide an attorney, the offender does have the right to obtain legal representation, if he or she should desire.

Third, the sentencing stage is when a judge either requires that the offender be incarcerated or, as in many cases where the violation is minor, that the offender continue their probation sentence but under more restrictive terms.

Lastly, it is not uncommon for offenders to have some sort of hearing or proceeding throughout their term of probation. The longer the period of probation, the more likely that this is to happen. Nevertheless, many do eventually finish their probation terms. For those offenders who do complete the terms of their probation (eventually meeting all of the requirements) termination of the sentence then occurs. These offenders are free in society without any further obligation to report to the justice system. It is at this last point that their experience with community corrections ends, presuming that they lead a conviction-free life throughout the remainder of their days.

Caseload Assignment Models

The **model of caseload delivery** has to do with the process whereby offenders are initially assigned their CSO. This is often determined by the agency size and the number of offenders under the agency's jurisdiction. Some models of caseload delivery may use some form of random offender assignment or they may base the assignment on the geographical location of offenders to make the task of face-to-face supervision easier for the CSO. However, other issues such as organizational culture and agency intent can affect the manner by which offenders are assigned to a given caseload. As previously mentioned, probation officer workload is associated with various caseload assignments. For instance, a CSO with a handful of hardcore offenders is likely to have the same overall workload as a CSO with numerous small-time offenders on his or her caseload. Finding an equitable match in officer workload and keeping things in equilibrium can be difficult. The intensity of the supervision status of each offender typically determines the amount of work that is required to supervise that offender. Unlike the workload assignment model, however, the concern with caseload assignments are more focused on ensuring that offender needs are met rather than addressing the workload of CSOs.

▲ **Photo 6.4**   Probation officer Rosalyn Horton looks over her reports of checking an offender on her caseload during the penalty phase of the trial involving the abduction, rape, and murder of a child named Carlia Brucia.

Champion (2002) identified three different types of caseload and management models as follows: the **conventional model**, the **conventional model with geographic consideration**, and the **numbers game model**. A brief overview of each will be provided simply to ensure comprehensiveness.

The conventional model of case management simply involves the random assignment of offenders to CSOs. This model of case assignment results in officers having a mix of different types of offenders, this having pros and cons to developing equity in workload among officers and in optimizing service coordination for offenders. Champion (2002) noted that the conventional model is probably the most frequently used model around the nation. This model is simple to use because in reality it is not even a model. It is simply assignment of offenders using a list of officers. There are no other logistical considerations, and offenders are assigned as they emerge. Though this is perhaps the most commonly used method of case assignment and management, it is somewhat haphazard in application and requires that CSOs act as a jack-of-all-trades in many respects. This can be dangerous for community safety when some of these offenders should be given more specialized supervision to optimize both security and treatment outcomes. This method of case management is also likely to be more stressful than others on CSOs since they essentially must learn to do it all and since their workload is determined more by luck and happenstance than a methodical and balanced approach based on evidence-based principles.

The conventional model with geographic consideration is actually common in many areas where it can be practically implemented. A prime determinant of this model is the amount of time that officers must spend traveling to various locations during their day-to-day routine of checking on offenders. This has benefits for both the officer and the agency since the officer's time traveling is minimized and since the agency can optimize the work efforts of the officer. Eliminating excessive travel time also provides the officer with more time for the visit itself and for the reams of paperwork that they must contend with. Thus, the consideration of geographic dispersal of an officer's caseload can help to reduce the stress of the job; this should undoubtedly improve morale of CSOs in the agency.

The next model is what Champion (2002) referred to as the numbers game model. The version of the numbers game model for this text consists of one where the agency defines a desired caseload per officer (such as 40 offenders per officer) and the agency makes its hiring decisions based on this formula. For example, an agency employs 7 CSOs and has a total of 400 offenders to supervise. This agency desires to have officer caseloads of 40 offenders per officer. This agency would need to then hire three more officers to meet its caseload objective. This type of model is more useful for agency administrators than it is for the individual CSO or the offender. Naturally, agencies will pick caseloads within their own budgetary considerations and, as such, the emphasis is on simply ensuring that numbers are distributed evenly, the only question being the specific number per officer who will be set by the agency. This approach is not too much different from the conventional model, but it does ensure that the agency routinely addresses the caseload issues since hiring decisions are directly linked to the caseload assignment process itself.

Generally speaking, the **specialized needs caseload model** is used when dealing with offenders in need of specialized services or treatment (Champion, 2002). Naturally, if and when it is possible, it would also be beneficial if the agency were to structure the caseload as geographically realistic as possible so that the supervision officer can reasonably make their visits. The specialized needs caseload model pertains to community supervision assignments to offenders who share common specialized needs such as substance abuse, sex offending, a given set of disabilities, and so on. This model is a derivative of the specialized caseload model presented in other works (Champion, 2002). With this model, the officer assigned to these offenders will have special skills or training related to these needs.

Further, supervision officers will typically have a close rapport with the therapists and the treatment program that is utilized. Indeed, the supervision officer and the therapist should have a close working relationship, even if this is largely conducted by phone. Informal ties between the two should be fostered by both agencies, and supervisors on both ends could accommodate work schedules so that both are even able to occasionally have lunch or other meetings with one another. The main idea is that both work together as a team. In order for specialized models to be correctly implemented, collaboration between different service providers is mandatory.

⬚ Public Probation and Private Probation Agencies

A good deal of attention has been given to public probation agencies and their services to the community, but no true mention has been made regarding the increased use of privatized probation services. This issue is actually one that is of no small import, as several states utilize private companies for community supervision of offenders on probation. Private probation is the same as other forms of probation but is administered by privately owned and operated companies that contract with courts to supervise misdemeanor cases. As an example of how widespread the use of private probation has become, consider that the state of Georgia passed legislation in the early 1990s that required various municipalities and counties to use alternative probation services as the state's DOC phased out its own supervision of probationers in many jurisdictions. As a result, the state of Georgia established the County and Municipal Probation Advisory Council to create rules and regulations regarding contracts and/or agreements for the provision of probation services through private providers. The state reserves the right to deny, suspend, and revoke a company's operation and the state conducts routine audits of companies providing such services (Office of the Auditor, 2007).

As with much of the corporate world, the state of probation, when administered under private corporations, tends to experience rapid change and continual development. To gain an understanding of how quickly the private arena of corrections can change, consider that in May of 2005, the private company Maximus bought out another company, National Misdemeanant Private Probation Operations (NMPPO), as part of an acquisition agreement (Maximus, 2003). NMPPO serviced more than 31,000 misdemeanant clients in over 200 courts and agencies each week. Maximus, one of the nation's largest government services companies providing state and local governments with program management, consulting, and information services, had over 5,300 employees located in more than 245 offices across the United States and even in other countries (Maximus, 2003). NMPPO, the company purchased by Maximus, had made public claims of a 90% probation completion rate, with 90% of fines, fees, and restitution collected. This would make probation a high profit business that also generates revenue for the community and provides full compensation to victims (Maximus, 2003). Maximus, through its acquisition of NMPPO, would be equipped to provide programming for offenders, including treatment groups, drug and alcohol testing, and education classes. NMPPO had operated several nonresidential programs for misdemeanants that included various forms of offender assessment, case management, and enforcement/supervision. Software used by NMPPO collected and maintained accurate and comprehensive information on probationers, their payment status, the court-ordered conditions that are required, and their progress and history while on supervision (Maximus, 2003).

Then, in October of 2006, a company named Providence Service Corporation bought out Maximus, acquiring all of the assets of the correctional services business affiliated with Maximus (Providence Service Corporation, 2006). Providence Service Corporation noted that its annual revenue was estimated to be around $8 million, and the chief executive officer for that company, when commenting on the acquisition of Maximus, stated,

> This acquisition further expands our human services delivery platform and will enable us to introduce probation services in those states where we operate that have privatized probation. . . . The number of felony arrests in America makes it impossible for most court jurisdictions to provide probation supervision for minor offenders. The acquired business has a great track record with its payer base and we believe will create a replicable service in many of our existing markets. The fit of human services staff and probation staff side by side should also be well received by our mutual payers. (Providence Service Corporation, 2006)

As of 2006, Providence Service Corporation maintained over 100 contracts, providing privatized misdemeanant probation services in the states of Georgia, Tennessee, South Carolina, Florida, and

Washington State (Providence Service Corporation, 2006). It should be clear that the world of private probation is one that is experiencing high growth and is constantly changing.

In the county of Athens-Clarke, Georgia, roughly 2,100 misdemeanant offenders are on probation during any given month. Private probation companies are contracted to supervise nearly 95% of the low-risk probationers in the dual county region. The local government of Athens-Clarke supervises the remaining offenders who are in the community. Generally, the private probation corporations in Athens-Clarke supervised offenders with convictions for crimes such as DUI, underage possession, marijuana possession, shoplifting, criminal trespass, and (when violent) simple battery.

The majority of offenders on probation are nonviolent, and the examples provided from Athens-Clarke reflect this fact. This then makes a strong case for the use of privatized probation services since, for the most part, public safety is genuinely not an issue. Though this is not meant to trivialize crimes that are nonviolent in nature, it does demonstrate that outsourcing may be a viable alternative to managing the burgeoning caseloads of many community supervision agencies. Further, the standard of supervision can be (and is) maintained through state audits, ensuring that companies provide suitable levels of follow-up with offenders. Given that companies have an obvious incentive to collect program fees, fines, and other monetary requirements from probationers, it is highly likely that private companies would provide appropriate follow-up and routine services. Further, the level of accountability, at least in terms of economic accountability, is likely to be further improved since these companies desire to generate profits from the fees and fines of the probationers under their supervision. This then has direct benefits for the community and the victim who is compensated. Since most of these offenders are nonviolent, and since most forms of victimization are likely to be property-related in nature, this can be a particularly productive alternative with low-risk and nonserious offenders.

If the points just presented are indeed true, then it would seem that the main question to be resolved is whether private probation services are able to adequately sustain themselves while maintaining public safety. Though this picture may provide an overly optimistic view of private probation services, it does seem to demonstrate that outsourcing of probation services may become more common in the future. From the information just presented, it would seem that such services provide better collection rates of compensation for victims, provide substantially more pay for probation staff employed in the agency, and have caseloads that are relatively close to recommended levels for low-risk and administratively supervised probationers (Burrell, 2006). All the while, the agency itself generates a profit margin that is likely to range from 12% to 19%, depending on the circumstances. While these figures will likely vary from region to region and from year to year, they do demonstrate the viability of private probation services.

Further, caseload management could be better improved in these circumstances since some relief could be provided by hiring combinations of assistant probation officers or part-time officers (roughly $20,000 could absorb another 120 offender cases, ensuring that caseloads do not exceed 230 offenders throughout the agency). It is worth mentioning that similar types of probation personnel are utilized in various parts of the United States, including Georgia. On the other hand, private companies could simply raise the probation fee by a mere $4.00 per month per probationer (at an 85% collection rate off of 2,100 offenders, this would generate an additional $85,000) to hire two additional officers (at which point caseloads would be right at 200 low-risk offenders per officer, exactly within suggested levels). The point is that with just some adjustment in charges, personnel allocation, collection rates, or accepted profit margins private companies can provide supervision services that are well within the recommended caseload levels, thereby avoiding burnout of employees while providing salaries that are well above average in their respective locations. And, as just pointed out, victims are all the better compensated while the community benefits from the lack of tax expenditures on probationer supervision.

Beyond the benefits just noted, it would be reasonable to consider the level of quality of private probation personnel. In this case, states can and do set standards that are equal to or exceed those required of state-level probation and/or parole personnel. For instance, in the state of Georgia (Georgia being our state of reference for this current subsection), passage of O.C.G.A. § 42-8-102 and Rule 503-1-.21(b) specifically articulates minimal personnel standards that Georgia courts and private probation agencies must adhere to when signing contracts for private probation services.

Thus, it is clear that all qualification and/or training requirements for private probation officers are equal or similar to those required of public probation officers. Further, it should be pointed out that private companies have much more latitude in hiring and firing decisions than do public service agencies and, therefore, may make more expedient and effective decisions regarding personnel retention when qualifications and/or professional performance criteria are an issue. The fact that these private agencies provide more income to their probation officers also means that it is likely that these companies are able to recruit quality personnel within their ranks.

While private probation supervision is not meant to be construed as a panacea for the challenges that face state or county probation systems, it is meant to demonstrate that such an option may be viable in the right circumstances. Certainly, cost-related figures presented in this section would be quite different in other states such as California or New York, but it would be presumed that revenue collected would be similarly inflated. In addition, programs such as those discussed would not necessarily be ideal for all supervision levels, though, at least hypothetically, more serious offenders could be supervised effectively by private agencies that have state-of-the-art technology and equipment. Naturally, costs would increase, fees would then increase, and overall profitability might go down. Regardless, the use of private agencies provides a set of opportunities that should not be overlooked.

⊠ Objectives and Advantages of Probation

As was noted previously, the two primary objectives of community supervision, or more specifically probation, is to protect the community from further criminal behavior (recidivism) while also reintegrating the offender. These two goals are both complementary to one another though they may seem to operate at cross-purposes. The means by which these competing goals are met most practically occurs on a case by case basis where the granting of probation is a highly individualized process. This allows the judge and the probation agency to provide the appropriate balance between these competing objectives so as to be best tailored to the specific conditions surrounding an offender. Naturally, the individualized nature of probation leads to some degree of variability and also requires a more detailed approach to supervising cases because of this variability.

Latessa and Allen (1999) noted that even though probation tends to have this individualized approach, there are several advantages to probation that are generally recognized among probation experts. According to Latessa and Allen (1999, p. 173), these advantages are as follows:

1. The use of community resources to reintegrate offenders who are thus forced to face and hopefully resolve their individual problems while under community supervision

2. Fiscal savings over imprisonment

3. Avoiding **prisonization**, which tends to exacerbate the underlying causes of criminal behavior

4. Keeping offenders' families off local and state welfare rolls or at least reducing the amount of needed assistance

5. A relatively successful process of correcting offending behavior, depending on the type of offender and the specific jurisdiction

6. A sentencing option that can permit selective incapacitation of those that genuinely require displacement from the community

While the disadvantages of probation naturally include the fact that offenders are able to reoffend in society since they are not incarcerated, it is the general notion that this can be minimized effectively enough so as to ensure that the advantages to the public outweigh the disadvantages. The previous points demonstrate that probation saves the public a great deal of money and resources when used correctly. The last part of the previous statement is particularly important, since a poor or haphazard use of this sentence can result in physical, emotional, and economic costs to the public.

It is important that the student understands that this argument is not presented as ideological support for the probation sanction. The mere fact that probation is used in approximately 60% of all sentences demonstrates that it has a great deal of utility. It is not the intent of this text to prove or disprove whether probation should be used. However, its use as leverage during negotiated pleas that are sought by the prosecutor, the range of special conditions that can be applied, and the types of treatment approaches that can be pursued make this sanction indispensable to the criminal justice system. In fact, students must understand that whether this be good, bad, or indifferent, the American criminal justice system simply could not operate without the existence of the probation sanction. This is a reality that students often fail to acknowledge, being given to beliefs that the justice system "ought to" do one thing or the other in an effort to eliminate what is perceived as a weak response to crime.

However, probation is a reality that is here to stay, and it is a necessary reality. This is similar to the reality of plea bargaining. In the vast majority of cases (upward of 90% of all cases), the final sentence is the result of a plea between the prosecution and the defense counsel. This is, of course, arranged before the judge even commences to sentencing. The use of plea bargaining is a critical element of our adversarial system of justice. In fact, plea bargaining occurs because of our emphasis on an adversarial system where both parties present their evidence, refute the evidence of the other party, and are generally expected to engage in a competitive process that allows judges or juries to sift through this parade of evidence (both real and testimony based) as a means of obtaining a truthful conviction.

If we did not have the probation sanction, none of this would be possible. The student of community corrections should make a point to keep this in focus. Without this flexibility in the criminal justice system, options would be limited, and the ability to provide restitution to victims would be much more difficult. Further, offenders in prison would not be likely to generate any true benefit for victims and would, in all likelihood, simply end up being a higher cost to society while at the same time failing to assume direct accountability to the victims of their crime(s). Thus, the benefit of community corrections to ensure offender accountability cannot be ignored.

Take, for example, the state of North Carolina regarding the costs involved with different levels of offender supervision. As these numbers will suggest, the costs for community supervision sanctions are much more effective than imprisonment. Indeed, even if one were to place an offender on ISP costing $11.47 a day, and if the offender were also placed on electronic house arrest costing $7.92 a day, along with additional community service requirements costing only $0.73 per day, as well the use of a fully integrated system of community partnerships for another $9.58 per day, the total daily cost is only $29.70 per day. This comes well under the $50.04 daily cost that is required for minimum custody within a prison facility. This is actually a very important point when drug offenders and other nonviolent offenders are among those being processed. In such cases, it is highly likely that a complete community supervision package will be just as effective as will a prison sentence where minimal levels of security and supervision are maintained. Further, the types of comprehensive services given to the inmate are likely to be much better in community-based programs. Lastly, the use of a full contingent of community supervision mechanisms can maintain security while at the same time allowing the offender to work and provide additional restitution to victims and/or state run compensation programs. When inmates are in prisons, they are not as likely to be able to provide any meaningful restitution.

Thus, it is clear that these types of programs have substantial economic benefits, but it is also clear that along with this saving of tax dollars these offenders (when correctly assessed and classified) are able to be much more productive to society and much more accountable to the victims of their crimes if they are made to fulfill their sentence in the community. Naturally, there will be exception to this since some offenders will simply refuse to work and/or comply with various requirements that are necessary for their sentence. In these cases, community supervision is not an appropriate sanction. However, in the majority of cases, offenders (particularly nonviolent offenders) will tend to comply at least at a bare minimum. The cost effectiveness of community supervision is also a compelling argument at the federal level. While the imprisonment of inmates in the Bureau of Prisons (the federal prison system) costs $63.57 per day, supervision by federal probation officers costs only $9.46 per day. Most federal inmates and/or offenders are, in fact, nonviolent, and this then makes the use of probation a much more appealing option for the federal system.

From the information just discussed, it should be clear that community-based sanctions have a very practical function within our criminal justice system. The use of probation is, in the simplest of sentences, a functional approach supervising the many offenders who are processed through the criminal justice system. Probation lends itself well as leverage for prosecutors when negotiating pleas is much less expensive than using overcrowded jails and/or prisons, provides more direct compensation for victims, and also provides better intervention services for the majority of offenders. Given these factual realities, it should be clear to the student that our current criminal justice system simply could not operate without the use of probation. The fact that roughly 60% of all convicted offenders in the United States are on probation tends to attest to the fact that, like it or not, probation is a pragmatic reality of criminal justice in America and that it is probably here to stay for quite some time to come.

◧ Conclusion

The institution of probation is one that is integral to our correctional system. As has been discussed, probation is complementary to our current adversarial system, which results in a negotiated form of justice. Further, private probation companies have emerged as a viable option to addressing the nation's burgeoning probation population. Though privatization is no panacea to the plight of probation, private companies can provide services that are equally as effective as public probation, with added benefits that are not realized among many public probation agencies (higher salaries for probation staff, cost effectiveness, and competitive caseloads).

Likewise, the use of probation allows our justice system to implement a great degree of flexibility, both in terms of the conditions associated with a sentence and in terms of the specific type of probation that can be given to an offender. The various types of probation can also provide numerous options for those who must supervise probationers and enforce the conditions of probation sentences. Having these various means of implementing probation sentences also brings to question the effectiveness of these sanctions. Though specific and comparable comparisons are not easily found, some basic characteristics of probation can be standardized to provide more effective evaluative information for future policy makers. The use of this evaluative process can be an effective guide for future probation agencies, both when enforcing probation terms and when making critical decisions at revocation proceedings. From this section, it is clear that there are many aspects of the probation sanction that work together to provide a unique blend of options for the justice system. These same aspects are continually examined as practitioners and scholars seek to improve the ability of probation agencies to achieve the two primary goals of public safety and offender reintegration.

⊠ Section Summary

- Probationers are criminal offenders who have been sentenced to a period of correctional supervision in the community in lieu of incarceration.
- At the close of 2008, the total probation population was 4,270,917.
- The use of probation has its origins in recognizance and suspended sentences.
- John Augustus is considered the father of probation.
- States incorporate various methods of managing the organizational structure of their probation and parole programs ranging from the state- and county-level executive branches to state- and county-level judicial branches.
- A large portion of probation officers' time is spent completing PSIs.
- The majority of probation agencies in the United States require that officers have at least a bachelor's degree.
- Because of the high demands of the job, many probation officers experience role identity confusion and ultimately job stress and burnout. High caseloads and paperwork appear to be the greatest source of stress.
- Both standard and special conditions may be set for the probationer.
- Probation may be revoked for technical or new offense violations.
- There are six advantages to the continued use of probation. To summarize, they are as follows: (1) community resources addressing individual problems; (2) fiscal savings; (3) avoidance of prisonization; (4) plan to keep families off welfare; (5) successful process in correcting offender behavior; and (6) a sentencing option for selective incapacitation.

KEY TERMS		
Conventional model	Preliminary hearing	Sentencing stage
Conventional model with geographic consideration	Private probation	Shock probation
	Probationers	Split sentencing
Hearing stage	Residential treatment home	Standard probation
Numbers game model	Role identity confusion	Technical violations

DISCUSSION QUESTIONS

1. How might the use of assistant probation officers help to improve public safety? Can you see any drawbacks to using assistant probation officers?

2. Given the current financial constraints of most publically run agencies, what are some of the pros and cons of using private probation services to alleviate these burdens? How might state, county, or local agencies incorporate the use of private services into their daily activities?

3. What is the average probation caseload size in your community/state? As a chief probation officer, how might you divide the caseloads to ensure community safety and increase job satisfaction?

4. The majority of states and the federal government require that probation officers have a minimum of a bachelor's degree before being employed. Why would agencies see this as a valuable requirement? Why would probation officer requirements differ so vastly from that of a correctional officer?

5. Throughout the text, we have discussed the merits of punishment (retribution, incapacitation, and deterrence) versus reformative strategies for community-level supervision. Given the current state of affairs in your community and state, which philosophy should be guiding probation administration? Why? What are some of the potential barriers to this strategy? Where might you as a probation officer garner support for your ideas?

WEB RESOURCES

American Probation and Parole Association:

http://www.appa-net.org/eweb/

Biographical Outline of August Aichhorn:

http://www.cyc-net.org/profession/pro-Augustaichhorn.html

Please refer to the student study site for web resources and additional resources.

READING

Because of the growing concern for diminished resources at the local level, many state, county, and local agencies are seeking ways to effectively supervise offenders in the community. One such alternative is the growing use of private agencies known as private service providers (PSPs) to assist in the process of supervision and program administration. Despite the movement toward these alternatives, little to no research has been conducted on either the appropriateness of the service or the perceptions of attorneys' responsibility for utilizing these agencies. Alarid and Schloss sought to fill a void in the literature by conducting one such

SOURCE: Leanne Fiftal Alarid & Christine S. Schloss (2009). Attorney views on the use of private agencies for probation supervision and treatment. *International Journal of Offender Therapy and Comparative Criminology, 53*(3), 278–291. Copyright © 2009 Sage Publications.

exploratory study in Kansas City, Missouri. A total of 73 (55.7%) of the attorneys surveyed responded to a questionnaire asking for their overall satisfaction with the use of PSPs to supervise misdemeanant defendants, cost effectiveness, program administration, reputation of providers, accessibility, ownership, and programming availability. Results of bivariate and multivariate analysis revealed that prosecutors and defense attorneys differed on their perceptions of the success of the program. Overall, prosecutors' primary concern was agency accountability while defense attorneys were more concerned about the costs to their clients. Likewise, having a contract was deemed important to both prosecutors and defense attorneys but the company reputation, employee reputation, and financial stability of the company were more important to prosecutors than defense attorneys. One concern that arose from the results was the lack of consistent representation in the courtroom for routine dockets. Both prosecutors and defense attorneys supported the use of these. Finally, prosecutors seemed to endorse the use of private program offerings more than defense attorneys. Overall the results of this study provide a continuation of the discussion of privatizing services both in institutions and in the community. The authors provide several policy implications to guide further discussion on the subject.

Attorney Views on the Use of Private Agencies for Probation Supervision and Treatment

Leanne Fiftal Alarid and Christine S. Schloss

Private-sector involvement in the correctional system has increased at a significant rate over the past 25 years (Gaes, Camp, Nelson, & Saylor, 2004; Lukemeyer & McCorkle, 2006; Pozen, 2003). Privatization refers to the shifting of public functions and responsibilities either partially or totally to for-profit or nonprofit private organizations (Joh, 2005). In the corrections system, when the state enters into a contract with a private company, a public agency retains oversight even though day-to-day management may be left to the private company. Correctional privatization includes government contracts with vendors to provide programs in public agencies for health services, substance abuse counseling, job placement, and food services, as well as classes for those caught driving while intoxicated. Privatization efforts in correctional facility construction and management have perhaps received the most attention (Culp, 2005; Price & Riccucci, 2005).

Two theoretical perspectives formed the basis of the privatization debate. The first perspective, termed the "prison-industrial complex" (Donziger, 1996, p. 81), assumed that the continued growth in the correctional system ensures bureaucratic survival. By sentencing a steady supply of prisoners to longer terms of incarceration, the criminal justice system, along with the assistance of private vendors and politicians, ensures its own existence despite a decline in crime rates (Christie, 2000; Shelden & Brown, 2000). "[Private] agency survival depends on criminal justice referrals and fees charged to offenders," especially for treatment providers (Lucken, 1997a, p. 376). In effect, punishment becomes a profitable market-driven enterprise that involves increasing system efficiency and building organizational dynasties that will outlive the founders (Kraska, 2004).

In contrast to the prison-industrial-complex perspective, postmodernism theory assumed that the government has been unable to adequately control crime or ensure the security of the general public.

Thus, responsibilities for public safety have been redistributed to the private sector out of necessity (Garland, 2001; Kraska, 2004). For example, Connecticut probation officers experienced increased caseloads of between 200 and 300 cases, and with continued staff shortages and a shrinking budget, services were privatized to alleviate the crisis (Bosco, 1998). In the postmodernism perspective, the focus is on the management of risk, predictability, and organizational accountability. Private agencies serve in a conduit role to provide supervision and treatment services for lower risk individuals (in minimum-security prisons and halfway houses and on misdemeanor probation) so that the public sector can focus on medium- and high-security risks (in medium- and maximum-security prisons and on felony probation). Correctional privatization has been shown to support elements of both perspectives—that of being a growth industry (Donziger, 1996) and of being focused on risk management (Feeley & Simon, 1992).

⊠ Privatization in Community Corrections

With all the attention paid to private prisons and jails, the issue of private correctional agencies in the community has been researched by only a small number of academics (McCarthy, Lincoln, & Wilson, 2000; Meyer & Grant, 1996). Ironically, nationwide there are more clients served by private, locally operating, community correctional agencies than there are prisoners in private jails and prisons. An estimated 100,000 prisoners are incarcerated in 200 private prisons nationwide (Alarid & Reichel, 2008), compared to a conservative estimate of 300,000 misdemeanor probationers being supervised in 10 states by private agencies (Schloss & Alarid, 2007). This number does not include the probationers who are court ordered to attend some form of outpatient private treatment center and the thousands of offenders in residential community correction facilities in all states (Alarid, Cromwell, & del Cannen, 2008). The Bureau of Prisons contracts with 250 community centers operated by the Salvation Army, Volunteers of America, and other private agencies (Center for Community Corrections, 1997).

The ability of local community correctional agencies to operate is due in part to the proliferation of community corrections acts (CCAs), which transfer the authority for operating correctional programs from the state to local or private agencies. Local agencies and community boards are responsible for developing a range of community-based correctional options. As of 2008, 28 states have CCAs that have established community corrections partnerships between state, local, and private agencies (Alarid et al., 2008). However, state appropriations for full funding of these partnerships have been slow to develop compared to the overall probation growth rate. States that lack CCA legislation or funding mechanisms have contract options for the use of private agencies.

Community-based private agencies tend to be smaller and to range widely from facilities that manage the payment of fines and track community-service hours to privately owned and operated residential facilities such as work-release and halfway houses (see Alarid et al., 2008). Technological innovations in electronic monitoring and global positioning systems have spawned studies on the supervision of high-risk probationers and parolees in the community (Finn & Muirhead-Steves, 2002; Padgett, Bales, & Blomberg, 2006; Renzema & Mayo-Wilson, 2005). State-licensed drug treatment programs that partner with drug courts and probation agencies offer group counseling to offenders as a part of the public health system (for a more complete review, see Taxman, Perdoni, & Harrison, 2007).

Even less attention has been paid to probation privatization. This is surprising given that probation is the most common correctional sanction. More than 4 million people serve a probation sentence, compared to 2.1 million in correctional facilities (Alarid et al., 2008). As the numbers of probationers have risen, about 10 states have turned to private probation agencies to supervise misdemeanants, while the county or state has continued to supervise felons (Schloss & Alarid, 2007). For example, in Maricopa County, Arizona, 34% of adults and 57% of juveniles utilized private service providers for an average duration of 1 month after sentencing. In Philadelphia, the average sentence with private providers was 2 months for juveniles and nearly 4 months for adults (Mulvey, Schubert, & Chung, 2007).

Most private probation agencies provide both supervision and treatment services and are therefore known more generally as private service providers, or PSPs. For the purposes of this article, a PSP is defined as any for-profit or nonprofit private organization that contracts with county-level or state-level government to provide probation supervision, independent probation treatment services, or both probation supervision and treatment under one roof. By offering supervision and treatment at a single agency, offenders who have multiple court-ordered conditions can avoid the "piling up of sanctions" that can lead to an increase in the revocation of probation (Lucken, 1997a, p. 373). Diversifying treatment services allows PSPs to remain competitive for contract renewal through government contracts and court-ordered payments. Although community treatment programs exist in a variety of forms, PSPs, as defined in this study, tend to be outpatient group sessions for specific problems related to legal troubles or to substance abuse that do not result in imprisonment. PSPs are not inpatient or residential programs or reentry programs for parolees, nor are they drug courts or mental health courts (for definitions of specialty courts, see Nolan, 2003, and Slate, 2003).

Offenders attend court-ordered classes or group counseling in a variety of areas that include drug and alcohol assessments, substance abuse traffic offender programs, anger management, domestic violence, literacy, job training, or community service. PSPs accept clients from a multitude of possible entry points, including misdemeanor probation, drug court, pretrial release, diversion, parole, and the public health system (Townsend, 2004). Probationers are a common client source for PSPs, and clients are also referred directly from attorneys or other agencies. For individuals serving community sentences, the court has some responsibility to identify individuals in need of services and to ensure that offenders receive these services (Casey, 1998). Thus, court officials (prosecutors, defense attorneys, and

municipal judges) play important roles in defining the type and prevalence of PSP use in the community (Meyer & Grant, 1996; Shillon, 1992). PSP representatives recruit clients by making attorneys aware of their services through attending professional conferences and sending agency representatives to court (Lucken, 1997a).

Statutes and regulations have not kept pace with the addition of the private sector in probation, leaving some jurisdictions devoid of standards for awarding contracts to private providers, hiring staff, and quality control for offender treatment services (Schloss & Alarid, 2007). This has produced inconsistencies as to which private agencies receive contracts, and there is no oversight regarding the quality of staff nor the types of services offered to offenders.

In the jurisdiction under study, each local court can enter into an exclusive contract with an agency that allows a single private agency to provide services to all defendants coming from that court. Although the substance abuse traffic offender programs provided by the agency must be certified by the state Department of Mental Health, most other types of treatment services have no certification, licensing, or oversight. Private probation agencies in this jurisdiction are not regulated by any outside entity (other than the courts). This has contributed to wide variation among the various private probation agencies (Schloss & Alarid, 2007).

To complicate the problem, there is also a dearth of program evaluations in private probation and no requirement in some jurisdictions to verify fees collected, making auditing difficult (Lucken, 1997b). Although most private agencies have appropriate benchmarks and quality standards, lack of mandates caused some private probation agencies to hire part-time workers with minimal training and to be partially responsible for a situation criticized by Oldfield (1994, p. 187) as the "McDonaldization" of probation services. Even the harshest critics of probation privatization declare that private probation services should not be abandoned. Instead, attention should be directed to how treatment service partnerships can function more effectively.

During any case-screening process, prosecutors are typically the first professionals to assess defendant eligibility for probation and are thus in a key position to link clients to PSPs. However, many prosecutors avoid getting heavily involved in community corrections for a number of reasons, including heavy caseloads, turf issues, and being wary of risk with too many offenders in the community (Shilton, 1999). Suggesting probation and/or treatment services as a sanction is partly dependent on the perceptions of courtroom attorneys to accept the PSP as a viable alternative. No study has been conducted to measure how attorneys view PSPs. A review of the available literature reflected that attorney perceptions have been previously measured on issues related to the pretrial or trial process, such as suspect lineups, witness credibility, client competence, and plea bargaining (Bonnie, Poythress, Hoge, Monahan, & Kisenberg, 1996; Foot, Stolberg, & Shepherd, 2000; Hoge, Bonnie, Poythress, & Monahan, 1992; Kramer, Wolbransky, & Heilbrun, 2007; Slinson, Devenport, Cutler, & Kraviu, 1996).

This research attempts to fill the gap in the literature and uncover concerns that attorneys may have in the use of private probation providers with the following research questions:

- Do prosecutors and defense attorneys differ in their beliefs about the use of PSPs?
- What is the effect of having standardized criteria for PSPs in order to alleviate attorney concerns?
- What other variables might explain concerns about using PSPs?

Method

Surveys were mailed to all municipal and district prosecuting and public defenders in a three-county area that encompassed the metropolitan area of Kansas City, Missouri. The respondent list was procured through the Kansas City Sentencing Commission, and there were MO attorneys on the list. The sampling frame initially contained more prosecutors than defense attorneys by a margin of 2 to 1. Attorneys were chosen for sample selection because they have "street-level influence" over the use of court programming and services (Maynard-Moody, Musheno, & Palumbo, 1990, p. 833). Street-level practitioners work closely with offenders and victims, and they are thus likely to know what will work in the local environment. Street-level workers also have access to treatment programs and other agencies to suggest as sanctions. Given the high number of negotiated criminal cases, prosecutors and defense attorneys routinely suggest sanctions and programs to judges, who ultimately decide punishment.

All survey instruments were submitted anonymously and numerically identified in the order received. Of the 140 surveys sent out, 78 were returned, for a response rate of 55.7%. Five surveys were not included in the analysis due to too much missing data, so the final sample was 73 respondents. Surveys were coded and analyzed using the SPSS statistical software program.

Measures

Dependent Variable

The dependent variable was a summated four-item scale that measured concerns attorneys had regarding private providers in offering supervision and treatment services. The respondents were asked to indicate whether each item was a concern regarding the use of PSPs in their jurisdictions (coded as $1 = $ yes and $0 = $ no), and the scale ranged from 0 to 4. The items listed were agency qualifications, agency accountability to the court, timeliness of reports to courts, and consistency between agencies. The four items loaded on a single factor and had an alpha reliability of .60.

Two other concerns (cost of services and location accessibility for offenders) were asked on the survey, but these loaded on a different factor than the other four items when factor analysis was used on all six variables simultaneously. These two items were not used due to low reliability (alpha level was only .38).

Independent Variables

There were three types of independent variables in the analysis that measured the importance of certain criteria for PSPs. The first was a dichotomous variable that asked respondents whether they were in favor of allowing PSPs space in the court-house to make initial contact with defendants coming to court. The possible responses were coded 1 (yes) and 0 (no). This variable was included to determine whether allowing PSPs a more active presence in the courthouse might alleviate concerns.

The second set of independent variables was also dichotomous (1 = yes, 0 = no) and asked respondents to consider 10 different criteria and whether each should be used in determining whether a PSP is awarded a contract with the court. The 10 criteria were reputation of the PSP company, reputation of PSP employees, length of time in business, financial stability of PSP, educational background of PSP employees, location of PSP offices, accessibility of PSP for clients, ownership of PSP, types of certified programs offered, and types of noncertified programs offered. Principal components factor analysis was used to determine factor loadings for all 10 of these items simultaneously. These items loaded on four factors:

Factor 1 (two variables): reputation of the PSP company and reputation of PSP employees

Factor 2 (two variables): length of time in business and financial stability of PSP

Factor 3 (two variables): ownership of PSP and types of noncertified programs offered

Factor 4 (four variables): educational background of PSP employees, location of PSP offices, accessibility of PSP for clients, and types of certified programs offered

The third set of independent variables used a Likert-type ordinal scale of importance (1 = most important, 5 = least important) to ask respondents about the importance that PSPs meet seven different criteria. Each criterion was considered independently and not rank ordered. We hypothesized that those who believe more strongly in minimum criteria will also have more concerns about PSPs. The criteria in the survey were the importance that PSPs operate with a city or county contract, that PSP employees meet specific educational criteria, that PSP programs utilize standardized curricula for each service offered, that PSPs be allowed to specialize in their treatment offerings, that PSPs be allowed to limit the number of programs offered, that PSPs have representatives in court for routine dockets, and that PSPs have representatives in court for probation violation hearings.

Control Variables

The three control variables used in the analysis were type of attorney (0 = prosecuting attorney, 1 = defense attorney), time in current position (in number of years), and overall view of the court system. To measure overall satisfaction, respondents were asked, "How satisfied are you with the overall operation of the court systems in the metropolitan area?" (Possible responses were 1 = very satisfied, 2 = satisfied, 3 = neutral, 4 = dissatisfied, and 5 = very dissatisfied.)

⊠ Sample Characteristics

Surveys of criminal prosecutors and defense attorneys, particularly in the area of community sentencing programs, are not conducted very often in academia. This is partially due to the tendency of prosecutors not to get overly involved in community corrections issues due to the potential for public criticism if offenders in the community recidivate (Shilton, 1999).

To obtain the maximum number of respondents, a decision was made to eliminate personal characteristic questions such as gender, race, and age. Respondents were asked whether they were currently a prosecutor or a defense attorney, how many years they had worked in their current position, and their opinion overall on the court system in which they work. Three fourths of the respondents (78%) were prosecutors, and the remaining (22%) were defense attorneys. More than half of the respondents (62%) had worked with the court system for 5 or more years. Forty-four percent of attorneys indicated they were satisfied overall with court system operations, 35% were neutral, and 20% were dissatisfied.

◤ Findings

Because there are no previous empirical studies on the issues presented here, the findings are exploratory for use in future research. The findings were organized into general concerns about PSPs. criteria in awarding PSP contracts, courtroom representation of PSPs, and treatment services offered by PSPs for offenders. Responses by prosecutors were compared to those of defense attorneys, and significant differences are reported. Where there were no differences, the two groups are reported together.

Attorney Concerns About Private Probation Agencies

Attorneys were asked. "What concerns do you currently have regarding the use of private providers in offering court services?" Agency accountability was the primary concern of prosecutors, and this was significantly different from the concern of defense attorneys. Defense attorneys were more concerned about the cost to their clients. Both groups of attorneys shared concerns about staff qualifications and that PSPs were consistent between various agencies. Of less concern to respondents were timeliness of reports from PSPs to the court and accessibility of agency locations for probationers. It is noteworthy that 7.0% of prosecutors and 12.3% of defense attorneys expressed no concerns whatsoever about PSPs.

Four of these concern items (agency qualifications, accountability of PSPs, report timeliness, and agency consistency) were summed into a Concern scale that was reliable at .60. This scale was used as the dependent variable in further multivariate analyses.

Criteria in Awarding Private Probation Contracts

A second area of study was in the awarding of contracts between PSPs and city government. Attorneys were asked to rank the importance of having a contract in place. Having a contract between PSPs and the city was most or very important according to 64% of attorneys, one fourth decided it was somewhat important, and 10% thought the issue was not important. Of the attorneys who believed a contract to hold some level of importance, the vast majority were comfortable with a 2- to 3-year length of time.

In the decision to award contracts to PSPs, more than 80% of attorneys agreed that certified programs offered for offenders and the education level of employees were the two most important criteria. About 7 of 10 attorneys indicated that program accessibility was next in importance.

Prosecutors significantly differed from defense attorneys on three points. Prosecutors (68%), compared to defense attorneys (31%), were more likely to select company reputation as important ($\chi^2 = 7.2$, $p < .01$). Nearly the same number of prosecutors were concerned with employee reputation: 58% of prosecutors compared to 25% of defense attorneys ($\chi^2 = 5.4$, $p < .02$). More than half of prosecutors (54%) thought that a company's financial stability is an important factor in awarding a PSP contract. Only one fourth of defense attorneys agreed ($\chi^2 = 4.32$, $p < .04$). The least important criteria overall were the number of noncertified programs and the issue of ownership, which coincidentally were the same two variables that loaded on the same factor.

Courtroom Representation

The PSPs generally do not have staff present in the courtrooms for regular dockets, as this practice is not widely accepted in the Kansas City Municipal Court. In other courts in the metropolitan area, however, PSP staff members are present on a regular basis. In a pilot domestic violence program in the Kansas City court, PSPs have victim advocates in court to meet with victims, and there are also staff people for referred offenders in order to expedite client participation in the required services (Camacho & Alarid, in press). In courts where PSPs are present in the courtrooms, the PSP staff is able to make immediate contact with referred clients and advise them of requirements, cost of services, and their first appointment date. This also allows the PSP to obtain offender contact information and employment information and to check on any active warrants. The staff member can also answer any questions the offender may have while the offender's attorney is still present.

The survey findings indicated that attorneys overwhelmingly supported the use of PSP representatives in court on a daily basis for routine dockets, with 87.5% believing representatives to be very important or important. About 92.0% of both defense attorneys and prosecutors endorsed the use of PSP representatives during probation violation hearings in court as witnesses or to corroborate reports. Nearly three fourths of the sample favored allowing PSP representatives office or meeting space in courthouses to make initial contact with individuals coming to court.

Treatment Services Offered

The last part of the survey asked attorneys questions about private treatment program offerings for offenders. Most attorneys recognized the state's reliance on PSPs, as 83% believed PSP offerings to be very important or important for court-ordered sanctions. Prosecutors, more so than defense attorneys, seemed to endorse the use of PSPs and to agree with allowing private agencies to specialize in their treatment offerings (79% of prosecutors vs. 69% of defense attorneys).

For PSPs to specialize, it is likely that there would have to be two changes in the present situation. First, PSPs would have to limit the number of programs offered under one roof. This concept was supported by 84% of prosecutors and 69% of defense attorneys. A second change is that PSP programs would utilize identical curricula for their treatment offerings so that treatment offered by one provider would be similar to that offered by another. Identical curricula were favored by 87% of attorneys.

◪ Multivariate Analysis

The findings presented thus far have been bivariate relationships regarding concerns about PSPs, which include criteria in awarding PSP contracts, courtroom representation of PSPs, and treatment services offered by PSPs. We wanted to determine what variables may predict attorney concerns about PSP agencies. Because the Concern scale was a continuous measure, we used ordinary least squares regression with three independent variables and three control variables. PSP company reputation was the most important factor that predicted attorney concerns. Attorneys who believed that PSP reputation was important were also more likely to express concerns about PSP qualifications, accountability, and consistency.

There was an inverse relationship between respondents who were in favor of allowing PSP representatives to make contact with defendants in court and those respondents who expressed concerns. Attorneys who were against having private court representatives were more likely to express concerns about PSPs than were attorneys who favored PSP representation.

An inverse relationship also existed with the belief in having standardized criteria in the PSP treatment curriculum. More specifically, as belief in standardized treatment curricula increased, attorneys were less concerned about private providers. These three variables together explained nearly one third of the variance in this model ($r = .29$). None of the control variables were significant. In the multivariate model, length of employment, type of attorney (defense or prosecutor), and overall satisfaction with court operations did not predict attorney concerns.

◪ Discussion

Rapid growth in a time of decreased resources (doing more with less) has necessitated the redistribution of probation supervision and treatment services to community-based PSPs. Providing policies and defined standards for the use of PSPs is essential to the future of private probation (Meyer & Grant, 1996; Schloss & Alarid, 2007). This research was conducted in a jurisdiction that uses PSPs but has few guidelines on awarding contracts and providing treatment services. Our findings point to suggestions on how policy can be implemented to lower concerns about PSPs.

First, involving attorneys as street-level decision makers is paramount to successful policy implementation, particularly in states without consistent standardization and legislation in the use of PSPs (Maynard-Moody et al., 1990). One limitation of this research is the use of respondents from one metropolitan area. Related to this, a small number of defense attorneys, compared to prosecutors, responded to the survey. Given that the sampling frame from which prosecutors were chosen was significantly larger than the pool of defense attorneys, having more prosecutors in the final sample was not surprising. The data are still important because this is the first study of its kind, and most studies of attorney perceptions survey prosecutors or defense attorneys (rather than both). Future studies may wish to collect multijurisdictional data, perhaps to compare findings from jurisdictions with detailed legislation governing PSPs to compare with jurisdictions that lack such policy.

The results from this study indicate that although some variation exists between prosecutors and defense attorneys, the two groups do not significantly differ overall in their beliefs about the use of PSPs. As a group then, PSP agency reputation was the strongest factor that explained attorney concerns about qualifications, accountability, and consistency. Attorneys seem to value having a contract in place between PSPs and the government for between 2 and 3 years at a time. When making decisions about the recipients of these PSP contracts, the three most important criteria for attorneys are the number and type of certified programs offered for offenders, the education level of employees teaching and supervising offenders, and the accessibility of the program (location, transportation, etc.). These findings support a previous study that identified the need for standardized criteria with private probation agencies (Schloss & Alarid, 2007). The presence of standardized criteria for private providers was predicted to lower the concerns of practitioners who recommend these programs to judges. These findings are important for judges and managers or owners of PSPs to consider as well.

Attorneys seem willing to support the use of PSP representatives in court on a daily basis for routine dockets and during probation violation hearings in court as witnesses or to corroborate reports. This finding is consistent with earlier observations (Lucken, 1997b) and ties in with alleviating attorney concerns about PSPs. This is important in light of the added value of representatives being able to make initial contact with referred clients to advise them of requirements and cost, to verify offender information and employment, and to answer any questions offenders may have while their attorneys are still present. It may take between 7 and 14 days post-sentencing for an offender to make the initial contact. The delay in treatment services may ultimately affect supervision outcome. In the future, it may be useful to compare the outcomes of probation cases that had a courtroom representative to those where a representative was not present.

The results also point to actions that may be considered to improve policies on offender treatment services (Meyer & Grant, 1996; Schloss & Alarid, 2007). Attorneys favor treatment specialization by PSPs. To move toward this goal, PSPs would likely have to limit the number of programs offered. A second change is that PSP programs may wish to utilize standardized treatment curricula so that treatment offered by one provider would be similar to that offered by another.

Our study revealed that attorneys recognize the importance of PSPs to lessen the burden on local and state government, but policies should be in place to legitimize PSPs and lessen concerns. The findings support a postmodernist theoretical perspective more than they support the perspective of the industrial growth complex (Garland, 2001; Kraska, 2004). PSPs provide supervision and/or treatment services for lower risk probationers so that the public sector can focus on medium- and high-security probationers.

The debate continues over whether community corrections can be successfully privatized. Critics identify other plausible concerns that were not studied here, such as the potential for private agencies to go bankrupt, the creation of a two-tier system (private and public), and the role of PSPs as both "the inventors and the administrators of screening/evaluation devices and treatment service types." PSP "treatment agencies in effect control definitions of who is to be punished or treated. . . . They also control the frequency, intensity, and duration of program participation" (Lucken, 1997b, p. 255). To address these concerns, future researchers could examine the court's relationship with other PSPs. More specifically, researchers could explore the process of court assistance for individuals in need of services, how the court coordinates with PSPs, and the extent of program choices open to individual offenders (Casey, 1998). A second line of inquiry involves broadening the definition of PSPs to include how providers are able to coordinate services for specialized populations such as offenders convicted of crimes of a sexual nature or offenders who are mentally ill (Conly, 1999).

◼ References

Alarid, L. P., Cromwell, P., & del Carmen, R. V. (20118). *Community-based corrections* (7th ed.). Belmont, CA: Wadsworth.

Alarid, L. P., & Reichel, R. L. (2008). *Corrections: A contemporary introduction*. Boston: Allyn & Bacon.

Bonnie, R. J., Poythress, N. G., Hoge, S. K., Monahan, J., & Eisenberg, M. (1996). Decision-making in criminal defense: An empirical study of insanity pleas and the impact of doubted client competence. *Journal of Criminal Law and Criminology, 87*(1), 48–62.

Bosco, R. J. (1998). Connecticut probation's partnership with the private sector. In National Institute of Corrections (Eds.), *Topics in community corrections: Annual issue 1998 privatizing community supervision* (pp. 8–12). Longmont, CO: National Institute of Corrections.

Camacho, C. M., & Alarid, L. F. (in press). The significance of the victim advocate for domestic violence victims in municipal court. *Violence and Victims.*

Casey, R. (1998). Court populations in need of services: Defining the court's role. *Behavioral Sciences and the Law, 16,* 137–167.

Center for Community Corrections. (1997). A call for punishments that make sense. Washington. DC: Author. Retrieved on February 4, 2008, from http://www.communitycorrectionsworks.org

Christie, N. (2000). *Crime control as industry: Towards gulags, western style* (3rd ed.). New York: Routledge.

Conly, C. (1999). *Coordinating community services for mentally ill offenders: Maryland's community criminal justice treatment program* (NCJ 175046). Washington, DC: National Institute of Justice.

Culp, R. F. (2005). The rise and stall of prison privatization: An integration of policy analysis perspectives. *Criminal Justice Policy Review, 16,* 412–442.

Donziger, S. A. (1996). *The real war on crime: The report of the national criminal justice commission.* New York: HarperCollins.

Feeley, M. M., & Simon, J. (1992). The new penology: Notes on the emerging strategies of corrections and its implications. *Criminology, 30,* 449–474.

Finn, M. A., & Muirhead-Steves, S. (2002). The effectiveness of electronic monitoring with violent male parolees. *Justice Quarterly, 19,* 293–312.

Foot, M. T., Stolberg, A. L., & Shepherd, R. (2000). Attorney and judicial perceptions of the credibility of expert witness in child custody cases. *Journal of Divorce and Remarriage, 33*(1/2), 31–45.

Gaes, G. G., Camp, S. D., Nelson, J. B., & Saylor, W. G. (2004). *Measuring prison performance: Government privatization and accountability.* Walnut Creek, CA: Altamira.

Garland, D. (2001). *The culture of control: Crime and social order in contemporary society.* Chicago: University of Chicago Press.

Hoge, S. K., Bonnie, R. J., Poythress, N., & Monahan, J. (1992). Attorney-client decision making in criminal cases: Client competence and participation as perceived by their attorneys. *Behavioral Sciences and the Law, 10,* 385–394.

Joh, E. E. (2005). Conceptualizing the private police. *Utah Law Review, 2,* 573–617.

Kramer, G. M., Wolbransky, M., & Heilbrun, K. (2007). Plea bargaining recommendations by criminal defense attorneys: Evidence, strength, potential sentence, and defendant preference. *Behavioral Sciences and the Law, 25,* 573–585.

Kraska, P. B. (2004). *Theorizing criminal justice: Eight essential orientations.* Long Grove. IL: Waveland.

Lucken, K. (1997a). The dynamics of penal reform. *Crime, Law and Social Change, 26,* 367–384.

Lucken, K. (1997b). Privatizing discretion: Rehabilitating treatment in community corrections. *Crime & Delinquency, 43,* 243–259.

Lukemeyer, A., & McCorkle, R. C. (2006). Privatization of prisons; Impact on prison conditions. *American Review of Public Administration, 36,* 189–206.

Maynard-Moody, S., Musheno, M., & Palumbo, D. (1990). Streetwise social policy: Resolving the dilemma of street-level influence and successful implementation. *Western Political Quarterly, 43,* 833–848.

McCarthy, C., Lincoln, R., & Wilson, P. (2000). *Privatising community corrections.* Queensland, Australia: Center for Applied Psychology and Criminology, Bond University. Retrieved on November 15, 2007, from http://epublications.bond.edu.au/hss_pubs/48

Meyer, J., & Gram, A. (1996) The privatization of community corrections: Panacea or Pandora's box? In G. Mays & T. Gray (Eds.), *Privatization and the provision of correctional services: Context and consequences.* Cincinnati, OH: Anderson.

Mulvey, E. P., Schubert, C. A., & Chung, H. L. (2007). Service use after court involvement in a sample of serious adolescent offenders. *Children and Youth Services Review, 29,* 518–544.

Nolan, J. L. (2003). Redefining criminal courts: Problem-solving and the meaning of justice. *American Criminal Law Review, 40*(4), 1541–1565.

Oldfield, M. (1994). Talking quality, meaning control: McDonalds, the market and the probation service. *Probation Journal, 41,* 186–192.

Padgett, K. G., Bales, W. D., & Blomberg, T. G. (2006). Under surveillance: An empirical test of the effectiveness and consequences of electronic monitoring. *Criminology and Public Policy, 5,* 61–92.

Pozen, D. (2003). Managing a correctional marketplace: Prison privatization in the United Stales and the United Kingdom. *Journal of Law and Politics, 19,* 253–284.

Price, B. E., & Riccucci, N. M. (2005). Exploring the determinants of decisions to privatize state prisons. *American Review of Public Administration, 35,* 223–235.

Renzema, M., & Mayo-Wilson, E. (2005). Can electronic monitoring reduce crime for moderate to high-risk offenders? *Journal of Experimental Criminology, 1,* 215–237.

Schloss, C. S., & Alarid, L. F. (2007). Standards in the privatization of probation services: A statutory analysis. *Criminal Justice Review, 32,* 233–245.

Shelden, R. G., & Brown, W. B. (2000). The crime control industry and the management of the surplus population. *Critical Criminology, 9*(1/2), 39–62.

Shilton, M. K. (1992). *Community corrections acts for state and local partnerships.* Lanham, MD: American Correctional Association. Retrieved on November 15, 2007. From http://www.nicic.org/pubs/1992/010132.pdf

Shilton, M. K. (1999). Prosecutors' participation. In Center for Community Corrections (Eds.), *Partnerships in corrections: Six perspectives* (pp. 35–58). Washington, DC: Center for Community Corrections. Retrieved on February 4, 2008, from http://www.communitycorrectionsworks.org/steve/ourresources/publications/partnerships.pdf

Slate, R. N. (2003). From the jailhouse to Capitol Hill: Impacting mental health court legislation and defining what constitutes a mental health court. *Crime & Delinquency, 49,* 6–29.

Stinson, V., Devenpon, J. L., Culler, B. L., & Kravitz, D. A. (1996). How effective is the presence of counsel safeguard? Attorney perceptions of suggestiveness. fairness, and correctability of biased lineup procedures. *Journal of Applied Psychology, 87,* 64–75.

Taxman, F. S., Perdoni, M. L., & Harrison, L. D. (2007). Drug treatment services for adult offenders: The state of the state. *Journal of Substance Abuse Treatment, 32,* 239–254.

Townsend, W. A. (2004). Systems changes associated with criminal justice treatment networks. *Public Administration Review, 64*(5), 607–621.

DISCUSSION QUESTIONS

1. According to the authors, what policies can be implemented to lower concerns about the use of PSPs?

2. What are the potential pros and cons of having both government-hired probation officers supervising felony offenders with PSPs supervising misdemeanant offenders?

3. Given the diminishing resources in a community, should more agencies seek to utilize PSPs to perform vital tasks for convicted defendants? If no, why not? If yes, what services should they perform?

4. What does the term *McDonaldization* of probation services mean?

READING

In this study, Applegate and his colleagues sought to explore a potentially unanswered question in the world of probation studies by examining the extent to which probationers believe the traditional goals of punishment are being met by the probation sanction (p. 80). A total of 369 probationers reporting for a face-to-face meeting with their probation officer in a southeastern United States county were selected for inclusion in the study. Respondents were asked a series of questions regarding not only their perception of probation but societies' safety with them being supervised. Overall the majority of probationers believed that the sentence of probation did foster personal growth (60%) and provide assistance (p. 87), although a slight majority did believe there was "no point" to being placed on probation. Although probationers did respond to a feeling of being incapacitated, they also reported that this feeling resulted in little to no harm. One interesting noteworthy finding was that the majority of respondents did not equate their increased level of supervision to community safety; therefore, the view of themselves as being a contributor to the "us versus them" phenomena did not exist. Furthermore, the authors provided a discussion of the limitations of the study. Overall, they reported that probationers do see their punishment as "restrictive and deserved, and that they believe it is doing them some good" (p. 92).

From the Inside

The Meaning of Probation to Probationers

Brandon K. Applegate, Hayden P. Smith, Alicia H. Sitren, and Nicolette Fariello Springer

Recent national estimates reveal that probation remains the most widely used sanction in the United States. At the end of 2006, more than 4.2 million people were serving probation sentences throughout the country. This figure is more than double the number of people incarcerated in U.S. prisons and jails (Glaze & Bonczar, 2007). Despite this widespread popularity, relatively little information about how probationers perceive their sentence has been systematically assembled. Policy makers assume, often implicitly, that offenders will think about their sanctions in a certain way, but research on the relative severity of sanctions has called such assumptions into question. The current study seeks to expand our knowledge of perceptions of probation by examining the extent to which offenders see probation as achieving the traditional goals of corrections: rehabilitation, deterrence, incapacitation, and retribution. We also examine whether probationers think that probation serves no purpose for them and whether they believe that their ultimate goal is to manipulate the system and their probation officers.

SOURCE: Brandon K. Applegate, Hayden P. Smith, Alicia H. Sitren, & Nicolette Fariello Springer (2009). From the inside: The meaning of probation to probationers. *Criminal Justice Review 34*(1), 80–95. Copyright © 2009 Sage Publications. Published on behalf of Georgia State University Research Foundation.

Literature Review

The existing literature on the purposes of punishment is largely restricted to philosophical debates, surveys of public preferences, and assessments of policies and practices that evince specific correctional goals. For example, Bentham (1789/2007) and Beccaria (1764/1963) provided early discussions about the goals of punishment. In the 1970s and 1980s, several volumes debuted the merits of a retributive justice model (e.g., von Hirsch, 1976) and rehabilitation (e.g., Allen, 1981; Cullen & Gilbert, 1982). And, during the later 1980s and 1990s, attention turned to discussions of harming and confining offenders (e.g., Clear, 1995; Zimring & Hawkins, 1995).

Assessments of public opinion also are widespread. Taken together, they reveal complex feelings, where people are open to a range of responses to criminals. The public supports deterrent and incapacitative punishments and believes that offenders deserve to be sanctioned while simultaneously embracing rehabilitative treatment (Cullen, Fisher, & Applegate, 2000). Researchers have also undertaken sustained efforts to assess the effectiveness of deterrence (e.g., Pratt, Cullen, Blevins, Daigle, & Madensen, 2006), incapacitation (Zimring & Hawkins, 1995), and rehabilitation (Cullen & Gendreau, 2000; MacKenzie, 2006). Analyses of offenders' views of their sanctions, however, are in far more limited supply.

The Relevance of Offenders' Perceptions

Past research has investigated elites' views on correctional goals. The relevance of the opinions of legislators, prison wardens, correctional officers, judges, and others is clear: They are in positions to design or carry out policies, and these policies may be promoted or not depending on one's correctional orientation. It may be less immediately clear, however, why offenders' viewpoints are also important. Careful consideration of traditional correctional goals reveals assertions and assumptions about how criminals think about their sanction. Moreover, it is ultimately in the perceptions

and future behaviors of offenders that punishment philosophies find their relevance.

Deterrence asserts that offenders alter their perceptions of the relative costs and benefits of committing future crimes based on their experience with punishment. A large body of literature has assessed this contention, finding that it holds up, at best, weakly (Paternoster, 1987; Pratt et al., 2006). It is notable, however, that these studies take for granted that the "punishments" being evaluated for their deterrent value are actually experienced as punitive by offenders. For more than a decade, we have known that offenders' perceptions of the relative severity of different punishments vary (see, e.g., Crouch, 1993; May & Wood, 2005; Petersilia & Deschenes, 1994; Spelman, 1995), and there is good reason to be suspicious about whether some of the sanctions investigated in the deterrence literature are truly experienced as unpleasant by offenders (Sitren & Applegate, 2006).

Criminals' perceptions also matter for rehabilitation and retribution. Retribution involves calculations of deserved punishment. Under this philosophy, society determines what sanctions are deserved for which transgressions. However, the offender is also relevant, in that perceptions of the sanctioning body's legitimacy are important. Behavioral psychologists point out that punishment can lead to anger, resentment, and retaliation if it is not perceived as legitimate and deserved (Spiegler & Guevremont, 2003). It has also been asserted that antisocial or "criminogenic" attitudes are an important predictor of continued criminal behavior and an appropriate target for rehabilitative efforts (Andrews & Bonta, 2003). An offender's belief that his or her sentence is providing valuable treatment—"buying into" therapy—would signal prosocial views. Furthermore, a client's willingness to invest in therapy is recognized as a critical component of the relationship, or "therapeutic alliance," between clients and treatment providers (Horvath & Luborsky, 1993). In a variety of settings, research has shown that the quality of that alliance is a significant predictor of successful treatment outcomes (Martin, Garske, & Davis, 2000).

We venture that, in the context of probation, offenders' perceptions are relevant even for incapacitation.

Penologists and criminologists have tended to regard the offenders' perspective as irrelevant to the goal of incapacitation; rather, what matters to these researchers is the reality and extent of the restrictions. Probation, however, does not provide nearly the physical incapacitation offered by imprisonment. Probationers are restricted by supervision and monitoring, but they are in frequent contact with the broader community, which may provide myriad opportunities for offending. The incapacitative ability of the sentence may depend, in part, on how restricted the probationer feels. Two probationers serving under near identical conditions may experience vastly different levels of incapacitation, based solely on personal perceptions of the level of constraint.

Research on Offenders' Perceptions

Perhaps the most extensive body of literature addressing offenders' sanction perceptions developed during the past 20 years has focused on how they view the relative severity of different punishments (Apospori & Alpert, 1993; Crouch, 1993; May & Wood, 2005; May, Wood, Mooney, & Minor, 2005; McClelland & Alperl, 1985; Petersilia, 1990; Petersilia & Deschenes, 1994; Spelman, 1995; Wood & Grasmick, 1999; Wood & May, 2003). This work was spurred by efforts to develop "intermediate sanctions"—such as intensive supervision probation, day fines, shock incarceration, and others—as fitting along a continuum between prison and regular probation (Morris & Tonry, 1991). One notable finding directly challenged assumptions about intermediate sanctions: Intensive supervision probation and some other community-based sanctions are often regarded by offenders as at least as punitive as short periods of incarceration (Petersilia & Deschenes, 1994; Spelman, 1995; Wood & Grasmick, 1999; Wood & May, 2003). For example, nearly one third of the Texas prison inmates in Crouch's (1993) study reported that they would prefer 1 year in prison to just 3 years on probation. Despite challenges to core presumptions about intermediate sanctions, these studies have confirmed that regular probation—with little supervision and minimal restrictions on behavior—is consistently seen as less punitive than a variety of other possible sanctions. Thus, the popular belief that probation is a nonpunishment gains some support from these studies. Even so, this body of work addresses only a single aspect of correctional efforts—punitiveness—excluding other possible dimensions of the meaning of probation. From this work, we know only that offenders tend to see probation as comparatively less harsh than other sentences; it tells us nothing about other aspects of how probation is interpreted by probationers.

We were able to uncover only two prior studies that examined the meaning of punishment from the offenders' perspective. One, conducted by Allen (1985), gauged the views of a group of federal probationers in 1983. The other study was conducted by Van Voorhis, Browning, Simon, and Gordon (1997) and assessed inmates' perceptions of prison. Although our focus here is on probation, this study still provides some insights.

Allen (1985) asked his respondents two sets of questions regarding the traditional goals of corrections. First, he asked that they report their level of agreement or disagreement with four statements about what "the main purpose of probation is" (p. 70). He then posed a single question to the probationers on what they believed "the main purpose of probation *should* be ideally" (p. 70, emphasis in the original). Seventy-eight percent agreed strongly or agreed that the main purpose of probation "is to keep tabs on the probationer to prevent further violation of the law" (p. 70). Somewhat fewer believed the main purpose to be rehabilitation or desert: 63% and 61%, respectively. Finally, only 41% strongly agreed or agreed that the main purpose was what Allen (1985) called the "justice model"—"to resolve the problem between the probationer and the victim in a fair and just manner" (p. 70). When asked what should be the main purpose, each probationer was allowed to provide multiple answers. Overall, 69% indicated rehabilitation. 55% deterrence, 17% desert, and only 7% justice. Thus, probationers expressed a preference for rehabilitation over other goals. In contrast, they perceived the reality of probation to be more focused on surveillance or "keeping tabs" on them.

Allen's (1985) study suffers from several limitations. First, his data were collected nearly 25 years ago.

The intervening decades have seen fundamental shifts in probation. Changes include the expansion of monitoring technologies, increases in the number of people on probation in the United States, and a swing in the overarching orientation of probation. In the early 1990s, Feeley and Simon (1992) argued convincingly that corrections, including probation, had tilted in favor of an emphasis on classification, risk management, and efficient processing of cases. More recently, Steiner, Wada, Hemmens, and Burton (2005) showed that between 1992 and 2002, the number of legislatively established punishment functions within community corrections increased, whereas rehabilitative functions decreased. Second, Allen sampled 87 probationers who were scheduled to have their probation terminated during his 3-month study period. This approach virtually guaranteed that his sample would be unrepresentative by including mostly probationers who would successfully complete their sentences. Indeed, Allen reported that the outcome for 79 of his respondents was "difficulty free" (p. 72). Those who successfully complete probation may have experiences quite different from those who fail. Third, by wording his interview items in the third person when he asked probationers what is the main purpose of probation, Allen treated the meaning of probation as a general one not an individual one. Generalized reports of a situation may paint a very different picture than the personalized experience of each individual.

In contrast to Allen (1985), Van Voorhis et al. (1997) purposely sought to measure "actual inmate experiences of the prison environment" (p. 159). In this regard, most of the survey items they presented to their minimum and maximum security inmates were worded in the first person. For example, to assess respondents' views that their sentence was rehabilitative, Van Voorhis et al. (1997) had them agree or disagree with these two statements: "This experience is helping me to grow" and "I can accomplish something here" (p. 145). Van Voorhis and her colleagues also examined a broader set of possible meanings than Allen (1985) had. They included statements to measure inmates' perceptions that the purpose of their sentence was rehabilitation, deterrence, retribution,

desert, incapacitation, to impress the parole board, and to "scam" the staff. They also included one item to determine if the probationers believed that their sentence served no purpose.

We are persuaded that Van Voorhis et al.'s approach provides a more meaningful and more complete assessment of how correctional clients perceive their sentence. Although our methodology differs somewhat from theirs, their exploration of prison inmates served as the basis for the current exploratory study of probationers. In this way, we were able to investigate several dimensions of how probationers make sense of their sentence. Do probationers consider their probation to be a deterrent? Do they experience it as punitive? Do they believe they deserve to be on probation? Do they believe the sentence to be a rehabilitating experience? Do they take probation seriously or something only to be endured? That is, do they think there is no point to them being on probation? Do probationers see it merely as a game where they must attempt to manipulate their probation officer into seeing them in a positive light?

We also explore possible correlates. The literature on offenders' perceptions of the relative severity of sentences has shown fairly consistently that Blacks and males are less favorable toward community-based sanctions than their demographic opposites (Crouch, 1993; May et al., 2005; Spelman, 1995; Wood & Grasmick, 1999; Wood & May, 2003). Prior experience with a particular sanction may also alter perceptions (Apospori & Alpert, 1993; McClelland &Alpert, 1985; Van Voorhis et al., 1997; Wood & Grasmick, 1999). We assess whether these variables predict how probationers understand the meaning of their probation sentence.

▧ Methodology

Sampling and Data Collection

We collected the data for this study between May and September 2006 through self-report surveys distributed to misdemeanor probationers in a large metropolitan area of the Southeastern United States.

Participants were invited to complete the survey as they waited to meet with their probation officer at the county probation office. This department serves all community corrections offenders in the county, and all face-to-face meetings with probation officers are conducted at this single location. The research reported here reflects a sample of 369 probationers who responded to the survey. Some of the analyses reported below, however, are based on fewer cases because of missing data on individual items.

In an effort to encourage candid responses, we informed each respondent that their answers would be kept completely confidential and would not be shared with their supervising officers. We also made a concerted effort to have the research team appear independent from the probation department. In this regard, researchers refrained from interacting with the staff as much as possible during data collection visits, and each researcher wore a prominent name badge emblazoned with a university logo. The questionnaire itself also clearly identified the study as being conducted by the University of Central Florida and emphasized confidentiality.

For several reasons, we were unable to randomly select respondents from the department's client rolls. Instead, we attempted to obtain a sample that was as representative as possible in two ways. First, we invited each and every person who arrived at the probation department during each data collection visit to participate, and only rarely did a probationer decline. Second, the days and times of data collection were varied. Still, by collecting data from individuals who were at the probation office for a contact visit with their officers, we excluded those on the lowest levels of supervision. That is, probationers who were supervised only through telephone contacts with their officers were not included in the study. According to the probation department, 24% of the active probation cases were on telephone supervision.[2] In addition, only an English version of the questionnaire was available to participants; therefore, those who could not read English were also excluded. The probation department reported that 6% of their clients were non-English speaking.

We were successful in recruiting a group of respondents who were diverse in terms of gender, race,

age, type of offense, and prior experience with probation. The majority of our respondents were serving a sentence with a modest level of supervision—one contact with their officer per month. Notably, the sample is very similar to the population of clients who were serving a probation sentence at the time of data collection. Of the 4,184 probationers being supervised, 80% were male, 23% were Black, and 46% were on probation for a DUI (driving under the influence) offense.[3] Moreover, the mean age of all probationers was 31.6 years—only a 1-year difference from the mean age of the respondents included in this study.

Operationalization

Although others have investigated what the public and various specialized groups believe should be the main goal of corrections (e.g., Applegate, Cullen, & Fisher, 1997; Cullen, Latessa, Burton, & Lombardo, 1993; Harris, 1968), as noted above, our intention was not to assess probationers' prescriptive beliefs. Rather, we sought to assess each probationer's individual understanding of what their probation experience meant to them. In short, we assessed what goals each probationer thought probation was serving, not what goals he or she believed it should strive toward. Within the context of a larger survey, each respondent was presented with 12 items operationalizing what purpose was being served by being on probation. These questions were adapted for the probation context from Van Voorhis et al.'s (1997) study of prison inmates. Two items each measured four traditional correctional orientations: rehabilitation, specific deterrence, incapacitation, and retribution. We also included two items to assess whether the respondent believed that being on probation simply meant trying to manipulate a probation officer or manage his or her impression. Two items also measured whether the respondent felt that there was no purpose to being on probation. For each item, probationers responded on a 4-point Likert scale, ranging from strongly agree to strongly disagree.

We also explored the possibility that probationers' perceptions were related to the characteristics listed previously. Data on race, supervision intensity, and previous experience with being on probation were gathered on the self-report questionnaire. Initially, race and Hispanic ethnicity were measured separately. The survey responses revealed, however, that the probationers did not make this distinction. They consistently marked "Other" for race and indicated in the subsequent question that they were of Hispanic origin. To be consistent with the probationers' conceptions of themselves, we combined our race and ethnicity variables into a single measure. Anyone who indicated that they were Hispanic was coded as such regardless of their answer to the first question, and anyone who did not mark White or Black on the first question and also did not mark Hispanic on the second question was coded as other.

Data on the remaining two independent variables were gathered from probation files. For 291 of the respondents, we were able to match their survey responses with probation department records on gender and current offense. The remaining files could not be matched because of missing or incomplete identification information.[4]

Results

The Meaning of Probation

The respondents thought that their sentence was serving a variety of purposes, but the largest portion of respondents believed that their sentence was a deterrent. More than 90% of the probationers agreed or strongly agreed that they had given up any future crime to avoid probation again. More than three quarters also agreed that being on probation increased the risk of being punished. Although scholars typically think of punishment and rehabilitation as being opposing goals, a large majority of the respondents thought that their sentence was not only a deterrent but was also rehabilitative. Upwards of 60% believed that probation fostered personal growth and provided assistance with problems. Many respondents also understood probation to be serving a retributive purpose. More than half of the probationers said that they felt their sentence was helping them repay society for their crime: just less than half thought that they deserved to be on probation.

Somewhat in contrast to these views, however, are the results for the items assessing whether the probationers felt there was no purpose in probation. A slight majority agreed or strongly agreed that there was "no point" in being on probation, whereas only 8% strongly disagreed with this statement. Furthermore, almost 44% indicated that they thought their probation experience was not doing "any good" for them personally or for society. The probationers did tend to believe that they needed to foster a positive impression while on probation. More than 8 in 10 agreed that they try to engage in activities that will make their supervising officer see them as productive. More than three fifths of the probationers revealed their belief that what their probation officer thinks of them matters. The results for the two items ostensibly measuring the remaining traditional correctional goal—incapacitation—are not consistent with each other. Although almost 80% indicated that they thought their supervision was not making society any safer, an almost equal portion reported that committing a crime while on probation would be difficult. Thus, the probationers acknowledged feeling the effects of incapacitation, yet claimed that being incapacitated did not prevent any real harm. We explore the implications of these beliefs later in the discussion section.

It appears that many probationers believed that their sentence served multiple purposes. To investigate these results further, we examined the interrelationships among these perceptions. Specific goals, particularly rehabilitation and retribution, predominate in the first factor. The highest loadings are revealed for the items measuring perceptions that probation is assistive and is allowing the probationer to pay society back. Substantial loadings are also shown for the first incapacitation item and the first deterrence item. On the second factor, the two highest loadings are for the items measuring perceptions that probation has no purpose Beliefs that committing a crime while on probation would be easy and that a probation officer's opinions do not matter also contribute meaningfully to this factor. To explore possible correlates of probationers' perceptions, we regressed each factor score on race, gender, age, employment status, the type of offense for which the respondent was on probation, supervision intensity, and prior experience with being on probation. Neither regression model was statistically significant.[5]

⬚ Discussion

At the outset of this article, we pointed out that very little is known about probation from the probationers' viewpoint. Prior research shows that probationers believe that probation is relatively less punitive than most other forms of criminal punishment, but studies assessing other dimensions of probationers' perceptions of their sentence are nearly nonexistent. We also raised the argument that probationers' views are a relevant topic for investigation. We did not contend that probationers should be asked what the purpose of their sentence should be. Indeed, it is highly improbable that many probationers would indicate a preference for severe punishment that would dissuade them from committing any more crimes. Instead, we argued that the traditional philosophies of corrections make implicit assumptions about how probation is experienced, thus, calling for understanding what probation means to probationers. In this regard, the findings reported above enhance our knowledge about the nature of probation as well as point out some issues ripe for future investigation.

Before discussing the results of this study, we wish to acknowledge its limitations. Care should be exercised in generalizing the findings of the study. As we noted above, we were unable to randomly select the sample of participants. Although our efforts to include a wide variety of participants appear to have been successful, and the sample mirrors the population of probationers within the jurisdiction we studied on several dimensions, sampling bias may exist. In particular, we did not include probationers on the lowest level of supervision (telephone contacts only), those who could not read English were excluded, and probationers who had absconded during the data collection period, by definition, were unavailable and could not be included in the study. Also, the sample was drawn from only a single jurisdiction that supervised exclusively misdemeanor probationers. Misdemeanants make up only about half of all people on probation nationwide (Glaze & Bonezar, 2007). Felony probationers may hold different views. Furthermore, the organizational context of community corrections departments can influence how officers perform their jobs, thereby affecting their clients' experiences (McCleary, 1992). The extent to which our results are unique to the agency studied here or can be generalized to other probation departments should be assessed by replicating the current project in other jurisdictions.

With these caveats in mind, this study produced some important insights. As we noted early in this article, traditional correctional goals make implicit, and sometimes explicit, assumptions "about what may or may not be going on in the minds of offenders" (Van Voorhis et al., 1997, p. 164). The current study provides evidence on the extent to which these assumptions are consistent with the way probationers view their sentence. Deterrence theorists propose that exposure to a criminal sanction will increase an offender's perception of the risks of future criminality and the unpleasantness of the consequences that follow.

An important underlying question, then, is whether offenders perceive probation as a punitive experience. Our results demonstrate that an overwhelming majority of probationers see an increased risk of punishment for any future crime, and they assert that the threat of probation will keep them crime free. Whereas the deterrent effectiveness of punishment is questionable (Pratt et al., 2006) and is beyond the scope of the current study, learning that offenders perceive probation as punitive is an important finding. It raises a challenge for those who believe that probation is a nonpunishment. Although probation may lack legitimacy as a punishment with scholars, policy makers, and the public (Roberts & Stalans, 1997), probationers see it differently. Spelman's (1995) interview results suggest that probation may be viewed as unpleasant because of the inconvenience it imposes. As one offender put it, compared to probation, jail is "easier on your work and lifestyle" (p. 124). Future studies could investigate perceptions of the particular components of probation further, but the broader point is that probation is felt as a punitive experience. Thus, probation has a place in any deterrence-based correctional policy.

Our findings also hold implications for other correctional goals. Retribution seeks to deliver a level of punishment that is deserved based on an offender's infraction. Although broader society typically determines what is deserved, an offender's perception may also be relevant. Punishments that are not felt as legitimate may be disintegrative (Braithwaite, 1989) and may lead to resentment and retaliation (Spiegler & Guevremont, 2003). Our results show that probationers as a whole are somewhat ambivalent on this issue. Approximately half of our sample believed that they were paying society back for their crime by being on probation and half thought that they deserved a probation sentence. The remaining probationers disagreed or strongly disagreed with these orientations. Thus, a substantial portion of probationers do not see their sentence as legitimate. Far more of them, however, embraced views consistent with rehabilitation: 6 in 10 thought that their experience was helping them grow, and more than 70% said that probation was helping them solve problems related to their criminality. Probation programs can build on these perceptions by providing programming that addresses criminogenic needs (Andrews & Bonta, 2003) and by fostering an assistive relationship between probation officers and their clients. Although community correction has shifted toward punishment functions during the past decade and more (Clear, 1995), rehabilitation remains an important goal of probation among legislators (Steiner et al., 2005). Probationers seem to embrace it as well.

A curious finding was the discrepancy in reactions to the two items intended to measure feelings of incapacitation. The small minority of respondents who said that society was safer because they were on probation contrasted sharply with the large majority who indicated it would be difficult for them to commit a crime while on probation. These items also loaded on different factors in the principal components analysis. Apparently, the respondents did not equate being personally prevented from breaking the law with a protective effect for the broader public. The divergent results for these incapacitation items suggest that the respondents felt that their offenses posed no risk to society; being incapacitated, they believed, did not gain any real protection for possible victims. In short, these probationers felt that they were not "real criminals" worthy of fear or distrust. These perceptions deserve further investigation, but on their face, the practical implication is clear. Probationers would benefit from restorative justice efforts that would increase their understanding of how their criminal activities affect victims.

Probation may be suffering from the situation of traditional criminal justice described by Umbreit, Coates, and Vos (2001): "The state has somehow stood in for the victim, and the offender has seldom noticed how his or her actions have affected real, live people" (p. 30). To the extent that this is true, victim-offender mediation—where victims and offenders are brought face-to-face to discuss the offense, its impact, and possible ways of repairing the harm—would be a useful component of probation. Assessments reveal that, among other outcomes, participation in victim-offender mediation helps offenders see the consequences of their crimes. Umbreit and Coates (1992) provide direct illustrations of how offenders' perceptions were changed by their experience with mediation. As one offender noted, "After meeting the victim, I now realize that I hurt them a lot . . . to understand how the victim feels makes me different" (p. 16).

Although these approaches show promise for addressing the views of probationers who have committed property and personal offenses, probationers convicted of victimless crimes made up a substantial portion of our sample. Those whose primary charge was DUI or a drug offense constituted more than half of our respondents. A different approach within the restorative justice paradigm may help these offenders recognize the harm that their crimes cause as well. Karp and Drakulich (2004) evaluated Vermont's "Reparative Probation" program, which they report works mostly with victimless crimes and with cases where the victim declines to participate in restorative justice efforts. Under this model, victims are welcome to participate, but even when they do not. "a board composed of trained volunteers convenes with the offender to discuss the impact of the offense and find a restorative resolution" (Karp & Drakulich, 2004, p. 659). One of the central goals of this board is to help the offender see the harmful consequences of his or her action, even when there is no clear individual victim. The authors did not assess whether the program changed offenders' views, but they did find that more than three fourths of victimless cases included a specific component (such as attending a victim impact panel, writing an essay, or delivering a public presentation) aimed at this goal. Our results suggest that probationers may need such efforts to address beliefs that their offenses do not pose a risk to community safety.

Beyond implications for individual correctional goals, it is also notable that the probationers in our sample tended to experience aspects of several goals, seemingly simultaneously. This result can be contrasted against the arguments of scholars that typically pit one goal against others or argue that the goals are incompatible. Some authors have begun to suggest that treatment and punishment may profitably coexist (e.g., Andrews & Bonta, 2003). Pursuing multiple goals discomfits retributivists who vehemently reject the utilitarianism underlying other traditional goals of corrections (e.g., American Friends Service Committee, 1971; von Hirsch, 1976). Other critics include those who embrace treatment and see no need to pursue policies of harsh punishment (e.g., Gendreau, Paparazzi, Little, & Goddard, 1993) and writers who support incapacitation and eschew treatment efforts (e.g., Wilson, 1975).

Apparently, probationers have no such concerns in terms of how they actually experience their sentence. Not only did large segments of the sample agree with multiple goals, but the responses to these goals also tended to be related. Those who expressed a belief that their sentence was rehabilitative also tended to feel that it was a deterrent, and it was incapacitative and deserved. These results are not completely unexpected. Allen's (1985) federal probationers also asserted multiple goals as "the main purpose of probation," and Van Voorhis et al.'s (1997) inmate respondents expressed a belief that their sentence met several ends.

A final aspect of our findings merits additional consideration. Among the correlates we investigated, none were related to the probationers' views of their sentence. Thus, men, women, Blacks, Whites, Hispanics, and probationers of other races all experienced their sentence similarly. This result is in contrast to other research showing differences in the perceived severity of various punishments, particularly a preference for prison over probation (Crouch, 1993; May et al., 2005; Spelman, 1995; Wood & Grasmick, 1999; Wood & May, 2003). We also found that probationers' views were not structured along lines of age, employment status, prior experience with probation, supervision intensity, or the type of offense for which the client had been placed on probation. In short, we were unable to distinguish any subgroups who perceived probation in a certain way. Future research should investigate other possible correlates.

⊠ Conclusion

When asked what corrections should be, it is not uncommon to find that professionals and the public alike endorse multiple goals (see, e.g., Applegate, Davis, Otto, Surene, & McCarthy, 2003; Kifer, Hemmens, & Slohr, 2003; McCorkle, 1993). When unencumbered by considerations of how pursuing different goals might lead to conflicting practices, people want offenders to be deterred and rehabilitated, to be punished only to the extent they deserve but also to be isolated to protect the public from their future offenses. Humans seek meaning within the complexity of the criminal act, so there is no reason that similar reasoning would be suspended in terms of punishment philosophy. Judging from what probationers report feeling because of their sentence, probation more or less is meeting all the philosophical goals. It appears that for many offenders probation is experienced as unpleasant—more than a "nonpunishment"—it feels restrictive and deserved, and probationers believe it is doing them some good.

◙ Notes

1. Although Allen identified this item as "deterrence." it does not imply that the person is dissuaded from committing further criminal acts because of any unpleasantness of the probation experience. Rather, this item seems to tap perceptions that being on probation serves an incapacitative function.

2. Nearly one third of the probationers on telephone-only supervision, however, hold this supervision level because they live outside the local area. Thus, their supervision status was not based on low risk levels, and apart from their location, it is unlikely that they differ substantially from those probationers who were included in our sampling strategy.

3. Data on other offense classifications were not available from the probation department for the full population.

4. These items were excluded from the questionnaire for two reasons. First, an examination of probation records prior to data collection suggested that they were accurately and reliably recorded in those files. Second, under the direction of our institutional review board, we sought to eliminate unnecessary questions from the survey to minimize the burden placed on respondents. As one reviewer noted, researchers collecting the surveys could have recorded "their best guess" as to each respondent's gender. We did not adopt this practice, however, so gender information is unavailable only for respondents whose surveys could be matched with their probation records.

5. See online appendix for table displaying these results.

◙ References

Allen, F. A. (1981). *The decline of the rehabilitative ideal: Penal policy and social purpose.* New Haven, CT: Yale University Press.

Allen, G. F. (1985). The probationers speak: Analysis of the probationers' experiences and attitudes. *Federal Probation, 49*(September), 67–75.

American Friends Service Committee. (1971). *Struggle for justice: A report on crime and punishment in America.* New York: Hill & Wang.

Andrews, D. A., & Bonta, J. (2003). T*he psychology of criminal conduct.* Cincinnati, OH: Lexis/Nexis-Anderson.

Apospori, E., & Alpert, G. (1993). The role of differential experience with the criminal justice system in the changes in perceptions of severity of legal sanctions over time. *Crime & Delinquency, 39,* 184–194.

Applegate, B. K., Cullen, F. T., & Fisher, B. S. (1997). Public support for correctional treatment: The continuing appeal of the rehabilitative ideal. *Prison Journal, 77,* 237–258.

Applegate, B. K., Davis, R. K., Otto, C. W., Surette, R., & McCarthy, B. J. (2003). The multifunction jail: Policymakers' views on the goals of local incarceration. *Criminal Justice Policy Review, 14,* 155–170.

Beccaria, C. (1963). *On crimes and punishments* (H. Paolucci, Trans.). New York: Bobbs-Merrill. (Original work published 1764)

Bentham, J. (2007). *An introduction to the principles of morals and legislation.* Mineola, NY: Dover. (Original work published 1789)

Braithwaite, J. (1989). *Crime, shame and reintegration.* New York: Cambridge University Press.

Clear, T. R. (1995). *Harm in American penology: Offenders, victims, and their communities.* Albany, NY: State University of New York Press.

Crouch, B. M. (1993). Is incarceration really worse? Analysis of offenders' preferences for prison over probation. *Justice Quarterly, 10,* 67–88.

Cullen, F. T., Fisher, B. S., & Applegate, B. K. (2000). Public opinion about punishment and corrections. In M. Tonry (Ed.). *Crime and justice: A review of research* (pp. 1–79). Chicago: University of Chicago Press.

Cullen, F. T., & Gendreau, P. (2000). Assessing correctional rehabilitation: Policy, practice, and prospects. In J. Homey (Ed.), *Criminal justice 2000: Vol. 3. Policies, processes, and decisions of the criminal justice system.* Washington, DC: National Institute of Justice.

Cullen, F. T., & Gilbert, K. E. (1982). *Reaffirming rehabilitation.* Cincinnati, OH: Anderson.

Cullen, F. T., Latessa, F. J., Burton, V. S., Jr., & Lombardo, L. X. (1993). The correctional orientation of prison wardens: Is the rehabilitative ideal supported? *Criminology, 31,* 69–92.

Feeley, M. M., & Simon, J. (1992). The new penology: Notes on the emerging strategy of corrections and its implications. *Criminology, 30,* 449–474.

Gendreau, P., Paparazzi, M., Little, T., & Goddard, M. (1993). Does "punishing smarter" work? An assessment of the new generation of alternative sanctions in probation. *Forum on Corrections Research, 8,* 31–34.

Glaze, L. E., & Bonczar, T. P. (2007). *Probation and parole in the United States, 2006.* Washington. DC: U.S. Bureau of Justice Statistics.

Harris, L. (1968). Changing public attitudes toward crime and corrections. *Federal Probation, 32*(4), 9–16.

Horvath, A. O., & Luborsky, L. (1993). The role of the therapeutic alliance in psychotherapy. *Journal of Consulting and Clinical Psychology, 61,* 561–573.

Karp, D. R., & Drakulich, K. M. (2004). Minor crime in a quaint setting: Practices, outcomes, and limits of Vermont reparative probation boards. *Criminology & Public Policy, 3,* 655–686.

Kifer, M., Hemmens, C., & Stohr, M. K. (2003). The goals of corrections: Perspectives from the line. *Criminal Justice Review, 28,* 47–69.

MacKenzie, D. L. (2006). *What works in corrections: Reducing the criminal activities of offenders and delinquents*. New York: Cambridge University Press.

Martin, D. J., Garske, J. P., & Davis, M. K. (2000). Relation of the therapeutic alliance with outcome and other variables: A meta-analytic review. *Journal of Consulting and Clinical Psychology, 68*, 438–450.

May, D. C., & Wood, P. B. (2005). What influences offenders' willingness to serve alternative sanctions. *Prison Journal, 85*, 145–167.

May, D. C., Wood, P. B., Mooney, J. L., & Minor, K. I. (2005). Predicting offenders generated exchange rates: Implications for a theory of sentence severity. *Crime & Delinquency, 51*, 373–399.

McCleary, R. (1992). *Dangerous men: The sociology of parole*. Albany, NY: Harrow and Heston.

McClelland, K. A., & Alpert, G. P. (1985). Factor analysis applied to magnitude estimates of punishment seriousness: Patterns of individual differences. *Journal of Quantitative Criminology, 1*, 307–318.

McCorkle, R. C. (1993). Research note: Punish and rehabilitate? Public attitudes toward six common crimes. *Crime & Delinquency, 39*, 240–252.

Morris, N., & Tonry, M. (1991). *Between prison and probation: Intermediate punishments in a rational sentencing system*. New York: Oxford University Press.

Paternoster, R. (1987). The deterrent effect of the perceived certainty and severity of punishment: A review of the evidence and issues. *Justice Quarterly, 4*, 173–217.

Petersilia, J. (1990). When probation becomes more dreaded than prison. *Federal Probation, 54*(1), 23–27.

Petersilia, J., & Deschenes, E. P. (1994). Perceptions of punishment: Inmates and staff rank the severity of prison versus intermediate sanctions. *Prison Journal, 74*, 306–332.

Pratt, T., Cullen, F. T., Blevins, K., Daigle, L., & Madensen, T. (2006). The empirical status of deterrence theory: A meta-analysis. In F. T. Cullen, J. P. Wright, & K. R. Blevins (Eds.). *Taking stock: The status of criminological theory*. New Brunswick, NJ: Transaction.

Roberts, J. V., & Stalans, L. J. (1997). *Public opinion, crime, and criminal justice*. Boulder. CO: Westview Press.

Sitren, A. H., & Applegate, B. K. (2006). Intentions to offend: Examining the effects of personal and vicarious experiences with punishment and punishment avoidance. *Journal of Crime and Justice, 29*, 25–51.

Spelman, W. (1995). The severity of intermediate sanctions. *Journal of Research in Crime and Delinquency, 32*, 107–135.

Spiegler, M. D., & Guevremont, D. C. (2003). *Contemporary behavior therapy*. Belmont. CA: Wadsworth.

Steiner, B., Wada, J., Hemmens, C., & Burton, V. S., Jr. (2005). The correctional orientation of community corrections: Legislative changes in the legally prescribed functions of community corrections 1992-2002. *American Journal of Criminal Justice, 29*, 141–159.

Umbreit, M. S., & Coates, R. B. (1992). *Victim offender mediation: An analysis of programs in four states of the U.S.* Minneapolis, MN: Center for Restorative Justice and Peacemaking.

Umbreit, M. S., Coates, R. B., & Vos, B. (2001). The impact of victim-offender mediation: Two decades of research. *Federal Probation, 65*(December), 29–35.

Van Voorhis, P., Browning, S. L., Simon, M., & Gordon, J. (1997). The meaning of punishment: Inmates' orientation to the prison experience. *Prison Journal, 77*, 135–167.

von Hirsch, A. (1976). *Doing justice: The dance of punishments*. Boston: Northeastern University Press.

Warner, R. M. (2008). *Applied statistics*. Thousand Oaks, CA: Sage.

Wilson, J. Q. (1975). *Thinking about crime*. New York: Basic Books.

Wood, P. B., & Grasmick, H. G. (1999). Toward the development of punishment equivalencies: Male and female inmates rate the severity of alternative sanctions compared to prison. *Justice Quarterly, 16*, 19–50.

Wood, P. B., & May, D. C. (2003). Racial differences in perceptions of the severity of sanctions: A comparison of prison with alternatives. *Justice Quarterly, 20*, 605–631.

Zimring, F. E., & Hawkins, G. (1995). *Incapacitation: Penal confinement and the restraint of crime*. New York: Oxford University Press.

DISCUSSION QUESTIONS

1. Discuss the overall findings of the study. Why is it important to understand probationer perspectives of a sanction?

2. According to the authors, "respondents did not equate being personally prevented from breaking the law with a protective effect for the broader public" (p. 90). What are the potential implications of this finding for both punishment and supervision?

3. According to the findings of this study, the majority of respondents were sentenced to probation for victimless crimes. Based upon this finding, how might probation officers approach punishment?

4. One observation made by the authors is that probationers appeared to experience the goals of punishment (rehabilitation, retribution, incapacitation, and deterrence) simultaneously. If probation officers adopt this finding and implement it into practice, how might this finding alter probation supervision and still meet the goals set forth by the public?

READING

The issue of stress in a criminal justice setting has been a long explored and well-researched topic. Wells, Colbert, and Slate filled a void in the literature by exploring whether differences exist between male and female probation officers in internal, external, job-related, personal, or physical stressors. Using a sample of 626 state probation officers in a southern state, the authors examined the degree to which male and female officers experienced stress and determined whether gender is a significant predictor of stress. Previous studies assessing the link between job performance and stress suggest that when stress levels increase so does absenteeism, turnover, loss of productivity in the workplace, and diminished health of employees. Results from the present study revealed a less than clear relationship between stress and gender. Female officers appeared to exhibit greater amounts of physical stress than their male counterparts; male officers reported higher levels of stress in all other categories. One interesting finding to note is that male officers were more likely to be in management level positions. When controlling for position, the significant differences between the groups disappeared. These findings suggest a need for continued study into the differences between male and female stressors and work place satisfaction.

Gender Matters

Differences in State Probation Officer Stress

Terry Wells, Sharla Colbert, and Risdon N. Slate

The effect of stress on organizations and the people who work in them can be costly in both economic and human terms. The long-reaching effects of stress cannot be underestimated, as it affects not only employees but also managers, executives, significant others, and families. The linkage of stress to lost productivity in the workplace, employee absenteeism and turnover, and the diminished health of employees is well documented (see Brandt & Nielsen, 1992; Cooper & Watson, 1991; DeCario & Gruenfeld, 1989; Dillon, 1999; "Does Stress Kill?" 1995; Elkin & Rosch, 1990; Falk, Hanson, Isacsson, & Ostergren, 1992; Homer, Sherman, & Siegel, 1990; Ivancevich, Matteson, & Richards, 1985; Johnson, Hall, & Theorell, 1989; Johnson & Johansson, 1991; Karasek & Theorell,

SOURCE: Terry Wells, Sharla Colbert, & Risdon N. Slate (2006). Gender matters: Differences in state probation officer stress. *Journal of Contemporary Criminal Justice, 22*(1), 63–79. Copyright © 2006 Sage Publications.

1990; Muntaner, Tien, Eaton, & Garrison, 1991; Palmer, 1989; Schnall, 1990; Schnall et al., 1990).

Although occupations within the criminal justice system are typically considered among the most stressed work environments, the primary research focus has been on stress levels of police and prison personnel (Patterson, 1992; Simmons, Cochran, & Blount, 1997; State, Johnson, & Wells, 2000; State & Vogel, 1997; Whisler, 1994). Probation officers, in the face of burgeoning caseloads, have responsibility for more offenders than most other criminal justice practitioners, yet few studies have examined the effects of current working environments on these responsibility-laden and often overloaded probation officers.

As noted by Cullen, Link, Wolfe, and Frank (1985), criminal justice organizations often are characterized by a male-dominated working environment. Such environments can serve as the breeding grounds for the manifestation and promulgation of gender and sexual harassment (Dantzker & Kubin, 1998; Stohr, Lovrich, & Mays, 1997) and can negatively affect employee stress (Morash & Haarr, 1995). Gender differences in terms of stress levels have been identified among employees in the criminal justice research literature. In this article, we sought to examine the relevant literature and apply it to the findings to enhance interpretation and understanding of significant differences between male and female probation officers.

⊠ A Review of the Relevant Literature

Stressors (those things that cause stress) of criminal justice practitioners can, for the most part, be characterized as intrinsic to the organization, job or task related, extrinsic to the agency, or personal in nature. Spielberger, Wesiberry, Grier, and Greenfield (1981) developed a stress survey that captures these four categories of stressors for police officers, and this survey has been used in studies of police stress (Thomas-Riddle, 1999; Violanti & Aron, 1994). Whisler (1994) modified the Spielberger et al. (1981) police survey to make the questions applicable to probation officers.

Internal Organizational Stressors

Administrative or organizational practices and the bureaucratic nature of agencies within the criminal justice system are frequently cited as contributors to employee stress (Abdollahi, 2002; Storch & Panzarella, 1996; Violanti & Aron, 1994; Winter, 1993; Zhao, He, & Lovrich, 2002). Characteristics of the organization have been found to be the major source of stress in policing (Abdollahi, 2002), corrections (Cheek, 1984; Slate & Vogel, 1997; Whitehead & Lindquist, 1986), and probation (Finn & Kuck, 2003). Frustration with the promotional or reward system has been determined to be a cause of stress for both police officers (Toch, 2002) and correctional personnel (Finn, 2000). Insufficient salaries and lack of promotional opportunities have been recognized as stressors for probation officers (Simmons et al., 1997; Whisler, 1994; Whitehead, 1986), as have relationships with supervisors (Simmons et al., 1997), role ambiguity (Brown, 1987; Whitehead, 1985, 1986), and the feeling that there is insufficient time to meet the demands of the job (Thomas, 1988).

Participation in Workplace Decision Making

Participation in workplace decision making was often specified as a potential internal organizational stressor in paramilitaristic criminal justice organizations. In particular, lack of participation in workplace decision making has been identified as a significant source of stress in policing (Abdollahi, 2002; Archambeault & Weirman, 1983; Kuykendall & Unsinger, 1982; Lawrence, 1984; Melancon, 1984; Morash & Haarr, 1995; Patterson, 1992; Reiser, 1974; Rodichok, 1995; Stinchcomb, 2004; Terry, 1983), corrections (Farkat, 2001; Honnold & Stinchcomb, 1983; Lasky, Gordon, & Strebalus, 1986; Lindquist & Whitehead, 1986; Patterson, 1992; Sims, 2001; Slate & Vogel, 1997; Slate, Vogel, & Johnson, 2001; Ulmer, 1992), and probation (Brown, 1986, 1987; Finn & Kuck, 2003; Holgate & Clegg, 1991; Simmons et al., 1997; Slate et al., 2000; Tabor, 1987; Whisler, 1994; Whitehead, 1981, 1986; Whitehead & Lindquist, 1985).

Job or Task Stressors

Some stressors were inherent to the job or task performed by criminal justice practitioners. Consistently referred to in the literature was the potential dangerousness of offenders and the inherent stress associated with practitioners' interactions with this element in policing (Abdollahi, 2002; Anshel, 2000; Zhao et al., 2002), corrections (Finn, 2000; Slate, 1993; Slate & Vogel, 1997), and probation (Finn & Kuck, 2005; Thomas, 1988). Excessive paperwork was often cited as an on-the-job stressor for criminal justice practitioners (Abdollahi, 2002; Brown, 1987; Finn, 2000; Finn & Kuck, 2005; Simmons et al., 1997; Thomas, 1988; Whisler, 1994). Coupled with being inundated with paperwork, probation officers were frequently faced with tight suspense dates on reports and with extremely high caseloads, which all translated into a lack of time to get the job done (Finn & Kuck, 2003, 2005; Simmons et al., 1997).

External Stressors

A too lenient judiciary has been cited as a source of stress external to the organization for both police and probation officers (Abdollahi, 2002; Finn & Kuck, 2003; Whisler, 1994). Lack of appreciation by the public and the media has been noted as a stressor for some police officers (Abdollahi, 2002), and Finn (2000) has indicated that a poor public image and low pay have been reported as primary sources of external stress for correctional personnel. Similarly, nationally publicized failures resulting in death of minors by sex offenders on probation has increasingly brought public scrutiny on probation officers and resulted in stringent legislation, with limited resources, restricting options of probation officers supervising these types of offenders (see Carlie's Law, 2005; Jessica Marie Lunsford Foundation, 2005).

Personal Stressors

Storch and Panzarella (1996) found police officers' relationships with nonpolice to be problematic, and Anshel (2000) reported that police experience a general lack of social support. Anderson (1994) noted that familial and social support were strongly correlated with physical health and occupational stress, and Wellbrock (2000) maintained that female police officers are more likely than male police officers to seek support from family and/or friends after stressful events. Toch (2002) stated that the families of police officers could serve as a bastion of support or could prove to be a burden. Abdollahi (2002) noted that familial support was often lacking for police officers, and Cullen et al. (1985) found lack of family support to be a significant source of stress for correctional officers. Furthermore, probation officers who were married had been found to be more satisfied with their jobs and less occupationally stressed than their unmarried counterparts (Simmons et al., 1997; Tabor, 1987).

✖ Physical Symptoms of Stress

According to the National Institute for Occupational Safely and Health (1995), more than 75% of the trips to primary care physicians involved stressed employees. Both physical and psychological symptoms of stress have been associated with police officers and include cardiac disorders, cancer, shortened lifespan, diabetes, chronic fatigue, backaches, alcoholism, suicide, and depression (Abdollahi, 2002; Mearns & Mauch, 1998; Stinchcomb, 2004). Likewise, when compared to the general population, correctional officers have been found to have significantly lower life spans and higher rates of alcoholism, suicide, heart attacks, ulcers, and hypertension (Check, 1984). The linkage between stress and chronic health problems has also been reported in the literature on probation officer stress (Brown. 1987).

It is estimated that more than half of all absences in the workplace are stress-related (Elkin & Rosch, 1990), amounting to more than 1 million stress-induced employee absences a day in the workplace (Dillon, 1999). Up to 85% of workplace accidents are stress related ("Stress: The Workplace Disease of the 1990s," 1995). Stress can serve to escalate costs to policing, corrections, and probation organizations in terms of sick days taken (Finn, 2000; Finn & Kuck, 2005; Toch, 2002; Torres, Maggard, & To, 2003), resulting in lack of staff to cover those absent and long-term insurance concerns for the agency. Employee turnover has also been linked to stress in policing (Snipes, 2005), corrections (Finn, 2000; Slate & Vogel, 1997), and probation (Simmons et al., 1997).

Gender Differences and Stress

There is a substantial amount of literature linking work-related stress to the physical health of men and women. Morash and Haarr's (1995) study of police officers found that women experienced the same stressors as men, yet women often face a stress-inducing situation that Hochschild (1989) referred to as the "Second Shift." This occurs when women are forced into a double duty of juggling family and work, working by day outside of the home and working by night performing household and childcare responsibilities. Hendrix, Spencer, and Gibson (1994) and DeCarlo (1987) noted that women are more likely than men to be given household and childcare duties in the home. Hochschild (1989) stated that "women worked roughly fifteen hours longer each week than men," which means that, compared with their male counterparts, each year women "worked an extra month of twenty-four-hour days" (p. 3).

These family-based outside stress factors can result in a higher level of absenteeism among women than men. Tripplett, Mullings, and Scarborough (1999) studied the relationship between work-related and home-related stress and found that the level of stress at work was higher when the level of work-home conflict was greater. Jick and Mitz (1985) performed an extensive review of the literature for sex differences and stress in the workforce and found that women generally report higher levels of psychological distress than men; yet men were more prone to physical illness. Further, Nelson and Quick (1985) found that employed women experienced greater stress than both nonemployed men and women because of particular stressors faced by employed women. Supporting this finding, Miller et al. (2000) found that men and women within the same level of occupation experience the same stressors but different levels of distress.

Gender Differences, Stress, and the Criminal Justice System

As women increasingly have entered into the traditionally male domain of law enforcement and corrections, there has been a corresponding increase in the study of gender differences among police and correctional officers (Armstrong & Griffin, 2004; Britten, 1997; Cullen et al., 1985; Griffin, Armstrong, & Hepburn, in press; Griffin & Hepburn, 2005; Morash & Haarr, 1995; Slate, 1993; Stohr et al., 1997; Walters, 1992; Wright & Saylor, 1991; Zupan, 1986). Early studies showed that women correctional officers reported greater job stress than men (Cullen et al., 1985; Voorhis, Cullen, Link, & Wolfe, 1991; Wright & Saylor, 1991; Zupan, 1986), yet others found no differences in job stress by gender (Armstrong & Griffin, 2004; Walters, 1992).

The effect of gender on other job-related factors also has been studied. Job satisfaction does not appear to vary by gender (Crouch, 1985; Cullen et al., 1985; Griffin, 2001; Jurik & Halemba, 1984; Walters, 1992), but there is some evidence that professional orientation does differ between men and women. Contrary to the traditional role expectation that females are more sensitive and intuitive than men, Zupan (1986) found no significant differences by gender in perceptions of inmate needs; however, many researchers (e.g., Crouch, 1985; Crouch & Alpert, 1982; Jurik, 1985; Jurik & Halemba, 1984; Kissel & Katsampes, 1980; Zimmer, 1986; Zupan, 1986) have found female correctional officers to be more supportive than male officers of a human service or rehabilitative approach to corrections. Danger in the workplace, which is a significant source of job stress (Spielberger et al., 1981; Violanti & Aron, 1994; Whisler, 1994), has been found to be a significant predictor of job stress for both men and women (Armstrong & Griffin, 2004). Although the risk levels of job assignments have been found to vary by gender, with women more likely than men to be assigned to less dangerous work assignments (Patterson, 1989; Slate & Vogel, 1997), the threat of victimization is an ever-present stressor for both men and women employed in criminal justice agencies.

Probation Officers

There were approximately 84,000 probation officers in the United States in 2002, and this number is projected to reach 97,000 by the year 2012 (Bureau of Labor Statistics, 2004). Yet there has been comparatively little research on this segment of criminal justice professionals. There has been much less research to date on the importance of gender differences among probation officers. In light of the fact that there are more felons receiving probation than ever before (Jones & Johnson, 1994), that probation officers "have contact with more offenders than most other justice employees" (Slate, Wells, & Johnson, 2003, p. 520), and that women are an increasingly larger segment of the probation officer workforce, attention to this growing segment of the criminal justice system is warranted.

Categorically, probation officers have been found to have higher stress levels than persons in the general population (Tabor, 1987). Brown (1987) discussed the linkage between stress and chronic health problems in probation officers, whereas Thomas (1988) linked the stress of probation officers to the dangers inherent to their job and having to make recommendations that result in custodial sentences. Some researchers maintained that causes of probation officer burnout may be due to role ambiguity and role conflict (Brown, 1987; Whitehead, 1985, 1986). Pettway and VanDine (2000) found paperwork to be the most frequently performed task reported by probation officers, whereas being overwhelmed with paperwork was identified as a stressor or source of burnout for probation officers in several studies (Brown, 1987; Simmons et al., 1997; Thomas, 1988; Whisler, 1994). Other sources of stress and burnout for probation officers include insufficient salaries, lack of promotional opportunities (Simmons et al., 1997; Whisler, 1994: Whitehead, 1986), and boredom (Whitehead, 1985).

In the limited focus on gender differences in the probation studies that have been reviewed, female probation officers have been found to demonstrate greater levels of stress than their male counterparts (Simmons et al., 1997; Thomas, 1998). Further, DeCarlo and Gruenfeld (1989) found that females across occupations are more likely than males to use sickness as a means of coping with occupational stress.

Defining Stress

Another noteworthy area for research in gender differences is occupational stress. Selye (1976) stated that stress is the nonspecific response of the body to any demand and that stress can be created by both positive and negative circumstances, and prolonged, intense stress can manifest itself in withdrawal from work and emotional exhaustion. A person can also produce *burnout*, which is a term often used interchangeably with the term *stress* and has been found to be a significant problem among "people-oriented professions" such as probation, prison, and police work (Whitehead, 1981, 1985). Burnout is psychological distress that may result in physical illness if no reprieve is in sight (Maslach, 1982).

◪ Purpose of the Study

Based on the above body of research, the authors believe that gender differences in probation officers do exist and that this relationship needs to be further explored and fleshed out to determine meaningful distinctions as women increasingly enter this profession. The purpose of this study is to assess the degree to which male and female probation officers differ in their level of stress and to determine the extent to which gender is a significant predictor of stress, independent of other stressors.

◪ Method

Sample

The data for this study were taken from the same data set collected for an earlier study of state probation officer stress (Slate et al., 2003). With the approval of state probation authorities, all 925 sworn probation officers in a southern state were surveyed. A postage-paid envelope addressed to the researchers was provided with each survey, and a total of 626 surveys (68.8%) were returned. Although the response rate is at an acceptable level, caution should be used in generalizing these findings to probation officers in other states.

Measures

Dependent Variables

In keeping with the literature review, most of the survey questions used in this study came from previous research. The four scales that measure internal stress, external stress, job stress, and personal stress were adapted from Whisler (1994), and each item of the scale was answered on a 6-point ordinal scale that varied from not stressful to very stressful. Internal stress was measured by a 26-item scale that asked respondents to indicate the degree of stress originating from such factors as poorly defined duties and responsibilities, getting along with supervisors, and the rules and regulations of the agency. External stress was measured by responses to a 14-item scale made up of such possible stressors as public criticism of probation, the ineffectiveness of the judicial system, and the ineffectiveness of the correctional system. Job stress, which focuses on specific aspects of the officer's job, was measured by respondent's self-reported stress as a result of 14 potential stressors, such as having insufficient time to complete the required work, making on-the-spot critical decisions, fear for one's safety, excessive paperwork, and inadequate equipment. Finally, seven items were used to assess personal stress, including family demands for more time at home, negative effects of the job on one's social life, and the ability of family to understand the difficulty of the job. Cronbach's alpha suggested that there was a high level of reliability for each scale: external stress, .89; internal stress, .94; job stress, .91; and personal stress, .85.

The Selye Health Scale was used to measure the respondent's level of physical stress. This 54-item Likert-type scale, developed by Cheek and Miller (1982a) to assess the severity of physical symptoms and illnesses among respondents, has been used in a number of studies with criminal justice personnel to assess their physical stress levels (Cheek, 1984; Cheek & Miller, 1982b; Slate & Vogel, 1997; Slate et al., 2001).

Cronbach's alpha measure of reliability for the scale was .96.

Independent Variables

Employee participation in workplace decision making has been touted by a number of researchers as a means of alleviating problems such as stress in criminal justice organizations (Brodsky, 1982; Katsampes, 1975; Poole & Regoli, 1983; Slate et al., 2001; Smith, Meister, & Klofas, 1985; Toch & Klofas, 1982). Although participation in workplace decision making has been measured as responses to a single question (Spielberger et al., 1981; Whisler, 1994), this study relied on a scale to measure this critical independent variable (see Slate, 1993; Slate & Vogel, 1997; Slate et al., 2001; Slate et al., 2003). This study employed a scale focusing on the perceptions concerning employee participation in workplace decision making. Two subscales were created from 12 questions, with answers in a 5-point Likert-type scale ranging from *strongly disagree* to *strongly agree*. The first subscale measured the atmosphere for participation in workplace decision making and included items such as "I am encouraged to offer my opinion at work," "There is opportunity for me to have a say in the running of this agency on matters that concern me." and "Management responds in a satisfactory manner to what I have to say." The second subscale measured attitudes about participation in decision making and included items such as "Participation in decision making tends to make one feel better about one's self" and "Participation in decision making tends to make individuals feel more a part of the team." Cronbach's alpha for the two subscales was .84 and .83, respectively.

A six-item Likert-type scale measured probation officer job satisfaction. Respondents indicated their agreement or disagreement on a 5-point scale to items such as "I would recommend this job to others," "I am proud of what I do for a living," and "I believe I will remain with this agency until I retire." Cronbach's alpha for this scale was .86.

The basic demographic variables were gender, age, ethnicity, and marital status. For analysis purposes, male officers were assigned a value of 1 and female officers were assigned a value of 0. Similarly, White officers were assigned a value of 1 and non-White officers, who made up 32.2% of the sample, were assigned a value of 0. Marital status was categorized as either married (1) or nonmarried (0), with nonmarried including single/never married, separated, divorced, and widowed. Other variables specific to this study included the length of probation officer experience, measured in number of years employed; the officer's current job in a managerial/supervisory position (1) or a nonmanagerial/nonsupervisory position (0); and the number of sick days taken in the past year. Education was not included as a variable, largely because all probation officers in the state were required to have a 4-year college degree.

Results

Although the criminal justice system has been characterized as male dominated, females ($n = 325$) outnumber males ($n = 301$) in this study. However, males were significantly more likely to be in supervisory positions than were females. Male officers also were significantly more likely than female officers to be White and to be married, yet female officers had a significantly greater mean number of sick days than did male officers.

The results of the t test revealed significant gender differences on four of the five stress measures. Physical stress was significantly greater among women than among men, but there were significantly higher levels of internal stress, job stress, and personal stress among men. There was no difference between male and female probation officers in the level of external stress, however.

It is noteworthy that managerial position, perceived atmosphere for officer participation in decision making, and job satisfaction are the only significant predictors of each of the four measures of stress. Internal stress, external stress, job stress, and personal stress are significantly greater among officers in managerial or supervisory positions and significantly lower when the officers felt there was a positive atmosphere for participation and when their job satisfaction is

high. Marital status, which had been hypothesized to be especially salient to personal stress, was not a predictor of any of the four stress measures. Most important, gender had no significant effect on any of the measures of stress.

Discussion and Conclusion

The gender-stress relationship is less than clear. In this study, female probation officers had a greater level of physical stress than male probation officers, but internal stress, job stress, and personal stress were greater among male officers than among female officers. Yet, gender was found to have no direct effect on internal stress, external stress, job stress, or personal stress when salient demographic and work-related factors were statistically controlled. These findings are somewhat in conflict with earlier studies examining gender and stress and present difficulties in the interpretation of findings in this study concerning relationships involving stress, gender, and factors associated with the organization.

Females have been found to be less susceptible than males to serious illness, but females have been determined to be more likely to suffer from mild psychological distress and to manifest more acute symptoms (DeCarlo & Gruenfeld, 1989). With the tendency for females to be more sensitive to the early indications of stress, females are more likely than men to undertake measures to try to remedy their distress. Much of the Selye Health Score is made up of many of these early signs and symptoms of stress, which may explain why female probation officers reported higher physical stress levels than their male counterparts. Also, the Selye Health Score is determined via self-report measures, and women are socialized to be more communicative and expressive, whereas men are expected to maintain a level of toughness and play things close to the vest; this phenomenon has been described as the John-Wayne Syndrome and has been said to permeate male-dominated criminal justice organizations (Bartol & Bartol, 1994; Reiser, 1974; Wrighisman, Nietzel, & Fortune, 1994). Simply, it may be that females are more prone to discuss their maladies than males.

Similarly, females were significantly more likely than males to use sick days. In fact, females used almost twice as many sick days as males. As noted by DeCarlo and Gruenfeld (1989), females are more apt than males to use sickness as a coping strategy. In addition, it is possible that female probation officers are being bombarded by stressors unique to women and the traditional roles they play as primary caregiver for the family. As noted by Greenhaus and Beutell (1985), "the role pressures from the work and family domains are mutually incompatible" (p. 77). In this study, however, the level of personal stress, thought to measure these competing demands outside the workplace, was greater among men. Further, marital status was not a significant predictor of any of the four types of stress studied.

In this study, men were more likely than women to hold a supervisory or managerial position, and managerial position was a significant predictor of stress. This finding suggests that the observed bivariate differences in stress between men and women may have been due, at least in part, to the differences between men and women in their position within the organization. The multivariate regression models support this interpretation: Controlling for managerial position, gender has no effect on any of the four measures of stress. What emerges is a suggestion that the effects of gender on stress among probation officers may be mediated by a number of gender-related factors, such as position in the organization, perception that the organization encourages one's participation in decision making, and satisfaction with the intrinsic and extrinsic aspects of the job. These findings illustrate the need for continued research that will decipher the nuances of stressors, especially those outside the workplace, among men and women employed in traditional male-dominated work environments.

⬕ References

Abdollahi, K. M. (2002). Understanding police stress research. *Journal of Forensic Psychology Practice, 2*(2), 1–24.

Anderson, E. M. (1994). *Stress and its correlates: An empirical investigation anions North Dakota peace officers.* Unpublished doctoral dissertation. University of North Dakota, Grand Forks.

Anshel, M. (2000). A conceptual model and implications for coping with stressful events in police work. *Criminal Justice and Behavior, 27,* 375–400.

Archambeault, W. J., & Weirman, C. L. (1983). Critically assessing the utility of police bureaucracies in the 1980s: Implications of management theory z. *Journal of Police Science and Administration, 11,* 420–429.

Armstrong, G. S., & Griffin, M. L. (2004). Docs the job matter? Comparing correlates of stress among treatment and correctional staff in prisons. *Journal of Criminal Justice, 32,* 577–592.

Bartol, C. R., & Bartol, A. M. (1994). *Psychology and law* (2nd ed). Pacific Grove, CA: Brooks/Cole.

Brandt, L. P. A., & Nielsen, C. V. (1992). Job stress and adverse outcome pregnancy: A causal link or recall bias. *American Journal of Epidemiology, 135,* 302–311.

Britton, D. M. (1997). Perceptions of the work environment among correctional officers: Do race and sex matter? *Criminology, 35,* 85–105.

Brodsky, C. M. (1982). Work stress in correctional institutions. *Journal of Prison and Jail Health, 2*(2), 74–102.

Brown, P. W. (1986). Probation officer burnout: An organizational disease/an organizational cure. *Federal Probation, 50*(1), 4–7.

Brown, P. W. (1987). Probation officer burnout: An organizational disease/an organizational cure, part II. *Federal Probation, 51*(3), 17–21.

Bureau of Labor Statistics, U.S. Department of Labor. (2004). *Occupational outlook handbook, 2004-05 edition: Probation officers and correctional treatment specialists.* Retrieved December 6, 2005, from http://www.bls.gov/oco/ocos265.htm

Carlie's Law. (2005). Retrieved September 4, 2005, from http://www.en.wikipedia.org/wiki/Carlie_Brucia.html

Cheek, F. E. (1984). *Stress management for Hanoi officers and their families.* College Park, MD: American Correctional Association.

Cheek, F. E., & Miller, M. D. (1982a). *Managerial stress in correctional facilities handbook.* Trenton: New Jersey Department of Corrections.

Check, F. E., & Miller, M. D. (1982b). *Prisoners of life.* Washington, DC: American Federation of State, County and Municipal Employees.

Cooper, C. L., & Watson, M. (1991). *Cancer and stress: Psychological, biological and coping studies.* New York: John Wiley.

Crouch, B. (1985). Pandora's box: Women guards in men's prisons. *Journal of Criminal Justice, 13,* 535–548.

Crouch, B. M., & Alpert, G. P. (1982). Sex and occupational socialization among prison guards. *Criminal Justice and Behavior, 9,* 159–176.

Cullen, F., Link, B., Wolfe, N., & Frank, J. (1985). The social dimensions of correctional officer stress. *Justice Quarterly, 2,* 505–533.

Dantzker, M. L., & Kubin, B. (1998). Job satisfaction: The gender perspective among police officers. *American Journal of Criminal Justice, 23*(1), 19–31.

DeCarlo, D. T. (1987) *Workplace stress: Trends, outlook and perspectives.* New York: American Insurance Association.

DeCarlo, D. T., & Gruenfeld, D. H. (1989). *Stress in the American workplace: Alternatives for the working wounded.* Fort Washington, PA: LRP Publications.

Dillon, P. (1999). The cost of stress is mind numbing. *Orlando Business Journal, 16,* 36–45.

Does stress kill? (1995). *Consumer Reports on Health, 7*(7), 73–77.

Elkin, A. J., & Rosch, P. J. (1990) Promoting mental health at the workplace: The prevention side of stress management. *Occupational Medicine: State of the Art Review, 5*(4), 739–754.

Falk, A., Hanson, B. S., Isacsson, S., & Ostergren, P. (1992). Job strain and mortality in elderly men: Social network, support, and influence as buffers. *American Journal of Public Health, 82,* 1136–1139.

Farkas, M. A. (2001). Correctional officers: What factors influence work attitudes? *Corrections Management Quarterly, 5,* 20–26.

Finn, P. (2000). *Addressing correctional officer stress: Programs and strategies* (NCJ No. 183474). Rockville, MD: National Institute of Justice in cooperation with corrections program office.

Finn, P., & Kuck, S. (2003). *Addressing probation and parole officer stress.* Cambridge, MA: Abt Associates.

Finn, P., & Kuck, S. (2005). *Stress among probation and parole officers and what can be done about it* (NCJ No. 205620). Rockville, MD: National Institute of Justice.

Greenhaus, J., & Beutell, N. (1985). Sources of conflict between work and family roles. *Academy of Management Review, 10,* 76–88.

Griffin, M. L. (2001). Job satisfaction among detention officers: Assessing the relative contribution of organizational climate variables. *Journal of Criminal Justice, 29,* 219–232.

Griffin, M. L., Armstrong, G., & Hepburn, J. R. (in press). Correctional officers' perceptions of equitable treatment in the "masculinized" prison environment. *Criminal Justice Review, 30.*

Griffin, M. L., & Hepburn, J. R. (2005). Side bets and reciprocity as determinants of organizational commitment among correctional officers. *Journal of Criminal Justice, 33*(6), 611–625.

Hendrix, W. H., Spencer, B. A., & Gibson, G. S. (1994). Organizational and extraorganizational factors affecting stress, employee well-being, and absenteeism for males and females. *Journal of Business and Psychology, 9*(2), 103–128.

Hochschild, A. R. (1989). *The second shift.* New York: First Band Printing.

Holgate, A. M., & Clegg, I. J. (1991). The path to probation officer burnout: New dogs, old tricks. *Journal of Criminal Justice, 19,* 325–337.

Homer, C. J., Sherman, J. A., & Siegel, E. (1990). Work-related psychosocial stress and risk of preterm, low birthweight delivery. *American Journal of Public Health, 80,* 173–177.

Honnold, J. A., & Stinchcomb, J. B. (1985). Officer stress: Costs, causes and cures. *Corrections Today, 47,* 46–51.

Ivancevich, J. M., Matteson, M. T., & Richards, E. P. (1985). Special report: Who's liable for stress on the job? *Harvard Business Review, 70,* 60–62, 66, 70, 72.

Jessica Marie Lunsford Foundation. (2005). Retrieved September 4, 2005, from http://jmlfoundation.com/legislation html

Jick, T. D., & Mitz, L. F. (1985). Sex differences in work stress. *Academy of Management Review, 10*(3), 408–420.

Johnson, J. V., Hall, E. M., & Theorell, T. (1989). Combined effects of job strain and social isolation on cardiovascular disease mortality in a random sample of Swedish male working population. *Scandinavian Journal of Work Environment and Health, 15,* 271–279.

Johnson, J. V., & Johansson, G. (Eds.). (1991). *The psychosocial work environment: Work organization, democratization and health.* New York: Baywood.

Jones, M., & Johnson, W. (1994) The increased felonization of probation and its impact on the function of probation: A descriptive look at county level data from the 1980s and the 1990s. *Perspectives, 18*(4), 42–46.

Jurik, N. (1985). An officer and a lady: Organizational barriers to women working as correctional officers in men's prisons. *Social Problems, 32,* 375–388.

Jurik, N., & Halemba, G. (1984). Gender, working conditions, and the job satisfaction of women in a nontraditional occupation: Female correctional officers in men's prison. *Corrections Today, 43,* 40–51.

Karasek, R. A., & Theorell, T. (1990). *Healthy work: Stress, productivity and the reconstruction of working life.* New York: John Wiley.

Katsampes, P. L. (1975). Changing correction officers: A demonstration study. *International Journal of Criminology and Penology, 3,* 123–144.

Kissel, P., & Katsampes, P. (1980). The impact of women corrections officers on the functioning of institutions housing male inmates. *Journal of Offender Counseling, Services, and Rehabilitation, 4,* 213–231.

Kuykendall, J., & Unsinger, P. C. (1982). The leadership styles of police managers. *Journal of Criminal Justice, 10,* 311–321.

Lasky, G. L., Gordon, B., & Strebalus, D. J (1986). Occupational stressors among federal correctional officers working in different security levels. *Criminal Justice and Behavior, 13*(3), 317–327.

Lawrence, R. A. (1984). Police stress and personality factors: A conceptual model. *Journal of Criminal Justice, 12,* 247–263.

Lindquist, C. A., & Whitehead, J. T. (1986). Burnout, job stress, and job satisfaction among southern correctional officers: Perceptions and causal factors. *Journal of Offender Counseling, Services and Rehabilitation, 10*(4), 5–26.

Maslach, C. (1982). *Burnout: The cost of caring.* Englewood Cliffs, NJ: Prentice Hall.

Mearns, J., & Mauch, T. G. (1998). Negative mood regulation expectancies predict anger among police officers and buffer the effects of job stress. *Journal of Nervous and Mental Disease, 186*(2), 120–125.

Melancon, D. D. (1984). Quality circles: The shape of things to come? *The Police Chief, 51*(11), 54–55.

Miller, K., Greyling, M., Cooper, C., Lu, L., Sparks, K., & Spector, P. (2000) Occupational stress and gender: A cross-cultural study. *Stress Medicine, 16*, 271–278.

Morash, M., & Haarr, R. N. (1995). Gender, workplace problems, and stress in policing. *Justice Quarterly, 12*(1), 113–140.

Muntaner, C., Tien, A., Baton, W. W., & Garrison, R. (1991). Occupational characteristics and the occurrence of psychotic disorders. *Social Psychiatry and Psychiatric Epidemiology, 26*, 273–280.

National Institute for Occupational Safety and Health. (1995). *Stress: The workplace disease of the 1990s* (U.S. Department of Health and Human Services, Centers for Disease Control and Prevention). Washington, DC: U.S. Government Printing Office.

Nelson, D. L., & Quick, J. C. (1985). Professional women: Are distress and disease inevitable? *Academy of Management Review, 10*(2), 206–218.

Palmer, S. (1989, August). Occupational stress. *Health and Safety Practitioner,* pp. 16–18.

Patterson, B. L. (1989). *A comparative analysis of job stress among police, correctional, and probation/parole officers.* Unpublished doctoral dissertation. University of New York at Albany.

Patterson, B. L. (1992). Job experience and perceived job stress among police, correctional, and probation/parole officers. *Criminal Justice and Behavior, 19*(3), 260–285.

Pettway, C., & VanDine, S. (2000). One moment in time: Using pagers to measure how parole/probation officers spend their time. Paper presented at the meeting of the American Society of Criminology, San Francisco, California.

Poole, E. D., & Regoli, R. M. (1983). Professionalism, role, conflict, work alienation and anomie: A look at prison management. *Social Science Journal, 20*(1), 63–70.

Reiser, M. (1974). Some organizational stresses on policemen. *Journal of Police Science and Administration, 2*, 156–159.

Rodichok, G. J. (1995). *A quantitative and qualitative survey of job stress among African-American police officers.* Unpublished doctoral dissertation, Temple University. Philadelphia. Pennsylvania.

Schnall, P. L. (1990). Heartbreaking work: How job strain may harm the ticker. *Prevention, 11*, 14.

Schnall, P. L., Pieper, C., Schwartz, J. E., Karasek, R. A., Schlussel, Y., Devereux, R. B., et al. (1990). The relationship between job strain, workplace diastolic blood pressure, and left ventricular mass index: Results of a case-control study. *Journal of the American Medical Association, 263*, 1933–1934.

Selye, H. (1976). *The stress of life.* New York: McGraw-Hill.

Simmons, C., Cochran, J. K., & Blount, W. R. (1997). The effects of job-related stress and job satisfaction on probation officers' inclinations to quit. *American Journal of Criminal Justice, 21*, 213–229.

Sims, B. (2001). Surveying the correctional environment A review of the literature. *Corrections Management Quarterly, 5*(2), 1–12.

Slate, R. N. (1993). *Stress levels and thoughts of quitting of correctional personnel: Do perceptions of participatory management make a difference?* Unpublished doctoral dissertation, Claremont Graduate School, Claremont, California.

Slate, R. N., Johnson, W. W., & Wells, T. (2000). Probation officer stress: Is there an organizational solution? *Federal Probation, 64*(1), 56–60.

Slate, R. N., & Vogel, R. E. (1997). Participative management and correctional personnel: A study of the perceived atmosphere for participation in correctional decision making and its impact on employee stress and thoughts about quitting. *Journal of Criminal Justice, 25*, 397–408.

Slate, R. N., Vogel, R. E., & Johnson, W. W. (2001). To quit or not to quit: Perceptions of participation in correctional decision making and the impact of organizational stress. *Corrections Management Quarterly, 5*(2), 68–78.

Slate, R. N., Wells, T. L., & Johnson, W. W. (2003). Opening the manager's door: State probation officer stress and perceptions of participation in workplace decision making. *Crime & Delinquency, 49*(4), 519–541.

Smith, S., Meister, E., & Klofas, J. (1985). Participation in planning. *Corrections Today, 47*, 140, 142, 146.

Snipes, D. E. (2005). Occupational wellness. Retrieved September 1, 2005, from http://www.policecouiuding.com/POLICE%20 COUNSELING%20OCCUPATIONAL.html

Spielberger, C. D., Westberry, L. G., Grier, K. S., & Greenfield, G. (1981). *The police stress survey: Sources of stress in law enforcement.* Tampa, FL: Human Resources Institute.

Stinchcomb, J. B. (2004). Searching for stress in all the wrong places: Combating chronic organizational stressors in policing. *Police Practice and Research, 5*(3), 259–278.

Stohr, M. K., Lovrich, N. P., & Mays, G. L. (1997). Service v. security focus in training assessments: Testing gender differences among women's jail correctional officers. *Women and Criminal Justice, 9*(1), 65–85.

Storch, J. E., & Panzarella, R. (1996). Police stress: State-trait anxiety in relation to occupational and personal stressors. *Journal of Criminal Justice, 24*, 99–107.

Tabor, R. W. (1987). *A comparison study of occupational stress among juvenile and adult probation officers.* Unpublished doctoral dissertation, Virginia Polytechnical Institute and State University, Blacksburg.

Terry, W. C., III. (1983). Police stress as an individual and administrative problem: Some conceptual and theoretical difficulties. *Journal of Police Science and Administration, 11*, 97–106.

Thomas, R. L. (1988). Stress perception among select federal probation and pretrial services officers and their supervisors. *Federal Probation, 52*(3), 48–58.

Thomas-Riddle, R. (1999). *The relationship between life stress, work stress, and traumatic stress and burnout and cynicism in police officers.* Unpublished doctoral dissertation, United States International University, San Diego, California.

Toch, H. (2002). *Stress in policing.* Washington, DC: American Psychological Association.

Toch, H., & Klofas, J. (1982). Alienation and desire for job enrichment among correction officers. *Federal Probation, 46,* 35–44.

Torres, S., Maggard, D. L., Jr., & To, C. (2003, October). Preparing families for the hazards of police work. *Police Chief Magazine.* Retrieved September 5, 2005. from http://policechiefmagazine.org/magazine/index.cfm?fuseaction=display_arch&article_id=l20&issue_ id=102003

Tripplett, R., Mullings, J. L., & Scarborough, K. E. (1999). Examining the effect of work-home conflict on work-related stress among correctional officers. *Journal of Criminal Justice, 27,* 371–385.

Ulmer, J. T. (1992). Occupational socialization and cynicism toward prison administration. *Social Science Journal, 29*(4), 423–443.

Violanti, J. M., & Aron, F. (1994). Ranking police officers. *Psychological Reports, 75,* 824–826.

Voorhis, P. V., Cullen, F. T., Link, B. G., & Wolfe, N. T (1991). The impact of race and gender on correctional officers' orientation to the integrated environment *Journal of Research in Crime and Delinquency, 28,* 472–500.

Walters, S. (1992). Attitudinal and demographic differences between male and female corrections officers: A study in three midwestern prisons. *Journal of Offender Rehabilitation, 18*(1/2), 173–189.

Wellbrock, K. D. (2000) *Stress, hardiness, social support network orientation, and trauma-related symptoms in police officers.*

Unpublished doctoral dissertation, California School of Professional Psychology, Los Angeles.

Whisler, P. M. (1994). *A study of stress perception by selected state probation officers.* Unpublished master's thesis, University of South Florida, Tampa.

Whitehead, J. T. (1981). The management of job stress in probation and parole. *Journal of Probation and Parole, 13,* 29–32.

Whitehead, J. T (1985). Job burnout in probation and parole: Its extent and intervention implications. *Criminal Justice and Behavior, 12*(1), 91–110.

Whitehead, J. T. (1986). Job burnout and job satisfaction among probation managers. *Journal of Criminal Justice, 14,* 25–35.

Whitehead, J. T., & Lindquist, C. A. (1986). Job stress and burnout among probation/parole officers: Perceptions and causal factors. *International Journal of Offender Therapy and Comparative Criminology, 29*(2), 109–119.

Winter, D. (1993). Slot rattling from law enforcement to lawbreaking: A personal construct theory exploration of police stress. *International Journal of Personal Construct Psychology, 6,* 253–267.

Wright, K. N., & Saylor, W. G. (1991). Male and female employees' perceptions of prison work: Is there a difference? *Justice Quarterly, 8*(4), 505–524.

Wrightsman, L. S., Nietzel, M., & Fortune, W. (1994). *Psychology and the legal system* (3rd ed.). Pacific Grove, CA: Brooks/Cole.

Zhao, J. S., He, N., & Lovrich, N. (2002) Predicting five dimensions of police officer stress: Looking more deeply into organizational settings for sources of police stress. *Police Quarterly, 5*(1), 43–62.

Zimmer, L. E. (1986). *Women guarding men.* Chicago: University of Chicago Press.

Zupan, L. L. (1986). Gender-related differences in correctional officers' perceptions and attitudes. *Journal of Criminal Justice, 14,* 349–361.

DISCUSSION QUESTIONS

1. According to the article, what does the term *John Wayne Syndrome* refer to in the criminal justice system? Why is it important for agencies to understand and address this phenomenon as a way to reduce stress in the workplace?

2. In the article, the authors point to a stress-inducing situation for women known as "second shift." What is this phenomenon? Why is it important in addressing gender specific needs in the workplace? How might the workplace be able to mitigate the second shift effect for both males and females?

3. Why is it important to understand the concept and existence of stress in the workplace? What are some of the cons of increasing levels of stress among employees?

4. According to the literature, what factors may contribute to increasing stress levels in criminal justice related professions? What might agencies do to reduce the level of stress in these environments?

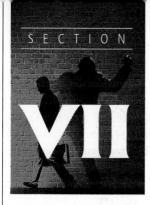

SECTION

VII

Community-Based Residential Intermediate Sanctions

Section Highlights

- Halfway Houses
- Community Residential Treatment Centers
- Shock Incarceration
- Conclusion

Learning Objectives

1. Understand the challenges facing jail facilities and the need for **jail diversion programs**.

2. Know the history of the development of halfway houses in America.

3. Be aware of the various types of community residential treatment programs that exist.

4. Understand the benefits that exist when using community residential treatment programs.

5. Be cognizant of the various offender needs and problems that residential facilities may address.

Currently, there is no single definition of **intermediate sanctions**, nor is there any such iron-clad agreement about what ought to be included within any definition of intermediate sanctions. Some researchers contend that almost anything between "regular" probation and a full prison term is an intermediate sanction; others deny inclusion to any sanction that involves incarceration. However, the growing popularity of residential facilities like **restitution centers, work release centers, and probation detention facilities,** some with capacities in the hundreds, make this distinction more important (McGarry, 1990).

What intermediate sanctions do have in common is the presence of features designed to enhance the desired sanctioning purpose. Indeed, regardless of whether the intent is to achieve punishment, incapacitation, rehabilitation, or specific deterrence, intermediate sanctions provide more options than simple probation. These sanctions also tend to vary in severity, leading to a continuum of sanctions that progress from the most restrictive (prison) to the least restrictive (suspended sentences, deferred adjudication, and so forth). This can then lead to increased surveillance and tighter controls on movement, while enhancing the integration of more intense treatment to address a wider assortment of maladies or deficiencies. The integration between supervision and treatment has been discussed in prior sections, and it is the use of intermediate sanctions that optimizes the mix between the two. Indeed, the use of intermediate sanctions should be perceived as a linking pin that integrates elements of both the security and the treatment spectrums, providing the glue between both orientations.

It was during the 1990s that intermediate sanctions truly came in vogue. The reasons for this were described before their use became commonly known among the public by McGarry (1990) in a report produced by the National Institute of Corrections. According to this report, overcrowding was not the only reason for the interest in intermediate sanctions. The rise of intermediate sanctions was also fueled by the following:

1. Public concern over the adequate supervision of probationers and parolees

2. The demands of victims and their communities to be made whole again following a crime

3. Changing and more available technologies that are challenging our notions of what is possible

4. The continuing desire of judges to tailor sentences to the offense and the offender

5. The rising failure rates of offenders on probation and parole

6. The impact of the drug abuse crisis that still exists around the United States

As was true then, it is still true now that communities suffering from the results of illegal drug use have little choice but to turn to the criminal justice system, particularly probation, to solve an immense societal problem. The community corrections section of the criminal justice system, often saddled with these offenders, was forced to adopt innovative options for processing large volumes of drug offenders. This was especially true during the war on drugs as more and more drug offenders appeared on community supervision officer (CSO) caseloads. At this time, probation and other forms of community supervision were viewed as being weak on crime, and the use of intermediate sanctions was thought to be a means of bringing respectable public perceptions to the field of community supervision (Hanser, 2007a). Though the suggestions provided by McGarry (1990) are roughly 20 years old since publication, these suggestions provide unusually insightful guidance on the proper use of these approaches. Even today these suggested actions serve as a good policy basis for agencies that implement intermediate sanctions. While these sanctions are now used by nearly every community supervision agency across the country, the effective evaluation of these sentences is often questionable. Agencies that follow the suggested actions by McGarry (1990) will find that outcomes associated with intermediate sanctions will be more predictable, effective, and easier to measure. Thus, there are actions that administrators can take to increase the chances of success of intermediate sanctions in their jurisdictions. The benefit is that in most cases implementing these actions do not require additional funding from budget-strapped community supervision agencies. Rather, improvements in job design and other considerations are all that are required to implement these actions.

The first of these is to articulate precisely why a jurisdiction needs intermediate sanctions. Upon questioning, most stakeholders in the sentencing process tend to indicate dissatisfaction with the choice of options available. The key is to get each stakeholder to specify precisely which offenders are now sentenced inappropriately and what would represent a more appropriate sanction. Typically, responses will range from those of presiding judges who want more restrictive, treatment-oriented programs for offenders they are now putting on probation to those of chief probation officers who may contend that their staff cannot provide appropriate control in the community for the many offenders that are in the local or regional jail. McGarry (1990) noted that "unless a jurisdiction has unlimited resources, any effort to implement intermediate sanctions must begin with the actors finding the areas of common agreement, whether types of offenders or categories of offenses, and building from there" (p. 4).

A second suggested action is to establish clear sanctioning goals: referred to as the why of sentencing. The individual actors and agencies within the criminal justice system commonly operate from different and unexamined philosophies of sentencing. The need for understanding of the different sentencing philosophies was discussed earlier in this text, and this is again conceptually revisited when considering intermediate sanctions. Often, the key actors in the justice system have ideologies and punishment philosophies that are at cross-purposes with one another. The individual goals of different court actors during the sentencing process may be different from case to case and may be directly contradictory to those of their peers or of another agency, potentially causing a number of problems. In addition to resolving contradictory efforts, choosing and defining goals is critical in the creation of either an individual sanctioning option or an entire sanctioning continuum. Further, the clarity in definition provides a better means of evaluating the program, an important element when attempting to refine services that are provided. However, regardless of evaluative considerations, the sanctioning goal should determine the features that will characterize the program; a day reporting center designed to offer rehabilitative services, for example, will look very different from one intended primarily to incapacitate or deter offenders (McGarry, 1990). The sentencing purpose should be the primary element in the continuum of sanctions and defines success for any individual program. The evaluative process, while best factored into the beginning planning stages of the program, should be secondary to ensuring that sentencing is carried out in a meaningful and balanced manner.

A third action in implementing effective and appropriate intermediate sanctions is to make available a continuum of sanctions scaled around one or more sanctioning goals. For example, the goal of incapacitation may be implemented through varying levels of surveillance or control of movement. Such a continuum permits the court or corrections authority to tailor sanctions that are meaningful with respect both to their purposes and to the kinds of offenders that come before them.

A current practice is to unload the complete list of sanctions on all offenders, setting up both offenders and the program for failure. A typical offender who is supporting two children, for example, is not likely to be able to pay restitution, perform extensive community service, and participate in frequent drug counseling. Targeting specific sanctions to specific offender profiles, on the other hand, increases the chances of success for both the program and the offender. This kind of policy-directed system can also be responsive to differing and changing behavior on the part of offenders.

The fourth action, as noted by McGarry (1990), is to collect and use good information about the jurisdiction's criminal justice system, including offender flow data, offender profiles, information about sentencing practices, about programs, and about what works and for whom. The availability of this kind of information makes possible much of the other action already described. It is impossible, for example, to create a program for a specific offender population if you do not know the characteristics of that population, the usual disposition for that group, or how many offenders fitting that profile pass through the court in any given period. In many jurisdictions, the problem does not lie in the information technology but rather with the awareness of how to use it.

Currently, as an alternative to the rising costs of incarceration, convicted offenders are being sentenced to community supervision with increasing frequency (Glaze & Palla, 2005). Despite supervising an overwhelming majority of offenders, community supervision (probation) departments have experienced budget cuts, which in turn have led to a reduction in staff and resources, regardless of the drastic increases of caseload sizes. Given the increased caseloads and decrease in program funding, the need for alternative means of supervision and treatment are at a premium. To this end, intermediate sanctions have become the order of the day.

When it comes to finding alternatives to punishment and rehabilitation for offenders, there is no shortage, particularly in terms of community-based rehabilitation. On a simplistic level, intermediate sanctions could simply be defined as alternatives to traditional incarceration that consist of sentencing options falling anywhere between a standard prison sentence and a standard probation sentence. Reflecting the versatile nature of intermediate sanctions, the National Institute of Corrections (1993) has also defined intermediate sanctions as "a range of sanctioning options that permit the crafting of sentences to respond to the particular circumstances of the offender and the offense; and the outcomes desired in the case" (p. 18). For this text, the definition of these sanctions will consist of a blend of both definitions. Thus, intermediate sanctions are a range of sentencing options that fall between incarceration and probation, being designed to allow for the crafting of sentences that respond to the offender and/or the offense, with the intended outcome of the case being a primary consideration. Table 7.1 provides an examination of the various intermediate sanctions, their philosophical underpinnings, and their intended purposes. As mentioned in Section I, this continuum of sanctions provides courts and communities the opportunity to supervise offenders effectively without referring them to a term of incarceration. Figure 7.1 provides an illustration of a continuum of sanctions offered by the state of Indiana's Community-Based Corrections Initiative.

The definition of intermediate sanctions, as just presented, provides a perspective that is highly consistent with the emphasis on reintegration that is found in this text. It is clear that these types of sanctions allow for a great deal of flexibility that can be adjusted to accommodate treatment considerations and supervision considerations. These sanctions are guided by the intent of the sentencing body but allow for consideration of the various needs, challenges, and issues associated with the offender and the type of offending that they are prone to committing. This allows for the calibration of sentences so that specific details are a better fit with the type of offense considered as well as the individual variables associated with the offender. This flexibility is what provides the field of community corrections with its greatest source of leverage among the offender population, both in terms of treatment and supervision.

This section will discuss the most commonly implemented and researched residential intermediate sanctions of halfway houses, restitution centers, work and study release, and **shock incarceration** (including boot camps). When considering the overcrowding problems in prison systems around the nation, it is

Table 7.1 Summary Listing of Coercive Intermediate Sanction Measures and Sentencing Options

Warning Measures [Notice of consequences of subsequent wrongdoing]	Admonishment/cautioning [administrative; judicial] Suspended execution or imposition of sentence	
Injunctive Measures [Banning legal conduct]	Travel [e.g., from jurisdiction; to specific criminogenic spots] Association [e.g., with other offenders] Driving Possession of weapons Use of alcohol Professional activity [e.g., disbarment]	
Economic Measures	Restitution Costs Fees Forfeitures Support payments Fines [standard; day fines]	
Work-related Measures	Community service [individual placement; work crew] Paid employment requirements	
Education-related Measures	Academic [e.g., basic literacy, GED] Vocational training Life skills training	
Physical and Mental Health Treatment Measures	Psychological/psychiatric Chemical [e.g., methadone; psychoactive drugs] Surgical [e.g., acupuncture drug treatment]	
Physical Confinement Measures	Partial or intermittent confinement	Home curfew Day treatment center Halfway house Restitution center Weekend detention facility/jail Outpatient treatment facility [e.g., drug/mental health]

(Continued)

Table 7.1 (Continued)

	Full/continuous confinement	Full home/house arrest
		Mental hospital
		Other residential treatment facility [e.g., drug/alcohol]
		Boot camp
		Detention facility
		Jail
		Prison
Monitoring/Compliance Measures [May be attached to all other sanctions]	Required of the offender	Mail reporting
		Electronic monitoring [telephone check-in; active electronic monitoring device]
		Face-to-face reporting
		Urine analysis [random; routine]
	Required of the monitoring agent	Criminal records checks
		Sentence compliance checks [e.g., on payment of monetary sanctions; attendance/performance at treatment, work, or educational sites]
		Third-party checks [family, employer, surety, service/treatment provider; via mail, telephone, in person]
		Direct surveillance/observation [random/routine visits and possibly search; at home, work, institution, or elsewhere]
		Electronic monitoring [regular phone checks and/or passive monitoring device—currently used with home curfew or house arrest, but could track movement more widely as technology develops]

clear that there is simply a pragmatic need for more space. As a result of the public's outcry for increased traditional sentencing of offenders coupled with legislative action as a response to the public, the use of intermediate sanctions has grown. Recent reports indicate that many parolees and probationers are supervised by some form of intermediate sanctioning (Camp & Camp, 2003). It must be remembered that as we discuss intermediate sanctioning, the applicability of such programming is dependent upon the potential for harm in local communities and the ability of intermediate sanctions to reduce recidivism.

Halfway Houses

The use of halfway houses has been traced back to the early 1800s in England. In the United States, the first use of a halfway house is thought to have occurred in 1817 when the Massachusetts Prison Commission

Figure 7.1 Indiana County Community Corrections Program Elements: A Continuum of Sanctions

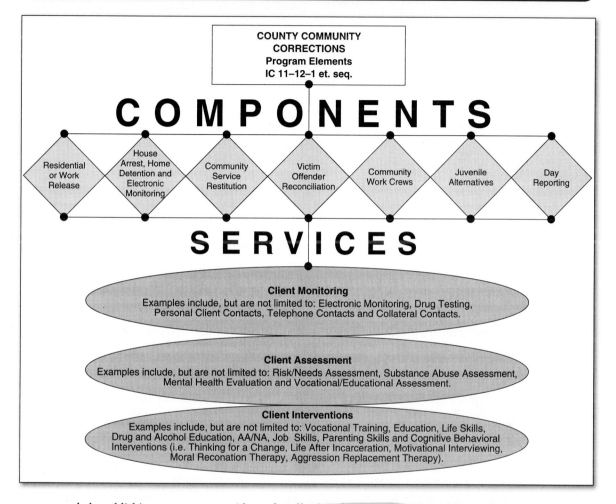

recommended establishing a temporary residence for offenders that were first released from prison (Latessa & Allen, 1999).The commission made this recommendation in the belief that offenders would need a supportive environment immediately after release to assist in the process of establishing a prosocial and law-abiding existence. Among other concerns was the fact that the community itself was (especially during the early 1800s) biased and unforgiving of prior offenders. Even at this time, the difficulty for offenders to find employment upon release was noted as a specific problem of concern (Cohn, 1973).

During the early 1800s, a type of penal system had been in practice, commonly referred to as the Pennsylvania System of prison operation. This model of prison management was first established by the Quakers and emphasized the need for prisoners to exercise a sense of penitence and reflection on the errors of their ways. In this model of imprisonment, offenders were kept in single cells and were given the Holy Bible to read and reflect on their sins, transgressions, and crimes. Offenders were kept in their cells and were not allowed to interact with other offenders also housed. These inmates did not work, talk, or recreate with one another. It was thought that if inmates were allowed to communicate they would essentially "contaminate" one another with their various negative influences and learned experiences. This is interesting because it is similar with the beliefs held by many of today's criminologists that prisons are actually schools of crime, thus lending to the possible validity of these concerns among prison workers in the early 1800s.

Unfortunately, recidivism rates were very high in Massachusetts during the early 1800s, and it did not seem that community corrections approaches were effective in lowering recidivism. Further, the influences of the Pennsylvania model of prison operations impacted the operation of halfway houses in Massachusetts. As a result, the Massachusetts legislature feared that those offenders released to halfway houses might contaminate one another if they were allowed to be housed together. This would, as it was thought at that time, reverse their prosocial learning and resistance to criminal behavior, thereby making their experience in prison all for naught. As a result, the use of the halfway house was discontinued in that state.

However, the concept did find a warm reception in other correctional systems. For instance, in 1845, the Isaac T. Hopper Home in New York City was opened (also by the Quakers) and is still in operation today as a home for female offenders seeking reentry into the community (Latessa & Allen, 1999). In 1864, the Temporary Asylum for Discharged Female Prisoners was opened in the Boston area (Champion, 2002; Cromwell, Del Carmen, & Alarid, 2002). This halfway house received less community opposition than did homes for men. According to Cromwell et al. (2002), the "reason for this difference was an underlying belief that, unlike male prisoners, women prisoners did not associate for the purpose of talking about criminal activity. Women prisoners were believed to contribute to their own rehabilitation" (p. 258). This is interesting because in many respects modern treatment providers note that female clients do tend to respond to therapeutic interventions in a more effective, trusting, and genuine manner than do male clients, particularly in the offender population. Though halfway houses during the early 1800s did not provide therapeutic services (only basic needs such as food and shelter were provided), it is fascinating that observations between the genders were just as distinct as they are today.

In 1896, the Hope House was established in New York City by Maud and Ballington Booth. The Hope House design spread to other cities such as Chicago, San Francisco, and New Orleans, being financially funded by philanthropic groups such as Volunteers of America (Latessa & Allen, 1999). Hope House was considered a premier service for its time and was among the first to provide additional services that went beyond food and lodging. Nevertheless, Hope House would not last due to the emergence of parole within many states. The use of parole in the early 1900s was implemented as a "means for controlling and helping ex-inmates after release from prison" (Latessa & Allen, 1999, p. 373). Parole systems across various states reduced or eliminated the need for halfway houses and, given that such facilities were underfunded and not provided substantive public support, it was only a matter of time until their demise would be witnessed. As funding became more difficult to obtain during the Great Depression and as public sentiment toward offenders become more skeptical during these economically hard times, halfway houses began to shut their doors (Latessa & Allen, 1999). It would not be until the 1950s that the halfway house would again emerge in the field of corrections. According to Cromwell et al. (2002), only one halfway house ultimately remained open throughout the Great Depression, the house called "The Parting of the Ways" in Pittsburgh. This, too, was a church-based program and operated off the donations and contributions of religious followers during that time. Otherwise, from about 1930 to the mid-1950s, halfway houses nearly disappeared from the correctional landscape.

In the mid-1950s, growing dissatisfaction with prisons began to emerge within the American public. This was further intensified by findings that parolees faced challenges in the transition from prison to free world living, with an understanding that supportive services and gradual integration was necessary if recidivism was to be reduced. In 1954, halfway houses began to reappear in various areas of the United States. Further, private religious organizations again surfaced to provide assistance to the offender population. During this revival of the halfway house concept, the use of individualized treatment, counseling, employment referral, and substance abuse counseling emerged as part of the services offered (Latessa & Allen, 1999). In 1961, halfway houses received governmental assistance for the very first time when Attorney General Robert F. Kennedy implored Congress to provide funds to open federal-level halfway houses for young offenders (Champion, 2002; Cromwell et al., 2002; Latessa & Allen, 1999). These developments eventually led to the passage of the Prisoner Rehabilitation Act of 1965, which authorized the Federal Bureau of Prisons to establish community-based facilities for the reintegration of young offenders. Further financial support continued due to the emphasis that was placed on reintegration during this period in community corrections history. In 1968, the Law Enforcement Assistance Administration provided additional funding for the establishment of nonfederal halfway houses, and the monetary support for these types of services lasted for over a decade, coming to a close in 1980 (Latessa & Allen, 1999).

Although government funding and support has decreased since the 1980s, private halfway houses continue to emerge as an alternative to prison. More will be provided on the use of various private organizations and facilities to offer halfway house services. As with the earliest of times in the history of corrections, the role of religious institutions continues to be instrumental in the role of many halfway house services. It would seem that religious institutions and organizations happen to be the primary sources of forgiveness and sincere reintegration for those persons phasing out from prison to the community at large. It is then ironic that an emphasis on the separation of church and state would be a potential impediment to providing services for offenders and for protecting the public from future increases in recidivism.

In 1964 occurred one of the most widespread and important developments in the history of halfway houses, the rise of the International Halfway House Association (IHHA) in Chicago. The fact that this organization is mentioned, in detail, among other leading texts on community corrections tends to underscore the importance of this organization within the developmental scheme of the halfway house concept. According to Latessa and Allen (1999), the IHHA was motivated by the absence of state and local support for halfway houses and sought to develop a voluntary and professional organization of halfway house administrators and personnel (p. 374; also see Wilson, 1985). The name of this organization was eventually changed to the **International Association of Residential and Community Alternatives (IARCA)** in 1989, reflecting the ambiguity in definitions that separate halfway houses and other forms of offender residential programs—the distinctions between these being more a matter of semantics than the actual operational function of such facilities. According to Cromwell et al. (2002), the IARCA represents roughly 250 private agencies operating nearly 1,500 programs around the world. Champion (2002) noted that even though halfway house programs were privately funded from the 1980s onward, the growth in their numbers was quite amazing during the decades that followed. As an example, he pointed out that in the United States and Canada, some researchers report that nearly 2,300 halfway house facilities are in operation with over 100,000 beds being available.

Regardless of how widespread these types of programs are, two things are for certain: (1) The halfway house concept is alive and well in the field of community corrections, and (2) these facilities are operating aside from and exclusive of government support in many cases. Though some of these facilities may obtain governmental grants, they are left to their own devices when stewarding their own future and the particular services that they will provide. Though this can provide managerial challenges, it also provides for a great deal of flexibility, as private halfway houses can make their own determinations as to whom they will house. This and other areas of pliability in the decision-making process allow these programs to maximize their service delivery and also serve to fill critical gaps that exist in state and county-level governmental community corrections programs.

At this point, much discussion has been provided in regard to halfway houses, but no true definition has been provided. This is because these facilities have often defied specification as to what it is that does and does not constitute a halfway house. For this text, halfway houses are defined as residential facilities for offenders that are either nearing release from prison or are in the initial stages of return to the community. In addition, halfway houses also consist of residential facilities that are designed as an intermediate sentencing option prior to prison, typically being applicable to serious probationers. Thus, halfway houses can be defined as either being halfway out or halfway in in scope of their function and operation.

It is this last point of the definition that has not been addressed so far in relation to halfway houses. During the past few decades, innovations in the operation of halfway houses have established such facilities as alternatives to jail or prison incarceration. Thus, it becomes clear that these facilities can actually be tied to jail diversion programs, particularly if the halfway house is designed for substance abuse treatment, co-occurring disorders, and/or primary diagnoses for mental illness. Indeed, many such facilities do specialize in such interventions, and this led to further blurring of the distinctions between halfway houses and other residential facilities that house the offender population. In fact, Champion (2002) went so far as to add that these facilities are sometimes referred to as community residential facilities. The fact that the IHHA changed its name to reflect residential and community alternatives underscores much of the blurring that exists within this component of community corrections. Nevertheless, the distinctions between halfway-in and halfway-out houses is important for students to remember since the severity of criminal behavior is typically different. Where one attempts to prevent further drift into an incarceration environment (halfway in), the other attempts to increase drift from the incarceration environment and with corresponding social "pulls and tugs" back in to the community.

⬚ Community Residential Treatment Centers

Community residential treatment centers are nonconfining residential facilities that are utilized as alternatives for adjudicated adults or juveniles who are not appropriate for probation and/or who need a period of readjustment after imprisonment. Most of these facilities serve the juvenile population, and some may specialize in either a type of offender (i.e., women) or type of treatment modality. The distinctions between community residential treatment centers may not be clear from those of the simple halfway house. However, the main point with residential treatment centers is that they are designed for persons who are not good risks for probation whereas halfway houses (at least halfway-out houses) are specifically designed for offenders who are expected to be released to the community. Halfway-in houses could be considered community residential treatment centers, but even in these cases, the person is still likely to be classified as being on probation.

With respect to community residential treatment centers, many have been created to address drug and/or alcohol problems. The most common facilities are those that are short-term and long-term in nature. Students may recall that different types of treatment programs were presented in relation to the use of reentry courts. In that case, the use of reentry courts were shown to be integrated with various treatment approaches, particularly in regard to substance abuse issues. Among these treatment approaches were the use of drug treatment programs in short-term and long-term residential facilities. This information is again provided in a different light, as community residential treatment facilities. This is not meant to be redundant but instead is intended to demonstrate the interlocking nature of many community corrections programs and processes. The connection between the courts, treatment modality, and the type of facility use are all interconnected in a means that reflects both treatment and security considerations. The longer term residential program, the type of halfway house (i.e., halfway-in house versus halfway-out house), and the type of jail program all reflect the likely seriousness of the offender and their prior behavior, thereby being a security consideration in most cases. The particular type of treatment program used may reflect either clinical issues or the type of offender. For instance, consider the use of diversionary treatment programs for mental health and/or drug treatment programs (type of clinical issue) or those designed for sex offenders, female offenders, and juvenile offenders (types of offenders). It is then clear that a great degree of variability and overlap exists when one takes into account both the security and the treatment aspects of offender processing.

As noted at the beginning of this subsection, many residential treatment facilities have been designed for drug treatment. This is one of the most common uses of residential

▲ **Photo 7.1** This residential treatment facility is informal in appearance and is located among other residences in a low income area of the community. Its decor is fairly relaxing. Also notice the metal stairs that serve as a fire escape. Refurbished facilities such as these must still meet state fire code and health regulations to remain open.

treatment facilities, though other types exist, particularly for juvenile offenders (see Section X for these particular types of programs). Since the 1980s, there has been an increased connection between drug courts and many community residential treatment facilities. This connection between these two functions demonstrates how different components of the criminal justice system may work in unison to provide a comprehensive means of processing. In these partnerships, short-term residential programs typically provide intensive but relatively brief residential treatment based on a modified 12-step approach. In most cases, offenders are kept in the program for no more than 90 days; often, their stay is for a period that is considerably less lengthy. On the other hand, long-term residential treatment provides housing in what are typically nonhospital-like settings. Within the field of addictions treatment, the most widely utilized form of residential treatment is the therapeutic community (TC). These programs tend to house drug offenders anywhere from 6 to 12 months. One example of the use of long-term residential TC treatment would be the Federal Bureau of Prison's Residential Drug Abuse Treatment Program attempts to identify, confront, and alter the attitudes, values, and thought patterns that led to criminal behavior and drug or alcohol abuse. This model program consists of three stages. First, there is a unit-based treatment program that exists within the confines of a prison where inmates undergo therapy for up to 12 months. Second, upon completion of the residential portion, offenders continue treatment for up to 12 months while in the general population of the prison, through monthly group meetings with the drug abuse program staff. In the third phase, inmates are transferred to community-based facilities prior to release from custody and are provided with regularly scheduled group, individual, and family counseling sessions (Inciardi, 1999b).

It is interesting to note that social reactions to long-term residential treatment centers, including those operating as therapeutic communities, have ranged from negative to positive, with community reactions often being negative. In many cases, it has been found that communities do express concern over having these types of treatment programs within their locale due to the perceived threat that members pose and due to effects on local real estate value fluctuations. This is unfortunate since it has been made clear throughout this text that the participation of the community itself is critical to the effectiveness of community corrections programs. While it is of course understandable why community members would be averse to having their property values diminished, it is perhaps the negative perception itself that ultimately results in the reduction of value in the first place. Though the process may be complicated, work with various local forms of government to ensure that zoning and/or home owner's insurance agencies do not penalize communities that work with community residential treatment facilities might be one effective means of offsetting community concerns. Further, employers in the area stand to gain from substantial tax breaks when they hire ex-offenders. These offenders seldom take jobs that would actually displace the nonoffending community member, particularly when considering the stigma that follows them in the hiring process. Thus, such offenders, while at residential facilities or immediately upon release, can fill an employment gap that may exist in a community. The point is that if done in an innovative, comprehensive, and coherent manner, the negative impact of integrating residential facilities into a community can be mitigated and, in some cases, the introduction of such facilities can even be a boon to that community.

▲ **Photo 7.2** Buildings such as this one demonstrate that residential facilities can be quite large in some cases. Such facilities come in all shapes and sizes, this one being brick and having a much different appearance from the facility illustrated in the previous photo.

Restitution Centers

Another type of residential treatment facility is the restitution center. Restitution centers are a type of facility that is designed primarily for first-time and/or property offenders. These offenders are required to pay victim restitution and/or provide community service as a means of fulfilling their sentence. While restitution centers may network with other treatment agencies, when such services are required for a given offender, their primary focus is on employment and providing economic amends to the victims of their crime. This is important because this once again demonstrates that residential facilities can provide benefits to the community. This is particularly true if the victim is in the very community in which the restitution center exists. In this respect, the offender has to replace the damage that is done to the victim—a much more productive use of the offender's time than is sitting in a jail or prison cell. As can be seen, there is a great deal of variation among residential facilities. In fact, some may be privately operated in some cases whereas others are part of an entire state system. Some residential programs may be privately based but funded by federal and/or state money. In most cases, residential facilities do receive some type of reimbursement for services either at the local county level and/or the state level. These facilities naturally tend to work in tandem with the local courthouse and the probation agency. This is particularly true since such facilities are designed for offenders who are not suitable for probation. However, residential facilities are also impacted by the region and/or socioeconomic characteristics of their area. In fact, this can have a very important bearing on how such facilities operate and the services that they provide. In particular, centers may find that they face differing challenges depending on whether they are located in a rural area, a midsized area, or a metropolitan area of the nation. It is with this in mind that we now turn our attention to the differing challenges that face both rural and urban residential centers.

Rural and Urban Residential Centers

Community residential centers in rural areas often had challenges that are not necessary to consider in many urban areas. The towns are smaller, and this also means that offenders have fewer educational and/or vocational options when compared to those in urban areas. Transportation may be an issue that serves as a serious impediment, as jobs may be far from the residential facility. The rural nature of these areas often require that offenders may have to travel greater distances to programs, services, and employment opportunities. Further, in small towns, the offender may be known to most of the people in the area. This lack of anonymity can also be an impediment, resulting in further challenges for the offender since stigmatization is more likely. In many cases, the offender may find it very difficult to overcome the obstacles that exist in such areas. Further, these residential facilities tend to be even further limited by budget, making the provision of comprehensive services even more difficult.

Conversely, urban residential centers have many advantages over those located in rural areas. These facilities will have a much wider array of social services to draw from. This alone serves as a very important benefit since it is the ultimate aim of these programs to reintegrate those offenders who are safe for such approaches. Though offenders in residential treatment facilities are not necessarily appropriate for probation, these offenders do eventually reenter the community, whether this be on probation or on some other form of modified sentence. This then means that full casework services are important for these offenders just as they are for offenders on community supervision. In many cases, these full casework services are not available to residential facilities located in rural areas but they are more frequently available in midsized or metropolitan areas. This results in a distinct advantage that these programs have over smaller rural-based operations. Further, transportation issues are often dealt with through mass transit availability. This alone makes various employment opportunities within easier reach of offenders since they have the benefit of more flexible mobility within urban areas.

Work Release and Study Release Programs

Work release programs are programs that are designed to equip offenders with the opportunity to seek employment and/or maintain employment, while also engaging in educational or vocational training, as well as other treatment services that might be available at the facility. These programs are often used in replacement of jail sentences. These programs most often provide day and night supervision, job referral services, and counseling for residents (Latessa & Allen, 1999). In many cases, offender unemployment or difficulties in maintaining substantive employment can be leading issues behind offender recidivism. Research throughout the nation clearly shows that offender employment tends to reduce recidivism. Because the basic needs of offenders must be met, it is critical that they obtain income that can accommodate those needs. It is this issue specifically that work release facilities seek to ameliorate.

The state of Washington has recently (in 2007) completed a study of its own work release program, examining a total of 15 work release centers that are operated by the state. The fact that this state has conducted recent research on the effectiveness of these programs is important because it demonstrates several points that are germane to this section and to this text as a whole. First, these programs have been implemented at a state level, demonstrating that like community restitution centers in Mississippi (discussed earlier), there is widespread use of community corrections alternatives in many states. Second, these programs are being put to the test with very reliable and competently designed forms of research evaluation. Third, this use of community corrections alternatives and the resulting research evaluations are occurring in the modern day, making the information all the more relevant to an argument on behalf of offender reintegration. These three points demonstrate that community residential programs are not just options utilized by private companies, faith-based groups, and other such independent actors but are often utilized by state correctional programs themselves. This adds to the credibility of these interventions, particularly when and if the research demonstrates recidivism reduction as well as other benefits such as lowered costs.

In the state of Washington, work release centers tend to be used with inmates who have already served some time in either a jail or prison facility. The work release program in Washington was first implemented in 1967 and was designed to enable selected offenders to serve up to 6 months of their prison sentence in a residential facility while employed in the community. Currently, the state of Washington has 15 such centers that house roughly 700 offenders throughout the state (Washington State Institute for Public Policy, 2007). While the state has its own criteria as to the types of offenders who may participate in work release, each facility has its own local criteria as well. As an example, some work release facilities may house male and female offenders while others are specific to only one gender. Likewise, some may be structured as therapeutic communities with substance abuse issues being an additional focus beyond employment considerations. Further, this state may also allow certain categories of sex offenders to enter work release programs, though specific forms of careful screening are implemented, identifying those that are not at the upper likelihood of recidivism.

Focus Topic 7.1

Work Release Programs in the State of Washington

Work release facilities enable certain offenders under the jurisdiction of the Washington State Department of Corrections (DOC) to serve up to six months of their prison sentence in a residential facility while employed in the community. Today, there are 15 work release facilities that house about 700 offenders statewide.

In 2007, the state legislature began to evaluate whether participation in Washington's work release facilities impacts recidivism. Our time period of study includes offenders released from DOC between January 1998 and July 2003. Findings from the study indicate participation in Washington's work release facilities:

- lowers total recidivism, by 2.8 percent
- has a marginal effect on felony recidivism; by 1.8 percent; and
- has no effect on violent felony recidivism.

Of the 15 facilities operating in 1998 to 2003, the state of Washington found that participation in some facilities was more effective than others in the reduction of recidivism. An economic model was utilized to determine if the marginal benefits of work release outweigh the cost. Based upon the felony recidivism findings, participation in work release generates $3.82 of benefits per dollar of cost. The benefits (about $2,300 per work release participant) stem from the future benefits to taxpayers and crime victims from the reduced recidivism.

For more information, see http://www.doc.wa.gov/facilities/workrelease/default.asp

Interestingly, this state uses private contractors to provide security for these facilities, food service, maintenance, and clerical functions. The actual state staff will typically consist of the work release supervisor, the case management staff, and their immediate administrative support (Washington State Institute for Public Policy, 2007). Thus, these facilities utilize a fusion between public and private employees to run and operate these facilities at a maximal level while also ensuring accountability to the state's DOC. This results in fiscal advantages while at the same time ensuring that these facilities are given appropriate public oversight.

While in these facilities, offenders are responsible for finding their own employment and are given roughly 10 days to do so once they arrive in the facility (Washington State Institute for Public Policy, 2007). Offenders are required to work 40 hours a week. In many cases, facilities have created informal agreements with local employers as a means of ensuring that offenders have the ability to obtain employment. In an effort to provide comprehensive employment services, these facilities sometimes have job specialists among the staff who are tasked with providing offenders with teaching résumé design, interviewing techniques, and job preparation. These specialists often are personnel who come from the state's employment services or are contracted professionals. The point to this is that offenders are given guidance on techniques in obtaining employment. Thus, these facilities link with outside employers while simultaneously providing a series of services that aid offenders in their job search and their ability to acquire a job. Further, employers get federal tax credits for hiring offenders and, when the employment is appropriate, the community benefits from the offender's work. When combined with restitution programs, this can provide money for specific victims or victim funds that are operated by the state. Thus, the community as a whole, the victims throughout the state, and the offender as well can benefit from these programs when they are run successfully.

As just noted, work release and restitution centers may have simultaneous functions and in many cases may be one in the same. This is not always true; some programs may have limited areas of focus, but when possible, it is recommended that facilities incorporate as many of these various objectives as possible. An emphasis on employment obviously has a logical connection to the ability for offenders to provide restitution. Likewise, it was noted that in the state of Washington, many work release programs provide additional focus on treatment issues, such as with substance abuse recovery. This is important since many of these offenders will tend to have problems with substance abuse, such challenges being extremely common among the offender population. Likewise, an emphasis on female offenders would necessitate services such as child care and even perhaps issues related to hiring disparity between men and women, with additional networking necessary to provide women with suitable employment in some industries. This can be particularly important in rural areas where much of the work may be male dominated and/or geared toward heavy labor. Thus, challenges facing locales and the type of offender involved can be quite diverse. Because of the variety of challenges that are likely to be encountered, it is probably most appropriate for work release centers to be multivaried in their services. This again demonstrates the overlap that exists within community corrections programs and provides further indication of the blurring in distinctions between one type of program and another within the field of community corrections.

A less known and less used variant of the work release center is the study release center or program. The **study release program** is similar to work release programs but is used to allow the offender to pursue educational goals. In fact, some states such as Arkansas may classify the criteria and the formal request process for study and work release options into the same category and requiring the same paperwork. Thus, these two programs do somewhat work hand in hand and should be viewed as being complementary of one another. The various types of study release can actually be quite relevant to the offender's ability to ultimately reintegrate effectively and to obtain employment. Study release programs may exist for basic adult education such as high school completion and/or high school equivalency (GED), technical or vocational education, and even college. These types of programs are fairly rare since many prison systems do offer similar educational opportunities. Nevertheless, study release may be a service that is offered in tandem with work release functions, thereby providing the offender with even more opportunities within the community.

Cost-Effectiveness and Actual Program Effectiveness of Community Residential Centers

Overall, it would appear that most forms of community residential centers are much more cost effective than are prisons. The general body of evidence clearly demonstrates that halfway houses and other community residential facilities are much more cost effective than prisons while also meeting the goals of reintegration by providing the offender with the ability to maintain community ties and to access community resources. Further, recent research from the Washington State Institute for Public Policy (2007) provides one of the most systematic and methodologically sound means of examining community-based residential centers that exists. These researchers conducted a cost–benefit analysis to determine the monetary benefits for offender placement into community residential treatment facilities. They factored into their model of evaluation that crime reductions would result in economic benefits to both the taxpayers and to crime victims. Overall, this group found that participation in work release generated $3.82 of benefits per dollar of cost (Washington State Institute for Public Policy, 2007). While most of these benefits were due to future benefits to the community and potential victims from recidivism reductions, it is nonetheless clear that these programs provide an economic incentive for society as a whole. Further, this does not even count the monetary considerations for restitution to victims. Thus, it is clear that residential centers provide cost effective services that are superior to the increased use of prisons.

In regard to recidivism, it would appear that in most cases, recidivism rates are typically no higher than for offenders who remain in prison and are later released directly into society. Latessa and Allen (1999) noted that issues related to determining recidivism are complex to address due to the variety of facilities, the diversity of offenders they service, and the differing regions of the United States (the external community being important to offender outcomes). Because of this variability, it is difficult to develop equivalent comparison groups. Citing 1990s research, Latessa and Allen (1999) noted that recidivism rates are low, being from 2% to 17%. When considering halfway houses in particular, Latessa and Allen (1999) noted that "on the whole, follow-up recidivism studies indicate that halfway house residents perform no worse than offenders who receive other services" (p. 393).

Even better results were found by more rigorous and more recent research provided by the Washington State Institute for Public Policy (2007). This group found that in the state of Washington, work release programs reduced overall recidivism (including misdemeanor and felony offenders) by about 2.8% and reduced recidivism for felony offenders by 1.8%. Though these reductions in recidivism are not great at all, it still should be pointed out that this is much better than if recidivism outcomes had gone in the other direction. When taken into consideration that these outcomes were achieved while also providing an economic benefit to society, it becomes clear that these programs are superior to pure forms of incarceration and that they do not place the public in jeopardy. Lastly, this same research did find that these programs did not have any effect on recidivism for violent offenders. This is important for two reasons. First, even with felony offenders, no increase in and no lowering of recidivism were detected as being significant on a mathematical (or statistically significant) level. Second, this research demonstrates why it is important to appropriately assess and classify offenders before placing them in these programs. It is clear that one would desire to include misdemeanant and felony offenders who are not violent since these offenders provide the greatest gains in monetary savings as well as slight reductions in recidivism. While violent offenders did not become more serious, they do not provide the same gains that other offenders do provide and therefore should not be considered as candidates for such programs—particularly in agencies that wish to optimize their outcomes and the use of their resources.

Lastly, the Washington State Institute for Public Policy (2007) conducted a comparison of research work release programs and recidivism. They found that, in general, programs are effective in reducing recidivism. Table 7.2 demonstrates that overall these programs have been successful when they have been evaluated based on recidivism. This is determined by the effect size found in each study. The effect size measures the degree to which a program has been shown to change an outcome for program participants relative to the comparison group. A negative effect size indicates a decrease in recidivism, and a positive effect size indicates an increase in recidivism. While 3 of the 4 studies found that work release programs reduce recidivism, the fourth study, which implemented more rigorous methodological approaches, failed to find any significant differences in outcomes. The researchers with the Washington State Institute for Public Policy noted that there is a dearth of current research on these programs and cited the need for further research on these programs.

Table 7.2 Rigorous Studies Evaluating the Impact of Participation of Work Release on Recidivism

	Jeffrey & Woollpert	LeClair & Guarino-Ghezzi	Turner & Petersilia	Waldo & Chiricos
Study Information				
Year published	1974	1991	1996	1977
Research design level[a]	3	3	5	5
Program Information				
State	California	Massachusetts	Washington	Florida
Number in work release	109	212	112	188
Number in comparison	92	211	106	93
Adjusted effect size	−0.172	−0.049	−0.049	0.021

Citations:
1) Jeffrey, R., & Woollpert, S. (1974). Work furlough as an alternative to incarceration. *The Journal of Criminology, 65*(3), 405–415.
2) LeClair, D. P., & Guarino-Ghezzi, S. (1991). Does incapacitation guarantee public safety? Lessons from the Massachusetts furlough and prerelease programs. *Justice Quarterly, 8*(1), 9–36.
3) Turner, S. M., & Petersilia, J. (1996). Work release in Washington: Effects on recidivism and corrections costs. *Prison Journal, 76*(2), 138–164.
4) Waldo, G. P., & Chiricos, T. G. (1977). Work release and recidivism: An empirical evaluation of a social policy. *Evaluation Quarterly, 1*(1), 87–108.

[a]Studies are rated based upon the Maryland scale of rigor—1 is the lowest quality and 5 is the highest quality, random assignment. In our analysis of the literature, we only report findings of studies rated a 3 or higher.

From the comments made by Latessa and Allen (1999) regarding halfway houses, the research by the Washington State Institute for Public Policy (2007) on work release, and the outcomes seen in Tennessee regarding restitution programs, it is clear that states are finding that, in general, community residential centers do "work," in both saving money and even reducing recidivism. Though the reductions in recidivism are often slight, the outcomes are nonetheless improvements that should not be ignored. It cannot be said that nothing works in the field of residential treatment, and practitioners who make such claims are simply not educated on current outcomes that exist across the nation. Even when recidivism is not reduced, these programs do not increase recidivism rates. Yet in all cases, there are substantive economic benefits that are realized among these programs, regardless of the impact on recidivism; thus, these programs do indeed work regardless of what might be otherwise contended by skeptics and laypersons.

Complex Offender Cases in Residential Facilities

Just as there are a variety of community-based residential treatment facilities, there are also a variety of offenders who may be encountered in those facilities. While the types of criminal offenses may vary, it is the recommendation of these authors that such facilities should generally exclude those offenders who have more than one violent crime. While some offenders may have an isolated incident where violence might occur, those with repeat offenses of simple assault, sexual assault, and more serious assaults are all too great a risk to the community as to be entrusted in such facilities. Further, these types of offenders are likely to have a negative impact on the informal culture and operations within a residential treatment facility, contaminating the positive effects that other offenders might otherwise realize. However, there is another reason why it is not necessary to even consider such offenders; they are a distinct minority of the correctional population. Given that offenders in this category include such a small percentage of the overall offender population, this should not even be an issue. Thus, community-based residential facilities can and should focus their attention on nonviolent, property, and drug-related offenders. There simply is no logical reason for these facilities to place their attention otherwise since this still leaves a very large offender base that can benefit from such services.

Even though careful selection is warranted, particularly with violent offenders, it is still the case that facilities will find themselves challenged with a variety of issues associated with complex offender concerns. As noted in previous sections with jail diversion programs, offenders may be selected based on problems with substance abuse and/or mental health issues. This is actually a recurring issue in many residential facilities, whether jail diversion or otherwise. Some offenders may simply be dealing with serious bouts of depression, and this obviously will affect their motivation levels when employed in the community and/or their ability to follow through with requirements. These offenders are also likely to require some sort of antidepressant medication, and unless medical staff are available at the facility, accommodations must be made to allow these offenders to have access to those medications. Naturally, this opens up a whole set of difficulties for the facility, both in terms of the offender's welfare and in terms of security of the drugs within the facility.

Other offenders may have a variety of personality disorders. In such cases, these offenders will tend to have a number of intractable thought processes that are maladaptive and difficult to work with. The attitudes and personalities may reflect pervasive problems with adjustment, self-perceptions, and understanding of the social environment around them. Some offenders may have challenges associated with intelligence; this being common since offenders in prisons tend to score roughly one standard deviation lower on IQ tests than do persons in the general community. Often, this may be due to a lack of educational access, but this also can be the result of neurological deficits that were inherent or even caused by long-term drug use. In addition, other offenders may have problems with anxiety, trauma, or any other set of disorders. The point is that the variety of mental health challenges can be great and just as jail staff must be prepared to address these issues so, too, should persons working at residential facilities.

Beyond mental health issues, there are a number of other factors dealing with adjustment and cognitive ability that are also relevant. For instance, some offenders may simply have low tolerances for frustration and ambiguity. This is often a sign of lower cognitive functioning, as ambiguity in social situations is more difficult to work with and interpret; this also leads to stress. Further still, offenders coping with new adaptations may find it difficult to meet demands placed upon them and may act out in both criminal and noncriminal means. This is particularly true with substance abusing offenders who may have depleted neural functioning, damage to their nervous systems, and/or negative social learning experiences that have affected their ability to deal with stressful and undefined circumstances. Because of this, these offenders will likely require more attention from residential staff and will also be prone to social problems within the facility. While these behaviors may not be criminal, they still place burdens on staff and other offenders in the facility.

The age of the offender may present certain challenges. For instance, juveniles are typically kept in separate programs and facilities, away from adult offenders. These offenders present an array of problems that are unique to adolescence and maturation. More will be discussed about juvenile offenders in Section X. On the other hand, offenders may be elderly, and this provides other challenges since such offenders are likely to be more prone to needing medical services on a routine basis. Further still, occupational options may be limited for these offenders since their health may restrict their ability to perform certain duties. In addition, it is common for elderly offenders to lack a support network since, over time, many of the persons to whom they were connected may have since given up on the offender or moved onward in life without the inclusion of the offender who has spent years behind bars; this is particularly true for offenders who have served time for several years and are just returning to the community after a long stint in prison.

One thing that should be mentioned is that unlike probation and parole, for residential facilities that house elderly offenders or persons with impediments, it is the facility that must take into account these various needs because the offender is in their custody. Thus, staff in these facilities must attend to day-to-day issues associated with these offender's livelihoods. While probation and parole staff may have to consider the challenges associated with such offenders, they typically are not charged with providing for the daily needs of these offenders. It is typically not within the scope of duty for most CSOs. Thus, residential staff must contend with the various complex needs of these and other offenders in a much more personal manner. This is one of the key distinctions between care for specialized offenders in residential facilities and those that are strictly supervised in the community. As with juvenile offenders, an additional section discusses the issues related to elderly offenders in more detail.

Lastly, some offenders may have medical challenges that impair their ability to function. Some may be physically disabled while others may have communicable diseases. Others still may have common medical problems such as hypertension whereas others may have a variety of health issues due to extensive prior addictions. Indeed, it is commonly true that offenders do tend to age more rapidly than do persons in the general community due to the ravages of their lifestyle on the streets as well as that experienced when in prison. In fact, prior inmates will often appear as if they were 10 years older than they actually may be chronologically, with their physiological functioning being impacted just as mush as their appearances are likely to be. In such cases, accommodations must be made and legal issues associated with the Americans with Disabilities Act may emerge as a consideration for residential staff and management.

Applied Theory Section 7.1

Differential Association and Treatment in Residential Facilities

Differential association serves as the precursor to many other types of criminological theory based on social learning elements. First postulated by Edwin Sutherland, this theory would be researched, tested, and modified by a number of scholars who would follow. In describing this theory, Cullen and Agnew (2006) provided a clear and effective explanation that follows:

> Crime is learned through associations with criminal definitions. Interacting with antisocial peers is a major cause of crime. Criminal behavior will be repeated and become chronic if it is reinforced. When criminal subcultures exist, many individuals can learn to commit crime in one location. (p. 6)

This notion that criminals teach one another how to engage in criminal activity is an important one in the field of corrections. Indeed, a number of studies have found that the longer an inmate spends in prison, the more likely they are to recidivate. The general notion is that prison breeds criminals and does not actually work to rehabilitate them. Thus, our nation's prisons encourage the development of inmate subcultures that ensure crime will continue. This, at least in part, explains the high recidivism rate among parolees and those released from prison.

It is for this reason that community-based residential treatment facilities are considered a much better option than prison, whenever such options are available and feasible for public safety. These facilities generate definitions that are conducive to treatment, not crime. Further, peers selected for such programs will also be in such programs for reintegrative purposes, thus diminishing the impact of pro-criminal peers that one is much more likely to find in prison. The environments associated with residential treatment facilities are designed to specifically counter those associations that are related to criminality. This is the specific charge of any effective treatment program, and staff at such facilities know to look for attitudes and behaviors among residents that might indicate a lack of recovery.

Thus, at their base, residential treatment facilities utilize the concepts of differential association. Indeed, Sutherland contended that both pro-criminal and anti-criminal definitions from other persons work to counteract against one another. When an excess of pro-criminal influences exists, the individual is more likely to engage in criminal behavior. Likewise, when an excess of anti-criminal definitions exist, the individual will be less likely to engage in criminal acts. This is the precise premise that is used in community-based residential treatment facilities. The offender is given gradual levels of freedom but is also surrounded by a regimen and group of staff and peers that support pro-social activities, eschewing further criminal activity. As has been noted, these programs have been found to be effective, and this is not surprising since differential association and its protégé, social learning theory (by Ronald Akers), have also received a great deal of empirical support.

Typical Staff in Residential Treatment Facilities

Typically, within residential facilities, staff will tend to play one of three roles. These roles are (1) the security role, (2) the treatment role, and (3) the auxiliary and/or support role. Each of these areas of operation is critical to residential facility operations. Though all of these individuals act within their own sphere of understanding, it is often the case that functions may overlap with security and/or treatment staff fulfilling other functions that are typically associated with auxiliary staff or other personnel. The point is that these facilities often require that staff work in a supportive manner and that the roles and functions may overlap, just as do the roles and functions of various community residential treatment programs throughout the nation. Nevertheless, these three types of residential staff are briefly presented in the following paragraphs to provide students with a general idea of the operations within many community residential treatment facilities.

Among staff, there are typically some that will fulfill a custodial role within the facility. As noted earlier, some residential facilities are privately operated while others may be overseen by the state or the county. In either event, the role of the custodial staff will typically be very similar. These staff will often be involved in the intake of new offenders by completing the proper paperwork, conducting inventories of the offender's personal property, as well as explaining and enforcing the rules of the facility to new residents. These staff will enforce rules by monitoring offender progress via telephone checks to ensure offender compliance while in the community. These same staff will also monitor activities at the facility through physical security checks. These are also the staff that will be tasked with collecting specimens for drug testing while also conducting random inspections of offenders and their living quarters to ensure that clients do not have contraband within the facility. Staff also write reports, monitor medications, and perform a sundry array of duties that encompass the day-to-day operations of the facility. This staff typically only requires a high school diploma or GED but requires persons who have good judgment and the ability to work in flexible rotating shifts that are necessary for facility operations.

Other staff might include correctional treatment staff and/or clinical staff. Regardless of the specific title that is given to these staff, they typically engage in various forms of case management and will engage in many of the same functions that correctional treatment specialists would fulfill. These staff will conduct group counseling and individual counseling sessions and a number of other tasks that are clinical in nature. Typically, these individuals will have graduate education at the master's or doctorate level and will be able to complete clinical work such as assessments, evaluation, and a variety of mental health interventions. These individuals may work in a variety of functions, providing substance abuse classes, psychoeducational classes, anger management, as well as individual sessions.

Lastly are the many auxiliary staff who fulfill various functions such as educational or vocational training, food service, religious programs, transportation, and a wide range of other services. These staff are often what actually make the residential facility operate in a smooth fashion, delivering competent and comprehensive services. Though these staff may not be central to the primary areas of interest in community supervision—security and treatment—they do nonetheless provide services that are important and integral to the smooth functioning of the facility. Without their assistance, residential treatment options would likely be impossible to provide.

▧ Shock Incarceration

For certain offenders, the mere subjection to a loss of freedom is all that is needed to get their lives in order. As a result, the mechanism used as for its stunning value is that of shock incarceration. Shock incarceration is the short term of incarceration followed by a specified term of community supervision in hopes of deterring the offender from recidivating. These sentences usually range between 30 and 90 days with the judge reducing the original sentence and allowing the offender to be released into the community. Because the brief stint of incarceration is to provide a sense of punitive reality to the offender, most shock incarceration programs are designed for juvenile offenders or first-time offenders who have never been incarcerated before. Given the basic tenets of shock incarceration, it is mostly used in the form of mixed sentencing. In this case, offenders are given a short term of confinement and then placed on community supervision to complete their term of probation or parole. If the sanction is followed by a term of probation it is referred to as shock probation. If it is followed by a term of parole then it is referred to as shock parole. This sanctioning is particularly controversial for three reasons: First, offenders may lose access to their mode of gainful employment. Second, community relationships are disrupted. Finally, the effects of labeling and brutalization may be experienced due to the incarceration alone.

More recently, the term *shock incarceration* is used interchangeably with boot camps. This definition, however, is too narrow. Boot camps are a form of shock incarceration but are not meant to be all inclusive of all types of programs. The use of split sentencing and boot camps will be discussed as the most frequently used forms of shock incarceration.

Split Sentencing

In split sentencing, more commonly known as shock incarceration, offenders are sentenced to a term of confinement only to be released after a set time and ordered to serve the remainder of their time on probation. The logic behind such action is that the offender will develop a natural dislike of incarceration and will seek to abstain from criminal behavior in hopes of avoiding such unpleasant incarceration. It is believed that shock incarceration was developed in 1965. Vito and Allen (1981) held that shock incarceration should be viewed as a viable intermediate sanction because it (1) allowed offenders the opportunity to realistically reintegrate into the community, (2) continued positive connections with existing family, (3) decreased the amount of time spent in prison, (4) decreased prison populations, and (5) decreased the amount of funding spent on prisons. Research has demonstrated that at least three fourths of all shock incarceration programs have demonstrated some sense of effectiveness.

Boot Camps

The use of boot camps, as a form of shock incarceration and an alternative to incarceration, experienced a resurgence in 1983 when the states of Georgia and Oklahoma were seeking an alternative means for dealing with prison overcrowding. The historical development of boot camps has been well documented (see MacKenzie & Armstrong, 2004, for a more extensive overview). For the purposes of this text, we will briefly describe the historical development, purposes of boot camps, and their effectiveness in reducing recidivism.

Historical Development of Boot Camps

The roots for creating and implementing boot camps can be traced back to the work of Zebulon Brockway, who was warden at the New York Elmira Reformatory. During the late 1800s and in response to the Progressive Movement (see Rothman, 1980), the 1870 National Prison Association at their annual meeting called for the removal of punitive measures from correctional institutions and for rehabilitation as a mechanism for reintegration to be the focus of incarceration (Cullen & Gilbert, 1982). Simultaneously organized labor unions and manufacturers banded together to eliminate the use of hard prison labor for the manufacturing and sale of prison goods. The passage of the "Yates Law" effectively eliminated the use of "hard labor" as a means for reforming the inmate behind institutional walls. In spite of this effort and because of the focus on reformation, Brockway created a hard-lined military style program emphasizing "obedience, attention, and organization into the prison environment" (Armstrong, 2004, p. 8). Although this program was met with some success, it was not widely adopted. Some have argued the influx of more rehabilitative programs focusing on education led to this lack of support and adoption on a wide scale basis. In spite of this lack of continued support on a national level, it was these programs from 1888 that served as the model for the creation and implementation of programs in the early 1980s (Armstrong, 2004; Caputo, 2004).

More specifically, during the 1980s, many states were experiencing a growing inmate proliferation in state institutions, the United States had approximately 10 years of getting tough on crime, and the focus on individual responsibility highlighted both enforcement and sentencing practice by the criminal justice system (Armstrong, 2004). Using examples from the 1960s whereby young men convicted of minor offenses were given an opportunity to choose between incarceration or military service and those choosing the military option often returned to their communities as reformed young men, the need for individual-level responsibility along with a regimented militaristic structure combined to form what we know as a correctional style boot camp.

Boot Camp Goals

Models of boot camps include both a punitive and punishment aspect. Also known as a "constructive punishment philosophy," boot camps are typically designed to use some form of strict discipline with rehabilitative measures (Armstrong, 2004, p. 9). Boot camps can be divided into three generations. First-generation boot camps were created as a short military-based program focused on military discipline, physical training, and manual labor. Second-generation boot camps included all of the first generation elements but added a therapeutic programming component that focused on not only addressing individual issues such as anxiety, problem solving, self-esteem, etc., but also included an intensive supervision component following release. The third-generation boot camps provide a combination of therapeutic programming, intensive supervision following release, and an aftercare services component (Duwe & Kerschner, 2008, p. 618). As Armstrong (2004) contended, there are five goals or motivations for the creation and maintenance of boot camps:

1. *Changing Inmates:* This includes altering attitudes to be more positive, less antisocial, and less impulsive (p. 12).

2. *Impact Recidivism:* The intention is to ideally reduce criminal activity and involvement in the justice system (p. 12).

3. *Impact on Community Supervision:* Second- and third-generation boot camps have begun to institute more regimented supervision post-boot camp release. Intensive supervision strategies post-boot camp release have included 3 months of electronic monitoring (EM) or post-residential placement for up to 60 days until the offender obtains gainful employment (pp. 12–13).

4. *Reducing Prison Crowding:* By focusing on eligibility requirements and completion or graduation rates, states seek to reduce the prison population, particularly for lower-risk offenders. States must seek to ensure that they are not widening the net of confinement in their efforts to utilize alternative methods of incarceration. Some research has suggested that boot camps often experience a 40% failure rate; therefore, for this alternative to be effective, judges should be 80% certain that the offender would have received imprisonment if not for the boot camp alternative (p. 13).

5. *Positive Environment Conducive to Change:* Finally, boot camps seek to enhance the quality of management in running and maintaining a boot camp program. Therefore, officers and management should be supportive of the idea of a "constructive punishment philosophy" (pp. 13–14).

Boot Camp Program Design

Boot camps are designed as a short-term alternative to incarceration. These programs require participants to spend 90 to 120 days in a strict military disciplined style environment. Programs are designed as either a front-end program, whereby offenders are referred directly by the courts or as a condition of probation, or as a back-end program, whereby offenders typically serve some short-term amount of incarceration and then either volunteer or are recommended for participation in a boot camp program followed by either a term of probation or parole (Caputo, 2004).

Again, thinking about the type of programs, they may be either military centered or treatment centered in their approach to dealing with offenders. Military-centered programs most often are back-end programs "designed not only to deter and punish, but also to transform participants into law-abiding and self respecting citizens" (Caputo, 2004, p. 67). Treatment-centered boot camps focus more on the underlying causes of behavior and include education and vocational components along with the regimented daily routine of the military-centered approach (Caputo, 2004).

Boot Camp Program Effectiveness

An ongoing debate exists in the field of criminal justice about the effectiveness of boot camps to achieve the five previously stated goals. Research on the ability of these programs to reduce recidivism, while not widening-the-net of incarceration, has received mixed results. For example, in a review of Pennsylvania's boot camp program, Kempinen and Kurlychek (2003) found that the recidivism rates were similar for those offenders sentenced to boot camp compared to offenders sentenced to traditional incarceration. Although there were no differences in recidivism rates, the authors did find that offenders' sentences were reduced by an average of 1 year therefore providing some support for the argument that the net was not widened in Pennsylvania. Likewise, Duwe and Kerschner (2008) found that the Minnesota Challenge Incarceration Program (CIP) reduced the amount of time under supervision by 40 days and saved the state of Minnesota at least $6.2 million between 1998 and 2002 (p. 635). Another issue generating concerns for opponents of the boot camp model is that it constitutes a violation of the offenders' Eighth Amendment protection against cruel and unusual punishment. Using the deliberate indifference and the malicious and sadistic test, Lutze and Brody (1999) examined the potential violations of boot camp programs. More specifically, they examined the involuntary nature of the program and the potential for abuses. Their review of previous court cases revealed that unless careful consideration is given for medical conditions and mental cruelty because of the "in your face" structure of the program, boot camps may be in violation of the Eighth Amendment protections thereby opening the facility for lawsuits. As MacKenzie (2006) contended, if the purpose of the boot camp programs is to reduce recidivism then an argument cannot necessarily be made to continue these programs. However, if the true goal is to reduce bed space or potential costs, as is suggested, then an argument may be made for continuing these efforts.

◪ Conclusion

This section provides an overview of several types of intermediate sanctions that are used around the country. In addition, specific examples have been provided to demonstrate the variety of sanctions that exist and their flexibility in being utilized. The flexibility of intermediate sanctions provides community supervision agencies with a range of potential responses to offender criminal behavior. This range falls along a continuum that ranges by the amount of liberty that is deprived the offender. These various penalties are interchangeable with one another and vary by level of punitiveness to allow community supervision agencies to calibrate the offender's punishment with their specific offense severity and/or tendency toward recidivism.

In addition, intermediate sanctions help to connect the supervision process with the treatment process. Lastly, as has been noted consistently throughout this text, the use of community partnerships is again emphasized. In this case, the community partnerships come by way of citizens monitoring the offender who is tasked with completing various activities to fulfill his or her sentence. The use of human supervision is again shown to be important, and intermediate sanctions are well suited to citizen involvement when ensuring offender compliance. It is in this manner that intermediate sanctions are yet one additional tool that provides external incentive for offenders to work their regimen within the community. These sanctions, when administered in a social vacuum, would not be expected to be effective. But when utilized against a backdrop of community involvement, agency collaboration, and solid case management processes, intermediate sanctions serve as another interlocking supervision mechanism that improves the overall prognosis of offender reintegration.

The term *community residential treatment* includes a variety of facilities that all have differing points of focus. From this section, we have found that these facilities exist at different points of the community corrections spectrum, with jail diversion programs existing at prebooking and postbooking points of offender processing, halfway houses being categorized as halfway in and halfway out, residential facilities being designed for persons who are not safe enough to release on probation, and other residential facilities being used as integrated treatment facilities to transition offenders back in the community. The fact that different forms of facilities provide very similar services and perform similar functions results in a blurring of the distinctions between the different types of programs. Added to this is the fact that some facilities may be privately operated (as the COMCORP example demonstrates) while others may be state run. Some programs may be small in operation whereas others may be part of an entire state's network (such as the restitution facilities in Mississippi). Thus, when we talk about community residential treatment, we actually refer to a number of different options that are available for offenders.

From the research that has been presented, it is clear that community residential treatment programs are, at least in a marginal sense, effective in reducing recidivism. Further, it is quite obvious that these options are much less expensive than the building of prison facilities. With these two points in mind, it can then be said that these options are considered generally successful in serving their intended purpose: reintegration of the offender while avoiding the ravages and criminogenic effects of prison. In addition, the research presented by this text is more recent than that which may be found in many other texts and thus is more relevant to programs in operation today. Further, this demonstrates that "something" works and that proponents of Martinson's outdated research are simply that: outdated. The weight of the research demonstrates the overall efficacy of these programs. When taken with research that also shows that prisons are criminogenic, breeding worse recidivists than do community-based programs, it becomes clear that alternatives to prison facilities just make good sense. It is on this note that we now close as we look toward the spectrum of intermediate sanctions that are available, many of which may dovetail and/or be used in tandem with the residential programs that have just been discussed in this current section.

⬙ Section Summary

- Intermediate sanctions are a range of sentencing options that fall between incarceration and probation, being designed to allow for the crafting of sentences that respond to the offender and/or the offense, with the intended outcome of the case being a primary consideration.

- Public concern over adequate supervision, demands of victims and communities, changes in technology, the continued rise of judges tailoring sentences to the offenders and the offense, the rise in failure rates of offenders, and the impact of the drug abuse crisis were all factors giving rise to the need for intermediate sanctions.
- Halfway houses are residential options for individuals who are either halfway-in (residential options used before prison) or halfway-out (residential options used for offenders transitioning back into the community post incarceration) facilities.
- Community residential treatment centers are another variation of halfway houses whereby persons who are not good risks for probation may receive special treatment or assistance while being detained.
- Restitution centers are specifically designed to assist the offender with maintaining gainful employment as a mechanism for paying back restitution to the victim. These programs/centers are typically used for first-time or property offenders.
- Work release centers are similar to restitution centers whereby they not only provide opportunities and assistance for offenders to work but they also provide educational and vocational training to participants.
- Study release programs are similar to work release, but they are used primarily for the offender to pursue educational goals.
- Shock incarceration is a sanction designed to "shock" offenders into compliance. These programs may include shock probation, shock parole, split sentencing, and boot camps.
- Boot camps are short-term programs based on military discipline. The current model originated in Georgia and Oklahoma in 1983. Three generations of boot camps exist.
- The goals of boot camp programs can be divided into five broad categories: (1) changing inmates, (2) impacting recidivism, (3) impacting community supervision, (4) reducing prison crowding, and (5) providing a positive environment conducive to change

KEY TERMS

Community residential treatment centers

Community service

Day reporting centers

Electronic monitoring (EM)

Intensive supervision

Intermediate sanctions

International Association of Residential and Community Alternatives (IARCA)

Jail

Jail diversion

Jail diversion programs

Long-term residential treatment

Restitution centers

Shock incarceration

Short-term residential programs

Study release program

Work release centers

DISCUSSION QUESTIONS

1. What is the definition and purpose of intermediate sanctions?

2. How does the concept of a continuum of sanctions apply to the use of intermediate sanctions? What are the pros and cons of having a continuum of sanctions?

3. Analyze the various means of ensuring offender compliance among substance abusers and sex offenders.

4. Compare the various means by which intermediate sanctions are used in a variety of states around the nation.

5. Describe the development history of halfway houses in the United States. What are the differences in purpose and scope of the various forms of halfway houses?

6. Be aware of the various types of community residential treatment programs that exist.

7. Discuss how the needs of offenders in community residential centers differ from those in traditional community-based sanctions.

8. Identify and discuss the five goals or motivations for the creation and maintenance of boot camps.

WEB RESOURCES

Family First Boot Camps:
http://familyfirstaid.org/alternatives.html

Office of Juvenile Justice and Delinquency Prevention History of Juvenile Boot Camps:
http://ojjdp.ncjrs.gov/pubs/reform/ch2_g.html

Correctional Boot Camps: Lessons Learned From a Decade of Research:
http://www.ncjrs.gov/pdffiles1/nij/197018.pdf

National Institute of Corrections: Effects of Correctional Boot Camps on Offending:
http://nicic.gov/Library/022761

Prison Boot Camps:
http://nicic.gov/Library/011016

Office of Justice Programs:
http://www.ojp.usdoj.gov/nij/pubs-sum/157639.htm

Bureau of Prisons: Boot Camp for Prisoners:
http://www.bop.gov/news/research_projects/published_reports/gen_program_eval/oreprbootcamp.pdf

Federal Bureau of Prisons Halfway Houses:
http://buildingbettertomorrows.org/fbophwh

Electronic Monitoring vs. Halfway Houses (BOP):
http://www.bop.gov/news/research_projects/published_reports/gen_program_eval/orepralternatives.pdf

National Institute on Chemical Dependency:
http://www.nicd.us/HALFWAY_HOUSES_LOCATOR_NATIONAL_STATE_TO_STATE_SEARCH.HTML

Increasing Public Safety Through Halfway Houses:
http://centerforcommunitycorrections.org/wp-content/3-halfway-houses-pub-safety.pdf

Please refer to the student study site for web resources and additional resources.

READING

In this article, Duwe and Kerschner evaluated the merits of Minnesota's CIP examining whether it reduced recidivism and saved the state money. This program serves as an example of the third-generation boot camp where rehabilitative services followed by long-term aftercare is essential to the success of the program. Those placed in the boot camp serve 180 days in the program followed by 12 months of aftercare. Failure to complete Phase I (the boot camp program) results in offenders being sent to a state facility where they are mandated to serve their prison time plus 90 days. Using a multistage sampling technique, the authors systematically reviewed the records for all offenders placed in the CIP and matched those offenders with a control group. A total of 1,347 CIP offenders (experimental group) and 1,555 matched prisons (control group) were included in the study. Overall, the study found that CIP did decrease the time to imprisonment and did save the state $6.2 million over the course of 10 years. Likewise program participation significantly reduced the number of new offenses (program participants were twice as likely to return to prison for a technical violation than the control group), and the time to rearrest was longer for CIP participants. Program participation lowered the time to first felony rearrest but did not reduce the likelihood of returning to prison. Overall, having prior prison commitments, age at first prison commitment, having a discipline history while confined, being male, being a minority, and being arrested in a metro-county area increased the risk for reoffending. Overall, results of this study did indicate support for the use of a rehabilitative focus. The authors concluded their study with recommendations for future programming and considerations.

Removing a Nail From the Boot Camp Coffin

An Outcome Evaluation of Minnesota's Challenge Incarceration Program

Grant Duwe and Deborah Kerschner

Correctional boot camps first appeared in the United States in the early 1980s in Georgia and Oklahoma. A successor to the "shock probation" and "scared straight" (i.e., shock education) programs from the 1960s and 1970s, boot camps were initially based on the premise that military regimentation, strict discipline, and strenuous physical activity could jolt offenders into reforming their criminal ways. Moreover, by providing early release to program graduates, boot camps were also conceptualized as a means to help alleviate the problem of prison overcrowding.

Boot camps were thus widely perceived to be a tough intermediate sanction that offered the promise of significant cost savings by reducing recidivism and

AUTHORS' NOTE: The views expressed in this study are not necessarily those of the Minnesota Department of Corrections.

SOURCE: Grant Duwe & Deborah Kerschner. (2008). Removing a nail from the boot camp coffin: An outcome evaluation of Minnesota's Challenge Incarceration program. *Crime & Delinquency, 54*(4), 614–643. Copyright © 2008 Sage Publications.

the size of prison populations. As a result, the boot camp concept gained a great deal of popular support during the 1980s and early 1990s. Indeed, by the mid-1990s, more than 100 boot camps were operating in federal, state, and local jurisdictions. Much of the growth occurred between 1990 and 1992, when at least 19 states first opened a boot camp (Camp & Camp, 1996, 2002).

Minnesota was one of the 19 states, for the state legislature mandated the Commissioner of Corrections to establish the Challenge Incarceration Program (CIP) in 1992. Although the earliest correctional boot camps contained little or no programming and aftercare for participants, Minnesota, such as a number of other states that implemented boot camps during the early 1990s, placed a much greater emphasis on rehabilitation during the creation and development of CIP. The enabling legislation stipulated, for example, that CIP would contain a 6-month institutional, or "boot camp," phase and two 6-month community phases in which offenders would be intensively supervised and required to participate in aftercare programming.

Although CIP has generally been well received in the state, the same cannot be said for boot camps nationwide. After reaching a peak in the mid-1990s, the number of boot camps operating in the United States has slowly declined. Most recently, the Federal Bureau of Prisons decided in January 2005 to close its 14-year-old boot camp program (i.e., the Intensive Confinement Center that operated in Pennsylvania, Texas, and California) that had, at one time, served more than 7,000 prisoners (Paulson. 2005).

Although some have attributed the decline to reported instances of physical and emotional abuse (Bottcher & Ezell, 2005), most have noted the failure of boot camp evaluations to demonstrate a reduction in offender recidivism. Of the more than 30 outcome evaluations since the 1980s, only a small minority have presented evidence showing a significant recidivism reduction among boot camp participants (Farrington et al., 2002; Jones, Olson, Karr, & Urbas, 2003; Kurlychek & Kempinen, 2006; MacKenzie & Souryal,

1994; Marcus-Mendoza, 1995). Although nearly every boot camp evaluation has examined offender recidivism, few have analyzed whether boot camps actually reduce costs. Despite the weak evidence regarding the ability of boot camps to lower recidivism, several studies have found significant reductions in prison beds and total costs (Clark, Aziz, & MacKenzie, 1994; Farrington et al., 2002; Jones et al., 2003; Marcus-Mendoza, 1995; State of New York, Department of Correctional Services, Division of Parole, 2005), whereas Austin and colleagues (2000) reported only modest savings.

The Present Study

Although it has been more than 14 years since CIP first opened in October 1992, it has yet to undergo a rigorous outcome evaluation. To this end, the present study evaluates CIP since its inception, focusing on two main questions: (a) Does CIP significantly reduce offender recidivism? and (b) Does CIP reduce costs?

Before examining these questions in more detail, the ensuing section describes CIP. Next, this study briefly reviews the boot camp and cost-benefit analysis literature, discusses the data and methods used to analyze recidivism, and presents the findings from the recidivism analyses. The methodology used for the cost-benefit analysis is then described, followed by a presentation of the results. This study concludes by discussing the implications of the findings for boot camps, in particular, and correctional program evaluations in general.

CIP: A Program Description

Consistent with the growing rehabilitative emphasis placed on boot camps that have opened since the early 1990s, CIP was created to be an intensive, structured, and disciplined program that not only protected public safety and punished offenders by holding them accountable, but also treated chemically dependent offenders and helped prepare them for successful reintegration into society. To meet these goals, CIP was designed to contain a 6-month institutional phase and two aftercare phases, each lasting at least 6 months. At 6 months, the institutional phase surpasses the national average of 4.6 months (Camp & Camp, 2002). Although data are not available on the lengths of aftercare for boot camps nationwide, it is unlikely that many exceed 12 months, the collective duration of Phases II and III. Thus, with three phases spanning a total of 18 months, CIP is arguably one of the longest boot camp programs in the country.

Unlike some boot camps in other states, where judges decide which offenders are eligible, Minnesota Department of Corrections (MDOC) staff determines which offenders will enter CIP by identifying those who meet the admission standards and are willing to participate. When CIP was originally created, the statutory criteria excluded offenders who have a history of violent offenses, have a term of imprisonment greater than 4 years,[1] were admitted as a supervised release violator, or received a dispositional departure. In April 2000, the admission standards were modified by expanding the list of prohibited offenses,[2] excluding offenders with more extensive criminal and institutional discipline histories,[3] and including for consideration factors such as gang affiliation, victim impact, community concern, and lack of residential ties within Minnesota. In general, the admission standards have been developed to identify nonviolent drug and property offenders who are perceived to be good candidates for early release.[4]

After meeting the eligibility requirements, incarcerated offenders are later transferred to MCF (Minnesota Correctional Facility)–Willow River (males) or MCF-Togo (females), where they enter Phase I, the "boot camp" phase. Since October 1992, CIP has accepted a group, or squad, of offenders at one time each month. During Phase I, offenders undergo a rigorous 16-hr daily schedule during which they are expected to maintain a high level of program activity and discipline. As with most correctional boot camps, military drill and

ceremony, rigorous physical training, and intensive manual labor are emphasized during Phase I. But in keeping with the rehabilitative emphasis of CIP, offenders also participate in a range of programming that includes critical thinking skills training, chemical dependency (CD) treatment, educational development, and transition planning. After successfully completing Phase I, offenders get released from MCF-Willow River (males) or MCF-Togo (females) and enter Phase II, the first of two community phases. Although in the community during Phase II, offenders are subject to intensive supervised release (ISR) conditions, which include contacting ISR agents daily, submitting to random drug and/or alcohol tests, maintaining full-time employment, abiding by assigned curfews, performing community service, and participating in aftercare programming.

After completing Phase II, offenders move on to Phase III, the final phase of CIP. During this phase, offenders remain in the community on ISR and are expected to maintain employment, perform community service and continue their participation in aftercare programming. Offenders are considered CIP graduates after they complete Phase III, at which point they are placed on regular supervised release until the expiration of their sentence.[5] However, if offenders voluntarily drop out or fail at any time during Phases I to III because of disciplinary reasons, they are required to serve the remainder of their term of imprisonment (i.e., two thirds of the pronounced sentence minus jail credit) plus the timespent in CIP in a Minnesota Correctional Facility.

◪ The Boot Camp Literature

Since the early 1980s, there have been three generations of correctional boot camps in the United States (Parent, 2003). The earliest, or "first generation," boot camps were short in duration and stressed military discipline, physical training, and manual labor. In response to disappointing evaluations of these programs, second-generation camps began placing a greater emphasis on rehabilitation by incorporating therapeutic programming during the "boot camp" phase and intensively supervising program graduates. Evaluations of the second-generation camps have generally been more positive in that findings have indicated that boot camp participation increases offenders' self-esteem, lowers their anxiety levels, reduces their antisocial attitudes, and improves their problem-solving skills (Austin et al., 2000; Gover, 2005; Kempinen & Kurlychek, 2002; MacKenzie, Gover, Styve-Armstrong, & Mitchell, 2001). Nevertheless, most studies of second-generation camps have failed to demonstrate a reduction in offender recidivism (Aloisi & LeBaron, 2001; Austin et al., 2000; Austin, Jones, & Bolyard, 1993; Burns & Vito, 1995; Kempinen & Kurlychek, 2003; Stinchcomb & Terry, 2001), whereas others have found that the increased intensity of postrelease supervision can produce a higher rate of technical violations (MacKenzie & Souryal, 1994).

The most promising recidivism findings tend to be associated with "third-generation" boot camps, which generally provide therapeutic programming, intensive postrelease supervision, and aftercare services (Jones et al., 2003; Kurlychek & Kempinen, 2006; MacKenzie, Wilson, & Kider, 2001; Wells, Minor, Angel, & Stearman, 2006). In particular, several recent studies suggest that the provision of aftercare programming may be a critical link in helping explain why few evaluations have found a recidivism reduction. For example, in an evaluation of a juvenile boot camp, Wells and colleagues (2006) found that boot camp graduates recidivated at a significantly lower rate than a matched control group during the 4-month aftercare phase. Moreover, in an evaluation of Pennsylvania's Quehanna Motivational Boot Camp, Kurlychek and Kempinen (2006) found that boot camp graduates who received aftercare services were significantly less likely to be rearrested than a control group of graduates who were not provided aftercare. Although not every study that has evaluated a boot camp with aftercare has found a reduction in reoffending (e.g., Bottcher & Ezell, 2005; Zhang, 2000), the findings suggest, on balance, that providing a continuum of care from the institution to the community increases a boot camp's chances of reducing the extent to which program graduates recidivate.

The present study does not attempt to isolate the impact of either aftercare or intensive postrelease supervision on recidivism. Instead, community supervision and aftercare are conceptualized here as essential program components for an effective boot camp. Although there is clearly value to be gained from trying to better understand the effects that specific program components have on reoffending, it is, nevertheless, true that there are relatively few existing evaluations of rehabilitative boot camps that have provided both intensive community supervision and lengthy aftercare services (Kurlychek & Kempinen, 2006). Minnesota's CIP thus offers a rare opportunity to evaluate one of the few boot camps in the country that has emphasized rehabilitation, intensively supervised graduates, and provided extensive aftercare since its beginning.

Like many prior boot camp evaluations, this study uses a retrospective quasiexperimental design. This evaluation is different, however, from the majority of existing boot camp studies in several important ways. First, by examining boot camps over the span of one or, at most, a few years—often shortly after inception—most studies have been short-term evaluations of "immature" boot camps. In contrast, by examining CIP during its first 10 years of operation, this study is a relatively long-term evaluation of a "mature" boot camp. Second, on a similar note, the follow-up period for recidivism has, with few exceptions (Bottcher & Ezell, 2005; Zhang, 2000), been relatively brief—usually 3 years or less. At 7.2 years, the average follow-up period in this study is the second longest to date, trailing only Bottcher and Ezell (2005) whose average was 7.5 years. By tracking offenders over an extended period of time, this study provides a more robust assessment of the impact of boot camp participation on recidivism. Third, apart from a few studies (Kempinen & Kurlychek, 2006; MacKenzie, Souryal, Sealock, & Kashem, 1997; Zhang, 2000), most evaluations have used control groups that have been only roughly comparable to the experimental group. This study, on the other hand, uses a sampling technique to produce a carefully matched control group that is not significantly different from the CIP group with respect to the variables used in the statistical analyses. Fourth, although many evaluations have relied on a single measure of recidivism (usually rearrest or reconviction), this study uses four different measures—rearrest, reconviction, reincarceration for a new crime, and any return to prison (for either a new offense or a technical violation). Fifth, unlike most previous evaluations, this study includes program dropouts in the analyses. Finally, as discussed in the next section, this study is one of the few boot camp evaluations to include a cost-benefit analysis.

⊠ Cost-Benefit Analysis

Boot camps can, in theory, reduce prison bed space needs in two ways: (a) offering program graduates a reduction in timeserved and (b) decreasing the amount of time offenders spend in prison following release. The reduction in bed space needs can cut costs by not only lowering the expenses involved with clothing, feeding, and housing inmates, but also by averting the need for the expansion of existing prisons or the construction of new ones. Previous research indicates that boot camps are more likely to reduce costs when they target prison-bound offenders, function as an early-release mechanism, graduate a high rate of offenders, decrease recidivism, have larger program capacities, use less restrictive entrance criteria, and are relatively short in duration (MacKenzie & Souryal, 1994; Parent, 2003). Some of these program characteristics conflict with one another, however, as efforts to lower recidivism can militate against meeting the goal of reducing bed space

needs, and vice versa. For example, lengthening a program to incorporate more therapeutic programming may help reduce recidivism, but it would also cut into the length of stay reduction, resulting in fewer bed spaces saved (Parent, 2003). Similarly, although expanding program capacity and softening the eligibility criteria might increase potential bed space savings by allowing more offenders to enter the boot camp, it may also lower the graduation rate through the admission of more high-risk offenders.

Of the boot camp evaluations that have performed cost-benefit analyses, most have focused on calculating the savings incurred from a reduction in time served for program graduates (Austin et al., 2000; Clark et al., 1994; Farrington et al., 2002; Marcus-Mendoza, 1995; State of New York, Department of Correctional Services, Division of Parole, 2005). Only two studies have tried to address the extent to which boot camps can reduce costs through a decrease in recidivism. For example, MacKenzie and Souryal (1994) generated prison bed savings estimates based on several different assumptions (as opposed to actual data) about the rate at which inmates would reoffend. In addition, Jones and colleagues (2003) attempted to account for recidivism in the cost savings analysis by deducting the amount of time served by technical violators from the overall cost savings. In the present study, however, we not only calculate the cost savings resulting from a discount in time served for program graduates, but we also use the data from the recidivism analyses to measure whether CIP decreased costs through a reduction in recidivism, which was defined as any return to prison (i.e., new offenses and technical violations).

In examining whether boot camps reduce costs, prior evaluations have generally identified the salient benefits that can be measured (e.g., prison beds saved because of early release), but have not included all of the relevant program costs, particularly the expenses involved with supervising program graduates. In this study, we include the costs resulting from both the incarceration of all Phase I participants and the supervision of Phase I completers. Moreover, consistent with the effort to avoid inflating CIP's cost savings, we use marginal costs in the cost-benefit analysis presented later. In contrast to fixed costs, which contain start-up costs associated with the construction and staffing of a prison, marginal costs include only food, clothing, medical, and other expenses that vary with the size of the inmate population. The choice of whether to use marginal or fixed costs depends on a key assumption one makes about the cost-benefit analysis. If the number of bed spaces saved is large enough to prevent the construction of a new prison, then fixed costs should be used. If not, then marginal costs should be used (Austin et al., 2000; Cohen, 2000; Lawrence & Mears, 2004).

This decision is not only a highly subjective one, but it is also a false dichotomy in that there are other options— besides construction or no construction—often available such as the expansion of existing facilities or the use of local jails or private prisons. Because the CIP population has historically represented about 1% of Minnesota's overall prison population, the number of bed spaces it has saved has never been large enough to prevent the construction of a new prison. Although we use marginal costs in our analyses, the findings shown later likely represent the most conservative cost savings estimate given that CIP's bed space savings might still be large enough to prevent the use of other measures besides new construction to deal with prison population growth.

⬚ Data and Method

In using a retrospective quasiexperimental design to compare the recidivism rates of CIP participants with a control group of offenders, this study examines all offenders who entered CIP from the time it opened, October 1992, through the end of June 2002. During this time, there were 1,347 offenders (1,216 male and 131 female) who entered CIP.[6] Given that Phase 1 of CIP lasts 6 months, nearly all of these offenders were released into the community by December 31, 2002. Similarly, the control group consists of offenders who were released from a MCF within a similar timeframe, January 1, 1993, to December 31, 2002.

Recidivism was operationalized as a rearrest, a felony reconviction, a return to prison for a new criminal offense (i.e., reimprisonment), and any return to prison (i.e., reincarceration because of a new crime or technical violation). It is important to emphasize that the first three recidivism measures contain only new criminal offenses, whereas the fourth measure is much broader in that it includes new crimes and supervised release violations.

For the first three recidivism measures, it was still necessary to account for supervised release violators in the recidivism analyses by deducting the amount of time spent in prison from their total at-risk period, or "street time." Failure to deduct time spent in prison as a supervised release violator would artificially increase the length of the at-risk periods for these offenders, particularly CIP participants, because they are generally subjected to more intense postrelease supervision (Bales, Bedard, Quinn, Ensley, & Holley, 2005). Therefore, the time that an offender spent in prison as a supervised release violator was subtracted from his or her "street" time (i.e., at-risk period), but only if it preceded a rearrest, felony reconviction, reincarceration for a new offense, or if the offender did not recidivate.

Operationalizing the concept of release is an important issue for the current study because it will have a bearing on how recidivism is measured and analyzed. To make the comparison among the experimental and control groups as even as possible, releases for the control group (i.e., the offenders who did not participate in CIP) are defined as the first instance in which they exit prison and are placed on some form of supervision such as supervised release, ISR, or work release. For the CIP group, releases are defined as any instance in which an offender has successfully completed Phase I of CIP (the institutional phase) and been released to the community. For those who fail during Phase I, their at-risk period begins when they are, like the control group, released to supervision from a MCF. Although offenders must complete Phases II and III to graduate from CIP and obtain the benefits of the term of imprisonment reduction, those who complete Phase I are, for the purposes of the recidivism analyses, considered program graduates because they are in the community during Phases II and III and, thus, have the opportunity to commit a new crime.

This study provides two different measures of boot camp participation. The first measure distinguishes between offenders who entered CIP (i.e., the experimental group) and those who did not (i.e., the control group). For this dichotomous variable, CIP participation was coded as 1, whereas the control group was coded as 0. The second measure, on the other hand, divides boot camp participation into three discrete categories: Phase I completers, Phase I failures, and the control group. For this measure, three dichotomous dummy variables were created: Phase I completers (1 = *Phase I completers*, 0 = *Phase I failures and control group offenders*), Phase I failures (1 = *Phase I failures*, 0 = *CIP graduates and control group offenders*), and control group (1 = *control group*, 0 = *Phase I failures and completers*). The control group variable serves as the reference in the statistical analyses.

Arrest, conviction, and incarceration data were collected on offenders in both the experimental and comparison groups through December 31, 2005. The average follow-up period for the 2,902 offenders was 7.2 years, with a minimum of 3 years and a maximum of 13. Data on arrests and felony convictions were obtained electronically from the Minnesota Bureau of Criminal Apprehension (BCA), whereas incarceration data were derived from the MDOC's Correctional Operations Management System database. The main limitation with using these data is that they measure only arrests, felony convictions, or incarcerations that took place in the state of Minnesota. Because neither measure includes arrests, convictions, or incarcerations occurring in other states, the findings presented later likely underestimate the true rearrest, reconviction, and reincarceration rates for the offenders examined here. Still, there is little reason to believe, however, that the omission of these data would affect offenders in the experimental group more than those in the comparison group, and vice versa.

As discussed shortly, a multistage sampling design was used to carefully select a control group that is as similar to the CIP group as possible. The control group was gathered by first selecting all offenders who were released from a MCF between January 1, 1993, and December 31, 2002, the same release timeframe for the CIP group. The CIP offenders were first removed from this sample, leaving a total of 28,644 released offenders. Next, offenders who had been incarcerated for sex and other person crimes were excluded because inmates imprisoned for violent offenses are ineligible to participate in CIP, lowering the size of the sample to 17,644 released offenders. Furthermore, offenders who were discharged, as opposed to being placed on supervised or ISR, were also removed because CIP participants are released to supervision, resulting in a total of 16,096 released offenders.

The goal of the multistage sampling procedure is to create a comparison group of offenders that matches the CIP group as closely as possible for the control variables used in the recidivism analyses. The dependent variable in the analyses is whether an offender recidivates (rearrest, felony reconviction, reimprisonment for a new offense, or any return to prison) at any point from the time of release through December 31, 2005. The principal variable of interest, meanwhile, is CIP participation because the central purpose of these analyses is to determine whether CIP significantly lowers the recidivism rates of its participants. The control variables included in the statistical model should therefore consist of those that might theoretically have an impact on whether an offender recidivates and, thus, might be considered a rival causal factor.

Previous boot camp research has suggested that the intensity of postrelease supervision and aftercare programming are important factors with respect to recidivism. As noted earlier, CIP Phase I completers are intensively supervised during Phases II and III, the first 12 months following release. Only 29 offenders in the control group, however, were released to intensive supervision. Instead, the vast majority was placed on work release or supervised release. As a result, it was not possible to include postrelease supervision as a control variable in the analyses because it was nearly perfectly collinear with program participation. Moreover, data were not available on the extent of aftercare services received by offenders in either group. The omission of these variables may be offset to some extent, however, by the relatively lengthy follow-up period used in this study. That is, if aftercare services and the intensity of postrelease supervision are significant predictors of recidivism, one might expect the beneficial impact to wear off over time, particularly after the first 12 months.

After violent offenders, CIP participants, and discharged offenders were removed from the control group, a multistage sampling design was used in which the control group was stratified by the control variables listed above. More specifically, at each stage, a simple random sample was drawn in proportion to the size of the strata (i.e., control variable) in the CIP population. For example, the first stage involved stratifying the control group by the offense type variable. Of the 1,347 CIP offenders in the experimental group, the offense type was drugs for 75%, property offenses for 21%, and other offenses for 4%. Accordingly, a simple random sample of the control group was drawn in which the offense type was drugs for 75% of the offenders in the sample, property for 21%, and other for 4%. This process was then repeated for most of the remaining control variables, resulting in a final control group sample of 1,555 offenders.[8] The multistage sampling technique was effective in producing a control group that is equivalent to the CIP population with respect to the control variables used in the recidivism analyses.

Of the boot camp evaluations that have used multivariate statistical methods, most have relied on binary logistic regression or Ordinary Least Squares regression. Only a few studies, however, have used survival analysis techniques to examine the recidivism rates of the experimental and comparison groups (Bottcher & Ezell, 2005; Kurlychek & Kempinen, 2006; MacKenzie, Brame, McDowall, & Souryal, 1995). In analyzing recidivism, survival analysis models are preferable in that they utilize time-dependent data, which are important in determining both whether and when offenders recidivate. As a result, this study uses a Cox proportional hazards model to analyze the recidivism of the CIP and control groups.

The Cox proportional hazards model uses both time and status variables in estimating the impact of program participation on recidivism. For the analyses presented here, the time variable measures the amount of time from the date of release until the date of first rearrest, reconviction, reimprisonment, return to prison, or December 31, 2005, for those who did not recidivate. For offenders who returned to prison as supervised release violators, the time they spent in prison was deducted from their total survival time when (a) recidivism was defined as either a rearrest, felony reconviction or reimprisonment for a new crime, (b) the supervised release return preceded a rearrest, reconviction, or reimprisonment, or (c) the offender did not have a rearrest, reconviction, or reimprisonment. The status variable used in the analyses was one of the four recidivism variables mentioned above, for example, rearrest, reconviction, reimprisonment for a new crime, and any return to prison.

▧ Recidivism Results

The findings reveal that the rearrest, felony reconviction, and reimprisoninent rates were lower for CIP offenders compared to those in the control group. For example, at the end of the follow-up period, 62% of the 1,347 CIP offenders were rearrested following release, 32% were reconvicted, and 22% were reincarcerated for a new crime. In comparison, 75% of the control group offenders were rearrested, 46% were reconvicted, and 34% were reincarcerated. Not surprisingly, Phase I completers had the lowest recidivism rates, as 60% were rearrested, 31% were reconvicted, and 20% were reimprisoned.

Unlike the above findings, offenders in the control and CIP groups returned to prison (whether for a new crime or for a technical violation) at virtually the same rate. The similar rate of return to prison is because of the fact that CIP offenders (both Phase I completers and dropouts) were more than twice as likely to return for a technical violation than the control group, who was, in turn, much more likely to return for a new crime. Indeed, 73% of the control group offenders returned to prison because of a new crime as opposed to 46% of CIP offenders. In contrast, 54% of the CIP offenders returned to prison for a technical violation compared to 27% of the control group.

When CIP offenders recidivated with a new crime, how did the severity of their offenses compare to that of the control group? Because the arrest and felony conviction data obtained from the BCA do not always include offense type information, reincarceration data are used to address this question. The results indicate that the control group was more likely to be reimprisoned for a crime against a person (19%) than CIP offenders (11%). Phase I dropouts, however, were more likely to recidivate with a property offense (42%), whereas Phase I completers were more likely to reoffend with a drug offense (44%).

The results presented thus far suggest that CIP offenders are, compared to the control group, less likely to reoffend with a new criminal offense. But are the lower reoffense rates for CIP offenders because of their participation in CIP? Or is the reoffense reduction because of other factors such as prior criminal history, discipline history, or offender race? To address this issue, a number of different Cox proportional hazards models with the aforementioned control variables were estimated across types of recidivism (e.g., rearrest, reconviction, reimprisonment, any return) and program participation (e.g., control vs. CIP and control, Phase I failure, and Phase I completer). In addition, to determine whether the effects of CIP are dependent on any of the control variables, interaction models were estimated for each measure of recidivism. Analogous to stepwise regression, all first-order interactions with CIP were examined and nonsignificant terms were removed until only the significant interactions remained in the model.

Rearrest

In Model 1, which is based on a binary measure of program participation (CIP = 1 and control = 0), the results indicate that, controlling for other factors, CIP significantly lowered the time to first rearrest. In particular, compared to the control group, CIP reduced the risk of timing to rearrest by 32%. Similarly, in Model 2, which divides CIP participants into completers and dropouts, the findings suggest that the risk of timing to rearrest for offenders who completed Phase I was 39% lower than the control group. Offenders who failed during Phase I, however, were not significantly different from the control group in terms of the rate at which they recidivated. This finding lends support to the notion that the CIP and control groups were very similar to each other, and that the recidivism reduction observed in both models is not because of a selection effect (i.e., CIP offenders differed in some unmeasured way from the control group).

The results from all three models further suggest that the number of prior arrests, offender race, county of commitment, age at first arrest, age at release, and length of stay were statistically significant predictors of rearrest. That is, the time to rearrest was significantly greater for offenders with prior felony convictions, minority offenders, inmates with a metro-area county of commitment, offenders younger at the time of first arrest and release, and inmates with shorter lengths of stay. The results in Model 3 indicate that the CIP × discipline and CIP × length of stay interaction terms were statistically significant, suggesting that CIP offenders' risk of timing to rearrest was dependent on both institutional disciplinary history and length of stay.

Felony Reconviction

CIP significantly lowered the time to first felony reconviction. In particular, compared to the control group, CIP reduced the risk of timing to reconviction by 32%. In Model 2, the findings suggest that the risk of timing to reconviction for offenders who completed Phase I was 37% lower than the control group.

The results from all three models further suggest that the number of prior felony convictions, offender race, county of commitment, and age at release were statistically significant predictors of felony reconvictions. Although discipline history was significant in Models 1 and 3, it failed to reach significance in Model 2. The results in Model 3 indicate that the CIP × release age, CIP × age at first conviction, and CIP × property offense interaction terms were each statistically significant.

Reimprisonment for a New Offense

The time to reincarceration for a new offense was, once again, significantly lower for CIP participants; that is, after controlling for the effects of the other independent variables, CIP decreased the risk of timing to reimprisonment by 35%. In addition, although Phase I dropouts' risk of timing to reimprisonment was not significantly different than the control group, it was 42% lower for Phase I completers.

Unlike the rearrest and reconviction analyses, metro area and release age were not significant predictors of reimprisonment for a new offense in any of the models. However, prior prison commitments, male offenders, and minority offenders significantly increased the risk of timing to reimprisonment in both models. The risk of timing to reimprisonment, however, was significantly lower for drug offenders than for other offenders. The results in Model 3 indicate that both the CIP × discipline and CIP × property offense interaction terms were statistically significant.

Any Return to Prison

Neither measure of CIP participation had a statistically significant impact on any return to prison when controlling for the other independent variables in the model. The results suggest, however, that prior prison commitments, age at first prison commitment, discipline history, male inmates, minority offenders, and those with a metro-area county of commitment all significantly increased the risk of timing to a return to prison for either a new crime or technical violation in both models.

Overall, the findings indicate that CIP significantly reduced offenders' time to reoffense, but it did not reduce their chances of returning to prison in general. The higher rate at which CIP offenders returned to prison as supervised release violators may be largely attributable to the fact that they were supervised not only more intensively than the control group (at least for the first 12 months), but also for a longer period of time. Because this study was unable to control for the intensity of postrelease supervision, it is possible that supervision intensity, rather than the boot camp itself, is the main reason why CIP offenders were less likely to reoffend but more likely to return as technical violators.

Still, if supervision intensity was largely responsible for the recidivism findings, one might expect the CIP reoffense rates to be lower, especially during the first 12 months following release, but to then converge with those from the control group over time. The recidivism findings do not support this pattern, however, as the differences between the two groups are fairly robust over time. In addition, if supervision intensity was the main causal factor, one might expect the return rate to be higher for CIP offenders during the first year after release when they are intensively supervised. Once again, however, the findings do not follow this pattern, as the control group actually had a higher return rate during the first year following release. Although the supervision intensity argument cannot be ruled out entirely, it is weakened to some extent by the relatively lengthy follow-up period used in this study.

✂ Does CIP Reduce Costs?

Early-Release Savings

In performing a cost-benefit analysis of CIP, we determine the savings resulting from (a) early release for program graduates (i.e., a length of stay reduction) and

(b) reduced recidivism (i.e., any return to prison). The early-release savings were calculated by first segregating CIP participants into 10 separate cohorts by the fiscal year in which they entered Phase I (FY 1993 to FY 2002). Next, program operating costs were determined by counting the total number of days each cohort spent in CIP and then multiplying by the full per diem associated with each phase for that fiscal year. For example, during FY 1993, the per diems were $75.63 for Phase I, $21.95 for Phases II and III, and $3.34 for supervised release; for example, "Phase IV."[9] Because the 81 offenders who entered CIP during FY 1993 spent 10.678 days in Phase 1, 18.177 days in Phases II and III, and 5,822 days in "Phase IV," the total program operating costs were $1.22 million.

As noted earlier, offenders who fail CIP are required to repeat the days spent in the program in a MCF. Thus, an offender who fails CIP Phase I after 90 days is required to serve the remainder of his or her term of imprisonment (i.e., two thirds of the pronounced sentence) plus the 90 days spent in CIP. The additional 90 days this particular offender would serve in prison would also be considered a program cost.

The calculation of days lost because of program failure is slightly different for Phase II and III failures. Offenders who fail during Phases II and III because of a new criminal offense are required to serve their new sentence, but are not required to serve over the time they spent in CIP. For these offenders, the time spent in prison for the new crime counts against the recidivism savings, not against the early-release savings.

But offenders who fail during Phases II and III because of a technical violation are required to redo the time they spent in CIP. Moreover, because these offenders are recidivists insofar as they return to prison after their release, the amount of return time they spend in prison must be partitioned into costs against both early-release and recidivism savings. More specifically, the number of days that Phase II and III failures spent in Phase I (usually 180 days) counts against the early-release savings because the Phase I time was spent in a correctional facility. Thus, the Phase I time that these offenders must serve over again

nullifies any cost savings that might have been gained from early release. However, the remainder of return time that Phase II and III failures spent in prison counts against the recidivism savings. For example, if an offender failed in Phase III after 400 days in CIP and returned to prison for 600 days, 180 of these days (the length of Phase I) would count against the early-release savings, whereas the remaining 420 would count against the recidivism savings.

The costs against the early-release savings thus consist of CIP operating costs and the Phase I days lost by offenders who failed during Phases I to III. Of the 81 offenders who entered CIP during FY 1993, there were 51 who failed during Phases I to III. The number of Phase I days these offenders had to redo was 2,364, which resulted in an additional cost of $137,986.68 (2,364 days multiplied by the estimated marginal per diem of $58.37 for FY 1993).[10] Adding this figure to the aforementioned $1.22 million produced a total cost of $1.36 million for FY 1993.

The early-release benefits, or savings, were calculated by first counting the total number of days for each CIP Phase III graduate from the time of release from Phase I until their original supervised release date (i.e., the time they were sentenced to serve in prison but were able to serve in the cominunity because of CIP's early-release provision). The total number of bed days saved for each cohort was then multiplied by the average marginal per diem for that fiscal year, resulting in total bed costs saved.[11] The total bed costs saved were subtracted by total CIP costs to produce the early-release savings for each fiscal year. For example, during FY 1993, the early-release provision saved 50 prison beds, which resulted in a savings of $1,059,415.50. However, because the operating costs were $1,363,238.15, CIP produced a cost, or savings deficit, of $303,822.65 during FY 1993.

The results suggest that the early-release savings from FY 1993 to FY 2002 amount to $2.8 million. It is interesting to note, however, that CIP did not begin to generate early-release savings until FY 1998. Indeed, from FY 1993 to FY 1997, the early-release deficit was $3.7 million. But from FY 1998 to FY 2002, the savings totaled $6.5 million.

The increased early-release savings are chiefly because of four factors. First, as CIP was developing and expanding during the mid-1990s, the per diems were comparatively high, resulting in higher operating costs. Since that time, however, per diems have decreased, which has reduced the costs associated with operating CIP. Second, graduation rates have increased since 1993, especially from FY 2000 to FY 2002. Although the graduation rate was 37% for the FY 1993 cohort, the rate was 68% for the 515 offenders who entered between FY 2000 and 2002. Third, along with higher graduation rates, increased program capacity has enabled more offenders to receive the length of stay reduction, resulting in an increase in early-release savings. Finally, modifications to statutory and departmental admission standards have augmented the number of bed days saved by program graduates. In particular, statutory changes during 1996 and 1997 removed the restriction on length of sentence (the upper limit was 54 months) and increased the maximum allowable length of stay from 36 to 48 months. Therefore, by expanding the admission standards to include eligible offenders with longer terms of imprisonment, the average number of bed days saved per CIP graduate increased significantly after FY 1996.

Recidivism Savings

The recidivism savings were calculated by making a comparison between the CIP and control groups with respect to how much time each group has spent, or will spend, in prison following the release that initiated their at-risk period. For the purposes of the cost-benefit analysis, recidivism is operationalized as any return to prison, whether for a new criminal offense or for a supervised release violation. As noted above, for offenders who fail Phases II and III because of a technical violation as opposed to a new crime, the return-time spent in prison (minus the Phase I days) counts against the recidivism savings.

The total number of prison days saved or lost for both the CIP and control groups was determined by first calculating the average number of days each group

(i.e., CIP and control) has spent, or will spend, in prison since the release that initiated their at-risk period. The difference (in days) in the averages for the two groups was then multiplied by the number of CIP offenders because of the uneven sizes of the CIP and control groups. For example, the difference in average prison return days between the CIP and control groups was 40.48 days, which was multiplied by 1,347 (the size of the CIP group) to produce a total of 54,527 prison days saved. The total number of prison beds saved (149) was then multiplied by the average marginal per diem ($63.08) over the 10-year period, resulting in the total recidivism savings of $3.4 million. Overall, the results indicate that CIP has saved the state of Minnesota $6.2 million. Given that the overall benefits amount to $40.7 million and the program costs total $34.5 million (a difference of $6.2 million), the benefit-cost ratio is 1.18. Thus, during the FY 1993 to FY 2002 period, CIP generated $1.18 of benefits for every $1.00 spent.

Although CIP and control group offenders returned to prison at virtually the same rate (47.6% vs. 47.0%), they returned for different reasons. Of the offenders who returned to prison, those in the control group were much more likely to return for a new crime (73.0%, or 34.4% of 47.0%) compared to CIP (46.0%, or 21.7% of 47.6%). CIP offenders, however, were much more likely to return for a technical violation (54.0%, or 25.9% of 47.6%) than comparison group offenders (27.0%, or 12.6% of 47.0%). Because of the legislative provision requiring CIP failures to redo their program time, the average amount of return prison time for a supervised release violation was 117 days higher (140 days minus 23 days) than the control group Furthermore, when CIP offenders did return to prison for a new crime, the average number of return days was 29 higher than the control group (1,136 days vs. 1,107 days). However, CIP offenders still served, on average, a little more than 40 fewer days (355 days vs. 396 days) in prison because the control group was significantly more likely to return for a new offense and, thus, have a longer stay in prison.

Although CIP has saved the state more than $6 million to date, this amount still likely underestimates the overall savings produced by the program. The lower reoffense rates for CIP participants leads to fewer victims, reduced victim restitution costs, and decreased use of law enforcement and court resources. Moreover, following their release from prison after the completion of Phase I, CIP participants produce added cost savings by working in the community and, thus, paying taxes. It is beyond the scope of this study, however, to calculate these additional cost savings.

◤ Conclusion

The results reported here indicate that CIP significantly reduced the rate at which offenders commit a new crime. But because of the fact that CIP offenders were more likely to come back as supervised release violators, they returned to prison at roughly the same rate as the control group. CIP still produced a recidivism savings, however, because offenders spent, on average, 40 fewer days in prison because of the shorter lengths of stay associated with supervised release violations. Although the total savings were relatively modest at $6.2 million over the 10-year period, the size of the savings, particularly those resulting from the early-release provision, increased nearly every year after FY 1998.

This study is limited in that it only evaluated a single boot camp, did not use an experimental design, and did not contain measures pertaining to community supervision and aftercare. But despite these limitations, this evaluation was rigorous to the extent that it used multiple measures of recidivism to compare boot camp participants with a carefully matched control group over a relatively long period of time. The findings from this study thus carry several implications for boot camps, in particular, and correctional program evaluations in general.

First, the evidence presented here suggests that boot camps can. indeed, deliver on the promise of reducing both recidivism and costs, but only under a fairly narrow set of conditions. As some evaluations have shown (Bottcher & Ezell, 2005; Zhang, 2000), a mixture of therapeutic programming, intensive postrelease supervision, and lengthy aftercare does not always lead to a recidivism reduction. But as this study and several recent evaluations (Kurlychek & Kempinen, 2006;

Wells et al., 2006) have demonstrated, this combination likely increases the chances that boot camp participation can produce a decrease in reoffending. The apparent significance of community supervision and aftercare does not necessarily imply, however, that boot camps have no effect on reoffending. On the contrary, the rigorous structure of a boot camp greatly minimizes offenders' idle time, whereas the repetition and organization of military life may foster an environment conducive to the effective delivery of programming such as CD treatment to offenders. Given the generally positive effects that rehabilitative boot camps have on participants' attitudes and perceptions (Kempinen & Kurlychek, 2002; MacKenzie et al., 2001), it is reasonable to infer that community supervision and, in particular, aftercare are critical in preserving the changes that occur in offenders during the boot camp phase. As such, future research should more closely examine whether outcomes for boot camp participants vary by the type, length, and quality of aftercare services provided.

Second, just as therapeutic programming, intensive supervision, and aftercare programming appear to be necessary (but perhaps not always sufficient) to decrease recidivism, so, too, are certain program characteristics likely needed to reduce costs. Most notably, the decisions to increase program capacity and accept offenders with longer sentences were instrumental in producing a reduction in costs. Still, the amount of the cost reduction was relatively modest, however, which is largely because of the small size of CIP and, by extension, the reliance on marginal costs. If, for example, fixed costs were used in the cost-benefit analysis, the total savings would have been slightly more than $18 million. Beginning in January 2007, MCF-Willow River will double its capacity by adding 90 prison beds. In doing so, CIP may begin to save enough prison beds (e.g., 500 per year) to justify the use of a fixed costs model.

The modest cost savings may also be because of the emphasis CIP has placed on lowering recidivism. Although the findings indicated that the recidivism reduction accounted for more than half of the cost savings, the average number of days saved (40) through decreased reoffending is less than that which would be saved by shortening the boot camp phase from 180 to 120 days. Of course, trimming the length of the boot camp by 2 months could also vitiate its effect on recidivism. As this evaluation has shown, boot camps can reduce reoffending, but it may come with a price in the form of smaller cost savings.

Third, the "growing pains" that CIP experienced from FY 1993 to FY 1997 imply that a great deal of caution should be exercised when conducting initial outcome evaluations of newly started boot camps or even correctional programs in general. Much like a new business that loses money before it begins to turn a profit, CIP did not reduce costs prior to FY 1998. Although Cox regression models limited to the FY 1993 to FY 1997 period reveal that CIP significantly reduced the extent to which participants reoffended (rearrest, reconviction, and reincarceration for a new offense) during this time, the recidivism savings would still not be enough to offset the early-release savings deficit. As a result, an outcome evaluation of CIP after its first 5 years of operation may have led to the premature—not to mention, erroneous—conclusion that it does not work insofar as it does not reduce costs.

Finally, the growing perception over the last decade that boot camps are largely ineffective has been based mainly on results showing that boot camp participants are no less likely to recidivate than a comparison group of offenders. But as this study illustrates, determining whether a program works should not be limited to a simple question of "Did they recidivate or not?" Rather, in assessing whether a program is effective, perhaps the focus should be not only on whether they recidivated, but also on why they returned and for how long.

Concentrating merely on whether offenders are rearrested, reconvicted, or reincarcerated following release is often the benchmark used in correctional program evaluations because it is, generally speaking, an easier or more feasible issue to address analytically. But results can vary significantly depending on how one measures recidivism. Moreover, even if multiple measures of recidivism are used, the issue of whether offenders recidivate does not tell the full story about whether a correctional program works. Instead, it is also critical to know why and how long offenders returned to prison because the answers to these two questions will provide a more complete picture as to whether a program is effective.

⊠ Notes

1. In 1992, offenders were required to be serving a sentence of 18 to 36 months. Recent legislation has increased the sentence length allowable to 48 months or less remaining.

2. In particular, the offenses added to the list were terroristic threats, felon in possession of a firearm, drive-by shooting, burglary of an occupied residence, simple robbery, theft from a person, criminal vehicular homicide, firearm-related crimes, gang-related crimes, and offenses committed by dangerous and repeat offenders.

3. The eligibility criteria excluded offenders with three or more prior incarcerations and those with four or more prior felony convictions.

4. Aside from the main original and modified requirements outlined above, admission to the Challenge Incarceration Program (CIP) is contingent on additional mandatory and discretionary criteria. Offenders are ineligible to participate in CIP if they are in close or maximum custody status; have prior CIP experience; have active warrants, detainers, or signed criminal complaints: have a history of escape; have recent extended incarceration disciplinary convictions; or have medical conditions such as diabetes, active seizures, hypertension, or pulmonary, cardiac, homozygous sickle cell, gastrointestinal, unstable neurological, or musculoskeletal diseases. Discretionary criteria include prior treatment and supervision failures, criminal history, discipline record, aggravated offense characteristics., upward durational departures, and mental and physical health status.

5. In 1980, the state of Minnesota implemented a sentencing guidelines system in which a recommended sentence is based on the severity of the offense and the offender's criminal history. Thirteen years later, the state abolished parole, replacing it with supervised release; as a result, the sentences for offenders who have committed crimes after August 1, 1993, have consisted of two parts: a minimum prison term equal to two thirds of the total executed sentence and a supervised release term equal to the remaining one third. Because of the early-release provision, CIP offenders who complete Phase III

serve less than the required two thirds of their executed sentence, thus creating bed-space savings.

6. There were 59 offenders who entered CIP more than once between FY 1993 and FY 2002. For these multiple-entry offenders, their last entry is the one considered here.

7. The "governing offense" is the crime carrying the sentence on which an offender's scheduled release date is based. Although offenders may be imprisoned for multiple offenses, each with its own sentence, the governing offense is generally the most serious crime for which an offender is incarcerated.

8. Following the removal of CIP participants, person offenders, and those not released to supervision, there were 16.0% offenders in the control group at the beginning of the multistage sampling process. After stratifying by offense type, there were 7,768 offenders in the sample. The control group sample was next stratified by length of stay, which removed 3,836 offenders, resulting in a total of 3,932. Stratifying by metro area eliminated 126 offenders, whereas age at release reduced the size of the sample by an additional 372 offenders. Stratifying by age at first felony conviction removed 115 offenders, whereas age at first prison commitment eliminated an additional 105, leaving 3,204 offenders at this stage. After stratifying by prior felony convictions, which removed 322 offenders, and prior prison commitments, which eliminated 567, there were 2,315 offenders left. Stratifying by institutional discipline convictions removed 403 offenders, whereas offender race eliminated an additional 259. After stratifying by offender sex, which removed 98 offenders, the final control group consisted of 1,555 offenders. Because there were, at this point, no statistically significant differences between the CIP and control groups, it was not necessary to stratify by either age at first arrest or prior arrests.

9. For CIP graduates, Phase IV is the period between the end of Phase III and the beginning of their supervised release period that they would have spent in prison had they not completed CIP. Because Phases II and III generally cover a period of 12 months, Phase IV time usually applies only to CIP graduates who earned a length of stay reduction in excess of 12 months. For example, a CIP graduate who received a 20-month reduction in his or her length of stay would spend 12 months in Phases II and III and 8 months in Phase IV. Because Phase IV represents time that offenders would have been incarcerated had they not completed CIP, it is necessary to account for the number of Phase IV days in both the benefits and costs.

10. For the full 10-year period, the provision requiring boot camp failures to serve more than the time they spent in Phase I resulted in a total cost of $2.9 million. Holding everything else constant, which may be a questionable assumption, removing this provision would have added $2.9 million to the early-release savings.

11. Because marginal per diems were not available prior to FY 2000, we generated estimates for the FY 1993 to FY 1999 period. During FY 2000 to FY 2002, the marginal per diem accounted for 76% of the full per diem. As a result, we multiplied this percentage by the full per diem for each year during FY 1993 to FY 1999 to produce marginal per diem estimates.

⊠ References

Aloisi, M., & LeBaron, J. (2001). *The Juvenile Justice Commission's Stabilization and Reintegration Program: An updated recidivism analysis.* Trenton: New Jersey Department of Law and Public Safety.

Austin, J., Camp-Blair, D., Camp, A., Castellano, T., Adams-Fuller, T., Jones, M., et al. (2000). *Multi-site evaluation of boot camp programs, final report.* Washington, DC: U.S. Department of Justice, National Institute of Justice.

Austin, J., Jones, M., & Bolyard, M. (1993). *Assessing the impact of a county operated boot camp: Evaluation of the Los Angeles County Regimented Inmate Diversion Program.* San Francisco: National Council on Crime and Delinquency.

Bales, W. D., Bedard, L. E., Quinn, S. T., Ensley, D. T., & Holley, G. P. (2005). Recidivism of public and private state prison inmates in Florida. *Criminology and Public Policy, 4,* 57–82.

Bottcher, J., & Ezell, M. E. (2005). Examining the effectiveness of boot camps: A randomized experiment with a long-term follow up. *Journal of Research in Crime and Delinquency, 42,* 309–332.

Burns, J. C. & Vito, G. F. (1995). An impact analysis of the Alabama boot camp program. *Federal Probation, 58*(1), 63–68.

Camp, C. G., & Camp, G. M. (1996). *The 1996 corrections yearbook.* South Salem, NY: Criminal Justice Institute.

Camp, C. G., & Camp, G. M. (2002). *The 2002 corrections yearbook.* Middletown, CT: Criminal Justice Institute.

Clark, C. L., Aziz, D. W., & MacKenzie, D. L. (1994). *Shock incarceration in New York: Focus on treatment.* Washington, DC: U.S. Department of Justice, National Institute of Justice.

Cohen, M. A. (2000). Measuring the costs and benefits of crime and justice. In *Measurement and analysis of crime and justice, criminal justice 2000* (Vol. 4, pp. 263–316). Washington, DC: U.S. Department of Justice, National Institute of Justice.

Farrington, D. P., Ditchfield, J., Hancock, G., Howard, P., Jolliffe, D., Livingston, M. S., et al. (2002). *Evaluation of two intensive regimes for young offenders.* London: Home Office Research, Development and Statistics Directorate.

Gover, A. R. (2005). Native American ethnicity and childhood maltreatment as variables in perceptions and adjustments to boot camps vs. "traditional" correctional settings. *Journal of Offender Rehabilitation, 40*(3/4), 177–198.

Jones, R. J., Olson, B. W., Kan, S. P., & Urbas, S. M. (2003). *Impact Incarceration Program: 2003 annual report to the governor and the general assembly.* Springfield: Illinois Department of Corrections.

Kempinen, C. A., & Kurlychek, M. C. (2002). *Pennsylvania's Motivational Boot Camp: 2001 report to the legislature.* University Park: Pennsylvania State College, Pennsylvania Commission on Sentencing.

Kempinen, C. A., & Kurlychek, M. C. (2003). An outcome evaluation of Pennsylvania's boot camp: Does rehabilitative programming within a disciplinary setting reduce recidivism? *Crime & Delinquency, 49,* 581–606.

Kurlychek, M. C., & Kempinen, C. A. (2006). Beyond boot camp: The impact of aftercare on offender reentry. *Criminology & Public Policy, 5*(2), 363–388.

Lawrence, S., & Mears, D. P. (2004). *Benefit-cost analysis of supermax prisons: Critical steps and considerations.* Washington, DC: Urban Institute.

MacKenzie, D. L., Brame, R., McDowall, D., & Souryal, C. (1995). Boot camp prisons and recidivism in eight states. *Criminology, 33,* 327–358.

MacKenzie, D. L. Gover, A. R., Styve-Armstrong, G., & Mitchell, O. (2001). *A national study comparing the environments of boot camps with traditional faculties for juvenile offenders.* Washington, DC: U.S. Department of Justice. National Institute of Justice.

MacKenzie, D. L., & Souryal, C. (1994). *Multi-site evaluation of shock incarceration.* Washington, DC: National Institute of Justice.

MacKenzie, D. L., Souryal, C., Sealock, M., & Kashem, M. B. (1997). *Outcome study of the Sergeant Henry Johnson Youth Leadership Academy (YLA).* College Park, MD: Department of Criminology and Criminal Justice.

MacKenzie, D. L., Wilson, D. B., & Kieler, S. B. (2001). Effects of correctional boot camps on offending. *Annals of the American Academy of Political and Social Science, 578,* 126–143.

Marcus-Mendoza, S. T. (1995). Preliminary investigation of Oklahoma's shock incarceration program. *Journal of the Oklahoma Criminal Justice Research Consortium, 2,* 44–49.

Parent, D. G. (2003). *Correctional boot camps: Lessons from a decade of research.* Washington, DC: U.S. Department of Justice. National Institute of Justice.

Paulson, A. (2005, December 1). Inmates try boot camp for kicking drugs. *Christian Science Monitor,* p. 2:1.

State of New York, Department of Correctional Services, Division of Parole. (2005). *The seventeenth annual shock legislative report.* New York: Author.

Stinchcomb, J. B., & Terry, W. C. (2001). Predicting the likelihood of rearrest among shock incarceration graduates: Moving beyond another nail in the boot camp coffin. *Crime & Delinqueny, 47,* 221–242.

Wells, J. B., Minor, K. I., Angel, E., & Stearman, K. D. (2006). A quasi-experimental evaluation of a shock incarceration and aftercare program for juvenile offenders. *Youth Violence and Juvenile Justice, 4,* 219–233.

Zhang, S. X. (2000). *An evaluation of the Los Angeles County Juvenile Drug Treatment Boot Camp.* San Marcos: California State University, San Marcos.

DISCUSSION QUESTIONS

1. Identify and describe the three generations of boot camps. What is the significance of adopting one style over another?

2. According to the research findings, CIP graduates were more than twice as likely to be returned to prison for technical violations compared to the control group. From a policy and administrative perspective, what is significant about this finding? How might this finding combined with the finding of a reduction in rearrest alter supervision strategies?

3. According to the study, why is it important to ask not only did an offender return to prison, but why as well?

4. What are some of the potential unaccounted for cost savings to the state by reducing recidivism for new crimes?

5. Based upon these findings, should the Minnesota DOC have continued to use the boot camp as an alternative to imprisonment? Why or why not?

READING

In their seminal work, McCollister and her colleagues conducted a cost-effectiveness analysis of a post-release substance abuse work release program compared to standard work release. Located in Delaware, the CREST Outreach Center was designed specifically to address the substance abuse needs of offenders. This program combines in-prison treatment, work release as a transitional TC, and outpatient aftercare services. Unlike traditional work release, this program includes an intensive 6-month process designed to address the specific needs of the offender and stop the criminal offending. Because of the extensive nature of a TC, it is essential to examine the overall cost effectiveness of this community-based intervention. In this study, the authors used a measure of reduced recidivism to define treatment success 18 months post-release. A total of 587 CREST participants ($n = 378$ CREST work release only; $n = 209$ aftercare participants) and 249 standard work release participants (comparison group) were identified for inclusion in the study. Overall, the study indicated that participation in CREST did reduce reincarceration. However, the cost savings to the state DOC was minimal. The authors did provide some explanations for this finding. Taken on its face value may imply that the TC program may not be justified. To this extent, the authors provided some valid arguments why long-term benefits may not yet be realized and why agencies may still consider this option in lieu of standard work release.

Post-Release Substance Abuse Treatment for Criminal Offenders

A Cost-Effectiveness Analysis

Kathryn E. McCollister, Michael T. French, James A. Inciardi,
Clifford A. Butzin, Steven S. Martin, and Robert M. Hooper

1. Introduction

During the past decade, the average annual growth rate of incarceration in the United States was 5.7%, primarily influenced by the increase in the Federal prison population (Bureau of Justice Statistics, 2001). By the end of 1999, 6.3 million people were under criminal justice supervision (incarcerated or on probation/parole), which translates to about 3.1% of the total US adult population (Bureau of Justice Statistics, 2001). The increasing rate of incarceration has numerous social and economic

AUTHORS' NOTE: This research was supported by the Robert Wood Johnson Foundation (grant number 041070) and the National Institute on Drug Abuse (grant numbers R01 DAI 1506, R01 DA06124, 3P50 DA07705).

SOURCE: Kathryn E. McCollister, Michael T. French, James A. Inciardi, Clifford A. Butzin, Steven S. Martin, & Robert M. Hooper. (2003). Post-release substance abuse treatment for criminal offenders: A cost-effectiveness analysis. *Journal of Quantitative Criminology, 19*(4), 389–407. Copyright © 2003 Springer, Netherlands.

consequences. In particular, criminal offenders can face a number of obstacles upon reentry to society such as finding a job and avoiding relapse into a criminal lifestyle.

An estimated 600,000 inmates were released in 2001, of which two-thirds were expected to return to prison for new offenses or parole violations (Travis et al., 2001). Parole violations accounted for more than a third of prison admissions in 1998 (Travis et al., 2001). Concurrently, federal spending on parole services has decreased while parole officers' caseloads have increased. With limited time available per case, parole officers tend to be less concerned with rehabilitative initiatives, such as enforcing drug treatment or job training activities, and more focused on detecting legal infractions (Travis et al., 2001).

Further complicating the rehabilitation of criminal offenders is the complementarity between crime and substance abuse. According to the Bureau of Justice Statistics, over 80% of State and 70% of Federal inmates reported past drug use, not including alcohol (Bureau of Justice Statistics, 1999). On average, one out of six criminal offenders reported committing a crime to obtain money for drugs (Bureau of Justice Statistics, 1999). Increasingly, the need for substance abuse treatment in correctional institutions is recognized, but often such programs are poorly implemented and not sufficient for addressing the host of issues associated with substance-abusing inmates. The Department of Justice estimated that while some form of treatment was available in 90% of the facilities examined, only 10–20% of inmates used these services (ONDCP, 1998). Further, it is estimated that only 25% of inmates requesting substance abuse treatment ever receive any care (McCaffrey, 2000).

The appropriate balance between punishing and rehabilitating criminal offenders is subject to considerable debate. A number of studies have shown that introducing treatment in prison is only the first step to effectively rehabilitate drug-abusing offenders. Perhaps more important is the establishment of a structured, transitional, post-incarceration program including work release and aftercare. Several recent studies have shown that offenders participating in a continuum of

treatment, including in-prison programs and community-based aftercare programs, have lower rates of drug relapse and criminal recidivism than non-treated offenders (Martin et al., 1999; Wexler et al., 1999a; 1999b; Lowe et al., 1998; Inciardi et al., 1997; Hiller et al., 1999; Griffith et al., 1999). Post-release programs (i.e., aftercare) appear to be a critical component in the rehabilitation process. Most studies have found that offenders receiving in-prison treatment (with no formal aftercare) had similar rates of recidivism and drug relapse as non-treated offenders (e.g., Inciardi et al., 1997; Knight et al., 1999).

To consider the potential economic importance of post-release treatment and socialization programs for incarcerated individuals, this research performed a cost-effectiveness analysis of work release treatment and aftercare programs for drug-abusing criminal offenders. Delaware's CREST Outreach Center, a work release therapeutic community (TC) and aftercare program for criminal offenders, served as the case study for the analysis. Standard work release participants were compared to CREST work release participants to determine differences in program cost and effectiveness, where effectiveness was measured by the number of days reincarcerated during the period 18-months post-release from prison. In addition, a secondary cost-effectiveness analysis was performed that compared two sub-groups within the CREST program. Specifically, treatment cost and days reincarcerated over the follow-up period were analyzed for CREST participants that continued treatment in the aftercare program and CREST work release-only participants.

Economic evaluations of substance abuse treatment for criminal offenders provide policy makers with information on the economic returns to investments in such programs—ultimately helping to direct scarce resources toward efficient services. This research offers a unique perspective on treatment in criminal justice settings, as it is to our knowledge the first study to consider the cost and effectiveness of post-release treatment, delivered through a work release program and aftercare component. The analysis addresses three primary research questions: (I) How much did the CREST work release TC and aftercare programs cost the Delaware Department of Corrections? (2) Was the number of days reincarcerated over follow-up significantly different across the study conditions? (3) In comparing treatment cost and reincarceration, (a) was CREST work release a cost-effective alternative relative to standard work release; (b) did the additional investment in aftercare services prove cost-effective relative to CREST work release-only? The results of this research offer important policy information for the Delaware Department of Corrections and provide a foundation for future economic evaluations of post-release treatment.

2. Review of Previous Research on Corrections-Based Treatment

Early evaluations of prison-based substance abuse treatment programs found little evidence to support the effectiveness of these programs (Lipton et al., 1975; Martinson, 1974). Lipton (1995) provided an updated review of in-prison treatment, and explained how advances in these treatment programs (from the 1970s through the 1990s) led to reductions in drug use and criminal behavior by treatment participants, thereby establishing a renewed interest in providing treatment for addicted inmates.

The Therapeutic Community (TC) model for drug abuse treatment has been highlighted as a potentially effective approach in criminal justice settings. In the last decade, the TC model has been modified and successfully adapted to correctional environments (Wexler, 1995; Wexler et al., 1991; Wexler and Lipton, 1993; Inciardi et al., 2001). The goal of the TC is a global change in lifestyle involving abstinence from drugs, elimination of antisocial activities, and the development of employable skills, prosocial attitudes, and values. TCs in prisons are distinguished from the general prison environment by several characteristics: (1) TC activities embody prosocial values and promote lifestyle change; (2) TC staff, some of whom are recovering addicts and former inmates, provide positive role models; and (3) TC concepts offer an optimistic view of the inmate and his/her potential for change.

Work release programs for offenders have evolved since the 1970s (Inciardi et al., 1994; Martin et al., 1995), but only in the past decade have formal work release plus aftercare programs for drug-abusing offenders been incorporated into the treatment process. Several treatment initiatives include in-prison treatment followed by some form of aftercare (e.g., Florida's Four Tiered Approach; California's Amity prison TC and Vista aftercare; Texas's ITC [In-prison TC] and TTC [Transitional TC]; Colorado's San Carlos prison [TC and aftercare]. Delaware, however, was the first state to implement a three-stage treatment initiative for criminal offenders including in-prison, work release, and aftercare programs modeled on the TC (Inciardi et al., 1997).

2.1. Economic Studies of Treating Criminal Offenders

Based on the results of the outcome evaluations discussed above, the benefits of prison-based treatment, and particularly post-release treatment programs, appear promising. To further clarify these potential returns to society, formal economic analyses of these programs and other types of criminal justice programs are necessary. A few economic cost, cost-effectiveness, and benefit-cost studies have been completed in this area, providing impetus for additional evaluations.

3. Delaware's CREST Outreach Center

In 1988, with the support of Project REFORM,[1] Delaware's Department of Corrections established

---

[1] Project REFORM was initiated in 1987 with funding from the Bureau of Justice Assistance within the U.S. Department of Justice. Project REFORM provided funding for corrections-based substance abuse treatment programs across 22 States. See Lipton (1995) for details.

the KEY—an in-prison TC program for males in Wilmington, Delaware. In 1991, with funding from the National Institute on Drug Abuse, researchers at the Center for Drug and Alcohol Studies at the University of Delaware established the CREST[2] Outreach Center—the first work release TC in the United States (Inciardi et al., 2001). The Delaware initiative for criminal offenders evolved into a three-stage TC treatment continuum, incorporating in-prison treatment (Stage 1), work release tailored as a transitional TC program (Stage 2), and aftercare services delivered on an outpatient basis (Stage 3).

CREST work release is a coeducational, 6-month TC program. Participants transition through five treatment phases, incorporating orientation, integration into the CREST community, community responsibilities, program leadership and mentoring roles, job seeking, and re-entry into society. The aftercare component to CREST was developed in 1996 to assist with fulfillment of probation requirements, and to continue access to counseling and other treatment services after reentering society. The aftercare program runs for six months, wherein aftercare participants attend both group and individual counseling sessions weekly, and are subject to urine testing for illegal drug use (Inciardi et al., 1997).

Data for the cost-effectiveness analysis correspond to the years 1997-98 and were provided by the original follow-up evaluations (at 6- and 18-months post-release) of Delaware's KEY-CREST[3] programs conducted by researchers at the University of Delaware (Inciardi et al., 1997; Inciardi, 1996; Martin et al., 1999). The outcome evaluations collected information on inmates' drug use, criminal activities, sexual behavior, history of drug abuse and other treatment, and psychological status. Eligibility for the study included offenders who: were from the general inmate population; were sentenced and had no additional open charges; were within 12–18 months of probation (or within 18–24 months of release for mandatory

sentences); had a history of substance abuse, and had no history of sexual offenses or arson charges (Inciardi et al., 1997).

The Comparison group was part of the original study design for evaluating outcomes from the CREST program. In this study, inmates in the Delaware correctional system reaching eligibility for work release status and with a correctional classification recommendation of needing "intensive drug treatment" were randomly assigned to either CREST treatment or to standard work release. Those assigned to standard work release became the Comparison group.

Most inmates were eligible for work release. Exceptions included violent felons and those with mandatory sentences to be served entirely in prison. Over 65% of those classified to work release also had the recommendation of needing intensive drug treatment. In the original study, these randomly selected groups were compared with non-randomly selected groups of in-prison treatment graduates (from the KEY program) who either went to standard work release or to CREST (Inciardi et al., 1997). Consequently, the Comparison group, although not truly random in terms of all respondents in this study, does represent a comparable group needing treatment that did not receive it through criminal justice programs.

The sample for the cost-effectiveness analysis comprised 836 criminal offenders that were released in 1997 to either standard work release (Comparison group, $N = 249$) or the CREST Outreach Center (CREST, $N = 587$). Some of the CREST participants came from the in-prison KEY program ($N = 161$). However, the majority of study participants ($N = 426$) entered the CREST program from the general correctional population. At follow-up, four study conditions were evaluated: all CREST work release participants ($N = 587$), CREST participants that only received CREST work release ($N = 378$), CREST participants that also received the aftercare component ($N = 209$), and the

---

[2] The term CREST is not an acronym. CREST expresses the idea that the participant is on the crest of a major life change, and is also always written in capital letters.

[3] The term KEY is not an acronym. KEY refers to offering the offender a "key" for change and is always written in capital letters.

Comparison group of standard work release participants ($N = 249$).

4. Methods

Although several complementary approaches exist for performing an economic evaluation of healthcare interventions (e.g., cost-effectiveness analysis, cost-utility analysis, benefit-cost analysis), a cost-effectiveness analysis (CEA) was selected as the most appropriate methodology for examining the 18-month post-release returns to the CREST programs. Unlike benefit-cost analysis (BCA), which estimates the dollar value of a collection of outcomes, CEA generally highlights one primary outcome. For example, a BCA of a substance abuse treatment program would consider the economic benefits to society from outcomes such as reductions in criminal activity, increased employment, and reduced utilization of healthcare services. However, consistent patterns in drug use or criminal activity may not form until several months after leaving custody. Employment may be difficult to obtain following release from prison. Also, access to healthcare and other services may be delayed until the parolee has had a chance to successfully navigate treatment options and insurance issues. Thus, it might be less important to assess the short-term economic benefits from treating criminal offenders, as it may take more than one year for most treatment benefits to materialize.

With CEA, one important outcome, such as reduced recidivism, is used to express treatment effectiveness, which is then compared with treatment cost. The results of the analysis are expressed as a cost-effectiveness ratio—typically with cost in the numerator and the effectiveness measure in the denominator (a lower cost-effectiveness ratio is better than a higher ratio).[4]

Effectiveness can also be described as a combination of outcomes using a common scale (e.g., change in quality-adjusted life-years) (French, 2000). Alternatively, the ratio of cost and effectiveness can be derived for a single program and then compared with an established benchmark ratio in the literature (Kenkel, 1997; Gold et al., 1996; Barnett et al., 2001). Each component of a CEA is described below, followed by a discussion of the empirical approach used in the present study.

4.1. Economic Cost Analysis

The foundation for economic evaluations of healthcare or addiction treatment programs is a comprehensive economic cost analysis (Gold et al., 1996). The cost data for the CREST work release and aftercare programs were collected using the Drug Abuse Treatment Cost Analysis Program (DATCAP; www.DATCAP.com). The DATCAP is a structured data collection instrument developed by French and colleagues, which considers both program revenues and costs (French, 2002a; French, 2002b). The instrument is used to collect resource utilization and other data to estimate total annual program cost, annual cost per client, and the cost per treatment episode. The DATCAP has been applied to a variety of treatment interventions such as methadone maintenance, outpatient drug-free, long-term residential, short-term residential, prison-based programs, and employee assistance programs (e.g., French et al., 1997; French and McGeary, 1997; McCollister and French, 2002; Salome and French, 2001; Roebuck et al., 2002).

Economists generally prefer to examine program costs from a societal perspective, which considers the value of all resources used in providing a treatment program, including the value of donated or subsidized resources. However, we chose a more narrow perspective for the CREST cost analysis (direct expenditures

---

[4] As explained later in this section, CEA is fundamentally an incremental analysis with a cost-effectiveness ratio equal to incremental cost divided by incremental effectiveness.

incurred by the Delaware Department of Corrections) for the following reasons. First, the only resource that was not directly purchased by the CREST programs was the facility that housed both the work release and aftercare components. This building was already owned by the Delaware Department of Corrections and was part of the standard work release campus when the CREST work release program was initiated. Although some minor retrofitting was necessary to prepare the facility for the CREST programs, these costs had relatively little impact on total program cost. Thus, the cost of the CREST facility was not part of the incremental costs specifically associated with the CREST work release and aftercare programs. Second, considering that our focus for the CEA in this study is on the short-run returns to the CREST programs, and given that we are evaluating a criminal justice outcome (incarceration), we chose to frame the cost analysis from the perspective of the Delaware Department of Corrections. Thus, direct program expenditures were used to estimate the costs of the CREST work release and aftercare programs.

4.2. Treatment Effectiveness

Treatment effectiveness was measured as the number of days reincarcerated for any reason over the 18-month follow-up period. Thus, fewer incarceration days implies greater effectiveness. This measure of effectiveness is most appropriate given the perspective of the analysis. Assessing the cost per avoided incarceration day ultimately gauges the avoided incarceration costs for the Department of Corrections by sending offenders through the CREST program. In addition, although the original outcome data covered multiple areas (psychological status, drug use, criminal activity, sexual behavior), cost-effectiveness analysis dictates the selection of one outcome of primary importance to assess program effectiveness. For the purposes of the research question addressed in this paper, reincarceration was the optimal outcome measure.

4.3. Cost-Effectiveness Calculations

A CEA calculates and compares ratios of incremental cost and incremental effectiveness between two or more study conditions. For the present analysis, mean values for treatment cost and days reincarcerated during the follow-up period for the treatment condition were subtracted from corresponding cost and effectiveness values for the comparison condition to determine if the treatment condition was cost-effective. In this context, the cost-effectiveness ratios report the marginal cost of achieving one fewer incarceration day in one study condition relative to another study condition.

⬛ 5. Results

Standard demographic information, completion of in-prison treatment, criminal justice measures, and the cost of CREST work release treatment and aftercare are included. Significant differences across study groups were found for age, ethnicity (African American and White), attending in-prison treatment (i.e., being a graduate from the KEY program), number of follow-up days incarcerated, and program costs. Although the total sample included both men and women, the majority of participants were male (71 to 81% across study conditions) and African American (67 to 75%).

CREST participants had a mean number of 74.39 days reincarcerated over the 18-month follow-up period. Within this group, CREST plus aftercare participants had an average of 42.60 days reincarcerated, and CREST work release only participants had an average of 91.96 days reincarcerated. The Comparison group had 104.20 days reincarcerated. Average program cost was $1937 for CREST participants and $2539 for the subgroup of CREST participants that also received aftercare. The Comparison group received no CREST or aftercare services and therefore had a program cost of $0.

The number of days in each program and the average (per client) cost are reported by study condition.

The total cost for the CREST programs for each client was calculated as the product of length of stay (in days) and unit cost of treatment per day (estimated with the DATCAP). Total program cost was comprised of personnel, program supplies and materials, contracted services, and equipment. These estimates represent the incremental costs associated with operating the CREST work release and aftercare programs relative to the costs of standard work release. The average annual cost per client was $4,261 for the work release program and $994 for the aftercare program.[5] This translates to an average daily cost of $11.68 for CREST work release and $2.72 for aftercare services.

The primary CEA examined all CREST participants relative to the Comparison group. Mean incremental treatment cost was $1937 and incremental effectiveness was 29.77 fewer days incarcerated over the follow-up period. Dividing incremental cost by incremental effectiveness produced a cost-effectiveness ratio of $65. This value represents the marginal cost of avoiding an incarceration day for the average CREST participant. Expressed differently, the Delaware Department of Corrections spent $1937 per offender for the CREST program, which led to ~30 fewer days of incarceration relative to the Comparison group over the follow-up period. Thus, on average, a day of reincarceration was avoided at a cost of $65.

A secondary CEA considered the CREST participants that also received aftercare ($N = 209$) relative to the CREST work release only group ($N = 378$). For this scenario, the difference in cost was $935 and the difference in effectiveness was 49.36 fewer days incarcerated for CREST work release plus aftercare participants. The incremental cost-effectiveness ratio was $19, suggesting that adding an aftercare component to CREST work release avoided an additional day of reincarceration at an average cost of $19. However, this result must be interpreted with caution because the aftercare participants volunteered from the CREST work release program rather than being randomly assigned to aftercare services. This group formation process implies a potential selection bias in the group that participated in aftercare. The issue of selection bias and other methodological qualifications are presented in the Discussion and Conclusion section that follows.

▧ 6. Discussion and Conclusion

The cost-effectiveness analysis presented here demonstrated that involvement in the CREST program reduced reincarceration days for substance abusing criminal offenders relative to standard work release participants. The estimated average cost per avoided incarceration day was $65. This cost per avoided incarceration day is actually slightly higher than the average daily cost of incarceration in Delaware ($57), suggesting that the CREST work release program was not cost effective. However, two issues should be highlighted in this regard. First, the 95% bootstrapped CI on the point estimate of the cost-effectiveness ratio is $42 to $169. Since the average daily cost of incarceration ($57) is included in this range, we cannot statistically conclude that the CREST work release program was not cost effective. Second, it is important to emphasize that the investment in CREST is not only buying reductions in incarceration in the first 18 months following release. Potential benefits include averted incarceration beyond the 18-month follow-up period examined here, reduced drug use, stable employment, improved relationships with family and the community, and a lessened dependence on the welfare system. These are potentially important outcomes resulting from treatment that were beyond the scope of measurement for this analysis.

The role of aftercare (post-work release) appears to be an important factor in the success of CREST

---

[5] The aftercare program was housed within the CREST work release facility. The program was just getting started in 1997, the year of the cost analysis, and only had program costs associated with personnel. In addition, aftercare services were delivered on a weekly basis rather than daily.

participants. The investment in aftercare services was associated with an additional 49 days of reduced incarceration relative to CREST work release only. Thus, if the Department of Corrections had to decide between sending another offender to CREST work release only or CREST work release plus aftercare, it would be substantially more cost-effective to select CREST plus aftercare. To explain this quantitatively, the cost per avoided incarceration day is $131 when comparing CREST work release only participants to the Comparison group, but the cost per avoided incarceration day is only $19 when comparing CREST work release only to CREST work release plus aftercare.[6] Of course, due to potential selection bias within the CREST intent-to-treat subgroups, this comparison must be expressed as a hypothetical interpretation of the potential for a continuum of post-release treatment in criminal justice populations. CREST participants were randomly assigned into the CREST work release program, but participation in aftercare was voluntary and subject to time-and space-availability. Essentially, the only policy lever the Department of Corrections could control was whether an individual entered CREST work release or standard work release. Thus, in terms of Delaware's criminal justice policy, promoting CREST participation and encouraging treatment completion should be the first priority. The importance of the aftercare program must be reexamined with longer-term data that are free of the potential selection bias associated with voluntary selection.

Other research qualifications should be noted and explained. First, one should guard against drawing general economic conclusions about treatment programs for criminal offenders based on this short-term CEA of the CREST programs. Currently, no widely accepted standard exists for providing treatment in criminal justice settings, so programs should be evaluated individually. Thus, this analysis is useful for assessing the short-term potential of the CREST

Outreach Center programs in Delaware and for providing the Delaware Department of Corrections with tangible results on which further funding decisions for corrections-based treatment can be considered. But, it is not clear that these findings would apply to other correctional systems.

Second, the Comparison group for this study did not perfectly reflect a "non-treated" sample. In fact, 56% of the Comparison group sample reported receiving some "treatment" services during follow-up, although specific details about these services were not available (Inciardi et al., 1997). Nevertheless, Comparison group participants did not receive TC treatment, which is an important distinguishing feature of the CREST Outreach Center.

Third, the primary effectiveness measure for this analysis was reincarceration days for any reason during follow-up. It is possible that the CREST group may have an inflated number of incarceration days because probation officers may have been more attentive to the CREST participants (because they had been through the CREST program). Evidence suggests that the aftercare process itself makes participants more at risk for urinalysis detection. For example. Knight et al. (1999) found that treatment participants underwent substantially more urinalysis testing than the Comparison group subjects. In this case, the CREST group may show a greater number of incarceration days than otherwise if both Comparison and CREST clients were scrutinized equivalently during the post-release period. Data are not available in this study to allow us to explore the possibilities of criminal over-identification in the treatment groups, but future evaluations could consider this situation when collecting data.

Finally, this study considered follow-up days incarcerated up to 18 months post-release. Many of the participants that were returned to custody during the follow-up period were still incarcerated at the 18 months postrelease anniversary. Forty-one percent of CREST dropouts and 33.1% of

---

[6] The CREST work release only group ($N = 378$) generated an average cost $1604 but only had 12.24 fewer days incarcerated than the Comparison group. Thus, the cost-effectiveness ratio for CREST work release only relative to the Comparison group was $131 per avoided incarceration day.

Comparison group individuals were still incarcerated at 18 months postrelease. These numbers highlight the importance of retention in treatment programs. This phenomenon will be addressed in future planned analyses of these data over longer timelines.

6.1. Conclusion

The most important estimates from this cost-effectiveness analysis are the average cost of the CREST work release program ($1937) and the fewer days incarcerated (30) relative to standard work release. This implies that for about $65 per day (per offender), the Delaware Department of Corrections can reduce reincarceration for substance abusing offenders by investing in the CREST program. More favorable than CREST alone may be the performance of aftercare in the success of CREST participants. The investment in aftercare services reduced follow-up incarceration by an additional 43% (49 days) relative to CREST work release only. Thus, if the Department of Corrections could choose between sending another offender to CREST work release only or CREST work release plus aftercare, it would be substantially more cost-effective to select CREST plus aftercare.

At the current stage of research on this topic, an important contribution to the literature would be a benefit-cost analysis of post-incarceration treatment programs. Naturally, analyses of long-term (i.e., 3-years post-release or longer) follow-up data would enhance any type of economic evaluation. If future studies could estimate and compare a more comprehensive range of costs and benefits (e.g., the value of reduced crime, increased employment, changing use of healthcare services, and family stability) over a longer follow-up period, policy makers would be equipped with a broad range of information to understand the impact of providing substance abuse treatment in criminal justice settings.

⊠ References

Aos, S., Phipps, P., Barnoski, R., and Lieb, R. (2001). *The comparative costs and benefits of programs to reduce crime: A review of national research findings with implications for Washington State*. Washington State Institute for Public Policy, Washington, D.C.

Barnett, P. G., Zaric, G. S., and Brandeau, M. L. (2001). The cost-effectiveness of buprenorphine maintenance therapy for opiate addiction in the U.S. *Addiction* 96(9): 1267–1278.

Bell, D. C. (1994). Connection in therapeutic communities. *Int. J. Addict.* 29: 525–543.

Bureau of Justice Statistics (1999). Substance Abuse and Treatment, State and Federal Prisoners, 1997. (Bureau of Justice Statistics Special Report). BJS website: http: www.ojp.usdoj.gov/bjs/

Bureau of Justice Statistics (2001). Prisoners in 2000. (Bureau of Justice Statistics Special Report). BJS website: http://www.ojp.usdoj.gov/bjs/

De Leon, G., and Ziegenfuss, L. J. (1986). *Therapeutic Communities for Addictions: Readings in Theory, Research, and Practice*. Charles C Thomas Publishing, Springfield, IL.

De Leon, G., and Rosenthal, M. S. (1989). Treatment in residential communities. In Karasu, T. B. (ed.), *Treatment of Psychiatric Disorders Volume II*. American Psychiatric Press, Washington, DC, pp. 1379–1396.

De Leon, G. (1995). Therapeutic communities for addictions: A theoretical framework. *Int. J. Addict.* 30: 1603–1645.

De Leon, G. (2000). *The Therapeutic Community: Theory, Model, and Method*. Springer Publishing Company, Inc., New York.

French, M. T. (2000). Economic evaluation of alcohol treatment services. *Eval. Prog. Plan.* 23(1): 27–39.

French, M. T. (2002a). Drug Abuse Treatment Cost Analysis Program (DATCAP): Program Version User's Manual Seventh edition. Medical University of South Carolina, Charleston, South Carolina.

French, M. T. (2002b). *Drug Abuse Treatment Cost Analysis Program (DATCAP): Program Version*, Seventh edition, Medical University of South Carolina, Charleston, South Carolina.

French, M. T., Dunlap, L. J., Zarkin, G. A., McGeary, K. A., and McLellan, A. T. (1997). A structured instrument for estimating the economic cost of drug abuse treatment: the drug abuse treatment cost analysis program (DATCAP). *J. Subst. Abuse Treat.* 14: 1–11.

French, M. T., and McGeary, K. A. (1997). Estimating the economic cost of substance abuse treatment. *Health Econ.* 6: 539–544.

French, M. T., McCoilister, K. E., Sacks, S., McKendrick, K., and De Leon, G. (2002). Benefit-cost analysis of a modified therapeutic community for mentally ill chemical abusers. *Eval. Prog. Plan.* 21(2): 137–148.

Gold, M. R., Siegel, J. E., Russell, L. B., and Weinstein, M. C. (1996). *Cast-effectiveness in Health and Medicine*. Oxford University Press, Oxford, UK.

Griffith, J. D., Hiller, M. L., Knight, K., and Simpson, D. D. (1999). A cost-effectiveness analysis of in-prison therapeutic community treatment and risk classification. *Prison J.* 79(3): 352–368.

Hiller, M. L., Knight, K., and Simpson, D. D. (1999). Prison-based substance abuse treatment, residential aftercare and recidivism. *Addiction* 94: 833–842.

Hoffman, P. B. (1983). Screening for risk: A revised salient factor score. *J. Crim. Justice* 11: 539–547.

Hoffman, P. B., and Beck, J. L. (1974). Parole decision-making: A salient factor score. *J. Crim. Justice* 4: 69–76.

Inciardi, J. A. (1996). A corrections-based continuum of effective drug abuse treatment. In *National Institute of Justice Research Preview*. Department of Justice, Office of Justice Programs, Washington, D.C.

Inciardi, J. A., Lockwood, D., and Martin, S. S. (1994). Therapeutic communities in corrections and work release: Some clinical and policy implications. In Tims, K, De Leon, G., and Jainchill, N. (eds.). *Therapeutic Community: Advances in Research and Application*, NIDA Research Monograph 144. U.S. Department of Health and Human Services, Rockville, MD, pp. 259–267.

Inciardi, J., Martin, S. S., Butzin, C. A., Hooper, R. M., and Harrison, L. D. (1997). An effective model of prison-based treatment for drug-involved offenders. *J. Drug Issues* 27(2): 261–278.

Inciardi, J. A., Martin, S. S., and Surratt, H. (2001). Therapeutic Communities in prisons and work release: Effective modalities for Drug-Involved Offenders. In Rawlings, B. and Yates, R. (eds.) *Therapeutic Communities for Drug Users*. Jessica Kingsley Publishers, London, UK, pp. 241–256.

Kenkel, D. (1997). On valuing morbidity, cost-effectiveness analysis, and being rude. *J. Health Econ.* 16: 749–757.

Knight, K., Simpson, D. D., and Hiller, M. L. (1999). Three-year reincarceration outcomes for in-prison therapeutic community treatment in Texas. *Prison J.* 79: 337–351.

Lipton, D. S. (1995). The Effectiveness of Treatment for Drug Abusers under Criminal Justice Supervision. Presentation at the 1995 Conference on Criminal Justice Research and Evaluation.

Lipton, D. S., Martinson, R., and Wilks, J. (1975). *The Effectiveness of Correctional Treatment*. Praeger Publishers, New York.

Lowe, L., Wexler, H. K., and Peters, J. (1998). *The R.J. Donovan in-prison and community substance abuse program: three-year return-to-custody data*. Sacramento, CA: Office of Substance Abuse Programs, Delaware Department of Corrections.

Martin, S. S., Butzin, C. A., and Inciardi, J. A. (1995). Assessment of a multistage therapeutic community for drug-involved offenders. *J. Psychoactive Drugs* 27(1): 109–116.

Martin, S. S., Butzin, C. A., Saum, C. A., and Inciardi, J. A. (1999). Three-year outcomes of therapeutic community treatment for drug-involved offenders in Delaware: From prison to work release to aftercare. *Prison J.* 79(3): 294–320.

Martinson, R. (1974). What works? Questions and answers about prison reform. *Pub. Interest* 35: 22–54.

McCaffrey, B. R. (2000). Drug abuse and the criminal justice system: Saving lives and preventing crime through treatment. *Connection*. Academy for Health Services Research and Health Policy, National Institute on Drug Abuse.

McCollister, K. E., and French, M. T. (2002). The Cost of Drug Abuse Treatment in Criminal Justice Settings. In Leukefeld, C., Tims, F., and Farabee, D. (eds.). *Treatment of Drug Offenders: Policies and Issues*, Springer Publishing Company, New York, pp. 22–37.

Mooney, C. Z., and Duval, R. D. (1993). *Bootstrapping: A Nonparametric Approach to Statistical Inference*. Sage Publications, Inc., Thousand Oaks, CA.

Office of National Drug Control Policy (1998) *Drug treatment in the criminal justice system*. ONDCP Drug Policy Information Clearinghouse Fact Sheet.

Roebuck, M. C., French, M. T., and McLellan, A. T. (2002). *DATStats: Summary Results from 85 Completed Drug Abuse Treatment Cost Analysis Programs (DATCAPs)*. Medical University of South Carolina Working Paper.

Salome, H. J., and French, M. T. (2001). Using cost and financing instruments for economic evaluation of substance abuse treatment services. In Galanter, M. (ed.), *Recent Developments in Alcoholism*, Volume XV, Plenum Press, New York, pp. 253–269.

StataCorp (1999). *Stata Statistical Software: Release 8*. College Station, TX: Stata Corporation.

Travis, J., Solomon, A. L., and Waul, M. (2001). *From prison to home: The dimensions and consequences of prisoner reentry*. The Urban Institute, Justice Policy Center, Washington, DC.

Wexler, H. K. (1995). The success of therapeutic communities for substance abusers in American prisons. *J. Psychoactive Drugs* 27: 57–66.

Wexler, H. K., Blackmore, J., and Lipton, D. (1991). Project REFORM: Developing a drug abuse treatment strategy for corrections. *J. Drug Issues* 21(2): 473–495.

Wexler, H. K., and Lipton, D. (1993). From reform to recovery: Advances in prison drug treatment. In Inciardi, J. (ed.), *Drug Treatment and Criminal Justice* (Volume 27). Sage Publications, Newbury Park, CA, pp. 209–227.

Wexler, H. K., De Leon, G., Thomas, G., Kressel, D., and Peters, J. (1999a). The Amity prison TC evaluation: reincarceration outcomes. *Crim. Justice Behav.* 26(2): 147–167.

Wexler, H. K., Melnick, G., Lowe, L., and Peters, J. (1999b). Three-year reincarceration outcomes for Amity in-prison therapeutic community and aftercare in Delaware. *Prison J.* 79(3): 321–336.

DISCUSSION QUESTIONS

1. According to the findings of the McCollister et al. article, a TC work release program only demonstrated minimal cost reductions compared to standard work release. Given these findings, why might the state of Delaware still want to invest in a TC program?

2. Why might measuring treatment failure as any reincarceration confound the effectiveness of the program?

3. Given the economic constraints most states are experiencing at this time, do you believe DOC should invest in therapeutic communities? Why or why not?

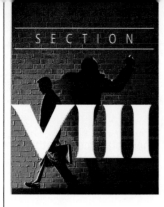

VIII

Community-Based Nonresidential and Economic Intermediate Sanctions

---

Learning Objectives

1. Know the definition and purpose of intermediate sanctions.

2. Identify the various types of intermediate sanctions and their placement within the continuum of sanctions.

3. Analyze the various means of ensuring offender compliance among substance abusers and sex offenders.

4. Compare the various means by which intermediate sanctions are used in a variety of states around the nation.

5. Understand both the security and treatment functions associated with intermediate sanctions.

This section of the text will cover the nonresidential intermediate sanctions. As you recall from Section VII, intermediate sanctions are a range of sentencing options that fall between incarceration and probation, being designed to allow for the crafting of sentences that respond to the offender and/or the offense, with the intended outcome of the case being a primary consideration. Like the residential intermediate sanctions covered in the last section, these options increase the level of supervision but still allow the offender to remain in the community. These sanctions include **intensive supervision probation (ISP)**, electronic monitoring (EM), **home detention**, and day reporting centers. This section will discuss the most commonly implemented and researched intermediate sanctions of ISP, day reporting centers, economic sanctions, home detention, EM, community service, and various methods of compliance assurance.

☒ Economic Sanctions

The use of economic sanctions to hold offenders accountable for their actions is not a new phenomenon. Public assistance programs estimate that the losses for victims total more than $105 billion per year. These losses include medical expenses, lost wages, counseling expenses, lost or damaged property, funeral expenses, and other direct out-of-pocket expenses (Office for Victims of Crime [OVC], 2002, p. 2). These sanctions are typically combined with another penalty such as probation, although they may be used separately. Ruback and Bergstrom (2006) argued there are three distinct reasons for the use of economic sanctions: (1) to punish offenders, (2) to deter future criminal offending, or (3) to restore justice principles. In spite of these goals, these sanctions are often criticized for being too harsh on the poor, too lenient on the wealthy, or simply unenforceable (Ruback & Bergstrom, 2006). Ultimately, economic sanctions are more difficult to enforce than any other alternative because the U.S. Constitution prohibits incarceration for failure to pay debt. Despite these difficulties, there are five distinct advantages to using economic sanctions. First, economic sanctions are cheaper than incarceration. When offenders are allowed to remain in the community, they are able to maintain their employment, not only saving the state resources that would be used to detain the offender but also providing the offender with an opportunity to repay the victim for damages caused. Second, these sanctions are easier to impose than incarceration. Economic sanctions can and in some states have been attached to every penalty. These sanctions may both increase revenue for the state or local criminal justice system while enhancing the deterrent effect of the offenses. Third, these sanctions are more punitive in nature than simple probation. Fourth, these sanctions are flexible allowing for an extended amount of time to repay the debt or even the amount owed. Finally, success on these programs is easy to determine based upon their ability to repay or to successfully pay the amount owed (Ruback & Bergstrom, 2006, p. 248).

Like other intermediate sanctions, economic penalties can and do also work on a continuum ranging from a simple fine to something more severe, such as restitution. Economic sanctions can also be used in both the criminal and civil court systems allowing an opportunity for victims to seek some remedy for damages caused by the offenders' actions. For the purposes of this section, fines, fees, and forfeiture and also restitution will be discussed.

Fines, Fees, and Forfeiture

Most all offenders convicted of a criminal offense are assessed a fine as a punishment for committing the offense. A fine can be defined as a monetary penalty imposed by a judge or magistrate as a punishment for being convicted of an offense. In most cases, the fine is a certain dollar amount established either by the judge or according to a set schedule dependent upon offense committed.

The historical development of the fine can be traced as far back as just after the Middle Ages and in the works of Jeremy Bentham. Bentham argued that fines met the goals of utilitarianism (deterrence) by taking away pleasure (money or goods) rather than enacting pain. He further argued that fines should be commensurate with the offender's income, therefore increasing the reduction in pleasure. This concept set the tone for what we know today as day fines (O'Malley, 2009). In most jurisdictions, the fines are assessed and paid in monthly increments to the receiving agency. In contemporary community supervision agencies, offenders are now able to pay their fines via credit or check cards. The feelings are mixed regarding the ability of an offender to pay their fees via credit or check card. Officers sometimes feel that this does not allow the offender to accept personal responsibility by delaying the effect of the monetary fine.

As the offense seriousness increases from misdemeanor to a felony, presumably the fine increases. This assessment of fines is totally dependent upon the independent judicial discretion. Gordon and Glaser (1991) have demonstrated that most offenders are more likely to pay their fines in totality and that their likelihood of recidivism is significantly less than that of those who are sentenced to traditional institutional incarceration after controlling for offender typologies and type of offense committed.

At both the federal and state level, fines are imposed. Traditionally there was one set fine for certain offenses regardless of the financial standing of the offenders. As time has evolved, many judiciaries are beginning to understand that one set fine is more punishing to the offender who happens to earn the least amount of money and a cakewalk to those offenders who happen to be financially blessed. Given this, there has been a push for graduated or structured fines dependent upon the income of the offender at time of sentencing.

Structured fines, also known as day fines, were first introduced in Sweden in 1920; the use of this alternative quickly spread to other Scandinavian countries. Western European countries have used this method as their sanction of choice since the late 1960s. The use of day fines originated in the United States in Richmond County (Staten Island), New York, in 1988 (Vera Institute of Justice, 2002). Unlike traditional fines that are set by statute or criminal code, day fines are meant to serve as a deterrent to criminal offending by basing the amount on the severity of the offense and the income of the offender. A two-step process is recommended. First, the court must "establish the number of day fine units based on the offense, then calculate the monetary value of the units based on the information about the offender's net daily income and number of dependents" (Vera Institute of Justice, 2002, p. 3). Although day fines are meant to be the ultimate equalizer based upon income, difficulty does arise for those with lower incomes and those who have no income such as homemakers, students, the disabled, and the unemployed. The Vera Institute of Justice (2002) set forth four approaches to dealing with this group of individuals. The first approach bases the fine on the household income. The second approach bases the fine on the potential income of the offender. A third approach looks at the household income but only holds the money that would go directly to the responsible party in question accountable. The last approach bases the level of the fine on the local community unemployment and welfare compensation rates. Regardless, this system is meant to hold the offender accountable in a more fair and proportionate manner.

As the use of community corrections becomes more contemporary, agencies will begin to experiment with alternative ways to pay fines. Today there are a host of private, for-profit companies that have contracted with community supervision agencies to handle their fee payments. There are those companies that are now allowing offenders to pay their fines online or anywhere there is web access. For several years in New York City, offenders have been able to pay fines at kiosks around the city as opposed to having to travel to a centralized location that may be miles from their residence or employment. In this day of drastic budget cuts and a push for alternatives to incarceration, fines are the order of the day. They allow the offender an opportunity to fund their treatment and punishment as opposed to the traditional method of placing the financial burden on the state.

The use of fees to cover costs for programming, treatment, and institutionalization is becoming a more common practice as communities fight for the few resources available. These fees are used to reimburse the state or agency for administrative costs. Many fees are set by state law and include basic elements such as supervision fees. In Indiana, for example, the Senate Enrolled Act 506 structured user fees for both adult and juvenile probationers. Adult probation fees range from $15 to $30 for felons and $10 to $20 for misdemeanants with an administrative fee of $100 for felons and $50 for misdemeanants. Fees for juveniles classified as delinquent range from $10 to $25 per month with a $100 administrative fee if the youth is supervised by a probation officer. These fees are typical for most states. The range may vary but is representative of most agencies. Interestingly enough, research indicates that probationers in rural counties are more likely to be charged fees than those in urban areas (Ruback & Bergstrom, 2006). One explanation for this might be the lack of resources in these communities that require creative sentencing.

Like fines and fees, the use of asset forfeiture continues to expand in the United States. Forfeiture is the seizing of property by the government "because it is illegal contraband, was illegally obtained, was acquired with resources that were illegally obtained, or was used in connection with an illegal activity" (Ruback & Bergstrom, 2006, p. 257). Within this context, the U.S. Supreme Court has ruled that "forfeiture is a fine within the meaning of the Eighth Amendment and, therefore, that if the amount of the forfeiture is grossly disproportionate to the gravity of the defendant's offense, the forfeiture would violate the excessive fines clause" (Ruback & Bergstrom, 2006, p. 257). The historical roots of forfeiture trace back to the days when the federal government seized boats from shippers who failed to pay. In 1970, these ideas were expanded into the federal Racketeer Influence and Corrupt Organizations Act and the Continuing Criminal Enterprise Act. Approximately 40,000 asset seizures occur annually in the United States. The majority of these forfeitures are uncontested. Estimates value these forfeitures at more than $1 billion per year. One reason for the lack of contesting forfeiture is due to the link between crime, drugs, and organized activities (Ruback & Bergstrom, 2006).

During the mid- to late 1990s, *USA Today* published all governmental asset forfeitures in Friday's paper. Since that time, these forfeitures have ceased to be published but continue to be at the forefront of many agency pursuits.

Restitution

Restitution is a form of restorative justice that requires the offender to pay monetary compensation to the victim, the victim's family, or an organization designated by the victim for the harm caused. The amount of restitution owed is based on the monetary harm caused by property loss, loss incurred because of bodily injury, and possibly lost wages. States will vary by the amount allowed to recover. Historically, restitution is one of the oldest known penalties. As Caputo (2004) noted, use of restitution can be traced as far back as to the time of tribes or clans and to the Middle Ages where it was used as a formal mechanism to minimize blood feuds between families (wergild or "man money") in England (p. 138). The use of restitution as a formal sanction lost favor with the government when focus switched from the victim and their family to the use of fines, which ultimately benefitted the government. It was not until the 1970s that restitution began to once again be used in the United States. More specifically, Law Enforcement Assistance Administration (LEAA) began to offer funding to local governments and courts for the development of restitution programs. As Caputo (2004) reported, the President's Task Force on Victims of Crime and the Victim Witness Protection Act of 1982 spurred the creation of restitution programs to compensate victims (p. 138). By 1990, all states had instituted some form of restitution (Ruback & Bergstrom, 2006). As of 2002, 32 states had some form of a victims' right constitutional amendment. Of those amendments, 18 states gave victims the right to restitution (OVC, 2002). The original programs were used primarily for property offenders in conjunction with other sanctions. Although this has been the traditional use it can be expanded effectively for use with violent offenders. These programs can and have been implemented as both front-end (combined with probation) and back-end (as a condition of parole) programs. Restitution, unlike fines, focuses solely on reparation to the victims (Ruback & Bergstrom, 2006).

Collecting restitution can create a variety of difficulties. Because, as previously noted, the U.S. Constitution does not allow for the imprisonment of individuals for debt, many sentencing courts rely on the work of victim's rights groups and community agencies to assist with collection. For those with limited resources, paying back this debt may be an onerous task (Caputo, 2004). Ruback and Bergstrom (2006) illuminated the four different ways restitution can be handled: "(a) as a component of victim/witness assistance programs, (b) through victim-offender reconciliation programs, (c) in conjunction with probation or parole supervision, and (d) through court-based employment programs" (p. 250). Opponents of these programs have argued that they are unfair to individuals who lack resources and are unable to pay; there is ambiguity regarding who is supposed to collect the restitution, and restitution is just one of several forms of monetary compensation the offender must pay.

In spite of the difficulties with restitution programs, restitution is a common practice throughout the world. Most European countries have used this form of sanction with much success. As Saiman (2008) contended, the United States appears to only have a scholarly interest in restitution rather than a true desire to implement this sanction on a larger basis. Likewise, research on the effectiveness of restitution programs in the United States reveals that bias does exist by judges on whom they order restitution. In a study by Outlaw and Ruback (1999) where restitution was ordered in conjunction with probation, they found that judges were most likely to order restitution where damages were easily quantifiable and it appeared that the offender had the means and would pay. Other research indicates that having a victims' advocate group located at the courthouse and notifying their offender of their requirement to pay the victim increased the likelihood that offenders would compensate their victims (Ruback & Bergstrom, 2006). Despite the difficulties in recovering compensation, there is support for the continued use and expansion of these programs in addition to other economic intermediate sanctions.

⚑ Community Service

Perhaps the most widely known yet least likely to be used form of intermediate sanctioning is that of community service. Community service is the work that one conducts in hopes of repaying their debt to society after being found at fault for committing a criminal or deviant offense. In most cases, community service is ordered by the sentencing judge and supervised by the community supervision officer (CSO). Most judges prefer that offenders sentenced to complete community service do so at a not-for-profit agency within their local jurisdiction. Types of community service range from your typical trash pickups to that of caring for animals at an animal shelter or participating in menial labor type jobs at the local public facilities.

A relatively new innovation in the criminal justice system, the first community service program, can be traced back to Alameda County, California (late 1960s). This program was utilized for traffic offenders who could not pay their fines (Caputo, 2004, p. 149). Judges began offering this as an alternative to incarceration for those who could not pay their fines. During the 1970s, the LEAA began offering grants for the creation and the expansion of these programs. One interesting development historically regarding fines is the shift in purpose from its origins to now. As Caputo (2004) noted, the idea of community service began as one of rehabilitation. During the 1970s and into the 1980s, correctional philosophy changed from a focus on reformation to a get tough approach. Despite this shift in philosophy, the use of community service as an alternative sanction did not diminish. Rather its intent and focus shifted from one of rehabilitation to incapacitation and reintegration, which explains the modern-day classification as a form of intermediate sanction (Caputo, 2004, p. 149). Due to the fact that many offenders are economically challenged, community service options began to spring up all around the country—particularly as an option for younger and less violent offenders.

At latest count, most states in the United States had some form of community service at either the juvenile or adult offender levels. There was an estimated 547 community service programs being run nationwide in the late 1990s (Bouffard & Mufti, 2007, p. 172). In most cases, offenders are required to complete a set amount of community service hours a month. Most all offenders placed on probation are required to complete some specified amount of community service inclusive of various other conditions of probation. Though there may be statutorily prescribed terms of community service ordered, the amount typically given out is very subjective, because it depends on the amount determined by the presiding judge.

The amount of community service varies, and in most cases the offenders must find time to complete their hours within the confines of their normal work week. For those offenders without employment, officers often require that they complete as many as 40 hours of community service per week until they have completed their hours. In certain jurisdictions, offenders have been known to be allowed to work off some of their fines by complete additional hours of community service. Most cases call for this subjective determination of the value of the hours to community service ratio by the directors of such agencies. The standard has been that the offenders are provided at least minimum wage credit for each hour of community service.

The question remains as to how effective community service is at meeting its intended objectives of rehabilitation and punitiveness. Used extensively in Europe, these sanctions have demonstrated some success at reducing recidivism. However, little to no research has been conducted on its effectiveness in the

United States. One potential reason for this is that programs are so varied in both their implementation and use; therefore, it's nearly impossible to compare effectiveness between programs and even within. The reality is no matter how effective they may or may not be, numerous nonprofit agencies are grateful to the massive amount of assistance that they receive from community service workers. For example, after Hurricane Katrina, one of the five most costliest and deadliest hurricanes in American history, community service offenders were responsible for manning hours of assistance in local shelters feeding, clothing, and assisting to the emergency needs of recently evacuated citizens of the Gulf Coast region. Anderson (1998) demonstrated that most offenders complete their community service conditions as directed by the court. Those offenders who are least likely to complete their hours have been shown to have an officer who does not stress the completion of the community service hours. Judges are very reluctant to provide an offender additional time to complete community service unless there is proof of extenuating circumstances, such as significant health and transportation concerns.

Due to the low cost of overhead in funding community service programs, coupled with the added use of much needed labor in communities, community service options will continue to be well utilized. One of the most pressing problems in evaluating community service is that the community service opportunities vary, and oftentimes offenders participate in multiple community service sites and types throughout their time under supervision. In most cases, community service is completed anywhere the offender can get the hours. For example, an offender may begin their community service at the local courthouse and complete their hours at the homeless mission. Despite the lack of research, community service is an integral part of intermediate sanctioning and provides a positive avenue through which offenders and the community can learn the rehabilitative and punitive ideals.

Intensive Supervision Probation

Perhaps the most commonly known form of intermediate sanction is that of intensive supervision. Intensive supervision is the extensive supervision of offenders who are the greatest risk to society and/or are in need of the greatest amount of governmental services (i.e., drug treatment). In most cases, intensive supervision is the option afforded to individuals who would otherwise be incarcerated for felony offenses. The early forms of intensive supervision operated under the conservative philosophy of increasing public safety via strict offender scrutiny all the while; today's ISPs are focused on a host of components.

In the early days, ISPs operated under the assumption that increasing an offender's contact with their supervising officer would increase public safety and simultaneously the offender's chances of rehabilitation. As an example, the California Special Intensive Parole Unit of the 1950s was created with an emphasis in increased supervision with a special interest in offender rehabilitation. A short time later, the field began to seek that optimal number of offender-officer ratio, which was to provide the most effective ratio of the offender-officer relationship. As a result of the inability to find that optimal level of offender-officer ratio effectiveness, intensive supervision suffered in credibility during the 1960s and 1970s.

If you were to examine today's intensive supervision units, it would be questionable whether or not ISPs of today are focused on public safety, punishment, and ultimately offender control and not so much on the offender's rehabilitation. Within the past 10 to 15 years, there has been a resurgence of the use of ISPs. Perhaps this may be a result of the massive number of offenders incarcerated in the United States, with the most recent numbers reflecting over 2 million prisoners.

In their early years, intensive supervision was afforded the luxury of smaller caseloads, mostly as a result of the smaller number of offenders being processed through the criminal justice system. Despite the enviable officer to offender intensive supervision ratio, the rates of offender rearrest and/or reconvictions remained significantly high. Given the old adage that history repeats itself, today's intensive programs have begun to shrink the offender-officer ratio while at the same time focusing on offender control and supervision. It should be noted that despite this current reverting to the old days of intensive supervision, the U.S. prison population continues to rise.

When examining the various facets of intensive supervision one would find that they are diverse. Some ISPs focus on specific offender offense types (i.e., sex offenders and younger offenders) to the level of supervision that ranges from 5 days per week to once every 2 weeks. The types of supervising officers vary from untrained CSOs to specialized officers who have been well trained in the supervision of at-risk offenders. In most cases, officers are afforded a less stringent caseload of approximately 10 to 20 offenders. Placement into intensive supervision is dependent upon the sentencing judge, supervision officer, and/or the parole board. In today's agencies, the decision to place an offender on intensive supervision is dependent upon the level of assessed offender risk of rearrest or needs for rehabilitative services.

There is a host of literature that regards ISPs as cost savers of public funds as opposed to institutional incarceration. It should be noted that this is difficult to determine because in order to determine the amount of money saved by ISPs as opposed to prison, one would have to actually decrease the prison operating cost, which would never happen. Research has demonstrated that ISPs are not significant predictors of a lowered rate of recidivism. This lack of influence may be a result of the reality that the ISP offenders may be a victim of increased scrutiny, which ultimately leads to increased chances of arrest. No research has been examined to date that examines the influence of ISPs on an offender's chances of recidivism. Petersilia and Turner (1993) found that ISP offenders who took part in a rehabilitative component of ISP were more likely to desist from criminal or addictive behavior.

Electronic Monitoring

Perhaps the most widely used but least understood intermediate sanction is that of EM. It was Ralph Schwitzgebel who first proposed the use of some form of monitoring apparatus for supervising offenders in the community with the first type developed and utilized on parolees, mental patients, and research volunteers in Boston (1968) (Illinois Criminal Justice Information Authority, 1988; McCarthy, McCarthy, & Leone, 2001). The legal liability of such monitoring was argued in the *Harvard Law Review* in 1966. Massachusetts has been credited with the first use of EM (Schwitzgebel, 1969). In the 1970s, the use, effectiveness, and liability often found debate among the legal and scholarly community (Ingraham & Smith, 1972; Szasz, 1975). Renzema (1992) conducted an analysis of the states that use EM and found that 44 states were utilizing the monitors. The National Institute of Justice (1999) revealed that there were over 100,000 offenders being supervised via EM in 1,500 programs.

EM includes the use of any mechanism that is worn by the offender for the means of tracking their whereabouts through electronic detection. There are two main types of EM: radio frequency (RF) and global positioning system (GPS). Each of these systems will be described.

Radio Frequency

EM includes both active and passive monitoring systems. Active systems require that the offender answer or respond to a monitoring cue (such as a computer-generated telephone call) whereas passive forms of monitoring emit a continuous signal for tracking. With both types of EM devices, offenders are provided an ankle bracelet with a tracking device. The active types are used in conjunction with the local telephone line. At random times throughout the day, the offender's home phone will ring; once it rings, the offender has a certain amount of time to answer. Once the offender answers the phone, a signal is transmitted to the phone to the bracelet at which time a response is sent to the phone, which validates that the offender is at home. With the passive type, the ankle bracelet transmits a continuous signal to a nearby transmitter that transmits the signal to a monitoring computer (also known as RF monitoring). With each type, the supervising officer is sent a readout each morning of the offender's compliance. It is not uncommon for an offender to be at home, and it appears that they are noncompliant. If an offender attempts to alter the connection, most devices have alarms that will sound and send an immediate alarm to the monitoring devices. Of the two EM types, the active system has the lowest rate of false alarms. Even though the passive system has the highest rate of false alarms, they are the fastest in determining noncompliance because they are assessing the offender's whereabouts a lot faster. Unlike other forms of intermediate sanction, EM programs were designed to be used in conjunction with other sanctions, such as home confinement, curfew, etc. (Meyer, 2004).

In a rare analysis of the effectiveness of various EM programs, Baumer, Maxfield, and Mendelsohn (1993) demonstrated that the effectiveness of such programming is depen-

▲ **Photo 8.1** Officer Jared Steward examines an electronic ankle bracelet. These types of devices are used with high-risk offenders, including sex offenders. Officer Steward is currently a graduate student in one of the author's courses.

dent upon the administrative philosophy and the offender typologies placed under supervision. Of all offenders, the pretrial offenders were the most likely to violate the conditions of EM but the most likely to be diverted from jail as a result of EM. In most cases, EM was provided for those offenders who had possessed stable employment. EM devices have come close to $50,000 to purchase with additional daily operating costs. Some jurisdictions have required that the offenders assist in paying for the use of GPS. This has raised concerns because the less fortunate offenders are not afforded an opportunity for independence from supervision unlike the more financially blessed individuals of the country.

Those who are "pro" EM are basing their argument on the ability to increase public safety due to the knowledge of whereabouts of each offender. Simply having knowledge of being personally tracked may deter offenders from committing crime. Proponents also argue that EM provides the least punitive alternative to incarceration, which allows for offenders, who can, to be supervised in the community. Undoubtedly EM is a viable intermediate sanction in terms of diverting offenders from incarceration. The question remains as to the ability of EM to assist offenders in the desistance from criminal behavior, supervision officer discretion, and the effects of community and family involvement on EM.

Focus Topic 8.1

Electronic Monitoring: A New Approach to Work Release

The telephone was ringing as electronic detention participant Jones returned home from work. Jones was half an hour late according to his approved movement schedule, and community correctional center staff had initiated response procedures to locate him. This scenario could be played out at any Illinois community correctional center on any given day, because the centers have a central role in the operation of the Department of Corrections' electronic detention (E.D.) program.

Working cooperatively with parole agents assigned to the Special Intensive Supervision Unit, the centers have served 1,540 E.D. participants between June 1989 and 1991. Of those 1,540 participants, 645 have successfully completed the program, and 384 have been returned to prison for technical program violations. There have been eight arrests for new crimes, but only two have led to prosecution by local law enforcement officials. The primary reason for this success is the personal involvement of the community correctional center staff in client screening, programming, and monitoring.

Program Requirements

The E.D. program is for offenders in work release status, and they are required to abide by the same guidelines as those who live at a center. These guidelines require participants to be involved in employment, education, and /or vocational training for more than thirty-five hours per week. Those not actively participating in programming must demonstrate that they are trying to become involved in it.

Offenders being considered for the E.D. program are initially screened by a center counselor who also orients them to the program. After conducting a needs assessment, the counselor helps the offender develop an individual program contract that defines specific goals. Prospective participants also sign an agreement to abide by the program rules—counselors clearly inform them that failure to abide by the agreement will result in their being returned to prison with the possible loss of good conduct credits.

Once in the program, the E.D. participant reports weekly to the center to meet with his or her counselor for thirty to forty-five minutes. During these meetings, counselors review participants' progress in accomplishing their program goals. The counselor also approves the next week's itinerary, which includes specific times for each activity so that the participant's movements can be monitored. Participants are aware that they may be tested for drugs or alcohol at any time.

They may be required to submit to urinalysis either during their weekly visits to the center or at any other time that their counselor determines that testing is necessary. Participants also must turn in their paychecks and work with the counselor to budget their incomes for living expenses.

Like center residents, E.D. participants must pay maintenance to the department at a rate of 20 percent of their earnings to a maximum of $50 per week. The most important result of the weekly counseling sessions is that they give E.D. participants an opportunity to identify with their counselors and the counselors a chance to know them.

Security

The role of the E.D. agent is to be a watchdog, acting as the community corrections center's eye in the community. Although center staff spot-check E.D. participants' movements by telephone, there are insufficient staff to allow physical visits or to follow up on those missing. E.D. agents are required to make face-to-face conduct with their clients at least twice a week. Agents are on call seven days a week, twenty-four hours a day to respond to alarms sounded when E.D. participants are missing. In these instances, the agent visits the host site and other areas where the offender might be, such as with other family members. If all efforts to locate the participant fail, he or she is placed on escape status. Department rules permit revocation of up to one year of good conduct credits for escape, and local law enforcement may prosecute as well.

Mr. Jones was fortunate. He was just a little late, but he made a mistake by not phoning the center to tell staff that he was late leaving work and would be late returning home. Since this was the first time it has happened and he hasn't had any other problems, Mr. Jones will probably just receive a lecture. But if it becomes a habit or he is unavailable for longer periods, he won't be allowed to stay in the program.

Accountability

Electronic monitoring fosters accountability. Participants are forced to schedule, plan ahead, and budget their earnings. This structured environment provides a support base that allows them to gradually reintegrate into their home communities. It is important to convince the public that safety is actually improved when participants learn to take on more responsibility at the same time they are being held accountable. The alternative, "cold turkey" release to both the freedom and responsibilities of the outside world, is often too much for the release to handle. The result may be a return to crime, reliance on drugs or alcohol, and ultimately another prison term.

Cost Savings

Agencies considering implementation of electronic monitoring programs must be careful not to be misled by dollar signs and promises of an easy and inexpensive way to solve a population crunch. However, electronic monitoring is economical. In Illinois, prison incarceration requires an estimated $16,200 per year per inmate, compared to an estimated $7,034 for electronic monitoring. This includes the cost of the monitor at about $3,285 and another $3,849 per participant for staff salaries and overhead costs.

For further information, contact Anthony Scillia, Logan Correctional Center, R.R. 3, Lincoln, Illinois 62566; (217) 735-5581.

Global Positioning System

In this new millennium, community supervision is beginning to utilize military capabilities to keep track of offenders. GPS uses 24 military satellites to determine the exact location of a coordinate. By using the satellite monitoring and remote tracking, offenders can be tracked to their exact location. This GPS

▲ **Photo 8.2** The equipment in this photo is used for GPS tracking. In some cases, equipment has specialized functions, such as the emission of alarms or noises that can be sounded by a CSO from a distance. When an offender cannot be found physically or when he or she enters a restricted or off-limits area, an alarm can be emitted by the probation officer merely pushing a button, even from a distance of several miles. The noise can be deafening and serves as a deterrent for most offenders and as a warning to community members.

tracking system used with offenders is joined with an ankle or wrist device that sends a signal to a tracking device that houses a micro transmitter and antenna, which sends a signal to the GPS system. The tracking device is capable of being placed in an offender's bag, and the offender must remain within 100 feet of the receiver. After receiving the signal, a continuous report is sent to a computer that tracks the whereabouts of the tracked offender. The GPS tracking device for offenders allows for supervising officers to place location restrictions on the offenders so that there can be certain places that are off limits. For example, sex offenders may be excluded from being within the vicinity of a school yard or church. If the offender enters a prohibited area, an alarm will sound. On the flip side, officers are allowed to program the offender's schedule for work and religious services and regular day-to-day whereabouts so that it can be easier to detect and verify where and when the offender does what he is supposed to. In some cases, the system can send notification via pager or telephone that the offender is near the victim or any other excluded location. The advantage of such a program is that the offender's whereabouts are known in a more real-time manner.

Given all of the new advances that GPS has provided for community corrections there are obvious disadvantages, such as expense and loss of signal. Just as with any other satellite device, the GPS offender tracking systems often lose their signal during bad weather or when an area is densely populated with trees. Of the disadvantages, the most noted one is the monetary concerns. Due to the extensive nature of the parties involved, GPS tracking is very expensive, and in this day of drastic budget cutbacks in community corrections, many agencies are not willing to provide funding for such contemporary and often extra unnecessary devices. Some have suggested that as a way to cut back on the operational costs of GPS devices agencies should request the offenders' whereabouts every 30 minutes or so as opposed to every minute. Others have suggested that GPS devices should be reserved for the most serious offenders within the community, such as child molesters and rapists. Across the country, there are approximately 150,000 offenders being supervised by EM devices. In the most recent analysis, there were only 1,200 offenders being monitored with GPS (Greek, 2002).

✂ Home Detention

Also known as house arrest, home detention is the mandated action that forces an offender to stay within the confines of their home or on their property until a time specified by the sentencing judge. It was the "father of modern science" Galileo who provides the example of the first offender who was ever placed on home detention after he proposed that the earth rotated around the sun. It was with the war on drugs that home detention gained notoriety. As a result of the massive numbers of drug offenders being sentenced to jail/prison, officials were seeking an alternative to supervision that would allow an offender to be supervised prior to trial or just before being placed into a residential treatment facility.

Offenders sentenced to home confinement are often required to complete community service or pay a host of fines, fees, and victim restitution while others are forced to wear electronic monitors or other detection devices to ensure that they are remaining in their residence during the specified amount of time. In a host of cases, home detention is used for offenders during the pretrial phase or just prior to an offender being released from prison on a work or educational release status. If an offender leaves their residence without permission or against the policies set forth, they are seen to have technically violated their conditions of supervision (U.S. Government Accounting Office, 1990).

Given the fact that home detention was designed as an alternative to incarceration, its use is very minimal, mostly as a result of the amount of work involved in supervising an offender under these conditions. Home detention is advantageous for those offenders who are not well suited for incarceration such as those with health concerns or pregnant offenders within days of delivery. EM devices are used to increase the level of offender surveillance for many offenders while on home detention.

The issue of net widening is the most damning argument against the use of home detention programs (Rackmill, 1994). This argument holds that since home detention programs are available, many offenders who would otherwise be ordered to pay a host of fines and complete community service would now be placed on home detention because the option is available. It should be noted that there is a lack of empirical research examining the effects of home detention in terms of recidivism, overall effectiveness, and of **process evaluations**. In an evaluation of the Florida Community Control Program, the National Council on Crime and Delinquency researchers demonstrated that home detention programs are effective in reducing prison overcrowding, reducing correctional funding allocations and offender recidivism. Overall the use of home detention is an intermediate sanction that has been widely adopted across the United States. Most home detention sentences are used in the juvenile court system where the youth are placed under the custody of their parents and for adult low-risk offenders.

◤ Day Reporting Centers

Day reporting centers are treatment facilities where offenders are required to report, usually on a daily basis. These facilities tend to offer a variety of services, including drug counseling, vocational assistance, life skills development, employment assistance, and so forth. The offenders who are likely to be required to report to day reporting centers may be of two types: either those who are placed on early release from a period of incarceration or those who are on some form of heightened probation supervision. Among those who are released early from a jail or prison term, the day reporting center represents a gradual transition into the community whereby they are supervised throughout the process. The advantage of day reporting centers is that they do not require the use of bed space and therefore save counties and states a substantial portion of the cost in maintaining offenders in their custody. Focus Topic 8.2 provides a very good example of a day reporting center operated by Hampden County, Massachusetts. This example demonstrates the various facets of day reporting centers The Hampden County facility is operated by that county's sheriff's department and therefore provides a strong integration between law enforcement efforts and those of community supervision agencies.

Day reporting centers are somewhat similar to residential treatment facilities except that offenders are not required to stay overnight. In some jurisdictions, the regimen of the day reporting center is designed so that offenders attend 8 to 10 hour intervention and treatment classes. This is an important element of the day reporting center since it provides added human supervision. As noted previously, the implementation of creative and versatile forms of human supervision serves to optimize both treatment and security characteristics of offender supervision, and day reporting centers facilitate this concept. Indeed, one staff person conducting some form of instruction class (i.e., a life skills class, a psychoeducational class on effective communication, or perhaps a parenting class) can essentially watch over several offenders at the same time. Further, the offender's time is spent in prosocial activities with little opportunity to engage in any form of undetected criminal activity. Thus, day reporting centers enhance security processes while filling up the leisure points of an offender's day and/or evening with activities that are constructive and beneficial to the offender and to society; little time is left for distractions or unregulated activity.

Focus Topic 8.2

An Example of a Day Reporting Center

The Hampden County Day Reporting Center: Three Years' Success in Supervising Sentenced Individuals in the Community

By Richard J. McCarthy

Public Information Officer, Hampden County, Massachusetts, Sheriff's Department

In Massachusetts, the county correctional system incarcerates both those in pre-trial detention and those sentenced to terms of two and one-half years or less for crimes such as breaking and entering, larceny, driving while intoxicated, and drug possession. Thus, each county facility is both a jail for pre-trial detainees and a house of correction for sentenced individuals. The sheriff of each county, an elected official, is the administrator of the jail and house of correction.

Sheriff Michael J. Ashe, Jr. has been in charge of the Hampden County Jail and House of Correction in Springfield, Massachusetts, for more than fifteen years. One of his early actions as sheriff was to choose not to live in the "Sheriff's House" that went with the job, but to turn it instead into a pre-release center. Inmates in residence at the center are within six months of release and are able to work and participate in community activities. These activities range from Alcoholics Anonymous and Narcotics Anonymous groups to individual counseling, religious services, "work-out" regimens at the YMCA, and community restitution.

In October 1986, faced like many other correctional administrators with worsening overcrowding, Sheriff Ashe instituted what the Crime and Justice Foundation refers to as the first day reporting center in the nation. The day reporting center was located in the county's pre-release center, so that the new operation could draw on the pre-release center staff's experience in supervising offenders in the community. In addition, pre-release center staff member Kevin Warwick was selected to direct the day reporting center.

Program Description. The Hampden County Day Reporting Center supervises inmates who are within four months of release and who live at home, work, and take part in positive activities in the community. Participants' behavior is monitored in several ways:

- They must report into the center daily to be observed by staff;
- They must call in daily at several specified times;
- They must be at home when scheduled to be there to receive random computer calls from an electronic monitoring system; and
- They must pass frequent random urinalysis tests that detect alcohol or drug use.

Participants also are monitored randomly by "community officers." Under this system, each participant is contacted between fifty and eighty times per week.

Day reporting center participants meet with their counselors at the beginning of each week to chart out a schedule of work and attendance at positive community activities. They are responsible for following this schedule to the letter.

It is important to note that the Hampden County day reporting center is not a "house arrest" program; participants spend a good deal of time out of their homes, re-entering the community. Day reporting is also not a diversion program. Sheriff Ashe was concerned that if used as a diversion program, day reporting would just "widen the net" so that offenders who would not have otherwise gone to jail would be sentenced to day reporting.

Day reporting participants are still on sentence, in the custody of the sheriff, and have earned their way into the day reporting program by positive behavior and program participation. Some participants "graduate" from pre-release center in-house status to day reporting. Others, on shorter sentences, come right from the main institution to day reporting. All have been assessed for entrance into the program based on the likelihood of their being accountable for their behavior in the community.

Program Success. Nearly 500 individuals have participated in the day reporting center program to date, and, because of the program's close supervision, none has committed a violent crime in the community while in the program. Eighty percent of participants have successfully completed the program. Twenty percent have been returned to higher security, usually for lack of accountability (e.g., not following the required schedule) or a failed urinalysis test. Under the program, one "dirty" urine (testing positive for either alcohol or drugs) results in a return to higher security. This strict policy was established because of the pre-release center's experience that alcohol or drug use was the primary reason that program participants caused problems in the community.

Pre-trial Participants. During the past year, the day reporting program has expanded to provide some supervision of pre-trial individuals, who are released by the court on personal recognizance with the provision that they report daily to the day reporting center, even though they are not in the custody of the sheriff. These individuals do not receive the full services or supervision of day reporting, but their daily reporting is seen by the court as preferable to a release on personal recognizance with no stipulations for reporting at all.

Benefits. Advantages of the day reporting center to our department are numerous. Cell and bed spaces are saved for those who need them the most. Costs of supervising participants in the day reporting program are considerably less than costs for twenty-four-hour lock-up. Day reporting is also the ultimate "carrot" in our institutional incentive-based program participation philosophy. Inmates who behave well in jail can serve the end of their sentences at home.

(Continued)

(Continued)

We have also found that individuals who earn the opportunity for house and community participation at the end of their sentences have an improved chance of successful community re-entry. When sentences are a continuum of earned lesser sanctions, the final step to productive and positive community living is much easier than when inmates are released from a higher-security setting. Day reporting also benefits the community, because participants work, pay taxes, and perform community service.

We in Hampden County would be happy to share information about our experience in implementing and operating the day reporting center with any interested jurisdictions. For more information, write to Richard McCarthy, Public Information Officer at the Hampden County Sheriff's Department, 79 York Street, Springdale, Massachusetts 01105, or call (413) 781-1560, ext. 213.

Effective day reporting centers will tend to be those that have a variety of classes, such as relapse prevention, educational development, individual counseling, group counseling (Hanser, 2007a), and employment assistance (Craddock, 2009). In addition, these programs may include structured bibliotherapy that require clients to complete assignments as homework, returning each day to discuss their bibliotherapy assignment in a classroom or group counseling setting. Naturally, this serves to keep the offender on track while they are home, and the staff person supervising the bibliotherapy component will be able to detect if the offender is working toward effective reform by the time and quality that the offender seems to put on their assignments. This again allows for another measure or observation of the offender's genuineness and motivation to reform. While such a system is not fail-safe, the use of multiple mechanisms and techniques provides a multilayered collection of interventions that keep the offender constructively busy, well supervised, and on task. Amidst their participation in the day reporting center program, offenders might also be subject to EM or even GPS tracking, depending on the offender and their offense history. The point is that the day reporting center is used in tandem with other sanctions, providing an interlocking set of tools to monitor the offender. At the same time, the day reporting center provides an environment that facilitates the ultimate reintegration of the offender into the community. Thus, the offender is immersed into a treatment regimen that accomplishes three key tasks:

a. The offender is supervised on a face-to-face basis.

b. The offender is kept busy and thus cannot be out on the street offending.

c. The offender is forced to comply with treatment and regardless of any inherent resistance, a certain amount of this will eventually be processed even if they are resistant.

Methods of Ensuring Compliance: Detecting Drug Use Among Offenders

The detection of offender drug use is accomplished through a number of testing procedures that use a variety of body samples. The most common of these is that obtained from the offender's urine, blood, hair, sweat, and saliva. According to Robinson and Jones (2000), urine testing is the most cost effective, reliable, and widely used drug testing procedure. Nevertheless, it is important that staff understand the drug use demographics of their own region and/or jurisdiction so that they can determine the most appropriate drug testing strategy to employ. This will vary according to the type of drug use that is most common among drug abusers in the region as well as other considerations. In general, there are five sources from which samples are drawn for drug testing. The description for each of these sources is taken from the government document published by the Office of Justice Programs and written by Robinson and Jones (2000) and is as follows:

1. **Urine Testing:** Due to price and accuracy of the testing process, urinalysis is considered the most suitable method for drug courts and most criminal justice agencies for detecting the presence of illegal substances. Generally, urine testing methods fall into two types: (1) instrumental and (2) noninstrumental. Both methods use some form of immunoassay technology to provide an initial determination of the presence of a drug (Robinson & Jones, 2000 p. 3).

2. **Blood Testing:** Testing blood for evidence of drug use is a highly invasive procedure. Blood tests can provide discrete information regarding the degree of an individual's impairment, but the invasiveness of the procedure and the potential danger of infection make blood testing inappropriate for drug court programs (Robinson & Jones, 2000 p. 3).

3. **Hair Testing:** The introduction of new, powerful instruments for hair analysis has increased interest in hair testing. Despite its increased popularity among agencies, caution should be used because hair analysis is subject to potential external contamination (Robinson & Jones, 2000, p. 3). Indeed, there are indications that hair analysis can produce tainted results, depending on the type of hair as well as the type of drug that is analyzed. For example, dark pigmented hair absorbs drugs more readily than blond or bleached hair. Male African American hair (black/brown) appears to absorb drugs more readily than hair of other groups, such as female African Americans (black/brown), male Whites (black/brown), female Whites (black/brown and blond) (Robinson & Jones, 2000, p. 3).

4. **Sweat Testing:** Sweat samples, which are obtained from patches that can be placed on a person for a number of days, have the advantage of providing a longer time frame for detection, and they are difficult to adulterate. They do not, however, provide a correlation regarding the degree of impairment, and they are subject to individual differences in sweat production (Robinson & Jones, 2000, p. 3).

5. **Saliva Testing:** Saliva samples permit a correlation with the degree of impairment and can be easily obtained. They are, however, subject to contamination from smoking or other substances (Robinson & Jones, 2000, p. 3).

▲ **Photo 8.3** The multidrug screen test allows CSOs to find a variety of drugs that may have been used by offenders.

▧ Testing Technologies: Immunoassay and Chromatography

The most widely used technology for testing the presence of drugs in the human system is the immunoassay. This system is typically used as a screening mechanism, with immunoassays using antibodies that bind to drugs and their metabolites (the chemical compounds that result after the body has metabolized a drug) in urine and other fluids (Robinson & Jones, 2000). The immunoassay drug-screening procedures have been widely used due to the fact that they are relatively inexpensive, provide rapid results, and are highly accurate when performed properly (Robinson & Jones, 2000).

Gas chromatography/mass spectrometry (GC/MS), on the other hand, is an analytical technique that can be used to confirm a positive initial drug screen (Robinson & Jones, 2000). Chromatography testing provides a method that is specific to a particular drug of interest and can distinguish a specific drug from other substances that may have similar chemical properties, such as a prescription medication (Robinson & Jones, 2000). This advanced technology allows technicians to identify and quantify atoms, isotopes, and the chemical composition of a given sample. Gas chromatography/mass spectrometry can be used to analyze urine, blood, hair, and other samples to determine the presence of drugs and other substances. Robinson and Jones (2000) noted that this process is currently the most definitive procedure available when attempting to pinpoint the use of specific types of drugs.

Testing Methods: Instrument Testing and Point-of-Contact Tests

Urine testing methods fall into two types: (1) instrumental and (2) noninstrumental. Both methods of analysis use some form of immunoassay technology to provide an initial determination of the presence of a drug, while chromatography is used to confirm the presence and quantity of a given drug (Robinson & Jones, 2000). It is critical that the integrity of the collection, testing, and reporting process is maintained to (1) ensure that the specimen is from the named defendant, (2) detect adulteration, and (3) ensure that no contaminants have been introduced that would affect the validity of the results (Robinson & Jones, 2000). Evidence of drug use may be present in the urine in the form of the parent drug and/or metabolites.

According to Robinson and Jones (2000), **instrument testing** is analysis that involves instrumentation (a machine) that will sample, measure, and produce a quantitative result that is given as a numeric amount on a scale. Instrumented analysis has the advantage of being automated, providing precise and accurate documentation, and lending itself to convenient storage of samples in the event that subsequent retesting may be required. Instrumental methods for testing urine rely on immunoassay technology for initial detection. These analyses have increased accuracy and precision in testing results and provide data printouts for review and courtroom presentation.

According to Robinson and Jones (2000), **point-of-contact testing** is analysis that involves devices that require manual sampling and manual observation to produce a qualitative result that includes both negative and/or positive values. Point-of-contact testing utilizes a noninstrument device to analyze a sample at the point of collection. Noninstrumental test devices have improved significantly in recent years and can be useful if handled by properly trained staff. Although noninstrument testing does not provide the detailed analysis that is obtained with instrumental readouts, these tests provide quick and relatively accurate results (Robinson & Jones, 2000). Lastly, staff training is essential to ensure that test results are interpreted correctly. Relying on a visual detection of a color result can lead to misinterpretation of results for a number of reasons, including color acuity, color perception, and lighting. Care must also be taken to ensure that staff are not color blind. In particular, skill in interpretation is required for those circumstances where positive indication of drug use is weak from the sample that is utilized, requiring greater judgment of the person interpreting the outcome (Robinson & Jones, 2000).

Applied Theory Section 8.1

Routine Activities Theory as Applied to Community Supervision

For the most part, the tenets of **routine activities theory**, by Cohen and Felson, reflect the general premise behind most intermediate sanctions. Cullen and Agnew (2006) provided a clear and effective synopsis of this theory by stating that

> Crime occurs when there is an intersection in time and space of a motivated offender, an attractive target, and a lack of capable guardianship. People's daily routine activities affect the likelihood they will be an attractive target and will encounter an offender in a situation where no effective guardianship is present. (p. 7)

Intermediate sanctions work to eliminate the likelihood that offenders will not have effective guardianship. In other words, an effective guardian will protect potential victims; this guardian is the use of surveillance devices and supervision programs utilized by community supervision agencies. Further, when agencies keep the community informed and when the community is encouraged to volunteer and partner with the agency, an additional layer of guardianship is added to the offender's supervision.

It is in this manner that the offender is released into the community yet members of an informed and involved community is able to modify their routines to reduce the likelihood of victimization. Further, the offender is deterred from likely recidivism due to the understanding that they are being supervised from a number of different persons and through a variety of potential mechanisms. Thus, heightened community vigilance and increased controls placed on the offender work to augment one another, providing an ethereal-like prison, when implemented correctly.

Amidst this process, it is hoped that the offender learns to modify his or her own activities. While under supervision, many are restricted from certain areas of the community (i.e., an alcoholic may be restricted from bars and nightclubs, a sex offender may be restricted from approaching an elementary school). Over time, graduated sanctions are lessened as offenders demonstrate that they are able to maintain their own behavior within the constraints of prosocial behavior. It is in this way that the reinforcement of routine activities theory leads to a form of internal social learning, being operantly reinforced upon the offender, whether they realize it or not (Lilly, Cullen, & Ball, 2007).

⬚ Conclusion

This section provides an overview of several types of intermediate sanctions that are used around the country. In addition, specific examples have been provided to demonstrate the variety of sanctions that exist and their flexibility in being utilized. The flexibility of intermediate sanctions provide community supervision agencies with a range of potential responses to offender criminal behavior. This range falls along a continuum that ranges by the amount of liberty that is deprived of the offender. These various penalties are interchangeable with one another and vary by level of punitiveness to allow community supervision agencies to calibrate the offender's punishment with their specific offense severity and/or tendency toward recidivism. In addition, intermediate sanctions help to connect the supervision process with the treatment process. Various intermediate sanctions, such as community service and the payment of fines, create a system of restoration while the use of flexible supervision schemes, such as EM and GPS tracking, allow the offender to engage in employment activities. Other programs, such as day reporting centers, ease the transition of offenders from incarceration to community membership and provide a series of constructive activities to ensure that the offender remains on task with respect to their reintegration process. Each of these sanctions can be used in conjunction with one another to further augment the supervision process—all the while being less expensive and more productive than is a prison term.

Lastly, as has been noted consistently throughout this text, the use of community partnerships is again emphasized. In this case, the community partnerships come by way of citizens monitoring the offender who is tasked with completing various activities to fulfill his or her sentence. The use of human supervision is again shown to be important, and intermediate sanctions are well suited to citizen involvement when ensuring offender compliance. It is in this manner that intermediate sanctions are yet one additional tool that provides external incentive for offenders to work their regimen within the community. These sanctions, when administered in a social vacuum, would not be expected to be effective. But when utilized against a backdrop of community involvement, agency collaboration, and solid case management processes, intermediate sanctions serve as another interlocking supervision mechanism that improves the overall prognosis of offender reintegration.

Various intermediate sanctions, such as community service and the payment of fines, create a system of restoration while the use of flexible supervision schemes, such as EM and GPS tracking, allow the offender to engage in employment activities. Other programs, such as day reporting centers, ease the transition of offenders from incarceration to community membership and provide a series of constructive activities to ensure that the offender remains on task with respect to their reintegration process. Each of these sanctions can be used in conjunction with one another to further augment the supervision process—all the while being less expensive and more productive than is a prison term.

◪ Section Summary

- Like residential intermediate sanctions, the alternatives provide options that seek to penalize the offender through economic sanctions or increased supervision in the community.
- Economic sanctions include the use of fines (both traditional and structured), asset forfeiture, fees, and restitution.
- Fines are the most common sanction used in the criminal justice system. Almost every penalty allows for some type of fine.
- Restitution is based on the principles of restorative justice whereby the offender is mandated to pay back to the victim monetary losses incurred through the crime.

- Community service is the work that one conducts in hopes of repaying their debt to society after being found at fault for committing a criminal or deviant offense.
- ISPs were created as an alternative to incarceration. Typically designed in a step-down manner these programs have high contact levels with their supervising officer.
- EM is another nonresidential community-based option. In these instances, offenders are supervised either through the use of an RF or GPS device. This monitoring can be restrictive to the point of not allowing the offender to leave their residences to providing opportunities for employment, education, medical care, etc., with a higher level of surveillance.
- Home detention is oftentimes used in conjunction with this alternative. These sanctions provide flexibility in allowing offenders to leave their home.
- Day reporting centers are treatment facilities where offenders are required to report, usually on a daily basis, for various forms of treatment or drug testing.

KEY TERMS

Blood testing	Global positioning system (GPS)	Saliva testing
Community service	Hair testing	Structured fines/day fines
Day reporting centers	Home detention	Sweat testing
Electronic monitoring (EM)	Instrument testing	Urine testing
Fine	Point-of-contact testing	

DISCUSSION QUESTIONS

1. What is the definition and purpose of intermediate sanctions?

2. Describe how the various forms of intermediate sanctions fit within the overall continuum of sanctions. Is one form of intermediate sanction used more frequently? Why or why not?

3. Describe how agencies/agency personnel ensure offender compliance among substance abusers and sex offenders? How effective are these compliance strategies?

4. Although all states utilize some form of intermediate sanction as an alternative to incarceration, the depth and breadth of these alternatives varies greatly. Describe the various means by which intermediate sanctions are used around the nation and provide an explanation for why these variances may exist.

5. Understand both the security and treatment functions associated with intermediate sanctions. Identify and describe the various security and treatment functions associated with intermediate sanctions. How do these two functions both complement and contradict one another in the supervision of offenders sentenced to intermediate sanctions?

WEB RESOURCES

Community Service (National Institute of Justice):

http://www.ojp.usdoj.gov/nij/topics/courts/restorative-justice/promising-practices/community-service.htm

Illinois Prison Talk:

http://www.reentrypolicy.org/program_examples/day_reporting_center_reentry_program

National Institute of Corrections:

http://nicic.gov/

National Institute of Justice Electronic Monitoring Resource Center:

https://emresourcecenter.nlectc.du.edu/

Please refer to the student study site for web resources and additional resources.

READING

In this study, Bouffard and Mufti acknowledged the lack of research in the United States assessing the effectiveness of community service programs. Used extensively in Europe these sanctions have demonstrated some success at reducing recidivism. Using a quasi-experimental design, Bouffard and Mufti sought to examine whether participation in a community service program lowered the likelihood of recidivism both while in the program and post-release. A sample of 200 offenders receiving a sentence of community service during 2003 were compared to a sample of 222 first-time DUI offenders who received only a sentence to pay a fine during this same time period. Results of the study revealed that the samples were essentially equivalent on key demographic variables; however, the community service sample was on average 3 years older than the comparison group. One other key difference was time at risk. The community service group was at risk 8 months less than the DUI offenders. Overall, the results indicated that community service offenders with a prior arrest record and more severe offense were more likely to recidivate. When comparing recidivism rates between the community service and the control groups, those offenders sentenced to community service recidivated at lower rates than those sentenced to the control group. Likewise, it appeared the harsher the sentence the less likely the individual was to reoffend. Overall, the results of this study provided support for the argument that community service is a viable alternative to incarceration. Additionally, some support does exist for the continued use or expansion of this program.

SOURCE: Bouffard, Jeffrey A., & Lisa R. Mufti. (2007). The effectiveness of community service sentences compared to traditional fines for low-level offenders. *The Prison Journal, 87*(2), 171–194. Copyright © 2007 Sage Publications.

The Effectiveness of Community Service Sentences Compared to Traditional Fines for Low-Level Offenders

Jeffrey A. Bouffard and Lisa K. Mufti

Community service (CS) emerged as an alternative sanction in the United States in the 1960s (McDonald, 1986) and was initially designed to meet the goal of providing an alternative to imprisonment or fines for less serious types of offenders, such as those convicted of traffic violations, petty theft, and other nonviolent offenses. By contrast, in Europe, CS sentences are more likely to be used as an alternative to periods of incarceration (Muliluvuori, 2001; Tonry, 1998). In the United States, CS can also be used in combination with other sanctions, for instance as an add-on to traditional probation or in addition to the imposition of fines. When compared to a traditional criminal fine, the use of CS sentences has the added benefit of providing direct service to the community through the provision of unpaid labor.

Although the process of sentencing less serious offenders to CS work has been employed in the U.S. criminal justice system for nearly four decades (McDonald, 1986), relatively little research has been conducted on the operation (including frequency, prevalence, and severity of CS sanctions) or effectiveness of such programs. It is estimated that in the late 1990s there were 547 CS and restitution programs being run nationwide (Development Services Group, 2006). However, there is a paucity of research that examines these programs. Delens-Ravier (2003) hypothesizes that the primary reason for the lack of evaluation research on CS programs is "because the objectives of CS are so varied and diverse" (p. 152), making the exact criteria against which CS sentencing programs are to be measured unclear. In fact, unlike programs in Europe and Asia, which tend to employ CS as one component of a restorative justice system, community service programs (CSPs) in the United States tend to derive from wide-ranging goals, including retribution, rehabilitation, and skill building and function as an alternative sanction (Delens-Ravier, 2003; Harris & Wing Lo, 2002; Wing Lo & Harris, 2004). In addition, the lack of consistent theoretical grounding for the goals of CS compounds the inability to determine what the programs' outcomes are or should be. As such, there are few studies that evaluate the outcomes of CSPs, in terms either of the likelihood of successfully completing a CS sentence or of post-program recidivism and those that do exist offer little guidance on the effectiveness of CS sentences in the United States, especially when compared to other community-based (nonincarceration) sanctions.

Although CS has been employed as a sanction for relatively less serious offenders in this country for nearly 40 years, it is still a comparatively new and under-researched form of correctional intervention. Even considering the relatively recent implementation of this sanction type, the number of studies examining its impact on recidivism, especially in the United States, is even smaller than one might expect given its use during the past several decades. Tonry (1998), noting the lack of sufficient research on the effectiveness of CS, suggests that it may also be the most underused alternative sanction in the United States. He notes that although CS is often simply used as a condition of probation in the United States, its use could be expanded as a stand-alone sanction for both minor and some types of moderate offenders, as it is in Europe. Tonry also anticipates that the public might even appreciate CS as a "tough" sanction that can be readily scaled to the severity of the crime, in addition to the fact that it is relatively inexpensive to administer and produces a valuable outcome in the form of unpaid labor provided to the wider community.

Finally, Tonry (1998) points out that the existing European and U.S. research (all of which compares

CS-sentenced offenders to those sentenced to some period of incarceration) suggests that CS does not reduce recidivism when used in lieu of short-term prison sentences. This finding may also suggest that some of these incarceration-bound offenders could be safely managed in the community using a CS sentence (with no increase in the likelihood of recidivism), thus reducing correctional crowding while still protecting public safety. On the other hand, in the United States, incarceration-bound offenders may not be an appropriate comparison group for those receiving CS sentences because there is a greater tendency to use incarceration as a criminal sanction, even for less serious offenses, than is the case in many European countries (Langan & Farrington, 1998; Lynch, 2002; Tonry, 1998).

In recognition of this issue, the current study examines the recidivism rate of offenders receiving CS sentences ($n = 200$) relative to that of a more appropriate comparison sample of offenders sentenced using a traditional community-based sanction, criminal fines ($n = 222$). Specifically, this study expands on previous research by asking three distinct questions. First, do CS offenders recidivate at lower rates (post-sentencing) than do fined offenders? Second, what factors are related to offending for offenders completing a CS sentence? Third, what impact does sentence type have on post-program recidivism?

Contributions of the Current Study

The research that does exist does not necessarily generalize to the United States (most of it is from European studies) and provides little guidance regarding the impact of CS compared with other community-based sanctions.[1] More importantly, the one study that has examined this type of sanction in the United States (McDonald, 1986) suffers from several methodological limitations and other weaknesses that reduce its usefulness. First, the Bronx program was evaluated nearly 20 years ago and compares CS sentences to jail terms, a potentially inappropriate comparison group. Second, the evaluation did not use any statistical procedures to control for initial group differences, did not report tests of statistical significance for differences in recidivism

outcomes, and combined in-program and post-program recidivism for the CS-sentenced offenders.

Given the paucity of outcome research on CS in the United States, one of the central contributions of the current study is its examination of a more recent CS sentencing program in the United States than was examined in McDonald's (1986) study. In addition, this study examines the impact of CS sentences relative to another traditional and nonincarcerative sentence type (criminal fines), which may be a more typically applied sanction for comparable offenders in the United States. Although the available literature would suggest that CS may not be effective compared to the use of short periods of incarceration, this type of sentence may not be a realistic comparison for CS if more serious offenders are consistently sentenced to short terms in prison or jail and are only rarely considered appropriate for CS sentences. Thus, this study examines whether CS is more effective than a sentence that is more directly comparable than jail or prison terms. If CS sentences are as effective or more effective than the imposition of criminal fines, some jurisdictions may wish to consider the additional community benefits (e.g., unpaid labor) that accrue from the use of CS.

Research Questions

In terms of specific research questions, this study first asks whether receiving a CS sentence is related to a lower probability of "any recidivism" post-sentence relative to similar offenders who receive monetary fines. Second, the study examines factors related to the likelihood of in-program recidivism among a sample of offenders sentenced to complete CS sentences. Finally, this study attempts to determine if receiving a CS sentence reduces reoffending rates post-program participation relative to the use of traditional fines, statistically controlling for initial differences between these two groups of offenders.

◤ Method

The current study utilizes a quasi experimental research design to compare the effectiveness of two types of community-based sanctions imposed on a sample of misdemeanants during calendar year 2003. Specifically, the recidivism rate for a sample of 200 offenders who received a CS sentence is compared to that for a sample of 222 offenders sentenced to pay a monetary fine after being convicted of a first-time driving under the influence (DUI) offense. To answer the central question posed in this study, data are analyzed using multivariate logistic regression models to determine whether there is evidence to demonstrate that being sentenced to CS affects the likelihood of any recidivism (and, in later models, post-program recidivism) relative to receiving a traditional monetary fine. Similar multivariate analyses are also used to examine the factors related to in-program recidivism among CS participants only.

Sample

As part of a larger program evaluation, data were collected on a sample of offenders ($N = 810$) monitored by RESTORE, Inc., a nonprofit, community-based corrections agency in the small metropolitan area (population of roughly 100,000) of Fargo, North Dakota. The agency's records contained information on 810 adult offenders who had been sentenced to complete CS hours during the period January 1, 2003, to December 31, 2003. This group of 810 offenders had engaged in more than 46,295 hours of CS during the 1-year study period, contributing an estimated total value of $296,000 worth of unpaid labor to local businesses and community agencies. During this period, 560 offenders (69.1%) successfully completed their CS sentence. Male offenders constituted almost two thirds of the total sample (65.1%), and the majority of these CS offenders were White (70.7%). Many of these CS-sentenced offenders had at least a high school education or higher (89.9%), with an average age of 23 years. Approximately half (51.0%) of the CS sample had a prior arrest record, with the majority sentenced to CS for a drug- or alcohol-related offense (74.2%). Nearly three fourths (74.3%) were referred from the local municipal court, with the remainder being sentenced by the county district court. On average, these

offenders were ordered to complete 57.6 CS hours and had been given an average of 93 days to complete their CS sentence.

Subsample of CS offenders for recidivism analyses. The data utilized in the recidivism analyses presented in this study were collected by a single police officer from the local department who volunteered personal time to gather this information. Because of limitations on the amount of time available for such data collection, a smaller sample of 200 offenders was randomly selected from among the entire group of 810 CS-sentenced offenders for use in the recidivism analyses. This sample of 200 offenders sentenced to CS included 100 offenders randomly selected from among the 560 who had successfully completed their sentence and another 100 offenders randomly selected from among those 250 who were terminated from the CS program (either for violation of program rules or for not working all of the required hours within the allotted time). In general, these randomly selected samples represented the larger groups of CS-sentenced offenders from which they were drawn.[2]

Fined-offenders sample. Data were collected on a comparison group of 222 first-time DUI offenders from the same jurisdiction as the CS sample. First-time DUI is classified as a Class B misdemeanor, as are the offenses included in the CS sample. These 222 DUI offenders were mandated by the municipal court to pay a monetary fine in calendar year 2003. The sentencing options available to the municipal court include CS, monetary fines, evaluation for substance use or domestic violence treatment needs, and/or jail. Probation is not a sentencing option for municipal court. As such, no offenders processed through the municipal court are supervised by probation.

This group of fined offenders paid a total of $107,100 in monetary fines to the municipal court during the course of 12 months. Offenders receiving a fine were overwhelming male (70.3%) and White (96.4%). The average age of fined offenders was 21.3 years (ranging from 18 to 25). Just more than one third of these first-time DUI offenders had a prior arrest record (35.6%). Almost all of these fined offenders (90.5%) paid their respective fine (usually at the time of imposition), with an average fine amount of $532 (range = $250 to $800).

Materials and Data Sources

CS program data. Information regarding demographic characteristics and program services received by the offenders ordered to this community corrections agency during the evaluation period was collected from the agency's electronic and paper files, including age, gender, race, employment status, education level, previous CS sentences, the number of hours to be completed under the CS sentence, the number of days given to complete the sentence, the referring agency (e.g., municipal court), the primary offense charge, and whether the offender successfully completed the CS sentence. To understand the operation of the CS program, interviews were conducted with the program director, all of the agency's case managers, and several other local criminal justice system officials (e.g., state's attorney).

Fined-offenders' data from the municipal court. Data containing information on 222 first-time DUI offenders who were sentenced by the court to pay a monetary fine were collected from the municipal court clerk's office. These data included the name of offender, date of offense, offense type (i.e., DUI), date of sentence, amount of fine, and amount of fine paid (additional data, such as education level and current employment status, that were available from the community corrections agency's files were not available from the court's database for the comparison sample). An interview was also conducted with the court clerk to understand the operation of the monetary fine process. To augment the data collected from the court clerk, data regarding each offender's gender, date of birth (used to calculate offender's age at time of sentence), and race were retrieved from the local police department's database.

Criminal histories and recidivism data. Officially recorded arrest histories and rearrest information were collected from the local police department on the 200 CS-sentenced offenders and 222 fined offenders described above. Each offender's name and date of birth were used to search various local, state, and regional criminal history databases, including the local police department's database (reflecting arrests in several local cities and counties) and the local states attorney's database. All arrest data were cross-referenced between each of these databases to ensure no arrest incident was counted more than once for each offender. The highest-level (most serious) offense was used in cases where there were multiple charges in any given arrest event.

An offender was considered to have a prior arrest record if he or she had one or more arrests that occurred before his or her current court date. A CS offender was considered to have recidivated post-program if he or she was rearrested after either his or her date of successful completion or his or her date of termination from the CSP. Fined offenders were considered to have recidivated post-program if they had another arrest after the date that their fine was imposed by the court. In-program recidivism for CS offenders was recorded as those instances in which the person's first rearrest after the current CS sentence date occurred prior to the date he or she was terminated from or completed the CS sentence according to the CS agency's records. Information was also collected on the date the rearrest occurred.

Description of the CS process. As previously mentioned, interviews with case managers and the program director and a review of written program materials (e.g., policy and procedure manuals, client forms) were used to document the operation of the CS program being studied. This community corrections program serves both adult and juvenile offenders (only adults are examined in this study because of restrictions on accessing juvenile data), primarily accepting referrals from the local municipal court, with smaller numbers also coming from the district court (including the juvenile court) and the local office of the state's adult parole and probation agency. On average, the program conducts 84 intake interviews with adult offenders referred from various local courts (66.7%

from municipal court, 15.5% from district court) and/or parole or probation agency (17.8%) during a typical month. During these in-person interviews, case managers screen the offender for program eligibility and evaluate the offender's skills, interests, abilities or disabilities, and circumstances that may interfere with work site placement. In addition, the case manager familiarizes the offender with the program's policies, procedures, and expectations, and offenders sign a program contract or agreement and medical release form.

Program guidelines instruct case managers to place offenders in various work site placements after considering the court's objectives, the offender's characteristics (i.e., offender interests, skills, and abilities, geographic location of work site), and the work site agency's needs. Successful work placements are described by the agency as those that match the offender's interests and skills while offering the offender a challenging and rewarding experience. The case manager also involves the work site in the process of assigning workers and communicates program expectations to the relevant work site supervisor, who then oversees the CS offender while working onsite. The offender is notified during the intake interview process of the date, time, and address where he or she is to report for CS work.

Throughout the duration of the offender's sentence, the case manager is responsible for monitoring the offender's progress, including evaluating the offender's performance, recording of the number of CS hours successfully completed, and quickly intervening if any problems develop. However, the offender is directly supervised by an individual at the workplace, not by the case manager. It is important to note that additional monitoring activities, such as verification of employment or stable housing, tracking the offender's location throughout the day, or drug testing (as might occur among offenders sentenced to probation supervision), are not conducted on these CS-sentenced offenders. On average, the case manager contacts the work site supervisor by telephone once a month to monitor the offender's progress. An offender who completes the required number of CS hours will be recorded as a "successful completion" of the CS sentence.

Those offenders who repeatedly fail to comply with the terms of the work site contract or court order are terminated from the CS program as "unsuccessful." In either case, the referring agency is provided written notification of the outcome for each offender. If the offender is cited for what is termed "incidental behavior" (e.g., minor infractions of program rules), the primary goal is to bring the offender in compliance rather than to immediately terminate the offender and return the case to the referring agency, although repeated instances of incidental behavior do result in the return of the case to the referring agency as an unsuccessful termination from the program.

Examples of incidental misbehavior while in the CS program can include marginal performance, personality conflicts with staff, or occasional lateness or absenteeism because of transportation problems (note that the subsample of 200 CS offenders used in the recidivism analyses presented here included 100 such unsuccessful offenders, randomly selected from among the 250 who were recorded as unsuccessful participants during 2003).

Overview of the fine process. In the local jurisdiction, adults arrested on a DUI charge are taken to the local jail. On posting bond (typically within 24 hours), arrestees are given a date to appear before a municipal court judge (typically 3 weeks following arrest). Convicted first-time DUI offenders in this jurisdiction are sentenced to pay a monetary fine (average for this sample = $532), although the judge also has the discretion to sentence offenders to lower (a mandatory minimum of $250 is imposed by state law for first-time offenders) or higher fine amounts. Although the majority of offenders pay their fine at the time of sentencing, fines may also be paid in installments, again at the discretion of the sentencing judge.

⊠ Results

Comparison of Offender Samples

The two samples of offenders utilized in the current study appear to have some important differences in individual characteristics; however, both groups share some important similarities as well (unless otherwise noted, all tests of statistical significance are reported at the one-tailed level). For instance, both samples are predominantly White (90.5% of CS offenders, 96.4% of fined offenders) and male (60.5% of CS offenders, 70.3% of fined offenders). The racial homogeneity of both samples reflects that of the wider community in which this study was conducted.[3] In terms of other individual characteristics, CS offenders and fined offenders exhibit some notable differences. For instance, offenders from the CS sample were, on average, 3 years older than offenders from the fined sample (24.3 years and 21.3 years, respectively; $t = -4.918, p < .001$). CS offenders also appear to have more serious criminal histories (51.0% with a prior arrest) compared to fined offenders (35.6%; $\chi^2 = 10.206, p < .001$). The majority of the CS offenders were arrested on a drug or alcohol offense (85.3%), whereas all offenders in the fined sample were charged with a current (first-time) DUI offense (100%; $\chi^2 = 34.897, p < .001$). Finally, the time at risk (i.e., number of months from date of sentence to the end of the data-collection period) for each group of offenders was significantly different ($t = 21,464, p < .001$). The follow-up time for fined offenders was, on average, almost 8 months longer than CS offenders (18.0 months vs. 10.5 months).

In general, these groups share important similarities in terms of race, gender, and current offense level (all misdemeanants), although the CS sample appears to be composed of somewhat more serious offenders (higher likelihood of prior arrests and age)[4] and to have experienced less time at risk than the fined sample. In light of these differences between the samples, multivariate models presented below include controls for the individual characteristics on which the two samples vary.[5]

Predictors of Any Recidivism

Bivariate analyses. Bivariate analyses reveal that several independent variables were related to the probability of any recidivism after the date that the CS sentence or fine was imposed, including race and criminal history. For instance, non-White offenders were more likely to reoffend compared to White offenders (63.0% vs. 33.0%; $\chi^2 = 9.986, p < .001$). As expected, offenders with a prior criminal record were significantly more likely to recidivate than were offenders with no prior criminal record (47.0% vs. 25.8%; $\chi^2 = 20.268, p < .001$). Variables that were not found to be significantly related to recidivism include age, gender, offense type (i.e., alcohol- or drug-related offense vs. violent or property offense), sentence severity (i.e., being at or above the median fine or CS hours amount), sentence type (CS or fine), and time at risk (i.e., number of months from date of sentence to the end of the data-collection period).

Multivariate analyses. A logistic regression model was computed to examine whether any of these variables are significantly related to the probability of an offender recidivating at any time after the imposition of the CS sentence or fine. Results of the model reveal that three variables were significantly related to any post-sentence recidivism, including race, prior criminal history, and offense type (i.e., alcohol- or drug-related offense vs. violent or property offense). Consistent with the results of the bivariate analyses, non-White offenders have a significantly higher likelihood of reoffending as do offenders with a prior criminal history. Interestingly, offenders charged with a violent or property crime (vs. a drug- or alcohol-related offense) are less likely to reoffend at any point after receiving their sentence. Variables not found to be significantly related to the probability of recidivism at the multivariate level include gender, age, sentence severity (being at or above the median fine or CS hours amount), sentence type (CS or fine), and time at risk (number of months from date of sentence to the end of the data collection period).

Additional Recidivism Analyses

McDonald (1986), in his evaluation of a CS program in New York City, examined the impact of a CS sentence on recidivism from the date of sentence imposition onward, including in his outcome measure any recidivism that occurred both while the offenders were completing their

CS hours and several months after they completed their sentence. He compared this to the recidivism rate of offenders sentenced to jail, after they had been released to the community. As presented above, the current study replicates this type of analysis and produces similar results. The next set of analyses attempts to examine the impact of sentence type on post-participation recidivism while also controlling for whether or not the offender completed his or her sentence (worked all his or her CS hours or paid his or her fine in full).

To examine the impact of successfully completing either type of sentence, a dependent variable that measures only recidivism that occurs after the offender participates in the intervention (whether successfully completed or not) must be employed to ensure correct temporal ordering This is necessary because in-program recidivism (among the CS participants) would negatively affect the likelihood of successfully completing an ongoing intervention (e.g., CS), leading to faulty conclusions about the relationship between these two variables. For fined offenders, post-intervention recidivism is simply measured as any recidivism after the date the fine is imposed because the deterrent impact of a fine may be expected to arise from the time of its imposition onward. On the other hand, among the CS offenders in this sample, post-participation recidivism means any recidivism either after the offender is terminated from the program (for violation of program rules or failing to complete all the hours as ordered, typically 3 months) or after the offender successfully completes all CS hours as ordered.[6]

In-program recidivism. Before examining the impact of CS sentences on post-participation recidivism, a multivariate regression model is used to examine the predictors of in-program recidivism among only those offenders receiving a CS sentence. This analysis is useful for examining the types of CS offenders who are more or less likely to succeed while in the community completing a CS sentence and thus contributes to an understanding of whether more serious offenders can in fact be equally well managed with CS programs. On average, CS offenders were given 3 months (93 days) in which to complete their CS order. Of the 200 CS-sentenced

offenders for which arrest records were collected, 28 (14.0%) were rearrested prior to completing or being terminated from the CSP. A logistic regression model was computed to analyze which independent variables were related to in-program recidivism among these CS offenders.

Although few independent variables exhibited significant effects on the likelihood of in-program recidivism, those that did are instructive in relation to calls for increased use of CS sentences for more serious types of offenders (e.g., Tonry, 1998). First, offenders with a prior arrest record were more likely to recidivate while in the process of completing their CS order. Severity of sentence was also found to be significantly related to in-program recidivism, with offenders who received a more severe sentence (i.e., a sentence that was at or above the median number of CS hours) having a higher likelihood of reoffending. Finally, age was found to be significantly related to in-program recidivism, with older offenders having a higher likelihood of reoffending. Thus, controlling for all other variables in the model, more serious offenders (i.e., older offenders who had a prior arrest record and were given more CS hours to complete) have a higher likelihood of recidivating before completion of their CS sentence. Conversely, another potential indicator of offense severity (those who committed misdemeanor property or violent crimes) did not increase the likelihood of recidivating during participation in the CS program. Overall, the pattern of results presented thus far suggests that those with criminal histories (even among those receiving a CS sentence and not necessarily prison or jail bound) may have difficulty successfully avoiding reoffending during their participation in such CS programs. However, those with non drug or alcohol offenses are not more likely to reoffend in program. It may be possible to improve the effectiveness or "appropriateness" of CS sentences for more serious offenders, however, through the use of additional supervision of these more serious offenders while they are serving a CS sentence in the community.

Post-program recidivism. In the following section, a logistic regression model predicting recidivism after program participation is presented. To reiterate, the post-intervention period for fined offenders is defined as any recidivism after the date the fine is imposed, whereas for CS offenders it is defined as any recidivism after the offender either completes or is terminated from the CS program. Again, in this model, CS cases in which the person recidivated during the time in the CS program are omitted. Although the examination of post-program recidivism is necessary to include a control for program completion (an important potential measure of the offender's inherent motivation), the removal of CS in-program recidivists could result in a comparison that is biased toward finding a crime-reducing effect for CS sentences, if those CS offenders who remain in the sample are less serious offenders. In this case, that does not seem to be the result. For instance, those CS offenders who remain in the sample (those not recidivating during the program) are still more likely to have a prior arrest (45.3%) than are the fined offenders (35.6%; $\chi^2 = 3.854$, $p < .05$) examined here. In addition, those CS offenders who recidivated in program reoffended 3 times more quickly (an average of 19.7 days after sentencing) than did even the group of "unsuccessful" offenders who were either terminated from the CS program or who failed to pay their fines (an average of 59.3 days after sentencing), whereas offenders who eventually completed either type of sentence lasted an average of 90.2 days from sentencing to first rearrest ($F = 52.67$, $p < .01$). This result for time to rearrest in particular suggests that these in-program recidivist CS offenders may be qualitatively different from those who do not recidivate while completing their CS sentence and may be fairly removed from the comparison. Note that despite the removal of the in-program recidivists from the CS sample, this comparison is still essentially a conservative estimate of the impact of CS on post-program recidivism relative to fines because the CS sample is still composed of offenders who are more likely to have a prior arrest.

A logistic regression model was computed to determine which independent variables were statistically significant predictors of post-program recidivism (excluding those CSP offenders who recidivated during the program), when controlling for a number of other individual-level variables. The other control variables used in this model include prior arrests (0 = no prior arrest, 1 = prior arrest), sentence severity (0 = below median, 1 = at or above the median fine or amount of CS hours), time at risk (in months), offense type (0 = non drug or alcohol offense, 1 = drug or alcohol offense), sentence completion (0 = did not complete all CS hours or did not pay fine in full, 1 = all CS hours completed or fine paid in full), sentence type (0 = fine, 1 = CS), and other demographic factors, including age, gender (0 = female, 1 = male), and race (0 = White, 1 = non-White). The dependent variable is the likelihood of recidivism among the sample of 172 CSP offenders and 222 fined offenders (because of missing data for 23 cases, some from each group were not included in the final model).

Results reveal that the likelihood of rearrest was again higher among offenders with a prior arrest record. Sentence severity appears to result in a deterrent effect, with offenders receiving sentences at or above their respective medians recidivating at significantly lower rates than those receiving more lenient CS sentences or fines. Of most interest in this study, sentence type was also found to be significantly related to recidivism, with offenders sentenced to complete CS work less likely to reoffend, controlling for all other variables in the model. Successfully completing either type of sentence was also related to a lower likelihood of repeat offending, suggesting at least some effect for offender motivation in addition to the "intervention" effect seen for CS sentences.

⬛ Discussion

Overall, the results for post-program recidivism presented in this study support the use of CS over another community-based sanction typically used with comparable types of less serious offenders, specifically traditional monetary fines. This conclusion is supported in both bivariate results and in multivariate analyses controlling for initial group differences and the successful completion of either sentence type. These results are especially noteworthy given that there are at least some indications that the CS sample (even when the in-program recidivists were removed) was composed of more serious offenders (more likely to have prior arrests), which would make this a relatively conservative test of the effectiveness of CS sentences compared to traditional fines at reducing post-program recidivism.

Although the statistical analyses of any recidivism fail to show significant reductions among CS-sentenced offenders, these analyses do not include controls for program completion (a potentially important measure of offender motivation). On the other hand, even in this model (which might arguably be seen as including less selection bias regarding the CS sample), the finding of no effect may suggest that CS sentences are at least as effective as traditional fines in terms of any post-sentencing recidivism. Given that the use of CS sentences also likely results in other benefits to the community that do not materialize with the use of fines, correctional officials may wish to consider the expanded use of this type of alternative sanction, at least for some types of low-level offenders. For instance, even in this small community, more than 46,000 hours of unpaid labor, valued at nearly $300,000, was provided back to local service agencies and other businesses.

More importantly, the positive effects demonstrated by this study were generated using a design and methodology that is a substantial improvement over the existing literature on CS effectiveness, most of which either lacks generalizability because it is outdated or was conducted overseas or lacks internal validity because it compares CS to incarceration or employs inadequate research methods. In fact, the current study's design is considerably stronger than the one previously published U.S. study of recidivism among those sentenced to CS (McDonald, 1986) in that it employs an appropriate comparison sample of offenders receiving community-based sanctions, controls for initial group differences, and employs statistical testing to examine differences in reoffending outcomes using a post-program measure of recidivism.

This study's results also provide some interesting, if preliminary, support for the claims of restorative justice scholars (e.g., Bazemore & Maloney, 1994), who suggest that CSPs could be designed to incorporate restorative principles (e.g., matching offenders to appropriate CS work experiences, as was done in this program) and that doing so would lead to positive program outcomes. These results also support the "principles of effective treatment," as outlined by correctional rehabilitation scholars (Andrews et al., 1990), especially in regard to the concept of "matching offenders' risks or needs," as is done in the program studied here. McDonald (1986) also advocated for the use of CS with low-level offenders, underlining the importance of matching offenders' risk or need level to the intensity of the intervention to which they are sentenced; however, the Bronx program he studied did not actually individualize work placements for offenders. Instead, all offenders were assigned to complete a fixed number of hours within a limited number of work types.

On the other hand, Gelsthrope and Rex (2004) conclude from their study of CS-sentenced offenders that for offenders to benefit from this type of sanction (i.e., reductions in recidivism, improvements in attitudes, self-perceived problems), offenders should be screened by CS program staff and matched to work experiences based on their needs (Gelsthrope & Rex, 2004). This concept of matching offenders with appropriate work experiences then is also consistent with both the "principles of effective intervention" (Andrews et al., 1990) and one of the central restorative justice suggestions made by Bazemore and Maloney (1994). Given these suggestive findings, future research more directly comparing different styles of delivering CS sentences also seems warranted.

At a broader level, the apparent success of this CS program at reducing recidivism underlines the utility of innovative, alternative sanctioning efforts in general, in contrast to the reliance on incarcerative sentences, which is often the predominant response to offenders of all levels of seriousness in the United States. If, as some authors (see Tonry, 1998) have suggested, community correctional programs can be relatively effective at reducing recidivism and maintaining public safety, then their increased usage as an appropriate and effective response to certain types of (nonviolent) offenders seems warranted. This is especially true if these community-based programs, such as CS, provide other additional benefits to the larger community (e.g., unpaid labor) that do not materialize as a result of placing offenders in jail or prison.

Limitations and Future Research

Although these results appear quite promising relative to the potential impact of CS sentences on reoffending, the research design employed here is not without limitations. For instance, although the offenders in both the CS and fined groups studied here are comparable in terms of the legal severity of their offenses (all misdemeanors), and although statistical procedures were used to control for initial group differences (e.g., prior arrest histories), the use of a true experimental design was not possible in this jurisdiction. As such, the possibility cannot be ruled out that other initial group differences actually accounted for recidivism differences but were not controlled with the data available for this study.

In addition, although these results were generated with a design that improved on the internal validity of the study, they may not generalize to other programs in other jurisdictions. Specifically, the community under examination here is in a relatively small urban area, with its own municipal court system and a relatively homogeneous populace in terms of racial composition. Similarly, although the evaluation of a CS program that incorporates at least some restorative justice principles suggests support for some of the claims about the potential benefits of this type of approach, no direct comparison to a more traditionally delivered CS program was included. Thus, it is not clear if the positive results seen in this program are from the restorative components included in the program, from the use of a similar sample of offenders sentenced to another community-based sanction (in contrast to what is seen in the existing literature finding no effects), or from some other unique but unaccounted for aspect of this particular CS program.

In terms of future research, the authors hope that this study, which suggests that CS sentences can be effective at reducing recidivism among relatively less serious offenders, will spur additional research into this type of alternative sanction. Specifically, future research should attempt to replicate these positive results among CS programs in more diverse jurisdictions (racially and in terms of population size), among CS programs that serve offenders from other than primarily municipal courts, and among other types of community-based sanctions (e.g., day-reporting centers, home confinement, or misdemeanor probation). As is the case in many correctional program evaluations, additional research should attempt to employ even more rigorous (i.e., experimental) designs to continue to examine the impacts of CS sentences on reoffending.

Finally, given that one of the aspects of this CS program that may have accounted for its positive results is the focus on implementing at least some restorative justice concepts, additional research directly comparing CS programs that are delivered in different styles (traditional vs. restorative) is also called for. Overall, the authors agree with other scholars writing about the underuse of CS as a viable alternative sanction (e.g., Tonry, 1998), especially in light of the benefits that are provided back to the wider community from the use of this type of sanction, as opposed to requiring offenders to simply pay a fine to the court. In the community studied here, offenders sentenced to complete CS hours not only were significantly less likely to recidivate (post-program, regardless of successful completion) but also annually provided thousands of hours and hundreds of thousands of dollars in unpaid work to their local communities. Hopefully, recognition of these types of benefits, along with the results of this initial study of the impact of CS sentences' impact on recidivism, will lead to more empirical and practical attention to this type of sanction.

Notes

1. The generalizability of the aforementioned European studies is limited largely because the context in which community service (CS) is implemented in Europe is markedly different than

the context in which CS is delivered in the United States. Largely, CS is one of many alternative sanctions imposed in European countries, while at the same time these nations often rely less on the use of incarceration for minor and first-time offenders than does the United States (Lynch, 2002).

2. Bivariate statistics (e.g., χ^2, t tests) were used to examine any differences in these randomly selected samples relative to their respective groups of CS completers and terminated offenders, including age, race, gender, education level, current offense type, previous experience with CS, and days given to complete the sentence. These results generally demonstrate that the randomly selected sample of 100 completers represented the entire sample of 560 completers, with the exception that the subsample of 100 appeared to include significantly more non-Whites (9%) than did the entire sample of 560 (2.9%, $\chi^2 = 8.729, p < .01$). No significant differences were found between the random sample of 100 terminated CS offenders and the entire sample of 250 terminated CS offenders.

3. The population of the local community from which the samples included in this study were drawn is predominately White (94.2%).

4. In the CS sample, age is correlated with offense type. Specifically, younger CS offenders were more likely to have been charged with less serious offenses (i.e., minor in possession), whereas older offenders were more likely to have been charged with property and violent offenses.

5. Although the authors recognize that these are not perfectly matched samples, in conversations with the clerks from the municipal court, these fined, first-time driving under the influence offenders were likely the most similar to the CS offenders who were available from within this court's jurisdiction.

6. One drawback of this type of comparison of post-intervention recidivism rates is the exclusion of those CS cases in which the offender recidivated during the program. This procedure might, for instance, result in "creaming off" those CS offenders who are most likely to fail in such a program, biasing the subsequent comparison of (some) CS to (all) fined offenders. To examine the potential for selection bias in this modeling procedure, a similar regression model was computed to analyze the impact of sentence type on any recidivism (including in-program recidivism among CS offenders). However, this supplemental model uses a three-category completion variable to control for whether the offender (a) recidivated during the program (coded 0), (b) avoided in-program recidivism (CS only) but did not successfully complete all of his or her CS hours or pay his or her fine (coded 1), or (c) successfully completed either sentence without in program recidivism (coded 2). Results for this model do not change the conclusions presented here that participation in the CS and completion of either sentence reduce the likelihood of post-program recidivism, relative to those CS

offenders who recidivated during the program. Results are available from the authors on request.

◼ References

Andrews, D. A., Zinger, I., Hoge, R. D., Bonta, J., Gendreau, P., & Cullen, F. T. (1990). Does correctional treatment work? A clinically relevant and psychologically informed metaanalysis. *Criminology, 28*(3), 369–404.

Bazemore, G., & Maloney, D. (1994) Rehabilitating community service: Toward restorative justice sanctions in a balanced justice system. *Federal Probation, 58*(1), 24–35.

Delens-Ravier, I. (2003). Juvenile offenders' perceptions of community service. In L. Walgrave (Ed.), *Repositioning restorative justice* (pp. 149–166). Portland, OR: Willan.

Development Services Group.(2006). Restitution/community service. Retrieved November 13, 2006 from http://wvvw.dsgonline .com/mpg_non_flash/restitution_community_ service.htm

Gelsthrope, L., & Rex, S. (2004). Community service as reintegration: Exploring the potential. In G. Mair (Ed.), *What matters in probation* (pp. 229–254). Portland, OR: Willan.

Harris, R. J., & Wing Lo, T. (2002). Community service: Its use in criminal justice. *International Journal of Offender Therapy and Comparative Criminology, 46*, 427–444.

Killisa, M., Aebi, M., & Ribeaud, D. (2000). Does community service rehabilitate better than short-term imprisonment? Results of a controlled experiment. *Howard Journal, 39*(l), 40–57.

Langan, P. A., & Farrington. D. P. (1998). *Crime and justice in the United States and in England and Wales, 1981-1996: Executive summary*. Washington, DC: Bureau of Justice Statistics.

Lynch, J. (2002). Crime in international perspective. In J. Q. Wilson & J. Petersilia (Eds.), *Crime: Public policies for crime control* (pp. 5–41). Oakland, CA: ICS Press.

McDonald, D. C. (1986). *Punishment without walls: Community service sentences in New York City*. New Brunswick, NJ: Rutgers University Press.

Muliluvuori, M. L. (2001). Recidivism among people sentenced to community service in Finland. *Journal of Scandinavian Studies in Criminology and Crime Prevention, 2*(1), 72–82.

Spaans, E. C. (1998). Community service in the Netherlands. Its effects on recidivism and net-widening. *International Criminal Justice Review, 8*, 1–14.

Tonry, M. (1998). *Sentencing matters*. Oxford, UK: Oxford University Press.

Wing Lo, T., & Harris, R. J. (2004). Community service orders in Hong Kong, England, and Wales: Twins or cousins. *International Journal of Offender Therapy and Comparative Criminology, 48*, 373–388.

DISCUSSION QUESTIONS

1. Given the findings of this study, what are the long-term policy implications for the increased use of community service as an alternative to imprisonment?

2. Using your own community, what type of projects or work needs might qualify for a community service project?

3. Thinking about your own community, is community service used?

4. Given the diminished resources most local governments are experiencing, how might the results of this study support the increased use of community service as a viable option?

READING

In this study, Craddock sought to evaluate the likelihood of completing a day reporting center program for 14 of North Carolina's 41 programs. More specifically, the author explored the impact of individual characteristics, program participation, and program characteristics on the likelihood of completion. It is important to note that North Carolina enacted legislation in 1994 in an attempt to reduce prison overcrowding particularly for less serious offenders. Therefore, successful completion of the program signifies to some extent success of the legislation. The 14 programs selected for inclusion in the study were chosen because they had demonstrated consistent admissions for at least 6 months. Of those chosen, semistructured interviews were conducted with program directors and observations of groups in each of the facilities, the Level of Service Inventory-Revised (LSI-R) scores were examined as a mechanism to obtain the risk and needs of offenders, and the Substance Abuse Subtle Screening Inventory (SASSI) provided information on the likelihood for drug dependence. Overall, the results indicated that 45.3% of those individuals who remained in the program for at least 2 weeks successfully completed. A measure of program intensity was developed as a means for determining the number of hours per week the participants spent in programming. The programs and level of intensity were coded as being low (less than 10 hours per week), medium (10 to 15 hours per week), and high (more than 15 hours per week). Craddock contends that day reporting centers appear to be less suited for minorities (p. 129). Likewise, those offenders "who had drug and/or alcohol problems, a poor living situation, and predominantly criminal companions were significantly less likely to complete the program than others" (p. 130). Finally, employment predicted successful completion of the program. Those facilities offering some form of job placement/assistance were more likely to have higher completion rates than those that did not offer this assistance. This study serves to advance the understanding of day reporting centers as an effective alternative to incarceration.

SOURCE: Craddock, Amy. (2009). Day reporting center completion: Comparison of individual and multilevel models. *Crime & Delinquency, 55*(1), 105–133. Copyright © 2009 Sage Publications.

Day Reporting Center Completion

Comparison of Individual and Multilevel Models

Amy Craddock

When states implement sentencing laws designed to incarcerate violent and repeat offenders, they may also establish or expand community corrections programs to help protect the public and provide viable rehabilitative programming options. For this approach to be successful, programs must provide services and interventions that are likely to yield positive outcomes and that do not increase risk to the community.

The literature tends to agree that programs that adhere to principles of risk, needs, and responsivity often have positive postprogram outcomes (see Lowenkamp & Latessa, 2005; Sherman et al., 1998). Most of these findings are predicated on the assumption or observation that offenders complete the programs. Although services that reflect these principles are important to positive outcomes, the literature is virtually silent on whether or how such components affect completion. In light of research findings that those who complete programs have better outcomes than those who do not, an important step in improving program outcomes is improving completion rates (see, e.g., Craddock, 2001; Craddock & Graham, 1996).

Just as in studies of postprogram outcomes, understanding program completion requires examination of individual and program-level factors. A low completion rate may signal that a program is not appropriate for the population being served or it may imply structural problems within the program (e.g., high staff/client ratio, poorly trained staff, poor relationship with other agencies). A low completion rate may also be related to individual offender characteristics and/or factors operating above the program level (e.g., state policy preventing offenders from participating in certain programs or services).

Most relevant research on program retention and completion is in the substance abuse treatment area.[1]

Treatment researchers have long recognized that maximizing retention and completion is important to positive outcomes. One can speculate about why community corrections research has not often addressed the dynamics of program completion, but the fact remains that almost all of the research addresses postprogram outcomes only. To help fill this gap in the research, the present study examines program completion in 14 day reporting centers (DRCs) in North Carolina that provide or broker various types of treatment and other services.[2]

To address the dynamics of program completion, it is useful to view clients in DRCs much like any other individuals who function within an organization. Within the context of the organization, individual outcomes are always a function of both individual- and organizational-level factors (Hall & Tolbert, 2005). The characteristics, policies, and practices of a corporation shape a work environment, for example, just as they shape the DRC program environment. Programs have behavioral expectations that clients must meet to complete the program, just as companies have behavioral expectations employees must satisfy to retain their jobs; personal characteristics of individuals influence how they perform these activities. (The larger social environment also influences individuals and organizations, but this is not the focus of the present study.)

Figure 8.1 presents a conceptual model that reflects this approach. The double-headed arrows indicate an expected correlation; single-headed arrows indicate prediction. As illustrated in this figure, a client's personal characteristics (demographic characteristics and risk/need factors) and program participation (measured as contact hours received in various programming areas) predict program completion. These two areas comprise the individual-level measures in the analysis. Organizational-level factors include the characteristics of the program and types of services offered. Program-level factors include the characteristics of the program and types of services offered. The choice of organizational-program-level characteristics is based on findings from the literature on postprogram outcomes, mentioned above. Variation in the first program characteristic listed (criminogenic needs addressed) will yield different components and opportunities for participation and possibly different chances for completion. The other characteristics of the program presented in Figure 8.1 are not directly related to program offerings and participation but may also affect the likelihood of completion. Because clients are grouped into different programs, a multilevel analytical approach is appropriate. Given that multisite evaluations of community corrections programs tend to ignore the clustering of these data, it is instructive to compare the results of an individual-level analysis to those of a multilevel analysis.

Rates and Predictors of Community Corrections Program Completion

Completion rates for DRCs vary, but they are generally not high. Parent, Byrne, Tsarfaty, Valade, and Esselman (1995) found an approximately 50% completion rate for a nonrepresentative national sample. McDevitt, Domino, and Baum (1997) studied a DRC that serves offenders released from relatively short incarceration terms in the Boston, Massachusetts, area. Almost 80% self-reported a serious substance abuse problem. Just over half were first offenders. This program had a 66.5% completion rate. Program services included substance abuse treatment with mandatory Alcoholics Anonymous and/or Narcotics Anonymous participation for those with drug or alcohol problems. The program also includes community service, education, random drug testing, and job training and other employment assistance. No data were available on correlates of program completion.

Several other small-scale studies have examined DRCs that serve more serious offenders and are generally of

longer duration than the Massachusetts program. An evaluation of the Fairfax County (Virginia) DRC revealed a 54% completion rate among the 244 offenders in the outcome study (Orchowsky, Lucas, & Bogle, 1995). Clients were primarily probationers who violated the terms of their supervision, but some were directly sentenced to the program. The program is operated by the Department of Corrections and includes the types of components often found to be associated with positive outcomes, including substance abuse treatment, life skills, community service, employability skills, and securing of employment. The average time spent in the program for successful completers was about 15 weeks, compared to 8 weeks for noncompleters. The most common reason given for failure to complete the program was continued substance abuse.

A quasi-experimental study of two programs in Wisconsin (one in a rural county and one in a small urban county) designed to serve high-risk and high-need probationers similar to those in the present study found that 61.3% of the 137 clients in the rural county completed the program, as did 41.1% of the 97 clients in the urban DRC. Probation officers in the rural county tended to refer the highest risk probationers to the DRC, whereas in the urban county, probation officers primarily referred their most troublesome supervisees (who also were usually of highest risk and need) to the DRC (Craddock & Graham, 1996).

The first published study of DRCs in North Carolina found a completion rate of about 13.5% (Marciniak, 1999). This program differs from the Massachusetts programs in important ways that can be expected to contribute to a lower completion rate. It is in a relatively small metropolitan county, of 12 months' duration, and aimed at more serious and primarily substance-abusing offenders with prior records—a substantial portion of whom would be prison bound if the DRC were not available. Because the evaluation included consideration of program completion during the early implementation of the program, the instability common in new programs may have contributed to the low completion rate. Statewide, the North Carolina

Figure 8.1 Conceptual Model of Program Completion

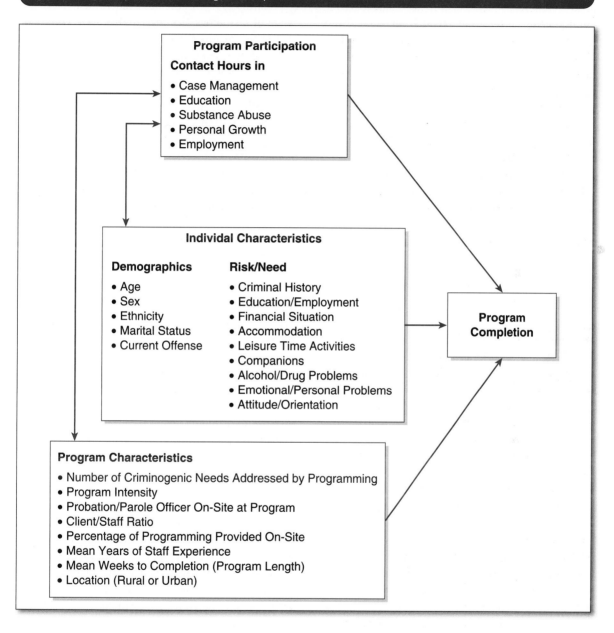

Division of Community Corrections (North Carolina Department of Correction [DOC], Annual Statistical Report Fiscal Year 2003-2004, 2005) reported a statewide DRC completion rate of 38% for fiscal year 2003–2004. This overall rate has remained fairly constant since about 1999.

Research on predictors of nonresidential community corrections program completion is rather sparse.

An exception is Lowenkamp and Latessa's (2002) study of more than 3,600 offenders in 15 nonresidential community-based correctional facilities in Ohio. These facilities had an overall 79% completion rate. Individual program completion rates ranged from 58% to 93%, and the average time spent in the programs by successful completers was approximately 20 weeks. Logistic regression analysis revealed that offenders who had a prior conviction for a sex offense, were unemployed at arrest, were younger, had a psychological problem, were Black, had a current conviction for a violent offense, and had a prior violation while on community control were significantly more likely to be unsuccessfully terminated from the program.

⊠ Program Completion in Relation to Program Participation and Program Characteristics

Program participation is a function of client involvement and program characteristics. Research in substance abuse treatment, in particular, has found that full participation is important to retention and ultimately to completion (see, e.g., Sung, Belenko, & Feng, 2001). One client who fully participates in a program of low intensity and another who minimally participates in a highly intensive program may have a similar number of program contact hours, however. Very little is known about whether offenders are more likely to complete programs of low or high intensity.

Community corrections research has fairly well established that certain program components tend to result in positive outcomes. The current study measures as many of these components as possible in an effort to determine whether they influence the likelihood of completion, as well. Several metaanalyses and reviews of research on the effectiveness of community-based correctional programs highlight the need to combine punishment with treatment interventions to achieve success generally (Andrews & Bonta, 1998; Cullen, Wright, & Applegate, 1996) and

for substance-abusing offenders specifically (Martin & Inciardi, 1993). These researchers discussed the range of characteristics that studies have shown to lead to successful outcomes. Although results have been mixed, some consistencies exist. Probably most important, programs should focus on assessed criminogenic risk and needs to address areas of the offender's life that lead to criminal behavior. Moreover, programs that focus on higher risk offenders achieve better results ("the risk principle"). The primary areas are antisocial attitudes and thinking, substance dependencies, criminal peer associations, life skills, and self-control and/or anger management. Treatment should teach the offender strategies to learn to avoid problems associated with criminogenic needs and, ideally, establish means to test these strategies in "real-world" settings. Introspective therapy that aims primarily at self-discovery is not helpful. Also, programs should be designed and staffed by individuals committed to the integrity of the therapeutic regimen. Lowenkamp and Latessa's (2002, 2005) examination of a wide array of community corrections programs in Ohio found that adherence to the risk principle indeed was associated with lower rates of recidivism.

Although the program must focus on criminogenic needs, it should be flexible enough to respond to individual circumstances (Palmer, 1996). It must also provide or broker other services that will enhance the offender's likelihood of success in reducing or eliminating criminal behavior (e.g., housing, education). Research does not recommend specific numbers but reports that such activities are best provided in programs with relatively small caseloads and a low staff-to-client ratio (Bonta, 1996; Gendreau, 1996; Sherman et al., 1998). Researchers focusing on substance-abusing offenders have echoed these findings and have stressed that treatment be of sufficient duration (generally at least 3 months) to have an impact (Prendergast, Anglin, & Wellisch, 1998). Such components can exist in many program structures, but research has not identified an optimum delivery structure. The DRC is a reasonable structure to use to provide these services. This approach may be helpful especially for substance-abusing offenders (McBride & VanderWaal, 1997).

North Carolina Criminal Justice Partnership Program

The present study examines programs established as part of the 1994 Structured Sentencing Act in North Carolina. The overall aim of the law is to reduce the traditionally heavy reliance on incarceration by reserving jail and prison space for violent and repeat offenders and by directing most others to community-based sanctions (Structured Sentencing Act, 1994).

Concomitant with this law, the legislature passed the State-County Criminal Justice Partnership Act to develop a system of community-based correctional programs for offenders who would likely heretofore have been sentenced to state prison. The act facilitated establishment of programs designed to both appropriately punish criminal behavior and provide effective rehabilitation services. Recognizing that the DOC itself and many North Carolina counties historically had little experience with community corrections programs that provide rehabilitative services, the act established the Criminal Justice Partnership Program (CJPP) within the DOC. With CJPP guidance, counties established advisory boards to facilitate the interagency cooperation required to develop local policies and programs (Smith, Cummings, & Lensing, 2000).

CJPP reflects scholars' recommendations to reduce the likelihood and extent of net widening by structuring the discretion of judges in determining assignments to community corrections programs (Tonry, 1999). The National Institute of Justice (NIJ) Executive Sessions on Sentencing and Corrections called for this type of system as a mechanism for corrections to advance public safety and help coordinate state and local needs and concerns (Smith & Dickey, 1999). The programs were envisioned as local or state collaborations designed to meet local needs, rather than broad attempts to simply duplicate or import model programs that conventional wisdom dictates may not be appropriate for all localities (Curtin, 1996). CJPP

determined that the primary program structure was to be the day reporting center. Some were established within local public agencies, whereas others were established by private nonprofit organizations. At every step, the guiding principle was to address local needs as identified by local agencies and then to bring together county and state resources to address these needs.

Sample Selection and Client Data Collection

Because all CJPP programs were fairly new, the study considered only those that had had a consistent flow of referrals for at least 6 months. Programs were selected based on admissions in the 6 months immediately prior to selection. Of the 41 programs, 13 had 10 or fewer admissions, primarily because they had not been operational for the entire 6 months. From the remaining 28 programs, 19 were selected that had fairly consistent admissions from month to month. Finally, 14 were chosen from these to achieve statewide geographic and population (urban/rural) representation.

All clients admitted to these 14 programs from June through December 1997 were asked to be in the study; fewer than 1% refused. The analysis excluded two groups from the original 396 participants. First, 14 clients who did not stay at least 2 weeks in the program were dropped. When evaluating program effectiveness, it is necessary that clients stay a sufficient length of time to receive services. An examination of the hours of programming received per week for those who stayed 2 months or less indicated that the weekly contact hours were similar for clients who stayed at least 2 weeks (and up to 2 months) than for those who stayed less than 2 weeks. These early dropouts received very few hours of programming services. So, 2 weeks appeared to be a natural cutoff point that signaled the beginning of greater than minimal participation in services. Those who dropped out early did not receive sufficient services to be deemed to have been treated.[3]

The analysis also excluded 18 clients who left the program due to circumstances external to their behavior in the program (e.g., moved to another county, developed severe health problems, probation supervision period ended while in the program) because they would not have had the opportunity to complete or to fail to complete the program. A total of 32 clients were dropped. The final sample for the present analysis included 364 individuals from 14 DRCs throughout the state. All but one program served a single county; the remaining program served a rural six-county region.

Measures of risk of reoffending and need for services came from the Level of Service Inventory-Revised (LSI-R) (Multi-Health Systems, Inc., 1995). The total LSI-R score can range from 0 (very low risk and need) to 54. The components of the total LSI-R score cover 10 areas that research has demonstrated to be associated with recidivism: criminal history, education and/or employment, financial situation, family, living situation, use of leisure time, companions, alcohol and/or drug problems, emotional problems, and attitude toward crime and sentence.

The Substance Abuse Subtle Screening Inventory (SASSI) (Miller, Roberts, Brooks, & Lazowski, 1997) provided information on chemical dependency. Data on probation supervision came from the DOC's management information system (MIS). Data on the current offense(s), sentence, and recidivism came from the records maintained by the Administrative Office of the Courts (AOC). Client participation information came from the CJPP's Offender Tracking Record (OTR), which contains information about the services received, results of urine tests, and program completion status. A client is discharged from the program when he or she has completed it (by fulfilling the program requirements) or failed to do so. The case manager indicates on the OTR whether the client completed the program or, if not, enters the reason(s) for a negative discharge.

Client Characteristics

It is evident that completers and noncompleters differ significantly on most characteristics (e.g., demographic, offense, criminal history) measured in the final analysis sample. Program completers are more likely to be younger, White, high school graduates, married, and of overall lower risk and need than non-completers. LSI-R scores in the study sample ranged from 2 to 43, with a mean score of 21.7. Completers had significantly lower risk and/or need than noncompleters in all areas of the LSI-R except for family situation and emotional problems.

Overall, 45.3% of CJPP clients who stayed at least 2 weeks completed the program. Among clients who failed to complete the program, 65.8% were removed for noncompliance with program requirements or rules, 16.6% absconded, 13.6% had their probation revoked for a new offense or technical violation, and 4% elected to serve their sentence rather than stay in the DRC program.[4]

Program Participation

In addition to characteristics of the individuals themselves, the study collected data on the contact hours each client received in each programming area offered. Also presented are case management contact hours.

One participation measure important to completion is the rate of positive drug and alcohol tests while in the program. The OTRs showed that among clients who had at least one positive test for either drugs or alcohol, only 31.5% completed the program, compared with 70.7% who had no positive tests ($p <$ .001). According to the OTR data, however, only about 55% of the clients in the sample were tested for drugs or alcohol while in the program. Given the proportion of clients who had no record of drug or alcohol tests, this variable was excluded from the analysis. In addition, the testing procedures were not necessarily random or consistent across or within programs. Information from site visits suggests that more clients were tested than OTRs indicated. In some cases, this may have occurred if clients were tested by a treatment provider that did not report the results of all tests to the DRC.

◤ Program Components and Dimensions

Systematic program-level data came from site visits that included semi-structured interviews with program directors and structured observations of program activities. Protocols contained items on whether the programs addressed LSI-R assessment areas and corresponded to the dominant findings in the literature on components of successful programs.[5] CJPP encouraged counties to design programs based on local needs, but the major components were fairly consistent.

Program activities and components were rated according to the extent to which they reflected components found to be important to effective programming, but it was beyond the scope of the study to conduct an evaluation of the quality of their implementation and operation.

Intensity Level

Program intensity measures were based on the number of hours per week of available programming. Programs typically had phases with required hours of participation that decreased over time as clients progressed. Programming assignments also varied based on the needs of the client. The final measure of intensity is the maximum number of programming hours per week to which any individual client could have been assigned at any given time. Intensity is not a measure of the number of hours of programming that a client actually received; this measure is referred to as "contact hours" and is discussed below. Intensity is a measure of how many hours the program makes available. Contact hours is a measure of the client's degree of participation in the available programming.

Several considerations entered into this measure. First, a client was normally assigned to only one of several similar programming options (e.g., assignment to either adult or youth intensive outpatient substance abuse treatment, but not both). In these cases, the measure included the hours for only one of these possible assignments. When the hours differed among similar components (e.g., substance abuse treatment), the measure used the highest number of hours.

Second, General Equivalency Diploma/Adult Basic Education (GED/ABE) programming and case management were relatively constant across sites. The local community college provided GED/ABE instruction (usually at the DRC) with fairly standard content and mechanisms of delivery. This activity is "constant" in that it would have almost the same number of available programming hours across all programs for any given client. Likewise, case management existed in all programs. Although meetings with the case manager often occurred on a similar schedule for all clients, this service was available on an as-needed basis as well, and most programs had no predetermined number of hours of case management. Because these requirements were either relatively constant across programs or provided primarily on an individualized basis, they were excluded from the development of the program intensity measure.

Finally, programs did not always have a high degree of internal consistency in scheduling. Some programming options were available sporadically, usually based on either the availability of staff or the existence of a sufficient number of clients at a particular time to warrant provision of the service. This phenomenon was observed in both rural and urban programs.

For the third, fourth, and final situations described above, the analysis used 1 hour per week for each type of service. For example, if a program offered individual substance abuse counseling as needed and job interview preparation instruction as needed, 1 hour was assigned to each component. Although this may underestimate or overestimate the number of hours actually available, the measure is consistent. This calculation was used only when the actual number of hours per week that a person could use these services was unavailable.

Because these characteristics of program service provision made it difficult to obtain a precise measure of the number of hours of programming offered per week, the analysis used an ordinal measure of program intensity: Low program intensity is defined as less than 10 hours of programming available per week, medium intensity is 10 to 15 hours per week, high intensity is more than 15 hours per week. (The number of hours used in this measure excludes the several hours per week of programming that is constant across programs.)

Criminogenic Needs Components

Several meta-analyses and other studies of multiple programs have identified components associated with successful outcomes, usually reductions in criminal behavior (e.g., Palmer, 1996). It is crucial that programming be directive and based on principles of behavioral psychology that include a system of rewards and punishments. As clients begin to learn new coping strategies, they must have opportunities to test these new skills in the community.

Components that address criminogenic needs are those that focus on antisocial attitudes and criminal thinking, substance abuse, criminal peer associations, life skills, self-control, anger management, education, and employment. If a program had more than one of the same area of programming, it was counted only once in the measure of criminogenic needs components. For example, offering both intensive and regular outpatient substance abuse treatment was considered to address one criminogenic need area. The study methodology could not ascertain the extent to which the program *formally* included opportunities to test new skills in the community, but anecdotal information from site visits indicated that this was an aspect of all programs. Also, all programs rewarded positive behavior and progress and punished negative behavior, but none used a reward schedule or other verifiable system of graduated (positive and/or negative) sanctions.

Client to Staff Ratio

This measure is the number of clients for each professional staff member. This and all other measures pertaining to staff exclude clerical personnel, volunteers, and professionals who may provide services at the DRC but who are not employed *by* the DRC. The professional program staff consists primarily of directors, case managers, and substance abuse counselors. Part-time positions are prorated. Volunteers are excluded because there was no way to accurately track their involvement. Only three programs used volunteers consistently. Two of these programs had about three volunteers each. One used them as GED/ABE tutors, whereas the other used them to help with seminars (e.g., life skills). Only one program (in the largest urban area) used volunteers extensively, primarily to facilitate seminars. The ratio is calculated as the number of clients divided by the number of full-time equivalent professional staff members.

Staff Characteristics

This measure considered the percentage of DRC staff with graduate degrees, years of experience in similar program settings, and whether the program offered training. Almost no professional staff member had a graduate degree, but almost all had a baccalaureate degree. Staff members in all programs participated in training provided by CJPP. Almost all DRCs offered other types of training, as well. Therefore, educational level and training were excluded from the analysis because they were virtually constant across programs. Even though a number of staff members had experience working with offenders in the community, almost none had prior experience working in a DRC or similar program. Therefore, the final measure of staff qualifications is the mean years of experience in substance abuse treatment and/or community corrections.

Across all programs, 42.3% of the professional program staff members were white, and the remainder were African American. Note that these figures include DRC program staff only. Outside vendors who provide services at the DRC or off-site are excluded.

Another measure is whether a probation or parole officer is located at the DRC. One reason that DRCs exist is to better coordinate services, and coordination with probation supervision is an important aspect of this mission. No direct evidence suggests that this approach is advantageous, but doing so may improve coordination of supervision and other types of services.

Programming Location

On-site programming is considered to be an important advantage, as well as a defining characteristic, of DRCs (Parent et al., 1995). This measure considers services provided by DRC staff, ancillary services, and the location of Probation/Parole Officers (PPOs) on-site.

Program Characteristics of Study Sample

Programs were designed to last approximately 6 months (about 25 weeks), but providers were free to vary from this length based on client needs and local CJPP Board of Directors policy. Average time spent in the program for completers across all programs is 35 weeks, 9 weeks longer than the 6-month target, and the standard deviations show that some programs have much more variation than others in the length of time in which individuals actually completed the program.

⌧ Discussion

The analysis presented here has two related purposes. Primarily, it examines program completion as an important aspect of program evaluation. In addition, it compares the results of a typical individual-level analysis to those of a multilevel analysis that accounts for the effects of variation across programs on individuals' likelihood of program completion.

The relatively small sample size and measurement issues notwithstanding, the MLM process reveals that ignoring the clustering of the data leads to somewhat different conclusions regarding predictors of program completion from those obtained in an individual-level analysis. What may appear to be an important predictor of completion may instead be an artifact of differences among programs. In a program evaluation, such differences may lead to erroneous conclusions regarding the types of clients who are most likely to complete the program and the types of services that should be provided or enhanced.

The conceptual model (see Figure 8.1) proposed three areas of influences on program completion: individual characteristics, program participation, and program characteristics. Three major findings regarding these areas are noteworthy. First, examination of individual demographic characteristics shows that minorities, in general, may not be well served by these programs. Even considering risk and need factors and the fact that most programs had a sizable proportion of minority staff members, ethnic minorities were still significantly less likely to complete the program than White/non-Hispanic clients.

Second, the risk and/or need area accommodation (living situation) specifically addresses the number of address changes in the past year, whether the client lives in a high-crime neighborhood, as well as factors related to the safety and stability of the client's living situation. Certainly, this score partially reflects the fact that many offenders live in low-income neighborhoods that may also have high-crime rates. Further analysis (not shown) revealed significant interactions among these variables, although their inclusion did not improve model fit. This analysis showed, not surprisingly, that clients who had drug and/or alcohol problems, a poor living situation, and predominantly criminal companions were significantly less likely to complete the program than others.

Given this observation, programs should consider providing more assistance with housing. Although no program listed housing assistance as a specific component, site visit information indicates that case managers routinely addressed clients' housing needs to some degree. Programs may need to be more proactive, though. The inclusion of a supervised housing component for high-risk clients is an option to consider. One program did offer a few clients the option of supervised drug-free housing, but similar services were not widely available elsewhere.

Another aspect of the relationship between drug and/or alcohol abuse and completion may relate to the handling of substance-abusing clients. About 56% of clients who were not chemically dependent (based on the SASSI) completed the program, compared with 46% of those who were chemically dependent (difference not statistically significant). Interviews with program staff in several counties indicated that some local probation officers were less tolerant of relapse to substance abuse than the program staff thought appropriate, based on PPOs' removal of clients from the program for positive urine tests. Substance-abusing clients in such counties may have been less likely to complete the program than similar clients in counties in which the PPOs and the program staff agreed on how to handle positive urine tests. The analysis could not examine this program-level characteristic directly, however.

Third, the finding regarding program participation is instructive. Examination of the results of individual-level models might lead a program to focus on case management and personal growth programming to improve completion rates. When accounting for the multilevel nature of the data, however, these variables are no longer significant. Rather, employment programming is the only component that predicts completion. Employment services chiefly consisted of job placement and job readiness programming. Job training was only offered by two programs.

Examination of the importance of specific program characteristics was hampered by the small number of level-two units (programs). Standard MLM techniques showed that although a fairly substantial amount of the variation in the likelihood of completion is related to characteristics of the program, it did not appear that any of those measured were important. If these results are to be accepted, then I would conclude that the program characteristics that research has shown to be important to recidivism (primarily those that address criminogenic needs) are not important to completion. However, other program characteristics measures were likewise not significant. However, it is just as likely that the finding reflects the small sample size.

In summary, this study has demonstrated the importance of personal characteristics, program participation, and program characteristics to DRC completion. Future research that includes a larger number of programs may shed more light on these relationships through a more detailed examination of these factors than was possible in the present study.

◪ Notes

1. Retention is defined as the length of time a client spends in a program from admission to (successful or unsuccessful) discharge.

2. The present analysis is part of a larger study that addressed recidivism of program clients and two comparison groups of probationers, but this article considers program completion only.

3. Concern may exist over whether the clients who dropped out early differ from those who did not. Bivariate analysis of the two groups showed no significant differences in age, race and/or ethnicity, sex, offense seriousness, Level of Service Inventory-Revised (LSI-R) scores, or chemical dependence.

4. Criminal Justice Partnership Program (CJPP) programs were intended to target offenders who need more services and intervention than probation supervision alone provides. The similarly situated comparison group of probationers in the larger study had a mean LSI-R score of 16.2 (median = 16, SD = 6.65). Scores differed significantly ($p < .001$) between the clients and the comparison group (Craddock, 2001). Based on this difference, it appears that the CJPP programs generally reached their target population.

5. The original project design included administration of the Correctional Program Assessment Inventory (CPAI), to assess programs based on characteristics found to predict successful outcomes (Gendreau & Andrews, 1996). This instrument was being revised and was not available for use during this study (P. Gendreau, personal communication, March 12, 1999).

6. The variance partition coefficient can also be interpreted as the extent to which the likelihood of completion is more similar among clients in the same program than among clients across all programs.

7. I also estimated a model with interaction terms. Although three interactions were significant, the R^2 increased by .01, indicating that the two models were virtually identical in predictive ability. Therefore, I chose to interpret the main effects model only.

References

Allison, P. D. (1999). *Logistic regression using the SAS System.* Cary, NC: SAS Institute.

Andrews, D. A., & Bonta, J. (1998). *The psychology of criminal conduct* (2nd ed.). Cincinnati, OH: Anderson.

Bonta, J. (1996). Risk prediction in criminal justice. In A. T. Harland (Ed.), *Choosing correctional options that work: Defining the demand and evaluating the supply* (pp. 33–67). Thousand Oaks, CA: Sage.

Craddock, A. (2001). *Offender outcomes under the North Carolina Criminal Justice Partnership Act* (Grant # 96-CE-VX-0004). Washington, DC: National Institute of Justice.

Craddock, A., & Graham, L. A. (1996). Recidivism as a function of day reporting center participation. *Journal of Offender Rehabilitation, 34*(1), 81–100.

Cullen, F. T., Wright, J. P., & Applegate, B. K. (1996). Control in the community: The limits of reform? In A. T. Harland (Ed.), *Choosing correctional options that work; Defining the demand and evaluating the supply* (pp. 69–116). Thousand Oaks, CA: Sage.

Curtin, E. L. (1996). Day reporting centers. In A. C. Association (Ed.), *Correctional issues: Community corrections.* Lanham, MD: American Correctional Association.

Gendreau, P. (1996). The principles of effective intervention with offenders. In A. T. Harland (Ed.), *Choosing correctional options that work: Defining the demand and evaluating the supply* (pp. 117–130). Thousand Oaks, CA: Sage.

Gendreau, P., & Andrews, D. A. (1996). *Correctional program assessment inventory* (CPAI, 6th ed.). Saint John, New Brunswick, Canada: University of New Brunswick, Department of Psychology.

Goldstein, H. (2003). *Multilevel statistical models.* London: Hodder Arnold.

Hall, R. H., & Tolbert, P. S. (2005). *Organizations: Structures, processes and outcomes.* Englewood Cliffs, NJ: Prentice Hall.

Hoffmann, D. A., & Gavin, M. B. (1998). Centering decisions in hierarchical linear models: Implications for research in organizations. *Journal of Management, 24*(5), 623–641.

Hox, J. (2002). *Multilevel analysis: Techniques and applications.* Mahwah, NJ: Lawrence Erlbaum.

Kreft, I. G. G., de Leeuw, J., & Aiken, L. S. (1995). The effect of different forms of centering in hierarchical linear models. *Multivariate Behavioral Research, 30,* 1–21.

Lowenkamp, C. T, & Latessa, E. J. (2002). Evaluation of Ohio's community based correctional facilities and halfway house programs: Final report. Unpublished manuscript.

Lowenkamp, C. T., & Latessa, E. J. (2005). Increasing the effectiveness of correctional programming through the risk principle: Identifying offenders for residential placement. *Criminology and Public Policy, 4*(2), 263–290.

Marciniak, L. M. (1999). The use of day reporting as an intermediate sanction: A study of offender targeting and program termination. *The Prison Journal, 79*(2), 205–225.

Martin, S. S., & Inciardi, J. A. (1993). Case management treatment program for drug-involved prison releases. *The Prison Journal, 73*(3/4), 319–331.

McBride, D., & VanderWaal, C. (1997). Day reporting centers as an alternative for drug using offenders. *Journal of Drug Issues, 27*(2), 379–397.

McDevitt, J., Domino, M., & Baum, K. (1997). *Metropolitan day reporting center: An evaluation.* Boston: Northeastern University.

Miller, F. G., Roberts, J., Brooks, M. K., & Lazowski, L. E. (1997). *SASSI-3 user's guide.* Bloomington, IN: Baugh Enterprises.

Multi-Health Systems, Inc. (1995). *Level of service inventory-revised: Manual.* Tonawanda, NY: Author.

North Carolina Department of Correction, Annual Statistical Report Fiscal Year 2003-2004. (2005). Raleigh: North Carolina Department of Correction.

Orchowsky, S., Lucas, J., & Bogle, T. (1995). *Final report: Evaluation of the Fairfax day reporting center (FDRC).* Richmond, VA: Virginia Department of Criminal Justice Services, Criminal Justice Research Center.

Palmer, T. (1996). Programmatic and nonprogrammatic aspects of successful intervention. In A. T. Harland (Ed.), *Choosing correctional options that work: Defining the demand and evaluating the supply* (pp. 131–182). Thousand Oaks, CA: Sage.

Parent, D., Byrne, J. M., Tsarfaty, V., Valade, L., & Esselman. J. (1995). *Day reporting centers, Vols. 1 and 2.* Washington, DC: Department of Justice, National Institute of Justice.

Prendergast, M. L., Anglin, M. D., & Wellisch, J. (1998). Community-based treatment for substance abusing offenders: Principles and practice of effective service delivery. In T. C. Castellano & B. J. Auerbach (Eds.), *Proceedings of the 1994 conference of the International Community Corrections Association (ICCA)* (pp. 75–115). Lanham, MD: American Correctional Association.

Rabash, J., Steele, F., Browne, W., & Prosser, B. (2004). *A user's guide to MLwiN Version 2.02.* Bristol, UK: Centre for Multilevel Modeling.

SAS Institute. (2005). SAS OnlineDoc® 9.1.3. Cary, NC: Author.

Sherman, L. W., Gottfredson, D. C., MacKenzie, D. L., Eck, J., Reuter, P., & Bushway, S. D. (1998). *Preventing crime: What works, what doesn't, what's promising.* Washington, DC: Department of Justice, National Institute of Justice.

Smith, M. E., & Dickey, W. J. (1999). *Reforming sentencing and corrections for just punishment and public safety.* Washington, DC: Department of Justice, National Institute of Justice.

Smith, W. R., Cummings, T. S., & Lensing, C. M. (2000, February). Local/state correctional partnerships that work. *Corrections Today,* pp. 22–25.

Snijders, T. A. B., & Bosker, R. J. (1999). *Multilevel analysis: An introduction to basic and advanced multilevel modeling.* London: Sage.

Structured Sentencing Act, North Carolina General Statutes, §§15A-1340.11-1340.23 (1994).

Sung, H., Belenko, S., & Feng, L. (2001). Treatment compliance in the trajectory of treatment progress among offenders. *Journal of Substance Abuse Treatment, 20*(2), 153–162.

Tonry, M. (1999). Community penalties in the United States. *European Journal on Criminal Policy and Research, 7,* 5–22.

DISCUSSION QUESTIONS

1. How do day reporting centers differ from traditional alternative sanctions?

2. What is significant about program intensity in reducing long-term recidivism rates of offenders?

3. Given the findings of the study, how might day reporting centers institute plans to increase completion rates?

4. Given the findings of the study and what we know about day reporting centers, should communities continue to utilize them as an alternative to incarceration? Why or why not?

READING

In this extensive work, the authors tested the effectiveness of both RF and GPS monitoring on 75,661 offenders placed in home confinement in Florida between 1998 and 2002. Unlike previous research, these authors used a proportional-hazard regression model, which allowed them to control for time variances in the independent and dependent variables. To measure the effectiveness of these alternative sanctions, the authors explored the likelihood of revocation and absconding from supervision (p. 63). Revocation was further defined as revocation for a new offense and revocation for a technical violation. Because of the statistical methodology used, the authors were unable to follow the program participants post-supervision; therefore, there was no measure comparing them to those released from incarceration. Additionally, Padgett and her colleagues examined the relative impact of net widening of this sanction and the risk to community safety should it be further expanded. Results of the study indicate that no differences exist between type of supervision. Therefore, those offenders placed on GPS were no more likely to be revoked or to abscond than those placed on RF supervision. The findings further revealed that because revocation did not differ compared to those on other forms of community supervision the argument for the net-widening effect was not supported. The authors offered three policy implications for the use of EM and supervision in the community. Overall, both RF and GPS supervision appear to be an effective means of supervision for violent, property, and drug offenders.

SOURCE: Padgett, Kathy G., Bales, William D., & Blomberg, Thomas. (2006). Under surveillance: An empirical test of the effectiveness and consequences of electronic monitoring. *Criminology & Public Policy, 5*(1), 61–92. Copyright © 2009 by the American Society of Criminology.

Under Surveillance

An Empirical Test of the Effectiveness and Consequences of Electronic Monitoring

Kathy G. Padgett, William D. Bales, and Thomas G. Blomberg

During the 1980s, the United States began to experience "exponential growth in incarceration" (Blumstein, 1998). Austin et al. (2003) report that between 1980 and 2000, the prison population more than tripled. In response to this unprecedented growth in imprisonment and its associated costs, various intermediate sanctions were promoted as less costly but still "tough" and effective alternatives to imprisonment (Clear and Braga, 1995; Morris and Tonry, 1990). Despite reservations by penal reform scholars and researchers, intermediate sanctions, including intensive supervision, home confinement with and without electronic monitoring (EM), day reporting centers, and boot camps, proved appealing to both liberal and conservative policy makers and quickly spread across the country.

In theory, intermediate sanction programs were to divert offenders from prison, while providing a greater level of offender accountability and surveillance than would be provided by traditional probation supervision. The end result, therefore, would be less penal control imposed on individual offenders and less expense to the taxpayer, without any compromise to public safety (Baumer et al., 1993; Clear et al., 1998). To date, however, the extent to which intermediate sanctions have fulfilled their formal goals of reducing prison populations and protecting public safety has yet to be established. Despite the absence of empirical proof regarding the effectiveness of electronic surveillance, this strategy is likely to become a national approach for managing high risk offenders in the community.

The widely publicized sexual battery and murder of nine-year-old Jessica Lunsford in early 2005, allegedly by a registered sex offender, prompted legislation in Florida that requires sex offenders who molest children to wear satellite tracking devices (global positioning system, or GPS, monitoring) for the rest of their lives once they leave prison. Despite an estimated fiscal impact on the state of $3.9 million, the legislation passed by unanimous vote, effectively ensuring that the number of offenders in Florida under electronic surveillance will more than double (from 720 to 1,920) within fiscal year 2005–2006. Whether prompted by the case of Jessica Lunsford and Florida's Jessica Lunsford Act or by the growing awareness of the capabilities and availability of GPS monitoring devices, legislation related to the EM of offenders in the community was proposed in at least 11 additional states and at the Federal level in the Spring 2005 legislative season, all of which provide for its increased use. Even if media attention to sex offenders in the community and the presumed public outcry for closer surveillance of these offenders subside, it seems likely that the use of EM devices will increase dramatically in the very near future. Alongside this anticipated increase, policy makers will surely face questions about their effectiveness in preventing or deterring further criminal activity, as well as concerns about the intensity of surveillance they afford and a subsequent increase in prison sentences or returns to prison for technical violations.

This study addresses the effectiveness of EM for serious offenders supervised in the community. Using data on 75,661 offenders placed on home confinement in Florida from 1998 to 2002. we estimate the effect of radio-frequency (RF) and GPS monitoring on the likelihood of revocation and absconding from supervision. During this time period in Florida, only a small percentage of offenders placed on home confinement was ordered to wear an EM device as a condition of the home confinement sentence, which allows for a comparison between those and other, like offenders who were not electronically monitored in terms of their likelihood of technically violating, reoffending, or absconding while on home confinement. In doing so. we can test for a potential net-widening effect of EM as well as its potential for protecting public safety. We also test for potential net-widening at the "'front end," or the point at which the decision is made to place an offender on EM as a condition of his or her home confinement sentence, with additional data on offender seriousness levels.

The Current Study

In 1983, Florida became the first state to legislate and implement a statewide home confinement program specifically designed to address the problem of exponential increases in prison admissions and the need for intermediate sanctions as an alternative to incarceration (Florida Department of Corrections [FDOC], 2001). As the program developed and admissions increased, it became apparent that even within the narrower category of home confinement, different offenders required different levels of supervision intensity and surveillance while on the program. Various approaches to case management were tried and revised, but the advent of RF technology as a viable option for closer surveillance of higher risk offenders reframed the issue and ushered in a second phase of home confinement supervision strategy in which EM became the primary differentiating factor in the treatment of offenders.

Since 1987, with legislative approval, the FDOC implemented RF monitoring as an additional surveillance technique for offenders on home confinement, and in 1998 the use of EM was expanded to include GPS monitoring for those offenders judged to be of higher risk to public safety and in need of an even higher level of surveillance while in the community. According to the FDOC (2003):

> The additional features of inclusive and exclusive boundaries, two-way communication with the victim or the offender, location mapping for archives retrieval, immediate tamper notification and remote laptop tracking with a wireless modem for constant communication with

the monitoring center, makes the GPS system the best available. It would seem logical that violations of home confinement would decrease because offenders would know in advance that violations are tracked in "near real time" 24 hours a day.

Methods

The data for this study were drawn from the FDOC's Offender-based Information System (OBIS). The sample comprises 75,661 offenders placed on home confinement from 1998 to 2002. These "placements" include original sentences to home confinement, split sentences (prison followed by supervision) to home confinement, post-prison sentences (Home Confinement-Parole), and sentences to home confinement for a violation of probation.

As noted, one method for assessing the effectiveness of EM as an alternative to incarceration versus an enhancement that results in net-widening has been the comparison of the relative "risk" to public safety of offenders sentenced to EM and offenders sentenced to community supervision without EM (Bonta et al., 2000; Gendreau et al., 2000; Renzema, 2003; Renzema and Mayo-Wilson, 2005). The logic underlying this kind of comparative analysis is that evidence of offenders who are sentenced to this new alternative being of no greater "risk" than offenders sentenced to the previously existing community supervision sanction lends support to a net-widening rather than an alternative-sentencing argument. Although Bonta et al.'s (2000) analysis uses the results of a self-reported questionnaire to measure "risk" as the Level of Service Inventory–Revised (LSI-R) score, they rely on a much broader definition of offender risk in making their case for a "net-widening" effect of EM. In their assessment of the prior research on EM and the relative risk of offenders placed on EM, Bonta et al. (2000) include factors such as prior record (Ball et al., 1988; Cadigan, 1991), violent versus nonviolent primary offense (Baumer et al., 1993; Maxfield and Baumer, 1990), DUI or traffic offenders only (Lilly et al., 1993), first offense or property offenders (Mortimer and May, 1997), or other "'low-risk" offenders (Beck et al., 1990; Ontario, 1991; Roy, 1997; Whittingdon, 1987) as indicators of relative risk. A more recent examination of EM and front-end net-widening (Renzema and Mayo-Wilson, 2005) follows this course as well, defining offender "risk" in terms of prior record and primary offense convicted of. For this study, we use primary offense type (violent/not violent) and Florida's sentencing guidelines scoring system as indicators of offender "risk" and contend that equal levels of risk for offenders on EM and offenders on home confinement without EM supports the net-widening argument as it applies to the imposition of harsher sentences, or "front-end" net-widening.

Although sentencing guidelines are just that—guidelines—from which judges can and do depart, Florida's sentencing guidelines scoring system has been shown to serve as a valid indicator of "offender seriousness" (Burton et al., 2004). The weighted score produced by this system takes into account an offender's primary offense and all additional offenses, his or her prior record and the seriousness of prior offenses, and other circumstances of the criminal event (victim injury, weapon use, supervision violation, etc.). In the absence of risk scores derived from psychological or other such inventories, this indicator of offender seriousness is the best available quantitative measure of the risk an offender poses to public safety.

To test the effectiveness of EM in reducing the likelihood of failure while on home confinement, three outcome measures—revocation for a technical violation, revocation for a new offense, and absconding—were modeled using proportional-hazards regression (survival) analysis. This statistical modeling technique allows for right-censoring and the inclusion of time-varying independent variables as well as taking into account "time to failure" in the estimation of maximum-likelihood coefficients. The time variable used is weeks from placement on home confinement to release, and cases were right-censored on the week of the release event. When the release event was due to something other than one of the three types of

supervision "failure" listed above—death, successful termination of supervision, sentence reduction to regular probation, etc.—the offender was considered "at risk" of failure for each of the weeks before that event and then right-censored, or dropped from the analysis. In the event of an offender remaining on active home confinement beyond 105 weeks (2 years) from placement, the case was censored at week 105.

Measures

Dependent Variables

As discussed, three outcomes of a period of supervision are modeled in the multivariate survival analysis—revocation for a new offense,[1] revocation for a technical violation, and absconding from supervision. In Florida, a revocation results from a court decision to terminate supervision for failing to meet the requirements of supervision. It is not, necessarily, an indicator of offender behavior, but an indicator of "getting caught" and the subsequent community supervision officer and judicial response. Both types of revocation—for a new offense or for a technical violation—are considered permanent releases, although many offenders are returned to community supervision with a new sentence. Absconding, on the other hand, does not in and of itself constitute a permanent release. FDOC (2005) defines absconding as follows: "Offender absconds from supervision; the whereabouts are unknown and the court issues a warrant for violation of supervision." Supervision may or may not be terminated upon return from absconding. In this analysis, absconding is treated as a separate "outcome," and an offender is still considered "at risk" for revocation after an absconding event.

For this study, a separate analysis was conducted for each of the three "outcome" measures—revocation for a technical violation, revocation for a new offense, and absconding. These outcome variables were dichotomized so that the value is zero for all weeks that an individual offender is at risk of the unsuccessful outcome but does

---

[1] For this analysis, we collapsed the categories of "revocation for a new misdemeanor" and "revocation for a new felony" into one outcome variable, "revocation for a new offense." Nearly three-quarters (71%) of revocations for a new offense are for a new felony offense.

not experience the event, and the value is 1 for the one week in which he or she does experience the unsuccessful outcome. As noted, for offenders who experience a release even other than one of these "failures," the outcome variable is coded 0 for all weeks up to the week of release, at which point the case is dropped from the analysis.

Independent Variables

The variable of primary interest in this analysis is whether the offender was placed on EM while on home confinement. Two dichotomous, time-varying variables were created to indicate time on EM in any given week—one for RF monitoring and one for GPS monitoring—to determine whether one device type has a greater or lesser effect on the outcome variables than the other. Comparing the relative effectiveness of the two types of EM is important because one type—GPS monitoring—involves considerably more intensive and precise surveillance than the other (RF monitoring), which means it should be more effective in deterring and incapacitating the offender and more likely to "catch" offenders violating the conditions of their community supervision. Unlike RF monitoring, which only provides surveillance when the offender is in his or her home, GPS monitoring tracks the location of offenders and maps their whereabouts for retrieval by the community supervision officer (FDOC, 2005).

Control Variables

Several variables were included in the analysis to control for any offender characteristics, criminal history, or current period of supervision circumstances related to the likelihood of an unsuccessful outcome. Each of the time-varying independent variables, like the dependent variables, was dichotomized so that its value is 1 for any week in which the condition applies to an individual offender and 0 for any week in which it does not.

In all, 62 independent variables are included in each proportional-hazards regression model, not counting the reference categories for the multinomial

variables. The control variables include indicators of community supervision success or failure in the following categories: sociodemographic characteristics of the offender and his/her criminal history and prior record; factors related to the offender's current term of community supervision, including any conditions and provisions of supervision or other sentence-event differences, the judicial circuit in which the offender was being supervised, and the primary offense for which the offender was convicted; and time-varying events that occurred within the period of supervision being examined that resulted in the offender avoiding surveillance by the community supervision officer (i.e., absconding), being subjected to a greater level of surveillance (i.e., participating in drug court), or being incapacitated (i.e., in a residential drug treatment facility or in the county jail) for a certain amount of time.

Sociodemographic Characteristics of the Offender. Age, race, and sex are included to control for the well-established relationship between these demographic characteristics and success or failure on community supervision. The two additional sociodemographic variables, permanence of residency and employment status, are included as measures of the offender's lifestyle stability.[2] Marital status, another measure of lifestyle stability, was not included in our models. Although data on marital status are collected for offenders committed to prison in Florida (however, it is worth noting that, on average, 36% of those data are missing), they are not collected for offenders placed on community supervision. It is expected that if data were available, the variable for marital status would have an effect on the likelihood of an offender being revoked or absconding: however, it does not necessarily follow that this effect would prove a source of spuriousness for the EM-revocation or EM-absconding relationship. Further research on the differences between offenders placed on EM and those not placed on EM is needed to determine whether lifestyle and stability measures have an effect

---

[2] Data on offender marital status and educational level were not available, nor were data on arrest history, prior county jail incarceration, or prior convictions in other states

on both the likelihood of placement on EM and the likelihood of revocation or absconding.

Current Primary Offense. Three aspects of the offender's current primary offense[3] were included in the multivariate models: primary offense category, whether the offender was the principle in a completed act (not an attempt), and the number of counts for which he or she was convicted. For this analysis, the "primary" offense was coded according to the nine-group categorization of offenses established and used by the FDOC: (1) murder/manslaughter, (2) sex offenses, (3) robbery, (4) other violent/personal offenses, (5) burglary, (6) theft, (7) drug offenses, (8) weapons offenses, and (9) "other" offenses. Current primary offense category dummy variables are included in the multivariate analyses to control for the known association between offense type and community supervision outcome.

Current Sentence. In addition to current offense, we include aspects of the current sentence as control variables in the multivariate models. Within the home confinement program as a whole, separate conditions are mandated for offenders placed on sex-offender home confinement and for post-prison releasees on home confinement-parole. The particular circumstances and characteristics of these offenders are controlled for with dummy variables for the type of home confinement to which the offender is sentenced. Similarly, offenders serving a split (prison then home confinement) sentence and those originally sentenced to probation and later placed on home confinement for a violation are taken into account with dummy variables for "split sentence" and "home confinement placement for VOP," respectively. Sentence length is controlled for with a continuous variable measuring the number of days the offender was sentenced. If the offender's sentence was mitigated, meaning that he or she "scored" to prison according to

the Florida's Sentencing Guidelines but was sentenced to home confinement instead, we take that into account with a dummy variable where mitigated is 1.

Conditions of Supervision. In addition to the standard conditions of home confinement, offenders can be held to several special provisions stipulated by the sentencing judge. These include participation in a treatment program (domestic violence, psychological, drug, and/or sex offender treatment), participation in an educational program, regular drug testing, and/or the completion of public service hours, all of which are controlled for with dummy variables to indicate whether the provision was court-ordered. Dates of attendance for outpatient treatment programs were not available, but time-varying variables reflecting weeks in which an offender was in residential drug treatment or participating in drug court were included to control for the incapacitation effect of residential drug treatment, at which point an offender would be at lower risk for reoffending or absconding, and for the more stringent conditions imposed on offenders in drug court, who would be at greater risk for technically violating during that time. A time-varying variable for "non-reporting status" is also included, as this status is assigned to offenders who are temporarily incarcerated in a county jail and, therefore, at lower risk for reoffending or absconding.

Circuit of Supervision. Finally, the judicial circuit in which the offender was being supervised is included to control for local-level discretion in "violation" policies and judicial decision making. If and when an offender was transferred from one circuit to another, the circuit variable was recoded to reflect that change for the week in which it took place and the weeks thereafter. The distribution of home confinement placements by circuit is available from the authors upon request.

The comparisons of risk, or seriousness, levels for home confinement offenders with and without EM show that for all five measures, EM offenders have

---

[3] Each placement on home confinement is associated—by a unique (to the offender) "prefix" code—to a particular sentencing event. An offense is designated as primary for that sentencing event by means of a formula that takes into account the seriousness of the offense (according to the offense code), the level of the charge (Capital Life; Life; 1st-, 2nd-, 3rd-degree felony, etc.), and the associated sentence length.

statistically significant ($p < 0.001$) higher levels than those for offenders not on EM. Additionally, offenders on the higher level surveillance EM modality of GPS have risk levels significantly higher ($p < 0.001$) than those under the less controlling RF monitoring mechanism on all five risk measures. Specifically, EM offenders are more likely to have committed a violent offense and more likely to have "scored" to prison, and their mean sentencing guidelines points scores, in terms of the total points and points for the primary offense alone, are significantly higher than those for offenders sentenced to home confinement without EM ($p < 0.001$).

Whether these offenders would have received a sentence to prison in the absence of the EM alternative is impossible to determine using secondary data. However, these findings do indicate that offenders on EM are, on average, more serious offenders, and their perceived risk to the community makes them more likely than offenders not on EM to be sentenced to prison in the absence of the EM alternative. Additionally, offenders sentenced to supervision under the enhanced level of offender control through GPS instead of RF are clearly more serious offenders and considered more of a risk to public safety.

Specifically, offenders on home confinement with EM of either type exhibit significantly higher risk scores on all four of the sentencing guidelines measures ($p < 0.001$). However, mixed results are found in comparisons of those offenders monitored under GPS versus RF for violent offenders. GPS offenders are found to be significantly more serious and pose a greater risk to the community ($p < 0.001$) than those under RF surveillance for the same four measures as for all offenders combined. For property offenders, however, the differences virtually disappear, indicating no greater risk to the community from offenders placed on the more intensive GPS monitoring than from those placed on RF monitoring.

For drug offenders, the picture is slightly different when comparing EM with non-EM offenders and RF with GPS offenders. Although drug offenders on EM are significantly more likely to have scored to prison for their primary offense and to have higher mean sentencing guidelines points for their primary offense, the differences disappear when the total sentencing points

are compared. Furthermore, regardless of statistical significance, differences for all four measures are considerably smaller for drug offenders than for violent or property offenders, both for EM vs. non-EM offenders and RF vs. GPS offenders.

This analysis of the differences in risk levels, or offender seriousness, between offenders on home confinement with and without EM and between those on RF versus the more intrusive GPS provides no clear evidence that, overall, the decision to monitor offenders on home confinement with enhanced electronic control mechanisms results in "front-end" net-widening. In other words, offenders sentenced to home confinement with EM seem to have posed a significantly higher risk to public safety and would have had a higher likelihood of receiving a prison sentence if not for the availability of EM as an enhanced control mechanism. However possible "front-end" net-widening for drug offenders is suggested by findings that show that non-EM drug offenders exhibit almost equivalent levels of risk to the public as those placed on the more controlling EM program.

Although the question of "front-end" net-widening remains somewhat elusive, relying on proxies to indicate the likelihood of a sentence to prison in the absence of qualitative data on judicial decision making, the question of "back-end" net-widening is more easily addressed and answered. With the introduction of intermediate sanctions into the continuurn of punishment alternatives came the concern that these more intensive forms of community supervision, with their stricter conditions and closer surveillance, would increase the likelihood of an offender violating those conditions and getting caught doing so. The fact that EM of offenders on home confinement constitutes the last option before prison, it seems likely that a violation while on EM would result in a sentence to prison, therefore, widening the net.

Unlike previous findings of a "surveillance" effect, our findings indicate that offenders on EM are less likely to be revoked for a technical violation. In fact, and surprisingly, offenders on RF monitoring are 95.7% less likely and offenders on GPS monitoring are 90.2% less likely than offenders on home confinement without EM to be revoked for a technical violation. However, the difference in the magnitude of these effects is statistically significant (z-score $= 2.962$). which partially supports the "surveillance effect" hypothesis, in that offenders on the more intense form of electronic surveillance are more likely than those on the less intense form to get caught violating the conditions of their home confinement sentence. Secondly, these findings show that the prohibitory effect of EM on technically violating holds true for offenders in all three primary offense categories and has virtually the same degree of effect across the three categories. This finding is of particular significance given that EM is used at a considerably higher rate for violent offenders (12.3%, compared with 5.7% and 4.7% for property and drug offenders, respectively) and that violent offenders are significantly less likely than property and drug offenders (the reference category) to be revoked for a technical violation, whether they are placed on EM.

Although one set of concerns related to the addition of EM to home confinement sentences is that it will widen the net of control, another set of concerns has to do with public safety and the effectiveness of EM in deterring or incapacitating offenders living in the community. The proportional hazards regression modeling of the likelihood of revocation for a new offense was our primary measure of risk to public safety.

For both outcomes, the results show that EM significantly reduces the likelihood of failure and that the degree to which that likelihood is reduced is about the same for revocation for a new offense and absconding. Where public safety is concerned, either form of electronic surveillance seems to significantly reduce the likelihood of reoffending for all three "types" of offender.

Absconding from supervision is an outcome measure that has not, to date, been addressed in the literature on EM and home confinement. However, its implications for public safety and the relative frequency of its occurrence suggest that absconding and the potential for EM to reduce the rate of absconding should be considered in any test of the effectiveness of EM. As of December 30, 2004, more than 40,000 of the 114,891 offenders on community supervision in Florida were classified as absconders, their "whereabouts unknown" (FDOC, 2005). In our sample of 75,661 offenders on home confinement, 11,857 (15.7%) absconded from supervision at some point within two years of placement, and 1,911 (16.1%) of those absconders were subsequently revoked for a new offense. This rate of reoffending is considerably

higher than that for the offenders who did not abscond (9.8%) and indicates an increased risk to public safety of offenders who escape surveillance.

These findings consistently demonstrate that either form of EM significantly reduces the risk to public safety from offenders living in the community. Moreover, our findings for the effect of EM on the likelihood of revocation for a technical violation indicate that rather than widening the net of penal control, the addition of electronic surveillance to a home confinement sentence may actually reduce the probability of eventual imprisonment and, therefore, effectively serve as a useful alternative sanction. Notwithstanding the limitations of using official data to represent the complex circumstances of offenders serving a sentence to home confinement and the complexities of officer discretion and judicial decision making, these findings suggest that the dual goals of reducing the number of admissions to prison while protecting public safety may, in fact, be achieved via the introduction of newer and more refined means of offender surveillance.

Summary and Discussion

The findings reported here have addressed two questions related to the net-widening effect and the public safety effectiveness of EM for offenders on home confinement. With regard to net-widening, the findings provide only scant support for a net-widening effect resulting from the addition of EM into Florida's home confinement program. Using primary offense type (violent or not) as the measure of offense seriousness, it was shown that those offenders on home confinement with EM were significantly more likely to have committed a violent offense as compared with those offenders on home confinement without EM. Additionally, those offenders on home confinement with GPS monitoring were even more likely than those with RF monitoring to have committed a violent offense. Furthermore, using sentencing guideline scores as an indicator of the likelihood of a prison sentence, offenders on home confinement with EM had a greater likelihood of a prison sentence than did offenders on home confinement without EM. Similarly, offenders on home confinement with GPS had a greater likelihood than those offenders on home confinement with RF of receiving a prison sentence in the absence of some form of home confinement. However, when all home confinement offenders were divided into primary offense type groups, the positive relationship between relative levels of control (i.e., No EM, RF, and GPS) and the likelihood of a prison sentence held true for violent and, to a lesser extent, property offenders, but significantly decreased for drug offenders, demonstrating that the net may, in fact, have widened for this group of offenders. With regard to "back-end" net-widening, EM was found to decrease rather than increase the likelihood of revocation for a technical violation, which contradicts the expectation of a surveillance effect.

In relation to public safety effectiveness, EM was found effective in reducing the likelihood of reoffending and absconding while on home confinement. Both RF and GPS significantly reduced the likelihood of revocation for a new offense and absconding from supervision, even when controlling for sociodemographic characteristics of the offender, current offense, prior record, and term of supervision factors and conditions. The use of GPS monitoring compared with the use of RF monitoring was found to be no more likely to reduce revocations or incidents of absconding. However, the use of either GPS or RF monitoring had virtually the same inhibiting effect on revocations and absconding for violent, property, and drug offender groups on home confinement.

Policy Implications

As for the policy implications of this research, it is important to note that the statistical modeling technique used in our analysis, proportional-hazards regression (survival analysis), takes into account the timing of an event and its occurrence in relation to the timing of placement on and removal from electronic monitoring. Therefore, our findings are limited to the effect of EM while the offender is actually being monitored, not after he/she completes the program. Although we agree with Kenzema (2003:9) that "Many agencies using EM neither build rehabilitation components into their programs nor expect an enduring impact," and the informational literature related to EM that has been produced by the FDOC indicates the same, further study of the long-term effects of EM is needed before drawing conclusions about a rehabilitative effect or basing policy decisions on such an effect. However, our findings do indicate that home confinement with EM can effectively serve an incapacitation and/or deterrence role in protecting public safety.

Additional policy implications of this research include decision making regarding which offenders should be placed on EM, which type of monitoring device will be the most cost-effective and efficient, and the potential for front-end net-widening if states adopt a practice of "Got 'em? Use 'em." The first two of these policy issues are addressed directly by the results of our analysis, whereas the third calls for further research and some monitoring of our own. Regarding decisions about which offenders should be placed on EM, our findings show that:

1. EM works for serious offenders—much of the previous research has looked at less serious offenders. Whereas we find an effect of EM on technical violations, reoffending, and absconding for a cohort of offenders judged too serious to be placed on regular probation. This overall finding bodes well for EM's anticipated use for sex offenders and other, more serious, offenders.

2. EM works equally well for all "types" of serious offenders, when offender type is defined as the category of the offender's primary offense (violent, property, or drug). Assuming that EM devices will not be available for every offender placed on community supervision, the decision about which offenders should be electronically monitored will need to be based on more than his or her primary offense. Further research should address the factors associated with success on EM.

As much of the new legislation related to EM is specific to sex offenders on EM after release from prison, it should be noted that our findings also indicate that sex offenders are less likely than all other types of offenders to have their supervision revoked for a new offense or to abscond and no more or less likely to have their supervision revoked for a technical violation, even when controlling for EM status, and that less than 3% of the offenders in our sample were on parole or serving the second half of a split sentence.

Regarding decisions about which type of monitoring device is most cost-effective and efficient, our findings show that RF is just as effective as GPS in reducing the likelihood of an offender absconding or being revoked for a new offense and slightly more effective than GPS in reducing the likelihood of revocation for a technical violation. Given these findings, policy makers should consider whether GPS monitoring is worth its price. Although this study did not include an in-depth cost analysis of RF versus GPS or EM versus imprisonment, raw cost figures for EM in the State of Florida indicate considerable differences per diem. According to the FDOC (Brooks, 2005), the current (as of July 1, 2005) per diem cost for active GPS monitoring is $8.97, as compared with $1.97 for RF monitoring. The per diem cost for prison is $51.22. At more than four times the cost, policy makers may want to reconsider their commitment to GPS over RF monitoring.

Finally, policy makers need to consider the potential for front-end net-widening as a result of states procuring great numbers of devices to meet the mandates of recent legislation and then keeping all of the devices "in service" regardless of real need. Lawmakers would do well to consider amendments to sentencing guidelines legislation that would specify a point range for which home confinement with EM would be the recommended sentence. In Florida, where there is no pre-trial risk-assessment instrument to guide the sentencing decision, such a point-range guideline would be preferable to blanket polices targeted at specific offender "types" or unlimited judicial discretion. Another option would be to limit the sentence of home confinement with EM to offenders who "score to prison" under the sentencing guidelines, thereby ensuring the use of EM only as a true alternative to incarceration. The adoption of the latter policy is unlikely, and in the end, we have to agree with Morris and Tonry (1990:218) that "all one can hope for is that the important desideratum of parsimony in punishment will restrain enthusiasms [for electronic 'tracking'] and respect autonomy."

Theoretical Implications

Such theoretical abstractions as net-widening, dispersal of discipline, transcarceration, carceral society, maximum security society, and culture of control have been proposed to capture and account for the reported negative and unintended consequences of various penal reforms. Whether concerned with the disparity between the ideas and the policies of penal reform strategies or what these patterned disparities have meant in terms of larger or master penal control shifts, the focus has been on what was believed to be ever expanding penal control. Moreover, it is important to acknowledge that these theoretical abstractions have not only been useful in understanding certain aspects and potentials of penal reforms but were informed by some degree of empirical support for their negative and unintended consequences.

However, and as demonstrated by this study's findings for Florida's statewide home confinement and EM program, also salient intended outcomes are associated with this particular penal reform. The question, therefore, is do these findings mean "bad news" for the leading theoretical interpretations of penal reform, which have been largely focused on negative and unintended consequences? Or, alternatively, do these findings provide evidence that must and can be successfully confronted and interpreted by modifying and refining some of the existing penal reform theories? We believe it is the latter, and the task at hand is to reconcile unexpected findings of intended consequences with the larger, theoretical issues surrounding the concept of social control. Lianos's (2003:412) observation that "the question of control presents itself inevitably in the light—or should one say in the shadow?—of its social utility" is especially relevant here. Although EM seems to effectively thwart offenders from reoffending or otherwise threatening public safety, it simultaneously affords a degree of surveillance that would likely offend the sensibilities of the average, "free" citizen of the Western world.

EM presents a new challenge for both theorists and policy makers. Not only is the EM of offenders in the community an intermediate sanction and, therefore, a subject for discussion and debate in that context, it is also surveillance made possible only by recent advances in computer and electronic technology. As such, the EM of offenders falls within the broader discussion of electronic surveillance in general. It seems likely that current and future developments in technology will result in ever increasing levels of personal transparency for both offenders and citizens alike. Certainly this possibility poses an increasingly urgent and important mandate—we need to confront these current and future control strategies and technologies with comprehensive and rigorous empirical, theoretical, and public policy scrutiny. The traditional "great divide" among research, theory, and public policy must be routinely bridged if responsible penal and public policies are to be implemented in this era of a technology-driven "culture of control."

In conclusion, this emerging technological culture of control poses both positive and negative outcome potentials. Various new forms of technology can be used to produce more refined forms of control and regulation for offenders and citizens alike that are capable of not only negative and unintended consequences but also of being used in a manner that produces maximum desired results with minimum imposition. Technology makes it possible to control subjects in more discerning, less heavy-handed ways. Greater technological control capacities need not always result in more control. Rather, it depends on the uses to which these technologies are put, which depends, in turn, on the pressure that is placed on the control agents and technological methods to be used so that they are in accord with our civil liberties and social values. Consequently, systematic and responsible research is fundamental if we are to maximize the positive and minimize the negative potentials associated with the uses and impacts of these technologies in our fast changing culture of control (Garland, 2004).

◢ References

Austin, James and Barry Krisberg 1981 Wider, stronger and different nets: The dialectics of criminal justice reform. *Journal of Research in Crime and Delinquency* 18:165–196.

Austin, James, John Irwin, and Charis E. Kubrin 2003 It's about time: America's imprisonment binge. In Thomas G. Blomberg and Stanley Cohen (eds.). *Punishment and Social Control.* 2d ed. New York; Aldine de Gruyter,

Ball, Richard A., Ronald C. Huff, and J. Robert Lilly 1988 *House Arrest and Correctional Policy: Doing Time at Home.* Newbury Park, Calif.: Sage.

Baumer, Terry L. and Robert I. Mendelsohn 1992 Electronically monitored home confinement- Does it work? In James M. Byrne, Arthur J. Lurigio, and Joan Petersilia (eds.), *Smart Sentencing: The Emergence of Intermediate Sanctions.* Newbury Park, Calif: Sage.

Baumer, Terry L., Michael G. Maxfield. and Robert I. Mendelsohn 1995 A comparative analysis of three electronically monitored home detention programs. *Justice Quarterly* 10: 121–142.

Beck, James, Jody Klien-Saffran, and Harold B. Wooten 1990 Home confinement and the use of electronic monitoring with federal parolees. *Federal Probation* 54:22–31.

Berry, Bonnie 1985 Electronic jails: A new criminal justice concern. *Justice Quarterly* 2:1–22.

Blomberg, Thomas G. 1977 Diversion and accelerated social control. *Journal of Criminal Law and Criminology* 68:274–282.

Blomberg, Thomas G. and Karol Lucken 1994 Stacking the deck by piling up sanctions: Is intermediate punishment destined to fail? *The Howard Journal* 33:62–80.

Blomberg, Thomas G. and Gordon P. Waldo 1987 Criminal justice reform and social control: Are we becoming a minimum security society? In John Lowman, Robert J. Menzies, and T. S. Palys (eds.). *Transcarceration: Essays in the Sociology of Social Control.* England: Gower Press.

Blomberg, Thomas G., William Bales, and Karen Reed 1993. Intermediate punishment: Redistributing or extending social control? *Crime, Law, and Social Change* 19:187–201.

Blomberg, Thomas G., Gordon P. Waldo, and Lisa C. Burcroff 1987 Home confinement and electronic surveillance. In Belinda R. McCarthy (ed.), *Intermediate Punishments: Intensive Supervision. Home Confinement and Electronic Surveillance.* Issues in Criminal Justice. Vol. 2. London: Willow Press.

Blumstein, Alfred 1998 U.S. criminal justice conundrum: Rising prison populations and stable crime rates. *Crime & Delinquency* 44:127–135.

Bonta, James, Suzanne Wallace-Captretta, and Jennifer Rooney 2000a Can electronic monitoring make a difference? An evaluation of three Canadian programs. *Crime & Delinquency* 46:61–75.

_____ 2000b A quasi-experimental evaluation of an intensive rehabilitation supervision program. *Criminal Justice and Behavior* 27:312–329.

Brooks, Murray 2005 Personal correspondence.

Brown, Michael P. and Preston Elrod 1995 Electronic house arrest: An examination of citizen attitudes. *Crime & Delinquency* 41:332–346.

Burton, Susan E., Matthew Finn, Debra Livingston, Kristen Scully, William D. Bales, and Kathy Padgett 2004 Applying a crime seriousness scale to measure changes in the severity of offenses by individuals arrested in Florida. *Justice Research and Policy* 6:1–18.

Cadigan Timothy P. 1991 Electronic monitoring in federal pretrial release. *Federal Probation* 55:26–30.

Clear, Todd and Anthony A. Braga 1995 Community corrections. In James Q. Wilson and Joan Petersilia (eds.), *Crime: Twenty-eight Leading Experts Look at the Most Pressing Problem of our Time.* San Francisco, Calif.: Institute for Contemporary Studies.

Clear, Todd and George F. Cole 2003 *American Corrections.* 6th ed. Belmont, Calif.: Thomson-Wadsworth.

Clear, Todd, Matthew White, and Kristen Presnell 1998 The offender in the community: Implications of the experience in the United States for the New Czech Republic. *Crime, Law and Social Change* 28:3–4, 243–268.

Cooprider, Keith W. and Judith Kerby 1990 Practical application of electronic monitoring at the pretrial stage. *Federal Probation* 54:28–35.

Corbett, Ronald and Gary T. Marx 1991 Critique: No soul in the new machine: Technofallacies in the electronic monitoring movement. *Justice Quarterly* 8:399–414.

Courtright, Kevin E., Bruce L. Berg, and Robert J. Mutchnick 1997 Effects of house arrest with electronic monitoring on DUI offenders. *Journal of Offender Rehabilitation* 24:35–51.

Erez, Edna, Peter R. Ibarra, and Norman A. Lurie 2004 Electronic monitoring of domestic violence cases: A study of two bilateral programs. *Federal Probation* 68:15–20.

Erwin, Billie S. 1990 Old and new tools for the modern probation officer. *Crime & Delinquency* 36:61–74.

Finn, Mary A. and Suzanne Muirhead-Steves 2002 The effectiveness of electronic monitoring with violent male parolees *Justice Quarterly* 19:293–312.

Florida Department of Corrections 2001 *A Report on Community Control, Radio Frequency (RF) Monitoring and Global Positioning Satellite (GPS) Monitoring: October 2001.* Tallahassee, FL: Florida Department of Corrections, Bureau of Research and Data Analysis.

_____ 2003 *A Report on Community Control, Radio Frequency (RF) Monitoring and Global Positioning Satellite (GPS) Monitoring: October 2003.* Tallahassee, FL: Florida Department of Corrections, Bureau of Research and Data Analysis.

_____ 2005 *Monthly Status Report.* Tallahassee, FL: Florida Department of Corrections, Bureau of Research and Data Analysis.

Frazier, Charles E. and Soon Rae Lee 1992 Reducing juvenile detention rates or expanding the official control nets: An evaluation of a legislative reform effort. *Crime & Delinquency* 38:204.

Gainey, Randy R. and Brian K. Payne 2003 Changing attitudes toward house arrest with electronic monitoring: The impact of a single presentation. *Journal of Offender Therapy and Comparative Criminology* 47:196–209.

Gainey, Randy R., Brian K. Payne, and Mike O'Toole 2000 The relationship between time in jail, time on electronic monitoring, and recidivism: An event history analysis of a jail-based program. *Justice Quarterly* 17:733–752.

Garland, David 2004 Personal correspondence.

Gendreau, Paul, Claire Goggin, Francis T. Cullen, and Donald A. Andrews 2000 The effects of community sanctions and incarceration on recidivism. *Forum on Corrections Research* 12:10–13.

Gowen, Daren 2001 Remote location monitoring: A supervision strategy to enhance. *Federal Probation* 65:38–41.

Hylton, John 1982 Rhetoric and reality: A critical appraisal of community corrections programmes. *Crime & Delinquency* 28:341–373.

Johnson, Byron R., Linda Haugen, Jerry W. Maness, and Paul P. Ross 1989 Attitudes toward electronic monitoring of offenders: A study of probation officers and prosecutors. *Journal of Contemporary Criminal Justice* 5:153–164.

Jolin, Annette and Brian Stipak 1992 Drug treatment and electronically monitored home confinement: An evaluation of a community-based sentencing option. *Crime & Delinquency* 38:158–170.

Klein, Malcolm W. 1979 Deinstitutionalization and diversion of juvenile offenders: A litany of impediments. In Norval Morris and Michael Tonry (eds), *Crime and Justice: An Annual Review of Research.* Chicago, IL: The University of Chicago Press.

Lemert, Edwin M. 1981 Diversion in juvenile justice: What hath been wrought. *Journal of Research in Crime and Delinquency* 18:34–46.

_____ 1993 Vision of social control: Probation considered. *Crime & Delinquency* 39:447–461.

Lianos, Michalis 2003 Social control after Foucault. *Surveillance and Society* 1:412–430.

Lilly, J. Robert, Richard A. Ball, G. David Curry, and John McMullen 1993 Electronic monitoring of the drunk driver: A seven-year study of the home confinement alternative. *Crime & Delinquency* 39:462–484.

Lucken, Karol 1997 Privatizing discretion: "Rehabilitating" treatment in community corrections. *Crime & Delinquency* 43:243–259.

Mainprize, Stephen 1992 Electronic monitoring in corrections: Assessing cost effectiveness and the potential for widening the net of social control. *Canadian Journal of Criminology* 34:161–180.

McMahon, Maeve 1990 Net-Widening: Vagaries of the use of a concept. *The British Journal of Criminology* 30:121–149.

Morris, Norval and Michael Tonry 1990 *Between Prison and Probation: Intermediate Punishments in a Rational Sentencing System.* New York: Oxford University Press.

Mortimer, E., and C. May 1997 *Electronic Monitoring in Practice: The Second Year of the Trials of Curfew Orders.* London: Home Office Research and Statistics Directorate.

Ontario 1991 *An Evaluation of the Electronic Monitoring Pilot Project: Mimico Correctional Centre, April 1989-October 1990.* North Bay, Canada: Ministry of Correctional Services of Ontario.

Payne, Brian K. and Randy R. Gainey 1999 Attitudes toward electronic monitoring among monitored offenders and criminal justice students. *Journal of Offender Rehabilitation* 29:195–208.

_____ 2000 Electronic monitoring: Philosophical, systemic, and political issues. *Journal of Offender Rehabilitation* 31:93–111.

Petersilia, Joan and Susan Turner 1990 Comparing intensive and regular supervision for high risk probationers. *Crime & Delinquency* 36:87–111.

Renzema, Marc 1991 The scope of electronic monitoring today. *Journal of Offender Monitoring* 4:6–11.

_____ 1992 Home confinement programs: Development, implementation, and impact. In James M. Byrne, Arthur J. Lurigio, and Joan Petersilia (eds.), *Smart Sentencing: The Emergence of Intermediate Sanctions.* Newbury Park, Calif: Sage.

_____ 2003 *Electronic Monitoring's Impact on Reoffending.* Revised March 24, 2003. Retrieved August, 2005. Available online: http//www.campbellcollaboration.org/doc-pdf/elec-monpdf.

Renzema, Marc and Evan Mayo-Wilson 2005 Can electronic monitoring reduce crime for moderate to high-risk offenders? *Journal of Experimental Criminology* 1:215–237.

Roy, Sudipto 1997 Five years of electronic monitoring of adults and juveniles in Lake County, Indiana: A comparative study on factors related to failure. *Journal of Crime and Justice* 20:141–160.

Schmidt, Annesley K. 1991 Electronic monitors: Realistically, what can be expected? *Federal Probation* 55:47–53.

SPEC Associates 2002 *Final evaluation report: Michigan department of correction's GPS pilot phase II.* Detroit, Michigan.

Stanz, Robert and Richard Tewksbury 2000 Predictors of success and recidivism in a home incarceration program. *The Prison Journal* 80:326–344.

Sugg, Darren, Louise Moore, and Philip Howard 2000 *Electronic monitoring and offending behavior: Reconviction results for the second year of trials of curfew orders.* London: Home Office Research, Development and Statistics Directorate.

Taxman, Faye S., and Lori Elis 1999 Expediting court dispositions: Quick results, uncertain outcomes. *Journal of Research in Crime and Delinquency* 36:30–55.

Tonry, Michael, and Michael J. Lynch 1995 Intermediate sanctions. In Michael Tonry (ed), *Crime and Justice: A Review of Research.* Vol. 20. Chicago, IL: University of Chicago Press.

Ulmer, Jeffrey T. 2001 Intermediate sanctions: A comparative analysis of the probability and severity of recidivism. *Sociological Inquiry* 71:164–193.

Vaughn, Joseph P. 1987 Planning for change: The use of electronic monitoring as a correctional alternative. In Belinda R. McCarthy (ed.), *Intermediate Punishments: Intensive Supervision, Home Confinement and Electronic Surveillance.* Issues in Criminal Justice. Vol. 2. London: Willow Press.

Vollum, Scott, and Chris Hale 2002 Electronic monitoring: A research review. *Correction Compendium* 27:1–1, 23–26, 27.

Wallers, R. 1996 Alternatives to youth imprisonment: Evaluating the Victorian youth attendance order. *The Australian and New Zealand Journal of Criminology* 29:166.

Whittingdon, Marie 1987 *Supervised Electronic Confinement Pilot Program October 1986-September 1987: Final Report.* Santa Ana, Calif.: Orange County Probation Department.

DISCUSSION QUESTIONS

1. According to the findings of this study, are there any differences in RF supervision versus GPS? Explain your response.

2. What are the pros and cons of using GPS and/or RF systems to supervise offenders in the community?

3. The authors discuss the impact of the increased use of EM on net widening both at the front and back end of the system. According to the results of this study, how does EM impact the net-widening of the system?

4. Because of the analytical methodology used in this study, the authors were unable to track the offenders post-supervision. Are there any potential problems with generalizing these findings to the population? Why or why not?

5. The authors offer three policy implications for the use of EM. Identify and discuss these three policy implications. How might these implications inform EM practices in your state/jurisdiction?

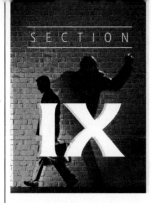

IX

Parole Management, Case Planning, and Reentry

Learning Objectives

1. Know and understand the basics regarding state **parole**, its organization, and its administration.

2. Be able to discuss the parole selection process, factors influencing parole decisions, and factors considered when granting and denying parole.

3. Know some of the subjective and objective inputs (including both victim impact statements as well as the **salient factor score**) that are included in the parole decision-making process.

4. Demonstrate knowledge of the entire supervision process from prerelease planning to the successful termination of parole supervision.

5. Be aware of the common conditions of parole and understand how parole effectiveness can be refined and adjusted to better meet supervision requirements that are based on the offender's behavior.

6. Understand how restorative justice paradigms can organize victim input and participation in the justice process, offender accountability in the reintegrative process, and community involvement in the supervision process.

Parole, as a mechanism for early release, is a function that has been eliminated at the federal level and has also been eliminated in many states throughout the nation. Nevertheless, a substantial number of inmates are released on parole throughout the Untied States, with some still serving sentences under the outdated federal system. Parole can be defined as the early release of an offender from a secure facility upon completion of a certain portion of his or her sentence As of 2008, the nation's parole population included 828,169 offenders, with mandatory releases from prison due to state statutes or good time provisions accounting for just over 49% of all entries, while only 27.6% were for discretionary release (Glaze & Bonczar, 2009). Because parolees comprise a significant portion of those offenders in the community, it is important to understand the historical development of parole, the current state of parole, its administration, types of parole, parole revocation, and liability of parole board members.

The Beginning of Parole

Two primary figures are attributed to the development of parole: Alexander Maconochie and Sir Walter Crofton. Alexander Maconochie was in charge of the penal colony at Norfolk Island, and Sir Walter Crofton directed the prison system of Ireland. While Maconochie first developed a general scheme for parole, it was Sir Walter Crofton who later refined the idea and created what was referred to as the **ticket-of-leave**. The ticket-of-leave was basically a permit that was given to a convict in exchange for a certain period of good conduct. Through this process, the convict could instead earn his own wage through his own labor prior to the expiration of his actual sentence. In addition, other liberties were provided so long as the convict's behavior remained within the lawful limits set by the ticket-of-leave system. The ticket-of-leave system is therefore often considered the antecedent to the development of parole.

During the 1600s and 1700s, England implemented a form of punishment known as banishment on a widespread scale. During this time, criminals were sent to the American colonies under reprieve and through stays of execution. Thus, the convicts had their lives spared, but this form of mercy was generally only implemented to solve a labor shortage that existed within the American colonies. Essentially, the convicts were shipped to the Americas to work as indentured servants under hard labor. However, the war of independence within the colonies put an end to this practice until 1788 when the first shipload of convicts were transported to Australia. Australia was the new dumping ground for convicts who were used as labor just as had been the case in the Americas. The labor was hard, and the living conditions were challenging. However, a ticket-of-leave system was developed on this continent in which different governors had the authority to release convicts that displayed good and stable conduct.

In 1837, Alexander Maconochie, a captain in the Royal Navy, was placed in command over the English penal colony in New South Wales at Norfolk Island, which was nearly 1,000 miles off the eastern coast of Australia. The convicts at Norfolk Island were the worst of the worst since they had already been shipped to Australia for criminal acts in England, only to be later shipped to Norfolk Island due to additional criminal acts or forms of misconduct that were committed while serving time in Australia. The conditions on Norfolk Island were deplorable—so much so that many convicts preferred to be given the death penalty rather than serve time upon the island (Latessa & Allen, 1999).

While serving in this command, Maconochie proposed a system where the duration of the sentence was determined by the inmate's work habits and their righteous conduct. Though this was already used in a crude manner through the ticket-of-leave process in Australia, Maconochie created a **mark system** in which "marks" would be provided to the convict for each day of successful toil. His system was quite well organized and thought out, being based on five main tenets, as described by Barnes and Teeters (1959):

1. Release should not be based on the completing of a sentence for a set period of time, but on completion of a determined and specified quantity of labor. In brief, time sentences should be abolished and task sentences substantiated.

2. The quantity of labor a prison must perform should be expressed in a number of "marks" which he must earn, by improvement of conduct, frugality of living, and habits of industry, before he can be released.

3. While in prison he should earn everything he receives. All sustenance and indulgences should be added to his debt of marks.

4. When qualified by discipline to do so, he should work in association with a small number of other prisoners, forming a group of six or seven, and the whole group should be answerable for the conduct of labor of each member.

5. In the final stage, a prisoner, while still obliged to earn his daily tally of marks, should be given a proprietary interest in his own labor and be subject to a less rigorous discipline, to prepare him for release into society. (p. 419)

Under this plan, convicts were given marks and moved through phases of supervision until they finally earned full release. Because of this, Maconochie's system is considered indeterminate in nature, with convicts progressing through five specific phases of classification. These phases included the following: (1) strict incarceration, (2) intense labor in forced work group or chain gang, (3) limited freedom within a prescribed area, (4) a ticket-of-leave, and (5) full freedom. This system, as devised by Maconochie, was based on the premise that inmates should be gradually prepared for full release. It is apparent that Maconochie's system utilized versions of intermediate sanctions and **indeterminate sentencing**. Indeterminate sentencing is sentencing that includes a range of years that will be potentially served by the offender. The offender is released during some point in the range of years that are assigned by the sentencing judge. Both the minimum and maximum times can be modified by a number of factors such as offender behavior and offender work ethic. The indeterminate sentence stands in contrast to the use of **determinate sentencing**, which consists of fixed periods of incarceration imposed on the offender with no later flexibility in the term that is served. This type of sentencing is grounded in notions of retribution, just deserts, and incapacitation. Due to the use of indeterminate sentencing and primitive versions of intermediate sanctioning, Maconochie's mark system is perhaps best thought of as a precursor to parole as well as the use of classification systems. In fact, the use of classification systems tended to be underdeveloped. Thus Maconochie provided a guide in predicting likelihood of success with convicts, making him a man who was well ahead of his time.

However, Maconochie appears to have been too far ahead of his time; many government officials and influential persons in both Australia and England believed that Maconochie's approach was too soft on criminals. His methods of reform drew increasing negative publicity from Australian and English citizens who perceived the system as being too lenient on convicts. Ironically, this is not much different from today where the common consensus among Americans is that prisons and punitive sanctions are preferred forms of punishment. Contrarily, Maconochie was fond of criticizing prison operations in England, his own belief being that confinement ought to be rehabilitative in nature rather than punitive (note that this is consistent with the insights of John Augustus and his views on the use of probation). Maconochie's ideas were not popular among government officials of the Crown nor the general populace of England, and he ultimately was dismissed from his post on Norfolk Island as well as other commands for being too lenient with convicts. Nevertheless, Maconochie was persistent, and in 1853, he successfully lobbied the **English Penal Servitude Act**, which established several rehabilitation programs for convicts.

The English Penal Servitude Act of 1853 applied to prisons in both England and Ireland. Though Maconochie had spearheaded this act to solidify, legalize, and make permanent the use of ticket-of-leave systems, the primary reason for this act's success had more to do with the fact that free Australians were becoming ever more resistant to the use of Australia as the location for banished English convicts. Though this act did not necessarily eliminate the use of banishment in England, it did provide incentive and suggestions for more extensive use of prisons. This law provided guidelines for the length of time that inmates should serve behind bars before being granted a ticket-of-leave. The law also included the power to revoke their license; the opportunity to remain in the community as long as they were conduct free; and that forfeiture of the license could occur for associating with those of bad character, the inability to obtain an honest living, etc., not just a new offense (Cromwell, Del Carmen, & Alarid, 2002, p. 166). It should be clear that these guidelines form the basis of modern-day parole. Because of this and other significant improvements in penal policies in England, as well as his contributions to early release provisions in England, Maconochie has been dubbed the father of parole.

During the 1850s, Sir Walter Crofton was the director of the Irish penal system. Naturally, since the English Penal Servitude Act of 1853 was passed during his term of office, he was aware of the changes implemented in prison operations, and he was likewise aware of Maconochie's ideas. Crofton used Maconochie's ideas to create a classification system that proved useful and workable within the Irish prison system. This classification system utilized three stages of treatment. The first stage placed the convict in segregated confinement with work and training being provided to the offender. The second stage was a transition period whereby the convict was set to the task of completing public work projects while under minimal supervision. During the third stage, and presuming that the offender proved reliable, he was eventually released on "license" (Dressler, 1962; Latessa & Allen, 1999).

In implementing this classification system, each inmate's classification level was specifically measured by the number of marks that they had earned for good conduct, work output, and educational achievement. This idea was, quite naturally, borrowed from Maconochie's system on Norfolk Island. It is also important to point out that the Irish system developed by Sir Walter Crofton was also much more detailed, providing specific written instructions and guidelines that provided for close supervision and control of the offender, using police personnel to supervise released offenders in rural areas and an inspector of released prisoners in the city of Dublin (Petersilia, 2003).

Release on license was contingent upon certain conditions, with violations of these conditions providing for the possibility of reimprisonment. "While on license, prisoners were required to submit to monthly reports and were warned against idleness and association with other criminals" (Latessa & Smith, 2007, p. 142). Thus, offenders released on license did have to report to either a police officer or other designated person, they had specific requirements that they had to meet, they had to curtail their social involvements, and they could be again incarcerated if they did not maintain those requirements (Latessa & Smith, 2007). This obviously resembled several aspects of modern-day parole programs. In fact, the impetus for parole in the United States was a paper delivered by Sir Walter Crofton at the 1870 National Prison Association annual meeting in Cincinnati. The results of this presentation were the incorporation of ideals of indeterminate sentencing and classification into the principles. Reformers ultimately coined the U.S. parole system as the "Irish System" (Petersilia, 2003, p. 58).

In 1876, Zebulon Brockway, warden of the Elmira, New York, prison facility for young men ages 16 to 30, first began incorporating these principles into practice in what he deemed a graded system of rewards and punishment. All offenders entered the prison at the second grade of classification. Inmates who behaved correctly for 6 months were moved up to first grade classification. Those who misbehaved or were disruptive could be moved down to third grade classification. An inmate who remained in the first grade classification could be released early under the jurisdiction of the authorities for 6 months whereby they were "required to report on the first day of every month to his appointed volunteer guardian" (Petersilia, 2003, p. 58). In 1927, New York became the first state to formally pass a law adopting all components of parole. "By 1927, only three states (Florida, Mississippi, and Virginia) were without a parole system, and by 1942, all of the states and the federal government had such systems" (Petersilia, 2003, p. 58). These mechanisms for release were based on discretionary decisions by the prison facility and the warden. Parole boards were instituted in the early 1900s to assist with these decisions. The implementation of parole, although progressive, has always been met with skepticism. Studies dating back to the 1930s report that American citizens believed parole was too lenient on offenders. As Rothman (1980) noted, the original parole board members made these discretionary release decisions based upon the seriousness of the offense and their institutional eligibility as opposed to readiness to reenter society. The move away from any form of rehabilitative ideal has become apparent with the abolition of discretionary release (parole) in 15 states and the federal government as it was originally intended. Most states still maintain some form of supervision following release but the release is mandatory less good time credits.

Good time credits allow for the early release of an offender based upon good behavior. These credits range from 1 day off for 1 day served to as much as 2 days off for 1 day served. The federal sentencing guidelines restrict good time to 85% of the sentence being served. This process of receiving credits for good behavior very closely resembles that used in the earliest forms of marks in the Irish system and that used by Brockway at the Elmira Reformatory. Merit credit time is another variation of this process that rewards offenders for program completion. In Indiana, for example, offenders can earn up to 6 months' early release per qualified program completion for things such as an educational degree (including the GED) substance abuse programming, cognitive programming, etc. Following release on a fixed sentence, all but sex offenders are supervised on parole for a maximum of 2 years not to exceed the original sentence. Sex offenders, when released, are required to be supervised for up to 10 years not to exceed the original sentence. Offenders receiving no time off for good behavior are required to serve their maximum fixed time with no supervised community release.

As you recall from Section VI, the focus of removing offenders from institutions centered on the rehabilitative ideal or the medical model (1930s to 1950s). This line of reasoning was followed by the community-oriented and reintegration efforts. The mid- to late 1970s saw a slowly emerging shift take place due to high crime rates that were primarily perceived as being the result of high recidivism rates among offenders. As you recall from Section IV, Robert Martinson's (1974) article stated that "with few and isolated exceptions, the rehabilitative efforts that have been reported so far have had no appreciable effect on recidivism" and served as an impetus for this shift (p. 22).

From this point forward, there was a clear shift from a community model of corrections to what has been referred to as a **crime control model of corrections.** During the late 1970s and throughout the 1980s, crime became a hotly debated topic that often became intertwined with political agendas and legislative action. The sour view of rehabilitation led many states to abolish the use of parole. Indeed, from 1976 onward, 15 states and the federal government abolished the use of parole. The state of Maine abolished parole in 1976, followed by California's elimination of discretionary parole in 1978, and the full elimination of parole in Arizona (1994), Delaware (1990), Illinois (1978), Indiana (1977), Kansas (1993), Minnesota (1980), Mississippi (1995), North Carolina (1994), Ohio (1996), Oregon (1989), Virginia (1995), Washington (1984), and Wisconsin (1999) (Petersilia, 2003, pp. 66–67; Sieh, 2006). In addition, the federal system of parole was also phased out over time. Under the Comprehensive Crime Control Act of 1984, the U.S. Parole Commission only retained jurisdiction over offenders who had committed their offense prior to November 1, 1987. At the same time, the act provided for the abolition of the Parole Commission over the years that followed, with this phasing out period being extended by the Parole Commission Phaseout Act of 1996. The Parole Commission Phaseout Act of 1996 extended the life of the Parole Commission until November 1, 2002, but only in regard to supervising offenders who were still on parole from previous years. Thus, though the U.S. Parole Commission continued to exist, continued use of parole was eliminated, and federal parole offices across the nation were slowly shut down over time (see Focus Topic 9.1 for further information on various developments in parole).

Focus Topic 9.1

Historical Developments in Parole

1840   Maconochie creates his "mark system" in Australian penal colony.

1854   Sir Walter Crofton establishes the ticket-of-leave system in Ireland.

1869   New York establishes indeterminate sentencing processes.

1870   The American Prison Association publicly endorses parole.

1976   Maine abolishes parole.

1984   Federal government abolishes granting additional forms of parole leniency.

1999   The state of Wisconsin becomes the 15th state to formally abolish parole.

In addition to the eventual elimination of parole, many states implemented determinate sentencing laws, truth-in-sentencing laws, and other such innovations that were designed to keep offenders behind bars for longer periods of time. The obvious flavor of corrections in the 1980s was toward crime control through incarceration and risk containment (Clear & Cole, 2003). This same crime control orientation continued through the 1990s and even through the beginning of the new millennium, with greater emphasis on drug offenders and habitual offenders during the 1990s. Also noted were developments in intensive supervision probation (ISP), more stringent bail requirements, and the use of three strikes penalties. The period during the last half of the 1990s and beyond the year 2000 had a decidedly punitive approach. The costs (both economic and social) have received a great deal of scrutiny even though crime rates had lowered during the new millennium. Though there was a dip in crime during this time, it was not necessarily made clear if this was, in actuality, due to the higher rate of imprisonment or due to other demographic factors that impacted the nation.

⊠ State of Parole Today

The state of parole and the characteristics of the population serving under that sanction have gone through some noticeable fluctuations and changes. For instance, while the parolee population has continued to grow each year from 1980 to 2008, this sanction experienced the highest rate of growth between the years of 1980 to 1990 during which time the number of entries to state parole supervision more than tripled, going from 113,400 to 349,000 parolees. These state parole entries continued to rise during the 1990s while parole discharges also increased during that same time period. Nevertheless, an overall growth pattern in the number of parolees released in the community continued to occur. However, during the years 2000 to 2008, the number of state parole cases that entered into the parole phase of supervision consistently exceeded the number of parolees that exited the system. All in all, the average percentage increase in state parolees has only been around 1.7% annually. As of 2008, the nation's parole population included 828,169 offenders, of which 91,395 were federal probationers (Glaze & Bonczar, 2009).

Among the parolee population, roughly 1 out of 8 (or about 12%) are female offenders. During the past decade, the proportion of female parolees has increased from 10% to 12%, making this a 20% increase in the proportion of female offenders represented in the parolee population. In addition, the percentage of parolees who are African American tends to be around 38%, with a slight downward trend having been noted during the past decade or so (in 1995, African American offenders made up 45% of the parolee population). Contrastly, the proportion of white American offenders has increased during the past several years, coming to 41% of the overall parole population. Roughly 19% of all parolees nationwide are Latino, with another 2% in other racial categories. Lastly, the largest percentage of parolees were convicted of drug offenses with 37% of the total parolee population having some drug-related conviction. Twenty six percent of all parolees had violent offenses while 23% had property offenses (Glaze & Bonczar, 2009).

As with probation, parole has differing levels of supervision. Roughly speaking, one can divide parole conditions between those that require active supervision and those that do not. Active supervision requires parolees to routinely report to their parole officer through personal contact, via mail, or by telephone. Active supervision is used with roughly 85% of all parolees, and this statistic has remained stable over time. On the other hand, parolees on inactive status are still carried on the caseload, but they are not required to report to their parole officers. Only about 4% of all parolees are placed on this type of release, making this a small group of offenders who are the least likely to pose any serious public safety risk. In addition, roughly 6% of all parolees have absconded during a given year. Lastly, during the past 10 to 12 years, the percentage of parolees who have successfully met the conditions of their parole sentencing requirements has remained stable at around 48%. However, this is lower than the rate of success that probationers have; probationers successfully completed the terms of their probation sentence in about 60% of all cases.

⚅ Tasks and Nature of Work for Parole Officers

First, it is important to note that parole differs from probation in some very distinct ways. The offender on parole has served a portion of his or her sentence in a correctional facility. This alone can have an impact on the type of security that must be maintained as well as the issues associated with reintegration. In these cases, the offender will likely need more support services since they have been subject to the effects of prisonization. For the most part, probationers have only served brief stints in jail and therefore do not tend to suffer the same level of emotional shock when introduced back into the free world. For the ex-prison inmate, it may have been years since they have seen their area of origin, family members, and/or friends. Spouses may have abandoned them, they may be cut off from much of their family, and progress in society may have drastically changed workforce requirements and/or other issues.

▲ **Photo 9.1** Two parole officers discuss their schedule for the upcoming week in an effort to maximize their field and office work. They work as partners in supervising a specified area (called a zone) of the city.

Latessa and Allen (1999) noted that in one study it was found that parole officers tend to review their caseloads in an effort to identify the presence of offenders that seem unpredictable and/or irrational. These offenders are likely to be more dangerous and in need of added supervision since they do not respond to threats or promises made by the supervision agency in a rational manner. In this regard, it would seem that parole officers tend to view their role as being one primarily concerned with public safety.

In many states, such as Colorado, Louisiana, and elsewhere, community parole officers are also Peace Officer Standards and Training (POST) certified. This is, quite naturally, similar to the previous discussion related to probation officers, where much of the training is similar to that provided to law enforcement. Parole officers must maintain offender records, and they often must maintain automated information systems that manage inmate records.

Unlike probation officers, parole officers almost always tend to work for the state, and they do not answer to a judge or set of judges. The parole office is an extension of the correctional system and is therefore run by the executive branch of the government. This makes for a less stressful situation since there tends to be much more uniformity in operations for parole officers. Also, parole officer caseloads tend to be a bit lighter than are encountered among probation officers. Though these caseloads are still challenging and are often considered too high to manage, they do still tend to be lower than those for probation officers. However, one thing should be kept in mind: All of the offenders on a parole officer's caseload tend to have more serious offenses than is the case for probation officers.

Essentially, the work of a parole officer is very similar to that of a probation officer; it is perhaps for this reason that the functions are combined among several state systems. Nevertheless, parolees are a distinct group from probationers, and in many states, they are supervised separately. Even though this may be true, the tasks performed by both types of supervision are fairly similar. Beyond this general description, parole officers in Colorado, Kansas, Louisiana, New Mexico, Pennsylvania, and elsewhere may conduct a pre-parole investigation (PPI) for the purpose of determining the suitability of an inmate's proposed parole plan. Such an investigation may include an examination of the proposed living conditions, the type of community surroundings, the plans for employment, input from regional law enforcement, as well as explanations from the person that has agreed to sponsor the parolee. This is somewhat similar to the presentence investigation report (PSI) that was noted when examining the job functions of probation officers.

In addition, just as with probation officers, parole officers make personal contact with the parolees on their caseload, though there is often a great deal of caution associated with this aspect of the supervision process. This is especially true in the states of Kansas and Texas where lower-ranking parole officers are given less discretion when conducting their jobs. In these cases, low-ranking parole officers may be assisted or directed by a higher-ranking parole officer, particularly when field visits and/or other tasks may be conducted in high danger areas of the state.

Though many parole officers view themselves as performing an enforcement function, many find themselves addressing issues such as marital discord, financial troubles, housing challenges, placement with vocational and/or educational training, referral for mental health counseling, as well as providing appropriate referrals to community service agencies for the previously mentioned issues as well as others that may emerge. Naturally, this resembles a casework function that has been similarly noted in Section VI. These parole officers will take reports from the parolees themselves and will also verify the validity of these reports by checking with employers, family, and other sources that have contact with the parolee.

As would be expected, the parole officer, by virtue of his or her job assignment, assumes responsibility for the proper maintenance of the offenders assigned to their caseload and is expected to ensure that offenders comply with the rules and regulations of their parole requirements. When violations are detected, these officers will be required to complete incident reports for major violations of parole conditions, but they may exercise some degree of discretion in the case of technical violations (technical violations are those that do not result in a new criminal offense but are noncompliant actions). It is the parole officer who typically makes the decision to issue a warrant for parole violations, which result in the offender being sent back to prison.

Parole officers, like probation officers, will frequently make regular and special home visits to the offender's domicile. The parole officer will also visit the parolee's family members, sometimes in separate circumstances and sometimes jointly. As noted with probation officers, this can be an unpleasant experience even if the family is welcoming and compliant. In many cases, the neighborhood will be able to identify the parole officer (particularly if they are driving a state-owned vehicle with state markings), and in criminogenic neighborhoods, it is often the case that local community members consider the parole officer's presence to be a bother or an intrusion. Aside from field visits, parole officers may visit prison facilities for the purpose of establishing personal contact with prospective parolees who will soon be released. Such decisions will often be made by what is referred to as an institutional parole officer (referred to as a facility parole officer in the state of New York), who is tasked with assessing inmates within the prison system and making determinations of suitability that go before the state parole board. In other cases, prison classification personnel may make this determination and will fill the role that institutional parole officers would perform.

Lastly and very important, parole officers will usually be expected to maintain an open line of communication with the law enforcement community in the area. This is also similar to the functions of probation officers but also reflects the need for collaborative functions between agencies, as discussed previously. However, this is an especially important function for parole officers, particularly in areas where released offenders may be prior or—unbeknownst to correctional staff—current gang members. Because gang offenders tend to recycle in and out of prison systems—going into the community, committing an offense, getting placed back in prison, and then again being paroled—this can have a revolving-door effect that is observed both by parole officers and police officers who routinely arrest and rearrest these offenders. Parole officers may also be instrumental in overseeing gang exit programs so that youth can safely and permanently break away from gang membership. Regardless, it is clear that parole officers (typically called aftercare officers when dealing with juvenile offenders) work closely with police in cases where this is beneficial or a necessity. This also fits with the self-image that parole officers tend to have of themselves where their primary function is one of enforcement and ensuring compliance among their parolee caseload.

⊠ Education, Training, and Qualifications for Parole Officers

For the most part, the education and qualifications for parole officers are similar (if not identical) to probation officers. Parole officers typically must have a bachelor's degree in criminology, criminal justice, social work, psychology, counseling, sociology, or some other related field. In addition, many areas of the nation (such as the state of New York) also require 3 to 5 years of relevant work experience in casework or some other related area of employment. In addition, most states require parole officers to be at least 21 years of age and also require the applicant to successfully pass a civil service examination.

Naturally, candidates must prove eligible through a full background investigation and after psychological screening. Depending on the specific state, the psychological screening can be quite extensive. Consider the state of Ohio, where a series of three personality tests are given to prospective parole officer candidates along with an in-depth interview. The assessment process is conducted by contract psychologists who either recommend the candidate for employment, recommend with reservations, or (when the applicant is not suitable) decide not to recommend the applicant for any future employment whatsoever.

Training for parole officers, as with probation officers, can vary. In states where probation and parole are combined, the training is naturally similar to that discussed with probation officers. Often this may include attendance in paramilitary and/or law enforcement styles of training (such as in the states of Louisiana where such officers are POST certified). In states where parole functions are not combined with probation, training can still require that parole officers be peace officer certified (as with the state of Texas where officers are Texas Commission on Law Enforcement Officer Standards and Education [TCLEOSE] certified). In other states (such as Ohio), parole officers are expected to be distinct from peace officers and thus are not given that capacity of training.

Lastly, as mentioned earlier, there is a growing emphasis on the professionalization of community corrections that includes both probation and parole. The American Probation and Parole Association (APPA) and the American Correctional Association (ACA) have been instrumental in advocating for continued training on everything from the use of technological equipment to understanding unique needs associated with specialized offenders. It is expected that this tendency will continue into the future as community supervision becomes an increasingly important function of the overall criminal justice system.

⊠ When Probation and Parole Are Combined Into One Department

In many states, probation and parole functions are combined. Although numerous states have abolished parole, some residual offender caseloads may exist from before the abolition of this sanction was implemented. The point in mentioning this fact is to illustrate that parole has had a diminished influence on the community corrections research, literature, and training developments since probationers greatly outnumber parolees across the nation and since parole is not even a continued practice in 19 states throughout the country. Thus, probation and parole services are often provided simultaneously, being a combined function in several states. In such states, it is the probation function that tends to consume most of the activities of these agencies that have combined forms of community supervision.

Also, the qualifications, functions, and type of work conducted for both probation and parole officers are very similar in most respects. There are numerous issues that similarly confront probation/parole officers, and because of this, as well as the similarity in functions that each performs, many texts and professional journals refer to these practitioners simply as POs. This text will again revert to using the term **community supervision officer (CSO)** to refer to both groups simultaneously. Throughout the remainder of the text, the term *CSO* will be used interchangeably with the terms *probation officer* and/or *parole officer* to identify persons who work in community supervision agencies and perform the supervision duties that are typically associated with probation and/or parole officers. The exceptions to this use of the term will occur where specific reference is made to parole officers exclusively. Even in these cases, reference may still sometimes be made by using the term *CSO*.

As noted earlier, CSOs do tend to have heavy caseloads, and this tends to impair their ability to effectively supervise offenders. Though CSOs with caseloads restricted only to parolees tend to have smaller caseloads (as mentioned earlier, parole officers tend to have slightly lower caseloads) this does tend to be a minority of the cases among CSOs. Thus, it is clear that caseload issues are a serious source of stress for most officers, and it should also be clear that the management of this caseload may require certain means of adaptation among various CSOs. In this regard, it has been found that CSOs tend to approach their jobs from different vantage points, much of this having to do with their own perceptions of their particular role in the community corrections process. This again ties into the dichotomy between the competing emphases on public safety and offender reintegration.

Daniel Glaser conducted research on parole officers and the orientation by which they approach their job. Glaser (1964) contended that CSOs tend to operate at differing points along two spectrums: (1) offender assistance and (2) offender control. These two spectrums work in seeming contradiction with one another, as they each tend to put officers at cross-purposes when trying to balance their job as reformer and public safety officer. This means that four basic categories emerge that describe the officer's general tendency when supervising offenders. Table 9.1 illustrates both the offender assistance and offender control spectrums as well as the four resultant categories of officer supervision styles.

Table 9.1   Role Orientations of Community Supervision Officers

Assistance Spectrum	Control Spectrum	
	High	**Low**
High	Paternal officer	Welfare worker
Low	Punitive officer	Passive agent

Paternal officers use a great degree of both control and assistance techniques (Clear & Cole, 2003). They protect both the offender and the community by providing the offender with assistance, as well as praising and blaming. This type of officer can seem sporadic at times. These officers are ambivalent to the concerns of the offender or the community; this is just a job that they do. Indeed, these officers may be perceived as being noncommittal by taking the community's side in one case then the offender's in another. The officer does not tend to have a high degree of formal training or secondary education, but they tend to be very experienced and thus are able to weather the difficulties associated with burnout within the field of probation.

Punitive officers see themselves as needing to use threats and punishment in order to get compliance from the offender. These officers may also view the offender as a "lower class" of individual and are likely to see punitive methods of control as the only type of mechanism that the offender population will or can understand. They will likely have a morally judgmental view of their caseload. These officers will place the highest emphasis on control and protection of the public against offenders, and they will also be suspicious of offenders on their caseload. This suspiciousness is not necessarily wrong or unethical however, as this is part and parcel of the supervision of offenders; however, these officers may in fact never be content with the offender's behavior until they find some reason to award some form of punitive sanction. In other words, the view is that those on the caseload are doing wrong but they are just not getting caught. The officer knows this to be true and makes it his or her duty to ensure that the offender gets away with as little as possible. Naturally, human relations between this officer and his or her caseload are usually fairly impaired and sterile.

The **welfare worker** will view the offender more as a client rather than a supervisee on their caseload. These individuals believe that ultimately the best way they can enhance the security and safety of the community is by reforming the offender so that further crime will not occur. These officers will attempt to achieve objectivity that is similar to a therapist and will thus avoid judging the client. These officers will be most inclined to consider the needs of their offender–clients and their potential capacity for change. This officer views their job more as a therapeutic service than a punitive service, though this does not mean that they will not supervise the behavior of their caseload. Rather, the purpose for their supervision is more likened to the follow-up screening that a therapist might provide to a client to ensure that they are continuing on the directed trajectory that is consistent with their prior treatment goals.

The **passive agent** tends to view their job as just that—a job. They will tend to do as little as possible, and they do not have passion for their jobs. Unlike the punitive officer and the welfare worker, they simply do not care about the outcome of their work so long as they avoid any difficulties. These individuals are often in the job simply due to the benefits that it may have as well as the freedom from continual supervision that this type of job affords.

Clear and Cole (2003) noted that it is debatable whether officers would best be served using one consistent type of approach or if they should attempt to use each orientation when they seem appropriate. Thus, the community supervision process can be greatly impacted by the approach taken by the CSO. Further, agencies can transmit a certain tendency toward any of these orientations through policies, procedures, informal organizational culture, or even through daily memos. The tone set by the agency is likely to have an effect on the officer's morale and subsequently their approach to the supervision process.

On the other hand, some agencies may be very clear about their expectations of CSOs. In this case, if the agency has a strict law-and-order flavor, the officer may be best served by utilizing the approach of a punitive officer to ensure that they are a good fit with agency expectations. In another agency, the emphasis might be on a combined restorative/community justice model coupled with community policing efforts that are designed to reintegrate the offender. In an agency such as this, the officer may find that a welfare worker approach is the best fit for that agency and that community. Thus, it is the culture of the community service organization that will have a strong impact upon the officer's orientation, and if the officer's personal or professional views are in conflict with the organizational structure, the likelihood of effective community supervision is impaired. This is an important point because it again comes back to the sense of stress that is encountered among most CSOs.

Beyond the other stressors mentioned earlier in this section, it has been found that much of the stress for CSOs is organizationally generated (Finn & Kuck, 2003). Indeed, it is common for officers to feel that their agency is the primary source of their stress, including the lack of consistency in priorities and orientations that are emphasized. Most telling is the fact that it tends to be the agency rather than the offender population that is the most reported source of stress for CSOs (Finn & Kuck, 2003). The specific organizational culture and the manner by which the organization treats its employees can be very important to ensuring that quality employees are retained and that turnover (which tends to be high in community supervision agencies) is minimized. Excellent research on organizational culture within community supervision agencies was conducted in 2006 by the National Institute of Corrections. This research, led by Stinchcomb, McCampbell, and Layman (2006), points toward the impact that an agency's culture can have on individual officer performance and their approach toward the completion of the job requirements.

Organizational culture is basically the personality of an organization. Just as an individual's personality tends to consist of behavioral tendencies, organizational culture defines and reinforces behaviors that are acceptable and fails to reinforce (or even perhaps punish) those that are not acceptable. Essentially, organizational culture defines how tasks are approached in a particular agency. Naturally, it can be understood that some officer typologies on the control spectrum and the assistance spectrum (see Table 9.1) may or may not fit with different agencies. This can seriously impact agency effectiveness, employee turnover, and offender outcomes.

Agencies that overemphasize a paramilitary approach, place distance between officers and supervisors, emphasize liability evasion, fail to give frequent positive reinforcers, and attempt to exert control will tend to have less loyalty among personnel, higher rates of employee absence, and high rates of turnover. Employee longevity will likely be less than would otherwise exist, and valuable experience will tend to be lost at critical points through employee competence and usefulness to the agency. Thus, when and where possible, agencies should be amenable to the means of coping that individual officers may take to adapt to their dichotomous roles of law enforcer and caseworker.

⊠ Firearms and the Community Supervision Officer

Similar to the proceeding discussion, the agency's emphasis on law enforcement functions can be seen in its policy orientation toward the use of firearms. However, there are two competing means by which agency firearm usage can be interpreted. On the one hand, this may be indicative of an agency that has an orientation based on offender control and the enforcement of supervision requirements. On the other hand, this can instead be interpreted as a desire to ensure that officers are protected and that they feel safe in some of the criminogenic areas that they must travel through when conducting their field visits.

Public safety is considered "job one" of this text. Thus, the use of firearms among CSOs is perhaps a necessary ingredient to ensuring their own safety. It is also the contention of this text that this does not necessarily contradict with the reintegrative aspects of community corrections. In fact, the use of firearms should be an irrelevant issue if offenders are not committing an action that would require an officer to unholster his or her weapon.

Critics of such a policy would be well served to keep in mind three key points. First, the use of firearms among community supervision personnel has more to do with the officer's personal safety rather than being a means of obtaining offender compliance. The means of obtaining offender compliance are most often effected through the power to arrest, and there are few critics who would contend that CSOs should have that power stripped from their repertoire of options.

Second, even in those cases where firearms might be used to obtain offender compliance, this is simply an aspect of the public safety charge to which community supervision agencies must be receptive and accountable. This is no different than the same responsibility that police officers assume when they agree to "serve and protect" the public, and this is the same charge for the CSO as well. In addition, it is clear that in many states CSOs already obtain the same level of entry level recruit training that peace officers also obtain (including firearms practice and proficiency), and this then would seem to make it more than reasonable to have such community service officers armed with an agency-approved firearm. In fact, it is the contention of this text that CSOs deserve the same respect attributed to standard peace officers. It would seem to be nearly a professional slight for agencies to be guarded against allowing the officer to carry a firearm, particularly when they have been trained to do so and even more so when one considers that they must come into contact with serious offenders during field visits.

Third, many CSOs in general and especially those who supervise parolees, view their function as being one primarily involved with enforcement. This is telling of both the agency culture that is likely to surround such officers, and this is also a statement of how the officer perceives his or her role in the community. With this in mind, it may not be inconsistent among CSOs' self-perceptions and the agency climate to have the inclusion of firearms among the officer's tools of the trade. Evidently, this does seem to be the general line of thought in many state agencies around the nation. The clear majority of states do have some sort of allowance for carrying firearms (at least with adult probation and parole), though there is still a large minority of states that do not make such an allocation.

Lastly, it should be noted that probationers and parolees can be and sometimes are dangerous. As was seen earlier in this section, probation and parole officers in New York, Pennsylvania, Texas, and Virginia all have reported dangerous circumstances associated with their jobs. The percentage of respondents reporting dangerous conditions was substantial enough as to seemingly justify the need for firearms among CSOs. Though this text's orientation is one geared toward reintegration of offenders, it would be a very naive outlook to not presume that some offenders are not only resistant to such opportunities but that they are an outright danger to society and to those who supervise them. A fair number of offenders (nearly 1.5 million) are on community supervision for felony level crimes, and among those offenders, almost 20% have committed some type of violent crime, whether that crime be homicide, sexual assault, robbery, assault, or some other type of violent offense. This alone should be sufficient grounds for CSOs to carry firearms, at least for those who have offenders on their caseloads who committed felony offenses. However, even the misdemeanant offenders include some violent offenders, and this completely overlooks that fact that there is a large dark figure of crime among these offenders. This means that offenders on supervision have probably committed numerous other offenses that were never detected prior to (and perhaps even during) their stint on community supervision. It is likely that some of their activities did entail acts of violence but that these acts never were (and never will be) detected by the criminal justice system. It is because of all of these considerations that this text takes a definitive standpoint on CSOs' use of firearms, and it is also the contention of this text that such an approach, whereby officer safety is placed as a top priority, does not impair an integrative orientation toward community supervision. This contention is true so long as the agency's organizational culture supports such an outlook as part of its organizational mission.

▧ Models of Parole Administration

The administration of parole tends to be much less complicated than with probation. Peak (1995) noted that few studies exist concerning the organization, administration, or other aspects regarding policy and practice of parole. At the point of writing this text, Peak's (1995) observations were still true and, in all fairness, it is not surprising that this is the case. Simply put, there is not much more need for such an examination due to the fact that parole is for the most part a static process throughout the nation. Aside from the fact that many states and the federal government eliminated the official use of parole, no other major and/or sweeping changes in parole administration have occurred in decades. Thus, among those states that have retained parole, most have combined it with probation. When added with those states that have eliminated parole altogether, it becomes clear that there are few occasions when parole administration occurs as a truly stand-alone function. Thus, much of the information pertaining specifically to probation in Section VI will tend to equally apply here as well. Rather than repeat that information, the student should simply keep in mind that there are substantial similarities among both forms of supervision, aside from the information that is presented in this section as well as the fact that parolees, quite obviously, have exited prison whereas most probationers have not.

Another point regarding the administration of parole is that it is much simpler to understand than is the administration of probation. This is because in all cases where parole exists it is administered by one single agency throughout the state. Thus, unlike probation, there are not multiple agencies or overlapping jurisdictions when administering parole, and as just noted, this is true in all of the states throughout the nation. Though there is some confusion with the choice of terms and vernacular, the use of parole in this textbook strictly refers to the use of post-incarcerative release from prison, not from jail. The releasing from these two different environments should not be confused.

Generally speaking, there are three basic services that tend to be provided by a parole agency. These are parole release, parole supervision, and executive clemency (Peak, 1995). Among various states that have abolished parole, parole officers still exist and continue to supervise these offenders (though again, a number of states have simply combined this function with the probation apparatus). Also, many states and even the federal government may award early release due to the use of "good time" incentives, and this may also result in post-incarcerative community supervision that is not at the discretion of a parole board. In these cases, the release dates are projected based on legislatively set timelines and standards and simply act as a release valve for prisons. Though the supervision in the community comes on the heels of an offender's being incarcerated, it is typically not referred to as parole. Further, this type of release is for much shorter periods of time than is parole, particularly due to truth-in-sentencing laws and mandatory minimums that have been passed in several states and the federal government. In 1973, the National Advisory Commission on Criminal Justice Standards and Goals (NACCJSG) succinctly identified two basic models for administering parole services. Though this may seem dated, the student is once again reminded that since the period of time when states abolished parole and/or consolidated it with probation, there has not been any serious change in parole administration or organization that has occurred. Thus, the two models identified by the NACCJSG still stand today as the only true models of parole administration. These two models are

1. *Independent Parole Administration Model:* This is where a parole board is responsible for determining release determinations from prison as well as overseeing the supervision processes of offenders who are released on parole (or good time). This type of administration is independent of any other state agency and reports directly and only to the governor of the state.

2. *Consolidated Parole Administration Model:* This is where the parole board is merely a semiautonomous agency that is connected to (and perhaps subservient to) a larger agency or governmental body. This larger organization will typically oversee the entire spectrum of correctional services, particularly the prison system. Supervision of persons on parole under this model is under the leadership and authority of that state's chief correctional executive officer (i.e., the commissioner or the director of corrections) with the parole board having no authority to direct post-incarcerative supervision.

In both of these models, probation services will sometimes be combined with parole services, just as has been discussed in prior sections of this text.

There have been critics and advocates for both models of parole administration. Critics of the independent model note that this model of parole tends to be indifferent to—or perhaps aloof from—institutional programs and that the parole board, when operating under this model, tends to place too much emphasis on concerns that do not dovetail with the needs or concerns of institutional corrections. On the other hand, critics of the consolidated model have noted that the parole board tends to be subjected to pressure and coercion from institutional management and institutional concerns regarding crowding and other issues that should, on the face of it, be restricted to appropriate risk assessment processes (remember Section V) rather than the fact that prisons are overcrowded. As can be seen, there are pros and cons to both forms of administration. Regardless, parole boards, when used at all, should be administered independently to ensure that release decision making and risk prediction are as pure as possible rather than being contaminated by political concerns and/or other concerns that truly do not actually hinge on the characteristics of the offender him- or herself.

The Financial Aspects of Parole

As has been discussed in other parts of this text, the use of community corrections holds substantial savings advantages when compared with incarceration. The advantages hold true for the use of parole just as with probation. Indeed, the state of Nebraska (as well as other states) notes that when comparing parole supervision and incarceration, it is clear that even the most stringent forms of parole are more cost effective than is incarceration. The lower costs are associated with the reduction in the need for secure facility settings as well as the fact that parolees pay for their own housing, food, and medical expenses. In such cases, the primary budgetary items associated with parole administration are simply that of paying for personnel, vehicles, and equipment.

To provide a clear idea of the difference in costs, consider the state of Idaho. In the Idaho corrections system, the cost for housing one inmate for one day in prison is $55.00, compared to the very low cost of $4.00 per day for those on community supervision. This makes it obvious that parole costs only a fraction of the cost that imprisonment entails. Thus, states could literally save millions of dollars each year if they were to use parole more frequently when inmates are eligible. However, it is important that the financial cost-cutting aspects are not allowed to cloud a parole system's judgment. Students must remember public safety is "job one," and community corrections holds a responsibility to ensure that the public is made as safe as is reasonably possible. Thus, if state correctional systems decide to increase the use of parole, they may find it more prudent to use more structured and intensive forms of parole supervision. More intensive forms of parole, such as those that use electronic tracking and/or global positioning system (GPS) surveillance, more frequent field visits from parole officers, as well as day reporting and intensive treatment program participation, will be more costly. But even in these cases, the cost is usually no more than $20.00 to $25.00 a day compared to the $55.00 cost noted by the state of Idaho. The savings are still less than half that associated with the daily cost of imprisonment.

In addition, it has been presented in other sections of this text that prolonged imprisonment can and does *increase* the likelihood of recidivism. This is compared with the resounding fact that, when implemented in a sound and effective manner, community corrections (including parole) produces *lower* recidivism rates. According to the Florida Correctional Commission, it stands to reason that if, in fact, parole does reduce recidivism, the savings are even greater when one considers the avoided cost of future incarcerations. Thus, it appears that there may be significant cost savings when using ISP that go beyond the simple comparison of daily costs to house and/or supervise offenders. In fact, it should be this long-term realization that should be the true philosophical basis for implementing a more widespread use of parole since this long-term effect is what essentially eliminates criminality and reforms the offender. In other words, the most cost-effective situation is one where neither supervision nor incarceration are necessary at all. Presuming that parole works better for the genuine reform of offenders, it would stand to reason that this option provides the greatest hope of achieving circumstances where states can safely say that no further supervision is necessary for a given offender. Such circumstances are, therefore, the most cost-effective outcomes for which one could hope.

Nevertheless, states around the nation find themselves considering the increased use of parole and/or early release due to problems with prison overcrowding (see Figure 9.1). State correctional systems may find it difficult to house the influx of offenders when their budgets are not increased to accommodate this continual flow of new inmates. The state of Arkansas is a very good example of how prison overcrowding has become a basis for the expansion of parole options. Indeed, in 2001, the Arkansas Board of Correction and Community Punishment implemented an accelerated parole scheme to release over 500 inmates, citing the need to free prison and jail space due to the state's record-breaking incarcerated population ("Arkansas Speeds Parole," 2001). The state's system is so backlogged that there were over 1,000 state inmates who were being held in county jails due to a lack of prison space ("Arkansas Speeds Parole," 2001). This same problem has been noted in other areas of the nation, such as Maricopa County, Arizona.

The state of Arkansas, in dealing with the overcrowding issue, lowered the security level of many cell blocks and facilities from maximum to medium security and from medium to minimum security since lower levels of security require fewer officers to supervise these inmates. In 2001, the state had a high number of correctional officer vacancies and simply could not effectively supervise its inmate population. It is clear that the policies implemented—artificially lowering inmate security levels—were dangerous and were not based on the security of the institution or society but were instead based on economics ("Arkansas Speeds Parole," 2001).

As noted before, this is a dangerous game to play and fails to live up to the notion that "public safety is job one," a primary tenet of this text. Further, the original purpose of community corrections was not to alleviate jail or prison overcrowding. Indeed, there were no legal protections for the incarcerated during the early correctional history of the United States or Europe. The true purpose of community corrections was consistent with that set forward by Alexander Maconochie and Sir Walter Crofton—to reform those offenders who

Figure 9.1   Parole Population Increases and Decreases by State (2002)

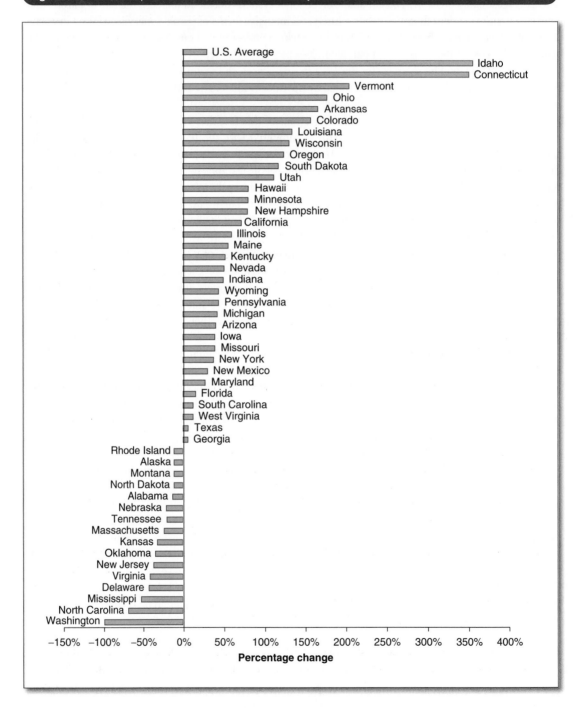

showed sufficient motivation and likelihood of being reformed. The entire point and purpose to both proba-tion and parole was reformation of the offender. This was even true for those persons who served their sen-tence in early penitentiaries, where it was the goal that offenders seek penitence for their crimes through introspective reflection and spiritual contemplation of their wrongdoings. The point is that while it is under-standable that state agencies may resort to more use of parole, it is important that they not do so simply due to financial incentives.

As Section V demonstrates, correctional systems must adhere to scientifically valid risk assessment processes when determining if inmates are eligible for parole. This determination must not be affected by financial concerns lest the validity of the determination becomes contaminated. If this contamination of the scientifically validated process is allowed, public safety is compromised, all in the interest of saving money and alleviating prison overcrowding. This is precisely what happens in a number of states when dangerous offenders are set loose under haphazard supervision schemes, sometimes resulting in heinous crimes against a member of society. This also (quite understandably) reduces the public support for parole and actually makes many members of society embittered against the idea of early release. This is a paramount issue and, regardless of dollars that can be saved, state officials must keep this in mind if they wish to avoid putting their citizenry in jeopardy. Also important for any politician is the desire to avoid embarrassment and scandal, an all-too-certain by-product of any media-catching criminal incident that happens during their tenure in office. Thus, it is in the best interests of state political officials (not just correctional officials) to pay closer attention to their correctional system budgets to ensure that those who should remain in prison do so and to likewise ensure that those who have a greater likelihood for reform are correctly identi-fied and given the appropriate means for pursuing that reform. The best means of doing this is by obtain-ing the most effective system of statewide risk prediction that money can buy. Such a system will pay for itself tenfold, both in dollars that are saved and in the reduction of public victimization that would other-wise occur.

Almost as if the state of Arkansas anticipated such criticism being leveled at their 2001 decisions to restructure their system, the state implemented plans that emphasized rehabilitative efforts during the year that followed ("Arkansas to Emphasize Rehabilitation," 2002). These plans, implemented in 2002, relied on drug court and community facilities for parole violators and included funding for a 300-bed facility for sex offenders ("Arkansas to Emphasize Rehabilitation," 2002). These programs demonstrate that officials with the state of Arkansas understood the connection between reformative efforts and lowered recidivism. The fact that Arkansas sought to avoid reincarceration of those already on parole demonstrates three points that are funda-mental: (1) Non-dangerous parolees are better off in the community than in prison; (2) the public is better off if non-dangerous parolees are not sent back to prison; and (3) specialized forms of treatment must be given for offenders who have specialized criminal tendencies, such as with the sex offender population.

What is also important is that these implemented processes did not allow for more expedient release of offenders from prison. Rather, quite intelligently, the state of Arkansas focused on those who were already in the community and had good prospects of reform. The goal in this case was undoubtedly to continue their path to reform and, in the process, refrain from further crowding the state prison system through the reincarceration of these identified parolees. This is an especially good policy if parolees commit technical violations and/or minor forms of crime. In addition, the separation of sex offenders into a specialized facil-ity allows these offenders the possibility of genuine change that is not obstructed by a prison subculture that tends to continually victimize these types of offenders. Such subcultures aggravate the mind-set of many sex offenders and can create a worse offender than had originally been encountered upon initial entry into the prison facility.

⊠ The Granting of Parole

In most states, offender cases are assigned to various individual parole board members who are tasked with reviewing the case so that they can formulate their initial recommendations. The recommendations that they provide are typically honored and accepted as written. Most states that do follow this process will have a formal hearing where parole board members may share their views. When the parole hearing is conducted with the offender seeking parole, it may be that all members involved with the decision may be present or just one member may be present. It is not always the case that all parole board members will meet with the inmate seeking parole but may be modified considerably from what is typically presented on television. Lastly, when parole hearings are conducted, the board may convene at the facility where the inmate is located (requiring the board to travel) or the inmate may be brought to the board, wherever the board is located (in many cases, the state capital).

The process and guidelines for parole selection tends to vary considerably from state to state. Some may have a minimum amount of time that must be served. Others may have stipulations on the types of crimes that were committed in the past. Naturally, some states may have both of these criteria as well as others to regulate the parole process. However, the actual decision by any parole review decision-making body is often one that is made by members who have a great deal of discretion. Indeed, it would appear that parole boards are influenced by a wide variety of criteria, many of which are not necessarily noted by statute or official agency guidelines. Institutional infractions, the age of the offender, marital status, level of education, and other factors may all weigh into the parole board's decision making.

Naturally, one of the key concerns with granting parole is the probability of recidivism. To a large extent, the prediction process has been little better than guesswork. For decades, the development of prediction devices has continued with an attempt to standardize risk factors. Psychometric tools and statistical analyses have ultimately rested upon actuarial forms of risk prediction. In most cases, it is the objective use of statistical risk prediction that turns out to be more accurate than that which allows for individual subjectivity. There are, of course, some exceptions, since the context surrounding the statistical data may be important and may provide alternate explanations as to why a certain set of numbers and/or statistical outcomes may have been obtained. However, this often simply results in the overprediction of likely reoffending. Nevertheless, this is costly to prison systems and, in some states, there may be a need to reduce prison system overcrowding. Indeed, parole mechanisms can serve as release valves for prison systems that become overstuffed with offenders. When this occurs, there may be a need for a certain amount of offender releases, and parole boards may have to make tough decisions that do not necessarily comport with the formal risk assessment that is based on a standardized instrument. This is where the difficulty tends to occur, and this demonstrates why, on the one hand, it is counterproductive for standardized risk assessment instruments to overpredict (as with the Wisconsin risk assessment system), yet on the other hand, subjective decision making is a necessary evil that is fraught with peril, resulting in mispredictions that ultimately lead to serious mistakes in determining an offender's likelihood to recidivate.

There are other factors that also affect the decision to grant parole. For instance, an inmate may (on a standardized instrument) have a high likelihood of reoffending. But the type of reoffending may be of a petty nature. In such instances, parole boards may decide to grant parole despite the fact that the offender is not considered a good risk based on a pure analysis of whether they will, or will not, reoffend. Thus, it is clear that the specific type of reoffending is also an important consideration among parole board personnel. As just noted, this may be an especially important consideration when parole boards are aware that the state's prison system is overcrowded and that a certain number of releases will assist prison administrators in maintaining their prison populations levels within required guidelines. Thus, it is better to release a person likely of relapsing on drugs and/or alcohol or who may commit some form of shoplifting than it is to release someone likely of committing some form of violent crime. It is with this next-best-solution approach that parole boards may be compelled (though not legally required) to make their releasing decisions.

Though not specifically germane to a Community Corrections course or textbook, it is important for students to appreciate the problems associated with prison overcrowding that go beyond the financial aspects of parole. Administrators in state prison systems are required by a variety of federal rulings and mandates to not exceed their intended capacity of inmates who may be held within the various facilities that comprise that system. Individual prisons and other types of correctional facilities must (and do) pay close attention to the number of inmates within their custody as compared to the maximum number that are allowed to be kept within their facility. Various federal court rulings during the 1970s and 1980s occurred that penalized many state prison systems and essentially forced these systems to honor a variety of civil rights standards when incarcerating inmates. Thus, the issue of overcrowding is not something that can be taken lightly by prison administrators, and state systems resort to a number of alternatives to alleviate this overcrowding. Some states are better than others at finding innovative means of housing and/or supervising offenders. But, among those states that still do use parole, it is an unquestionable fact that this option is one of the means by which state prison systems resolve their overcrowding problems, meaning that these state correctional systems rely on their community corrections system to augment and support their institutional correctional system. Thus, parole boards may play a key role in bridging these two components in an effort to ameliorate challenges facing a state correctional system.

The fact that parole boards may play such a critical linking-pin role should not be underestimated. They may, in fact, be under some pressure to assist the overall state system. Further, consider that these boards are often constructed by the governor of a given state. In some cases, state politics and state priorities may come into play, affecting the decision making of some parole board cases. This is particularly true when the parole board's administration is consolidated rather than independent in nature. In times past, parole boards were subject to differing degrees of corruption and/or disparity in decision making due to the influences of political and/or other concerns. While this is an issue that warrants attention even today (a degree of ethical oversight is always good to have), the point to this section is not to insinuate that parole boards are given to capricious decision making. Rather, the point is to demonstrate that parole boards do not operate in a complete vacuum. The influences of the surrounding contextual reality are inevitable, and these influences come from a number of directions. Indeed, prison wardens, state offices, victims, the parolee's family, and the public media may all have an impact upon the discretion that is employed by parole board members, individually and collectively.

Other points that may lead to premature release may be more relevant to the individual offender's circumstances. For instance, the offender may have been convicted when very young but may have committed a very serious crime (i.e., a multiple shooting) that carried a very lengthy sentence. It may be that the parole board simply considers the maturation of that offender and, as much of the criminological research demonstrates, considers that the offender is less likely to reoffend and that they are more likely to remain crime free in the later years of their lives. In addition, an occasional situation may develop where the offender considered for parole has extenuating circumstances in outside society such as an ill or dying family member that is close to the offender or perhaps children of the offender that are in need of parental contact. In these cases as well, it may be that the parole board will grant priority in releasing that offender from incarceration while noting that appropriate levels of community supervision should be maintained. Lastly, there are various circumstances where offenders are given compassionate release. Hanser (2007a) noted that this is one option that is given to numerous inmates who are terminally ill. Hospice programs and other forms of medically related release programs have been implemented in a number states, even those that typically adopt a hardened stance on crime and offender processing (Hanser, 2007a).

One of the key factors that may be held against offenders seeking parole is their behavior while within the institution. Inmates who have had continual infractions—and especially violent infractions—are quite naturally not likely to receive parole. Latessa and Allen (1999) noted that parole boards are very sensitive to public criticism and thus are likely to be very reluctant to release any offender who has the potential to commit an act of violence, even if there is only a very small likelihood that violent recidivism might occur. Just one incident can generate substantial public media attention and thus acts as a strong deterrent to releasing such offenders. This may be the case even if all other indicators show that the offender is highly likely to be successful on parole.

✂ Subjective and Objective Indicators in Parole Determinations

While Section V has provided an overview of subjective and objective characteristics associated with risk prediction, this subsection serves as a simple reminder to students that both contextually and statistically based factors are used when making decisions to release or to reincarcerate. In fact, subjective factors, such as terminal illness, likelihood of committing to treatment programs, impressions during interviews, and so forth, have been discussed previously in this section. These factors undoubtedly come into play when making determinations. Recall from Section IV that the use of subjective and objective indicators should be separated according to different purposes. Indeed, this section will also follow along that notion, with the contention being that all public safety determinations be based solely on objective assessment instruments and that subjective criteria be avoided when issues of public safety are at stake. For parole boards, often sensitive to bad publicity from the media, reliance on mathematical principles provides a precise, consistent, and effective means of protecting public safety and provides board members with a quantifiable rationale for their decisions. Further, statistical models tend to simply be more accurate than subjective models of risk prediction. While there will be some degree of overprediction in the likelihood of recidivism, this will nonetheless minimize the amount of error that is made by the board and the amount of corresponding criticism that is leveled at the board. On the other hand, just as noted in Section V, subjective criteria are best used when making determinations regarding treatment progress, and the use of subjective criteria from the specific primary treatment provider should be utilized more than any other form of assessment. Many of the issues in determining offender genuineness and effective completion of treatment goals will require individual observation that cannot be adequately appraised by some form of standardized process. Thus, subjective indicators should only be considered after the board has objectively determined that the offender is a safe release risk.

Naturally, from our previous discussion, this is not the case with many parole boards. In fact, parole boards may actually release offenders who are likely to reoffend, but their likely crimes are not expected to be serious in nature. Further, parole boards (as noted earlier) may release for other reasons such as terminal illness and so forth. These all lead to exceptions in a process that tends to overpredict success (remember that many instruments are prone to false positives). The point to this discussion is that both subjective and objective indicators have their own primary roles, yet, at the same time, they each overlap one another in their uses. Indeed, though objective indicators may provide one recommendation, subjective or contextual issues may simply be used to override the statistical risk assessment that is utilized. On the other hand, there may be cases where the contextual or subjective observations seem to indicate that an offender is genuinely making effort to reform, but due to the nature of the prior offense and the mathematical risk calculations that are generated, the offender may be denied parole. Thus, both types of indicators have their time and place, and each one tends to enhance the other in some offender cases yet each one can serve as a basis to override the other type of indicator when other types of offenders may be involved. This demonstrates that a balancing act exists when using both types of indicators and points toward the need for sound judgment and the use of effective discretion among parole board members.

Other types of contextual information may also be used by parole boards, providing yet an additional layer of subjective influence in the release process. One example is the inclusion of victim participation. Prior to an offender's early release, it is common practice for states to notify the victim, if the victim desires to know. Once notified, numerous states also allow these victims or members of the victim's family to appear before the parole board prior to an offender's release. These persons, along with others who may be permitted to provide written statements, are allowed to share their thoughts and feelings regarding the offender's release. This is typically referred to as a **victim's impact statement**, where the victim is able to express their own views on the appropriateness of the parolee's release and is also allowed to voice their sense of trauma and victimization that resulted from the criminal actions of the offender. The actual impact that these statements have on parole boards has not been well studied. However, the fact that the use of such statements has become widespread, along with the modern emphasis on victim's rights, indicate that parole boards do consider these powerful and moving statements in their decision making, at least to some extent.

Parole boards also use a variety of objective indicators. The various forms of assessment noted in Section V include most all instruments that are used by both probation and parole with one exception for parolees, the salient factor score. The salient factor score has been used by the U.S. Parole Commission (though federal parole was abolished, some early release mechanisms still remain) and some states around the nation. This simple instrument enjoyed widespread use for years due to its practicality and simplicity in administration. The salient factor score measures offender risk along six items, with each of these six items being measured with a value that ranges from 0 (zero) to 3 with inverted indications of risk (meaning that the lower the number the higher the likelihood that the offender will recidivate). The categories of consideration include the following: prior convictions, prior commitments, age, recent period being commitment free, on community supervision at the time of the offense, and history of heroin/opium dependence.

After considering all of the points listed throughout the previously mentioned categories, scores for each are obtained and then these scores are summed. The summed total of the scores are then used to assess the offender's likelihood of recidivism (Champion, 2002; Torres, 2005). The maximum number of points on the salient factor scale is a total of 10, with a score of 8, 9, or 10 representing a low risk of recidivism and thereby being judged a good candidate for parole. Table 9.2 provides a clear presentation of the scoring outcomes of the salient factor score.

Table 9.2 Scoring of the Salient Factor Score

Sum of Scores	Likely Success on Parole
8–10	Very Good
6–7	Good
4–5	Fair
0–3	Poor

In addition, federal parole officers would use this score when determining the level and type of supervision that the offender would be given. Parolees with scores of 9 or 10 might be given minimal levels of supervision while those with scores of say 3 or below would be given very strict levels of intensive supervision (Torres, 2005).

The salient risk factor score has been popular because of its utility and ease in administration. Though this is certainly a plus for agencies choosing to adopt a particular tool for assessment, this does not necessarily speak well of the validity or reliability of this instrument. While the six factors of the salient risk factor score are (on their face) relevant to recidivism and thus possess a good degree of face validity, this instrument has been normed on federal offenders (typically, federal inmates are not convicted of nearly as many violent offenses as are state inmates), and it is therefore unlikely that this instrument would be effective in predicting recidivism from these offenders (depending on the state, of course). Thus, to some extent, the external validity is questionable, depending upon the region of the United States and the particular type(s) of offenders involved (i.e., male or female, mentally ill, and so forth). This flies in the face of our prior discussion where it was made clear at the outset that effective assessment tools must be normed on the population to which it is administered and that such tools must have (at a minimum) strong inter-rater reliability and good face validity.

Further, the instrument does nothing to consider other variables that may, perhaps, mitigate, contradict, or offset the six factors that are included, such as drug abuse or addiction for anything other than heroin or opium. Thus, the assessment provides only a piece of the overall recidivism puzzle and is not necessarily reflective of the vast drug abusing offender population. This is a pretty serious oversight when one considers that over half of all offenders test positive for drugs or alcohol at the point of arrest (Hanser, 2007a).

In reality, the salient factor score is comprised of variables that are the most basic of predictors; therefore, the instrument is only valid or reliable along a few specific criteria. Thus, this instrument is not an all-encompassing predictive instrument and so narrowly defines the predictive indicators as to overpredict in some areas while failing to predict at all in others (i.e., history of stimulant abuse, especially if no conviction has ever occurred in relation to this drug use; perhaps due to plea bargaining, alternate diagnoses). This instrument, when placed in the balance, is definitely found wanting.

⊠ Prerelease Planning and Institutional Parole Officers

Institutional parole officers, often referred to as case managers, will work with the offender and a number of institutional personnel to aid the offender in making the transition from prison life to community supervision while on parole. As a profession, some states, such as Texas and New York, may heavily rely on institutional parole officers. Institutional parole officers in the state of Texas are primarily involved with making assessment determinations regarding parole suitability rather than eligibility. These officers use various assessment instruments to weigh both static and dynamic factors associated with the inmate's risk of recidivating. From this point,

> institutional Parole Officers compute a Parole Guidelines Score (which combines assessed risk and severity classification factors) online and document the results in a Decision Summary Form, which is transmitted electronically to members of the Board of Pardons and Paroles along with

each inmate's case file. Board members then vote electronically to grant or deny parole. (Texas Board of Pardons and Paroles, 2001, p. 1)

This same or a similar process tends to be used in most other states (whether electronic or otherwise) where institutional parole officers are used. These professionals are often referred to as caseworkers as well as institutional parole officers, denoting their reintegrative role in the parole process and the fact that this professional's job function follows the theoretical casework tenets that were presented earlier. Thus, this professional serves both a security function (assessing suitability for parole) and a reintegration function (providing casework services inside the prison and providing networks that extend beyond the prison). Much of the information presented in this section regarding prerelease planning and the role of the institutional parole officer follows information from the state of Oklahoma's Pre-Release Planning and Re-Entry Process guidelines (Jones, 2007).

During prerelease planning, prison staff will work together to provide a bridge of services that connect the offender to the outside world. A great deal of work can go into the planning and preparation process of an inmate's exit from prison. Upon determining that an inmate is suitable for parole, the institutional parole officer will begin the prerelease planning process that attends to the offender's transition from prison to the community. This process typically begins about 6 months prior to release and involves a shift from institutional case planning to individual community preparedness. Further, a range of wrap-around services are provided (see Section III). Prior to exiting the prison, the goal of a good reintegration program should be to ensure that the offender has the support, information, and contacts necessary to begin anew, without having to do self-exploration during the initial 3- to 6-month period of leaving the prison. Even small details must be attended to, such as providing offenders with essentials, such as proper clothing and shoes that are appropriate for the season and are not marked as being inmate clothing, proper identification, and appropriate referrals to community agencies that can assist with other services.

The use of one or two personable and involved volunteers can make a substantial difference in assisting the offender. Indeed, if such a volunteer were able to assist with some of the more mundane issues that emerge from simple day-to-day living, a world of difference can be made. Even further, if that volunteer should go so far as to be a genuine friend to the soon-to-be released inmate, this can provide further emotional support that will greatly improve the prognosis of the released offender. If the offender should be so fortunate, it is often typical that the institutional parole officer will maintain contact with this volunteer as well.

Throughout the process, agency administration will tend to track the offender's progress, keeping a careful eye on them 6 months prior to release. At this point, the offender may experience problems with anxiety due to nervousness over their newly expected freedom, the responsibilities of the outside world, and the effects of prisonization inside the facility. A good prerelease program will address these issues in advance, preparing the inmate psychologically for their release. Aside from their initial entry into prison, this period is often one of the most stressful points for the inmates coping with prison life since so much of their future is unexpected and since they will be held to expectations that they have not had to meet in years.

Various forms and checklists will be completed during this time as interviews are completed as part of the review case plan that notes the offender's approach toward release. These interviews will seek to identify various needs that the offender might have upon release. As you may recall from Section V, the use of needs-based assessment instruments perform this function and are used to determine an offender's treatment needs. Identified needs can be many but often may consist of some program that the offender did not complete while in prison, such as educational plans or substance abuse treatment programs. Other needs may be related to the payment of restitution, ensuring transportation, making provisions for child support, etc. The prerelease plan must, at a minimum, include information on their place of residence, their financial obligations, and any program referrals (Jones, 2007). Beyond this, staff should note any unique circumstances in the prerelease plan that might provide challenges to the successful reintegration of the offender. This will typically be included in the "Adjustment Review" and will also be included with what is often referred to as the Offender Accountability Plan. The Offender Accountability Plan addresses needs for restitution, the need to respect the rights and privacy of prior victims, any particular arrangements that have been made with the victim, as well as provisions that might be included to ensure the offender's responsibility to the community at large.

The actual day of release is an important milestone for the offender and is actually critical to the offender's successful reintegration. Activities should focus on the last few tasks that are required for the seamless transition to the community. In addition, the offender should be provided a portfolio of the various services available, requirements of parole, and so forth, allowing the offender to keep the information and requirements organized. Organizational skills may be somewhat impaired given the newness of the release experience and the likely euphoria that will be experienced. Torres (2005) pointed out that although release from the prison facility can be a euphoric experience it can also subsequently result in unexpected disappointment and frustration for the offender. The majority of life as the offender knew it has changed. Family members and peers have moved on, the offender must resume responsibilities, and the days of living in a structured environment have come to an end. Institutional parole officers are cognizant of the situation that faces upcoming parolees. They must ensure that the offender has the full range of support that is necessary to face what can be actually traumatic as an adjustment demand. The offender will come to grips with issues that most people do not consider. Offenders may (or may not) themselves realize the full range of emotional experiences that they will have upon release, and it is the job of the institutional parole officer to, among other duties and responsibilities associated with the offender's release, ensure that appropriate support for coping is provided to the offender that may be disappointed and/or overwhelmed by their experience.

Supervision From Beginning to End of Sentence

The actual community supervision process begins when the offender is placed on the caseload of a parole officer. This initial point of community supervision is referred to as a case assignment and will typically either be handled according to the offender's particular type of criminal activity (e.g., sex offender, gang-related offender) or the geographic location of the offender. For the most part, it is the geographic location where the offender intends to reside that first determines the agency and the likely parole officer that they receive. This is particularly true in rural areas or in small towns that do not have enough supervision officers to allow for highly specialized caseloads. However, urban areas will further segment geographical regions by the type of offense, with parole officers who have received specialized training overseeing specialized offender typologies.

Overall, the use of geographic considerations assists both the offender and the supervision officer since the amount of travel time is reduced. In rural jurisdictions, the caseload may be smaller to account for the added travel time that will be required as offenders are located in far-flung areas of the parole region. These factors are balanced against the type of offender, with specialized offenders being classified by their specific needs and/or security requirements. These requirements may naturally limit the offender's range of options in the community, will likely require that more activities be met, and will produce additional work for the parole officer. Thus, this factor will also come into play when determining caseload and the work that is entailed with that particular offender caseload.

⊠ Conditions of Parole

The terms and conditions for parolees, in most cases, are identical to many of those included for offenders on probation, such as not associating with known offenders, parole fees, curfews, etc. Parolees may be revoked for the same reasons as probationers: technical violations and new offenses. If possible, the offender will be kept on supervision (depending on the nature of the violation) but will experience a graduated set of increasingly restrictive sanctions and requirements that will become additional conditions to their parole requirements. Because this aspect of parole is so similar to that associated with probation and because the issue related to terms and conditions have been fully discussed in Section VI (addressing legal issues related

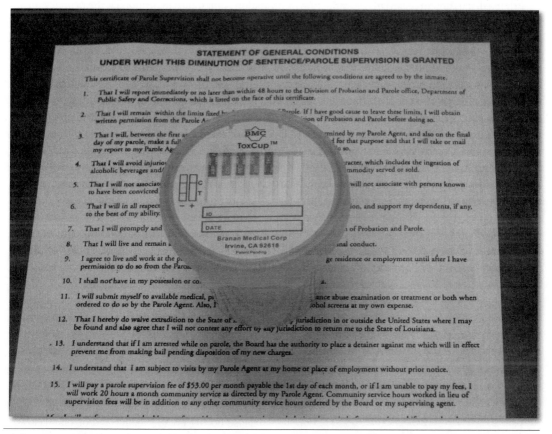

▲ **Photo 9.2** The sheet of paper underneath this urinalysis cup clearly identifies the conditions of an offender's parole. In this case, the parole officer is making it clear that the offender is expected to remain drug free by placing the urinalysis specimen cup directly on top of the list of parole conditions.

to the setting of terms and conditions of community supervision) there is no pressing need to provide further discussion on this issue. Again, the similarity between conditions with parole and those with probation should not be surprising since many agencies combine both functions and since each type of supervision may occur under the same officer. The terms and conditions, for the most part, tend to be very similar from state to state. Similarly, the use of additional conditions that are unique to the offender are not as frequently used aside from additional fines and/or community service, unless the offender happens to be in a specialized category of population typologies (such as with sex offenders), but even in these cases, restrictions tend to be similar to most others required of other sex offenders.

Thus, terms and conditions of parole tend have much more consistency throughout the nation when compared with probation. This should not be surprising since, as we have seen, parole is administered from a single agency in each state and since there are not hundreds of independent judges throughout the nation that are setting conditions for this type of community supervision (as with county-based probation).

⬛ Evaluation of Compliance and Modifications to Parole

As with the discussion in regard to the evaluation of probation compliance in Section IV, the primary means of determining success is simply by determining if offenders have recidivated. Indeed, as was pointed out with the salient risk factor scale, the central focus given to the prediction of success tends to revolve around the simple likelihood of recidivism. But, as noted earlier, this provides a very singular measure of risk prediction that does not necessarily define the type of recidivism likely to occur nor does it take into account other aspects that might mitigate variables that place the offender at risk.

In a similar fashion, it may be a bit shortsighted to simply focus on "yes" and "no" categories of reoffending. As noted in Section IV, the definition of reoffending can be quite fluid, and one act of recidivism is not necessarily equal to all others. So with the variability of potential infractions (consider again the issue of technical violations, as discussed with probation) there should also be variability in the types of response. As it turns out, there typically is quite a bit of variability in options.

The use of partial incarceration actually has a dual benefit. It is able to work as a sanctioning tool and, at the same time, a preventive tool. Indeed, it may well be that there are certain points in the day or the week where the offender is more at risk of reoffending, such as with Friday and Saturday evenings. Aside from the punitive aspects associated with the brief period of incarceration, such forms of brief incarceration can be seen as tools that prevent the offender from engaging in criminal behavior. This might be used for a variety of offenders, such as substance abusers who tend to have strong urges toward relapse during evening hours and/or on weekends. This might even include persons who are trying to avoid associations with prior friends who still engage in criminal activity (such as prior gang associates).

▲ **Photo 9.3** In many states, when offenders are placed on community supervision they are fingerprinted. In this photo, a probation and parole employee trains another community supervision worker on the proper process of obtaining offender fingerprints and identification.

The offender is essentially prevented from the physical ability to relapse while in custody and is shielded from other criminals who may continue to exert pressure on him or her to rejoin the criminal subculture.

Though this may seem a bit odd as a form of therapeutic intervention, it is consistent with other gang-exit strategies that exist (Hanser, 2007a). This is a particularly useful tool if the offender cannot (or will not) consider moving to another area or location. The offender may wish to remain due to mutual locations with family and other friends or perhaps due to the fact that their only source of housing and/or place of employment are located in a particular area. Thus, the issues can be complicated, and examples such as these again demonstrate how both punitive and reintegrative approaches may actually be one in the same in many cases. The use of evening and weekend incarceration is very similar to the use of an **intermittent sentence** in probation, which is simply a sentence that requires some form of temporary confinement throughout intermittent and partial periods of an offender's sentence. The key difference in this case is that it is the parole agency, as a modification of the initial sentence, who has applied this type of sanction, most often as a condition in response to some sort of detected violation to the offender's initial parole agreements.

As with probation, offenders on parole may have a number of requirements or conditions of their supervision that, if not met, can result in a technical violation. Most states require offenders to comply with any substance abuse treatment and/or mental health treatment requirements that might be relevant to their particular circumstances on supervision. Offenders who fail to meet these requirements might incur a technical violation of their parole, at which point other sanctions might be added. The use of additional fines may also be imposed, depending on the type of violation. Fines are used extensively in community supervision sanctions and can be adjusted over the duration of an offender's supervision. However, it has often been the case that offenders just trying to start anew while on parole lack the true ability to pay such fines. Further, efforts to collect fines can be strained since community supervision cannot be revoked by an offender's inability to pay his or her fines. Thus, fining of offenders, though a plausible option in some circumstances, may not be a good solution in a number of cases. On the other hand, the use of community service can be used to effectively sanction offenders. In fact, rather than fining offenders a specific dollar amount, it is perhaps best to look at community service as a form of bartered fine where a set amount of time and labor is exchanged for monetary compensation. The use of community service also enhances a number of therapeutic and/or reintegrative goals since this type of service engages the offender in prosocial activities.

Applied Theory Section 9.1

Braithwaite's Crime, Shame, and Reintegration as Related to Parole

Unlike most labeling theorists, Braithwaite does not suggest noninterventionist approaches when addressing offenders. Rather, Braithwaite holds that shaming is necessary for social control and the offender. However, the important issue is what follows shaming: reintegration or stigmatization. Reintegration is essential because shamed individuals are considered to be at a turning point in their lives. It is at this point where the offender can become reacquainted with society or find themselves further entrenched in the criminal subculture. It is when quality social relations exist that they provide the means through which offenders are given the forgiveness and support needed to become a member of the community (Lilly, Cullen, & Ball, 2007).

(Continued)

(Continued)

According to Cullen and Agnew (2006), "restorative justice programs most closely mirror Braithwaite's admonition to meld shaming with reintegration" (p. 277). Restorative justice programs seek to restore and heal the victim, repair the damage to the community, and reintegrate the offender after they have made their commitment to the victim. From this point, "repentant offenders potentially are granted a measure of forgiveness by victims and are reaccepted by their family and community" (p. 277). These attempts at shaming and further reintegration provide much more effective alternatives to stigmatizing sanctions that are used in the criminal justice system.

In this chapter, the mention of reintegration is particularly important since these offenders will be coming back into the community after serving years in prison. In addition, the "measure of forgiveness" that Cullen and Agnew refer to is also important, since this will be a necessary ingredient if offenders are to have a chance at reintegrating into the community. Thus, Braithwaite's work specifically applies to the reintegration of paroled offenders and explains that though reconnection with the community is the primary end goal, there is a shaming element that is both proper and necessary. In other words, there must be a genuine consequence to aberrant and/or illegal behavior if the learning mechanisms are to be taking place. However, once those consequences have been meted out and once the offender has experienced the full impact of those consequences, society has an ethical obligation to cease and desist from applying additional consequences to the offender; to do so is unethical, disproportional, and unproductive. In fact, excessive consequences that go beyond the norm are likely to produce more crime.

Given that there are serious labeling implications for ex-cons well after they have served their term in prison, it is clear that the consequences continue to follow them well after they have completed the duration of their sentence. This is true even after they finish their parole or early release obligations when coming out of prison. Further, these additional consequences affect the prior offender's ability to obtain jobs and necessary resources to function in society. Because of these additional consequences, the punishments are perhaps excessive, and it is therefore to be expected that recidivism rates would be high.

The primary point to Braithwaite's work is that a shaming process is indeed necessary and this shaming process should be public and should hold the offender accountable. However, once that process of accountability has been fulfilled, society must then assume the burden of reintegrating the offender back within the community. Otherwise, we should not be at all surprised when individuals turn back to criminal behavior. In fact, when we fail to offer the chance for reintegration, we essentially have contributed to the recidivism. As a society, it could be argued that if we continue to add consequences beyond the sentence and if we do this with the knowledge that this is likely to increase recidivism then we essentially make a knowing choice that encourages further criminality among those in need of our support and guidance.

⊠ Liability of Parole Board Members for Violation of Substantive or Procedural Rights

For the most part, it is clear that parole boards are not typically liable for violations of substantive or procedural rights when determining initial parole decisions. This should not be confused with decisions during parole revocation hearings. During revocation hearings, the Supreme Court case of *Morrissey v. Brewer* (in 1972) clearly established a number of rights related to due process through a prompt informal inquiry before some form of impartial hearing officer. However, initial decisions to grant parole are simply a privilege to which an inmate has not constitutionally secured this right. Though inmates do not have a right to parole, they do, however, have a right not to be discriminated against on the bases of race, religion, sex, creed, and so forth, when such determinations are being made. One case, *United States v. Irving*, was filed under Section 1983 of 42 U.S. Code in the Seventh Circuit. In this case, the offender alleged systematic racial **discrimination** against African American inmates with respect to parole board decisions for release. Interestingly, the circuit court did hold that the parole board members themselves had **absolute immunity** when faced with such suit. However, the Seventh Circuit noted that the offender could still sue of declaratory relief (essentially requesting an **injunction** that the parole board change their practices) due to the fact that the Seventh Circuit did find evidence that tended to demonstrate discrimination on the part of the parole board.

Thus, it may be that individual parole board members are immune from liability when performing their functions. Yet, on the other hand, offenders do still retain certain civil rights under the Fourteenth Amendment that must be honored by parole boards just as they must be honored by custodial corrections officials. This is a reasonable point since, after all, the desire to eliminate bias and discrimination among government officials was the actual reason that Section 1983 forms of redress were created. Just as prison officials must provide constitutional treatment of prisoners, so should parole granting bodies.

One additional point of interest regarding parole board liability revolves around the rights of offenders who are released on parole, only later to find out that such a release was a mistake on the part of the parole board itself. While such instances are not common, they have occurred frequently enough to be ruled on by more than one federal court. Indeed, two lower courts have held that the protections in *Morrissey* also confer some substantive protections for inmates who are mistakenly released. In both *Ellard v. Alabama Board of Pardons and Paroles* and *Kelch v. Director, Nevada Department of Prisons*, it was determined that once a state confers a right to be released, the inmate's due process rights go beyond the contours set by *Morrissey*. Indeed, it was determined that the grant of freedom places substantive limits on a state's power to reincarcerate an inmate who has been mistakenly released. In the *Ellard* case it was held that a mistakenly released inmate could not be reincarcerated unless the release violated some sort of state law and that this departure from state law substantially undermined that state's penological interests (see the U.S. Supreme Court case, *Turner v. Safely*, for a discussion on legitimate penological interests). A similar ruling was found in the *Kelch* case as well, demonstrating a consistency among circuit court rulings and thereby lending support for the point that parolees do not have a right to parole, prior to the parole granting decision. However, this changes when they are actually released on parole, with *Morrissey* protections affecting revocation proceedings for those legitimately on parole and a subsequent expectation of parole surfacing when offenders are mistakenly and prematurely released from the prison environment by parole board officials.

When considering the procedural elements of the parole granting process, it is important to remember that parole boards are given a great deal of discretion that is statutorily granted to the parole board body.

Indeed, it was held in *Partee v. Lane* that parole boards enjoy absolute immunity from Section 1983 suits when processing requests for parole. In other federal cases, it is equally clear that parole boards are considered to have absolute immunity when making decisions that grant, deny, or revoke parole. For instance, in *Walker v. Prisoner Review Board*, it was found that the court did have absolute immunity for their official actions. This was despite the fact that the board had not allowed the inmate to have access to critical files relevant to his parole determination, and this was despite the fact that the district court in *Walker* found this to be a violation of the inmate's civil rights. In such cases, inmates have a right to another parole board hearing and/or determination, and some form of injunctive determination may be imposed against the parole board, but the board members themselves cannot be held legally liable for these actions. The *Walker* case was, in actuality, only a district court level case, but this court correctly pointed to the Seventh Circuit's precedence that has held parole board review functions to be adjudicatory in nature, and being that they were judicial in nature, absolute immunity was considered to extend to board members just as is the case with judicial judges.

This issue has, at least in part, been addressed during an earlier case. Specifically, it is the public duty doctrine that holds that community supervision personnel (including parole board members) are not liable for failing to protect a member of the public from injuries inflicted by an offender on community supervision. As noted before, this is because general functions of public safety and security are owed to the public as a whole but not necessarily to any one individual in particular. However, does this change when the decision makers are tasked with protecting the entire public when making the ultimate decision to release or not to release?

The answer to this question is both "yes" and "no." When considering these answers, it is important that the distinction between **tort** cases and Section 1983 cases are kept squarely in mind. Currently, some federal circuit courts have indicated that liability can occur in cases where gross or reckless **negligence** is found (*Grimm v. Arizona Board of Pardons and Paroles*). While there is no concrete answer as to when members are reckless or grossly negligent in granting parole release, courts have tended to consider the standard of duty that is owed by parole boards as well as the predictability of the potential danger (Del Carmen, Barnhill, Bonham, Hignite, & Jermstad, 2001). This is a rather nebulous set of criteria that ultimately is decided by the circumstances of each case. Thus, it is possible for state parole boards to be found liable for their release decisions if they are shown to have committed reckless or **gross negligence** where the standard of duty to the public is broadened by that state's own laws to create potential liability to individuals and if the danger that occurs is judged to be foreseeable. Despite this possibility, it is rare that such suits are ever successful.

The unlikely success of these suits is exemplified in the case of *Santangelo v. State*, where it was found that the release decision did not include a rigorous or even suitable examination of the parolee's background or character (Del Carmen et al., 2001). No psychological or psychiatric reports were utilized in this decision. Further, prior to being released, the release decision-making body never did interview the parolee nor had he appeared before the releasing body for any reason other than to have the conditions of his release explained to him. This offender ultimately ended up raping a woman who brought suit against the state. However, it could not be proven that the releasing body would have made a different releasing determination if such precautions had been implemented, and since liability for negligence requires that the negligent actions must be shown to be the cause of the injury, it was found that the releasing body was not liable.

Beyond state-level parole boards, the Fifth Circuit court also found that federal agencies could be sued via tort claim (just as with state torts) through the Federal Tort Claims Act. In *Payton v. United States*, the U.S. Parole Commission was itself sued via tort claim for releasing what should have been an obviously dangerous inmate who later, when released on parole, kidnapped, raped, and murdered three women (Del Carmen et al., 2001). However, the Fifth Circuit held that the decision to release was discretionary and thus fell under the realm of judicial absolute immunity.

Another case, perhaps the most important case on this issue, was decided by the U.S. Supreme Court. The case of *Martinez v. California*, involved a 15-year-old girl who was murdered by a parolee only 5 months after being released from prison. The offender also had a history of sexual offending. The parents of the girl brought suit under Section 1983, and this case eventually reached the U.S. Supreme Court. The court held that the parole board members were not liable under federal law because, among other things, the parole board was not aware that a particular person (remember the "special relationship" exception to the public duty doctrine) as distinguished from the larger general public was in any special danger. Further, the parole board's decision was not a proximate cause of the girl's death; in other words, the girl's death was too remote a possibility for the parole board to know that such might occur. Being that the girl's death was such a remote consequence of the parolee's release, the parole board members could not be held directly responsible under a Section 1983 suit.

⬚ The Use of Objective Instruments as a Safeguard From Liability

As has become quite clear, parole board members are largely insulated from liability when performing their discretionary acts of release determination. So long as parole board members maintain a judicial function and so long as these discretionary acts are within the purview of this function, there is not likely to be any liability issue that will emerge. Indeed, any CSO, when performing judicial related functions, is likely to be given absolute immunity. This has, of course, been made clear throughout this section and is one of the reasons that probation officers enjoy such immunity when completing their PSI reports. However, the issue of liability regarding risk prediction does not simply stop with the parole board. Further, the use of discretion is authorized and legally protected for parole board members due to their responsibilities reflecting a judgment or judicial function.

The use of such discretion, however, is not equally protected for probation and/or parole officers and the agency supervisors that must make decisions regarding the enforcement of probation and/or parole conditions related to revocation. It is important to point out that individual probation and/or parole officers simply do not have to worry about potential liability issues related to decisions to release. The reason for this is simple; individual officers are not tasked with this responsibility. Rather, it is the court judge who will make such decisions regarding probation, and it is the parole board/committee or other such post–incarcerative-releasing body that will be tasked with this function. All of these individuals empowered with such discretionary powers are granted absolute immunity.

However, it is often the case that probation and/or parole officers may make another type of discretionary decision that addresses the offender's likelihood to be supervised in the community—this occurs when officers must make discretionary decisions to revoke an offender's probation or parole. Though this is not necessarily a function that the individual officer will make alone (though they may), it still requires a degree of discretion that can perhaps open up liability for the officer. Consider, for example, a situation where the offender commits a minor infraction and the probation officer (aware that the local jail is already overcrowded and also having a general idea of the probationer's supervision ethic) decides to provide a warning and to strengthen some of the sanctioning restrictions on the offender. If this same offender should again commit some act (regardless of whether it may be similar to the previous violation), this can place the supervision officer in a position where suit or at least questioning of his or her judgment may take place from members of the general public. For the most part, as we have noted, CSOs will be granted **qualified immunity** in these circumstances (presuming that they acted in good faith within the scope of their duty).

However, the officer making such recommendations may indeed be called to task and may be denied qualified immunity in some cases where the circumstances are warranted. Though this may be a moot issue in cases where revocation may automatically require that the offender be reincarcerated, it is often the case that offenders are simply given stricter conditions for their current community supervision sentence. This can be an issue in some cases where qualified immunity is concerned. This is particularly true considering that qualified immunity is extended for those cases where a discretionary act (not a mandatory act by agency policy) is at issue and where the officer must indicate sincere belief that their action was correct under the circumstances (and again, without the benefit of a mandatory regulation given force of agency authority).

In these specific cases, officers would be well served to base their discretionary decisions on the results of any objective assessment tools that are available. Because the officer will have no true policy, per se, to rely upon and because a sincere belief in the correctness of their action will be an issue, the use of such instruments, based on the findings of other assessment professionals, can substantially bolster the officer's determination and can add a great degree of confidence to their decisions. Though this is a specialized set of circumstances and limited use of these instruments, it can make a considerable difference in those instances where qualified immunity may not be assured for the officer. This can also serve as a substantial area of consideration for juries and judges that must make decisions regarding liability should the officer find himself or herself in court. The use of objective assessment indicators can provide the officer with additional protection to shield them from being found liable. Further, knowledge of these assessment tools and their outcomes can provide additional ammunition when supervision officers seek to have certain modifications added and/or required to a particularly problematic offender under their supervision. CSOs should strive to become fairly conversant in the use of these tools since this knowledge can bolster their decisions regarding offender community supervision revocation. Further, even if this knowledge does not prove necessary as a means for protecting from liability, this knowledge helps to improve the day-to-day competence of the officer. This in itself is a laudable goal.

◤ Parole Revocation Proceedings

This section, to some extent, is a bit redundant when considering information that has already been covered in Section VI. The legal issues surrounding parole revocation will only be discussed topically and briefly since this was discussed in considerable depth in Section VI. Nevertheless, no discussion pertaining to parole would be complete without at least noting some of the issues associated with the revocation of that sentencing option. As discussed earlier in Section IV, the revocation process is often a two-stage process that was initially set forth in the Supreme Court ruling of *Morrissey v. Brewer* in 1972. The first hearing is held at the time of arrest or detention and is one where the parole board or other decision-making authority will determine if probable cause actually does, in fact, exist in relation to the allegations against the parolee that are made by the parole officer. The second hearing then is tasked with establishing the guilt or innocence of the parolee. During this hearing, the parolee possesses a modified version of due process, namely being provided with written notice of the alleged violations, having disclosure of evidence to be used against them (similar to discovery), the right to be present during the hearing and to provide his or her own evidence, the right to confront and cross-examine witnesses, the right to a neutral and detached decision-making body, and the right to a written explanation of the rationale for revocation.

One interesting development in response to revocation procedures is that of the **parole revocations officer**. In some states such as South Carolina, the parole revocations officer is primarily tasked with the routine holding of preliminary parole revocation hearings by reviewing allegations made by parole officers against parolees. These hearings are administrative and not near as formal as those held by a judge in a true court of law. Typically, these courts are routine in nature, but some situations may have rulings and findings of fact that vary. Though most hearings are not complicated, a degree of discretion is required on occasion when determining if the evidence has been presented well and/or to determine if the violation requires a true revocation of parole, as opposed to more restrictive sanctions. The position of parole revocations officer does not require formal legal training but instead simply requires that the hearing officer know the laws and regulations surrounding that state's parole system.

While the issue of legal liabilities was addressed in Section IV, issues surrounding the role of parole revocations officers were not brought up. In *King v. Simpson* (in 1999), the court did rule that parole officers and parole revocation officers have absolute immunity when acting in a quasi-judicial or prosecutorial role. The initiation of parole revocation proceedings and the task of presiding over those meetings are considered quasi-judicial in nature. Thus, in the majority of cases, the parole revocation officer is likely to have absolute immunity in the vast majority of the functions that they perform (Cromwell et al., 2002).

Lastly, Cromwell et al. (2002) pointed out that that the process of revocation is actually a bit more in-depth and takes longer than many people may realize. In considering Burke's (1997) research throughout the nation, it was found that the average time required to complete the revocation process, from the point of violation detection to the disposition by the parole revocation decision-making body, took anywhere from 44 to 64 days to complete. When taken in total with the safeguards afforded parolees during the revocation process, and the fact that many are returned to some more stringent form of parole (rather than prison), there is clearly an effort to work with offenders on parole. It is clear that, whenever possible, only dangerous offenders or those who simply will not generally comply with their conditions are returned back to prison. Further, this demonstrates that parolees do, in many cases, have the time to formulate their defense and/or to demonstrate that they are indeed working in earnest on meeting their supervision requirements, despite violations that might be detected. The main point to these last few statements is that there is minimal likelihood that parolees, for the most part, experience revocation due to capricious and arbitrary reasons. Rather, it would seem that the system of post-incarcerative supervision is quite balanced in many respects, particularly when one considers that these offenders are, after all, prior convicted felons.

Regardless of whether the decision-making body consists of the parole board itself or a parole revocations officer, there are some situations where the offender may be entitled to some form of legal counsel. In 1971, in *Gagnon v. Scarpelli* it was held that parolees do have a limited right to counsel during revocation proceedings, as determined by the decision-making person or body over the proceedings and to be determined on a case by case basis. This is, quite naturally, relevant only to those circumstances where the parolee contests the allegations of the parole officer and at the parolee's own expense; there is no obligation on the part of the state to provide such representation.

Lastly, Cromwell et al. (2002) noted that the time that is taken to complete the parole revocation process varies from one jurisdiction to another. However, this time period is probably much longer than most people realize. In a national study by Burke (1997), it was found that when counting from the moment the violation was detected until disposition by the parole board or parole revocation officer, roughly 44 to 64 days tended to transpire. Thus, it is clear that parole officers must go through considerable effort when proceeding with revocation processes, and it is also clear that offenders on parole are not devoid of the ability to protect themselves legally while also having adequate time to make preparations for that defense. The point to this is that arbitrary capriciousness does not tend to occur in these proceedings since the process is slow, parolees are given several rights, and since they are able to obtain a lawyer, if they should so choose.

⊠ Conclusion

This section demonstrates that the use of parole, for the most part, concerns state-level offenders more than it does federal offenders. Likewise, it is clear that unlike probation, the organization and administration of parole systems tend to have more similarities than differences when compared on a state by state basis. Likewise, it has been made clear that there are a number of subjective and objective forms of assessment that go into the parole decision-making process. One subjective element that is not often considered as part of the assessment process in many textbooks on community corrections is the use of victim input via the victim impact statement. The use of this information is becoming more important over time, and the inclusion of this input also dovetails well with a restorative justice approach. Likewise, the salient factor score is presented, with updates from *28 CFR Part 2* (Reilly, 2002) being included. Though the salient factor score has been used extensively in the federal system, there are some pitfalls in this instrument that may make it less effective with state offenders throughout many areas of the nation, particularly since state inmates tend to be considerably different from federal inmates.

The parole supervision process has been discussed, with substantial emphasis being given to the rapport that is developed between the parole officer and the parolee. The importance of this relationship cannot be overemphasized as it can be instrumental in setting the tone between a reintegrative experience and one that is punitive in nature. Though parole officers must naturally enforce the terms and conditions of parole, they do have a degree of discretion in relation to that enforcement, and they also have a great deal of choice in how they approach the supervision process. The individual parole officer stands second only to the parolee him- or herself in terms of the impact that they can have on that parolee's success or failure on parole. Regardless of the parole officer's orientation, it is ultimately the parolee that is responsible for their behavior and, if that behavior is not kept in compliance, revocation proceedings will likely be generated against the parolee. These proceedings progressively increase the sanctions against the parolee up to and including reincarceration of the offender.

Lastly, restorative justice approaches have been presented as a useful paradigm from which victim input can be maximized while at the same time supporting reintegration efforts for offenders. However, restorative justice approaches must be grounded in the reality of the practitioner, not the theorist, and must have a strong supervision element that ensures the safety of the public. In addition, the use of community service, restitution, and other such mechanisms of compensation emphasizes offender accountability. It is the clear contention of this text that such forms of accountability are not punitive (contrary to the claims of other researchers and/or authors) but that they are actually rehabilitative and/or reintegrative in nature, if implemented correctly. This then demonstrates that these sanctions are consistent with restorative justice approaches that seek to reintegrate the offender. In a like manner, victim impact statements used in the parole decision-making process and the supervision process are also consistent with restorative justice paradigms. The last component—the community—has been presented as a critical component in the community supervision process in prior sections and demonstrates again the utility that restorative justice holds for parole in particular and community supervision in general.

◪ Section Summary

- The origins of parole stem from the work of Alexander Maconochie in England and Sir Walter Crofton's Irish marks system.
- Zebulon Brockway is considered the father of parole and indeterminate sentencing in the United States. The first form of parole was used in the United States in 1876 at the Elmira Reformatory.
- As of 2002, 15 states and the federal government had abolished the use of discretionary parole.
- The tasks and nature of work for parole officers greatly resemble that of probation officers. Many states now combine these services into one office.
- Parole administration is governed by two models: the **independent parole administration model** and the consolidated parole administration model.
- For states still issuing parole through the use of discretionary parole, the salient factor score is the most widely used prediction instrument.
- The use of preplanning instruments provide an opportunity for the institution and community to assess the readiness for reentry. These instruments include information on the residence, employment options, and opportunity for treatment.
- The parole revocation process is similar to that of probation.

KEY TERMS

Consolidated parole
  administration model

Good time credits

Independent parole
  administration model

Intermittent sentences

Mark system

Merit time credits

Offender Accountability Plan

Parole

Parole revocations officer

Salient factor score

Ticket-of-leave

Victim's impact statement

Wraparound services

DISCUSSION QUESTIONS

1. What are the basics regarding state parole, its organization, and its administration?

2. How are offenders selected for release? What are the factors influencing parole decisions, and what are the factors considered when granting and denying parole?

3. What is the difference between discretionary and mandatory release? What are the different issues confronting parole officers based upon the differences in release?

4. What is good time and merit time? What role do each of these play in determining release of an offender?

5. What is the salient factor score? What are some of the pros and cons for using the measure for early release?

6. Demonstrate knowledge of the entire supervision process from prerelease planning to the successful termination of parole supervision.

7. What are the common conditions of parole? How can parole effectiveness be refined and adjusted to better meet supervision requirements that are based on the offender's behavior?

WEB RESOURCES

American Probation and Parole Association (APPA):

http://www.appa-net.org/eweb/

Center for Court Innovation Parole Reentry Courts:

http://www.courtinnovation.org/index.cfm?fuseaction=Page.ViewPage&PageID=595&currentTopTier2=true

Policy Brief—Role of Parole:

http://www.crjustice.org/rolparol.htm

Research Series on Salient Factor Scoring:

http://www.ussc.gov/publicat/RecidivismSalientFactorCom.pdf

Please refer to the student study site for web resources and additional resources.

READING

In this study, the authors compared the recidivism rates of offenders released on parole via discretionary versus mandatory release from imprisonment. Schlager and Robbins recognized that the rates of recidivism for offenders' post-incarceration have been well documented. The method of release, however, has not been explored. Using a random sample of 500 offenders released from the New Jersey prison system in 2001, the authors examined the rates of rearrest, reconviction, and reincarceration for the population. Of those identified in the sample, 173 were released by maxing out their sentence, while 307 were released via discretionary parole. Technical violations were omitted from the study. These variables were assessed at a multitude of intervals ranging from 3 months to 4 years' post-release. Results of this study reveal those offenders who maxed their sentence were more likely to have served time on parole previously, more likely to have a violent instant offense, and more likely to be rearrested and reincarcerated earlier (24% within the first 3 months). These findings offer policy implications for post-release supervision even for those offenders who have maxed out their sentence.

SOURCE: Schlager, Melinda D. & Robbins, Kelly (2008). Does parole work?—Revisited: Reframing the discussion of the impact of postprison supervision on offender outcome. *The Prison Journal, 88*(2), 234–251. Copyright © 2008 Sage Publications.

Does Parole Work?–Revisited

Reframing the Discussion of the Impact of Postprison Supervision on Offender Outcome

Melinda D. Schlager and Kelly Robbins

Problem Statement

The steady but significant increase in the number of people incarcerated in U.S. prisons and jails over the past three decades has resulted in an inevitable surge in the number of ex-prisoners returning to communities either on completion of the sentence or under community supervision (Petersilia, 2003). Unfortunately, until recently, little was written about the phenomenon known as offender reentry. Practitioners and scholars are just beginning to understand and recognize the nature and complex array of issues that affect the offender, their families, and the communities to which they return. Nowhere is testimony to the importance of offender reentry more apparent than in the burgeoning scholarship on the subject (see Petersilia, 2003; Travis, 2005; Travis & Visher, 2005; and the August 2001 issue of *Crime & Delinquency* for comprehensive and excellent overviews of the issues subsumed under the umbrella term offender reentry).

This new interest in the period in time when an offender leaves jail or prison and returns to the community has resulted in a reevaluation of current release practice; it has forced scholars and practitioners to think about offender release in new contexts, stirring old debates on several traditional corrections issues. In particular, the intense focus on offender reentry has fueled the age-old discussion of the viability of parole as an effective method of community supervision (Lynch & Sabol, 2001; Petersilia, 2003).

Although alarmingly high rates of recidivism among released prisoners have been well documented over the past 10 years, limited research has been carried out to evaluate offender outcomes by release decision type (Petersilia, 1999; Tonry, 2000; U.S. Department of Justice, 2001). That is, little scholarship exists that attempts to determine whether the way in which an offender is released (i.e., whether an offender is released from prison unconditionally on completion of sentence or whether an offender is released conditionally on parole or under the guise of mandatory release) affects outcome. Certainly, any dialogue on effective offender reentry practice must also include an informed discussion about the ways in which offenders are released from prison and what potential effect a given method of release may have on recidivism.

Literature Review

A review of the literature reveals relatively few studies that have directly assessed release from prison according to release type and recidivism. A recent Bureau of Justice Statistics (BJS) study completed in 2001 evaluated trends in state parole and directly compared offenders who were released from prison by discretionary means with those released from prison under mandatory release guidelines or at the expiration of sentence (U.S. Department of Justice, 2001). Results from this study concluded that offenders released from prison on discretionary parole were more likely to successfully complete parole supervision compared with those released from prison to parole via mandatory release (U.S. Department of Justice, 2001). Between 1990 and 1999, offenders released from prison by the discretion of a parole board successfully completed parole 50% to 56% of the time, whereas offenders released to parole via mandatory release successfully completed parole 24% to 33% of the time (U.S. Department of Justice, 2001).

⊠ Justification of Research

There are several limitations to the existing research on recidivism, especially when considering outcome by release type. First, conclusions from existing research are based on data reported in the aggregate. Travis and Visher (2005) argued that one cannot divorce disparate state-level policy and practice from outcome, thereby suggesting that cross-state comparisons of rates of recidivism are difficult and not particularly useful. Moreover, conclusions about parole practice drawn from aggregate data do not adequately account for significant interstate variation in parole populations and supervision guidelines (U.S. Department of Justice, 2001) or political will.

Piehl and LoBuglio (2005) also noted that there is significant interstate variability with regard to many characteristics of released offenders that do not necessarily present in the aggregate. Furthermore, technical violations and the parole revocations process—processes that affect parole supervision and practice—vary greatly from state to state and are more representative of how individual states choose to respond to crime than of underlying criminal behavior (Blumstein & Beck, 2005; Travis & Visher, 2005). Consequently, assessments of recidivism at the state level, especially as they pertain to differences in outcome by release type, are particularly desirable as states attempt to determine the viability of discretionary release and to develop release policies and practice that meet local needs.

Another limitation to the existing recidivism research is that the data employed in these studies are at least a decade old, making it difficult to draw conclusions about the efficacy of current (or relatively current) release practice. Modifications to criminal justice practice over the past 10 years, including changes in

sentencing guidelines, ideological shifts in the purpose of parole, the increasing reliance on technical violations, and new technologies such as electronic monitoring, have individually and in aggregate significantly affected and substantially changed the landscape of release practice from what it was in the 1990s (Lynch & Sabol, 2001; Petersilia, 2003).

In all fairness, significant time must pass for a recidivating event to occur, requiring that researchers sometimes wait for years before an evaluation of recidivism can take place. However, those analyses must then be extremely sensitive to changes in practice, legislation, ideology, and their collective effect on outcome. Reporting older data in the aggregate likely reduces the sensitivity of statistical tests to account for subtle, but very important individual state differences—differences that may very well affect states' corrections and parole policies, procedures, and practice.

Recent research also makes clear the need for additional assessments of recidivism that take into consideration differences in methods of release. Rosenfeld, Wallman, and Fornango (2005) in their work on the contributions of ex-prisoners to crime rates noted that although understanding the issues surrounding the ratio of prison admissions to releases is important, so too is understanding the conditions under which an offender is released. Moreover, the documented increase in the number of offenders released via mandatory parole and at the expiration of sentence compared with those released to discretionary parole makes examining the impact of this shift in release practice necessary (U.S. Department of Justice, 2001).

Although the conclusions of the UI report illustrate the success (or lack thereof) of parole at the national level, the report's most important conclusions indicate how little scholars actually know about parole practice at the state level. Therefore, it seems prudent to conduct a more detailed state-level analysis of offender release practice and outcome. To that end, this research addresses some of the limitations of previous research by providing an analysis of offender release in New Jersey. Specifically, this study seeks to discern whether there are demographic differences between offenders on parole compared with offenders released from prison without supervision. Furthermore, this research assesses whether offenders released to parole present with lower rates of recidivism compared with those released from prison to the community at the expiration of sentence and evaluates the effect of time at risk on the outcome.

✎ Method

The sample utilized for this analysis was a random sample of 500 offenders taken from a sampling frame of 14,780 offenders—the total number of offenders who were released from prison in New Jersey in the calendar year 2001. Ultimately, 11 offenders were not included in the final analysis due to missing case files or state police interstate information index (III) information. The remaining 489 offenders included in this analysis were released from New Jersey Department of Corrections facilities between January 1, 2001, and December 31, 2001, and were followed through March 12, 2005. A cursory review of offenders by release type for the sample of 489 offenders revealed that only 9 offenders from this sample were released from prison to parole via mandatory release. This discovery made evaluating the efficacy of mandatory parole release impossible. Therefore, this research focused on assessing differences in outcomes between 480 offenders released from prison via discretionary release and offenders who were released from prison at the expiration of sentence (max outs).

Data for analysis were obtained from several sources, including judgments of conviction, offender parole files, and official state data management systems, including the New Jersey State Parole Board automated parole information system and the New Jersey Department of Corrections automated offender management system. Outcomes data were derived from state police criminal case history reports that capture rearrest, reconviction, and reincarceration data within the state and from III reports that capture these outcomes nationwide.

The following criterion variables were utilized to assess outcome. Rearrest was defined as an arrest by municipal, state, or federal law enforcement personnel after the offender was released in 2001. Reconviction was defined as a municipal (a conviction for a term less than 365 days) or a state (a conviction for a term more than 365 days) conviction resulting from a first arrest after release in 2001. Convictions resulting from a second or a later arrest after release in 2001 were not followed. Reincarceration was defined as a county or state incarceration that resulted from the first arrest and conviction after release in 2001.

Technical violations and parole revocations were not considered in this analysis due to inherent problems in the measurement and reliability of these variables as indicators of criminal behavior as opposed to parole policy or officer management style. Intervals developed for the observation of outcomes for this analysis include 3 months, 6 months, 6-12 months, 1 year inclusive, 1-2 years, 2 years inclusive, 2-3 years, 3 years inclusive, 3-4 and 4 years inclusive.

✎ Results

Given that one of the primary purposes of this study was to assess whether differences in outcome were observed between offenders who were paroled in New Jersey compared with those who maxed out, by-group differences were assessed for a variety of descriptive characteristics. Although several of the analyses revealed no statistically significant differences between max outs and parolees, some statistically significant results were noted and merit discussion.

With respect to demographic information, no statistically significant differences in gender and ethnicity were found between max outs and parolees. Moreover, no statistically significant differences between max outs and parolees were detected for several other descriptive variables, including sentence length, number of instant offenses, number of arrests previous to the current offense for which the offender was incarcerated, number of felony convictions previous to the current offense for which the offender was incarcerated, total number of felony convictions ever, whether an offender had been previously paroled, the number of parole violations ever, whether the offender had previously maxed out on an adult sentence, whether the offender had a juvenile record, whether the offender had ever committed violent crime, the number of violent crimes ever committed, and if the offender was rearrested, reconvicted, or reincarcerated, whether it was for a violent crime.

However, statistically significant differences between max outs and parolees were found with respect to several characteristics. Data show that there were statistically significant differences between max outs and parolees with respect to age, with max outs presenting with a mean age of 38 compared with parolees who had a mean age of 36 ($t = 2.5, p = .01$).

Furthermore, max outs also presented with statistically more significant number of arrests (ever) compared with parolees, with max outs having a mean of 10.1 arrests compared with parolees who had a mean of 8.6 total arrests ($t = 2.3, p = .02$). Differences were also found between max outs and parolees with regard to the number of times an offender was incarcerated prior to the instant offense for which they were most recently incarcerated. Prior to the instant offense for which they were most recently incarcerated, max outs were incarcerated a mean of 1.7 times compared with parolees who were incarcerated a mean of 1.1 times ($t = 4.2$, $p = .001$). Max outs and parolees also differed with respect to the number of times an offender was paroled prior to the instant offense for which they were incarcerated. Max outs were previously paroled a mean of 1.4 times compared with parolees who were paroled a mean of 0.8 times, $t = 5.0 (475), p = .001$.

The variable that captured the instant offense for which the offender was most recently incarcerated included 63 criminal offenses that were collapsed into seven offense types, including drug-related offenses, theft/burglary offenses, fraud/forgery offenses, violent crime/assault offenses, escape offenses, weapons offenses, and nonviolent offenses. Dummy variables were created for this variable to assess differences in offense type by release type. Results indicate that offenders in the

parolee subgroup were incarcerated for drug offenses more than offenders in the max-out subgroup, $\chi^2 = 7.1$ (1), $p = .008$. Conversely, offenders in the max-out sample subgroup were incarcerated for more violent crime/assault offenses than offenders in the parolee sample subgroup, $\chi^2 = 4.1 (1), p = .04$. For offenders who were rearrested after their release to the community in 2001, max outs were found to have a statistically significantly higher number of postrelease arrests (mean of 2.3 times) compared with parolees who were rearrested a mean of 1.7 times ($t = 2.7, p = .001$).

In addition to assessing similarities and differences in sample subgroups, this research evaluated differences in base rates of max outs compared with parolees. Base rates represent the presence or absence of the particular event in question. In this instance, outcome measures for this analysis included rearrest, reconviction, and reincarceration.

Overall, offenders who maxed out were rearrested and reconvicted at statistically significant rates greater than parolees. Seventy percent of max outs were rearrested, and 44% of max outs were reconvicted compared with 60% of parolees who were rearrested and 34% who were reconvicted up to 4 years after release, $t = 2.2 (376), p = .03; t = 2.1 (343), p = .04$.

Further analysis of base rates when evaluated by time interval revealed that max outs were rearrested statistically significantly more often than parolees (a) within 3 months, 0.24 for max outs compared with 0.14 for parolees, $t = 2.3 (215), p = .02$; (b) within 6 months, 0.43 for max outs compared with 0.27 for parolees, $t = 2.7 (235), p = .006$; (c) within 1 year, 0.68 for max outs compared with 0.48 for parolees, $t = 3.6$ (267), $p = .003$; and (d) within 2 years of release from prison, 0.88 for max outs compared with 0.78 for parolees, $t = 2.3 (290), p = .02$. Interestingly, parolees were rearrested statistically significantly more often than max outs between Year 1 and Year 2 of release, 0.30 for parolees compared with 0.19 for max outs, $t = 2.2 (280), p = .03$, and between Year 2 and Year 3 of release, 0.13 for parolees compared with 0.03 for max outs, $t = 3.3 (292), p = .001$. There were no statistically significant differences in rearrest between max outs and parolees within 3 years of release from prison or during year 4.

With respect to reconviction and reincarceration, the results show that the reconviction for the max outs were statistically more significant than parolees within 3 months after release, 0.09 for max outs compared to 0.02 for parolees; $t = 2.0$ (99), $p = .05$. No other differences between max outs and parolees and reconviction were observed. For offenders who were reincarcerated, max outs were reincarcerated significantly more often than parolees within 2 years of release, 0.71 for max outs compared to 0.52 for parolees, $t = 2.2$ (110), $p = .03$, and within 3 years of release from prison, 0.94 for max outs compared to 0.73 for parolees; $t = 3.4$ (115), $p = .001$. Parolees, on the other hand, were reincarcerated statistically significantly more than max outs within 4 years of release from prison, 0.25 for parolees compared to 0.06 for max outs; $t = 3.0$ (117), $p = .003$.

Discussion

Descriptive analyses indicated that there were several characteristic differences between the max out and parolee sample subgroups, including age, total number of arrests ever, the number of times an offender was incarcerated prior to the instant offense, the number of times an offender was paroled prior to the instant offense, and the instant offense for which the offender was most recently incarcerated. Although several of these differences (age, the total number of arrests ever, the number of prior incarcerations) mirror correlates found to be consistent indicators of recidivism (Petersilia, 2003), the others require more detailed explanation.

This research indicates that, compared with parolees, offenders in the max-out sample subgroup were more likely to have been on parole at some point previous to the instant offense. Yet these data also show no difference between max outs and parolees with regard to the number of parole violations experienced by each group. This finding suggests that although parole board members may have been willing to take a chance by granting parole to the max-out sample

subgroup at some point in the past, the board members were not willing to chance it again, either because of the nature of the instant offense or because of past participation on parole.

The other prearrest characteristic of interest is the instant offense for which the offender was incarcerated. When the instant offense for which the offender was incarcerated was collapsed into one of seven crime type categories, differences were seen between parolees and max outs with respect to drug offenses and violent crime/assault offenses. Interestingly, the instant offense of record was more likely to be a drug offense for offenders who were eventually paroled in contrast to the instant offense of record for offenders who ultimately maxed out, which was more likely to be a violent crime. Although these results may suggest inherent differences in the two sample subgroups at the outset, subsequent Cox regression analyses indicated that these differences in the instant offense type did not significantly impact survival, the ability of the offender to remain free from rearrest, reconviction, or reincarceration.

Logically, some scholars argue that inherent selection bias between those offenders who are selected for discretionary release compared with those who max out may exist. It is not unreasonable to postulate that offenders released to parole are chosen precisely because they are believed to have a better chance for success on parole compared with those released at the expiration of sentence or via mandatory release (Rosenfeld et al., 2005). Yet these data suggest that inherent differences in individual-level characteristics between max outs and parolees released in New Jersey either do not exist or, if they do exist, do not seem to impact outcome.

Moreover, even if individual-level differences in subgroup characteristics sway parole board members to vote one way or the other, these characteristics may not be representative of the overall risk that an offender actually poses to the community. Gendreau, Little, and Goggin (1996) have established that although static factors of risk are important to consider when ascertaining how much risk an offender poses to the community, so too are dynamic risk factors such as attitudes, peer relationships, and housing. As this research was unable to account for these potential confounding factors, future research on release practice in New Jersey should consider assessing risk by release type and outcome using an objective risk instrument. In this way, the impact of static and dynamic factors on outcome when stratified by release type may be more fully elucidated.

Despite unanswered questions about the role that characteristic differences in sample subgroups play in impacting outcome, in keeping with previous research, this analysis found that offenders who were released from prison to parole demonstrated more successful outcomes than other release types (Rosenfeld et al., 2005; U.S. Department of Justice, 2001). Moreover, data from this study indicate that offenders released from prison at the expiration of sentence were more likely to be rearrested and reincarcerated earlier and more often compared with offenders released to parole. Specifically, max outs were likely to be rearrested very soon after release: 24% of max outs were rearrested in the first 3 months after release from prison and 43% of max outs were rearrested within 6 months of release. These data support the conclusions from the 2001 BJS Study that determined that on a national level, if offenders fail, they are more likely to fail in the first 12 months after release (U.S. Department of Justice, 2001).

These data not only argue that offenders who are released to discretionary parole are able to remain free from rearrest, reconviction, and reincarceration longer than offenders released from prison at the expiration of sentence but also show that if parolees were rearrested this event was more likely to occur between Year 1 and Year 2 or between Year 2 and Year 3 of release from prison. This finding has particular relevance for practitioners in New Jersey and other states that may have experienced this phenomenon.

Knowing this, parole policy and practice in New Jersey should enhance strategies that focus on identifying and servicing the needs of parolees during this critical period; further reductions in recidivism might be possible if a supervision strategy that takes this phenomenon into account were developed.

Unfortunately, efforts to determine which specific factors influenced the ability of parolees to remain free from rearrest, reconviction, and reincarceration longer than max outs fell short. Analyses assessing sentence length and the impact of the type of parole supervision on outcome indicated that there were no statistically significant differences between the two sample subgroups with regard to these variables. Furthermore, data on whether the offender was a first-time offender were not captured, making evaluation of this potential confounding factor impossible.

Yet, one explanation for the observed differences in outcomes between parolees and max outs may be tied to the very function of supervision. It may be that the mere existence of supervision is enough to increase the ability of parolees to remain free from rearrest, reconviction, and reincarceration longer than max outs. In this scenario, exposure to supervision through access to a parole officer, the inherent responsibilities and conditions that come with parole, and the services that offenders are often required to obtain may serve as protective factors, extending the time to failure (rearrest, reconviction, or reincarceration) for offenders on parole compared with those who leave prison at the completion of sentence. Furthermore, although it is true that the quality of supervision and service may vary significantly by officer and service provider, one could argue that offenders on parole must have greater access to services compared with offenders who max out, simply because they are made aware of the existence of these services. Lack of access to or knowledge of available services may potentially impact outcome.

However, prior research has shown that exposure to supervision often results not in success but in failure, precisely because supervision exposes an individual to a heightened level of scrutiny not ordinarily experienced by those not under supervision or those subject to less stringent supervision. The 1993 study by Petersilia and Turner, a nine-state randomized study of intensive supervision probation/parole programs (ISP) compared with standard supervision, found that ISP resulted in more technical violations and that overall there was little difference in rearrest rates between offenders assigned to standard supervision compared with those in the ISP group (Petersilia & Turner, 1993).

The possibility exists that practitioners and scholars may be confusing the potentially positive effects of supervision (an umbrella term that encompasses elements of casework and case management and law enforcement) with the decidedly negative effects of too much surveillance. This contention is supported by results from a study by Sherman and colleagues (1997) that found that supervision that includes elements of treatment or rehabilitation reduced recidivism more than supervision alone. Future research might consider reframing evaluations of supervision to include the possibility that supervision may serve as a protective factor, might evaluate the role of the parole officer as service provider, might assess the impact of exposure to service on outcome, and analyze whether differences in parole officer attitudes and practice impact offender outcome.

Although the results of this study have perhaps raised more questions than provided answers, this research does confirm the contention of Travis and Visher (2005) that national evaluations sometimes obscure state-level policy and practice. Hopefully, this research has demonstrated the need for future state-level analyses in New Jersey and elsewhere that result in critical appraisals of policy and practice and substantive change where necessary. In fact, this critical evaluation has already begun in earnest in New Jersey with the formation of the New Jersey State Parole Board Evidence-Based Practices Initiative that has been endorsed and supported in part by the National Institute of Corrections. This initiative's primary aim is to evaluate current parole policy and practice in an effort to improve outcome.

Ultimately, statistical significance that shows that parolees in New Jersey are able to remain free from rearrest, reconviction, and reincarceration longer than max outs must be reconciled with the practical reality that 88% of max outs and 78% of parolees were rearrested within 2 years of release from a New Jersey prison. These outcomes are staggering and should be unacceptable under any circumstances. Discretionary parole release may work in New Jersey, but there is great potential for it to work better.

✉ References

Blumstein, A., & Beck, A. J. (2005). Reentry as a transient state between liberty and recommitment. In J. Travis & C. Visher (Eds.), *Prisoner reentry and crime in America* (pp. 50–79). New York: Cambridge University Press.

Gendreau, P., Little, T., & Goggin, C. (1996). A meta-analysis of the predictors of adult offender recidivism: What works! *Criminology, 34,* 575–607.

Lynch, J. P., & Sabol, W. J. (2001). *Prisoner reentry in perspective.* Washington, DC: The Urban Institute Press.

Petersilia, J. (1999). Parole and prisoner reentry in the United States. In M. Tonry & J. Petersilia (Eds.), *Prisons* (pp. 479–529). Chicago: University of Chicago Press.

Petersilia, J. (2003). *When prisoners come home: Parole and prisoner reentry.* New York: Oxford University Press.

Petersilia, J., & Turner, S. (1993). Intensive probation and parole. In M. Tonry (Ed.), *Crime and Justice: An Annual Review of Research* (pp. 281–335). Chicago: University of Chicago Press.

Piehl, A., & LoBuglio, S. F. (2005). Does supervision matter? In J. Travis & C. Visher (Eds.), *Prisoner reentry and crime in America* (pp. 105–138). New York: Cambridge University Press.

Rosenfeld, R., Wallman, J., & Fornango, R. (2005). The contribution of ex-prisoners to crime rates. In J. Travis & C. Visher (Eds.), *Prisoner reentry and crime in America* (pp. 80–104). New York: Cambridge University Press.

Sherman, L. W., Gottfredson, D., MacKenzie, J., Eck, J., Reuter, P., & Bushway, S. (1997). *Preventing crime: What works, what doesn't, and what's promising.* Washington, DC: National Institute of Justice.

Solomon, A. L., Kachnowski, V, & Bhati, A. (2005). *Does parole work? Analyzing the impact of postprison supervision on rearrest outcomes.* Washington, DC: The Urban Institute Press.

Tonry, M. (2000). Fragmentation of sentencing and corrections in America. *Alternatives to Incarceration, 6,* 9–13.

Travis, J. (2005). *But they all come back: Facing the challenges of prisoner reentry.* Washington, DC: The Urban Institute Press.

Travis, J., & Visher, C. (2005). Introduction: Viewing public safety through the reentry lens. In J. Travis & C. Visher (Eds.), *Prisoner reentry and crime in America* (pp. 1–14). New York: Cambridge University Press.

U.S. Department of Justice. (2001). *Trends in state parole, 1990–2000* (special report). Washington, DC: National Institute of Justice.

DISCUSSION QUESTIONS

1. Given that many states are moving in the direction of eliminating or reducing discretionary parole, what are the potential implications of these findings?

2. Why might states want to continue to supervise those offenders who have maxed out their sentences?

3. Why are these findings potentially not surprising?

4. Using your own state, what method of release is provided for offenders? How many offenders on parole recidivate in a given year? How might your state benefit from the findings of this study?

◈

READING

In this article, Steen and Opsal analyzed parole revocation data from four different states for the individual predictors of success. More specifically, the authors were interested in identifying those factors that explain why someone either succeeds or fails on parole. Using the National Corrections Reporting Program, Steen and Opsal sampled individuals exiting parole in Kentucky, Michigan, New York, and Utah in 2000. A total of 30,766 offenders were included in the sample. Measures of demographic categories, offense type, prior felony convictions, and length of time on parole were included in the analysis. This study was designed as exploratory in nature. Results of the study reveal that being black, being male, and being older (over 30) are predictive of those who are most likely to fail on parole. Legal factors also pose particular problems with this group of offenders. Having prior convictions and being convicted of a violent offense are the strongest predictors of being arrested for a new offense. Likewise, the longer an individual is on parole the more likely they are to reoffend. Overall, these findings have implications for supervision on parole. Although exploratory in nature, this study does point the need for more research examining the individual level predictors of revocation.

SOURCE: Steen, Sara, & Opsal, Tara (2007). "Punishment on the Installment Plan": Individual-level predictors of parole revocation in four states. *The Prison Journal, 87*(3), 344–366. Copyright © 2007 Sage Publications.

"Punishment on the Installment Plan"

Individual-Level Predictors of Parole Revocation in Four States

Sara Steen and Tara Opsal

Between 1980 and the end of the 20th century, the number of people entering prison for parole violations increased dramatically. Whereas in 1980 parole violators represented 17% (27,000) of prison admissions, by 1999 they represented 35% (203,000) of admissions. During this period, the number of offenders admitted to prison for new offenses increased by approximately 350%, whereas the number of offenders admitted for parole violations increased by almost 750%. Stated differently, the number of parole violators admitted to prison in 1999 was greater than the total number of offenders admitted in 1980 (Travis & Lawrence, 2002). Travis and Lawrence argued that "we have, in essence, created a separate path to prison for large numbers of former prisoners" (p. 24). Although there is an extensive research literature on the more common path to prison (i.e., research identifying the predictors of incarceration for new offenders), little is known about the circumstances under which individuals are returned to prison for violating the conditions of their parole (for an excellent review of what is known, see Petersilia, 2003). Furthermore, despite large differences between states in rates of parole revocation, little is known about either the nature or the causes of these differences. For those concerned with recent increases in prison populations, a more complete understanding of the parole revocation process should be paramount.

The question driving this research is not new: We are interested in why some people are sentenced to spend time behind bars while others are allowed to remain in the community. What is new about our research is our study population. Rather than identifying predictors of incarceration for "new" offenders, we hope to identify predictors of reincarceration for individuals who have been in prison and subsequently released on parole. It seems possible that the factors most relevant to revocation decisions are different from those most relevant to initial decisions to incarcerate. In particular, assessments of risk, of paramount importance in today's criminal justice system, may occur differently when all of the offenders under consideration have been incarcerated. This may be especially true in the current climate, where, as Garland (2001) claimed. "The assumption today is that there is no such thing as an 'ex-offender'— only offenders who have been caught before and will strike again" (pp. 180–181).

Of particular interest to us is the role of race in the decision making process. There is a voluminous literature exploring the impact of race on arrest, charging, and sentencing decisions that we draw from to develop predictions about how race will affect decisions about parole revocations. Because of the almost complete absence of research on the revocation decision, we start by looking at whether race has a direct effect on revocation. We then move into an exploration of whether race matters more under certain circumstances than others. By looking at White and Black offenders separately, we are able to assess the relative impact of various demographic and legal factors on parole revocation for members of each group.

In this article we first provide a brief history of parole, explaining both how parole revocation differs from other types of criminal justice decisions and how recent changes in the goals of parole have placed revocation "at the very center of the practice" (Simon, 1993, p. 218). We next review the research literature on revocations, which we supplement with research on recidivism (because one of the forms of revocation arises when a parolee reoffends). In our section on theory, we identify likely main effects on revocation decisions and develop hypotheses regarding legal and extra-legal factors that may contextualize the effect of race.

Theory and Research Hypotheses

In this article, we are interested in identifying factors that explain why some individuals fail on parole whereas others do not. We are further interested in understanding the role of race in parole revocation decisions. In particular, we are interested in whether race will matter more under certain circumstances than others. Our analyses are therefore structured so that we can look at the main effects of variables on parole revocation and at the differential effects of variables on parole revocation for Black and White offenders.

Based on the literature on recidivism, we expect that the variables that predict recidivism will also predict parole revocation, particularly for new offense revocations. Because little is known about the factors contributing to technical violation revocations, we are unsure whether these same variables will help explain variation in these decisions. However, given that Hughes et al. (2001) identified these as factors associated with parole failure (their study does not include controls and does not distinguish between new offense and technical violation revocations), and absent any reason to believe otherwise, we predict that these variables will affect both technical violation and new offense revocations.

> *Hypothesis 1:* Minorities, male individuals, younger offenders, property offenders, and offenders with prior felony incarcerations will be more likely to have their parole revoked than their counterparts.

Based on recidivism findings, we also predict the following:

> *Hypothesis 2:* Parolees who have recently been released from prison will be more likely to have their parole revoked than parolees who have spent more time on parole.

This may be particularly true for new offenses (as Langan and Levin's, 2002, results apply only to recidivism, not to revocation), but we expect it to hold true for technical violations as well, as it seems likely that parolees will have less difficulty following conditions of parole after they have had time to settle back into their lives outside prison.

Beyond these main effects, we are also interested in how race contextualizes the effects of legal and extralegal variables on revocation. We look to theoretical work on racial stereotyping to develop predictions about the circumstances under which race will matter. Much of the theoretical work on discretion focuses on how culturally derived stereotypes link certain groups of offenders to notions of dangerousness, culpability, and threat of criminality. In a theoretical statement about judicial discretion, for example, Albonetti (1991) explained that judges develop "patterned responses" using stereotypes that link individual characteristics (such as race, age, or gender) to expectations about criminal responsibility and dangerousness (p. 247). Steffensmeier, Ulmer, and Kramer (1998) took this idea a step further, arguing that it is the combination of indicators of threat that will have the largest impact on sentencing. Their analyses suggest that the effects of offender race are contextualized by both age and gender, with young male Blacks receiving the harshest treatment. The first possibility we consider, then, is that minority status will affect decision making when it is associated with other status characteristics associated with threat, such as age and gender.

> *Hypothesis 3:* The positive effect of minority status on the likelihood of parole revocation will be largest for male and younger offenders.

Whereas Steffensmeier et al. (1998) demonstrated that race is most likely to be salient for particular kinds of offenders, Spohn and her colleagues (Spohn & Cederblom, 1991; Spohn & DeLone, 2000) have argued that the salience of race will depend in part on legal factors. In their 1991 article, Spohn and Cederblom tested the "liberation hypothesis" (Kalven & Zeisel, 1966), which suggests that in less serious cases . . . the appropriate sentence is not necessarily obvious; consequently judges arc liberated from the constraints imposed by the law, by other members of the courtroom work group, and by public opinion, and are free to take into account extralegal considerations such as race. (Spohn & Cederblom, 1991, p. 323)

Their findings strongly support this argument, with race being significant only in cases involving less serious offenses and offenders with no prior felony convictions. Based on their findings, we predict the following:

Hypothesis 4: The positive effect of minority status on the likelihood of parole revocation will be largest for offenders convicted of less serious offenses (i.e., offenses other than violent or sex offenses) and for offenders with no prior felony incarcerations.

A third (and related) possibility is that race will matter most when the appropriate decision is ambiguous (Unnever & Hembroff, 1988). This possibility leads us to predict that the effects of race will depend largely on the type of revocation. Revocation decisions involving technical violations are more ambiguous than those involving new offenses for a number of reasons. First, in cases involving technical violations, parole officers are more likely to have discretion than when a new criminal offense occurs. Second, under the new model of parole, one of the primary functions of parole officers is to assess and manage risk. Because risk assessment is largely subjective, it generally involves a large amount of discretion (though attempts to objectify risk assessment have likely decreased discretion at this stage). Parole decisions regarding technical violations, then, likely involve a larger element of risk assessment than do decisions regarding new offenses. Thus, we predict the following:

Hypothesis 5: The positive effect of minority status on parole revocation will be larger for technical violation revocations than for new offense revocations.

✄ Method

Sample

Our sample consists of individuals exiting parole in four states in 2000. The four states—Kentucky, Michigan, New York, and Utah—were selected according to the following set of criteria. First, each sample state reported to National Corrections Reporting Program (NCRP) parole release data in the year 2000. Second, each state distinguishes between revocations for new offenses and for technical violations, a distinction that is central to our analyses. Third, none of the states reports more than 5% of its cases as falling into categories other than successful completion of parole, revocation for a new offense, or revocation for a technical violation (other categories include discharged as absconder or under warrant, returned to prison with revocation or charges pending, transferred to another jurisdiction, and death).

The states were also selected based on the degree to which they contributed to variation of the sample. We looked for geographical variation and therefore included states from the Northeast, the Midwest, the West, and the South. We also looked for variation in parole trends. Specifically, for variation in experiences with crime and justice, we looked at prison population size. The four states in our sample range from a prison population rate of 254 per 100,000 citizens in Utah to a rate of 480 per 100,000 citizens in New York. Success rates among parolees (the percentage of parole discharges that were because of successful completion) range from 19% in Utah (the lowest success rate in the nation in 2000) to more than 50% in New York and Michigan.

Although our sample states satisfy the requirements for this study and provide a geographically diverse sample, it is important to note that these were virtually the only states that met our requirements. Although there were a few other states that we could have chosen (particularly in the Northeast), we had no other choices in the South or West.

The parole release mechanisms in our four study states are similar. All four states authorize a parole board to evaluate prisoners and allow discretionary release after a minimum sentence has been served. New York, however, as a result of the Sentencing Reform Act of 1998 (commonly referred to as Jenna's Law), eliminated discretionary release for all violent offenders. These offenders, after serving six sevenths of their sentence, must serve a period of court-imposed postrelease supervision. Finally, prisoners can also be released from New York prisons as a result of completing their entire sentence; these offenders have no supervision following release.

Information regarding the details of states' revocation policies is not as accessible as release information. It is our understanding, however, that the four states in this study operate within a similar revocation framework. All offenders on parole in these states are assigned to a community parole officer. These officers are responsible for supervising the offender as they reenter their community by ensuring they are following the conditions set forth by their parole agreement. If the offender violates one or more of the conditions in this agreement, the parole officer may file for revocation of parole.

In each of our study states, offenders have the right to two hearings if a revocation is filed. A probable cause hearing establishes whether there is enough evidence to follow through with the revocation. Two decisions are made at the revocation hearing itself: whether to revoke and what the new sentence will be. In Kentucky, Michigan, and Utah, a hearing officer that represents the parole board hears the probable cause hearing; New York uses either a hearing officer or some type of supervisor. In Utah and Kentucky the parole board conducts the final hearing, whereas in New York and Michigan the hearing officer makes the final decision. New York appears to be the only state that uses guidelines which govern the parole revocation process. These guidelines require revocation and the resultant punishment to be determined by an offender's criminal history, number of prior parole violations, and crime of conviction.

Data

The data used for this research come from the NCRP. NCRP data are collected and compiled every calendar year by the Bureau of the Census through an agreement with the Bureau of Justice Statistics and include information on all individuals entering and exiting correctional custody and correctional supervision in the United States. The NCRP data are divided into three separate data sets; prison admissions, prison releases, and parole releases. For the project presented here, we look only at the parole releases data set, as we are trying to better understand why certain parolees exit parole because of successful completion, whereas others exit because of revocation. The dependent variable in our study is parole release type, which compares individuals who are released from parole because of successful completion (reference category) to individuals who are released because of revocation for a new offense and individuals who are released because of revocation for a technical violation.

Information that is not included in the NCRP data includes the type of new offense or technical violation for which an offender has been revoked. This information would add greatly to our understanding of the revocation process. Unfortunately, it is not only unavailable in the NCRP data, it is often unavailable even at the state level. We also have only rough measures of offense seriousness (we can categorize offenses into types, but we cannot distinguish the seriousness of offenses within these types) and of prior record (we know only whether someone has previously been incarcerated for a felony and therefore cannot distinguish among offenders with lengthy prior records; we also know nothing about the criminal history of those without prior felony incarcerations—these individuals could be repeat offenders but simply never before been in a state prison). Although these are serious limitations, we hope that this study can provide some general information about parole revocation decisions and perhaps prompt data gathering that would allow for more nuanced analyses.

Measures

Demographic variables in the study include race (Black and White offenders only, other races excluded), sex, age at the time of release from prison onto parole (coded in three categories: 18–29, 30–49, and 50 and older), and education (highest level of schooling completed by the offender, coded in four categories: less than high school degree, high school degree or equivalent, some college, college degree or higher). We measure offense type by looking at the most serious offense for which an offender was convicted (for the original incarceration) and recode offenses into five categories: property, drug, violent, sex, and public order. The NCRP includes general information about each individual's criminal history, measured only roughly by whether an offender has any prior felony incarcerations. Finally, we include a variable measuring the length of time an offender has spent on parole prior to revocation (in years).

It is important to conducting multivariate analyses to understand the relationships between race, demographic, and legal variables as they affect the likelihood of parole revocation. For example, offense type differs between Black and White offenders, with White offenders more likely to have committed property, sex, or public order offenses and Black offenders more likely to have committed violent or drug offenses. Black offenders are also more likely to have prior felony incarcerations (59%) than White offenders (50%).

Analysis

The dependent variable in our analyses, parole outcome, is polychotomous, with the following outcomes: "Successful completion of parole," "Parole revocation on a new offense," and "Parole revocation on a technical violation." Because the dependent variable is nominal, we use multinomial logistic regression for our analyses. This type of logistic regression is appropriate when it cannot be assumed that the slopes for each logit are the same across each level of the dependent variable. The reference category in each model is "completed parole successfully."

Results

The discussion of results is organized as follows. First, we discuss the results of the full sample analyses. We then focus on the race-specific models for the full sample to discuss differential effects of legal and demographic variables by race. In doing this, we first discuss the effects of demographic factors, then move to a discussion of legal factors.

Full Sample

Most of the demographic variables have significant effects on the likelihood of revocation in the predicted directions. Being Black has a significant positive effect on revocation for new offenses (Blacks are 19% more likely than Whites to have their parole revoked for a new offense) and technical violations (Blacks are 50% more likely than Whites to have their parole revoked for a technical violation). Female individuals are significantly less likely than male to fail on parole, and this effect is larger for new offenses (48% less likely than male offenders) than for technical violations (26% less likely than male). Older offenders are much less likely than younger offenders to fail on parole. Compared to 18- to 29-year-olds, offenders between 30 and 49 are 26% less likely to fail because of a new-offense, and offenders 50 and older are 59% less likely to come back on a new offense and 40% less likely to fail because of a technical violation. With the exception of the insignificant effect of being between 30 and 49 on the likelihood of revocation for a technical violation, these findings are all consistent with Hypothesis 1.

Legal factors are also significant predictors of parole revocation, in the predicted directions (consistent with Hypothesis 1). Offenders with prior felonies are much more likely than offenders who have not previously been incarcerated for a felony to have their parole revoked. Offenders with priors are 121% more likely to have their parole revoked for new offenses and 80% more likely to have their parole revoked for technical violations. Offense type is also an important predictor of parole success. Compared to property offenders (excluded category), all other offenders are less likely to be revoked for a parole violation. For revocation for new offenses, property offenders are followed by drug offenders (the difference is not significant), violent offenders (34% less likely to be revoked), public order offenders (51% less likely), and sex offenders

(73% less likely). These findings are generally consistent with research on recidivism and Hypothesis 1, which suggest that property offenders are the most likely to recidivate and sex offenders the least likely. For technical violations, property offenders are followed by sex offenders (the difference is not significant), violent offenders (11% less likely to be revoked), drug offenders (15% less likely), and public order offenders (49% less likely). Differences in parole failures for technical violations are likely influenced by the different levels of surveillance for different offenders. Offenders classified as high-risk offenders will likely be under tighter surveillance, even if the perceived risk is not related to actual likelihood of reoffending. Sex offenders, for example, although unlikely to commit a new offense, may be under more intense supervision than public order offenders, thereby increasing the odds they will get caught violating a condition of their parole.

Time on parole is also a significant predictor of parole revocation. As predicted in Hypothesis 2, the longer an offender has served on parole, the more likely he or she is to succeed. The magnitude of this effect is somewhat smaller for new offenses (for each year on parole, an offender is 33% less likely to be revoked for a new offense) than for technical violations (revocation is 40% less likely for each year on parole).

Finally, the state effects are all significant and large (compared to the excluded category, New York). Although we would need to collect much more data to discuss the reasons for these differences (e.g., interviews with decision makers, analysis of policy differences), it is important to point out that states appear to operate very differently in terms of their use of revocation. The fact that New York is the only state in our sample with parole revocation guidelines suggests that perhaps one fruitful avenue for research would be to look at these policy differences and the impact they have on rates of revocation.

◪ Race-Specific Models

The race-specific models allow us to look at differences in the magnitude of effects on revocation for

Black and White offenders. The columns to the right of the regression results indicate significant differences between Black and White offenders. Gender and age have significantly different effects on the likelihood of revocation for Black and White offenders. First, the negative effect of being female on the likelihood of revocation for a technical violation is significantly larger for female Blacks (who are 56% less likely to be revoked than male Blacks) than for female Whites (where the difference is 38%). This difference also exists for technical violation revocations, with no significant gender difference for White offenders, and female Blacks being 37% less likely than male Blacks to have their parole revoked.

There are also significant differences in the effects of age on the likelihood of revocation for Black and White offenders. The difference between the youngest (ages 18–29) and oldest (ages 50 and older) Black offenders in terms of likelihood of revocation for a new offense (older offenders are 65% less likely to be revoked) is significantly larger than the difference for White offenders (older offenders are 51% less likely to be revoked). The opposite, however, is true for revocation for technical violations, where the oldest White offenders are 50% less likely to be revoked and the oldest Black offenders are only 32% less likely.

The difference in likelihood of revocation for a new offense between property (excluded category) and public order offenders is significantly larger for Blacks (58% less likely to be revoked) than Whites (49% less likely to be revoked), whereas the difference in likelihood of revocation for a technical violation between these two types of offenders is larger for Whites (53% less likely to be revoked) than Blacks (43% less likely to be revoked). There is also a significant difference in the magnitude of the difference between property and violent offenders for new offense revocations, with a larger difference existing for Whites (41% less likely to be revoked) than Blacks (32% less likely to be revoked).

Years on parole has a significantly larger effect for Whites than Blacks. For new offense revocations, each year on parole renders White offenders 37% less likely to be revoked, compared to 31% for Black offenders; for technical violations, each year on parole renders White offenders 44% less likely to be revoked, compared to 38% for Black offenders. Finally, the positive effect of prior felony incarcerations is much larger for Whites than for Blacks. For Whites, having a prior felony incarceration leads to a 184% increase in the likelihood of being revoked for a new offense (compared to 81% for Blacks) and a 133% increase in the likelihood of being revoked for a technical violation (compared to 50% for Blacks).

Without further analysis, however, we cannot determine whether these results support or refute Hypotheses 3 and 4, which predict that the positive effects of race on revocation will be larger for certain groups of offenders than others. We cannot determine from the findings whether the significant differences by race are because of larger effects for the groups predicted (i.e., male offenders, younger offenders, offenders convicted of less serious offenses, and offenders with no prior felony incarcerations) or smaller effects for the counterparts of these groups.

In regard to gender, the negative effect of being female on the likelihood of revocation is significantly larger for Blacks than Whites. We cannot, however, determine from these results whether the larger differences for Black offenders are a result of lenient treatment of female Blacks relative to female Whites, harsh treatment of male Blacks relative to male Whites, or both. Looking first at new offense revocations, it appears that the significant race differences result more from relatively lenient treatment of female Blacks (for whom the revocation rate is 4.4%, compared to a rate of 6.5% for female Whiles) rather than relatively harsh treatment of male Blacks (indeed, the revocation rates for male Blacks are slightly lower, at 8%, than those for male Whites, at 9.5%). Turning to technical violations, however, we see that for both female Blacks and Whites the revocation rate is approximately 33%, suggesting that the difference lies in relatively harsh treatment of male Blacks. Indeed, the revocation rate for male Blacks is 42%, compared to 35% for male Whites. These results show mixed support for Hypothesis 3 (i.e., differences for new offense revocations contradict Hypothesis 3,

whereas differences for technical violation revocations support Hypothesis 3).

Similar patterns can be observed regarding the relative rates of revocation for different age groups for Black and White offenders, although, for revocation for technical violations, the difference between young (18–29 years old) and old (50 and older) offenders is larger for Whites than Blacks. The results suggest that, for technical violation revocations, the difference between Black and White offenders increases with age, with age appearing more important for Whites (for whom the likelihood of revocation decreases more sharply by age) than for Blacks.

This is contradictory to our prediction in Hypothesis 3 that differences in the likelihood of revocation between young and old offenders would be larger for Black than for White offenders.

Turning now to Hypothesis 4, it may be observed that for property and public order offenders, Blacks are significantly more likely to have their parole revoked for a technical violation than are Whites. This finding does not allow us to make the kind of argument we made with gender, that the differences are clearly caused by more severe treatment of the group predicted (in this case, public order offenders) rather than less severe treatment of the comparison group (in this case, property offenders). To test Hypothesis 4, we can however examine whether the differential treatment is larger for less serious cases, which it is. The race difference in revocation rates for property offenders (more serious) is 7.5%, whereas the difference for public order offenders (less serious) is 10.5%. These results begin to address Hypothesis 4, which suggests that the positive effect of minority status on the likelihood of parole revocation will be largest in less serious cases. Because the difference is quite small, however, our findings provide only tentative support for Hypothesis 4.

The significantly larger effect of prior felony incarcerations for Whites than for Blacks is driven entirely by harsher treatment of Blacks with no felony incarcerations compared to their White counterparts. The revocation rate for offenders with prior felony incarcerations is remarkably similar (45% for White offenders,

46% for Black offenders). For offenders with no prior felony incarcerations, however, the rate for Black offenders (35%) is considerably larger than the rate for White offenders (25%). These results provide clear support for Hypothesis 4.

To conclude this section, we turn to Hypothesis 5, in which we predict that the positive effect on minority status on revocation will be larger for technical violations than for new offenses. Although Black offenders are 19% more likely than White offenders to be revoked for new offenses, they are almost 50% more likely to be revoked for technical violations. Whether this is because of a higher percentage of violations being committed by Blacks, a higher level of supervision of Blacks than Whites (controlling for their offense type), or differences in the way decision makers behave in revocation decisions is a question we hope to pursue in future work.

Discussion and Conclusions

Before embarking on a discussion of our findings, we repeat the caution that this study is exploratory. The NCRP data do not allow us to control for what might be very significant explanatory variables, such as the type of new offense or technical violation for which an individual is being revoked. Because of this, we put this study forward as a call for more detailed data collection and continued research into the factors that predict parole revocation than as a conclusive statement about what factors explain the likelihood of failure or success on parole.

With these caveats in mind, several findings stand out as noteworthy. First, race has a significant impact on the likelihood of revocation. In the full sample, Black offenders are 19% more likely than White offenders to have their parole revoked for a new offense and are 50% more likely than Whites to have their parole revoked for a technical violation, controlling for other demographic and legal factors. We argue here that this effect may be a result of the relatively large amount of discretion available in decisions about whether to file for a revocation when an offender violates parole and about whether to revoke such an offender. In particular, the

larger difference in revocations for technical violations than for new offenses could provide support for Unnever and Hembroff's (1988) argument that race will matter most in decisions where the appropriate outcome is relatively ambiguous. It is also possible, however, that Black offenders are more likely to violate the conditions of their parole (by committing a new offense or technical violation) or to be detected in such violations. The available data simply do not allow us to parse these different explanations. To look at whether differential revocation rates are because of differences in parolee behavior or in parole officer decision making, one would need much more detailed information about the behavior of parolees, information that is in many states available only in offender case files. We are currently in the process of collecting such information for one state so that we can begin to address this important question.

The second important finding is that the size of both legal and demographic effects on the likelihood of revocation varies, often dramatically, depending on whether the revocation is for a new offense or a technical violation. This finding suggests the importance of separating these two different types of revocation and of thinking about them as different kinds of decisions. That some effects are larger for new offense revocations whereas others are larger for technical violation revocations suggests the need for more detailed information about the behavior for which an offender is being revoked. That is, it is impossible to know why race matters more for technical violation revocations than new offense revocations without better understanding what kinds of technical violations offenders are being revoked on (and whether the violations are similar for Black and White offenders).

Third, time on parole is a significant predictor of parole success. The longer offenders spend on parole, the more likely they are to succeed (this finding differs from Kassebaum's, 1999, findings). This effect is large, with each year on parole reducing the likelihood of a new offense revocation by 33% and of a technical violation revocation by 40%. These findings support the argument that the longer an offender has spent in the community, the better integrated he or she will be and the less likely to engage in unlawful behaviors. It is interesting that this effect is significantly larger for White offenders than for Black offenders (for both new offenses and technical violations), raising important questions about whether White offenders are more successfully reintegrated than Black offenders.

Fourth, the magnitude of many of the effects uncovered differs between White and Black offenders. The significantly larger effect of gender on Black offenders is entirely because of a higher likelihood of revocation for male Blacks than male Whites. Our analyses demonstrate that the strength of gender as a predictor of revocation decisions for White offenders is much smaller than it is for Black offenders, supporting the argument that indicators of threat such as gender and race act in concert to significantly impact the treatment of minority offenders.

Fifth, prior felony incarcerations are more relevant in determining revocation for Whites than they are for Blacks. This difference arises from a higher likelihood of revocation for Blacks with no priors (compared to similar Whites) rather than a higher likelihood of revocation for White offenders with priors (compared to similar Black offenders). If this difference arises because of differences in decision making (rather than differences in behavior), it would support the notion that race will matter more in less serious cases (Spohn & Cederblom, 1991).

Finally, the significant differences between the states included in our analysis strongly suggest the importance of looking at parole revocation decision making in the context of jurisdictions rather than trying to look at them in the aggregate. Although our analyses allowed us to get only to the level of the state, it would be instructive to explore parole revocation decision making at the level of the county, the parole agency, and even the parole agent to detect differences that likely exist. Research that looks at the intricacies of this decision point (e.g., by breaking it into separate decisions of whether to file for revocation and whether to revoke) will help us to better understand why revocation rates vary so much over time and place.

The parole revocation decision is extremely important—as important, one might argue, as the original incarceration decision, given that it is a decision that results in the deprivation of an individual's freedom based on a decision by the state. That we know so little about it is troublesome, not only because it provides a unique window into the exercise of discretion in criminal justice decision making but also because decisions to revoke offenders' parole have contributed greatly to the explosion in prison populations across the country. Our hope is that this research will provide a useful jumping-off point for future research on this decision.

✂ References

Albonetti, C. A. (1991). An integration of theories to explain judicial discretion. *Social Problems, 38,* 247–266.

Burke, P. (1997). *Policy-driven responses to probation and parole violations.* Silver Spring, MD: Center for Effective Public Policy.

Caplow, T., & Simon, J. (1999). Understanding prison policy and population trends. In M. Tonry & J. Petersilia (Eds.), *Prisons: Crime and justice: A review of research* (Vol. 26). Chicago: The University of Chicago Press.

Clarke, S., Yuan-Huei, W. L., & Wallace, W. L. (1988). *Probation and recidivism in North Carolina: Measurement and classification of risk.* Chapel Hill: University of North Carolina, Institute of Government.

Feeley, M., & Simon, J. (1992). The new penology: Notes on the emerging strategy of corrections and its implications. *Criminology, 30,* 449–474.

Garland, D. (2001). *The culture of control.* Chicago: University of Chicago Press.

Hughes, T., Wilson, D. J., & Beck, A. J. (2001). *Trends in state parole, 1990–2000.* Washington, DC: Bureau of Justice Statistics.

Irish, J. (1989). *Probation and recidivism.* Mineola, NY: Nassau County Probation Department.

Kalven, H., Jr., & Zeisel, H. (1966). *The American jury.* Boston: Little, Brown.

Kassebaum, G. (1999). *Survival on parole: A study of post-prison adjustment and the risk of returning to prison in the state of Hawaii.* Honolulu: Social Science Research Institute and Department of the Attorney General State of Hawaii.

Kassebaum, G., & Davidson-Corondo, J. (2001). *Parole decision making in Hawaii: Setting minimum terms, approving release, deciding on revocation, and predicting success and failure on parole.* Honolulu: Social Science Research Institute and Department of the Attorney General State of Hawaii.

Knapp, K. (1993). Allocation of discretion and accountability within sentencing structures. *University of Colorado Law Review, 64,* 679–705.

Langan, P., & Levin, D. (2002). *Recidivism of prisoners released in 1994*. Washington, DC: Bureau of Justice Statistics.

Messinger, S., & Berecochea, J. (1992. June). Don't stay too long but do come back soon: Reflections on the size and vicissitudes of California's parole population. Paper presented at California Conference on Growth and Its Impact on correctional policy. University of California at Berkeley.

Petersilia, J. (1985). Granting felons probation: Public risks and alternatives. *Crime and Delinquency, 31,* 379–392.

Petersilia, J. (2003). *When prisoners come home: Parole and prisoner reentry*. New York: Oxford University Press.

Simon, J. (1993). *Poor discipline: Parole and the social control of the underclass. 1890-1990*. Chicago: University of Chicago Press.

Spohn, C., & Cederblom, J. (1991). Race and disparities in sentencing: A test of the liberation hypothesis. *Justice Quarterly, 8,* 305–327.

Spohn, C., & DeLone, M. (2000). When does race matter? An analysis of the conditions under which race affects sentence severity. *Sociology of Crime, Law and Deviance, 2,* 3–37.

Steffensmeier, D., Ulmer, J., & Kramer, J. H. (1998). The interaction of race, gender, and age in criminal sentencing: The punishment cost of being young, Black, and male. *Criminology, 36,* 762–798.

Travis, J., & Lawrence, S. (2002). *Beyond the prison gates: The state of parole in America*. Washington, DC: Justice Policy Center.

Unnever, J. D., & Hembroff, L. A. (1988). The prediction of racial/ethnic sentencing disparities: An expectation states approach. *Journal of Research in Crime and Delinquency, 25,* 53–82.

DISCUSSION QUESTIONS

1. How might the results of this study impact who receives parole and when?

2. What are the implications of this study for supervision of individuals released in the community?

3. What are some of the benefits and some of the potential limitations of examining parole revocation in four states?

4. Given what we know about recidivism and overcrowding, should states revoke offenders for more technical violations? Why or why not?

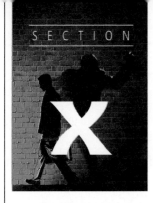

SECTION

X

Juvenile Offenders

Learning Objectives

1. Know the early origins of juvenile probation.

2. Know and understand the processes involved with juvenile probation.

3. Demonstrate knowledge of the juvenile court system and its effect on community corrections with juvenile offenders.

4. Understand how risk factors and protective factors affect the likelihood for continued offending among juveniles.

5. Identify the different forms of residential and nonresidential programs that exist in juvenile corrections and the types of therapy they both employ.

6. Be aware of the basic dynamics associated with juvenile gang offenders and understand the difficulties in getting youth out of gang life.

7. Be aware of the informal and alternative approaches to juvenile processing, including restorative justice, family conferences, and teen courts.

The juvenile justice system is one that is complicated and quite different from that of the adult criminal justice system. It is also a major component of the work involved in community supervision. Since the young tend to commit more crimes than those who are later in life, and since most juveniles are not incarcerated for long periods of time (if at all), this means that there is a substantial population of juvenile offenders on probation throughout the United States. This means that the juvenile population is one that must be given specific attention and consideration when discussing various aspects of community supervision. Though it is impossible to fully describe and detail the entire juvenile justice system in one chapter of a text, this chapter seeks to fill in some of the gaps in information that might otherwise exist, thereby integrating information specific to juvenile offenders as it fits within the whole scheme of this text. In this manner, the information in this section augments the other information so that the student will be fully aware of community supervision issues when dealing with both the adult and the juvenile offender populations.

⬛ The Early History of Juvenile Probation

As with most issues pertaining to juvenile justice, **juvenile probation** traces its roots back to those precepts that were established in England during the Middle Ages under the principle of **parens patriae**. Parens patriae is a Latin term that denotes that the king, as father of his country, is empowered and obligated to protect the welfare of the country's children. However, it is John Augustus who is revered as the father of juvenile probation, just as he is held to be the father of adult probation. Indeed, it was not uncommon for John Augustus to supervise juvenile offenders. This is particularly true when one considers that laws back then were different in relation to adulthood, child protection, and the general coming of age into majority.

Thus, even the adult offenders who John Augustus might have supervised were probably juveniles by today's standards. John Augustus' work was instrumental in legislation that established probation for juveniles in 1878. During this same time period, the Society for the Prevention of Cruelty to Children was also established in 1875. Later, in 1899, this group would be instrumental in forming the first juvenile court in Cook County, Illinois.

The Cook County juvenile court emerged from the concerns of a group of compassionate and wealthy women in Chicago who advocated for the rights of disadvantaged children who were found errant of the law. These women, commonly referred to as the child savers, fought for these needy children to have the same care, custody, and treatment as their natural family would have presumably provided. The creation of the juvenile court was one project that was thought to help toward this objective, integrating individualized treatment approaches, serving needs of the youth, and providing guidance to avoid engaging in further deviant behavior. It was at this time that the concern with stigmatization of youth emerged within the treatment of juveniles, a concept that is still alive and well today. In order to avoid the negative effects of labeling, informal court proceedings were utilized where the full gamut of constitutional safeguards would not be necessary—the point to the court being one of reintegration rather than punishment.

Thus, juvenile court proceedings were informal and conducted without any of the typical constitutional protections secured by adults, with the goal to protect and serve the best interests of the child. Interestingly, juvenile court records were sealed as a means of ensuring that youth were not negatively labeled as a result of their contact with the court. The whole idea revolved around the notion that youth, unlike adults, were not yet lost and that reintegrative efforts would tend to have optimal likelihoods of success. This line of thought also considered youth to be more impressionable and open to positive change, if only given the appropriate guidance. The use of constitutional safeguards were thought to be impediments to the informal helping approach that was desired since these safeguards were rooted in an adversarial mentality that juvenile advocates sought to avoid.

After the first juvenile court was established, these courts spread throughout the nation until in 1927 all but two states had enacted legislation for both juvenile courts and juvenile probation. It is important to point out that probation is largely an extension of the courts in many respects, even though it is presented in this text (and in others) as a branch of corrections. Thus, any developments in the juvenile court also transferred to eventual changes in the nature of juvenile probation. Thus, juvenile probation quite naturally implemented the helping approach with youth, just as did those courts that processed juveniles. According to Latessa and Allen (1999), "the theoretical assumption of juvenile probation was that providing guidance, counseling, resources, and supervision would assist low-risk juveniles to adapt to constructive living," and in the process, these youth could avoid the detrimental effects of institutionalization.

⊠ The Nature of Juvenile Probation

Juvenile probation is a judicial disposition under which youthful offenders are subject to certain conditions imposed by the juvenile court while being allowed to remain in the community during the duration of their sentence. Probation is the most widely used judicial disposition used in juvenile courts around the country. The three primary functions of juvenile probation are intake, investigation, and supervision. During the intake stage of the court proceedings, the probation officer will typically decide whether or not to file a petition on a child referred to the court. Investigation consists of the compilation of a social history of the juvenile to assist the judge in making decisions. Lastly, supervision focuses mainly on crime control elements to ensure that juveniles do not reoffend.

During the intake stage of the juvenile process, the probation officer screens youth who are referred to the court and conducts a preliminary investigation, which includes an interview where the probation officer will advise the youthful offender of their rights. If the parents or legal guardians have not yet been notified of the juvenile's status, the probation agency will inform them and will ensure that they are advised of their legal options and their right to secure an attorney. In addition, the probation officer conducting the intake may find it useful to interview the family, witnesses, victims, and other personnel to determine if detention or other considerations may be necessary for the youthful offender. Naturally, the juvenile's school will likely be contacted to gain information and to also make appropriate educational arrangements for the youth while they are being processed. Lastly, if the youth has been in court before or is already on probation, the intake officer will find it necessary to update himself or herself with the previous reports that are on file.

The investigation stage is roughly 60 days in length, but if the courthouse combines the adjudicatory and disposition stages, it may be required that the officer finish the investigation prior to the youth's appearance in court. This investigation is often referred to as the **social study**, which details the youth's personal background, family, educational progress, previous violations, employment, and so forth. This social study will end with the probation officer's diagnosis and treatment plan, as well as the probation officer's ultimate recommendation to the court. With this report, the probation officer provides final determination of whether the youth should be returned to the community as well as the specific conditions for the recommended probation sentence.

The **supervision stage** includes the casework, surveillance, and various aspects of security management to track the behavior of the juvenile. This stage is, at least in the most basic terms, a key function of the probation department. In the process of performing this function, it is common for juveniles to actually develop a strong connection with their juvenile probation officer. Despite the fact that juvenile probation officers may be responsible for supervising the security elements of the youth's sentence, the other functions of juvenile probation tend to mitigate the relationship and provide for a blend between mentor and rule monitor. The strong focus on rehabilitation tends to weigh out in most cases and reflects the general operational focus of the juvenile probation officer.

Probation supervision is used in the majority of cases where juveniles are adjudicated. This form of sentence is considered appropriate for youth who are not violent and are not seen as being in serious need of intensive services, such as might be encountered with drug addicted youth or those with serious mental health concerns. In such cases, these youth would be sent to residential community treatment centers, most of which will be designed for youthful offenders. Even though the youth may have emotional and/or behavioral problems, they can still end up on probation due to a lack of effective inpatient services being available in a given area. This might be true in some rural communities where residential facilities may not exist. In such cases, youth are typically required to participate in a number of activities and/or treatment-related functions as a means of accommodating their corollary (but important) issues. Further, during the supervision of the youth, there are often added requirements that the youthful offender obey their parents/guardians, that they attend school, that they return home at a specified time during the day, and that they avoid other known youthful offenders. During this process, the probation officer will often work with the youth, attempting to dialogue about problems facing the young offender, including the pushes toward crime and the potential lack of pulls to keep them from returning to crime.

There are many theories that speculate on the causal factors associated with delinquency, but nearly all agree that the presence of adult supervision is important and that the existence of family influences are perhaps the most instrumental forms of socializing elements available. Thus, probation officers who oversee juveniles will likely be engaged in a number of functions that also involve the families of the juvenile offender. Addressing these factors can become quite complicated since it may be that the parents themselves are not high functioning and/or may be ill-equipped to handle the youth's behavior, both at home and in their school or community. Indeed, some parents may be in need of parenting classes and may be misguided on effective parenting techniques to aid their child. In these cases, it may seem that to some extent the entire family is on probation, particularly if family therapy is warranted and/or it is determined that the parents have been neglectful or abusive of the youth. It is common for many juvenile offenders to report disproportionate levels of abuse in their past histories, leading researchers to conclude that abusive experiences aggravate the likelihood of offending and compound the likelihood of recidivism. Thus, returning youth to these homes may not be the best option. However, many youth are returned to homes that are not the best option due to a lack of resources. Though juvenile probation officers will tend to monitor the family system's progress, this can still have negative effects on the youth and their overall ability to break out of criminal behavior. This is particularly true when the juvenile does not wish to be separated from their family, regardless of how toxic that family might be.

On the other hand, it may be that the parental system is actually quite well functioning and that the youthful offender engages in delinquent actions due to other factors. One primary factor can be peers who are selected. The impact of a teen's friends is great, and if the youth befriends other youngsters who are delinquent, a certain pull toward criminogenic behavior is likely. The impact of delinquent peers is actually a commonly studied phenomenon (Cox, Allen, Hanser, & Conrad, 2008; Hanser, 2007a). In fact, as youth progress from early childhood to adolescence, they tend to place more importance on the judgment from their peers than that which they receive from their parents; that is a natural process of autonomy seeking, a process common to youth who are maturing into adults. This then means that some may go through periods of storm and stress where parents seem to have lost much of the influence and impact that they once had in guiding their child's life. Add to this the various physiological changes that occur during the teenage years and it becomes clear that these individuals can be inherently challenging for even the best of parents. Thus, it cannot be said that youthful delinquency is simply a product of poor parenting.

Further, others may see problems with juveniles on probation stemming from an inability and/or unwillingness to relate in a constructive manner with authority figures (Abadinsky, 2003). Abadinsky (2003) claims that "parents, school officials, and others who have represented authority to the young person have caused him or her to develop a negative, even hostile, attitude toward authority in general" (p. 143). While it is true that many youth on juvenile probation may have a natural distrust of authority (particularly adult authority), the general claim that school officials and parents serve as the cause of these problems is something that should be refuted. Indeed, some youth will have a variety of behavioral disorders, such as oppositional defiant disorder, hyperactivity disorder, or the even more serious conduct disorder (Hanser, 2007a). These disorders tend to appear with disproportional frequency among those youth processed through the juvenile justice system than is the case among youth not processed. Often, when youth have these types of diagnosable disorders, the fault does not lie with parents or school officials. In such cases, the causal factors are complicated and are often due to personal characteristics of the young person that are biopsychosocial in nature.

Even in such cases where treatment-resistant diagnoses are involved, probation officers can have an overall positive impact by role modeling healthy reactions to the youth's aberrant behavior while also enforcing consequences for illegal behavior. Further, the use of other role models who are important to the young person should be utilized, when feasible. In some cases, juvenile probation officers may incorporate such persons into the overall supervision plan, and this helps to provide a meaningful bond for the young person and, as it turns out, provides an additional source of human supervision that is based in well-intended purposes for the youth. Throughout the course of the helping process, the probation officer will often involve the family and will meet the juvenile probationer at different times and places. The juvenile probation officer is likely to network with school officials (counselors, teachers, and administrators) and may even serve as an advocate for the child to secure public school placements (Abadinsky, 2003). In fact, many youth processed through the juvenile justice system may have learning disabilities and other challenges, and this can add to the list of problems that they face. In most cases, the worse these youth do at school, the more likely they are to engage in problematic behaviors. In frustration and perhaps due to diagnosable problems, these youth may exhibit disruptive behavior, making school administrators hesitant to accommodate the young person. Thus, the juvenile probation officer may find that they are indeed the youth's most passionate advocate when resolving problems that face the individual. In some cases, probation officers may have to arrange for placement of juveniles into a foster home and/or adoption. This is particularly true if the family conditions are deplorable. Thus, juvenile probation officers find themselves often working in tandem with other social service agencies. The partnerships between these agencies and the probation officer are often critical to ensuring that the young person receives the appropriate help that they need.

The Juvenile Court System

Neubauer (2002) noted that while all states today have juvenile courts their organizational relationship to other judicial bodies varies greatly. Indeed, it would seem that only a few states have created juvenile courts that are completely separate from other judicial bodies in their jurisdiction (Neubauer, 2002). In fact, juvenile courts have a great deal of difference from state to state, falling within one of three general categories: (1) that of a separate court, (2) a part of the family court, or (3) a component of the local trial court system.

When a juvenile court operates as its own separate statewide entity, this means that it will have its own administrators, judges, probation officers, clerks of the court, and other personnel. This type of system is actually rare, falling within the states of Connecticut, Rhode Island, and Utah. However, in a few large metropolitan areas, the juvenile court is kept completely separate from other court systems. Most jurisdictions do not separate juvenile courts because the operation of juvenile courts is thought to be more expensive when administered separately. Because of this, it is more common for such courts to be connected to other court systems and/or functions.

A second and more common form of juvenile court organization is to include juvenile courts within the broader scope of the family court system. Family courts have jurisdiction over almost all family matters, which are often civil in nature. Further, since family issues obviously tend to include issues pertaining to children, the integration of juvenile court proceedings into these services is even more pragmatic in nature. In many cases, family courts oversee matters concerning delinquency, status offenses, and child-victim or **child abuse** cases (a topic that follows this subsection).

The most common means for juvenile courts to operate is as part of the broader trial court system. Though the most common means of administration, this is also a very interesting means of handling juvenile justice. Indeed, when going beyond the legal considerations of the jurisdiction, the question of where juvenile cases are heard tends to be more a function of the courthouse caseload within a given jurisdiction. Neubauer (2002) stated that "in rural areas with few cases, they most often are a type of case on the judge's calendar much like tort and contract cases" (p. 506). This demonstrates that juvenile cases may be worked in with the common court caseload in a rather informal and potentially haphazard manner. The quality of such proceedings is perhaps speculative, at best. In most other areas, there do tend to be sufficient cases to warrant one or more specific judges who devote themselves fully to the juvenile caseload. While this separation of the juvenile court is grounded in the need to more effectively process the volume of juvenile cases in these jurisdictions, it is also rooted in the fact that juvenile cases are shielded from the public eye. In other words, it is easier to keep juvenile proceedings from public view or scrutiny when they are conducted in separate sections of the court or (even better) in an entirely separate courthouse.

▧ Juvenile Records

Juvenile records tend to include various types of information. Among these records there is likely to be a composite of the criminal history, family and personal information, abuse history, truancy records, as well as other identification information such as fingerprints and/or photographs. Other information, such as driving records, HIV/AIDS testing, status offense records, substance abuse history, and so forth may also be included. In addition, if the juvenile has committed a violent crime, there is likely to be information regarding the victim and witness notification process as a means of protecting those persons from the juvenile offender.

Importantly, some states such as Texas may have a central repository for juvenile records whereas other states may have local jurisdictions that maintain the records of juveniles who are processed within their jurisdiction. Obviously, the more centralized the records, the more likely they are to be useful for public safety purposes. However, juvenile records do tend to be confidential in nature, and only the juvenile offender, the juvenile's parents/legal guardian(s), or the attorney of record is typically given access. State social service and/or various law enforcement agencies also tend to have the right to access these records, given appropriate justification. The general public, however, is not given access to these records. It is clear that centralized record systems are superior to those maintained by far-flung jurisdictions, particularly when agencies must share information in the interest of public safety. Given the recent concern with violent juvenile offenders, in general, and juvenile sex offenders, in particular, issues related to interagency information sharing have become an increasing area of concern. Effective information systems on juvenile offenders tend to be fingerprint-based systems. This tends to address issues related to the reliability and accuracy of juvenile records. Since fingerprints are the biometric standard for identification of persons who are classified in criminal justice computerized systems, this basis makes good simple sense.

▧ Adjudication Processes and Difference From Adult Courts

The juvenile court system consists of unique legal characteristics that are reflected in the very terms that are used. Where adults are arrested, tried, and sentenced to prison, juveniles are summoned, have a hearing, and are committed to residential placement (Neubauer, 2002). According to Neubauer (2002), juvenile courts differ from adult courts in four important means: (1) These courts are informal in nature, (2) their legal basis is in civil law, (3) they tend to have closed proceedings, and (4) they do not usually have jury trials. These differences provide for more fluid options, both in terms of processing and sentencing, reflecting the desire of the juvenile courts to reform the juvenile, when practical.

In helping the child, the juvenile courts emphasize informality, which, as noted earlier in this section, contrasts with the formal and adversarial nature of the adult court. Although some elements of due process have been added to juvenile proceedings in recent years, juvenile proceedings continue to rely on less formal proceedings. As a result, the rules of evidence and procedural laws have little relevance in many juvenile proceedings (Neubauer, 2002). As an extension from the premise that juvenile courts are designed to help the child, the early shapers of the juvenile court system viewed procedural safeguards as unnecessary and, even more important, they viewed these safeguards as harmful to the outcome for most juveniles. The concern was that a legal technicality might keep a child from receiving the appropriate help and/or assistance that they might need (Neubauer, 2002). "In essence, the substance of the decision (helping the child) was more important than the procedures used to reach that decision" (Neubauer, 2002, p. 504).

Further highlighting the differences between adult and juvenile courts is that while adult prosecutions are conducted in criminal courts, juvenile court proceedings are based on civil law. This is the primary reason for the differences in terminology that exist between the two types of proceedings. A primary premise behind the use of civil law is that in using civil law rather than criminal law, the notions of rehabilitation would be emphasized instead of those associated with punishment. As Neubauer (2002) pointed out, it is for this reason that a child's juvenile court record is not admissible in adult court. "Regardless of the frequency or severity of the offenses committed by a juvenile, once he or she becomes an adult in the eyes of the criminal law, the person starts over with no prior record" (Neubauer, 2002, p. 504). This demonstrates how earnest the intent is within the juvenile court system to ensure that youth are not permanently stigmatized by the effects of their actions that are committed during an early phase of their life. This also is thought to aid in reducing the likelihood of recidivism since these youth will be able to avoid the negative impact of public recording of their crimes.

In what seems to be a recent trend, the U.S. Supreme Court and various state courts and legislatures have modified various procedural due process aspects of the juvenile court, resulting in a blend between both courts. The intent in these cases has been benevolent, providing safeguards to juveniles while still attempting to maintain the informal nature of much of the court process. Given the fact that juveniles are being tried in adult courts with more frequency, this latest development is perhaps expected. The hope is that juveniles can be afforded more safeguards in juvenile court while simultaneously ensuring that the pro-treatment aspect of juvenile courts is maintained.

This pro-treatment characteristic of juvenile courts is further reflected in the fact that juvenile court proceedings are typically closed from public view. Essentially, this means that crime victims and/or ordinary citizens wishing to view these proceedings are restricted from doing so. Thus, public audiences within the juvenile court are not a usual occurrence as is found within adult courts. Further still, most jurisdictions prohibit law enforcement and juvenile court personnel from releasing the identity of juvenile offenders to the media (Neubauer, 2002). Further reinforcing this is the fact that even when media personnel are able to find out the identities of juvenile offenders, the ethics governing bodies within the journalism industry prohibit the revealing information from being printed, broadcast, or otherwise disseminated (Neubauer, 2002). There are both advocates and critics of these closed proceedings. Advocates tend to view the closed nature of these proceedings as being necessary for effective interventions while critics contend that such secrecy prevents public scrutiny—something that most critics believe would work to perhaps deter juveniles from future crime while also providing victims with rights to information regarding the juvenile perpetrator who has victimized them.

On another front, juvenile courts also differ in the manner by which the offender is tried. While offenders in adult court have the right to trial by a jury of their peers, juveniles have no such constitutional right. The reason for this is to ensure that juvenile proceedings remain informal in nature. The absence of jury trials also strengthens the control and flexibility that juvenile court personnel have when maintaining supervision of the offender. This greatly aids both judges and probation officers in juvenile courts who are entrusted to act in the best interests of the child.

⊠ The Role of Child Protection

In many cases, juvenile youth are victims of various forms of neglect or abuse. This is a very important aspect of juvenile offending, particularly in community corrections. In many cases, community supervision officers (CSOs) will find themselves networking with child protection agencies, and they will likewise tend to have offenders on their caseloads who are in need of parenting assistance, whether the offender realizes it or not. Further, one must consider that over 70% of female offenders on community supervision are also the primary caretakers of their children. This is an important observation, especially when one considers that the proportion of female offenders on community supervision is much higher than those who are incarcerated. This means that CSOs are likely to come across issues related to the welfare of children on a fairly frequent basis. Further still, among a high number of delinquent youth, disproportionate rates of abuse and neglect occur. This then further demonstrates that CSOs who supervise juvenile offenders are likely to contend with neglect and abuse issues with young offenders on their caseload. **Child neglect** and abuse can then be relevant to CSOs who supervise either adult or juvenile offenders.

In discussing these issues, we first turn our focus to child neglect since such maltreatment is often a precursor to later forms of abuse and since neglect also often occurs in conjunction with abusive treatment. Child neglect occurs when a parent or caretaker of the child does not provide the proper or necessary support, education, medical or other remedial care that is required by a given state's law, including food, shelter, and clothing. Child neglect also occurs when adult caretakers abandon a child they are legally obligated to support (Cox et al., 2008). Neglect is typically divided into three types: (1) physical, (2) emotional, and (3) educational (Cox et al., 2008). **Physical neglect** includes abandonment, the expulsion of the child from the home (being kicked out of the house); a failure to seek or excessive delay in seeking medical care for the child; inadequate supervision; and inadequate food, clothing, and shelter (Cox et al., 2008). **Emotional neglect** includes inadequate nurturing or affection, allowing the child to engage in inappropriate or illegal behavior such as drug or alcohol use, as well as ignoring a child's basic emotional needs (Cox et al., 2008). Lastly, **educational neglect** occurs when a parent or even a teacher permits chronic truancy or simply ignores the educational and/or special needs of a child (Cox et al., 2008).

The impact of neglect is not as readily observable as is abuse. Over time, however, the long-term effects to the child can be just as damaging as they are when a child is overtly abused. Among the offender population, child neglect is not at all uncommon. In cases where either the male or female parent is a serious drug abuser, it may be common for the child to be neglected. In fact, there are some circumstances where the oldest child may be *parentified* and delegated responsibility of caring for younger siblings while also taking care of the parent as well. The **child parentification** occurs when he or she is placed in a position within a family system whereby they must assume the primary caretaker role for that family, often taking care of both children and adults within that family system. This is common in single head-of-household families where the adult caretaker is an alcoholic or drug abuser and even in some dual adult household families, particularly those that are criminogenic in nature.

Interestingly, children who are neglected, including those who are parentified, often do not realize that they are necessarily being mistreated. Even if they do, many have no recourse, and when coupled with the emotional bonds that they may have with their siblings, they are unlikely to leave or report such maltreatment on their own. These inappropriate family circumstances lead to very poor socialization in many cases, with children observing negative behaviors and developing criminogenic mind-sets. Thus, these toxic family systems help to breed a new generation of persons who are susceptible to further perpetuation of the criminal lifestyle. It is because of this that CSOs overseeing juvenile offenders must take into account the family situation, encouraging family involvement when the family is functional and recommending family interventions when the family is not functional.

Beyond child neglect, acts of abuse are even more serious forms of maltreatment and include both physical or psychological forms. Child abuse occurs when a child (defined as a youth under the age of 18 in most states) is maltreated by a parent, an immediate family member, or any person responsible for the child's welfare (Cox et al., 2008). Child maltreatment can include physical, sexual, and emotional abuse as well as physical, emotional, and even educational neglect from the caretaker (Cox et al., 2008). There are varying degrees of abuse and, in many cases, multiple forms of abuse may have been inflicted against the child. Further, these youth may also come from homes where there is domestic abuse between spouses or significant others. Research has shown that among juvenile sex offenders, the existence of child abuse is a common characteristic among such offenders in the United States as well as other countries (Hanser & Mire, 2008). The existence of abuse in a youth's background is an important observation to attend to, since aberrant behaviors are likely to have been learned from other dysfunctional family members. In some cases, the youth's behavior may be a form or acting out against the stress and frustration of their toxic family environment.

According to Cox et al. (2008), **physical abuse** "can be defined as any physical acts that cause or can cause physical injury to a child" (p. 266). These authors go on to describe child abuse as a vicious cycle that involves parents who have unrealistic expectations of their children, thereby getting easily frustrated with the shortcomings that they perceive their children to have. It is not uncommon for such parents to have themselves been abused as children, resulting in an intergenerational transmission of violence through their abusive behavior. The extent of the harsh discipline tends to depend on the level of frustration that the parent feels, their ability to regulate their own emotions, and their views on appropriate parenting and discipline practices. The level of parenting skills and the age of the child often affect the type of abuse and frequency of abuse that is inflicted since younger children are less able to defend themselves and/or perhaps run away.

Further, this type of treatment can greatly exacerbate any potential diagnoses that the young person might have (such as those just discussed in prior subsections), and this further complicates potential treatment approaches for that child. In fact, it may well be that the adult family members themselves have a number of mental health issues, and this adds further difficulty to the family situation. Within such family environments, it is unlikely that the youth will be able to ever achieve any sense of normalcy or positive support. The parent's own challenges will tend to aggravate those problems facing the youth, and the youth's behavior will in turn serve as a further aggravating factor for their own maladaptive parenting. The two then will tend to continually fuel the dysfunction within the family system, thereby ensuring that the maladaptive system continues. In such cases, it is not likely that the juvenile should remain within the family system, and it should be considered that the youth's behavior is perhaps a symptom of what is an unhealthy family grouping.

Psychological abuse is the third most frequently reported form of child abuse, with physical abuse and child neglect being the first and second most common types of abuse. Psychological abuse is somewhat vague and hard to define. Definitions that are too narrow are not likely to capture the various aspects of psychological abuse that might exist within an adult–child relationship that is abusive. On the other hand, definitions that are too broad may be nearly impossible to clearly identify in quantitative terms for research and/or in a legally substantive manner that could aid law enforcement and prosecutors. Because of these difficulties, this is the most difficult form of abuse to prosecute, being somewhat elusive when put to rigorous examination. Further, the difficulty in proving this abuse makes it likely that much of it goes unreported since it is so difficult to detect, prove, and document.

Psychological abuse is also sometimes referred to as emotional abuse and includes actions or the omission of actions by parents and other caregivers that could cause the child to have serious behavioral, emotional, or mental impairments. In some instances of psychological abuse, there is no clear or evident behavior of the adult caregiver that provides indication of the abuse. Rather, the child displays behavior that is impaired and/or has emotional disturbances that result from profound forms of emotional abuse, trauma, distance, or neglect. This is an issue that should be seriously considered when children have diagnosable disorders, particularly those that are obsessive/compulsive, dissociative, anxiety-based, and/or oppositional/defiant in nature.

When considering children with disorders such as those just previously indicated, it should be taken to mean that the caregiver is not necessarily the cause of the disorder, though that likelihood can certainly exist as well. Rather, it may well be that the child has these disorders and, due to frustration, the parent resorts to punishments that are bizarre or unorthodox in nature. For example, parents of a strongly oppositional child may resort to locking the child in a dark closet as a means of containing the child and also depriving them of stimuli that may heighten the child's emotionality. While this may have a basis of logic to it, this type of punishment is not appropriate yet may occur for long periods of time. In the process, the child's short-term behavior may be adjusted, but their sense of long-term maladjustment is further aggravated; in short, the parents contribute to the emotional disturbances that the child exhibits. On the other hand, parents who are psychologically abusive may also actually be a causal factor in a child developing any variety of emotional or adjustment disorders. Children who are psychologically abused may have depression, anxiety, dissociative, and so forth. In such cases, the treatment from the caregiver negatively impacts that child's ability to thrive, resulting in an emotionally impaired child.

When neglect or abuse is detected within the home of a juvenile on a CSO's caseload and/or when an adult offender is thought to be neglecting or abusing his or her children, the officer is under a legal obligation to report these actions to child protection services within that state. In reality, most all citizens are required to report this activity anytime they observe it occurring, but CSOs are especially liable and required to make such reports when they encounter child maltreatment. In essence, the CSO is required to intervene. Intervention officially begins when the officer reports the neglect or abuse and the child protection agency proceeds to the investigatory stage. This stage usually involves a home visit and interviews with all parties involved in the behavior and who know about the circumstances. Child protection officials typically then generate a risk assessment and make a decision regarding the best type of action to take that meets the best interests of the child.

If it is determined that abuse has indeed occurred, the police and the investigator for the child protection agency will take the case to the local prosecutor so that it can be charged. Even with the official determination of neglect or abuse, these proceedings can be difficult and challenging. First, the juvenile may be quite ashamed, unable, or even afraid to leak information regarding their abuse. Cox et al. (2008) noted that

> in many cases, even though they are being regularly and severely abused, children will not tell others because of the fear (sometimes instilled by their abusers) that their parents will be taken away from them if they do seek help. (p. 274)

This is a very important observation since these children often know no other way to live, their current abusive situation being normalized as part of their life. In addition, among some cases that do go to court, the child may be unable to effectively testify due to fear, trauma, and anxiety that impedes their ability to provide information effectively to the court. Lastly, even in those cases where the child is able to provide effective testimony, judges and/or family protection agencies may still be hesitant to remove the youth from a home due to objections from the family members, often including objections from the very juvenile who has been abused. Lastly, when youth are enmeshed in such toxic systems and when their socialization is such that they are not even personally aware that they should, in fact, seek refuge from their abusive family system, it is important that states exercise that right that was mentioned earlier in this section—the right of parens patriae. The state should protect the welfare of the juvenile, both as a moral obligation and even as a public safety obligation. Indeed, it is in this manner that the state protects the welfare of the child while aiding future crime prevention within the community, since a reduction in maltreatment of these youth will translate to a reduction in future delinquency. In such cases, intervention simply makes good sense.

When maintenance of the family is not a viable option and it is not in the juvenile's best interest, it may be that the juvenile probation officer will place the juvenile in a foster home. Typically, foster homes are used for children who have been victims of abuse or neglect. Among those youth who are persistently delinquent, the use of residential treatment facilities are generally more appropriate (Cox et al., 2008). Foster homes are intended to provide the appropriate supervision and care that, in the case of juvenile offenders, is likely to have been missing from their own family life. The care and attention provided by foster homes naturally go beyond that which the probation officer can provide and therefore are critical resources for youth that truly have no where else to turn.

Though juvenile courts are careful when selecting foster home placements, it is inevitable that some juveniles will simply be too difficult to control. This places difficulty on the foster parents who attend to such youth, and this also can negatively impact other youth staying at the foster home. In some cases, difficult juveniles may victimize the other children staying at the home, and this then creates a risk that makes further placement unlikely, resulting in the youth's placement in residential treatment. It is clear that the complexities with raising these needy youth can be quite challenging and stressful for foster parents, so careful screening is typically conducted of those persons that apply to be foster parents. As Cox et al. (2008) noted,

> assuming responsibility for a delinquent, abused, or neglected juvenile placed in one's home requires a great deal of commitment, and many juveniles who might benefit from this type of setting cannot be placed due to the lack of available families. (pp. 246–247)

◤ Family Services and Family Interventions

In many communities, there tends to exist a number of programs that provide for family services; CSOs who have juvenile offenders on their caseloads will likely become familiar with these agencies over time. Such services can be important in reducing delinquency and in providing the juvenile probationer with some degree of grounding since these agencies tend to have a variety of healthy and prosocial programs for youth. This range of services can include recreational activities, after-school programs, access to therapeutic services for families, services for domestic violence victims (adult and juvenile), Planned Parenthood and/or teenage pregnancy services, as well as a number of other important functions and activities.

◤ Risk Factors and Protective Factors for Juveniles

When implementing any program for preventing or treating juvenile offenders, the risk factors that lead to juvenile delinquency must be understood. Risk factors may be found in the individual, the environment, or the individual's ability to respond to the demands or requirements of the environment. Research has indicated a number of factors that have a high likelihood of leading to delinquent behavior (McCall, 1994; Moffitt, 1993). Further, each of these factors, when added together, can have a cumulative effect on the likelihood of future delinquency (McCall, 1994). For instance, while poor parenting is a risk factor, this becomes more pronounced when it is coupled with a child's poor academic performance. Further, the environment can serve to compound this, such as when a child attends a school where rules of conduct are lax and teachers are dissatisfied; in these cases, the chances of the child engaging in delinquency increase (McCall, 1994).

Risk factors are many and occur along a continuum within the child's development. Table 10.1 shows some risk factors that could be used to predict the onset of juvenile offending. It should be pointed out that these risk factors simply serve to increase the likelihood of future delinquency; they do not cause delinquency. As Table 10.1 demonstrates, these risk factors fall within one of five primary domains: (1) individual, (2) family, (3) school, (4) peer group, and (5) community. These domains include a number of factors that, depending on whether youth possess these factors, helps to determine the likelihood of future juvenile offending.

▲ **Photo 10.1**   The Caddo Correctional Center is a large jail facility with numerous types of programs for offenders. This facility houses gang offenders, violent offenders, and a number of other types of offenders who are provided different kinds of in-house programming. The Caddo Correctional Center is well integrated with external agencies, including probation and parole offices.

Protective factors, on the other hand, serve to counter the effects of risk factors that may exist for the individual, within the family, school, peer group, or community. In essence, protective factors are variables that serve as the opposite of risk factors. For instance, a community risk factor might be the existence of crime and drugs within a neighborhood. In contrast, a protective factor would then be if a program were implemented that taught youth to avoid crime and drugs, providing alternate activities for youth to engage in. While both the risk factor and the protective factor may exist within that same community, each works against each other in the young person's environment. Amidst these community-level risk and protective factors, the individual domain and the family domains might also either mitigate or aggravate the likelihood of juvenile offending.

In regard to protective factors, there is some disagreement among experts that attempt to specifically define and identify these factors. This is because protective factors have been viewed both as the absence of risk and as something conceptually distinct from risk (Wasserman & Miller, 1998). The former view typically places risk and protective factors on the opposite ends of a continuum. While this is an oversimplification of how offending may take place (Table 10.1 is not all-inclusive) this should provide the student with a clear understanding of how there are various factors that work with and against one another across a variety of domains. Throughout this interplay between risk factors and protective factors, a final analysis is derived where the likelihood of future juvenile delinquency can be estimated. Again, this is not all encompassing.

On the other hand, the view that protection is conceptually distinct from risk defines protective factors as characteristics or conditions that interact with risk factors to reduce their influence on juvenile offending (Stattin & Magnusson, 1996). For example, low family socioeconomic status is a risk factor for juvenile offending, and a warm, supportive relationship with a parent may be a protective factor. The warm relationship does not improve the child's economic status, but it does buffer the child from some of the adverse

Table 10.1 Risk Factors for Juvenile Offending

Domain	Risk Factors	Protective Factors
Individual	1. Antisocial attitudes	1. Intolerant attitude to criminality
	2. Low IQ	2. High IQ
	3. Being male	3. Female gender
	4. Negative social orientation	4. Positive social orientation
	5. Willingness for risk taking	5. Sanctions/punishment taken seriously
	6. Substance abuse	
Family	1. Harsh or lax discipline	1. Warm relationship with adult caretaker
	2. Poor adult supervision	2. Peer group accepted by parents
	3. Low parental involvement	3. Parental monitoring
	4. Low socioeconomic status	
	5. Abusive home	
School	1. Poor attitude or performance	1. Commitment to school
	2. Academic failure	2. Engages in conventional school activities
Peer group	1. Antisocial peer group	1. Friends engage in conventional behavior
	2. Weak social ties	
Community	1. Neighborhood crime and drugs	1. Crime and drug-free neighborhood

effects of poverty. Protective factors may or may not have a direct effect on juvenile offending but instead moderate or buffer the effects of risk that are likely to increase the likelihood of juvenile offending (Davis, 1999). Thus, protective factors offer an explanation for why children and adolescents who face the same degree of risk may be affected differently.

The concept of protective factors is familiar in public health. Identifying and measuring the effects of protective factors is relatively new in juvenile research, and information about these factors is limited. Because they buffer the effect of risk factors, protective factors are an important tool in the prevention of juvenile offending. Like risk factors, proposed protective factors are grouped into individual, family, school, peer group, and community categories. Just as risk factors do not necessarily cause an individual child or young person to become violent, protective factors do not guarantee that an individual child or young person will not become violent. They reduce the probability that groups of young people facing a risk factor or factors will engage in juvenile delinquency.

Lastly, it is important to note that this interplay among individual, family, school, peer group, and community domains provides important possibilities for community supervision agencies. When considering the previous examples and discussion, it becomes clear that juvenile community supervision agencies are well served to maximize their partnerships with local schools, family social services, and community programs that provide youth with healthy and/or prosocial activities. One primary theme throughout this text has been the need for community supervision agencies to maximize the use of partner agencies and community volunteers within the community when providing comprehensive supervision and treatment services. The current examination of risk and protective factors further supports this concept when providing services to juveniles at risk of offending and for those that have committed some offense. Thus, programs that include family interventions or support activities are actually responding to the various and complex interplays between risk factors and protective factors within the family domain. At the same time, after-school programs respond to this interplay within the school domain, while community recreational services may do so at the community level. Taken together, these various programs can enhance the ability of community supervision agencies to better supervise juvenile offenders and to provide better alternative options for that youth, all with the intent of countering the likelihood of future juvenile offending.

Applied Theory Section 10.1

Developmental Theories, Juvenile Delinquency, and Community Responses

The advent and expansion of longitudinal studies in criminology and criminal justice have provided researchers and practitioners with opportunities to examine and effectively influence the outcomes of behavior beginning early in an individual's life. One such example is exemplified by the work of the Office of Juvenile Justice and Delinquency Prevention's (OJJDP) Study Group on Serious and Violent Juvenile Offenders. The results of the research conducted in Pittsburgh, Rochester, New York, and Denver have influenced community responses to preventing crime and delinquency, particularly violent offenses before they begin. Known as Developmental Theories of Crime, these researchers have identified a variety of predictors, as noted in this section, that can either exacerbate or mitigate delinquent activity (Loeber & Farrington, 1998).

Modern-day developmental theorists have sought to understand why some youths' delinquent behavior peaks at an early age and then levels off while others continue to persist thought out their life course. The Pittsburgh youth study in particular has been instrumental in expanding our understanding of the developmental pathways into delinquency. A pathway is defined as "a group of individuals that shares a behavioral

(Continued)

(Continued)

development that is distinct from the behavioral development of another group of individuals." (Thornberry, Huizinga, & Loeber, 1995, p. 222)

In their longitudinal study of youth in the Pittsburgh area, they identified three major pathways to chronic and serious delinquency (see Figure 10.1 for an overview of the Pathways to Delinquency; Thornberry, Huizinga, & Loeber, 2004, p. 6).

Figure 10.1   Developmental Pathways to Serious and Violent Offending

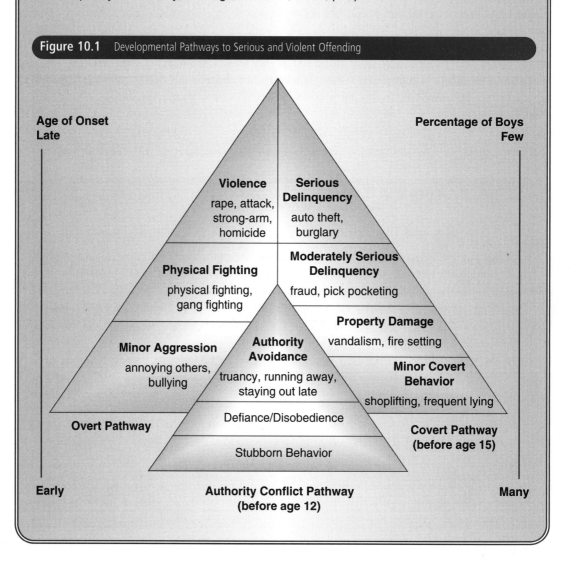

These pathways include overt pathways, which range from minor aggression, such as bullying and annoying others, to violence, such as rape and attacks. Covert pathways range from minor covert behavior, such as shoplifting and frequent lying, to moderate and serious delinquency, such as fraud, burglary, and serious theft. The final pathway is the authority conflict pathway, which occurs before age 12 and ranges from stubborn behavior to authority avoidance (e.g., truancy and running away) (Houston & Barton, 2005, pp. 46–47). Research has indicated that delinquency was highest for those youth who participated in behavior in all three pathways but particularly for those who partake in overt and covert behavior. To address these individuals and prevent future delinquent activity, community-based workers must distinguish between those who persist in this type of activity and those who experiment. The key to preventive strategies must be the development of programs meant to address minor transgressions that keep a youth from participating in more serious types of offending. Likewise, programs should be prepared to address the multitude of factors that confront youth and that have been shown to serve as risk factors, as noted in this section, as well as making efforts to enhance those protective factors that keep youth from going down the wrong pathway.

◪ Juvenile Intensive Probation Supervision

As was noted previously, probation tends to be the most common sanction given to juvenile offenders. While this may be true, there are those juvenile offenders on probation who do not necessarily require institutionalization but are still in need of stricter forms of supervision. It is with this in mind that juvenile intensive supervision is often utilized for certain juvenile offenders. The use of intensive supervision probation (ISP) have become more widely used since there is a desire to keep juveniles out of institutions and since there is more acceptance of community corrections programs and processes. Juvenile Intensive Probation Supervision (JIPS) is a regimented program of supervision that requires much greater supervision contact than regular probation and also serves as an alternative to incarceration while maintaining acceptable levels of public safety. Currently, juvenile JIPS is used in roughly half of all programs around the nation. Though JIPS is a tool for any juvenile probationer that requires strict forms of supervision, it is typically only used with those youth who have residential placement as their only other alternative.

The main distinction between JIPS and standard probation is the number of supervision contacts throughout the week that the juvenile is required to make and the extent to which those contacts occur. Further still, most CSOs who have JIPS caseloads tend to also network with other agencies and services as a means of providing the child with needed assistance while also further increasing the number of human contacts that occur. This is of course similar to discussions in past sections where adult probation programs employ similar techniques to ensure that offenders are well supervised. However, JIPS will have services that in many cases are more readily available and/or more specific to juvenile issues. For example, groups such as Big Brothers/Big Sisters may be involved, foster grandparent programs may be utilized, and alternative education programs may be part of the services delivered. These types of services would typically be nonexistent in most adult supervision programs.

JIPS typically requires nearly daily supervision by a juvenile probation officer. At a minimum, six face-to-face contacts per month should occur between the probation officer and the juvenile offender. In addition, it is recommended that juvenile probation officers make at least three face-to-face contacts with the youth's parents, and at least two contacts with school officials. With such intensive contact and with other requirements added to the probation sentence, it is clear that the juvenile probation officer will be quite busy maintaining their caseload and tracking the various corollary activities that may be mandated by the court. On the other hand, the juvenile offender is also kept busy, with additional requirements for community service, drug and alcohol counseling, anger management classes, educational services, restitution activities, and psychoeducational programs placing high demands on these probationers. Research indicates that this type of supervision is best used with serious hardcore offenders rather than younger offenders who have committed only petty crimes. The regimen is simply not necessary among less serious offenders.

In some cases, such as in the state of Arizona, juvenile offenders on JIPS are supervised by teams of probation personnel. Typically, one probation officer will be utilized, and other staff called surveillance officers will also be included. These are often either two-person or three-person teams. For two-person teams, the state of Arizona sets the caseload at no more than 25 juvenile offenders while three-person teams may supervise no more than 40 juveniles at a time. According to the Arizona State Supreme Court website (2008), JIPS probation officer teams are tasked with the following duties:

1. Keep complete identification records for each youth supervised.

2. Meet with each probationer at least four times a week and make weekly contact with the juvenile's parents or guardian, school, employer, and treatment program.

3. Closely monitor each juvenile's conduct including evening and weekend activities.

4. Monitor the juvenile's payment of restitution.

Generally speaking, JIPS has been found to be fairly effective. For instance, a study by Wiebush (1993) was conducted that examined the 18-month recidivism of juvenile felony offenders who were placed into an intensive supervision program as an alternative to institutionalization. This study compared the outcomes of JIPS participants with other juveniles who were institutionalized and then released to parole, as well as a third group that was given standard probation (Wiebush, 1993). The results of this study were promising since it was found that recidivism rates for youth were lower than those who were institutionalized and since this type of supervision provided better controls than did standard probation. However, it was found that JIPS was not necessarily cost-effective unless large-scale diversion programs were implemented. Apparently, the reduction in recidivism was not so great as to offset that added expense except in cases where substantial numbers of juveniles were diverted (Wiebush, 1993).

◪ Residential Treatment Programs

Residential treatment programs are facilities that offer a combination of substance abuse and mental health treatment services while youth are kept under 24-hour supervision in a highly structured and secure environment. These programs typically are designed for youth with significant psychiatric or substance abuse problems and who are not otherwise appropriate for foster care services, day treatment programs, or other less secure programs. Although these treatment centers must be licensed by their respective states, they are frequently owned and operated by private companies, with treatment approaches and admissions criteria varying widely among institutions throughout the nation.

The specific modalities of treatment may vary, but they all tend to include various forms of therapy, psychoeducational counseling, behavioral management, group counseling, and other such services. Settings come in a variety of types, including hospital-like environments, group homes, and even halfway houses (see Section VII). Though there are a variety of approaches, research regarding the effectiveness of these facilities is quite mixed yet these facilities do continue to be an important component of the juvenile correctional process. It is for this reason that they are presented in this section.

Wilderness camps (sometimes called challenge programs) are residential programs where juveniles engage in a series of physically challenging outdoor activities, such as backpacking, canoeing, or even rock climbing. These programs do

▲ **Photo 10.2** This juvenile detention center is new and modern in appearance. Many such buildings may not even seem like detention facilities. Indeed, if the sign at the entry did not note the purpose of this building, it might be difficult to know the true purpose of its existence. To some extent, this may be reflective of the fact that the juvenile system seeks to avoid the labeling of delinquent youth in the community.

vary considerably in their settings, types of activities, and therapeutic goals, but their treatment perspectives are usually based on an experiential learning approach that is designed to stimulate personal growth and build a sense of self-efficacy (Office of Juvenile Justice & Delinquency Prevention [OJJDP], 2007). These programs raised a number of concerns during the 1980s and early 1990s due to the risks that youth encountered and due to a number of incidents around the country where youth were either injured or died accidentally. Since that time, programs have been designed to be less physically intensive and extreme while still allowing youth to engage in activities designed to build personal confidence.

One researcher conducted a meta-analysis of 29 different studies that examined wilderness programs (Lipsey, 2000). This study involved over 3,000 juvenile offenders and found that youth in these programs have recidivism rates that are about 8% lower than juveniles in other programs. However, this study was not able to adequately account for the various differences in programming among the programs in the various studies, leaving much open to speculation. However, Lipsey (2000) did find that programs that included intense physical activity along with therapeutic interventions such as individual counseling, family therapy, and group counseling were more effective than those that involved little or no therapeutic content.

Perhaps one of the most widely known wilderness programs in the United States is VisionQuest (OJJDP, 2007). This program provides alternatives to incarceration for serious juvenile offenders. Youth in this program spend from 12 to 15 months engaged in a variety of challenging outdoor activities coupled with various therapeutic treatment programs. A normal treatment course often includes a 3-month stay at a wilderness orientation program where they typically camp outdoors; a 5-month adventure program during which time juveniles participate in activities such as wagon train journeys, cross-country biking, or ocean voyages; and staying in a 5-month community residential/therapeutic program (OJJDP, 2007). Interestingly, this program also includes an aftercare program called HomeQuest that offers support to youth and families upon reentry. This follow-up care helps to make the entire process one that is transitional in nature, providing support for the juvenile that is transitioned back into the community. Controlled studies of VisionQuest have consistently demonstrated its effectiveness in lowering juvenile recidivism rates (OJJDP, 2007).

Juvenile boot camps are residential facilities that are run in a military fashion with drill instructors and other staff using strict regimen and intensive interventions during a short period of time, usually lasting between 90 and 120 days. These programs were widely touted as innovative treatment programs during the 1990s but since that time have consistently failed to demonstrate any positive impact on juvenile offenders' recidivism rates. Further, these programs tend to be much more expensive to operate than simply incarcerating youth in secure facilities. Thus, these programs, though intuitively seeming to make good sense, are actually failures at treatment and in terms of fiscal considerations. In 2000, the Koch Crime Institute conducted a study on the number of juvenile boot camps in the United States. At that time, at least 21 states reported at least one boot camp in operation. The majority were

> designed for male offenders, ages fourteen to seventeen, who had committed nonviolent offenses. The average reported costs were approximately $87.00. The range however, was from a reported low of $20.00. . . . to a high of $134.25 per day. (Houston & Barton, 2005, p. 206)

Compared to traditional sentencing, these boot camp alternatives cost approximately $14,000 less per year to detain a youth than traditional confinement (see Table 10.2 for more detailed information on the boot camps).

Table 10.2   Juvenile Boot Camps by State*

State	No. Boot Camps	Type of Program	Sex	Age	Program Duration	Program Aftercare Duration
Alabama	1	Residential	M	12–18	13 weeks	9 months
Arizona	1 (closed)	Residential	M/F	14–17	1 year (4 months secure, 8 mo. aftercare)	8 months
California	1	Residential	M/F	14+	365 days	7–7.5 months
Colorado	1	Residential	Varies by judicial district	Varies by judicial district	60 days	avg. 90 days
Florida	8	6 Residential (R) 2 Non-Residential (NR)	M/F	14–18 (R) 10–16 (NR) 14–17 (NR)	4 mo. boot camp/ 4 mo. transition (R) 22 hours 2 Saturdays (NR) 1 year (NR)	4 months
Georgia	1 open 5 closed	Residential	M	Juveniles	90 days	N/A
Illinois	1	Residential	M	13–19	6 months	6–12 months
Indiana	1	Residential	M	13–17	120 days	Determined by parole services

Table 10.2 (Continued)

State	No. Boot Camps	Type of Program	Sex	Age	Program Duration	Program Aftercare Duration
Kansas	1	Residential	M/F	Juveniles	6 months	Provided by community corrections until released by probation
Kentucky	1	Residential	M/F	14–17	4 months residential, 4 months intensive aftercare	4 months
Louisiana	1	Residential	M	15+	90-120 days	Varies
Maryland	2 (closed)					
Michigan	1		M	15–18	18 weeks	4–6 months
Minnesota	1 (closed)					
New Jersey	1	Residential	M/F	13+	6 months	Varies according to length of sentence
New York	1	Residential	M/F	Juveniles	6 months	6 months
North Carolina	2	Residential	M/F	1 designated for 16–30; other open	90-120 days 81–120 days	15 months 18 months
Oklahoma	1	Residential	M/F	Level I through L	90 days	Varies
Oregon	1	Residential	M/F	Youth offenders	4 months	8 months
Pennsylvania	1	Residential	M/F	Juveniles	15 weeks	Varies
South Dakota	1	Residential	M	14–18	120 days	6–12 months
Texas	5 open 2 closed	All residential	Court referred Males	Court referred 15–17 13–17 Type B violent offenders Youth	2–12 months N/A 6 months 9–12 months 9–2+ years	No aftercare N/A N/A 3 months at Halfway House No aftercare
Virginia	2	Residential	M/F	14–18 Youth	5 months 120 days	6 months 6 months
Washington	1		M/F	12–19	120 days	At least 12 weeks or maximum sentence

* See the Koch Crime Institute report for a more in-depth discussion of the program selection criteria as well as date program established and costs per day per youth. This table just presents a summary overview of the criteria. For example, many states restrict program participation to type of offense committed as well as sex and age.

⊠ Group Homes

Group homes are residential placement facilities for juveniles that operate in a homelike setting with unrelated children living together for varied periods of time, depending on their individual circumstances. Group homes usually serve 5 to 15 youth, who are placed there as result of a court order or through interactions with public welfare agencies (OJJDP, 2007). These homes may utilize a single set of "house parents" or they may have rotating staff.

The primary treatment approach used in group homes today is the Teaching-Family Model (OJJDP, 2007). This model relies heavily on structural behavior interventions and highly trained staff who act as parents and live in the group homes 24 hours a day (OJJDP, 2007). Other group homes rely more on individual psychotherapy and group interaction (Surgeon General, 2001). Studies suggest that adolescents placed in group homes do experience positive treatment effects *while they are in these homes*, but little evidence exists to suggest that treatment outcomes are sustained over time (OJJDP, 2007). When compared with foster homes, research has demonstrated that foster homes offer several advantages over group homes. For example, foster homes require lower costs, have less recidivism, and result in more frequent reunifications between the juvenile and their family (OJJDP, 2007). One reason for the difference in outcomes between these two programs is that group homes are frequently used as the last stop before juveniles are placed in secure detention; thus youth referred to these facilities often suffer from more serious mental or behavioral problems than those who are referred to foster homes (OJJDP, 2007).

◪ Nonresidential Programs

Home confinement, or house arrest, is an intermediate community corrections sanction in which offenders are restricted to their residence except during specifically designated times where they are authorized to attend vocational, educational, treatment-based, or social functions. This sanction allows offenders to remain in their homes, go to work, run errands, attend school, and maintain other responsibilities (OJJDP, 2007). However, their activities are closely monitored (either electronically and/or by frequent staff contacts) to ensure that they are complying with the conditions set by the court. Offenders placed under home confinement are restricted to their residence for varying lengths of time and are required to maintain a strict schedule of daily activities (OJJDP, 2007).

Day treatment facilities are highly structured, community-based, nonresidential programs for serious juvenile offenders. The goal of day treatment is to provide both intensive supervision to ensure community safety while exposing the juvenile offender to a wide range of services that he or she might not otherwise access. The intensive supervision is fulfilled by requiring the offender to report to the facility on a daily basis at specified times for a specified length of time. In most cases, these programs are open throughout the week during both the day and/or evening, with special weekend activities often included to ensure that youth are kept busy while completing their sentence (OJJDP, 2007). Treatment services in day treatment facilities tend to be fairly comprehensive and may include individual and group counseling, recreation, education, vocational training, employment counseling, education, life skills and cognitive skills training, substance abuse treatment, as well as community resource referrals (OJJDP, 2007).

Aftercare can be defined as reintegrative services that prepare juveniles released from an institution for reentry into the community by establishing collaboration between agencies, the community, and available resources to maximize reintegrative processes (Altschuler and Armstrong, 2001). Aftercare requires the creation of a seamless set of systems across formal and informal social control networks as well as the creation of a continuum of community services to prevent the reoccurrence of antisocial behavior. It can also involve public–private partnerships to expand the overall capacity of youth services. Effective aftercare is very important due to the stigmatizing effect that institutionalization can have upon youth. As was noted previously with the VisionQuest program, the use of effective aftercare can greatly

reduce any agency's recidivism rates that they encounter within their jurisdiction.

▧ Treatment Programs and Types of Therapy

Wraparound is [a] complex, multifaceted intervention strategy designed to keep delinquent youth at home and out of institutions whenever possible. As the name suggests, this strategy involves "wrapping" a comprehensive array of individualized services and support networks "around" young people, rather than forcing them to enroll in predetermined, inflexible treatment programs (Portland State University Research and Training Center, 2003). Although one of the central features of the wraparound approach is individual case management, wraparound interventions should not be confused with traditional case management programs. Conventional case management programs merely provide youth with an individual case manager (or probation officer) who guides them through the existing social services or juvenile justice system (Burchard et al., 2002). (OJJDP, n.d.)

▲ **Photo 10.3** The Ouachita Parish Juvenile Court is a smaller facility than the Caddo Parish Juvenile Complex. Nevertheless, this facility provides court, detention, and aftercare services to youth who are processed through the juvenile justice system.

Numerous public agencies and research organizations, including the U.S. Surgeon General's Office and the Substance Abuse and Mental Health Services Administration (SAMHSA), have offered their own definitions of what constitutes a wraparound program. While these definitions vary slightly, the OJJDP (2007) notes that true wraparound services feature several basic elements, including

- A collaborative, **community-based interagency team** that is responsible for designing, implementing, and overseeing the wraparound initiative in a given jurisdiction. This team usually consists of representatives from the juvenile justice system, the public education system, and local mental health and social service agencies. In most cases, one specific agency is designated the lead agency in coordinating the wraparound effort.
- A **formal interagency agreement** that records the proposed design of the wraparound initiative and spells out exactly how the wraparound effort will work. At a minimum, this agreement should specify who the target population for the initiative is, how they will be enrolled in the program, how services will be delivered and paid for, what roles different agencies and individuals will play, and what resources will be committed by various groups.
- **Care coordinators** who are responsible for helping participants create a customized treatment program and for guiding youth and their families through the system of care.

From these basic elements of wraparound services, it is clear that this concept mirrors the same premise that has been presented throughout this text. Again, as has been stated in prior sections, there is a need for interagency partnerships that are community-based in orientation. The use of formal interagency agreements helps to ensure that there is accountability within these partnerships. Further, the use of care coordinators helps to organize the various programs and services, reflecting many of the concepts that were initially presented in Section VIII on case management. However, as previously noted, wraparound services are not just the utilization of typical case management processes but are much more comprehensive, interlaced, and multidimensional in scope. This is considered superior to many other forms of intervention and is particularly suitable for juveniles due to the fact that they are thought to be at an impressionable point in their lives, being much more malleable to the treatment programming.

Perhaps the most widely used form of therapy in the criminal justice system is cognitive behavioral therapy (CBT). CBT is a problem-focused approach designed to help people identify and change the dysfunctional beliefs, thoughts, and patterns of behavior that contribute to their problems. Its underlying principle is that thoughts affect emotions, which then influence behaviors. This type of therapy combines both cognitive and behavioral types of therapy into one of the most empirically validated treatment orientations that exist. Cognitive therapy concentrates on thoughts, assumptions, and beliefs . With cognitive therapy, offenders are encouraged to recognize and to change faulty or maladaptive thinking patterns. Cognitive therapy is a way to gain control over inappropriate repetitive thoughts that often feed or trigger various presenting problems.

Behavioral therapy, on the other hand, concentrates on specific actions and environments that either change or maintain behaviors. Behavioral interventions target behavior on a mechanistic level with a more direct training approach using observable reinforcements, punishments, and stimuli (Van Voorhis, Braswell, & Lester, 2000). Behavioral interventions may also incorporate elements of social learning and models in learning new behavior (Hanser, 2007a). They may also utilize techniques such as role-playing, performance feedback, and imitation. This type of therapy is used extensively with almost all types of offender–clients and is one of the favorites in criminal justice agency because it can be easily observed and measured (Hanser, 2007a). The empirical evidence shows that CBT is associated with significant and positive changes, particularly when therapy is provided by experienced practitioners (Waldron & Kaminer, 2004). According to OJJDP (2007),

> Cognitive Behavioral Therapy has been successfully applied across settings (e.g., schools, support groups, prisons, treatment agencies, community-based organizations, churches) and across ages and roles (e.g., students, parents, teachers). It has been shown to be relevant to people with differing abilities and from a diverse range of backgrounds. The strategies of CBT have been successfully used to forestall the onset, ameliorate the severity, and divert the long-term consequences of problem behaviors among young people. Problem behaviors that have been particularly amenable to change using CBT have been 1) violence and criminality, 2) substance use and abuse, 3) teen pregnancy and risky sexual behaviors, and 4) school failure. Across the range of continuum-of-care, many model programs have successfully incorporated the strategies of CBT to effect positive change. (p. 3)

Cognitive behavioral treatments for juvenile offenders are designed to correct dysfunctional thinking and behaviors associated with delinquency, crime, and violence. CBT has been successfully implemented in a host of correctional systems such as residential juvenile facilities and boot camps and in numerous other venues such as schools and job training programs (Little, 2005; OJJDP, 2007). Further, meta-analyses of various treatment programs for criminal offenders have consistently shown cognitive behavioral treatment modalities to be highly effective in reducing recidivism rates (Little, 2005; OJJDP, 2007).

Another common form of treatment that is often very effective with juvenile offenders is family therarpy. Family therapy consists of therapeutic approaches that include the juvenile's family members in the treatment plan through ongoing counseling sessions (OJJDP, 2007). Among the various family therapy approaches, one in particular has been shown to be highly effective with juvenile offenders; this is multisystemic family therapy (MSFT), which targets chronic, violent, or substance-abusing juvenile offenders (ages 12–17) who are at risk for out-of-home placement (OJJDP, 2007). This type of family therapy is delivered in the home, school, and community rather than in a clinic or residential treatment setting. Emphasis is placed on promoting behavior change in the youth's own environment and also addresses the behaviors and interactions of other family members. Services are more intensive than traditional family therapies and include several hours of treatment per week rather than the traditional 50 minutes (OJJDP, 2007). With this type of therapy, "the emphasis is on developing a support network for the family in which the family is empowered to handle difficulties with the offending youth, and the youth is empowered to cope with family, peer, school, and neighborhood problems" (OJJDP, 2007, p. 3).

⊠ The Juvenile Gang Offender

According to OJJDP (2007), the average age of gang members is 17 to 18 years old, with gang members being older, on-the-average, in cities where gangs have existed longer. The typical range in age for juvenile gang offenders tends to be from 12 to 24 years (OJJDP, 2007). The median age at which youths start hanging around gangs is roughly 13 years old, and the median age for joining a gang is 14 (OJJDP, 2007; Valdez, 2005). Although female gang membership is increasing, male gang members outnumber females by a wide margin (Valdez, 2005). Certain offenses are related to different racial/ethnic gangs, though the drug trade tends to be involved with all groups due to its being so lucrative (Valdez, 2005). It is important to point out, however, the disproportionate representation of minority groups in gangs is not a result of a predisposition toward gang membership but rather that minorities tend to be overrepresented in areas overwhelmed with gang activity (Valdez, 2005).

There are other ways to classify gangs other than by ethnicity. One way is viewing gangs along a continuum by degree of organization (Valdez, 2005). Indeed, further, gangs in the community tend to have one of two different forms of organizational structure. These two types of organizational structure are the vertical/hierarchical organization and the horizontal organizational structure (Bureau of Justice Assistance, 1999; Valdez, 2005). Gangs with a vertical/hierarchical organizational structure are likely to indulge in group, as opposed to individual, violence; however, these gangs generally avoid using violence at all. This type of gang tends to focus on making money, which typically overrides individualistic acts of violence. This type of gang is fairly high functioning, and when juvenile members are involved, they tend to work under the leadership of adult gang leaders. In addition and because of the intermix between adult and juvenile gang members, these gangs are able to exert greater control over their members (older veteran gang members maintaining power over younger less acclimated members). On the other hand, gangs that have a horizontal structure tend to have less control over their members (Bureau of Justice Assistance, 1999). While some of these gangs may include cliques or subgroups that can be very organized and able to control their members, the gang as a whole is a loose collection of factions with limited organizational coordination (Bureau of Justice Assistance, 1999).

Gang members commit a disproportionate number of offenses and commit serious and violent offenses at a rate several times higher than non-gang members (Hanser, 2007a). Further, gang members are much more likely than their non-gang peers to commit certain types of crime, such as assaulting others; carrying concealed weapons in school; stealing cars and committing other theft; intimidating or assaulting victims and witnesses; participating in drive-by shootings and homicides; and using, selling, and stealing drugs—even when the two groups have grown up under similar circumstances (OJJDP, 2007). Thus the nature of gangs and their involvement in serious crime and violence produces many risk factors for youth. Likewise, the greater the number of risk factors to which youths are exposed, the greater their risk of joining a gang (Hanser, 2007a). It should be noted that many young gang offenders report that they view their gang as their actual family. This should not be surprising since earlier in this section it was made clear that many of the more serious juvenile offenders come from homes that are chaotic, neglectful, and abusive. It is only natural then that these youth would then turn to others like themselves as a source of support and protection. Thus, it is understandable why many of these youth become gang members.

✖ Establishing an Effective Youth Gang Exit Program

According to Evans and Sawdon (2004), anti-gang programs should not just include law enforcement sweeps and gang suppression efforts but they should also include community advocacy to facilitate cohesive neighborhoods that are not intimidated by gang threats and activity. In Toronto, Canada, a program does just that and is targeted toward young gang members. This gang exit program strategy has three components: (1) assessment and intake, (2) intensive training and personal development, and (3) case management process.

Gang member assessment and intake is the phase that identifies interest and motivation of the gang member, the amount of gang involvement, and the member's family and social history (Evans & Sawdon, 2004). During this phase, members are provided an orientation to the program. The next phase is the gang member intensive training and personal development phase. This phase implements two separate curricula— one for the male gang member and another for female gang members. Each curriculum involves up to 60 hours of intensive training. Topics during this training include anger management, aggression, sexism, racism, homophobia, and bullying. Communication skills training is also given during this phase. The last phase is the gang member case management phase, which involves both individual support for the member but also requires ongoing group meetings for the ex-gang member. The intent is to reinforce what was learned at intake and to provide a proactive intervention when life takes some unforeseen turn for the prior gang member.

This program utilizes prior members that successfully complete the exit program as future facilitators with future members of the program. These prior gang members are tasked with being active in establishing community contacts and outreach. Participants visit local community centers and other youth services to provide information about the program. From this point, many prior members will engage in community presentations to help generate support (financial and otherwise) for the anti-gang program. This program trains these prior members who are "passing the word" with leadership skills training, empathy building, counseling, and the development of their own "personal stories," which are stories that explain how they became involved in gangs and why they have chosen to cease involvement with the gang. This "story" is told in schools and other areas where the ex-gang member tries to warn against joining the gang life.

If it is possible to extract youth from the gang-oriented environment, then this option should be given priority. Indeed, the youth is much less likely to recidivate when away from the adverse peer group. In the absence of such an intervention, the next best strategy is to inoculate him or her from the effects of the gang world and to also replace the prior peer group with a new prosocial peer group. This is specifically what the gang exit program attempts to do all the while working against the backdrop of the prior gang family's pressure to return. This is what makes the task so difficult for the offender and the CSO and it is the strong tug of a subculture that eschews any attempt at reform made by the prior member.

⧄ Restorative Justice Techniques, Family Conferences, and Teen Courts

As you recall from Section III, restorative justice, family conferencing, and teen courts as an alternative sanction were discussed in more detail. However, because of their importance to processing juvenile offenders it is relevant to briefly revisit their definitions and usefulness as an alternative in processing juvenile offenders.

Restorative justice seeks to restore the victim and the community to its state of functioning prior to the criminal act, often involving numerous persons in the community in the reintegration of offenders and holding them accountable for their behavior. By bringing together victims, offenders, families, and other key stakeholders in a variety of settings, restorative justice helps offenders understand the implications of their actions and provides an opportunity for them to become reconnected to the community. Thus, restorative practices, while emphasizing the need for victim compensation and/or community healing, are essentially reintegrative approaches for the offender. Students should recall that the most common forms of restorative justice are community service and restitution. Community service requires the offender to perform some form of work that will benefit the community. It is not uncommon for elements of shaming to be utilized whereby youth will perform work in situations whereby their peers or respected members of their community may witness their actions. This act of shaming is meant to serve as a deterrent to future offending. Monetary restitution on the other hand, requires the offender to pay back monetary losses incurred during the commission of the act or at a minimum a percentage of the total that is agreed upon by the judge, the victim, the offender, and the prosecutor.

Family group conferences, as you may recall from Section III, are discussions that are facilitated and bring the victim, the victim's family, the offender, and the juvenile offender's family together to discuss the impact of a crime committed by the juvenile so that the group can decide how the juvenile is to be held accountable (Hanser, 2007a; OJJDP, 2007; Umbreit, 2000). While teen courts are much like traditional courts in that there are prosecutors and defense attorneys, offenders and victims, and judges and juries, the difference is that other youth rather than adults fill these roles and these youth even determine the disposition of the case (OJJDP, 2007). Similar to restorative justice precepts, the primary goal of teen courts is to hold young offenders accountable for their behavior while requiring reparation for the harm inflicted against the victim and the community (OJJDP, 2007). These alternatives are mechanisms by which youths may be held accountable for their actions while maintaining community safety and the goal of reintegration.

⧄ Conclusion

Juvenile offenders are a large subgroup of the community corrections population and therefore warrant specific and detailed coverage. In addressing the juvenile offender population on community supervision, it is important to understand the historical background and philosophical basis behind the juvenile justice system in general and the use of community sanctions with juveniles in particular. The concept of parens patriae serves as an ancient and fundamental principle behind juvenile supervision and ensuring the welfare of youth processed by the state. In cases where youth are acting outside of the scope of the law and/or in cases where parents or guardians fail to maintain adequate supervision of their children, the state has an obligation to intervene and take charge of the juvenile. In many (but certainly not all) cases, the juvenile youth who are processed through the courts also have issues at home and/or may come from criminogenic family systems that require criminal justice intervention with the young offender and his or her family. In many cases, serious juvenile offenders come from abusive and/or neglectful family systems, making family interventions all the more important.

Juvenile probation, though similar to adult probation, does have some fundamental differences that are interlaced with the juvenile court's concern with stigmatization. Basically, the goal is to ensure that youth are accountable for their actions, but at the same time, permanent stigmatization is to be avoided. Often the relationship between the probation officer and the youngster may have much more depth than the mere supervision of the youngster. In some cases, the probation officer may be a mentor and/or even a counselor to the youth, the desire for reintegration of the youthful offender being an important goal in juvenile community corrections. The juvenile probation officer will conduct a social investigation and, similar to a presentence investigation report (PSI), will provide this inquiry to the judge prior to disposition of the case. The very use of different terminology in juvenile court (as opposed to adult court) belies the difference in orientation and underscores the fact that juvenile courts are civil in nature, not criminal.

The effects of risk factors on a juvenile's likely recidivism are very important. Effective prevention programs will address these issues in advance, when possible. Intervention programs will likewise attempt to reduce the severity of risk factors as a means of lowering the likelihood of future recidivism. Further, protective factors tend to be at the other end of the spectrum. These factors tend to insulate the youth from delinquent or criminal acts. Treatment programs often work to specifically improve or develop these protective factors to make youth resistant to likely recidivism. By working on both ends of the spectrum, it is hoped that youth will be discouraged from further acts of criminality.

There are a number of residential and nonresidential programs for juvenile offenders. Residential programs may include day residential treatment facilities, boot camps, group homes, or wilderness programs. Each of these have their own specific focus, but all are based on the premise that youth can change if given the appropriate guidance to do so. Nonresidential programs might include home confinement, day treatment centers, or aftercare. All of these are more intensive than the basic probation sentence, but each allows the juvenile to return home each evening and maintain their own domicile that is separate from their treatment program. Each of these types of programs utilize a variety of therapeutic methods, with CBT and MSFT being two of the most effective and most commonly used therapeutic orientations. Further, the use of effective gang exit strategies is important when dealing with juveniles in gangs. Each of the prior discussed treatment programs and therapeutic orientations should be used, but the integration of gang exit techniques is imperative if this specific group of juvenile offenders is expected to avoid future criminality.

Lastly, juvenile community corrections use a number of alternate means of processing juvenile cases. Among these are restorative justice principles, family conferences, and teen courts. Restorative justice approaches ensure that the victim and the community are made whole and that the offender is held accountable to the victim and/or the community for their actions. Family conferences follow a similar method of processing offender-victim issues but integrate the family members of both the victim and the offender, as well as other family members. Each of these approaches are moderated and supervised by trained personnel. Lastly, teen courts are similar to common juvenile courts except other youth actually fill the roles of the typical adult courtroom actors. The disposition itself is decided by these youth, and it is in this manner that the juvenile is truly tried by his or her own peers. Each of these approaches demonstrate the unique orientation of the juvenile justice system and of juvenile community supervision—a system that is quite distinct from the adult system of justice.

◪ Section Summary

- John Augustus is considered the father of juvenile probation as well as adult probation. The first law recognizing probation for juveniles was created in 1878.
- The first juvenile court was established in Cook County, Illinois, in 1899.
- Juveniles may be sentenced to either a term of formal or informal probation.
- Juvenile records are quite extensive and are typically confidential.
- Child protection plays a central role in supervising offenders and maintaining their safety from abuse and neglect by either their parents or caregivers.
- Risk factors for delinquent activity can be collapsed into individual, family, school, peer group, and community.
- JIPS is used in roughly half of all programs in the United States. These programs increase the number of contacts between the probation officer and youth. These programs are an attempt to keep the youth in the community as opposed to institutionalization.
- A variety of other options exist for handling youth, such as residential treatment programs, juvenile boot camps, group homes, home confinement, day treatment facilities, aftercare, and wraparound programs.
- Youth gang membership continues to be a major concern for many communities. The ability to identify those at greatest risk for involvement and providing services for youth to leave the gangs are gaining more support in communities.
- Restorative justice, family conferences, and teen courts continue to be used as alternative mechanisms for handling youth in the system.

KEY TERMS

Aftercare	Formal interagency agreement	Physical neglect
Beliefs	Group homes	Psychological abuse
Care coordinators	Home confinement	Residential treatment programs
Child abuse	Involvement	
Child neglect	Juvenile boot camps	Restorative justice
Child parentification	Juvenile Intensive Probation Supervision (JIPS)	Social study
Cognitive behavioral therapy (CBT)		Supervision stage
Community-based interagency team	Juvenile probation	Teen courts
	Juvenile records	Wilderness camps
Community service	Monetary restitution	Wraparound
Educational neglect	Parens patriae	
	Physical abuse	

DISCUSSION QUESTIONS

1. How did the early origins of juvenile probation differ from that of adult probation?

2. How do the processes of juvenile probation differ from adult probation?

3. How do risk and protective factors affect the likelihood for continued offending among juveniles? How might the juvenile justice system work with communities to prevent future delinquency?

4. Identify the different forms of residential and nonresidential programs that exist in juvenile corrections and the types of therapy they both employ.

5. What are the basic dynamics associated with juvenile gang offenders? What are some of the difficulties in getting youth out of gang life?

6. What are some of the informal and alternative approaches to juvenile processing used in your local community?

7. How does the organization and administration of juvenile courts and probation differ from the adult system in your community/state?

WEB RESOURCES

Office of Juvenile Justice and Delinquency Prevention:
http://ojjdp.ncjrs.org

National Association of Youth Courts:
http://www.youthcourt.net/

Please refer to the student study site for web resources and additional resources.

READING

In 1997, Ventura County, California received $4.5 million in grant funding to create an ISP program for youth between the ages of 12 and 18 who scored at least a 12 on a locally adopted risk assessment instrument. Using an experimental design, youth were referred to either regular probation (control group) or to the ISP program over a 3-year time period. This program was originally designed to serve 500 youth (250 in the control group and 250 in the experimental group). The argument for the creation of this program was based in the literature stating that therapeutic approaches addressing the causes of crime through the youths' family and peers would result in a reduction in recidivism. By creating an environment more conducive to treatment rather than punitive in nature, the youths would be more apt to respond to the intervention. A cross-training model or approach was implemented whereby youth were assigned a mentor, a probation officer, and case managers.

SOURCE: Brank, Eve, Lane, Jodi, Turner, Susan, Fain, Terry, & Sehgal, Amber. (2008). An experimental juvenile probation program: Effects on parent and peer relationships. *Crime & Delinquency, 54*(2), 193–224. Copyright © 2008 Sage Publications.

A "Challenge Plan" was created by the team members for each of the participants. The control caseload received typical probation services while the experimental group received extra services. The team assigned to the experimental participant was required to meet at least one time per week. Probationers met with their officers in a community service center as opposed to the normal probation office. At the completion of the program, a total of 151 experimental probationers and 163 control group members were identified for inclusion in the study. Interviews were conducted with each of the youths as a mechanism to assess parent–child and peer relationships. Overall, the results indicated no significant differences between the groups. The only difference between the groups was the control group was more likely to eat dinner with parents. The authors provided some explanations for why there was a finding of no difference between these two groups. Additionally, there were concerns given regarding the intensity of the family focus of the program. Research indicates that those programs having the greatest intensity between youth and their families were most effective.

An Experimental Juvenile Probation Program

Effects on Parent and Peer Relationships

Eve Brank, Jodi Lane, Susan Turner, Terry Fain, and Amber Sehgal

During the 1990s, juvenile crime was one of the top policy concerns nationwide. Policymakers and practitioners faced rising juvenile violence rates and worried that the problem would only increase as the juvenile population swelled later in the decade. To curb the expected rise in crime, leaders looked for new solutions including both front-end and back-end prevention strategies. In the midst of this national concern, California developed the Juvenile Crime and Accountability Challenge Program, designed to fund multiagency collaborations at the county level in an attempt to keep juveniles from eventually entering the California Youth Authority, the state's juvenile prison system. In 1997, Ventura County received about $4.5 million to implement the South Oxnard Challenge Project (SOCP) to serve juveniles on probation over a 3-year period. They later received an additional year of funding. This project brought together probation, drug and alcohol counselors, a mental health counselor, police, recreation and community services staff, mediators, and mentors (called Navigators) to work

together in one location in the heart of South Oxnard, the area with the highest juvenile crime rate in the county.

SOCP staff used Corrections of Place (COP) principles (Clear, 1996; Clear & Corbett, 1998) as a guide to develop a program and treatment approach with a wider range of services to youth and their families than was available for those on routine probation. Each case was assigned to a team of service providers with a case manager in charge of coordinating services. For formal probation youth, the case manager was a probation officer. For informal probation youth, the case manager was a nonprobation employee called a service coordinator. The probation officers for the SOCP were all recruited from their current positions as probation officers within formal or informal juvenile units. The probation officers who applied to be part of SOCP did so because of interest and fit in the project. They were selected through an interview process by a team of probation department leaders who were instrumental in writing and obtaining grant funding. All of those selected had been through the traditional probation officer training programs and had at least a few years of experience working as a probation officer. In addition, they participated in specific SOCP training about their roles in the team and in the project overall.

In addition to the service coordinator and probation officers, each youth had a mentor called a Navigator. A Navigator was a paid, full-time staff person who assisted the youth in "navigating" through the justice system and other areas of their lives. The Navigators' primary role was to develop a consistent relationship with the youth. The Navigators were told to give clear messages of what was expected from youth and were there to facilitate and motivate success. The Navigators' role on the team was to share this information and to act in support of the plan. Each Navigator had a caseload of approximately 15 youth. The need for additional team members (e.g., alcohol and drug treatment specialist, mental health social worker) beyond the service coordinator, probation officer, and Navigator was based informally on information the service coordinators knew about the youth and their families.

An individual service plan, called a Challenge Plan, was developed by the team in connection with the family for each youth referred to SOCP. Team members would meet together at least once per week to discuss the cases, with more spontaneous collaborations occurring daily (Lane & Turner, 1999). During the scheduled meetings, the team members would discuss the cases and contribute ideas for how to better facilitate the youth and their families. One characteristic of this team approach was the inclusion of the special service providers and their involvement in making suggestions for youth during these meetings. Therefore, even if a youth did not have direct contact with an alcohol and drug treatment specialist, that specialist often provided input during team meetings concerning the youth's treatment and the Challenge Plan. Those on the control caseloads received typical probation services—i.e., a probation officer (not a team) who met with them approximately once a month to monitor terms and conditions. The family was not a focus of control group intervention and therefore had no input in developing goals for the youth.

The contact with the youth also took place in a more comfortable and inviting context than a typical probation office; the SOCP was located in a community center that included a library and recreation facility. SOCP youth and their families on average received 14 contacts per month with the members of the SOCP staff (Lane, Turner, Fain, & Sehgal, 2005). Routine probation officers without the help of Navigators and other support personnel averaged one contact with their juveniles (Lane et al., 2005). Evidencing the comfortable atmosphere, SOCP probation officers informally reported incidences of youth coming to the community center after school just to visit with their probation officers.

Earlier research (Lane et al., 2005) on this intervention demonstrated significantly different services provided by SOCP as compared to the routine probation program. For instance, 47% of SOCP youth received drug and alcohol treatment. In contrast, only 29% of the traditional probation youth received these same services. Likewise, 76% of the SOCP youth received some form of family services, but only about 6% of the routine probation youth received family services. The number and length of contacts with the youth differed significantly also. SOCP probation officers spent on average about 365 more minutes per month with their youth than did the routine probation officers.

Throughout the project, the evaluators were able to informally talk with the probation officers and repeatedly heard from them how different the SOCP was from the traditional probation system. In fact, similar to the reports of some of the youth coming to the community center to spend time after school, there were also incidences of SOCP probation officers spending more time with their youth than they would normally do in a traditional probation program. For instance, it became common for youth or their parents to call their SOCP probation officers to report when they had earned good grades in school. One of the SOCP probation officers even went running regularly with one of his youth. Others also participated in nontraditional activities with their youth (see Lane et al., 2005).

The SOCP combined the team approach, service availability, and a comfortable setting to encourage youth and their parents to actively participate in the justice process and improve family relationships at the same time (see Karp, Lane, & Turner, 2002; Lane et al., 2005; Lane, Turner, Fain, & Sehgal, 2007). SOCP staff was aware of research (see Clark & Shields, 1997; Cottle, Lee, & Heilbrun, 2001; Loeber & Dishion, 1983; Simourd & Andrews, 1994) indicating that family relationships were key factors in the ability to avoid crime. They also knew through experience that many of the youth on their caseloads had problems in their family environment. Consequently, one of SOCP's stated goals was to reduce recidivism by improving family relationships.

Multisystemic Therapy (MST) was available to only a few youth in SOCP. In fact, only 11 experimental youth were assigned to MST and only one completed it. This low number was due in part to the intensity of MST and the resulting small caseloads (five youth at a time) of mental health counselors, but also to the more informal focus on the family. Most of the youth received more informal attention to their family relationships. Specifically, SOCP hoped to better include families in the justice process by asking families to participate in the development of the Challenge Plan, maintain an active relationship with the service providers, attend SOCP events (including community meetings), and work together to improve family relationships. The idea was to use the restorative/community justice philosophy of focusing on healing everyone (but not simply in terms of clinical healing) rather than just focusing on the offender. For example, in families where the parents were struggling with their own issues, SOCP staff sometimes helped the family so that the youth might succeed. In one family, a youth rarely attended school because the mother was often abusing drugs or asleep and did not regularly wash the child's uniform, so SOCP staff helped by ensuring the youth had clean uniforms— sometimes by washing the uniforms themselves—and by making sure the youth had a ride to school. Other families had little furniture or food, so staff helped them obtain these necessities in hopes that relieving stress over basic living conditions would improve the likelihood that they could focus on helping the youth work through the issues that had gotten them in trouble.

The probation officers knew through their own experiences and through research that peer relationships were another key element related to choices about whether to participate in conforming or delinquent behavior. Although the project did not address peer relationships in their official list of goals, much of the daily work with the youth was focused on helping them choose better peers. Gangs were considered a serious problem in South Oxnard during the mid- to late 1990s, and many of the SOCP clients lived in areas where gang activity was present. Therefore, questions were also included in the current project to gauge gang or tagging crew activity.

SOCP was designed as a randomized experiment, and eligible youth had an equal chance of being randomly assigned to either SOCP or routine probation. The authors were evaluators on the project and were involved from the beginning, participating in the initial program and evaluation design. Prior articles have addressed SOCP's effects on official outcomes (Lane et al., 2005) and self-reported outcomes (Lane, Turner, Fain, & Sehgal, in press) as well as the experience of implementing COP ideas (Karp et al., 2002; Lane et al., 2007). Those studies generally found few differences between experimental youth in SOCP and control youth on routine probation. The current article examines data from youth interviews conducted with both experimental and control cases at 1 year post random assignment and focuses on youth's perceptions of their parent and peer relationships during the previous year. The research question addressed in this article is, "Did SOCP significantly improve family and peer relationships for involved youth compared to the control group?"

With such clear evidence supporting the deleterious effects of delinquent peers, juvenile justice programs often attempt to target peer relationships and encourage more beneficial friendships. Likewise, the role parents play is also often a focus because of the wealth of research demonstrating the importance of healthy parent-child relationships. The current research was able to assess the nature of these relationships by asking both experimental and control group juveniles about their parents and their friends 1 year after random assignment.

Because the SOCP staff specifically intended to encourage better parent and peer relationships, it was hypothesized that the groups would differ after a year's time. We hypothesized that juveniles who participated in the SOCP would report more quality relationships with their parents than the control group juveniles. The relationship was assessed through questions that asked about the daily life of the family, including enjoyment in being together, eating dinner together, cooperation, trust, and other similar questions (discussed in detail in the results section below). Because parental behaviors are also important, we asked the juveniles about the parents' monitoring behaviors. In addition, we hypothesized that compared to control group juveniles, SOCP juveniles would report healthier peer relationships with less criminal activity by their peers. The peer relationships were assessed through questions that focused on the criminal activity, drug use behaviors, gang membership, and other related issues of the friends (see results section for questions). The juveniles' recidivism rates are not the focus of the current research, but earlier research demonstrated that they were not significantly different between the control and experimental group (Lane et al., 2005, in press).

⊠ Method

Sample and Evaluation Design

SOCP targeted youth between 12 and 18 years old who had a citation (arrest) or violation of probation, lived in South Oxnard or the small neighboring town of Port Hueneme, and scored at least 12 points on a locally adapted risk assessment.[1] The evaluation used an experimental design with random assignment, one of the strongest scientific methods for studying program impact (see Baird, 1991; Boruch, 1997; Campbell & Stanley, 1966; Cook & Campbell, 1979; Farrington, 2003; Palmer, 1992). The initial design called for 500 youth (250 experimental and 250 control) who met the above eligibility criteria to be randomly assigned to either SOCP or routine probation over an 18-month period beginning January 1, 1998. When more funding was awarded, random assignment was continued until February 29, 2000. Trained probation officers in multiple units completed risk assessments when a youth received a citation or violation of probation. If the youth scored at least 12 points

on the assessment, the probation officer called evaluation staff for random assignment to either SOCP or routine probation. Evaluation staff used equal probability assignment, and youth had a 50% chance of being assigned to SOCP and a 50% chance of being assigned to routine probation. A total of 539 youth were assigned to the study, 264 to SOCP and 275 to routine probation.

SOCP planned to serve youth on informal (not court-ordered) probation for 7 months and youth on formal (court-ordered) probation for 9 months. SOCP decided on these intervention periods for two reasons. First, they believed that formal probation cases by definition were more serious and required a longer intervention period. Second, the granting agency (the California Board of Corrections) required that each youth be followed for 18 months post intervention, and ending the intervention at this point allowed for the lengthy follow-up during the funding period.

At 1 year post random assignment, evaluation staff conducted lengthy interviews covering multiple topics with the majority of study youth. The evaluators chose this time period to ensure that the interview periods were consistent across both informal and formal probation, to gauge attitudes after the intervention period, and to include some part of the follow-up period. Evaluators obtained both parental consent and youth assent before conducting the interviews, which lasted approximately 1 hr and were conducted at times and places convenient to the youth. Participating youth were paid $25 to complete the interview. Although there were multiple topics on the interview, this article examines youth perceptions of their parental and peer relationships during the year after random assignment. Given SOCP's specific efforts to improve both parent and peer relationships, we hypothesized that these youth would perceive significantly more improvement in these two aspects of their lives.

By the end of the study, evaluators had interviewed 151 (57.2%) of experimental (E) youth and 163 (59.3%) of control (C) youth.[2] There were no significant differences between the youth interviewed and the entire study sample on personal characteristics (e.g., age, gender, ethnicity, prior record). The interview sample was mostly male (E = 78.8%, C = 73.6%), mostly Hispanic

(E = 85.4%, C = 77.9%), and mostly 17 or older at the time of interview (E = 73.5%, C = 65.1%). Close to half of both groups lived with both parents (E = 47.7%, C = 49.7%), and about a third lived with their mother only (E = 36.4%, C = 33.1%). About a third of each group was referred for property offenses (E = 33.8%, C = 31.9%), about a fifth for violent offenses (E = 22.5%, C = 19.6%), and very few were referred for drug offenses (E = 3.3%, C = 1.8%). Over 40% of each group was referred for offenses that fell into other categories (e.g., violation of probation, public order; E = 40.4%, C = 46.6%). Only about a third of each group had a prior sustained petition at the time of referral (E = 35.3%, C = 33.7%). Most youth in both groups were on informal probation (E = 67.5%, C = 68.7%) rather than formal probation. There were no statistically significant differences between the interviewed groups on the characteristics outlined above.

Measures

Parent relationships. Our first set of questions regarding the family was designed to gauge what daily life in their family was like. The stem read, "What is it usually like when you are around members of your family? Tell me how often there is:"This was followed by six questions: (1) a feeling of cooperation, (2) enjoyment in being together, (3) an interest in listening and helping one another, (4) fighting or loud arguments, (5) complaining about one another, and (6) boredom-nothing happening. We also asked the participants, "How often do you and your family spend leisure time together?" They were given a response card with the following answer options—never, sometimes, about half the time, usually, always. The answer options were coded 1 (never) through 5 (always). We also asked, "How many times a week do you generally eat dinner with your family?" (coded 0 = none to 7 = every night).

We then asked another set of questions asking specifically about their relationships with their mother and their father. For each parent, we asked the following five questions: (1) How often do you trust him or her? (2) How often do you feel you can talk to him or her about your problems? (3) How often do you think he or she is genuinely interested in you? (4) How often do you feel he or she supports you? (5) How often are you afraid of your mom or dad? The youth answered these questions with the same response card used earlier, and the response options were coded 1 (never) through 5 (always).

The last set of questions about parents asked two yes/no questions (coded 1 = yes, 0 = no), asking, "During the 12 months after [random assignment date], only the time when you were on probation/in the Challenge Project:" (1) Did you get along better with your parents (or guardians) than you did before [random assignment date]? (2) Did you find it easier talk to your parents (or guardians) about important things?

Peer relationships. We also asked a series of questions about peer relationships. We first asked them how many close friends—"that is, people you can really depend on"—that they had. Then, we asked how many close friends they had "with whom you can talk about private matters." Then, we asked more detailed questions about the characteristics of these close friends. First, we asked how many of these friends (1) look to you as a leader, (2) agree with your ideas, (3) laugh at or make fun of you, and (4) cause trouble. Youth were given a response card with the following options: none, some, half, most, and all. The codes for these options ranged from 1 (none) to 5 (all).

The next set of peer questions addressed delinquent behaviors and experiences of the participants' close friends during or at 12 months after the youth was randomly assigned to the program. We asked, during the 12 months after the youth was randomly assigned, "Did your close friends do things that are against the law?" We also asked how many of them had been in local residential facilities (juvenile hall, Colston Youth Center, and the Juvenile Restitution Project [JRP]), boot camp, the California Youth Authority or prison, or on probation by the interview date. We also asked how many of their closest friends were gang members or hung out with gangs. The next set of questions asked about drug behaviors of their close friends. We asked (1) How many of these close friends use drugs now? (2) How many of your friends have used drugs and alcohol in the past but don't use now? All of these questions were again coded from 1 (none) to 5 (all). If their friends used drugs either now or in the past, we also asked the youth if he or she used drugs with the friends (coded $1 = $ yes, $0 = $ no). Another question asked, "During the 12 months after [random assignment date], how many of your friends helped you to quit drugs?" Finally, the last drug-related question asked, "How many of your close friends who do not use illegal drugs could you call and talk to right now?" These questions were again coded from 1 (none) to 5 (all).

The final set of peer-related questions asked about gang-related or tagging crew activity they had participated in during the previous 12 months and at the time of interview.[3] We asked (1) Did you associate ("kick it") with any gang members or a tagging crew? (2) Have you ever been jumped in? (3) Did you claim a gang or tagging crew? and (4) Do you have a moniker (nickname)? If they said they claimed a gang/tagging crew, we asked the following questions: Does your gang (1) Get into fights with other gangs? (2) Steal cars? (3) Rob other people? (4) Steal things? Are there (1) initiation rites, (2) established leaders, (3) symbols or colors, or (4) hand signs?

The next set of questions asked participants about help they may or may not have received to get out of negative peer relationships. These questions were designed to determine if SOCP staff were more active than routine probation officers in encouraging more positive peer relationships. For those who claimed a gang or tagging crew, we asked if during the previous 12 months while they were on probation or in SOCP: (1) Did anyone talk to you about leaving the gang/tagging crew? (2) Did anyone help you choose friends outside the gang/tagging crew? If so, (3) Was the help useful to you? For all youth, even those who did not claim a gang/tagging crew, we asked: (1) Did anyone help you choose friends who do not break the law? (2) Was this help useful to you? (3) Did anyone help you choose friends who do not use alcohol and/or other drugs? If so, (4) Was this help useful in helping you not use alcohol and/or drugs?

▨ Results

Family Relationships

There were no significant differences between SOCP and control youth on these questions, except that control youth ate dinner with their families significantly more nights (a little over three) than did SOCP youth (slightly less than three). Youth in both groups indicated that their families experienced a feeling of cooperation, enjoyment in being together, and interest in listening to and helping one another about half the time. Fighting occurred somewhere between sometimes and half the time. They generally indicated that they sometimes complained about each other or were bored.

There are no significant differences between the two groups on participants' perceptions about their relationships with their parents, but the results are interesting generally. Youth generally indicated that they usually trusted both their mother and father, although they indicated that they talked to them about their problems about half the time. They also believed their parents usually were genuinely interested in them and supported them. Youth said they were only sometimes afraid of either parent.

The perceptions about their relationships with their parents during the 12 months since random assignment illustrate only one statistically significant finding—SOCP youth were more likely than control youth to say that the help received from staff improved their family relationship (E $= 49.3\%$, C $= 30.3\%$). In contrast to this more general question, less than half of both groups indicated that they got along better with their parents, found it easier to talk to their parents, or that their parents monitored their behavior more. Although not statistically different, a higher percentage of control youth than experimental youth indicated improvements on these three more specific questions.[4]

Peer Relationships

The concept of peer relationships was addressed by our question of whether SOCP made a significant difference in decreasing negative peer relationships for their clients. Table 10.4 presents the characteristics of the close friends. Once again, SOCP youth were not significantly different from those on routine probation in the types of friends they had during the time since they were randomly assigned.

Generally, the results demonstrated that some of the friends met the criteria asked about in each question. Youth in both groups generally indicated that some of their friends looked to them as a leader, while about half of their friends agreed with their ideas. Some of their friends also laughed at them or made fun of them (see Table 10.3).

Interestingly, when we asked about problem or delinquent behaviors or experience with justice system punishments, youth generally indicated that only some of their friends caused trouble or did things that were

Table 10.3   Mean and Percentage Comparison of Close Friend Characteristics for South Oxnard Challenge Project (SOCP) and Control Youth

Survey Questions (response scale: 1 = none, 5 = all)	Mean Ratings	
	SOCP	Control
How many of your close friends:		
• Look to you as a leader?	2.0	2.1
• Agree with your ideas?	2.7	2.8
• Laugh at or make fun of you?	1.8	1.9
• Cause trouble?	2.3	2.5
• Did things that are against the law?	2.3	2.1
• Had been in juvenile hall, Colston, or JRP?	1.9	1.8
• Had been in boot camp?	1.4	1.4
• Had been in CYA or prison?	1.2	1.2
• Were on probation?	2.3	2.1
• Were gang members?	2.0	1.9
• Hung out with gang members?	2.3	2.2
• Use drugs now?	2.3	2.2
If so, did you use with them? (% yes)	68.6	70.8
• Used drugs in the past, but don't use now?	2.1	2.1
If so, did you use with them? (% yes)	61.6	70.8
• Help you quit drugs?	2.4	1.4
Of close friends who do not use illegal drugs:		
• How many could you call and talk to right now?	2.3	2.4

NOTE: JRP = Juvenile Restitution Project; CYA = California Youth Authority.

against the law. Some of them had also been on probation, but fewer had been in institutions, especially those that were not locally run. Youth in both groups indicated that some of their friends were gang members and some of their friends used drugs either now or in the past. If their friends used drugs, most of the youth indicated that they had used drugs with these friends. SOCP youth were more likely, but not statistically significantly, to say they had close friends who tried to help them quit drugs. Youth in both groups said that they had some friends who did not use drugs whom they could call and talk to (see Table 10.3).

Peer relationships specific to gang activity were addressed by asking the youth if they associated or claimed a gang or tagging crew. If the youth said yes (33 experimental cases and 33 control cases), we then asked about their gangs.[7]

Still, there were some intriguing results. Almost half of both groups indicated that they associated with gang members or a tagging crew during the 12 months since random assignment, and most of these were still associating with the group at the time they were interviewed. Still, less than 10% had been "jumped in"; yet, about 20% of youth in both groups said they "claimed" a gang. Of those who claimed, most had a moniker/nickname, and most said their gangs fought with other gangs, stole cars, robbed people, stole things, had initiation rites, had symbols or colors, and had hand signs. About a third of those in both groups who claimed gangs said their gangs had established leaders. If they still claimed a gang at the time of interview, we asked the youth, "Do you plan to stay in the gang/crew or are you considering getting out?" There are again no significant differences across groups on this measure, and about a third of both groups planned to stay in.

The first three questions were asked only of those youth who claimed a gang. The results again indicated that there were no significant differences between the two groups regarding someone talking to them about leaving the gang, helping them choose friends outside the gang, or the usefulness of this help. The next two questions were asked of all youth surveyed. Again, there were no significant differences

between the groups regarding help choosing friends who did not break the law or use alcohol and drugs. If someone did help them choose different friends, control youth were more likely to say this help was useful to them.

Discussion

Summary of Results

Our research examined the impact of SOCP on parent and peer relationships. We found that there were generally no significant differences between SOCP and control youth on our measures. Control group youth ate dinner with their families significantly more times per week (3.4 vs. 2.8), and experimental youth who received help on family issues were significantly more likely to say that the help actually improved their relationships. These were the only findings that were different across groups, but they should be considered with great caution. These differences could be attributed to statistical chance or question wording issues rather than substantive differences. Although an initial reaction may be to say that SOCP improved the parent-child relationships, this is more likely a result that represents experimental youth responding to the intensive program and the focus that was clearly directed toward their relationships with their parents. In support of this interpretation there were no other differences with regard to specific questions about their daily life experiences in the family, their relationships with their parents, characteristics of their close friends, gang participation or gang-related activities, or help getting out of the gang.

Based on the current literature that relates family and peer relationships with juvenile offending, the SOCP was positioned to provide noteworthy changes in the lives of the experimental youth. Previous studies have consistently demonstrated the importance of family and peer influences on juvenile offending. Although research has indicated that these microsystem relationships play a large part in a juvenile's offending, we have less empirical information about attempts by programs such as SOCP in altering those relationships. We expected to see a change in the targeted relationships and in turn those differences may be useful in predicting reductions in recidivism. Unfortunately, the results are overall unsupportive of an effect on parent or peer relationships, which naturally removes the possibility of differentially predicting recidivism. The following sections will address the possible reasons why the experimental and control group juveniles had no significant differences on their reports of parent and peer relationships.

Why No Significant Differences?

Family intervention lacked necessary intensity. A number of researchers who have studied the role parents play in their child's delinquency have also postulated that programs developed to address delinquency should focus on shaping more appropriate parent-child relationships (Barnow, Lucht, & Freyberger, 2005; Ge, Best, Conger, & Simons, 1996). In fact, family-centered interventions appear to have some of the greatest potential with reductions in delinquency and recidivism (Sherman et al., 1997). These family-focused interventions often involve intensive family therapy or skills training (Mulvey, Arthur, & Reppucci, 1993). Additionally, Lipsey, Wilson, and Cothern (2000) examined through meta-analysis serious juvenile offender programs and found that family counseling provided mixed but generally positive effects. Programs such as Functional Family Therapy (FFT; Gordon, Graves, & Arbuthnot, 1995), Problem-Solving Skills Training (PSST), Parent Management Training (PMT; Kazdin, Siegel, & Bass, 1992), and MST (Henggeler, Melton, & Smith, 1992; see also Henggeler, Melton, Brondino, Scherer, & Hanley, 1997) are intensive family interventions that have had notable success at reducing juvenile antisocial behaviors and recidivism rates. The current intervention was one that lacked this kind of intensive focus on the family or the parents for the whole group. While the staff clearly had the goal of influencing family relationships, the results seem to indicate that the intensity of the interventions was likely not adequate. SOCP staff had hoped to provide MST to experimental youth, but the mental health counselor was limited to serving five youth at a time due to the intensity of services she was to deliver. Consequently, most youth did

not receive MST and even fewer completed it. Many youth did receive other forms of services including drug and alcohol, counseling, education, family, vocational, mentoring, and recreational services (see Lane et al., 2005, for a complete comparison of percentages between routine probation and SOCP for these services).

Based on the previous literature where success was demonstrated, the current program may not have focused enough on family involvement to be able to obtain the desired significant changes (see Mulvey, Arthur, & Repucci, 1993). While this answer may appear as a simple, even vacuous, explanation to the null findings, there are deeper ramifications to this interpretation. State legislators have been moving toward a juvenile justice system that places a greater weight and responsibility on juveniles' parents.

Often referred to as parental responsibility laws or parental involvement laws (Brank, Kucera, & Hays, 2005; Davies & Davidson, 2001), these statutes place expectations or even requirements of parental involvement in a youth's case. For instance, in Arizona, the court may order parents to participate in a diversion program or complete counseling, treatment, or an educational program (Treatment, service, restraining and protective orders, 2006, § 8–234[F]). Similarly, in North Carolina, parents can be ordered to attend parental responsibility classes when their child is adjudicated undisciplined or delinquent (Parental responsibility classes, 2005). Parents of delinquent youth in Oregon may also be ordered to attend parental education or counseling programs (Court may order education or counseling, 2003).

Parental involvement laws, rightly or wrongly, place an emphasis on the parent's role and the parent-child relationship. Notably, legal scholars have pointed out that these laws, however, do not address implementation (much less evaluation) of the required parental involvement (Ebenstein, 2000). These laws relate to the current study because SOCP was a program that had the goal of improving parent-child relationships to reduce recidivism, but was unable to do either probably because of the lack of focus and intensity on those relationships. These Parental Involvement Laws speak of the parent-child relationship as an answer to the juvenile crime problem without considering the implementation difficulties or the needed intensity. They are "symbolic politics"

(Tomaszewski, 2005) in the sense that they allow for a response to juvenile crime without any financial commitment from the legislature. The current study suggests that such responses to juvenile crime may not be focused or intensive enough to have the intended consequences.

Peer Intervention

The authors know of little research that addresses the specific issue of interventions that focus on peer relationships. Clearly, there is a link between delinquent behaviors and peer delinquent involvement (Brendgen, Vitaro, Tremblay, & Wanner, 2002; Dishion, McCord, & Poulin, 1999; Mrug, Hoza, & Bukowski, 2004; Vitaro, Brendgen, & Tremblay, 2000); however, research in this area has primarily focused on this association or the negative effect of aggregating delinquent youth together in intervention programs (Dishion et al., 1999; Gifford-Smith, Dodge, Dishion, & McCord, 2005; Mahoney, Stattin, & Magnusson, 2001; O'Donnell, 2003). Although the staff was certainly aware of the effects peer relationships can have on delinquency, the program did not have the primary goal of influencing these relationships. In line with the research in the area, the program only had minimal aggregation of the juveniles; there were only a few opportunities for the juveniles to be together with other participants during their program. It may be that there were no significant differences on some of the gang-related questions because of the small number of youth who were in a gang and therefore answered these dependent questions. In general, the peer relationships were likely not affected for the same reason the family relationships did not see a vast improvement, that is, a lack of intensity of the program on this issue. In addition, there were several implementation issues with undertaking such a program. The following section will address these difficulties.

Implementation difficulties. These authors have consistently reported the problems faced by the SOCP while implementing such an ambitious program (see Lane & Turner, 1999; Karp et al., 2002; Lane et al., 2005; in press). The program set out to deliver a multiagency, comprehensive program to juvenile probationers,

because they believed that addressing multiple factors in youths' lives was their best chance at making a difference. A key stumbling block was that because of time limits on grant funding, all of these components were implemented simultaneously, rather than phased in over time. The challenge of putting so many new program components in place together was difficult on the best days. This difficulty was compounded by the newly developed multiagency collaboration. Although all parties were motivated and interested in the new ideas included in the project, they often spoke different languages and had different visions of what those ideas meant in practice (see Karp et al., 2002). Participants were faced with the challenge of overcoming these differences while they built the new program from scratch.

Another issue that may have resulted in these findings was staff discomfort with the requirements and expectations of the new SOCP program, which was designed based on Clear's COP model (see Clear, 1996) and built from restorative justice principles. Consequently, the SOCP program called for a different approach to doing business (see Clear, 1996; Clear & Karp, 1999), and staff often felt they had no clear guidelines regarding what COP and restorative justice principles meant in practice. For probation officers especially, often the philosophy (helping in atypical ways) was contradictory to their training (surveillance, accountability). Many of them were energetic about helping youth, but they struggled with balancing the unique helping approach of the program with what they perceived to be their obligations to the court (see Authors, 2002). In other words, even though the SOCP probation officers desired to focus on the families, they knew they still had an obligation to the court to provide the judge with the typical probation reports.

Many staff were also not experts on family matters, so it may be unreasonable to expect them to have had big impacts on family relationships that were likely more strained than those in the "typical" family (e.g., because of involvement in the criminal justice system and living in a high-crime neighborhood). Probation officers, mentors, and others were not trained in dealing with the complexities these families faced. Rather, the project had mental health counselors on site who specialized in this area. However, because they were to deliver MST, they had very few youth on their caseloads at one time (a maximum of five). This meant that they were not able to spend much time helping the majority of youth in the project. There were also parent-child mediations available, which were conducted by an on-site mediator, but very few of the interviewed SOCP ($n = 17$) or control youth ($n = 2$) reported having participated in these mediations. These factors together lead the authors to believe that few of the families likely got the intensity of services they probably needed to really make differences in their lives (see Mulvey et al., 1993).

Similarly, few of the staff had specific training regarding how to improve peer relationships. Rather, as in most probation programs, they were expected to encourage youth to choose different peers and to talk to them about the benefits and costs of choosing offending friends. Navigators were there to guide them toward better choices and the program created an environment for choosing "better" friends through positive peer activities. But, again, it may have been too much to expect staff to be able to reach the core issues underlying their choices of friends without providing more mental health counselors or others specifically trained to address these needs. The program was already expensive and included many components, which were difficult to implement en masse, so it may have been unreasonable to expect the project to be able to hire even more staff and focus even more on each of the included components.

Although the research did employ an experimental design, no preintervention measures are available for comparison. Baseline information about family and peer relationships may have provided some useful information for pre- and postintervention comparisons; however, careful care was taken to ensure random assignment into the two conditions. Earlier examinations of these data (Lane et al., 2005) confirm that the two groups were not statistically different on demographic characteristics. Although it is impossible to know without the pretest information, the assumption is that the two groups were not statistically different on the relationship questions before the intervention because they were randomly assigned to the conditions. Nonetheless, adding a baseline would be helpful in future research endeavors such as this.

In addition to the inclusion of a baseline measure, an additional recommendation would be to more closely monitor the behaviors of the team members, especially the probation officers. Informal observations indicated that the team members were following the recommendations for their roles and the goals of the program; however, there is no substitute for empirical data collection and analyses on the topic.

⊠ Conclusion

The current research was based on random assignment of juveniles to either a traditional probation program or an intensive experimental one. While the researchers have some methodological concerns about the implementation (see Discussion section), the strength of the research design enables us to make some conclusions that we might not otherwise be able to make. We encourage those involved with future probation programs desiring to influence family and peer relationships to carefully consider the results from this study. Although we generally found that SOCP did not have an effect on the juveniles, there is much that can be gleaned from this project. First, intensive family interventions will take an enormous commitment of time and resources. The current program tried to influence family relationships, but was likely not focused enough on that portion of the intervention for it to be successful. A phasing in of different components will be useful so that the service providers and probation officers can become acclimated to each new component one at a time. In addition, it would be helpful to more closely control the actions of the probation officers and other team members.

Second, general questions about family relationships may illicit false perceptions, or at least incomplete perceptions, from the youth. In the current study, youth said that they got along better with their families, but when questioned more specifically about that relationship it appeared that there was not a true improvement as compared to the traditional probation youth. Future studies investigating family relationships will need to be careful to employ in-depth scales about those relationships to ensure that an accurate measure of family relationships is obtained.

Third, legislators and policymakers should give careful consideration when implementing parental involvement programs in their statutes. The results from the current project imply that a simple inclusion of such language in the statutes (without the focused, intensive programs to back them up) will likely not result in the intended impact or any impact at all.

Notes

1. During the summer of 1997, a local screening and selection committee comprised of agency leaders and personnel adapted (revised scoring categories) and pretested a validated risk instrument to ensure that it would "capture" youth who, based on probation agency experience, were actually at medium to high risk of committing crime in the near future. The committee was aware of research indicating that programs are more successful when they target youth who are at medium to high risk (see Lipsey & Wilson, 1998; Wilson & Howell, 1995). The committee determined that a score of at least 12 on their assessment would capture these youth in their community. The final sample, however, was primarily informal probation cases, indicating that this assessment did not necessarily capture high-risk youth.

2. Youth may not have been interviewed because parents or the youth refused consent, interviewers were unable to establish contact, or the study ended before they were contacted.

3. The researchers recognize that a tagging crew is not the same as a gang. Tagging crews are involved in graffiti only, while gangs have a much larger scope. The participants were asked the name of their tagging crew or gang if they indicated involvement. Although we could have determined from the name provided and the police files to which group the youth belonged, we decided not to do so. We decided not to make the distinction in the current research because it was not important to do so for our study's purpose and the proportion of respondents who indicated involvement in either group was quite small.

4. Youth were also asked whether they got along better with their siblings and whether they found it easier to talk with their siblings about important things than they did before (random assignment date). There were no significant differences between the SOCP and the routine probation youth. For those youth who had siblings, approximately 30% of both groups believed they were getting along with their siblings better than before and were finding it easier to talk to them about important things.

5. The lower numbers for some of these questions are the result of the father/male guardian or mother/female guardian not being a regular part of the youth's life. If that was the case, then the youth did not answer the questions regarding them.

6. The information provided in this table is also presented in Lane, Turner, Fain, & Sehgal (2007).

7. The lack of significant differences on gang-related questions displayed in the following tables may be because of the small number of youth who responded that they were in a gang or tagging crew and therefore answered the dependent gang questions.

References

Agnew, R. (1991). The interactive effects of peer variables on delinquency. *Criminology, 29,* 47–72.

Akers, R. L. (1998). *Social learning and social structure: A general theory of crime and deviance.* Boston: Northwestern University Press.

Baird, C. (1991). Intensive supervision programs for high-risk juveniles: Critical issues for program evaluation. In T. L. Armstrong (Ed.), *Intensive interventions with high risk youths: Promising approaches in juvenile probation and parole* (pp. 295–315). Monsey, NY: Criminal Justice Press.

Barnow, S., Lucht, M., & Freyberger, H.-J. (2005). Correlates of aggressive and delinquent conduct problems in adolescence. *Aggressive Behavior, 31,* 24–39.

Boruch, R. F. (1997). *Randomized experiments for planning and evaluation: A practical guide.* Thousand Oaks, CA: Sage.

Brank, E. M., Kucera, S. C., & Hays, S. A. (2005). Parental responsibility statutes: An organization and policy implications. *Journal of Law and Family Studies, 7,* 1–55.

Brendgen, M., Vitaro, F., Tremblay, R. E., & Wanner, B. (2002). Parent and peer effects on delinquency-related violence and dating violence: A test of two mediation models. *Social Development, 11,* 225–244.

Bronfenbrenner, U. (1979). *The ecology of human development: Experiments in design and nature.* Cambridge, MA: Harvard University Press.

Browning, K., & Huizinga, D. (1999). *Highlights of findings from the Denver Youth Survey* (Fact Sheet No. 106). Washington, DC: U.S. Department of Justice, Office of Juvenile Justice and Delinquency.

Browning, K., & Loeber, R. (1999). *Highlights of findings from the Pittsburgh Youth Study* (Fact Sheet No. 95). Washington, DC: U.S. Department of Justice, Office of Juvenile Justice and Delinquency.

Campbell, D. T., & Stanley, J. S. (1966). *Experimental and quasi-experimental designs for research.* Chicago: Rand McNally.

Caprara, G. V., Scabini, E., Barbaranelli, C., Pastorelli, C., Regalia, C., & Bandura, A. (1998). Impact of adolescents' perceived self-regulatory efficacy on familial communication and antisocial conduct. *European Psychologist, 3,* 125–132.

Clark, R. D., & Shields, G. (1997). Family communication and delinquency. *Adolescence, 32,* 81–92.

Clear, T. R. (1996). Toward a corrections of "place": The challenge of "community" in corrections. *National Institute of Justice Journal, 231,* 52–56.

Clear, T. R., & Corbett, R. P. (1998). The community corrections of place. In *Crime and place: Plenary papers of the 1997 conference on criminal justice research and evaluation* (pp. 69–80). Washington, DC: National Institute of Justice.

Clear, T. R., & Karp, D. R. (1999). *The community justice ideal: Preventing crime and achieving justice.* Boulder, CO: Westview Press.

Conger, K. J., & Conger, R. D. (1994). Differential parenting change in sibling differences in delinquency. *Journal of Family Psychology, 8,* 287–302.

Cook, T. D., & Campbell, D. T. (1979). *Quasi-experimentation: Design and analysis issues for field settings.* Chicago: Rand-McNally.

Cottle, C. C., Lee, R. J., & Heilbrun, K. (2001). The prediction of criminal recidivism in juveniles: A meta-analysis. *Criminal Justice and Behavior, 28,* 367–394.

Court may order education or counseling. Or. Rev. Stat. § 419C.573 (2003).

Davies, H. J., & Davidson, H. A. (2001). *Parental involvement practices of juvenile courts.* Report to the Office of Juvenile Justice and Delinquency Prevention U.S. Department of Justice. Washington, DC: American Bar Association.

Deater-Deckard, K. (2001). Annotation: Recent research examining the role of peer relationships in the development of psychopathology. *Journal of Child Psychology and Psychiatry, 42,* 565–579.

Dishion, T. J., Eddy, J. M., Haas, E., Li, F., & Spracklen, K. (1997). Friendships and violent behavior during adolescence. *Social Development, 6,* 207–223.

Dishion, T. J., McCord, J., & Poulin, F. (1999). When interventions harm: Peer groups and problem behavior. *American Psychologist, 54*(9), 755–764.

Dishion, T. J., Nelson, S. E., & Bullock, B. M. (2004). Premature adolescent autonomy: Parent disengagement and deviant peer process in the amplification of problem behavior. *Journal of Adolescence, 27,* 515–530.

Ebenstein, E. P. (2000). Criminal and civil parental liability statutes: Would they have saved the 15 who died at Columbine? *Cardozo Women's Law Journal, 7,* 1–28.

Farrington, D. P. (1989). Early predictors of adolescent aggression and adult violence. *Violence and Victims, 4,* 79–100.

Farrington, D. P. (2003). A short history of randomized experiments in criminology: A meager feast. *Evaluation Review, 27,* 218–227.

Finkenauer, C., Engels, R. C., & Baumeister, R. F. (2005). Parenting behavioural and emotional problems: The role of self-control. *International Journal of Behavioral Development, 29,* 58–69.

Florshim, P., Tolan, P. H., & Gorman-Smith, D. (1996). Family processes and risk for externalizing behavior problems among African American and Hispanic boys. *Journal of Consulting and Clinical Psychology, 64,* 1222–1230.

Ge, X., Best, K. M., Conger, R. D., & Simons, R. L. (1996). Parenting behaviors and the occurrence and co-occurrence of adolescent depressive symptoms and conduct problems. *Developmental Psychology, 32,* 717–731.

Gifford Smith, M., Dodge, K. A., Dishion, T. J., & McCord, J. (2005). Peer influence in children and adolescents: Crossing the bridge from development to intervention science. *Journal of Abnormal Child Psychology, 33,* 255–265.

Gordon, D. A., Graves, K., & Arbuthnot, J. (1995). The effect of functional family therapy for delinquents on adult criminal behavior. *Criminal Justice and Behavior, 22,* 60–73.

Gottfredson, M. R., & Hirschi, T. (1990). *A general theory of crime.* Stanford, CA: Stanford University Press.

Griffin, K. W., Botvin, G. J., Scheier, L. M., Diaz, T., & Miller, N. L. (2000). Parenting practices as predictors of substance use, delinquency, and aggression among urban minority youth moderating effects of family structure and gender. *Psychology of Addictive Behaviors, 14,* 174–184.

Guo, J., Hawkins, J. D., Hill, K. G., & Abbott, R. D. (2001). Childhood and adolescent predictors of alcohol abuse and dependence in young adulthood. *Journal of Studies on Alcohol, 62,* 754–762.

Harris, J. R. (1995). Where is the child's environment? A group socialization theory of development. *Psychological Review, 102,* 458–489.

Heaven, P. C. L., Newbury, K., & Mak, A. (2004). The impact of adolescent and parental characteristics on adolescent levels of delinquency and depression. *Personality and Individual Differences, 36,* 173–185.

Henggeler, S. W., Melton, G. B., Brondino, M. J., & Scherer, D. G. (1997). Multisystemic therapy with violent and chronic juvenile offenders and their families: The role of treatment fidelity in successful dissemination. *Journal of Consulting and Clinical Psychology, 65,* 821–833.

Henggeler, S. W., Melton, G. B., & Smith, L. A. (1992). Family preservation using multisystemic therapy: An effective alternative to incarcerating serious juvenile offenders. *Journal of Consulting and Clinical Psychology, 60,* 953–961.

Hirschi, T. (1969). *Causes of delinquency.* Berkeley, CA: University of California Press.

Karp, D. R., Lane, J., & Turner, S. (2002). Ventura County and the theory of community justice. In D. R. Karp and T. R. Clear (Ed.), *What is community justice? Case studies of restorative justice and community supervision* (pp. 3–33). Thousand Oaks, CA: Sage.

Kazdin, A. E., Siegel, T. C, & Bass, D. (1992). Cognitive problem-solving skills training and parent management training in the treatment of antisocial behavior in children. *Journal of Consulting and Clinical Psychology, 60,* 733–747.

Kiesner, J., Kerr, M., & Stattin, H. (2004). Very important persons: In adolescence: Going beyond in-school, single friendships in the study of peer homophily. *Journal of Adolescence, 27,* 545–560.

Laird, R. D., Pettit, G. S., Bates, J. E., & Dodge, K. A. (2003). Parents' monitoring-relevant knowledge and adolescents' delinquent behavior: Evidence of correlated developmental changes and reciprocal influences. *Child Development, 74,* 752–768.

Lambert, S. F., & Cashwell, C. S. (2004). Preteens talking to parents: Perceived communication and school-based aggression. *Family Journal, 12,* 122–128.

Lane, J., & Turner, S. (1999). Interagency collaboration in juvenile justice: Learning from experience. *Federal Probation, 63,* 33–39.

Lane, J., Turner, S., Fain, T., & Sehgal, A. (2005). Evaluating an experimental intensive juvenile probation program: Supervision and official outcomes. *Crime and Delinquency, 51,* 26–52.

Lane, J., Turner, S., Fain, T., & Sehgal, A. (2007). Implementing "Corrections of Place" ideas: The perspective of clients and staff. *Criminal Justice & Behavior, 34,* 76–95.

Lane, J., Turner, S., Fain, T., & Sehgal, A. (in press). The effects of an experimental intensive juvenile probation program on self-reported delinquency and drug use. *Journal of Experimental Criminology.*

Le, T. N., Maonfared, G., & Stockdale, G. D. (2005). The relationship of school, parent, and peer contextual factors with self-reported delinquency for Chinese, Cambodian, Laotian or Mien, and Vietnamese youth. *Crime and Delinquency, 51,* 192–219.

Lipsey, M. W., & Wilson, D. B. (1998). Effective intervention for serious juvenile offenders: A synthesis of research. In R. Loeber & D. P. Farrington (Eds.), *Serious and violent juvenile offenders: Risk factors and successful interventions* (pp. 313–345). Thousand Oaks: Sage.

Lipsey, M. W., Wilson, D. B., & Cothern, L. (2000, April). *Effective intervention for serious juvenile offenders* (Juvenile Justice Bulletin). Washington, DC: U.S. Department of Justice, Office of Juvenile Justice and Delinquency Prevention.

Loeber, R., & Dishion, T. J. (1983). Early predictors of male delinquency: A review. *Psychological Bulletin, 94,* 68–99.

Loeber, R., & Farrington, D. P. (2000). Young children who commit crime: Epidemiology, developmental origins, risk factors, early interventions, and policy implications. *Development and Psychopathology, 12,* 737–762.

Longshore, D., Chang, E., & Messina, N. (2005). Self-control and social bonds: A combined control perspective on juvenile offending. *Journal of Quantitative Criminology, 21,* 419–437.

Mahoney, J. L., Stattin, H., & Magnusson, D. (2001). Youth recreation centre participation and criminal offending: A 20-year longitudinal study of Swedish boys. *International Journal of Behavioral Development, 25,* 509–520.

McCord, J. (1979). Some child-rearing antecedents of criminal behavior in adult men. *Journal of Personality and Social Psychology, 37,* 1477–1486.

McCord, J. (1991a). Family relationships, juvenile delinquency, and adult criminality. *Criminology, 29,* 397–417.

McCord, J. (1991b). The cycle of crime and socialization practices. *The Journal of Criminal Law and Criminology, 82,* 211–228.

Mounts, N. S., & Steinberg, L. (1995). An ecological analysis of peer influence on adolescent grade point average and drug use. *Developmental Psychology, 31*(6), 915–922.

Mrug, S., Hoza, B., & Bukowski, W. M. (2004). Choosing or being chosen by aggressive-disruptive peers: Do they contribute to children's externalizing and internalizing problems? *Journal of Abnormal Child Psychology, 32,* 53–65.

Mulvey, E. P., Arthur, M. W., & Reppucci, N. D. (1993). The prevention and treatment of juvenile delinquency: A review of the research. *Clinical Psychology Review, 13,* 133–167.

Nofziger, S., & Kurtz, D. (2005). Violent lives: A lifestyle model linking exposure to violence to juvenile violent offending. *Journal of Research in Crime and Delinquency, 42,* 3–26.

O'Donnell, C. R. (2003). Culture, peers, and delinquency: Implications for the community-peer model of delinquency. *Journal of Prevention and Intervention in the Community, 25,* 79–87.

Palmer, T. (1992). *The re-emergence of correctional intervention.* Newbury Park: Sage.

Parental responsibility classes. N.C. Gen. Stat. § 7B-2701 (2005).

Patterson, G. (1986). Performance models for antisocial boys. *American Psychologist, 41,* 432–444.

Patterson, G., DeBaryshe, B. D., & Ramsey, E. (1989). A developmental perspective on antisocial behavior. *American Psychologist, 44,* 329–335.

Patterson, G. R., & Stouthamer-Loeber, M. (1984). The correlation of family management practices and delinquency. *Child Development, 55,* 1299–1307.

Poulin, F., Cillessen, A. H. N., Hubbard, J. A., Coie, J. D., Dodges, K. A., & Schwartz, D. (1997). Children's friends and behavioral similarity in two social contexts. *Social Development, 6,* 224–236.

Richards, M. H., Miller, B. V., O'Donnell, P. C, Wasserman, M. S., & Craig, C. (2004). Parental monitoring mediates the effects of age and sex on problem behaviors among African American urban young adolescents. *Journal of Youth and Adolescence, 33,* 221–233.

Rubin, K. H., Lynch, D., Coplan, R., Rose-Krasnor, L., & Booth, C. L. (1994). "Birds of a feather . . .": Behavioral concordances and preferential personal attraction in children. *Child Development, 65,* 1778–1785.

Scalora, T. (1997). Creating problems rather than solving them: Why criminal parental responsibility laws do not fit within our understanding of justice. *Fordham Law Review, 66,* 1029–1074.

Sherman, L. W., Gottfredson, D., MacKenzie, D., Eck, J., Reuter, P., & Bushway, S. (1997). *Preventing crime: What works, what doesn't, what's promising. A report to the United States Congress.* Prepared for the National Institute of Justice, Washington, DC.

Sigfusdottir, I. D., Farkas, G., & Silver, E. (2004). The role of depressed mood and anger in the relationship between family conflict and delinquency behavior. *Journal of Youth and Adolescence, 33,* 509–522.

Simourd, L., & Andrews, D. (1994). Correlates of delinquency: A look at gender differences. *Forum on Corrections Research, 6,* 26–31.

Slaby, R. G., Braham, J. E., Eron, L. D., & Wilcox, B. L. (1994). Policy recommendations: Prevention and treatment of youth violence. In Eron, L. D., Gentry, J. H., & Schlegel, P. (Eds.), *Reason to hope: A psychological perspective on violence and youth* (pp. 447–456). Washington, DC: American Psychological Association.

Smith, C., & Thornberry, T. P. (1995). The relationship between childhood maltreatment and adolescent involvement in delinquency. *Criminology, 33,* 451–481.

Snyder, J., & Patterson, G. R. (1987). Family interaction and delinquent behavior. In H. C. Quey (Ed.), *Handbook of juvenile delinquency* (pp. 216–243). New York: John Wiley.

Sutherland, E. H. (1947). *Criminology* (4th ed.). Philadelphia: Lippincott.

Thornberry, T. P. (1994). *Violent families and youth violence* (Fact Sheet No. 21). Washington, DC: U.S. Department of Justice, Office of Juvenile Justice and Delinquency Prevention.

Tomaszewski, A. L. (2005). From Columbine to Kazaa: Parental liability in a new world. *University of Illinois Law Review, 2005,* 573–595.

Treatment, service, restraining and protective orders, Ariz. Rev. Stat. § 8-234 (2006).

Urberg, K. A., Değirmencioğlu, S. M., & Pilgrim, C. (1997). Close friend and group influence on adolescent cigarette smoking and alcohol use. *Developmental Psychology, 33*(5), 834–844.

Vitaro, F., Brendgen. M., & Tremblay, R. E. (2000). Influence of deviant friends on delinquency: Searching for moderator variables. *Journal of Abnormal Child Psychology, 28,* 313–325.

Vitaro, F., Brendgen, M., & Wanner, B. (2005). Patterns of affiliation with delinquent friends during late childhood and early adolescence: Correlates and consequences. *Social Development, 14,* 82–108.

Warr, M. (1998). Life-course transitions and desistance from crime. *Criminology, 36,* 183–216.

Wan, M. (2005). Making delinquent friends: Adult supervision and children's affiliations. *Criminology, 43,* 77–105.

Widom, C. S. (1989). The cycle of violence. *Science, 244,* 160–166.

Wilson, J. J., & Howell, J. C. (1995). Comprehensive strategy for serious, violent, and chronic juvenile offenders. In J. C. Howell, B. Krisberg, J. D. Hawkins, & J. J. Wilson (Eds.), *A sourcebook: Serious, violent, and chronic juvenile offenders* (pp. 36–46). Thousand Oaks: Sage.

Zingraff, M. T., Leiter, J., Myers, K. A., & Johnson, M. C. (1993). Child maltreatment and youthful problem behavior. *Criminology, 31,* 173–202.

DISCUSSION QUESTIONS

1. The primary finding of no difference between the groups on recidivism rates was particularly disturbing to the program administrators. What reasons did the authors of the study offer for these findings? How might these problems be addressed in the future?

2. How might having an increased level of supervision actually harm rather than help the success of the program?

3. The authors provide at least three explanations for why this program may not have had the desired effect. What are those explanations and can they be remedied? Explain your response.

4. What are some of the potential problems of using random assignment in this type of environment?

READING

One of the trends experienced in both the adult and juvenile criminal justice system is the growing number of women and girls coming to the attention of the courts and correctional systems. Of particular interest is the growing trend toward administering harsher penalties/sentences for girls for lesser offenses simply because alternatives are not available. In this article, Hubbard and Matthews reviewed the literature to ascertain to what extent female criminality exists and should be reconciled differently from males. More specifically, the authors

SOURCE: Hubbard, Dana Jones, & Matthews, Betsy. (2008). Reconciling the differences between the "gender-responsive" and the "what works" literatures to improve services for girls. *Crime & Delinquency, 54*(2), 225–258. Copyright © 2008 Sage Publications.

recognized competing philosophies on how to address the growing trends of girls committing more serious types of delinquency with gender-specific arguments explaining behavior versus gender-responsive approaches to the phenomenon. The authors further contended that the disparities between the gender responsive literature and the traditional what works approach diverge on six differing categories. First, the authors argued that the theoretical foundation explaining delinquency is offered at the micro-level using pathology to explain behavior rather than at the macro-level that uses societal issues for causes. Second, the authors explored the differences in program goals between the need to reduce recidivism and the need to focus on programming that seeks to empower girls rather than demean them. Third, the researchers contended that the concept of risk is overutilized when it comes to explaining female criminality. The mere definition of risk places girls in more confined settings because instead of their actual risk being high it is their need for treatment. Therefore, placement in these higher risk programs may serve to exacerbate the problem rather than diminish it. Fourth, the efficacy of the actuarial instruments used to assess and classify juveniles was questioned because these instruments are normed and validated on a male population and therefore may not be reflective of female delinquency. Fifth, classification instruments aimed at addressing the individual "dynamic" needs of offenders fail to address societal issues that particularly confront girls. This body of literature and work fails to recognize that girls have a higher rate of mental health issues than boys and are more likely to be victims of abuse (p. 236). Finally, those advocating for a gendered response to the therapeutic environment are less favorable toward the ordinary cognitive behavioral approaches that are oppressive in nature and fail to empower girls. Instead they argue that therapeutic approaches should be based on techniques that are "(a) trauma informed and (b) based on the relational model" (p. 238). Following a review of these differences, the authors provided a "blueprint" for how to work effectively with girls that includes elements of addressing gender specific needs of offenders (p. 227).

Reconciling the Differences Between the "Gender-Responsive" and the "What Works" Literatures to Improve Services for Girls

Dana Jones Hubbard and Betsy Matthews

During the past 20 years, we have witnessed startling patterns in official rates of female delinquency. From 1980 to 2000, the female juvenile arrest rate increased 35% compared to a decline of 11% for males (Child Welfare League of America, 2003), and by 2003, girls accounted for 29% of all juvenile arrests (Bureau of Justice Statistics [BJS], 2006). What is particularly disconcerting is that the crimes that girls are being arrested for are becoming increasingly more violent. There was an almost 60% increase in girls' arrests for assault in the past decade (Chesney-Lind, 2003). Not surprisingly, the number of girls in custody increased 52% during the same period (BJS, 2006). Some researchers question the extent to which these statistics are reflective of true changes in girls' behaviors, suggesting that it is the official response to and perceptions of girls' behavior that has changed (Chesney Lind & Okamoto, 2001; Mahan, 2003;

Steffensmeier, Schwartz, & Zhong, 2005). Nonetheless, concern over these recent statistics is making the development of effective girls' programming a priority with juvenile justice agencies that have traditionally neglected this population of offenders.

There are two main bodies of literature that help guide practitioners in the formation of correctional rehabilitation for girls. First, there is the "gender-specific" or "gender-responsive" literature, based primarily on a feminist perspective, that focuses on explaining the increase in the amount and seriousness of girls' delinquency (see Chesney-Lind & Brown, 1999; Mahan, 2003; Steffensmeier & Allan, 1998; Steffensmeier et al., 2005), identifying its underlying causes (see Belknap, 2001; Chesney-Lind, 1997; Gilligan, 1982; Howell, 2003; Steffensmeier & Allan, 1998), discussing the sexist and paternalistic response of the juvenile justice system (see Belknap, 2001; Chesney-Lind & Sheldon, 2004; Feinman, 1986; Fox, 1984; Freedman, 1974; Odem & Schlossman, 1991), and putting forth principles on how to best prevent female delinquency and support girls involved in the criminal justice system (see Acoca, 1999; Acoca & Dedel, 1998; Bloom & Covington, 2001; Bloom, Owen, & Covington, 2003; Chesney-Lind & Sheldon, 2004; Covington, 2002; Morgan & Patton, 2002; Peters, 1998). This literature emphasizes the unique experience of being a girl in the United States and asserts that girls need qualitatively different types of programs and services to adequately address their delinquent behavior (Belknap, 2001; Belknap & Holsinger, 1998; Bloom, 2000; Chesney-Lind, 1997). Second is the "what works" literature, emanating from the work of Canadian psychologists. This literature has emerged from quantitative reviews of studies on correctional programs and has identified certain principles of effective intervention that are associated with a reduction in recidivism (Andrews, Zinger, Bonta, Gendreau, & Cullen, 1990; Cullen & Gendreau, 2000; Gendreau, 1996; Latessa, Cullen, & Gendreau, 2002). These researchers assert that these core evidence-based principles are applicable to males and females alike.

These categories of literature and their respective scholars may not be as distinguishable from each other as portrayed here, that is, there are some researchers who have a foot in both camps. Furthermore, we do not mean to imply that all "gender-specific" researchers and all "what works" researchers are in full agreement with all that is written within these broad categories of literature. We do assert, however, that there is dissension between these two general groups of scholars that has been observed in several arenas. First, articles by the gender-responsive group demonstrate mistrust in the data and policy implications being promulgated by the what works group (see Bloom, 2000; Kendall, 1994). Second, conflicting viewpoints between the two groups have been highlighted at professional conferences (e.g., the 2002 annual meeting of the American Society of Criminology; also see McMahon, 2000). Third, the authors of this article have witnessed firsthand, through focus groups and training, the uncertainty that the disagreements between these two bodies of literature create for juvenile justice practitioners. As these groups of scholars battle over differences in philosophy, practitioners are left confused, with little clarity as to what effective girls' programming should look like in practice.

The purpose of this article is to make sense of these seemingly irreconcilable differences within the literature. Through a thorough examination of the literature, we will demonstrate that these "camps" are more complementary than competitive, and that taken together, they provide a blueprint on how to effectively work with girls. In this article, we will present the main points of contention between these two bodies of research, make sense of these differences by providing our own synopsis of the evidence, and suggest ways to translate the current state of knowledge into practice. To do this however, it is important to begin with a discussion of the trends in female delinquency and to provide some explanations as to why we have seen an increase in crime for girls.

▧ Girls, Crime, and Juvenile Justice

Taken at face value, increases in the rates and severity of female delinquency have led to media portrayals of girls as "mean," as "behaving badly" or as "going wild." This spotlight on girls' delinquency has brought with it a much needed focus on girls' programming. It has also contributed to more formal controls being placed on girls, a trend of key concern to many feminist scholars who assert that the achievement of any real improvements in girls' programming rests on understanding the story behind the official statistics and putting them in their proper context (Chesney-Lind, 2003; Steffensmeier et al., 2005).

On closer examination of national delinquency trends, the Office of Juvenile Justice and Delinquency Prevention's Girls' Study Group concluded that the recent trends are more indicative of changes in juvenile justice processes than girls' behavior (Zahn, 2005). This conclusion was based on two key findings from comprehensive data analyses conducted by Steffensmeier et al. (2005). First, a comparison of data sources on trends in girls' delinquency reveals different patterns. Official data reported in the Uniform Crime Reports (UCR) show that girls accounted for 16% of violent juvenile arrests in 1988 and 25% of violent juvenile arrests in 2003. However, data reported in the National Crime Victimization Survey and the Monitoring the Future study, which include self-reported data from victims and youth, respectively, revealed relative stability in the percentage of violent juvenile arrests attributable to girls during that same time period. Second, when assaults were omitted from the violent crime index, the female delinquency trends were fairly stable, and girls accounted for only 10% of violent juvenile crime. These findings suggest that the increases in girls' violent delinquency reported in the UCR stem more from changes in the laws and the actions of officials rather than from changes in the behavior of girls. Indeed, what were once considered normal fights between family members are now classified as assault that attract formal police intervention and more frequently result in arrest (Chesney-Lind, 2003).

Even if these reported increases accurately reflected changes in behavior, it is important to remember that girls still account for a very small proportion of delinquency. According to the UCR, girls constitute only 1 in 4 of all juvenile arrests and less than 1 in 5 of juvenile arrests for violent crimes (BJS, 2006). For most categories of offenses, girls account for 15% or less of juvenile arrests (Steffensmeier & Allan, 1998). These percentages are largest for prostitution and minor property crimes and smallest for more serious crimes. Moreover, when girls are involved in violent crime, it is usually in the form of a simple assault against someone they know rather than unprovoked violence against a stranger (BJS, 2006).

Based on the reported statistics and the nature of girls' violence, it has been argued that girls present a very low risk to public safety and, as such, are not in need of the types of controls applied to boys (Belknap, 2001; Belknap, Holsinger, & Dunn, 1997). Comparisons of juvenile court dispositions for boys and girls, however, suggest that in recent years, girls have experienced harsher penalties for less serious crimes (Beger & Hoffman, 1998; MacDonald & Chesney-Lind, 2001). Beger and Hoffman (1998) attribute this differential treatment to a lack of alternatives for girls within a juvenile justice system that has adopted the "get tough" policies associated with adult courts.

Other inequities in the treatment of girls concern the greater likelihood of their being arrested and detained for running away (Potter, 1999). This more stringent response to running away, and other status offenses committed by girls, is believed to stem from the efforts of a patriarchal court to control girls' sexuality (MacDonald & Chesney-Lind, 2001; Mahan, 2003). Legislation providing for the deinstitutionalization of status offenders has curtailed the incarceration of girls for the status offense; but once in the system, girls find it hard to get out (Belknap, 2001; Chesney-Lind, 1997). In their attempt to escape adverse circumstances at home, they run away again, violate their probation, and become eligible for institutionalization. Moreover, several studies have demonstrated that responses to girls' probation violations are more stringent than those experienced by boys (Beger & Hoffman, 1998; MacDonald & Chesney-Lind, 2001).

This focus on gender bias in the juvenile justice system highlights one of the key differences between the gender-responsive and what works scholars. The former insists that we cannot begin to address the needs of girls in the juvenile justice system until we understand the sociological and systemic forces that carry them to its doorstep. The latter emphasizes the individual differences that influence girls' responses to these sociological forces and determines whether they will choose an antisocial or prosocial pathway. The next section of this article explores additional differences in how each group views girls' delinquency and methods of intervention.

⊠ The "Gender-Responsive" and "What Works" Literature: Substantive Differences

Both groups of researchers have promulgated a set of principles to guide program development. A quick review of these two sets of principles highlights the major difference between the two agendas. The gender-responsive agenda starts with the belief that boys and girls are different and the unique needs of girls should be central to the principles for developing gender-responsive programs. The what works agenda starts with an attempt to identify a common core of program characteristics that contribute to positive behavioral change for all offenders. The recognition that girls and other subgroups require a different approach is encompassed by the "responsivity principle." This principle is based on the idea that certain "responsivity" factors (e.g., cultural background, gender, personality, learning styles) can lessen or enhance offenders' amenability to particular types of intervention (Bonta, 1995; Kennedy, 2000). As such, the responsivity principle directs agencies to match offenders to interventions and program staff that can best accommodate these factors.

One's strength is the other's weakness. The gender-responsive literature provides a stronger advocacy for girls, but because of the recency of the perspective and the high cost associated with drawing the large samples of girls that are needed for statistical analysis (Howell, 2003), longitudinal empirical support for many of the principles is limited to qualitative research based on small samples of girls. The what works literature suffers from the opposite problem: A growing body of scientific literature attests to the validity of the principles of effective correctional intervention (see Andrews, Zinger, et al., 1990; Gendreau & Ross, 1987; Lipsey & Wilson, 1998; Sherman et al., 1997), but most of the research has not involved girls (Krisberg, 2005). These researchers are charged with the criticism that neither can their male-focused, quantitative methods of inquiry possibly uncover the complex nature of female offending nor can they demonstrate their utility within girls' programming (Belknap, 2001; Bloom & Covington, 2001; Chesney-Lind, 2000).

In addition to these overriding disparities between the two approaches for developing and researching girls' programs, there are several other differences worth noting.

Theoretical Foundation

As implied earlier, one of the differences between the what works and gender-responsive literature rests on the theoretical foundation or root of girls' problems. The gender-responsive literature supports a macro-level explanation that attributes girls' delinquency to societal issues such as sexism, racism, and classism that triply marginalize girls and create an environment where they are apt to get involved in destructive behaviors (Belknap, 2001; Covington & Bloom, 1999). These authors criticize traditional theories of delinquency for their focus on individual-level factors that blame and pathologize girls instead of recognizing the roles that society and the criminal justice system play in girls' crime.

In contrast, the what works literature is rooted in traditional micro-level theories of crime (Andrews & Bonta, 1999). The authors of this literature draw heavily on social learning, social bond, and general strain theories from sociology and on cognitive-behavioral theories from psychology. Their chosen theoretical framework focuses on individual-level factors such as antisocial attitudes and antisocial peers as the root of criminal behavior.

Program Goals

The second difference lies in goal definition. The what works literature emphasizes the reduction of recidivism as the ultimate goal of correctional and juvenile justice interventions; other intermediate goals (e.g., improved education, reduced drug and alcohol abuse, increased self-control) are only important as they relate to recidivism (Latessa et al., 2002). In contrast, the gender-responsive group argues that the focus should be more encompassing and that programs should aim to empower girls and improve their overall quality of life (Peters, 1998). Although a reduction in recidivism or delinquency is important to advocates of gender-responsive programming, it is their view that it should not take primacy over other important goals.

Consideration of Risk

The concept of "risk" dominates the delinquency literature. According to the what works literature, a youth's level of risk indicates his or her likelihood of recidivism.

Once determined through assessment, this information on a youth's level of risk should be used to determine the intensity and duration of services that the youth needs, This "risk principle" is based on research that demonstrates that high-risk offenders require intensive levels of services to reduce recidivism and that low-risk offenders can be made "worse" by inappropriately assigning them to intensive services/sanctions (Andrews, Bonta, & Hoge, 1990; Lowenkamp & Latessa, 2004; Van Voorhis, 2004).

Advocates of the gender-responsive literature take issue with how the concept of risk is applied to girls on two accounts. First, they argue that although girls may be high "need" they are not high risk; the lower rate of delinquency among girls and the type of offenses committed by girls suggest that they are not a danger to society (Bloom, 2000; Covington & Bloom, 2003; Hannah-Moffat & Shaw, 2003). Furthermore, they argue that the types of behaviors in which girls commonly engage (runaway, drug abuse, prostitution or promiscuity) present more danger to themselves than to others. Second, they claim that as applied, the risk principle can hurt girls inappropriately categorized as high risk by locking them up and exacerbating some of the very problems that got them into trouble in the first place (e.g., depression, sexual abuse, disruptions in relationships) (see Holtfreter & Morash, 2003). What girls need, these advocates argue, are services in the community.

Assessment and Classification

Major differences exist in the two bodies of literature on the most appropriate techniques for the assessment and classification of girls in the juvenile justice system. Increasingly, juvenile justice agencies are moving from more traditional social histories to the use of more actuarial, or objective, assessment instruments to identify youth's risks and needs and guide program placement (Howell, 2003). Although this shift in practice has been driven largely by resource constraints, legal challenges, and a push for more equitable treatment (Jones, 1996), it is also a response to the principles of effective intervention that view good assessment and classification as the engine that drives program development (Andrews, Bonta, et al., 1990; VanVoorhis, 2004). This view stems from research that has shown that actuarial assessment instruments are

superior to clinical approaches for predicting the likelihood of recidivism (Gottfredson, 1987; Jones, 1996).

Despite the evidence regarding the superiority of actuarial approaches to risk assessment, the gender-responsive group argues that the current instruments were developed using White male samples and are therefore "gendered and racialized" and suffer from several specific limitations (Hannah-Moffat, 1999). First, these assessments often do not reflect factors that are gender specific and believed to be more commonly associated with females such as depression, low self-esteem, and sexual victimization. Second, these assessments put the sole responsibility of crime on the individual by ignoring macro-level sociological factors such as poverty, sexism, racism, and heterosexism that are believed to promote girls' antisocial behaviors (Covington & Bloom, 2003). Third, the assessment protocols proposed by the what works group are perceived as deficiency based and as depicting girls as pathological beings that must be fixed (Hannah-Moffat & Shaw, 2003). The gender-responsive group asserts that it is more important to identify strengths that can be used to empower girls toward adaptive ways of coping with a sexist society (Hannah-Moffat & Shaw, 2003). Finally, the gender-responsive group asserts that quantitative methods of predicting risk cannot possibly capture the nuances of girls' lives that lead to their problematic behavior (Bloom, 2000). In contrast to the standardized, actuarial instruments supported by the what works group, the gender-responsive group prefers qualitative, interview-based assessments that tap into the female experience.

"Criminogenic" Needs

Another salient difference between the two bodies of literature revolves on the issue of service or treatment needs. The what works literature distinguishes between general needs and "criminogenic" needs (Andrews, Bonta, et al., 1990; Van Voorhis, 2004). General needs reflect areas that, although important for programs to consider and address, have not emerged in research as strong correlates of delinquency. These needs can range from the basics of food and shelter to problems with anxiety or depression. Criminogenic needs are dynamic factors that are proven correlates of delinquency (i.e., they are a subset of risk factors). They exist within five broad domains including individual, family, school, peers, and community domains (Howell, 2003). Given this distinction, the "needs principle," as set forth in the principles of effective intervention, suggests that targeting these criminogenic needs must be a priority for programs interested in reducing the risk of recidivism.

The gender-responsive group takes issue with the "needs principle" on two related accounts. First, they take issue with the very notion of "criminogenic," suggesting that it places the problem of crime within the individual and ignores the role of societal factors (Covington & Bloom, 1999). Second, they assert that limiting the targets of intervention to a select number of criminogenic needs ignores the problems that underlie girls' delinquent behavior and the realities of the social context in which they live (Covington & Bloom, 1999; McMahon, 2000).

Another point of contention in the area of treatment needs centers on the similarities and differences among the criminogenic needs (i.e., dynamic risk factors) of boys and girls. The what works researchers rest their laurels on studies showing that the major risk factors are similar for boys and girls. Simourd and Andrews (1994) conducted a meta-analysis, which found that the most important risk factors for crime were antisocial attitudes and associates, personality/temperament, problems with educational/vocational achievement, and poor parent/child relations and that they were equally correlated with delinquency for boys and girls. A more recent study by Farrington and Painter (2004) arrived at similar conclusions. This longitudinal study looked at brothers and sisters within 397 families and found that the important risk factors for each gender were similar in that convicted parents, poor parental supervision, parental conflict, and harsh or erratic discipline all predicted early and frequent offending.

The gender-responsive researchers remind us that aside from these few studies, the bulk of studies on risk factors have been conducted on boys. Also, they assert that despite a lack of empirical evidence identifying low self-esteem, sexual abuse, and mental health problems as predictors of delinquency, there is enough evidence to suggest that these needs are more prevalent among girls than boys involved in the juvenile justice system and among delinquent than nondelinquent

girls. Studies of adjudicated delinquents and detainees have revealed that girls are more likely than boys to have mental health problems and a history of physical and sexual abuse (McCabe, Lansing, Garland, & Hough, 2002; Teplin, 2001). Another study found that girls in the juvenile justice system were 3 times more likely than girls in the general population to have clinical symptoms of depression or anxiety (Kataoka et al., 2001). Moreover, Obeidallah and Earls (1999) reported that compared to nondepressed girls, depressed girls were more likely to commit violent and property crimes, and Khoury (1998) found that compared with girls who had higher self-esteem, early adolescent girls with low self-esteem were less likely to delay the use of substances. Covington and Bloom (1999) assert that combined, these and other similar studies provide enough evidence to suggest that these factors underlie girls' antisocial behaviors in some fashion.

Therapeutic Approach

Given the aforementioned differences, it should come as no surprise that the two groups of researchers disagree on the most appropriate therapeutic approach for girls. The what works group has amassed a large body of literature suggesting that cognitive-behavioral models of treatment are most effective in addressing antisocial behaviors among offender populations (Andrews, Zinger, et al., 1990; Cullen & Gendreau, 2000; Gendreau, 1996; Lipsey & Wilson, 1998; McGuire, 2000; Wilson, Allen Bouilard, & Mackenzie, 2005). These models, it is argued, are effective because they target important cognitive characteristics that are prevalent among offender populations and strongly associated with criminality, that is, they target important criminogenic needs.

There are two types of cognitive-behavioral approaches. The first type, cognitive restructuring, is rooted in the idea that our beliefs, values, and attitudes prompt and maintain our behaviors (Lester & Van Voorhis, 2004). If youth believe that stealing is okay, and does no harm to victims who can cover their losses with insurance, they are likely to steal. Also, how youth interpret events or circumstances within their environments determines how they will respond to them (Ellis, 1991). For example, if a girl perceives a poor grade on a test as unfair, she may give up on her studying rather than use the feedback to improve her grade on the next test. The second type, cognitive skills training, recognizes poor critical thinking and problem-solving skills as sources of maladaptive behavior. Both approaches include a behavioral component in recognition of the fact that beliefs, values, attitudes, and cognitive skills are learned by observing the actions of significant others. Once observed, the behavior is imitated, and whether the behavior is repeated is dependent on whether the actor is rewarded or punished.

Cognitive-behavioral therapies are directive approaches that are more educational than therapeutic, that is, they are structured, goal-oriented approaches that focus on values enhancement and skill development through the use of modeling and reinforcement techniques. In practice, these approaches look and sound very different from the psychoanalytical approach that emphasizes expression of emotion and the resolution of past trauma.

The application of cognitive-behavioral approaches to female offenders is one of the most contentious areas in programming for female offenders. The what works group has amassed a significant number of studies attesting to the efficacy of cognitive-behavioral programming in treating a variety of offender populations and in a broad spectrum of problem areas (see Lipsey & Wilson, 1998; McGuire, 2000; Wilson et al., 2005). According to Cameron and Telfer (2004), this research has contributed to an almost unilateral adoption of cognitive-behavioral approaches for offenders within the United Kingdom, Canada, Australia, and the United States. They caution that this widespread application may be premature given a lack of available research that specifically examines the efficacy of cognitive-behavioral treatment with specific offender groups, including female offenders.

The gender-responsive group asserts that the antisocial attitudes targeted in much of the cognitive restructuring programs are more characteristic of male offenders and argue that the cognitive-behavioral models designed to challenge these antisocial attitudes have limited applicability to female offenders (Covington & Bloom, 1999). Kendall and Pollack (2003) assert that cognitive-behavioral approaches ignore the structural

aspects of crime and pathologize females' "rational responses to unjust circumstances" (p. 75). Additionally, they argue that cognitive-behavioral approaches are oppressive in that they try to teach women what and how to think. In contrast to the deficit-based approach used in many cognitive-behavioral programs and other male-oriented treatment, they assert that the best approach for girls is a strengths-based approach that is designed to empower females and help them gain control over their lives (Covington, 2002; McClellan, Farabee, & Crouch, 1997; Wald, Harvey, & Hibbard, 1995). Finally, they argue that the structured, present-oriented, psychoeducational model of group therapy applied to contemporary cognitive-behavioral models of treatment for offenders does not accommodate girls' needs for establishing connections with others. Instead, they propose a therapeutic model that allows girls to explore common problems in their lives and develop a sense of self-worth through intimate communication with others (Covington, 2002; Wald et al., 1995).

The gender-responsive group suggests that more important than the therapeutic approach (e.g., cognitive-behavioral, psychoanalytic) or the targets of intervention (e.g., substance abuse, antisocial attitudes) is the manner in which it is delivered. They support therapeutic approaches that are (a) trauma informed and (b) based on the relational model. Being trauma informed requires service providers to be aware of consumers' history of past abuse, to understand the role that abuse plays in victims' lives, and to use this understanding to create services that facilitate their participation in treatment (Harris & Fallot, 2001, p. 4). Trauma-informed services conduct universal screening on intake to identify consumers with a history of abuse, use a strengths-based approach to help consumers recognize the skills that have helped them survive their abuse, and help them transfer these skills to achieve important treatment goals (e.g., improved decision making, reduced substance abuse).

The relational model is based on the recognition that girls' healthy development is dependent on affiliation with others through positive interpersonal relationships (Gilligan, 1982; Miller, 1986). According to Covington (2000), many of the problems girls experience can "be traced to disconnections or violations within relationships" (p. 197), and thus, positive change for girls is dependent on developing mutually trusting and empathetic relationships that prevent them from undergoing the same experiences again. Both the trauma theory and the relational model emphasize the importance of a collaborative approach that gives girls a voice in all phases of service delivery.

As can be seen, there are significant differences between the what works and gender-responsive groups in their perspectives on the causes of girls' delinquency and on the appropriate interventions for addressing the needs of girls in the juvenile justice system. Although valuable knowledge has been generated by both academic camps, we believe that in their attempt to highlight their particular positions each group discounts, or remains silent, on the important contributions of the other, and as such, they amplify the areas of disagreement, downplay the areas of agreement, and leave practitioners confused. In the paragraphs that follow, we expand our discussion of the literature and provide our own synopsis of the evidence to demonstrate that the two perspectives are more complementary than competitive.

Irreconcilable Differences?

The bulk of this discussion centers on a key question that we believe is the crux of the differences between the two groups: How different are the risks/needs of boys and girls in the juvenile justice system? Then, given the evidence, we will address two additional questions about girls' programming that are particularly contentious: Are current trends in risk assessment and classification appropriate for girls? and What is the most appropriate therapeutic approach for girls?

How Different Are the Risks/ Needs of Boys and Girls in the Juvenile Justice System?

Just the small glimpse into the literature on the risk factors or criminogenic needs of boys and girls makes it easy to see why juvenile justice professionals are left scratching their head and feeling that the more they learn the

more elusive the truth is about similarities and differences between boys and girls. We assert that uncovering the truth lies in (a) conducting more longitudinal research on girls; (b) clarifying what exactly the studies cited by both camps tell us, or do not tell us, about the relationship between these factors and girls' delinquency; and (c) a closer examination of the specific factors embedded within these broad categories of risk factors. Given the significance of this issue to the ongoing debate about the best approach for system-involved girls, the last two points are addressed below in some depth.

What is and is not known about the risks/needs of girls. There are three interrelated methodological issues that limit our knowledge about the similarities and differences between the factors associated with boys' and girls' delinquency. First, the basis of the what works groups' assertion that the major risk factors, or predictors, of delinquency are similar for boys and girls are studies done to develop or validate risk assessment instruments. Because these studies are usually retrospective, they are limited to what information or measures are available. What is typically available has been driven by programming for and research on boys. This, and the fact that the regression models used in these studies explain very little of the variation in recidivism for boys or girls (see Gottfredson & Snyder, 2005), begs the question What other factors underlie delinquent behavior? Could it be that the variables more predictive of girls' delinquency (and boys' for that matter) have not yet been examined?

In their 2002 meta-analysis of studies on the factors associated with female delinquency, Hubbard and Pratt were particularly interested in examining factors thought to be associated with female delinquency (e.g., sexual abuse, low self-esteem) but not readily available in prediction studies. Similar to findings generated by the what works group, they found that factors such as antisocial peers and antisocial personality were the strongest predictors of delinquency. However, the findings also suggested that school and family relationships and a history of physical and/or sexual assault, although less powerful predictors, were still robust predictors of female offending. The results of this study, while adding to the growing body of findings regarding the similarity of major risk factors among boys and girls, support the need for the continued study of these less examined factors.

Second, studies that have been conducted to examine the risks/needs of boys and girls are commonly cross-sectional studies; thus, the only conclusion that can be drawn is that there are statistically significant correlations, or associations between the major risk factors and delinquency. The exact nature of these relationships is unknown. How can we explain the findings regarding the higher prevalence rates of sexual abuse, low self-esteem, depression, and posttraumatic stress disorder among delinquent girls and yet, simultaneously, explain their weak correlations with delinquency? Are there unmeasured or mediating factors that mask the important role that these factors play in girls' delinquency?

A study by Horwitz, Spatz Widom, McLaughlin, and Raskin White (2001) speaks of this conundrum. Numerous studies have demonstrated that childhood sexual abuse contributes to poor mental health outcomes and crime in adulthood and that negative effects are even stronger for women (Bailey & McCloskey, 2005; Herrera & McCloskey, 2003; McClellan et al., 1997). In an effort to disentangle the relationship between sexual abuse and later mental health outcomes, Horwitz et al. (2001) conducted a prospective, longitudinal study that compared the mental health outcomes of participants with documented cases of childhood abuse and neglect and a matched control group of participants who did not have documented cases of abuse and neglect. They also examined the differential impact of victimization on males ($n = 586$) and females ($n = 562$). The results indicated that adult men and women who experienced early victimization had more symptoms of dysthymia and antisocial personality disorder than matched controls; adult women who experienced early victimization also had more symptoms of alcohol abuse than matched controls. The results also show, however, that when a measure of lifetime stressors (e.g., unemployment, unstable employment, financial problems, homelessness, divorce, family involvement in drug or alcohol abuse or arrest) and demographic variables (parents on welfare, age, race) were entered into the regression models, whether

participants were a member of the abused or neglected group or the control group explained less than 2% of the variance in mental health outcomes. Based on these findings, the authors conclude that the impact of childhood victimization "is likely to stem from a matrix of disadvantage that abused and neglected children suffer from, only one part of which consists of the abuse and neglect itself" (p. 195) and that "childhood victimization has stronger indirect than direct effects on adult mental health" (p. 197). Horwitz et al. suggest that uncovering the mediating and protective factors that help some victims of child abuse and neglect avoid problem outcomes is an important area for future research.

Studies on the role of depression in girls' problem behaviors also speak of this issue. Because depression is difficult to distinguish from typical adolescent behaviors (e.g., intensity of emotions, increased need for sleep, irritability), it is often left undiagnosed and untreated, opening the door for later problem behaviors. For example, there is some evidence to suggest that girls' entry into substance abuse often is preceded by depression (King, William, & McGue, 2004). Also, depression has been found to contribute to problems with academic functioning and interpersonal relationships (Obeidallah & Earls, 1999). Thus, it appears that depression leads to other negative outcomes known to increase a youth's risk of delinquency.

In many ways, the findings reported in these studies are consistent with the arguments of the what works group: Despite the fact that abuse and mental health disorders co-occur more often with girls' delinquency than with boys, they have not been found to be significant predictors of delinquency; thus, we should focus our interventions on changing the more proximal, and perhaps mediating, factors such as cognitive skills and learning environments.

Third, how generalizable are the results of these studies? Many of the studies conducted to examine the risks/needs of youth are conducted on system-involved youth, and thus, the findings may not be representative of differences among boys and girls in the general population. For example, a recent study of cognitive distortions among delinquent and nondelinquent youth revealed that although self-serving and self-debasing distortions were more prevalent among delinquent youth, there were no differences in the types of cognitive distortions invoked across genders (Barriga, Landau, Stinson, Liau, & Gibbs, 2000). However, other studies of youth in the general population have demonstrated important differences in the distortions and coping mechanisms enacted by boys and girls (Achenbach, Howell, Quay, & Connors, 1991). It may be that there are more gender differences in predelinquent risks/needs and that these differences diminish as youth move further along the continuum to chronic and serious delinquency.

Specifying factors within broad risk/need domains that contribute to boys' and girls' delinquency. A closer examination of research on specific factors within the broad categories of risk factors touted by the what works group reveals truths within both research camps. For example, in support of the what works group, a comprehensive review of the extant literature led Bennett, Farrington, and Huesmann (2005) to conclude that although more prevalent among boys, problematic social cognitive processes resulted in similar maladaptive outcomes (i.e., crime, violence) for boys and girls. In support of the gender-responsive group, there is a sufficient amount of evidence to suggest that there are important gender differences in these problematic social cognitive processes and that these differences are believed to contribute to the gender differences in the rates of antisocial behavior. For example, girls have been found to have lower rates of hyperactivity and poor impulse control (Moffitt, Caspi, Rutter, & Silva, 2002), stronger moral evaluations of behavior that enhance their ability to counteract negative peer influences (Mears, Ploeger, & Warr, 1998), greater empathy and more guilt proneness (Mears et al., 1998), and a greater tendency to engage in self-debasing distortions (e.g., self-blame, negative thoughts about self) that lead to internalizing behaviors and self-harm, whereas boys are more likely to engage in self-serving distortions (e.g., externalization of blame, rationalizations) and externalizing behaviors that harm others (Achenbach et al., 1991). Also, girls have a stronger sociotropic cognitive style than boys, that is, they have a stronger desire for affiliation and

acceptance. This desire and eagerness to please contributes to negative emotional (e.g., stress) and behavioral outcomes (e.g., risky sexual behavior) (Donabella Sauro & Teal Pedlow, 2005). Although these differences do not diminish the value of cognitive-behavioral treatment with girls as supported by the what works group, they do reiterate the importance of differentiated treatment for boys and girls, a point that is strongly advocated by the gender-responsive group.

When other domains of risk factors are examined, similar distinctions emerge. Although not incongruent with the findings of the what work group, most of these distinctions highlight points that are emphasized in the gender-responsive literature: the importance of relationships in girls' lives and the sociotropic cognitive style (i.e., the desire to be accepted) that is so prevalent among girls. For example, recent studies have revealed that many of the family factors long associated with delinquency have a stronger influence on the emotional and behavioral outcomes of girls: Kaker, Friedemann, and Peck (2002) found stronger correlations between a lack of emotional bonding with parents and substance abuse for girls, and Farrington and Painter's (2004) longitudinal analyses of brothers and sisters revealed that low praise by the parents, harsh or erratic discipline, poor parental supervision, parental conflict, low parental interest in education, and low paternal interest in the children were stronger predictors of sisters' later delinquency.

Although important in the etiology of offending for both boys and girls, schools provide another context in which relational factors appear to create special challenges for girls. Studies by the American Association of University Women (AAUW, 1992, 1998) uncovered gender bias within schools in the form of girls receiving less attention in the classroom, lower scores in math and science, and curricula that ignore or stereotype women. Other studies have found that girls experience high rates of sexual harassment within the school setting (Fineran, 2002) and that girls' emotional safety is often threatened when participating or speaking in class (Schoenberg, Riggins, & Salmond, 2003). These negative experiences contribute to reduced self-esteem, increases in truancy, reductions in school achievement, and lower career aspirations (AAUW, 1992, 1998)—all factors that have been found to increase the likelihood of delinquency.

Consistent with the claims of the what works group, the peer group has a powerful influence on the behaviors of adolescent girls. But a closer examination of this relationship reveals that different dynamics may be at work beyond the presence of antisocial peers. In particular, there are two factors about girls' peer groups that seem to contribute to girls' problem behaviors. First, research has revealed that girls who report having a mixed-sex friendship group are significantly more likely to engage in delinquency than girls with a same-sex friendship group (Giordano, 1978). The reasons for this are unclear. Is it because, as the what works group would suggest, boys are more likely to be antisocial influences for girls? Is it because of the way boys make girls feel about themselves (e.g., anxious, uncertain, eager to please). Or, is it because girls with more male friends are missing out on the greater degree of social controls that are provided by female friendships (McCarthy, Femlee, & Hagan, 2004)? Second, according to Brown (2003), girls undermine the development of the supportive friendships they so desperately need by engaging in "girlfighting," or the emotional and discreet bullying of other girls (e.g., gossip, manipulation, teasing, exclusion). Brown describes this as "horizontal aggression" that serves as a protective factor, as a safe avenue for girls to express their fears and gain power within a sexist culture. But this type of aggression among girls' friendship groups has been shown to interfere with the development of self-esteem and the ability to experience intimate relationships (Brown, 2003; Prinstein, Boergers, & Vernberg, 2001). It undermines the development of the cohesive friendship networks that are needed for girls' healthy development (Bearman & Moody, 2004; Hazier & Mellin, 2004). Also, because this girlfighting often occurs in the school setting, it can lead to increased truancy and interfere with student engagement in learning (Kochenderfer & Ladd, 1996; Olweus, 1978), both of which are known risk factors for delinquency.

In sum, our knowledge about the development of girls' antisocial behaviors is constrained by a lack of longitudinal research and by methodological issues associated with existing studies. There is enough evidence, however, to support both sides of the argument: Research reveals both similarities and differences in the factors that contribute to boys' and girls' delinquency. It may be that factors such as depression, that are more prevalent among delinquent girls, prompt or initiate delinquent behavior but that self-serving and other antisocial attitudes, that are more similar to boys, maintain and escalate the behavior. If this is the case, then the targets of intervention may need to change depending on whether services are being offered as primary, secondary, or tertiary prevention. The key point of the what works group, with which we agree, is that programs for delinquent girls that focus on the self-esteem and mental health problems at the exclusion of the major, more proximal, risk factors may empower girls and improve their overall quality of life but they are not likely to reduce recidivism. We also believe, however, that conclusions regarding the similarity of major risk factors for boys and girls are overly simplistic and impede the development of differentiated treatment that adequately addresses the needs of girls. What then, does this mean for girls' programming? In the following sections, we will discuss what we believe are the most appropriate methods of assessment and intervention for girls based on our synopsis of the evidence.

Are Current Trends in Risk Assessment and Classification Appropriate for Girls?

Both groups agree that overclassifying and overtreating female offenders causes harm. There is sufficient evidence, both anecdotal and empirical, to support this concern (see Holtfreter & Morash, 2003; Lowenkamp & Latessa, 2004). Both groups also support the use of community-based services over incarceration. Despite this, and the fact that girls on average present a lower risk than boys, there are some high-risk girls who are engaging in serious and chronic delinquency and may need to be separated from society at large. The real issue lies in whether the current methods of risk assessment appropriately categorize girls.

It is difficult to refute the gender-responsive group's arguments against the use of actuarial risk assessment instruments with girls. The development of gender-specific actuarial assessment instruments is severely constrained by small samples of girls within the juvenile justice system. This statistical fact alone may account for the absence of the sociological and individual risk factors believed to promote girls' delinquency. There is growing evidence, however, to suggest that these risk instruments predict the subsequent delinquency of males and females equally well (Flores, Travis, & Latessa, 2004; Ilacqua, Coulson, Lombardo, & Nutbrown, 1999; Schwalbe, Fraser, Day, & Arnold, 2004). A study of one of the more popular risk/need instruments in use today, the Youthful Level of Services/Case Management Inventory, found a statistically significant correlation between the youth's risk score and a variety of correctional outcomes (i.e., technical violations, rearrest, rearrest seriousness, and reincarceration) for both boys ($n = 1,321$) and girls ($n = 358$) (Flores et al., 2004).

It is our contention that current actuarial instruments reflect the state of knowledge about factors that increase the likelihood of recidivism for boys and girls and that, as such, they are congruent with an overriding goal of the juvenile justice system—to reduce the recidivism of youth under its care. We also believe that these objective instruments serve to minimize, rather than amplify, the gender bias that is of concern to the gender-responsive group and the overclassification that is of concern to both groups. We agree that there is a disconnect between the popular "strengths-based approach" and the risk and need factors that appear in actuarial risk assessment instruments. At this juncture, however, there is considerable debate as to whether strengths, or protective factors, are just the flip side of the risk factors already measured by these instruments, or whether they represent a completely different set of factors (Farrington, 2000; Rutter, 1985). Furthermore, we assert that the common factors within these instruments (i.e., individual, family, and school-based factors) reflect the domains in which juvenile justice programs and practices can make a difference. Although the broader sociological concerns of feminist scholars (e.g., sexism, intergenerational poverty) are important to acknowledge, changes in these factors are beyond the scope of what professionals in the juvenile justice system can realistically accomplish, that is, they are far more likely to be successful in changing the way girls interpret and respond to their environment than they are to change the environment itself. Whether this approach is perceived as "fixing" girls or "empowering" girls is left to the reader's interpretation.

Based on the sources of contention about assessment practices for girls, what is known about the correlates of crime, and what is known about girls' unique needs, we recommend that first, and foremost, agencies use a validated, actuarial risk assessment instrument to measure girls' risk of recidivism. These instruments should be normed on female offenders and appropriate cutoff levels should be established. In addition, it is recommended that agencies (a) conduct other standardized, objective measures of problem areas known to be prevalent among girls (e.g., standardized mental health assessments), (b) measure girls' strengths and assets, and (c) conduct an in-depth interview with each girl on intake.

We believe that the proposed protocol reflects the best approach for discovering what girls need to reduce their likelihood of recidivism and improve their overall quality of life. It gives the empirical knowledge about actuarial assessment and risk factors its due credit while elevating the importance of assessing factors that appear to be more prevalent and influential in the lives of girls. The consistent use of other standardized instruments will allow us to conduct further research that enhances our understanding of how these factors affect girls' delinquency.

What Is the Most Appropriate Therapeutic Approach for Girls?

At this juncture, this question cannot be answered with any degree of certainty because of a lack of outcome studies on girls' programming within the juvenile justice system. We assert that an integrated approach or one that recognizes the value of both perspectives is needed to work effectively with girls. Based on the evidence, it appears that the best approach would reflect both the relational model advocated by the gender-responsive group and the cognitive-behavioral model supported by the what works group.

In support of the relational model, an essential element of girls' programming is the promotion of healthy connections for girls with persons both internal and external to the program. Within the program, the focus should be on developing a therapeutic or helping alliance. The therapeutic alliance has been conceptualized as the collaborative relationship that develops within a helping relationship and provides the foundation for positive psychological change (Horvath & Luborsky, 1993). According to Bordin (1980), the working alliance is what "makes it possible for the patient to accept and follow treatment faithfully" (p. 2). In the counseling profession, the therapeutic alliance has long been viewed as an intermediate criterion of counseling effectiveness, that is, stronger alliances contribute to better outcomes (Frieswyk, Allen, Colson, & Coyne, 1986; Horvath & Symonds, 1991; Stiles, Agnew-Davies, Hardy, Barkham, & Shapiro, 1998). Although important when working with boys, we assert that in concert with the relational model, a strong helping alliance is particularly relevant when working with girls. The three primary characteristics of a high-quality therapeutic alliance include (a) agreement between the change agent and the client on the goals of intervention, (b) collaboration on the development and completion of tasks devised to achieve the goals, and (c) a trusting and respectful relationship that provides a safe context for self-examination and personal growth (Florsheim, Shotorbani, & Guest-Warnick, 2000). In essence, a strong working alliance gives girls a voice in their treatment, a position strongly supported by the gender-responsive group.

Interventions also should be aimed at promoting healthy connections with persons and organizations external to the program. Programs for girls should build on the risk and protection framework and emphasize the importance of building positive connections in the domains of family, peers, school, and community. The goal is to surround girls with social support that insulates them from adverse circumstances that may lead to risky or antisocial behavior. Studies show that social support protects youth from adverse circumstances by providing them with a sense of felt security (Bretherton, 1985) and counteracting

psychological and physical consequences of stress (Unger & Wandersman, 1985; van der Kolk, 1994).

Potential avenues for promoting these connections include family interventions that aim to decrease conflict, improve communication, and increase the monitoring and supervision of girls. School-based interventions for girls should focus primarily on helping girls feel safe by connecting them with caring adults within the school setting and by promoting academic self-efficacy. Promising peer interventions that promote healthy relationships among girls include social competency training and cognitive interventions that target negative beliefs about the self or others. Three other promising strategies for connecting girls with prosocial activities and others within the community include recreational programming, faith-based programming, and mentoring. It should be noted that in addition to recognizing the important role that relationships play in girls' lives, these types of interventions help to establish social bonds, expose girls to positive role models, and provide girls with a source of positive reinforcement for prosocial behaviors, all of which are elements supported in the principles of effective intervention proffered by the what works group.

Within the context of the helping alliance, we support the use of cognitive-behavioral approaches with girls. This support is based on the research suggesting that cognitive distortions and processing deficits contribute to a range of maladaptive behaviors among girls (see Bennett et al., 2005; Owens & Chard, 2001; Simourd & Andrews, 1994; Young, Martin, Young, & Ting, 2001). Additionally, there is a sufficient amount of research to suggest that these approaches are effective in treating depression and eating disorders among adolescent girls (Schapman-Williams, Lock, & Couturier, 2006; Wood, Harrington, & Moore, 1996).

In support of the responsivity principle and the evidence suggesting some differences in the general and problematic cognitive processes of boys and girls, we suggest that the cognitive-behavioral approaches be modified from those approaches typically used with male populations in two key ways. First, as noted by Cameron and Telfer (2004), cognitive-behavioral groups for girls should conform to their need for greater support, safety, and intimacy versus the confrontational tendencies of male-oriented groups. Second, cognitive-behavioral approaches for girls must target the types of cognitive distortions and processes that are more common among girls including the self-debasing distortions and internalizing behaviors referenced previously.

Finally, both the what works and gender-responsive groups recognize the importance of understanding differences that affect the way girls relate to others and the way they respond to interventions. Some of the most important of these differences include mental health disorders, sexual preference, and cultural backgrounds.

Although mental health disorders are not strong predictors of delinquency, they are responsivity factors that interfere with a person's amenability to treatment. Thus, prior to addressing girls' criminogenic needs, it may be necessary to treat disorders that undermine potential treatment gains. Another difference that must be clearly understood when working with girls is their sexual orientation. Studies show that lesbian, bisexual, and transgender girls are at greater risk for delinquency and other antisocial behaviors (see Anhalt & Morris, 1998). Juvenile justice agencies can enhance services for lesbian, bisexual, and transgender girls by avoiding language and assumptions that present alternative sexual orientations as pathological states, pro-viding visible role models, being familiar with resources for girls with alternative sexual orientations, and matching them to staff that view their lifestyles as valid and are comfortable with their own sexuality. Finally, it is important to acknowledge race, ethnic, and class differences in girls' programming. The gender-responsive group emphasizes the need to understand how gender, race, and class intersect to create worldviews that influence girls' relationships with others (Belknap, 2001; Covington & Bloom, 1999). According to Sue and Sue (1999), a failure to understand and value cultural differences in counseling or psychotherapy can impede the development of rapport and strong alliances that are needed for effective helping relationships.

The proposed therapeutic approach integrates the key principles from each body of work. Although it recognizes the merit of cognitive-behavioral interventions, it emphasizes the relational aspect as the foundational, essential ingredient for working effectively with girls.

☒ Future Research and Development

Longitudinal, prospective research is needed to document the pathway to girls' delinquency from early childhood through late adolescence. This pathway is now just speculation and does not provide solid footing for program development. According to life course theory, the factors predictive of problem behaviors change over time (Sampson & Laub, 1993); knowing how these factors change for girls will ensure that programs are targeting the most relevant factors at each developmental stage. Practitioners can facilitate research on the risks and needs of girls in the juvenile justice system by following the assessment protocol outlined above. Given the focus on cognitive-behavioral interventions, instruments should be included that measure the cognitive processes that contribute to girls' problem behaviors. This area of inquiry would lend itself to the development of gender-responsive cognitive-behavioral programs.

The next step in the process of integrating these two bodies of literature is to translate this knowledge into concrete practices. According to Porporino and Fabiano (2005), the calls for gender-responsive approaches have been largely unanswered in practice. Part of our intention here was to set forth a framework from which these practices could be developed, implemented, and tested through program evaluation.

Despite the success of the what works group in translating their principles into practice, there is an ongoing struggle with getting into the "black box" of correctional interventions, that is, the "program" as a whole is tested, but little is known about the unique contributions of particular program elements to its overall success (or failure) or to its success among various subgroups (e.g., girls). Two specific elements that could be tested within the proposed framework are the therapeutic alliance and the gender-responsive cognitive-behavioral model. The more knowledge we gain about the importance of building strong relationships with youth, especially girls, the more likely we are to challenge the current culture of many modern-day juvenile justice agencies—a culture that appears to impede the development of helping alliances. Additionally, a greater investment must be made in developing and testing various models of cognitive-behavioral interventions for girls.

⊠ Conclusion

Valuable knowledge has been generated by both academic camps (i.e., the what works and gender-responsive groups). Having sorted through extensive amounts of both bodies of literature, we assert that the perspectives and findings therein are more complementary than competitive and that each makes valuable contributions to our understanding of girls' delinquency. In our opinion, the two major contributions of the gender-responsive group include their (a) explication of how the social context of being a girl in the United States facilitates girls' delinquency and (b) research and discussions on the need for gender-responsive treatment to reflect the differences in the socialization and development of boys and girls. The major contributions of the what works literature includes (a) their empirical basis for program development and (b) their success in translating this research into practical applications for correctional and juvenile justice agencies.

Despite their vastly different approaches to addressing the needs of girls, both these sources of knowledge have value for girls' programming. Ignoring the relevance of either body of literature to working effectively with girls involved in the juvenile justice system is tantamount to knowledge destruction. The gender-responsive group can no longer afford to ignore the mounting evidence for the efficacy of programs rooted in the principles of effective intervention. At the same time, the what works group could benefit from recognizing the important contributions of the gender-responsive group. Their knowledge about what it is like to grow up as a girl adds clarity to the responsivity principle as it applies to girls.

It is essential that staff working with girls have a basic understanding of both bodies of literature. In this article, we have attempted to integrate the two bodies of literature into essential elements to be included in

prevention and/or treatment programs for girls by recognizing the value in each "camp" and reflecting that knowledge in specific program components. Taken separately, neither body of literature is very instructive as to what specific elements and approaches are needed to improve the lives of girls and reduce their propensity for delinquency. Together, however, they provide a blueprint for effective girls' programming.

⊠ References

Achenbach, T. M., Howell, C. T., Quay, H. C, & Conners, C. K. (1991). National survey of problems and competencies among four- to sixteen-year-olds: Parents' reports for normative and clinical samples. *Monographs of the Society for Research in Child Development, 56*, 5–120.

Acoca, L. (1999). Investing in girls: A 21st century strategy. *Juvenile Justice, 6*(1), 3–13.

Acoca, L., & Dedel, K. (1998). *No place to hide: Understanding and meeting the needs of girls in the California juvenile justice system.* Washington, DC: National Council on Crime and Delinquency.

American Association of University Women. (1992). *How schools shortchange girls: The AAUW report.* Washington, DC: Author.

American Association of University Women. (1998). *Gender gaps: Where schools fail our children.* Washington, DC: Author.

Andrews, D. A., & Bonta, J. (1999). *The psychology of criminal conduct.* Cincinnati, OH: Anderson.

Andrews, D. A., Bonta, J. D., & Hoge, R. D. (1990). Classification for effective rehabilitation: Rediscovering psychology. *Criminal Justice and Behavior, 17*, 19–52.

Andrews, D. A., Zinger, I., Bonta, J. D., Gendreau, P., & Cullen, F. T. (1990). Does correctional treatment work? A psychologically informed meta-analysis. *Criminology, 28*, 369–404.

Anhalt, K., & Morris, T. L. (1998). Developmental and adjustment issues of gay, lesbian, and bisexual adolescents: A review of the empirical literature. *Clinical Child and Family Psychology Review, 7*, 215–230.

Bailey, J., & McCloskey, L. (2005). Pathways to adolescent substance abuse among sexually abused girls. *Journal of Abnormal Child Psychology, 33*, 39–53.

Barriga, A., Landau, J., Stinson, B., Liau, A., & Gibbs, J. (2000). Cognitive distortion and problem behaviors in adolescents. *Criminal Justice and Behavior, 27*, 36–56.

Bearman, P. S., & Moody, J. (2004). Suicide and friendships among American adolescents. *American Journal of Public Health, 94*, 89–95.

Beger, R. R., & Hoffman, H. (1998). Role of gender of detention dispositioning of juvenile probation violators. *Journal of Crime and Justice, 21*, 173–188.

Belknap, J. (2001). *The invisible woman: Gender, crime, and justice.* Belmont, CA: Wadsworth.

Belknap, J., & Holsinger, K. (1998). An overview of delinquent girls: How theory and practice have failed and the need for innovative changes. In R. Zaplin (Ed.), *Female offenders: Critical perspectives and effective intervention* (pp. 31–59). Gaithersburg, MD: Aspen.

Belknap, J., Holsinger, K., & Dunn, M. (1997). *Moving toward juvenile justice and youth-serving systems that address the distinct experiences of the adolescent female: A report to the governor.* Columbus, OH: Office of Criminal Justice Services.

Bennett, S., Harrington, D. P., & Huesmann, L. R. (2005). Explaining gender differences in crime and violence: The importance of social cognitive skills. *Aggression and Violent Behavior, 10*, 263–288.

Bloom, B. (2000). Beyond recidivism: Perspectives on evaluation of programs for female offenders in community corrections. In M. McMahon (Ed.), *Assessment to assistance: Programs for women in community corrections* (pp. 107–138). Lanham, MD: American Correctional Association.

Bloom, B., & Covington, S. (2001, November). *Effective gender-responsive interventions in juvenile justice: Addressing the lives of delinquent girls.* Paper presented at the annual meeting of the American Society of Criminology, Atlanta, GA.

Bloom, B., Owen, B., & Covington, S. (2003). *Gender-responsive strategies: Research, practice, and guiding principles for women offenders* (NIC Publication No. 018017). Washington, DC: National Institute of Corrections.

Bonta, J. (1995). The responsivity principle and offender rehabilitation. *Forum on Corrections Research, 7*(3), 34–37.

Bordin, E. S. (1980). *Of human bonds that bind or free.* Pacific Grove, CA: Society for Psychotherapy Research.

Bretherton, I. (1985). Attachment theory: Retrospect and prospect. *Monographs of the Society for Research in Child Development, 50*(1/2), 3–35.

Brown, L. M. (2003). *Girlfighting: Betrayal and rejection among girls.* New York: New York University Press.

Bureau of Justice Statistics. (2006). *Juvenile offenders and victims: 2006 National Report.* Washington, DC: U.S. Department of Justice, Office of Juvenile Justice and Delinquency Prevention.

Cameron, H., & Telfer, J. (2004). Cognitive-behavioural group work: Its application to specific offender groups. *Howard Journal of Criminal Justice, 43*, 47–64.

Chesney-Lind, M. (1997). *The female offender: Girls, women, and crime.* Thousand Oaks, CA: Sage.

Chesney-Lind, M. (2000). What to do about girls? Thinking about programs for young women. In M. McMahon (Ed.), *Assessment to assistance: Programs for women in community corrections* (pp. 139–170). Lanham, MD: American Correctional Association.

Chesney-Lind, M. (2003, October). Gender and justice: What about girls? Presentation at the National Girls' Initiative Symposium, Washington, DC.

Chesney-Lind, M., & Brown, M. (1999). Girls and violence: An overview. In D. Flannery & C. Huff (Eds.), *Youth violence: Prevention, intervention, and social policy* (pp. 171–199). Arlington, VA: American Psychiatric Publishing.

Chesney-Lind, M., & Okamoto, S. K. (2001). Gender matters: Patterns in girls' delinquency and gender responsive programming. *Journal of Forensic Psychology Practice, 1*(3), 1–28.

Chesney-Lind, M., & Sheldon, R. (2004). *Girls, delinquency, and juvenile justice* (3rd ed.). Belmont, CA: Wadsworth.

Child Welfare League of America. (2003). *The CWIA National Girls Initiative: Growing girls for greatness.* Washington, DC: Author. Retrieved April 9, 2005, from www.cwla.org/conferences/2003ngirecap.htm

Covington, S. (2000). Helping women recover: Gender-specific treatment for substance abuse in community corrections. In M. McMahon (Ed.), *Assessment to assistance: Programs for women in community corrections* (pp. 171–233). Lanham, MD: American Correctional Association.

Covington, S. (2002). Helping women recover: Creating gender-responsive treatment. In S. L. A. Straussner & S. Brown (Eds.), *The handbook of addiction treatment* (pp. 52–72). San Francisco: Jossey-Bass.

Covington, S., & Bloom, B. (1999, November). Gender-responsive programming and evaluation for females in the criminal justice system: A shift from what works? to what is the work? Paper presented at the 51st Annual Meeting of the American Society of Criminology, Toronto, Canada.

Covington, S., & Bloom, B. (2003). Gendered justice: Women in the criminal justice system. In B. Bloom (Ed.), *Gendered justice: Addressing female offenders* (pp. 3–24). Durham, NC: Carolina Academic Press.

Cullen, F. T., & Gendreau, P. (2000). Assessing correctional rehabilitation: Policy, practice, and prospects. In J. Homey (Ed.), *Policies, processes, and decisions of the criminal justice system: Criminal justice 2000* (Vol. 3, pp. 109–175). Washington, DC: National Institute of Justice/NCJRS.

Donabella Sauro, M., & Teal Pedlow, C. (2005). The role of stress and personality factors on health and high-risk behaviors in young women. *Women, Girls, and Criminal Justice, 6*(6), 87–88, 93.

Ellis, A. (1991). The revised ABC's of rational-emotive therapy (RET). *Journal of Rational-Emotive and Cognitive Behavior Therapy, 9*, 139–172.

Fanington, D. (2000). Explaining and preventing crime: The globalization of knowledge—The American Society of Criminology 1999 Presidential Address. *Criminology, 38*, 1–24.

Farrington, D., & Painter, K. (2004). *Gender differences in risk factors for offending.* Research, Development and Statistics Directorate, UK. Retrieved May 11, 2005, from www.homeoffice.gov.uk/rds

Feinman, C. (1986). *Women in the criminal justice system.* New York: Praeger.

Fineran, S. (2002). Adolescents at work: Gender issues and sexual harassment. *Violence Against Women, 8*, 953–967.

Flores, A. W., Travis, L. F., & Latessa, E. J. (2004). *Case classification for juvenile corrections: An assessment of the Youth Level of Service/Case Management Inventory* (JLS/CMI). Final report (Grant No. 98-JB-VX-0108). Washington, DC: National Institute of Justice.

Florsheim, P., Shotorbani, S., & Guest-Warnick, G. (2000). Role of the working alliance in the treatment of delinquent boys in community based programs. *Journal of Clinical Child Psychology, 29*(1), 94–107.

Fox, J. G. (1984). Women's prison policy, prisoner activism, and the impact of the contemporary feminist movement: A case study. *Prison Journal, 64*(1), 15–36.

Freedman, E. (1974). Their sisters' keepers: An historical perspective on female correctional institutions in the United States: 1870–1900. *Feminist Studies, 2*, 77–95.

Frieswyk, S., Allen, J., Colson, D., & Coyne, L. (1986). Therapeutic alliance: Its place as a process and outcome variable in dynamic psychotherapy research. *Journal of Consulting and Clinical Psychology, 5*, 483–489.

Gendreau, P. (1996). The principles of effective intervention with offenders. In A. Harland (Ed.), *Choosing correctional options that work: Defining the demand and evaluating the supply* (pp. 117–130). Thousand Oaks, CA: Sage.

Gendreau, P., & Ross, R. (1987). Revivification of rehabilitation: Evidence from the 1980's. *Justice Quarterly, 4*, 349–409.

Gilligan, C. (1982). *In a different voice.* Cambridge, MA: Harvard University Press.

Giordano, P. (1978). Girls, guys, and gangs: The changing social context of female delinquency. *Journal of Criminal Law and Criminology, 69*, 126–132.

Gottfredson, S. (1987). Prediction and classification. In D. Gottfredson & M. Tonry (Eds.), *Prediction and classification: Criminal justice decision making* (pp. 1–20). Chicago: University of Chicago Press.

Gottfredson, D. M., & Snyder, H. N. (2005). *The mathematics of risk classification: Changing data into valid instruments for juvenile courts* (NCJ 209158). Washington, DC: Office of Juvenile Justice and Delinquency Prevention.

Hannah-Moffat, K. (1999). Moral agent or actuarial subject: Risk and Canadian women's imprisonment. *Theoretical Criminology, 3*, 71–94.

Hannah-Moffat, K., & Shaw, M. (2003). The meaning of "risk" in women's prisons: A critique. In B. Bloom (Ed.), *Gendered justice: Addressing female offenders* (pp. 69–96). Durham, NC: Carolina Academic Press.

Harris, M., & Fallot, R. D. (2001). Envisioning a trauma-informed service system: A vital paradigm shift. In M. Harris & R. D. Fallot (Eds.), *Using trauma theory to design service systems* (pp. 3–22). San Francisco: Jossey-Bass.

Hazler, R. J., & Mellin, E. A. (2004). The developmental origins and treatment needs of female adolescents with depression. *Journal of Counseling and Development, 82*, 18–24.

Herrera, V., & McCloskey, L. (2003). Sexual abuse, family violence, and female delinquency: Findings from a longitudinal study. *Violence and Victims, 18*, 319–334.

Holtfreter, K., & Morash, M. (2003). The needs of women offenders: Implications for correctional programming. *Women and Criminal Justice, 14*(2/3), 137–160.

Horvath, A., & Luborsky, L. (1993). The role of the therapeutic alliance in psychotherapy *Journal of Consulting and Clinical Psychology, 61*, 561–573.

Horvath, A. O., & Symonds, D. B. (1991). Relationship between working alliance and outcome in psychotherapy: A meta-analysis. *Journal of Counseling Psychology, 38*, 139–149.

Horwitz, A. V., Spatz Widom, C., McLaughlin, J., & Raskin White, H. (2001). The impact of childhood abuse and neglect on adult mental health: A prospective study. *Journal of Health and Social Behavior, 42*, 184–201.

Howell, J. C. (2003). *Preventing and reducing juvenile delinquency: A comprehensive framework.* Thousand Oaks, CA: Sage.

Hubbard, D. J., & Pratt, T. C. (2002). A meta-analysis of the predictors of delinquency among girls. *Journal of Offender Rehabilitation, 34*(3), 1–13.

Ilacqua, G. E., Coulson, G. E., Lombardo, D., & Nutbrown, V. (1999). Predictive validity of the young offender level of service inventory for criminal recidivism of male and female young offenders. *Psychological Reports, 84*, 1214–1218.

Jones, P. (1996). Risk prediction in criminal Justice. In A. Harland (Ed.), *Choosing correctional options that work: Defining the demand and evaluating the supply* (pp. 33–68). Thousand Oaks, CA: Sage.

Kaker, S., Friedemann, M., & Peck, L. (2002). Girls in detention: The results of focus group discussion interviews and official records review. *Journal of Contemporary Criminal Justice, 18*, 57–73.

Kataoka, S., Zima, B., Dupre, D., Moreno, K., Yang, X., & McCracken, J. (2001). Mental health problems and service use among female juvenile offenders: Their relationship to criminal history. *Journal of the American Academy of Child and Adolescent Psychiatry, 40*, 549–555.

Kendall, K. (1994). Therapy behind prison walls: A contradiction in terms? *Prison Service Journal, 96*, 2–11.

Kendall, K., & Pollack, S. (2003). Cognitive behavioralism in women's prisons: A critical analysis of therapeutic assumptions and practices. In B. Bloom (Ed.), *Gendered justice: Addressing female offenders* (pp. 69–96). Durham, NC: Carolina Academic Press.

Kennedy, S. (2000). Treatment responsivity: Reducing recidivism by enhancing treatment effectiveness. *Forum on Corrections Research, 12*(2), 19–23

Khoury, E. L. (1998). Are girls different? A developmental perspective on gender differences in risk factors for substance use among adolescents. In W. A. Vega & A. G. Gil (Eds.), *Drug use and ethnicity in early adolescence* (pp. 95–123). New York: Plenum.

King, S. M., William, I. G., & McGue, M. (2004). Childhood externalizing and internalizing psychopathology in the prediction of early substance use. *Addiction, 99*, 1548–1559.

Kochenderfer, B., & Ladd, G. (1996). Peer victimization: Cause or consequence of school maladjustment? *Child Development, 67*, 1305–1317.

Krisberg, B. (2005). *Juvenile justice: Redeeming our children.* Thousand Oaks, CA: Sage.

Latessa, E., Cullen, F., & Gendreau, P. (2002). Beyond correctional quackery: Professionalism and the possibility of effective treatment. *Federal Probation, 66*(2), 43–49.

Lester, D., & Van Voorhis, P. (2004). Cognitive therapies. In P. Van Voorhis, M. Braswell, & D. Lester (Eds.), *Correctional counseling and rehabilitation* (pp. 109–126). Cincinnati, OH: Anderson.

Lipsey, M., & Wilson, D. (1998). Effective intervention for serious juvenile offenders: A synthesis of research. In R. Loeber & D. P. Farrington (Eds.), *Serious and violent juvenile offenders: Risk factors and successful interventions* (pp. 313–335). Thousand Oaks, CA: Sage.

Lowenkamp, C., & Latessa, E. (2004). Understanding the risk principle: How and why correctional interventions can harm low-risk offenders. In *Topics in community corrections* (pp. 3–7). Washington, DC: U.S. Department of Justice, National Institute of Corrections.

MacDonald, J. M., & Chesney-Lind, M. (2001). Gender bias and juvenile justice revisited: A multiyear analysis. *Crime and Delinquency, 47*, 173–195.

Mahan, S. (2003). Pregnant girls and moms in detention. *Justice Policy Journal: Analyzing Criminal and Juvenile Justice Issues and Policies, 1*(2), 41–58.

McCabe, K., Lansing, A., Garland, A., & Hough, R. (2002). Gender differences in psychopathology, functional impairment, and familial risk factors among adjudicated delinquents. *Journal of American Academy of Child & Adolescent Psychiatry, 41*, 860-867.

McCarthy, B., Felmlee, D., & Hagan, J. (2004). Girl friends are better: Gender, friends, and crime among school and street youth. *Criminology, 42*, 805–835.

McClellan, D. S., Farabee, D., & Crouch, B. M. (1997). Early victimization, drug use, and criminality: A comparison of male and female prisoners. *Criminal Justice and Behavior, 24*, 455–476.

McGuire, J. (2000). Can the criminal law ever be therapeutic? *Behavioral Sciences & the Law, 18*, 413–426.

McMahon, M. (2000). Assisting female offenders: Art or science?—Chairperson's commentary. In M. McMahon (Ed.), *Assessment to assistance: Programs for women in community corrections* (pp. 279–328). Lanham, MD: American Correctional Association.

Mears, D., Ploeger, M., & Warr, M. (1998). Explaining the gender gap in delinquency: Peer influence and moral evaluations of behavior. *Journal of Research in Crime and Delinquency, 55*, 251–266.

Miller, B. J. (1986). *Toward a new psychology of women.* Boston: Beacon.

Moffitt, T., Caspi, A., Rutter, M., & Silva, P. (2002). Sex differences in antisocial behavior: Conduct disorder, delinquency and violence in the Dunedin longitudinal study. *Psychological Medicine, 32*, 1475–1476.

Morgan, M., & Patton, P. (2002). Gender responsive programming in the justice system- Oregon's guidelines for effective programming for girls. *Federal Probation, 66*(2), 57–65.

Obeidallah, D. A., & Earls, F. J. (1999, July). *Adolescent girls: The role of depression in the development of delinquency.* Washington, DC: National Institute of Justice.

Odem, M., & Schlossman, S. (1991). Guardians of virtue: The juvenile court and female delinquency in the early 20th century Los Angeles. *Crime & Delinquency, 37*, 186–203.

Olweus, D. (1978). *Aggression in the schools: Bullies and whipping boys.* Washington, DC: Hemisphere.

Owens, G., & Chard, K. (2001). Cognitive distortions among women reporting childhood sexual abuse. *Journal of Interpersonal Violence, 16*, 178–191.

Peters, S. (1998). *Guiding principles for promising female programming: An inventory of best practices.* Washington, DC: U.S. Department of Justice, Office of Juvenile Justice and Delinquency Prevention.

Porporino, F. J., & Fabiano, E. (2005). Is there an evidence base supportive of women-centered programming in corrections? *Corrections Today, 67*(6), 26–27, 101.

Potter, C. C. (1999). Violence and aggression in girls. In J. M. Jenson & M. O. Howard (Eds.), *Youth violence: Current research and recent practice innovations* (pp. 113–138). Washington, DC: NASW Press.

Prinstein, M., Boergers, L., & Vernberg, E. (2001). Overt and relational aggression in adolescents: Social-psychological adjustment of aggressors and victims. *Journal of Clinical Child Psychology, 30*, 479–491.

Rutter, M. (1985). Resilience in the face of adversity: Protective factors and resistance to psychiatric disorder. *British Journal of Psychiatry, 147*, 598–611.

Sampson, R. J., & Laub, J. H. (1993). *Crime in the making: Pathways and turning points through life.* Cambridge, MA: Harvard University Press.

Schapman-Williams, A. M., Lock, J., & Couturier, J. (2006). Cognitive-behavioral therapy for adolescents with binge eating syndromes: A case series. *International Journal of Eating Disorders, 39*, 252–255.

Schoenberg, J., Riggins, T., & Salmond, K. (2003). *Feeling safe: What girls say.* New York: Girl Scouts of the USA.

Schwalbe, C., Fraser, M., Day, S., & Arnold, E. M. (2004). North Carolina assessment of risk (NCAR): Reliability and predictive validity with juvenile offenders. *Journal of Offender Rehabilitation, 40*(1/2), 1–22.

Sherman, L. W., Gottfredson, D. C., MacKenzie, D. L., Eck, J., Reuter, P., & Bushway, S. (Eds.). (1997). *Preventing crime: What works, what doesn't, what's promising.* Washington, DC: National Institute of Justice.

Simourd, D. J., & Andrews, D. L. (1994). *Correlates of delinquency: A look at gender differences.* Ottawa, Ontario, Canada: Carleton University, Department of Psychology.

Steffensmeier, D., & Allan, E. (1998). The nature of female offending: Patterns and explanation. In R. T. Zaplin (Ed.), *Female offenders: Critical perspectives and effective interventions* (pp. 5–24). Gaithersburg, MD: Aspen.

Steffensmeier, S., Schwartz, J., & Zhong, H. (2005). An assessment of recent trends in girls' violence using diverse longitudinal sources: Is the gender gap closing? *Criminology, 43,* 355–405.

Stiles, W. B., Agnew-Davies, R., Hardy, G. E., Barkham, M., & Shapiro, D. A. (1998). Relations of the alliance with psychotherapy outcome: Findings in the second Sheffield Psychotherapy Project. *Journal of Consulting and Clinical Psychology, 66,* 791–802.

Sue, D. W., & Sue, D. (1999). *Counseling the culturally different: Theory and practice* (3rd ed.). New York: John Wiley.

Teplin, L. (2001, March). *Mental health: An emerging issue.* Paper presented at the American Correctional Health Services Association Multidisciplinary Training Conference, Atlanta, GA.

Unger, D. G., & Wandersman, A. (1985). The importance of neighbors: The social, cognitive, and affective components of neighboring. *American Journal of Community Psychology, 13,* 139–169.

van der Kolk, B. A. (1994). *Trauma and development in children.* Albany: State-wide Grand Rounds, Sponsored by the New York State Department of Mental Health, Bureau of Psychiatric Services.

Van Voorhis, P. (2004). An overview of offender classification systems. In P. Van Voorhis, M. Braswell, & D. Lester (Eds.), *Correctional counseling and rehabilitation* (5th ed., pp. 133–162). Cincinnati, OH: Anderson.

Wald, R., Harvey, S. M., & Hibbard, J. (1995). A treatment model for women substance users. *International Journal of the Addictions, 30,* 881–888.

Wilson, D. B., Allen Bouffard, L., & Mackenzie, D. L. (2005). Quantitative review of structured, group-oriented, cognitive-behavioral programs for offenders. *Criminal Justice and Behavior, 32,* 172–204.

Wood, A., Harrington, R., & Moore, A. (1996). Controlled trial of a brief cognitive behavioral intervention in adolescent patients with depressive disorders. *Journal of Child Psychology and Psychiatry, 87,* 737–746.

Young, T. M., Martin, S. S., Young, M. E., & Ting, L. (2001). Internal poverty and teen pregnancy. *Adolescence, 36,* 289–305.

Zahn, M. (2005, July). *Girls study group: Preliminary findings.* Paper presented at the NIJ Conference, Washington, DC.

DISCUSSION QUESTIONS

1. In the article by Hubbard and Matthews, they discuss how different the needs are for boys than for girls. What are these differences? Why is it important to understand these?

2. Why is it important to understand the differences between a gender-response versus a gender-specific approach to dealing with girls in the system?

3. Assume you are an administrator of a coed juvenile residential facility. Given what we know about gendered-response approaches to juvenile delinquency, how would this alter how girls and boys are treated and monitored in the facility?

4. The authors further argue that "interventions also should be aimed at promising healthy connections with persons and organizations external to the program." As a program administrator, how might you accomplish these goals?

SECTION

XI

Specialized and Problematic Offender Typologies in a Changing Era

Learning Objectives

1. Identify different types of adult sex offenders.

2. Understand various methods of supervision for sex offenders as well as common treatment techniques.

3. Identify and understand substance abusers.

(Continued)

545

(Continued)

4. Understand the concept of co-occurring disorders.

5. Identify and discuss different types of treatment programs for substance abusers.

6. Understand and discuss the mentally ill offender.

7. Identify different types of **mental illness** common to the offender population.

8. Understand various classifications of mental retardation.

Specialized and problematic offenders often suffer from symptoms, disorders, and illness not commonly or fully understood by most employees of community corrections agencies. As a result, it is critical that employees of community corrections agencies identify resources within their communities that have the expertise and capabilities of providing needed services to certain offenders. In order for community corrections agencies to maximize their ability to effectively supervise specialized offenders, supervision efforts should coincide with appropriate psychological and emotional counseling provided by licensed professionals within the community. This section will review four of the most frequently supervised specialized and problematic offender: the sex offender, the substance abuser, the mentally ill offender, and the mentally retarded offender. Each of these offender groups will be discussed along with possible alternatives to referral and supervision.

✄ Adult Sex Offenders

This section addresses the issue of **sexual assault** against adult (not child) victims. Before proceeding, however, it is necessary to define sexual assault. First, the reader should understand that the term *sexual assault* is used as a blanket term that refers to a number of sexually related forms of offending. Sexual assault includes all types of sexual offenses that involve touching or penetration of an intimate part of a person's body without consent (LeBeau & Mozayani, 2001). Thus, sexual assault includes forced sodomy, forced oral copulation, child molestation, and any form of undesired sexually related touching (LeBeau & Mozayani, 2001). For purposes of this chapter, sexual assault is the act of forced penetration of any bodily orifice (vaginally, anally, or orally), or forced cunnilingus or felatio, involving violation of the survivor's body and psychological well-being. The assault is accomplished by the use of force, the threat of force, or without force when the survivor is unable to physically or mentally give their consent.

Sex Offender Typologies: Victim Chosen Is Adult

Throughout North America, sex offenders make up an increasing proportion of persons who are convicted and later incarcerated. In some states, it has been found that the largest group of offenders is that of sex offenders (Morris & Tonry, 1990). The most common demographic feature is that rapists tend to be young.

When examining the Uniform Crime Reports (UCR) data, over half of rapists arrested are under 25 years of age, and a full 80% are under the age of 30. Further, the National Crime Victimization Survey estimates that roughly one fourth of all combined rapes and attempted rapes that occur at any point in the year are committed by offenders who are between the ages of 12 and 20. Additionally, it has been shown that a high number of rapes of adult victims have been committed by juvenile offenders. This underscores the finding that roughly half of all adult sex offenders report that their first sexual offense occurred during their teens (Bartol, 2002).

Bartol (2002) noted that roughly half of all men arrested for rape tend to be employed in working-class occupations, with another approximate third being unemployed. Of the convicted rapists, only 20% had a high school education and the overwhelming majority came from labor-oriented occupations (Bartol, 2002). Thus, few white-collar or professional workers are convicted of rape. There is, however, substantial evidence that

▲ **Photo 11.1** This community supervision officer (CSO) is assigned solely to a sex offender caseload. He holds a miniature tracking device, typically referred to as an MTD in the field. This piece of equipment works in conjunction with global positioning system (GPS) surveillance technology.

most charges for rape are dropped or pleaded out of court to a lesser charge for those men who are more affluent. Likewise, the majority of these offenders are not under correctional supervision before their initial arrest for their sex offense and most have some establishment within the community. Further, it has been found that sex offenders do not share the same tendency to "age out" of their crimes as do offenders who are fond of committing other types of offenses (Abel & Rouleau, 1990). Thus, one can deduce that sex offenders start their offending at a young age, and they are likely to continue offending throughout their life span if some form of intervention is not successful.

It should also be noted that most sex offenders do not have a serious mental illness. Although a diagnosis of **antisocial personality disorder (ASPD)** is very common among sex offenders, it is generally not considered sufficient to justify classifying the offender as mentally disordered (Rice, Harris, & Quinsey, 2002). Moreover, despite sensationalism from the media, most sex offenders do not have a major mental disorder such as schizophrenia or some other psychoses (Sturgeon & Taylor, 1980).

Many researchers have attempted to classify various kinds of rapists (Holmes & Holmes, 2002). However, the chosen typology that will be used for this text and for this section was originally devised by Knight and Prentky (1990). This typology divides rapists into four categories: (1) power reassurance, (2) power assertive, (3) anger retaliation, and (4) sadistic. In addition, two more categories have been provided to more adequately discuss the various types of adult-on-adult sex offenders and their motives for committing their crimes. These two additional categories are the sexual gratification rapist and the opportunistic rapist.

Power Reassurance Rapist

The **power reassurance rapist** is probably the least violent of the types that will be considered. Typically, these offenders are socially incompetent and may be quite introverted in thought and behavior. These individuals tend to have a low sense of self-esteem and suffer from profound feelings of inadequacy, both socially and sexually. Aggression is not a key factor of motivation. Rather these offenders seek to prove their sexual prowess and adequacy through fantasies in which they imagine eagerly yielding victims who succumb to their sexual coercion enjoying the experience so much that they actually begin to desire further sexual intercourse. Such fantasies are soothing to their sense of insecurity and incompetence.

Knight and Prentky (1990) pointed out that many of these offenders come from single-parent homes, tend not to do well in school, and have an average educational level of 10th grade. They are typically single adults who continue to live with their parents. This offender is not likely to be athletic, is likely to be passive, and will generally have few if any friends. He is, however, likely to be a stable and reliable worker but typically employed in a menial occupation due to his lack of desire for achievement.

Power reassurance rapists are not likely to be mentally ill, but they may have other sexual disorders such as transvestism (cross-dressing) or fetishism. They may engage in exhibitionism, voyeurism, and so on, as this may be part of the method by which they select victims in their own neighborhoods for future sexual assaults. These offenders may watch their victim intensely over time until they feel secure in their decision to assault. They typically will case the home of their victims and are most likely to commit the act within the home of the victim when the opportunity presents itself. The main purpose of rape for this type of offender is to improve his sense of self-respect. The primary aim is sexual in nature and not necessarily about power over his victim.

Sexual Gratification Rapist

For the **sexual gratification rapist,** aggression is simply instrumental and used to gain compliance. However, unlike the power reassurance rapist, this offender is not necessarily withdrawn or reclusive. Rather, this offender may simply desire sex and may be in a situation where he feels that force or coercion could successfully get the sexual intercourse that he wants. This type of rape is most reflected by date rape and similar forms of sexual assault. It may or may not be a repetitive behavior, depending on how any previous attempts at coercion have ended. It is unlikely that this type of offender will allow the coercion or aggression to escalate to the point of serious injury to the victim.

This type of offender may have a high degree of social and interpersonal competence, and the sexual offense is likely to reflect more sexualization in both activity and interaction. Further, the offender is likely to express his interest in the victim as a sex object. However, he may use any means of cajoling, flattery, or pleading while using the gentlest of force necessary to encourage the victim to submit to his desire. Within this group of offenders are those who drug their victims (e.g., with Rohypnol or excessive alcohol, or by providing the drug Ecstasy), and there is often no use of physical violence against the victim. The offender simply has sex with the victim without the person's consent. This is still clearly rape, but it is also not based on attempting to cause pain to the victim as much as it is designed to gratify the sexual urges of the offender.

The offender who is successful in this type of rape is likely to repeat the act with other victims as well. Further, it should be noted that many victims will fail to report the act because they know the offender (perhaps very well), or there may be a sense of guilt or shame. In addition, the intoxicated state of the victim does not help her sense of credibility, in her mind if nothing else. Thus, the act tends to go unreported. This method of rape is a primary tactic used on many college campuses and among individual students as well as student groups that may rape, such as members of fraternities or athletic groups or teams.

Opportunistic Rapist

The **opportunistic rapist** demonstrates neither strong sexual nor aggressive features but engages in spontaneous rape when an opportunity presents that makes it look like an easy prospect. This form of rape is usually conducted during the commission of another crime, such as robbery or burglary. The victim simply happens to be at the scene, or the victim of the crime resists and this provokes the idea of assaulting the victim. In most cases, this offender is likely to have a history of criminal offenses (not necessarily all of the crime being detected by police, however) beside rape. In fact, the offender may have never committed a prior rape, and they may not even rape again after the isolated opportunity that had presented itself. In order to fall within this category, the offender must show both callous indifference to the welfare and comfort of the victim and they must use no more force than would be necessary to obtain compliance from the victim.

Power Assertive Rapist

With the **power assertive rapist**, rape is an attempt to express the person's virility and sense of dominance over the victim. This offender has a sense of superiority that is based on "hypermasculinity" in which he believes he is entitled to sexual access simply because he is a man. For this offender, rape is an impulsive act of predatory victimization that the female deserves because she is female and is fair game for subjugation (Holmes & Holmes, 2002). The aggression exhibited in the rape is intended to secure the compliance of the victim rather than necessarily cause harm to the victim. To be sure, the power assertive rapist is not concerned with whether the victim is injured in the process, but this is not their primary motivation when using force against a victim. Their primary motivation is to simply obtain and maintain control over the victim. Thus, unlike the power reassurance rapist, this rapist is indifferent to the comfort of his victim; he simply is concerned with ensuring compliance from the victim. The power assertive rapist commits sexual assault so as to feel a sense of dominance and control over a female victim due to heightened beliefs regarding the roles and rights of men and women (Holmes & Holmes, 2002).

Holmes and Holmes (2002) noted that about 70% of these rapists have been raised in single-parent households and roughly a third of these offenders have stayed in foster homes. In addition, the majority (three fourths) of these offenders have suffered from prior abuse as children (Holmes & Holmes, 2002; Knight & Prentky, 1990). This type of rapist generally has many domestic problems and has often been involved in numerous failed marriages. Obviously, these marriages are replete with negative incidents, including (or especially) domestic violence.

The attack of the power assertive rapist consists of a mixture of verbal and physical violence. If he is resisted, he will physically overpower his victim. The level of aggression of these rapists tends to escalate as their raping continues. Power assertive rapists are not typically considered to be amenable to treatment. In fact, Holmes and Holmes (2002) clearly pointed out that the power assertive rapist is likely to be the most difficult of rapists to interview and interrogate. These rapists are simply unlikely to provide any cooperation even when intimidation, pleas for aid, and/or appeals for the victim's welfare are used.

Holmes and Holmes (2002) noted that "the power assertive rapist . . . may be considered to be close to the clinical evaluation of having a character disorder" (p. 153). In fact, these authors stated that this category of rapist is likely to be psychopathic in nature. Further, the power assertive rapist feels no remorse for their actions (reflective of their common underlying disorders of ASPD, narcissism, and tendencies toward psychopathy) or the victim's welfare (Holmes & Holmes, 2002). They simply care about having power over the victim or the situation. With investigators, the fact that they have information desired by investigators itself becomes a form of power that they are likely to relish.

Anger Retaliation Rapist

The **anger retaliation rapist** strongly desires to harm women. This offender seeks to "get even" with women who have embarrassed or humiliated him in his past. These causes for embarrassment or humiliation may be real or imagined, but this type of offender essentially views women as bad, even evil, and thus deserving of harm. Unlike the power reassurance rapist, the anger retaliation rapist is socially competent (Holmes & Holmes, 2002). This type of rapist usually comes from a noxious family of origin where abuse or neglect was commonplace. There is a high likelihood that male role models were abusive to the mother of the offender and that the mother was, in turn, abusive to the offender when he was a child (Holmes & Holmes, 2002). These abusive mother–child interactions may be a substantial part of why this type of offender harbors resentment for women.

For this type of offender, the act of rape is meant to humiliate the victim—especially when the victim is chosen because she seems to be promiscuous or because she is seen as deserving of the abuse (Holmes & Holmes, 2002). When acting alone, this type of offender is likely to use verbal insults toward the victim, and he is likely to rip off her clothing in a demonstration of force. This type of offender will also be likely to use weapons of opportunity to assault the victim. This rapist will tend to commit his crimes near home and will usually stalk victims who are of his own race and near to his own age. It should also be noted that this type of offender is not likely to attempt further contact with the victim after the assault is over (Holmes & Holmes, 2002).

Sadistic Rapist

The **sadistic rapist** is the most dangerous and the most likely to kill or permanently maim his victim. The primary desire of this offender is to cause pain to the victim. This offender will seek to express sexually aggressive fantasies that have formed from an extended history of the classically conditioned pairing of sexual excitement and violence. Indeed, graphic pairings such as that presented in "snuff" pornographic films are an integral part of their day-to-day thoughts and lifestyle in many cases. This offender derives ultimate pleasure when inflicting pain and psychological terror upon his victim. Sadistic rapists will often use restraining, blindfolding, paddling, spanking, whipping, pinching, beating, burning, electrically shocking, cutting, strangulating, mutilating, and performing any other imaginable act of torture and abuse to their rape victim (American Psychiatric Association, 2000). Indeed, he has difficulty obtaining sexual satisfaction without inflicting harm upon the object of his desire.

When sexual sadism is severe and especially when it is associated with ASPD, these individuals are likely to kill their victims. According to the American Psychiatric Association (2000), the diagnostic criteria for the mental disorder of sexual sadism is as follows:

A. Over a period of at least 6 months, recurrent, intense sexually arousing fantasies, sexual urges, or behaviors involving acts (real, not simulated) in which the psychological or physical suffering (including humiliation) of the victim is sexually exciting to the offender.

B. The person has acted on these sexual urges with a non-consenting person, or the sexual urges or fantasies cause marked distress or interpersonal difficulty. (p. 573)

Because it is unlikely that this type of crime can go unreported by the victim due to the nonsexual injuries that would require hospitalization, this offender is more likely than any other to murder his victim so that they will be silenced. Similar to the power assertive rapist, the prognosis for this group of offenders is extremely poor. These types of offenders are also not good security or treatment risks for community supervision programs.

Sex Offender Typologies: Child as Victim

According to the *DSM-IV-TR* (American Psychiatric Association, 2000), **pedophilia** involves sexual activity with a prepubescent child (generally age 13 and younger). The individual with pedophilia must be at least 16 years of age and at least 5 years older than the child who was the victim. Pedophiles most often report a stronger attraction to children within a certain age range. Those most attracted to females usually prefer 8- to 10-year-olds. Those attracted to males usually prefer slightly older children. Pedophilia involving female victims is reported more often than pedophilia involving male victims.

These offenders may limit their activities to their own children, stepchildren, or relatives, or they may victimize children outside their families. Some individuals with pedophilia threaten the child to prevent disclosure. Others, particularly those who routinely victimize children, develop complex techniques for obtaining access to their victims, which may include winning the trust of a child's mother; marrying a woman with an attractive child; trading children with other individuals with pedophilia; or as in some rare cases, adopting children from underdeveloped countries or even abducting the children from strangers.

The pedophile may be attentive to the child's needs in order to gain the child's affection, interest, and loyalty and to prevent the child from reporting the sexual assault. Pedophiles start to notice their urges in adolescence in most cases, but some report that they did not become aroused by children until middle age. The recidivism rate for those having a preference for males is roughly twice that for those who prefer females (American Psychiatric Association, 2000).

While there is considerable variability in age of child molesters, most who are convicted are between the ages of 36 and 40. This is in stark contrast to the rapists who choose adult victims where, as mentioned, about 75% are under age 30. Despite the statistical finding that child molesters tend to be older than most other sex offenders, there seems to be a pattern of victim preference that is based on the age of the pedophile (Bartol, 2002). It has been found that older pedophiles (over the age of 50) seek immature children who are 10 years old or younger. On the other hand, younger pedophiles (under the age of 40) tend to select girls who are between the ages of 12 to 15 years of age (Bartol, 2002). These latter pedophiles are referred to as *hebophiles*, which simply denotes a type of pedophile that prefers preteen and teenaged children rather than prepubescent children. Most child molesters do not have a mental illness of any sort other than the pedophilia disorder as listed in the *DSM-IV-TR* (American Psychiatric Association, 2000). Pedophiles typically do not finish high school and most have poor work histories in unskilled employment backgrounds.

Adult Sex Offenders in the Community

When addressing sex offenders on community supervision, the first concern that comes to mind is public safety. This concern is the overriding and understandable priority when considering the suitability of community supervision for sex offenders. Thus, understanding the true recidivism rates for sex offenders, and understanding recidivism rates for different types of sex offenders, is critical if an agency is to make effective and safe decisions about early release. In 2003, the U.S. Department of Justice published a study that examined recidivism among sex offenders released in 1994 and tracked their reoffending rates during the subsequent 3 years. This study looked at prison systems in 15 states that released a total of 9,691 male sex offenders. These offenders comprised two thirds of all the male sex offenders released from state prison systems throughout the entire United States in 1994 (Bureau of Justice Statistics, 2003). The 9,691 were divided by type of sex offender, and the breakdown was as follows:

- 3,115 released rapists
- 4,295 released child molesters
- 6,576 released sexual assaulters
- 443 released statutory rapists.

It should be noted that the study included the "big four" among state correctional systems (California, New York, Texas, and Florida). The other remaining states were selected due to their representativeness of the overall U.S. correctional population. These states released 272,111 prisoners in 1994, meaning that the 9,691 sex offenders consisted of about 3.6% of all those released on community supervision (Bureau of Justice Statistics, 2003). On average, the 9,691 sex offenders served 3.5 years of an average 8-year sentence before being released in 1994 (Bureau of Justice Statistics, 2003).

This study found that within the first 3 years following their release from prison, 5.3% (517 of the 9,691) of released sex offenders were rearrested for a sex crime. The rate for the 262,420 released non-sex offenders was lower—1.3%. For sex offenders, it was found that in the first 12 months following their release from a state prison, roughly 40% recidivated. In comparison, an average of 4,295 child molesters were released after serving about 3 years of an approximate 7-year sentence. With child molesters, the first 3 years following release from prison resulted in 3.3% (141 of 4,295) of released child molesters being rearrested for another sex crime against a child (Bureau of Justice Statistics, 2003).

While recidivism studies typically find that the older the prisoner when released, the lower the rate of recidivism this was not the case with sex offenders. Overall, of the 9,691 released sex offenders, 3.5% (339 of the 9,691) were reconvicted for a sex crime during the 3-year follow-up period. From these results, it can be seen that sex offenders have a higher likelihood of recidivism (3.5%) than do non-sex offenders (1.3%).

Thus, many community supervision programs utilize what is referred to as the **containment approach**, which has been publicized by the American Probation and Parole Association. The containment approach is based on the idea that multiple dimensions of supervision are necessary to optimize public safety, and this therefore requires numerous actors within the criminal justice and community setting. When utilizing the containment approach, the supervision team will consist of at least three persons, each with his or her own specific role in the process (Center for Sex Offender Management [CSOM], 2001). The Center for Sex Offender Management (CSOM) points toward three personnel who are commonly involved with the containment approach in supervision: (1) the community supervision officer (CSO), (2) **sex offender therapist**, and (3) **polygraph examiner**. First, the CSO is responsible for monitoring the offender's behavior in the community and assesses their compliance with court mandates. These officers of the court maintain regular contact with the offender (usually through some form of intensive supervision coupled with electronic monitoring) and routine conversations with the treatment therapist. This agent represents the authority of the court and is responsible for initiating court action if the offender does not comply with the terms of their supervision. Second, the sex offender therapist usually sees the offender once a week in a group counseling setting. These therapists are highly trained and experienced in working with the sex offender population. Advanced training is usually required in most states before a therapist can provide services. The therapist maintains close contact with the CSO, and both work collaboratively to identify potential problems in the offender's compliance with their community supervision requirements. When the sex offender therapist and the CSO work together, the offender is less able to hide relevant issues from the therapist or the treatment group. Finally, because sex offenders are generally very manipulative and superficially compliant, the polygraph examiner, uses techniques to detect deception in offenders. Sex offenders are very adept at withholding information and keeping secrets; therefore, the expertise of the polygraph examiner is very useful. The information gained from **polygraph** examinations is forwarded to the therapist and CSO.

In essence, these three supervising agents work together to "contain" the offender's risk to the community. In addition to the three-pronged supervision, there are a number of other supervision requirements that are likely to be mandated to ensure compliance. For instance, the sex offender will usually be required to submit to routine polygraph testing and, incidentally, the offender will be made to pay for this testing. The polygraph is usually given every 3, 6, or 12 months, depending on the jurisdiction.

Further, depending on the type of sex offender, there may be conditions with their potential contact with children. Most offenders are initially restricted from having contact with children. This is of course often the case with pedophiles. However, some offenders may be allowed to have supervised contact with their own children if they had not been victims and if the offender does not seem to be a risk to the children. As the offender's progress in treatment continues, the conditions of this restriction may be modified as seems practical with that offender. Further, these offenders are almost always restricted from residing near a school or day care center, and they cannot go to places commonly known to have children. Lastly, it is common that sex offenders are restricted from purchasing pornography or frequenting sexually oriented businesses. Restrictions on Internet usage is also becoming a common condition as well.

Sex Offender Notification Programs and Community Partnerships

Currently, every state has some type of notification process when sex offenders are released into the community. This is true regardless of whether the sex offender is on probation (having not been incarcerated) or has been released on parole (after serving a prison term). Commonly, the term used for these requirements are **Megan's Laws**, which are attributed to the brutal rape and murder of a 7-year-old New Jersey girl named Megan Kanka. The victim's parents pushed for legislation in the state of New Jersey to mandate reporting of sex offenders who are released into the community, and in 1994, New Jersey was the first state to pass such legislation. The following year, the federal government passed similar legislative requirements. Since that time, other states have followed suit, with these laws often being informally referred to as Megan's Laws in respect to the crime victim who served as the catalyst for this reporting requirement.

The CSOM is operated by the U.S. Department of Justice and is perhaps the leading national warehouse for training on sex offender-related issues. This organization is a federally operated program that provides a vast array of curricula that are available to the general public and that are ideal for community training. The CSOM notes that in addition to the typical notification programs that exist throughout the United States, there are many occasions where public agencies (such as police, prosecutors, and community supervision agencies) are required to provide specific information pertaining to individual sex offenders. This is conducted through a variety of means, including door-to-door citizen notification, public meetings, as well as the distribution of written and printed notices.

Further, the CSOM notes that as more comprehensive and collaborative approaches to the management of sex offenders emerge, community members, victims, the victim's family, the offender's family, and other community members are invited to become partners in the sex offender management process (CSOM, 2008). Naturally, this dovetails with this text's emphasis on community partnerships and citizen involvement with the offender supervision and treatment process. Students may recall that a similar discussion was provided in Sections II, VIII, and IX of this text, noting that community partnerships are the key in filling in gaps in both supervision and treatment objectives. At this point, it should be clear to the student that there are a number of sources, particularly federal sources, that constantly refer to this same theme. Indeed, this text draws from a substantial array of federal publications and documents as source material. The reason for this is because these sources are generally considered valid by most all of the practitioner and the academic communities, thus referencing from these sources adds to the legitimacy of this text. Because these sources continually point toward the community as a means of improving offender reintegration (both in terms of security and treatment) it should be clear that this text's orientation is then likewise valid and legitimate.

Naturally, the ability for agencies to collaborate with community members will be specific to that region and/or location, as some areas are more amenable to such forms of notification and offender tracking than are others. Such agency-community programs require that staff involved in such programs exercise sensitivity to the context and needs of individuals, families, and communities that are involved (CSOM, 2008). This process, while entailing a very important community education component, also requires a great deal of care since victim reactions can be quite varied.

Thus, this aspect of ensuring compliance consists of two parts: First, the notification process by which the community is made aware of the existence of a sex offender in their community; second, the community's involvement, which ensures that the offender is monitored by human observation, interaction, and general community awareness. This provides a strong preventive component for the offender and also ensures that other potential victims are vigilant to the potential threat that exists within their community. Nevertheless, these programs must also educate community members on the dynamics of sex offending and the likelihood of recidivism. For instance, in most cases, sex offenders do not recidivate; the majority of all sex offenses are actually not committed by an offender with a prior sex offending history. This is important for community members to understand because it will lend to the efficacy of reintegrative approaches while (at the same time) improving overall supervision of the offender. According to the CSOM, community supervision staff tasked with establishing community partnerships should do the following:

1. Inform community members about their state's sex offender registration and community notification laws and local supervision and treatment efforts to safely manage these offenders.

2. Acknowledge community member's interest in their own safety and the safety of their neighborhoods. Explain that stability is a key ingredient in preventing reoffense. If the offender is intimidated, harassed, or threatened because of citizen overreaction, it can lead to the offender "going underground," or hiding from the criminal justice professionals charged with his or her supervision, avoiding helpful therapeutic opportunities and even disengaging from positive other activities, such as work.

3. Explain the potential consequences of abuse of the law, through harassment of the offender. Explain that vigilantism is against the law and that if citizens take matters into their own hands they can be prosecuted.

4. Provide a brief description of the specific efforts that are underway to safely manage the offender, emphasizing the supervision methods, special conditions, and therapeutic interventions being employed with this offender.

5. Provide contact information for community members if they have further questions about the offender.

6. Provide information about the sex offender subject to community notification as required by statute and policy in the agency's jurisdiction. This probably will include a general description (or photograph) of the offender, address at which the offender will reside, and the crime of conviction.

It is with these mechanisms in place that compliance of sex offenders can be optimized. This also can be effective in providing a sense of control and empowerment within the community; as members become more aware and proactive they then have a sense of control or influence over their community environment. Further, the legal parameters that citizens have in regard to offender supervision will be clarified, and this can generate productive results in citizen confidence and understanding of their own role in the partnership as well as that of the community supervision agency. It is in this manner that citizen involvement aids in ensuring that sex offenders comply with various intermediate sanctions that may have been imposed upon them, such as with community service requirements and/or requirements associated with house arrest.

Treatment Strategies for Sex Offenders

While most readers (particularly students of criminal justice) are aware that a variety of offenders may be given treatment they are not typically aware of how these treatment techniques are utilized. This last section is used to simply provide a brief overview of some of the techniques used in sex offender treatment. Specifically, the reader will be given a list of various methods of intervention that are used with the sex offending population to ensure a more direct understanding of how interventions are applied. Treatments may be categorized as follows: (1) cognitive behavioral therapy (CBT), (2) interrogation-oriented, and (3) drug administrative treatment.

Cognitive Behavioral Techniques

These treatments are geared toward reducing and/or eliminating the deviant sexual arousal. There are many techniques commonly used by clinicians, each with a different rationale to their use. These techniques are designed to teach impulse control, arousal reduction, and empathy.

The first cognitive behavioral technique, impulse control, utilizes three processes to alter behavior. These include **thought-stopping**, **thought-shifting**, and **impulse-charting**. The process of thought-stopping is used to disrupt a deviant-thinking pattern. The offender is given pictures of arousing images and is forced to stop his thoughts when the image is seen. The use of group confrontation, observation, and journaling assist in ensuring that this is accomplished (Knopp, 1989). The second process, thought-shifting, requires that the offender shift his thoughts to aversive imagery. The sex offender may be allowed to view or think about some arousing image but then is trained to think about something aversive, like an approaching police officer. Again, the use of group confrontation, observation, and journaling assist in ensuring that this is accomplished (Knopp, 1989). Finally, impulse-charting is a method used to track points and times when certain thoughts and or desires seem more intense. The time of day, location, and number of times per week are all important. The offender will usually also be required to report the level of intensity of the impulse (i.e., 1 to 10 scale), and this will be tracked through a journaling process with the therapist (Knopp, 1989).

The second cognitive behavioral technique, arousal reduction, includes five interventions: (1) **scheduled overmasturbation**, (2) **masturbatory reconditioning**, (3) **aversion therapy**, (4) **spouse monitoring**, and (5) **environmental manipulation**. The first intervention, scheduled overmasturbation, requires that the client routinely masturbate on a progressively more frequent schedule throughout the week. This is intended to reduce sexual drive and to make control easier for the offender. This exercise also teaches that the client does have some measure of control over his sexual arousal and use of sexual energy (Knopp, 1989). The second intervention, masturbatory reconditioning, involves having the client masturbate to an appropriate fantasy until he has an ejaculation (Knopp, 1989). The third intervention, aversion therapy, teaches offenders to associate unpleasant stimuli with presently desirable yet unacceptable behaviors (Van Voorhis, Braswell, & Lester, 2000). A wide range of physical or overt aversive stimuli has been used to treat sex offenders. Most notable are electric shock, foul odors and tastes, drugs that temporarily paralyze, and drugs that induce vomiting. Because of ethical and constitutional considerations, some of the more extreme forms of aversive stimuli are not used as frequently as they were some 20 to 30 years in the past. The fourth intervention, spouse monitoring, involves supervision on the part of the spouse (if and when available, though other family members may be able to assist) or significant other to complete a daily checklist on the offender's compliance with the treatment and to ensure that any therapeutic homework given to the client is being completed at the prescribed times in the week. This increases the overall supervision that the offender has (Knopp, 1989). The final arousal reduction intervention, environmental manipulation, assists the offender with removing himself out of high-risk situations away from potential victims. The offender should train himself to move out of the house, not the victim (Knopp, 1989).

The third and final technique used in CBT, empathy training, includes three approaches to recognizing the harm caused to the victim: (1) **victim counselors**, (2) **cognitive restructuring**, and (3) **role-playing**. The first approach involves inviting victim counselors to attend the group meeting. In fact, the victim may colead the group. Offenders may be required to visit a victim advocate center and, at their own expense, ask a victim counselor to explain their feelings on sex crimes. The second approach involves cognitive restructuring whereby the offender constructs scenes that cast him or significant others in the role of the victim. The client then focuses on typical rationalizations he uses to justify the assault (Knopp, 1989). Scenes are constructed where he utilizes and internalizes the rationalization. These scenes are then paired with aversive imagery. Lastly, alternate scenes are constructed where the offender catches himself in the distortion and counters with a reality-grounded message in which it is acknowledged that these actions do not end in the way that the offender hopes (Knopp, 1989). The final approach, role-playing, requires the offender to reenact their own crime scene(s) with another offender taking on the role of their victim. The remaining group offenders observe and later critique the role-play and allow for group processing of the effects on the victim.

Interrogation-Oriented Techniques

Interrogation-oriented techniques are designed to ensure that the offender is being honest in their feedback that they are providing program treatment staff. This is important since sex offenders are notorious for lying and manipulating. These tools assist the therapist and community supervision staff in determining whether progress is being made in the program. The two techniques typically used with ensuring compliance are polygraphs and the **penile plethysmograph (PPG)**. Most students should be familiar with the use of the polygraph technique. Just like the one used in law enforcement, this is the standard lie detector used to measure biological responses to deception. The polygraph is used in sex offender supervision for three primary reasons: (1) to break through offender denial of the offense, (2) to assess honesty in sexual history, and (3) to monitor offender's compliance with probation conditions (Hunt County CSCD, 2004). The PPG is a technique used to identify deviant sexual patterns. An electronic transducer is placed around the penis of the offender while he is being shown non-pornographic materials and given auditory stimuli. An electronic recorder then monitors the patterns of erection. The argument is successful completion of programming should be reflected in the pattern of response (Hunt County CSCD, 2004; Lester & Hurst, 2000).

Drug Administered Techniques

Chemical Castration: With **chemical castration**, sex offenders are injected with drugs (most commonly Depo-Provera) to reduce the amount of testosterone in the offender's body. This achieves the sex drive reduction of surgical castration but does not require the controversial surgery. Some side effects include fatigue, weight gain, loss of body hair, and depression. Sex offenders typically regard this as the least preferred intervention (Rice et al., 2002).

The use of these drugs has been found to generally work but only if the offender dutifully maintains their schedule of intake. Programs can monitor this by having the offender report to a clinic that works with the community supervision agency to receive their injection. Nonetheless, this drug will not be effective for all sex offenders. For instance, sadistic rapists and pedophiles are not necessarily motivated by sex alone. Rather, the infliction of pain is their primary source of arousal. Thus, this treatment would not be effective with this group of offenders.

✂ Substance Abusers

American culture promotes high consumption of legal and illegal drugs. This high rate of drug use factors into the rate of criminal behavior. To illustrate this fact, consider that in 1999 it was reported that at least 50% of adult male arrestees tested positive for at least one drug (Bartol, 2002). In fact, as much as 64% of all arrested adult males and 67% of all arrested adult females tested positive for the use of drugs (Bartol, 2002). It would appear that marijuana was the drug of choice among most male arrestees, with cocaine being the next highest choice. With arrested adult females, cocaine, marijuana, and methamphetamines were found to be the most common (Bartol, 2002). The use of multiple drugs was also common, with more than one quarter of the adult male arrestees testing positive for two or more drugs (Bartol, 2002).

Thus with respect to the connection of drug use and criminal activity, there are three broad commonalities that can be stated. First, drug abusers are more likely to commit crime than non-drug abusers. Second, many arrestees are under the influence while committing crimes. And third, drugs and violence tend to occur together in many reported violent incidents (Hanson, Venturelli, & Fleckenstein, 2002).

Other demographics on drug abusers are not always easy to determine. Of those that exist, most are based either on arrests or admissions into detox or treatment programs. One such variable is age. The age of the drug offender often shapes the dynamics of their drug abuse, including their drug of choice. For children under the age of 12, experimentation is found with those who are neglected, abused, or isolated, as well as those with undiagnosed

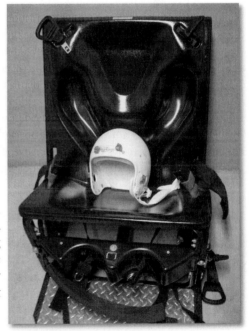

▲ **Photo 11.2**   This chair looks as if it might be used for punishment, but, in reality, it is used in some jails to safeguard a detainee from harming him- or herself. The risk of suicide for arrested offenders on drugs is high during the first 48 hours. Equipment such as this actually is intended to save the life of the offender.

behavioral or learning disorders (Myers & Salt, 2000). The abuse of inhalants and vapors from glues, paints, and solvents is of particular concern at this age (Myers & Salt, 2000). For adolescents, the individual risk factors of substance abuse are compounded by the confluence of developmental conflict and demands that occur during adolescence, as well as a number of other risk factors toward general delinquency that may covary with the substance abuse risk factors. For middle-aged and elderly drug offenders, issues surrounding loss of body image, friends and family, and other normal life span losses may be pertinent. Further, elderly offenders may not necessarily have drug abuse problems with illegal drugs but are more likely to have dependencies on prescription drugs that have resulted in usage levels that violate federal drug laws (Myers & Salt, 2000).

The gender of the drug offender is also an important consideration. When assessing female drug offenders, it is particularly important to explore relationships with significant others, support systems, and issues related to domestic abuse and prior childhood sexual abuse. Female drug abusers are prone to being involved with a male drug abusing spouse or boyfriend. Female drug offenders tend to stay with their addicted partners, and the most important reason for their use and increase in use is the intimate relationship to which they belong (Myers & Salt, 2000). This is a particularly relevant issue when one considers that female offenders tend to become involved in crime with a romantic partner who was typically the primary active criminal.

Considerable research demonstrates that some social, racial, and/or cultural groups have a **drug of choice** in their drug using habits. A drug of choice is a drug that is consistently used with greater frequency than other types of drugs by a certain identifiable demographic group. For instance, crack cocaine is typically considered a drug of choice among the urban poor African American underclass, whereas heroin is more often associated with Latino Americans. Perhaps equally intriguing is the fact that the majority of drug offenders using methamphetamine and/or Ecstasy tend to be white Americans who are most often of middle-class status (Hanson et al., 2002). Likewise, Latino American women are more likely than Latino American men to be shamed within their own cultures for substance abuse (Van Voorhis et al., 2000). Also, while African American males do not seem to differ from other ethnic groups in their symptoms of drug abuse, black males convicted of drug offenses as a group experienced the largest increase in incarceration rates during the 1980s (Van Voorhis et al., 2000).

Regardless of public concern over hard drugs, it is the use of alcohol that is the most problematic for society. In fact, alcohol is responsible for more deaths and violence than all of the other drugs combined (Bartol, 2002; Hanson et al., 2002). Roughly one third of all offenders who commit violent crime were drinking at the time of the offense, and many were highly intoxicated (Bartol, 2002). Despite the fact that alcohol is so debilitating, and the fact that alcohol is the most common drug to be associated with violent crime, there is still widespread cultural support for the continued social use of alcohol (Hanson et al., 2002). This makes the screening and assessment of such use all the more difficult.

Screening and Placement Criteria

Every form of treatment program involves some sort of screening. According to Myers and Salt (2000), screening serves two major purposes:

1. It attests to the presence of a condition that may go unrecognized if not detected.

2. It provides data to decide whether a client is appropriate for a specific treatment program or vice versa.

In the first use of screening, social, health, and criminal justice workers determine if there are sufficient grounds for referral of a client to a particular drug/alcohol treatment program. This screening is very important because the earlier that the intervention takes place, the better the prognosis for the client. Obviously, the likelihood of reforming a drug experimenter (as described previously) is much better than when treating a compulsive user. The second use of screening is to determine client appropriateness for a given treatment modality. It should be pointed out that the discretion in placement may not only consider the client's individual characteristics but it may also include the ability of a given agency to provide these services (i.e., fiscal constraints may be a factor despite the fact that the treatment program may be ideal for the client). In either case, it is this use of screening that provides the placement criteria for drug offenders in the criminal justice system.

Placement criteria are very important when processing drug offenders. The initial placement is important for both public safety and for treatment-oriented concerns. When deciding upon placement criteria, a match must be made between the severity of the addiction to the level of care needed, ranging from medical inpatient care, nonmedical inpatient care, and intensive outpatient care to outpatient care (Hanson et al., 2002). Further, matching the client's profile to a treatment modality is more likely to achieve lasting success translating to the enhanced evaluation of program effectiveness. For example, a client with attention-deficit/hyperactivity disorder might be unsuited for the regimentation of a therapeutic community (TC). Conversely, a person with low self-esteem, insecurities, and a fragile sense of self-worth would not be appropriate for a highly confrontational style of intervention.

Substance Abuse Treatment Programs

The primary modality of treatment implemented in most jails is chemical detoxification. Detoxification is designed for persons dependent on narcotic drugs (i.e., heroin, opium) and is typically found in inpatient settings with programs that last for 7 to 21 days. The rationale for using detoxification as a treatment approach is grounded in two basic principles (Hanson et al., 2002; McNeece, Springer, & Arnold, 2002; Myers & Salt, 2000). The first is a conception of "addiction" as drug craving accompanied by physical dependence that motivates continued usage, resulting in a tolerance to the drug's effects and a syndrome of identifiable physical and psychological symptoms when the drug is abruptly withdrawn. The second is that the negative aspects of the abstinence syndrome discourage many addicts from attempting withdrawal, which makes them more likely to continue using drugs. The main objective of chemical detoxification is the elimination of physiological dependence through a medically supervised procedure.

While many detoxification programs address only the addict's physical dependence, some provide individual or group counseling in an attempt to address the problems associated with drug abuse. Many detoxification programs use medical drugs to ease the process of overcoming the physical symptoms of dependence that make the detoxification process so painful for the addicted substance abuser. For drug offenders in jails or prisons, the mechanism of detoxification varies by the client's major drug of addiction. For opiate users, methadone or clonidine is preferred. For cocaine users, desipramine has been used to ease the withdrawal symptoms. Almost all narcotic addicts and many cocaine users have been in a chemical detoxification program at least once (Inciardi, 1999a). However, studies show that in the absence of supportive psychotherapeutic services and community follow-up care nearly all are certain to suffer from relapse (Ashford, Sales, & Reid, 2001).

In all detoxification programs, inmate success depends upon following established protocols for drug administration and withdrawal. In a recent assessment of research literature on the effectiveness of detoxification, there appear to be promising rates of program completion (McNeece et al., 2002). Yet many clinicians note that mere detoxification from a substance is not drug abuse "treatment" and does not help people stay off drugs. This in no way ensures that relapse will not occur; thus, it is important for any program to have much more than a simple detoxification process. In essence, detoxification should be viewed as an initial step, after the intake process, of a comprehensive treatment process. As you recall from Section VII, other alternatives for dealing with substance abusers include the use of the TC and drug courts.

Beyond the detoxification phase of "treatment," the residential TC is the next full service form of treatment provided to incarcerated substance abusers. The TC is a total treatment environment in which the primary clinical staff are typically former substance abusers—"recovering addicts"—who themselves were rehabilitated in TCs (Inciardi, 1999a; Myers & Salt, 2000). The treatment perspective of the TC is that drug abuse is a disorder of the whole person—that the problem is the person and not the drug, that addiction is a symptom and not the essence of the disorder. In this view of recovery, the primary goal is to change the negative patterns of behavior, thinking, and feeling that predispose a person to drug use. The overall goal is a responsible, drug-free lifestyle. Recovery through this form of treatment depends on positive and negative pressures to change. This pressure is brought about through a self-help process in which relationships of mutual responsibility are built. In addition to individual and group counseling, this process has a system of explicit rewards that reinforce the value of earned achievement. As such, privileges are earned. In addition, TCs have their own rules and regulations that guide the behavior of residents and the management of their facilities. Their purposes are to maintain the safety and health of the community and to train and teach residents through the use of discipline.

Social reactions to TCs have ranged from negative perceptions from the local community to highly supportive by various governmental programs. Many communities frown upon these types of treatment programs being within their locale due to the perceived threat that members pose and due to effects on local real estate value fluctuations. Despite this, some organizations have held that TCs hold an irrefutable value to society. For instance, the Ford Foundation Drug Abuse Survey Project has held TCs in high regard. Further, there are hundreds of treatment programs that mostly follow the TC model (Myers & Salt, 2000).

As you may recall from Section II, drug courts were established in response to the growing number of individuals processed through the court system, which resulted in prison overcrowding. This court was designed as a non-adversarial approach to integrating substance abuse treatment with criminal justice case processing. See Section II for a more in-depth discussion of these alternative placements.

Substance Abusers on Community Supervision

The main method of monitoring offenders who have been released to the community is probation. With regular probation, an offender lives at home and receives periodic monitoring. Many offenders with substance abuse problems are sentenced to intensive supervised probation (ISP), a more restrictive type of probation. ISP requires that the offender and probation officer keep in close contact, which generally includes random home visits to ensure compliance with the minimum criteria of the program.

In addition, drug offenders on probation may be required to submit to drug screens to ensure compliance with treatment. Court and corrections officials will generally want to know if the offender is complying with treatment and remaining abstinent from drug usage. In programs in which access to treatment may be limited by available space or funding, those who do not comply may be discharged from treatment. Those who do not successfully complete treatment and continue to have positive drug screens may be sent back to court for further sentencing. While drug testing does appear to serve a useful purpose in monitoring offenders with substance abuse problems, this testing alone is not sufficient to keep offenders from using drugs and reoffending. The best approach may be to combine random drug testing with forms of rehabilitative drug treatment to address the addiction and minimize the likelihood that the individual will engage in future criminal behavior.

Drug offenders on probation are placed in what are termed *outpatient treatment programs*, which usually include individual and group therapy, and some programs offer family therapy and relapse prevention support. An increasing number of drug-free outpatient treatment programs are including case management services as an adjunct to counseling. The basic case management approach is to assist clients in obtaining needed services in a timely and coordinated manner. The key components of the approach are assessing, planning, linking, monitoring, and advocating for clients within the existing nexus of treatment and social services.

Evaluating the effectiveness of drug-free outpatient treatment is difficult because programs vary widely from drop-in "talk" centers to highly structured arrangements that offer counseling or psychotherapy. Some likewise include a strong "faith-based" element to their intervention that represents a blend between therapy and religious instruction. A number of studies have found that outpatient treatment has been moderately successful in reducing daily drug use and criminal activity. However, the approach appears to be inappropriate for the most troubled and the antisocial users.

The number of rigorously designed studies of corrections-based outpatient programs is quite small. One of the few examples involves a relatively well-funded and designed program known as "Passages"—an 8-hour-per-day, 5-day-per-week, 12-week nonresidential program for women incarcerated in the Wisconsin correctional system. Although the treatment staff and correctional administrators agreed that the program improved clients' self-esteem, their subsequent reduced drug use and criminal activity was not reported (McNeece et al., 2002).

Self-Help Groups

Self-help groups, also known as 12-step programs, are composed of individuals who meet regularly to stabilize and facilitate their recovery from substance abuse. The best known is Alcoholics Anonymous (AA), in which sobriety is based on fellowship and adhering to the 12 steps of recovery (Hanson et al., 2002; Inciardi, 1999a; Myers & Salt, 2000). The 12 steps stress faith, confession of wrongdoing, and passivity in the hands of a "higher power." The steps move group members from a statement of powerlessness over drugs and alcohol to a resolution that they will carry the message of help to others and will practice the AA principles in all affairs. In addition to AA, other popular self-help 12-step groups are Narcotics Anonymous (NA), Cocaine Anonymous, and Drugs Anonymous (Hanson et al., 2002; Inciardi, 1999a; Myers & Salt, 2000). All these organizations operate as stand-alone fellowship programs but are also used as adjuncts to other modalities. Although few evaluation studies of self-help groups have been carried out, the weight of clinical and observational data suggest that they are crucial to recovery.

Research has failed to demonstrate that anonymous fellowship meetings by themselves are effective with heavy drug users. According to Inciardi (1999a), there are few known evaluations of prison-based self-help programs for a variety of reasons: Prison administrators tend to prefer other types of programs, the model contains variables that are extremely difficult to operationalize and measure, members and leaders often view scientific studies of their groups as intrusive threats to anonymity and therapeutic processes, and evaluation research funding is more often available for innovative programming than for such well-established services. Nonetheless, self-help programs are widely used in community correctional agencies.

There is a widely held belief that they work (Inciardi, 1999a). The meetings are organized and run by volunteers at no cost to the prison authorities, and the meetings appear to help inmates make the transition from correctional to community-based settings (Inciardi, 1999a).

The success of self-help programs in general, and AA in particular, may be explained by its comprehensive network, which supports abstinence and recovery; frequent attendance at AA meetings, where role modeling, confession, sharing, and giving support take place; and participation in the member network between meetings, including obtaining and relying on a senior member or sponsor. Al-Anon, a fellowship for relatives and significant others of alcoholics, was founded in 1951, although it did not take off as a movement until the 1960s. NA, the third of the three major 12-step fellowships, was founded in 1953. It was relatively small throughout the 1950s and 1960s but obtained a great deal of popularity during the 1970s and 1980s. The atmosphere of NA meetings is more emotional than is AA, and this is due to the fact than many members attended drug treatment programs that emphasize interpersonal interaction in group sessions (Myers & Salt, 2000).

Applied Theory Section 11.1

Individual Trait Criminological Theories and Criminal Activity

Cullen and Agnew noted that research has suggested that genetic factors and biological harms of a nongenetic nature, such as with head injuries, may increase the likelihood that individuals will develop traits that make them more prone to criminal activity. Among these are traits such as impulsivity and/or sensation seeking behaviors. David Rowe (2002) argued that physiological factors account for a substantial amount of criminal activity due to the effects of genetics and/or injury to various segments of the central nervous system.

In particular, Rowe has focused on the chemical messengers, called neurotransmitters, that exist within our nervous systems and transmit electronic signals between the billions of neurons in our brain. The neurotransmitters are many, but serotonin and dopamine are particularly important because they affect our mood, emotional stability, and because even slight changes in the amount of each in our bloodstream can lead to different levels of emotional response and/or behavior. Further, Rowe (2002) and others have examined critical hormones such as testosterone, which help to regulate various impulses such as our sex drive and reaction to stressors that are presented.

This research is not just important from a mental health perspective but it also ties in with many of the substance abuse issues presented in this section. Indeed, most illicit drugs impact our serotonin and dopamine levels of release. In fact, it is this release of neurotransmitters that actually gives persons their sense of high and/or release when using the substance. This provides direct reinforcement to the cerebral areas that are affected and many drug users experience additional social reinforcers due to social contact with other drug users and acceptance within that crowd.

Though it may seem far-fetched, there has been substantial research that has demonstrated a connection between nervous system functioning and criminal activity (Bartol, 2002). This is true for juvenile and adult offenders and is also true for nonviolent and violent offenders. Numerous cases exist where offenders were found to have various forms of imbalance in their neurochemistry. Andrea Yates, a female offender who drowned her own children during a serious bout of postpartum depression, might be one classic example. Others abound throughout the literature, particularly in regard to the study of the classic psychopath whose central nervous systems do not process anxiety-related impulses, making them less able to acquire empathy for their victims. Indeed, brain imaging with MRIs and PET scans have pinpointed specific biological deficits involved in criminal dispositions among a variety of offender typologies; these deficits appear to be in the frontal cortex area of the brain, an area that regulates higher order functioning.

Given the confluence between these physiological factors, mental illness, substance abuse, and criminal activity, the individual trait theories are important to consider. These theories are grounded in medical science and study specific physiological effects, producing results that are much more valid and reliable than survey-based research attributed to most social-based theories. In effect, these theories seem to point toward inherent risk factors that are possessed by the person before any social learning can take place. Naturally, these theories hold serious implications for society and also impact how we might assess offenders in the future.

◪ Mentally Ill Offenders

There are special challenges involved with addressing mental disorders within the offender population. Often the problems associated with mentally disordered offenders have less to do with their actual threat to society and more to do with the bizarre nature of their behavior. Most mentally ill do not commit crimes—especially when intent is considered. However, many mentally ill may act strange by public standards or may act in a manner that would be considered "irresponsible" from a common citizen's standpoint.

Bartol (2002) noted that the media has portrayed the mentally ill as not only criminal but outright violent. This is often the case on television and in newspapers. Most violent crime (particularly murder), however, is impulsive and committed by non–mentally disordered persons who are simply stressed to the point of using violence among their repertoire of behavioral responses.

Mental disorders are manifested in a variety of behaviors, ranging in severity from what many might refer to as "crazy behavior" to conduct that is simply unusual. Crazy behavior

▲ **Photo 11.3** This hospital once used a variety of case management and mental health interventions that would now be considered outdated. As research and evaluation continues, older facilities and outdated modes of intervention are refined and improved. A newer facility now exists not too far from this original site.

▲ **Photo 11.4**   Mental health interventions are becoming more frequent as community corrections is tasked with supervising mentally unstable offenders. The sign in this photo refers to a local mental health facility that routinely works with local courts and state facilities.

is that which is obviously strange and cannot be logically explained (Bartol, 2002). The concept of mental disorder includes behaviors that are bizarre, dramatic, harmful, or mildly unusual behaviors, and the classifications for individuals exhibiting these behaviors can be found in the *Diagnostic and Statistical Manual of Mental Disorders IV Text Revision (DSM-IV-TR).* For the purposes of this chapter, mental illness is defined as any diagnosed disorder contained within the *DSM-IV-TR,* as published by the American Psychiatric Association (2000). Mental illness causes severe disturbances in thought, emotions, and ability to cope with the demands of daily life. Mental illness, like physiological forms of illness, can be acute, chronic, or under control and in remission.

Common Types of Mental Disorders in the Criminal Justice System

Specific types of disorders have been found to be more problematic than others among the offending population. Among these are the **mood disorders, schizophrenic disorders,** and **personality disorders.** As a backdrop against these disorders is the reality that a large number of offenders also have addiction or substance abuse disorders that are comorbid with the primary diagnosis (Sacks, Sacks, & Stommel, 2003). This is commonly referred to as **dual diagnosis** within the treatment community, and this simply denotes the fact that the offender has two or more disorders. In most cases, when an offender is said to have a dual diagnosis, the clinician is referring to a primary disorder accompanied by a substance abuse-related disorder. The frequency of the dual diagnosis among the offending population is specifically the reason for the eventual development of mental health courts.

Mood disorders are those disorders such as **major depressive disorder,** bipolar disorder, and dysthymic disorder. Major depressive disorder is characterized by one or more major depressive episodes (i.e., at least 2 weeks of depressed mood or loss of interest accompanied by at least four additional symptoms of depression). Major depressive disorder is the most common mood disorder associated with the offender population. Bipolar disorder is characterized by one or more manic episodes, which is usually accompanied by major depressive episodes. The individual afflicted with bipolar disorder will have mood swings that go back-and-forth between manic and depressive states. Dysthymic disorder is characterized by at least 2 years of depressed mood for more days than not, accompanied by additional depressive symptoms that do not meet the criteria for a major depressive disorder.

According to the *DSM-IV-TR* (American Psychiatric Association, 2000), the degree of impairment associated with major depressive disorder varies, but even in mild cases, there must be either clinically significant distress or some interference in social, occupational, or other important areas of functioning. The afflicted person will likely have decreased energy, tiredness, and fatigue without physical exertion. Even the smallest tasks may seem to require substantial effort. Further, these individuals often have a sense of worthlessness or guilt that may include unrealistic negative evaluations of one's worth or guilty preoccupations or ruminations over minor past failings. Such individuals often misinterpret neutral or trivial day-to-day events as evidence of personal defects and have an exaggerated sense of responsibility for untoward events (American Psychiatric Association, 2000, p. 350). The National Institute of Mental Health (2002) noted that a person experiencing major depression is likely to have

- a persistent sad, anxious, or "empty" mood;
- feelings of hopelessness, pessimism;
- feelings of guilt, worthlessness, helplessness;
- loss of interest or pleasure in hobbies and activities that were once enjoyed, including sex;
- decreased energy, fatigue, being "slowed down";
- difficulty concentrating, remembering, making decisions;
- insomnia, early-morning awakening, or oversleeping;
- appetite and/or weight loss or overeating and weight gain;
- thoughts of death or suicide and/or suicide attempts;
- restlessness, irritability; and
- persistent physical symptoms that do not respond to treatment, such as headaches, digestive disorders, and chronic pain.

Among those persons with bipolar depression, manic symptoms will also typically occur, with a cycle between bouts of depressive symptoms and manic symptoms that occur back and forth. These manic symptoms are taken from the National Institute of Mental Health (2002) and are listed here:

- Abnormal or excessive elation
- Unusual irritability
- Decreased need for sleep
- Grandiose notions
- Increased talking
- Racing thoughts
- Increased sexual desire
- Markedly increased energy
- Poor judgment
- Inappropriate social behavior

Schizophrenic disorders, according to the *DSM-IV-TR* (American Psychiatric Association, 2000), have five characteristic symptoms, and at least two must be present before the diagnosis can be given to an individual. These symptoms are as follows: (1) delusions, (2) hallucinations, (3) disorganized speech, (4) grossly disorganized behavior, and (5) inappropriate affect. Further, the social, self-care, and/or occupational life of the individual must show signs of being well below the level achieved prior to the onset of the illness. Lastly, these symptoms must have existed for 6 months or longer.

Personality disorders are disorders that are characterized by an enduring pattern of inner experience and behavior that deviates markedly from the expectations of the individual's culture, is pervasive and inflexible, has an onset in adolescence or early adulthood, is stable over time, and leads to distress or impairment. The focus of this section will be on specific personality disorders that are most frequently seen as problematic within the offender population. The following list contains these disorders with the exception of ASPD. ASPD is so problematic and is encountered so frequently among the offender population that an entire section is devoted to this disorder and its link with violent actions by offenders so that the disorder can be given the full attention that it deserves.

Borderline personality disorder is a pervasive pattern of instability of interpersonal relationships, self-image, and affects, and marked impulsivity beginning by early adulthood and present in a variety of contexts as indicated by five (or more) of the following:

1. Frantic efforts to avoid real or imagined abandonment

2. A pattern of unstable and intense interpersonal relationships characterized by alternating between extremes of idealization and devaluation

3. A markedly and persistently unstable self-image or sense of self

4. Impulsivity in at least two areas that are potentially self-damaging (e.g., spending, sex, substance abuse, reckless driving, binge eating)

5. Recurrent suicidal behavior, gestures, or threats, or self-mutilating behavior

6. Affective instability due to a marked reactivity of mood

7. Chronic feelings of emptiness

8. Inappropriate, intense anger or difficulty controlling anger

9. Transient, stress-related paranoid ideation or severe dissociative symptoms

Histrionic personality disorder is a pervasive pattern of excessive emotionality and attention seeking, beginning by early adulthood and present in a variety of contexts, as indicated by five or more of the following:

1. Uncomfortable in situations in which he or she is not the center of attention

2. Interaction with others often characterized by inappropriate sexually seductive or provocative behavior

3. Display of rapidly shifting and shallow expression of emotions

4. Consistent use of physical appearance to draw attention to self

5. A style of speech that is excessively impressionistic and lacking in detail

6. A show of self-dramatization, theatricality, and exaggerated expression of emotion

7. Suggestible—that is, easily influenced by others or circumstances

8. A consideration of relationships to be more intimate than they actually are

Among the offending population, this disorder is seen among female offenders most frequently. This is not surprising because female offenders often engage in criminality while under the guidance or due to the influence of a male partner. Because of the codependent nature of their relationship and the often-noted low self-esteem found among female offenders, this disorder seems to develop from the need to have attention. Likewise, these offenders are easily suggestible. This works well for their male counterparts, such as drug runners using the female to carry drugs, the pimp involving the female offender into prostitution, or the male offender who implicates the female by asking for assistance or for help with alibis and other peripheral support.

Narcissistic personality disorder is a pervasive pattern of grandiosity (in fantasy or behavior), need for admiration, and lack of empathy, beginning by early adulthood and present in a variety of contexts, as indicated by five (or more) of the following:

1. Has a grandiose sense of self-importance (e.g., exaggerates achievements and talents or expects to be recognized as superior without commensurate achievements)

2. Is preoccupied with fantasies of unlimited success, power, brilliance, beauty, or ideal love

3. Believes that he or she is "special" and unique and can only be understood by, or should associate with, other special or high status persons or institutions

4. Requires excessive admiration

5. Has a sense of entitlement (i.e., unreasonable expectations of especially favorable treatment or automatic compliance with his or her expectations)

6. Is interpersonally exploitative (i.e., takes advantage of others to achieve his or her own ends)

7. Lacks empathy: unwilling to recognize or identify with the feelings and needs of others

8. Is often envious of others or believes that others are envious of him or her

9. Shows arrogant, haughty behaviors or attitudes

Prevalence rates within the clinical population range from 2% to 16%. Since most offenders are given a clinical screening and are more frequently diagnosed than the general population, the expectation is that the offender population will have higher percentages of this disorder. Possession of this disorder will result in a person who is likely to be tough-minded, glib, superficial, exploitative, and unempathetic. However, they are not likely to have characteristics of impulsivity, aggression, and/or deceit that is associated with ASPD individuals. The *DSM-IV-TR* (American Psychiatric Association, 2000) noted that vulnerability in self-esteem makes the disordered individual very sensitive to "injury" from any form of criticism or defeat. Such experiences may not be apparent outwardly, but they are likely to feel humiliated, degraded, hollow, and empty. Reactions may range from disdain to rage and to defiant counterattack. Violent offenders occasionally have this disorder and make note that their violence was sparked by a display of insult from the other party. Family violence batterers also have a tendency to have this disorder.

Anxiety and Stress-Related Disorders

Generalized anxiety disorder is characterized by excessive anxiety and worry (apprehensive expectation), occurring more days than not for at least 6 months, about a number of events or activities. The individual also must report that it is difficult to control the worry to the point that it causes clinically significant distress or impairment in social, occupational, or other areas of functioning. And the anxiety and worry are associated with three (or more) of the following six symptoms (with at least some symptoms present for more days than not for the past 6 months):

1. Restlessness or feeling keyed up or on edge

2. Being easily fatigued

3. Difficulty concentrating or mind going blank

4. Feeling irritable

5. Having muscle tension

6. Difficulty falling or staying asleep, or restless unsatisfying sleep

A number of offenders may have this disorder, though it may be difficult to determine because many of them will have objectively sound reasons for their anxiety. The hallmark of this disorder is when the individual worries when there is no specific reason for this worry. This is not necessarily a common disorder among offenders but for those who have particularly difficult backgrounds (i.e., abuse) or for those who had difficulty adjusting to their experiences within the criminal justice system. This disorder is most prevalent in female offenders because the disorder is more prevalent among females in the general population. In addition, this disorder tends to coexist with mood disorders and/or with addiction disorders. Often, the addiction disorder may be a direct attempt to medicate the sense of anxiety.

Antisocial Personality Disorder, Psychopathy, and Other Mentally Disordered Offenders

The offender with ASPD is the offender who is of most concern to the criminal justice system and to the public at large. This is the offender who is likely to be violently dangerous and is likely to be a recidivist. It is this group of offenders who make it hard to plead mercy and leniency for other offenders with other forms of mental disorder. The essential feature of ASPD is a pervasive pattern of disregard for, and violation of, the rights of others that begins in childhood or early adolescence and continues into adulthood. Diagnosis with this disorder occurs if the individual has three (or more) of the following symptoms:

1. Failure to conform to social norms with respect to lawful behaviors as indicated by repeatedly performing acts that are grounds for arrest

2. Deceitfulness, as indicated by repeated lying, use of aliases, or conning others for personal profit or pleasure

3. Impulsivity or failure to plan ahead

4. Irritability and aggressiveness, as indicated by repeated physical fights or assaults

5. Reckless disregard for safety of self or others

6. Consistent irresponsibility, as indicated by repeated failure to sustain consistent work behavior or honor financial obligations

7. Lack of remorse, as indicated by being indifferent to or rationalizing having hurt, mistreated, or stolen from another

Additional symptoms, as outlined in the *DSM-IV-TR* (American Psychiatric Association, 2000), include stealing, fighting, truancy, and resisting authority that are typical childhood symptoms. Those with ASPD lack empathy and tend to be callous, cynical, and contemptuous of the feelings, rights, and sufferings of others (Bartol, 2002). Furthermore, those with ASPD frequently engage in precocious and aggressive sexual behavior, excessive drinking, and the use of illicit drugs. These individuals also seem to lack the ability to maintain lasting and meaningful relationships with family, friends, or intimate partners.

For the most part, those with ASPD rarely become independent and responsible adults. They spend much of their lives in some form of institutional setting or dependent on family members. It should be noted that this disorder is much more prevalent in males versus females with base rates in the community being roughly 3% for males and 1% for females (Gacono, Nieberding, Owen, Rubel, & Bodholdt, 2001). However, it is estimated that up to 30% of all males in secure correctional facilities suffer from ASPD, with it being progressively found as the level of institutional security increases (Gacono et al., 2001).

Mentally Ill Offenders in the Community

Long-term inpatient or hospitalization of the mentally disordered has largely ceased to occur. As a result, the mentally disordered individual has become more prevalent within society. This trend from hospitalization to community release was first set in motion in 1959 when nearly 559,000 mentally ill patients who were housed in state mental hospitals were progressively released over time due to a shift to "deinstitutionalize" mentally ill persons (National Institute of Corrections, 2004). By the late 1990s, the total number of persons housed in public psychiatric hospitals dropped to approximately 70,000. This is despite the fact that the U.S. population (and the mentally ill population as well) has grown considerably since 1959. Thus, more people are mentally ill, but fewer and fewer of them are placed in secure facilities. Rather, these individuals are returned to the community. Some mentally ill persons experience difficulty adjusting to life in the community and, as a result, may come into increasing contact with the criminal justice system.

More specific to the court process is the issue of trial and sentencing. Jurisdictions utilizing either mental health courts or their own hybrid system should ensure that certain factors are taken into account within the court system (see Section II for a discussion of mental health courts). Specifically, judges and other parties involved in the court process should be cognizant of the effects that mental illness can have on a person's behavior, particularly when criminal behavior is at issue. Such an understanding should go beyond merely determining competency to stand trial. Instead other factors should be considered as well, such as training for the defense bar on mental health issues. Also, the mentally ill should be given access to defense counsel adept in working with those with mental health disorders, judges should have access to mental health records of the accused in order to determine competence to stand trial, and state criminal codes should permit judges to divert nonviolent offenders from incarceration into the appropriate treatment facilities (The Sentencing Project, 2002, p. 19).

Services for mentally ill probationers can be most effective when they are provided through special programs staffed by officers with specialized training and experience (The Sentencing Project, 2002). For probation services to be successful with the mentally ill, they must address the broad range of offenders' needs and work in collaboration with other agencies and services to ensure that these needs are met. Specifically, community service agencies should do the following:

1. Increase access to mental health professionals.

2. Provide specialized cross-training to parole and probation officers pertaining to characteristics of mental illness, the effects that these illnesses have on daily functioning, and the goals of treatment programs. Also, core functions of the therapeutic process such as crisis intervention, screening, counseling, discharge planning and community follow-up in case management are very helpful.

3. Fully understand the requirements of confidentiality statutes and mental health law.

4. Ensure increased communication between community supervision and other provider agencies. This should result in a collaborative effort between the therapist/treatment facilitator and the client's probation officer. Each should know each other on a "first name" basis.

5. Provide training for culturally competent community corrections services.

6. Ensure that caseloads for individual probation officers are reasonable.

The last recommendation is critical since this is one of the primary complaints for individual probation officers. Lurigio (1996) noted that probation officers struggling with large caseloads were likely to avoid mentally disordered probationers because of their problematic or bizarre behavior. Further, officers often do not feel equipped to address the problems associated with emotional instability. Because of this, specialization among probation and parole officers is becoming a common strategy for handling probationers and parolees with particular needs or elevated risk for continued criminality (Lurigio, 1996).

⬛ Mentally Retarded Offenders

Defining mental retardation has been something of a controversial issue. However, the definition provided by the American Association on Mental Retardation (AAMR) is the definition of choice among the courts of America. According to this definition, "mental retardation refers to significantly subaverage general intellectual functioning existing concurrently with deficits in adaptive behavior and manifested during the developmental period."

Usually, to be considered mentally retarded the individual must have an IQ of less than 70. Further, the person must also demonstrate impairments in adaptive behavior as well. These impairments may come in many forms such as slow overall emotional maturation, poor personal responsibility, or low social skills that are below that normally expected of a person their age. Third, the individual must have the disorder during their formative years, typically well before the age of 18.

Generally speaking, it is estimated that mental retardation has a prevalence of 3% in society with roughly 89% having mild retardation. Similar percentages have been found to exist in the correctional population as well. Offenders with severe or profound retardation are often either unlikely to commit crime or they are diverted in the early stages of processing through the criminal justice system.

It is often difficult to identify mildly retarded offenders since their handicap is not especially pronounced so as to be easily identified. This is further compounded among the offender population when one considers that the offender population tends to have intellectual scores (IQ) that are slightly lower than the majority of the nonoffending population (much of this is due to lower socioeconomics and lack of education among the majority of the lower income offending population within the correctional system).

Moderately retarded offenders are more easily identifiable. Their deficits usually manifest in early childhood periods and exhibit some delayed muscular–motor development. These persons can usually learn to take care of themselves and can do simple tasks. However, they often have difficulty with more complex tasks. They can usually progress to the 3rd or 4th grades of academic ability. These offenders do require fairly extensive training for community living and often need some form of structured employment setting.

Offenders with severe retardation often show marked delays in motor development early in life and are extremely hindered from functioning independently. These offenders need constant supervision to just function and communicate. These individuals often need constant nursing care and often have other existing physical and/or mental impairments beyond their mental retardation. These individuals need extensive training for the simplest of basic skills. Because of this, they are seldom kept in the institutional or community correctional systems. Offenders with this level of impairment are extremely rare.

It is important to provide a clear distinction between mental retardation and mental illness. In technical terms, mental illness is a disease, whether temporary, periodic, or chronic. Mental retardation, on the other hand, is a developmental disability and therefore not considered a disease. A person suffering from mental illness may recover; however, the state of mental retardation is a permanent characteristic that will limit the individual's ability to learn indefinitely.

Distinguishing between the two impairments is further confounded when one considers that these two handicaps are not necessarily exclusive of one another. There are offenders in the correctional system who are dually diagnosed. This "dual diagnosis" means that the offender may have both a mental illness and they may also be mentally retarded. These offenders, for instance, may have mild retardation and may also suffer from some form of personality, mood, or adjustment disorder (see Section II for further information on types of disorders). These offenders do not often receive the specialized services they need due to the plethora of needs that they may have and the difficulty in providing the needed services for this severely challenged group of offenders.

Mentally Retarded Offenders in the Community

The vast majority of offenders with mental retardation can be managed in the community supported by the social, probation, and specialist psychiatric services. Many continue to live with their families while attending local programs, but some require an out-of-home placement either because they need more structure and support or because of disruptive family relationships.

The same principles of treatment and care apply in the community corrections setting as in the institution system. The key to success often has more to do with effective interagency coordination within the community. Obviously, probation personnel and any peripheral treatment personnel must be well versed on the needs of these types of offenders. One successful community-based program is the Special Offenders Service in Lancaster County, Pennsylvania (Day & Berney, 2001). This program provides services to both juvenile and adult offenders suffering from mental retardation. This program emphasizes personal responsibility and accountability, increasing self-esteem and improving social competence. The team sees clients at first on a daily basis then later on a weekly basis for counseling services and other forms of support. This program is intensive and includes work orientation, social skills training, time management, and, where appropriate, involvement of the family. This program is considered highly successful since it has a recidivism rate of only 5% as compared with the national average of 60% with this type of offender (Day & Berney, 2001; Wood & White, 1992).

✄ Conclusion

In this section, we have examined various types of sex offenses and their typologies. The method of perpetration is important as this can tell us a great deal about the offender and their motivation. We also noted important distinctions and characteristics between those offenders who choose adults as their victims and those who choose children. Research shows that sex offenders have a higher recidivism rate when compared to other types of offenders, but this rate of recidivism has not been determined to be high enough to preclude their ultimate release into the community. Some sex offenders (those with sadistic sexual disorders and/or psychopathic characteristics) are perhaps untreatable, and it is recommended that they be incarcerated indefinitely. Lastly, methods of supervision in the community need to be collaborative in nature to ensure compliance from these offenders.

Substance abuse offenders require numerous special services if the addiction is to be successfully overcome. Regardless of personal or professional viewpoints on treatment efficacy, it is clear that alcohol and drugs are strongly correlated with other criminal behavior. This correlation is so common that it could well be argued that substance abuse offenders are in fact not a "special" needs offender but that they are instead a "common" needs offender. Thus, any program that overlooks drugs or alcohol is overlooking a primary component behind most offender's repertoire of behaviors. Substance abuse programs have been shown to work among both court-mandated and voluntary clients.

Regarding mentally ill offenders it should be clear they are somewhat misunderstood by the general public, particularly when the effects of the media on public perception are considered. For the most part, offenders who are mentally ill simply have either bizarre behaviors (if they have some form of psychosis) or they have extremes in mood or personality development. Though this is the case, a select group of offenders with ASPD do pose an elevated risk to society and they are particularly resistant to treatment. With all mentally ill offenders the dual diagnosis of substance abuse exacerbates the illness, and it is this duality in diagnoses that creates the truly dangerous mentally ill offender.

The ability to distinguish between those mentally ill offenders who are violent and dangerous and those who are simple nuisances and non-dangerous is critical, both for public safety and when planning methods of intervention within the institution and the community. Various jurisdictions around the country are becoming more aware of this need within the criminal justice and mental health systems and are thus re-tailoring various criminal justice responses to better address the specialized needs of the mentally ill offender. It becomes clear that these offenders have a multiplicity of problems and that a one size fits all approach to mental illness is not appropriate for treatment or effective for public safety.

Similar to mentally ill offenders, mentally retarded offenders are often misportrayed in the public media. There are definitely cases in which the mentally retarded have committed terrible crimes, but these are isolated and tend to receive a disproportionate amount of media attention. For the most part, the mentally retarded should be considered treatable and should also be given some form of intervention within the community since they are so susceptible to victimization within a prison facility. Placement and intervention should be conducted by qualified professionals.

⊠ Section Summary

- Specialized and problematic offenders often suffer from symptoms, disorders, and illness not commonly or fully understood by most employees of community corrections. This section of the text focused specifically on four categories of offenders: (1) adult sex offenders, (2) substance abusers, (3) the mentally ill, and (4) the mentally retarded.
- Sex offender typologies have been created for adult victims. More specifically, six broad categories of rapist have been identified: (1) power reassurance, (2) sexual gratification, (3) opportunistic, (4) power assertive, (5) anger retaliation, and (6) sadistic.
- The act of pedophilia defines the typology of a sex offender when the victim is a child.
- The containment approach is one effort to supervise sex offenders in the community. This multimodal approach calls for three designated officers to work with and supervise the offender in the community. These individuals include the CSO, the sex offender therapist, and the polygraph examiner.
- Sex offender notification laws have been created as a mechanism to notify the public when a person convicted as being a sex offender resides in their community.
- Cognitive behavioral techniques, interrogation-oriented, and drug administrative treatments have successfully been used to supervise and treat sex offenders in the community.
- The majority of all persons arrested test positive for some form of drug or narcotic. This growing population generates great concern in the field for supervision and reductions in recidivism.
- Much effort has been given to screening and appropriately placing offenders in treatment programs or detoxification centers. One response has been the use of TCs and self-help groups.
- A significant portion of individuals convicted of crimes have mental health disorders. Common disorders include the following: mood disorders, depression, schizophrenia, personality disorders, and anxiety disorders. Each of these requires a specific diagnostic technique and consideration for placement.
- The handling of individuals diagnosed as mentally retarded is of a growing concern as well. These offenders present a different set of challenges particularly for group settings and treatment.

KEY TERMS

Anger retaliation rapist

Antisocial personality disorder (ASPD)

Aversion therapy

Borderline personality disorder

Chemical castration

Cognitive restructuring

Community supervision officer (CSO)

Containment approach

Detoxification

Drug of choice

Dual diagnosis

Environmental manipulation

Generalized anxiety disorder

Histrionic personality disorder

Impulse-charting

Major depressive disorder

Masturbatory reconditioning

Mental illness

Mental retardation

Mood disorders

Narcissistic personality disorder

Opportunistic rapist

Pedophilia

Penile plethysmograph (PPG)

Personality disorders

Polygraph

Polygraph examiner

Power assertive rapist

Power reassurance rapist

Role-playing

Sadistic rapist

Scheduled overmasturbation

Schizophrenic disorders

Self-help groups

Sex offender therapist

Sexual assault

Sexual gratification rapist

Spouse monitoring

Thought-shifting

Thought-stopping

Victim counselors

DISCUSSION QUESTIONS

1. What are the different types of adult sex offenders?

2. What are the various methods of supervision for sex offenders as well as common treatment techniques?

3. How do substance abusers differ from other offenders?

4. What is meant by the concept of co-occurring disorders?

5. Identify and discuss different types of treatment programs for substance abusers.

6. Why is it important to understand the issues presented with the mentally ill offender? How might a community officer deal with offenders with varying disorders?

7. Identify different types of mental illness common to the offender population.

8. What are the various classifications of mental retardation? How might a community-based officer deal differently with these offenders?

WEB RESOURCES

American Psychological Association:
http://www.apa.org/

National Institutes of Health:
http://www.nih.gov/

National Institute of Mental Health Juvenile Sex Offender Protocol Manual:
http://www.csom.org/pubs/JSOAP.pdf

National Center on Sexual Behavior of Youth:
http://www.ncsby.org/pages/Assessment.htm

Please refer to the student study site for web resources and additional resources.

READING

In this study, Warner and Kramer examined the impact of drug treatment programs on offenders who were originally targeted for incarceration. This study further explores whether rates of recidivism differ by types of traditional sentencing including state incarceration, county jail, and probation (p. 93). The comparison sample was drawn from offenders sentenced 1 year prior to the start of the RIP/D&A program who would have been eligible for participation had the program been available. A total of 3,290 cases (1,552 treatment cases and 1,738 comparison cases) were reviewed during a 36-month follow-up period measured at the 12-, 24-, and 36-month time periods. The researchers used rearrest as their outcome variable. Using a Cox proportional hazards model, the findings revealed that those who completed the RIP/D&A program had a 61% lower risk for rearrest than traditionally sentenced offenders (p. 98). When compared with those sentenced to a traditional penalty, those who were sentenced to the RIP/D&A program but did not complete were more likely to fail than all other groups. However, when comparing these groups to those incarcerated in state facilities both completers and failures in the RIP/D&A were at a higher risk for rearrest than those serving time in a state facility at all time intervals. When compared to local jails and probationers (separately), those completing the RIP/D&A program had lower rearrest rates, but there were no differences for noncompleters and both the probation and the jail populations. The researchers provided three plausible explanations for these findings.

Closing the Revolving Door?

Substance Abuse Treatment as an Alternative to Traditional Sentencing for Drug-Dependent Offenders

Tara D. Warner and John H. Kramer

By the mid-1970s, the rehabilitative ideal of sentencing had come under attack. Research such as that reviewed by Robert Martinson (1974) in his article on treatment effects led to the conclusion that "nothing works," contributing to rehabilitation losing credibility as a guiding principle of sentencing. The retributive model moved to the forefront as the focus of sentencing, and determinate models were proposed to enhance fairness, resulting in harsher sanctions (Tonry & Lynch, 1996). This move was most strongly reflected in the passage of mandatory minimums, the prime target of which were drug offenders, who in turn contributed disproportionately to prison population increases (Tonry, 1995).

In the early 1990s, research such as the Arrestee Drug Abuse Monitoring Program (ADAM) and the

AUTHORS' NOTE: This project was supported by Pennsylvania Commission on Crime and Delinquency (PCCD) Subgrant 2003-DS-19–14576. Points of view or opinions within this document are those of the authors and do not necessarily represent any official position, policy, or view of PCCD.

SOURCE: Warner, Tara D., & Kramer, John H. (2009). Closing the revolving door? Substance abuse treatment as an alternative traditional sentencing for drug-dependent offenders. *Criminal Justice and Behavior, 36*(1), 89–109. Copyright © 2009 Sage Publications. Published on behalf of the American Association for Correctional and Forensic Psychologists.

Drug Use Forecasting Program (DUF) showed that a large proportion of offenders were drug users (Martin, Maxwell, White, & Zhang, 2004). In response to these data, prison overcrowding, and repeat offending, criminal justice researchers debated the effectiveness of incarceration as a deterrent, especially among drug-dependent offenders, who were perceived by the justice system as repeat offenders driven by addiction and/or unable to remain in treatment (Kassebaum & Okamoto, 2001; Longshore et al., 2001; Spohn, Piper, Martin, & Frenzel, 2001). Scholars argued that incarceration was ineffective for drug-dependent offenders because it did not address the specific needs of these offenders, namely, the social and psychological correlates of drug addiction (Broome, Knight, Knight, Hiller, & Simpson, 1997; Senjo & Leip, 2001; Wormith & Oliver, 2002). When research emerged indicating that substance abuse treatment was in fact effective at reducing drug use and drug-related crimes—challenging the claim that "nothing works" and reviving rehabilitation (Cullen, 2005)—state policy makers sought to revise their sentencing guidelines to provide a more effective means of sanctioning drug-dependent offenders. Rehabilitation was resuscitated in many ways, one of which was the development of intermediate punishments (Tonry, 1998). This study evaluates the effectiveness of an intermediate punishment in Pennsylvania at reducing recidivism among drug-dependent offenders.

Intermediate Punishments in Pennsylvania

Pennsylvania was among the first states to modify its sentencing guidelines to incorporate intermediate punishments as an alternative to incarceration, in an effort to address prison overcrowding by rehabilitating drug-dependent offenders. Act 193 of 1990, the Intermediate Punishment Act, created a postconviction alternative to incarceration for eligible offenders. It was incorporated into the state's guidelines during the 1994 revisions and further expanded during the 1997 revisions. Restrictive Intermediate Punishment (RIP) programs were required to house offenders full- or part-time, or significantly restrict their movement and monitor their compliance with the program(s) (Dupont-Morales & Sims,

2001). Through this narrowly defined concept, these sanctions were both considerably more severe than traditional probation and relatively equivalent to incarceration. Examples of RIP sanctions include drug and alcohol treatment, house arrest with electronic monitoring, or boot camps. These sanctions provide for sufficient surveillance and offender accountability.

The development of restrictive intermediate punishments provided an avenue for dealing with drug-dependent offenders, who were contributing to the growing prison populations in Pennsylvania (Kramer, Williams, & Williamson, 2006). Drug- and/or alcohol-dependent offenders are considered for a substance abuse treatment-based restrictive intermediate punishment (hereafter referred to as RIP/D&A) in lieu of incarceration, which is the focus of the current analysis. Eligible offenses are nonviolent offenses within Levels 3 and 4 of the Pennsylvania Commission on Sentencing's Guideline Matrix (Kramer & Ulmer, 2002). Ineligible offenses are violent offenses including, but not limited to, homicide, aggravated assault, kidnapping, rape or sexual assault, robbery, and arson. Offenders eligible for substance abuse treatment-based RIP/D&A undergo diagnostic assessment by qualified personnel (e.g., from the Pennsylvania Department of Health's Bureau of Drug and Alcohol Programs) to assess their drug dependence (Dupont-Morales & Sims, 2001). At this time, an initial recommendation is made regarding level of care needed. The levels of care include outpatient, halfway house, short-term residential/detox, and long-term residential. Requests for evaluation of an offender's RIP/D&A eligibility can be made by the district attorney's office, the Probation Department, or the court. RIP/D&A is not limited to *drug offenders*. Nonviolent Level 3 and 4 offenders are eligible if they are determined to be *drug dependent*.

Evaluating Treatment for Drug-Dependent Offenders

Over the past 15 years, the criminal courts have recognized that the sentencing of drug-abusing offenders merges a criminal issue (drug offending) with a public health issue (drug addiction); however, this poses a difficult dilemma for the courts. The movement to connect drug treatment to sentencing has been explicitly set in some jurisdictions through the establishment of drug courts, whereas in other jurisdictions it has been developed as a sentencing option, either as a condition of probation or as an intermediate punishment. Regardless of their organization, these approaches rely on the coercive nature of the court to place and keep the offender in drug treatment. The foundation for the use of drug treatment in sentencing is the idea that traditional sentencing is a revolving door for drug-dependent offenders because, inasmuch as it does not treat the addiction, these offenders will continue to commit crimes to support their drug use, and/or their likelihood of committing other crimes is increased (Longshore et al., 2001; Lurigio, 2000). The premise of the drug treatment model is that addiction is a multiple relapse disease (Senjo & Leip, 2001), and treating and punishing a relapse as a new offense undermines the rehabilitative component of drug treatment sentences. Therefore, treatment facilities are able to adjust offender's treatment plans as needed (e.g., after a relapse), and the court is able to sanction offenders when necessary (e.g., after failure to comply with treatment or new arrests).

This study evaluates drug treatment effects on offenders targeted for incarceration who were diverted to a drug treatment alternative to incarceration by the court. As noted above, drug treatment sentences rely on the coercive power of the court to keep the offender in treatment longer. This raises an important question about the effectiveness of *coerced* treatment. Historically it was often argued that if an offender did not volunteer for treatment, the treatment was unlikely to be successful. However, research has challenged this argument. Farabee, Prendergast, and Anglin (1998) reviewed the effectiveness of coerced treatment for drug-abusing offenders and concluded that the findings were somewhat mixed but supportive of the effectiveness of coercive measures at increasing the likelihood of offenders remaining in treatment. Baird and Frankel (2001) reached a similar conclusion based on their evaluation of two residential drug treatment programs; this study was limited to clients referred to treatment from two coercive environments, either county jail or state prison.

It is important to examine whether these sentencing alternatives are effective in achieving both their rehabilitative goals (eliminating drug use, increasing

legitimate opportunities, encouraging prosocial behavior, etc.) and their criminal justice goals (decreasing the risk of recidivism). A variety of methodologies has been used to evaluate the effectiveness of treatment interventions for drug-dependent offenders. The three most common approaches involve (a) comparing offenders randomly assigned into treatment and comparison groups, (b) comparing program participants to eligible offenders sentenced prior to program implementation, and (c) comparing program participants to nonparticipants who select out of the study (e.g., refuse treatment) or are not selected for the treatment program.

Although the sentencing of offenders into RIP/D&A does not take place in drug courts, those specialized courts display many of the same characteristics of the RIP/D&A program, and as such the abundant literature on drug courts provides helpful guidance when evaluating similar programs (see Rodriguez & Webb, 2004; Senjo & Leip, 2001; Wenzel, Longshore, Turner, & Ridgely, 2001; Wilson, Mitchell, & Mackenzie, 2006; Wolfe, Guydish, & Termondt, 2002). For example, offenders diagnosed as drug dependent are threatened with incarceration or drug treatment, the type of treatment is linked to the assessment of the severity of the addiction, and relapses are not perceived and punished as new offenses. The major difference between RIP/D&A and drug courts is the active oversight that drug court judges give to the offender, including monthly appearances before the judge.

A majority of the studies on drug court outcomes compare those who enter drug court to those who do not. Although the most methodologically rigorous, few studies have been able to use random assignment (Lum & Yang, 2005). Among those few are Gottfredson, Najaka, and Kearley (2003) and Turner, Petersilia, and Deschenes (1992). In their well-known evaluation of the Baltimore Drug Treatment Court, Gottfredson et al., found that treatment participants were significantly less likely to be rearrested than control group participants (66.2% vs. 81.3%) and had significantly fewer rearrests (1.6 vs. 2.3) than the control group. Less promising results were found by Turner et al. in their study of drug-involved offenders randomly assigned to an intensive supervision probation/parole program (ISP). ISP participants had more technical violations but did not differ on rearrests from offenders sentenced to traditional probation or parole.

When random assignment is not possible, using offenders sentenced prior to the drug treatment program implementation as a comparison sample may be the most appropriate method, because it limits the selection bias that could be present when comparing program participants to nonparticipants (Harrell, Mitchell, Hirst, Marlowe, & Merrill, 2002; Ulmer & Van Asten, 2002; Wolfe et al., 2002). In their evaluation of the Breaking the Cycle pretrial monitoring program, Harrell and colleagues (2002) compared treatment participants to those who would have been eligible for the program but were sentenced before its implementation. In a sample of 245 program participants and 137 comparison offenders, the average number of rearrests for treatment participants was substantially lower than that of comparison offenders, but this effect was for Whites only. Spohn et al. (2001) compared 285 drug court participants to two comparison samples: 194 traditionally sentenced offenders and 232 participants in a diversion program who were sentenced prior to the drug court's implementation. The likelihood of arrest was lowest among drug court participants, highest among diversion program participants.

Other studies comparing participants to eligible offenders sentenced prior to program implementation have found that participation in treatment was not significantly associated with a lower likelihood of rearrest (Ulmer & Van Asten, 2002). However, Wolfe and colleagues (2002) found that among program participants only, the rearrest rate for graduates was 19% compared to 53% for nongraduates; being female and older decreased the likelihood of rearrest. In a previous evaluation of Pennsylvania's RIP/D&A program, Ulmer and Van Asten (2002) compared recidivism rates for all offenders sentenced to RIP/D&A in 1998 to a stratified random sample of RIP/D&A eligible offenders sentenced in 1996 before the program was available. They did not find a significant effect of RIP/D&A on recidivism, as measured by likelihood of rearrest and reconviction. However, they noted that the higher odds of rearrest among RIP/D&A participants may not represent a failure of the program but may, instead, represent addiction as a multiple relapse disease (Dynia & Sung, 2000; Harrison, 2001; Kassebaum & Okamoto, 2001; Senjo & Leip, 2001).

Many evaluations of drug treatment programs compare participants to nonparticipants. Some studies using this method of evaluation have found that treatment participants were less likely to be rearrested than nonparticipants and that length of time in treatment was a strong predictor of success in avoiding rearrest (Anglin, Longshore, & Turner, 1999; Dynia & Sung, 2000). Dynia and Sung (2000) studied the effectiveness of the Drug Treatment Alternative-to-Prison program (DTAP), where 184 offenders arrested for felony drug sales facing mandatory imprisonment were diverted into therapeutic communities for 15 to 24 months. Although they narrowed the treatment sample to drug offenders, the current RIP/D&A study parallels this evaluation because it diverted *felony, prison-bound* offenders to drug treatment. However, the current study differs from Dynia and Sung's because their comparison samples (those who opted into treatment but failed to complete treatment, $n = 88$; and those who rejected the treatment offer, $n = 215$) were developed through self-selection. At 3 years, the *completers* had a rearrest rate of 23%, whereas the *nonparticipants'* and *failures'* rearrest rates were 47% and 52%, respectively. Another similar study is Hepburn's (2005) evaluation in Maricopa County, Arizona, which compared eligible drug offenders diverted into treatment to offenders who failed the treatment program or refused treatment. Results indicated that offenders who completed treatment did better than those who failed, and both of these groups did better than those who refused treatment.

It appears that drug treatment as a sentencing alternative may be effective, but the findings are clouded by the various methodologies used to evaluate such programs. Although prior research on the effectiveness of drug treatment is encouraging, the methodological weaknesses prevent strong conclusions about the effectiveness of drug treatment. From a rehabilitative standpoint, one is hopeful about such programs, but it is clear that advancements in methodology, sample sizes, comparison groups, and controls are needed to further develop the findings of previous research.

The Current Study

The current study expands on a previous analysis of Pennsylvania's RIP/D&A program (Ulmer & Van Asten,

2002) by including additional years of the program and a new comparison sample. Based on the findings of previous evaluations of sentencing alternatives, and to expand on previous literature, the current study proposed the following research questions: (a) Is the RIP/D&A program effective at reducing the risk of rearrest among participants, compared to traditionally sentenced offenders? and (b) Do the effects of RIP/D&A on the risk of rearrest vary across the different types of traditional sentencing: state incarceration, county jail, and probation?

▧ Method

Participants

We evaluated the effectiveness of RIP/D&A on reducing recidivism by comparing all offenders sentenced to RIP/D&A to a sample of comparable offenders sentenced 1 year prior to the program's implementation. We used Cox proportional hazards models to compare the risk of rearrest between these two groups at 12, 24, and 36 months postrelease during a 36-month follow-up period. The RIP/D&A treatment sample consisted of all offenders sentenced to RIP/D&A between 1998 and 2001 as identified in the offender database maintained by the Pennsylvania Commission on Sentencing (PCS). This sample was drawn from the first 12 counties to receive funding for drug and alcohol treatment services: Allegheny, Philadelphia, Centre, Berks, Lycoming, Cumberland, Lehigh, Tioga, Schuylkill, Westmoreland, Montgomery, and Delaware. Although the 1994 Pennsylvania sentencing guideline revision introduced RIP/D&A, the program did not receive state funding supporting full implementation until fiscal year 1997. It would not be beneficial to collect data on the 1st year of implementation, because any effects observed may actually be the result of the new program, but not necessarily the treatment. Although the PCS database was our primary sampling method, once data collection began, treatment facilities provided participant names and information not contained in the database; therefore, an additional snowball sample of offenders sentenced to RIP/D&A between 1998 and 2001 was also obtained.[1]

The comparison group consisted of a simple random sample of offenders from the 1997 PCS database,

sentenced in one of the 12 counties originally funded for RIP/D&A.[2] Based on their offense gravity score (OGS, a measure of offense severity) and prior record score (PRS), these offenders would have been eligible for RIP/D&A had the program been available at that time. Instead, they were sentenced to state incarceration, county jail, or probation.[3] RIP/D&A is available and intended for drug-dependent offenders but not drug offenders exclusively; therefore, because the RIP/D&A population contained various offense types, we did not believe it appropriate to limit the comparison sample to drug offenders. These 1997 offenders were chosen as the comparison group instead of offenders not sentenced to RIP/D&A between 1998 and 2001, because those not chosen for RIP/D&A may differ from those chosen for RIP/D&A in important ways and are therefore subject to selection bias (Ulmer & Van Asten, 2004).

All data for offenders in the comparison sample were obtained from the PCS database. Information on RIP/D&A cases was obtained from the PCS database (for 1998 and 1999 cases) and from County Clerk of Courts records (for 2000 and 2001 cases).[4] Additional data on treatment history and detailed demographic characteristics (e.g., education, marital status, drug dependence) were obtained from treatment facilities for all RIP/D&A cases (not used in the current analyses). RIP/D&A offenders missing an OGS (6.85%) and PRS (7.32%) were excluded from analyses, as we were unable to ascertain RIP/D&A eligibility for these cases (because this is based on OGS and PRS). To assess not only the effectiveness of sentencing to RIP/D&A ("dosage effects") but also the effect of successful program completion, RIP/D&A offenders missing program discharge status were excluded from analyses (4.70%). Results of ancillary analyses including these cases did not differ substantively from the current analyses excluding them. Cases missing rearrest information because their rap sheets could not be identified were also excluded from this analysis (6.75%). RIP/D&A and comparison group cases from Delaware County (6.26%) were removed from all analyses due to excessive missing information. These percentages were not cumulative, and resulted in an overall 13.31% case loss, after which 3,290 cases remained; 1,552 treatment cases and 1,738 comparison cases (221 state incarcerated offenders, 892 county jail offenders, and 625 probationers).

Measures

Dependent Variable: Rearrest

Rearrest information was obtained from criminal history rap sheets maintained by the Pennsylvania State Police. Rearrests were coded as any arrest occurring after the sampled sentence date, that being the date at which that person was sentenced to RIP/D&A or probation or was released from state incarceration or county jail. Listwan, Sundt, Holsinger, and Latessa (2003) have argued that rearrest may be a more accurate measure of recidivism than reconviction, because it is temporally closer to the crime and less subject to the discretions within court processing.

Independent Variables

RIP/D&A treatment. Information on the alcohol and drug treatment sentence for RIP/D&A offenders was obtained from the case files maintained by each treatment facility. If the person successfully completed all requirements of his or her RIP/D&A sentence, that person "graduated" from RIP/D&A, was labeled a successful completion, and the file was closed. Participants were labeled "unsuccessful" if they were discharged from a treatment facility prior to completion, left against medical advice, or were discharged after being rearrested.

Basic offender characteristics. Demographic information obtained from the PCS database and County Clerk of Courts offices included age, race/ethnicity, gender, and county of processing. Age of the offender was measured as age at the time of the sampled offense. Race/ethnicity was coded as two dummy variables for Black and Hispanic, with White as the reference category. County was coded with a series of dummies for Montgomery; Allegheny; Lehigh; Berks; and "Other Rural," as Centre, Lycoming, Cumberland, Tioga, Schuylkill, and Westmoreland Counties were combined due to small sample sizes (to allow for meaningful comparisons). Philadelphia County was the reference category.

Offense characteristics. OGS for these offenders ranged from 1 to 8, increasing with the severity of the offense. PRS, based on the type and number of prior convictions, ranged from 0 to 6. Offenders missing offense type (14.29%) were assigned to drug offense, because these cases were all part of the RIP/D&A sample. We controlled for this assumption in the analyses with a dummy variable for missingness. Supplemental analyses did not reveal any substantive differences when we relaxed this assumption and retained the missing cases with a dummy variable alone. We obtained the number of prior arrests and number of prior convictions from the criminal history rap sheets of each offender, maintained by the Pennsylvania State Police; these were used to describe the sample but were not used in the multivariate analyses, due to their collinearity with PRS.

Analyses

We evaluated the overall effectiveness of RIP/D&A by comparing all offenders sentenced to RIP/D&A drug and alcohol treatment between 1998 and 2001 to the comparison sample of offenders sentenced to state incarceration, county jail, or probation in 1997, who would have been eligible for RIP/D&A had the program been available at that time. We used Cox proportional hazards models to test for significant differences in risk of rearrest between these "treatment" and "no-treatment" conditions and across each specific type of traditional sentencing at the 12-, 24-, and 36-month follow-up points.

Cox proportional hazards models are especially appropriate for modeling recidivism, because the risk of recidivating depends on the amount of time an offender has been out of jail or incarceration. Using logistic regression to predict whether an offender recidivates assumes that a rearrest on the 1st day of release from treatment or incarceration is the same as a rearrest on the last day of the follow-up period (Banks & Gottfredson, 2003). It does not control for differential exposure time between offenders. Because various methodologies were needed to calculate exposure time across the RIP/D&A and comparison groups, a discussion of these calculations is warranted.

Exposure time, or "street time," represents the length of time offenders were at risk of offending because they were not incapacitated by incarceration.[5] Exposure time was calculated at three points during the 36-month follow-up period to test for differences in risk of rearrest between groups: 12 months postrelease, 24 months postrelease, and 36 months postrelease. Offenders not rearrested by the 36-month end of the follow-up period were right-censored, that is, coded as not rearrested, and their exposure time was set to 36 months. For offenders in RIP/D&A and those sentenced to probation, exposure time was calculated as the date of the first rearrest minus their sentence date. For offenders who were not rearrested, exposure time was calculated as the date their rap sheet was requested from the State Police minus their sentence date.

The measure of exposure time for state incarcerated offenders controlled for time incarcerated due to parole violations. A parole violation was not considered a failure because it was not a rearrest for a new offense. Therefore, exposure time for state incarcerated offenders was the sum of exposure times between any time served for parole violations. For offenders not rearrested, exposure time was calculated as the date their rap sheet was requested minus their release date, censored at 36 months. Exposure time for offenders in county jail was the date of rearrest minus release date or, for offenders not rearrested, the date their rapsheet was requested minus their release date.

Release dates were estimated for state incarcerated and county jail offenders when this information could not be found (66 state incarcerated and 386 county jail offenders). Among our county jail sample, actual time served did not differ significantly from the estimated time served based on the incarceration minimum; therefore, release dates were estimated using the minimum sentence. Release dates were predicted for state incarcerated offenders using the amount of time between arrest date and sentence date, incarceration minimum, incarceration maximum, OGS, and PRS. Because of the possible inaccuracies of these calculations, the findings for the state incarcerated and county jail samples should be interpreted with caution.

Cox proportional hazards models do not control for this exposure time, per se, but these models explicitly incorporate differential exposure times into the calculation of risks, so that as the risk set changes (i.e., some offenders are rearrested), the model adjusts the risks to reflect that fact. That is, once an offender is rearrested, he or she is censored and no longer in the analyses. This provides a more accurate prediction of risk of rearrest because the estimation uses only the characteristics of the population still at risk (Allison, 1995; Banks & Gottfredson, 2003).

We could not model *time to rearrest* in the current analysis because exposure time was based on release dates that were estimated for some offenders in the state incarcerated county jail samples. It would be inappropriate to model time as the dependent variable here because it was imputed for some offenders. In a Cox proportional hazard model, time is not the dependent variable; instead, the dependent variable is the log odds of rearrest, *adjusted* for time. These models allow us to understand differences between groups in terms of the risk of rearrest, not the timing of rearrest.

⬧ Results

Sample Descriptives

Approximately 16% of the RIP/D&A sample was female. Similarly, 17% of the probation sample was female. This is not surprising—it can be expected that females are more likely than males to be sentenced more leniently, rather than be sentenced to jail or prison. Black offenders make up more than 50% of each of the four groups. The RIP/D&A sample consists primarily of drug offenders, even after accounting for offenders coded as drug offenders due to missing information. The majority of RIP/D&A participants were sentenced to short-term or long-term residential treatment. Slightly less than half of the treatment participants (46%) successfully completed their program. Not surprisingly, successful treatment completion was more likely among offenders sentenced to outpatient treatment or halfway houses, with approximately 60% of these offenders successfully completing, compared to approximately 42% of residential treatment patients (not shown).

Mean exposure time varies across groups from approximately 22 to 28 months. The percentage of offenders rearrested by the end of the 36-month follow-up was highest among county jail offenders (58%), followed by probationers (56%), and RIP/D&A treatment participants (53%), with the lowest percentage among state incarcerated offenders (39%). Chi-square analyses indicated that the percentage rearrested at 12, 24, and 36 months were significantly different between the RIP/D&A and comparison group ($p < .10$ at 36 months, data not shown).

Multivariate Analyses

We used Cox proportional hazards regression to evaluate the effectiveness of RIP/D&A at reducing the risk of rearrest, compared to traditionally sentenced offenders at 12, 24, and 36 months postrelease. According to the bivariate model, at 12 months offenders sentenced to RIP/D&A had a risk of rearrest approximately 20% lower than traditionally sentenced offenders. This percentage is obtained by subtracting one from the hazard ratio and multiplying by 100 ([{0.802 − 1} = −0.198] × 100 = −20%). The negative percentage indicates that risk is lower among the RIP/D&A sample than the comparison sample.

Approximately 46.9% of the RIP/D&A sample successfully completed their treatment sentence. When we controlled for this, those who did not complete RIP/D&A had a risk of rearrest 19% *higher* than traditionally sentenced offenders ([1.189 − 1] × 100 = 19%).

Offenders who successfully completed RIP/D&A had a 61% *lower* risk of rearrest than traditionally sentenced offenders. To interpret combined effects (i.e., sentencing to RIP/D&A and successful completion), hazard ratios must be multiplied ([{1.189 × 0.328} − 1] × 100 = −61%). These results suggest that merely being sentenced to RIP/D&A may not be effective at reducing the risk of rearrest, but successfully completing the program leads to a much lower risk of rearrest. Even after controlling for the offender, offense, and county characteristics that can be expected to influence the risk of rearrest (Model 3), offenders who successfully completed treatment were almost 50% less likely to be rearrested. These findings were consistent at 24 and 36 months postrelease, where offenders successfully completing RIP/D&A were 35% and 30% less likely to be

arrested than those traditionally sentenced, respectfully. Female offenders were less likely to recidivate than males, and Black offenders were more likely to recidivate than White offenders. Furthermore, recidivism declined with age, such that for every year older, the risk of rearrest at 36 months declined by 2.5%.

Because the RIP/D&A program is aimed at diverting offenders from state incarceration, county jail, and probation, it is both helpful and necessary to compare RIP/D&A to each type of traditional sentence. The state incarceration, county jail, and probation samples represent diverse sentencing decisions. For example, state incarcerated offenders were less likely to be female, or White, and more likely to be Hispanic and have higher OGS scores. We compared the RIP/D&A sample to each of these samples separately, while controlling for the characteristics that make these groups different.

State Incarceration

RIP/D&A was compared to state incarcerated offenders at 12, 24, and 36 months. The models comparing RIP/D&A to traditional sentencing in general show that offenders who did not successfully complete RIP/D&A were more likely to be rearrested, but offenders successfully completing RIP/D&A had a much lower risk of rearrest compared to traditionally sentenced offenders. However, the results were quite different when RIP/D&A sentenced offenders were compared to state incarcerated offenders. According to the bivariate model (Model 1), at 12 months RIP/D&A participants had a 61% higher risk of rearrest than state incarcerated offenders. When controlling only for successful discharge (Model 2), offenders who did not complete RIP/D&A had a risk of rearrest 141% *higher* than state incarcerated offenders. Offenders who successfully completed RIP/D&A had a 22% lower risk of rearrest at 12 months than state incarcerated offenders.

After controlling for offender, offense, and county characteristics (Model 3), we found that offenders who successfully completed RIP/D&A had a risk of rearrest approximately 5% higher than state incarcerated offenders (those not completing RIP/D&A had a rearrest risk 214% higher). As in the previous models, older and female offenders had a lower risk of rearrest, and offenders in all counties had a lower risk of rearrest than offenders in Philadelphia County. Hispanic offenders had a lower risk of rearrest than White offenders at 12 and 36 months, although this was significant at the .10 level. PRS was positively associated with risk of rearrest, as was being convicted of a personal offense, compared to a property offense. These results were consistent at 24 and 36 months postrelease. At 24 months, successful RIP/D&A completers had a 42% higher risk of rearrest than state incarcerated offenders; at 36 months, their risk of rearrest was 39% higher.

It appears that successful RIP/D&A participants were more likely to be rearrested than state incarcerated offenders 12 months postrelease; however, they had a much higher likelihood of rearrest 24 and 36 months postrelease. State incarcerated offenders in our sample may have engaged in treatment programs while incarcerated, and because program completion is often a factor in release, the low rearrest may reflect the effectiveness of prison treatment programs.

County Jail

When comparing RIP/D&A to county jail sentenced offenders at 12 months, the bivariate model (Model 1) indicated that offenders sentenced to RIP/D&A had a 25% lower risk of rearrest than offenders sentenced to county jail. After controlling for successful discharge (Model 2), unsuccessful RIP/D&A participants did not differ from county jail offenders; however, those successfully completing RIP/D&A had a risk of rearrest that was 64% lower than offenders sentenced to county jail. Their risk of rearrest remained lower (54%) after controlling for offender, offense, and county characteristics at 12 months (Model 3). At 24 months postrelease, RIP/D&A successful completers had a 44% lower risk of rearrest, and their risk of rearrest was 40% lower than county jail offenders at 36 months postrelease (after controlling for offender, offense, and county characteristics). On the other hand, offenders who did not complete RIP/D&A had a higher risk of rearrest than county jail offenders at 24 and 36 months (after controlling for offender, offense, and county characteristics).

Again, age and female gender were negatively associated with risk of rearrest at all time points during follow-up. Blacks had a slightly higher risk of rearrest than White offenders (significant at $p < .10$). Interestingly, OGS was slightly negatively associated with risk of rearrest, as were drug and personal offenders, compared to property offenders. Finally, offenders sentenced in Philadelphia County were significantly more likely to recidivate than offenders sentenced in all other counties, except Allegheny County. The relatively poor performance of offenders released from jail may reflect the lack of treatment programs in county jails, which are often insufficiently funded for such programs.

Probation

A probation sentence is a departure below the guideline recommendation, implying that although the offender's OGS and PRS make him or her eligible for state incarceration or county jail, the court believed this was too severe, or unnecessary, to adequately sanction the offender.[6] As a result of this departure, one may expect that probationers should be the most successful at avoiding rearrest, assuming some validity in the court's decision to reduce their sentence. At 12 months postrelease, unsuccessful RIP/D&A participants did not differ significantly from offenders sentenced to probation in terms of risk of rearrest (Model 2), but those who successfully completed treatment had a 64% lower risk of rearrest. After controlling for offender, offense, and county characteristics, we found that successful completers had a 56% lower risk of rearrest than probationers and unsuccessful RIP/D&A participants had a 31% higher risk of rearrest than probationers. These results were maintained at 24 and 36 months. Consistent with the previous models, older and female offenders were less likely to be rearrested. Blacks were slightly more likely to be rearrested than White offenders, although this was significant only at $p < .10$ at 24 and 36 months. Parallel to the findings of the comparison to county jail, OGS was negatively associated with rearrest. In the models comparing RIP/D&A to probation, PRS was positively associated with rearrest at 24 and 36 months. There were no significant differences in risk of rearrest by offense type.

Offenders in all other counties had a much lower risk of rearrest than offenders in Philadelphia County.

Discussion

Drug addiction is a critical issue facing our criminal justice system. The link between drugs and crime has driven policy makers in the criminal justice system to attempt to cope with this through mandatory minimums, treatment sentencing alternatives, and numerous intervention programs. Although each of these may have slowed some drug use, they have certainly not solved the drug abuse problem. This study focused on the effectiveness of community-based treatment programs for drug-dependent offenders. Of particular importance for this public policy is that the RIP/D&A program targets midlevel or more serious offenders (for whom the guidelines prescribe incarceration) than are typically targeted for drug treatment diversion programs and drug court programs. The RIP/D&A program views traditional incarceration as a revolving door for substance-using offenders and recognizes addiction as a correlate for crime.

To evaluate the effectiveness of RIP/D&A, we compared offenders sentenced to the program to a simple random sample of comparable offenders sentenced to state incarceration, county jail, or probation. This comparison sample was selected from the year prior to the RIP/D&A program's availability. Offenders sentenced to RIP/D&A had a risk of rearrest lower than traditionally sentenced offenders at 12 months, without controlling for offender, offense, and county characteristics, as well as discharge status. Once discharge status was controlled for, however, RIP/D&A was effective at reducing the risk of rearrest, but only for participants who successfully completed the program. Offenders successfully completing RIP/D&A had a risk of rearrest 49% lower than traditionally sentenced offenders at 12 months, 35% lower at 24 months, and 30% lower at 36 months, controlling for offender, offense, and county characteristics. Noteworthy is the finding that drug offenders had a lower risk of rearrest than property offenders. Although this finding may represent treatment success at curbing drug addiction

and motivation, it may also be that property offenses usually involve a victim; they are more visible, more likely to be reported, and more likely to be traced back to the offender than are drug offenses.

Examining each type of sentencing provides a fuller picture of the effects of RIP/D&A compared to "business as usual." For example, compared to traditionally sentenced offenders in general, unsuccessful RIP/D&A participants had a risk of rearrest approximately 51% higher (net of offender, offense, and county effects) 12 months postrelease. However, when compared to state incarcerated offenders, unsuccessful RIP/D&A participants did much worse, with a risk of rearrest 214% higher. Successful completers were only slightly more likely to be rearrested than state incarcerated offenders at 12 months. This distinction is lost in the analyses pooled across the three types of traditional sentences. State incarcerated offenders had a much lower risk of rearrest than RIP/D&A participants within the first 12 months after release.

There are several plausible explanations for the low risk of rearrest among the state incarcerated offenders. First, it is possible, but not likely, that we have a sample of low-risk offenders who responded positively to state prison by changing their criminal patterns. The severity of their offense may have gotten them sentenced to state incarceration, but their PRS indicates offenders who are unlikely to reoffend. Second, we are sure that some of our state incarcerated offenders received drug treatment while incarcerated, or participated in a therapeutic community. Unfortunately, the Pennsylvania Department of Corrections did not maintain that information on offenders in our 1997 sample, and consequently we were unable to determine if offenders had received any type of treatment while incarcerated. Last, recidivism that is measured by rearrest for state incarcerated offenders who are under state parole supervision once released is likely an underestimate of recidivism. Many offenders under state parole who commit a new offense are sanctioned as technical parole violators rather than rearrested for a new charge (Bucklen, 2005). Although we were able to adjust the exposure time for offenders reincarcerated for parole violations, we were not able to check whether these violations included a new offense.

Compared to county jail and probation sentenced offenders, RIP/D&A sentenced offenders fared better. Offenders who successfully completed RIP/D&A had a risk of rearrest 54% lower at 12 months, decreasing to 40% lower at 36 months, compared to county jail offenders (and net of offender, offense, and county effects). The results are similar when we compare successful completers to probationers. However, offenders who did not complete RIP/D&A had rearrest risks that were higher than offenders sentenced to county jail or probation.

Limitations

Although this study illustrates the possible benefits of RIP/D&A at reducing rearrest, some limitations should be noted. Although the comparison sample was identified based on eligibility for RIP/D&A, we do not know the proportion of offenders within this sample who were in fact drug dependent. Additionally, readers should be cautious about recidivism measures based on administrative data, which measure rearrest but may not accurately capture offending behavior (e.g., as might be captured in self-report or drug-testing data). Also, because we collected data from administrative records and treatment facility case files, we encountered much missing data. Our analysis controlled for missing data, but the potential for bias remains because of differences between the counties in terms of recordkeeping. This speaks to the need for consistent, centralized recordkeeping to best evaluate program effectiveness.

Finally, a major assumption in our analysis is that the quality of treatment is equal within each treatment type, treatment facility, and across all counties. Yet this and other program characteristics likely vary across these categories, further suggested by the differences in RIP/D&A effects across counties. Future analyses of RIP/D&A and other similar programs would benefit from evaluating treatment levels of care separately, and possibly within counties, to identify and control for some of these differences in delivery. Additionally, given the differences between RIP/D&A completers and noncompleters, an analysis of the factors associated with successfully completing RIP/D&A is warranted.

Notwithstanding these limitations, overall, we find that RIP/D&A is successful for offenders who complete the program. One may be tempted to attribute the relationship between successful program completion and lower risks of rearrest to a simple selection effect: Offenders who are motivated to succeed will both successfully complete the RIP/D&A program and successfully avoid rearrest, independent of any real effect of the program. Whereas motivation is related to treatment success (Brocato & Wagner, 2008), we have no measure of offender motivation, so we cannot assume that all successful RIP/D&A completers were motivated upon entering the program. Also, if these findings were due simply to selection effects, we would expect those individuals who did not complete RIP/D&A to be no different from traditionally sentenced offenders. However, we can see that unsuccessful RIP/D&A participants had a higher risk of rearrest than state incarcerated, county jail, and probation offenders.

We should examine the effectiveness of the program at reducing the likelihood of rearrest, independent of offender motivation. We do this by controlling for the characteristics that likely affected the judge's decision to sentence to RIP/D&A and the offender's ability to avoid rearrest: race, age, gender, offense type and severity, prior record, and county of processing. A primary goal of any treatment program should be to treat the untreatable; motivating the unmotivated offender to commit to and successfully complete the program is the key to the success of the program and the offender.

✎ Notes

1. The majority of these cases (215, 13.85% of the drug and alcohol treatment based Restrictive Intermediate Punishment [RIP/D&A] sample) were from Philadelphia County, which frequently does not submit sentencing forms to the Pennsylvania Commission on Sentencing (PCS), resulting in severe underreporting of the use of RIP sentences. There were no additional differences between these cases and the cases reported to the PCS beyond the characteristics controlled for in the multivariate analyses.

2. Because funding for RIP/D&A was not available until September of 1997, the comparison group is limited to offenders sentenced prior to this date.

3. All presumptive guideline recommendations were for sentencing to either a county or state facility. Probation sentences

reflect departures below the sentencing guidelines, meaning, based on the offender's offense gravity score (OGS) and prior record score (PRS), the prescribed sentence should have been state incarceration or county jail, but because of some potential mitigating circumstance, probation was sentenced.

4. Data collection preceded completion of the 2000 and 2001 PCS databases; offense information for these cases had to be obtained directly from the respective County Clerk of Courts.

5. Although RIP/D&A offenders in inpatient treatment are confined, supervision is much lighter than for those incarcerated in county jails or state prison; therefore, the time in inpatient treatment is counted as "street time."

6. The reason for departing below the guidelines was missing from the majority of probation cases; however, "plea agreement" was reported for 13.7% of the cases.

◪ References

Allison, P. D. (1995). *Survival analysis using the SAS system: A practical guide.* Cary, NC: SAS Institute.

Anglin, M. D., Longshore, D., & Turner, S. (1999). Treatment alternatives to street crime: An evaluation of five programs. *Criminal Justice and Behavior, 26,* 168–195.

Baird, F. X., & Frankel, A. J. (2001). The efficacy of coerced treatment for offenders: An evaluation of two residential forensic drug and alcohol treatment programs. *Journal of Offender Rehabilitation, 34,* 61–80.

Banks, D., & Gottfredson, D. (2003). The effects of drug treatment and supervision on time to rearrest among drug treatment court participants. *Journal of Drug Issues, 33,* 385–412.

Brocato, J., & Wagner, E. F. (2008). Predictors of retention in an alternative-to-prison substance abuse treatment program. *Criminal Justice and Behavior, 35,* 99–119.

Broome, K., Knight, D. K., Knight, K., Hiller, M., & Simpson, D. D. (1997). Peer, family and motivational influences on drug treatment process and recidivism for probationers. *Journal of Clinical Psychology, 53,* 387–397.

Bucklen, K. B. (2005). The Pennsylvania Department of Correction's Parole Violator Study (Phase 1). *Research in Review, 8,* 1–17.

Cullen, F. T. (2005). The twelve people who saved rehabilitation: How the science of criminology made a difference. *Criminology, 43,* 1–42.

Dupont-Morales, T., & Sims, B. (2001). *Assessment of county restrictive intermediate punishment programming.* Harrisburg: Pennsylvania Commission on Crime and Delinquency.

Dynia, P., & Sung, H. E. (2000). The safety and effectiveness of diverting felony drug offenders to residential treatment as measured by recidivism. *Criminal Justice Policy Review, 11,* 299–311.

Farabee, D., Prendergast, M., & Anglin, M. D. (1998). The effectiveness of coerced treatment for drug-abusing offenders. *Federal Probation, 62,* 3–10.

Gottfredson, D., Najaka, S., & Kearley, B. (2003). Effectiveness of drug treatment courts: Evidence from a randomized trial. *Criminology, 2,* 171–196.

Harrell, A., Mitchell, O., Hirst, A., Marlowe, D., & Merrill, J. (2002). Breaking the cycle of drugs and crime: Findings from the Birmingham BTC demonstration. *Criminology, 1,* 189–216.

Harrison, L. (2001). The revolving prison door for drug-involved offenders: Challenges and opportunities. *Crime & Delinquency, 47,* 462–485.

Hepburn, J. R. (2005). Recidivism among drug offenders following exposure to treatment. *Criminal Justice Policy Review, 16,* 463–481.

Kassebaum, G., & Okamoto, D. (2001). The drug court as a sentencing model. *Journal of Contemporary Criminal Justice, 17,* 89–104.

Kramer, J. H., & Ulmer, J. T. (2002). Downward departures for serious violent offenders: Local court "corrections" to Pennsylvania's sentencing guidelines. *Criminology, 40,* 897–932.

Kramer, J. H., Williams, T. D., & Williamson, C. (2006). *Evaluation of RIP/D&A treatment: Final report* (Subgrant No. 2003-DS-19-14576). State College: Pennsylvania Commission on Sentencing, Pennsylvania Commission on Crime and Delinquency.

Listwan, S. J., Sundt, J., Holsinger, A., & Latessa, E. (2003). The effect of drug court programming on recidivism: The Cincinnati experience. *Crime & Delinquency, 49,* 389–411.

Longshore, D., Turner, S., Wenzel, S., Morral, A., Harrell, A., McBride, D., et al. (2001). Drug courts: A conceptual frame work. *Journal of Drug Issues, 31,* 7–26.

Lum, C., & Yang, S. (2005). Why do evaluation researchers in crime and justice choose non-experimental methods? *Journal of Experimental Criminology, 1,* 191–213.

Lurigio, A. J. (2000). Drug treatment availability and effectiveness: Studies of the general and criminal justice populations. *Criminal Justice and Behavior, 27,* 495–528.

Martin, S., Maxwell, C., White, H., & Zhang, Y. (2004). Trends in alcohol use, cocaine use, and crime: 1989–1998. *Journal of Drug Issues, 34,* 333–359.

Martinson, R. (1974). What works? Questions and answers about prison reform. *The Public Interest, 35,* 22–54.

Rodriguez, N., & Webb, V. J. (2004). Multiple measures of juvenile drug court effectiveness: Results of a quasi-experimental design. *Crime & Delinquency, 50,* 292–314.

Senjo, S., & Leip, L. (2001). Testing and developing theory in drug court: A four-part logit model to predict program completion. *Criminal Justice Policy Review, 12,* 66–87.

Spohn, C., Piper, R. K., Martin, T., & Frenzel, E. D. (2001). Drug courts and recidivism: The results of an evaluation using two comparison groups and multiple indicators of recidivism. *Journal of Drug Issues, 31,* 149–176.

Tonry, M. (1995). *Race, crime, and punishment in America.* Oxford, UK: Oxford University Press.

Tonry, M. (1998). Intermediate sanctions in sentencing guidelines. *Crime and Justice, 23,* 199–253.

Tonry, M., & Lynch, M. (1996). Intermediate sanctions. *Crime and Justice, 20,* 99–144.

Turner, S., Petersilia, J., & Deschenes, E. (1992). Evaluating intensive supervision probation/parole (ISP) for drug offenders. *Crime & Delinquency, 38,* 539–556.

Ulmer, J. T., & Van Asten, C. (2002). *Restrictive intermediate punishments and recidivism in Pennsylvania.* State College: Pennsylvania Commission on Sentencing.

Ulmer, J. T, & Van Asten, C. (2004). Restrictive intermediate punishment and recidivism in Pennsylvania. *Federal Sentencing Reporter, 16,* 182–187.

Wenzel, S. L., Longshore, D., Turner, S., & Ridgely, M. S. (2001). Drug courts: A bridge between criminal justice and health services. *Journal of Criminal Justice, 29,* 241–253.

Wilson, D. B., Mitchell, O., & Mackenzie, D. L. (2006). A systematic review of drug court effects on recidivism. *Journal of Experimental Criminology, 2,* 459–487.

Wolfe, E., Guydish, J., & Termondt, J. (2002). A drug court outcome evaluation comparing arrests in a two-year follow-up period. *Journal of Drug Issues, 32,* 1155–1172.

Wormith, J. S., & Oliver, M. (2002). Offender treatment and attrition and its relationship with risk, responsivity, and recidivism. *Criminal Justice and Behavior, 29,* 447–471.

DISCUSSION QUESTIONS

1. Based upon the findings of this study, what might account for the differences in rearrest between those confined to a state institution versus those participating in the RIP/D&A program?

2. What policy implications might be derived from these findings?

3. As a sentencing judge or court administration, what are the benefits of this type of a program? What are the potential cons?

4. Using your local community or state, does a program such as the one described in this study exist? If so, how is that program administered? If not, would this program be a viable alternative given the current court structure?

5. How might a program such as the RIP/D&A program address the issue of limited resources in any given community?

READING

In this study, Willis and Grace sought to explore the planning mechanisms for release of child molesters into their communities post incarceration. Using a retrospective design, the researchers examined the post-release planning process for 30 recidivists and 30 non-recidivists. The sample was drawn from males who completed a 32- or 12-week prison-based program between 1994 and 2000 (p. 496). This program is voluntary. Participants are assigned a reentry coordinator to assist with the transition from prison into the community. Of particular interest to these researchers were the mechanisms in planning that either mitigated or exacerbated recidivism post-incarceration. A variety of static and dynamic factors were used to predict success or failure once released. Measures of both static and dynamic variables were created. These included factors

SOURCE: Willis, Gwenda M. & Grace, Randolph C. (2009). Assessment of community reintegrative planning for sex offenders: Poor planning predicts recidivism. *Criminal Justice and Behavior, 36*(5), 494–512. Copyright © 2009 Sage Publications. Published on behalf of the American Association for Correctional and Forensic Psychologists.

such as accommodation (support person available, housing, relationship to offender, etc.), community-based treatment referrals, employment, motivation, supervised access to children, and recidivism (violent and general). Overall, the findings indicated that the quality of reintegration planning was predictive of future child molesting. Those individuals recidivating were more likely to have a poorer plan when released from the program. More specifically they were less likely to have a strong social support network, had difficulty obtaining gainful employment, and had difficulty obtaining housing. These findings have a variety of implications for research on treatment. The use of recidivism as the indicator of success may be confounded with the planning process post-release. Additionally, as these findings suggest, those programs, such as Megan's Laws, which are intended to inform the public of a sex offender's whereabouts, may have the reverse effect. The authors concluded their research with an overview of the limitations of the present research design.

Assessment of Community Reintegration Planning for Sex Offenders

Poor Planning Predicts Recidivism

Gwenda M. Willis and Randolph C. Grace

The challenges that offenders face when reentering the community after release from prison have been well documented in research articles, news headlines, and the popular media. Typically, such challenges include securing housing and employment (e.g., Graffam, Shinkfield, Lavelle, & McPherson, 2004), maintaining prosocial support networks (e.g., Taxman, Young, & Byrne, 2002), and addressing drug and alcohol abuse and other mental and physical health problems (Hammett, Roberts, & Kennedy, 2001; Lurigio, Rollins, & Fallon, 2004). Although many researchers have noted the importance of comprehensive prerelease planning (Graffam et al., 2004; Hammett et al., 2001; Petersilia, 2003; Seiter & Kadela, 2003; Taxman, 2004), few attempts have been made to develop measures of planning quality and examine its impact on recidivism outcomes. If poor release planning is a risk factor for recidivism, correctional staff and relevant community agencies may be in a position to reduce reoffending through more effective reintegration of offenders into the community.

Child molesters represent an offender population that faces particularly acute challenges in terms of community reintegration. Public fear evoked by such offenders returning to the community has resulted in cases of shunning, pickets and vigils, and evictions (Petrunik & Deutschmann, 2008). Such responses are not surprising given the well-documented negative correlates of childhood sexual abuse (e.g., Colman & Widom, 2004; Roberts, O'Connor, Dunn, & Golding, 2004; Widom, 1999; Widom, Marmorstein, & Raskin White, 2006) and thus may be understandable attempts to eradicate the potential for further harm. The problem, however, is that child molesters do not return to prison when forced out of communities. Rather, they are left potentially homeless or in unstable living conditions, which have been linked with recidivism for general offenders (see Zambie & Quinsey, 1997).

Risk factors for recidivism by sexual offenders have been extensively studied in recent years and have been categorized as *static* and *dynamic*. Static risk factors are unchangeable aspects of an individual's history that indicate long-term propensities toward sexual offending

(Hanson, 1998). Examples include the number of prior convictions for sexual offenses and preferences for stranger and male victims (e.g., Hanson & Bussiere, 1998). Static risk measures provide a key component of overall risk assessment (Beech, Fisher, & Thornton, 2003), with the Static-99 (Hanson & Thornton, 1999) being the most widely used and validated such measure for sexual offenders (Ducro & Pham, 2006; Hanson & Thornton, 2000; Looman, 2006).

By contrast, dynamic risk factors represent the broad range of potentially changeable predictors of recidivism. These have been divided into *stable* and *acute* dynamic risk factors (Hanson, 1998). Stable dynamic risk factors are relatively enduring tendencies that may be amenable to change through treatment, such as sexual deviancy, antisocial orientation, and self-regulation problems (Hanson & Morton-Bourgon, 2005). Thus, it might be expected that prosocial change on such factors during treatment would reduce recidivism risk. However, research in this area is inconclusive (e.g., see Beech & Ford, 2006; Hudson, Wales, Bakker, & Ward, 2002). Acute dynamic risk factors are those that can potentially change rapidly and precipitate recidivism, such as negative mood states. Because of their transitory nature, acute factors are difficult to measure; thus, not surprisingly they have been rarely studied compared to other types of risk factors. In a pioneering study, Hanson and Harris (2000) found from interviews with parole officers that recidivists' mood significantly decreased, and anger, substance abuse, and victim access significantly increased in the month immediately prior to their reoffending, compared to a matched group of nonrecidivists.

The "risk factors perspective" summarized above emphasizes those aspects of an individual's history or personality that increase the likelihood of reoffending. By contrast, if behavior is viewed from an ecological perspective (e.g., Bronfenbrenner, 1979), interactions with environmental systems such as family, community, and employment might be paramount in preventing sexual recidivism. According to this view, activation of acute dynamic risk factors may be associated with specific environmental contexts. If so, then poor reintegration planning may increase recidivism risk. Moreover, poor reintegration may threaten the maintenance of treatment gains related to stable dynamic risk factors. Effective treatment generalization requires an environment that supports and reinforces newly learned concepts, for example, restructuring of offense-supportive beliefs (see Ward & Nee, in press).

Limited research based on an ecological perspective has examined poor reintegration as a risk factor for sexual recidivism. However, research on dynamic risk factors has identified some variables that might be relevant for reintegration. For example, employment instability was identified as a significant predictor of sexual recidivism in Hanson and Morton-Bourgon's (2005) meta-analysis. Hanson and Harris (2000) found that recidivists had significantly fewer positive peer influences and more negative peer influences than nonrecidivists while on community supervision. Andrews, Bonta, and Wormith (2006) listed antisocial associates as one of the "big four" risk factors for general recidivism. Poor performance at school or work, low levels of involvement in anticriminal leisure activities, and substance abuse featured in Andrews and colleagues' "central eight" major risk factors—all potentially related to problematic experiences of community reintegration.

Recently, Willis and Grace (2008) developed a coding protocol to evaluate the quality and comprehensiveness of release planning for child molesters. The protocol included items related to planning for accommodation (a place to live), employment, social support, "good lives model" (GLM; Ward & Stewart, 2003) secondary goods, and community-based treatment. The GLM is a contemporary strengths-based model of offender rehabilitation that emphasizes the promotion of primary goods or human values, such as relationships with others, as treatment targets, through secondary goods, which are socially acceptable and personally meaningful goals.

Willis and Grace (2008) applied the coding protocol to 39 recidivists and 42 nonrecidivists, matched for static risk level and time since release, from the Kia Marama Special Treatment Unit at Rolleston Prison near Christchurch, South Island, New Zealand. As predicted, recidivists had significantly poorer overall reintegration planning scores compared to nonrecidivists and lower scores as well for accommodation, employment, and GLM secondary goods items. However, when IQ and a psychometrically derived measure of stable dynamic risk were tested as covariates (see Allan, Grace, Rutherford, & Hudson, 2007), only the accommodation planning score remained significantly worse for recidivists.

Thus, a major goal of the present study was to validate Willis and Grace's (2008) finding that poor release planning was a risk factor for sexual recidivism with an independent sample. A secondary aim was to improve the coding protocol by using revised items for social support and community-based treatment planning. These items had not shown significant differences in Willis and Grace's study. The response scale for the revised social support item was increased to differentiate offenders with only one person in their planned support network. In terms of community-based treatment planning, the frequency and types of community-based treatment referrals were examined for any differences between recidivists and nonrecidivists. If poor community-based treatment planning was a risk factor for recidivism, recidivists should have fewer referrals than nonrecidivists. Details of these revised items, and the original items, are described in the Method section.

We hypothesized that recidivists would have poorer release planning than the nonrecidivists, and provided this was true, analyses were planned to see whether this difference remained significant after controlling for potential confounding variables. In addition, survival analyses were conducted to determine whether poor planning was associated with a reduced time to reoffend, to identify the subset of items that comprised the best predictive model for recidivism, and to estimate the strength of the relationship between planning quality and recidivism.

◼ Method

Participants

The sample for this study was drawn from males who completed the 32- or 12-week prison-based treatment programs at the Te Piriti Special Treatment Unit between 1994 and 2000. Te Piriti is a self-contained unit for males convicted of sexual offending against children, located within Auckland Prison. All men had provided written consent for their file information to be used for research and evaluation purposes. The recidivist group was drawn from all males who had been reconvicted of a sexual offense (as of December 2007) since leaving Te Piriti ($n = 35$). Sufficient file information was available for 30 of these men. An equal number of nonrecidivists were selected to form the comparison group (total $N = 60$). Nonrecidivists were individually matched on static risk level (see below) and time at risk with the recidivist group.

Reintegration Planning at Te Piriti

Similar to Kia Marama (Hudson, Wales, & Ward, 1998), the primary goal of the Te Piriti treatment program is to reduce an offender's risk of recidivism in the community. In line with this aim, offenders voluntarily enter the program toward the end of their sentence to facilitate the transition to living in the community. A reintegration coordinator oversees reentry planning for each inmate at Te Piriti and liaises between the offender, his support network, and community agencies. Throughout treatment, reintegration plans are discussed, refined, and detailed in reports written to the Parole Board or Community Probation Service as the offender's release approaches. At a minimum, conditions of release typically include residing at an approved address, regular meetings with the Community Probation Service, and regular attendance at a monthly follow-up support group. For further information about the Te Piriti program, see Larsen, Robertson, Hillman, and Hudson (1998) or the evaluation conducted by Nathan, Wilson, and Hillman (2003).

Measures

Static risk level. The Automated Sexual Recidivism Scale (ASRS; Skelton, Riley, Wales, & Vess, 2006) was used to measure static risk. The ASRS is based on the Static-99 (Hanson & Thornton, 2000), which is the most widely used and validated measure of static risk for sexual offenders (Ducro & Pham, 2006; Hanson & Thornton, 2000; Looman, 2006). The ASRS is scored by a computer from information stored in the database maintained by the Department of Corrections and includes 7 of the 10 items from the Static-99 (excluded were Item 6, any unrelated victim; Item 7, any stranger victim; and Item 10, single or ever lived with a lover for at least 2 years, as this information is not recorded). The overall ASRS score is divided into four risk bands, which correspond closely to those associated with the Static-99 (ASRS: 0 = *low,* 1 or 2 = *medium low,* 3 or 4 = *medium high,* 5+ = *high).* Skelton et al. demonstrated that the ASRS had comparable predictive validity to the Static-99 for sexual recidivism in a sample of male sex offenders *(N* = 1,133), with areas under the receiver operating characteristic curve (AUCs) from .70 to .78. They also found that when offenders were sorted into risk bands, survival curves were very similar to those of the Static-99 reported by Hanson and Thornton (2000).

Time at risk. Time at risk was measured from the date participants were released from Te Piriti until criminal history records were obtained in December 2007.

Recidivism. Criminal history information was obtained from the National Intelligence Application computer database maintained by the New Zealand Police in December 2007.

Any convictions for sexual, violent, or general offenses that occurred postrelease were noted. Sexual recidivism was defined as Category A offenses according to the Static-99 scoring criteria (A. Harris, Phenix, Hanson, & Thornton, 2003), that is, an offense with an identifiable victim (e.g., incest, sexual assault, exhibitionism). Category B offenses (i.e., no identifiable victim) were excluded, except for possession of child pornography. Violent recidivism was recorded when the offender had been convicted for a nonsexual offense against a person (e.g., assault, robbery, kidnapping). General recidivism was defined as an offense that was neither sexual nor violent (e.g., possession of cannabis). The time at large prior to each reconviction, or to the end of the follow-up period, was calculated for each offender.

Release planning. Five of the six items of the coding protocol developed by Willis and Grace (2008) were used to rate release planning. These were accommodation planning, social support planning, employment planning, idiosyncratic risk factors (whether these were indicated and an attempt had been made to minimize

them through release planning), and motivation. The structure of Te Piriti reports meant that insufficient information was available to rate the GLM secondary goods item, so this item was omitted.

Revised items were included in an attempt to improve the release planning coding protocol. In the Willis and Grace (2008) study, planning for social support was rated on a 4-point scale: 0 = *no planned social support network,* 1 = *suggested social support network* (not confirmed), 2 = *confirmed social support network from one system* (friends, family, or volunteers), and 3 = *confirmed social support network from more than one system* (e.g., friends and family). More than half (53.1%) of participants received a rating of 2 for the social support item; however, some of these participants had only one confirmed person in their support network, whereas others had multiple people (but all from the same system). The current study included a revised social support item with a 5-point scale to differentiate participants with only one confirmed support person.

The idiosyncratic risk factors item of the Willis and Grace (2008) study was designed to investigate whether high-risk situations and warning signs of relapse for individual offenders had been documented and whether an attempt had been made to minimize these through community-based treatment planning. It was expected that when idiosyncratic risk factors (e.g., substance abuse, anger problems) were followed up through referrals to appropriate services, recidivism risk would be reduced. However, scores on this item did not significantly differ between recidivists and nonrecidivists, and the majority (85.2%) of participants scored 2 (on a 0-3 scale) on this item, meaning idiosyncratic risk factors had been documented and some, but not all, had been connected with release planning through referral to community agencies. The main reason participants did not score a 3 (meaning all idiosyncratic risk factors had been connected with release planning) was because no attempt had been made to minimize exposure to the high-risk situation of unsupervised access to children. Because this could not be readily accomplished through community-based treatment referrals, in the current study a separate item was included that rated whether any attempt had been made to minimize unsupervised access to children. To determine whether poor planning for community-based treatment was a risk factor for recidivism, community-based treatment referrals were recorded separately for each participant and grouped according to whether they were conditional (e.g., at the request of an offender's probation officer) or unconditional (e.g., as a condition of parole). Community-based treatment referrals were further grouped according to four broad areas of dynamic risk: social inadequacy, sexual interests, lifestyle impulsivity, and emotional functioning. The revised items were piloted on a random selection of reports written by Te Piriti staff nearing an offender's release and adjusted accordingly depending on the information typically available.

The original and revised items were rated for each participant. The items from the original protocol are summarized below, with the scale for each indicated in parentheses:

1. Accommodation (0–2). This item measured the extent of accommodation planning. The proposed type of accommodation was recorded, for example, with support people.

2. Social support (0–3). This item measured whether a social support network had been established and, if so, how many systems it comprised.

3. Idiosyncratic risk factors (0–3). This item assessed whether high-risk situations and/or warning signs were indicated and, if so, whether these had been connected with reintegration planning.

4. Employment (0–3). This item measured the extent of employment planning.

5. Motivation (0–1). This item indicated motivation to follow through with postrelease plans, as stated by the therapist.

The revised items are outlined below, with the scale for each item indicated in parentheses:

6. Social support (0–4). This item was similar to the original social support item but differentiated support networks of one person from support networks of multiple people who were all from the same system.

7. Social support A' (total number of people in an offender's planned support network).

8. Unsupervised access to children (0–1). This item indicated whether any attempt had been made to minimize the likelihood of unsupervised access to children.

9. Community-based treatment referrals (0–1 for each conditional and unconditional referral type).

Procedure

Files held by the Department of Corrections Psychological Service were sourced for each participant, and the report written for each participant by Te Piriti staff to the Parole Board or Community Probation Service nearing release was rated for release planning. These reports typically contained details relating to the offender's conviction, a summary of assessment findings and treatment outcomes, an indication of current risk level, a list of high-risk situations and warning signs, and an outline of release plans. All reports contained sufficient information to rate each item described above, except for the motivation item. When an offender's motivation to continue with his postrelease plans was not indicated, this item was coded as missing.

The first author scored all files, and a research assistant scored 45% of these to obtain a measure of interrater reliability. Data coders were blind to the recidivism outcome for each participant and rated release plans independently of each other. For each report, data coders were instructed to

1. read the report in its entirety before conducting any ratings,

2. reread the report and record ratings (coders were instructed to be conservative in any event of uncertainty), and

3. ensure that all ratings and comments relating to qualitative aspects of release planning have been recorded.

All disagreements between coders were resolved by consensus. Data analyses were conducted using

SPSS (Version 14.0). Two sets of analyses were planned: a validation of the Willis and Grace (2008) findings and an extension of results combining the Kia Marama and Te Piriti data to explore whether reintegration planning predicted time to reoffend, to identify the best reintegration planning model for predicting sexual recidivism, and to determine its accuracy in terms of the AUC. The AUC ranges from .5 to 1.0, with higher values indicating greater accuracy, and is recommended as a measure of predictive validity for recidivism studies because it is independent of base rate (Rice & Harris, 1995). All significance tests used the .05 level, unless otherwise indicated.

⬙ Discussion

The primary goals of the present research were to determine whether poor planning for community reintegration was related to sex offender recidivism and to estimate the strength of the relationship between planning quality and reoffending. Consistent with the results of Willis and Grace (2008), the overall quality of reintegration planning was poorer for child molesters who were released from prison and who subsequently reoffended, compared with a matched group who did not reoffend. In addition to the total reintegration score, planning for both employment and social support was significantly worse for recidivists. These differences in reintegration planning were not confounded with differences in static risk level or in dynamic risk as assessed by a psychometric battery. Thus, the present data confirm Willis and Grace's results with an independent sample of child molesters released from a different treatment unit (Te Piriti).

Pooling data from both Willis and Grace (2008) and the current study, we can see that planning for accommodation, employment, and social support combined to give the best predictive model for predicting sex offender recidivism. The accuracy of this model in predicting recidivism (AUC = .71) was in the same range as that obtained using static risk models (e.g., Barbaree, Seto, Langton, & Peacock, 2001; G. T. Harris et al., 2003). Given that static risk was controlled for in the present study, this suggests that reintegration planning

and static models may predict reoffending with equal accuracy. Moreover, because there were no significant correlations between reintegration planning and static risk scores, our results suggest that assessment of reintegration planning may represent an independent and equally valid source of predictive validity for recidivism.

The best predictive model of reintegration planning yielded a scale of planning quality that ranged from 0 to 8, which discriminated well between recidivists and nonrecidivists. The percentage of recidivists decreased steadily with increases in planning quality, and results indicated that there were three approximate ranges: poor quality (0–1), average quality (2–5), and good quality (6–8), which differed in terms of their risk for recidivism. Although the percentages of recidivists across the ranges were inflated because the overall base rate was artificially set at 50%, this suggests that the total reintegration planning score may have practical utility in terms of risk assessment as an adjunct to static models. Future research should address whether the quality of reintegration planning produces significant increments in predictive accuracy above static risk measures. Such analyses were not possible in the present study because the matching procedure used to obtain the nonrecidivist group ensured that there was no correlation between static risk and recidivism.

The present results have implications for research on treatment outcome because variation in the quality of reintegration planning may make it harder to detect a link between treatment and recidivism. Although reintegration planning is incorporated into prison-based programs such as Kia Marama and Te Piriti, its quality varies and it is not a core treatment module. In contrast to modules such as arousal reconditioning, victim empathy, and mood management (Hudson et al., 1998), which target stable dynamic risk factors at the individual level, reintegration planning requires the involvement of environmental systems. The present results suggest that incorporating a systems framework may increase the effectiveness of sex offender treatment. The Circles of Support and Accountability (COSA) model of professionally facilitated volunteerism in the community-based management of sex offenders is one example of a systems-based initiative

(Wilson, Huculak, & McWhinnie, 2002), and a recent COSA evaluation study found that rates of recidivism for sex offenders involved in COSA were significantly lower compared to a matched comparison group (Wilson, Picheca, & Prinzo, 2007).

Findings of the current study may be especially pertinent in countries and states that enforce community notification and residency restriction legislations. Originally enacted to enhance community safety and reduce sex offender recidivism, such legislation may increase the same risk they intended to deter. Job loss, housing disruption, social isolation, and stress have been associated with community notification, commonly known as Megan's law in the United States (Levenson & Cotter, 2005a; Levenson, D'Amora, & Hern, 2007). Likewise, residency restrictions have been shown to prevent sex offenders from living with supportive family members and to increase social isolation (Levenson & Cotter, 2005b). Thus, community notification and residency restriction legislations may hinder quality reintegration planning. Not surprisingly, there is little empirical evidence that community notification contributes to a reduction in sexual recidivism (Levenson et al., 2007). Residency restrictions are a more recent initiative, and research has yet to examine their impact on sexual recidivism (Mercado, Alvarez, & Levenson, 2008).

Several revised items were investigated in an attempt to improve the Willis and Grace (2008) reintegration planning coding protocol. The revised social support item, together with the accommodation and employment items, produced the best predictive model of recidivism for the Te Piriti data. The AUC value for this model was .78, compared to .74 when the original social support item was used. As predicted, having multiple people from one support system (i.e., friends, family, or volunteers) was superior to having only one person in a support network. The revised item and the original item were both superior to the number of people in a planned social support network, indicating that having support from different systems or groups was more important than the number of people involved.

Some limitations of the current study should be acknowledged. First, the results do not provide a strong basis for inferring a causal linkage between reintegration planning and recidivism. Although groups were matched in terms of static risk and no significant differences in IQ or dynamic risk were found, the possibility that some other confounding variable might have influenced the results cannot be ruled out. Also, the study was retrospective, and whether offenders were successful at implementing their plans remains unknown. A prospective study that examines the relationship between planning and experience of reintegration and reoffending outcomes could provide stronger evidence of a causal link between poor planning and recidivism. Finally, the study was based on a relatively small sample size, which may limit the generalizability of the results, including the ability to compare different types of child molesters (e.g., intrafamilial vs. extrafamilial).

It is important to consider how quality reintegration planning may promote desistance from crime. Prosocial relationships and employment have frequently been cited as major turning points in criminal careers (e.g., Hepburn & Griffin, 2004; Kruttschnitt, Uggen, & Shelton, 2000) and are consistent with basic human needs or "primary goods," described by Ward and Stewart (2003) as necessary for a fulfilling and offense-free life. More specifically, prosocial relationships may allow the primary good of relatedness to be achieved, and employment may fulfill several primary goods including excellence in play and work, knowledge, and agency (see Ward & Stewart, 2003). Thus, findings of the present study support a strengths-based approach to treatment in which offenders' values are built on and realized through prosocial means, such as the approach of the GLM.

Reintegration planning should be a core component in treatment programs for sexual offenders because effective planning may contribute to reductions in recidivism. Accommodation, prosocial support, and employment all reflect needs that occupy the lower steps of Maslow's (1943) well-known hierarchy of needs. According to Maslow, physiological, safety, and social needs must be secured before higher order values such as self-esteem, respect of others, and morality can be realized. It seems unrealistic to expect released sex offenders to live as law-abiding, respectful members of society while they struggle to attain basic human needs. Assisting sex offenders to develop effective reintegration plans may help to ensure that their basic needs are met after release and in turn contribute to a reduction in sex offender recidivism.

Notes

1. 1 = *primary only or less*, 2 = *Form 3–4*, 3 = *Form 5*, 4 = *school certificate*, 5 = *Form 6*, 6 = *university entrance*, 7 = *Form 7*, 8 = *polytechnic diploma/teacher's college*, 9 = *university undergraduate*, 10 = *bachelor's*, 11 = *master's/postgraduate diploma*, 12 = *doctorate*.

2. An appendix reporting all demographic and psychometric comparisons is available from the authors by request.

References

Allan, M., Grace, R., Rutherford, B., & Hudson, S. (2007). Psychometric assessment of dynamic risk factors for child molesters. *Sexual Abuse: A Journal of Research and Treatment, 19,* 347–367.

Andrews, D. A., Bonta, J., & Wormith, J. S. (2006). The recent past and near future of risk and/or need assessment. *Crime & Delinquency, 52,* 7–27.

Barbaree, H. E., Seto, M. C., Langton, C. M., & Peacock, E. J. (2001). Evaluating the predictive accuracy of six risk assessment instruments for adult sex offenders. *Criminal Justice and Behavior, 28,* 490–521.

Beech, A., & Ford, H. (2006). The relationship between risk, deviance, treatment outcome and sexual reconviction in a sample of child sexual abusers completing residential treatment for their offending. *Psychology, Crime & Law, 12,* 685–701.

Beech, A. R., Fisher, D. D., & Thornton, D. (2003). Risk assessment of sex offenders. *Professional Psychology: Research and Practice, 34,* 339–352.

Bronfenbrenner, U. (1979). *The ecology of human development: Experiments by nature and design.* Cambridge, MA: Harvard University Press.

Colman, R. A., & Widom, C. S. (2004). Childhood abuse and neglect and adult intimate relationships: A prospective study. *Child Abuse & Neglect, 28,* 1133–1151.

Ducro, C., & Pham, T. (2006). Evaluation of the SORAG and the Static-99 on Belgian sex offenders committed to a forensic facility. *Sexual Abuse: A Journal of Research and Treatment, 18,* 15–26.

Graffam, J., Shinkfield, A., Lavelle, B., & McPherson, W. (2004). Variables affecting successful reintegration as perceived by offenders and professionals. *Journal of Offender Rehabilitation, 40,* 147–171.

Hammett, T. M., Roberts, C., & Kennedy, S. (2001). Health-related issues in prisoner reentry. *Crime & Delinquency, 47,* 390–409.

Hanson, R. K. (1998). What do we know about sex offender risk assessment? *Psychology, Public Policy, and Law, 4,* 50–72.

Hanson, R. K., & Bussiere, M. T. (1998). Predicting relapse: A meta-analysis of sexual offender recidivism studies. *Journal of Consulting and Clinical Psychology, 66,* 348–362.

Hanson, R. K., & Harris, A. J. R. (2000). Where should we intervene? Dynamic predictors of sexual assault recidivism. *Criminal Justice and Behavior, 27,* 6–35.

Hanson, R. K., & Morton-Bourgon, K. E. (2005). The characteristics of persistent sexual offenders: A meta-analysis of recidivism studies. *Journal of Consulting and Clinical Psychology, 73,* 1154–1163.

Hanson, R. K., & Thornton, D. (1999). *Static-99: Improving actuarial risk assessments for sex offenders* (User Report 1999–02). Ottawa: Department of the Solicitor General of Canada.

Hanson, R. K., & Thornton, D. (2000). Improving risk assessments for sex offenders: A comparison of three actuarial scales. *Law and Human Behavior, 24,* 119–136.

Harris, A., Phenix, A., Hanson, R. K., & Thornton, D. (2003). *STATIC-99 coding rules revised-2003.* Ottawa: Department of the Solicitor General of Canada.

Harris, G. T., Rice, M. E., Quinsey, V. L., Lalumiere, M. L., Boer, D., & Lang, C. (2003). A multisite comparison of actuarial risk instruments for sex offenders. *Psychological Assessment, 15,* 413–425.

Hepburn, J. R., & Griffin, M. L. (2004). The effect of social bonds on successful adjustment to probation: An event history analysis. *Criminal Justice Review, 29,* 46–75.

Hudson, S., Wales, D., & Ward, T. (1998). Kia Marama: A treatment program for child molesters in New Zealand. In W. L. Marshall, Y. M. Fernandez, S. Hudson, & T. Ward (Eds.), *Sourcebook of treatment programs for sexual offenders* (pp. 17–28). New York: Plenum.

Hudson, S. M., Wales, D. S., Bakker, L., & Ward, T. (2002). Dynamic risk factors: The Kia Marama evaluation. *Sexual Abuse: A Journal of Research and Treatment, 14,* 101–117.

Kruttschnitt, C., Uggen, C., & Shelton, K. (2000). Predictors of desistance among sex offenders: The interaction of formal and informal social controls. *Justice Quarterly, 17,* 61–87.

Larsen, J., Robertson, P., Hillman, D., & Hudson, S. (1998). Te Piriti: A bicultural model for treating child molesters in Aotearoa/New Zealand. In W. L. Marshall, Y. M. Fernandez, S. Hudson, & T. Ward (Eds.), *Sourcebook of treatment programs for sexual offenders* (pp. 385–398). New York: Plenum.

Levenson, J. S., & Cotter, L. P. (2005a). The effect of Megan's law on sex offender reintegration. *Journal of Contemporary-Criminal Justice, 21,* 49–66.

Levenson, J. S., & Cotter, L. P. (2005b). The impact of sex offender residence restrictions: 1,000 feet from danger or one step from absurd? *International Journal of Offender Therapy and Comparative Criminology, 49,* 168–178.

Levenson, J. S., D'Amora, D. A., & Hem, A. L. (2007). Megan's law and its impact on community re-entry for sex offenders. *Behavioral Sciences & the Law, 25,* 587–602.

Looman, J. (2006). Comparison of two risk assessment instruments for sexual offenders. *Sexual Abuse: A Journal of Research and Treatment, 18,* 193–206.

Lurigio, A. J., Rollins, A., & Fallon, J. (2004). The effects of serious mental illness on offender reentry. *Federal Probation, 68,* 45–52.

Maslow, A. H. (1943). A theory of human motivation. *Psychological Review, 50,* 370–396.

Mercado, C. C., Alvarez, S., & Levenson, J. S. (2008). The impact of specialized sex offender legislation on community reentry. *Sexual Abuse: A Journal of Research and Treatment, 20,* 188–205.

Nathan, L., Wilson, N., & Hillman, D. (2003). *Te Whakakotahitanga: An evaluation of the Te Piriti Special Treatment Programme for child sex offenders in New Zealand.* Wellington, New Zealand: Psychological Service, Department of Corrections. Retrieved April 23, 2008, from http://www.coiTections.govt.nz/public/pdt/research/tepiriti/tewhaka.pdf

Petersilia, J. (2003). *When prisoners come home: Parole and prisoner reentry.* New York: Oxford University Press.

Petrunik, M., & Deutschmann, L. (2008). The exclusion-inclusion spectrum in state and community response to sex offenders in Anglo-American and European jurisdictions. *International Journal of Offender Therapy and Comparative Criminology, 52,* 499–519.

Reynolds, C. R., Willson, V. L., & Clark, P. L. (1983). A four-test short form of the WAIS-R for clinical screening. *Clinical Neuropsychology, 5,* 111–116.

Rice, M. E., & Harris, G. T. (1995). Violent recidivism: Assessing predictive validity. *Journal of Consulting and Clinical Psychology, 63,* 737–748.

Roberts, R., O'Connor, T., Dunn, J., & Golding, J. (2004). The effects of child sexual abuse in later family life: Mental health, parenting and adjustment of offspring. *Child Abuse & Neglect, 28,* 525–545.

Seiter, R. P., & Kadela, K. R. (2003). Prisoner reentry: What works, what does not, and what is promising. *Crime & Delinquency, 49,* 360–388.

Skelton, A., Riley, D., Wales, D., & Vess, J. (2006). Assessing risk for sexual offenders in New Zealand: Development and validation of a computer-scored risk measure. *Journal of Sexual Aggression, 12,* 277–286.

Taxman, F. S. (2004). The offender and reentry: Supporting active participation in reintegration. *Federal Probation, 68,* 31–35.

Taxman, F. S., Young, D., & Byrne, J. M. (2002). *Offender's views of reentry: Implications for processes, programs and services.* College Park: University of Maryland, Bureau of Governmental Research.

Ward, T., & Nee, C. (in press). Surfaces and depths: Evaluating the theoretical assumptions of cognitive skills programmes. *Psychology, Crime, & Law.*

Ward, T., & Stewart, C. A. (2003). The treatment of sex offenders: Risk management and good lives. *Professional Psychology-Research and Practice, 34,* 353–360.

Widom, C. S. (1999). Posttraumatic stress disorder in abused and neglected children grown up. *American Journal of Psychiatry, 156,* 1223–1229.

Widom, C. S., Marmorstein, N. R., & Raskin White, H. (2006). Childhood victimization and illicit drug use in middle adulthood. *Psychology of Addictive Behaviors, 20,* 394–403.

Willis, G. M., & Grace, R. C. (2008). The quality of community reintegration planning for child molesters: Effects on sexual recidivism. *Sexual Abuse: A Journal of Research and Treatment, 20,* 218–240.

Wilson, R. J., Huculak, B., & McWhinnie, A. (2002). Restorative justice innovations in Canada. *Behavioral Sciences and the Law, 20,* 363–380.

Wilson, R. J., Picheca, J. E., & Prinzo, M. (2007). Evaluating the effectiveness of professionally-facilitated volunteerism in the community-based management of high-risk sexual offenders: Part two-A comparison of recidivism rates. *Howard Journal of Criminal Justice, 46,* 327–337.

Zamble, H., & Quinsey, V. L. (1997). *The criminal recidivism process.* New York: Cambridge University Press.

DISCUSSION QUESTIONS

1. Given the findings of this study, how might a community work to assist with reintegration of sex offenders?

2. What are some of the potential difficulties of reintegration of sex offenders/child molesters into a community?

3. Why should communities be concerned with successful reintegration of convicted child molesters?

4. What are some of the long-term policy implications of these findings?

Glossary

Absolute immunity: Exists for those persons who work in positions that require unimpaired decision-making functions. Judges and prosecutors have this type of immunity.

Activities: Services or functions carried out by a program (i.e., what the program does). For example, treatment programs may screen clients at intake, complete placement assessments, provide counseling to clients, etc.

Aftercare: Reintegrative services that prepare juveniles released from an institution for reentry into the community by establishing collaboration among agencies, the community, and available resources to maximize reintegrative processes.

Anger retaliation rapist: This rapist desires to harm women. This offender seeks to "get even" with women who have embarrassed or humiliated him in his past.

Antisocial personality disorder (ASPD): A personality disorder characterized by pervasive antisocial tendencies, excessive risk-taking behaviors, and a lack of empathy or remorse.

Assertive community treatment case management: An intensive case management model with low caseloads and frequent, community-based contact with clients.

Aversion therapy: Behavioral technique often used in varying degrees within sex offender programs. The aim of aversive techniques is to teach offenders to associate unpleasant stimuli with presently desirable yet unacceptable behaviors.

Baseline interviews: Consists of gathering data related to each variable we are attempting to measure at the time of entry into the program.

Behavioral therapy: Holds that long-term change is accomplished through action and that disorders are learned means of behaving that are maladaptive.

Beliefs: This refers to a general *lack* of beliefs that counter delinquent behavior. In essence, it is not the possession of pro-delinquent beliefs

as much as it is a lack of beliefs regarding the inappropriateness of delinquency.

Benefit of clergy: This benefit was the pardoning of a person from the commission of a crime. The benefit of clergy was originally implemented for members of various churches, including clerics, monks, and nuns who might be accused of crimes.

Blood testing: A highly invasive procedure that can provide discrete information regarding the degree of an individual's impairment. However, the invasiveness of the procedure and the potential danger of infection make blood testing inappropriate for many drug programs.

Boot camps: Short-term forms of incarceration in an environment that is similar to basic training in the military. This sanction is primarily used with youthful offenders and is intended to have an emphasis on disciplining the offender.

Borderline personality disorder: A disorder characterized by a pervasive pattern of instability of interpersonal relationships, self-image, and affects, and a marked impulsivity beginning by early adulthood.

Broker/generalist case management: Narrow in scope of action, the broker/generalist model focuses primarily on rapid linkage and referral. The case manager provides limited direct services, other than the initial assessment to determine service needs, service referrals, and occasional monitoring of service provision.

Care coordinators: Those responsible for helping participants create a customized treatment program and for guiding youth and their families through the system of care.

Case management: The process whereby an offender is provided fully comprehensive and coordinated services that address the offender's vocational, social, educational, and mental health functions. The goal is to address the offender's needs so that he or she can be a fully functioning member of society.

Caseload management: The process we use to assign supervision workloads to community supervision officers. This takes into account the number of offenders, the security risk of those offenders, and the specialized needs that those offenders may have. The more serious the security risk or the more profound the needs, the more intensive that offender is to supervise, resulting in fewer offenders in a caseload, under a balanced system of caseload management.

Certification: Implies a certain level of oversight in that a minimum standard of competency exists. This is particularly relevant to mental health professionals, such as counselors.

Chemical castration: Method of reducing violent behavior in which sex offenders are injected with drugs (most commonly Depo-Provera) to reduce the amount of testosterone in their bodies.

Child abuse: Maltreatment of a child (being a youth under the age of 18 in most states) by an immediate family member or any person responsible for the child's welfare.

Child neglect: Occurs when a parent or caretaker of the child does not provide the proper or necessary support, education, or medical or other remedial care that is required by a given state's laws, including food, shelter, and clothing.

Child parentification: Occurs when a child is placed in a position within a family system in which he or she must assume the primary caretaker role for the family, often taking care of both children and adults within that family system.

Client-centered therapy: Therapy technique whose central point is that the therapist must be genuine, accepting, and empathetic to the offender–client.

Clinical/rehabilitation case management: Approach to case management in which those providing case management services deliver the clinical treatment as well, providing both in an integrated manner.

Cognitive behavioral therapy (CBT): A problem-focused approach designed to help people identify and change the dysfunctional beliefs, thoughts, and patterns of behavior that contribute to their problems.

Cognitive restructuring: Therapy technique in which the offender constructs scenes that cast him or her or significant others in the role of the victim. The client then focuses on typical rationalizations he or she uses to justify the assault.

Cognitive therapy: Approach based on the belief that faulty thinking patterns and belief systems cause psychological problems and that changing our thoughts improves our mental and emotional health and results in changes in behavior.

Collective efficacy: Refers to a sense of cohesion within a given community whereby citizens have close and interlocking relationships with one another.

Community-based interagency team: The team of people responsible for designing, implementing, and overseeing the wraparound initiative in a given jurisdiction.

Community corrections: Includes all non-incarcerating correctional sanctions imposed upon an offender for the purposes of reintegrating that offender into the community.

Community justice: Simultaneously a philosophy of justice, a strategy of justice, and a combination of justice programs.

Community policing: Employs methods of creating partnerships between the police and the community. Examples include programs such as Neighborhood Watch and Citizens on Patrol.

Community residential treatment centers: Nonconfining residential facilities for adjudicated adults or juveniles who are not appropriate for probation or who need a period of readjustment after imprisonment.

Community service: Work performed by an offender for the benefit of the community as a component of that offender's sentence.

Community supervision officer (CSO): A term used to identify persons who work in community supervision agencies and perform the supervision duties that are typically associated with probation or parole officers.

Consolidated parole administration model: Model in which the parole board is merely a semiautonomous agency that is connected to (and perhaps subservient to) a larger agency or governmental body.

Containment approach: Based on the idea that multiple dimensions of supervision are necessary to optimize public safety, and this therefore requires numerous actors within the criminal justice and community setting.

Content analysis: The systematic analysis and selective classification of the contents of mass media.

Conventional model: Involves the random assignment of offenders to community supervision officers. This model of case assignment results in officers having a mix of different types of offenders, which has both pros and cons as far as developing equity in workload among officers and in optimizing service coordination for offenders.

Conventional model with geographic consideration: A prime determinant of this model is the amount of time that officers must spend traveling to various locations during their day-to-day routine of checking on offenders. This model takes into account such geographic factors.

Counselors: Professionals who typically have training in particular mental health areas, such as a substance abuse counselor. Many counselors have a master's degree and full licensure; in these cases, the counselor is referred to as a licensed professional counselor.

Crime control model of corrections: Model of corrections that seek to simply incapacitate the offending population with no concern for the reentry issues that will follow for the community or the offender.

Cultural competence: Possession of knowledge and information pertaining to individuals and groups that entails skills, services, and techniques that match an individual's culture and improve the relevance of services to the person receiving them.

Day reporting centers: Treatment facilities that offenders must report to on a daily (or near daily) basis. These are similar to residential treatment facilities except that offenders on intensive supervision are not required to stay overnight.

Day treatment facilities: Highly structured, community-based, nonresidential programs for serious juvenile offenders.

Determinate sentencing: Consists of fixed periods of incarceration imposed on the offender with no later flexibility in the term that is served. This type of sentencing is grounded in notions of retribution, just deserts, and incapacitation.

Deterrence: Discouraging people from lawbreaking by example.

Detoxification: Treatment designed for persons who are dependent on narcotic drugs (e.g., heroin, opium). This treatment is typically found in inpatient settings with programs that last for 7 to 21 days.

Diagnostic and Statistical Manual of Mental Disorders (DSM-IV-TR): Manual that allows mental health practitioners to label, or diagnose, an individual (in this case an offender) so that the person can be better categorized for further treatment interventions. This is a necessary process when attempting to match a client with the correct treatment modality.

Discrimination: Refers to differential and negative treatment of an individual or group without reference to the behavior or qualifications for that treatment.

Disparity: Refers to the unequal treatment of one group by the criminal justice system, compared with the treatment accorded other groups.

Dispositional needs assessment: Provides additional information within one or more given need dimensions regarding the specific program or treatment that would benefit the offender.

Diversion: A process whereby someone—either an adult or child—is referred to a program (usually external to the official system) for counseling or care of some form in lieu of referral to the official court.

Drug of choice: A drug that is consistently used with greater frequency than other types of drugs by a certain identifiable demographic group.

Dual diagnosis: A term that denotes the fact that the offender has two or more disorders.

Dynamic risk factors: Those characteristics that can change and are more or less influenced or controlled by the offender, such as employment, motivation, drug use, and family relations.

Educational neglect: Neglect that occurs when a parent or even a teacher permits chronic truancy or simply ignores the educational or special needs of a child.

Electronic monitoring: Includes the use of any mechanism that is worn by the offender for the means of tracking the person's whereabouts through electronic detection. Electronic monitoring includes both active and passive monitoring systems. Active systems require that the offender answer or respond to a monitoring cue (such as a computer-generated telephone call), whereas passive forms of monitoring emit a continuous signal for tracking.

Emotional neglect: This neglect includes inadequate nurturing or affection, allowing the child to engage in inappropriate or illegal behavior such as drug or alcohol use, and ignoring a child's basic emotional needs.

English Penal Servitude Act: Alexander Maconochie lobbied for this act in 1853, which established several rehabilitation programs for convicts in both England and Ireland.

Environmental crime prevention: Component of a community justice orientation that determines why certain areas of a jurisdiction are more crime prone than others.

Environmental manipulation: Getting the offender out of situations that are high risk for him and his potential victims. The offender should train himself to move out of the house rather than the victim.

Ethnicity: A concept that takes into account cultural characteristics, such as language and religion, as a means of identifying different groups of people.

Faith-based therapy: Forms of therapy that are often a blend of cognitive and behavioral techniques that are grounded in scriptural instructions on the appropriate form of cognition or behavior.

False negative: Data result implying that the offender is predicted to not reoffend but the prediction turns out to be false.

False positive: When an offender is predicted to be likely to commit a crime but later, despite this prediction, the offender is released to community supervision and is found to never reoffend.

Family systems therapy: Therapy that looks at the entire family as a system with its own customs, roles, beliefs, and dynamics that affect and impact the offender more routinely than does any other group.

Female offenders: Defined as both juvenile and adult female offenders who have committed a criminal offense that has been either adjudicated or criminally processed. These offenders include women in facilities as well as those in community corrections settings.

Feminist theory: Contends that traditional criminology has typically generated theories that are suited for the male population, with little or no regard for the corresponding female offender.

Feminist therapy: Therapy that focuses on empowering women. This type of therapy often aids in strengthening women's communication skills, sense of assertiveness, self-esteem, and relationships.

Fine: Monetary penalty imposed by a judge or magistrate as a punishment for being convicted of an offense.

Five essential elements of specialized courts: Include the use of (1) immediate interventions; (2) non-adversarial adjudication; (3) hands-on judicial involvement; (4) treatment programs with clear rules and structured goals; and (5) a team approach that brings together the judge, prosecutors, defense counsel, treatment provider, and correctional staff.

Formal interagency agreement: Agreement that records the proposed design of the wraparound initiative and spells out exactly how it will work.

General deterrence: Intended to cause vicarious learning whereby observers see that offenders are punished for a given crime and therefore are discouraged from committing a like-mannered crime due to fear of similar punishment.

Generalized anxiety disorder: Characterized by excessive anxiety and worry (apprehensive expectation), occurring more days than not for at least 6 months, about a number of events or activities.

Global positioning system (GPS): This type of system uses 24 military satellites to determine the exact location of a coordinate. By using the satellite monitoring and remote tracking, offenders can be tracked to their exact location.

Goals: Desired states of affairs that outline the ultimate purpose of a program. These are the end toward which program efforts are directed. For example, a goal of many criminal justice programs is a reduction in criminal activity.

Gross negligence: A failure to exercise the standard of care and attention that is even less than that which would be expected from someone who was already careless in his or her duty.

Group homes: Residential placement facilities for juveniles that operate in a homelike setting with unrelated children living together for varied periods of time, depending on their individual circumstances.

Hair testing: The introduction of new, powerful instruments for hair analysis has increased interest in hair testing. Hair testing is used to detect trace amounts of drugs in the person's body. Despite its increased popularity among agencies, caution should be used because hair analysis is subject to potential external contamination.

Halfway house: Residential setting for offenders who are court-ordered to stay at the facility while on community supervision. Offenders who are exiting prison will often be required to stay at one of these facilities. It is also defined as residential facilities for offenders who are either nearing release from prison or in the initial stages of return to the community.

Hearing stage: Stage of disposition of an offender that allows the probation agency to present evidence of the violation while the offender is given the opportunity to refute the evidence offered.

Histrionic personality disorder: A pervasive pattern of excessive emotionality and attention seeking, beginning by early adulthood and present in a variety of contexts.

Home confinement: An intermediate community corrections sanction where offenders are restricted to their residence except during specifically designated times when they are authorized to attend vocational, educational, treatment-based, or social functions.

Home detention: The mandated action that forces an offender to stay within the confines of his or her home or on the offender's property until a time specified by the sentencing judge.

Hypothesis: An affirmative statement about the relationship between two variables.

Impulse-charting: Method used to track points and times when certain thoughts or desires seem more intense. The time of day, location, and number of times per week are all important.

Incapacitation: Deprives the offender of liberty and removes him or her from society with the intent of ensuring that society cannot be further victimized by that offender during the offender's term of incarceration. Also, the physical restriction is to prevent further opportunities for lawbreaking.

Independent parole administration model: Supervision model in which a parole board is responsible for making release determinations from prison as well as overseeing the supervision processes of offenders that are released on parole (or good time releases).

Indeterminate sentencing: Sentencing that includes a range of years that will be potentially served by the offender. The offender is released during some point in the range of years assigned by the sentencing judge.

Injunction: A court order that requires an agency to take some form of action(s) or to refrain from a particular action or set of actions.

Instrument testing: Analysis that involves instrumentation (a machine) that will sample, measure, and produce a quantitative result that is given as a numeric amount on a scale.

Intake screening of needs: Leads to a series of judgments that subdivide offenders into broad categories of basic needs or deficits. This then points case managers in the general direction for referral of offenders to generalized service areas.

Intensive needs assessment: Highly detailed intervention plan within a priority need area. Identifies areas of need that require increased involvement of specialized professionals, such as job placement programs, educational institutions, medical services, or mental health treatment services.

Intensive supervision: The extensive supervision of offenders who pose the greatest risk to society or are in need of the greatest amount of governmental services. In most cases, intensive supervision is the option afforded to individuals who would otherwise be incarcerated for felony offenses.

Intensive supervision probation (ISP): Form of sanction usually viewed as the most effective alternative to imprisonment. This type of supervision requires more face-to-face contact between the officer and the offender. In addition, the supervision officer may visit the offender at home and work on a routine basis. The requirements of ISP are much stricter than those for traditional probation.

Intermediate sanctions: A range of sentencing options that fall between incarceration and probation, being designed to allow for the crafting of sentences that respond to the offender or the offense, with the intended outcome of the case being a primary consideration.

Intermittent sentence: A sentence that requires some form of temporary confinement throughout intermittent and partial periods of an offender's sentence.

International Association of Residential and Community Alternatives (IARCA): Established in 1989, this organization advocates for the use of various types of intermediate facilities for offender reentry. The name of the organization reflects the ambiguity in definitions that separate halfway houses and other forms of offender residential programs.

Involvement: Concept conveying that if youth are involved in conventional activities, they will be unable or less likely to engage in delinquent behavior.

Jail: A confinement facility, usually operated and controlled by county-level law enforcement, that is designed to hold persons charged with a crime who are either awaiting adjudication or serving a short sentence of one year or less after the point of adjudication.

Jail diversion programs: Programs that are designed to divert mentally ill offenders and offenders with drug abuse issues from the jail facility as a means of enhancing therapeutic treatment aspects related to the challenges that face these offenders.

John Augustus: A cobbler and philanthropist of Boston, often recognized as the Father of Modern Probation.

Judicial reprieve: A judicial sanction used to suspend sentences whereby judges believed incarceration was not proportionate to the crime committed.

Juvenile Intensive Probation Supervision (JIPS): A regimented program of supervision that requires much greater supervision contact than regular probation and also serves as an alternative to incarceration while maintaining acceptable levels of public safety.

Juvenile probation: A judicial disposition under which youthful offenders are subject to certain conditions imposed by the juvenile court while being allowed to remain in the community during the duration of their sentence.

Juvenile records: Records that include a composite of the youth's criminal history, family and personal information, abuse history, and truancy records, as well as other identification information such as fingerprints or photographs.

Labeling theory: Contends that individuals become stabilized in criminal roles when they are labeled as criminals. As a result, they are stigmatized, develop criminal identities, are sent to prison, and are excluded from conventional roles.

Level of Service Inventory–Revised (LSI-R): A well-regarded, quasi-objective clinical inventory that is used to determine offender likelihood of recidivism and suitability for community supervision.

Licensure: Professional certification that provides the legal right to see clients and receive third-party billing. Third-party billing is when insurance companies, employment assistance programs, or state programs are billed to reimburse the therapist. Licensure is important for the therapeutic practitioner working in private practice or in a nonprofit but private facility.

Long-term residential programs: Treatment programs that provide care 24 hours per day, generally in nonhospital settings. The best-known residential treatment model is the therapeutic community (TC), but residential treatment may also employ other models, such as cognitive behavioral therapy (CBT). These programs tend to house drug offenders for anywhere from 6 to 12 months.

Major depressive disorder: The afflicted person will have decreased energy, tiredness, and fatigue without physical exertion. Even the smallest tasks may seem to require substantial effort. Further, these individuals often have a sense of worthlessness or guilt that may include unrealistic negative evaluations of their worth or guilty preoccupations over minor past failings.

Mark system: Created by Alexander Maconochie, a system whereby "marks" were provided to the convict for each day of successful toil. Under this plan, convicts were given marks and moved through phases of supervision until they finally earned full release.

Martinson report: A landmark report released in 1974 that noted with few and isolated exceptions the rehabilitative efforts that had been reported thus far had had no appreciable effect on recidivism. This report generated substantial controversy in the field of corrections.

Maryland Addictions Questionnaire (MAQ): A substance abuse assessment instrument that is typically administered at intake. It provides the evaluator with an idea of the severity of the addiction, the motivation of the client offender, and the likely risk of relapse for the offender.

Masturbatory reconditioning: Treatment technique that involves having the client masturbate to an appropriate fantasy until he has an ejaculation.

Megan's Laws: A blanket term used to refer to various state notification laws addressing the release of sex offenders in the community. This term is attributed to the brutal rape and murder of a 7-year-old girl named Megan Kanka. The victim's parents pushed for legislation to mandate reporting of sex offenders who are released into the community. These laws have now been adopted by all states, though each may use different names for its own particular legislation.

Megargee offender classification system: System of classification that is known to provide solid empirical support for classification and placement decisions. This system is especially effective in assisting criminal justice practitioners in dealing with an offender population that includes mentally ill or disordered individuals within its ranks.

Mental illness: Defined as any diagnosed disorder contained within the *DSM–IV–TR*, as published by the American Psychiatric Association.

Minnesota Multiphasic Personality Inventory–2, or MMPI-2: An objective personality adjustment inventory test that can be given to large numbers of offenders at the same time or individually as desired.

Minnesota Multiphasic Personality Inventory–2 Criminal Justice and Correctional Report, or MMPI-2 CJCR: Designed to identify those offenders who may suffer from thought disorders, serious depression, and substance abuse problems; identifies those who may need mental health treatment as well as those who are most likely to be hostile, predatory, bullied, or victimized while incarcerated. This report also includes predictor items related to self-injury and suicide.

Model of caseload delivery: Process whereby offenders are initially assigned their community supervision officer. This is often determined by the agency size and the number of offenders under the agency's jurisdiction.

Monetary restitution: A process by which offenders are held partially or fully accountable for the financial losses suffered by the victims of their crimes.

Mood disorders: Disorders such as major depressive disorder, bipolar disorder, and dysthymic disorder. Major depressive disorder is characterized by one or more major depressive episodes.

Narcissistic personality disorder: A pervasive pattern of grandiosity (in fantasy or behavior), need for admiration, and lack of empathy, beginning by early adulthood and present in a variety of contexts.

Needs assessment: Refers to those aspects of offender classification that seek to identify or determine the condition or state of individuals relative to some preestablished functional criteria.

Needs-principled assessment: Type of assessment that deals with the subjective and objective needs of the offender to maximize his or her potential for social reintegration and to reduce the likelihood of future recidivism.

Negative punishment: The removal of a valued stimulus when the offender commits an undesired behavior.

Negative reinforcers: These are unpleasant stimuli that are then removed when a desired behavior occurs.

Negligence: Defined as doing what a reasonably prudent person would not have done in similar circumstances or failing to do what a reasonably prudent person would have done in similar circumstances.

Numbers game model: Caseload model in which the agency defines a desired caseload per officer (such as 40 offenders per officer) and the agency makes its hiring decisions based on this formula.

Objectives: Specific results or effects of a program's activities that must be achieved in pursuing the program's ultimate goals. For example, a treatment program may expect to change offender attitudes (objective) in order to ultimately reduce recidivism (goal).

Opportunistic rapist: Demonstrates neither strong sexual nor aggressive features but engages in spontaneous rape when there appears an opportunity that makes the rape an easy prospect. This form of rape is usually perpetrated during the commission of another crime, such as robbery or burglary.

Outpatient drug-free treatment: Treatment option that typically costs less than residential or inpatient treatment and often is more suitable for individuals who are employed or who have extensive social supports.

Parens patriae: Latin term that originally meant that the king, as father of his country, is empowered and obligated to ensure the welfare of the country's children. In modern times, this means that the state is empowered and obligated to ensure the welfare of children, even when this might result in the removal of a child from the family home.

Parole: Defined as the early release of an offender from a secure facility upon completion of a certain portion of his or her sentence, based on good behavior or other factors.

Parole revocations officer: The officer tasked with the routine holding of preliminary parole revocation hearings by reviewing allegations made by parole officers against parolees.

Passive agent: An officer who views the job as just that—a job. This officer will tend to do as little as possible, and he or she does not have passion for the tasks. Officers who are passive agents do not tend to care about the outcome of their work so long as they avoid any difficulties.

Paternal officers: Officers who use a great degree of both control elements and assistance techniques in supervision.

Pedophilia: Crime involving sexual activity with a prepubescent child (generally age 13 or younger).

Penile plethysmograph (PPG): Treatment technique utilized with sexual offenders that uses a cup or band that is placed around the penis while the offender is in a private room. This instrument is designed to measure sexual arousal, particularly when stimuli such as pictures of children are presented to the offender.

Personality disorders: Psychological disorders that are characterized by an enduring pattern of inner experience and behavior that deviates markedly from the expectations of the individual's culture, is pervasive and inflexible, has an onset in adolescence or early adulthood, is stable over time, and leads to distress or impairment.

Physical abuse: Any physical acts that cause, or have the potential to cause, some sort of physical injury to children or adults.

Physical neglect: Encompasses abandonment; the expulsion of the child from the home (being kicked out of the house); a failure to seek or excessive delay in seeking medical care for the child; inadequate supervision; and provision of inadequate food, clothing, and shelter.

Point-of-contact testing: Analysis using devices that require manual sampling and manual observation to produce a qualitative result that includes both negative and positive values.

Policy: A governing principle pertaining to goals, objectives, or activities. It is a decision on an issue not resolved on the basis of facts and logic only. For example, the policy of expediting drug cases in the courts might be adopted as a basis for reducing the average number of days from arraignment to disposition.

Polygraph: The standard lie detector apparatus used to measure biological responses to deception.

Polygraph examiner: This individual operates the polygraph machine, which is able to detect the likelihood of untruth through a measure of physiological indicators. Because sex offenders are generally very manipulative, superficially compliant, and adept at keeping secrets, the polygraph examiner is invaluable when interviewing or interrogating the sex offender.

Positive punishment: When a stimulus is applied to the offender in response to the offender committing an undesired behavior.

Positive reinforcers: Rewards for a desired behavior.

Power assertive rapist: A rapist who is characterized by a sense of superiority that is based on "hypermasculinity" in which he believes he is entitled to sexual access simply because he is a man. For this offender, rape is an impulsive act of predatory victimization that the female deserves simply because she is female and is fair game for subjugation.

Power reassurance rapist: The least violent of the types considered in this text. These offenders are typically not socially competent and may be quite introverted in thought and behavior. They typically have a low sense of self-esteem and suffer from profound feelings of inadequacy, both socially and sexually.

Preliminary hearing: Examines the facts of the arrest to determine if probable cause exists for a violation.

Presentence investigation report (PSI): File that will typically include demographic, vocational, educational, and personal information on the offender, as well as records on his or her prior offending patterns and the probation department's recommendation as to the appropriate type of sentencing and supervision.

Prisonization: A process whereby inmates become dependent upon institutional routines and guidance as a means of functioning on a day-to-day basis. This is an overadaptation to prison life that is dysfunctional among the social community outside of prison.

Private probation: This type of probation is similar to other forms but is administered by privately owned and operated companies that contract with courts to supervise misdemeanor cases.

Probation: An alternative sanction to incarceration whereby the offender is supervised in the community with specific conditions. It is usually used in conjunction with a suspended sentence.

Probation with community service and restitution: This sanction requires the offender to provide a certain number of designated hours of free labor to a given cause determined by the court.

Probationers: Criminal offenders who have been sentenced to a period of correctional supervision in the community in lieu of incarceration.

Process evaluations: Refers to assessments of the effects of the program on clients while they are in the program, making it possible to assess the institution's intermediary goals.

Prognosis: Refers to the likelihood that an offender will successfully reform and simultaneously refrain from further criminal activity. There is both a treatment component and a public safety component contained within an offender's prognosis.

Psychiatrists: This is a medical doctor who has the ability to prescribe medication for anxiety, depression, anger, and other disorders. It distinguishes them from the other categories of mental health provider.

Psychological abuse: This is sometimes referred to as emotional abuse and includes actions or the omission of actions by parents and other caregivers that could cause a child to have serious behavioral, emotional, or mental impairments.

Psychologists: These professionals have doctorates in psychology and have extensive education in research, theories of human behavior, and therapeutic techniques. In addition, most also specialize in the administration of psychological tests and assessments.

Punitive officers: Officers who see themselves as needing to use threats and punishment in order to get compliance from the offender.

Qualified immunity: Requires that the community supervision officer (CSO) demonstrate certain key aspects prior to invoking this form of defense against suit.

Quasi-experimental design: Used to approximate the advantages of random selection. An example of such a design might be to identify a comparison group that is similar to the treatment group in those characteristics thought to be capable of influencing the outcome under examination.

Race: A concept that is based on biological factors such as skin color and other physical features as a means of distinguishing among different groups of people.

Reality therapy: Uses forms of involvement between counselor and client to teach client to be self-responsible.

Recognizance: This practice involves the use of an obligation entered into by a defendant who is bound to refrain from engaging in crime for a stipulated period and to appear in court on a specified date for final disposition of the case. In exchange, the defendant is not required to remain in jail while waiting for his or her court date.

Reentry courts: Courts that provide comprehensive services to offenders who return from prison to the community by utilizing comprehensive services provided by a network of agencies in the surrounding area.

Rehabilitation: This implies that an offender should be provided the means to fulfill a constructive level of functioning in society, with an implicit expectation that such offenders will be deterred from reoffending due to having worthwhile stakes in legitimate society—stakes that the offender will not wish to lose due to criminal offending. Also, it is meant to change the offender's behavior or circumstances to reduce the possibility of further lawbreaking.

Reliability: A concept that describes the accuracy of a measure, which in turn describes the accuracy of a study.

Residential treatment home: Facility designed to house the offender, but the offender is not ordered by the court to stay at the facility. These facilities may also have "day students" who use the facility as a day reporting center (see day reporting centers).

Residential treatment programs: Facilities that offer a combination of substance abuse and mental health treatment services while youth are kept under 24-hour supervision in a highly structured and secure environment.

Restitution: Compensation to the victim and/or community for crimes committed.

Restitution center: A type of facility that is designed primarily for first-time or property offenders. These offenders are required to pay victim restitution and/or provide community service as a means of fulfilling their sentence.

Restorative justice: A term for interventions that focus on restoring the health of the community, repairing the harm done, meeting the victim's needs, and emphasizing that the offender can and must contribute to those repairs. Restorative justice considers the victims, communities, and offenders as participants in the justice process.

Retribution: Often referred to as the "eye for an eye" mentality, this term simply implies that offenders committing a crime should be punished in a like fashion or in a manner that is commensurate with the severity of the crime that they have committed.

Risk-principled assessment: For this type of assessment, the main concern revolves around the protection of society. The risk-principled assessment system will ensure that hardcore offenders are not in the same treatment regimen as less serious offenders.

Role identity confusion: Occurs when an officer is unclear about the expectations placed upon him or her as the officer attempts to juggle between the "policing"-oriented nature of his or her work and the "reform" orientation.

Role-playing: A therapy technique in which the offender reenacts his or her own crime scene(s) with another offender, and they take turns playing the role of their victim.

Routine activities theory: A theory based on three simplistic notions. First, in order for a crime to occur, a motivated offender must converge with a suitable target. Second, this theory contends that the likelihood of such an occurrence is affected by the routine activities that both victims and offenders engage in. Third, the area of occurrence must be absent of capable guardians that might thwart criminal behavior.

Sadistic rapist: The most dangerous of sex offenders. The primary desire for these offenders is to cause pain to their victim.

Salient factor score: An instrument that measures offender risk along six items, each of which is measured with a value that ranges from 0 (zero) to 3 with inverted indications of risk (i.e., the lower the number, the higher the likelihood that the offender will recidivate).

Saliva testing: Saliva samples permit drug testing and even HIV/AIDS testing to be easily administered. These samples are subject to contamination from smoking or other substances.

Sanctuary: Sanctuary existed historically through the identification of various cities or regions (most often cities) that were set aside as a sort of neutral ground, protected from criminal prosecution. Accused criminals could escape prosecution by fleeing to these cities.

Scheduled overmasturbation: Intervention requiring the client to routinely masturbate on a progressively more frequent schedule throughout the week. This is intended to reduce sexual drive and to make self-control easier for the offender.

Schizophrenic disorders: According to the *DSM–IV–TR,* such disorders have five characteristic symptoms and at least two must be present before the diagnosis can be given to an individual.

These symptoms are as follows: (1) delusions, (2) hallucinations, (3) disorganized speech, (4) grossly disorganized behavior, and (5) inappropriate affect.

Screening: The process by which an offender is determined to be appropriate for admission to a given intervention program.

Self-help groups: As the term is used in this text, these are 12-step programs, composed of individuals who meet regularly to stabilize and facilitate their recovery from substance abuse. The best known is Alcoholics Anonymous (AA).

Sentencing stage: When a judge requires either that the offender be incarcerated or, as in many cases where the violation is minor, that the offender continue his or her probation sentence but under more restrictive terms.

Sex offender therapist: This therapist usually sees the offender once a week in a group counseling setting. These therapists are highly trained and experienced in working with the sex offender population.

Sexual assault: Includes all types of sexual offenses that involve touching or penetration of an intimate part of a person's body without consent.

Sexual gratification rapist: For this rapist, aggression is instrumental and is designed to gain compliance. This offender simply desires sex and may be in a situation where he feels that force or coercion could successfully get him the sexual intercourse that he wants.

Shock incarceration: Short term of incarceration followed by a specified term of community supervision in hopes of deterring the offender from recidivating.

Shock probation: A process of placing an offender in prison and later releasing him or her on probation at some unknown date and time. The shock of incarceration is expected to have a deterrent impact on the offender, with a corresponding sense of gratitude when the offender is released from the facility to probation.

Short-term residential programs: Programs that typically provide intensive but brief residential treatment based on a modified 12-step approach. In most cases, offenders are kept in the program for no more than 90 days.

Social learning theory: Contends that offenders learn to engage in crime through exposure to and the adoption of definitions that are favorable to the commission of crime.

Social study: Second stage of juvenile supervision, following the intake. Also called the investigation stage. This is similar to a presentence investigation report (PSI) and details the youth's personal background, family, educational progress, previous violations, employment, and so forth.

Solution-focused therapy: This treatment begins from the observation that most psychological problems are present only intermittently. Solution-focused therapy assists the client in noticing when symptoms are diminished or absent and helps him or her to use this knowledge as a foundation for recovery.

Specialized needs caseload model: Pertains to community supervision assignments to offenders who share common specialized needs around such areas as substance abuse, sex offending, a given set of disabilities, and so on.

Specific deterrence: The infliction of a punishment upon a specific offender in the hope he or she will be discouraged from committing future crimes.

Split sentencing: A sentence by a judge that consists of a fixed period of incarceration, which is expected to be followed by an additional fixed term of probation supervision. Felony-level offenders are more likely to receive split sentences than are misdemeanants.

Spouse monitoring: This involves supervision on the part of the spouse (if and when available, though other family members may be able to assist) or significant other to complete a daily checklist on the offender's compliance with the treatment.

Stakeholders: In the context of community corrections evaluations, this group would include the agency personnel, the community in which the agency is located, and even the offender population that is being supervised.

Standard probation: The basic form of supervision that is administered by most agencies. This type of sentence is actually little more than a baseline starting point for sanctioning.

Static risk factors: Characteristics that are inherent to the offender and are usually permanent in nature.

Strengths-based perspective case management: Case management in the strengths-based model involves assisting clients to examine and identify their own strengths and assets as the vehicle for resource acquisition and goal attainment.

Study release program: Similar to a work release program but designed to allow the offender an opportunity to pursue educational goals.

Subcultural theory: Theory that many individuals tend to simultaneously learn to commit crime in one location, and this results in crime rates becoming disproportionately high in such areas where criminal behavior is learned as a valued norm.

Subjective assessment process: The use of interviewing and observation methods to determine the security and treatment needs of the offender. Professionals use their sense of judgment and experience to determine the offender's possible dangerousness and treatment needs.

Subjective structured interview: A process whereby an interviewer will ask a respondent a set of prearranged and open-ended questions so that the interview seems informal in nature, yet because of the prearranged questions, a structure evolves throughout the conversation that ensures certain bits of desired data are gathered.

Substance Abuse Relapse Assessment (SARA): A structured interview designed as a treatment planning instrument for treatment professionals who work with substance abusers. It is helpful in developing relapse prevention goals for clients who tend to use multiple substances and in monitoring the achievement of these goals during treatment.

Substance Abuse Subtle Screening Instrument (SASSI): A substance abuse screening instrument that provides interpretations of client profiles and aids in developing hypotheses that clinicians or researchers may find useful in understanding persons in treatment.

Substance abuse treatment: A form of treatment targeting a variety of different forms of substance abuse. These treatments may address specific substances or they may address a multitude of problems.

Supervision stage: This stage of juvenile supervision includes casework, surveillance, and various aspects of security management to track the behavior of the juvenile. This stage is a key function of the probation department.

Sweat testing: Uses sweat samples obtained from patches that can be placed on a person for a number of days. This type of testing has the advantage of providing a longer time frame for detection of drug use, and it is difficult to adulterate the testing results.

Technical violations: Actions that do not comply with the conditions and requirements of a probationer's sentence, as articulated by the court that acted as the sentencing authority. Technical violations are not necessarily criminal and would likely be legal behaviors if the offender were not on probation.

Teen courts: Much like traditional courts in that there are prosecutors and defense attorneys, offenders and victims, and judges and juries, but youths rather than adults fill these roles, and these youths even determine the disposition of the case.

Theory: A concept that describes a set of interrelated constructs that purport to explain some phenomenon.

Therapeutic jurisprudence: The study of the role of the law as a therapeutic agent. Essentially, therapeutic jurisprudence focuses on the law's impact on emotional life and on psychological well-being.

Thought-shifting: This requires that the offender shift his thoughts to aversive imagery. The sex offender may be allowed to view or think about some arousing image but then is trained to think about something aversive, like an approaching police officer.

Thought-stopping: This is used to disrupt a deviant thinking pattern. The sex offender is given pictures of arousing images and is forced to stop his thoughts when the image is seen.

Ticket-of-leave: A permit that was given to offenders on Norfolk Island and Australia in exchange for a certain period of good conduct. Through this process, convicts could earn their own wage through their own labor prior to the expiration of their actual sentence.

Tort: A legal injury in which the action of one person causes injury to the person or property of another as the result of a violation of one's duty that has been established by law.

True negative: Implies that an offender is predicted not to reoffend and that prediction turns out to be true.

True positive: Implies that the offender is predicted to reoffend and that this prediction later turns out to be true.

Urine testing: Due to low cost and reasonably high accuracy of the testing process, urinalysis is considered the most suitable method for drug courts and most criminal justice agencies for detecting the presence of illegal substances.

Validity: A concept that describes whether the instrument used is measuring what it is intended to measure.

Victim counselors: These persons are counselors who were prior victims of some type of traumatic crime, such as domestic abuse or sexual assault.

Victim wraparound services: Complex, multifaceted intervention strategy designed to keep delinquent youth at home and out of institutions whenever possible. Services are provided to offenders transitioning to the community with the aid of a team of support individuals that may include the offender's family, clergy, social service workers, probation and/or parole officers, and other parties.

Victim's impact statement: This allows the victim to express his or her own views on the appropriateness of the parolee's release, and it also allows the victim to voice his or her sense of trauma and victimization that resulted from the criminal actions of the offender.

Welfare worker: Name for an officer who views the offender more as a client than as a supervisee on his or her caseload. This officer believes that the best way to enhance the security and safety of the community is by reforming the offender so that further crime will not occur.

Wilderness camps: Residential programs where juveniles engage in a series of physically challenging outdoor activities, such as backpacking, canoeing, or even rock climbing.

Wisconsin risk assessment system: One of the best-known risk assessment systems, it examines 10 specific factors. This form of structured assessment has become the prototype for many probation and parole systems in the United States.

Work release programs: Programs designed to equip offenders with the opportunity to seek or maintain employment while also engaging in educational or vocational training, as well as other treatment services that might be available at the facility.

References

Abadinsky, H. (2003). *Probation and parole: Theory and practice* (8th ed.). Upper Saddle River, NJ: Prentice Hall.

Abel, G. G., & Rouleau, J. L. (1990). The nature and extent of sexual assault. In W. L. Marshall, D. R. Laws, & H. L. Barbaree (Eds.), *Handbook of sexual assault: Issues, theories, and treatment of the offender* (pp. 9–20). New York: Plenum.

Alarid, L., & Del Carmen, R. V. (2011). *Community-based corrections* (8th ed.). Belmont, CA: Wadsworth.

Alarid, L. F., Del Carmen, R. V., & Cromwell, P. (2007). *Community-based corrections* (7th ed.). Belmont, CA: Wadsworth.

Altschuler, D. M., & Armstrong, T. L. (2001). Reintegrating high-risk juvenile offenders into communities: Experiences and prospects. *Corrections Management Quarterly, 5*(1), 79–95.

American Psychiatric Association. (2000). *Diagnostic and statistical manual of mental disorders.* Washington, DC: Author.

Anderson, D. (1998). *Sensible justice: Alternative to prison.* New York: New Press.

Andrews, D. A., & Bonta, J. (1994). *The psychology of criminal conduct.* Cincinnati, OH: Anderson Publishing Company.

Andrews, D., & Bonta, J. (2003). *Level of supervision inventory–revised (LSI-R).* Retrieved from http://www.mhs.com/LSI.htm

Andrews, D. A., & Dowden, C. (2002). A meta-analytic investigation into effective correctional intervention for female offenders. *Forum on Corrections Research, 11*(3), 18–21.

Anthony, W., Cohen, M., & Farkas, M. (1990). *Psychiatric rehabilitation.* New York: Center for Psychiatric Rehabilitation.

Arizona State Supreme Court. (2008). *Juvenile intensive probation supervision (JIPS).* Retrieved from http://www.supreme.state.az.us/jjsd/JIPS/jips.htm

Arkansas speeds parole to ease jam. (2001, November 30). *Corrections Digest, 32*(48), 2.

Arkansas to emphasize rehabilitation in drive to curb crowding, cut costs. (2002, July 12). *Corrections Digest, 33*(28), 1.

Armstrong, G. S. (2004). Boot camps as a correctional option. In D. L. MacKenzie & G. S. Armstrong (Eds.), *Correctional boot camps: Military basic training or a model for corrections?* (pp. 7–15). Thousand Oaks, CA: Sage.

Ashford, J. B., Sales, B. D., & Reid, W. H. (Eds.). (2001). *Treating adult and juvenile offenders with special needs.* Washington, DC: American Psychological Association.

Austin, J. (2006). How much risk can we take? The misuse of risk assessment in corrections. *Federal Probation, 20*(2). Retrieved from http://www.uscourts.gov/fedprob/September_2006/risk.html#basics

Babcock, J. (2006). *Does batterer treatment work? New directions to improve its efficacy.* Paper presented at the annual meeting of the American Society of Criminology (ASC). Retrieved from http://www.allacademic.com/meta/ p127404_index.html

Barnes, H. E., & Teeters, N. D. (1959). *New horizons in criminology.* Englewood Cliffs, NJ: Prentice Hall.

Bartol, C. R. (2002). *Criminal behavior: A psychosocial approach* (6th ed.). Upper Saddle River, NJ: Prentice Hall.

Baumer, T., Maxfield, M., & Mendelsohn, R. (1993). A comparative analysis of three electronically monitored home detention programs. *Justice Quarterly, 10,* 121–142.

Bazemore, G., & O'Brien, S. (2002). The quest for a restorative model of rehabilitation: Theory-for-practice and practice-for-theory. In L. Walgrave (Ed.), *Restorative justice and the law.* Portland, OH: Willan Publishing.

Bazemore, G., & Seymour, A. (1998). *Victims, judges, and restorative justice partnerships.* Fort Lauderdale: Balanced and Restorative Project, Florida Atlantic University.

Bazemore, G., & Umbreit, M. (2001). *A comparison of four restorative conferencing models.* Washington, DC: U.S. Department of Justice.

Begnaud, C. (2007). *Parole and probation in the United States.* New York: Associated Content. Retrieved from http://www.associatedcontent.com/article/151400/parole_and_probation_in_the_united.html

Bonczar, T. P. (1995). *Characteristics of adults on probation.* Washington, DC: U.S. Department of Justice.

Bouffard, J. A., & Mufti, L. R. (2007). The effectiveness of community service sentences compared to traditional fines for low-level offenders. *The Prison Journal, 87*(2), 171–194.

Boulton, J. (2006). Restorative practices as a tool for organizational change. *Reclaiming Children and Youth, 15*(2), 89–91.

Braithwaite, J. (1989). *Crime, shame, and reintegration*. New York: Cambridge University Press.

Braithwaite, J. (2000). Shame and criminal justice. *Canadian Journal of Criminology, 42*(3), 281–298.

Braithwaite, J. (2002). Setting standards for restorative justice. *British Journal of Criminology, 42*(3), 563–577.

Braithwaite, J. (2006). Crime, shame, and reintegration. In F. T. Cullen & R. Agnew (Eds.), *Criminological theory: Past to present* (3rd ed., pp. 277–285). Los Angeles: Roxbury.

Bureau of Justice Assistance. (1999). *Addressing community gang problems: A model for problem solving*. Washington, DC: Office of Justice Programs. Retrieved from http://www.ojp.usdoj.gov

Bureau of Justice Statistics. (2003). *Recidivism of sex offenders released from prison in 1994*. Washington, DC: U.S. Department of Justice.

Burke, P. B. (1997). *Policy-driven responses to probation and parole violations*. Washington, DC: U.S. Department of Justice, National Institute of Corrections.

Burrell, B. (2006). *Caseload standards for probation and parole*. Washington, DC: National Institute of Corrections.

Butts J., Buck, J., & Coggeshall, M. (2002). *The impact of teen court on young offenders*. Washington, DC: The Urban Institute.

Camp, C., & Camp, G. (2003). *The 2002 corrections yearbook: Adult corrections*. Middletown, CT: Criminal Justice Institute.

Caputo, G. A. (2004). *Intermediate sanctions in corrections: Number 4 in the North Texas crime and criminal justice series*. Denton: University of North Texas Press.

Center for Sex Offender Management. (2001). *Training curricula*. Washington, DC: U.S. Department of Justice.

Center for Sex Offender Management. (2008). *Training curricula*. Washington, DC: Office of Justice Programs, U.S. Department of Justice.

Champion, D. (2002). *Probation, parole and community corrections* (4th ed.). Upper Saddle River, NJ: Prentice Hall.

Clear, T. R., & Cole, G. F. (2003). *American corrections* (6th ed.). Belmont, CA: Thompson/Wadsworth.

Clear, T. R., & Dammer, H. R. (2000). *The offender in the community*. Belmont, CA: Wadsworth.

Clear, T. R., & Karp, D. R. (2000, October). Toward the ideal of community justice. *NIJ Journal*, 20–28.

Clements, C. B., McKee, J. M., & Jones, S. E. (1984). *Offender needs and assessment: Models and approaches*. Washington, DC: National Institute of Corrections.

Cohn, J. (1973). *A study of community-based correctional needs in Massachusetts*. Boston: Massachusetts Department of Corrections.

Connolly, M. M. (2003). A critical examination of actuarial offender-based prediction assessments: Guidance for the next generation of assessments. (Doctoral dissertation, The University of Texas at Austin, 2003). Retrieved from http://www.ncjrs.org/pdffiles1/nij/grants/202982.pdf

Cox, S. M., Allen, J. M., Hanser, R. D., & Conrad, J. L. (2008). *Juvenile justice: A guide to theory, policy, and practice* (6th ed.). Thousand Oaks, CA: Sage.

Craddock, A. (2009). Day reporting center completion: Comparison of individual and multilevel models. *Crime & Delinquency, 55*(1), 105–133.

Cromwell, P. F., Del Carmen, R. V., & Alarid, L. F. (2002). *Community-based corrections* (5th ed.). Belmont, CA: Wadsworth.

Cullen, F. T. (2007). Make rehabilitation corrections' guiding paradigm. *Criminology & Public Policy, 6*(4), 717–728.

Cullen, F. T., & Agnew, R. (2003). *Criminological theory: Past to present* (2nd ed.). Los Angeles: Roxbury.

Cullen, F. T., & Agnew, R. (2006). *Criminological theory: Past to present* (3rd ed.). Los Angeles: Roxbury.

Cullen, F. T., & Gilbert, K. E. (1982). *Reaffirming rehabilitation*. Cincinnati, OH: Anderson Publishing.

Davis, L. E. (1999). *Working with African American males: A guide to practice*. Thousand Oaks, CA: Sage.

Davis, S. F., & Palladino, J. J. (2002). *Psychology* (3rd ed.). Upper Saddle River, NJ: Prentice Hall.

Day, K., & Berney, T. (2001). Treatment and care for offenders with mental retardation. In J. B. Ashford, B. D. Sales, & W. H. Reid (Eds.), *Treating adult and juvenile offenders with special needs* (pp. 199–220). Washington, DC: American Psychological Association.

Del Carmen, R. V., Barnhill, M. B., Bonham, G., Hignite, L., & Jermstad, T. (2001). *Civil liabilities and other legal issues for probation/parole officers and supervisors*. Washington, DC: National Institute of Corrections.

Demuth, S., & Steffensmeier, D. (2004). The impact of gender and race-ethnicity in the pretrial release process. *Social Problems, 51*(2), 222–242.

DiMascio, W. M (1997). *Seeking justice: Crime and punishment in America*. New York: Edna McConnell Clark Foundation.

Dressler, D. (1962). *Practice and theory of probation and parole*. New York: Columbia University Press.

Drummond, R. J. (1996). *Appraisal procedures for counselors and helping professionals* (3rd ed.). Englewood Cliffs, NJ: Prentice Hall.

Duwe, G., & Kerschner, D. (2008). Removing a nail from the boot camp coffin: An outcome evaluation of Minnesota's Challenge Incarceration Program. *Crime & Delinquency, 54*(4), 614–643.

Dzur, A. W., & Wertheimer, A. (2002). Forgiveness and public deliberation: The practice of restorative justice. *Criminal Justice Ethics, 21*(1), 3–20.

Eddy, J. M., & Reid, J. B. (2003). The adolescent children of incarcerated parents: A developmental perspective. In J. Travis & M. Waul (Eds.), *Prisoners once removed: The impact of incarceration and reentry on children, families, and communities* (pp. 233–258). Washington, DC: The Urban Institute Press.

Enos, R., & Southern, S. (1996). *Correctional case management.* Cincinnati, OH: Anderson Publishing.

Evans, D. G., & Sawdon, J. (2004). The development of a gang exit strategy. *Corrections Today, 66*(6), 78–82.

Finn, P., & Kuck, S. (2003). *Addressing probation and parole officer stress.* Washington, DC: National Institute of Justice.

Firshein, J. (1998). Does treatment work? Retrieved from http://www.thirteen.org/closetohome/policy/html/treat work.html

Froland, C., Pancoast, D. L., Chapman, N. J., & Kimboko, P. J. (1981). *Helping networks and human services.* Beverly Hills, CA: Sage.

Gacono, C. B., Nieberding, R. J., Owen, A., Rubel, J., & Bodholdt, R. (2001). Treating conduct disorder, antisocial, and psychopathic personalities. In J. B. Ashford, B. D. Sales, & W. H. Reid (Eds.), *Treating adults and juvenile offenders with special needs.* Washington, DC: American Psychological Association.

Gaes, G. G., Flanagan, T. J., Motiuk, L. L., & Stewart, S. (1999). Adult correctional treatment. In M. Tonry & J. Petersilia (Eds.), *Prisons. Crime and justice: A review of research* (Vol. 26, pp. 361–426). Chicago: University of Chicago Press.

Gendreau, P., Smith, P., & Thériault, Y. L. (2009). Chaos theory and correctional treatment: Common sense, correctional quackery, and the law of fartcatchers. *Journal of Contemporary Criminal Justice, 25*(4), 384–396.

Gerkin, P. M. (2009). Participation in victim-offender mediation: Lessons learned from observations. *Criminal Justice Review, 34*(2), 226–247.

Glaser, D. (1964). *The effectiveness of a prison and parole system.* Indianapolis, IN: Bobbs-Merrill.

Glaze, L. E., & Bonczar, T. P. (2007). *Probation and parole in the United States, 2005.* Washington, DC: U.S. Bureau of Justice Statistics.

Glaze, L. E., & Bonczar, T. P. (2009). *Probation and parole in the United States, 2008.* Washington, DC: U.S. Bureau of Justice Statistics.

Glaze, L. E., & Palla, S. (2005). *Probation and parole in the United States, 2004.* Washington, DC: United States Department of Justice.

Goffman, E. (1961). *Asylums: Essays on the social situation of mental patients and other inmates.* Garden City, NY: Anchor Books.

Gordon, M., & Glaser, D. (1991). The use and effects of financial penalties in municipal courts. *Criminology, 29,* 651–676.

Greek, C. (2002). The cutting edge: Tracking probationers in space and time: The convergence of GIS and GPS systems. *Federal Probation, 66,* 51–53.

Grinnel, F. W. (1941). The common law history of probation. *Journal of Criminal Law and Criminology, 32*(1), 15–35.

Hanser, R. D. (2006a). Restorative justice applications to sex offenders and domestic abusers in Canada. *Crime and Justice International, 22*(90), 31–35.

Hanser, R. D. (2006b). *Special needs offenders.* Upper Saddle River, NJ: Pearson/Prentice Hall.

Hanser, R. D. (2007a). *Special needs offenders in the community.* Upper Saddle River, NJ: Prentice Hall.

Hanser, R. D. (2007b). Restorative justice paradigms as applied to nonviolent and violent special needs offenders. *International Journal of Restorative Justice, 3*(1), 54–65.

Hanser, R. D. (2009). *Community corrections.* Thousand Oaks, CA: Sage.

Hanser, R. D., & Mire, S. M. (2008). Juvenile sex offenders in the United States and Australia: A comparison. *International Review of Law and Technology, 22*(1 & 2), 101–114.

Hanson, K. R., Gordon, A., Harris, A. J., Marques, J. K., Murphy, W., Quinsey, V. L., et al. (2002). First report of the collaborative outcome data project on the effectiveness of psychological treatment for sex offenders. *Sexual Abuse: A Journal of Research and Treatment, 14*(2), 169–194.

Hanson, G. R., Venturelli, P. J., & Fleckenstein, A. E. (2002). *Drugs and society* (7th ed.). Sudbury, MA: Jone & Bartlett.

Harris, P. (1994). Client management classification and prediction of probation outcomes. *Crime and Delinquency, 40*(1), 154–174.

Harris, M. K. (1996). Key differences among Community Corrections Acts in the United States: An overview. *The Prison Journal, 76*(2), 192–238.

Heck, C., & Roussell, A. (2007). State administration of drug courts: Exploring issues of authority, funding, and legitimacy. *Criminal Justice Policy Review, 18*(4), 418–433.

Hepburn, J. R., & Harvey, A. N. (2007). The effect of the threat of legal sanction on program retention and completion: Is that why they stay in drug court? *Crime and Delinquency, 53*(2), 255–280.

Holmes, R. M., & Holmes, S. T. (2002). *Profiling violent crimes* (3rd ed.). Thousand Oaks, CA: Sage.

Houston, J., & Barton, S. M. (2005). *Juvenile justice: Theory, systems, and organization.* Upper Saddle River, NJ: Prentice Hall.

Hunt County CSCD. (2004). *Why sex offenders on probation?* Retrieved from http://www.koyote.com/users/hunt/page9.html

Hurley, M. H. (2009). Restorative practices in institutional settings and at release: Victim wrap around programs. *Federal Probation, 73*(1), 16–22.

Illinois Criminal Justice Information Authority. (1988). *Electronically monitored home confinement in Illinois.* Chicago, IL: Author.

Inciardi, J. A. (1999a). Drug treatment behind bars. In P. M. Carlson & J. S. Garrett (Eds.), *Prison and jail administration: Practice and theory.* Gaithersberg, MD: Aspen Publications.

Inciardi, J. A. (1999b). Prison-based therapeutic communities: An effective modality for treating drug-involved offenders. In K. C. Haas & G. P. Alpert (Eds.), *The dilemmas of punishment* (pp. 403–417). Prospect Heights, IL: Waveland.

Ingraham, B., & Smith, G. (1972). Electronic surveillance and control of behavior and its possible use in rehabilitation and parole. *In Issues in Criminology, 7,* 35–52.

Jones, J. (2007). *Pre-release planning and re-entry process: Addendum 02.* Tulsa: Oklahoma Department of Corrections.

Kempinen, C. A., & Kurlychek, M. C. (2003). An outcome evaluation of Pennsylvania's boot camp: Does rehabilitative programming within a disciplinary setting reduce recidivism? *Crime & Delinquency, 49*(4), 581–601.

King, W. R., Holmes, S. T., Henderson, M. L., & Latessa, E. J. (2007). The community corrections partnership: Examining the long-term effects of youth participation in an Afrocentric diversion program. *Crime & Delinquency, 47*(4), 558–572.

Knight, R. A., & Prentky, R. A. (1990). Classifying sexual offenders: The development and corroboration of taxonomic models. In W.L. Marshall, D. R. Laws, & H. L. Barbaree (Eds.), *Handbook of sexual assault: Issues, theories, and treatment of the offender* (pp. 9–20). New York: Plenum.

Knopp, F. H. (1989). Northwest treatment associates: A comprehensive community-based evaluation and treatment program for adult sex offenders. In P. C. Kratcoski (Ed.), *Correctional counseling and treatment* (2nd ed., pp. 364–380). Prospect Heights, IL: Waveland Press, Inc.

Krauss, D. A., Sales, B. D., Becker, J. V., & Figueredo, A. J. (2000). Beyond prediction to explanation in risk assessment research. *International Journal of Law and Psychiatry, 23*(2), 91–112.

Krauth, B., & Linke, L. (1999). *State organizational structures for delivering adult probation services.* Washington, DC: National Institute of Corrections.

Latessa, E. J., & Allen, H. E. (1999). *Corrections in the community.* Cincinnati, OH: Anderson Publishing Company.

Latessa, E. J., Cullen, F. T., & Gendreau, P. (2002). Beyond correctional quackery: Professionalism and the possibility of effective treatment. *Federal Probation, 66*(2), 43–49.

Latessa, E. J., & Smith, P. (2007). *Corrections in the community* (4th ed.). Cincinnati, OH: LexisNexis.

Latimer, J., Dowden, C., & Muise, D. (2005). The effectiveness of restorative justice practices: A meta-analysis. *The Prison Journal, 85*(2), 127–144.

LeBeau, M., & Mozayani, A. (2001). *Drug-facilitated sexual assault.* San Diego, CA: Academic Press.

Lehman, J., Beatty, T. G., Maloney, D., Russell, A., Seymour, A., & Shapiro, C. (2002). *The three "R's" of reentry.* Washington, DC: Justice Solutions.

Lester, D., & Hurst, G. (2000). Treating sex offenders. In P. VanVoorhis, M. Braswell, & D. Lester (Eds.), *Correctional counseling and rehabilitation* (4th ed., pp. 251–264). Cincinnati, OH: Anderson Publishing Company.

Lightfoot, E., & Umbreit, M. (2004). An analysis of state statutory provisions for victim-offender mediation. *Criminal Justice Policy Review, 15*(4), 418–436.

Lipsey, M. W. (2000, July 16–19). *What 500 intervention studies show about the effects of intervention on the recidivism of juvenile offenders.* Paper presented at the Annual Conference on Criminal Justice Research and Evaluation, Washington, DC.

Lipsey, M. W. (2009). The primary factors that characterize effective interventions with juvenile offenders: A meta-analytic overview. *Victims and Offenders, 4*, 124–147.

Lipsey, M. W., Wilson, D. B., & Cothern, L. (2000). *Effective intervention for serious juvenile intervention.* Washington, DC: Office of Juvenile Justice and Delinquency Prevention.

Little, G. L. (2005). Meta-analysis of moral reconation therapy: Recidivism results from probation and parole implementations. *Cognitive-Behavioral Treatment Review, 14*, 14–16.

Lowenkamp, C. T., & Whetzel, J. (2009). The development of an actuarial risk assessment instrument for U.S. Pretrial Services. *Federal Probation, 73*(2), 33–36.

Lowry, K. D. (2000). United States probation/pretrial officer's concerns about victimization and officer safety training. *Federal Probation, 64*(2), 51–59.

Lurigio, A. J. (1996). Responding to the mentally ill on probation and parole: Recommendations and action plans. In A. J. Lurigio (Ed.), *Community corrections in America: New directions and sounder investments for persons with mental illness and codisorders* (pp. 166–171). Washington, DC: National Institute of Corrections.

Lutze, F. E., & Brody, D. C. (1999). Mental abuse as cruel and unusual punishment: Do boot camp prisons violate the eighth amendment? *Crime & Delinquency, 45*(2), 242–255.

MacKenzie, D. L. (2006). *What works in corrections: Reducing the criminal activities of offenders and delinquents.* New York: Cambridge University Press.

MacKenzie, D. L., & Armstrong, G. S. (Eds.) (2004). *Correctional boot camps: Military basic training or a model for corrections?* Thousand Oaks, CA: Sage.

Martinson, R. (1974, Spring). What works?—Questions and answers about prison reform. *Public Interest*, 22–54.

Maximus. (2003). *MAXIMUS acquires misdemeanor probation outsourcing firm.* Reston, VA: Gale Group.

McCall, R. B. (1994). *Preventing school failure and antisocial behavior in the U.S.A.* Pittsburgh, PA: University of Pittsburgh Office of Child Development.

McCarthy, B. R., McCarthy, B. J., & Leone, M. C. (2001). *Community-based corrections* (4th ed.). Belmont, CA: Wadsworth.

McCoy, T. (2000). Probation officer safety: The results of the National Association of Probation Executives Probation Safety survey. *Executive Exchange*, 4–11.

McGarry, P. (1990). *NIC focus: Intermediate sanctions.* Washington, DC: National Institute of Corrections.

McNeece, C. A., Springer, D. W., & Arnold, E. M. (2002). Treating substance abuse disorders. In J. B. Ashford, B. D. Sales, & W. H. Reid (Eds.), *Treating adult and juvenile offenders with special needs* (pp. 131–169). Washington, DC: American Psychological Association.

Megargee, E. I. (2004). *MMPI-2 criminal justice and correctional report.* Upper Saddle River, NJ: Pearson.

Meyer, J. F. (2004). Home confinement with electronic monitoring. In G. A. Caputo (Ed.), *Intermediate sanctions in corrections. Number 4: North Texas crime and criminal justice series* (pp. 97–123). Denton: University of North Texas Press.

Mika, H., Achilles, M., Halbert, E., Amstutz, L., & Zehr, H. (2004). Listening to victims—A critique of restorative justice policy and practice in the United States. *Federal Probation 68*(1), 32–38.

Miller, E. J. (2007). The therapeutic effects of managerial reentry court. *Federal Sentencing Reporter, 20*(2), 127–135.

Moffitt, T. E. (1993). Adolescence-limited and life-course persistent antisocial behavior: A developmental taxonomy. *Psychological Review, 100*, 674–701.

Monchick, R., Scheyett, A., & Pfeifer, J. (2006). *Drug court case management: Role, function, and utility*. Alexandria, VA: National Drug Court Institute.

Morris, N., & Tonry, M. (1990). *Between prison and probation: Intermediate punishments in a rational sentencing system*. New York: Oxford University Press.

Myers, P. L., & Salt, N. R. (2000). *Becoming an addictions counselor: A comprehensive text*. Sudbury, MA: Jones & Bartlett Publishers.

National Association of Pretrial Services Agencies (NAPSA). (2008). *Performance standards and goals for pretrial diversion/intervention*. Retrieved from http://napsa.org/publications/diversion_intervention_standards_2008.pdf

National Center for Victims of Crime. (1988). *Responding to workplace violence and staff victimization in probation, parole, and corrections: A training and resource manual*. Arlington, VA: Author.

National Center for Women and Policing. (2001). *Equality denied: The status of women in policing in 2001*. Beverly Hills, CA: National Center for Women and Policing.

National Criminal Justice Resources and Statistics. (1999). *Reentry courts: Managing the transition from prison to community*. Washington, DC: Author. Retrieved from http://www.ncjrs.org/pdffiles1/ojp/sl000389.pdf

National Institute of Corrections. (1993). *The intermediate sanctions handbook: Experiences and tools for policymakers*. Washington, DC: National Institute of Corrections.

National Institute of Corrections. (2004). *Mentally ill persons in correctional settings*. Retrieved from http://www.nicic.org/resources/topics/MentallyIll.aspx

National Institute of Justice. (1998). *What can the federal government do to decrease crime and revitalize communities?* Washington, DC: Author.

National Institute of Justice. (1999, October). *Keeping track of electronic monitoring*. National Law Enforcement and Corrections Technology Center Bulletin.

National Institute of Mental Health. (2002). *Depression*. Bethesda, MD: Author.

National Institute on Drug Abuse. (2005). *Types of treatment*. Washington, DC: Office of National Drug Control Policy. Retrieved from http://www.whitehousedrugpolicy.gov/treat/treatment.html

Nelson, K. E., Ohmart, H., & Harlow, N. (1978). *Promising strategies in probation and parole*. Washington, DC: U.S. Government Printing Office.

Neubauer, D. W. (2002). *America's courts and the criminal justice system* (7th ed.). Belmont, CA: Wadsworth/Thomson Learning.

Nored, L. S., & Carlan, P. E. (2008). Success of drug court programs: Examination of the perceptions of drug court personnel. *Criminal Justice Review, 33*(3), 329–342.

Office for Victims of Crime. (2002). *Ordering restitution to the crime victim. Legal Series Bulletin #6*. Washington, DC: Office of Justice Programs.

Office of Juvenile Justice. (n.d.). Wraparound/case management. Retrieved November 13, 2010 from OJJDP Model Programs Guide: http://www.ojjdp.gov/mpg/progTypesCaseManagementInt.aspx

Office of Juvenile Justice & Delinquency Prevention (2007). *Model programs guide*. Washington, DC: Author. Retrieved from http://www.dsgonline.com/mpg2.5/mpg_index.htm

Office of the Auditor (2007). *Probations services for Athens-Clarke County state and municipal courts: Report to the mayor and commission*. Athens-Clarke County, GA: Unified Government of Athens-Clarke County.

O'Keefe, M. L., Klebe, K., & Hromas, S. (1998). *Supervision inventory (LSI) for community-based offender in Colorado: Phase II. State of Colorado*. Retrieved from http://www.doc.state.co.us/AlcoholDrug/pdfs/PHASE2.pdf

O'Malley, P. (2009). Theorizing fines. *Punishment & Society, 11*(1), 67–83.

Outlaw, M. C., & Ruback, R. B. (1999). Predictors and outcomes of victim restitution orders. *Justice Quarterly, 16*(4), 847–869.

Palmer, T. (1975). Martinson revisited. *Journal of Research in Crime and Delinquency, 12*, 133–152.

Panzarella, R. (2002). Theory and practice of probation on bail in the report of John Augustus. *Federal Probation, 66*(3), 38–42.

Parke, R. D., & Clarke-Stewart, K. A. (2003). The effects of parental incarceration on children: Perspectives, promises, and policies. In J. Travis & M. Waul (Eds.), *Prisoners once removed: The impact of incarceration and reentry on children, families, and communities* (pp. 189–232). Washington, DC: The Urban Institute Press.

Parsonage, W. H., & Bushey, W. C. (1987). The victimization of probation and parole workers in the line of duty: An explanatory study. *Criminal Justice Policy Review, 2*(4), 372–391.

Peak, K. J. (1995). *Justice administration: Police, courts, and corrections management*. Upper Saddle River, NJ: Prentice Hall.

Perlman, H. H. (1957). *Perspectives on social casework*. Philadelphia: Temple University Press.

Petersilia, J. (2003). *When prisoners come home: Parole and prisoner reentry*. New York: Oxford University Press.

Petersilia, J., & Turner, S. (1993). *Evaluating intensive supervised probation/parole results of a nationwide experiment*. Washington, DC: U.S. Department of Justice.

Pretrial diversion abstract. (1998). Milwaukee, WI: National Association of Pretrial Services Agencies. Retrieved from http://napsa.org/publications/diversionabstract.pdf

Pretrial Justice Institute (2009, August). *2009 survey of pretrial services programs*. Washington, DC: Author. Retrieved from http://www.pretrial.org/Docs/Documents/PJI's%20Survey%20of%20Pretrial%20Programs%202009.2.pdf

Providence Service Corporation. (2006). *Providence Service Corporation acquires MAXIMUS Correctional Services Business.* Tucson, AZ: Author.

Rackmill, S. (1994). An analysis of home confinement as a sanction. *Federal Probation, 58,* 45–52.

Rapp, C. A. (1998). The active ingredients of effective case management: A research synthesis. *Community Mental Health Journal, 34*(4), 363–372.

Reilly, Jr., E. F. (2002). *28 CFR Part 2: Paroling, recommitting, and supervising federal prisoners: Prisoners serving sentences under the United States and District of Columbia codes.* Washington, DC: Department of Justice, Parole Commission.

Renzema, M. (1992). Home confinement programs: development, implementation, and impact. In J. Bryne, A. Lurigio, & J. Petersilia (Eds.), *Smart sentencing: The emergence of intermediate sanctions* (pp. 41–53). Thousand Oaks, CA: Sage.

Rice, M. E., Harris, G. T., & Quinsey, V. L. (2002). Research on the treatment of adult sex offenders. In J. B. Ashford, B. D. Sales, & W. H. Reid (Eds.), *Treating adult and juvenile offenders with special needs.* Washington, DC: American Psychological Association.

Robinson, J. J., & Jones, J. W. (2000). *Drug testing in a drug court environment: Common Issues to address.* Washington, DC: Office of Justice Program, Drug Courts Program Office. Retrieved from http://www.ncjrs.gov/pdffiles1/ojp/181103.pdf

Rothman, D. (1980). *Conscience and convenience: The asylum and its alternatives in progressive America.* Boston: Little, Brown.

Rothman, D. J. (2002). *Conscience and convenience: The asylum and its alternatives in progressive America* (Rev. ed.). Piscataway, NJ: Aldine Transactions.

Ruback, R. B., & Bergstrom, M. H. (2006). Economic sanctions in criminal justice: Purposes, effects, and implications. *Criminal Justice and Behavior, 33*(2), 242–273.

Sabol, W. J., West, H. C., & Cooper, M. (2009). *Prisoners in 2008.* Washington, DC: U.S. Bureau of Justice Statistics.

Sacks, S., Sacks, J. Y., & Stommel, J. (2003). Modified therapeutic community programs: For inmates with mental illness and chemical abuse disorders. *Corrections Today, 65*(6), 90–100.

Sahagun, L. (2007, June 2). A mother's plight revives sanctuary movement. *Los Angeles Times.* Retrieved from http://www.latimes.com/news/printedition/california/la-me-beliefs2jun02,1,1213380.story?coll=la-headlines-pe-california.

Saiman, C. (2008). Restitution in America: Why the US refuses to join the global restitution party. *Oxford Journal of Legal Studies, 28*(1), 99–126.

Sarre, R. (2001). Beyond "what works?": A 25-year jubilee retrospective of Robert Martinson's famous article. *The Australian and New Zealand Journal of Criminology, 34*(1), 38–46.

Sarri, R., & Vinter, R. (1975). Juvenile justice and injustice. *Resolution, 18,* 45.

Saum, C. A., & Hiller, M. L. (2008). Should violent offenders be excluded from drug court participation? An examination of the recidivism of violent and nonviolent drug court participants. *Criminal Justice Review, 33*(3), 291–307.

Schmidt, A. (1994). An overview of intermediate sanctions in the United States. In U. Zvekic (Ed.), *Alternatives to imprisonment: A comparative perspective* (pp. 349–362). Chicago: Nelson Hall.

Schneider, A., & Finkelstein, M. (1998). *National directory of restitution and community service programs.* Washington, DC: U.S. Office of Juvenile Justice & Delinquency Prevention.

Schultz, E. (2006). The Second Chance Act. *Corrections Today, 68*(5), 22–23.

Schwitzgebel, R. L. (1969, April). A belt from big brother. *Psychology Today, 2,* 45–47.

The Sentencing Project. (2002). *Mentally ill offenders in the criminal justice system: An analysis and prescription.* Washington, DC: Author.

Seymour, A. (2000). Providing victim services within a restorative justice paradigm. *Corrections Management, 4*(3), 21–29.

Shusta, M., Levine, D. R., Wong, H. Z., & Harris, P. R. (2005). *Multicultural law enforcement: Strategies for peacekeeping in a diverse society* (3rd ed.). Upper Saddle River, NJ: Prentice Hall.

Siegel, L. J. (2003). *Criminology: Theories, patterns, and typologies* (7th ed.). Belmont, CA: Wadsworth.

Sieh, E. W. (2006). *Community corrections and human dignity.* Sudbury, MA: Jones & Bartlett Publishers.

Smith, P., Goggin, C., & Gendreau, P. (2002). *The effects of prison sentences on recidivism: General effects and individual differences.* Saint John, Canada: Centre for Criminal Justice Studies, University of New Brunswick.

Stattin, H., & Magnusson, D. (1996). Antisocial development: A holistic approach. *Development and Psychopathology, 8,* 617–645.

Steadman, H. J., Cocozza, J. J., & Veysey, B. M. (1999). Comparing outcomes for diverted and nondiverted jail detainees with mental illnesses. *Law and Human Behavior, 23*(6), 615–627.

Steen, S., & Bandy, R. (2007). When the policy becomes the problem: Criminal justice in the new millennium. *Punishment & Society, 9*(1), 5–26.

Stinchcomb, J. B., McCampbell, S. W., & Layman, E. P. (2006). *Future force: A guide to building the 21st century community corrections workforce.* Washington, DC: National Institute of Corrections.

Sturgeon, V. H., & Taylor, J. (1980). Report of a five-year follow-up study of mentally disordered sex offenders released from Atascadero State Hospital in 1973. *Criminal Justice Journal, 4,* 31–63.

Surgeon General. (2001). *Youth violence: A report of the Surgeon General.* Washington, DC: Office of the Surgeon General.

Szasz, T. (1975). The control of conduct: Authority vs. autonomy? *Criminal Law Bulletin, 11.*

Takagi, P., & Shank, G. (2004). Critique of restorative justice. *Social Justice, 31*(3), 147–163.

Texas Board of Pardons and Paroles. (2001). Parole guidelines score: Offender information system. Austin, TX: Author. Retrieved from www.reentrypolicy.org/reentry/Document_Viewer.aspx?DocumentID=300

Tonry, M. (1999). Parochialism in U.S. sentencing policy. *Crime & Delinquency, 45*(1), 48–65.

Torres, S. (2005). Parole. In R. A. Wright & J. M. Mitchell (Eds.), *Encyclopedia of criminology*. New York: Routledge.

Umbreit, M. (2000). *Family group conferencing: Implications for crime victims*. St. Paul: University of Minnesota, School of Social Work, Center for Restorative Justice and Peacemaking.

U.S. Bureau of Labor Statistics. (2006). *Occupational outlook handbook, 2006–07 edition, Probation officers and correctional treatment specialists*. Retrieved from http://www.bis.gov/oco/ocos265.htm

U.S. Courts Probation and Pretrial Services. (2010a). *Beginnings of probation and pretrial services*. Retrieved from http://www.uscourts.gov/fedprob/history/beginnings.html

U.S. Courts Probation and Pretrial Services. (2010b). *Milestones in system history*. Retrieved from http://www.uscourts.gov/fedprob/history/milestones.html

U.S. Government Accounting Office. (1990). *Intermediate sanctions*. Washington, DC: Author.

Valdez, A. (2005). *Gangs: A guide to understanding street gangs*. San Clemente, CA: LawTech Publishing.

Van Voorhis, P., Braswell, M., & Lester, D. (2000). *Correctional counseling and rehabilitation* (4th ed.). Cincinnati, OH: Anderson Publishing Company.

Vera Institute of Justice. (2002). *How to use structured fines (day fines) as an intermediate sanction: Monograph*. Washington, DC: Bureau of Justice Assistance, Office of Justice Programs.

Vito, G., & Allen, H. (1981). Shock probation in Ohio: A comparison of outcomes. *International Journal of Offender Therapy and Comparative Criminology, 25*, 70–76.

Waldron, H. B., & Kaminer, Y. (2004). On the learning curve: The emerging evidence supporting cognitive-behavioral therapies for adolescent substance abuse. *Society for the Study of Addiction, 99*, 93–105.

Walker, J. S., & Schutte, K. (2003). *Individualized service/support planning and wraparound: Research bibliography*. Portland, OR: Portland State University, Research and Training Center on Family Support and Children's Mental Health.

Walker, L., Sakai, T., & Brady, K. (2006). Restorative circles—A reentry planning process for Hawaii inmates. *Federal Probation, 70*(1), 33–37.

Walsh, J. (2000). *Clinical case management with persons having mental illness*. Belmont, CA: Brooks/Cole.

Washington State Institute for Public Policy. (2007). *Does participation in Washington's work release facilities reduce recidivism?* Washington, DC: National Institute of Corrections. Retrieved from http://nicic.org/Library/022723

Wasserman, G. A., & Miller, L. S. (1998). The prevention of serious and violent juvenile offending. In R. Loeber & D. P. Farrington (Eds.), *Serious and violent juvenile offenders: Risk factors and successful interventions* (pp. 197–247). Thousand Oaks, CA: Sage.

Wemmers, J., & Cyr, K. (2005). Can mediation be therapeutic for crime victims? An evaluation of victims' experience in mediation with young offenders. *Canadian Journal of Criminology and Criminal Justice, 47*(3), 527–544.

Wenzel, M., Okimoto, T. G., Feather, N. T., & Platow, M. J. (2008). Retributive and restorative justice. *Law and Human Behavior, 32*, 375–389.

Wexler, D. B., & Winick, B. J. (2008). Thereapeutic jurisprudence. In A. W. Graham (Ed.), *Principles of addiction medicine* (4th ed., pp. 550–552). Chevy Chase, MD: American Society of Addiction Medicine.

Whitehead, J. T. (1986). Job burnout and job satisfaction among probation managers. *Journal of Criminal Justice, 14*(1), 25.

Wiebush, R. G. (1993). Juvenile intensive supervision: The impact on felony offenders diverted from institutional placement. *Crime & Delinquency, 39*(1), 68–89.

Wilson, G. (1985). Halfway house programs for offenders. In L. F. Travis (Ed.), *Probation, parole, and community corrections* (pp. 151–164). Prospect Heights, IL: Waveland Press.

Wood, H. R., & White, D. L. (1992). A model for habilitation and prevention for offenders with mental retardation-The Lancaster County (PA) Office of Special Offenders Services. In R. Conley, R. Luckasson, & G. Bouthilet (Eds.), *The criminal justice system and mental retardation* (pp. 153–165). Baltimore: Brookes.

Woodahl, E. J., & Garland, B. (2009). The evolution of community corrections: The enduring influence of the prison. *The Prison Journal, 89*(1), 81S–104S.

Yacus, G. M. (1998). Validation of the risk and needs assessment used in the classification for parole and probation of Virginia's adult criminal offenders. (Doctoral dissertation, Old Dominion University, 1998).

Youth violence: A report of the surgeon general. (2002). *Surgeon general executive summary*. Retrieved from http://www.mentalhealth.org/youthviolence/surgeongeneral/SG_Site/chapter4/sec1.asp

Credits and Sources

Section I: History and Development of Community-Based Corrections

Applied Theory box 1.1:

Davis, S. F., & Palladino, J. J. (2002). *Psychology* (3rd ed.). Upper Saddle River, NJ: Prentice Hall.
Smith, P., Goggin, C., & Gendreau, P. (2002). *The effects of prison sentences on recidivism: General effects and individual differences.* Saint John, Canada: Centre for Criminal Justice Studies, University of New Brunswick.

Photo 1.2: © Robert D. Hanser

Section II: Pretrial Release and Diversion

Applied Theory box 2.1:

Sampson, R. J., Raudenbush, S. W., & Earls, F. (1997). Neighborhoods and violent crime: A multilevel study of collective efficacy. *Science, 277,* 918–924.

Section III: Restorative Justice

Applied Theory box 3.1:

Cullen, F. T., & Agnew, R. (2006). *Criminological theory: Past to present* (3rd ed.). Los Angeles: Roxbury.
Lilly, J. R., Cullen, F. T., & Ball, R. A. (2007). *Criminological theory: Context and consequences* (4th ed.). Thousand Oaks, CA: Sage.

Focus Topic box 3.1:

Iowa Department of Corrections. (2007). *Victim services.* Des Moines, IA. Retrieved from http://www.doc.state.ia.us/VictimServices.asp

Photo 3.1: © Getty Images

Section IV: The Viability of Treatment Perspectives

Table 4.1:

Latessa, E. J., Cullen, F. T., & Gendreau, P. (2002). Beyond correctional quackery: Professionalism and the possibility of effective treatment. *Federal Probation, 66*(2), 45.

Figure 4.1:

Walters, S. T., Clark, M. D., Gingerich, R., & Meltzer, M. L. (2007). *A guide for probation and parole: Motivating offenders to change.* Washington, DC: National Institute of Corrections.

Table 4.2:

Walters, S. T., Clark, M. D., Gingerich, R., & Meltzer, M. L. (2007). *A guide for probation and parole: Motivating offenders to change.* Washington, DC: National Institute of Corrections.

Figure 4.2:

Hanser, R. D. (2006). *Special needs offenders.* Upper Saddle River, NJ: Pearson/Prentice Hall.

Applied Theory box 4.1:

Gaes, G. G., Flanagan, T. J., Motiuk, L. L., & Stewart, S. (1999). Adult correctional treatment. In M. Tonry & J. Petersilia (Eds.), *Prisons. Crime and justice: A review of research* (Vol. 26, pp. 361–426). Chicago: University of Chicago Press.

MacKenzie, D. L. (2006). *What works in corrections: Reducing the criminal activities of offenders and delinquents.* New York: Cambridge University Press.

Ross, R., & Fabiano, E. (1985). *Time to think: A cognitive model of crime and delinquency prevention and rehabilitation.* Johnson City, TN: Academy of Arts and Sciences.

Photo 4.2: © Claire White

Section V: Assessment and Risk Prediction

Figure 5.1:

Kansas Sentencing Commission. (2004). *Kansas sentencing guidelines: Presentence investigation report.* Topeka, KS: Author. Retrieved from http://www.kspace.org/bitstream/1984/69/7/Appendix_D_2004_PSI_Form.pdf

Figure 5.2:

This assessment form was adapted from the following U.S. government publication: Prentky, R., & Righthand, S. (2003). *Juvenile sex offender assessment protocol-II (J-SOAP-II) manual.* Washington, DC: Office of Juvenile Delinquency and Prevention. Retrieved from http://nicic.org/Library/019361

Table 5.2:

Harris, P. (1994). Client management classification and prediction of probation outcomes. *Crime and Delinquency, 40*(1), 154–174; and Yacus, G. M. (1998). Validation of the risk and needs assessment used in the classification for parole and probation of Virginia's adult criminal offenders. (Doctoral dissertation, Old Dominion University, 1998).

Figure 5.4:

Pennsylvania Board of Probation and Parole website: http://www.pbpp.state.pa.us/pbpp/site/default.asp

Focus Topic box 5.1:

Haas, S. M., Hamilton, C. A., & Hanley, D. (2006, July). *Implementation of the West Virginia Offender Reentry Initiative: An examination of staff attitudes and the application of the LSI-R.* Charleston, WV: Mountain State Criminal Justice Research Services.

Applied Theory box 5.1:

Lilly, J. R., Cullen, F. T., & Ball, R. A. (2007). *Criminological theory: Context and consequences* (4th ed.). Thousand Oaks, CA: Sage.

Table 5.3:

Clements, C. B., McKee, J. M., & Jones, S. E. (1984). *Offender needs and assessment: Models and approaches.* Washington, DC: National Institute of Corrections.

Photo 5.1: © Robert D. Hanser

Photo 5.2: © Ima Stewart

Section VI: Probation Management and Case Planning

Figure 6.1:

Allegheny County Probation Department. Retrieved from http://www.alleghenycourts.us/downloads/organization%20charts/adult_probation.pdf

Applied Theory box 6.1:

Lilly, J. R., Cullen, F. T., & Ball, R. A. (2007). *Criminological theory: Context and consequences* (4th ed.). Thousand Oaks, CA: Sage.

Photo 6.2: © Robert D. Hanser

Section VII: Community-Based Residential Intermediate Sanctions

Table 7.1:

National Institute of Corrections (1993). *The intermediate sanctions handbook: Experiences and tools for policymakers.* Washington, DC: National Institute of Corrections.

Focus Topic box 7.1:

Washington State Institute for Public Policy (2007). *Does participation in Washington's work release facilities reduce recidivism?* Washington, DC: National Institute of Corrections. Retrieved from http://nicic.org/Library/022723

Table 7.2:

Washington State Institute for Public Policy. (2007). *Does participation in Washington's work release facilities reduce recidivism?* Washington, DC: National Institute of Corrections. Retrieved from http://nicic.org/Library/022723

Applied Theory box 7.1:

Cullen, F. T., & Agnew, R. (2006). *Criminological theory: Past to present* (3rd ed.). Los Angeles: Roxbury Publishing Company.
Lilly, J. R., Cullen, F. T., & Ball, R. A. (2007). *Criminological theory: Context and consequences* (4th ed.). Thousand Oaks, CA: Sage.

Section VIII: Community-Based Nonresidential and Economic Intermediate Sanctions

Focus Topic box 8.1:

Scillia, A. (1994). *Electronic monitoring: A new approach to work release.* Washington, DC: National Institute of Corrections. Retrieved from http://www.nicic.org/pubs/1991/period17.pdf

Focus Topic box 8.2:

McCarthy, R. (2006). The Hampden County Day Reporting Center: Three years' success in supervising sentenced individuals in the community. Washington, DC: National Institute of Corrections. Retrieved from http://www.nicic.org/pubs/1990/period74.pdf. Used with permission.

Applied Theory box 8.1:

Cullen, F. T., & Agnew, R. (2006). *Criminological theory: Past to present* (3rd ed.). Los Angeles: Roxbury Publishing Company.
Lilly, J. R., Cullen, F. T., & Ball, R. A. (2007). *Criminological theory: Context and consequences* (4th ed.). Thousand Oaks, CA: Sage.

Photo 8.1: © Robert D. Hanser

Section IX: Parole Management, Case Planning, and Reentry

Table 9.1:

Glaser, D. (1964). *The effectiveness of a prison and parole system.* Indianapolis: Bobbs-Merrill.

Figure 9.1:

Travis, J., & Lawrence, S. (2002). *Beyond the prison gates: The state of parole in America.* Washington, DC: Urban Institute Justice Policy Center.

Applied Theory box 9.1:

Cullen, F. T., & Agnew, R. (2006). *Criminological theory: Past to present* (3rd ed.). Los Angeles: Roxbury Publishing Company.
Lilly, J. R., Cullen, F. T., & Ball, R. A. (2007). *Criminological theory: Context and consequences* (4th ed.). Thousand Oaks, CA: Sage.

Section X: Juvenile Offenders

Table 10.1:

U.S. Public Health Services. (2002). *Youth violence: A report of the Surgeon General.* Retrieved from http://www.mentalhealth
.org/youthviolence/surgeongeneral/SG_Site/chapter4/sec1.asp

Figure 10.1:

Thornberry, T. P., Huizinga, D., & Loeber, R. (2004). The causes and correlates studies: Findings and policy implications. *Juvenile Justice Journal, 9*(1), 3–19.

Applied Theory box 10.1:

Houston, J., & Barton, S. M. (2005). *Juvenile justice: Theory, systems, and organization.* Upper Saddle River, NJ: Prentice Hall.
Loeber, R., & Farrington, D. P. (Eds.) (1998). *Serious & violent juvenile offenders: Risk factors and successful interventions.* Thousand Oaks, CA: Sage.
Loeber, R., & Hays, D. F. (1994). Developmental approaches to aggression and conduct problems. In M. Rutter & D. F. Hays (Eds.), *Development through life: A handbook for clinicians* (pp. 488–516). Oxford, UK: Blackwell Scientific.
Thornberry, T. P., Huizinga, D., & Loeber, R. (1995). The prevention of serious delinquency and violence: Implications from the program of research on the causes and correlates of delinquency. In J. C. Howell, B. Krisberg, J. D. Hawkins, & J. J. Wilson (Eds.), *Serious, violent, & chronic juvenile offenders: A sourcebook* (pp. 213–237). Thousand Oaks, CA: Sage.
Thornberry, T. P., Huizinga, D., & Loeber, R. (2004). The causes and correlates studies: Findings and policy implications. *Juvenile Justice Journal, IX*(1), 3–19.

Table 10.2:

Koch Crime Institute. (2000, March). *Juvenile boot camps and military structured youth programs.* Topeka, KS: Author.

Section XI: Specialized and Problematic Offender Typologies in a Changing Era

Applied Theory box 11.1:

Bartol, C. R. (2002). *Criminal behavior: A psychosocial approach* (6th ed.). Upper Saddle River, NJ: Prentice Hall.
Cullen, F. T., & Agnew, R. (2006). *Criminological theory: Past to present* (3rd ed.). Los Angeles: Roxbury Publishing Company.
Rowe, D. (2002). *Biology and crime.* Los Angeles: Roxbury Publishing Company.

Photo 11.1: © Robert D. Hanser

Index